AMERICAN DECADES

1940 - 1949

AMERICAN DECADES

1940-1949

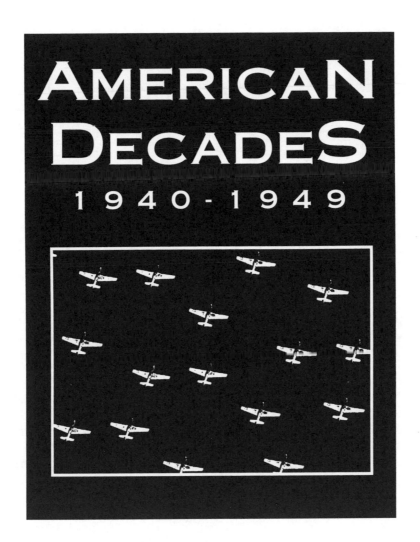

EDITED BY

VICTOR BONDI

A MANLY, INC. BOOK

 **Gale Research Inc.** • DETROIT • WASHINGTON, D.C. • LONDON

AMERICAN DECADES
1940-1949

Matthew J. Bruccoli and Richard Layman, *Editorial Directors*
Karen L. Rood, *Senior Editor*

Printed in the United States of America

Published simultaneously in the United Kingdom
by Gale Research International Limited
(An affiliated company of Gale Research Inc.)

CONTENTS

INTRODUCTION

A Canceled Exhibit. In 1995 curators at the Air and Space Museum of the Smithsonian Institution in Washington, D.C., attempted to install an exhibit commemorating the fiftieth anniversary of the end of World War II. Centered on the last dramatic acts of the conflict, the atomic bombings of Hiroshima and Nagasaki, the exhibit simultaneously attempted to memorialize the struggle and to integrate recently recovered historical evidence, hoping to provoke "a more profound discussion of the atomic bombings" (as exhibit planners told *The New York Times*). The plans alone spurred intense public discussion. Veterans' groups, peace activists, historians, journalists, and politicians debated American objectives during World War II, the merit of the Hiroshima bombing, and the causes of the Cold War, all as part of an effort to influence the Smithsonian's presentation of the exhibit. Five times the curators revised the exhibit to meet the concerns of interested parties. Finally, unable to reconcile often-conflicting perspectives, the Smithsonian canceled the exhibit. Yet the debate over the history of the 1940s continues. Two generations after the end of the war, the events of midcentury are alive in the minds of much of the American public.

Hard-Won Victory. The controversy over the Smithsonian exhibit suggests the vital importance of the 1940s to Americans of the war generation and after. For those who lived through the war, it was a period of sacrifices and struggles, of lives disrupted and lost, of total war and partial peace. For subsequent generations the 1940s were equally important; for the history of the decade includes critical lessons: the barbarism of fascism and militarism, the dehumanization of racism and the Holocaust, the thralldom of ideological dogmatism. Many refuse to forget the 1940s for fear of repeating the past; others cling to the decade as the source of identity and meaning. What we as a people believed ourselves to be before the 1940s is not what we believe ourselves to be after that decade. The Blitz, Stalingrad, Corregidor, the Warsaw Ghetto, Auschwitz, Okinawa, and Hiroshima made us aware of human cruelty and brutality on a scale scarcely imagined before the 1940s. Equally, perhaps, the war broadened the spectrum of human endurance, heroism, and bravery, but in the intellectual postmortem after the war, few celebrated wartime achievements, and

the vast majority searched for a means to prevent another such war. Nothing quite like World War II has ever occurred again; yet a glance at any contemporary newspaper suffices to note how many lessons of the 1940s remained unlearned.

A World Torn Apart. The 1940s were a decade in which history dramatically transformed the lives of millions, radically altering basic suppositions about the character and possibility of life itself. The period following the war brought an explosion of monographs on religion, psychological studies of authoritarianism, and novels dissecting the war experience. Existentialism, with its demand for activism to overcome the absurdity of life, is a poignant product of the war; Reinhold Niebuhr's neo-orthodox assessment of humanity's innate evil was similarly shaped by reactions to the war. While intellectuals revised basic social and political assumptions, average people grappled with the disruption of established norms caused by the war. This disruption was less notable in America than elsewhere in the world. Americans never experienced the terror of air bombardment, the loss of homes, the suspension of justice — the sheer devastation that visited Russia, China, Japan, and most of Europe. Instead, Americans emerged from the war as citizens of the most powerful nation on earth, far more prosperous than they were before it. People's ambitions, their expectations and desires, however, had been altered irrevocably. Americans spent the first five years of the decade watching the world pull their lives apart; they spent the next five years of the decade trying to put their lives back together. But nothing was ever the same.

A World Power. In the 1940s Americans became worldly. Sixteen to seventeen million Americans served in the military, the majority overseas. The rest of the nation was in nightly radio contact with London, Rome, Tokyo, Moscow, Addis Ababa, and Tehran. Postcards and letters from all over the world circulated; rationing and sacrifices on the home front in America had effects oceans away. Newsreels brought the war home to millions; Hollywood took home to the soldiers abroad. Families charted the maneuvers of generals and learned the names of places they never dreamed existed. Soldiers brought wives home from the Philippines, Germany, and

Italy; families joined occupying troops in Japan, Germany, and Korea. As the 1940s began, isolationism, the belief that America was somehow disconnected from the rest of the world, was the most popular political movement in America; the decade ended with the United States signing unprecedented military alliances with foreign powers. Isolationism was irrevocably dead. America stepped on the world stage to fight a world war; Americans became citizens of the world in the process.

A National Mind. The United States became a global power, but Americans were not accustomed to thinking in global terms. Their interpretations of the world could be surprisingly simplistic and one-dimensional. Newsreels presented pictures of faraway places, but they were only images. Wartime France was not the "real" France, and the American army by necessity did not so much experience foreign cultures as roll right over them. The American military had a job to do they really did not care for; they wanted to get it done and go back home.

The Face of the Enemy. The simplistic assumptions Americans had about the world are exemplified in commonly held generalizations about the enemy. "A Jap's a Jap," said Gen. John DeWitt, and, accepting that axiom, many Americans collapsed all distinctions between the Tokyo government and the Japanese people, the Japanese and Asians generally, and the Japanese enemy and Japanese Americans. The demands of total war fostered such propagandistic stereotypes, images of the enemy that lumped them all into a slightly dehumanized category. Humanitarian considerations were all but abandoned when carpet bombing Stuttgart, Cologne, or Dresden. For most Americans the moral issue was simple: German civilians made weapons for German soldiers who killed American boys. No one was innocent. Similarly, after the war few Americans distinguished between the communism of Joseph Stalin and that of Marshall Tito, Chairman Mao, or Ho Chi Minh, no matter how long the histories of animosity among them. Nor for that matter could many Americans distinguish communism from the postwar French socialism of Léon Blum or the British Labourism of Clement Atlee. President Harry S Truman dispensed with President Franklin D. Roosevelt's subtlety and cosmopolitan assurance in foreign affairs and returned American society to a world outlook bound by cultural arrogance and simplistic aphorisms. "The only thing the Russians understand is force," he said, right after Winston Churchill announced the dawn of the Cold War in the American heartland of Fulton, Missouri. Such simplicity cost Truman dearly. Lacking a true understanding of the complexities of Chinese politics, the American people concluded that the Truman administration "lost" China when Mao Tse-tung won the Chinese civil war in 1949. Assuming Truman was soft on communism, they handed him his hat before the 1952 election even began.

The World in Fine. For all their nationalist arrogance, however, Americans did become more worldly, did begin to think more globally in the 1940s. In some ways they had no choice. The world got smaller. Aircraft routinely circumnavigated the globe by the end of the decade. The development of nuclear weapons and ballistic missiles meant that two oceans no longer adequately protected the United States. Foreign ideas penetrated American borders with impunity. Propaganda broadcasts from the enemy were received on the front lines and in the heartland during the war. American broadcasters carefully monitored their programs and canceled weather reports so their transmissions would be useless to an enemy listening a continent away. In the 1940s, moreover, the world came to America. In the receiving and transmitting of information, refugee scientists recognized no national boundaries. British military strategists and Latin American diplomats converged on Washington. Madame Chiang Kai-shek toured America by train. In 1944 European economists met their American counterparts in Bretton Woods, New Hampshire, and mapped out the structure of postwar trade. In 1945 the world sent representatives to San Francisco to establish the United Nations, which took up permanent residence in New York City. American ports shipped goods from every continent. American corporations penetrated nearly every world market. American educators rebuilt the school systems in Germany and Japan. In the 1940s America *was* the world.

New York. More precisely, New York City was the world. Even before the war the city had been teeming with millions from all points of the compass: Asians, South Americans, Eastern Europeans, Italians, Irish, Poles, and Russians. London, already struggling before the war to maintain its position as the world financial center, finally gave way to Wall Street. Berlin, the academic and intellectual capital of the West before the Nazis, relocated to Morningside Heights. Paris, long the artistic center of the West, shipped its talent en masse to Greenwich Village, which replaced the Left Bank as the premiere site for artistic display and sale. Paris almost lost its reputation as the world's fashion center as well; it recovered by 1950, but New York became at least its equal. Nothing demonstrated New York's primacy in science better than the fact that the American atomic bomb was conceived within the five boroughs; the massive program to develop it, of course, was named the Manhattan Project. Not only, however, did the world come to New York, but New York went to the world. The Americanization of Europe began on Broadway, on 52nd Street, in Midtown. American communications, cinema, and publishing companies, located in Manhattan, shipped the culture of the United States abroad. Bebop, swing, blues, and country music, the giants of American literature, Abstract Expressionism, modern dance, the Broadway show — even baseball and basketball — were exported through New York. Millions of soldiers and sailors passed through New York on their way to and from the war; they took the tastes and sights of cosmopolitan

New York home with them. The television industry was born in New York, as was the urban superhighway, the modern American suburb, and the gray-flannel suit. The blacklist got its start in New York, as did the Beat writers of the 1950s, and the black nationalism of the 1960s. New York hammered the regional and ethnic cultures of the United States into nationally recognizable form: the South of Erskine Caldwell, Carson McCullers, and Tennessee Williams passed through New York publishing houses and production companies to the rest of America; Milton Berle and a host of New York television and publishing figures took Brooklyn Judaism to the heartland; Sinatra and New York–based record companies took the Italian American style of Hoboken and the Bronx to the nation. The crossroads of American and European culture, New York became the center of innovative hybrids of high and low culture; it was the richest and largest city in the world, the only major world center unscathed by war; a place teeming with vitality, diversity, and style.

Creative Fusions. New York and the rest of the United States in the 1940s were the laboratory for exciting, creative fusions in the arts and sciences, the birthplace of a new, cosmopolitan perspective. When the aesthetic sensibility of high European modernism met the expressive preoccupations of American democracy, the result was the creation of the world's first international culture. Abstract Expressionism, the style of modern painting pioneered in postwar New York, projected this fusion perfectly. The result of a combination of European advances in formal composition and native American vigor, Abstract Expressionism was internationalism on canvas, a universal portrait of postwar anxiety and aspiration. Much the same fusion of European and American ideas was exhibited in postwar architecture and fashion. American fashion of the late 1940s was actually a combination of American practicality and European flair. Film noir, the most distinctive style of postwar cinema, fused German expressionism to the American detective story. Modern dance linked jazz to ballet; European composers experimented with jazz; jazz musicians experimented with composition. The atomic bomb was an international effort, as were innovations in radar, aviation, antibiotics, and medical technology. The Nuremberg trials were the product of a burgeoning movement in international jurisprudence; so, too, was the United Nations. Even Keynesian economics, the basis of much postwar prosperity, was the result of an American adaptation of a British theory. Like antibiotics, Abstract Expressionism, and the international style in architecture, Keynesian economics claimed to be applicable almost anywhere. Such a universalism was at the center of the new international culture, embracing, in hidden form, an assumption that had been part of the United States since the moment of its birth: American aspirations are the aspirations of the world; American hope, the hope of mankind.

Liberalism Ascendant. Such universal aspirations had always been implicit in American liberalism, and the United States was unmistakenly more liberal. The broad goals of liberalism — the emancipation of humanity from tyranny and ignorance — were in a sense the goals of the Atlantic Charter, signed by Winston Churchill and Franklin D. Roosevelt in 1941. Victory over the Nazis in the war was a triumph for the liberalism the charter enunciated. In religion, law, education, culture, and politics, liberalism was ascendant. Religious life in the late 1940s was more liberal, less given to interfaith intolerance, dogmatic fundamentalism, and institutional authoritarianism than at any previous time in American history. Legal realism triumphed over stare decisis and strict constitutionalism, opening the way for the legal revolutions of the 1950s and 1960s. American education became more liberal, professional, and modern, less disposed to doctrinaire instruction. Although censorship was still common, the culture tolerated a greater range of expression, embracing previously forbidden discussions of marital infidelity, sexuality, and substance abuse in popular music, literature, and cinema. Most important, the politics of the period were dominated by the liberal coalition of finance capital, big labor, and ethnic and racial minorities forged by Franklin Roosevelt and the New Deal Democrats. In the 1940s the liberalism of the New Deal was consolidated and institutionalized. Government supervision of American trade, labor disputes, and the business cycle was an accomplished fact. Social Security and other welfare-state compensations for the more socially corrosive aspects of capitalism were in place. Wealth was more evenly distributed than at any time in American history. The introduction of African Americans into political life was proceeding, though at an often frustratingly slow pace. The Four Freedoms Roosevelt articulated in the Atlantic Charter — freedom of speech, freedom of religion, freedom from want, and freedom from fear — seemed nearly realized by the end of the decade. Historians often discuss the 1940s as the decade in which a long postwar "ideology of liberal consensus" was formed — a bipartisan movement to administer prosperity through welfare and military spending. The high-minded idealism of the New Deal and American liberalism had won World War II and sustained a prosperous peace that seemed nearly unassailable.

Liberalism Assailed. In retrospect, however, the success of liberalism in the 1940s was more apparent than real. The decade of liberal ascendancy also contained the first manifestations of liberalism's later decline. Even as the war consolidated some New Deal measures, it hopelessly compromised others. Dollar-a-year men who volunteered for government service from the ranks of business during the war turned government priorities toward business after the war. The ideological clarity with which Roosevelt approached politics in 1936 and 1937, clearly distinguishing his populist programs from those of the businessmen he termed "economic royalists," was hopelessly blurred by his association with these same businessmen during the war. American labor's efforts to build industrial democracy in the United States were crushed in the General Motors strike of 1945–1946; big labor suffered a further erosion in power with the passage of the Taft-Hartley Act in 1947. The Roosevelt political coalition could not find a successor for him after his death in 1945. Henry Wallace's 1948 presidential bid floundered on the issue of anticommunism, an issue which killed the left wing of the New Deal coalition. Harry S Truman was a logical successor to Roosevelt in domestic policy, being an ardent New Dealer who had supported Roosevelt for years. Three important parts of Truman's Fair Deal — federal aid to education, national health insurance, and support for civil rights — were attempts to extend the New Deal into the 1940s. Truman's rhetoric during the 1948 "give 'em hell" campaign echoed Roosevelt's in 1936, but Truman lacked Roosevelt's finely tuned sense of politics. Roosevelt was apt to do only the politically possible; Truman often pushed the politically impossible and only furthered the resistance to his proposals. Of the three Fair Deal objectives listed above, only support for civil rights was accomplished — and even that goal was achieved only partially and accompanied by political resistance so severe that Southern Democrats bolted the party.

The End of Ideology. Already political opinion in America was changing. Because they were out of power, conservatives nurtured angry grudges against liberal society, establishing the roots of the conservatism that would blossom in the 1970s. The flower of a later conservatism was being seeded: Friedrich Hayek's 1944 economic study, *The Road to Serfdom*, argued that welfare-state liberalism led to totalitarianism; neo-Thomist educators insisted that progressive education was undermining the moral structure of society; Dixiecrats objected to unwarranted federal interference in the peculiar institution of Jim Crow. Simultaneously, the Old Left in American politics died, expiring from Stalinist abuses, the Nazi-Soviet pact, and postwar prosperity. Even as the Right grumbled on the sidelines and the Left disintegrated, the rhetoric of political debate became more volatile, filled with ugly implications that would have been impossible before World War II. The examples of Nazi Germany and Stalinist Russia were cited so often as to become virtually meaningless. Conservatives charged liberals with "fellow-traveling," immorality, and the abandonment of certainty, all of which supposedly led to cultural barbarism and totalitarianism. Liberals reversed the charges and suggested that conservatives were paving the way toward an all-American brand of fascism. The center held, but only by becoming ever more apolitical. The New Deal demanded a type of ideological thinking that exalted the common man and disapproved of concentrations of wealth. In the charged atmosphere of the late 1940s, however, ideologies were discredited. As political scientist Daniel Bell suggested in a 1948 essay, ideological thinking was becoming bad form. In new suburbs around the old cities, millions of Americans abandoned the New Deal and public politics to indulge their private concerns, bolstered by postwar prosperity.

The Birth of Modern America. Increasingly, Americans tied their futures after the war to economic prosperity rather than New Deal politics. That association, more than any other, would be responsible for the decline of liberalism in the 1970s. In their rise to the ranks of the middle class, working-class Americans forgot that New Deal policies were the basis of their prosperity. The GI Bill, governmental support for collective bargaining, federal support for housing construction, Social Security, military purchases, and highway construction — all were responsible for the creation of the modern middle class. Even more important was the historically unprecedented position of the United States in global trade after World War II, when the United States alone maintained a fully functional economy. After the war the suburbs seemed to spring into existence without any historical, economic, or political context. Most Americans had been poor before the war; by the 1950s it seemed that most Americans had always been middle class. Women had been working in factories since industry first developed in the United States, and during World War II 60 percent of women were working. After the war, however, women were portrayed as if they had always been housewives and mothers. Psychology textbooks posited an "eternal female" who was necessary to sustain the "traditional family." Even in the nineteenth century, however, the United States had the highest divorce rate of any industrialized society in the world.

Tradition and History. The suburbs assumed the values of a traditional world that was disappearing as America became worldly and liberal; in fact, suburbanites invented a traditional world as a refuge from the pressure of modernity, the possibility of nuclear war, and the demands of global leadership. The model American family — prosperous, white, Protestant, churchgoing, car-loving Americans — hardly reflected the often-impoverished, diverse, secular, horse-drawn reality of the American past. The model distorted actual American traditions; but accuracy was not its function. Historian Elaine Tyler May, borrowing a metaphor from the politics of the period, has suggested that a sort of "containment," a type of willful forgetting, went on in the American suburbs of the postwar period. After the ideological warfare of midcentury, few cared to reiterate the often-violent tradition of class warfare in the United States. After the separation of families during the Depression and war, few wished to ponder the unorthodox family arrangements common in American history. After years of struggle during the Depression, few wanted to analyze the precarious historical and political context of economic prosperity. In the rush to embrace a safe tradition, postwar suburbia neglected the rich and often troubling relationship of Americans to their actual past, a past equally filled with courage and cowardice, tragedy and triumph.

PLAN OF THIS VOLUME

This is one of nine volumes in the *American Decades* series. Each volume will chronicle a single twentieth-century decade from thirteen separate perspectives, broadly covering American life. The volumes begin with a chronology of world events outside of America, which provides a context for American experience. Following are chapters, arranged in alphabetical order, on thirteen categories of American endeavor ranging from business to medicine, from the arts to sports. Each of these chapters contains the following elements: first, a table of contents for the chapter; second, a chronology of significant events in the field; third, Topics in the News, a series, beginning with an overview, of short essays describing current events; fourth, anecdotal sidebars of interesting and entertaining, though not necessarily important, information; fifth, Headline Makers, short biographical accounts of key people during the decade; sixth, People in the News, brief notices of significant accomplishments by people who mattered; seventh, Awards of note in the field (where applicable); eighth, Deaths during the decade of people in the field; and ninth, a list of Publications during or specifically about the decade in the field. In addition, there is a general bibliography at the end of this volume, followed by an index of photographs and an index of subjects.

ACKNOWLEDGMENTS

This book was produced by Manly, Inc. Karen L. Rood and Darren Harris-Fain were the in-house editors.

Production coordinator is James W. Hipp. Photography editor is Bruce Andrew Bowlin. Photographic copy work was performed by Joseph M. Bruccoli. Layout and graphics supervisor is Penney L. Haughton. Copyediting supervisor is Laurel M. Gladden. Typesetting supervisor is Kathleen M. Flanagan. Systems manager is George F. Dodge. Julie E. Frick is editorial associate. The production staff includes Phyllis A. Avant, Charles D. Brower, Ann M. Cheschi, Patricia Coate, Denise W. Edwards, Joyce Fowler, Stephanie C. Hatchell, Erica Hennig, Kathy Lawler Merlette, Jeff Miller, Pamela D. Norton, Laura S. Pleicones, Emily R. Sharpe, William L. Thomas, Jr., and Jonathan B. Watterson.

Walter W. Ross and Robert S. McConnell did library research. They were assisted by the following librarians at the Thomas Cooper Library of the University of South Carolina: Linda Holderfield and the interlibrary-loan staff; reference librarians Gwen Baxter, Daniel Boice, Faye Chadwell, Cathy Eckman, Gary Geer, Qun "Gerry" Jiao, Jean Rhyne, Carol Tobin, Carolyn Tyler, Virginia Weathers, Elizabeth Whiznant, and Connie Widney; circulation-department head Thomas Marcil; and acquisitions-searching supervisor David Haggard.

AMERICAN DECADES
1940 - 1949

WORLD EVENTS: SELECTED OCCURRENCES OUTSIDE THE UNITED STATES

1940

- Max Beckmann paints *Circus Caravan*.
- T. S. Eliot's long poem *East Coker,* the second part of his *Four Quartets,* is published.
- Graham Greene's novel *The Power and the Glory* is published.
- Carl Jung's *Psychology and Religion* is published.
- Arthur Koestler's novel *Darkness at Noon* is published.
- Igor Stravinsky composes his Symphony in C Major.
- Dylan Thomas's *Portrait of the Artist as a Young Dog,* a collection of largely autobiographical short stories, is published.

14 Jan.	Japanese premier Gen. Abe Nobuyuki resigns. Adm. Yonai Mitsumasa forms a new cabinet.
27 Jan.	In Rangoon, Burma, a riot breaks out between Hindus and Muslims.
9 Feb.	The Irish Supreme Court upholds a law authorizing the internment without trial of suspected members of the Irish Republican Army.
12 Feb.	The Dominican Republic announces a contract to resettle one hundred thousand European refugees.
16 Feb.	The British destroyer *Cossack* attacks the German ship *Altmark,* liberating some three hundred English prisoners. Norway protests the attack, which violated Norwegian territorial waters.
18 Feb.	President José Félix Estigarribia of Paraguay announces he is assuming dictatorial powers.
21 Feb.	In the small Polish village of Auschwitz, construction begins on a German concentration camp.
22 Feb.	In Tibet a six-year-old boy is crowned the fourteenth Dalai Lama.
28 Feb.	In Egypt the twenty-eight-hundred-year-old sarcophagus of Pharaoh Psusennes is opened, revealing treasures that rival those found in the tomb of Tutankhamen.
1 Mar.	Italian laws restricting the professional practices of Jews go into effect.

12 Mar.	Defeated in the Soviet-Finnish war, the Finns sign a treaty ceding the Karelian Isthmus and the Rybachi Peninsula to the Soviet Union and granting it lease rights to the Hango Peninsula in return for their continued independence.
18 Mar.	At a meeting on the Italian side of the Brenner Pass, Benito Mussolini informs Adolf Hitler that Italy will enter the war against Britain and France.
19 Mar.	U.S. ambassador to Canada James Cromwell declares in an official address that Hitler is bent on the destruction of American social and economic order.
20 Mar.	French premier Edouard Daladier resigns; the next day Paul Renaud forms a new cabinet and creates a war council in expectation of a German invasion.
26 Mar.	The Mexican government announces the expropriation of 1.5 million acres of land held by three American corporations.
30 Mar.	Wang Ching-wei establishes a Chinese government under the supervision of occupying Japanese troops.
9 Apr.	Germany invades Denmark and Norway. Belgium refuses to allow the British to move their troops through the Low Countries.
10 Apr.	King Haakon VII of Norway repudiates the puppet government of Norwegian Nazi Vidkun Quisling.
18 Apr.	In India the All-India National Congress calls for civil disobedience against British rule.
10 May	Germany invades Belgium and Holland, beginning its blitzkrieg (lightning war) through the Low Countries into France. Neville Chamberlain resigns as British prime minister and is succeeded by Winston Churchill.
13 May	Churchill announces to the House of Commons, "I have nothing to offer but blood, toil, tears, and sweat."
14 May	The Dutch army surrenders to Germany. Authorities report that 100,000 Dutch troops, more than one-fourth of their army, have been killed in the fighting. The official capitulation papers are signed the next morning.
17–18 May	German troops take Brussels and Antwerp in Belgium.
20 May	The German army takes Amiens, France.
26 May	German troops take Calais.
27 May	The British begin to evacuate Dunkirk, France. By 4 June their flotilla of warships, private yachts, and fishing boats has removed nearly 350,000 troops. They leave 2,000 guns, 60,000 trucks, 76,000 tons of ammunition, and 600,000 tons of fuel in France. England is left practically disarmed by the defeat, but in the House of Commons on 4 June Churchill declares, "We shall defend our island whatever the cost may be, we shall fight on the beaches, we shall fight on the landing grounds, we shall fight in the fields and in the streets . . . we shall never surrender."
28 May	King Leopold III of Belgium surrenders his country to the Germans.
30 May	Reich commissioner Arthur Seyss-Inquart assumes office as civil administrator of the occupied Netherlands.
3 June	German planes bomb Paris.

7 June	King Haakon VII and his Norwegian government go into exile in London.
9 June	An armistice is signed in Norway.
10 June	Italy declares war on Britain and France. The next day its planes bomb British bases on Malta and in Aden, while the British hit Italian air bases in Libya and Italian East Africa.
11 June	President Getulio Vargas of Brazil reasserts his country's neutrality.
12 June	The heaviest single Japanese bombing attack on Chungking, China, kills 1,500 people and leaves 150,000 homeless. Between 18 May and 14 August Japanese planes drop 2,500 tons of bombs on the city, killing more than 2,000 civilians and injuring nearly 3,500.
14 June	The German army enters Paris; Hitler orders a three-day celebration of the victory. The French government relocates to Bordeaux. The Soviet Union occupies the small Baltic nation of Lithuania; two days later it takes over neighboring Estonia and Latvia, demanding that all three countries put themselves under Soviet protection.
16 June	Italian planes bomb British bases in Egypt.
17 June	French premier Reynaud resigns and is replaced by World War I hero Marshal Philippe Pétain, who calls for surrender to the Germans.
18 June	German planes raid the east coast of England. In a radio broadcast from London, Gen. Charles de Gaulle of France calls on his countrymen to rally behind him as he continues to oppose Germany from exile.
22 June	The French government signs an armistice with the Nazis at the same site in the Compiègne Forest where Germany surrendered to the Allies in World War I. Germany occupies three-fifths of France, leaving the southern portion as a so-called Free Zone. De Gaulle announces the formation of the French National Committee in London to continue fighting alongside the British Empire.
24 June	France and Italy sign an armistice.
26 June	Turkey declares itself a nonbelligerent.
28 June	The Soviet Union occupies Bessarabia and northern Bucovina, in Romania.
30 June	The Germans occupy the Channel Islands.
2 July	The French government establishes itself at Vichy. On 10 July it abolishes the Third Republic and adopts a new constitution creating an authoritarian government and investing full power on the chief of the French State, Pétain.
6 July	Hitler makes peace overtures to Britain.
10 July	German aircraft bomb South Wales.
14 July	Fulgencio Batista defeats Ramon Grau San Martin for the presidency of Cuba.
16 July	Hitler issues Directive 16, ordering the invasion of Great Britain. During the Battle of Britain, which lasts from early August to November, the British lose 827 aircraft, but they shoot down 2,409 German planes.
21 July	The Soviet Union annexes Latvia, Lithuania, and Estonia.

22 July	Prince Konoye Fumimaro of Japan forms a new government. At the second Pan-American conference, meeting in Havana, U.S. secretary of state Cordell Hull proposes a collective trusteeship of European possessions in the New World; the proposal is adopted on 28 July.
25 July	The United States places severe restrictions on the export of scrap metal, petroleum, and petroleum products, and it bans the export of aviation fuel and lubricating oil outside the Western Hemisphere; the measure is aimed chiefly at Japan, which relies heavily on American oil.
2 Aug.	Italian troops invade British Somaliland, occupying the capital, Berbera, on 19 August; British forces are evacuated.
6 Aug.	Germany orders the expulsion of all Jews from Kraków, Poland.
15 Aug.	The Minseito Party, the last remaining political party in Japan, dissolves itself, making the nation an authoritarian state.
17 Aug.	Germany announces a "total" naval blockade of the British Isles.
20 Aug.	Reflecting on the conduct of the Royal Air Force (RAF) in the Battle of Britain, Churchill declares, "Never in the field of human conflict was so much owed by so many to so few."
24 Aug.	The first German bombing of London occurs.
25 Aug.	The RAF bombs Berlin, an event Luftwaffe head Hermann Göring had assured Hitler could never happen.
7–15 Sept.	The London Blitz, massive German bombardment of London, occurs.
13 Sept.	Italian troops invade Egypt from Libya.
22 Sept.	Vichy France accedes to a Japanese ultimatum demanding bases in northern Indochina near the Chinese border.
25 Sept.	After meeting heavy resistance from Vichy French forces, British and Free French forces led by General de Gaulle abandon an invasion of Dakar, in French West Africa.
27 Sept.	Germany, Italy, and Japan sign the Tripartite Pact in Berlin, committing themselves to providing each other with military assistance in case of attack by any nation not already at war against them.
1 Oct.	Military delegations from several Latin American nations visit Washington, D.C., for consultations.
2 Oct.	All Jews in occupied France are required to register with police.
7 Oct.	German troops move into Romania.
12 Oct.	Hitler postpones "Operation Sealion," a German invasion of Britain, until spring 1941.
18 Oct.	Vichy France bars Jews from positions in government, the teaching profession, the armed forces, the press, film, and radio. On 30 October Pétain announces a policy of collaboration with Germany.
28 Oct.	Italian troops invade Greece.
8 Nov.	Italian troops begin retreating from Greece.

11 Nov.	British fighter planes cripple much of the Italian fleet in an engagement at Taranto.
14 Nov.	The English automotive center of Coventry is carpet-bombed by 449 German aircraft. The attack creates a firestorm that kills more than 550 people and destroys the city's fourteenth-century cathedral.
20 Nov.	Hungary joins the Axis.
23–24 Nov.	Romania and Slovakia sign the Tripartite Pact with the Axis.
24 Nov.	Slovakia joins the Axis.
26–27 Nov.	The RAF conducts heavy night raids on Cologne.
30 Nov.	Japan formally recognizes the puppet government of Wang Ching-wei in China.
9–11 Dec.	The British crush the Italians at Sidi Barrani, Egypt, wiping out four divisions and taking more than twenty thousand prisoners.
17 Dec.	In North Africa the British take Sidi Omar and Sollum from the Italians.
25 Dec.	The Germans suspend bombing of London until 27 December.
29 Dec.	The Germans drop incendiary bombs on the center of London, causing the worst damage to the city since the fire of 1666.

1941

- Bertolt Brecht's play *Mother Courage and Her Children* premieres in Zurich.
- Benjamin Britten composes his opera *Paul Bunyan.*
- Noel Coward's play *Blithe Spirit* premieres in London.
- T. S. Eliot's long poem *The Dry Salvages,* the third part of his *Four Quartets,* is published.
- Erich Fromm's *Escape from Freedom,* an analysis of fascism, is published.
- Franz Werfel's novel *The Song of Bernadette* is published.

10 Jan.	Germany and the Soviet Union announce what the German government calls the largest grain deal in history.
21 Jan.	The British suppress publication of the Communist newspaper *Daily Worker.*
22 Jan.	Tobruk, Libya, falls to British and Free French forces.
26 Jan.	British forces invade Somaliland.
28 Jan.	The Free French announce the capture of Murzuk, in southern Libya.
2 Feb.	Three days of riots between soldiers and anti-British demonstrators come to an end in Johannesburg, South Africa.
6 Feb.	British forces capture Bengasi, in eastern Libya.
9 Feb.	British warships shell Genoa, Italy.
10 Feb.	Great Britain breaks off diplomatic relations with Romania because German troops have been deployed there.

12 Feb.	Gen. Erwin Rommel arrives in Tripoli to take command of German and Italian forces in Libya.
24 Feb.	In a speech to the Japanese Diet, Foreign Minister Matsuoka Yosuke demands the cession of Oceania to Japan.
1 Mar.	Bulgaria joins the Axis.
3 Mar.	The Soviet Union denounces Bulgaria for allying itself with the Axis powers.
5 Mar.	Nazis in Amsterdam sentence eighteen Dutch resistance fighters to death.
7 Mar.	The British recapture Somaliland.
25 Mar.	Yugoslavia joins the Axis; anti-Nazi riots erupt in Belgrade, and on 27 March the pro-Axis government is overthrown in a military coup.
28–29 Mar.	The British navy destroys much of the remaining Italian fleet off Cape Matapan, Greece.
3 Apr.	Italian and German troops force the British to evacuate Bengasi, Libya.
4 Apr.	The German army invades the Balkan Peninsula; it then crosses into Yugoslavia and Greece on 6 April.
10 Apr.	The Danish envoy to Washington, D.C., announces an agreement to provide American protection for Greenland; the government of Nazi-occupied Denmark declares the agreement void on 12 April.
13 Apr.	The Soviet Union and Japan sign a neutrality pact.
17 Apr.	The Yugoslavian army surrenders to the Axis.
19 Apr.	The British land troops in Iraq to protect the oil fields after the Baghdad government has displayed an increasingly pro-Axis bias. Military exchanges between the British and Iraqis follow.
27 Apr.	German forces occupy Athens.
5 May	Following the British conquest of Ethiopia, Emperor Haile Selassie returns to assume the throne lost in the Italian conquest of 1936.
8 May	Nazi air raids flatten Hull, England.
9 May	The RAF conducts devastating air raids on Hamburg and Bremen.
10 May	Rudolf Hess, Hitler's personal deputy, parachutes into Scotland.
10–11 May	Nazi bombers blitz London, damaging the House of Commons, Westminster Abbey, and Big Ben.
16 May	The RAF bombs German airfields in Syria.
20 May	The Germans launch an invasion of Crete, completing their conquest of the island on 1 June.
21 May	The U.S. ship *Robin Moor* is torpedoed and sunk by a German U-boat off the coast of Brazil.
24 May	The British battle cruiser *Hood* is sunk by the 35,000-ton German battleship *Bismarck* between Greenland and Iceland.
27 May	The British navy sinks the *Bismarck* off the French coast.

31 May	British forces enter Baghdad, and the Iraqi government agrees to an armistice.
8 June	British and Free French troops invade Syria, taking Damascus on 21 June.
18 June	Germany and Turkey sign a ten-year friendship treaty.
22 June	Germany and Italy declare war on the Soviet Union as Germany launches a massive attack on three fronts. Turkey declares its neutrality. Britain assures the Soviets of aid, as does the United States, as President Franklin D. Roosevelt declares on 25 June that the neutrality act does not apply to Russia.
26 June	Finland joins the Axis attack on the Soviet Union; German troops are already within fifty miles of Minsk, which falls to them on 30 June.
27 June	Hungary declares war on the Soviet Union.
1 July	The Germans capture Riga, the capital of Lithuania; the next day the Nazis capture 160,000 Russian troops near Bialystok.
3 July	Soviet premier Joseph Stalin announces a "scorched earth" defense; two days later German mechanized troops reach the Dnieper River, three hundred miles from Moscow.
7 July	The United States occupies Iceland with naval and marine forces; the Icelandic parliament approves the occupation on 10 July.
8 July	The Nazi advance into Russia stalls. An estimated 9 million men are engaged in the war between Germany and Russia.
18 July	Japanese premier Konoye forms a new cabinet, which includes four generals and three admirals.
19 July	Bolivia announces the uncovering of an Axis plot and ousts the German diplomatic minister.
23 July	Vichy France accedes to Tokyo's demand for military bases in Indochina.
24 July	German troops advance to the outskirts of Leningrad and Smolensk. Japanese troops arrive in southern Indochina.
25 July	The United States and Great Britain freeze all Japanese assets; Japan retaliates the next day by freezing American and British assets.
31 July	Japan formally apologizes for sinking the American gunboat *Tutuila* in Chungking, China, on 30 July.
1 Aug.	President Roosevelt places an embargo on the export of all motor fuel oils outside the Western Hemisphere except to the British Empire.
8 Aug.	Vichy military observers estimate the casualties from the first forty-eight days of the German invasion of the Soviet Union to be 1.5 million Axis troops and 2 million Russians.
19 Aug.	German troops lay siege to Odessa.
21 Aug.	In Paris two Communists are executed, and thousands more so-called Communists and anarchists are arrested as the Germans crack down on the Resistance. By the end of the month eleven more suspected Resistance members are executed, and in Paris alone thousands of Jews are rounded up for deportation to Nazi concentration camps.

25 Aug.	Responding to increasing Axis infiltration, Soviet and British troops invade Iran.
28 Aug.	The Vichy regime executes three more suspected Resistance fighters; on 29 August they will execute eight more men.
29 Aug.	German troops occupy Tallinn, Estonia.
4 Sept.	German U-boats attack the U.S. destroyer *Greer* en route to Iceland; the *Greer* counterattacks with depth charges.
5 Sept.	German artillery begins shelling Leningrad.
10 Sept.	German authorities in Oslo place the city under martial law after several strikes have broken out; on 12 September they begin mass arrests of trade unionists.
11 Sept.	President Roosevelt authorizes American ships to protect themselves by shooting first if they feel threatened by Axis warships; the next day Berlin announces that it will take appropriate countermeasures.
14 Sept.	The first Russian-based RAF wing arrives in the Soviet Union. In Zagreb, Yugoslavia, the central telephone exchange is bombed, and Axis authorities arrest and execute fifty Resistance fighters.
16 Sept.	Under pressure from the Allies, ailing Reza Shah Pahlevi of Iran abdicates in favor of his twenty-one-year-old son, Mohammed Reza Pahlevi.
18 Sept.	Stalin orders the conscription of all Soviet workers between the ages of sixteen and fifty for after-hours military training.
21 Sept.	German troops enter Kiev and reach the Sea of Azov, cutting off the Crimea.
28 Sept.	German authorities announce the arrest of Czech premier Alois Elias on charges that he had plotted high treason with the Czech government in exile in London. Many other arrests and executions follow, including Mayor Otokar Klapka of Prague, convicted on 3 October. Two days later German radio reports 159 executions and 900 arrests so far.
2 Oct.	Hitler announces a final drive against Moscow.
15 Oct.	The Germans capture Kalinin, one hundred miles northwest of Moscow. Soviet troops begin their final evacuation of Odessa.
16 Oct.	Axis troops capture Odessa. In Japan premier Konoye resigns. On 18 October Lt. Gen. Tojo Hideki forms a new cabinet, making himself premier, minister of war, and home minister.
17 Oct.	The U.S. destroyer *Kearny* is torpedoed and damaged off the coast of Greenland.
19 Oct.	The Germans lay siege to Moscow.
21 Oct.	In reprisal for the slaying of a German officer, fifty French citizens are executed in Nantes, and the Germans warn they will execute fifty more if the killers of the officer are not turned over by 23 October. On 22 October the Nazis seize one hundred people in Bordeaux after the killing of another German officer; fifty are killed immediately and fifty are held hostage, as in Nantes. Because of an international outcry, execution of the Nantes and Bordeaux hostages is first postponed and then suspended indefinitely on 30 October.
22 Oct.	In Zagreb, Yugoslavia, newspapers report the execution of two hundred citizens in reprisal for an attack on two German officers.

30 Oct.	The U.S. destroyer *Reuben James* is sunk off the coast of Iceland.
6 Nov.	The United States announces $1 billion in lend-lease aid to the Soviet Union.
9 Nov.	In Vienna Nazi authorities announce the execution of twenty Czechs.
17 Nov.	Special envoy Kurusu Saburo delivers Japanese premier Tojo's ultimatum to President Roosevelt. Tojo demands American withdrawal from China and the lifting of the U.S. economic embargo in return for peace in the Pacific.
18 Nov.	Britain begins an invasion of Libya that drives Rommel's forces back to the point at which he began his invasion of Egypt.
19 Nov.	The United States and Mexico sign trade and financial agreements designed to stabilize currency and resolve nationalization claims.
24 Nov.	The United States dispatches troops to Dutch Guiana to help Dutch troops protect its bauxite mines.
28 Nov.	Reports from Shanghai indicate that transports carrying some 30,000 Japanese troops are moving southward from China toward Haiphong in Indochina.
30 Nov.	In an inflammatory speech, Japanese premier Tojo declares that Anglo-American exploitation of Asia must be purged.
2 Dec.	In Trieste sixty people go on trial on various charges, including espionage and involvement in a 1938 plot to assassinate Mussolini; on 14 December nine are sentenced to death, and others receive long prison terms.
6 Dec.	The Soviet army begins a counteroffensive along the Moscow front.
7 Dec.	In a surprise attack Japanese planes bomb U.S. naval and air bases at Pearl Harbor, Hawaii, destroying two battleships and four other capital vessels. Japanese air forces simultaneously attack U.S. bases in the Philippines, Guam, and Wake Island and British bases in Hong Kong and Singapore, while also invading Malaya and Thailand by land and sea. A Japanese declaration of war on the United States is delivered after the attack.
8 Dec.	The United States, Great Britain, the Free French government, and the Dutch government in exile in London declare war on Japan, as do Canada, Costa Rica, Honduras, San Salvador, Guatemala, Haiti, and the Dominican Republic. Thailand capitulates to the Japanese.
11 Dec.	Germany and Italy declare war on the United States; the U.S. Congress unanimously responds by declaring war on Germany and Italy — as do Cuba, Costa Rica, Nicaragua, Guatemala, and the Dominican Republic; Mexico severs relations with both nations.
13 Dec.	Japanese forces take Guam.
14 Dec.	Turkey and Ireland declare neutrality in the U.S./Japanese war.
16 Dec.	A Japanese submarine shells the Hawaiian port of Kahului, one hundred miles southwest of Honolulu.
22 Dec.	Prime Minister Churchill and other British officials visit Washington, D.C., to establish a combined American-British military command for the war.
23 Dec.	Japanese forces complete their invasion of Wake Island.

25 Dec.	The British garrison at Hong Kong surrenders to the Japanese.
30 Dec.	Mohandas K. Gandhi resigns from the All-India National Congress Party because it has abandoned civil disobedience.

1942

- Albert Camus's novel *The Stranger* is published.
- T. S. Eliot's *Little Gidding*, the fourth part of his *Four Quartets*, is published.
- Dmitry Shostakovich composes his Seventh Symphony, his homage to Leningrad.

1 Jan.	In Washington, D.C., twenty-six Allied nations, including the United States, Great Britain, the Soviet Union, and China, sign a pact agreeing not to make separate peace with Germany.
2 Jan.	The Japanese take Manila.
14–15 Jan.	The RAF conducts heavy bombing raids on port facilities at Hamburg and Rotterdam, beginning a long series of air attacks on port and factory cities in Germany and occupied Europe.
15–28 Jan.	Foreign ministers of the Western Hemisphere nations, including the United States, meet in Rio de Janeiro. With the exception of Argentina and Chile, they sever diplomatic relations with Axis nations and agree to collective-security arrangements.
17 Jan.	The Japanese invade Burma.
20 Jan.	Leading Nazi officials meet in Wannsee, near Berlin, to plan a "final solution" to the "Jewish problem."
21 Jan.	In North Africa Rommel begins a counteroffensive that drives the British back into Egypt within two weeks.
26 Jan.	The first U.S. troops arrive on British soil.
29 Jan.	The Soviet Union, Great Britain, and Iran conclude a treaty providing for wartime occupation of Iran. The Soviets station troops in the northern section of the country, the British in the south, to guard Iranian oil reserves and vital supply lines from the Persian Gulf to the Soviet Union.
15 Feb.	Japan occupies Singapore and Malaya.
3 Mar.	The RAF bombs the Renault works outside Paris, destroying the factory, which has been manufacturing tanks and aircraft engines for the Germans.
7 Mar.	The Japanese complete their invasion of Java.
23 Mar.	British envoy Sir Stafford Cripps arrives in India to offer postwar dominion status; the terms of the offer are rejected by the Indian Congress on 11 April. The British respond by imprisoning Indian Nationalists.
28 Mar.	The RAF bombs Lübeck, Germany, inflicting heavy damage in the important Baltic port.
2 Apr.	Dr. William Temple, archbishop of York, becomes archbishop of Canterbury.
18 Apr.	"Doolittle's Raiders," a squadron of U.S. Army Air Corps bombers led by Brig. Gen. James H. Doolittle, raid Tokyo and other Japanese cities.

23–26 Apr.	The RAF bombing of the Baltic port of Rostock is the heaviest on any city since the beginning of the war. The Germans begin reprisal raids on British cities.
1 May	The Japanese take Mandalay, forcing the British to begin withdrawal from Burma to India.
4–9 May	American and Japanese naval forces trade blows in the Coral Sea.
6 May	U.S. forces surrender the Philippines to the Japanese.
7 May	The Allies take Bizerte and Tunis.
26 May	Great Britain and the Soviet Union sign a twenty-year alliance. Rommel begins a new offensive in the western Sahara.
27 May	Reinhard Heydrich, second in command of the Gestapo, is shot in Czechoslovakia; he dies on 3 June. In retaliation the Nazis kill thousands of Czechs, including everyone in the town of Lidice.
30 May	More than one thousand Allied bombers level Cologne, the major railway center of western Germany.
3 June	Japanese aircraft attack a U.S. naval base in the Aleutian Islands. A few days later they land troops on Attu and Kiska, in the western Aleutians.
4–6 June	The United States cripples the Japanese fleet at the battle of Midway.
9–28 June	Rommel's victories in North Africa force the British to retreat to El Alamein, east of Alexandria, Egypt.
18 June	The United States declares war on Bulgaria.
25 June	Maj. Gen. Dwight D. Eisenhower is appointed commander in chief of Allied military forces.
1–9 July	Rommel's troops attack El Alamein, attempting to reach and gain control of the Suez Canal, but they are turned back by British forces.
16–17 July	During the Rafle du Vel' d'Hiver (Roundup of the Winter Velodrome) more than twelve thousand Jews are arrested and held in a Paris sports arena for deportation to Germany and the occupied countries of eastern Europe.
26–29 July	The Allies conduct one of their most successful bombing raids on Hamburg.
7 Aug.	The United States lands troops on Guadalcanal, where the Japanese have been building an airstrip since early July ; on 12–15 November American naval forces score a costly victory in a major sea battle for control of this strategically important island in the Solomon Islands, but the Japanese fight on until February 1943.
12–15 Aug.	Churchill, Stalin, and American representative Averell Harriman meet in Moscow to discuss the progress of the war against Germany.
25 Aug.	German troops reach the outskirts of Stalingrad.
27 Aug.	British scientists announce the discovery of penicillin.
14 Sept.	The German siege of Stalingrad begins.
5 Oct.	Prof. Gilbert Murray helps to found Oxfam to help relieve starvation in occupied Europe.

1943

23–26 Oct.	The British Eighth Army, under the leadership of Lt. Gen. Bernard L. Montgomery, defeats Rommel's forces at El Alamein.
8 Nov.	Allied troops under Gen. Dwight D. Eisenhower land in French North Africa to support the British offensive in Egypt. The United States and Vichy France break off diplomatic relations. In a speech in Munich Hitler announces, incorrectly, that Stalingrad is "firmly in German hands."
9–11 Nov.	German troops occupy the so-called Free Zone of France.
11 Nov.	The Allies take Algiers, Oran, Casablanca, and Rabat.
13 Nov.	Tobruk is retaken by the British.
19–22 Nov.	A Soviet offensive lifts the siege of Stalingrad, but heavy fighting in the area continues until February 1943.
20 Nov.	The British retake Benghazi.

- Aram Khachaturian composes his *Ode to Stalin*.

- Harold Laski's political study *Reflections on the Revolution of Our Time* is published.

- Thomas Mann's novel *Joseph the Provider* is published.

- Jacques Maritain's *Christianity and Democracy* is published.

- Henri Michaux's *Exorcismes*, a collection of war poems, is published.

- Henry Moore sculpts his *Madonna and Child*.

- Sean O'Casey's play *Red Roses for Me* premieres in Dublin.

- Sergey Prokofiev composes his opera *War and Peace*.

- Jean-Paul Sartre's philosophical work *Being and Nothingness* is published.

- Dmitry Shostakovich composes his Eighth Symphony.

- The Aqua-Lung is invented.

- Hitler suppresses publication of the *Frankfurter Zeitung*.

14–27 Jan.	Churchill and Roosevelt confer with the joint chiefs of staff at Casablanca and demand unconditional surrender by the Axis powers.
22 Jan.	American and Australian forces overrun the last pockets of Japanese troops in New Guinea.
23 Jan.	The British Eighth Army takes Tripoli.
31 Jan.	On the outskirts of Stalingrad, the Germans under Gen. Friedrich Paulus capitulate. Stalin announces the capture of more than 45,000 prisoners, including thirteen generals, and the deaths of 146,700 Germans. The remaining German troops in the area, including eight more generals, surrender on 2 February.
9 Feb.	The last Japanese forces retreat from Guadalcanal.
20 Feb.	At the Kasserine Pass in Tunisia, Allied troops are forced to retreat by Rommel's Afrika Korps. On 25 February Allied troops retake the pass.

2–4 Mar.	The Japanese are defeated by the United States in the battle of the Bismarck Sea, losing a convoy of 22 ships and more than 50 aircraft.
20 Apr.	The Nazis massacre Jews in the Warsaw ghetto.
7–9 May	After the Allies take Tunis and Bizerte, the German forces in Tunisia surrender unconditionally.
11 May	American forces land on Attu. They complete their invasion of the island on 2 June, and the Japanese abandon Kiska without a fight by 27 July.
22 May	Moscow announces it has dissolved the Third Communist International (Comintern), formed in 1919.
3 June	French generals de Gaulle and Henri Giraud form the French Committee of National Liberation (CFLN) to coordinate the French war effort.
4 June	A military coup in Argentina is staged by generals Arturo Rawson and Pedro Ramirez.
10 July	The Allies invade Sicily, overcoming the last remaining forces on the island at Messina on 17 August.
19 July	Allied forces bomb Rome for the first time.
25 July	Mussolini resigns. Italian king Victor Emmanuel III asks Marshal Pietro Badoglio to form a new government.
1 Aug.	The Japanese grant independence to Burma, which declares war on the United States and Great Britain.
14–24 Aug.	Allied representatives meet in Quebec to plan a war strategy.
8 Sept.	Eisenhower announces the unconditional surrender of Italy to the Allies. Stalin permits the reopening of many Soviet churches.
9 Sept.	Allied troops land near Salerno, Italy.
10 Sept.	Germany announces the occupation of Rome and northern Italy.
12 Sept.	German commandos led by Capt. Otto Skorzeny rescue Mussolini from house arrest in San Grasso and take him to northern Italy, where he forms a new Fascist government.
30 Sept.	The Allies occupy Naples.
13 Oct.	The Italian government led by Badoglio declares war on Germany.
14 Oct.	The Japanese declare the Philippines independent.
19–30 Oct.	The Allies confer in Moscow and agree that Germany will be stripped of all territory acquired since 1938.
1 Nov.	American forces land at Bougainville in the Solomon Islands.
6 Nov.	The Russians retake Kiev.
19 Nov.	Sir Oswald Mosley, a British Fascist leader imprisoned since May 1940 as a security risk, is released on the grounds of failing health.
22–26 Nov.	Churchill, Roosevelt, and Chinese Nationalist leader Chiang Kai-shek meet at Cairo to plan a postwar Asian policy.

1944

28 Nov.– **1 Dec.**	Stalin, Churchill, and Roosevelt meet in Teheran to discuss war strategy and plan the structure of the postwar world.

- Béla Bartók composes his Sonata for Solo Violin Concerto.

- Max Beckmann paints his *Self-Portrait in Black.*

- Paul Hindemith composes his opera *Herodias.*

- Max Horkheimer and Theodor Adorno's *Dialectic of Enlightenment,* a study of western Marxism and authoritarianism, is published.

- Aldous Huxley's novel *Time Must Have a Stop* is published.

- Somerset Maugham's novel *The Razor's Edge* is published.

- Henry Moore sculpts the first version of his *Family Group.*

- Jean-Paul Sartre's play *No Exit* premieres in Paris.

11 Jan.	Moroccan nationalists demand independence from France.
22 Jan.	Allied troops land at Anzio, Italy, in an attempt to outflank German defense positions in central Italy. Progress is slow, as they meet stubborn resistance.
27 Jan.	The German siege of Leningrad ends.
30 Jan.	At Brazzaville, in the Congo, African leaders discuss the postwar decolonization of Africa.
24–25 Feb.	President Ramirez of Argentina is overthrown in a coup led by Gen. Edelmiro Farrell.
4 Mar.	American planes bomb Berlin.
6 Mar.	In a daylight raid American bombers drop 2,000 tons of bombs on Berlin.
15 Mar.	The Soviet Union officially replaces "The Internationale" with "Hymn of the Soviet Union" as its national anthem.
4 June	Allied forces enter Rome.
6 June	D day: Allied forces establish beachheads in Normandy, France, and begin the liberation of western Europe. The operation, code-named "Overlord," involves more than 4,000 ships, 3,000 planes, and 4 million troops.
13 June	The Germans begin attacking Britain with their V-1 rockets, launching more than seven thousand against England by 24 August.
15 June	American long-range Superfortress aircraft begin bombing operations against the Japanese home islands.
1 July	The Allies confer in Bretton Woods, New Hampshire, hoping to establish a stable postwar economic system.
3 July	The Soviets announce their recapture of Minsk.
18 July	Tojo resigns as Japanese prime minister.

20 July	At Hitler's East Prussian headquarters, a bombing assassination attempt fails. Plotters, including Col. Claus von Stauffenberg, chief of staff of the Home Army, are executed during the night.
12 Aug.	Allied troops take Florence.
21–29 Aug.	In Washington, D.C., at the Dumbarton Oaks conference, the Allies begin discussions on the formation of the United Nations.
25 Aug.	Allied troops liberate Paris.
4 Sept.	Allied troops liberate Brussels.
8 Sept.	The Germans begin V-2 rocket attacks on England.
12 Sept.	Romania signs an armistice with the Allies.
17–28 Sept.	Allied efforts to secure Rhine bridges and outflank the Germans at Eindhoven and Arnhem fail.
19 Sept.	Finland signs an armistice with the Allies.
29 Sept.	The Soviet Union invades Yugoslavia.
9–20 Oct.	Churchill and Stalin confer in Moscow.
20 Oct.	American forces led by Gen. Douglas MacArthur land in the Philippines.
23–26 Oct.	During the Battle of Leyte Gulf, the largest naval battle of World War II, American forces destroy the remainder of the Japanese fleet.
16 Dec.	German general Karl von Rundstedt launches an unsuccessful German offensive in the Ardennes. This "Battle of the Bulge" is the last major German military offensive of World War II.

1945

- Martin Buber's theological study *For the Sake of Heaven* is published.
- Carlo Levi's autobiographical work *Christ Stopped at Eboli* is published.
- Jean Giraudoux's play *The Madwoman of Chaillot* premieres in Paris.
- George Orwell's novel *Animal Farm* is published.
- Karl Popper's *The Open Society and Its Enemies*, a study of authoritarianism, is published.
- Jean Renoir's movie *The Southerner* is released.
- Roberto Rossellini's movie *Open City*, filmed in postwar Rome, is released.
- Dmitry Shostakovich composes his Ninth Symphony.
- Igor Stravinsky composes his Symphony in Three Movements.
- Evelyn Waugh's novel *Brideshead Revisited* is published.
- In France women gain the right to vote.

Jan.	Part one of Sergey Eisenstein's movie *Ivan the Terrible* is released and achieves instant success, earning Eisenstein a Stalin Prize. Completed in February 1946, part two, however, is denounced by the Central Committee of the Communist Party for its unflattering portrayal of Ivan and his bodyguard and is promptly banned. It is not publicly released until 1958.
1 Jan.	In Egypt elections boycotted by the nationalist Wafd result in the election of Ahmed Maher Pasha as premier.
18 Jan.	The Soviets announce the liberation of Warsaw.
20 Jan.	The provisional Hungarian government of Gen. Bela Miklos signs an agreement of unconditional surrender to the Allies.
22 Jan.	British troops retake Monywa, in Burma, reopening the land route to China.
26 Jan.	Soviet troops reach the Prussian coast at Elbing, severing East Prussia from the rest of Germany.
27 Jan.	The Red Army liberates Auschwitz.
29 Jan.	Soviet troops cross the 1939 border between Poland and Germany, entering the province of Pomerania in northeastern Germany. By 2 February they control most of East Prussia.
31 Jan.	Soviet troops cross the Oder River, coming within fifty miles of Berlin.
4–11 Feb.	Roosevelt, Churchill, Stalin, and other Allied leaders confer at Yalta, in the Crimea, on issues of postwar international organization. They agree to divide Germany into separate Allied occupation zones.
13 Feb.	The Soviets capture Budapest after a fifty-day seige.
14 Feb.	The Allies firebomb Dresden.
19 Feb.	U.S. Marines land at Iwo Jima, 750 miles south of Tokyo. The island falls to the Americans on 17 March, at a cost of 4,000 American and 20,000 Japanese lives.
21 Feb.	The Inter-American Conference convenes in Mexico City to discuss economic issues such as conversion to a peacetime economy.
24 Feb.	U.S. troops drive the last Japanese forces from Manila. After announcing the Egyptian declaration of war on Germany and Japan, Premier Ahmed Maher Pasha is assassinated in Cairo.
6 Mar.	U.S. troops capture Cologne.
7 Mar.	The American First Army crosses the Rhine at Remagen.
9 Mar.	American Superfortress bombers drop more than 2,300 tons of incendiary bombs on Tokyo.
19 Mar.	The Soviet Union formally denounces a 1925 nonaggression treaty with Turkey and demands diplomatic revisions.
30 Mar.	The Soviets capture Danzig.
1 Apr.	American forces invade Okinawa, 360 miles south of Tokyo.
9–13 Apr.	The Red Army enters Vienna.

12 Apr.	President Roosevelt dies at Warm Springs, Georgia. He is succeeded by Vice-president Harry S Truman. American troops liberate Buchenwald concentration camp.
21 Apr.	Soviet troops reach the outskirts of Berlin.
25 Apr.	Advancing armies of the United States and the Soviet Union meet at Torgau, on the Elbe River in Germany. The United Nations conference opens in San Francisco. The delegates complete the UN charter on 26 June.
28 Apr.	In Como, Italy, Mussolini is executed by Italian partisans.
29 Apr.	The U.S. Seventh Army enters Munich and liberates the concentration camp at Dachau. German troops in Italy surrender to the Allies.
30 Apr.	Hitler commits suicide at his bunker in Berlin.
2 May	The Germans surrender Berlin to the Soviets.
8 May	V-E Day. German military authorities formally surrender to the Allies, ending World War II in Europe.
19 May	Demonstrations erupt in Lebanon and Syria following the landing of French troops sent to reestablish colonial control.
22 May	Yonabaru, the key Japanese position on Okinawa, is taken by American forces. The Japanese surrender the island on 21 June, at a cost of 13,000 American and 100,000 Japanese lives.
23 May	French authorities report 1,300 casualties in a nationalist uprising staged by Berber tribesmen in Algeria.
29 May	French artillery shells Damascus after street fighting breaks out between Syrians and French troops.
3–25 June	French troops are withdrawn from Beirut and Damascus, as France requests UN mediation.
11 June	The Liberal Party, led by Prime Minister Mackenzie King, wins in the Canadian elections, but King loses his seat in the House of Commons.
5 July	The United States completes the reoccupation of the Philippines, at a cost of nearly 12,000 men.
16 July	The United States successfully detonates the first atomic bomb at Alamagordo Air Force Base in New Mexico.
17–26 July	Truman, Stalin, Churchill, and other Allied representatives meet in Potsdam, a suburb of Berlin, and issue the Potsdam Declaration, demanding unconditional surrender from Japan.
26 July	Elections in Britain result in a Labour Party landslide; Clement Attlee succeeds Churchill as prime minister.
6 Aug.	The U.S. Superfortress bomber *Enola Gay* drops an atomic bomb on the Japanese city of Hiroshima, killing more than 50,000 people and leveling four square miles of the city.
8 Aug.	The Soviet Union declares war on Japan and attacks Japanese forces in Manchuria the next day.

9 Aug.	The United States detonates an atomic bomb on the Japanese city of Nagasaki, killing more than 40,000 people and destroying a third of the city.
10 Aug.	The Japanese Supreme Council votes to accept the surrender terms of the Potsdam Declaration.
14 Aug.	The Soviet government concludes a treaty with the Chinese Nationalist government of Chiang Kai-shek.
15 Aug.	V-J Day. The Allies accept the unconditional surrender of the Japanese. The French sentence Pétain to death as a Nazi collaborator; the sentence is later commuted to life imprisonment.
28 Aug.	U.S. troops land on the home islands of Japan to supervise the disarmament of the Japanese military.
2 Sept.	In ceremonies aboard the U.S.S. *Missouri,* moored in Tokyo Bay, the Japanese formally surrender to the Allies, ending World War II. In Hanoi Vietnamese nationalist leader Ho Chi Minh declares Vietnamese independence, using a copy of the American Declaration of Independence supplied by the Office of Strategic Services.
20 Sept.	The All-India Congress Committee, led by Gandhi and Jawaharlal Nehru, convenes. It rejects British proposals for national autonomy and calls for the removal of Britain from India.
11–12 Oct.	Gen. Eduardo Avalos seizes control in Argentina. His government is overthrown on 17 October by Col. Juan Perón.
21 Oct.	Elections for the French Constituent Assembly result in significant gains for the Communists.
10 Nov.	The United States, Great Britain, and the Soviet Union recognize the Communist government of Albania, led by Col. Enver Hoxha.
13 Nov.	The Constituent Assembly of France unanimously elects Charles de Gaulle as head of the French government.
18 Nov.	Antonio de Oliveira Salazar's National Union Party wins the Portuguese elections, which are boycotted by the opposition.
20 Nov.	In Nuremberg the trials of top Nazi leaders for crimes against humanity begin.
14 Dec.	The U.S. government sends Gen. George C. Marshall as envoy to China to mediate in the civil war between the Communists and Nationalists.
15 Dec.	The Allied Control Commission abolishes Shintoism as the state religion of Japan.
27 Dec.	Allied foreign ministers, meeting in Moscow, call for the establishment of a provisional democratic government in Korea. Soviet forces occupy Korea north of the thirty-eighth parallel while U.S. troops occupy the southern portion of the country.

1946

- Simone de Beauvoir's novel *All Men Are Mortal* is published.
- Benjamin Britten composes his opera *The Rape of Lucretia.*
- Marcel Carné's movie *Les Portes de la Nuit* is released.

- Ernst Cassirer's *The Myth of the State,* a study of political science, is published.

- André Gide's *Journal, 1939–42* is published.

- David Lean's movie *Great Expectations* is released.

- Michael Polanyi's *Science, Faith and Society,* an analysis of scientific method and medicine, is published.

- Bertrand Russell's *A History of Western Philosophy* is published.

- Dylan Thomas's *Deaths and Entrances,* a collection of poems, is published.

- Women gain the right to vote in Italy.

24 Feb. Perón, leader of a Fascistic political movement, is elected president of Argentina.

2 Mar. British troops complete their evacuation of Iran, but Soviet troops remain, violating the Anglo-Russian treaty of 1942, by which the two countries agreed to remove all troops from Iran within six months of the end of the war. Following diplomatic pressure from the United States and Great Britain, the Soviet Union completes the withdrawal of its troops by 9 May.

5 Mar. In a speech at Westminster College in Fulton, Missouri, Churchill warns that in Europe "an iron curtain [of Communism] has descended across the continent."

22 Mar. Great Britain recognizes the independence of Transjordan, which came under British mandate after World War I.

18 Apr. The League of Nations conducts its final assembly in Geneva, turning over its assets to the United Nations.

3 June Italians vote to replace their monarchy with a republic.

1 and 25 July The United States conducts atomic-bomb tests at Bikini Atoll in the Pacific Ocean.

4 July The United States grants independence to the Philippines.

8 Sept. Bulgarian voters reject their monarchy in favor of a republic; on 15 September Bulgaria is declared a people's republic.

13 Oct. French voters approve a new constitution, which establishes the Fourth Republic.

16 Oct. At Nuremberg, as a result of their convictions for war crimes, ten leading Nazis are executed. Nazi chief Hermann Göring, scheduled to hang with the others, commits suicide two hours before the executions.

10 Nov. French Communists score significant electoral gains, resulting in political deadlock in the French Assembly.

22 Nov. French authorities, seeking the surrender of Vietnamese nationalists, bombard the cities of Haiphong and Hanoi, killing 6,000.

16 Dec. Socialists led by Léon Blum form a new French government.

1947

- Benjamin Britten composes his opera *Albert Herring.*

- Albert Camus's novel *The Plague* is published.

- Charlie Chaplin's movie *Monsieur Verdoux* is released.

- Anne Frank's *The Diary of a Young Girl* is published.

- Erich Fromm's *Man for Himself,* a psychological study of ethics, is published.

- Alberto Giacometti sculpts *Man Pointing.*

- Le Corbusier begins the Unité d'habitation, an apartment complex intended to function as a self-sufficient community, in Marseilles.

- H. R. Trevor-Roper's historical work *The Last Days of Hitler* is published.

1 Jan.   The British and Americans join their German occupation zones into a single economic unit.

29 Jan.   American envoys, led by General Marshall, abandon efforts to negotiate an end to the Chinese civil war.

10 Feb.   The Allies sign formal peace treaties with Italy, Bulgaria, Romania, Hungary, and Finland, officially ending the hostilities of World War II.

3 Mar.   Martial law is declared in Palestine after increased incidences of Zionist attacks against British personnel.

4 Mar.   France and England sign a fifty-year military alliance.

12 Mar.   Speaking to a joint session of the U.S. Congress, President Truman requests $500 million in military and economic assistance for the governments of Greece and Turkey.

29 Apr.   The Constituent Assembly of India outlaws untouchability, affirming equal rights for all, regardless of race, religion, caste, or sex.

3 May   A new Japanese constitution, drafted by the Americans, goes into effect.

June   France is paralyzed by a series of strikes.

27 June   Soviet, British, and French representatives meet in Paris to discuss American proposals for economic assistance to Europe. Talks break down on 2 July when Soviet foreign commissar Vyacheslav Molotov denounces the Americans' "Marshall Plan" as politically motivated and refuses to participate in the reconstruction program.

15 Aug.   India and Pakistan become independent nations, ending nearly 350 years of British colonial rule on the Indian subcontinent.

2 Sept.   Nineteen Western Hemisphere nations, including the United States, sign the Rio Pact, committing themselves to collective defense against aggression.

5 Oct.   The Soviet Union announces that during a secret meeting in Warsaw in September, the Communist parties of the Soviet Union, Bulgaria, Czechoslovakia, France, Hungary, Italy, Poland, Romania, and Yugoslavia created the Communist Information Bureau (Cominform) to coordinate the activities of European Communist Parties and trade unions.

26 Oct.   India annexes Kashmir, provoking war with Pakistan; on 30 December the conflict will be referred for settlement to the United Nations.

30 Dec.	After King Michael of Romania abdicates, the Romanian parliament abolishes the monarchy and proclaims the nation a people's republic.

1948

- The first volume of Winston Churchill's memoir, *The Second World War*, is published.

- Graham Greene's novel *The Heart of the Matter* is published.

- Aldous Huxley's novel *Ape and Essence* is published.

- Laurence Olivier stars in a screen version of *Hamlet*.

- Vittorio de Sica's movie *The Bicycle Thieves* is released.

- Belgium grants the right to vote to women.

1 Jan.	The Benelux Customs Union is established.
4 Jan.	Burma becomes an independent nation.
20 Jan.	Gandhi is assassinated.
4 Feb.	Ceylon becomes independent.
25 Feb.	Communists seize control of the Czechoslovakian government. Czech nationalist Jan Masaryk dies on 10 March after falling from a window. Reported as a suicide, his death arouses suspicion in the West.
1 Mar.	British and American authorities establish a central bank to serve their occupation zones of Germany.
17 Mar.	France, the United Kingdom, and the Benelux countries sign the Brussels Pact, a fifty-year military alliance.
3 Apr.	The U.S. Congress appropriates $6 billion for the Marshall Plan.
1 May	North Korea proclaims itself a people's republic and adopts a Soviet-style constitution.
14 May	The state of Israel is declared, as the British mandate in Palestine comes to an end. At midnight troops from Egypt, the Transjordan, Syria, Lebanon, and Iraq invade Palestine; the United Nations effects a truce on 15 July.
26 May	The United Party, led by Premier Jan Smuts, loses control of the South African House of Assembly after running on a platform that included a gradual increase in the rights of native Africans. The victorious Nationalist Party and its coalition partner, the Afrikaner Party, advocate a policy of strict apartheid.
18 June	France merges its German occupation zone with the Anglo-American zone, forming a single West German political unit.
20 June	A new currency, the deutsche mark, is established for West Germany.
24 June	Soviet authorities halt all surface traffic from West Germany into Berlin, blockading the city. Western authorities respond with an airlift to supply the western sections of Berlin with vital necessities.
28 June	The Soviet Union expels Yugoslavia from the Cominform, signaling hostile relations between the two Communist governments.

25 July Britain ends the rationing of bread.

Aug. Soviet scientists who disagree with the environmental evolutionary theories of geneticist T. D. Lysenko are purged from the Russian scientific establishment.

15 Aug. South Korea formally proclaims itself the Democratic Republic of Korea.

22 Aug. In Amsterdam 147 Protestant and Orthodox denominations from forty-four countries found the World Council of Churches.

12 Nov. An American military tribunal finds Tojo and six other Japanese defendants guilty of war crimes and sentences them to death. They are executed on 23 December.

27 Dec. Cardinal József Mindszenty is arrested by the Communist government of Hungary on charges that he had furnished western powers with information about Soviet-Hungarian relations and urged western intervention in Hungary. On 8 February 1949 he is sentenced to life imprisonment for high treason.

1949

- Simone de Beauvoir's feminist work *The Second Sex* is published.

- T. S. Eliot's play *The Cocktail Party* premieres in Edinburgh.

- George Orwell's novel *Nineteen Eighty-Four* is published.

- Paul Tillich's theological study *The Shaking of the Foundations* is published.

20–23 Jan. Representatives of nineteen Middle Eastern, Far Eastern, and Australasian nations meet in New Delhi to discuss Asian affairs and issue a statement critical of Dutch efforts to prevent the Netherlands East Indies from becoming the independent nation of Indonesia.

25 Jan. The Soviet Union and Communist countries of Eastern Europe announce that they have established the Council for Mutual Economic Assistance.

8 Mar. France agrees to recognize the independence of Vietnam within the French Union and to reinstall Vietnamese emperor Bao Dai.

4 Apr. Twelve nations, including the United States and the Brussels Pact nations, form the North Atlantic Treaty Organization (NATO), committing themselves to mutual military assistance.

18 Apr. The Republic of Ireland is officially proclaimed.

5 May Ten Western European states form the Council of Europe to promote peace and foster European cooperation.

11 May Israel is admitted to the United Nations.

12 May Soviet authorities, announcing they have completed road and rail "repairs," end the Berlin blockade.

29 June American occupation forces are withdrawn from Korea. South Africa signals a hardening of apartheid restrictions by banning mixed marriages and automatic citizenship for immigrants from Commonwealth countries.

5 Aug. The United States terminates all military and economic assistance to the Nationalist Chinese government of Chiang Kai-shek.

14 Aug.	The conservative Christian Democratic Party, led by Konrad Adenauer, garners 31 percent of the vote in the first postwar parliamentary election conducted in the new Federal Republic of Germany (West Germany).
23 Sept.	American, British, and Canadian officials announce that the Soviet Union has successfully detonated an atomic bomb.
1 Oct.	The Communist People's Republic of China is proclaimed.
7 Oct.	The eastern, Soviet-occupied zone of Germany declares itself the German Democratic Republic.
24 Oct.	In New York the permanent headquarters of the United Nations is dedicated.
8 Nov.	Cambodia becomes an independent nation within the French Union.
26 Nov.	India adopts a federal constitution and opts to remain within the British Commonwealth.
16 Dec.	The British Parliament further restricts the powers of the House of Lords.
27 Dec.	Led by President Sukarno, the United States of Indonesia becomes an independent nation.

THE ARTS

by DAVID MCLEAN

CONTENTS

Sidebars and tables are listed in italics.

1940

Movies
Doctor Ehrlich's Magic Bullet, starring Edward G. Robinson; *Fantasia*, Walt Disney feature-length animation; *Foreign Correspondent*, directed by Alfred Hitchcock; *The Grapes of Wrath*, starring Henry Fonda, directed by John Ford; *The Great Dictator*, directed by and starring Charlie Chaplin; *Knute Rockne, All-American*, starring Ronald Reagan; *The Mortal Storm*, starring Jimmy Stewart and Margaret Sullivan; *My Little Chickadee*, starring W. C. Fields and Mae West; *The Philadelphia Story*, starring Katharine Hepburn, Cary Grant, and Jimmy Stewart; *Rebecca*, starring Laurence Olivier, directed by Alfred Hitchcock; *The Road to Singapore*, starring Bob Hope and Bing Crosby; *The Thief of Baghdad*, starring Sabu and Conrad Veidt.

Fiction
Erskine Caldwell, *Trouble in July;* Willa Cather, *Sapphira and the Slave Girl;* Walter von Tilburg Clark, *The Ox-Bow Incident;* William Faulkner, *The Hamlet;* Ernest Hemingway, *For Whom the Bell Tolls;* Sinclair Lewis, *Bethel Merriday;* Richard Llewellyn, *How Green Was My Valley;* Carson McCullers, *The Heart is a Lonely Hunter;* Upton Sinclair, *World's End;* William Carlos Williams, *In the Money;* Thomas Wolfe, *You Can't Go Home Again* (published posthumously); Richard Wright, *Native Son.*

Popular Songs
"Along the Santa Fe Trail," Glenn Miller and his Orchestra with Ray Eberly; "Amapola," Jimmy Dorsey and his Orchestra; "Boog-it," Cab Calloway and his Orchestra; "Can't Get Indiana Off My Mind," Kate Smith; "Devil May Care," Bing Crosby; "Dream Valley," Sammy Kaye and his Orchestra; "I Can't Love You Any More," Benny Goodman with Helen Forrest; "In an Old Dutch Garden," Glenn Miller and his Orchestra; "Java Jive," The Ink Spots; "Just to Ease My Worried Mind," Roy Acuff; "Love Lies," Tommy Dorsey and his Orchestra with Frank Sinatra; "Practice Makes Perfect," Bob Chester and his Orchestra; "San Antonio Rose," Bing Crosby; "Strange Fruit," Billie Holliday; "Trade Winds," Bing Crosby; "We Three," The Ink Spots; "Well All Right!," The Andrews Sisters.

26 Jan.
The Italian Art Masterpiece exhibit opens at the Museum of Modern Art in New York. It is the first time most of the work is shown in the United States.

3 Feb.
President Franklin D. Roosevelt pledges his support to the $1-million drive to save the Metropolitan Opera House in New York.

14 May
A Mexican art exhibit covering two thousand years of Mexican history opens at the Museum of Modern Art.

12 June
American artists vote to withdraw from the Venice Art Exhibit because of the war.

13 Oct.
Benny Goodman signs a contract to play with the New York Philharmonic.

22 Oct.
Piet Mondrian arrives in New York, in exile from the war in Europe.

31 Oct.
The Hollywood film industry pledges facilities to produce army training films.

13 Nov.
Fantasia opens in New York with Leopold Stokowski conducting the orchestra.

14 Nov.
The American Academy of Arts and Letters gives the Howells Medal for Fiction to Ellen Glasgow for the most distinguished work of the past five years.

18 Nov.
A giant "battle of the swing bands," featuring twenty-eight of the biggest bands in the country and lasting from eight in the evening to four in the morning, is held at New York's Manhattan Center.

21 Dec.	F. Scott Fitzgerald, age forty-four, dies in Hollywood.

1941

Movies	*Buck Privates*, starring Abbott and Costello; *Citizen Kane*, directed by and starring Orson Welles; *Dumbo*, Walt Disney film; *The Great Lie*, starring Mary Astor and Bette Davis; *High Sierra*, starring Humphrey Bogart; *Hold That Ghost*, starring Abbott and Costello; *How Green Was My Valley*, directed by John Ford, starring Donald Crisp; *The Maltese Falcon*, directed by John Huston, starring Humphrey Bogart; *Meet John Doe*, directed by Frank Capra; *Sergeant York*, starring Gary Cooper; *Suspicion*, directed by Alfred Hitchcock, starring Cary Grant and Joan Fontaine; *The Two-Faced Woman*, starring Greta Garbo.
Fiction	William Attaway, *Blood on the Forge*; A. J. Cronin, *The Keys of the Kingdom*; Edna Ferber, *Saratoga Trunk*; F. Scott Fitzgerald, *The Last Tycoon* (published posthumously); Ellen Glasgow, *In This Our Life*; James Hilton, *Random Harvest*; Carson McCullers, *Reflections in a Golden Eye*; John P. Marquand, *H. M. Pulham, Esq.*; Vladimir Nabokov, *The Real Life of Sebastian Knight*; Robert Nathan, *They Went Together*; William Saroyan, *Fables*; Upton Sinclair, *Between Two Worlds*; Marguerite Steen, *The Sun Is My Undoing*.
Popular Songs	"Absent Minded Moon," Jimmy Dorsey with Bob Eberly; "Aurora," The Andrews Sisters; "Boogie Woogie Bugle Boy," The Andrews Sisters; "By-U, By-O," Woody Herman and his Orchestra with Muriel Lane; "Confessin' the Blues," Jay McShann and his Orchestra; "Everything Happens to Me," Tommy Dorsey with Frank Sinatra; "Frenesi," Artie Shaw and his Orchestra; "Hawaiian Sunset," Sammy Kaye with Marty McKenna; "The Hut-Sut Song," Freddie Martin and his Orchestra; "I Don't Want to Set the World on Fire," The Mills Brothers; "I Wonder Why You Said Goodbye," Ernest Tubb; "Jump For Joy," Duke Ellington with Herb Jeffries; "Maria Elena," Jimmy Dorsey with Bob Eberly; "This Love of Mine," Tommy Dorsey with Frank Sinatra; "'Til Reveille," Bing Crosby; "When My Blue Moon Turns Gold Again," Gene Autry.
4 Jan.	Charlie Chaplin declines the New York Film Critics' Circle Award, saying that actors should not compete with one another.
10 Jan.	James Joyce dies in Zurich.
16 Jan.	Will Hays denies Sen. Burton Wheeler's charge that the film industry is interventionist.
27 Jan.	William Randolph Hearst's art collection, of some ten thousand items, is put on private display in New York.
10 Feb.	Paramount Pictures purchases screen rights to *Lady in the Dark* for a record price of $283,000.
17 Mar.	President Roosevelt opens the National Gallery of Art in Washington, D.C.
28 Mar.	Virginia Woolf drowns herself in Lewes, Sussex, England.
2 May	The Federal Communication Commission (FCC) authorizes full commercialization of television broadcasting to begin 1 July.
6 June	The American Writers' Congress presents the Randolph Bourne Memorial Award for "distinguished service to the cause and culture of peace" to Theodore Dreiser.

1 Sept.–
26 Sept.   The congressional committee chaired by Sen. Gerald Nye investigates Hollywood's "interventionist propaganda."

15 Oct.   Sculptor Jo Davidson says the United States is on the verge of an art renaissance due to Works Progress Administration (WPA) art projects.

1942

Movies   *Casablanca*, starring Humphrey Bogart, Ingrid Bergman, and Paul Henreid; *The Glass Key*, starring Alan Ladd and Veronica Lake; *In Which We Serve*, written by Noel Coward; *Johnny Eager*, starring Robert Taylor and Van Heflin; *The Magnificent Ambersons*, directed by Orson Welles; *Mrs. Miniver*, starring Greer Garson and Walter Pidgeon, directed by William Wyler; *The Pied Piper*, starring Anne Baxter; *Pride of the Yankees*, starring Gary Cooper; *Random Harvest*, starring Ronald Colman and Greer Garson; *Road to Morocco*, starring Bob Hope, Bing Crosby, and Dorothy Lamour; *This Gun for Hire*, starring Alan Ladd and Veronica Lake; *Wake Island*, starring William Bendix; *Woman of the Year*, starring Katharine Hepburn and Spencer Tracy; *Yankee Doodle Dandy*, starring James Cagney.

Fiction   Nelson Algren, *Never Come Morning* ; Louis Bromfield, *Until the Daybreak*; Pearl S. Buck, *Dragon Seed* ; James Gould Cozzens, *The Just and the Unjust* ; Marcia Davenport, *Valley of Decision*; William Faulkner, *Go Down, Moses*; Rachel Field, *And Now Tomorrow*; Nancy Hale, *The Prodigal Woman*; Zora Neale Hurston, *Dust Tracks on the Road*; John Steinbeck, *The Moon Is Down*; Eudora Welty, *The Robber Bridegroom*; Franz Werfel, *The Song of Bernadette*.

Popular
Songs   "All I Need Is You," Dinah Shore; "Back to Donegal," Bing Crosby; "Daybreak," Tommy Dorsey with Frank Sinatra; "Der Fuehrer's Face," Spike Jones and his Band; "I Had the Craziest Dream," Harry James with Helen Forrest; "I Lost My Sugar in Salt Lake City," Johnny Mercer; "I'll Always Be Glad to Take You Back," Ernest Tubb; "I'll Be Around," The Mills Brothers; "It Won't Be Long," Roy Acuff; "The Lamplighter's Serenade," Glenn Miller with Ray Eberly; "Lonely River," Gene Autry; "Lover Man," Billie Holliday; "Praise the Lord and Pass the Ammunition," Kay Kyser and his Orchestra; "Private Buckeroo," Gene Autry; "Strip Polka," The Andrews Sisters; "Take Me," Tommy Dorsey with Frank Sinatra; "When the Lights Go On Again," Vaughn Monroe and his Orchestra; "White Christmas," Bing Crosby.

16 Jan.   Carole Lombard, her mother, and twenty others die in a plane crash near Las Vegas.

8 Feb.   Mark Rothko holds his first solo exhibition at the Artists' Gallery in New York.

3 Mar.   John Cage's *Imaginary Landscape No. 3*, a percussive orchestral piece, is premiered at the Chicago Arts Club.

6 Mar.   Artists in Exile exhibit begins at the Pierre Matisse Gallery in Manhattan.

9 Apr.   In Madison Square Garden Igor Stravinsky's *Circus Polka* debuts with the Ringling Brothers circus. The ballet that accompanies the music is performed by fifty elephants and fifty showgirls and is choreographed by George Balanchine.

16 Apr.   The New York Drama Critics' Circle gives no award for best play of 1941–1942 season.

28 Apr.	20th Century–Fox buys rights to *The Moon Is Down* for a record three hundred thousand dollars.
2 May	Aaron Copland's *Lincoln Portrait* premieres, played by the Cincinnati Symphony Orchestra, Andre Kostelanetz, directing; William Adams, narrator.
4 July	*This Is the Army*, a soldier revue with a cast of three hundred army men, opens at a Broadway theater in New York.
8 July	James Petrillo, president of the American Federation of Musicians, announces a ban on recording because of a dispute with American Society of Composers, Authors and Publishers (ASCAP).
1 Aug.	The American Federation of Musicians, led by president James C. Petrillo, begins its yearlong strike against the recording industry.
3 Sept.	*The World at War*, a film survey written and produced by the Office of War Information, opens in New York.
23 Sept.	A Dial Press poll names Carl Sandburg the "greatest living American writer." Ernest Hemingway and Willa Cather finished second and third.
22 Oct.	The Art of This Century Gallery opens in New York.
26 Oct.	Agnes de Mille's ballet, *Rodeo*, premieres in New York, danced by the Ballets Russes de Monte Carlo and featuring a score composed by Aaron Copland.
18 Nov.	Thornton Wilder's *The Skin of Our Teeth* opens in New York.
25 Dec.	A *Motion Picture Herald* poll shows Abbott and Costello as the leading box-office attraction of 1942.
31 Dec.	Roy Harris's Symphony no. 4 (*Folksong*) is performed for the first time by the New York Philharmonic-Symphony Orchestra and New York High School Choruses, directed by Dimitri Mitropoulos.

1943

Movies	*Action in the North Atlantic*, starring Humphrey Bogart; *For Whom the Bell Tolls*, starring Gary Cooper and Ingrid Bergman; *Guadalcanal Diary*, starring William Bendix; *Hitler's Children*, starring Robert Watson and Tim Holt; *The Human Comedy*, starring Mickey Rooney and Frank Morgan; *Mission to Moscow*, starring Walter Huston; *Mr. Lucky*, starring Cary Grant; *The North Star*, written by Lillian Hellman; *The Outlaw*, starring Jane Russell; *The Ox-Bow Incident*, directed by William Wellman, starring Henry Fonda; *Since You Went Away*, starring Claudette Colbert and Jennifer Jones; *Song of Bernadette*, starring Jennifer Jones; *Stormy Weather*, starring Lena Horne; *Tender Comrade*, starring Ginger Rogers, screenplay by Dalton Trumbo; *Victory Through Air Power*, Walt Disney Studios; *Watch on the Rhine*, starring Paul Lukas and Bette Davis.
Fiction	Sholem Asch, *The Apostle;* Louis Bromfield, *Mrs. Parkington;* Erskine Caldwell, *Georgia Boy;* John Cheever, *The Way Some People Live;* John Dos Passos, *Number One;* James T. Farrell, *My Days of Anger;* Arthur Koestler, *Arrival and Departure;* Sinclair Lewis, *Gideon Planish;* John P. Marquand, *So Little Time;* William Saroyan, *The Human Comedy;* Betty Smith, *A Tree Grows in Brooklyn;* Wallace Stegner, *The Big Rock Candy Mountain;* Robert Penn Warren, *At Heaven's Gate;* Eudora Welty, *The Wide Net.*

Popular Songs

"Comin' In on a Wing and a Prayer," The Song Spinners; "Don't Believe Everything You Dream," The Ink Spots; "Don't Sweetheart Me," Lawrence Welk and his Orchestra with Wayne Marsh; "G.I. Jive," Louis Jordan and his Tympany Five; "Goodbye Sue," Perry Como; "Home in San Antone," Bob Wills and his Texas Playboys; "Hot Time in the Town of Berlin," Bing Crosby; "I'll Be Home for Christmas," Bing Crosby; "I've Had This Feeling Before," Johnny Long and his Orchestra; "Johnny Zero," The Song Spinners; "The Prodigal Son," Roy Acuff; "Rainbow Rhapsody," Glenn Miller and his Orchestra; "Rusty Dusty Blues," Count Basie and his Orchestra with Jimmy Rushing; "That Ain't Right," The King Cole Trio; "Travelin' Light," Billie Holiday; "Velvet Moon," Harry James and his Orchestra.

18 Jan. The Whitney Museum of Art announces it will consolidate with the Museum of Modern Art.

7 Feb. John Cage performs compositions at the Museum of Modern Art in New York, including *First Construction* and *Amores.*

14 Mar. Aaron Copland's *Fanfare for the Common Man* debuts with the Cincinnati Symphony Orchestra, conducted by Eugene Goossens.

30 Mar. *Oklahoma!* opens in New York.

16 Apr. The Book-of-the-Month Club reveals it has been pressured by the *Daily Worker* to suppress publication of an English translation of Mark Aldanov's anti-Soviet novel *The Fifth Seal.*

5 May Howard Walls, the curator for the Library of Congress's new film collection, announces plans to restore five thousand pictures made between 1897 and 1917.

5 June Noel Coward's *Blithe Spirit* closes in New York after 650 performances.

19 Sept. Decca Records reaches an agreement with the American Federation of Musicians, becoming the only record label currently recording.

20 Oct. The Juilliard School of Music announces Benny Goodman will conduct a five-week clarinet course in popular and classical music.

4 Nov. Shostakovich's Eighth Symphony is given a world premiere in Moscow.

9 Nov. Jackson Pollock's first solo show opens at the Art of This Century Gallery.

7 Dec. *Carmen Jones,* a musical comedy by Oscar Hammerstein II, based on Georges Bizet's *Carmen,* opens in New York with an all-black cast.

9 Dec. Frank Sinatra is declared 4-F, unable to fight in World War II because of a punctured eardrum.

1944

Movies

Double Indemnity, directed by Billy Wilder; *The Fighting Seabees,* starring John Wayne ; *Gaslight,* starring Ingrid Bergman; *Going My Way,* starring Bing Crosby; *Hail the Conquering Hero,* directed by Preston Sturges; *Henry V,* directed by and starring Laurence Olivier; *Laura,* starring Gene Tierney and Dana Andrews; *Lifeboat,* directed by Alfred Hitchcock; *Meet Me in St. Louis,* starring Judy Garland and Margaret O'Brien; *National Velvet,* starring Elizabeth Taylor; *Since You Went Away,* starring Claudette Colbert and Joseph Cotten; *Thirty Seconds Over Tokyo,* starring Van Johnson, screenplay by Dalton Trumbo; *To Have and Have Not,* starring Humphrey Bogart and Lauren Bacall; *Up In Arms,* starring Danny Kaye; *Wilson,* starring Alexander Knox.

Fiction	Saul Bellow, *Dangling Man;* Kay Boyle, *Avalanche;* Harry Brown, *A Walk in the Sun;* Erskine Caldwell, *Tragic Ground;* A. J. Cronin, *The Green Years;* Isak Dinesen, *Winter Tales;* Howard Fast, *Freedom Road;* John Hersey, *A Bell for Adano;* Charles Jackson, *The Lost Weekend;* D. H. Lawrence, *The First Lady Chatterley;* Somerset Maugham, *The Razor's Edge;* Anaïs Nin, *Under a Glass Bell;* Katherine Anne Porter, *The Leaning Tower and Other Stories;* Jean Stafford, *Boston Adventure;* Lillian Smith, *Strange Fruit.*
Popular Songs	"Ac-cent-tchu-ate the Positive," The Andrews Sisters; "Be-bop," Dizzy Gillespie; "Blues in My Mind," Roy Acuff; "Each Minute Seems a Million Years," Eddy Arnold; "G.I. Blues," Floyd Tillman; "Gonna Build a Big Fence Around Texas," Gene Autry; "Good, Good, Good," Xavier Cougat and his Orchestra; "Groovin' High," Dizzy Gillespie; "I Can't See For Lookin'," The King Cole Trio; "I'm Making Believe," Ella Fitzgerald; "Just a Prayer Away," Bing Crosby; "Little Brown Book," Duke Ellington and his Orchestra; "Sentimental Journey," Les Brown and his Orchestra with Doris Day; "Solo Flight," Benny Goodman and his Orchestra; "That Ole Devil Called Love," Billie Holiday; "You Always Hurt the One You Love," The Mills Brothers.
1 Feb.	Piet Mondrian dies in New York.
20 Mar.	The Boston Board of Retail Merchants bans the sale of Lillian Smith's novel *Strange Fruit.*
2 Apr.	Shostakovich's Symphony no. 8 is played by the U.S. Philharmonic in Carnegie Hall.
10 Apr.	*The First Lady Chatterley* by D. H. Lawrence is published in New York.
2 May	The Museum of Modern Art purchases its first works by Jackson Pollock (*The She-Wolf*) and Robert Motherwell (*Pancho Villa Dead and Alive*).
14 May	*Strange Fruit* is banned from the mails by the United States Postal Service.
29 May	New York magistrate Charles G. Kentgen declares Lawrence's *The First Lady Chatterley* obscene and orders Dial Press to trial.
17 June	*Arsenic and Old Lace* closes on Broadway after 1,444 performances.
7 Aug.	The Justice Department files suit ordering motion-picture producers to end theater ownership and restore competition.
1 Sept.	Helsinki reports the original manuscripts of Jean Sibelius destroyed in an Allied bombing of Leipzig.
1 Nov.	Justices Nathan D. Perman and George DeLucca rule that *The First Lady Chatterley* is not obscene.
15 Dec.	Glenn Miller dies in a plane crash, traveling from London to Paris.
16 Dec.	Boston police arrest a bookseller for selling Erskine Caldwell's *Tragic Ground.*
28 Dec.	Judge Elijah Adlow rules in Boston that *Tragic Ground* is not obscene.

1945

Movies *Anchors Aweigh,* starring Frank Sinatra and Gene Kelly; *The Bells of St. Mary's,* starring Bing Crosby and Ingrid Bergman; *The Lost Weekend,* starring Ray Milland and Jane Wyman; *Mildred Pierce,* starring Joan Crawford; *Objective Burma,* starring Errol Flynn; *The Picture of Dorian Gray,* directed by Albert Lewin; *Spellbound,* starring Gregory Peck and Ingrid Bergman; *The Story of G.I. Joe,* starring Burgess Meredith; *They Were Expendable,* directed by John Ford and starring John Wayne; *A Tree Grows in Brooklyn,* directed by Elia Kazan; *The Woman in the Window,* directed by Fritz Lang.

Fiction Nancy Bruff, *The Manatee;* T. B. Costain, *The Black Rose;* F. Scott Fitzgerald, *The Crack Up* (published posthumously, edited by Edmund Wilson); Chester Himes, *If He Hollers Let Him Go;* Sinclair Lewis, *Cass Timberlane;* John P. Marquand, *Repent in Haste;* George Orwell, *Animal Farm;* John Steinbeck, *Cannery Row;* Irving Stone, *The Immortal Wife;* James Ramsey Ullman, *The White Tower;* Jessamyn West, *The Friendly Persuasion;* Richard Wright, *Black Boy.*

Popular Songs "All That Glitters Is Not Gold," Dinah Shore; "Beulah's Boogie," Lionel Hampton and his Orchestra; "Choo Choo Ch'Boogie," Louis Jordan and his Tympany Five; "Gotta Be This or That," Benny Goodman and his Orchestra; "The Gypsy," The Ink Spots; "Her Bathing Suit Never Got Wet," The Andrews Sisters; "Homesick – That's All," Frank Sinatra; "I Think I'll Go Home and Cry," Roy Acuff; "I'll Be Back," Gene Autry; "I'm Tired," Private Cecil Grant; "Let It Snow! Let It Snow! Let It Snow!" Vaughn Monroe and his Orchestra; "Till the End of Time," Perry Como; "Waitin' for the Train to Come In," Peggy Lee.

28 Mar. W. H. Auden wins the American Academy of Arts and Letters poetry prize.

31 Mar. Tennessee Williams's *The Glass Menagerie* opens on Broadway.

8 Apr. The U.S. Senate's Small Business Committee begins an investigation of the motion picture studios' monopoly that forces independents out of business.

5 May Ezra Pound is arrested by U.S. armed forces in Genoa on charges that he made treasonous radio broadcasts from Italy during the war.

21 May Humphrey Bogart and Lauren Bacall marry in Mansfield, Ohio.

30 Oct. Martha Graham's modern dance, *Appalachian Spring,* debuts in Washington, D.C., with music composed by Aaron Copland.

11 Nov. Metropolitan Museum of Art director William C. Osborn announces plans for a $10-million construction program.

26 Dec. Bernard Shaw proposes a new phonetic alphabet with only one sign for each sound in the English language.

1946

Movies *Anna and the King of Siam,* starring Irene Dunn and Rex Harrison; *The Best Years of Our Lives,* directed by William Wyler; *The Big Sleep,* starring Humphrey Bogart and Lauren Bacall; *The Blue Dahlia,* starring Alan Ladd and Veronica Lake; *Brief Encounter,* directed by David Lean; *Henry V,* directed by and starring Laurence Olivier; *It's a Wonderful Life,* directed by Frank Capra, starring Jimmy Stewart; *Notorious,* directed by Alfred Hitchcock; *The Postman Always Rings Twice,* starring John Garfield and Lana Turner; *The Razor's Edge,* starring Tyrone Power; *The Stranger,* directed by Orson Welles; *To Each His Own,* starring Olivia de Havilland; *The Yearling,* starring Gregory Peck and Jane Wyman.

Fiction	Kay Boyle, *Thirty Stories;* Taylor Caldwell, *This Side of Innocence;* Daphne Du Maurier, *The King's General;* Pat Frank, *Mr. Adam;* Alfred Hays, *All Thy Conquests;* Francis Parkinson Keys, *River Road;* Carson McCullers, *The Member of the Wedding;* Erich Marie Remarque, *The Arch of Triumph;* J. D. Salinger, *The Catcher in the Rye;* Robert Penn Warren, *All the King's Men;* Eudora Welty, *Delta Wedding;* William Carlos Williams, *The Build Up;* Edmund Wilson, *Memoirs of Hecate County.*
Popular Songs	"All Alone in the World," Eddy Arnold; "Atomic Power," The Buchanan Brothers; "The Christmas Song," Nat King Cole; "Coax Me a Little Bit," The Andrews Sisters; "The Frim Fram Sauce," Ella Fitzgerald and Louis Armstrong; "A Hundred and Sixty Acres," Bing Crosby and The Andrews Sisters; "Kentucky Waltz," Bill Monroe; "Laughing on the Outside," Dinah Shore; "Long Time Gone," Tex Ritter; "No One to Cry To," The Sons of the Pioneers; "One-Z Two-Z I Love You-Z," Phil Harris and his Orchestra; "Rainbow at Midnight," Ernest Tubb; "Route 66!" The King Cole Trio; "Something Old, Something New," Frank Sinatra; "Sonata," Perry Como.
3 Jan.	Evelyn Waugh's *Brideshead Revisited* is published in New York.
20 Feb.	The Daughters of the American Revolution ban Eddie Condon's jazz band from Constitution Hall because of "the type of audience which would attend."
13 Mar.	Bennett Cerf agrees to include twelve Ezra Pound poems in the new edition of *An Anthology of Famous English and American Poetry* after first announcing that none would be included.
30 Mar.	A poll of the Metropolitan Opera Guild's 123,000 listeners reveals their favorite operas as *Aida, Carmen, La Traviata, Hansel and Gretel,* and *Boris Godunov.*
30 Mar.	Critic Robert Coates uses the term *Abstract Expressionism* to describe the New York modernists.
14 Apr.	The first film to have a world premiere aboard a scheduled airline flight, *So Goes My Love,* is shown on a PanAm clipper from New York to Ireland.
1 July	*Oklahoma!* breaks the record for the longest run by a musical with its 1,405th performance.
26 Aug.	George Orwell's *Animal Farm* is published and becomes a Book-of-the-Month Club selection.
31 Aug.	*The New Yorker* devotes an entire issue to John Hersey's account of Hiroshima after the atomic bomb.
9 Oct.	*The Iceman Cometh,* Eugene O'Neill's first production in twelve years, opens in New York.
11 Dec.	Hank Williams cuts his first single, "Calling You," b/w "Never Again (Will I Knock on Your Door)" for the New York–based independent label, Sterling.
13 Dec.	Walt Disney's *Song of the South* is called "an insult to the Negro" by the National Negro Congress.

1947

Movies   *The Bachelor and the Bobbysoxer*, starring Cary Grant and Myrna Loy; *A Double Life*, starring Ronald Colman; *The Farmer's Daughter*, starring Loretta Young; *Forever Amber*, directed by Otto Preminger, starring Linda Darnell; *Gentleman's Agreement*, directed by Elia Kazan, starring Gregory Peck; *The Ghost and Mrs. Muir*, starring Gene Tierney and Rex Harrison; *Great Expectations*, directed by David Lean; *Life With Father*, directed by Michael Curtiz; *Miracle on 34th Street*, starring Edmund Gwenn and Natalie Wood; *Monsieur Verdoux*, directed by and starring Charlie Chaplin; *The Secret Life of Walter Mitty*, starring Danny Kaye.

Fiction   Saul Bellow, *The Victim*; John Horne Burns, *The Gallery*; Erskine Caldwell, *The Sure Hand of God*; Theodore Dreiser, *The Stoic* (published posthumously); John Gunther, *Inside U.S.A*; Chester Himes, *Lonely Crusade*; Laura Hobson, *Gentleman's Agreement*; James Michener, *Tales of the South Pacific*; Kenneth Roberts, *Lydia Bailey*; Jean Stafford, *The Mountain Lion*; John Steinbeck, *The Pearl* and *The Wayward Bus*; Lionel Trilling, *The Middle of the Journey*.

Popular Songs   "Anniversary Song," Tex Beneke and the Glenn Miller Orchestra; "As Sweet As You," Art Lund; "Christmas Dreaming," Frank Sinatra; "The Dum Dot Song," Frank Sinatra; "Footprints in the Snow," Bill Monroe; "Free," Billy Eckstine; "Heartaches," Ted Weems and his Orchestra; "Here Comes Santa Claus," Gene Autry; "I Want to Cry," Dinah Washington; "I've Only Myself to Blame," Doris Day; "Mam'selle," Art Lund; "Move It On Over," Hank Williams; "Near You," The Andrews Sisters; "Open the Door, Richard," Count Basie and his Orchestra; "Peg O' My Heart," The Harmonicats; "Pianissimo," Perry Como; "Snatch It and Grab It," Julia Lee and Her Boyfriends; "Wedding Bells," Hank Williams.

24 Jan.   Sixty British masterpieces on loan from George VI go on display at the Metropolitan Museum of Art.

29 Jan.   Arthur Miller's play *All My Sons* opens in New York.

24 Apr.   Willa Cather dies at age seventy.

7 May   At Columbia University, Virgil Thomson debuts his opera based on the life of Susan B. Anthony, *The Mother of Us All*.

22 May   Poet Archibald MacLeish is inducted into the American Academy of Arts and Letters.

31 May   The Art of This Century Gallery closes.

5 June   Aaron Copland's Third Symphony is voted best orchestral work of the year by the New York Music Critics.

29 Sept.   *Annie Get Your Gun* is banned in Memphis because of its integrated cast.

13 Oct.   The Hollywood Ten begin appearing before the House UnAmerican Activities Committee (HUAC).

22 Oct.   *Forever Amber* opens in New York. Francis Cardinal Spellman and the Catholic Legion of Decency condemn it, but it brings in a record first-day gross of more than twenty-five thousand dollars.

3 Dec.   The Screen Directors' Guild bars Communists from holding office.

3 Dec.   Tennessee Williams's *A Streetcar Named Desire* opens on Broadway.

1948

Movies   *The Babe Ruth Story*, starring William Bendix; *A Foreign Affair*, directed by Billy Wilder, starring Marlene Dietrich; *Joan of Arc*, starring Ingrid Bergman; *Johnny Belinda*, starring Jane Wyman and Lew Ayres; *Hamlet*, starring Laurence Olivier; *Key Largo*, starring Humphrey Bogart and Lauren Bacall; *Red River*, starring John Wayne; *The Red Shoes*, directed by Michael Powell and Emeric Pressburger; *The Snake Pit*, starring Olivia de Havilland; *The Treasure of the Sierra Madre*, directed by John Huston, starring Humphrey Bogart.

Fiction   Pearl Buck, *Peony*; Erskine Caldwell, *This Very Earth*; Truman Capote, *Other Voices, Other Rooms*; Willa Cather, *The Old Beauty and Others* (published posthumously); James Gould Cozzens, *Guard of Honor*; John Dos Passos, *The Grand Design*; William Faulkner, *Intruder in the Dust*; Martha Gelhorn, *Wine of Astonishment*; Zora Neale Hurston, *Seraph on the Suwanee*; Norman Mailer, *The Naked and the Dead*; Thomas Mann, *Doctor Faustus*; Carl Sandburg, *Remembrance Rock*; Irwin Shaw, *The Young Lions*; Upton Sinclair, *One Clear Call*; Elizabeth Spencer, *Fire in the Morning*; Gore Vidal, *City and the Pillar*; Thornton Wilder, *The Ides of March*.

Popular Songs   "Ah, But It Happens," Frankie Laine; "Am I Asking Too Much?," Dinah Washington; "Black Coffee," Sarah Vaughan; "Blue Christmas," Ernest Tubb; "Bouquet of Roses," Eddy Arnold; "Buttons and Bows," Dinah Shore; "Confess," Patti Page; "The Deck of Cards," Tex Ritter; "Faraway Places," Bing Crosby and the Ken Darby Choir; "Gloria," The Mills Brothers; "Honky Tonkin'," Hank Williams; "The Huckle Buck," Frank Sinatra; "Mañana," Peggy Lee; "Mansion on the Hill," Hank Williams; "Oklahoma Waltz," Patti Page; "The Pretty Mama Blues," Ivory Joe Hunter.

7 Jan.   Ring Lardner, Jr., sues 20th Century–Fox for $1.4 million and Edward Dmytryk sues RKO Radio for $1.8 million because they were dismissed after their convictions for contempt of Congress.

11 Mar.   Zelda Fitzgerald, widow of F. Scott Fitzgerald, and eight others die in a hospital fire in Asheville, North Carolina.

27 Mar.   Following nearly a year's imprisonment on a narcotics charge, blues singer Billie Holiday performs at New York's Carnegie Hall.

28 Apr.   Igor Stravinsky conducts the first performance of his ballet *Orpheus* in New York.

29 May   *Oklahoma!* closes on Broadway after a record 2,246 performances and a $7-million gross.

4 Aug.   New York's Metropolitan Opera cancels the 1948–1949 season after three of twelve unions representing the employees refuse to accept contracts renewing the previous year's terms.

7 Aug.   Hank Williams joins the country-music radio program *Louisiana Hayride*.

23 Aug.   Unions accept renewal and the Metropolitan Opera season is reinstated.

6 Oct.   The Museum of Modern Art purchases its first work by Willem de Kooning (*Painting*).

25 Oct.   The Supreme Court upholds a New York obscenity ban on Edmund Wilson's *Memoirs of Hecate County*.

30 Oct.   RKO Studios agrees to separate its film production and distribution from its theater holdings, in compliance with a Justice Department antitrust suit.

4 Nov.	T. S. Eliot is awarded the Nobel Prize for literature.
29 Nov.	The Metropolitan Opera season opens with Verdi's *Otello*. It is the first time a Met production is shown on television.
30 Dec.	*Kiss Me Kate*, with songs by Cole Porter, opens in New York.

1949

Movies *Adam's Rib*, starring Spencer Tracy and Katharine Hepburn; *All the King's Men*, starring Broderick Crawford; *Battleground*, starring Van Johnson; *The Champion*, starring Kirk Douglas; *The Heiress*, starring Olivia De Havilland and Montgomery Clift; *In the Good Old Summertime*, starring Judy Garland and Van Johnson; *Letter to Three Wives*, directed by Joseph L. Mankiewicz; *Madame Bovary*, starring James Mason and Jennifer Jones; *Portrait of Jenny*, directed by William Dieterle, starring Joseph Cotten and Jennifer Jones; *Samson and Delilah*, directed by Cecil B. DeMille; *Sands of Iwo Jima*, starring John Wayne; *She Wore a Yellow Ribbon*, directed by John Huston, starring John Wayne; *White Heat*, starring James Cagney.

Fiction Nelson Algren, *The Man With the Golden Arm*; Paul Bowles, *The Sheltering Sky*; Pearl Buck, *Kinfolk*; Truman Capote, *A Tree of Night and Other Stories*; William Faulkner, *Knight's Gambit*; John Hawkes, *The Cannibal*; Shirley Jackson, *The Lottery*; Sinclair Lewis, *The God-Seeker*; Robert Lowry, *The Wolf That Fed Us*; John P. Marquand, *The Point of No Return*; John O'Hara, *A Rage to Live*; Harold Robbins, *The Dream Merchants*; Upton Sinclair, *Oh Shepherd, Speak!*; Eudora Welty, *The Golden Apples*.

Popular Songs "Baby, It's Cold Outside," Dinah Shore and Buddy Clark; "Bali Ha'i," Perry Como; "The Blossoms on the Bough," The Andrews Sisters; "Bluebird on Your Windowsill," Doris Day; "Boogie Chillin'," John Lee Hooker; "Cabaret," Rosemary Clooney; "Careless Hands," Mel Torme; "A Dreamer's Holiday," Perry Como; "Happy Talk," Juanita Hall; "He Calls Me Crazy," Billie Holiday; "I'm So Lonesome I Could Cry," Hank Williams; "Land of Love," Nat King Cole; "A Marshmallow World," Bing Crosby; "Sittin' By the Window," Vic Damone; "Smokey Mountain Boogie," Tennessee Ernie Ford; "Some Enchanted Evening," Ezio Pinza; "Who Do You Know in Heaven?" The Ink Spots; "A Wonderful Guy," Mary Martin.

11 Jan.	In New York City John Cage premieres his *Sonatas and Interludes*, performed by Maro Ajemian.
22 Jan.	In San Francisco Billie Holiday is arrested for possession of opium; she will later be acquitted of the charges.
10 Feb.	Arthur Miller's *Death of a Salesman*, directed by Elia Kazan, opens on Broadway.
19 Feb.	Ezra Pound receives the Bollingen Prize for the *Pisan Cantos*.
25 Apr.	Jean-Paul Sartre's *Nausea* is published by New Directions Press.
28 Apr.	Leonard Bernstein wins the Boston Symphony Orchestra Merit Award for his *Age of Innocence*.
5 May	Thomas Mann is given the Award of Merit Medal of the American Academy of Arts and Letters.

23 May   The Hollywood Ten, dismissed for refusing to tell the House Un-American Activities Committee whether or not they were Communists, file suit against Hollywood producers.

4 June   Hank Williams's "Lovesick Blues" hits number one on the hillbilly chart of *Billboard* magazine.

11 June   Hank Williams joins the country-music radio program *Grand Ole Opry*.

9 Aug.   *Life* magazine asks the question, "Jackson Pollock: Is He the Greatest Living Painter in the United States?"

19 Aug.   The Library of Congress discontinues all prizes for art, music, and literature on the recommendation of Congress following Ezra Pound's winning of Bollingen Prize.

16 Nov.   U.S. academics recommend twenty American literary works for a UNESCO publication of the world's great classics.

OVERVIEW

Shaken. The United States entered the 1940s a shaken nation. The Depression years had been difficult nationwide. Poverty and unemployment had led to labor strife and the rise of socialist and communist sentiment, and to questions about the overall structure of American society. As a result many artists had become socially aware and active. Artists and writers of the 1930s were stark and realistic, focused on the common man. Social justice at home was their primary concern, but they also kept a cautious eye on Europe, where fascism was on the rise and war had broken out as Germany expanded. These artistic concerns continued into the 1940s, but Americans' creative endeavors also began to reflect a shift in American society, as World War II stimulated the economy and brought the nation out of the Depression. Prosperity replaced poverty. The film industry was presenting a darker view of the world, not simply providing light entertainment. American painters had discovered abstraction, and America's writers had left realistic, community concerns for introspection and an examination of form. American life began to stratify into a society of rigid, materialistic conformity and an underclass. During the 1940s the majority of American artists pursued individual concerns rather than social movements or popular entertainment.

War. World War II divided and defined the decade. The war brought about discernible changes in American films, art, music, fiction, and drama. Social movements and concern for the working class ended to some extent on 7 December 1941, with the bombing of Pearl Harbor. For the next three and a half years the nation concentrated on the war effort. The emphasis was on unity to defeat fascism and Nazism. America seemed to live two lives. One was overseas, where events were followed closely. The other was at home trying to live a "normal" life. Once fascism was defeated, the energy of mass movements was dissipated. Social criticisms were blunted by prosperity. There was little left for which artists could campaign. The inevitable result was that the artist turned inward. Art seemed less ambitious and more introspective. The universal was no longer found in the nation or group, but in the individual. Politics solidified this interest in the self by discouraging activity of the Left. The Cold War began and essentially silenced art that argued

for social causes. Communism was literally outlawed, and most members of the Left, disillusioned by the Soviet Union, abandoned radicalism for an exploration of form and self.

Modernism. The movement inward was best characterized by the term *modernism*. The ideas of modernism originated in Europe. While modernism was introduced in the United States, it took some time taking hold there. While American artists were struggling financially and socially through the 1930s, new forms of expression were rising in Europe. Modernism infused all of the American arts during the 1940s. The works of Franz Kafka and James Joyce and their implications seemed finally to interest American writers. American painters, influenced by European exiles, began seriously exploring abstract art in the form of Cubism, Surrealism, and finally Expressionism. They, more than any other creative people in the decade, turned away from political themes to individual expression. Existentialism arrived and influenced writers such as Saul Bellow. Music moved away from big bands toward the individual singer interpreting a song or a jazz instrumentalist discovering new variations on an old riff or chord structure. Mass thought seemed exhausted, as though the only hope for the individual lay in his individuality, which, according to the existentialists, was also the center of his loneliness and anxiety. Bellow's *Dangling Man* may be the most appropriate title to sum up postwar artists and mankind.

Hollywood Stumbles. In many respects the 1940s could be seen as Hollywood's finest moment. The most public and influential of art forms took to the fight against fascism with unique zeal both literally, in the number of Hollywood stars that enlisted and the industry's cooperation with the government, and figuratively, in the number of war films to entertain the audiences at home. Despite Hollywood's support of the war, its abuses were attacked when the war ended. The Justice Department challenged the industry's monopoly of movie distribution. Anticommunists attacked Hollywood as full of subversive elements. The Hollywood Ten went to prison for defying Congress. Television arrived, and for the first time Hollywood had competition for the attention of the public. In form, the film industry took on the dark tone of film noir, a new form unique to American cinema. Directors such as Billy Wilder, John Huston, and Fritz Lang began to reveal a violent, dark underside to American urban life. By decade's end noir was the dominant form in a shrinking Hollywood. Film attendance dropped by about 25 percent from a midwar high and the industry blacklisted hundreds of writers, actors, and technicians.

The New York School. While the film industry suffered from a postwar lethargy, American art flourished as never before. New York City was the center of it all, and by decade's end it had unseated Paris as the art capital of the world. Drawn together in the 1930s by the Federal Arts Project and tutored by the best minds of Europe, who were exiled by the war, the young painters of New York flourished. Mark Rothko, Jackson Pollock, William Baziotes, Arshile Gorky, Barnett Newman, Robert Motherwell, and Ad Reinhardt were just some of the painters who forged America's first international movement in the arts. Abstract Expressionism, as the movement came to be called, influenced sculpture and photography as well. The ideas of the New York School were remarkably free of the influence of the war. The painters eschewed politics for paint and dived inward into their own subconscious minds. More than any other artists, these painters embraced the modernism of Europe and made it their own. With Pollock becoming internationally famous for his "drip" paintings, Abstract Expressionism was becoming the dominant form for the next decade.

New Voices. Fiction in the 1940s was changing. Ernest Hemingway, the most influential American writer of his time, remained almost silent after 1940. William Faulkner's reputation flowered overseas, but he fell out of print by middecade. He won a Nobel Prize in 1949 as his reputation finally began to grow at home. The Lost Generation of the 1920s had grown old and had not yet been replaced, but the realists — Sinclair Lewis, Upton Sinclair, and John Dos Passos — continued to produce. Southern writers flourished. Eudora Welty, Carson McCullers, Tennessee Williams, and Robert Penn Warren were dominant voices of the decade, still working in a realistic style. Modernism arrived in the imported forms of Kafka, Albert Camus, and Thomas Mann. These Europeans would exert more influence on the young novelists of the 1940s than Americans. Bellow was an important modernist voice, and by the end of the decade the young John Hawkes had mastered the new forms. Meanwhile war narratives began to emerge. Norman Mailer, James Gould Cozzens, John Horne Burns, Irwin Shaw, and Robert Lowry forged strong statements about war

and society from their own experiences. When the decade ended, fiction had made the move forward toward modernism and voices such as Truman Capote, Paul Bowles, and Gore Vidal were setting the stage for the rich spectacle that would follow in the 1950s.

Smaller Stage. Theater became smaller in the 1940s. While Broadway musicals such as *Oklahoma!, South Pacific,* and *Brigadoon* were playing spectacularly, the stage drama moved sluggishly forward. Little of the work written and produced would enter the canon of American classics. Lillian Hellman, among the most successful playwrights of the 1930s, carried over into the 1940s. William Saroyan, Maxwell Anderson, Elmer Rice, and Thornton Wilder were other playwrights of a previous generation who continued to produce during the decade. But like other forms, the stage, so dominated by social movements in the 1930s, moved away from the theater of the proletariat. It did not, however, embrace the innovations of modernism. While concerning itself with some of modernism's approaches to the individual, the stage remained stuck in a realistic approach. Aside from Wilder, there was little technical innovation. Plays were interested in families, postwar prosperity, private disillusionment, and frustration. The content, on the whole, was negative after the war, a kind of theater of pessimism. Commercially, Broadway downsized and became more conservative. New plays were often tried in the new Off-Broadway venues that opened in response to Broadway's increasing economic crunch. By 1950 only two new voices had truly emerged: Tennessee Williams and Arthur Miller.

Blacks. The 1940s saw nascent movements in civil rights. Blacks fought in the war but remained segregated. Hollywood's idea of the "Negro" was Hattie McDaniel's patient maternalism in *Gone With the Wind,* or the ridiculous, primitive comedic figure of Stepin Fetchit. American black artists fought such images. With the publication of Richard Wright's *Native Son* in 1940, black writers made a leap forward. Wright's work ranked with his white contemporaries' in power and vision. A statement had been made, an angry one. Meanwhile, black musicians were highly successful on the swing-jazz circuit. Duke Ellington was chosen favorite musician in one poll. Beneath the mainstream a young man named Charlie Parker was redefining all jazz music, while Billie Holiday and Sarah Vaughan were popular singing stars. Black art discovered a tradition with the publication of James A. Porter's *Modern Negro Art* in 1943. Still, actual progress was hardly noticeable. Wright fled for more racially tolerant France in 1947 and began to explore international issues of racial prejudice.

TOPICS IN THE NEWS

AMERICAN ART ARRIVES

New Ideas. American artists were wrestling with abstraction when the 1940s opened. Cubism and Surrealism had been at the forefront of European art for over two decades but had not really arrived in the United States. Through the 1930s social realism and regionalism dominated the American art scene. This naturalist painting was the style of Thomas Hart Benton, Grant Wood, and John Stuart Curry. Edward Hopper had made some gestures toward abstraction, and Stuart Davis was a crossover artist creating work somewhere between figure painting and abstraction. The focus of their work was depiction of place and people, a kind of folkloric representation of American life, the texture and the color of its objects. Though Georgia O'Keeffe and Arthur Dove had worked abstractly in their own style through the 1920s, the American painters as a whole were looking backward. Modernism had not really arrived.

Art in Exile. A small number of American painters had begun to show an interest in abstract art in the 1930s. An American Abstract Artists Association had developed in New York. The idea was to make New York the center of abstract art. With the help of fascism in Europe, the association succeeded. As events in Europe came to a head, artists began leaving Europe for New York, bringing their ideas with them. Piet Mondrian, the most influential of these artists in exile, arrived in 1940. Hans Hofmann had come earlier. In 1941 the father of Surrealism, French poet and critic André Breton, arrived along with André Masson. Other artists in exile included Marc Chagall, Max Ernst, Salvador Dalí, and Robert Matta. They brought with them the experimental styles of Surrealism, Cubism, and Expressionism. They began teaching, attracting young American painters to their ideas. They began to exhibit their work in the new galleries that were opening in New York to accommodate them. The Museum of Non-Objective Painting had opened in 1939. It would eventually take the name of its founder, Solomon Guggenheim. In January 1942, Mondrian, age sixty-nine, held his first and only solo exhibition at the Valentine Dudensing Gallery. An Artists in Exile exhibit opened at the Pierre Matisse Gallery in March of that year, and in

Peggy Guggenheim and Jackson Pollock at her home in front of a mural he painted for her, 1946

October 1942 Peggy Guggenheim opened the Art of This Century Gallery on West 57th Street.

Federal Arts Project. The stage was set in New York because of the Federal Arts Project, a division of the New Deal's Works Projects Administration (WPA) system designed to employ artists and provide painting and sculpture for public buildings. Like any other workers affected by the Depression, artists were in need of federal support. The art market had bottomed out in the 1930s. The WPA Federal Arts Project was centered in New York. Thus, in the years before the Europeans flocked to

ROTHKO AND GOTTLIEB ISSUE A MANIFESTO

On 6 June 1943 critic Edward Alden Jewell singled out Mark Rothko's *The Syrian Bull* and Adolph Gottlieb's *Rape of Persephone* in a review of the Federation of Modern Painters and Sculptors third annual exhibition. Jewell confessed "befuddlement" and wrote that "this department" could not "shed the slightest enlightenment" on either work. Rothko and Gottlieb responded in a letter which Jewell published in his column for Sunday, 13 June. The letter, not intended to be a defense, was, however, a kind of manifesto stating the thinking behind the nascent and still unnamed Abstract Expressionist movement. They listed five "aesthetic beliefs" that they were trying to demonstrate in their work:

1. To us art is an adventure into an unknown world, which can be explored only by those willing to take the risks.

2. This world of the imagination is fancy-free and violently opposed to common sense.

3. It is our function as artists to make the spectator see the world our way — not his way.

4. We favor the simple expression of the complex thought. We are for the large shape because it has the impact of the unequivocal. We wish to reassert the picture plane. We are for flat forms because they destroy illusion and reveal truth.

5. It is a widely accepted notion among painters that it does not matter what one paints as long as it is well painted. This is the essence of academicism. There is no such thing as good painting about nothing. We assert that the subject is crucial and only that subject-matter is valid which is tragic and timeless. That is why we profess spiritual kinship with primitive and archaic art.

Jewell remained unenlightened, but a public controversy ensued, thus explaining the theory and providing publicity for the new painters.

Sources: James E. B. Breslin, *Mark Rothko* (Chicago: University of Chicago Press, 1993);

Edward Alden Jewell, "'Globalism' Pops into View," *New York Times*, 13 June 1943, IV: 9.

Piet Mondrian (with glasses) at the opening of the Masters of Abstract Art Exhibit, 1 April 1942

Mark Rothko, Ad Reinhardt, and David Smith. They would subsequently emerge as the New York School, the first true American art movement, the movement whose distinctive Abstract Expressionism would finally break America's dependence on Europe for ideas and inspiration. As a whole the WPA provided not only economic support, but also a kind of unity and shared experience. Artists were asked to submit an oil painting every four to eight weeks. The paintings were then donated to public buildings. The artists were allowed to work at home and were generally free to follow their own ideas. Rothko would later refer to the project as a "Godsend to so many artists who needed help." Pollock was "grateful to the WPA for keeping me alive during the thirties." The project not only freed artists from economic concerns but also created a community that encouraged artists, provided new ideas for them, and allowed them opportunities for formal training and study. The Americans were ready when the exiled Europeans began arriving.

Art of This Century. The year 1942 was crucial in the drive toward what would become known as Abstract Expressionism. Early in the year Mondrian's exhibit appeared. John Graham showed a combined exhibit of European and American painters at McMillen, Inc. In February Rothko had his first solo exhibition at the Artists' Gallery. The Artists in Exile exhibit opened a few weeks later and Breton's *First Papers of Surrealism* appeared in the fall. Also that fall Peggy Guggenheim, heiress and

the city, American artists had come. In 1937 approximately twenty-one hundred artists were in New York participating in the project and two thousand more were on a waiting list. Among those working for the WPA were William Baziotes, Willem de Kooning, Arshile Gorky, Philip Guston, Lee Krasner, Jackson Pollock,

Mark Rothko and Clyfford Still, 1946

wife of surrealist Max Ernst, opened the Art of This Century Gallery. Her gallery, which showed her private collection of modernist art, also provided exhibition space for contemporary New York painters. The gallery's collection impacted the New York scene and became a gathering place for artists. Guggenheim also encouraged the young American artists, giving the thirty-one-year-old Pollock a solo exhibition in November of 1943, thirty-two-year-old William Baziotes a showing in October of 1944, and twenty-nine-year-old Robert Motherwell an exhibition just weeks after that of Baziotes. She also exhibited influential European Hans Hofmann for the first time in New York. Other galleries were exhibiting the "new" art, but none so forcefully as Guggenheim's Art of This Century Gallery. Such galleries were instrumental in attracting attention to the artistic breakthrough of the New York School artists: Abstract Expressionism.

Abstract Expressionism. The tag Abstract Expressionism is not entirely comprehensive. The art it describes is neither exclusively abstract nor always expressive. But Abstract Expressionism, a term coined by critic Robert Coates in a *New Yorker* review in March 1946, has come to represent the group of painters in New York during the 1940s. To some extent the Abstract Expressionists were successful because of the praise heaped on them by art critics such as Coates, Clement Greenburg, and Harold Rosenberg. Not all critics, however, championed the modernists. In 1943 Edward Alden Jewell, a critic for the *The New York Times,* expressed "befuddlement" over paintings by Rothko and Adolph Gottlieb. Mark Rothko and Gottlieb responded in a letter to the

Times that became something of a manifesto for the New York modernists. While not defending their work, which they felt did not need defending, the letter explained the thinking behind the style: "It is our function as artists to make the spectator see the world our way — not his way." By 1946 they were succeeding. The Museum of Modern Art purchased its first works by Pollock and Motherwell that year. Pollock had succeeded enough to buy a house on Long Island, where he moved with his wife, painter Lee Krasner, in 1945. The Art of This Century Gallery closed in 1947, but the Abstract Expressionists were now well entrenched, though not yet widely popular or accepted.

Abstract Expressionist Styles. Abstract Expressionism had developed into three areas by 1948. "Action" painting described the work of Pollock, de Kooning, and Franz Kline. Rothko, Barnett Newman, and Clyfford Still were being referred to as "Color-Field" painters. Artists such as Gottlieb, Motherwell, and Philip Guston were not easily categorized but belonged to the movement as a whole. All shared certain traits. They were generally not figurative painters. They were artists who looked inward, influenced by modern ideas regarding psychology, myth, and dreams. The exploration of the unconscious through an "automatism" of expression became one method of working. Their work, considering the social movements of the 1930s and the national unity of the war years, was remarkably interior and individual, as Abstract Expressionists insisted on exploring their own psyches. They were essentially romantic, pursuing the lonely struggle of the studio instead of trying to improve society. For the first time in American art history, American artists claimed for themselves the social and political independence often demanded by European artists. New York in the 1940s became the center of the art world and would remain so for at least another two decades.

Action Painting. In the fall of 1947 Pollock, who had established himself as a successful painter, began the work that would make him an international star. In the barn at his Long Island home he began to lay huge swatches of canvas on the floor and proceeded to pour paint on them in a controlled way. Pollock had always been interested in myth and the unconscious. Like other modern painters he looked inward, exploring his mind through spontaneous application of paint. But when he began working on his drip paintings, he climbed inside the work. Their huge scale was meant to dominate the viewer, to envelop him. Pollock poured paint off a brush in controlled arcs. It was physical and dynamic work. He approached the canvas from all sides like a Native American sand painter of the Southwest. Pollock and the painting became one, he would say. Critic Harold Rosenberg would later coin the phrase *action painting* as a means of describing Pollock's most original work. Action painting became a general term for describing any artist who physically attacked the canvas, such as de Kooning.

Jacob Lawrence with panel 44 of his *Migration* series, 1941

De Kooning was a quiet member of the New York School through the 1940s but was as influential as any of them. His series of Woman paintings have become world famous as well as repellent and controversial to many. He was and is an aggressive painter interested in the gesture with the brush. The action painters were often only interested in paint. They disregarded lines and figures entirely. In work such as *Lavender Mist* (no. 1, 1950) Pollock needed no image beneath his beautiful arcs of paint. The paint was both the subject and the content of the work. The canvas was not divided spatially by lines and edges as in the Cubists' work. He offered no references in real figures as with the Surrealists. The surface of the painting was uniform and even bled off of the canvas, as if never ending. Pollock became internationally famous after *Life* magazine published a feature article on him in 1949.

Color-Field Painting. Seemingly opposite of Pollock were the color-field painters led by Mark Rothko, Ad Reinhardt, and Barnett Newman. Unlike the physical action of the action painter, color field appears as a quiet, contemplative work. The line, traditionally a major tool of the artist, disappears in a color-field work. Huge washes of color bleed together creating a flat, barely divided surface. The attempt is to convey meaning and feeling through unified fields of color. As in action painting, figures often disappear entirely, leaving bands of color interacting. They are romantic paintings, often simply beautiful. Rothko felt that figure painting was simply inadequate to the human experience in the aftermath of World War II. Rothko had always trusted silence, and the still contemplation of his fields of color were meant to impact emotionally as well as morally. Newman aimed for a similar feeling, though his fields of color were often

divided by a single strip of tape, pulled up after the painting was completed, appearing as a zip in the work. The zip implied creation for Newman, something forming in a void, attempting to organize the field of color. The zip did not so much divide the canvas as unify it. Like the action painters, the color-field painters often worked on a huge scale. The sheer impracticality of the work suggested the romantic impulse behind it. As the 1940s came to a close, the abstract expressionists as a group had made their collective statement to the world, laying the ground for a generation to follow in the 1950s and the postmodernism of the 1960s. The group was breaking into its component parts as each painter — de Kooning, Rothko, Pollock, Newman, Gottlieb, Reinhardt, Still, and Motherwell — developed in individual ways. America had finally achieved its own art.

Blacks. In 1943 *Modern Negro Art* by James A. Porter appeared to widespread acclaim. The book was the most comprehensive historical and contemporary survey of the art of African Americans published at that time. While the 1940s are known as the decade when Abstract Expressionism developed in New York, it should also be known as the time when black artists began to flourish. Black painters had been working for years, unbeknownst to most critics. The Harmon Foundation, founded in 1926 to support black art, helped painters develop. When the WPA arrived in New York in the 1930s, it supported black artists just as it had the seminal artists of the New York School. The Harlem Renaissance, a cultural revolution of writing, music, and art, had flourished quietly through the 1920s and 1930s. Porter's book gave voice and history to the black artist of the 1940s. A painter himself, Porter and other artists exhibited in New York, Chicago, and Washington, D.C. After the war, opportunities arose for travel and study of art. The most prominent black painters of the 1940s include Jacob Lawrence, Hale Woodruff, Alma Thomas, Palmer Hayden, Romare Bearden, William Johnson, Beauford Delaney, and Lois Jones. Sculptors included William Edmondson, Richmond Barthe, and Elizabeth Catlett. Though depiction of black life in a realist or social realist style was the dominant form of painting, some artists like Bearden and Delaney experimented with abstraction. Another popular style was the "consciously naive" style which showed a flat, two-dimensional, purposefully folkloric style of painting that depicted scenes of black life. The 1940s were a threshold period for black art, though it remained relatively ignored by art historians until the 1960s.

Jacob Lawrence. The most prominent and prolific of black artists in the 1940s was Jacob Lawrence. He was twenty-three when the decade opened, and he began his epic journey to tell the story of black Americans through his series of panel paintings. He was one of the few black painters fully taught and influenced by other black artists. His first and most famous series, *The Migration of the Negro,* consists of sixty paintings and tells the story of southern American blacks migrating north to the cities to

Robert Capa on D-Day

JAMES A. PORTER

In 1930, tired of hearing that "the American Negro has no pictorial or plastic art," James A. Porter began a journey of discovery that would culminate with *Modern Negro Art*, published in 1943. Porter was a painter and a student of art. He was also a thorough scholar, and *Modern Negro Art* is still considered an authoritative work on African-American art.

Porter discovered a rich tradition of painting, sculpture, and folk art that could be traced back to West Africa, from where most of the slaves brought to America were taken. Although two previous volumes had appeared on the subject (both by Alain LeRoy Locke of Howard University, in 1936 and 1940), neither of them had approached the depth of Porter's research. Porter's book offered critical assessment and, more important, the self-affirmation of racial identity in the art of black America. Porter's book provided a tradition that had remained relatively unknown. In a sense he gave a voice to black artists. In the 1940s and 1950s the number of fellowships awarded, exhibitions, and opportunities to travel and study painting increased markedly for African-American artists. Porter's book began the process toward acceptance in a field that was dominated by white academic critics looking to Europe for influences in American art. Slowly, but more quickly thanks to Porter, black American painters have begun entering the canon of American art.

Source: James A. Porter, *Modern Negro Art* (New York: Dryden Press, 1943).

form contemporary urban communities. The paintings were done in 1940 and 1941 and exhibited to wide acclaim at New York's Downtown Gallery. Lawrence followed up with *The Life of John Brown* (twenty-two panels), *Harlem* (thirty panels), *War* (fourteen panels), *The South* (ten panels), and *Hospital* (eleven panels). In 1947 he taught at the influential Black Mountain College in North Carolina, and by the end of the decade he was established as the foremost black painter of the twentieth century and among the most important American artists.

Sculpture. Abstract Expressionism also influenced the sculpture of the 1940s. Many of the same ideas of Abstract Expressionist painting — interior exploration, automatism of creation, the grand scale of productions, avoidance of the mere figure art, concern with myth and psychology, Surrealism — reached sculpture. David Smith was the foremost American sculptor of the era. Like many of his contemporaries, Smith was a constructivist, building sculpture out of material rather than shaping already existing blocks of stone or wood. Smith had learned welding while working at an auto plant in 1925.

He was not formally trained in art. He was influenced in his direct metal sculpting by the Surrealists of the 1930s but in the 1940s began an exploration that could only be called Abstract Expressionist. The move made him the foremost sculptor of postwar American art. Other notable sculptors include Reuben Nakia, who became known for his work with terra-cotta, expressionist explorations of classical mythology; Theodore Roszak, another geometric constructivist who moved into abstraction with natural forms. Ibram Lassaw showed the influence of Pollock's poured paintings in his lacy metal work. Joseph Cornell, a Surrealist, produced "box constructions," wooden boxes, glass fronted, filled with icons and fragments. And Isamu Noguchi, a pure abstractionist, became known after the war for his work in polished stone.

Photography. World War II, of course, was the dominant subject matter for photographers during the first half of the 1940s. The social realism of the 1930s had kept photography stark, simple, and reportorial. The war

Scene from Antony Tudor's *Pillar of Fire*, 1941

necessitated much of the same, with photography, like the film of the newsreel, acting as the public's eyes in the days before television coverage. But during and after the war, photographers moved toward abstraction, led by Robert Capa. His camera provided no simple reporting but seemed to focus on the personal and the tragic, as though the photograph were an expression of the photographer, not a shot of the external world. Another brilliant photographer of the decade was Minor White, the editor of *Aperture* magazine. White found abstraction in normal things using "straight" photography. Where Capa's blurred images suggested expression, White's clear straight photography revealed shapes and lines, like the black-and-white paintings of de Kooning. In the same vein was Aaron Siskind, whose flat-surface photographs of walls and graffiti showed an interest in surface texture, not unlike the Abstract Expressionists. Ansel Adams was photographing his grand, romantic, straight depictions of nature. He was also busy establishing the Department of Photography at the Museum of Modern Art. Another nature photographer, though more spare than Adams's grand vision, was Eliot Porter. Harry Callahan was also influenced by Adams in his simple photographs of unspoiled nature. The overall trend was to find near-abstract images in natural scenes and photograph them simply.

Sources:

H. Harvard Arnason, *History of Modern Art: Painting, Sculpture, Photography,* third edition (Englewood Cliffs, N.J.: Prentice-Hall, 1986);

James E. B. Breslin, *Mark Rothko: A Biography* (Chicago: University of Chicago Press, 1993);

Emile De Antonio and Mitch Tuchman, *Painters Painting: A Candid History of the Modern Art Scene, 1940-1970* (New York: Abbeville Press, 1984);

Anna Moszynska, *Abstract Art* (New York: Thames & Hudson, 1990);

Regenia Perry, *Free Within Ourselves* (Washington, D.C.: National Museum of American Art, Smithsonian Institution, in association with Pomegranate Artbooks, 1992);

James A. Porter, *Modern Negro Art* (New York: Dryden Press, 1943).

Martha Graham in *Cave of the Heart,* 1946

DANCE

World Leader. The 1940s were the crucial decade for American dance in this century, crystallizing the experiments of the two previous decades and establishing the dominant forms of the medium until the 1970s. It was an age of remarkable cross-fertilization. Various forms heretofore distinct were imaginatively combined: ballet was fused with modern dance; modern dance with burlesque and vaudeville. Jazz, tap, and swing music influenced everything; popular dances and steps from Harlem nightclubs, such as the jitterbug, found their way to the performance hall and the Broadway stage. The giants of modern American dance — George Balanchine, Martha Graham, Helen Tamiris, Jerome Robbins, Agnes de Mille, Fred Astaire, and Gene Kelly — established or consolidated their reputations during the decade; classic musicals such as *Oklahoma!* (1943), *Pal Joey* (1940), *Annie Get Your Gun* (1946), and *Anchors Aweigh* (1945) were scored in the 1940s. For dance it was a time of movement and sound and vigor. In the 1940s American dance perfectly reflected the ascendancy and vibrancy of America's new world leadership.

Broadway. Broadway prospered tremendously during the 1940s. During the war New York City was a magnet for off-duty servicemen, whose presence in Broadway theaters provided huge profits and whose expectations established, in a sense, the form of the stage musical for the next twenty years. In 1943 eleven million people attended Broadway shows, and they brought with them a taste for spectacle, glamour, and flash. They were not disappointed. Smash shows with patriotic themes such as Irving Berlin's *This Is the Army* (featuring a cast of three

hundred soldiers), *Winged Victory,* or *Something for the Boys,* starring Ethel Merman, usually culminated in a high-kicking number sure to boost morale. Spectacle and all-Americanism was also the key to choreographer de Mille's hits during the 1940s: *Rodeo* (1942), *Oklahoma!,* and *Fall River Legend* (1947), all of which also integrated the expressionism and innovations of modern dance into a more popular setting. A similar fusion was evident in the smashes Tamiris choreographed for Richard Rodgers and Oscar Hammerstein. One hit musical, *On The Town* (1944), established the reputation of men who would become forces in their fields in subsequent decades: choreographer Jerome Robbins, set designer Oliver Smith, and composer and conductor Leonard Bernstein. The war nurtured and promoted such talent; it helped Broadway come of age.

Ballet. The war not only invigorated Broadway, it also brought new popularity to ballet. New York enjoyed an influx of European refugees who infused ballet in America with new energy. The Ballets Russes de Monte Carlo, featuring Russian dancers, was especially popular. Ballet in New York also owed an debt to three patrons, Lucia Chase, Edward Warburg, and Lincoln Kirstein, who financed and publicized ballet and dance during the 1930s and 1940s. Chase organized the American Ballet Theater in 1939, which amassed critical support quickly, producing ballet landmarks such as Antony Tudor's *Pillar of Fire* (1941) and *Dark Elegies* (1943). Warburg and Kirstein were the chief patrons of Balanchine, a Russian choreographer brought to New York in 1933 for the express purpose of establishing an American ballet school and company. Balanchine had trained with the Imperial Ballet in Saint Petersburg before the Russian Revolution, and then, under the supervision of modern ballet master Serge Diaghilev, he spent time in Paris, integrating circus acrobatics and commercial dance styles into his choreography. Despite the help of Warburg and Kirstein, ballet was a limited financial success during the Depression, and Balanchine also worked in vaudeville, on Broadway, and in Hollywood — he even choreographed a dance for fifty elephants for the Ringling Brothers Circus (to music commissioned of Igor Stravinsky). Balanchine integrated dance movements derived from these popular idioms into ballet and gained a popular audience. In 1948, under his direction, the New York City Ballet was formed and became for many years the premier dance company in America. New York audiences during the decade were treated to numerous ballet classics, especially in the form of opera ballets: *Swan Lake, Carmen, The Marriage of Figaro, La Traviata,* and *Don Giavanni.* Balanchine achieved critical acclaim with his abstract, nonnarrative choreography for *The Four Temperaments* (1946, music commissioned of composer Paul Hindemith), *Symphony in C* (1947, to music by Maurice Ravel), and *Orpheus* (1948, music commissioned of Stravinsky). New York's daring integration of popular influences was perhaps best expressed in the New York City Ballet production of

The Four Step Brothers in *Greenwich Village*, 1944

Stravinsky's *Firebird* (1949), with choreography by Balanchine and costumes by artist Marc Chagall. Colorful, dramatic, and energetic, it was an enormously popular hit and began a great period of popularity and experimentation for New York ballet in the 1950s.

Modern Dance. The indigenous American art form of modern dance achieved worldwide acclaim in the 1940s. Unlike classical ballet, modern dance was spontaneous, expressionistic, jazzy. Spurred by innovative compositions by masters such as Doris Humphrey, Graham, and Tamiris, modern dance gained a wide audience not only in the United States, but also in Europe and Latin America. Martha Graham specialized in psychoanalytically influenced studies of classical mythology and the unconscious, such as *Cave of the Heart* (1946), *Night Journey* (1947), and *Herodiade* (1944). Her marvelous paean to the pioneer spirit, *Appalachian Spring* (1944), featuring music composed by Aaron Copland, was one of the decade's artistic highlights. Humphrey took the basis of human motion, the uncertain balance between walking and falling, and constructed a rigorous dance technique around it. With her partner Charles Weidman she founded the premier modern dance company in the world and produced acclaimed pieces such as *Inquest* (1944), *Sing Out, Sweet Land* (1944), and *Fables For Our Time* (1947), a suite of comedies based on the writings of James Thurber. Tamiris fused the expressionism of Graham and Humphrey to the flamboyance of Broadway for her triumphs, the revival of the 1927 musical *Showboat* and *Annie Get Your Gun* (both 1946). Deeply engaged in political causes, Tamiris also choreographed an unusual Elia Kazan play, attempting to popularize meat rationing, *It's Up to You* (1943), and a barnstorming revue to help reelect Franklin Roosevelt, *The People's Bandwagon* (1944), which featured performances by actor Will Geer and folksinger Woody Guthrie.

Jazz and Tap. The 1940s were also the heyday of jazz and tap dancing. Swing music and the dances it inspired, such as the jitterbug, remained as popular as when they were introduced in the 1920s and 1930s. Urban ballrooms, such as the Roseland or the Savoy in New York, could be counted on to be packed any weekend during the war. Ballroom dancing was so popular that two thousand war plants provided dancing facilities to their employees. The big swing bands that played these clubs and rooms — Count Basie, Benny Goodman, Duke Ellington — featured great tap dancers such as Jimmy Slyde, Cholly and Dolly, and Peg Leg Bates as part of their revues. The Depression-era Hollywood musical got even more popular, and some of the greatest jazz, tap, and show dancing was captured on film during the decade. Top-flight dancers, such Bill Robinson, Ann Miller, Fred Astaire, and Gene Kelly, were featured in movies such as *Holiday Inn* (1942), *Anchors Aweigh* (1945), *Easter Parade* (1948), and *On The Town* (1949). Tap and show dancing were so popular, however, that even B movies were filled with toe-tapping musical numbers, especially in the "Jivin' Jacks and Jills," series, featuring young stars like Peggy Ryan and Donald O'Conner, who challenged each other to competitive dances. The competitive challenge had been brought to the silver screen from black nightclubs such as Harlem's Cotton Club, where fiery, acrobatic tappers such as the Four Step Brothers sought to outdance each other before delighted audiences. The Four Step Brothers featured the hottest tappers in the country, such as Prince Spencer and Maceo Anderson. They played radio, made films such as *Greenwich Village* (1944), toured America to sold out houses (including the Apollo in Harlem and Radio City Music Hall), and in 1947 stormed Europe. But tap dance was not limited to nightclubs and movies. One of the most innovative dancers of the era was Paul Draper, who tapped in symphonic halls to the music of Bach, Tchaikovsky, and Brahms, often in concert with classical harmonica player Larry Adler. Draper's work exemplified the extraordinary cross-fertilization dance experienced during the decade. Jazz, show, modern, ballet — from Balanchine to the Four Step Brothers — dance stepped lively in the 1940s.

Marlon Brando, Kim Hunter, and Jessica Tandy in the 1947
Broadway production of *A Streetcar Named Desire*

Sources:

Agnes de Mille, *America Dances* (New York: Macmillan, 1980);

Rusty E. Frank, *Tap: The Greatest Tap Dance Stars and Their Stories, 1900–1955* (New York: Morrow, 1990);

Margaret Lloyd, *The Borzoi Book of Modern Dance* (New York: Knopf, 1949);

Don McDonagh, *George Balanchine* (Boston: Twayne, 1983);

Moira Shearer, *Balletmaster: A Dancer's View of George Balanchine* (London: Sidgwick & Jackson, 1986).

DRAMA DOWNSIZES

Downsizing. Theater diminished in the 1940s. Although attendance rose on Broadway during the war years, audiences sought musicals and spectacles — escape, not drama. Dramatic theater, in fact, was downsizing and entering a period of decline. In the 1930s, with the advent of the Federal Theater Project, a division of the WPA, the sheer number of plays being produced and actors being employed reached an all-time high nationwide. The volume of production led to a theater of mass consciousness that reflected the politics of the times. Social realism was the norm, as it was in fiction and painting during the decade. The proletarian plays of Clifford Odets or the socially conscious melodrama of Lillian Hellman were the dominant forms on stage. Utopian ideas about working people entering a new era were common, including an often rhapsodic, tragic, and beautiful portrayal of mass movements. These ideas began to dissi-

The single most publicized event of the American stage during the 1940s was the return of Eugene O'Neill. O'Neill had not allowed any of his new work to be produced in twelve years when *The Iceman Cometh* opened in New York on 9 October 1946. It was an international event.

O'Neill was and is still considered America's greatest playwright. *Life* magazine reported that O'Neill was the "second most widely read playwright ever" behind William Shakespeare. He had dominated the American stage in the 1920s and won the Nobel Prize in 1936, topping off a career that had earned him three Pulitzer Prizes.

O'Neill had lived quietly on the West Coast during his absence from the public eye. He wrote prolifically. *The Iceman Cometh* had actually been finished in 1939. O'Neill returned to New York in May 1946 to prepare the production. The pre-opening ticket sales topped three hundred thousand dollars. Inevitably, the hoopla drowned the drama. The play disappointed many critics. The review in *Life* was headlined "too long, too wordy, but deeply absorbing." Other reactions were similarly mixed, though all agreed the play had merit. The American theater was glad to have any work from its most prominent voice. The play was later revived with great success.

Sources: "Broadway Goes Hollywood," *Life*, 21 (28 October 1946): 109–111;

Tom Prideaux, "Eugene O'Neill," *Life*, 21 (14 October 1946): 102–116.

pate in the 1940s. Labor unions became less confrontational and more cooperative with the forces of Capital. Russia's purge trials and short-lived non-aggression pact with Hitler disillusioned idealists in America. The result in the theater was a shrinking of the scope of the stage and its themes. Postwar drama focused on families, not unions, on the individual in conflict with himself, not social forces clashing against one another. Theater became a quieter, more intimate peek into manners, lives, personal morality, and individual responsibility than it had been in the 1930s. By 1950 it had also become more pessimistic.

Optimists. Two playwrights early in the decade provided optimistic dramas for theatergoers. Thornton Wilder's *Our Town* defied the theater of the proletariat in 1938 by shedding all sense of mass struggle in favor of the individual life. Wilder was an experimenter on the stage, content to show human beings surrounded by the incomprehensible wonder of existence. His experiments in

THIS IS THE ARMY

No single cultural artifact of World War II better expresses the spirit of the war effort than did Irving Berlin's musical *This Is The Army*. Originally a 1942 Broadway hit, the show toured the country, ending in Hollywood, where it became a smash 1943 film featuring a cast that included future president Ronald Reagan. The show was so popular that it was shipped overseas, winding its way through the various war theaters to entertain the troops. Irving Berlin's lyrics reassured Americans that this was the last time they would be called to war. His show-stopping tunes, "This Is the Army, Mr. Jones" and "The Army's Made a Man out of Me," were hummed by millions.

The show had something for everyone. Billed as an "all soldier musical," it nonetheless had characters such as Eileen, the girl left behind on the home front, who stoically endured separation from her beau because "We're all in this fight together." Joe Louis, the fighter, was recruited for the film to pitch the war cause to African Americans.

The show was conceived as a wartime morale booster, and the army created a special company comprised of talented soldiers to man the musical. The Broadway contingent had to stand muster every morning for roll call and duty assignments. The touring company carried its own props, costumes, and sets around the world, pitching the play on makeshift stages from the Middle East to the Pacific. Ultimately the show gave 1,238 performances to 2,468,005 people across four continents and three oceans.

---

technique, the stripping away of the realist facade, had great influence in Europe, while *Our Town* became a classic modern play. In 1942 he premiered *The Skin of Our Teeth*, a play which merges all history into a middle-class moment in time. Wilder took the long view of life. He believed in human life on a small scale, in the "things that repeat and repeat in the lives of millions," as he later put it. William Saroyan had a similar outlook, though he was less of an innovator on stage. With *My Heart's in the Highlands* (1939), *The Time of Your Life* (1940, Pulitzer Prize winner), and *Hello, Out There* (1941), Saroyan enjoyed meteoric success as the decade opened. He, too, found the good and the personal that lurked behind the faceless masses of men. He was a brash, lyric optimist who had written himself out by 1945. His later work never approached his energy of the early 1940s.

Tennessee Williams. The great find of the decade was Tennessee Williams. He wrote arguably the two best plays of the era. The first, *The Glass Menagerie,* appeared in 1945 and opened the door to the late-1940s theater of the negative, of disillusionment. Williams was very much an American dramatist in an American idiom. His characters lived a brutal existence that belied their romantic illusions. He presented his character studies in a stark, realistic style. With the production of *A Streetcar Named Desire* in 1947, Williams established himself as a major figure in American drama. His intense, compulsive characters reveal his unique insight into and empathy with anguished and frustrated people. The same themes would appear in his later work such as *Cat on a Hot Tin Roof* (1955), another of his American classics.

Arthur Miller. The other major playwright to emerge during the 1940s was Arthur Miller, who, like Williams, contributed two works to the canon of American literature during the decade. While Williams was showing the fragility of personal illusion, Miller was exposing the illusions inherent in the American Dream. He called capitalism and the morality it imposes on people into question. *All My Sons,* produced in 1947, deals with the theme of personal responsibility in a world that values the dollar or the deal, that values personal success over the success of the whole. Miller's greatest work, *Death of a Salesman* (1949), expands his themes of disillusionment. The play made Miller's reputation as a playwright, and Willy Loman became one of the most recognizable figures in American literature. Miller again pointed the finger at the illusions fostered by postwar prosperity and its materialism. The work is powerful theater and got Miller branded as anti-American. He would become one of the most prominent targets of the House Un-American Activities Committee in the 1950s.

Other Notables. Other playwrights produced satisfying if not spectacular work. Lillian Hellman carried over her success of the 1930s with *Watch on the Rhine* (1941), *The Searching Wind* (1944), and *The Autumn Garden* (1951). *Watch on the Rhine* was chosen best play of 1941 by the New York Drama Critics' Circle. Older playwrights who had thrived in the 1920s and early 1930s produced several good works. Maxwell Anderson (*Candle in the Wind,* 1940; *The Eve of St. Mark,* 1942), Elmer Rice (*Dream Girl,* 1945), and Philip Barry (*Without Love,* 1942; *Foolish Notion,* 1945) closed out their careers with solid work. Robert Sherwood won his third Pulitzer Prize in 1941 with *There Shall Be No Night* before moving to Hollywood. Even Eugene O'Neill, the grand theatrical voice of American letters, produced a new play. *The Iceman Cometh* (1946) was the most widely publicized production of the year. The hit comedy *Mister Roberts* (1946), by Thomas Heggen, was one of the few productions that dealt with World War II. All of these plays reflected the almost bland realism of the times. There was neither great experimentation nor great poetry, Williams and Miller excepted, appearing on the stage.

Off Broadway. One prominent and promising development during the decade was the rise of the Off-

Broadway theater. Broadway drama was declining. Fewer plays made a profit, and fewer were produced. The pressure for every production to be a smash hit grew due to rising costs. As a result theater often took the safe route of old familiars such as Henrik Ibsen and Anton Chekhov rather than risk a new play. New artists were forced to find new venues. Broadway had begun outpricing its larger audience. The result was a growth in the number of small "fringe" theaters that used little or no set design. Budgets were often kept below one hundred dollars per production. The focus was on ideas and language. The settings were small theaters, high-school gymnasiums, or any small space where people could sit to watch actors perform. There was little chance for profit Off Broadway. Groups such as On Stage and Abbé Practical Workshop produced new plays. Erwin Piscator's Dramatic Workshop produced Marlon Brando. Broadway was waning but theater remained vital. Plays such as Jean-Paul Sartre's *The Flies,* Robert Penn Warren's *All the King's Men,* and Barrie Stavis's *Lamp at Midnight* were produced Off Broadway when Broadway would not touch them. The small stage seemed to flourish, a fitting scale for the new, intimate plays of the 1940s.

Sources:

John Gassner, ed., *Best American Plays: Third Series, 1945–1951* (New York: Crown, 1952);

Allan Lewis, *American Plays and Playwrights of the Contemporary Theatre* (New York: Crown, 1965).

FICTION IN TRANSITION

Social Realism Exhausted. The 1940s were an in-between era for American fiction. The decade marked an end and also a beginning. Social realism was the trend coming to a close. The 1930s had seen a rise in social concern among fiction writers. Novelists such as James T. Farrell, Erskine Caldwell, and Theodore Dreiser had aimed for socially significant fiction that portrayed working people fighting against the machine of capitalism. Novelists such as Sinclair Lewis, Upton Sinclair, and Willa Cather had for three decades presented a realistic fiction entrenched in American landscapes and language. They were often political writers with a political agenda. In 1939, with the publication of John Steinbeck's *The Grapes of Wrath,* social realism reached its peak. Steinbeck's novel, which followed the journey of Oklahoma's poor to the "promised land" of California, only to see them crushed by forces beyond their control, was the ultimate statement of social realism. It garnered Steinbeck a Pulitzer Prize. After *The Grapes of Wrath* social realism seemed exhausted in form and content. The social movements of the 1930s were coming to an end, and the fiction that had described them was spent.

Old Lions. Another group of writers was also winding down. The Lost Generation of the 1920s, who had left America for Paris to become the most celebrated group of writers back home, was also declining in stature. F. Scott Fitzgerald died in 1940. Ernest Hemingway published

Richard Wright in Paris, 1948

For Whom the Bell Tolls in 1940 and then remained nearly silent for an entire decade. Two other major American novelists had also become silent. Thomas Wolfe died in 1938, though his *You Can't Go Home Again,* appeared in 1940. William Faulkner, a prolific writer in the 1930s, published *The Hamlet,* the first volume of his Snopes Trilogy, in 1940 and *Intruder in the Dust,* generally regarded as a minor novel, in 1948; his production and his critical reputation diminished significantly during the 1940s. Just five years before his Nobel Prize in 1949 (awarded in 1950), Faulkner was essentially out of print and forgotten by the public while he struggled unhappily as a Hollywood screenwriter. American fiction was looking for new energy, new ideas, and new themes to follow up two fruitful decades of work.

Modernism Arrives. As in American art, the source of the energy for new developments would be Europe. The modernism that had developed in Europe in the 1920s and 1930s finally began to influence American writers in the 1940s. Modernism was the antithesis of social realism and regionalism in America. The works of Europeans that influenced American literature of the 1940s — that of Jean-Paul Sartre, Albert Camus, Simone de Beauvoir, Thomas Mann, and especially Franz Kafka — looked not at social commentary or working people, but at the individual instead. The reportorial style of realism gave way to subjective viewpoints. The thematic novel suddenly seemed old-fashioned. Modernism tried to reinvent the world and force the reader to do the same. The familiar was made unfamiliar. Abstraction increased. Novelistic methods of narrative, characterization, and plotting were replaced or remade, but modernism did not come easily to American writers. The old lions, whose influence on younger writers was tremendous, actually acted as a barrier to modern ideas. Though Faulkner had already adopted modern techniques, he had never attained popu-

HEMINGWAY LEARNING TO WRITE AGAIN

In 1940 Ernest Hemingway published *For Whom the Bell Tolls,* his most ambitious novel, when he was forty-one years old and at the peak of his powers. He was the best known writer in the world, and in 1945 readers awaited his fictional treatment of World War II, which he had covered as a reporter. He had written novels set during World War I and the Spanish Civil War in the 1930s.

But Hemingway had sustained two major concussions during World War II. As a result, he suffered from headaches and had trouble concentrating. Worst of all, his memory became impaired, and he had difficulty writing words. He had always been a disciplined writer and he began a strict program to resume his work. It was first necessary for him to limit his alcohol consumption. According to Hemingway's biographer Carlos Baker, he began by writing letters. He then wrote short stories. When he was ready to write longer fiction, he began a sequence of novels about the sea, the air, and the land. This project was interrupted by work on *Across the River and Into the Trees* (1950). (Work-in-progress on the sea-air-land novels was posthumously published in 1970 as *Islands in the Stream.*) The reception of *Across the River and Into the Trees* was mixed, but most critics condemned the novel as imitation Hemingway. A victim of his own stature, Hemingway was not allowed to fail. He would produce only one more fictional work of great standing, *The Old Man and the Sea* (1952), which many saw as an answer to his critics.

Source: Malcolm Cowley, *A Second Flowering* (New York: Viking, 1974).

larity. One of the first of the "new" novelists was twenty-eight year old Saul Bellow, destined to be among the foremost writers of the post–World War II era. In 1944 his novel *Dangling Man* appeared. As the title suggests, Bellow was interested in the individual man in the modern world. He showed the influence of the French existentialists and Kafka in his depiction of an individual attempting to determine his place in the world. Bellow followed up with *The Victim* in 1947 and established himself as an influential voice. Other new voices followed Bellow, among them Truman Capote, Paul Bowles, John Hawkes, and Chester Himes. Modernism was in its youth in America in the 1940s, hardly a dominant form. While Bellow and Hawkes led the movement slowly forward, many other novelists wrote and exerted their influence on other styles. Though regionalism and realism were waning, writers produced a notable body of work in these veins — Warren's *All the King's Men* (Pulitzer Prize winner, 1946), John Hersey's *A Bell for Adano* (Pulitzer Prize winner, 1944), the work of Southern regional writers Carson McCullers and Eudora Welty, William Carlos Williams' Stecher Trilogy, Nelson Algren's *The Man with the Golden Arm* (the first National Book Award winner, in 1949), and the stories of John O'Hara (the creator of the so-called *New Yorker* short story). But modernism was the style that would influence the following generations. In the 1940s it was being done more quietly, against the grain of popular opinion.

The Combat Novel. World War II would of course influence fiction as it did all other aspects of life. In the final years of the war and in the late 1940s, the first fictions describing the war began to appear, but they were not simply reportorial accounts of what had been seen in combat. They became a genre in themselves that would endure through the 1950s, 1960s, and 1970s. In a sense they were accounts of the societies that produced the war. The war became a microcosm of America. The military company came to stand for the whole nation. The novels described men in combat or the military mindset about conflict, whether war was actually depicted or not. Harry Brown's *A Walk in the Sun* (1944) was the first of this group of novels to appear. Novelists such as Norman Mailer (*The Naked and the Dead,* 1948), John Horne Burns (*The Gallery,* 1947), James Gould Cozzens (*Guard of Honor,* 1949), Irwin Shaw (*The Young Lions,* 1948), Robert Lowry (*The Wolf That Fed Us,* 1949), and John Hawkes (*The Cannibal,* 1949) looked at the war culture and the world in its aftermath. Hawkes as a modernist innovator and Mailer as a major new force in American letters were the most influential of the group.

Blacks. The 1940s marked a new beginning for black writers. With the Harlem Renaissance of the 1920s and early 1930s, American black culture had thrived, but it had been largely ignored by white America. In 1940, with the publication of Richard Wright's *Native Son,* black America gained a voice that could not be ignored. The next generation of black writers would refer to Wright as their "father" because *Native Son,* and his subsequent autobiography (*Black Boy,* 1945), placed Wright among his contemporaries as a prominent American writer, regardless of racial distinctions. Wright's energy and the anger in his voice opened up new channels of discussion for American black authors, many of whom disagreed with his portrayal of blacks. Zora Neale Hurston, whose *Their Eyes Were Watching God* (1937) is now an American classic, published her autobiography *Dust Tracks on the Road* in 1942 and *Seraph on the Suwanee* in 1948. William Attaway, Chester Himes, and Hurston were the preeminent black writers of the decade. The decade would end with promise. Himes and Attaway were established. James Baldwin had begun his work. Wright had given black Americans a voice. In the late 1940s and the 1950s they would begin to speak with that voice.

Gary Cooper, front, in *Sergeant York,* 1941

Sources:
Edward Margolies, *Native Sons* (New York: Lippincott, 1968);

Frederick R. Karl, *American Fictions, 1940-1980* (New York: Harper & Row, 1983).

FILM BEFORE THE WAR

Sitting Pretty. Hollywood was at its peak when the 1940s opened. The industry had exploded into the American consciousness during the previous two decades and held a unique grip on the American imagination that would only begin to dissolve in the late 1940s when television would become more widespread and the studio monopoly of production and distribution would be shattered by the U.S. Justice Department. Eight studios controlled the entire industry (Warner Bros., M-G-M, RKO Radio, 20th Century–Fox, United Artists, Paramount, Universal, and Columbia) and signed a stable of directors, technicians, and actors, controlling their careers exclusively during the life of the contract. The system has often been compared to a form of servitude, though perhaps baseball's reserve clause is a better analogy. Actors were not free to pursue projects outside the studio. Studios often released one picture a week either as a head-

liner or as a B film. Quality did not matter because the studios owned a majority of the theaters in densely populated areas. Ninety-five percent of all reel rentals went to the big eight studios. Overseas markets were also huge and often accounted for the profit margin in films. Overseeing the production of movies was the Production Code Association (PCA), or the Hays Office, named for Will H. Hays and presided over by the strict Joseph Breen. Censorship was not a dirty word in Hollywood. The Hays Office screened all movies for general release and held fast to its pristine code for the content of films. The movies were entertainment, light or fantastic. The good guys always won. Social issues were not discussed. Too much was at stake to risk controversy. Estimates are that eighty million Americans, or two-thirds of the population, bought a movie ticket every week.

Royalty. In return for the limited options of the studio system, actors were treated as royalty by the public and the press. Stars such as Clark Gable, Alan Ladd, Katharine Hepburn, and Betty Grable drew people to the movies. Stories often did not matter. Through the 1930s only New York and Washington, D.C., had more press correspondents stationed in them than were in Hollywood.

The eyes of the world watched Hollywood for laughter, love, and fashion. Directors such as Frank Capra, John Ford, and Preston Sturges provided all three, as well as adventure, mystery, and fantasy (and a spate of gangster films). A survey of 530 feature films of 1940 reveals only 27 containing political ideas. But by the late 1930s a small ripple of unrest had appeared in Hollywood. Like the other arts, Hollywood had socially conscious participants who were keeping an eye on events developing in Europe.

The Great Debate. By 1940 Hollywood was asking the same question as the rest of the nation: Where should America's place be in a European war? Most Americans were divided into isolationist and interventionist camps. Hollywood was no different. Many movie producers were Jewish and were concerned about the Nazi treatment of Jews in Europe. But Hays and Breen feared intervention. Breen, the head of the PCA, was suspicious of Jews and leftists. The studios feared closure of markets if they made obviously antifascist films. When the Nazis demanded the firing of all "non-Aryan" employees in Germany, studios with production facilities in Europe capitulated. Some films about Europe did get made, however. William Dieterle directed the first, *Blockade,* a film about the Spanish Civil War, in 1938. Conservatives branded the movie "leftist propaganda." The real breakthroughs came in 1939 with *Confessions of a Nazi Spy* and in 1940 with Charlie Chaplin's *The Great Dictator. Confessions of a Nazi Spy,* directed by Anatole Litvak, was a Warner Bros. melodrama based on a real incident in New York. It was promptly banned in Germany, Italy, Spain, and many neutral countries. Chaplin, declaring that "Hitler must be laughed at," portrayed him as a raving madman in *The Great Dictator,* a movie made with little support from the studio system. Interventionists were beginning to win the debate in Hollywood. Hollywood's interventionist bent was starting to show through. In mid 1940 the Hays Office formed the Motion Picture Committee Cooperating for Defense, a bureau that helped the armed forces make short training films. On 17 August Germany banned American films from areas under its control. The ban removed Hollywood's excuse for timidity and sparked a wave of anti-Nazi films that year (including *The Mortal Storm, Four Sons,* and *I Married a Nazi*).

Sergeant York. With the release of *Sergeant York* on 1 July 1941, Hollywood issued its manifesto — America should enter the war. The film industry was no longer just Nazi-bashing. It seemed intent on making the moral case for intervention. The movie was released to huge fanfare. A parade that included Alvin York (the war hero depicted in the film), Eleanor Roosevelt, and Wendell Willkie (the 1940 Republican nominee for president) marched down Broadway in New York. York met President Franklin D. Roosevelt. The army produced an eight-page recruitment pamphlet to be released with the film. York served as a metaphor for conscience. The movie tells the story of how the God-fearing, reluctant warrior, played by Gary Cooper, finally chose to fight and became America's most celebrated hero of World War I. The message was an obvious one and was not missed in the nation's capital.

Hearings. The isolationists had had enough. Sen. Gerald Nye, a Republican from South Dakota, accused the film industry of trying to "rouse the war fever in America." He blamed Roosevelt and Hollywood's monopoly control over its own industry. In September 1941 he presided over congressional hearings investigating Hollywood's interventionist policies. He pointed at films such as *Sergeant York* and *The Great Dictator* as evidence of Hollywood's grand design. The film industry chose Wendell Willkie to act in its defense. He did so brilliantly, not by denial, but by assertion. "We abhor everything which Hitler represents," he told the committee, and produced overwhelming statistics in the industry's favor: less than 5 percent of all films released during the previous two years had been war related. Hollywood notables, such as producers Harry M. Warner and Darryl F. Zanuck, testified as well. The hearings did nothing for the isolationist cause. They were adjourned on 26 September 1941 and officially abandoned on 8 December as America entered the war.

The Other Hollywood. Most of Hollywood was not participating in the debate. As Willkie had pointed out in the congressional hearings, 95 percent of films made were nonpolitical. Walt Disney's monumental *Fantasia,* starring Mickey Mouse in an animated film with classical music played by a full orchestra, appeared in 1940. Alfred Hitchcock's *Rebecca* and *The Philadelphia Story,* starring Cary Grant, James Stewart, and Katharine Hepburn, were hits. *The Grapes of Wrath,* based on John Steinbeck's Pulitzer Prize–winning novel of the Depression years, was brilliantly filmed by John Ford. In 1941 two comedians, Bud Abbott and Lou Costello, scored three major hits (*Buck Privates, Hold That Ghost,* and *Keep 'em Flying*) and were among the year's biggest box-office attractions. Greta Garbo's *The Two-Faced Woman* (1941) was banned in Boston, and a twenty-five-year-old prodigy by the name of Orson Welles released his first film. *Citizen Kane* won the New York Film Critics Circle Award as best film of 1941 and is still often chosen as the greatest film ever made.

MOVIES DURING THE WAR

Government Work. Hollywood, ever fearful of any conflict that might upset their system of production and generally aligned politically with the president, had worked with the government prior to the war. In August 1940 President Roosevelt asked Nicholas Schenck, the president of M-G-M, to make a film on foreign policy and defense. Schenck produced *Eyes of the Navy.* In February 1941 a filmed message was shown of President Roosevelt thanking Hollywood for its efforts and cooperation with the "expansion of our defense force." By mid

Henry Travers and Greer Garson in *Mrs. Miniver,* 1942

1941 government propaganda offices such as the Office of the Coordinator of Information (COI) were being formed. Robert E. Sherwood, a Pulitzer Prize–winning playwright and a screenwriter, joined COI, whose job was to counter anti-American propaganda in Europe. Sherwood set up the Foreign Information Service (that eventually would become Voice of America) and promptly recruited notable writers, including Thornton Wilder, Stephen Vincent Benét, and John Houseman, to help. The work was usually pro-American, not anti-Nazi, in tone. The single largest cooperation ever between the government and America's entertainment industry was under way.

Coordination. The government did not actively censor Hollywood during the war. Instead it worked with the studios to coordinate Hollywood and government efforts to the benefit of both. Ten days after Pearl Harbor, Roosevelt appointed Lowell Mellett as coordinator of government films. Mellett traveled to Hollywood and cut a deal. The government would not interfere with Hollywood's production and distribution in return for a guarantee to show all films released with a War Action Committee seal. Mellett knew Hollywood would cooperate if their box office remained unaffected. By June 1942 Roosevelt had created the Office of War Information

(OWI), a government propaganda agency which promptly set up an office in Hollywood headed by Nelson Poynter, a newspaper editor. Sherwood's COI became OWI's foreign branch, and the Bureau of Motion Pictures, headed by Mellett, joined as well to oversee production of government newsreels or "Victory" shorts. Former radio newsman Elmer Davis became the head of all OWI offices.

Celluloid Battles. Encouraged by the government to produce movies with a war theme, Hollywood rushed in with abandon, if not with subtlety. The industry released some seventy war-related films within six months of the bombing of Pearl Harbor. Most of the films were simply typical Hollywood themes grafted onto a war scenario. The gangster film, the comedy, and the musical were all given wartime twists. In *The Daring Young Man* (1942), racketeers become Nazi spies. An aging Johnny Weissmuller acted out Tarzan's battle against Nazis in Africa. Another theme was even easier — Japan-bashing. Anti-Japanese feeling raged in the United States. Japanese Americans had been interned by executive order in February 1942. The films and their advertisements revealed the mood of the country. Movies such as *Menace of the Rising Sun* and *Remember Pearl Harbor* had no purpose other than to portray the Japanese as cruel and

HOLLYWOOD ENLISTS

On 12 August 1942 Clark Gable was sworn in as a forty-two-year-old private in the U.S. Army. Gable claimed that he had "no interest in acting as long as the war is going on." His wife, Carole Lombard, had been killed in a plane crash earlier in the year. She was flying back from a war-bond rally, Hollywood's first "casualty" of war.

Gable joined the ranks of many of Hollywood's elites who had enlisted voluntarily in the first months of the war. Hollywood stars were a kind of royalty providing the role-model behavior and the occasional scandal worthy of the princes and princesses of Europe. Gable withstood the rigors of Officers Candidate school and contributed to an army air force film, *Wings Up* (1943), about the training program.

Within weeks of the bombing of Pearl Harbor, stars such as James Stewart and Douglas Fairbanks, Jr., had joined up. Director Frank Capra volunteered, as did Henry Fonda, Tyrone Power, and Darryl Zanuck, among the many. Hollywood prepared for other sacrifices: private planes were grounded, and the navy considered commandeering private yachts and pleasure boats. Executives prepared to lose 35 to 50 percent of their manpower to the armed forces. Those who did not or could not join tarnished their reputations. Actor Lew Ayres claimed conscientious-objector status, and within days theater owners in Chicago prohibited his films from being shown. Frank Sinatra, the popular singing star, was declared 4-F due to a punctured eardrum. By war's end his popularity had plummeted.

Sources: Thomas Doherty, *Projections of War* (New York: Columbia University Press, 1993);

Otto Friedrich, *City of Nets* (New York: Harper & Row, 1986);

"Hollywood to the Colors: One of Biggest War Time Assets is Set for All-Out Effort," *Newsweek*, 18 (22 December 1941): 59–60.

---

bloodthirsty. Caricatures of the Japanese as fanged, buck-toothed monkeys were common and reflected in the language of the movies, where the Japanese were the target of American contempt and hatred. They were "brutes," or "animals," and needed "to be exterminated" in the most extreme cases. The OWI office of Poynter was troubled by the trend immediately upon his arrival in May 1942. He did not think the war was being treated seriously and visited studio heads to convince them to change their tactics.

The Manual. Officially OWI had no censorship power. Poynter emphasized this fact to the studios. The government was looking for cooperation. He wanted Hollywood to make positive films. While censors usually delete material, the OWI wanted to insert the government view of the country and the war into the films. To speed up the process and save the studios money, he asked that scripts be submitted to the OWI so that changes could be made before shooting. Some in Hollywood howled at the suggestion, but the studios ultimately complied. The industry had been censoring itself for years, so occasional complaints of OWI pressure were somewhat hypocritical. Poynter was not a movie man and often suggested ridiculous changes, but to some extent Hollywood listened and complied with OWI's manual. The emphasis in the manual was on the positive. The manual asked questions such as "Will this picture help win the war?" and "If it is an 'escape picture,' will it harm the war effort by creating a false picture of America, her allies, or the world we live in?" OWI's belief was that fascism was the enemy, not the German or the Japanese people. Poynter tried to restore some balance into films by suggesting "good" Germans be shown anguishing over Nazi tactics and that multi-ethnic unity be portrayed.

Mrs. Miniver. The film that Poynter cited as an example of what OWI wanted was William Wyler's *Mrs. Miniver* (1942). Set in Great Britain during the early stages of the war and portraying the "home front" during the Battle of Britain, *Mrs. Miniver* combined all of the elements that OWI viewed as necessary to a positive portrayal of the war effort. Greer Garson portrays a middle-class woman presiding over a country house near the English Channel. As war breaks out, she demonstrates the fortitude needed at home. Mr. Miniver (played by Walter Pidgeon) helps night patrols and assists in the evacuation of Dunkirk. The oldest son, Tony, becomes an RAF pilot fighting in the skies above Britain. Class distinctions drop away magically, and the village unites smoothly in the war effort while also trying to keep life as normal as possible. The film ends with the impassioned speech of a priest describing the war as "the people's war" for freedom. The movie won the Academy Award for Best Picture in 1942. OWI praised *Mrs. Miniver* profusely and asked Hollywood to produce similar films set in the United States or in Allied countries such as China and the Soviet Union. Other movies honored a variety of contributions to the war. *Tender Comrade* (1943) portrayed women without men, working in a wartime factory and living together in a democratic, unified way while waiting for the men to come home. *Action in the North Atlantic* (1943) showed the contribution of the merchant marine. *The Fighting Seabees* (1944) portrayed the patriotism of construction workers helping the war effort. OWI's favorite word was *unity*.

OWI Exerts Pressure. Despite OWI pleas, not everyone in Hollywood portrayed the homefront as unified and democratic. Studios resented the intrusiveness of government officials who admittedly knew little about the film industry. During the summer of 1942, 20th Century–Fox embarassed the government by releasing *Little*

Gen. George C. Marshall and Col. George Capra planning the *Why We Fight* film series, 1942

Tokyo, U.S.A., an anti-Japanese B movie that portrayed the internment of Japanese Americans earlier in the year. OWI objected strenuously, but the studio rightly pointed out that it was only portraying government policy in action. OWI responded to the movie by pushing for more script supervision, which became a large part of its work. Their second response, however, was much more effective. Hollywood had been ignoring much of OWI's code of conduct, using military approval as a rubber stamp to get films through the government agencies. The military was happy to offer equipment and services to any film that portrayed them in a positive light. Democratic unity was not an issue for them. With army approval for a film, the studios felt no need to please OWI. So in the fall of 1942, OWI decided to get tough. Ulric Bell was appointed liaison between OWI and the film industry in November. Though the government again claimed no power of censorship, it did justifiably control information that would be leaving the United States. Since most Hollywood films made their profit margin on overseas distribution, Bell began exerting economic pressure to force studios to comply with OWI. Films deemed inappropriate by OWI simply would not be released overseas be-

cause of the potentially detrimental effect on the war effort. OWI was saying, "Comply by our rules or choose to lose money." Hollywood began to comply more readily. By early 1943 OWI was reviewing scripts more regularly and offering suggestions. By the end of the war OWI had read 1,652 Hollywood scripts and had effected changes in nearly 70 percent of them.

Capra. Not all of Hollywood was resisting the war effort or the government. Shortly after the bombing of Pearl Harbor, Frank Capra, one of the film industry's star directors, enlisted in the army. He was made a colonel and immediately put to work making short training and educational films for troops. But Capra's greatest contribution to the war effort was in his *Why We Fight* series. Made for wider release, the series, consisting of seven separate films, attempted to portray the events leading up to the war and explain whom the United States was fighting and exactly why. Capra was a virtuoso director. After initially balking at the plan, he proceeded to pull out all the stops and produce a monumental documentary. He used maps, diagrams, optical printing, archival footage, double exposures, and, in select cases, reenact-

Stars were often the main point of movies in the 1940s. Under the studio system films were often cobbled together as vehicles for presenting the personalities the public wanted. The annual poll of the *Motion Picture Herald* revealed the stars with the most staying power. Bing Crosby headed the list for five consecutive years in the 1940s. With films such as *Going My Way* (1944) and *The Bells of St. Mary's* (1945), Crosby, who was equally popular as a singer, scoring hit after hit, was one of the decade's stars among the stars.

1944	1945	1946	1947	1948
1. Bing Crosby	Bing Crosby	Bing Crosby	Bing Crosby	Bing Crosby
2. Gary Cooper	Van Johnson	Ingrid Bergman	Betty Grable	Betty Grable
3. Bob Hope	Greer Garson	Van Johnson	Ingrid Bergman	Abbott and Costello
4. Betty Grable	Betty Grable	Gary Cooper	Gary Cooper	Gary Cooper
5. Spencer Tracy	Spencer Tracy	Bob Hope	Humphrey Bogart	Bob Hope
6. Greer Garson	Humphrey Bogart and Gary Cooper (tie)	Humphrey Bogart	Bob Hope	Humphrey Bogart
7. Humphrey Bogart	Humphrey Bogart and Gary Cooper (tie)	Greer Garson	Clark Gable	Clark Gable
8. Abbott and Costello	Bob Hope	Margaret O'Brien	Gregory Peck	Cary Grant
9. Cary Grant	Judy Garland	Betty Grable	Claudette Colbert	Spencer Tracy
10. Bette Davis	Margaret O'Brien	Roy Rogers	Alan Ladd	Ingrid Bergman

ment of events. He had first come to realize the power of the documentary from Nazi Germany, the master of propaganda. Capra had first seen Leni Riefenstahl's homage to the Nazis, *Triumph of the Will,* in early 1942. The sheer power of the images from the German director's camera stunned and horrified Capra. He would eventually incorporate footage from the films into his own work, turning the tables on Riefenstahl. The first film in the series, *Prelude to War,* won an Oscar for best documentary of 1942. Other segments followed: *The Battle of Britain, The Battle of Russia, The Nazi Strike,* and *Divide and Conquer* in 1943 and *War Comes to America* in 1945. Not all of the films were released commercially. *Prelude to War* was delayed in release until 1943 and did not fare well at the box office. Dollars aside, however, Capra had triumphed over Riefenstahl as a filmmaker and counterpropagandist. Other directors followed Capra into war and contributed to recording what has been called the most documented event in human history. John Ford personally filmed *The Battle of Midway Island* (1943) while standing on a beach. The raw, disturbed footage, blurred and shaken because Ford had used a hand-held camera, became a technical innovation worth copying for effect in later films. John Huston made a documentary (*Let There Be Light*) showing shell-shocked veterans. The army would not allow it to be released. Disney studios estimated that 94 percent of its wartime work was for the war effort. Its *Victory Through Airpower* was a documentary supporting the air war against the Axis. The film did well at the box office, due in large part to its stunning animated visuals.

Other War Films. For all of the poorly made films that the studios cranked out during the war years, a few films met OWI standards and became timeless movies of the war years. David O. Selznick's *Since You Went Away* (1944) became the ultimate home-front statement. Selznick, who had produced *Gone With the Wind* in 1939 and *Rebecca* in 1940, wrote the script for *Since You Went Away* himself. John Cromwell directed. The film starred Claudette Colbert, Jennifer Jones, Shirley Temple, and Agnes Moorhead and portrayed life at home while father fights in the war. The whole family pitches in, though, and unlike *Mrs. Miniver, Since You Went Away* has a happy ending. OWI loved the film. Another happy ending of a different kind occurred in Michael Curtiz's *Casa-*

blanca (1942), now considered one of the truly great films of the war years. Humphrey Bogart plays Rick, a cynical idealist trying to survive in refugee-laden Casablanca. Bogart mastered his "tough guy with a soft heart" persona in *Casablanca*. He resists getting involved in the politics of the time but ultimately risks his life and sacrifices his love for the larger good. His speech at the airport as he forces Ingrid Bergman to board the plane without him concisely sums up the war-era feelings OWI tried to promote. The problems of "two little people" don't amount to a "hill of beans," Rick tells Ilsa as his dormant idealism emerges. Rick has chosen the better good over personal triumph. OWI loved it, as did the American public. The film won an Oscar for best picture in 1943. Another popular war-era film was Preston Sturges's *Hail the Conquering Hero* (1944), a satire of the home front. OWI did not like the movie, but they underestimated the American public's willingness to laugh at itself.

Russia. Ironically, the effort to please OWI led to a series of films about Russia, America's ally against Germany. Though Joseph Stalin had fallen out of favor among American leftists in the late 1930s due to his purge trials and nonaggression pact with the Nazis, he had regained some American sympathies during his years as America's ally. At the request of OWI, Hollywood produced pro-Soviet films that depicted Russians as remarkably similar to Americans and on the side of right. In 1943 *Mission to Moscow* (directed by Michael Curtiz) was released. A controversy ensued, but the film was a hit. Based on a book by Joseph Davies, the former ambassador to the Soviet Union, *Mission to Moscow* portrayed Stalin as a strong, moral leader; by 1947 it became an embarrassment as the Cold War spread. Warner Bros. destroyed all of its release prints, and *Mission to Moscow*, like other films such as *Song of Russia* (M-G-M, 1943) and *The North Star* (1943, with screenplay by Lillian Hellman, music by Aaron Copland and lyrics by Ira Gershwin) became a focal point of Washington's anti-Communist hearings after the war. Jack Warner, producer of *Mission to Moscow*, denounced the movie before the House Un-American Activities Committee and then named his screenwriter Howard Koch a Communist.

Aftermath. The war in Japan ended in two flashes in August 1945. The nuclear age arrived, and the United States and its film industry would never be the same. On 31 August 1945 President Harry Truman disbanded the Office of War Information. Hollywood was again free to produce movies without government intervention. Within two years, however, despite its cooperation during the war years, Hollywood was again the target of Washington investigations. As life returned to normal following the war, focus on the laws of the land also returned, and the Justice Department began its investigation into the studio system and the Hollywood monopoly. The investigation concluded with a Supreme Court decision that effectively stripped the studios of their theater chains. The decision, in tandem with a high personal

THE MALTESE FALCON: B MOVIE TO FILM HISTORY

George Raft could have had the part but did not want it. "Not an important picture," he said. The 1931 film version of the novel had been a flop. He had Bogart removed from *Manpower* (1941) so he could take a starring role in the film. Bogart was free, then, to become Sam Spade for Hollywood's third attempt at filming Dashiell Hammett's 1930 novel, *The Maltese Falcon*. The other two versions had failed miserably, in part because they had taken too much license with Hammett's tightly plotted work.

The film was John Huston's first as a director. He wrote the script, staying true to the novel. Warner Bros. had low expectations for *The Maltese Falcon*. They liked it as a low-budget production. Bogart was not yet a major star, though *High Sierra*, released earlier in 1941, had increased his stature. Mary Astor was reconstructing a shaky career ruined by scandal in 1936. Sidney Greenstreet was a sixty-one-year-old Englishman who had never appeared in a movie. Peter Lorre was a struggling character actor. They began an unlikely assembly preparing to make another low-grade production. Instead they made film history. *The Maltese Falcon* is today considered a classic and is often referred to as the first real film noir, a strictly American style of film making that reached its peak in the late 1940s and early 1950s.

Sources: Jonathan Coe, *Humphrey Bogart: Take It and Like It* (New York: Grove Weidenfeld, 1991);

"The Maltese Falcon," *Newsweek*, 18 (13 October 1941): 66–67.

income tax rate that hit Hollywood stars hard, spelled doom for the studio system. Stars such as Bing Crosby and Bob Hope agitated to be released from their studio contracts and to be allowed to form their own independent production companies to avoid the high income tax. Independent theaters limited the studios' profitability. When HUAC began investigating Hollywood in 1947, the studio system was on its last legs; the introduction of television the following year hurt the studios even more. Although Hollywood as a place continued to produce films, and the studios remained in operation, the factory system of cinema production, which had ushered the nation through war, disappeared.

MOVIES AFTER THE WAR

Film Noir Develops. In 1941 Warner Bros. released *The Maltese Falcon*, directed by John Huston and starring Humphrey Bogart and based on the 1930 novel of the

Humphrey Bogart, Peter Lorre, Mary Astor, and Sidney Greenstreet in *The Maltese Falcon,* 1941

same name by Dashiell Hammett. The movie was an unexpected hit. No one then knew that the film would become a Hollywood classic the first of a host of dark detective movies. In 1946 critic Nino Frank, noticing this trend, coined the phrase *film noir,* or black film. He saw a similarity between this loose group of films and the hard-boiled detective fiction of the 1920s and 1930s. Pulp fiction had made it to the screen. Detective novelists such as Hammett, Raymond Chandler (*The Big Sleep*; movie version, 1946), and James M. Cain *(The Postman Always Rings Twice*; movie version, 1946) were seminal noir writers who also adapted their books for the screen. French critics had called the novels *serie noire,* or "black series" novels. Frank adapted the phrase for films in the 1940s. These movies were often morally ambivalent, moody and claustrophobic. Noir was without real precedent, save its relationship to pulp fiction. It exploded in stature after the war and remained a loose genre of film until about 1958.

Defining Noir. The noir figure was new to American film. In many ways film noir came to represent the un-

derlying mood of postwar America. The war had ended; fascism had been defeated. America was experiencing unprecedented economic prosperity. Veterans returned home to well-paying jobs and normal family life. America's position in the world was at a peak. But disturbing currents ran beneath the surface of this prosperity. The Cold War began and, with it, a paranoia fomented that led to the anti-Communist inquisition. Noir captured these currents. Technical developments during the war helped solidify the noir style. Fine-grained negatives allowed for darker filming, and smaller camera dollies allowed for more camera movement to produce mood. Portable generators allowed for more location shooting. Orson Welles's *Citizen Kane* had handed all film directors a basketful of new filming ideas and techniques. The war had helped generate the early noir simply out of practicalities. The government limited location shoots for fear of showing too much detail of American cities on the landscape. As a result more films were shot strictly with interior scenes, which could lend a sense of claustrophobia to the screen. These developments, along

Chairman J. Parnell Thomas (standing at right with hand raised) swearing in a witness to testify before the House Un-American Activities Committee, 1947

with the mood of the country, created noir. The noir figure was usually a dangling man at the mercy of fate. He was often a returning war veteran with shell shock or an alienated idealist. The settings were always urban and stark. Existential and Freudian thought had reached Hollywood. The mass movements of the 1930s were over, and the individual stood alone against fate and often against himself to meet his predetermined destiny. Noir figures were obsessive, driven, sometimes mad. Typically a male noir "hero" was done in by a fatal obsession with a femme fatale whom he could never see through. The film viewer participated with the noir victim. Roving cameras and strange angles brought the viewer into the noir hero's mind. Audiences loved it. The run of noir hits — *The Glass Key* (from the novel by Hammett, 1935, remade in 1942), *Journey into Fear* (from the novel by Eric Ambler, 1942), *Double Indemnity* (from the novel by Cain, 1944), *Murder My Sweet* (from the novel *Farewell, My Lovely,* by Chandler, 1944) — lasted into the 1950s. They drew crowds with their suspense and violence and were inexpensive to make. Also, as the studios lost their monopoly grip on the distribution of films, competition caused them to produce quality movies. Major directors tried their hands at noir — John Huston, Billy Wilder, Alfred Hitchcock, Welles, and Edward Dmytryk were among the many. Some of the elements of noir reached into genre films such as Westerns (*Blood on the Moon,* 1948), gangster films (*White Heat,* 1949), and comedy (*Arsenic and Old Lace,* 1944), but by and large the films were of

their own characterization, free of the other Hollywood genres. Film noir was a relatively brief phenomenon in film, originating on the American screen. The techniques have often been borrowed, especially with the noir revival begun in the 1970s, but noir is a product of its time, a dark vision of America heading out of a decade that closed the first half of the century and remade the world for the second half to come.

The Cold War in Hollywood. The second half of the 1940s were turbulent in Hollywood. The industry seemed to have peaked in glamour prior to the war and peaked in popularity during the war. Unprecedented prosperity should have sent people flocking to the theaters in greater numbers than ever. But while noir flourished as a form, attendance at the movies declined. Television had begun to cut into the film-going audience. The number of television sets in the United States rose from some sixty-five hundred in 1945 to eleven million in 1950. The Justice Department broke up the studios' monopoly of theater ownership. Hollywood could no longer force popular stars and poor-quality movies onto the public because of the increased competition. And while the postwar films began to glorify the wartime heroes and welcome them home (as in *The Best Years of Our Lives,* 1946), Hollywood itself was tarnished by the House Un-American Activities Committee. HUAC descended on Hollywood with subpoenas in May 1947 and held hearings in Washington the following October. Nothing was really accomplished. The committee seemed more inter-

OLD MR. HEARST AND YOUNG MR. WELLES

Orson Welles made *Citizen Kane* (1943) in near secrecy. He had been granted unheard-of freedom by RKO Studios to produce, direct, star in, and edit his first film without studio interference. The film's actors were allowed to read only script pages for scenes in which they would appear, but RKO lawyers, checking for libel, were allowed to see the entire script.

Thus, when Welles showed a "rough cut" of the film to several reviewers, the sensational news leaked out: Welles, age twenty-five, the enfant terrible of radio and theater, was attacking the eighty-year-old newspaper publisher William Randolph Hearst with a story that paralleled his life. Hearst was incensed. He immediately ordered all mention of RKO Studios and anyone associated with the studio to be banished from Hearst newspapers. He canceled advertising deals with RKO and sent his Hollywood columnist, Louella Parsons, to demand a screening. She watched the film with two lawyers and wordlessly left the screening room.

Threats followed. Not only did Heart threaten a lawsuit against RKO, but Hearst newspapers also appeared to be poised to attack Hollywood as a whole. The fear was that Hearst's inflammatory editorialists would pump up publicity about Hollywood's employment of illegal aliens, the risqué nature of some scripts, and the scandalous private lives of Hollywood producers or stars.

Debate raged over whether RKO should release the picture. Welles's alienation from the film industry through his sheer talent and audacity would follow. He was bucking the studio system of production and creating resentment all through Hollywood. *The Hollywood Reporter* sided with Hearst. Ironically, the film was released only to a limited market and lost money despite nine Academy Award nominations (resulting in one Oscar) and critical raves. Most of the public did not even see the film, and only in the late 1950s did its reputation as the greatest movie ever made begin to build.

Sources: "Hearst vs. Orson Welles," *Newsweek,* 17 (20 January 1941): 62–63;

James Howard, *The Complete Films of Orson Welles* (New York: Citadel, 1991);

Michael Sage, "Hearst Over Hollywood," *New Republic,* 104 (24 February 1941): 270–271.

screenwriters with leftist sympathies, argued bitterly with the committee, refusing to acknowledge the right even to be questioned about their involvement with the Communist Party. The owners of the studios readily and meekly capitulated to the committee while leftist screenwriters, John Howard Lawson and Dalton Trumbo among them, shouted back. The hearings were dropped on 30 October and the Ten were cited for contempt of Congress. They were fined; eight were sentenced to a year in jail, two to six months; and at the studios' own prompting the Ten were blacklisted from ever working in Hollywood again. The committee had essentially succeeded in intimidating the powers of Hollywood. The blacklisted Ten were followed by hundreds of other actors, writers, and technicians, who were barred from working in their professions for about a decade. Initial support for the Ten waned due to their ugly confrontations with the committee. The Cold War, present beneath the surface of noir and pervading the ethos of American life, had also reached deeply into Hollywood's off-screen life.

Blacks. Black Americans did not fare well in the Hollywood films of the 1940s. While black performers triumphed in music and black authors began to assert their voices in fiction and poetry, black actors, by and large, were marginal, often comedic figures in film, in the rare instances that they made it to the screen. There were no black producers or filmmakers, nor were there any "serious" or lead actors. Hattie McDaniel became the first black American to win an Academy Award for her role in *Gone With the Wind* (1939), but even then she played an iconic figure, the patient, serving woman. Segregation was still commonplace nationwide. Even movie theaters were "whites only" in many places, and black theaters often did not receive first-run films. Hollywood occasionally made a gesture toward a kind of equality. Though the real army was segregated, some films, such as *Bataan* (1943), showed mixed-race companies of men. Sam, played by Dooley Wilson, the piano player and friend to Bogart's Rick in the movie *Casablanca,* is the strongest role for a black man in the war films. Black soldiers were ignored by the newsreels for much of the war, though Col. Frank Capra oversaw Stuart Heisler's documentary *The Negro Soldier* (1944). Hollywood did improve, in part through the influence of the OWI office, which pushed for unity. Walter White, president of the National Association for the Advancement of Colored People (NAACP), lobbied Hollywood producers personally in hopes of effecting change. The effects came slowly, however, usually reflecting the racial sensitivity of an individual producer or writer, not Hollywood as an institution. Trumbo, for instance, published an article in *Negro Digest* complaining of his colleagues' habits of stereotyping blacks. The oft-quoted statement is worth quoting again, as it summarizes Hollywood's portrayal of blacks so well: "We have made tarts of his daughters, crap shooters of his sons, obsequious Uncle Toms of his fathers, superstitious and grotesque crones of his mothers,

ested in the publicity it could generate than in rousting subversives. The so-called Hollywood Ten, prominent

Billie Holiday with the Art Tatum Trio

After Pearl Harbor, Rep. J. Parnell Thomas, hearkening back to World War I, urged songwriters to pen stirring anthems to the war effort. "What America needs today is a good five cent war song," he declared. America's songwriters did not waste time answering his call. Musician Burt Wheeler debuted his tune "We'll Knock the Japs Right into the Laps of the Nazis" at a nightclub on the evening of the Pearl Harbor attack; by next morning songwriter Max Lerner had finished "The Sun Will Soon Be Setting on the Land of the Rising Sun." The soon-to-be-popular "You're a Sap, Mr. Jap" was copyrighted three hours before Congress declared war.

As is obvious from the titles of these tunes, early war songs were usually chauvinistic and antagonistic toward the enemy, perhaps a natural response after the surprise attack on Hawaii. But anti-Japanese songs also tended toward racism in songs such as "When Those Little Yellow Bellies Meet the Cohens and the Kelleys" and "Slap the Jap Right Off the Map." Anti-German songs focused on Nazi leaders, such as "Lets Knock the Hit out of Hitler" and "Der Fuehrer's Face," originally sung by Donald Duck and featuring a tongue-sputtering raspberry. Later tunes tended to be more rousing and upbeat, especially "We Did It Before and We Can Do It Again" and "Praise the Lord and Pass the Ammunition." Patriotic standards made a comeback, especially Kate Smith's recording of "God Bless America," a prewar hit that made a timely comeback. Perhaps the most popular war tunes were hot swing numbers such as "GI Jive" and "The Boogie-Woogie Bugle Boy of Company B," infectious enough to get soldiers and nonsoldiers alike jitterbugging.

Source: Richard R. Lingeman, *Don't You Know There's A War On?: The American Home Front, 1941-1945* (New York: Putnam, 1970).

strutting peacocks of his successful men, psalm singing mountebanks of his priests and Barnum and Bailey side shows of his religion." The situation would not really improve for another two decades.

Sources:
Thomas Doherty, *Projections of War* (New York: Columbia University Press, 1993);

Otto Friedrich, *City of Nets* (New York: Harper & Row, 1986);

Clayton Koppes and Gregory Black, *Hollywood Goes to War* (New York: Free Press, 1987);

Alain Silver and Elizabeth Ward, *Film Noir: An Encyclopedic Reference to the American Style,* third edition (Woodstock, N.Y.: Overlook Press, 1992).

MUSIC

A Dynamic Decade. An explosive growth in the variety of musical styles marked American music during the 1940s. Electric blues, hard bop, serial music, folk opera, country swing, and show jazz were all innovations of the decade. Technology was in some way the catalyst of this growth, as a host of advances in musical media brought heretofore neglected styles to a broader audience, or, as in the case of the increased use of electric guitar, changed the instrumental presentation of existing musical styles. The boundaries between musical genres was fluid, and musicians swapped and fused styles. Musical experiments begun in the previous decade — especially in classical music — were completed in the 1940s. The impact of World War II on music was significant: classical music blossomed, infused with a host of expatriate European

talent; swing became the soundtrack of the war; Broadway expanded to meet the demands of an enormous off-duty GI audience; jazz, swing, and country suffered from the impact of the draft; and great talent, such as Glenn Miller's, was lost in the war. The postwar consumer boom also transformed American music. Prosperity brought firmer backing to classical music and a tonier audience to jazz; consumer buying fueled rhythm and blues and country and western. Music's first teen idol, Frank Sinatra, set bobby-soxers swooning during the war; nightclub singers such as Billie Holiday thrilled thousands. The 1940s were the heyday of swing and the crucible of bop and country. It was a dynamic, exciting decade for American music.

Tommy Potter, Charlie Parker, and Miles Davis, 1948

Swing and Pop. As the 1940s began, the most popular music in the United States was played by large swing-jazz orchestras. Swing was a style of blues and jazz orchestration, developed in the 1930s, that was bold, exciting, and danceable. Swing could be found on three- to four-minute 78-rpm records, in the dance-hall, on the radio, and in the movies. Commercial recordings by swing bands were big sellers, and swing groups led by men such as Tommy Dorsey, Earl Hines, Louis Armstrong, Cab Calloway, Harry James, Les Brown, and Benny Goodman (featuring the terrific arrangements of Fletcher Henderson and Eddie Sauter) crisscrossed America on successful tours. Big-band swing featured highly structured, rhythmically dynamic compositions with solo improvisation often by acclaimed musicians such as saxophonists Lester Young and Coleman Hawkins, vibraharpist Lionel Hampton, guitarist Charlie Christian, and trumpeter Cootie Williams. Blues and pop singers such as Billie Holiday, Helen Forrest, the Andrews Sisters, Bing Crosby, Dinah Shore, and Frank Sinatra were associated with swing bands and were frequently accompanied by them in live performance and on record. After the decline of swing following World War II, such singers and lesser lights such as Perry Como, Rosemary Clooney, Dick Haymes, and Vaughn Monroe became the staple of pop music — usually with the punch and rhythm of swing replaced by string orchestration.

Jazz Composition. In the 1940s many swing musicians who had formerly considered themselves entertainers began to take their music seriously and ventured into less-than-commercial territory, experimenting with composition and solos. Jazz pianist Art Tatum blended blues and swing to classical music. Count Basie took the jazz convention of the riff and placed it into a structured, orchestral setting. Gil Evans explored jazz orchestration with classical instruments. Jazz composer Duke Ellington produced some of the more radical departures of the era. Such Ellington pieces as *Harlem Airshaft* (1940) and *Jack the Bear* (1940) featured a remarkable mixture of melody and rhythmic texture that in their depth and complexity were the equal of classical composition. Classical composers worked in the opposite direction. In 1946 Igor Stravinsky acknowledged the depth and richness of jazz by composing his Ebony Concerto for Woody Herman's band; Aaron Copland did the same with his Concerto for Clarinet and String Orchestra (1948) for Benny Goodman; Marc Blitzstein by composing a "jazz opera," *Regina* (1949).

Thelonious Monk, Howard McGee, Roy Eldridge, and club manager Teddy Hill in front of Minton's Playhouse

Bebop. At the same time jazz was conquering audiences in the concert hall, jazz in the nightclubs was undergoing a revolution called bebop. Unlike swing, bebop was played in stripped down, five-and four-man combos and featured fast, shimmering, undanceable rhythms and dynamic, riffing horn solos. Developed by a host of creative, uncommercial musicians who gathered at Manhattan nightclubs such Minton's Playhouse, The Spotlite, Birdland, and Monroe's Uptown House, the style was widely scorned when it debuted around 1944–1945. Gradually, however, bebop became acclaimed. Bebop's players were undeniably talented and led jazz into a more improvisational, visceral direction. Led by soloists such as Lester Young, Theodore "Fats" Navarro, and Charlie Parker, bebop owed a debt to tough, urban, Kansas City blues. Parker's unpredictable saxophone improvisations in masterpieces such as "Cherokee," "Ko Ko," "Scrapple from the Apple," and "Ornithology" became hallmarks of the genre. The explosive, snare-punctuated drumming of players such as Kenny Clarke, Jo Jones, Art Blakey, and Max Roach also defined the style. Bebop featured propulsive string bass playing by pioneers such as Jimmy Blanton and Oscar Pettiford, and bebop quintets often highlighted cascading piano playing from pacesetters such as Earl "Bud" Powell and Thelonious Monk. In 1945 Parker joined a South Carolina trumpet player, John Birks "Dizzy" Gillespie, to form the All Star Quintet, which was instrumental in demonstrating the new style nationwide. Parker also played in his own quintet, which in 1947 featured the trumpet playing of a young Julliard student, Miles Davis. Davis went on to lead a revolution against the frenetic rhythms of bebop, ushering in the dominant jazz style of the 1950s: cool jazz.

Blues. Like jazz, blues was also undergoing a transformation in the 1940s, expanding a host of changes that began the decade before. The most profound of these changes was the reworking of rural and delta blues into an urban format. As African Americans migrated from the rural South into the urban, industrial centers of the North (at the turn of the century nine out of ten blacks lived in the country; at the end of World War II over half of all blacks lived in cities), rural forms of the blues fused with big-band jazz. Boogie-woogie — a musical fad of the late 1930s and early 1940s — was the best example of this fusion, a combination of barrelhouse-piano blues and swing jazz. Following such precedents, musicians added horns and drums for punch or a percussive piano to delta blues to make them tough and urban. Chicago blues shouters such as John Lee "Sonny Boy" Williamson, Big Bill Broonzy, Muddy Waters, and Big Joe Turner of Kansas City developed a raucous style of singing capable of being heard over a loud (and increasingly electrified) band. Such innovations were picked up and advanced by other blues stylists in the 1940s, especially "jive" artists such as saxophonist Louis Jordan or white pianist Harry "the Hipster" Gibson. Jive artists specialized in outrageously flamboyant recordings such as Jordan's *The Chick's Too Young to Fry* (1945) or Gibson's *Who Put the Benzedrine in Mrs. Murphy's Ovaltine?* (1944). The volume and flamboyance of the blues shouters and jive artists anticipated the rock 'n' roll of the next decade, as did the increasingly prominent electric blues guitarist, such as T-Bone Walker, Clarence "Gatemouth" Brown, or Sam "Lightin'" Hopkins.

Rhythm and Blues. The most important aspect in the transition from delta blues to urban blues to rock 'n' roll was a change in the business setting of the blues. The popularity of urban blues among African Americans caused many record labels to issue records by bluesmen. Before the Depression record manufacturers had sold "race" records to the black community, but with the Depression and the subsequent popularity of white swing bands, most companies dropped their race labels. In the 1940s the blues were back on wax, now in the form of so-called rhythm and blues (R & B) records, often produced by specialty labels such as Chess or Bluebird in Chicago, and Savoy or Atlantic in New York. A change in Federal Communications Commission (FCC) rules for radio, resulted in an expansion of stations willing to play R & B records, now in the new, disc jockey–dominated radio format. The development of the magnetic tape recorder meant that companies could now easily and cheaply record new talent. Thus a tremendous increase in the numbers and quality of records being released made the differences between musical genres increasingly blurry. Blues musicians heard jazz musicians, who heard country musicians and vice-versa. By the late 1940s there were several R&B, boogie-woogie, or "jump blues" records issued which fused these different influences into something like rock 'n' roll: Arthur Crudup's "That's All

Bob Wills and his Texas Playboys

Right" (1946), Amos Milburn's "Down the Road Apiece" (1946), Roy Brown's "Good Rockin' Tonight" (1947), Stick McGhee's "Drinkin' Wine Spo-Dee-O-Dee" (1949), or the Delmore Brothers' "Hillbilly Boogie" (1945).

Country. The Delmore Brothers' "Hillbilly Boogie," along with other protorock-country records such as Freddie Slack and Ella Mae Morse's "House of Blue Lights" (1946) or Tennessee Ernie Ford's "Smokey Mountain Boogie" (1949), evidences the degree to which country music in the 1940s paralleled the blues. Both musical styles were evolving toward rock 'n' roll. Like blues musicians, country players borrowed from swing, and country-swing bands such as Bob Wills and the Texas Playboys, Ray Whitley's Rhythm Wranglers, Spade Cooley, Tex Williams, and Jimmy Wakely's Cowboy Band proved popular. Both blues and country were for the most part ignored by major record companies until they proved commercially successful at the end of the 1940s. Both musicals forms benefited from the expansion of radio in the 1940s and the emergence of the upstart music-licensing agency, Broadcast Music Incorporated (BMI). Most important, both musical styles reflected the experiences and ambitions of rural people migrating to cities. (Chicago had been as important to country in the 1930s as it was to blues in the 1940s.) Country particularly expressed the feelings of Southern and Appalachian whites who mi-

grated to defense centers during the war, especially in such cities as Los Angeles, Baltimore, Cincinnati, and Mobile. "Hillbilly" (as country was often called) songs by Jimmie Davis, Ernest Tubb, and others could be found on jukeboxes in many bars in these cities. Northern, working-class soldiers, on the other hand, developed a taste for country during their basic training, which often took place in the South. Responding to the demand for country music, the Special Services Division of the European Theater of Operations sent hillbilly bands abroad to entertain the troops, and one of the most popular country radio programs, *Grand Ole Opry*, sent a tour around the country to military bases in 1941–1942. By the end of the war country star Roy Acuff was as popular among servicemen as Frank Sinatra.

Honky-Tonk. After the war the lines between pop music and the heretofore marginalized hillbilly music began to blur. Pop star Bing Crosby recorded songs by country songwriters, such as Dick Thomas's "Sioux City Sue" (1946), and country singer Eddy Arnold set aside his drawl and in songs like "Bouquet of Roses" (1947) began to croon like Crosby. Like the blues, however, the sound of country was getting tougher. Electric guitars and pedal steel guitars became featured instruments on many country records, including hits such as Arthur Smith's "Guitar Boogie" (1947). Bluegrass music experienced a resurgence, and like bebop it highlighted the

Hank Williams

improvisational solos of superb musicians such as guitarist Lester Flatt and banjoist Earl Scruggs. Most important, however, the themes in country music got gritty and hard, perhaps reflecting the difficulties many rural folk experienced adjusting to their new urban environment or to postwar suburban success. Gone were the days when country focused on optimistic sing-a-longs such as "You Are My Sunshine" or "San Antonio Rose." In its place came honky-tonk songs filled with themes of betrayal and anxiety. Hank Thompson's 1947 hit "Whoa Sailor," a song about a fickle bar girl who wants an off-duty sailor for his money, exemplified the genre. It was based on Thompson's own experience, but that was not necessarily the case with other honky-tonk hits: "Pistol Packin' Mama," by Al Dexter (1943), or "One Has My Name, the Other Has My Heart," a 1948 hit for Jimmy Wakely. Perhaps the best of the honky-tonk tunes was written by Los Angeles songwriter Cindy Walker. Bob Wills, moving away from country swing, had a hit with her tune, "Bubbles in My Beer" in 1948. The song addressed the heretofore rarely addressed (or often censored) theme of drunkenness and marital discord with poignant regret, anticipating the classics of the genre that would appear in the 1950s. The greatest of all country singers, Hank Williams, would achieve fame with such themes in songs such as "I'm So Lonesome I Could Cry," "Honky Tonk

Blues," "Cold, Cold Heart," and "Your Cheatin' Heart" in the late 1940s and early 1950s. Williams's tremendous skill as a songwriter easily transcends the honky-tonk genre; his short life (1923–1953), alcoholic, violent, and lonely, did not. In the 1940s, however, Williams's star was on the rise. Ironically, his first national hit, "Lovesick Blues" (1949), was a cover (a recording in a different musical style than the original) of a forty-year-old Tin Pan Alley song. Its tremendous success inspired noncountry covers of his tunes, such as Tony Bennett's version of "Cold, Cold Heart" (1950). In the 1950s such covers would become commonplace, but Williams demonstrated that country music had arrived commercially and could become "popular music" on its own terms.

Folk and Gospel. Folk music in the 1940s was at a low point, midway between the rousing protest songs of the 1930s and the resurgence of folk in the later 1950s. Folk, in fact, seemed out of date by the 1940s. Much of the initial impetus of folk had been oriented toward documenting and preserving indigenous local musics of Americans, a goal that had seen folklorists such as Howard W. Odum, Lawrence Gellert, Robert W. Gordon, and John A. Lomax combing the American heartland for musical traditions. Another impetus to folk had been political: Communists and socialists in the 1930s sought out "authentic" popular musics that reflected and advanced social struggle. In the 1940s neither goal made much sense. Much folklorist documentation had already been accomplished; and folk musicians, exposed to a variety of music on the radio, were quickly developing new musical styles, none of which had the "pure" or "uncontaminated" qualities sought by folklorists. Even gospel music, as a folk style derived from spirituals and committed to tradition, changed in the 1940s. Popular gospel singers such as Rosetta Tharpe or the Staples Sisters were influenced by blues singers such as Bessie Smith. The increasing availability of gospel records made stars such as Mahalia Jackson ("Move On Up a Little Higher," 1945) million-sellers and thus commercial prospects. Politically, the beginning of the decade saw left-wingers and their protest songs enlisting in the war effort (even Pete Seeger's Almanac Singers, a labor-song troupe, broadcast for the Office of War Information); at the end of the decade protest singers were marginalized as part of the anti-Communist hysteria. Thus, what folk there was in the 1940s was a style of relatively primitive or simple music which was characterized as "folk" and was, when present in the culture, another commercial genre of American music — indistinguishable, really, from blues, country, or even pop, as in the case of the Mills Brothers or the Ink Spots. *Billboard* magazine's chart of hit folk songs was in fact dropped in 1949, replaced by its country and western chart. Huddie "Leadbelly" Ledbetter, acclaimed as a folk "discovery" in the 1930s, achieved popular acclaim with his "Goodnight, Irene" (1943). A similar popularization visited Woody Guthrie, the best known of the leftist singers, whose "This Land Is Your

Pete Seeger and Woody Guthrie at the Highlander Folk School, 1940

Land" (1944) was a patriotic anthem rather than a protest song during World War II. After the support of some protest singers for Henry Wallace's 1948 presidential bid and a brief period of commercial success for the Weavers, folk music virtually disappeared until the early 1960s, when it would be resurrected as a commercial genre by the Kingston Trio, Joan Baez, Bob Dylan, and Peter, Paul and Mary.

Folk Takes the Stage I. Where folk music made an impact in the 1940s was on the Broadway stage and within the symphonic concert hall. In the 1930s, classically trained composers began experiments integrating classical music with folk hymns, work songs, and jazz and blues. The experiments were motivated in part by New Deal funding, which financed many such endeavors, and by the excursions of European composers into their own national folk heritage — folk/classical fusions, in other words, were increasingly prominent expressions of nationalism during an extremely nationalistic era. Broadway, keyed to the commercial possibilities of such experiments, had already produced composers such as George Gershwin who recognized the popular potential in integrating blues, country, and jazz figures into a classical format. The great Broadway hits of the 1940s all repeated this fusion — usually with the addition of a libretto or plot derived from a folk source. Such was the key to Richard Rodgers and Oscar Hammerstein's 1943 smash, *Oklahoma!,* based on the Americana play *Green Grow the*

Lilacs, by Lynn Riggs; Rodgers and Lorenz Hart's *Pal Joey* (1940), based on urban short stories by John O'Hara; and Irving Berlin's *Annie Get Your Gun* (1946), based on Annie Oakley, the sharpshooting star of Buffalo Bill's Wild West Show. Such syntheses of Broadway and folk proved enormously popular, especially with the wartime audiences filled with off-duty servicemen, and they established many conventions in Broadway musicals for the next several decades.

Folk Takes the Stage II. Folk music proved alluring to classical composers as well as to Broadway showmen. Composers such as Aaron Copland had long been concerned with establishing American classical music in a fashion that he termed not "too European in derivation." Working on the problem in the 1930s, Copland's solution was to integrate American popular music and culture into a classical setting. His 1938 score for the ballet *Billy the Kid* began a period wherein Copland accomplished his goals in spectacular fashion. *Rodeo* (1942) freely adapted American folksongs such as "If He'd Be A Buckaroo by His Trade," "Sis Joe," and "Old Paint." Copland returned to the formula with a piece commissioned by Martha Graham for her dance *Appalachian Spring* (1944), which integrated the Shaker hymnal "Tis the Gift to Be Simple." In these works and others Copland brilliantly demonstrated what he called his "accessible style" — open textures, sweeping orchestration, elegance, and melodiousness, deeply evocative of prairie skies and pio-

Lee Dixon, Celeste Holm, Alfred Drake, Joan Roberts, Betty Garde, and Joseph Buloff (kneeling) in *Oklahoma*, 1943

neer vistas. An approach similar to that taken by Copland was pursued by Roy Harris with his Symphony no. 4, subtitled the *Folksong Symphony* (1940; 1942). It featured interludes of folk songs common since the Civil War. Harris returned to the Civil War for his Symphony no. 6, subtitled *Gettysburg* (1944), in which he hoped to recapture the spirit of America contained in the Gettysburg Address. Samuel Barber also hoped to revive the spirit of the past in his work *Knoxville: Summer of 1915* (1948), based on James Agee's novel *A Death in the Family*. Opera composer Virgil Thomson explored American history too, interweaving gospel hymns and popular songs into his opera *The Mother of Us All* (1947), whose cast of characters includes historical figures such as Susan B. Anthony, Ulysses S. Grant, and Lillian Russell.

Exiles. Copland, Barber, and Harris were committed in their folkish compositions and their other works to tonality and conventional restrictions of counterpoint and melody. A similar commitment was typical of several other American composers of the period, including Paul Creston, William Schuman, Howard Hanson, Walter Piston, and Roger Sessions. During World War II, however, atonal European composers found refuge in the United States and disseminated the innovations in compositions they pioneered on the Continent. Foremost among them was Arnold Schoenberg, the Viennese modernist who originated the twelve-tone composition system. His method, which he developed in the first decade of this century, was dissonant, unsettling, and, to more conservative ears, unmusical. It was, nonetheless, rigorous, intellectually challenging, and in some ways perfectly

keyed to unsettled times. By the 1920s Schoenberg was an acknowledged master of composition and was appointed to the Prussian Academy of Fine Arts in Berlin. Dismissed by the Nazis for his Jewish background, Schoenberg made his way to Paris, then to Los Angeles, where he taught, first at the University of Southern California then at the University of California, Los Angeles. Other European exiles included Russian composer Igor Stravinsky; Italian maestro Arturo Toscanini; pianists Arthur Rubinstein and Artur Schnabel; German composer Paul Hindemith; Hungarian composer Béla Bartók; German composer and songwriter Kurt Weill; the Parisian teacher of composition Nadia Boulanger; violinist Adolf Busch; harpsichordist Wanda Landowska; musicologists Alfred Einstein, Hugo Leichtentritt, Curt Sachs, and Karl Geiringer; conductors Bruno Walter, William Steinberg, George Szell, and Erich Leinsdorf; the composers Hans Eisler, Ernst Toch, Erich Korngold, Ernst Krenek, Darius Milhaud, and Bohuslav Martinu. Many of these people were forced to flee Europe because of their Jewish lineage or their political beliefs. Many, including Stravinsky, Hindemith, and Bartók, left because their art itself was too radical for the Nazis. These men were especially influential with American composers, but none more than Schoenberg, whose work is apparent in several classical American compositions, such as

John Cage, 1947

Wallingford Riegger's Symphony no. 3 (1948), and a host of serial music pieces composed by a variety of artists during the 1950s and 1960s.

Experiments. Schoenberg's most important student was the Californian John Cage. An unschooled pianist with a brilliant mind and a rebellious attitude, Cage began composing with Schoenberg's disciples Richard Buhlig and Adolf Weiss. In 1935 he began classes with the master himself but soon quit. Schoenberg's emphasis was on musical tradition — counterpoint, harmony — no matter that his approach was radical. Cage was interested in percussion, noise, space. He was inspired by the non-traditional activities of West Coast composers such as Harry Partch, experimenting with percussion on pieces of junkyard scrap. Cage also believed that noise and music should integrate this-worldly experiences rather than lead to otherworldly escape. His abusive compositions, based on percussion, were designed to direct the listener into a confrontation with fundamental musical and existential assumptions. By 1940 Cage had established a reputation as a master of percussive composition and had advanced the use of prepared piano (introduced by Henry Cowell), altering the sound quality of a piano by affixing bolts, nuts, and wires to the piano strings. He perfected this technique in 1943 with a compelling six-movement suite for piano that inspired many New York artists, *The Perilous Night*. Cage's compositions during the 1940s, *The Unavailable Memory Of* (1944), *The Seasons* (1947), *Suite for Toy Piano* (1948), and *Sonatas and Interludes* (1949), are similarly experimental, a fusion of noise and music, often reflecting Cage's interest in Eastern thought. Cage also began to consider the randomness with which he prepared his pianos — leading him to the experiments in time and silence (*4'33"*, 1952) that made him famous.

New York. With John Cage's excursions into silence, American music in the 1940s expressed almost every shade of the aural spectrum. Silence, harmony, noise, percussion, color, melody, timbre, syncopation, riff, improvisation, texture, phrasing — few sounds existed that were not being expressed by Cage, Copland, Rodgers, Acuff, Williams, Waters, Parker, Ellington, Holiday, Sinatra, Crosby, or Goodman. New York during the 1940s became the world's capital of music, much as Paris or Berlin had been before, except that in New York not only was the grand tradition of classical music subverted by noisy revolutionaries like Cage, it was expanded by the presence of American musical traditions derived from the heartland. In New York, moreover, there existed a communications and distribution infrastructure for music like none previous in world history. Gigantic media and music corporations, such as RCA, CBS, ASCAP, and BMI, spread American music from New York to every point on the globe. Transient musical expressions which were basically unpublishable in standard classical scorings — like Billie Holiday's phrasing — could be recorded and, in a sense, immortalized using the new recording technology. Perhaps most exciting was the fact that despite the richness of American music in the 1940s, there were musical horizons anticipated yet unexplored. Rock 'n' roll, perhaps the most popular form of music ever created, was yet to be born. Cage's random experiments anticipated the serial innovations and electronic music of subsequent decades. The folk-music research and collection techniques which promoted (and ex-

Duke Ellington, in hat, outside a Washington, D.C., record shop, 1942

ploited) so much country and blues would later bring global folk expressions such as calypso, bossa nova, juju, reggae, flamenco, Balinese, Indian, Yemenite, and African music to light. Most important, the spirit of innovation, cross-fertilization, and defiance of musical genre would continue, producing wonderful new styles of music. It was the spirit of New York in the 1940s; perhaps the spirit of American music anywhere, anytime.

Sources:

Patrick Carr, ed., *The Illustrated History of Country Music* (Garden City, N.Y.: Doubleday, 1980);

Gilbert Chase, *America's Music: From the Pilgrims to the Present,* revised, third edition (Chicago: University of Illinois Press, 1987);

Francis Davis, *The History of the Blues* (New York: Hyperion, 1995);

Bill C. Malone, *Country Music, U.S.A.* (Austin: University of Texas Press, 1985);

Paul Oliver, Max Harrison, and William Bolcom, *The New Grove Gospel, Blues and Jazz* (New York: Norton, 1986);

David Revill, *The Roaring Silence: John Cage: A Life* (New York: Arcade, 1992).

HEADLINE MAKERS

HUMPHREY BOGART

1899-1957

ACTOR

Unlikely Origins. He made his name as a sensitive tough guy on the screen. He came to define an everyman sensibility and cynicism with his edgy, slightly slurred urban delivery. In the 1940s and early 1950s he was among Hollywood's biggest box-office stars. But Humphrey Bogart's origins belie the screen persona he was to become. He was born into affluence on Riverside Drive in New York City. His mother, Maud Humphrey, was a well-known illustrator. Her "Maud Humphrey Baby" became a popular figure in advertising. The portrait was of the infant Humphrey Bogart. Bogart attended Trinity School in New York City and the prestigious Phillips Academy in Andover, Massachusetts. He was a poor student and left the school early to join the navy. He reported to the USS *Leviathan* in October 1918, and World War I ended sixteen days later. In June 1919 Bogart was discharged. The navy gave him one thing — his distinctive speech. While serving as a military policeman, he was hit in the mouth with handcuffs by a prisoner attempting escape. The blow left a scar and the slight slur that would be imitated worldwide by the 1940s.

Struggling on Stage. Out of the navy, Bogart procured work in odd jobs and on the stock exchange. A family friend, William Brady, helped Bogart become involved in the New York stage. He appeared briefly in *Drifting* (1922) and then took the lead in a comedy called *Swifty* (1922). He spent the next five years alternating successes, such as *Cradle Snatchers* (1925), with disasters such as *Baby Mine* (1927). He also began drinking and married twice. He appeared on film for the first time in 1929 in a

ten-minute Warner Bros. Vitaphone Corporation production called *Broadway's Like That*, which featured Joan Blondell.

Struggling on Film. One year later he signed with Fox Studios and began an undistinguished run as a supporting actor. He drifted back and forth from Hollywood to New York looking for stage and screen work. He filmed *Up the River* (1930) with Spencer Tracy. Within a decade both would be legendary. Tracy coined the name "Bogie," which Humphrey came to prefer. Despite steady work Bogart was in dire straits financially. His father died, leaving Humphrey in debt. Bogart began drinking heavily and hit the bottom of his career in 1934. That year, however, while appearing in *Invitation to Murder,* an undistinguished stage mystery, he was spotted by Arthur Hopkins, who decided to cast Bogart in *The Petrified Forest,* a Robert Sherwood play about random murder in an Arizona cafe. Bogart played Duke Mantee, a brooding, suicidal killer, and gained recognition for the role in 1935.

Stability. The star of *The Petrified Forest,* Leslie Howard, insisted that Bogart be given the same role in the screen production. Warner complied with the demand and thus affirmed Bogart's film appeal. He signed with Warner and became a staple of the gangster films of the 1930s as one of the "tough guys," along with Edward G. Robinson, George Raft, and James Cagney. For four years Bogart appeared in films such as *Bullets or Ballots* (1936), *Angels With Dirty Faces* (1938), and *Brother Orchid* (1940). This period peaked in 1941 with *High Sierra,* in which Bogart played a killer but also displayed the tragic tenderness that lay beneath the tough figures he would play.

"Bogie" Arrives. The Humphrey Bogart of legend arrived in 1941 as Sam Spade in John Huston's *The Maltese Falcon,* based on Dashiell Hammett's novel. George Raft had turned down the part, seeing it as not important enough. Bogart was ambivalent but took the role. The studio considered it a B movie. Bogart and Huston made it a hit, and it is often considered the first legitimate film noir movie. Bogart played Sam Spade, a tough private eye with a tender, not completely cynical style. He had played tough guys for years but was beginning to explore the underlying idealism of the roles. His exploration of this character type reached its peak in *Casablanca*, filmed in 1942. Bogart's Rick, the tough, cynical, bitter idealist, is the strongest statement of the Bogart role. He was nominated for an Academy Award for the picture and throughout the 1940s was among the top five box-office draws.

Versatility. In 1944, with his third marriage on the rocks, Bogart filmed *To Have and Have Not.* The film marked Lauren Bacall's screen debut, and she and Bogart promptly fell in love, creating one of Hollywood's most famous romances. She was nineteen, and he was forty-five. They were married in 1945 and had two children. In 1947 he traveled to Washington, D.C., to show support for the Hollywood Ten, who were testifying before the House Un-American Activities Committee. Bogart's most versatile acting followed the war years. He began branching out into more-complex roles. He again teamed with Huston in *The Treasure of the Sierra Madre* (1948) in which he played a man driven mad with greed. In 1957 he teamed with Katharine Hepburn in *The African Queen* and won an Academy Award for his role as the drunken and comedic Charlie Allnut. *The Caine Mutiny* followed in 1954 with one of his greatest roles. He filmed *The Harder They Fall* in 1956, but he was already showing the effects of cancer. On 14 January 1957 Humphrey Bogart died, leaving behind a distinguished body of film work and one of the greatest of Hollywood's legends.

Source:
Jonathan Coe, *Humphrey Bogart: Take It and Like It* (New York: Grove Weidenfeld, 1991).

MARTHA GRAHAM

1895-1991

MODERN DANCE INNOVATOR

Picasso of Dance. Martha Graham was to modern dance what Pablo Picasso was to modern art: the single greatest innovator of this century. Like Picasso, hers was a sweeping talent defined by a variety of styles and interests. In Graham's work Grand Kabuki, Greek theater, German expressionism, psychoanalysis, Native American ritual, Puritanism, and American history and poetry combined in explosive fashion. The 1940s were her heyday. She produced dances of transcendent splendor and worked with some of the world's most famous composers. During the de-

cade, her experimentation, earlier acclaimed in New York dance circles, became widely known; as modern dance was popularized, her name became synonymous with the form.

Background. Graham was born in Pittsburgh, Pennsylvania, into a wealthy family who traced their lineage back to Miles Standish. In 1909 the family relocated to Santa Barbara, California. Graham maintained she was drawn to dance from an early age. At age sixteen she attended a dance performance by Ruth St. Denis of the Denishawn dance troupe and quickly joined the group. One of the first American dance companies and schools, Denishawn specialized in that which was novel and exotic to American sensibilities: Greek pageants, Japanese sword dances, sexy Spanish flamencos. While touring with Denishawn, Graham studied the expressionistic dances of Isadora Duncan and Mary Wigman. Following their innovations, Ted Shawn, choreographer of Denishawn, wrote *Xochitl,* based on a Mexican legend, for Graham. It brought Graham to the attention of New York producers, and she left Denishawn for a short stint in the *Greenwich Village Follies.* Dissatisfied with commercial dance, Graham taught for a time at the Eastman School of Music in Rochester, New York, where she began the choreographic experiments that made her famous.

New York Diva. As a choreographer Graham initially returned to simple and primitive movements — walking, running, and skipping — and built short "mood" dances from these fundamentals. Such dances, composed in collaboration with pianist Louis Horst, established her reputation in New York dance circles. More-ambitious pieces featuring the dynamic music of modern composers, such as *Lamentation* (1930), *Dithyrambic* (1931), and *Primitive Mysteries* (1931), formalized the Graham style: highly theatrical expressions, angular stances, explosive, stylized gestures in the limbs, spare and abstract stage settings. Graham sought to integrate motifs and innovations in modern art and psychology into dance. Compelled by Sigmund Freud's and Carl Jung's analysis of the unconscious, she attempted to fuse abstracted gestures to psychological states, and her work was noted for its tension and unsettling qualities. Graham received twenty-three curtain calls after the debut of *Primitive Mysteries.* As dance companies toured behind her work, Graham's fame rapidly spread from New York.

Triumph. Beginning in 1938, with *American Document,* Graham crystallized the innovations begun earlier and reached the height of her powers with a series of dynamic, highly ambitious dances. *American Document* was nothing less than a condensed history of the United States, expressed via the conflict between the individual and society. Probing her own Puritan ancestry, *American Document* featured the juxtaposition of hellfire sermons by Jonathan Edwards and highly erotic dance. Graham returned to these themes with *Letter to the World* (1940), based upon the life and poetry of Emily Dickinson. *Letter* *to the World* reflected the tension between poet and community enshrined in Dickinson's verse: "This is my letter to the world / that never wrote to me." In 1944 Graham returned to her exploration of the American character with a triumph: *Appalachian Spring*. Featuring music by Aaron Copland (who won a Pulitzer Prize for the score in 1945) and sets by Isamu Noguchi, *Appalachian Spring* was an evocative celebration of pioneer life, a commemoration of the American spirit. Graham turned to less nationalistic, more intensely private themes with her next dances: *Herodiade* (1944), *Cave of the Heart* (1946), *Night Journey* (1947), and *Death and Entrances* (1943; revived, 1947). *Herodiade*, originally a poem by Stéphane Mallarmé set to music by composer Paul Hindemith, became in Graham's hands a ceremony of eternal feminine patience. *Cave of the Heart*, featuring music by Samuel Barber, and the stage again set by Noguchi, was a venture into Greek mythology and was as ambitious as classical tragedy. Under the influence of Jung, Graham wrote the dance to express her belief in a collective "motor memory" in the body, a primordial genius of the senses she sought to evoke. A noted psychoanalytically influenced dance was *Night Journey*, Graham's retelling of the Oedipus legend. *Death and Entrances* was perhaps the most ambitious of the psychological cycle, an attempt to probe, simultaneously, the inner life of the famous Brontë sisters and that of the dancers on stage. Graham used small portable objects to signify the icons of memory, both collective and individual; the dance itself was filled with tense body gestures, indicative of tortured repressions. At its most ambitious, *Death and Entrances* aimed less at expression than at therapy. Graham had become not only dance's Picasso, but also its Freud.

Honors. Graham completed her probing of the psyche through mythology with *Clytemnestra* in 1958. A retelling of Aeschylus's meditation on remembrance, revenge, and regret, the evening-long dance was a highly acclaimed pageant of color, motion, and violence. Graham, still starring in her own dances, was sixty-four, and she began to put her more famous dances on film, including *Appalachian Spring* (1959) and *Night Journey* (1960). Her fame was such that in the next twenty years she received numerous honors, including the Medal of Freedom and the French Legion of Honor. Nonetheless, her overwhelming dominance in modern dance inevitably called forth challengers to her position, especially former students intent on overthrowing her highly structured, overly psychological style. Former associates such as Merce Cunningham took modern dance into a spontaneous, decidedly non-Graham direction in the 1960s and 1970s. In 1969 Graham danced her last role, but she continued to choreograph new works, including two in 1975 starring Rudolph Nureyev, *Lucifer* and *The Scarlet Letter*. Despite the eclipse of her style, Graham continued through the Martha Graham Dance Company to choreograph new works, including the *Maple Leaf Rag*,

with music by Scott Joplin and costumes by Calvin Klein, in 1990. She died on 1 April 1991.

Sources:

Martha Graham, *Blood Memory* (Garden City, N.Y.: Doubleday, 1991);

Agnes de Mille, *Martha: The Life and Work of Martha Graham* (New York: Random House, 1991).

LILLIAN HELLMAN
1906-1984
PLAYWRIGHT, MEMOIRIST

Moralist. "I cannot and will not cut my conscience to fit this year's fashion," wrote Lillian Hellman in 1952 in a letter addressed to the House Un-American Activities Committee (HUAC). She had been called before the HUAC, like so many before her, in order to name names, to admit fault, and to plead forgiveness. Some had done so. Others, like the Hollywood Ten, had gone to jail for pleading protection under the First and Fifth Amendments and being found in contempt of Congress. Hellman's tactic was to write a letter displaying a willingness to discuss her own beliefs but refuse to name names had been tried before, but she released her letter to the press and used public opinion as an ally. The tactic stumped the committee but still got her blacklisted for nearly ten years. Had the panel of congressmen been familiar with her plays, they would have expected no less. Hellman referred to herself as a "moralist" who used drama, on screen and stage, to illuminate the individual conscience in the face of social conformity.

Accidental Writer. Writing was not a calling for Hellman. Born on 20 June 1906 in New Orleans, Louisiana, she was raised as the only child of a shoe merchant of modest means. She spent her childhood shuttling between her mother's family home in New York and her father's sister's boardinghouse in New Orleans. In 1922 she began attending New York University but quit after three years. She began reading manuscripts for Boni and Liveright, a prestigious New York publisher. The publishing life introduced her to the bohemian New York crowd of the 1920s. In 1925 she married press agent Arthur Kober and began dabbling in book reviews and play reading. In Paris in the late 1920s she published two short stories in *Paris Comet* (edited by her husband) and traveled briefly to Germany. By 1930 she was in Hollywood, where Kober worked as a screenwriter for Paramount while Hellman read scenarios for M-G-M. She met Dashiell Hammett, who would become her lifelong companion after she divorced Kober in 1932.

First Success. In 1933 Hammett suggested a chapter of William Roughhead's book *Bad Companions* (1930) as the basis of a play. Hellman wrote it, and *The Children's Hour* opened at Maxine Elliot's Theater in New York in 1934. It ran for 691 performances. Hellman was immediately recognized for her ability to draw characters concisely and to cut lean the exposition in a play. The play, about how a single lie can destroy lives, had the social realist edge of the 1930s. It also had lesbian overtones and was banned in Boston, London, and Chicago. *The Children's Hour* brought Hellman fame and fortune and got her hired as a screenwriter by Sam Goldwyn. She wrote the film *Dark Angel* in 1935, adapted *The Children's Hour* for the screen in 1936 (altering it markedly, removing the lesbian theme and calling it *These Three*), and began her second play, *Days To Come* (1936). That play failed miserably and closed after seven performances.

Hitting Stride. She wrote another screenplay (*Dead End*, 1937 starring Humphrey Bogart) before returning to the stage. She hit stride in 1939 with *The Little Foxes*, a portrait of a southern family set in 1900. The play, an exposure of greed and rivalry within the Hubbard family, was explosive theater, called by some a chronicle of the rise of the industrial South. The Left saw it as an attack on capitalism, and Hellman was acclaimed by the Communist Party. Her next play, *Watch on the Rhine*, won the New York Drama Critics' Circle Award for 1941. In this openly anti-Fascist play, Hellman begins her exploration of personal complacency in the face of a rising tide of political danger. The play documents the confrontation of an anti-Nazi and a political opportunist, all against the backdrop of a comfortable Washington, D.C., home. The themes resonated in the prewar atmosphere as interventionists and isolationists were debating nationwide America's position on the war in Europe. Hammett wrote the screenplay for *Watch on the Rhine* in 1942, and the film was released in 1943, garnering an Oscar for Paul Lukas for best actor. Hellman followed up *Watch on the Rhine* with an original screenplay called *The North Star* (1943), set in the Soviet Union during the Nazi invasion. The movie industry was in a mood to portray America's ally in a favorable light, a stance that would cause trouble after the war. Hellman debuted another play in 1944, *The Searching Wind*, which again looked at individual passivity, this time in 1920s Germany, and followed that up with *Another Part of the Forest* (1947), in which she made her debut as a director.

Public Politics. Though she claimed she never joined a political party, Hellman was public with her political opinions, which were expressed in more personal than ideological terms. She had seen fascism firsthand in Germany. She had written political plays. Her playwriting declined after the war, but she remained a public figure. She was a supporter of Henry Wallace, an internationalist who spoke against the Cold War. She traveled to the Soviet Union for five months in 1944 and met Serge Eisenstein. She visited a concentration camp in Poland. In 1948 she visited

Belgrade for the opening of *The Little Foxes*, met Marshal Tito, and praised him in an interview. She remained liberal in the face of the McCarthy years, continuing to write or adapt plays dealing with political conscience and private morality (*Montserrat* [1949], from a French play by Emmanuel Robles, *The Lark* [1955], based on Jean Anouilh's Joan of Arc story *L'Alouette*). Her Chekhovian play *The Autumn Garden* (1949) is among her finest, and her 1960 play *Toys in the Attic* won her another New York Drama Critics' Circle Award.

Her Craft. She was not a prolific writer. She is not easily categorized. Lillian Hellman spans the bridge of social realists in the 1930s through the middle-class conformity of the 1950s. In the 1960s and 1970s she wrote memoirs of her extraordinary life (*An Unfinished Woman, Pentimento: A Book of Portraits*, and *Scoundrel Time*, about the McCarthy years). Above all else, she was a craftswoman. Her plays are marked by character portraits; straightforward, unpoetic dialogue; and plots that rise to inevitable and explosive confrontations. "I am a moral writer, often too moral a writer, and I cannot avoid, it seems, the summing up," she claimed, though at the end of her life she was brought to task for self-serving lapses of memory in her accounts, notably by Mary McCarthy and Dianna Trilling.

Sources:

Carol MacNicholas, "Lillian Hellman," in *Twentieth-Century American Dramatists, Part 1: A-J*, volume 7 of *Dictionary of Literary Biography* (Detroit: Bruccoli Clark, 1981);

William Wright, *Lillian Hellman: The Image, the Woman* (New York: Simon & Schuster, 1986).

BILLIE HOLIDAY

1915-1959

JAZZ SINGER

Childhood. The facts of Billie Holiday's early life are uncertain. She was born Eleanora Fagan, probably in Baltimore. There are conflicting reports about whether her thirteen-year-old mother, Sadie Fagan, and fifteen-year-old father, Clarence Holiday, ever married, but if they did, they did not live together for any significant period. Clarence Holiday played guitar and banjo professionally and joined jazz-band leader Fletcher Henderson in the early 1930s, so he was on the road much of the time, and he was not conceivably a family man, in any case. Eleanora had a delinquent adolescence. She was sent to a reformatory at the age of ten and had become a prostitute by the time she was twelve. In Baltimore (or perhaps later) she assumed the first name of her favorite movie star, Billie Dove, and the last name of her father, and practiced to be a singer, taking Bessie

Smith and Louis Armstrong as models. She moved to New York City with her mother in 1928 or 1929, and together they struggled to make a living during the Depression, working as domestics when they could get no other work. When her father came to town, Billie Holiday confronted him on his jobs, threatening to call him daddy in front of his girlfriends unless he gave her money.

"Lady Day." Billie Holiday began singing in New York clubs as a teenager, and by the time she was old enough to drink legally she had established a reputation as a stirring jazz singer. She was a natural talent with excellent musical instincts and an earthy voice that matched the searching honesty of her songs. By the age of eighteen her fans included singer Mildred Bailey; Benny Goodman, with whom she recorded in 1933; and record producer-promoter John Hammond, who observed that "she sang popular songs in a manner that made them completely her own." Her nickname in Harlem was "Lady"; saxophonist Lester Young, an admirer, added the appellation "Day." She was "Lady Day," the hottest singer in Harlem before she was twenty.

Career Peak. The best early Billie Holiday recordings were organized by Hammond with pianist Teddy Wilson. After the success of those sessions, Hammond was devoted to promoting Holiday's career. He arranged for her to appear with the best musicians of the day. By the end of the 1930s she had sung in the bands of Count Basie and Artie Shaw, but life with a big band was too restrictive for her, and in 1938 she became a solo act. In January 1939 she opened at the new Greenwich Village club Cafe Society, where she sang for nine months and introduced her classic protest against lynching, "Strange Fruit." Holiday was a success, but she was also living her music with disastrous effects. In August 1941 she married Jimmy Monroe, and by the time of their breakup soon afterward, she was an opium user and a heroin addict. She was making one thousand dollars a week in the early 1940s and spending her money on her habit. She was also at the peak of her career. In 1943 she was voted the best jazz vocalist in the *Esquire* magazine readers' poll. With that acknowledgment of her greatness, Decca Records began making a series of thirty-six recordings that are regarded among the finest jazz vocals of the time. "Lover Man," "Porgy," "Now or Never," and a duet with Louis Armstrong on "My Sweet Hunk of Trash" are among those releases that mark the last of the good times for her.

Hard Times. In 1945 Holiday married trumpet player Joe Guy, and together they ran a band that lost large sums of money. Business woes, added to her chronic depression and dependence on drugs, brought her career to an abrupt halt. In 1947 she was arrested on a drug charge and voluntarily accepted placement in a federal drug-rehabilitation center for a year and a

day. Ten days after her release she appeared before a packed house at Carnegie Hall, but she was not allowed to play in Manhattan establishments that served alcohol because her cabaret license had been suspended. The years of drinking and the ravages of drug addiction took their toll on her talent as well. Her voice lost its resiliency, and she appeared on stage when she was unable to perform well.

Last Days. She toured Europe in 1954 and appeared triumphantly at Royal Albert Hall before an audience of six thousand. But increasingly the power of her performance was attributable to the pity the audience felt for a great talent that had destroyed itself, as if her music described a life too terrible to endure. That image was reinforced by her candid autobiography *Lady Sings the Blues* (1956), which did not hide the embarrassments of her life. In the mid 1950s her marriage to Louis McKay soured, as all her relationships with men did, and she was unable to drag herself from the world of drug abuse. By 1958 she was on her last slide downward. She died on 15 July 1959 in a hospital bed where she had been under house arrest since 12 June for possession of narcotics. She had $750 taped to her leg, an advance from a magazine for a series of articles about her life.

Sources:
Billie Holiday, *Lady Sings the Blues* (Garden City, N.Y.: Doubleday, 1956);

Colin Larkin, ed., *The Guinness Encyclopedia of Popular Music* (London & Chester, Conn.: Guinness, 1992).

DWIGHT MACDONALD

1906-1982

MAGAZINE EDITOR, POLITICAL COMMENTATOR

Iconoclast. In the 1940s Dwight Macdonald was a leading voice of intellectual dissent in America. A writer of satire and biting criticism, he published nearly singlehandedly a magazine called *Politics*, the only American intellectual journal to oppose U.S. participation in World War II. An ardent pacifist, Macdonald also championed equality for African Americans and homosexual rights.

Early Years. Macdonald was born in New York City. His father was a lawyer from a middle-class background, and his mother was the daughter of a wealthy Brooklyn merchant. Looking back at his parents' happy marriage, Macdonald later spoke of "the calm, affectionate atmosphere of my boyhood home." Indeed, Macdonald enjoyed a secure, privileged childhood. He attended private elementary schools in New York City, where he began to write, and then went to Phillips Exeter Academy, where he edited the student literary magazine and became class poet. He also helped found a club called "The Hedonists," whose cultural heroes were Oscar Wilde and H. L. Mencken. In 1924 Macdonald went on to Yale University, where he majored in history and continued to pursue his literary interests. He won literary prizes, and edited the *Yale Literary Magazine*, the *Yale Record*, and wrote columns for the *Yale Daily News*.

Working for Fortune. After Macdonald graduated in 1928, he wanted to begin his career as a literary critic, but his father's death in 1926 forced him to provide financial help to his mother. He joined the executive training program at Macy's department store in New York but after six months realized he was poorly suited for retailing. With the help of a friend from Yale, Macdonald got a job as associate editor of *Fortune* magazine, which was just being launched by Henry R. Luce, another Yale graduate. The magazine flourished despite the stock market crash of 1929, and while Macdonald did not share Luce's uncritical commitment to capitalism, his years at *Fortune* provided him with a valuable apprenticeship in journalism. Macdonald resigned from the *Fortune* staff in 1936.

From Capitalist to Revolutionary. Macdonald embraced revolutionary politics in the 1930s as he began reading Karl Marx, Vladimir I. Lenin, and Leon Trotsky. He later said of his political evolution, "the speed with which I evolved from a liberal into a radical and from a tepid Communist sympathizer into an ardent anti-Stalinist still amazes me." In 1937, with Philip Rahv, William Phillips, F. W. Dupree, and George L. K. Morris, he helped to revive the leftist literary magazine *Partisan Review*, which had been founded in 1934 and suspended publication in 1936. Taking an anti-Stalinist position while favoring revolutionary socialism, the new *Partisan Review* was more politically independent than the old, which had been closely linked to the Communist Party. Macdonald disagreed with his fellow editors at *Partisan Review* on involvement in World War II, which he firmly condemned, and resigned from the magazine in 1943.

Publishing Politics. In February 1944 Macdonald published the first issue of *Politics*, a magazine that he owned, published, edited, and proofread. Initially, he was also its chief contributor. According to Macdonald, the aim of *Politics* was "to create a center of consciousness on the Left, welcoming all varieties of radical thought." In its first two years, Macdonald explained, the magazine "forsook the true Marxist faith to whore after the strange gods of anarchism and pacificism. This was partly a matter of my own evolution . . . my thinking took its natural bent toward individualism, empiricism, moralism, estheticism." *Politics* went from a monthly to a bimonthly, and in its five years of existence it published articles of political, literary, and moral opinion. Macdonald stopped publishing *Politics* in 1949, in part to spend more time on his own writing.

Later Career. Macdonald continued to write for magazines such as *The New Yorker, Encounter,* and *Partisan Review,* earning a reputation as a satirist and championing a "radical humanist" outlook based on anti-authoritarianism. *Against the American Grain* (1962) is a collection of his cultural and literary criticism. In it he criticizes American mass culture, "which thrives not on aesthetic merit, but on marketability." During the years 1960–1966 Macdonald was a staff writer for *The New Yorker* and movie critic for *Esquire.* Later in the decade he spoke out against the Vietnam War. He remained a prolific writer and independent thinker until his death in 1982.

Sources:

Stephen J. Whitfield, *A Critical American: The Politics of Dwight Macdonald* (Hamden, Conn.: Archon, 1984);

Michael Wreszin, *A Rebel in Defense of Tradition: The Life and Politics of Dwight Macdonald* (New York: Basic Books, 1994).

CARSON McCULLERS

1917-1967

WRITER

Prodigy. By the time she was twenty-nine years old, Carson McCullers had already produced three novels (*The Heart is a Lonely Hunter* [1940], *Reflections in a Golden Eye* [1941], and *The Member of the Wedding* [1946]). The first and last of the three are her most memorable and guaranteed her a place in the literature of the 1940s as well as in American literary history. Poor health and a tumultuous emotional life cut short her work in full flower, but by her twenty-third birthday she had already fulfilled her mother's prediction that Carson would one day become famous.

Prelude. She was born Lula Carson Smith in Columbus, Georgia, on 19 February 1917. Childhood was to become a major theme in her work, especially in *The Member of the Wedding.* She was a tall girl (5'8" by age thirteen) and was seen as freakish by her peers. Her mother considered her destined. She gained early proficiency at the piano and was heading toward a career in music. At seventeen she went north to New York to attend The Juilliard School of Music and take writing classes at Columbia University. She had shown little literary bent but had been influenced deeply by her charismatic, storytelling mother. When she lost her tuition money for Juilliard on a New York subway, fate seemed to have chosen writing for her. She found odd jobs and began studying writing at Columbia under Whit Burnett. She wrote "Wunderkind," and Burnett published the story in his popular *Story* magazine. In 1937 she married

Reeves McCullers, who would become her on-again, off-again companion through life. The marriage became a distant union as her writing career flourished while his foundered.

Flowering. Marriage gave her the personal security to write, and within two years she had completed *The Heart is a Lonely Hunter*. The novel gained immediate critical attention. It contained the themes of alienation and solitude, often self-imposed, that would mark McCullers's work. It is the story of John Singer, a deaf-mute who, because he is without voice, becomes the receptacle of confidences of the lonely people around him. The novel is "contrapuntal," in McCullers's words, with Singer receiving the voices of others. Her musical education showed through. Her second novel, *Reflections in a Golden Eye*, displayed McCullers's penchant for the grotesque characters that would mark all of her work. The plot involves bisexuality and masochism, and the book was uniformly panned as sensationalistic. Despite suffering the first of several cerebral strokes in 1941, McCullers continued writing prolifically. Her marriage had disintegrated. She had begun a long association with Yaddo, a writers' conference in Saratoga, New York. Both she and her husband had begun experimenting with bisexuality. What many call her finest work, "The Ballad of the Sad Cafe", appeared in *Harper's Bazaar* in 1943. It was followed by *The Member of the Wedding* in 1946. The story is of Frankie Addams, a young tomboy on the edge of adolescence. Like most of McCullers's characters, she is alone, yet seeking attachment, in her case in the form of her relationship with her brother Jarvis and his fiancée Janice Williams. The novel is realistic and lyrical, lacking the Southern Gothic character of her early work and undoubtedly her best full-length work.

Playwright. McCullers was a great friend and companion of playwright Tennessee Williams. In 1946 Williams suggested that *The Member of the Wedding* could be adapted for the stage. McCullers began to work on it, though she knew little of drama and had seen only a few Broadway plays herself. Another stroke slowed her down, but in 1949 the play opened to rave reviews in New York, running for 501 performances. The play won the New York Drama Critics' Circle Award for the 1948–1949 season and was sold to Hollywood, giving McCullers financial stability for the first time in her life. She was thirty-two years old.

Health. But her career was essentially over. Her health was terrible. A spastic arm made writing difficult for her. She had trouble working. She became depressed with Reeves and left him in Paris as he tried to convince her to commit suicide with him. He killed himself weeks later. She was still writing, but it was laborious. A second and final play, *The Square Root of Wonderful*, opened in October 1956 and closed weeks later after forty-five performances. The failure of the play, an attempted homage to her mother and a working out of her husband's suicide, sent her reeling into depression. She survived with the help of a friend, Dr. Mary Mercer, and completed one final novel, *Clock Without Hands*. It failed critically, not coming close to the work of her prodigious years. It is again southern and freakish, as though McCullers, in failing health, was trying to return to the character of her finest work. She lived for seven more years in terrible health. She worked very little but watched as John Huston filmed *Reflections in a Golden Eye* and as Edward Albee adapted "The Ballad of the Sad Cafe" for the stage. On 20 September 1967 Carson McCullers died. She was fifty years old.

Themes and Legacy. McCullers's place is as a regionalist writer of southern grotesque works. Her legacy is a compassionate look at the lonely, whether neurotic adults or undefined children seeking connection. Her characters recognize their state but seem unable to change. In fact they further isolate themselves with their erratic behavior. Her imagination bore fruit early and fast, as though cognizant of the short time it had to produce, and gained McCullers a firm place in American literary history.

Sources:

Virginia Carr, *The Lonely Hunter: A Biography of Carson McCullers* (Garden City, N.Y.: Doubleday, 1975);

Robert F. Kiernan, "Carson McCullers," in *American Novelists Since World War II*, volume 2 of *Dictionary of Literary Biography* (Detroit: Bruccoli Clark, 1981).

EZRA POUND

1885-1972

POET

Champion of Modernism. Ezra Pound's odyssey of ideas took him far from his birthplace in Idaho and changed American literature irrevocably. He had an uncanny eye for talent. During the 1910s and 1920s he was a champion of innovative new writers such as D. H. Lawrence, Robert Frost, T. S. Eliot, James Joyce, H. D. (Hilda Doolittle), and William Carlos Williams. During the 1940s and 1950s Pound's ongoing epic poem, *The Cantos* (1917–1969), had a major influence on a whole new generation of poets. Yet the American public read little of his poetry and knew of him mainly as the poet who had been arrested for treason.

Expatriate in Wartime. When World War II broke out, Pound had been living in Europe since 1908 and in Rapallo, Italy, since 1924. During the 1930s he began dabbling in economics and political theory. His obsession with these subjects caused him to mistake the rise of Benito Mussolini's Fascist government in Italy for civilization remaking itself, moving beyond modern capitalism. He remained in Italy during the war, broadcasting pro-Fascist, anti-Semitic, and anti-American propaganda to American troops from 1941 until the Allied occupation of Italy in 1943. In 1945 he was charged with treason, arrested by the U.S. Army, and held prisoner in an outdoor cage at the U.S. Army Disciplinary Training Camp near Pisa. There he wrote *The Pisan Cantos* (1948), in which he cast himself a man facing execution and recalling in a elegiac tone his life as an expatriate in Paris during the early 1920s.

The Most Famous Patient at St. Elizabeths. Pound was returned to the United States for trial, but in February 1946 a U.S. federal court ruled that he was insane and committed him to St. Elizabeths Federal Hospital for the Insane in Washington, D.C., until such time as he was deemed competent to stand trial. Before long, poets of wide-ranging political persuasions were making pilgrimages to St. Elizabeths, as his wife, Dorothy Pound, began a long legal battle to have him released to her custody on the grounds that he was permanently insane and could never be tried.

Literary Politics. The publication of *The Pisan Cantos* in July 1948 involved Pound in further controversy. The following November the current Poetry Consultant to the Library of Congress, Léonie Adams, and that year's Fellows in Literature met to select the winner of the Bollingen Prize, a new prize to be awarded by the library for the best volume of poetry published in 1948. There were eight votes for *The Pisan Cantos* — including votes from W. H. Auden, T. S. Eliot, Robert Lowell, and Allen Tate; three votes for William Carlos Williams's *Paterson (Book Two)* — including votes from Conrad Aiken, Karl Shapiro, and Katherine Garrison Chapin (whose husband happened to be the U.S. attorney general who had indicted Pound for treason); and two abstentions. Chapin complained to her husband, Francis Biddle, who in turn "recommended strongly against the decision" in a letter to the Librarian of Congress, Luther H. Evans. He ruled that the prize jury should vote again. Pound won the second vote too, and on 19 February 1949 the jury announced that he would be awarded the $10,000 prize. Rather than helping Pound to win public sympathy, as friends such as Eliot and Tate had hoped, the awarding of the prize to Pound caused a public outcry and hurt his chances for release. The headline in *The New York Times* read: "POUND, IN MENTAL CLINIC, WINS PRIZE FOR POETRY PENNED IN TREASON CELL." By August 1949 the Joint Committee of the House and Senate on the Library of Congress had ruled that the library could no longer award any prizes. (Yale University took over the granting of the Bollingen Prize.)

Release. In the mid 1950s Archibald MacLeish spearheaded lobbying efforts to gain Pound's release — enlisting support from Frost, Ernest Hemingway, and Eliot in particular. In 1958, responding to the assertion that Pound had been in St. Elizabeths longer than he would have been imprisoned if he had been tried and found guilty of treason, a federal judge released Pound and allowed him to return to Rapallo, where he lived out the final fourteen years of his life. He wrote and published

little, giving up all idea of completing *The Cantos* by the late 1960s. The American champion of modernism died in silence at the age of eighty-seven.

Source:
Humphrey Carpenter, *A Serious Character: The Life of Ezra Pound* (Boston: Houghton Mifflin, 1988).

FRANK SINATRA

1915-

POPULAR SINGER, ACTOR

Climbing Up. Once stardom arrived for Frank Sinatra in the early 1940s, it came quickly and in a fashion never really seen in popular music before 1942. But fame had taken its time finding Sinatra. He could never be accused of not paying his dues in his rise to popular singer, Academy Award–winning actor, and eventually legend. He came from a working-class family in Hoboken, New Jersey. Although he grew up singing, it was only at eighteen, after seeing a Bing Crosby concert, that he decided to become a professional singer. His family resisted the career choice but helped him anyway, providing a car and an amplifier and even helping him find work through his mother's political connections. In 1935 he joined the Hoboken Four and went on the road for the first time. The experience was a difficult one, but Sinatra quickly learned that he was the star of the group and that the group was going nowhere.

First Break. In 1939 he was back in New Jersey singing at the Rustic Cabin, a club near the town of Alpine. The work was steady, but more important, it was broadcast on the radio. Sinatra knew that radio was his only chance for real exposure and a chance to sign on with a band. In 1939 Harry James, a trumpet player recently of the Benny Goodman Orchestra, signed Sinatra as a vocalist for James's newly formed big band. On 30 June of that year Sinatra made his first appearance with James's band at the Hippodrome Theatre in Baltimore. In July he recorded for the first time. The band had modest success during the year, and soon Sinatra had attracted the attention of music critics. James knew he could not keep Sinatra and was happy to release him from his contract when Tommy Dorsey approached Sinatra. By January 1940 Sinatra was singing with Dorsey's band. The band was more talented and more widely known than James's band, and exposure came quickly. The Dorsey band was also more geared toward vocalists. Alex Stordahl was the band's arranger and was a great influence on Sinatra's singing style. The touring was grueling — long bus rides crossing the country and up to nine forty-five-minute shows a day. Dorsey's band scored a number one hit with "I'll Never Smile Again" in summer 1940, but by then

Sinatra had begun to outgrow them. By May 1941 Sinatra was rated as the number one vocalist in the annual college music survey of *Billboard* magazine. By December he had surpassed Crosby in a *Down Beat* poll. The stage was set for a big break.

Going Solo. Sinatra began recording as a solo artist in January 1942, when Crosby was the only truly successful solo artist. It was the height of the big band and swing era, and singers had to rely on bands for support. To go solo was to take a risk. By July 1942 he was singing on his own. He had a hit with "There Are Such Things" and in December 1942 he appeared at New York's Paramount Theatre. In what *Life* magazine would call "the proclamation of a new era" Sinatra made music history when he stepped on stage and sent the girls in the audience into a frenzy. Within four years the big bands began fading out in favor of the solo singer crooning a song. Sinatra sang at the Paramount for eight weeks, at the end of which he was the most successful singer in the country. His big smile and skinny vulnerability made him a sex symbol. He would later say it was the war — most of the boyfriends were overseas, and the girls latched onto him as a substitute. But it was also the voice and the style that would become legendary. For the next five years Sinatra was the biggest singing star in the country. He followed up with a string of hit records and entered the film industry with *Reveille with Beverly* (1943), *Higher and Higher* (1943), *Step Lively* (1944), and *Anchors Aweigh* (1945).

Breakdown. But in 1947 Sinatra's career began to unravel. Personal problems had led to difficult relations with the press. His record during the war was questioned — he had been declared 4-F and unable to serve due to a hole in one eardrum. His marriage came to an end. His political beliefs were called into question at a time when liberal thought was becoming more and more suspect. He had campaigned for Franklin D. Roosevelt in 1944 and was associated with "fellow travelers," or Communist sympathizers. As damaging, his friendships with underworld figures were reported, tarnishing his image. Sinatra's battle with the press culminated with a charge of battery for a fight with Hearst newspaper man Lee Mortimer. Between 1948 and 1952 Sinatra's star plummeted. By 1952 he had no recording contract, and his shows were sometimes only one-third to one-half full. His career had hit bottom.

Eternity. The break came with the filming of James Jones's popular novel *From Here to Eternity* (1953). Playing the character of Angelo Maggio gave back to Sinatra his confidence on the screen. He won an Academy Award for Best Supporting Actor for the part and launched the second, more serious phase of his acting career. He appeared in numerous films through the 1950s and became a box-office star. More important, he gained a recording contract and relaunched his singing career. By 1954 he was again the top male vocalist in America. In the next six years he would star in seventeen films and record his

most famous albums. He became the most sought-after night-club performer in the country. The man who had redefined pop stardom in the 1940s rode a wave of successes through the next three decades to become an American legend of music and popular culture.

Source:
John Howlett, *Frank Sinatra* (London: Plexus, 1980).

ORSON WELLES
1915-1985

Secret History. At the time of his death in 1985, Orson Welles was most widely recognized for a series of television commercials selling wine. His delivery of the line "We will sell no wine before its time" and his substantial girth made him fodder for comedians. In many ways it was a fitting end to a genius who had never really been fully appreciated for his work while he was producing it. Although he was given an honorary Academy Award in 1970 "for superlative artistry and versatility in the creation of motion pictures," an American Film Institute Life Achievement Award in 1975, and a British Film Institute fellowship in 1984, Welles's contribution remained relatively unknown to a wider public. Little was known about this prodigy of theater and stage.

Boy Genius. Born in 1915 in Kenosha, Wisconsin, he displayed a precocious talent, becoming an accomplished pianist and beginning his stage career at age five in *Samson and Delilah* in Chicago. His mother, a professional musician, died when he was nine, and Welles was sent to the Todd School in Woodstock, Illinois. There he met Roger "Skipper" Hill, who encouraged Welles to read Shakespeare and produce plays for the school. At sixteen Welles traveled alone to Ireland. He audaciously walked into the Gate Theatre and presented himself as a nineteen-year-old with membership in New York's Theater Guild. He was given a role in *Jew Süss* and was called an overnight sensation in the *The New York Times*. He returned to Todd School as a drama coach and wrote a play, never produced, called *Marching Song,* which bore a resemblance to his later opus *Citizen Kane.* In 1938 Hill and Welles wrote a book about Shakespeare (*Everybody's Shakespeare*) that became a standard reference text. Through a meeting with Thornton Wilder, Welles wound up with Katharine Cornell's theater company. He began distinguishing himself as an actor. He was nineteen years old in 1934, when he made his New York stage debut as Tybalt in *Romeo and Juliet.*

Mercurial. In 1935 Welles was approached by John Houseman, who was working in the new Federal Theater Project. Welles joined the project, and the two promptly made a splash with an all-black production of *Macbeth* at the Harlem Theater. The "voodoo" production was a hit, and the company, now called Project 891, moved to the Maxine Elliot Theater. Joseph Cotten and Arlene Francis were among the players. Welles began broadcasting on radio and became a star. Project 891 lost its federal funding with a now-famous prounion production of Marc Blitzstein's *The Cradle Will Rock*. They were locked out of the theater on opening night and promptly walked with the audience to a nearby theater, where the play was performed in the audience so as not to break union rules. Welles now starred in *The Shadow* on radio and formed the Mercury Theater in 1937. His modern-dress, anti-Fascist version of *Julius Caesar* caused a sensation and confirmed Welles's status as an actor. He made the cover of *Time* magazine in 1938. The Mercury Theater went on the air, and on 30 October 1938 produced the legendary radio broadcast *The War of the Worlds*. Many believed the docudrama broadcast of a Martian invasion to be real, and an overnight panic gripped the country. In the morning Welles apologized before newsreel cameras. He was twenty-three and nationally notorious.

Citizen Kane. Offered a film contract by RKO Radio in 1939, Welles made a ridiculous list of demands and was promptly granted all of them. He had total control over his filmmaking, an unheard-of situation at the time. After starting and abandoning a film version of *Heart of Darkness*, Welles made *Citizen Kane* from a screenplay he had written with Herman Mankiewicz and Houseman. The film was seen as an attack on William Randolph Hearst, who promptly banned all mention of Welles and *Citizen Kane* from his newspapers. *Citizen Kane*, with its unusual, multiple points of view, its monumental visuals, and its camera technique, is continually voted as the greatest film ever made. It won an Oscar for best screenplay despite limited release and won the New York Film Critics' Circle Award as best film of 1941. Welles was twenty-five years old.

Trouble. In a sense the rest was downhill for Welles. His success caused resentment. His costly vision caused the studios to assert more control over his films. RKO Radio released his next project, *The Magnificent Ambersons*, while Welles was in Brazil. It failed miserably, in part because the studio editors had butchered it. For the next two decades Welles made a handful of films through sheer will, often with little studio support. He was the first independent filmmaker and often had trouble finishing projects for lack of finances. He filmed *Othello* and won the 1952 Cannes Film Festival Grand Prize. He had already filmed *Macbeth*, another of his famous productions. Meanwhile he continued acting in the films of others, creating many memorable roles such as Harry Lime in *The Third Man* and Rochester in *Jane Eyre*.

Drifter. Through the 1950s and 1960s Welles wandered. He wrote two novels, *Une Grosse Legume* (1953) and *Mr. Arkadin*, (1956) the latter of which he also filmed. He lived in England and performed in London's West End, triumphing as Othello and as Ahab in his own magnificently staged *Moby Dick*. He filmed *King Lear* for television, but still Hollywood would hardly approach him. In a 1955 production of *King Lear* in New York, Welles broke both ankles on opening night and finished the production in a wheelchair. Other film roles such as Cardinal Wolsey in *A Man for All Seasons* kept his fame alive, but his greatest work was behind him. He is often seen as a megalomaniac who had trouble finishing his work. More likely he was too independent for Hollywood's rigid studio system, and much of his greatest work was undercut by those who lacked his vision. *Citizen Kane* was enough, however, to mark Orson Welles's place in film history.

Source:
James Howard, *The Complete Films of Orson Welles* (New York: Citadel, 1991).

RICHARD WRIGHT

1908-1960

Going North. Richard Wright came from the rural South and became the first African American to write of ghetto life in the North. His formal schooling ended at age fifteen, yet he became the foremost black author in American history up to his death. Wright was the first black novelist/essayist in American history to achieve the status of a major American writer. He was a remarkable man from humble beginnings who began the process of self-education in the mid 1920s as a teenager. He read H. L. Mencken, Sinclair Lewis, Crane, and Dreiser. In the late 1920s he went to Chicago and discovered Gertrude Stein, Marcel Proust, and the Chicago school of sociologists (led by Robert Park and Louis Wirth). Wright also discovered the Communist Party and officially joined in 1932. He was active in the party, writing poems, stories, and essays for leftist magazines. He clashed with the rigid party dictates, was branded an intellectual, and finally quit in 1944, by which time he was already famous.

First Fiction. Two books brought him fame and critical notice. In 1938 he entered a book-length manuscript of four stories into a *Story* magazine contest for writers associated with the Federal Writers' Project. He won. The book was called *Uncle Tom's Children* and served notice to the literary world that a new talent had arrived. The stories are harsh and violent, melodramatic with a

Communist bent, but the anger and energy behind them impressed most critics. All of the stories deal with the oppression of blacks, violence against blacks, and how the two lead in turn to black violence born of frustration.

Native Son. Wright was not happy with himself. He sensed the melodrama in *Uncle Tom's Children* and decided to write his next book "so hard and deep" that "no one would weep over it." *Native Son* was just that book. The novel relates the story of Bigger Thomas, a Chicago black man who commits murder. Bigger is not a likable protagonist. He is a force, a fury of energy who ultimately finds murder has freed him, has defined him. The man who was less than a man commits murder, burns the corpse, and attempts blackmail, until the charred body is found. But the acts are his first conscious acts, and he is condemned for them. The novel put Wright at the upper echelons of the social realist writers of his time.

Black Boy. Wright then stepped away from fiction. His next story was his own. *Black Boy,* an autobiography, was published in 1945. Many critics call it his best book. He again looks at human will, oppression of the southern black, and blacks' acceptance of oppression. The story evokes the rural South of the early part of the century and condemns the black church as complicit in black oppression. For Wright, Christianity was a form of white hegemony. The book is sometimes viewed as a nonfiction novel in which Wright invented some scenes. Completely true or not, it is his strongest statement, not simply of black life, but of his developing sensibility and personality as an artist.

To Paris. In 1946, his position among American writers firmly set, Wright traveled to France at the invitation of the French government. In 1947 Wright returned to Paris and made it his home until his death in 1960. He entered the existentialist circle of Jean-Paul Sartre and Simone de Beauvoir and began to incorporate their themes into his work. The social realist was approaching modernism just as younger writers such as Saul Bellow and John Hawkes had begun doing in the United States. His next novel, *The Outsider* (1953), was among the first existential novels written by an American. The story moves away from Wright's themes of race. He is interested in the individual in *The Outsider.* Protagonist Cross

Damon is believed killed in a subway accident and is suddenly free of his entire past. He must reinvent himself and proceeds to join the Communist Party and commit three murders. It is a novel of ideas, of modern man, but it was not well received. Many thought Wright was dabbling too much in philosophy and not writing true fiction. His 1944 novella, "The Man Who Lived Underground," may have been a better statement of similar themes.

To Africa. Wright remained busy writing nonfiction. He became active in Ghana and other newly independent African nations. His books *Black Power* (1954), *The Color Curtain* (1956), and *White Man, Listen!* (1957) are considered excellent works of reporting about the Third World and colonial powers. Wright overtly stated that race was the major conflict between the new nations and the former colonial powers. The books were well received with some reservations. Many thought he overstated his claims, but his uncomfortable truths were not likely to be socially accepted.

Final Work. Wright wrote one more novel, *The Long Dream* (1958). He returns to his roots in the American South in telling the story of Fishbelly, the son of a black crime lord in a small town. The novel was given mixed reviews. Many found faults repeated from his early work — melodrama, lack of synthesis. The faults arose in later criticism, though Wright perhaps is difficult to judge from the usual standards of aesthetics. He was self-educated and, like Jack London, displayed awkward, clumsy technique at times. What drives Wright is sheer energy, anger, and a passion that more than compensates for structural faults. Through the 1950s Wright fell out of favor with new black writers such as James Baldwin and Ralph Ellison. They rejected his naturalism and his philosophical and ideological approach. Baldwin especially felt a need to "kill the father" in a critical assessment of Wright, while also acknowledging his power as a writer. Although he recognized the doors Wright opened for all African American writers, Baldwin refused to put Wright on a pedestal.

Source:
Addison Gayle, *Richard Wright: Ordeal of a Native Son* (Garden City, N.Y.: Anchor/Doubleday, 1980).

PEOPLE IN THE NEWS

On 22 December 1946 **Humphrey Bogart** signs a record fifteen-year contract with Warner Bros.

Novelist **Willa Cather** is given the gold medal by the National Institute of Arts and Letters on 27 January 1944.

On 8 May 1944 **Charlie Chaplin** is ordered to stand trial in a paternity suit filed by Joan Berry. On 4 April he is acquitted of a Mann Act violation, and a mistrial is declared on 4 January 1945. On 17 April 1945 Chaplin is named the father of Joan Berry's daughter.

On 16 October 1942 **Aaron Copland**'s ballet *Rodeo* is performed in New York City by the Ballets Russes de Monte Carlo.

W. E. B. DuBois becomes the first black elected to the National Institute of Arts and Letters on 18 December 1943.

On 23 January 1943 **Duke Ellington** debuts his fifty-minute-long tone poem for jazz orchestra, *Black, Brown, and Beige,* at Carnegie Hall in New York City.

Edna Ferber's unpublished novel *Saratoga Trunk* is sold to Warner Bros. for a record $175,000 on 25 March 1941.

On 13 October 1943 **Errol Flynn** is named in a paternity suit in Los Angeles by Shirley Evans Hassan, age twenty, who claims he is the father of her baby, born in 1940.

M-G-M grants a $150,000 novel award to **Esther Forbes** for her forthcoming book, *The Runner of the Tide,* on 17 December 1947.

On 14 November 1940 the American Academy of Arts and Letters awards the Howells Medal for Fiction for the most distinguished work of the past five years to **Ellen Glasgow**. On 4 May 1942 she is awarded the Pulitzer Prize in fiction for *In This Our Life.*

On 8 May 1945, V-E day, folksinger **Woody Guthrie** is drafted.

Screen star **Rita Hayworth** marries Prince Aly Khan, son of Muslim leader Aga Khan, on 27 May 1949.

On 16 May 1947 Philadelphia narcotics police raid the hotel room of blues singer **Billie Holiday.** Pleading guilty to a charge of narcotics possession, she is imprisoned in the Federal Reformatory for Women at Alderson, West Virginia, for nearly a year.

On 1 June 1943 Hollywood actor **Leslie Howard** and sixteen others are lost after an overseas airliner is attacked by an enemy plane.

The 26 June 1948 issue of *The New Yorker* featured **Shirley Jackson**'s story "The Lottery," a chilling parable of the Holocaust. A tale of a New England farming community that practices ritual human sacrifice, the story shocked many readers and was widely anthologized in the 1950s and 1960s.

During a 1943 concert at the Paramount theater in New York by **Harry James** and his swing band, jitterbugging teenagers cause a riot.

Henry Kallem's painting *County Tenement* is awarded first prize in the thirty-five-thousand-dollar Pepsi-Cola Painting of the Year contest on 30 September 1947.

Eleven-year-old **Loren Maazell** conducts the NBC Summer Symphony in a program of Felix Mendelssohn and Richard Wagner without using a score on 5 July 1941.

Thomas Mann joins the Library of Congress staff on 17 January 1942 as a consultant in German literature. On 23 June 1944 Mann and his wife become United States citizens. His novel *Doctor Faustus* is published on 29 October 1948 and is chosen as a Book-of-the-Month Club selection. He is given the Award of Merit of the American Academy of Arts and Letters on 5 May 1949.

On 20 July 1948 **Percy McKaye** is awarded a five-thousand-dollar fellowship by the American Academy of Poets for his dramatic tetralogy *Hamlet, the King of the Danes.*

Robert Mitchum is sentenced to sixty days in prison for marijuana possession on 9 February 1949.

War hero **Audie Murphy** signs a movie contract with Cagney Productions on 11 July 1946.

On 11 July 1941 **James Petrillo,** president of the American Federation of Musicians, orders 138,000 members to play "The Star-Spangled Banner" at the beginning and end of every concert. On 8 July 1942 he announces a union ban on recording.

Edith Piaf opens a variety revue in New York on 30 October 1947.

The Italian-born Metropolitan Opera basso **Ezio Pinza** is taken to Ellis Island and held as an enemy alien on 12 March 1942. He is released on 28 May.

On 9 November 1940 **Serge Rachmaninoff** holds a recital at Carnegie Hall. At the end of the recital, the crowd refuses to leave, and Rachmaninoff plays for thirty minutes more. On 28 March 1943 he dies in Beverly Hills.

When **Richard Rodgers** and **Oscar Hammerstein II** debut their new Broadway musical, *Oklahoma!*, on 31 March 1943, some critics doubt their unprecedented combination of show tunes, folk music, and dance will catch on. One critic scoffs that the show had "No legs, no jokes, no chance." By the end of its run of 2,212 performances, *Oklahoma!* breaks every record on Broadway.

The original manuscript of **Edgar Allan Poe**'s *Murders in the Rue Morgue* is sold on 18 October 1944 to dealer **Charles Sessler** for thirty-four thousand dollars.

Leopold Stokowski conducts the opening of *Fantasia* in New York on 13 November 1940. On 24 January 1941 Stokowski announces that he will train the eighty-five-piece army band to develop a more "typically American" music.

On 13 December 1945 **Chief Justice Harlan Stone** accepts custody of two hundred paintings brought to the United States from German museums. The works are assigned to the National Gallery of Art in Washington, D.C.

In the fall of 1941 composer **Igor Stravinsky** is repeatedly hounded at concert halls by protesters opposed to his arrangement of "The Star-Spangled Banner," which he hoped would replace the original melody.

Booth Tarkington is awarded the Howells Medal by the American Academy of Arts and Letters on 7 March 1945.

On 31 January 1943, while directing the NBC Symphony Orchestra, **Arturo Toscanini** substitutes "Italy Betrayed" for "Italy My Country" in Verdi's *Hymn of Nations*. On 6 January 1944 the Office of War Information announces that he has finished the film *Hymn of Nations*.

Dalton Trumbo's novel *Johnny Got His Gun* is chosen by the American Booksellers' Association as the most original novel of 1939 on 13 February 1940.

Alfred Wallenstein, the forty-four-year-old conductor, is elected permanent conductor of the Los Angeles Philharmonic Orchestra, becoming the first American-born conductor of a major American orchestra.

On 13 September 1941 **H. G. Welles** is elected the international president of P.E.N., but he declines.

When **Hank Williams** appears on the stage of the Grand Ole Opry on 11 June 1949, singing his hit single "Lovesick Blues," the crowd is so enthusiastic that it refuses to let him finish the song, and he struggles a half-dozen times to wrap up the closing lyrics. According to witnesses, when he finally finished, the applause lasted over five minutes.

P. G. Wodehouse is discovered in a Paris hotel on 31 August 1944 and arrested for making anti-Allies broadcasts from Berlin. On 23 November he is released but ordered to stay in contact with the French authorities.

AWARDS

PULITZER PRIZES

1940
Fiction: *The Grapes of Wrath,* by **John Steinbeck**
Drama: *The Time of Your Life,* by **William Saroyan**
Poetry: *Collected Poems,* by **Mark Van Doren**

1941
Fiction: no award
Drama: *There Shall Be No Night,* by **Robert E. Sherwood**
Poetry: *Sunderland Capture,* by **Leonard Bacon**

1942
Fiction: *In This Our Life,* by **Ellen Glasgow**
Drama: no award
Poetry: *The Dust Which Is God,* by **William Rose Benét**

1943
Fiction: *Dragon's Teeth,* by **Upton Sinclair**
Drama: *The Skin of Our Teeth,* by **Thornton Wilder**
Poetry: *A Witness Tree,* by **Robert Frost**
Music: Secular Cantata no. 2, ("A Free Song"), by **William Schuman**

1944
Fiction: *Journey in the Dark,* by **Martin Flavin**
Drama: no award
Poetry: *Western Star,* by **Stephen Vincent Benét**
Music: Symphony no. 4, op. 34, by **Howard Hanson**

1945
Fiction: *A Bell For Adano,* by **John Hersey**
Drama: *Harvey,* by **Mary Chase**

Poetry: *V–Letter and Other Poems,* by **Karl Shapiro**
Music: *Appalachian Spring,* by **Aaron Copland**

1946
Fiction: no award
Drama: *State of the Union,* by **Russel Crouse** and **Howard Lindsay**
Poetry: no award
Music: *The Canticle of the Sun,* by **Leo Sowerby**

1947
Fiction: *All the King's Men,* by **Robert Penn Warren**
Drama: no award
Poetry: *Lord Weary's Castle,* by **Robert Lowell**
Music: Symphony no. 3, by **Charles E. Ives**

1948
Fiction: *Tales of the South Pacific,* by **James A. Michener**
Drama: *A Streetcar Named Desire,* by **Tennessee Williams**
Poetry: *The Age of Anxiety,* by **W. H. Auden**
Music: Symphony no. 3, by **Walter Piston**

1949
Fiction: *Guard of Honor,* by **James Gould Cozzens**
Drama: *Death of a Salesman,* by **Arthur Miller**
Poetry: *Terror and Decorum,* by **Peter Viereck**
Music: *Louisiana Story,* by **Virgil Thomson**

ACADEMY OF MOTION PICTURE ARTS AND SCIENCES AWARDS (THE OSCARS)

1940
Actor: **James Stewart,** *The Philadelphia Story*
Actress: **Ginger Rogers,** *Kitty Foyle*
Picture: *Rebecca,* **Selznick International**

Director: **John Ford,** *The Grapes of Wrath*

1941
Actor: **Gary Cooper,** *Sergeant York*
Actress: **Joan Fontaine,** *Suspicion*
Picture: *How Green Was My Valley,* **20th Century–Fox**
Director: **John Ford,** *How Green Was My Valley*

1942
Actor: **James Cagney,** *Yankee Doodle Dandy*
Actress: **Greer Garson,** *Mrs. Miniver*
Picture: *Mrs. Miniver,* **M-G-M**
Director: **William Wyler,** *Mrs. Miniver*

1943
Actor: **Paul Lukas,** *Watch on the Rhine*
Actress: **Jennifer Jones,** *The Song of Bernadette*
Picture: *Casablanca,* **Warner Bros.**
Director: **Michael Curtiz,** *Casablanca*

1944
Actor: **Bing Crosby,** *Going My Way*
Actress: **Ingrid Bergman,** *Gaslight*
Picture: *Going My Way,* **Paramount**
Director: **Leo McCarey,** *Going My Way*

1945
Actor: **Ray Milland,** *The Lost Weekend*

Actress: **Joan Crawford,** *Mildred Pierce*
Picture: *The Lost Weekend,* **Paramount**
Director: **Billy Wilder,** *The Lost Weekend*

1946
Actor: **Frederic March,** *The Best Years of Our Lives*
Actress: **Olivia de Havilland,** *To Each His Own*
Picture: *The Best Years of Our Lives,* **Goldwyn, RKO**
Director: **William Wyler,** *The Best Years of Our Lives*

1947
Actor: **Ronald Colman,** *A Double Life*
Actress: **Loretta Young,** *The Farmer's Daughter*
Picture: *Gentleman's Agreement,* **20th Century–Fox**
Director: **Elia Kazan,** *Gentleman's Agreement*

1948
Actor: **Laurence Olivier,** *Hamlet*
Actress: **Jane Wyman,** *Johnny Belinda*
Picture: *Hamlet,* **Two Cities Film, Universal Studios**
Director: **John Huston,** *Treasure of the Sierra Madre*

1949
Actor: **Broderick Crawford,** *All the King's Men*
Actress: **Olivia de Havilland,** *The Heiress*
Picture: *All the King's Men,* **Columbia**
Director: **Joseph L. Mankiewicz,** *Letter to Three Wives*

DEATHS

Robert Ingersoll Aitken, 70, sculptor specializing in public monuments, 3 January 1949.

Ivy Anderson, 45, blues singer, 28 December 1949.

Sherwood Anderson, 64, short-story writer, author of *Winesburg, Ohio,* 8 March 1941.

George Arliss, 77, British actor and playwright, 5 February 1946.

Gertrude Franklin Atherton, 90, novelist (*The Conqueror,* 1902), 14 June 1948.

Philip Barry, 53, playwright (*The Philadelphia Story*), 3 December 1949.

John Barrymore, 60, Shakespearean actor, 29 May 1942.

Béla Bartók, 64, Hungarian composer and pianist, 26 September 1945.

Amy Marcy Cheney Beach, 77, pianist and composer, 27 December 1944.

Noah Beery, 62, character actor, 1 April 1946.

Wallace Beery, 63, Academy Award–winning actor (*The Champ,* 1931), 15 April 1949.

Stephen Vincent Benét, 44, author, acclaimed for *John Brown's Body* (1928) and *The Devil and Daniel Webster* (1937), winner of Pulitzer Prize for verse, 13 March 1943.

Richard Bennett, 72, actor of Eugene O'Neill plays and film actor (*The Magnificent Ambersons*), 22 October 1944.

Jules Bledsoe, 44, singer ("Ol' Man River" in *Showboat* on stage and screen), 14 July 1943.

Carl Oscar Borg, 68, painter, 8 May 1947.

Gutzon Borglum, 70, sculptor of Mount Rushmore, 6 March 1941.

Tom Breneman, 45, vaudevillian and former partner of Jack Benny, 28 April 1948.

George DeForest Brush, 85, portrait painter of American Indians, 24 April 1941.

Harry Thacker Burleigh, 82, black singer and composer ("Little Mother of Mine" and "Deep River"), 12 September 1949.

Alexander Sterling Calder, 74, sculptor of the Washington Square arch in New York, 6 January 1945.

Harry Carey, 57, actor of Westerns and *Mr. Smith Goes to Washington,* 5 June 1947.

Earl Carroll, 54, theatrical producer noted for his comedies and revues, 17 June, 1948.

Buddy Clark, 44?, radio singer, 1 October 1949.

Colin Clements, 53, playwright (*Harriet,* 1943), 29 January 1948.

George M. Cohan, 64, singer, actor, and composer ("Over There"), 5 November 1942.

Fannie Cook, 55, author, painter, and worker for interracial understanding, 25 August 1949.

Will Marion Cook, 75, black composer and orchestra leader (*Saint Louis 'Ooman,* all-black opera), led the American Syncopated Orchestra, 19 July 1944.

Courtney Ryley Cooper, 53, adventure writer and writer of circus tales for magazines, 29 September 1940.

Laura Hope Crews, 62, Shakespearean actress; appeared in *Arsenic and Old Lace* on Broadway in 1942, 13 November 1942.

Countee Cullen, 42, black poet and leader in the Harlem Renaissance of the 1920s, 9 January 1946.

Harry Davenport, 83, film actor (Dr. Mead in *Gone With the Wind*), 9 August 1949.

Edwin Willard Deming, 82, painter of American Indians and animal life, 15 October 1942.

Theodore Dreiser, 74, social-realist author (*An American Tragedy,* 1925), 28 December 1945.

Gus Edwards, 64, songwriter ("By the Light of the Silvery Moon," "In My Merry Oldsmobile"), 7 November 1945.

Serge Eisenstein, 50, legendary Soviet director (*Potemkin*) and Bolshevist, 10 February 1948.

Maud Howe Elliot, 93, Pulitzer Prize–winning author, 19 March 1948.

Maxine Elliot, 69, stage actress and theater owner, 5 March 1940.

Julian Eltinge, 58, silent-film star and female impersonator, 7 March 1941.

Frederick Faust (Max Brand), 51, writer of Westerns and Dr. Kildare series, 12 May 1944.

Rachel Field, 47, novelist and children's story writer (*Time Out of Mind*, 1935), 15 March 1942.

Lew Fields, 73, vaudevillian and partner of Joe Weber, 20 July 1941.

W. C. Fields, 66, actor and comedian, 25 December 1946.

F. Scott Fitzgerald, 44, novelist (*The Great Gatsby*, 1925, and *This Side of Paradise*, 1920) 21 December 1940.

Michel Fokine, 62, developer of modern ballet; choreographed *The Dying Swan*, 22 August 1942.

Wanda Hazel Gag, 53, author, illustrator, and translator of children's books; credited with creating the first modern children's picture book, 27 June 1946.

Ellen Glasgow, 71, author and Pulitzer Prize winner in 1941 for *In This Our Life*, 21 November 1945.

Susan Glaspell, 65, novelist and Pulitzer Prize winner in 1931 for *Allison's House;* the founder of Provincetown Players, first producers of Eugene O'Neill, 27 July 1948.

Earle Graser, radio actor and voice of the Lone Ranger whose identity was not known until his death, 8 April 1941.

David Wark Griffith, 68, innovative film director who made the controversial *The Birth of a Nation*, 23 July 1948.

Sam Harris, 69, partner of George M. Cohan and U.S. theatrical producer (*Animal Crackers*), 3 July 1941.

Lorenz "Larry" Hart, 48, lyricist, who, with Richard Rodgers composed Broadway hits such as *Babes In Arms* (1937) and *I Married An Angel* (1938), 22 November 1943.

Marsden Hartley, 66, artist famous for his impressionistic portraits of the Maine landscape, 2 September 1943.

Thomas Orlo Heggen, 29, best-selling novelist (*Mr. Roberts*), 19 May 1949.

Alice Corbin Henderson, 68, poet and cofounder of *Poetry* magazine, 18 July 1949.

DuBose Heyward, 54, author of *Porgy* (1925), 16 June 1940.

Phillips Holmes, 33, film actor of the 1920s and 1930s, 12 August 1942.

Louise Homer, 76, star singer of the Metropolitan Opera, 6 May 1947.

Leslie Howard, 49, director and actor (*Gone With the Wind*), 1 June 1943.

Willie Howard, 62, vaudeville comedian, 12 January 1949.

William Roderick James, 50, winner of the Newbery Award in 1926 for *Smoky*, 3 September 1942.

William Gary "Bunk" Johnson, 70, trumpet player and jazz band leader, 7 July 1949.

James Joyce, 58, famed Irish author of *Dubliners* (1914) and *Ulysses*, (1922) 13 January 1941.

Jerome Kern, 60, composer (*Showboat*), 11 November 1945.

Joyce Kilmer, 53, author of the famous poem "Trees," 1 October 1941.

Elissa Landi, 44, Italian-born actress (*The Sign of the Cross*), 21 October 1948.

Carole Landis, 29, film actress (*One Million B.C.*), 5 July 1948.

Harry Langdon, 60, silent-screen comedian and rival of Buster Keaton and Ben Turpin, 22 December 1944.

Huddie "Leadbelly" Ledbetter, 64, blues and folk musician known for songs such as "Rock Island Line," "Boll Weevil," and "Goodnight Irene," 6 December 1949.

Josef Lhévinne, 69, Russian-born pianist who taught at Juilliard, December 2, 1944.

Jonas Lie, 79, painted the Panama Canal construction and president of the American Academy of Design, 10 January 1940.

Ross Lockridge, Jr., 33, writer of the best-seller *Raintree County* (1948), 6 March 1948.

John Avery Lomax, 80, scholar and collector of folk songs, 26 January 1948.

Carole Lombard, 34, actress and wife of Clark Gable, 16 January 1942.

Louis Lumière, 83, French movie pioneer who invented the motion picture, 6 June 1948.

Katherine Mayo, 73, travel writer and author of *Mother India* (1927), 9 October 1940.

Samuel Sidney McClure, 92, publisher and founder of *McClure's* magazine who publicized Rudyard Kipling, Mark Twain, and Arthur Conan Doyle, 21 March 1949.

John McCormack, 61, Irish-born opera singer, 16 September 1945.

Claude McKay, 58, radical black poet and leader in the Harlem Renaissance of the 1920s, 22 May 1948.

Alice Duer Miller, 68, suffragette and author (*The White Cliffs*), 22 August 1942.

Glenn Miller, 35, swing band leader famed for "Moonlight Serenade"; presumed dead after his flight from England to Paris was announced missing, 24 December 1944.

Frederick Mills, 79, composer ("Meet Me in St. Louis, Louis"), 5 December 1948.

Margaret Mitchell, 49, author of the Pulitzer Prize–winning *Gone With the Wind* (1936), 16 August 1949.

Tom Mix, 60, former Texas Ranger turned Western actor, 12 October 1940.

Piet Mondrian, 71, Dutch cubist of the de Stijl school in 1940; immigrated to the United States and influenced Abstract Expressionists, 1 February 1944.

Lucy Maud Montgomery, 67, Canadian author of *Anne of Green Gables* (1909), 24 April 1942.

Helen Morgan, 41, stage, screen, and radio singer, 8 October 1941.

Karl Muck, 80, German composer and conductor who headed the Boston Symphony (1906–1908), 4 March 1940.

Edvard Munch, 80, Norwegian painter and founder of expressionism ("The Scream"), 25 January 1944.

Charlie Murray, 69, one of the Keystone Kops; star of *Cohens and the Kellys* series, 29 July 1941.

Paul Nash, 57, postimpressionist British painter, 11 July 1946.

Conde Nast, 68, founder of *Vogue* and *Vanity Fair* magazines, 19 September 1942.

Fred Niblow, 74, film director (*Ben Hur*, 1925) and co-founder of the Academy of Motion Picture Arts and Sciences, 11 November 1948.

Edward J. H. O'Brien, 50, author and editor who began the Best Short Stories series in 1915, 25 February 1941.

Andrew O'Connor, 67, sculptor of the Lincoln statue in Springfield, Illinois; student of Auguste Rodin and John Singer Sargent, 11 June 1941.

Rose Cecil O'Neill, 69, artist and creator of the Kewpie doll, 6 April 1944.

Edna May Oliver, 59, Broadway comedian and film actress (*Pride and Prejudice*), 9 November 1942.

José Clemente Orozco, 65, Mexican muralist, 7 September 1949.

Frank Packard, 65, Canadian author of Jimmie Dale books, 17 February 1942.

Ignace Jan Paderewski, 80, Polish pianist and composer, 29 June 1941.

Joe Penner, 36, vaudeville and radio comedian, 10 January 1941.

Edwin S. Porter, 70, motion-picture pioneer who produced *The Great Train Robbery*, 30 April 1941.

Ernie Pyle, 44, Depression-era journalist and war correspondent, 18 April 1945.

Sergei Rachmaninoff, 70, Russian-born pianist and composer, 28 March 1943.

Max Reinhardt, 70, Austrian-born theatrical producer, 31 October 1943.

Lola Ridge, 57, poet and winner of the Shelley Memorial Prize for Poetry in 1934, 19 May 1941.

Luther Bill "Bojangles" Robinson, 71, tap and dance star featured in many films, 25 November, 1949.

Romaine Rolland, 78, pacifist author, winner of the Nobel Prize for literature in 1915, 30 December 1944.

Damon Runyon, 62, journalist and short-story writer (*Guys and Dolls*), 10 December 1946.

Janet Scudder, 67, sculptor and painter, 9 June 1940.

Al Shean, 81, partner in the vaudeville team of Gallagher and Shean, featured in the Ziegfeld Follies, 12 August 1949.

Winfield Sheehan, 59, movie producer who discovered Tom Mix, Will Rogers, and Shirley Temple, 25 July 1945.

Edward Brewster Sheldon, 60, author of the controversial play *The Nigger* (1909), 1 April 1946.

Walter Richard Sickert, 81, British impressionist, 23 January 1942.

Oley Speaks, 72, composer ("On the Road to Mandalay"), 27 August 1948.

Antoine de St. Exupéry, 44, French author (*The Little Prince, Night Flight*), 9 August 1944.

Gertrude Stein, 72, expatriate author known for her highly individual experiments in language and style, 27 July 1946.

Leo Stein, 75, brother of Gertrude Stein; author and art critic who was one of the first to buy paintings by Pablo Picasso, Henry Matisse, and Georges Braque, 29 July 1947.

Herbert Stothart, 73, composer and music arranger who won an Academy Award for *The Wizard of Oz,* 1 February 1949.

Richard Strauss, 85, Austrian composer and conductor, 8 September 1949.

James Everett Stuart, 88, U.S. landscape painter, 1 January 1941.

Sir Rabindranath Tagore, 80, Indian poet and winner of the Nobel Prize for literature (1913), 7 August 1941.

Ernest Lawrence Thayer, 77, journalist who wrote "Casey at the Bat," 21 August 1940.

Ben Turpin, 71, vaudevillian and silent-film comedian, 1 July 1940.

Paul Valéry, 74, French poet and philosopher, 20 July 1945.

Conrad Viedt, 50, British-born actor (*Casablanca*), 3 April 1943.

Henry Bethule Vincent, 68, conductor for the Federal Music Project (1936–1937), 7 January 1941.

Thomas "Fats" Waller, 39, musician and composer ("Ain't Misbehavin'," "Honeysuckle Rose"), 15 December 1943.

Mark Warnow, 47, orchestra leader famous for conducting the NBC program *Your Hit Parade*, 17 October 1949.

Frederick Judd Waugh, 79, seascape painter, 10 September 1940.

John Lee "Sonny Boy" Williamson, 34, blues harmonica player and shouter, 1 June 1948.

Grant Wood, 50, American realist painter (*American Gothic*), 12 February 1942.

Samuel Wood, 65, film director (*A Night at the Opera, Goodbye Mr. Chips*), 22 September 1949.

Virginia Woolf, 58, English novelist-feminist (*To The Lighthouse*), 28 March 1941.

PUBLICATIONS

Alfred H. Barr, Jr., *Fantastic Art, Dada, Surrealism* (New York: Museum of Modern Art, 1947);

Barr, *Picasso: Fifty Years of His Art* (New York: Museum of Modern Art, 1946);

Saul Bellow, *Dangling Man* (New York: Vanguard, 1944);

Alice Browning, *Lionel Hampton's Swing Book* (Chicago: Negro Story Press, 1946);

E. E. Cummings, *50 Poems* (New York: Grosset & Dunlap, 1940);

T. S. Eliot, *Four Quartets* (New York: Harcourt Brace, 1943);

William Faulkner, *Go Down, Moses* (New York: Random House, 1942);

Henri Focillon, *The Life of Forms in Art* (New York: Wittenborn, Schultz, 1948);

Lloyd Frankenberg, *Pleasure Dome: On Reading Modern Poetry* (Boston: Houghton Mifflin, 1949);

Robert Frost, *A Witness Tree* (New York: Holt, 1942);

Naum Gabo, *A Retrospective View of Constructive Art* (New York: Philosophical Library, 1949);

Clement Greenberg, *Joan Miro* (New York: Quadrangle Press, 1948);

Peggy Guggenheim, *Out of This Century: Informal Memoirs* (New York: Dial, 1946);

John Hawkes, *The Cannibal* (New York: New Directions, 1949);

Ernest Hemingway, *For Whom the Bell Tolls* (New York: Scribners, 1940);

Charles F. Hoban, *Movies That Teach* (New York: Dryden Press, 1946);

Leon Howard, *The Connecticut Wits* (Chicago: University of Chicago Press, 1943);

Margaret Lloyd, *The Borzoi Book of Modern Dance* (Princeton, N.J.: Princeton Book, 1949).

Robert Lowell, *Land of Unlikeness* (Cummington, Mass.: The Cummington Press, 1944);

Lowell, *Lord Weary's Castle* (New York: Harcourt Brace, 1946);

Norman Mailer, *The Naked and the Dead* (New York: Rinehart, 1948);

F. O. Matthiessen, *American Renaissance: Art and Expression in the Age of Emerson and Whitman* (New York: Oxford University Press, 1941);

Carson McCullers, *The Heart is a Lonely Hunter* (Boston: Houghton Mifflin, 1940);

Milton Mezzrow and Raymond Wolfe, *Really the Blues* (New York: Random House, 1946);

Raymond Moley, *The Hays Office* (Indianapolis & New York: Bobbs-Merrill, 1945);

Piet Mondrian, *Plastic Art and Pure Plastic Art* (New York: Wittenborn, Schultz, 1945);

Robert Motherwell, *The Dada Painters and Poets: An Anthology* (New York: Wittenborn, Schultz, 1951);

Movie Lot to Beach Head: The Motion Picture Goes to War and Prepares for the Future (Garden City, N.Y.: Doubleday, Doran, 1945);

Beaumont Newhall, *The History of Photography from 1839 to the Present Day* (New York: Museum of Modern Art, 1949);

W. V. O'Connor, *Sense and Sensibility in Modern Poetry* (Chicago: University of Chicago Press, 1948);

James A. Porter, *Modern Negro Art* (New York: Dryden Press, 1943);

Ezra Pound, *Cantos LII–LXXI* (Norfolk, Conn.: New Directions, 1940);

Pound, *The Pisan Cantos* (New York: New Directions, 1948);

Ernie Pyle, *Last Chapter* (New York: Holt, 1946);

John Crowe Ransom, *The New Criticism* (Norfolk, Conn.: New Directions, 1941);

Charles Seymour, *Tradition and Experiment in Modern Sculpture* (Washington, D.C.: American University Press, 1949);

John Steinbeck, *Cannery Row* (New York: Viking Press, 1946);

Allen Tate, *Reason in Madness: Critical Essays* (New York: Putnam, 1941);

W. R. Valentiner, *Origins of Modern Sculpture* (New York: Wittenborn, Schultz, 1946);

Robert Penn Warren, *All the King's Men* (New York: Harcourt Brace, 1946);

Warren, *Eleven Poems on the Same Theme* (Norfolk, Conn.: New Directions, 1942);

Edward Weston, *Fifty Photographs: Edward Weston* (New York: Duell, Sloan & Pearce, 1947);

Richard Wright, *Native Son* (New York: Harper Bros., 1940);

Darryl F. Zanuck, *Tunis Expedition* (New York: Random House, 1943);

American Artist, periodical;

American Cinematographer, periodical;

ARTnews, periodical;

Billboard, periodical;

Down Beat, periodical;

Georgia Review, periodical;

Harper's, periodical;

Hollywood Reporter, periodical;

Hudson Review, periodical;

Jazz Review, periodical;

Metronome, periodical;

Motion Picture Herald, periodical;

Partisan Review, periodical;

Poetry, periodical;

Sewanee Review, periodical;

U.S. Camera, periodical;

Variety, periodical.

CHAPTER THREE

BUSINESS AND THE ECONOMY

by PHILLIP G. PAYNE

CONTENTS

Sidebars and tables are listed in italics.

1940

1 Jan.	U.S. agriculture secretary Henry Wallace announces that the war in Europe will hurt American farmers.
2 Jan.	The U.S. Supreme Court rules that National Labor Relations Board (NLRB) decisions cannot be appealed.
9 Jan.	A federal circuit court in Chicago rules that Inland Steel Corporation does not have to recognize the Steel Workers Organizing Committee of the Congress of Industrial Organizations (CIO) as a sole bargaining agent.
30 Jan.	The Associated Press reports that American business profits increased 67 percent from 1938 to 1939.
26 Feb.	The U.S. Supreme Court rules that only the NLRB, not labor unions, can enforce NLRB rulings.
8 Mar.	American Federation of Labor (AFL) president William Green calls for talks with the CIO.
24 Oct.	The forty-hour workweek begins as a result of the Fair Labor Standards Act, passed in 1938.
21 Nov.	John L. Lewis resigns as head of the CIO in protest over President Franklin D. Roosevelt's election to a third term. Philip Murray succeeds him as president of the CIO.

1941

3 Jan.	In anticipation of war the federal government calls for the construction of two hundred merchant vessels.
7 Jan.	President Roosevelt creates the Office of Production Management to supervise defense production, with industrialist William S. Knudsen as its head.
22 Jan.	Strikes at the Allied Chalmers plant initiate a series of defense-industry labor disputes.
24 Feb.	The Office of Production Management makes the manufacture of aluminum and machine tools a top priority.
19 Mar.	The National Defense Mediation Board is established to settle labor disputes in defense industries, with Clarence A. Dykstra as its first chairman.
11 Apr.	The Ford Motor Company signs its first union contract, settling a strike in which the CIO calls out 85,000 workers at the River Rouge plant.
11 Apr.	Congress establishes the Office of Price Administration and Civilian Supply (OPA) to recommend price-control measures.
14 Apr.	Steelworkers receive a 10¢-per-hour wage increase as a measure against future strikes.
16 Apr.	The OPA announces a freeze on the price of steel.
17 Apr.	The automobile industry agrees to cut production by 20 percent beginning on 1 August in order to increase capacity to manufacture war materials.
1 May	U.S. Defense Savings Bonds go on sale.
16 May	General Motors gives its workers a 10¢-per-hour wage increase to prevent strikes. In return the CIO drops its demand for a closed shop.

18 May Secretary of State Cordell Hull in a radio address suggests a postwar reconstruction program giving nations access to raw materials and abolishing trade barriers.

9 June President Roosevelt orders troops to take over the Los Angeles plants of the North American Aviation Company to replace striking workers.

25 June President Roosevelt issues Executive Order 8802, designed to end racial discrimination in government agencies, job-training programs, and industries with defense contracts. The order establishes the Committee on Fair Employment Practices to investigate racial violations of the order. The action prevented a march on Washington being organized by A. Philip Randolph of the Brotherhood of Sleeping Car Porters from taking place.

24 July The AFL and the Office of Production Management sign a no-strike pledge.

3 Aug. A gasoline curfew goes into effect, closing gasoline stations from 7 P.M. to 7 A.M.

23 Dec. An industry/labor conference agrees that there will be no lockouts or strikes and that all disputes will be settled peacefully.

27 Dec. The OPA announces rubber rationing. Civilian consumption of rubber declines by 80 percent.

1942

1 Jan. The Office of Production Management bans the sale of new cars and trucks.

16 Jan. President Roosevelt establishes the War Production Board by executive order, replacing the Office of Production Management. Donald M. Nelson is placed in charge.

30 Jan. President Roosevelt signs the Price Control Bill into law, giving the OPA the power to establish prices for all products except farm goods.

17 Mar. William Green of the AFL and Philip Murray of the CIO announce a no-strike agreement.

18 Apr. The War Power Commission is established under the direction of Federal Security Administrator Paul V. McNutt.

28 Apr. The OPA stabilizes rents.

5 May Sugar rationing begins.

15 May Gasoline rationing begins in seventeen eastern states. People are limited to three gallons a week for nonessential driving.

13 June President Roosevelt establishes the Office of War Information to control official news and propaganda. Elmer Davis, a newspaper writer and radio commentator, is placed in charge.

22 July A coupon system of rationing begins.

1 Oct. The Bell Aircraft Corporation tests the first jet airplane, the XP-59.

Oct. The Revenue Act of 1942 increases the number of people paying income taxes from 39 million to 42.6 million.

7 Oct. The United Mine Workers (UMW) withdraws from the CIO.

29 Nov.	Coffee rationing begins.
1 Dec.	Nationwide gasoline rationing begins.
4 Dec.	President Roosevelt cancels the Works Projects Administration by executive order.

1943

18 Jan.	The U.S. Supreme Court finds that the American Medical Association's practice of preventing the activities of cooperative health groups is in violation of antitrust laws.
7 Feb.	Shoe rationing begins, limiting civilians to three pairs per year.
9 Feb.	President Roosevelt orders a minimum forty-eight-hour workweek in war plants.
1 Mar.	Rationing of canned goods begins.
25 Mar.	Chester C. Davis is appointed U.S. food administrator and is given the task of alleviating food shortages.
29 Mar.	Rationing of meat, fat, and cheese begins.
17 Apr.	The War Manpower Commission prohibits 27 million essential workers from leaving their jobs.
1 May	The national government seizes coal mines after 530,000 miners refuse to obey a War Labor Board order to return to work.
5 May	Congress gives Fuel Administrator Harold Ickes the authority to seize coal for use in war plants and for emergency civilian purposes.
19 May	The UMW petitions for admission into the AFL.
27 May	The Office of War Mobilization is established, with James F. Byrnes as its chief executive, to coordinate war efforts on the home front.
10 June	President Roosevelt signs the Current Tax Payment Bill, allowing taxes to be deducted from paychecks.
20 June	Race riots hit Detroit as African Americans enter jobs in the war industries. In two days of rioting thirty-five people are killed and more than five hundred people are wounded, most of them black.
27 Dec.	The federal government, by presidential order, seizes the railroads in order to stop a nationwide rail strike.

1944

19 Jan.	The federal government returns the railways to their owners after settling a wage dispute.
29 Feb.	OPA director Chester A. Bowles announces that black marketeers are squeezing an estimated $1.2 billion from consumers.
19 Apr.	The House of Representatives extends the Lend-Lease program to 30 June 1945.

26 Apr.   Federal troops seize the Montgomery Ward plant after company chairman Sewell Avery refuses to extend the company's contract with the CIO as ordered by the War Labor Board.

3 May   The OPA ends meat rationing, except for steak and choice cuts of beef.

5 June   The U.S. Supreme Court rules that insurance companies are subject to the Sherman Anti-Trust Act.

1 July–
30 July   Diplomats at the Bretton Woods Conference establish the World Bank, the International Monetary Fund, and the General Agreement on Tariffs and Trade.

14 Aug.   The War Production Administration allows manufacturers to resume the production of consumer goods.

1945

15 Jan.–
8 May   A nationwide dimout is ordered to conserve fuel supplies.

2 Mar.   Striking workers close ten Chrysler and Briggs plants.

19 Mar.–
28 Aug.   The OPA freezes prices on clothing.

25 Apr.   In San Francisco the United Nations Conference on International Organization opens.

30 Apr.   Sugar rations are cut by 25 percent to preserve a diminishing supply.

10 May   The War Production Board lifts bans on seventy-three more consumer items.

12 May   The United States ends Lend-Lease aid to the Soviet Union.

25 May   Military aircraft production is reduced by 30 percent.

21 June   Pan Am airlines announces a round-the-world flight, which takes eighty-eight hours to complete and costs seven hundred dollars per passenger.

28 June   Ford Motor Company completes the last of its war contracts. During the war Ford manufactured a total of 8,600 bombers, 278,000 jeeps, and 57,000 aircraft engines.

30 June   The U.S. House of Representatives extends the Office of Price Administration for one more year.

1 July   The New York State Commission Against Discrimination, the first such agency in the United States, is established. The commission works to prevent "discrimination in employment because of race, creed, color, or national origins."

14 Aug.   The War Manpower Commission lifts all controls on wages.

15 Aug.   Rationing of gasoline and fuel oil ends.

17 Aug.   In New York State 100,000 war workers are laid off.

18 Aug.   President Harry S Truman orders the full restoration of civilian consumer production, collective bargaining, and the return of free markets.

20 Aug.   The War Production Board lifts consumer production controls on 210 products.

2 Oct.	Coal shipments are restricted in the eastern part of the United States to cope with shortages brought about by the coal strike.
4 Oct.	President Truman orders the government to seize twenty-six oil-producing companies.
5 Oct.	Bell workers disrupt telephone service for six hours in a show of strength.
17 Oct.	John L. Lewis, president of the UMW, orders the coal miners back to work.
30 Oct.	Shoe rationing ends.
19 Nov.	President Truman supports the creation of national health care.
21 Nov.– **3 Dec.**	The United Auto Workers union, 180,000 workers strong, begins a strike at all General Motors plants.
23 Nov.	Meat and butter rationing ends.
3 Dec.	President Truman asks Congress for a law to curb strikes.
6 Dec.	The United States forgives $25 billion in Lend-Lease loans.
20 Dec.	Tire rationing ends.
31 Dec.	The National War Labor Board is replaced by the National Wage Stabilization Board.

1946

3 Jan.	President Truman goes on nationwide radio to call on people to put pressure on Congress to act on labor legislation.
25 Jan.	The AFL votes to admit the UMW as a member under John L. Lewis, electing Lewis a vice-president.
27 Jan.	In Pittsburgh 800,000 steelworkers strike.
14 Feb.	President Truman eases wage and price controls in response to labor problems.
15 Feb.	The steel strike is settled with a 18.5¢-per-hour pay raise.
20 Feb.	The Employment Act creates the Council of Economic Advisers.
21 Feb.	President Truman creates the Office of Economic Stabilization under Chester A. Bowles to oversee reconversion to a peacetime economy.
27 Feb.	Ford increases wages by 18¢ an hour to end a strike.
13 Mar.	A strike at General Motors ends with a 18.5¢-per-hour pay raise for employees.
1 Apr.	More than 400,000 coal miners go on strike demanding wage increases and health insurance.
29 Apr.	Farm prices reach the highest point in the United States since the 1920s.
17 May	The federal government seizes the railroads to prevent a strike.
23 May	Railroad workers strike.

26 May	The federal government lifts its control of railroads as part of an agreement to end the strike.
11 June	President Truman vetoes a bill that would have established federal mediation in labor disputes.
14 June	In New York shipping comes to a stop as 200,000 dockworkers strike.
8 Aug.	President Truman approves a $24-billion bill for GI pay leave.
12 Aug.	In Philadelphia the bread supply is exhausted as an AFL strike continues.
5 Sept.	The worst maritime strike in history stops all shipping in the United States.
16 Sept.	The AFL and the CIO clash over settlement of the maritime strike.
24 Sept.	Reports circulate that New Yorkers are eating horse meat as a result of high meat prices.
15 Oct.	Price controls on meats are lifted.
16 Oct.	The OPA removes price controls on margarine.
19 Oct.	The cost of Lend-Lease reaches $51 billion.
23 Oct.	The OPA lifts price controls on all foods and beverages except sugar and rice.
9 Nov.	Wage and price controls end except for those on rent, sugar, and rice.
15 Nov.	John L. Lewis calls a coal strike in defiance of the government, which had seized the mines to prevent a strike.
21 Nov.	The Justice Department seeks a contempt citation against Lewis as 400,000 coal miners strike.
29 Nov.	Lewis and the UMW are indicted for contempt of court.

1947

7 Jan.	President Truman names George C. Marshall as his secretary of state.
27 Jan.	United States Steel demands the open shop.
6 Mar.	The U.S. Supreme Court upholds John L. Lewis's contempt conviction.
7 Mar.	Lewis declares that only a totalitarian regime can prevent strikes.
31 Mar.	Lewis calls a strike in sympathy for the miners killed in the Centralia, Pennsylvania, explosion.
7 Apr.	In the first nationwide telephone strike, 300,000 workers walk out.
17 Apr.	The U.S. Senate approves significant legislation to weaken the Wagner Labor Relations Act, which protects unions' right to collective bargaining.
20 Apr.	United States Steel and the steelworkers agree on a 15¢-per-hour pay raise, setting the standard for the industry.
9 May	The World Bank opens, loaning France $250 million for reconstruction.
13 May	The U.S. Senate passes the Taft-Hartley labor bill, which limits the powers of labor unions.

5 June	U.S. Secretary of State George Marshall announces the Marshall Plan, intended to help Europe recover from the damage of the war.
9 June	Marshall supports the idea of a unified Europe as a condition for American aid.
11 June	Sugar rationing ends.
23 June	Congress passes the Taft-Hartley Act over President Truman's veto.
12 July	European leaders meet to accept the Marshall Plan aid. Communist leaders are absent.
20 Aug.	President Truman predicts that the government will end the year with a $47-billion surplus.
12 Sept.	An eight-day steel strike ends with a wage increase of 15¢-per-hour.
8 Nov.	The Truman administration proposes $17 billion in aid to Europe as part of the Marshall Plan.
17 Nov.	President Truman asks Congress for wage and price controls.
1 Dec.	The National Labor Relations Board indicts the UMW for violating the Taft-Hartley Act.
12 Dec.	John L. Lewis removes the United Mine Workers from the AFL.

1948

1 Jan.	The General Agreement on Tariffs and Trades goes into effect, lowering international trade barriers.
2 Jan.	The University of Chicago, in cooperation with seven individual corporations, announces that it will engage in atomic research for industrial development.
2 Feb.	The AFL and the CIO decide not to support Henry A. Wallace's bid for the presidency.
10 Feb.	The CIO purges all members who oppose the Marshall Plan.
15 Mar.	The U.S. Supreme Court nullifies a section of the Taft-Hartley Act limiting political spending by labor unions.
15 Mar.–12 Apr.	More than 200,000 soft-coal miners go on strike demanding a better pension plan.
20 Apr.	John L. Lewis ends a coal strike but is still fined $20,000.
10 May	A judge grants an injunction to the federal government averting a nationwide railroad strike. President Truman threatens to order the army to seize the railroads.
25 May	The United Automobile Workers and General Motors sign the first sliding-scale wage contract. Wages are adjusted based on the cost of living.
21 June	The U.S. Supreme Court rules that unions may not be prevented from publishing political opinions.
31 June	President Truman dedicates the Idlewild International Airport, the largest airport in the world to date, in New York City.

25 July   The Federal Trade Commission warns Congress of the growing power of monopolies.

16 Aug.   Congress passes the Anti-Inflation Act.

16 Aug.   The Federal Reserve System attempts to slow down installment buying by raising interest rates.

25 Aug.   The consumer price index reaches a record high.

8 Oct.   The UMW endorses Republican presidential candidate Thomas Dewey.

14 Nov.   The AFL urges Congress to repeal the Taft-Hartley Act.

15 Nov.   General Electric and American Locomotive Companies test the first American-built electric locomotive.

1949

3 Jan.   The U.S. Supreme Court rules that states may ban closed shops.

14 Jan.   The Department of Justice files an antitrust lawsuit against the American Telephone and Telegraph Company (AT&T) in an effort to separate AT&T from its manufacturing subsidiary, Western Electric.

1 Feb.   President Truman says he favors a planned economy to prevent depressions.

13 Feb.   The American Medical Association supports a plan for medical care in opposition to President Truman's proposal for national health care.

25 Feb.   General Motors announces the first cuts in the price of automobiles since the end of the war.

11 Mar.   Lewis orders the UMW on a two-week walkout of the soft-coal mines to protest the appointment of James Boyd as director of the Bureau of Mines.

20 May   The AFL rejects a bid by the United Mine Workers to rejoin the organization.

1 Oct.–
11 Nov.   More than 500,000 steelworkers go on strike, which ends when the steel companies agree to the workers' pension demands.

26 Oct.   President Truman signs a minimum-wage bill into law, setting a minimum wage of 40¢ to 75¢ an hour for certain industries engaged in interstate commerce.

18 Nov.   Crucible Steel, the last holdout, signs a contract with the United Steelworkers.

5 Dec.   The U.S. Supreme Court upholds an Arkansas law prohibiting the use of violence by striking workers to keep strikebreakers from their jobs.

OVERVIEW

Silver Lining. The 1940s were one of the pivotal decades in the development of American business. During the decade the economy rebounded from depression; big business recovered its tarnished public reputation; wages and earnings reached new heights; and powerful new sectors of the economy developed, especially in the production of consumer goods and military hardware. Close cooperation with government (and in some instances outright government control) and labor unions produced a stable domestic climate for business, and business and government worked to build markets and advantageous trade overseas. American business in the 1940s was dominated by preparation for World War II, by the war itself, and in the late years of the decade by the Cold War. The silver lining among these storm clouds of war was the positive effect of war on the American economy. By the end of the decade Americans never had it so good.

Shadow of the Depression. As the decade began American business was still struggling with the effects of the Great Depression. The Depression had brought unprecedented hardship to millions of impoverished Americans, and despite assistance from President Franklin D. Roosevelt's New Deal programs, that hardship continued. With wages low and unemployment widespread, American business had few buyers for its goods. Abroad, markets once open to the United States closed with the rise of German and Japanese imperialism. Businessmen had a poor reputation with the public, a consequence of their callousness at the beginning of the Depression and of their continuing opposition to popular New Deal relief programs. The New Deal, initially attempting to cooperate with big business, shifted left after corporate America funded Roosevelt's political opponents. Powerful labor interests, which had become increasingly militant since the development of the sit-down strike in 1936, gained the lion's share of administration support. Although recovery surfaced briefly in 1937, budget balancing by the Roosevelt administration plunged the nation back into depression in the next year. Nothing the New Dealers did ushered back prosperity. By the end of the 1930s the American economy looked much as it had at the beginning of the 1930s: laggard, fragmented, and broken.

Arsenal of Democracy. The outbreak of World War II in Europe in 1939 began America's climb out of the depths of the Depression. American businesses profited from increased orders for military and nonmilitary goods by European nations engaged in the conflict. Businesses such as steel sold war goods to all parties and reaped a handsome profit. Later, as the Europeans ran short of cash, the Roosevelt administration developed a policy of American funding for allied purchases. The policy, announced as a means whereby the United States would become the "arsenal of democracy," was designed to advance American political and economic interests without involving the nation in World War II. But even policy supporters within the Roosevelt administration doubted America could stay out of the conflict and began preparing the United States for war. The government increased its purchases of military goods from private industry, spurring production and creating jobs. The depression cycle of high unemployment and low production was broken.

Isolationism. Ironically, the Roosevelt administration's cautious engagement in the European conflict stemmed in part from political forces created by American business. During the 1930s congressional investigations revealed business efforts to pressure the United States to enter World War I. The reputation of American business, already suffering as a result of the Wall Street crash, reached a new low among the public. By 1940 many Americans believed that bankers, munitions makers, and other "merchants of death" had in 1917 led the United States into World War I to protect loans to European governments and market shares. This belief, coalescing into a political movement known as isolationism, made direct American engagement in Europe politically impossible, even after France fell to the Nazis and Britain was devastated by German bombs. For many American businessmen, however, German seizure of Europe and Japanese aggression in Asia raised the alarming prospect of German and Japanese economic blocs closed to American trade. Organized into groups such as the carefully named Committee to Defend America by Aiding the Allies, such businessmen became advocates of intervention, but only circumspectly, especially in the election year of 1940. The December 1941 attack by the Japanese on Pearl Harbor came almost as a relief to interventionists within and without the Roosevelt administration. Isolationism evaporated overnight. American business could get into the business of full wartime production without any distractions.

"Dr. Win-the-War." The war emergency was an occasion not only for the recovery of American business but for its political rehabilitation. Public-relations experts presented armaments manufacturers as patriotic, and Washington was swamped with dollar-a-year men volunteering for public service from the ranks of big business. The dollar-a-year men served in government agencies at the salary of one dollar a year while returning their salaries from their companies. Their expertise was sorely needed, and the Roosevelt administration set aside much of its combativeness toward big business in order to advance the war effort. The same men Roosevelt denounced in 1936 as "economic royalists" in 1942 restructured the economy toward war production. Roosevelt explained the change in policy to the public by suggesting that "Dr. Win-the-War" had replaced "Dr. New Deal."

Cost-Plus. Roosevelt believed that political compromise with big business was vital to the war effort and set aside proposals for the nationalization of industry as too divisive. Instead, the government granted lucrative contracts on profitable terms to entice American business to war. Many of the government war orders were done on a cost-plus basis, meaning that the government guaranteed that the manufacturer would receive the cost of producing an item plus a prearranged profit. As Secretary of War Henry Stimson, a Republican who had joined the Roosevelt administration, remarked, when "you go to war in a capitalist country, you have to let business make money out of the process or business won't work." This became the administration's philosophy in cooperating with the very business leaders Roosevelt had battled during the Depression. The Roosevelt administration believed that the speed and volume of production was more important than the efficiency or cost of production and was willing to overlook a host of sins, such as price gouging and economic inefficiency, so long as the arsenal of democracy churned out goods. When it was revealed that the Standard Oil Company had violated antitrust laws and the national interest by making a 1941 deal with German petrochemical conglomerate I. G. Farben not to manufacture synthetic rubber — at a time when the Japanese were seizing the rubber plantations of Southeast Asia — the company was given a minimal fine, and the government began at taxpayer expense a crash program to manufacture synthetic rubber. By 1944, 800,000 tons of synthetic rubber were produced, and following the war lucrative patents and manufacturing plants were turned over to private interests. During the war, it seemed, American business could do no wrong.

Government Oversight. Despite the Roosevelt administration's friendly attitude toward big business, an unregulated marketplace approach to the war economy was impossible. Shortages and allocation of vital raw materials required economic oversight and coordination. By executive order Roosevelt therefore created a variety of new agencies to oversee mobilization. Among these agencies were the War Production Board (WPB), which coordinated war-related industries; the Office of Price Administration (OPA), which set prices on thousands of items to control inflation; and the National War Labor Board (NWLB), which set wages, monitored working conditions, and, if necessary, seized industrial plants in the event of labor strife. Roosevelt also converted older agencies that had been used in the war against the Depression to the new war against Fascism. The Reconstruction Finance Corporation (RFC) made loans to small businesses and home owners during the Depression; during the war the RFC loaned money at excellent terms to industries expanding to meet wartime demand.

Miracles of Production. The administration's combination of private capitalism and public stimulus accomplished exactly what the government intended: it made the United States the largest arms manufacturer in world history. Americans built nearly 300,000 airplanes, nearly 400,000 pieces of artillery, 47 million tons of artillery ammunition, 44 billion rounds of small arms ammo, nearly 87,000 warships, 86,000 tanks, and 6,500 ships. Many of these planes, tanks, and ships were used in the European and Pacific theaters of war, often with Russian, British, or other Allied soldiers using them. Often the infusion of American-made matériel proved decisive in battle. Even a Communist leader such as Soviet premier Joseph Stalin was impressed; at the Tehran Conference in 1943 he credited American production with the advancing victory.

Victory. At the end of the war American business and the economy were radically different than they were before Pearl Harbor. Americans enjoyed unprecedented prosperity. Corporate profits were simply astonishing. In 1943 alone earnings jumped $2.1 million over the prewar level. Workers' wages on average doubled, increasing from almost $25 a week to $50 a week, and many people earned hefty overtime bonuses. Even farm income increased, an incredible 250 percent, despite the loss of nearly 800,000 agricultural workers during the war. The character of corporate and working America also changed. Despite administration attempts to distribute the benefits of government contracts broadly, 71 percent of all contracts went to the hundred largest American corporations. By the end of 1942 there were 300,000 fewer small companies than there had been before the war. Small farmers also lost out. Labor also got bigger. The total labor force increased by 22 percent during the war, which along with the draft eliminated unemployment. Labor unions grew from 10.5 million members in 1939 to 14.75 million members in 1945. An acknowledged power in the American marketplace, big labor insured that many of the wage and benefit gains of the war years would continue into the next decades. Because of wartime labor shortages, moreover, the workforce was more diverse than before. Almost 60 percent of women in the United States were employed during the war. Industry, which for so long had closed its doors to African Americans, now employed 1.2 million. Sixty thousand African Americans migrated to Detroit alone during the war. Even teenagers worked during the war, and their earnings opened up a new consumer market after the war — one geared toward music and automobiles and other status symbols of adolescence. The one problem with all this prosperity was that it was purchased with government deficits justified by the pressure of war. With victory the new Truman administration was faced with a significant economic problem: how to maintain wartime prosperity without a war.

Consumer Revolution. The Truman administration sought to reconvert the American industry to its nonmilitary bases as quickly and as painlessly as the Roosevelt administration had converted it to war production. One way of accomplishing this goal was to use some of the government agencies overseeing war production to supervise the peacetime conversion of American industry. The Office of War Mobilization, retitled in 1944 the Office of War Mobilization and Reconversion, continued to coordinate manpower, production, and resources after the war. Rations on scarce goods remained in place long after armistices were signed. These wartime agencies and restrictions came under political pressure during peacetime. Truman hoped that the Office of Price Administration and Civilian Supply (OPA), for example, would continue to regulate production and prices in order to check runaway inflation. The OPA, however, faced criticism from businessmen who wanted to raise prices and from individuals who chafed at its limitations on consumer items. In June 1946 Congress extended the life of the OPA but stripped it of much of its power. Truman vetoed the bill, and when price controls expired on 1 July 1946 prices skyrocketed and the cost-of-living index rose 6 percent in one month. By 1947 the cost-of-living index had risen twenty-four points — twenty points more than it had risen in the previous year. The rise reflected not only the artificial depression of prices the government had maintained during the war but also the enormous consumer demand spiked by high wartime wages and wartime product shortages. This demand ultimately evened out the economic dislocations of reconversion. The postwar period was notable, in fact, for an unprecedented consumer revolution, as Americans rushed to buy houses, cars, appliances, and luxuries in record numbers.

Demobilization. The biggest single economic problem the Truman administration faced was the demobilization of its 17 million troops. Administration officials feared a rapid demobilization of the military would plunge the nation back into depression, yet the political pressure from American families for rapid demobilization was enormous, especially after 1946. The problem was partially solved by the Serviceman's Readjustment Act of 1944, commonly known as the GI Bill, which funneled many returning veterans into college, thus delaying their entry into the labor force and improving their working skills. Government, business, and labor-union policies, furthermore, favored the hiring of returning vets, forcing tens of thousands of working women and teenagers out of the labor market. There was also an enormous increase in the number of new industries in America following the war. Often sparked by wartime government research, industries such as television, aviation, and chemical and metallurgical processing absorbed many of the demobilized troops. Finally, the government maintained a larger military force after the war than it had ever maintained in American history during peacetime. Troops were needed as occupying forces in Europe and Asia, and American naval and air fleets remained enormous. The large standing army, the GI Bill, and new industries nonetheless failed to prevent widespread labor dislocations following the war. From 1946 to 1948, as unemployment rose and the American economy slowed, strikes became commonplace, and the Truman administration struggled with popular discontent with its economic policies.

Trade and Cold War. American economic planners also hoped that a revival in American international trade and the reconstruction of European economies would increase American production and absorb the veteran labor force. Even before Pearl Harbor international bankers and interventionists viewed the war as an opportunity to prevent the creation of world economic blocs closed to American trade. With the end of the war they constructed international institutions to accomplish this goal. The World Bank, the International Monetary Fund (IMF), and the General Agreement on Tariffs and Trade (GATT) were designed to insure American access to colonial markets formerly closed to American trade. These agreements were also designed to help Europe rebuild and resume trade with the United States. This goal was even more explicit in the 1947 Marshall Plan, whose guidelines specified the terms of renewed trade on a basis favorable to American corporations — often accompanied by a surprising degree of American interference in the domestic economies of European states. The Europeans, devastated and bankrupted by the war, rarely objected to the conditions of Marshall Plan assistance and by 1950 had resumed domestic production and American trade on a greater basis than before the war. The Soviet Union, however, committed itself to a policy of economic self-sufficiency and independence. Twice spurned in its requests for less restrictive loans by the United States, it rejected Marshall Plan funds and chose to reconstitute its economy by integrating it, rather poorly to that of Eastern Europe. The Soviets in effect created an economic bloc and closed it to American trade — anathema to American internationalists. The actions of the Soviets, as well as the economic restrictions of American assistance, form the economic backdrop to the Cold War. The political, cultural, and military repercussions of this economic confrontation in turn transformed the American domestic economy and by 1949 resolved the problems plaguing postwar industry. The potential military confrontation with the Soviet Union not only cemented American economic ties with Western Europe and increased American trade but also provided a viable rationale for increased military expenditures. By the end of the decade prosperity was insured by the twin forces of expansive American trade and the growth of what Dwight D. Eisenhower would later term "the military/industrial complex."

TOPICS IN THE NEWS

BUSINESS: MOBILIZATION FOR WORLD WAR II

Impact of War. World War II was an event of enormous consequence for business and industry. Before the war, caught in a deflationary spiral, industry longed for customers and closed plants for lack of demand. As the 1940s began, Europeans, desperate for goods with which to wage the already-raging war, paid for millions of dollars' worth of goods. Factories reopened, and new workers were hired to meet the demand. Government programs to mobilize and supply the American military furthered the recovery. Yet the marketplace proved poorly responsive to the political and military emergency. As business recovered, for example, more and more industries devoted their production to meet increased consumer demand at the very time government officials were seeking greater military production. Shortages of raw materials were common; so too were strikes and labor disputes. All of these factors combined to retard the production necessary to supply the American military completely. While some within the Roosevelt administration favored the wholesale appropriation of private industry in order to meet war priorities, the president, following the precedent of the New Deal, favored government oversight of private industry as the best way to mobilize for war. Government and industry created a mixed public/private economy to advance war production. Even before the attack on Pearl Harbor, the character of American business had changed radically.

Bureaucracy. The Roosevelt administration, concerned over the ease with which continental Europe had fallen to the Nazis, was determined to prepare America's economic and industrial base for the possibility of war. Spending on military preparedness soared, reaching $75 million a day by December 1941. On the model of the New Deal, the administration also established a host of agencies to oversee the economy. Some New Deal agen-

THE SPRUCE GOOSE

Howard Hughes made a fortune in the aviation business. In particular, he made a fortune during World War II building planes for the military. However, his war contracts became the subject of a public scandal as he was charged with plying top military officials and President Franklin D. Roosevelt's son with bribes. At the center of the controversy was the Spruce Goose, an $18-million airplane constructed of wood that stood five stories tall. In theory the Spruce Goose was to be a combination of boat and airplane. Testifying before the Senate, Hughes vowed that the plane would fly or he would leave the country. On 2 November 1947, almost by a miracle, the Spruce Goose took off from the water and flew almost one mile before landing in Long Beach Harbor. This was one of Hughes's last public appearances.

Source: Michael Drosnin, *Citizen Hughes* (New York: Holt, Rinehart & Winston, 1985).

cies simply shifted their work toward war preparedness. The Reconstruction Finance Corporation (RFC), originally established to provide low-cost loans to small businesses, began financing the construction of defense plants. Other agencies were created to facilitate preparedness, such as the Office of Production Management (OPM). Headed by production genius William S. Knudsen, industrialist Edward R. Stettinius, labor leader Sidney Hillman, and New Dealer Leon Henderson, the OPM attempted to coordinate the distribution of raw materials to industry and set production goals for vital war goods such as steel. Later that year the Supply Priorities and Allocations Board (SPAB) assumed some of

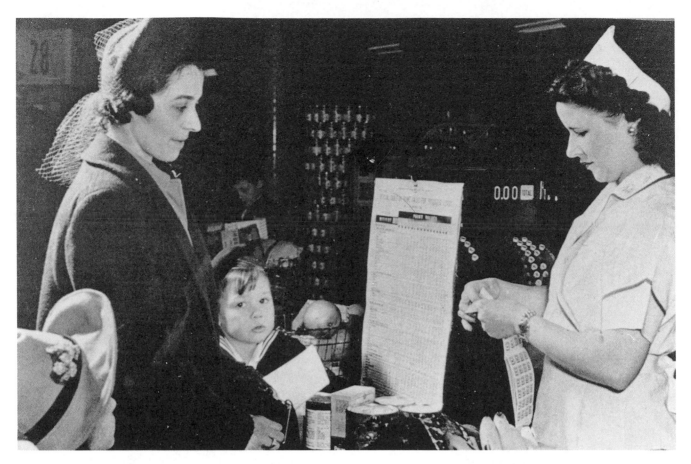

Grocery-store cashier tearing off ration stamps presented by customer purchasing canned goods

these duties. In March the administration created the National Defense Mediation Board, designed to mediate labor/management disputes in vital industries. In April the Office of Price Administration and Civilian Supply (OPA) was created to prevent inflation and protect consumers. In the wake of Pearl Harbor more bureaucracies were created. The War Production Board (WPB) had many of the same duties as the OPM but more-sweeping powers to accomplish its goals. Likewise, the new National War Labor Board (NWLB) took over from the National Defense Mediation Board and had the power to order arbitration rather than simply recommend it. When even these powers proved inadequate to the task of increasing war production, Roosevelt created a production czar to coordinate the varied problems of a mixed economy. Donald Nelson, a former executive with Sears Roebuck, reshaped the WPB and made himself the most powerful man in the American economy. Although critics charged he was a virtual dictator, the affable Nelson was a conciliator, and WPB was staffed with dollar-a-year men determined to use the board to advance the cause of private industry and retard government centralization of the economy.

Rationing. Despite Nelson's and the WPB's management of the economy, a persistent problem during the war was the scarcity of vital raw materials such as rubber, access to which was cut off in many cases by the enemy.

To fill the orders for these raw materials (a B-17 bomber used half a ton of rubber) the WPB, the OPA, and the rest of the government turned to the public, engaging them in the pervasive home-front activity of rationing. The government deemed many everyday items as essential to the war effort, ranging from gasoline to ketchup. The OPA limited the amounts of these items consumers could purchase via a series of rather complex red and blue ration books. Meat, sugar, butter, canned goods — all were rationed. Gasoline was apportioned via rating stickers on the windows of cars. Cars used for pleasure got an A rating and limited gas; emergency vehicles received an E rating and unlimited fuel; the remainder of cars received a B, C, or D rating, with different amounts of gasoline for each. The OPA's rationing system was cumbersome, necessitating sixty thousand full-time employees and fifty-five hundred local rationing boards to administer it. It generated a terrific amount of grumbling among the public and a lively traffic in black-market goods. A friendly grocer might slide favored customers extra meat with their ration; organized crime sometimes hijacked goods and sold them for exorbitant prices. Authorities tended to be tolerant of small-scale abuse of the rationing system, but the government did alter the type of ration books printed midway through the war in order to thwart counterfeiters.

Shortages and Scrap. Consumers also endured shortages in favorite goods during the war. Coffee was scarce because the ships that normally carried the beans north from Latin America were carrying goods to the front. Cigarettes were difficult to find, as they too made their way to the battlefield. Alcohol, used in explosives, was less available to distillers (one whiskey maker marketed Olde Spud, a product fermented from waste potatoes). Spectacles, two-thirds of which were formerly imported from Germany, naturally became scarce. Women compensated for the lack of silk stockings (silk was used in parachutes) by keeping their legs shaved and drawing seams down their calves with eyeliner to give the appearance of hosiery. The worst shortage of all was in housing, especially near the booming defense plants. Americans routinely doubled up, sharing small rooms in cramped apartments, or lived in makeshift trailers and other forms of substandard housing. While Americans tolerated such shortages, they also participated in a voluntary austerity program by limiting their purchases of consumer items. In a widespread publicity campaign the Office of Civilian Defense (OCD) suggested that limiting purchases would help win the war. The government also urged the public to grow victory gardens and supply themselves with food, a habit many had already cultivated in the Depression. Officials also solicited public help in acquiring used and scrap goods that could be reused in the war. Children especially participated in "scrap drives," saving bacon grease (used in ammunition) and old newspapers (to conserve paper) and hunting for bits and pieces of cardboard, scrap metal, tin cans, tinfoil, and old rubber. The cumulative economic and production effects of these sacrifices were less important than their ability to knit the nation to a common cause. Mobilization on the home front gave Americans a sense of participating in the struggle and diffused criticism of the war. For the most part, however, shortages, rationing, and patriotism meant most American worked overtime and saved their money ($140 billion by 1945), building a base for the boom in consumer purchases after the war.

Boom. By 1943 the combination of government oversight and incentive and of rationing and resource allocation resulted in astonishing advances in production. Production of raw materials was unprecedented. During the war the United States Steel Corporation alone made 414 million ingot tons of steel, more than Germany and Japan combined. Direct war production was also enormous, nearly two-thirds the total production in the United States. American industry turned out 2.4 million military trucks, 86,000 tanks, nearly 30,000 aircraft, 15 million rifles and machine guns, 64,000 landing craft, and 6,500 ships. U.S. Steel made 21 million helmets for the army, each capable of withstanding a hit from a .45-caliber bullet. The quality of other war goods also improved. Aircraft became faster and more powerful; jeeps (the name was soldier slang for "GP," or general-purpose vehicle) more rugged; tanks more impenetrable. The engineering advances spurred by the war became invaluable in the postwar economic environment, as did improvements in manufacturing techniques, which speeded up production. Indirect war production was also considerable, laying the foundation for the postwar economy. U.S. Steel made 31.4 million kegs of nails, enough steel fencing to stretch from New York City to San Francisco, and 90,500 tons of barbed wire. They cast 1,250 miles of pipe, manufacturing the "Big Inch" pipeline that supplied Texas oil directly to New Yorkers. Walter Kidde and Company increased its sales of carbon dioxide fire extinguishers and fire detectors during the war; sales rose from $2 million in 1938 to $60 million during the war as the company's equipment was used in tanks, ships, and planes. Its workforce grew from 450 to 5,000 people. Lights, Inc., experienced similar growth. The company made lights used in aircraft and automobiles. Its sales went from $150,000 to $50 million annually. Such success stories were commonplace. The war precipitated boom times in nearly every sector of the American economy. By 1944 American manufacturers were itching for the war to end so they could convert their industries fully to civilian production. The industrial infrastructure was in place, profits were high, and the workforce was trained. All that remained was victory.

Recovery. War mobilization rescued American industry from the worst crisis in its history. Massive government expenditures spurred tremendous growth, modernized aging physical plants, and insured high wages and speedy production lines. War profits after taxes reached $10.8 billion by 1944. The war also, in a sense, created the modern corporation, because government contracts did not go to small and large businesses equally; large companies benefited disproportionately. The government set aside antitrust suits as disruptive of production. Ten companies received 30 percent of the total $240 billion spent on defense contracts. The Kaiser shipbuilding company alone received 30 percent of defense outlays in 1943. Large companies further restructured their organizations to operate effectively within the new economic

Senators Harry S Truman, Ralph Brewster, and Homer Ferguson at a Senate hearing on wartime manpower resources, 24 March 1943

environment. Administration engaged more directly in politics; large corporations, such as General Motors, established planning divisions to anticipate future needs on the model of the WPB's allocation bureau; and research and development divisions became commonplace. The mixed economy of the war was so successful that many businessmen, heretofore opponents of government intervention into the economy, came to accept federal regulation, oversight, and expenditures. Other businessmen, however, ironically argued that the war vindicated private enterprise. Chafing at the bit of wartime regulation, they sought an immediate end to federal oversight after victory — whatever the temporary dislocations to the economy. The tension between these two groups fueled the political conflicts of the Truman administration. By the end of the decade, however, businessmen generally agreed that government participation in private business was beneficial. The mixed economy synthesized during the war became a model for subsequent decades: generous government defense spending; government expenditures to "prime the pump" of consumer spending during economic downturns; government mediation of labor disputes and generally high wages; and government toleration of gigantic American corporations. War mobilization ushered in thirty years of American prosperity.

Sources:

William Chafe, *The Unfinished Journey: America Since World War II* (New York: Oxford University Press, 1986);

John Harris Howell, *The Right to Manage: Industrial Relations Policies of American Business in the 1940s* (Madison: University of Wisconsin Press, 1982).

DEFENSE SPENDING UNDER SCRUTINY: THE TRUMAN COMMITTEE

Origins. The Truman Committee, officially known as the Senate Special Committee to Investigate the National Defense Program, was organized by Sen. Harry S Truman of Missouri. He wanted to contribute to the war effort, but he was too old to serve as an artillery officer, as he had during World War I. Concerned that the money spent on war preparedness was being wasted in corruption and inefficiency, he began his investigation in 1940 by driving thousands of miles to visit military bases and other projects to investigate complaints. Concluding that his concerns were accurate, on 10 February 1941 he delivered a speech to the Senate describing the waste he had uncovered.

Corruption. The Senate then established a special investigative committee to examine all aspects of war production, placing Truman in charge. While serving on the committee, he approached the issue of war funding with tenacity and caution, vigorously pursuing government officials and businessmen who wasted taxpayer money while also taking care not to hurt the incipient war effort or to damage the Roosevelt administration politically. Beginning in 1941 and continuing well into World War II, the committee investigated the construction of army camps and uncovered evidence that $100 million of a $1-billion budget was being wasted. The main problem was the cost-plus system, in which contractors were paid for their expenses plus an agreed-upon percentage as profit and which contractors abused in order to increase profits. Another major problem was that businesses were claiming to be meeting both domestic and defense needs but were focusing on more-profitable domestic production while accepting money for defense contracts. Further, some companies, in arrangements with German companies, delayed or curtailed essential production of war materials. The result of the investigation was increased oversight, and often outright control, of military production in the private sector. In addition to aiding in mobilization, some estimates placed the savings as a result of the Truman Committee in the billions.

Centralization. Truman focused attention on the need for a centralized administrative authority over the war effort. "The influence from above must be always toward unity," he said. Instead of trying to reduce the power of the executive branch, as Congress often did, he and his committee fought to create a single agency responsible for overseeing the war effort. Believing that bureaucratic red tape slowed the war effort and killed American soldiers, the committee worked to eliminate conflicts between departments and duplication of efforts that hindered construction of defense housing and the synthetic rubber program, among other projects. The Truman Committee proved to be a tremendous success despite its criticism of powerful government officials and private businesses. In 1944 the press chose Truman as one of the top ten most valuable men in Washington — the only congressman on the list.

Sources:

David McCullough, *Truman* (New York: Simon & Schuster, 1992);

William E. Pemberton, *Harry S. Truman: Fair Dealer and Cold Warrior* (Boston: Twayne, 1989).

THE ECONOMY: WAR TAXES AND FINANCING

War Deficits. The economic recovery of World War II was the result of massive federal expenditures for defense. The government spent approximately $360 billion on the war, at times as much as $250 million a day. A little under half of these expenditures were raised by taxes; bond sales and deficit spending accounted for the rest. Throughout the war the government operated in the red; by 1945 the national debt was a staggering $260 billion.

Taxes. Taxation was the government's best means of raising revenue, but tax policy was a complicated political construction, the product of numerous compromises between interest groups and their representatives on Capitol Hill. The Roosevelt administration hoped for a heavily progressive tax geared toward the wealthy. Such taxes would raise the greatest revenues and dampen inflationary pressures by reducing disposable income. From the experience of World War I, Roosevelt was also concerned about excess profits and price gouging by large corporations and wealthy individuals. He proposed an excess-profits tax on corporations and a cap on personal incomes of $25,000 to prevent this — impossible ideas politically, but ideas the administration used to gain tax concessions from privileged interests. The 1942 Revenue Act, the basis of wartime financing, was a compromise. The tax structure was unprecedentedly progressive, with the highest personal incomes taxed at a rate of 91 percent and a corporate tax rate of 40 percent; but the tax base was widened, and for the first time in American history low-income earners were taxed. The number of people who paid income taxes grew from 3.9 million in 1939 to 42.6 million in 1945. The government collected most of their personal income taxes through the new method of payroll deduction — automatic taxation of the weekly paycheck. Payroll deduction was intended to be a temporary war measure, but it became permanent after the war. Wartime prosperity and higher taxes made the income tax a reality for many Americans for the first time.

Bonds. Much of the war effort was financed by the selling of war bonds. Approximately 60 percent of the war cost was funded through borrowing. War bonds could be purchased in denominations ranging from $25 to $10,000. Banks and financial institutions bought much of the $135 billion total bond sales during the war, but $36 billion was purchased by smaller bondholders in lower denominations. Buying war bonds became an act of patriotism, a way for people on the home front to help the men and women fighting the war. Bond drives and rallies became civic celebrations, featuring publicity stunts such as auctioning off Kentucky Derby winner Man o' War's horseshoes or bidding for a kiss from movie star Hedy Lamarr. A marathon radio program featuring singer Kate Smith earned nearly $40 million in pledges. War bonds also helped hold down inflation because they took money out of circulation. Instead of spending

Advertisement by the Sparton radio company urging Americans to buy war bonds, 1944

money on scarce consumer goods, thus driving up prices through increased demand, people invested their money in government bonds, resulting in substantial savings for many after the war.

Redistribution. The war reversed a long-term trend of the rich becoming richer. Wartime tax policies, demands by organized labor for better wages, and redistributive programs such as Social Security shifted wealth, for the first time in American history, from the top 5 percent of income earners to the rest of America. In 1939 people in the top 5 percent income bracket controlled 23 percent of the nation's disposable income, but in 1945 they controlled only 17 percent of disposable income. Wartime tax policy, with its progressive income brackets, continued until 1964. Combined with the inordinate advantages America had in world trade, the churning production underwritten by defense expenditures, and continued high wages earned by unions, this situation insured that the new American middle class prospered in the postwar era.

Sources:

John Morton Blum, *V Was for Victory: Politics and American Culture during World War II* (New York: Harcourt Brace Jovanovich, 1976);

John Maynard Keynes in his office at the Treasury
Department, 1946

Robert Higgs, ed., *Arms, Politics, and the Economy: Historical and Contemporary Perspectives* (New York: Holmes & Meier, 1990);

Donald Nelson, *Arsenal of Democracy: The Story of American War Production* (New York: Harcourt, Brace, 1946);

Harold G. Vatter, *The U.S. Economy in World War II* (New York: Columbia University Press, 1985).

KEYNESIAN ECONOMICS

The Crisis of Capitalism. Although a citizen of Great Britain, economist John Maynard Keynes had a tremendous impact on American business practices and in particular the role of the government in the economy. Keynes theorized that the Depression was not a result of overproduction, the most commonly given cause, but rather a problem of distribution. Although Keynes's ideas were initially rejected during the 1930s, in the 1940s they became widely accepted.

Priming the Pump. Essentially, Keynes argued, the Depression was caused by a shortage of money that made it difficult to move goods from one location to another. The cure, as he saw it, was for the government to prime the economy's pump with deficit spending. An increase in government spending without accompanying tax increases would put more money in circulation and start the economy moving again. His theories were first put before President Franklin D. Roosevelt during the Depression, but at first Roosevelt rejected them because of his reluc-

tance to use deficit spending to end the Depression. However, after the recession of 1936–1937 the Roosevelt administration halfheartedly adopted Keynesian economic policies. Before World War II the administration did not commit the nation to sufficient spending to end the Depression. In fact, Roosevelt had caused the economic slump by cutting spending in an effort to balance the budget. The result was increased unemployment and a slowing of the economy.

Acceptance. Prosperity returned to the United States in the 1940s because, as Keynes had predicted, federal spending for military programs had produced growing deficits. The massive amount of money the government spent to prepare for and fight World War II validated his ideas. During the 1940s many business leaders accepted a larger role for the government in the economy to provide economic stability and to prevent the return of another depression. Americans, largely because of the Cold War, accepted his prescription for deficit spending to stimulate the economy but did not subscribe to his belief that the government should have a budgetary surplus during good times to slow inflationary growth. This approach to government spending became known in economic circles as military Keynesianism. Yet another approach to Keynesian economics was to cut taxes without cutting spending. All of these approaches were widely accepted by government officials and enjoyed bipartisan support from the 1940s to the 1980s.

Source:
Robert M. Collins, *The Business Response to Keynes, 1929–1964* (New York: Columbia University Press, 1981).

THE MILITARY-INDUSTRIAL COMPLEX

Containment. As World War II was winding down, the alliance between the Soviet Union and the United

American soldier at a Coca-Cola cooler, Guam, July 1944

States, brought together by a common foe, was deteriorating. Tensions between the two nations had existed since the Russian Revolution of 1917, and within a few years after World War II the two powers were engaged in a cold war. Following the war, the Truman administration made containment the cornerstone of all American foreign policy toward the Soviet Union. The policy of containment was originally devised by George Kennan, chargé d'affaires at the American embassy in Moscow. He argued that the United States and the Soviet Union could not coexist because the Soviet Union was by its very nature expansionist. The goal of the United States, according to Kennan, should be to apply counterpressure against Soviet attempts to expand, thus containing the Soviet empire. Successful containment of the Soviet Union, according to the plan, would mean its eventual collapse. This policy remained in effect for the next forty-five years and was the rationale behind American involvement in the Korean and Vietnam Wars.

Funding. The Cold War dramatically changed the American economy and the role of the federal government in business. Containment meant that the United States committed itself, for the first time in American history, to a large standing army and to large peacetime defense expenditures, things many Americans had historically feared. One of the first steps in the Cold War was taken during the Truman administration when the United States granted $400 million to Greece and Turkey to fight Communist rebels within their borders. Additionally, America's spending on the military skyrocketed, resulting in higher taxes and perpetual deficit spending.

Garrison State. In 1948 President Truman submitted the second largest peacetime budget in American history to Congress, justifying it as necessary to meet the threat of totalitarianism in the world. The budget came to $39.6 billion, with around $18 billion earmarked for military spending and international affairs. Such spending created a new industry in the United States devoted to the pro-

THE BRETTON WOODS AGREEMENT

With World War II coming to a close, American leaders wanted to ensure that past mistakes would not be repeated and that the United States would assume a place of global leadership. To these ends, American diplomats spent the final years of the war working to consolidate the gains American companies had made during the war by institutionalizing international free markets. The Bretton Woods Agreement negotiated in 1944 provided for three new institutions that were to help rationalize and open the world economy. They were the International Monetary Fund (IMF), the World Bank (International Bank of Reconstruction and Development), and the General Agreement on Tariffs and Trade (GATT). In a major triumph for both Truman and internationalists, the Bretton Woods Agreement passed Congress in mid 1945.

Because the United States had survived the war intact and prosperous, it had the resources to dominate the monetary fund and the World Bank. American control meant that both institutions operated on an open-door policy of free trade. The GATT essentially lowered trading barriers between member countries. Under the IMF, member governments agreed to rationalize how currency was converted to other nations' currency and to avoid the competitive devaluation of currency. Furthermore, resources were set aside to provide a large fund to help stabilize exchange rates by assisting countries in need. The World Bank had the same membership as the IMF and loaned money to governments and to government agencies at "conventional financial terms" — that is, it charged interest on its loans.

Sources: Michael J. Hogan, *The Marshall Plan: America, Britain, and the Reconstruction of Western Europe, 1947–1952* (New York: Cambridge University Press, 1987);

William E. Pemberton, *Harry S. Truman: Fair Dealer and Cold Warrior* (Boston: Twayne, 1989).

Sources:
Robert Higgs, ed., *Arms, Politics and the Economy: Historical and Contemporary Perspectives* (New York: Holmes & Meier, 1990);

Paul A. C. Koistinen, *The Military-Industrial Complex: A Historical Perspective* (New York: Praeger, 1980).

NEW MARKETS: AMERICAN BUSINESS FOLLOWS THE FLAG

Capital. During the 1940s many American businesses became truly international. During World War II American businesses expanded dramatically and acquired enormous wealth that could be used as investment capital after the war. In 1947 American investments abroad reached an all-time high of $26.7 billion, with a net outflow of $5.8 billion in loans and investments occurring in the first six months of 1947 alone. Both the private and the public sectors invested in overseas facilities; $16 billion in private capital and $10.7 billion in public capital went to foreign projects. Much government investment took place in new international agencies such as the International Monetary Fund, the World Bank, and the Reconstruction Finance Corporation of the Marshall Plan.

Open Markets. The American policy was to open foreign markets as part of an effort to contain communism and to prevent another global economic disaster such as the Depression. Also, many American businesses took advantage of the collapse of the European imperial system resulting from the war, particularly the empires of France and Great Britain. One of the constant tensions between the United States and Great Britain during the 1940s was the fate of the British Empire. American leaders, especially President Franklin D. Roosevelt, wanted to dismantle the empire and its barriers to trade, while the British wanted to preserve the empire as a closed economic system. This dispute proved to be one of the major sticking points in implementing the Marshall Plan and the European Common Market in the late 1940s.

Joint Ventures. American businesses expanded throughout the world in a series of cooperative efforts with the American government, with old and newly created foreign governments in the aftermath of the war, and with other companies. Robert W. Woodruff, the president of Coca-Cola, was a perfect example of how some businessmen used the war to practice their patriotism while furthering their companies' ends. Before the war Coca-Cola was the most widely distributed mass-produced item in the United States. With the outbreak of war the company faced an obvious problem: sugar, along with many other commodities, was being rationed by the government. However, Woodruff overcame the problem during the war, convincing government officials that Coca-Cola was the perfect drink for GIs and industrial workers. Soon Coca-Cola went where American troops went, following the flag into foreign lands. Woodruff kept the price of Coca-Cola at a nickel a bottle and created a worldwide market for his product,

duction of goods to supply weapons and other materials to the Pentagon. This industry, which became known as the military-industrial complex, became one of the largest industries in the United States and a crucial part of the economy. In a pattern similar to World War II mobilization, entire companies were supported solely by government spending. Unlike World War II, however, there was no end in sight. As long as the Soviet Union continued to exist there was a reason for the military spending. However, by 1961 outgoing president Dwight D. Eisenhower warned the nation of the danger the military-industrial complex posed to the future.

President Harry S Truman, George C. Marshall, Paul Hoffman, and Averell Harriman, architects of the Marshall Plan, November 1948

setting the stage for a remarkable expansion of the company after the war. Other manufacturing firms also expanded into global markets in search of profits and resources. American reserves of high-grade iron ore were depleted, so the Bethlehem Steel Corporation spent $37.5 million to develop iron ore deposits in Latin America, which included building railroads and other facilities necessary to use the ore. The M. A. Hanna Company struck a similar deal in Brazil, exploiting an iron range with an estimated 160 million tons of ore. Other examples abound. American investors also financed the building of a $60-million steel plant in Egypt, the nation's first. The Anaconda Copper Mining Company invested $150 million in Chilean copper mines. Two American tire manufacturers opened plants in South Africa, and a group of British and American investors formed the American-Anglo-Transvaal Corporation to invest in the country. The Ford Motor Company spent $3.25 million to build in Australia, and General Motors matched that effort with a $3-million investment.

Sources:
Michael J. Hogan, *The Marshall Plan: America, Britain, and the Reconstruction of Western Europe, 1947–1952* (New York: Cambridge University Press, 1987);

Daniel Yergin, *The Prize: The Epic Quest for Oil, Money and Power* (New York: Simon & Schuster, 1992).

THE PLAN THAT MARSHALL BUILT

Rebuilding Europe. In June 1947 U.S. secretary of state George Marshall proposed what became known as the Marshall Plan, in which suffering European nations trying to rebuild would receive American aid. The program, according to Marshall, would be "directed not against any country or doctrine but against hunger, poverty, desperation, and chaos." European nations, including the Soviet Union, responded quickly to the American offer. The Soviets and their allies withdrew after the first meeting, but the sixteen remaining countries reached an agreement with the United States. These countries initially asked for $29 billion in aid, but the United States cut this amount to $17 billion over four years, with $5 billion going to Europe in the first year of the program.

Motives. Marshall's proposal represented the culmination of much debate in Washington as to the best foreign-policy approach to the postwar world. Essentially, those who supported and worked for the Marshall

Postwar filling station, just after gas rationing had ended

Plan were New Dealers who had carried intact their political faith through the war. According to Marshall and his backers, World War II had two basic causes. First, they believed the United States had shirked its responsibilities by not embracing internationalism at the end of World War I, evident in its refusal to join the League of Nations and its virtual withdrawal from European affairs. Second, these liberals believed that the Depression was in part created by the failure of the United States to address international problems such as war debts. As a result Europe in general and Germany in particular had suffered unnecessarily under the Versailles Treaty and others that ended World War I. The desperate economic climate that developed in Germany gave rise to fascism and Adolf Hitler. This, in turn, helped to cause World War II.

Europe Made the American Way. Marshall's plan attempted to prevent such a scenario from repeating itself. Under the Marshall Plan the United States would help Europe rebuild. Those who developed the Marshall Plan wanted to impose New Deal–style regulations on the European economy. In addition, supporters of the plan wanted to turn Europe into one interconnected market without internal trade barriers.

Integrated Europe. The integration and restoration of Europe was important for several reasons. Following the war, most of Western Europe was politically and economically unstable, with strong Communist movements. France and Italy had developed large Communist parties outside established governments. Many Americans feared that the postwar climate in Europe could lead to the triumph of communism and to the spread of Soviet power, much like fascism had spread after World War I. Additionally, many American leaders recognized that a restored Europe could purchase a greater quantity of American goods. The Marshall Plan helped to lay the groundwork for the European Common Market and other efforts at a unified Europe.

Source:
Michael J. Hogan, *The Marshall Plan: America, Britain, and the Reconstruction of Western Europe, 1947–1952* (New York: Cambridge University Press, 1987).

SUPPLYING NEW DEMANDS AND FINDING NEW SOURCES FOR OIL

Oil Czar. During World War II the United States supplied the Allies with the bulk of the oil needed to fight the war, and oil was one of the most important strategic resources of the war. During the war U.S. secretary of the interior Harold Ickes also assumed the position of director of the Petroleum Administration for War, thus becoming an oil czar with unprecedented power over the oil industry. He increased domestic production and rationing civilian use of gasoline and other oil products to meet war needs. During the war American leaders in both the public and private sectors redefined the importance of oil and of overseas oil fields, particularly those in the Middle East.

Running Out of Oil. In the December 1943 *American Magazine* Ickes published an article titled "We're Running Out of Oil!" In it he expressed concern about the rapid depletion of America's oil reserves, writing that the "law of diminishing returns is becoming operative. As new oil fields are not being formed and the number is ultimately finite, the time will come sooner or later when the supply is exhausted." For the first time in its history the United States would become an importer of oil rather than an exporter, which would have serious implications for national security. As Ickes and others saw it, the United States had to gain access to foreign oil to avoid further depletion of the domestic supply. With President Franklin D. Roosevelt's support he then began pursuing a wide variety of options, including a national oil company and public-private joint ventures with companies investing in the Middle East.

New Reserves. Every American oil company ventured overseas in search of new oil reserves during the 1940s. Often they were involved in some type of joint effort to secure oil concessions, particularly rights to the oil fields of the Middle East. Foreseeing a dramatic increase in the demand for oil, economists and public officials predicted that by 1951 the world demand for oil would reach 3.75 billion barrels of crude oil, a 35 percent increase in demand over the war year of 1945. Standard Oil was the most aggressive company in seeking new sources of oil, spending $100 million to construct refineries, pipelines, and towns in Venezuela and $140 million to build refineries in England. Other investments were shared with separate oil companies when the risks and costs were too expensive for one company. For instance, several hundred million dollars were spent to build pipelines in the Middle East. Such international efforts placed the oil companies in close cooperation with the State Department and the Department of the Interior.

Cars. Oil consumption did not decline with the end of the war but instead increased dramatically as Americans entered into a new age of economic growth and prosperity. Oil became the primary source of energy in the United States. By 1950 there were 40 million cars on the

road, up from 26 million in 1945. With more cars on the road, the demand for oil was 42 percent greater than in 1945. Prices reflected the new demand as the cost of gasoline more than doubled from 1945 to 1950. Despite Ickes's predictions of doom during the war, new oil discoveries (especially in foreign oil fields) meant that there was a glut of oil. Oil company executives worried that a global glut would destroy the market even as consumers became angry at rising prices and local shortages. The problem was not in supply but in distribution and processing. Americans, with their continually rising demand for oil, would soon become very familiar with the virtues and problems of foreign oil.

Source:
Daniel Yergin, *The Prize: The Epic Quest for Oil, Money, and Power* (New York: Simon & Schuster, 1992).

THE TAFT-HARTLEY ACT

During the 1930s and World War II, organized labor made progress on many fronts. Various labor unions also formed an alliance with the Democratic Party, then in control, and promoted legislation and government regulation to cement these gains. However, in the 1946 election the Republican Party won control of Congress and set about to eliminate or roll back what they perceived to be the excessive power of labor unions. The Republican-controlled Congress passed the Taft-Hartley Act over the veto of President Harry S Truman, reducing or eliminating many labor union advantages provided for in the National Labor Relations Act of 1935. These included the unconditional closed shop; the checkoff system, which enabled unions to collect dues from all employed members; the unconditional right to strike at any time; and immunity from employer lawsuits over breaches of contract and strike damages.

Sources: Melvyn Dubofsky and Warren Van Tine, *John L. Lewis: A Biography* (Urbana: University of Illinois Press, 1986);

William E. Pemberton, *Harry S. Truman: Fair Dealer and Cold Warrior* (Boston: Twayne, 1989).

UNIONS: THE HEYDAY OF ORGANIZED LABOR

Power. During the 1940s the power of organized labor in the United States was at its height; at no other time in American history did labor unions exercise so much power and influence. Much of this power came from labor's close relationship with the Democratic Party and the labor shortages created by World War II. During the war membership in unions expanded dramatically, aided by the National War Labor Board (NWLB). In 1941, 10.5 million workers belonged to a labor union; by 1945

John L. Lewis, 20 April 1948, after being fined $20,000 by a federal judge for defying a federal injunction against a United Mine Workers strike

the number of union members had reached 14.7 million men and women.

Manpower Shortage. The largest labor organizations, the American Federation of Labor (AFL) and the Congress of Industrial Organizations (CIO), both agreed to a nonbinding no-strike pledge for the duration of the war, but labor leaders soon became disenchanted with the NWLB as the agency implemented wage controls as an inflation-fighting tool. Further, labor leaders charged that representatives from big business dominated the NWLB and other wartime agencies. Labor leaders argued that a cap on workers' wages when wartime spending was driving inflation higher was unfair to working people. Eventually the NWLB allowed a 15 percent increase in wages. In addition, most workers made more money from overtime, which helped to increase take-home pay in some industries by as much as 70 percent during the war even as labor leaders sought more for their followers. During 1942 fewer that 1 million men went on strike, but that number rose as 3.1 million men took part in work stoppages in 1943. John L. Lewis led the way when 400,000 members of the United Mine Workers went on strike in direct violation of the no-strike pledge. The strike was incredibly unpopular among the general populace because coal was the main source of fuel, and Lewis soon became one of the most hated men in America. Members of the Roosevelt administration began talking about seizing the mines. In response Congress passed the War Labor Disputes Act, which would have made it illegal to encourage strikes in plants taken over by the government. Roosevelt vetoed the bill but asked Congress for the authority to draft the miners in order to make them work. Lewis then called off the strike, and President Roosevelt ordered Secretary of the Interior Harold Ickes to take over the mines to ensure an adequate supply of coal. Ickes continued bargaining with miners even as they stayed off the job. Eventually he approved a new system of computing wages that did not technically violate wage ceilings.

National Service. The conflict between Roosevelt and Lewis threatened not only to disrupt the war effort but also to jeopardize Roosevelt's alliance with labor. In January 1944 Roosevelt proposed national service as a solution to the deepening manpower crisis. Originally the proposal would have placed all citizens at the government's disposal for assignment to whatever job seemed necessary. The Roosevelt administration eventually settled on a less drastic version, but organized labor opposed any form of national service. Union leaders described the plan as a form of involuntary servitude that would damage unions. Business leaders joined organized labor in protesting Roosevelt's plan for national service: businessmen did not want to be told whom to hire any more than union members wanted to be told where to work.

Strike. The tensions within the ranks of labor that had been building throughout the war erupted at its end. A rash of strikes broke out in 1946 as automobile, steel, electrical, and communication workers walked off their jobs in an effort to win higher wages and to hold on to wartime gains. In 1946, 4.6 million workers went on strike, more than ever before in American history. Strikes by railroad workers and coal miners presented severe challenges to the Truman administration. In both cases unions refused to accept arbitrated settlements. Exasperated with both sides, President Truman took over the mines and railroads in the name of national security to put an end to the strikes. However, the unions persisted in the strikes even as the government operated the mines and railroads. Truman then harshly denounced the railroad workers, called for legislation authorizing him to draft strikers, and spoke of the need to "hang a few traitors and make our country safe for democracy." He obtained a court injunction against the United Mine Workers, under which the union had to pay a stiff fine. Despite the conflict, labor organizations continued to attract more members, and Truman was able to repair the rift between his administration (as well as the Democratic Party) and organized labor.

Sources:

Melvyn Dubofsky and Warren Van Tine, *John L. Lewis: A Biography* (Urbana: University of Illinois Press, 1986);

Dubofsky and Van Tine, eds., *Labor Leaders in America* (Urbana: University of Illinois Press, 1987);

Nelson Lichtenstein, *Labor's War at Home: The CIO in World War II* (New York: Cambridge University Press, 1982);

William Serrin, *Homestead: The Glory and Tragedy of an American Steel Town* (New York: Random House, 1993).

HEADLINE MAKERS

ELIZABETH ARDEN

1884-1966

COSMETIC EXECUTIVE

Entrepreneur. Elizabeth Arden reached heights of business success traditionally reserved for men by building a business that relied upon women for support. She astutely tapped into several important trends of the twentieth century when she entered the cosmetic business, taking advantage of the rise of a growing youth culture and consumerism and the increasing presence of women in the workforce. A strong-minded, driven woman who fit the classic image of the American entrepreneur, she relied on implementing good ideas, innovation, and invention to make her business prosper.

Background. Florence Graham, the future Elizabeth Arden, was the fourth of five children born in Canada to immigrant tenant farmers; her mother was from England, her father from Scotland. Upon reaching adulthood she tried a variety of jobs, working as a dental assistant, cashier, and stenographer before she moved to New York City with her brother. There she took a clerical job with Eleanor Adair, who operated a beauty salon, and began her education in the use of facials and cosmetics. She realized that there was little chance of advancement for her as long as she worked in someone else's salon, so she entered into a partnership and opened a salon in 1909. When the partnership broke up she adopted the name Elizabeth Arden from Alfred Tennyson's poem "Enoch Arden." She entered the cosmetic business just as it was about to explode, and soon she was opening branch salons. While other businesses, often owned by women, sold beauty creams, Arden was among the first to make the salon a widespread success. Instead of selling products to women to take home and use, Arden provided on-site services, such as manicures and facial peels, in her salons. The women who worked at the salons took advantage of advancements made in dermatology to claim professional status. By the 1930s she had hundreds of salons throughout North America, South America, and Europe.

Contra Roosevelt. During the early 1940s Arden enjoyed her wealth even as her business empire expanded and engaged in a wide variety of high-priced endeavors. She developed a reputation as a blue-blooded Republican and disliked President Franklin D. Roosevelt and his New Deal, campaigning for Republican Wendell Willkie in 1940. After the election the Federal Trade Commission (FTC) investigated Arden for violating the Robinson-Patman Act by inadequately training her employees in the use of the products they sold. She believed that the Democrats were punishing her for campaigning against Roosevelt and appealed the FTC decision against her to the U.S. Supreme Court. Though the court ruled against Arden, it did so in such a way that allowed her to continue her business practices with little change.

Women at Work. With the mobilization for war, women entered the workforce at a rate previously unseen in American history. Arden took advantage of the movement of women into an increasingly diverse array of jobs formerly held by men by offering an Arden career course, which provided help in selecting clothes and career orientation in addition to tips on exercise and grooming. The war also allowed her to expand her business horizons as the fall of France to Germany meant that Parisian fashion designers could no longer dominate the American industry; she began offering an exclusive designer line of clothes at her salons, and her success continued after the war. During the 1940s her sales reached $60 million annually. In addition to her chain of salons, by 1947 she had opened health and beauty resorts in Maine and Arizona. She also took up horse racing, with *Time* magazine running a cover story on her success. In 1947 Jet Pilot, her horse, won the Kentucky Derby.

The Promotion of Beauty. Throughout her life Arden never stopped working on her businesses. She pushed her message, "Hold fast to life and youth," in a vigorous advertising campaign. At the time of her death she left a multimillion-dollar business empire and a legacy worth $4 million to be divided among her employees in addition to inheritances divided among surviving relatives. While Arden made a fortune, she believed that she had dedicated her life to the promotion of beauty and business.

Sources:
Lois W. Banner, *American Beauty* (New York: Knopf, 1983);

Alfred Allan Lewis and Constance Woodworth, *Miss Elizabeth Arden* (New York: Coward, McCann & Geoghegan, 1972).

WILLIAM EDWARD BOEING

1881-1956

INNOVATOR IN THE AVIATION INDUSTRY

Industrial Warfare. William Edward Boeing went from being a general businessman to a giant in the aviation business during the 1940s. Most of this success came as a result of the need for new weapons. World War II was the first major war to be fought with the extensive use of airplanes in a variety of capacities, and airplanes were what Boeing provided.

Background. Born in Detroit, Boeing studied at the Sheffield Scientific School at Yale University but left after two years without graduating. He then moved to Seattle, where he became a prominent timberman, landowner, and yachtsman. Inspired by the new field of aviation, he organized the Boeing Airplane Company in 1915 with a friend, Conrad Westervelt, hoping to build better airplanes than the wooden ones then being used. The Boeing Company began manufacturing airplanes in a seaplane hanger in Seattle, where he copied the designs of European planes used in World War I. Two of Boeing's seaplanes attracted the attention of the U.S. Navy, which encouraged Boeing to develop a new plane that would be used to train pilots. With America's entry into World War I the Boeing facilities expanded rapidly, but the company stagnated in the period between the wars. The company continued to have close ties to the military, and its reputation was based on building fighters during the 1920s and the 1930s. In 1934 his efforts were rewarded when he received the Daniel Guggenheim Medal for successful pioneering and achievement in aircraft design and manufacturing.

The Flying Fortress. During World War II the Boeing Company utilized technological innovations made during the 1930s. Boeing had begun expanding his factories in 1936 in anticipation of war, and the number of employees in the Seattle plants increased to 2,960 by the end of 1938, reaching 28,840 at the time of the Japanese attack on Pearl Harbor in December 1941. Boeing produced three basic types of planes for the military: the B-17 (designed in 1934), the B-29 (designed in 1938), and the Kaydet trainer. The B-17 Flying Fortress and the B-29 Superfortress were the foremost symbols of America's capacity to wage industrial warfare. Both bombers proved decisive in winning the war, particularly in the Pacific theater, where vast amounts of territory had to be covered. (A Boeing Superfortress carried the first atomic bomb dropped on Japan.) At the end of the war Boeing's contracts to produce the bombers ended as well. The company laid off temporary war workers, many of whom were women. He tried to diversify the company's products by experimenting with manufacturing other consumer goods, including furniture, but he quickly realized the difficulty of using airplane factories to manufacture other commodities.

A New Industry. During the 1950s the Boeing Company prospered, though Boeing's health failed and he no longer had any financial connection with it. In the years of prosperity that followed World War II the Boeing Company profited from the expansion of the commercial airline industry by building the Boeing 707 passenger plane. Furthermore, with the advent of the Cold War the government continued to place enough orders to keep weapons manufacturers in business. At the time of Boeing's death in 1956 the company that he had founded had made America's largest jet bomber, the B-52.

Source:
Peter M. Bowers, *Boeing Aircraft Since 1916* (Annapolis, Md.: Naval Institute Press, 1989).

SIDNEY HILLMAN

1887-1946

LABOR LEADER AND GOVERNMENT BUREAUCRAT

Politician. Unlike most labor leaders, Sidney Hillman assumed a place in the Roosevelt administration, both through a series of official appointments and as a confidant of the president, that allowed him to operate at the highest levels of government. Hillman became a power in the Democratic Party and was a participant in the shaping of domestic economic and social policy throughout the 1930s and 1940s.

Immigrant. In 1887 Hillman was born to a Russian-Jewish family living in Zagare. His family had a strong rabbinical tradition and intended for him to follow a religious calling. Against his father's wishes he began to read books on Western social thought, and he soon became politically active. In 1905 he was arrested for participating in a public protest in support of the Russian revolution of 1905. In 1907 he immigrated to the United States, where he became involved in the New York Jewish socialist community.

Pragmatic Labor Leader. Hillman's reputation came not as an ideologue but as a pragmatic labor organizer and a reasonable and fair negotiator. He helped to found and became the first president of the Amalgamated Clothing Workers of America in 1914. During World War I he made contacts with progressives in the government and became convinced of the benefits of state intervention on labor's behalf. During the 1920s he urged the American Federation of Labor (AFL) to reform and accept industrial unionism and public ownership of utilities. With the Depression he became an important New Dealer and an early advocate of sweeping reforms and the adoption of Keynesian economic policies.

Democrat. In 1940 Hillman cemented his relationship with President Franklin D. Roosevelt and helped firmly commit the Congress of Industrial Organizations (CIO) to the Democratic Party. Not only was he becoming an important person in the Democratic Party, he was also a personal friend of Roosevelt. As the only labor representative on the National Defense Advisory Commission, Hillman was a supporter of the administration's preparedness policies. He had a difficult time persuading the leadership of the CIO that preparedness was necessary, since many labor leaders feared that war preparation would be used as a pretext for eliminating the gains made by organized labor over the previous five years. During World War II he served on various government agencies. Roosevelt expected Hillman, as a labor leader, to prevent strikes and other labor disputes during the war — a thankless and virtually impossible task. Roosevelt also made him associate director of the Office of Production Management, which was under the direction of William S. Knudsen of General Motors. Unfortunately for Hillman, 1941 proved to be a bad year for labor relations. During his first year on his new job he faced strikes in shipyards, repair shops, aircraft plants, lumberyards, and many other businesses. The year saw more strikes than in any other year of American history except for 1937 and 1919. Furthermore, his position as a government official undermined his credibility with other labor leaders. For example, he sided with Roosevelt and Knudsen in the use of army troops to break a wildcat United Automobile Workers strike against the North American Aviation Company in June 1941. Even though it was a strike the CIO had itself condemned, the CIO in turn condemned Hillman for supporting the use of troops to end it.

Honest Broker. As the person unofficially in charge of mobilizing manpower for the war, Hillman tackled two major problems. The first was that of labor peace and plentiful workers. To promote these ends he pushed for an understanding between the AFL and the CIO that would end the feuding between the two major labor organizations. He also recognized that the Depression had undermined the skills of the American workforce and that such skills were needed for war industries. He worked closely with Owen Young of General Electric to create a vast vocational education program that drew on every government agency in any way related to mobilization and also stressed a "training within industry" program of worker training. On 12 April 1942 Roosevelt created the War Manpower Commission to oversee labor during the war and appointed Paul McNutt, the former governor of Indiana, as director. Hillman had been performing the responsibilities of the commission by himself and had expected to be appointed director. He finally succumbed to the pressure under which he had been working and suffered a heart attack. It was six months before he returned to work.

Politician. Although Hillman's influence as a labor leader was in decline during the last few years of his life, his political influence continued to be considerable. He played an important part in the Democratic Party national convention in 1944 and in choosing Harry S Truman as its vice-presidential nominee when most insiders realized that Roosevelt would not live out a fourth term. Hillman died in 1946 at age fifty-nine.

Source:
Steven Fraser, "Sidney Hillman: Labor's Machiavelli," in *Labor Leaders in America*, edited by Melvyn Dubofsky and Warren Van Tine (Urbana: University of Illinois Press, 1987), pp. 207–233.

Henry Kaiser

1882-1967

Industrialist

Political Connections. Henry Kaiser was one of the industrialists who most benefited from America's mobilization for World War II. He headed the Liberty Ship program, which incorporated techniques of prefabrication and mass production to speed ship production. During the war his companies also built roads, boats, and shelters for the government, but primarily they built ships. His contacts allowed him access to the government officials who oversaw the allocation of resources, particularly steel, and they also provided him with access to the officials who supervised labor contracts and the allocation of materials.

Propagandist. Kaiser's production techniques fit in with President Franklin D. Roosevelt's belief that speed and energy were more important than efficiency in producing quality war goods. Kaiser was originally from the West, where he had developed a reputation for taking risks, for getting things done, and for receiving generous government contracts. His reputation for speed was belied by his physical appearance: he was a large, lumbering man of about 250 pounds who tended to bully people. He was also a braggart who loved public attention and who became possessive of the companies and agencies with which he associated, once referring to a company of which he owned 7.5 percent as "my engine company." Much to the irritation of his business partners, he often took personal credit for accomplishments for which he was only partly responsible, going so far as to proclaim himself "at least a joint savior of the free-enterprise system." A contemporary biography described Kaiser as a "catalyst" upon the economy who was "bubbling over with ideas" and "endowed with dynamic energy."

Background. Kaiser dropped out of school in the eighth grade in his native Sprout Brook, New York. He then went to work as a cash boy in a dry-goods store located in nearby Utica. Eventually he went into sales, which led him to move to Spokane, Washington. There he entered sales in the gravel and cement business and in 1914 established the Henry J. Kaiser Company, which successfully won contracts and built roads in British Columbia, California, Washington, and Idaho and made $25 million between 1921 and 1930. Before the war he had made a fortune on government contracts, a trend that only increased during the war. Kaiser, as part of a consortium called the Six Companies, won the contract to build the Boulder, Hoover, Bonneville, Grand Coulee, and Shasta Dams. The profits from building Boulder Dam alone exceeded $10 million. During this time Kaiser developed a reputation for borrowing capital against future earnings, for organizing workers, and for sticking to a schedule. He also became well connected with the government and skilled at public relations.

Liberty Ships. With the war Kaiser used his government contacts to acquire war contracts, many of which were on a cost-plus basis. He used prefabrication techniques to build ships at a speed previously considered impossible, sacrificing quality to achieve quantity, as the ships his companies built were less sturdy than ships manufactured by conventional methods. However, enemy submarines sank so many American ships during 1942 and 1943 that a high volume of production seemed more important than sturdiness or longevity. In 1941 it took on average 355 days to produce one Liberty Ship, the basic cargo carrier of the war. For that year a little more than one million naval tons were delivered by the nation's shipyards. Roosevelt wanted that volume increased eightfold in 1942. Kaiser cut the average delivery time to 56 days, with one ship being completed in 14 days. By June 1942 his four West Coast shipyards had been assigned one-third of the war contracts. His yard in Vancouver, Washington, built and launched a 10,500-ton ship in a record 4 1/2 days. In addition to Kaiser's Liberty Ships, the Six Companies built small aircraft carriers, tankers, troop ships, destroyer escorts, and landing ships. By 1943 the company was responsible for 30 percent of the nation's total tonnage and had received more than $3 billion in contracts. Kaiser used his connections with Roosevelt to overrule the navy's objections to putting flight decks on cargo-ship hulls to make a fleet of baby flattops to use against German submarines, which proved extremely successful.

Competition. One of the difficulties Kaiser and the Six Companies encountered was the jealousy of their competitors. United States Steel and Bethlehem Steel were also in the shipbuilding business, and these companies began withholding steel shipments from Kaiser's shipyards. Kaiser again used innovation and government contacts to get around the problem by deciding to integrate his shipyards vertically — that is, by producing the materials needed for shipbuilding rather than acquiring them from other steel companies. Kaiser went to the War Production Board and gained permission to build his own steel plant, then secured a $20-million loan from the Reconstruction Finance Corporation (RFC) against future profits at his shipyards and began to produce the steel his shipyards needed.

Gambler. Kaiser was involved in a variety of projects during the war, including a cooperative venture with Howard Hughes in the use of magnesium (again with a loan from the RFC) for the purpose of building a light transport plane to be used after the war. The venture eventually failed. Kaiser, however, had already begun several postwar ventures in automobiles, prefabricated housing, and helicopters, most of which were financed by the profits he made during World War II. Kaiser Community Homes, for instance, built eighty houses a week in

1947. He eventually abandoned the daring style he used during the war, especially after his plan for a Kaiser-Frazer automobile company failed. Kaiser wanted to build automobiles and sold $53 million worth of stock before producing one, but he lacked the necessary steel. He charged that the steel industry was conspiring to keep him out of the automobile industry and asked for public assistance. This time the tactic he used so successfully during the war failed. Eventually Kaiser bought his own sheet-metal mill and briefly became the fourth largest manufacturer of cars in the United States.

Sources:

John Morton Blum, *V Was for Victory: Politics and American Culture during World War II* (San Diego: Harcourt Brace Jovanovich, 1976);

B. C. Forbes, ed., *America's Fifty Foremost Business Leaders* (New York: Forbes & Sons, 1948).

JOHN L. LEWIS

1880-1969

PRESIDENT OF THE UNITED MINE WORKERS

Leader. John L. Lewis was the most controversial labor leader and perhaps the most controversial political leader of the 1940s. As a labor leader he brought industrial unionism to many workers who had been previously ignored by trade unions and the American Federation of Labor (AFL), forever changing organized labor in the United States. During the 1940s he did not join the government or the Democratic Party as the newly organized industrial workers and their leaders did, instead charting a different course as an independent. In doing so he became one of President Franklin D. Roosevelt's most vocal critics and a lone voice among labor leaders in opposition to the expansion of the federal government.

Individualist. Lewis's background was different from those of many other labor leaders, who had often studied socialist and Marxist thought. In 1948 he said that "there are two great material tasks in life that affect the individual and affect great bodies of men. The first is to achieve or acquire something of value or something that is desirable, and then the second task is to prevent some scoundrel from taking it away from you." Throughout his career Lewis followed his own advice, applying it to himself and to the coal miners he led as president of the United Mine Workers (UMW). A man with a tremendous ego, which in part helps explain his falling-out with Roosevelt in the years leading up to World War II, he transformed the Washington headquarters of the UMW into a constant reminder of his importance by placing a photograph of himself in every passageway, corridor, wall, and office in the building.

Background. During the 1920s Lewis had been a Republican and held a romantic view of rugged individualism. He feared that the state could become too powerful, and he did not bring the UMW into the New Deal coalition, countering the trend of most other labor leaders, who supported Roosevelt and the Democratic Party. He eventually became one of Roosevelt's harshest critics, particularly concerning Roosevelt's drive for war preparations in the late 1930s. In 1939 Lewis used his influence in the labor movement and among left-wing political groups to oppose a third term for the president. At the golden anniversary convention of the UMW held in January 1940 he denounced Roosevelt by saying, "let no politician believe or dream that he is going to solve the unemployment question by dragging America into war."

Critic. In the summer of 1940 Lewis officially refused to support Roosevelt's bid for a third term by promising to resign as president of the Congress of Industrial Organizations (CIO) if Roosevelt won. He even took the UMW out of the CIO to protest the CIO's increasingly close ties to the Roosevelt administration and the Democratic Party. Lewis's political maneuvering took yet another — and this time more surprising — turn when he endorsed the Republican presidential candidate Wendell L. Willkie. Two weeks after Roosevelt was reelected in 1940, Lewis stepped down as head of the CIO and was replaced by Philip Murray, one of his longtime lieutenants in the UMW. In May 1942 Lewis denounced Murray and ordered all UMW affiliates and officials to withdraw from the CIO.

Activist. After ending his association with the CIO Lewis was free to vent his hostility toward Roosevelt and against the increasing power of the state in American life, becoming the only major labor leader to speak out against government wartime regulations and spending that favored the wealthy and large corporations. He led the UMW in a series of coal strikes in 1943 in an attempt to end government-imposed wage restrictions. His actions were popular among the miners, who staged an unprecedented wave of unauthorized wildcat strikes in 1944 and 1945. However, the leadership of both the CIO and the AFL condemned his militancy. Political leaders did more than condemn his struggle to liberate organized labor from state restraints: Congress increased government control over unions, first through the War Labor Disputes Act of 1943 and then through the Taft-Hartley Act of 1947. In the postwar era Lewis continued to use strikes to manipulate the state into advancing the welfare of miners. By creating a national emergency in 1946, for example, he forced the government to seize the mines but got the government to grant the union a welfare and retirement fund, a concession that the private operators had refused to make. Following a series of long and bitter coal strikes in the late 1940s, in which the UMW's adversaries were more often federal officials than coal operators and in which Lewis and his union were legally punished for activities that had been permissible even in the midst of World War II, the elderly labor leader executed a surprising about-face in his labor relations strategy. After three decades during which coal strikes came as predictably as the seasons, a calm came over the coal fields.

A Conservative. During the 1950s Lewis continued to disavow the New Deal and even called for the repeal of the Wagner Act as well as the Taft-Hartley Act, arguing that both were unneeded intrusions into the role of the union. He did believe, however, that the government should promote the health of the industry — and thus the miners — by such actions as coal purchases by the Tennessee Valley Authority. He retired as head of the UMW in 1960 and died on 11 June 1969.

Sources:

Melvyn Dubofsky and Warren Van Tine, *John L. Lewis: A Biography*, abridged edition (Urbana: University of Illinois Press, 1986);

Dubofsky and Van Tine, "John L. Lewis and the Triumph of Mass-Production Unionism," in *Labor Leaders in America*, edited by Dubofsky and Van Tine (Urbana: University of Illinois Press, 1987), pp. 185–206.

PHILIP MURRAY

1886-1952

PRESIDENT OF THE CONGRESS OF INDUSTRIAL ORGANIZATIONS AND LABOR LEADER

Early Years. Born in Blantrye, Scotland, in 1886, Philip Murray arrived with his family in the United States on Christmas Day 1902. At the time of their arrival he was a coal miner and a union member like his father, who was president of a local coal miners' union in Scotland. He remembered attending union meetings at age six. He began working in the mines when he was ten and as a result had little formal education. His family was Roman Catholic and tutored him on both religious and social issues.

Early Involvement. Working as a coal miner in western Pennsylvania, Murray became a labor activist because, as he explained, a "coal miner has no money. He is alone. He has no organization to defend him. He has nowhere to go. It is not inadequacy of the State law. The law is there, but the individual cannot protect himself because he has no organization. He has no one to go to." He joined the United Mine Workers (UMW), and in 1905 he was elected president of his local. He quickly moved up through the UMW bureaucracy by hard work and making contacts with labor leaders such as John L. Lewis. From 1919 to 1940 Murray served as a vice-president of the UMW under Lewis.

Labor Leader. Murray also served on a variety of government agencies that dealt with labor issues. During World War I he served on the War Labor Board, and in the 1930s President Franklin D. Roosevelt appointed him to the Labor and Industry Advisory Board of the National Recovery Administration. Although he was involved in government activities, Murray did not give up his union activities. He served as Lewis's right-hand man and helped in the creation of the Committee (later Congress) of Industrial Organizations (CIO) in 1935–1936. Lewis placed Murray in charge of the Steel Workers Organizing Committee. He successfully organized the steelworkers and became the president of United Steel Workers of America. In 1940 Murray was elected president of the CIO, a position he would hold throughout the decade.

Class Warfare. Like other union leaders, Murray gave a no-strike pledge during the war years, and following the war he successfully gained two wage increases for the steelworkers. Throughout the 1940s he also feuded with former CIO president Lewis. Murray enthusiastically supported Roosevelt and his efforts to prepare the nation for war; once war came, he shared the attitudes of rank-and-file members when he supported the war effort completely. He declared, "This is our war!" and suspected that business leaders were more interested in profits than in defeating fascism.

A Proposal. Murray proposed his own plan for mobilizing the economy for war, the Industrial Council Plan, in 1941. He wanted to create councils for every major industry. The council would consist of an equal number of representatives from both labor and management and would be chaired by a federal official. Roosevelt and other leaders considered the plan radical because it treated the industry, not the particular business, as important and elevated union leaders to an equal status with business leaders.

Dealing with Strikes. Following the war Murray fought public backlash against organized labor's strikes in 1946. After the passage of the Taft-Hartley Act, which restricted the powers of labor unions, he began to argue that labor should not be so entangled with the government, even as he increasingly relied on the intervention of the national government in negotiations with management. In 1946 and 1949 the CIO struck entire industries rather than one company in order to prompt federal intervention. President Harry S Truman's intervention in the 1949 dispute between the United Steel Workers and the steel industry was particularly beneficial to the CIO. Murray also purged the CIO of all Communists or people with left-leaning politics. In 1942 he stopped a movement at the CIO convention to add "or political behavior" to a clause in the United Steelworkers' constitution prohibiting discrimination based on "race, creed, color, or nationality." To bring the CIO into mainstream Cold War politics further, he often publicly denounced the Soviet Union.

Source:
Nelson Lichtenstein, *Labor's War at Home: The CIO in World War II* (New York: Cambridge University Press, 1982).

DONALD NELSON

1888-1959

BUSINESS EXECUTIVE AND GOVERNMENT BUREAUCRAT

The War Production Board. During World War II Donald Nelson assumed the responsibility for the entire mobilization effort, making him one of the most powerful men in the country. Many of the nation's leaders, including President Franklin D. Roosevelt and Sen. Harry S Truman, saw a need for a single centralized authority to coordinate economic mobilization. To this end Roosevelt created a variety of agencies but finally vested much of the power over mobilization in the War Production Board (WPB), with Nelson in charge of the agency.

Good Relations. Nelson was a gregarious, likable man, which proved to be both his strength and his weakness as an administrator. During the period that he was in the government, his easygoing nature endeared him to the New Dealers in the Roosevelt administration at a time when many veterans in the administration were suspicious and resentful of dollar-a-year businessmen who had previously been its enemies. His personality and style also made his relations with Congress remarkably good, especially after he personally took up the popular cause of preserving small business in a period dominated by big business. Unfortunately for him, some people took advantage of his good nature. He allowed the army and the navy to control their own procurement and Roosevelt to sidestep his authority. Nelson also experienced difficulty in managing the allocation of natural resources and often tolerated insubordination from people working in the WPB.

Background. Nelson was born in Hannibal, Missouri, and graduated from the University of Missouri in 1911. Looking for money to attend graduate school in chemistry, he took a job in a testing laboratory with Sears, Roebuck and Company. Instead of pursuing his original plan of studying for a doctorate, he stayed with Sears, where he was rapidly promoted. In 1927 he was appointed general merchandising manager of the company, in 1930 vice-president in charge of merchandising, and in 1939 executive vice-president and chairman of the executive committee.

In Charge. Prior to his appointment as head of the WPB, Nelson had worked in the government as a dollar-a-year man in the Treasury Department as the acting director of the procurement division. Then Roosevelt picked him to be the coordinator of national-defense purchasing in cooperation with the advisory commission of the Council of National Defense. In the name of centralization and efficiency the various agencies were reorganized into the Office of Production Management. Again Nelson was appointed executive director of the division on purchasing and thus assumed complete responsibility for buying billions of dollars of material for the defense program. On 13 January 1942 Roosevelt announced that he would create the new War Production Board and appointed Nelson executive director, in charge of converting the nation's industries to war production. Upon his promotion to the directorship of the WPB Nelson resigned his $70,000-a-year position at Sears for a $15,000 salary with the government. Between January and June 1942 he stopped the production of most nonessential civilian goods and worked to facilitate the flow of raw materials to war plants. With the war effort beginning to wind down in 1944, he became involved in a bitter struggle with the War Manpower Commission over his efforts to continue to limit the production of civilian goods. His book *The Arsenal of Democracy* (1946) tells his side of the story. In August 1944 he resigned from the WPB before Roosevelt sent him to China as his special representative to Chiang Kai-shek.

Private Business. After his return from China, Nelson left the government. From 1945 to 1947 he served as the president of the Society of Independent Motion Picture Producers. He also served on the board of directors of several mining and chemical companies throughout the 1950s.

Source:
John Morton Blum, *V Was for Victory: Politics and American Culture during World War II* (San Diego: Harcourt Brace Jovanovich, 1976).

PHILIP K. WRIGLEY

1894-1977

CHEWING GUM EXECUTIVE AND SALESMAN

Opportunity. During World War II Philip K. Wrigley, the chewing gum manufacturer, seemed an unlikely candidate for success. Initially it seemed that the war would temporarily halt the production of chewing gum, but Wrigley managed to turn it into an opportunity to introduce his company and his product to more people.

Background. Philip Wrigley was the second child and first son of William Wrigley, Jr. He worked in the family soap factory and eventually moved into sales, where he excelled. In sales, according to Paul M. Angle, his "salient traits — unbounded confidence, flair, imagination, industry, and persistence — paid off." He assumed control of the Wrigley Company in February 1932. In coping with the Depression he departed from his father's politics and cautiously embraced President Franklin D. Roosevelt's New Deal, making the Wrigley Company one of the first to sign up with the National Recovery Administration. Wrigley also continued to take an interest in sales. Prior to the war the company had emphasized the taste and the "healthful" nature of its Doublemint gum, but a new sales pitch would be necessary during the 1940s.

War Years. Certainly, chewing gum was not an essential war commodity. Gum consisted of 50 percent sugar, which was rationed, and chicle, the rubbery sap of trees, found in Malaysia, Borneo, and South America. The Japanese occupation of Malaysia and Borneo cut off Wrigley's Asian supply of chicle; the South American supply was plentiful, but transportation was difficult, as most ships were committed to transporting war materials. He found a way to overcome obstacles to wartime business and to come out ahead. Rubber trees also grew in South America, and rubber was definitely a war material in short supply, so Wrigley directed his employees in South America to tap both rubber trees and chicle trees. Then he managed to ship some chicle on the same ships that carried the rubber from South America. He shipped about twelve thousand tons a year, enough to keep him in business. He then found a way to obtain sugar. The key to gaining access to sugar was to convince the military that chewing gum was essential to the war effort. Fortunately for Wrigley, the army requested that each K ration, the meal packet issued to many GIs, contain one stick of gum. The Subsistence Research Laboratory of the Chicago Quartermaster came to the conclusion that chewing gum would relieve thirst and serve as a substitute for tobacco at times when smoking was inadvisable. During the early years of the war Wrigley gained little profit from supplying gum for the K rations, but the factories continued to operate, and an increasing number of people used his product. Initially Wrigley used his advertising time on the radio to update listeners on the war. As the war progressed he began glorifying war workers so that those in the factories could hear a show about people like themselves. As the war continued, Wrigley's profits increased. In preparation for the postwar years he stopped his previous advertising campaign and spent more than $2 million on advertisements designed to promote his chewing gum to civilians as a patriotic company manufacturing war materials. Wrigley then went to work on employers, arguing that chewing gum would "help your workers feel better — work better." In a fifteen-minute film for his employees Wrigley depicted thirst and nicotine as agents of Adolf Hitler, with the narrator stating, "Monotony . . . fatigue . . . false thirst . . . nervous tension. Yes — these are the agents of the Axis." Wrigley funded research to help prove that chewing gum relieved tension. He also promised that workers who chewed gum would take fewer trips to the water fountain or to the smoking area. To further the war effort and his company he promised to distribute five sticks of gum to each worker in an essential war industry, but he did so only if the order was accompanied by a letter from a company official on letterhead "stating the need for chewing gum in that particular plant."

Other Ventures. Besides his chewing gum business, Wrigley was best known as the owner of the Chicago Cubs and in the later decades of his life would become chagrined that people were not aware of his other ventures, especially when the Cubs did not do well. Still, he was deeply committed to both baseball and Chicago. His commitment to baseball prompted him to start the All-American Girls' Baseball League in 1943 for fear that with four thousand male baseball players in the military the professional game would come to an end. The league peaked in 1948, fielding ten teams and attracting one million fans. However, the league never expanded beyond the Midwest. The players did not earn anything near what their male counterparts did, but they did earn good money for the time — $40 to $100 a week.

Success. After the war the Wrigley Company experienced a record demand for Spearmint, Doublemint, and Juicy Fruit gums. In the 1950s he aggressively marketed his products overseas, especially in Europe. With a pervasive campaign Wrigley finally managed to overcome the perception that chewing gum was a crude activity.

Sources:
Paul M. Angle, *Philip K. Wrigley: A Memoir of a Modest Man* (Chicago: Rand McNally, 1975);

Susan M. Hartmann, *The Home Front and Beyond: American Women in the 1940s* (Boston: Twayne, 1982);

Roland Marchand, *Advertising the American Dream: Making Way for Modernity, 1920–1940* (Berkeley: University of California Press, 1985).

PEOPLE IN THE NEWS

William Balderston became president of the Philco Corporation in June 1948. Philco manufactured radio receivers, and under Balderston the company moved into the manufacture of televisions and refrigerators.

During the 1940s **Hilland G. Batcheller** served on the War Production Board and the Committee of Nineteen that assisted U.S. secretary of commerce Averell Harriman in determining European needs under the Marshall Plan. Batcheller was the president of the Allegheny Ludlum Steel Corporation, one of the foremost manufacturers of stainless steel.

Dave Beck served as the president of the Western Conference of Teamsters, an affiliate of the American Federation of Labor's International Brotherhood of Teamsters. In that capacity he organized national union drives during the late 1940s.

Chester A. Bowles advised Presidents Franklin D. Roosevelt and Harry S Truman. During World War II he served as director of the Office of Price Administration, and during the Truman administration he played a crucial role in the development of Cold War policy.

Concerned with America's rising debt, **Warren Randolph Burgess** wrote *Our National Debt* (1949). He was vice-chairman and director of the National City Bank of New York.

Although an insurance company executive, **Fred G. Clark** made the news as chairman of the American Economic Foundation. He campaigned for an "uncontrolled economy" that would eliminate friction in society.

John Hancock was an alternate for the United States delegation to the United Nations Atomic Energy Commission in 1946. He was also a partner in Lehman Brothers for twenty-five years and responsible for reorganizing much of the company.

A career politician and reformer from Indiana, **Paul McNutt** served as director of the War Power Commission in the Roosevelt administration.

Frances Perkins was the first female cabinet member as the U.S. secretary of labor under President Franklin D. Roosevelt from 1932 to 1945. She had worked as a social worker and administrator for Roosevelt when he was governor of New York.

Walter Reuther rose to prominence as a labor activist during the 1940s by recognizing that during the war the state would be the major arena of battle between labor and management. He led the United Automobile Workers union and was a prominent liberal activist in the Democratic Party.

Paul Anthony Samuelson's *Foundations of Economic Analysis* (1947) laid the basis for understanding the connection between the consuming household and the producing company and became a standard college text. He later won the Nobel Prize in economics in 1970.

As the president of Coca-Cola, **Robert W. Woodruff** took advantage of America's dominant position in the world to expand the company into a truly international organization during World War II and its aftermath.

DEATHS

Earle Bailie, 50, investment banker who served the Treasury Department as a dollar-a-year man, 15 November 1940.

Asa George Baker, 73, former president and chairman of the board of the G. and C. Merriam Company, publisher of Webster's dictionaries, 10 September 1940.

Herbert Baker, 59, president of the American Can Company, 25 November 1940.

George L. Berry, 66, labor activist and union official, 4 December 1948.

Charles Boettcher, 96, industrialist, 2 July 1948.

William J. Bowen, 80, labor leader, 27 July 1948.

Thomas A. Buckner, 77, president of New York Life Insurance Company (1931–1936) and chairman of the board (1936–1941), 8 August 1942.

Patrick Henry Callahan, 74, president of the Glidden Varnishing Company and later the Louisville Varnishing Company, innovator in employee profit, director of the Reconstruction Finance Corporation and the National Labor Relations Board during the 1930s, 4 February 1940.

Louis Chevrolet, 56, former race-car driver who in 1911 built and designed, with William Durant, the first Chevrolet automobile, 13 December 1941.

Walter Percy Chrysler, 65, former vice-president in charge of operations of General Motors, founder of Chrysler Motors, 18 August 1940.

Samuel Harden Church, 85, vice-president of the Pennsylvania Railroad who made headlines with his 1940 offer of $1 million for the capture of Adolf Hitler, 11 October 1943.

Joshua S. Cosden, 59, president of Cosden Oil Company, 17 November 1940.

Stuart Warren Cramer, 72, who served during World War I on the U.S. Council for National Defense and on President Herbert Hoover's commission on relief for the unemployed and the commission on home ownership during the 1920s, 2 July 1940.

Norman Hezekiah Davis, 65, sugar manufacturer and adviser to Presidents Woodrow Wilson and Franklin D. Roosevelt, 2 July 1944.

A. Felix Du Pont, 69, business executive, 29 June 1948.

William C. Durant, 86, founder of the Buick Motor Car Company in 1905 and General Motors in 1908, 18 March 1947.

Richard T. Ely, 89, economist and critic of laissez-faire capitalism, 4 October 1943.

Edsel Bryant Ford, 49, son of Henry Ford and president of the Ford Motor Company, 26 May 1943.

Henry Ford, 83, pioneer automobile manufacturer who employed the assembly line method of production, 7 April 1947.

Thomas Sovereign Gates, 75, president of the Philadelphia Trust Company and a partner in the banking firm J. P. Morgan and Company, 8 April 1948.

Amadeo Giannini, 79, San Francisco banker who founded the Transamerica Corporation and the Bank of America, 3 June 1949.

John Robert Gregg, 80, inventor of a shorthand system widely used in American business, 23 February 1948.

Solomon R. Guggenheim, 88, art patron, mining magnate, and financier associated with the Kennecott Copper Corporation and American Smelting and Refining, 3 November 1949.

Edward Stephen Harkness, 66, financier and philanthropist, 29 January 1940.

Basil Harris, 58, shipping official and president of the United States Lines, 18 June 1948.

August Heckscher, 92, zinc and real estate magnate, 26 April 1941.

Milton S. Hershey, 88, confectioner and philanthropist, chairman of the board of the Hershey chocolate company, 13 October 1945.

Louis Warren Hill, 76, son of railroad magnate James J. Hill who became president of the Great Northern Railroad when his father retired in 1907 and chairman of the board in 1912, 27 April 1948.

Sidney Hillman, 59, prominent labor leader and key figure in Roosevelt administration bureaucracies overseeing the New Deal and war mobilization, 10 July 1946.

Hale Holden, 71, railway executive with Southern Pacific, 22 September 1940.

John Maynard Keynes, 63, British economist whose theories on deficit spending were influential among American government officials, 14 May 1946.

William S. Knudsen, 69, industrialist, president of General Motors, head of the Office of Production Management during World War II, 27 April 1948.

Walter Jodok Kohler, 66, manufacturer and politician elected as governor of Wisconsin in 1928, 21 April 1940.

Claude W. Kress, founder and president of the Kress chain of discount stores, 18 November 1940.

Thomas William Lamont, 80, engineer, president of American Steel Foundries, U.S. secretary of commerce (1929–1932), 19 February 1948.

Jesse Lauriston Livermore, 63, well-known stock market investor, 28 November 1940.

William H. Luden, 90, confectioner and maker of menthol cough drops, 8 May 1949.

Gates W. McGarrah, 77, prominent banker, 5 November 1940.

George Jackson Mead, 57, engineer and industrialist, cofounder of Pratt and Whitney Aircraft Company, 20 January 1949.

Harry Alvin Millis, 75, labor negotiator who headed the National Labor Relations Board during World War II, 25 June 1948.

John Pierpont Morgan, 75, perhaps the most powerful banker and financier in the United States, 13 March 1943.

Charles W. Nash, 84, cofounder of the Buick Motor Company and president of General Motors until 1916, when he created Nash Motors, 6 June 1948.

Lewis Nixon, 79, designer of battleships and shipbuilder, 23 September 1940.

Charles O'Neill, 61, spokesman for the coal industry, prominent negotiator in labor disputes, 28 February 1949.

Gustave Pabst, 76, famous brewer, 29 May 1943.

George Nelson Peek, 70, industrialist and agriculture expert, administrator of the Agricultural Adjustment Administration under President Franklin D. Roosevelt, 17 December 1943.

Charles Ponzi, 72?, Italian-born promoter who organized a famous mail fraud in Boston, 15 January 1949.

Allan A. Ryan, 60, Wall Street financier, 26 November 1940.

Fred Wesley Sargent, 64, president of the Chicago and Northwestern Railroad, 4 February 1940.

Lewis-Baxter Schwellenbach, 53, U.S. secretary of labor (1945–1948), 10 June 1948.

Edward E. Shumaker, 67?, industrialist and president of the Victor Company, known for making phonographs before merging with Radio Corporation of America in 1930, 3 November 1949.

Edward R. Stettinius, Jr., 49, former vice-president of General Motors, chairman of the board of United States Steel, U.S. secretary of state (1944–1945), 31 October 1949.

Charles W. Taussig, 51, industrialist and expert in Caribbean affairs, member of President Franklin D. Roosevelt's "brain trust," 10 May 1948.

Henry H. Timkin, Sr., 72, cofounder of the Timkin Roller Bearing Company, 14 October 1940.

Harry Dexter White, 55, economist whose work was instrumental in the development of the Bretton Woods agreement and the establishment of the International Monetary Fund, 16 August 1948.

Wendell L. Willkie, 52, public-utility magnate, 1940 Republican candidate for president, 8 October 1944.

PUBLICATIONS

William Beveridge, *Full Employment in a Free Society* (New York: Norton, 1945);

Ralph Bradford, *Along the Way* (Washington, D.C.: Judd & Detweiler, 1949);

Robert Brady, *Business as a System of Power* (New York: Columbia University Press, 1943);

Melvin de Chazeau and others, *Jobs and Markets: How to Prevent Inflation and Depression in the Transition* (New York: McGraw-Hill, 1946);

John Flynn, *As We Go Marching* (Garden City, N.Y.: Doubleday, Doran, 1944);

Alvin Hansen, *Fiscal Policy and Business Cycles* (New York: Norton, 1941);

Seymour Harris, *The New Economics: Keynes's Influence on Theory and Public Policy* (New York: Knopf, 1947);

Donald Nelson, *Arsenal of Democracy: The Story of American War Production* (New York: Harcourt, Brace, 1946);

David Novick, Melvin Anshen, and W. C. Truppner, *Wartime Production Controls* (New York: Columbia University Press, 1949);

Paul Anthony Samuelson, *Foundations of Economic Analysis* (Cambridge, Mass.: Harvard University Press, 1947);

Henry A. Wallace, *Sixty Million Jobs* (New York: Simon & Schuster, 1945);

EDUCATION

by ROBERT T. LAMBDIN, LAURA C. LAMBDIN, and VICTOR BONDI

CONTENTS

Sidebars and tables are listed in italics.

1940

- Students numbering 12,640,000 are enrolled in the federal lunch program at a cost of around $12 million.

- The United States census lists nearly ten million adults as virtually illiterate.

30 Mar. The New York Supreme Court upholds a taxpayer suit to revoke the appointment of British philosopher Bertrand Russell to the faculty of City College of New York. Russell does not receive the appointment.

June The U.S. Supreme Court affirms a Pennsylvania law that allows any schoolchild who refuses to salute the American flag to be expelled.

Nov. The New York commission on secondary-school curriculum publishes the results of curricular experiments begun in 1933.

1941

- The Progressive Education Association publishes a pamphlet, *New Methods vs. Old in American Education,* proclaiming progressive-education techniques a success.

1 July Deferment of military service for college students is eliminated.

July Georgia governor Gene Talmadge fires University of Georgia dean of education Walter Dewey Cocking, a promoter of racial equality, which leads to widespread resignations and the loss of accreditation for the university.

16 Dec. Around five hundred liberal arts colleges decide to offer three-year degrees, with classes taken during the summer, allowing graduation before the draft age of twenty-one.

1942

- Correspondence courses sponsored by the U.S. Armed Forces Institute, located at the University of Wisconsin–Madison, begin.

Jan. The College Entrance Examination Board decides to replace its traditional essay test with achievement tests measuring skills in reading and problem-solving as well as general knowledge.

July U.S. education commissioner John Ward Studebaker estimates a shortage of fifty thousand teachers across the United States.

Sept. Thirty thousand American high schools begin preparing their graduates for military service.

1943

- The Council of Allied Ministries and Education compiles a report, "Education and the United Nations," that leads to the establishment of the United Nations Educational, Scientific, and Cultural Organization (UNESCO).

- The U.S. Supreme Court reverses an earlier decision allowing students who refuse to salute the American flag to be expelled from school.

- *The New York Times* publishes the results of a 1942 study that finds an enormous ignorance about American history among college students.

- The National Interfraternity Council, in response to vast losses in membership in campus fraternities caused by the war, announces that "the college fraternity, whose pattern has been woven into the fabric of American education for 118 years, is girding its loins to meet the terrific dislocation of a nation at total war."

Jan. In an address to Duke University, Wendell L. Willkie notes that the destruction of the tradition of the liberal arts in the United States would be as deplorable as the Nazi book burnings.

Jan. Second, third, and fourth graders in Seattle are taught to prepare simple dishes such as oatmeal, scrambled eggs, and butterscotch pudding because many of their mothers are busy with wartime jobs.

Apr. Education Commissioner Studebaker vigorously promotes education at all levels for blacks.

Oct. The Thomas-Hill Bill, providing federal supplements to state education, is defeated in the Senate due to a provision requiring that the funds be disbursed equally to all races.

Nov. President Franklin D. Roosevelt establishes the Vocational Rehabilitation Act, a precursor to the GI Bill of Rights.

1944

- More than 275 courses are offered to veterans from the United States Armed Forces Institute.

- Harvard University president James B. Conant suggests that the federal government provide college scholarships for promising high-school students.

- The Progressive Education Association changes its name to the American Education Fellowship.

Jan. *The Races of Mankind,* a forty-six-cent YMCA pamphlet attacking Nazi racial doctrines, is deemed controversial by many people because it opposes racism; the YMCA is ordered to stop distributing it at USO clubs, even though fifty thousand copies have been sold.

22 June The Serviceman's Readjustment Act is established and signed into law by President Roosevelt.

3–4 Oct. The White House sponsors a conference on rural education to assess the prospects for federal education assistance to state governments.

1945

- Harvard University releases a report called *General Education in a Free Society* encouraging interaction among three broad academic areas: the natural sciences, the social sciences, and the humanities.

- Columbia University announces the formation of a Russian institute and a school of international studies.

20 Feb. The U.S. Office of Education publishes an article urging the formation of schools specializing in foreign studies.

June Inspired by the military's success in teaching servicemen through movies about subjects such as machine guns, camouflage, and venereal disease, Virginia allocates $1,176,000 toward making educational movies for use in public schools.

July Vannevar Bush publishes the results of a year-long study of federal science education, *Science: The Endless Frontier*. It urges increased federal expenditures for science education.

Aug. Scientists meeting at the Conference on Science, Philosophy and Religion in New York urge the integration of ethics and humanities scholars into atomic weapons research.

Sept. The University of Maryland alters its curricular requirements, making courses in American history mandatory.

1–16 Nov. The United Nations Educational, Scientific, and Cultural Organization (UNESCO) is founded following a conference of international scholars.

1946

• Approximately 800,000 veterans are enrolled in correspondence courses through the United States Armed Forces Institute.

• Congress appropriates $75 million to upgrade the physical plants of American universities.

• Fifty-three percent of all college students are veterans.

May At the American Council on Education conference in Chicago, Gen. Omar Bradley announces that 1.6 million veterans have applied for benefits under the GI Bill.

July At the annual meeting of the National Education Association in Buffalo it is revealed that 350,000 teachers have left the profession since 1941.

13 July President Harry S Truman appoints the National Commission on Higher Education, headed by George F. Zook, to survey the situation in higher education.

30 July President Truman signs a bill authorizing American participation in UNESCO.

Aug. U.S. senator James W. Fulbright introduces and Congress passes Public Law 584, known as the Fulbright Act, to enable a cultural exchange of scholars from different countries.

1947

• UNESCO's educational efforts in developing countries are curtailed due to the growing Cold War.

• Allen Zoll's National Council for American Education produces the pamphlet *The Commies Are After Your Kids*.

Feb. The U.S. Supreme Court confirms the constitutionality of a statute allowing private-school students to be transported in publicly owned buses.

2 Feb. Teachers numbering 2,400 in Buffalo, New York, go on a week-long strike for higher pay.

May New York governor Thomas E. Dewey declares strikes by teachers and other public employees illegal. Similar laws are enacted in Ohio, Pennsylvania, and Texas.

Harvard University makes its coeducational arrangement with Radcliffe College permanent.

July	The National Conference for the Improvement of Teachers issues a teachers' "Bill of Rights," calling for higher salaries, a forty-hour workweek, tenure, and retirement plans.
Sept.	Students numbering 75,000 nationwide receive no schooling due to teacher shortages.
Oct.	The President's Committee on Civil Rights condemns segregated education.

1948

- Oregon junior high schools begin mixed classes in sex education via educational movies, which are considered necessary since pamphlets, slides, and lectures by embarrassed teachers failed to provide the necessary instruction.

- New Jersey desegregates its public schools.

- The National Student Association severs its ties with the International Student Union, which failed to condemn the Czech Communist coup.

- The President's Commission on Education issues its report *Higher Education for American Democracy,* calling for doubling the size of college enrollments, eliminating racial discrimination in education, and removing economic barriers to general education.

Jan.	The Smith-Mundt Act, providing for foreign academic exchanges, becomes law.
12 Jan.	In *Sipuel* v. *Oklahoma* the U.S. Supreme Court orders Oklahoma to provide law education to Ada L. Sipuel. Rather than admit her to the University of Oklahoma Law School because she is black, the state opens a one-pupil law school for her. She returns to court.
Mar.	Minneapolis teachers strike for twenty-seven days for salary increases.
8 Mar.	In *McCollum* v. *Board of Education* the U.S. Supreme Court rules that there may be no religious instruction or activity in public-school facilities.
1 Apr.	The Senate passes a bill to provide $300 million in federal education assistance to states. The bill is defeated in the House.
15 July	John W. Studebaker resigns as U.S. education commissioner. He had held the post since 1934.
11 Oct.	Fourteen governors from southern states meet and establish the Board of Control for Regional Education.

1949

- The first campus of the New York state university system, eventually consisting of thirty small institutions, is established.

- The Committee for Cultural Freedom is reactivated by scholars to provide an anti-Communist alternative to the Cultural and Scientific Conference for World Peace.

- The House Committee on Un-American Activities proposes that educators be required to submit for inspection lists of books used in courses.

- The first baby-boom children reach kindergarten age. Educators estimate a 39 percent increase in school attendance in the coming year.

- The cost of the federal lunch program for schoolchildren reaches $92 million.

- A businessmen's group, the National Citizens Commission for Public Schools, is organized by Roy E. Larsen, president of Time, Inc.

12 Apr.   Washington and Lee University in Virginia, the nation's seventh oldest university, celebrates the bicentennial of its founding.

June   The National Education Association, meeting in Boston, votes 2,882 to 5 to bar Communists from the organization.

Summer   Spurred by controversy over public funds used for parochial school students, a debate is held between Francis Cardinal Spellman, archbishop of New York, and Eleanor Roosevelt over the issue of separation of church and state.

Sept.   Students numbering 340 are enrolled in the Board of Control for Regional Education.

OVERVIEW

Transition. The 1940s were a decade of profound change at all levels of American education. Primary and secondary education, for the most part underfunded, poorly organized, and inefficient, became more standardized, better organized, and properly funded. Higher education, divided between progressive educational advances and the lingering traditions of nineteenth-century "gentleman's" education, became definitively modern. The new university offered students unprecedented social and academic freedom, restructured its pedagogy to emphasize the sciences, professionalized its humanities curriculum, and integrated its activities with government and industry. American education was in a decade of transition, well on its way to becoming standardized, professional, scientific, and national.

World War II. The major catalyst for these changes was World War II. The war exposed the deficiencies of American education. Millions of draftees were rejected by the army because they were illiterate, and as the army inducted men from around the nation, the degree of variance in their literacy and numeric skills was striking. By war's end, more than five million young men had been rejected for educational and nutritional deficiencies. At the more specialized level, America's universities were found wanting. Foreign-language and scientific training were inadequate, and America's college graduates were ill-equipped for global leadership. Clearly, American education was unorganized and too variable. Educators took notice of the military's complaints, determined to correct the situation after the war.

Impact on Curriculum. The war itself provoked a crisis in education. The many soldiers going off to war left a significant number of service jobs vacant, so the need for technical or vocational training was enormous. While community colleges had existed earlier as feeders to universities, their roles as trade schools expanded after World War II, and two-year degree programs increased. Both the army and navy offered specialized instruction in ballistics, cartography, metallurgy, cryptanalysis, and aeronautics and paid for the advanced education of service personnel at vocational and academic schools. Military necessity, as well as the technological breakthrough of the atomic bomb, led many colleges to revamp and expand their scientific and technical training after the war.

Impact on Teachers. Before the war, teaching was one of the more dismal professions in the United States. Teaching standards varied from state to state, often more dependent upon political contacts than competence, pay was exceedingly low, and social prestige was often lacking. During the war, teachers long dissatisfied with the low pay and minimal benefits of the profession left for more-lucrative work in the military or defense industries. By 1944 authorities estimated that nearly one hundred thousand had left the profession. Many primary and secondary schools closed: two years after the war seventy-five thousand students still had no classes to attend. On the other hand, schools in towns with booming defense industries found themselves badly overpopulated. The schools in Mobile, Alabama, estimated that the influx of defense workers had doubled their prewar enrollment of twenty-two hundred, creating an acute teacher shortage. Many state governments compensated for the drain and shortage of teachers by issuing emergency teaching certificates, but this failed to stem the exodus of teachers from the profession and badly lowered the quality of instruction. After the war overworked, undertrained, and poorly paid teachers would organize into powerful labor unions and strike for better contracts from state and local governments. Their efforts rarely met with public understanding and fueled the "Red Scare" of the late 1940s.

Impact on Universities. The national government, concerned about the decline of the educational infrastructure, responded by integrating education into the war effort, especially at the university level, and pioneered joint government/university/industry projects such as the Radiation Laboratory at Massachusetts Institute of Technology and the Metallurgy Laboratory at the University of Chicago, which became models for postwar coordinated research. The federal government spent $117 million on radar research at MIT alone. Such wartime cooperation vastly increased university revenues and suggested to many educators, such as Vannevar Bush and James B. Conant, an increased role for the federal government at all levels of education following the war.

GI Bill. The end of the war also presented challenges for American educators. Millions of veterans needed to be reintegrated into civilian life, so Congress passed the Serviceman's Readjustment Act, or GI Bill of Rights, to give servicemen training and education following the war. The GI Bill paid the college tuition of millions of veterans, who often became the first members of their families to receive a college education. So successful was the program (7.8 million veterans participated) that it packed classrooms after the war, pushing the limits of existing college resources and the patience of college professors. But the program was invaluable in providing professional and vocational education to millions of Americans who might not otherwise have received it.

Secularization. Not all educational issues in the 1940s were connected to the war. Earlier controversies in education continued, such as the debate over religious training in the schools and the differing assessments of progressive education. In the 1940s secularization of the schools had become widespread, but much public sentiment remained favorably disposed toward religious instruction in public education. Many school boards, apprehensive about the distinction between church and state in education, offered religious instruction under the semiofficial contrivance of "released time." In 1945, however, the Supreme Court ruled in *McCollum* v. *Board of Education* that any religious instruction by a public school was unconstitutional. The controversy over progressive education received no such definitive conclusion. Progressive education, a pedagogical idea most closely associated with pragmatic philosopher John Dewey, stressed the active participation of the child in the classroom, plural curriculum and educational tracking, and instruction in science and by scientific methods. In the 1930s progressives had opposed educational conservatives who stressed rote memorization and authoritarian instruction in the classroom, as well as educational romantics, some often calling themselves progressives, who saw in the child-centered approach of the progressives license for wholesale social experimentation. In the 1940s the debate became charged with the political disputes of the period, with progressives being accused by the Left as fascistic and authoritarian and by the Right as libertine and communistic.

Segregation. Another continuing problem in education during the 1940s was the continuing segregation of black students from white, and the poor quality of education often found in black segregated schools. School boards, especially in the segregated South, badly underfunded black schools, and the conditions within many classrooms were deplorable. The National Association for the Advancement of Colored People (NAACP) had begun a program to challenge segregation in the schools in the 1930s. In the 1940s they continued their efforts, seeking a court ruling invalidating segregated schools. NAACP cases such as *Sweatt* v. *Painter* (1949) set legal precedents that would culminate in the 1954 *Brown* v. *Board of Education of Topeka, Kansas* decision invalidating segregation.

Changes. While the debate over progressive education and the problem of segregation remained relatively unaffected by the war, for the most part American education after World War II continued to grapple with the changes set in motion by the conflict. The increased federal role in education was seen by most educators as salutary, and they sought increased federal expenditures for education after the war. They were blocked by conservatives, reeling from the *McCollum* decision and determined to use the long tradition of local funding of schools as an opportunity to oppose the influence of secularization and progressive education in the public schools. Such conservatives often pointed to the centralized education in authoritarian states such as Germany and Russia as examples to be avoided in America. But progressives also pointed to the war experience in advancing their educational agenda, arguing that the war demonstrated clearly the need for a well-educated polity, versed in social, economic, and political theory. Progressives also increased their efforts to standardize and systematize America's anarchic educational system. There was an increasing need for sociological and educational research to supply data for decisions in such areas as school policies, curricula, and student development. Various sociological measurements were developed to chart the influences of the educational experience upon students. Other educators, noting how little American education prepared its students for the experience of war, advocated a more realistic curriculum in the postwar era. Secondary-school educators and women's-college administrators proposed a "lifestyle adjustment" and "domestic science" curriculum, keyed toward the concerns of the emerging suburbs.

Purges and Loyalty Oaths. Among the more malevolent side effects of World War II was a certain suspicion that one's neighbor, friend, or coworker might secretly be aligned with the enemy and working to undermine democracy from within. While during the war the suspicion was that teachers might be indoctrinating their students in fascism, after the war the fear was that teachers were inculcating Communist ideology among their pupils. In some areas the goal of purging educational institutions of educators and administrators suspected of disloyalty to the United States became a witch hunt. Many teachers in institutions ranging from elementary schools to universities were forced to sign loyalty oaths or risk losing their jobs. The situation became worse during the 1950s, undermining progressive education and often rolling back teachers' union demands for better pay and benefits.

UNESCO. As American educators struggled to rationalize the educational system at home, they also made important contributions to education abroad. The United Nations Educational, Scientific, and Cultural Organization (UNESCO), an "international agency for education to promote understanding and cooperation among the peoples of the world as a guarantee of peace," was created as a result of interest in a meeting of the Council of Allied Ministries and Education in London in 1942. UNESCO supplied funds for libraries and museums, but it also sought to promote global harmony by encouraging dialogue among scientists, educators, and students from all countries. American universities began to offer systematic instruction to foreign cultures. By 1945 several universities, such as Columbia, Stanford, Princeton, and Yale, had established schools of international relations and institutes specializing in the study of Russia, Asia, Latin America, France, or Germany. In 1945 American educators opened colleges in Florence, Italy; Biarritz, France; and Shrivenham, England, to minister to the needs of American veterans and to act as research centers for scholars. American educators were also instrumental in reconstructing the school systems of Germany and Japan after the war, launching reeducation programs to counter the authoritarian propaganda of the war years. As the decade ended, American educators were setting the cultural agenda of the United States and the world.

TOPICS IN THE NEWS

ACADEMIC FREEDOM

A Contested Issue. In the 1940s the principle of academic freedom — that university teachers should be free to teach whatever their training and conscience command them to teach — was challenged. Several sensational academic freedom cases developed, signifying increasing political pressure on academia. Some cases were directly related to the volatile politics of the time, especially the anti-Communist hysteria of the late 1940s, but other cases reflected long-standing public suspicions of academia and of intellectuals, especially in terms of their sexual restraint and racial attitudes.

The Bertrand Russell Case. As the decade opened, the Bertrand Russell case was the most sensational academic freedom dispute. Russell was an acclaimed British philosopher and mathematician scheduled to teach classes in logic and mathematics at the City College of New York. A vocal advocate of socialism and sexual permissiveness, Russell became a lightning rod for conservatives. Conservative newspapers denounced him as an "anarchist and moral nihilist," and Catholic theologians mounted a vigorous opposition to him as a "propagandist against religion and morality." Although the New York Board of Education certified him to teach at City College, opponents filed suit in the state supreme court to block the appointment on the grounds of Russell's purported sexual immorality. The conservative judge John McGeehan forbade Russell's appointment, partially on the ludicrous grounds that Russell, one of the world's foremost logicians, was unqualified to teach at the college. The decision was a significant blow to academic freedom, a denial of the right of academics to judge and certify the work of

FASCISM, ANTICOMMUNISM, AND AMERICAN SCHOOLS

Prior to and during World War II there was a great deal of controversy over the political thrust of American education. Some were concerned that innovations in the curriculum were inspired by radicals; others feared that traditional curricula amounted to intellectual fascism. By 1947–1948 there was a host of private groups such as Allen Zoll's National Council for American Education, which produced the pamphlet *The Commies Are After Your Kids,* and journals such as Lucille Cardin Crain's *Educational Reviewer,* which charged textbooks with subversion, that accused American teachers of Communist indoctrination. There were frequent attempts to purge educational institutions of particular educators and administrators suspected of disloyalty to the United States. The most celebrated case was at the University of California in March 1950, when the regents refused to give up their demand that faculty members sign a special oath of loyalty or forfeit their jobs.

Sources: David Caute, *The Great Fear: The Anti-Communist Purge under Truman and Eisenhower* (New York: Simon & Schuster, 1978);

Mary Spering McAuliffe, *Crisis On the Left* (Amherst: University of Massachusetts Press, 1978);

Joel Spring, *The Sorting Machine* (New York: McKay, 1976).

their peers. American academics moved to appeal the Russell case, but their efforts were rendered moot when

NUNS IN THE PUBLIC SCHOOLS

In 1947 North Dakota found itself considering the separation of church and state because the state employed seventy-five nuns who taught in public schools in the heavily Catholic western portion of the state. When school boards could not find teachers, nuns often filled the gaps. The sisters' annual taxpayer-paid salaries averaged about one thousand dollars. When Protestants took the issue to court, the North Dakota Supreme Court determined that the simple fact of a teacher wearing religious garb did not constitute a violation of the separation of church and state.

Mayor Fiorello La Guardia, fearing the political fallout of the case, withdrew the salary for the position from the City College budget. John Dewey, in the past often Russell's philosophical opponent, deplored the decision. "As Americans," he said, "we can only blush with shame for this scar on our repute for fair play."

The Nation Case. A similar instance of political figures sacrificing academic freedom by bowing to conservative pressure groups occurred in the Newark and New York schools in 1948. At issue was a banning of the political journal the *Nation* from school libraries. The *Nation* had printed articles highly critical of Roman Catholic authorities in the New York City area. When Catholic authorities protested, the journal was pulled from many public schools. A group of more than one hundred educators and intellectuals, including President Isaiah Bowman of Johns Hopkins University, Eleanor Roosevelt, and the German author Thomas Mann, protested the ban as "a violation of the most fundamental principles of American equality." Political figures from Catholic districts, however, upheld the ban.

Coercive Authority. Other academic freedom cases in the 1940s concerned the independence of college faculty from coercive administrators. In 1941–1942 academics at the University of Georgia had to fend off an attack by Gov. Eugene Talmadge, who sought to integrate the school into a political patronage system. At the University of Chicago in 1944, the faculty senate protested a plan submitted by UC president Robert M. Hutchins to reorganize the campus and abolish academic rank. More than half the members of the faculty senate signed a protest to Chicago's board of trustees, and the case was given wide publicity in the nation's press. Hutchins abandoned the reorganization plan.

Communism and the Schools. The most pressing academic freedom issue throughout the decade, however, was the question of whether professed Communists should be allowed to teach in the nation's schools. The answer was, for the most part, a resounding no. Although Communist teachers, especially in New York, had proven themselves no better or worse than teachers of any other political persuasion, many Americans feared that teachers would use their influence with students to indoctrinate them subtly with Communist ideology. As early as 1941 the American Federation of Teachers withdrew the charters of two teachers' unions in New York for Communist activities. Nonetheless, conservatives feared the presence of hidden Communists in the schools, and feared as well that liberal and progressive educators undermined the moral fiber of students, leaving them easy marks for Communist recruitment. As Allen Zoll, one of the most vitriolic anti-Communist critics put it, "so-called progressive education . . . has had a very deleterious effect upon the original character of American education."

Investigations. Throughout the decade, investigations of the schools were constant. In 1941 the New York assembly appointed the Rapp-Coudert Committee to ferret out Fascist influence in the state's schools, but they quickly turned to Red hunting. Although no evidence of Communist indoctrination in the classroom was ever produced, twenty instructors were fired and eleven more resigned as a result of the Rapp-Coudert investigation. A similar committee in California, led by anti-Communist zealot Jack Tenney, raised charges of Communist subversion in the schools in 1946 and 1947; unlike the cases in New York, no dismissals followed. As in most Communist cases, no evidence existed to confirm suspicions of Communist conspiracies. Nonetheless, private organizations such as the Anti-Communist League of America and the National Council for American Education, led by Zoll, continued to maintain that Communists and Communist sympathizers had infiltrated American schools. Their pressure was such that in 1947 the Truman administration's Office of Education began a program termed "Zeal for American Democracy," designed to instill the proper anti-Communist mentality into the minds of students. In 1949 the House Un-American Activities Committee announced they would begin inspecting textbooks for evidence of Communist subversion. The National Education Association voted to ban Communist members in 1949. By 1951 thirty-six states required loyalty oaths of its teachers, requiring that they disavow membership in the Communist Party.

Communism and the Universities. The anti-Communist hysteria did not reach American universities until 1947–1948, but its impact on academic freedom was just as pronounced as it was in the nation's secondary schools. Despite the fact that its president, James B. Conant, had been a leader in the nation's national security apparatus and had coordinated the building of the atomic bomb, Harvard University was a favorite target for anti-Communists, less because there were actual Communist Party members on the faculty than for the fact that there were vocal, leftist professors on the campus who made life miserable for conservatives. Many charged with being Communists were supporters of Henry Wallace's Pro-

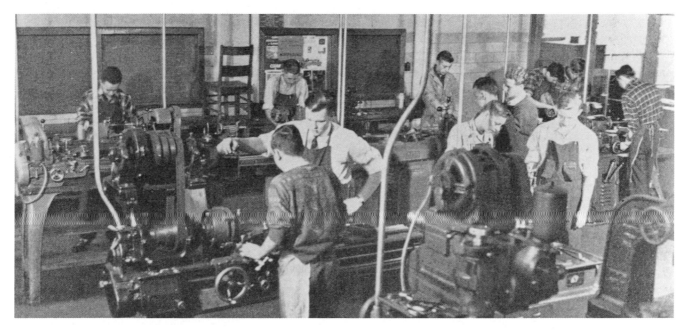

Vocational machine shop at Grosse Pointe High School in Michigan, 1945

gressive Party 1948 presidential campaign, including literary critic F. O. Matthiessen, astronomer Harlow Shapley, and historian H. Stuart Hughes. The Asian specialist John K. Fairbank was accused of communism because he accurately forecast that the Communists were gaining support in China. Harvard's prestige generally protected faculty from the more onerous consequences of the Red hunt, and this was also the case at the University of Chicago, where Hutchins successfully parried an anti-Communist attack in 1949. Academic prestige failed to protect faculty at the University of Washington. In 1948 several were expelled from the university for refusing to cooperate with anti-Communist investigators. Western Illinois State College fired two "liberalists" as a result of anti-Communist pressures. Oklahoma began a loyalty oath for university instructors in 1949. A similar measure passed in California in 1949, leading to the dismissals of thirty-one professors the following year. Such cases did far more than ruin the careers of academics; they cast a pall over free thought and academic innovation in education generally and prepared the way for the gray conformism of American education in the 1950s.

Sources:

Ronald W. Clark, *The Life of Bertrand Russell* (New York: Knopf, 1975);

Richard M. Fried, *Nightmare in Red: The McCarthy Era in Perspective* (New York: Oxford University Press, 1990);

James G. Hershberg, *James B. Conant: Harvard to Hiroshima and the Making of the Nuclear Age* (New York: Knopf, 1993).

AMERICAN EDUCATION ABROAD

UNESCO. The United Nations Educational, Scientific, and Cultural Organization (UNESCO) was an "international agency for education to promote understanding and cooperation among the peoples of the world as a guarantee of peace." Aside from peacekeeping initiatives and its efforts to prevent the bombing of university cities such as Oxford and Heidelberg, it also aided, through U.S. military occupation, governments in the postwar recovery of schools in Japan, Germany, and their allies. The aim of UNESCO was to restructure the educational foundations of toppled governments so as to facilitate the rebuilding process. The constitution of UNESCO was adopted in November 1945 by representatives of forty-four countries who met in London. In 1946 the organization became a standing agency of the United Nations. UNESCO provided funds for renovation to 362 libraries destroyed in the war. It also funded the reconstruction of four Belgian museums; the rebuilding of 1,326 churches in Yugoslavia; and the restructuring of 1,500 schools in France. One of the aims of UNESCO was the disestablishment of Shintoism in Japan and the denazification of Germany. With this aim the army employed under the Marshall Plan many scientists, educators, and students with the primary goal of teaching world peace. Toward this goal of global harmony UNESCO sought to promote the arts throughout the world and to ease racial tensions, encourage human rights, stimulate democracy, preserve the earth's natural resources, and encourage research designed to better human living conditions in all countries. However, most UNESCO peacekeeping efforts were abandoned by 1947 with the rise of the Cold War.

The Fulbright Act. Following the war, the international implications of American national decisions and attitudes became more apparent. In August 1946 Congress passed Public Law 584, initiated by Sen. James W. Fulbright of Arkansas, a former Rhodes Scholar and president of the University of Arkansas from 1939 to 1941. The Fulbright Act, as the law became known, sent

American students and scholars to study and teach overseas with all of their expenses paid. This program encouraged interaction among countries and proved so successful that it is still in operation half a century later.

Sources:

James Bowen, *A History of Western Education,* volume 3 (New York: St. Martin's Press, 1981);

W. F. Connell, *A History of Education in the Twentieth Century World* (New York: Teachers College Press, 1980).

THE CORE CURRICULUM AND THE GREAT BOOKS PROJECT

The Core Concept. In the period after World War II American universities debated a proposal to restructure postsecondary and secondary curricula around a "core" of courses devoted to the humanities. The foremost proponent of this idea, University of Chicago president Robert M. Hutchins, hoped it would cultivate a public familiarity with what he called "the tradition of the West." Educational curricula prior to the 1940s included many humanities disciplines — literature, art, music, political and social philosophy — but the dominant curricular tendency was toward the sciences, economics, and psychology. Curricula at the time also tended toward specialization and fragmentation; many progressive educators, for example, argued that education could be streamlined by having engineers study engineering rather than take classes in music appreciation. Hutchins criticized such a philosophy as simplistic, arguing that narrow, specialized education undermined tradition and led to a technical, mercantile culture without a strong set of values. His core-curriculum idea was designed as a corrective to what he believed to be an overly materialistic society. It was designed to instill a sense of values in a culture preoccupied with sheer monetary advancement.

Great Books. Hutchins and several associates, including Clifton Fadiman, Mark Van Doren, Scott Buchanan, Jacques Barzun, and philosophy professor Mortimer Adler, hoped that Hutchins could introduce the core curriculum to the University of Chicago, one of the nation's centers of specialized study. Adler, who had studied with Columbia University literature professor John Erskine, suggested a core curriculum much like Erskine's classes — one oriented around the "Great Books," the classics of Western culture. Erskine had his students read a classic a week — literature, philosophy, theology, political theory — for the duration of a semester. Hutchins and his associates argued that a similar curriculum would provide the necessary common experience to bind educated people to the traditions and values of Western culture. Hutchins proposed a two-year core curriculum at Chicago, followed by specialized graduate study. The faculty at Chicago vetoed the project, but the Great Books idea did become a regular course at the university, and Hutchins's colleague Stringfellow Barr left Chicago and took the idea to Saint John's College in Annapolis, Maryland, where it became the basis of the school's cur-

---

THE GREAT (BOOKS) EXPERIMENT

In 1949, 127 young male students completed their college educations at Saint John's College in Annapolis, Maryland. Their curriculum consisted of reading and studying one hundred "Great Books." Saint John's College, which had a total student population of 231, allowed these students to participate in the brainchild of the college's president, Stringfellow Barr, who had abolished electives, survey courses, standard texts, and books about books from the course of study. He continued this program until he left in 1947, leaving these students as the sole products of his experiment. Of these graduates, 55 percent went on to postgraduate work and trained to become doctors, ministers, and professors.

---

riculum. Barr also abolished electives, survey courses, standard texts, and books about books from the course of study. While the core curriculum was not adopted nationally, it became a model of instruction to which educators in the future often turned.

Tactics. During and after World War II Hutchins and his associates changed their argument in support of the core curriculum. In some celebrated books, including Hutchins's *Education for Freedom* (1943), Van Doren's *Liberal Education* (1943), and Adler's *How to Read a Book: The Art of Getting a Liberal Education* (1940), supporters of the Great Books concept argued that fascism had descended upon Germany and communism upon Russia precisely because both societies had lost their educational compass, sacrificing the humanities to a utilitarian, science-oriented curriculum. Perhaps out of a sense of frustration with their inability to advance the core-curriculum idea, Hutchins and his associates also began to attack progressive educators, arguing that progressive education would lead to authoritarianism. In an incendiary speech, "God and the Professors," given at a 1940 New York conference on philosophy, Adler charged John Dewey and other progressive educators with subverting American society. He argued that Dewey and the progressives' rejection of fixed ends in philosophy and espousal of experimentation in education would lead to disaster, equating these concepts with moral bankruptcy and nihilism. "Democracy," he charged, "has much more to fear from the mentality of its teachers than from the nihilism of Hitler. It is the same nihilism in both cases; but Hitler's is more honest and consistent, less blurred by queasy qualifications and hence less dangerous." That Adler would deliver this address after Hitler had stormed through France shocked many and occasioned a sharp rebuke from Dewey and other educators, such as Sidney Hook. But the tactic was persuasive, and it stuck. After the war educational traditionalists unconnected to the core-curriculum project would make similar charges against progressive education — this time inverting the formulation and charging the progressives with Communist subversion.

Problems. Though the attack on progressive education opened the way for later Red-baiting, it failed to gain the field for the core-curriculum idea, in no small measure due to inherent flaws in the concept. First, the issue of which books were classics, as well as seemingly endless lists of candidates for inclusion among the classics, generated disputation among instructors. Adler was scarcely troubled by this problem, arguing that a classic was that which endured the test of time and gave insight into the unchanging characteristics of human nature. A chronic list maker who described his habit as an "anal-erotic compulsion — the need to order and arrange things and keep them rigidly fixed in the order I have imposed on them," Adler generated a list of 175 titles to govern the teaching of the Great Books course at Chicago. Critics were not reassured, attacking the program for the works it included (they wondered about the universal value of Michael Faraday's three-volume *Experimental Researches in Electricity* [1839, 1844, 1855]) and those it omitted (there were almost no classics from the twentieth century). Second, critics argued that the proposal was elitist, an attempt to force a select set of values on all students, an attempt which was only available to wealthy individuals capable of attending expensive schools such as Chicago.

Great Books, Door-to-Door. The charge of elitism deeply troubled Hutchins, a committed democrat. He responded by farming the Great Books idea out to junior colleges and off-campus extensions of universities in an attempt to reach larger groups of people. He also attempted to popularize the concept by getting Britannica to publish the Great Books as a reference set, available to the general public. In 1943 Gen. Robert Wood, head of Sears Roebuck, had given Britannica, which it owned, to the University of Chicago as a gift. Hutchins set the Britannica staff to work compiling the Great Books to be published along with the encyclopedia set. Adler assembled a staff of graduate students to prepare an index to the series. The result, publicized with a seven-page spread in a 1948 *Life* magazine article, was less than astonishing. Adler's index cited the 102 great ideas of Western civilization, which, according to him, could be found in 432 Great Books written by 71 men from Homer to Sigmund Freud. Britannica was contracted to print 54 volumes of the Great Books, as well as Adler's *The Great Ideas: A Synopticon of Great Books of the Western World* (1952). The book subdivided the 102 basic great ideas into no more than 30 subdivisions, a technique one reviewer found akin to "a footnote that went berserk for two thousand pages." The divisions only highlighted the arbitrariness that so maddened Adler's critics. "Woman, not a main idea," noted *Life* sardonically, "is included in

Family, Man and Love." The series was initially a financial disaster, ultimately saved by being marketed, like the *Encyclopaedia Britannica,* door-to-door. Hutchins's ambition to make the Great Books idea into the foundation of a more humanistic, civilized culture disintegrated into the type of mercantilism he despised. The Great Books concept, born in high-minded idealism, died a coffee-table concept and middlebrow fad.

Sources:

Mortimer J. Adler, *Philosopher at Large: An Intellectual Autobiography* (New York: Macmillan, 1977);

Harry S. Ashmore, *Unseasonable Truths: The Life of Robert Maynard Hutchins* (Boston: Little, Brown, 1989);

Russell Jacoby, *Dogmatic Wisdom* (New York: Doubleday, 1994);

"The 101 Great Ideas," *Life,* 24 (26 January 1948): 92–102.

FEDERAL AID

Property and Funding Given to Schools. Traditionally, American schools were locally funded, but that began to change during the Franklin D. Roosevelt presidency. Following World War II the U.S. government sold approximately 106,000 acres of land and 2,500 buildings at an average cost of less than 3 1/2 percent of the fair value of the property to establish 5,500 schools and universities. Surplus military equipment, including such windfalls as 27,000 surplus typewriters, was also given to schools.

The School Lunch Program. In 1940 the federal government provided more than $12 million in meals for elementary and secondary school students; this grew to some $92 million in 1949. There were abuses in this program, such as price gouging and kickbacks, but the program was defended by former president Herbert Hoover, who coordinated the European Food Program after World War II and recognized the correlation between nutrition and education.

Educational Facilities for Defense. Education was needed for military personnel in order to promote war research and technical training. Federal funds for these areas of study at the university level in 1939 amounted to more than $160 million. However, by the mid 1940s the

Students in a school cafeteria supported by the school lunch program

government realized that too much money was being diverted into defense research and that there was not enough money going to nonmilitary educational facilities, so a policy was designed to promote military research at colleges and universities. During this time there was a significant cooperative effort among university research facilities, defense contractors, and the military, such as at the Radiation Laboratory at the Massachusetts Institute of Technology. Similarly, foreign-language institutes and cultural-analysis schools, such as Harvard University's Institute of East European Studies, poured money into the American educational system before and after World War II.

Mainstreaming the Vets. Additionally, the government opened military schools that stressed nonmilitary education to help veterans be mainstreamed back into civilian culture after the war. One such school was the United States Armed Forces Institute; by the middle of 1944 more than 275 courses were offered through the institute. By 1 February 1946 approximately 800,000 vets had enrolled in correspondence courses.

Continuing Controversy. The success of government assistance to education during the war stimulated postwar proposals to make such assistance permanent. Every year after the war Congress considered continuing federal aid to education; every year after the war funding bills were defeated in Congress. Several controversial issues prevented the passage of the bills. Conservatives concerned with progressive education and local control of the schools opposed the bill. But liberals also objected to federal control of local schools, and the National Teachers' Association opposed funding bills that failed to have provisions against federal interference. Many southerners opposed the proposals, afraid of the effects of federal intervention on segregated classrooms. Catholic educators, concerned that federal funding would shortchange their fund-raising activities, opposed the proposals unless federal funds went to parochial schools as well; liberals opposed any funding for parochial schools, so as not to violate the separation of church and state. By far the most strident controversy arose around the funding of the Barden Bill, a 1949 proposal for $300 million in federal assistance to state education. Sponsored by North

Carolina congressman Graham Barden, the bill extended federal assistance to public schools but excluded parochial assistance. Cardinal Francis Spellman expressed his opposition to the bill by characterizing its sponsors as "bigots" and "unhooded Klansmen" — an unwarranted and hyperbolic statement. Liberals responded by attacking Catholic education, leading to a rift between Eleanor Roosevelt and Spellman, formerly political allies. But other educators and political figures, such as Herbert Hoover, Columbia University president Dwight D. Eisenhower, and President Harold W. Dodds of Princeton University, opposed the bill because they feared it would lead to federal control of education. Despite the support of President Truman, the bill was defeated, and the decade ended without any federal assistance to state education.

Sources:

S. E. Frost, Jr., and Kenneth P. Bailey, *Historical and Philosophical Foundations of Western Education* (Columbus, Ohio: Merrill, 1973);

Edgar W. Knight, *Education in the United States* (New York: Macmillan, 1951).

GI BILL OF RIGHTS

Reason for Development. The GI Bill of Rights was established for two main reasons. First, it was considered appropriate to compensate veterans of World War II for their services and sacrifices. Second, it was absolutely necessary to reintegrate military personnel into the civilian economy. Even before servicemen had been sent to Europe and the Pacific during the war, it became obvious that some plan would have to be developed to absorb the sixteen million veterans after the war was over. Thus, the seventy-eighth U.S. Congress enacted the Servicemen's Readjustment Act of 1944, or the GI Bill of Rights, which President Franklin D. Roosevelt signed into law in June.

Options. Originally Congress desired simply to reward each veteran with a bonus payment, but a more ambitious plan emerged from debate: the establishment of a program to help veterans help themselves. The Servicemen's Readjustment Act provided for tuition, fees, books, and a monthly subsistence payment while veterans were in school; it also provided the vets with the opportunity to set up their own businesses, buy their own homes, and receive financial aid. The GI Bill was much more far-reaching than any other plan for veterans' benefits previously drafted by Congress. It benefited able-bodied veterans, and it used nonmilitary institutions throughout the country without federal intervention in admission or educational policies.

Provisions. The provisions of the bill were staggering: any veteran who had served at least ninety days after 16 September 1940 and had received anything other than a dishonorable discharge could take advantage of this benefit. Veterans were entitled to one full year of training plus a period equal to their time in the service, up to a maximum entitlement of forty-eight months. During this

Advertisement for a training program developed to meet the needs of veterans taking advantage of the GI Bill

period the act was carried out by the Veterans Administration, which paid tuition, laboratory and library fees, and other school costs up to a maximum of $500 a year for the duration of a veteran's entitlement. Additionally, the bill provided a monthly stipend of $50 for single veterans and $75 for a veteran with dependents. In December 1945 Public Law 268 was passed to increase the allowances. Veterans without dependents who were receiving full-time training could receive $65; those with dependents could get $90 per month. These limits were raised again two years later.

Application. Millions of veterans participated, slightly more than half of those eligible, and the average length of time during which a veteran received support was nineteen months. Up to the entitlement cutoff date of 25 July 1947, the total cost of the program came to $14.5 billion. Historians have praised the GI Bill as one of the most enlightened pieces of legislation ever enacted by the U.S. Congress.

Difficulties. There were occasional abuses of the program. For instance, while 1947 was a record-setting year in terms of enrollment at American colleges and universities, tuition prices also reached record highs. The United States Office of Education reported that tuition had increased 27 percent in private schools, 29 percent in public schools, and 46 percent in law schools since 1939 and warned that once the government stopped doling out millions of dollars under the GI Bill, colleges and universities would have to slash their prices or admit only the affluent. Still, the greatest difficulty administering the GI Bill resulted from the sheer number of students it attracted. American colleges, universities, and vocational training institutions were in many instances unable to handle the enormous influx of new students. They did not have enough professors, nor did they have the variety of educational and training courses that were suddenly demanded. New programs were begun, including night classes and year-round programs. The increased demand for higher education also spurred the growth of junior colleges and community colleges.

Junior Colleges. The first junior college was opened in Joliet, Illinois, in 1902. Subsequently, the idea spread, first to California, then to other states that saw the benefit of postsecondary schooling providing vocation-based training usually lasting two years. In 1940 there were 456 junior colleges in the United States among the 1,708 institutions of higher learning, and by the end of the decade another 52 junior colleges were established. They served some 217,000 students by 1950, about 10 percent as many students as were at four-year colleges and universities. Education at a junior college was less expensive than at a college or university, so they drew a wider variety of students than more expensive institutions.

Community Colleges. As they grew, the junior colleges began to add to their previous functions; while they continued to provide courses capable of being transferred for university credit, they also increased opportunities for training or retraining adults in the many technical jobs needed after the war — a purpose most have retained. Those schools that are publicly funded and have evolved into ends in themselves rather than stepping-stones to universities have tended since the late 1940s to be called community colleges.

Special High Schools. Many battle veterans of Europe and the Pacific were just a few credits short of a high-school diploma. So that they would not have to attend high school with teenagers, the Detroit School Board, with money allocated by the GI Bill, set up special classes at schools where vets could choose what courses they needed and move through them as quickly as possible. These servicemen were given condensed texts and teachers trained specifically for this purpose.

Investigation of Problems. Even with the rapid growth of institutions of higher education, however, difficulties with the GI Bill eventually became so numerous that on 28 August 1950 the Select Committee to Investigate the Educational and Training Program under the GI Bill was established. The Korean conflict and the need

FOREIGN LANGUAGES

During World War II thousands of GIs learned to speak even difficult languages, such as Thai, quickly by listening to records. While many American language teachers laughed at the army's methods, they seem to have been effective. Therefore, in 1947, 225 colleges and 300 high schools began using the army's records in their language courses. Cornell University had students listen to the records to the point of near-exhaustion and found that students could learn twice as quickly in this manner as compared to the old method. The records dealt only with commonplace needs, such as ordering meals, seeing sights, and locating restrooms.

for more military personnel made this committee's task vital. The select committee was directed in January 1951 "to conduct a full and complete investigation, evaluation, and study of the alleged abuses in the education and training and loan guaranty programs of World War II veterans, and of action taken, or the lack of action taken . . . to prevent abuses. . . ."

Benefits of the Bill. Despite all of the problems, the GI Bill was still an important way for the government to compensate military personnel for their services. When veterans were able to further their educations, they became more marketable and received better-paying jobs, which resulted in more taxes to finance the government. The GI Bill created a massive socio-economic shift upward for the American working class.

Sources:
S. E. Frost, Jr., and Kenneth P. Bailey, *Historical and Philosophical Foundations of Western Education* (Columbus, Ohio: Merrill, 1973);

John D. Pulliam, *History of Education in America* (Columbus, Ohio: Merrill, 1982).

HIGH-SCHOOL CURRICULUM

Disorganization. The curriculum for high schools before the 1940s was highly disorganized and variable. Student bodies of every race, cultural background, and religion defied singular, unified curricular planning. Although every state by law compelled attendance in high school through the age of sixteen, depending upon the state in which one lived, education could be rigorously academic, insufficiently academic, or fundamentally vocational. In 1941 high schools nationally offered no fewer than 274 subjects, although only 59 of these were traditional academic courses. During the New Deal, moreover, educators and New Deal administrators debated whether New Deal programs or high schools should be responsible for the nation's youth. Professional administrators were furthermore divided among those who favored a college-preparatory curriculum in high schools and those who favored vocational training. Finally, a mania for progressive education had many curriculum proponents arguing that their ideas were "progressive" — whether it had anything to do with John Dewey's rigorous philosophy of progressive education or not. The American high-school curriculum was, in other words, in a state of disarray.

Unskilled and Delinquent. The disorganization of American high schools reached a crisis level during World War II. The Naval Officers' Training Corps found that 62 percent of its candidates failed fundamental arithmetic reasoning tests and that only 23 percent had more than one and a half years of math in high school. The army reported similarly high levels of illiteracy among its inductees, rejecting millions for lack of any reading skills and spending valuable time shaping the literate and numerate skills of millions more up to speed. The war naturally enough precipitated an increase in high-school dropouts, as young men enlisted and other young men and women quit to take advantage of the high earnings in the defense industries. Authorities estimated that nearly three million teenagers left school for work. These teens formed a new adolescent consumer group, one whose mores were to some degree independent of adult influence. Moreover, as their parents joined the military or took positions in the defense plant, more and more teenagers went without supervision — and without schooling. A rise in juvenile delinquency alarmed educators and the public. In 1942 alone the rate of juvenile delinquency rose 8 percent among boys and 31 percent among girls, accompanied later by sensational incidents of teen violence, such as riots at Frank Sinatra and Harry James concerts and the zoot suit riots in Los Angeles. Unsupervised teenagers, even more than the poor academic skills of students, became a preoccupation with postwar planners. Commissioner of Education John W. Studebaker noted with alarm toward the end of the war

that only seven of ten high-school students were going on to grades eleven and twelve. Concerned with juvenile delinquency and with the possible consequences of this group competing with returning veterans for jobs, Studebaker was determined to use the curriculum to reduce the number of dropouts and improve the "holding power" of high schools.

Problems. While some educators focused on improving academic skills after the war, movement toward this goal took place slowly. High schools after the war were badly understaffed and underfunded, and it was difficult to find properly trained teachers who would put up with large classrooms and low pay. Educators hoped that the federal government would fund improvements in high-school education, but funding bills were repeatedly blocked in Congress by conservatives opposed to federal interference in state education. Even state increases in teacher salaries rarely kept pace with the soaring rate of postwar inflation. As late as 1948 authorities estimated that two million schoolchildren were receiving below-standard education. Increasingly, educators searched for a curriculum which would improve skills at low cost and would keep teens in school, out of the labor market and under the supervision of adults. In the "lifestyle adjustment curriculum" educators found the solution to their many problems.

The Lifestyle Adjustment Curriculum. The lifestyle adjustment curriculum was to a great extent the brainchild of Charles A. Prosser, an educator and administrator who had worked with the National Youth Administration during the New Deal. He introduced the concept publicly at an educational conference in 1945; by 1947 the U.S. Commission for the Education of Youth had endorsed the curriculum for use in high schools. Prosser saw high schools as having three fundamental missions. For the brightest 20 percent high school was preparation for college, and for a mechanically inclined 20 percent high school provided vocational training for industry. Prosser felt that 60 percent of high-school students were poorly served by the high schools, incapable of academic success or vocational competence. For them and the other two groups he proposed a basal curriculum oriented not toward academic achievement or industrial skills but toward "individual effectiveness and happiness." Prosser's lifestyle adjustment curriculum emphasized "communication skills" rather than literature and grammar; "the simple science of everyday life" instead of physics or chemistry; "civic problems of youth" in place of history; applied arithmetic and business math instead of mathematics; and fine and practical arts designed to produce well-rounded individuals. Prosser believed his curriculum would be more economical by directing academic resources toward those students who could make use of it. Because the curriculum more directly met the needs of the 60 percent majority, and was less intellectually daunting, he argued that more students would stay in school; in other words it would increase high-school holding power.

The emphasis the curriculum placed on social adjustment, moreover, would combat juvenile delinquency. Many educators agreed, and the lifestyle adjustment curriculum began to sweep through high schools.

Objections. To critics, however, the lifestyle adjustment curriculum led to intellectual torpor and caused high schools to abandon their true purpose: intellectual training through academic subjects. A history professor at the University of Illinois, Arthur Bestor, objected to the program because of its anti-intellectual qualities. He felt that all of the attention paid to problem solving was trivial and that there was little emphasis upon in-depth study of mathematics, science, history, or foreign languages. Bestor damned the ephemerals he culled from the state of Illinois's pamphlet on high-school youth, which cited as important "the problem of improving one's personal appearance," "the problem of selecting a family dentist," and "the problem of developing and maintaining wholesome boy-girl relationships." A more telling critic of the curriculum was historian Richard Hofstader, who, noting the rise of a suburban consumer culture after World War II, found the key to the success of the life adjustment curriculum in the degree to which it fit the cultural values of the moment: "what it aims to do is not primarily fit [students] to become a disciplined part of the world of production and competition, ambition and vocation, creativity, and analytical thought, but rather to help them learn the ways of the world of consumption and hobbies, of enjoyment and social complaisance — in short, to adapt gracefully to passive and hedonistic style summed up in the significant term adjustment."

The Results. Because of protests against the lifestyle adjustment curriculum, it failed to achieve a total revolution in high schools, and many schools continued to give college preparation and vocational education precedence. The curriculum for high schools in fact looked much as it had at the beginning of the decade: no national unity had been brought to the school system, and instruction was variable. The low state of academics and science, so bemoaned by the military during the war, would return as an important curricular issue following the launching of the Soviet satellite *Sputnik* in 1957.

Sources:
H. Warren Button and Eugene F. Provenzo, Jr., *History of Education and Culture in America* (Englewood Cliffs, N.J.: Prentice-Hall, 1983);

Richard Hofstadter, *Anti-Intellectualism in American Life* (New York: Knopf, 1963);

Edgar J. Knight, *Education in the United States* (New York: Macmillan, 1951);

Joel Spring, *The Sorting Machine* (New York: McCay, 1976).

PROBLEMS IN HIGHER EDUCATION

Increased Enrollment. Late in the 1940s administrators determined that schools needed larger facilities to accommodate increased enrollments. Of course, higher enrollment figures meant the need for additional faculty,

---

COLLEGE MADE FASTER

In June 1941 a group of American colleges announced a plan to give students a college education in three years so that students could be graduated before the draft age of twenty-one. The presidents of these schools, which included the Ivy League, felt that this initiative was needed since so many of the students would be called away or drafted before finishing their requirements for graduation. Since there were few deferments for men, administrators realized that few of the veterans would want to return to school because of their age after serving in the war. Ironically, many did under the GI Bill.

In November 1942 the National Education Association suggested that bright young men might skip from junior high into college, thus earning both high-school diplomas and college credits simultaneously. The suggestion was modified one month later by Edmund Ezra Day, the president of Cornell University, when he announced a plan through which bright male high schoolers would be allowed to advance into college during their senior high-school year and earn both high-school diplomas and freshman college credits at the same time. The purpose of the plan, he said, was to "give young men a 'toe hold' in college before they enter military service. . . . If we don't do this, college education for the duration is the privilege of the women and the 4-F men."

---

but there was no money budgeted with which to pay them, and there simply were not enough qualified individuals to fill the demand. Further burdening the system was the diminishing funding for endowments, as fewer gifts were given to the schools because of increasing taxes. By the end of 1949 the number of grants for research began to increase with the money coming from government and industry, mostly in the sciences, but this was the only bright spot concerning funding for higher education.

Government Scholarships and Fellowships. Federal scholarships for undergraduate students and fellowships for graduate students were recommended in late 1947 and early 1948 by President Harry S Truman's Commission on Higher Education. Guy E. Snavely, executive director of the Association of American Colleges, protested the proposed fellowships because he believed, as did others, that they would lead to federal control of higher education. Further, he felt that funding college education for all set a poor precedent when, he argued, it is obvious that certain people have higher scholastic aptitudes than others. It seemed clear to him and others that

Taking note of the rising tide of nationalism in the world, in 1944 Fisk University's white president, Thomas Elsa Jones, argued that African Americans had an important role to play as American envoys to the new independent states sure to emerge after World War II. Paraphrasing Horace Greeley's famous advice to young men, he said, "For effective living in a world community, the Negro has the dual advantage of being an American and a person who has pigment in his skin. His identification with members of darker races should be advantageous. For the Negro, the slogan should be 'Go south, east, and west.'"

not everyone needs or is capable of attaining a college education. The United States must have people for a variety of roles, their argument ran, if the country is to run smoothly. Not all can be white-collar workers; some have to be blue-collar laborers willing and able to do manual work.

The Business of Making Money. To solve their financial difficulties some colleges and universities purposefully turned their halls into businesses, with the goal of bringing in as many student dollars as possible. This also encouraged abuse of the tax-exempt status of educational institutions. Various colleges and universities became involved in moneymaking ventures such as cattle ranches, farms, and stores, often blatantly defying a 1938 U.S. Supreme Court ruling that established taxes on any university's commercial ventures.

Sources:
H. Warren Button and Eugene F. Provenzo, Jr., *History of Education and Culture in America* (Englewood Cliffs, N.J.: Prentice-Hall, 1989);

Joel Spring, *The American School: 1642–1985* (New York: Longman, 1986).

RESEARCH AND EDUCATIONAL SOCIOLOGY

Research Concerning Education. Educational research in the 1940s indicated a need for the reformation of high schools and the expansion of junior and community colleges. Responding to such studies, traditional educators demanded substantial amounts of further research; before initiating major changes schools needed to be sure that such reforms would produce the desired results, they maintained. Thus, research on American education became a growth industry in the 1940s, as well as the subject of many philosophical debates over the role of American education.

Research Areas. The bulk of the burgeoning discipline of educational research during the decade addressed four areas: school administration, curricula, student development, and pedagogy, or teaching methods. Debates soon formed over the changes and implementation of ideas posited in these four areas. The war had demonstrated the need for an expanded scientific community, but educators argued that overemphasis on science in the schools would come at the expense of a liberal education.

Educational Sociology. Researchers attempted in the 1940s to develop appropriate sociological techniques with which to study various aspects of education. One of the leaders of the movement was British scholar Karl Mannheim, who published several influential works of research about education, the last of which was *Diagnosis of Our Time* (1943). The ultimate goal of education, Mannheim reasoned, was to produce citizens capable of fitting smoothly into a particular national culture; therefore, the type of education stressed in the schools should reflect the type of society for which students were being educated. During World War II the global conflict was between democracy and totalitarianism; Mannheim stressed that in such a sociological climate educators were crucial in creating a future generation of democratically trained and inclined individuals.

Cultural Bias? In 1944 *Who Shall be Educated?*, by W. L. Warner, R. J. Havinghurst, and M. B. Loeb, reported research done at schools in the Midwest, the South, and New England to prove that middle-class white children did better in school because tests were biased in their favor; the solution, they suggested, was for teachers to increase their efforts to make the classroom more democratic and offer greater opportunities for social mobility.

Stereotyping. Later, Allison Davis's *Social Class Influence upon Learning* (1949) documented the stages by which elementary students became aware of social class. Her argument was that teachers and schools tended to reinforce the beliefs and habits of the white middle class to the exclusion of other cultural attitudes. Thus educators were blamed for the high failure rate of black and/or lower-class students. Davis found that the educational system tended to increase stereotyping, but she was uncertain about what actions would best alleviate the situation. As is often the case with educational sociology, the problem was noted, but no solution was offered.

Source:
I. L. Kandel, *The New Era in Education: A Comparative Study* (Boston: Houghton Mifflin, 1955).

SECULARIZATION OF PUBLIC EDUCATION

Changes in Focus. Education had always been linked with religion in Western culture. After World War II, however, educators became more interested in secular issues and concerned themselves with teaching democracy and other sociological ideas. Secularization became widespread, although there was much protest from reli-

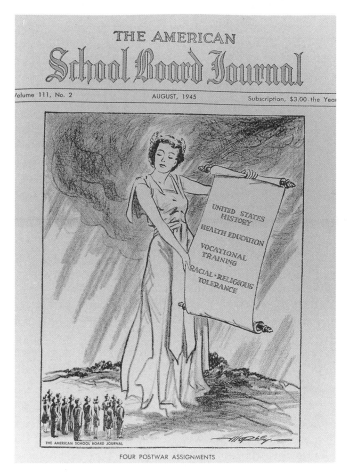

THE AMERICAN
School Board Journal

Volume 111, No. 2   AUGUST, 1945   Subscription, $3.00 the Year

UNITED STATES
HISTORY

HEALTH EDUCATION

VOCATIONAL
TRAINING

RACIAL · RELIGIOUS
TOLERANCE

THE AMERICAN SCHOOL BOARD JOURNAL

FOUR POSTWAR ASSIGNMENTS

Cover for a professional journal identifying postwar
educational concerns

gious communities. The debate over the role of religion in American education was long-standing, and it was made greater by the impact of the war. Although many American universities have their roots in a particular religious institution, most had become secular by the twentieth century. Curricula in American public schools up through the 1920s usually included Bible study and religious instructional practices that drew objections from progressives. After the war progressives pointed to the success of Fascist indoctrination (such as the Hitler Youth) and the Holocaust to argue that religious instruction was doctrinaire and intolerant. Traditionalists argued the opposite: to them, totalitarianism and other social ills were in part related to secular education. Eleanor Roosevelt attacked progressive education in February 1947, saying, "All over this country people are troubled . . . at the way delinquency extends down to even small children. I sometimes wonder if what is commonly called progressive education, in the effort to make children enjoy school and develop their individual personalities, has not done away with some of the essential disciplines. These disciplines made education in the old days . . . seem somewhat harsh at times, but even children came to recognize that . . . they were valuable." Roman Catholic educators in particular called for a return to religious

instruction and government support for private education.

McCollum and Religious Instruction. In 1945 the question of whether religion should be taught in public schools was argued before the U.S. Supreme Court in the case of *McCollum* v. *Board of Education.* Vashti McCollum, a mother who felt that her son was embarrassed and ostracized because she refused to allow him to attend his school's religious classes, sued the school board of Champaign, Illinois, to have all religious training in the schools shut down. She argued three points: that the classes wasted taxpayers' money, that the classes discriminated against minority religious faiths, and that the classes were an unconstitutional mix of church and state.

Presentation of Testimony by Different Beliefs. In the lower courts McCollum's lawyer produced several representatives of different faiths, including a Presbyterian, a Methodist, a Lutheran, a Jehovah's Witness, a Quaker, a fundamentalist Protestant, and a Christian Scientist to testify that the school system's classes of religious teaching were discriminatory; however, several of the witnesses claimed the opposite. The school board countered that their instruction was ecumenical and that the issue at stake was religious discrimination. The board called McCollum's father, Arthur C. Cromwell, president of the Rochester (New York) Society of Free Thinkers. He had been responsible for the abolishment of religious training in three upstate New York towns. Cromwell caused a stir by announcing that he would only swear to "affirm the truth," as he was opposed to "swearing by God." He then testified that he felt the story of Adam and Eve was fictitious, that the Flood was scientifically impossible, and that the Resurrection was physically impossible. Further, he declared himself proud to be an atheist. Terry McCollum, Vashti's son and the boy whose education was in question, was then called to the stand. After "affirming to tell the truth" he was prodded to state that he was an atheist and that, after one visit to Sunday school, he never returned because he felt funny. He then explained his definition of atheism and ended his testimony by saying atheism was fun in some ways, but in others it was not. Vashti McCollum was then called. Under questioning she noted, "I have not accepted belief in God myself, but I have never consciously ridiculed religion." She then noted that she had simply gone to court because she felt that the church and the state must be separate. The case was decided in her favor.

Separation of Church and State Upheld. The school board's appeals reached the Supreme Court in 1948, and the court held that religious instruction or activity in public-school facilities was unconstitutional. The exclusion of religious classes was naturally disturbing to those who historically believed religion and education went hand in hand. However, to others it was a welcome relief to find more school time spent on technical, scientific, or liberal arts topics. Secularization was encouraged by the increased interest in sciences following World War II. Further, teachers now tended to encourage students to take an interest in political and economic trends in the hope that an increased awareness of international affairs would help to avoid warfare in the future. While religious discussions were limited, there was an interest in creating ethically responsible citizens; the notion that scientists must not only know how to make an hydrogen bomb but must also know how to prevent the technology behind it from destroying the world became a rallying cry at universities. The educational shift was not simply toward technical training; it also reflected a greater interest in the humanities and the liberal arts.

Sources:

"The Bible and Stuff," *Time,* 46 (24 September 1945): 66–67;

Russell Jacoby, *Dogmatic Wisdom* (New York: Doubleday, 1994);

Edgar W. Knight, *Education in the United States* (New York: Macmillan, 1951).

SEGREGATION IN THE SCHOOLS

Segregation. Segregation in education meant separating black and white schoolchildren from one another, forcing them to attend black- or white-only schools. A national issue, segregation was most prominent in the South, where it was enforced by law and where it fit into a broader pattern of social segregation and political oppression of African Americans known as Jim Crow. The Jim Crow school system was patently unfair to the educational aspirations of millions of southern blacks. In many cases no institution of high training would accept black students; at the primary and secondary levels, white school boards badly underfunded black-only schools, failing to provide adequate facilities, textbooks and instructional materials, or qualified teachers. In 1949, for example, Clarendon County, South Carolina, spent $179 on each white child enrolled in school but only $43 on each black student. While public education was generally in dismal condition throughout the Deep South, the conditions in black schools were often appalling. Black students generally had to make do with used textbooks and broken school furniture, hand-me-downs from better-funded white schools. Black classes were often held in

dilapidated, aged buildings, with inadequate heat and light. In 1947 students at the all-black R. R. Moton High School in Farmville, Virginia, took their instruction, with winter coats on for lack of heat, in overflowing class-rooms made of tar paper and plywood. Black teachers were poorly paid and often acted as teacher, principal, building janitor, and bus driver. These conditions were illegal, violating the equal protection clause of the Fourteenth Amendment. But the Supreme Court decision *Plessy* v. *Ferguson* (1896) interpreted the Fourteenth Amendment in such a way that so long as school boards maintained the pretense of providing black students an education equal to that of white students, segregation was legal in the South. By the 1940s it was an established southern custom, enforced by law, public opinion, and political compromise.

The NAACP Challenge. The National Association for the Advancement of Colored People (NAACP), a civil rights organization, was determined to improve the school environment of southern black children. Under the leadership of a brilliant legal scholar, Charles Houston, the NAACP organized a team of lawyers to combat Jim Crow in every part of southern life but especially in education. The NAACP reasoned that if they defeated Jim Crow in the schools, they could defeat Jim Crow in the courthouse, department store, hiring office, and voting booth. Toward this end the NAACP began a series of legal challenges to Jim Crow in the 1930s, the most important of which was *Missouri ex. rel. Gaines* v. *Canada* (1938), which forced the creation of a black law school in the state of Missouri. They would continue such suits in the 1940s.

Advances. In the 1940s many Americans began to embrace the cause of racial equality, in part because the war against the Nazis invalidated in the minds of many the doctrines of white supremacy and racial superiority. The NAACP and other civil rights leaders scored major victories with the desegregation of the defense industries (1941) and with *Smith* v. *Allwright* (1944), which abolished southern laws that excluded blacks from voting. In 1946 President Truman established a civil rights commission to investigate Jim Crow; in 1948 he desegregated the military. That same year, African Americans filed suit in Virginia, Louisiana, and Oklahoma for equalized school facilities and equal teacher pay. In 1947, following the leadership of Father Joseph E. Ritter of Saint Louis, Catholic schools in the United States desegregated. New Jersey desegregated its schools in 1948. That same year, African Americans were admitted for the first time to graduate school at the Universities of Maryland, Delaware, Missouri, and Arkansas. In 1949 the National Interfraternity Council voted to admit blacks to college fraternities, as did the American Association of University Women. The Universities of Texas and Kentucky admitted African Americans for the first time, and Wesley A. Brown became the first black graduate from the U.S. Naval Academy to receive a commission. Although

President Harry S Truman on the steps of the Lincoln Memorial addressing the annual convention of the National Association for the Advancement of Colored People on 29 June 1947

at the white university but in empty rooms adjoining the main class or behind a sheet hung to segregate him from the white students. He filed suit to end the practice. His case, decided in 1950, as well as *Sweatt* v. *Painter* (1949) set the important legal precedent that segregated education, even when equal, conferred a psychological or professional stigma of inferiority upon the student. Substantially, this was the reasoning behind the case which finally overturned *Plessy* v. *Ferguson, Brown* v. *Board of Education of Topeka, Kansas,* which stated unequivocally that "separate education is inherently unequal."

Sources:

Taylor Branch, *Parting the Waters: America in the King Years, 1954–63* (New York: Simon & Schuster, 1988);

John D. Pulliam, *History of Education in America* (Columbus, Ohio: Merrill, 1982);

Joel Spring, *The Sorting Machine* (New York: McKay, 1976).

TEACHER SHORTAGES AND STRIKES

Poor Conditions. Teacher shortages during the 1940s were caused by poor salaries and bad working conditions. Most small communities could not afford to pay even minimal teacher salaries; the average pay was thirty-seven dollars a week. This, coupled with the idea that most teachers were usually responsible for additional activities such as overseeing clubs, athletics, or other social events, made the profession unappealing to most people. After the war there were massive shortages in all fields, so the prospect of teaching was unattractive to all but those who felt called to the profession. (Anyone smart enough to learn a skill could earn more money in another field.) This situation led to an educational crisis and general alarm about the poor quality of teachers. As one Harvard University professor noted, he had "yet to find a first-class person who was preparing to teach in the public school system."

Schools Closed. *The New York Times* estimated that more than six thousand schools would close in 1947 due to the lack of instructors and that seventy-five thousand students would have no schooling as a result. In 1947 teachers on average had one year of education less than their counterparts of the 1930s. One commissioner of education summed up the crisis by saying, "We no longer ask whether an applicant can read or write. If she looks as though she is able to stand up, we take her."

Striking Students. In November 1946 students of the small town of Rogersville, Tennessee, went on strike, refusing to return to the classroom until their demands for higher-quality teachers were met. Although he had interviewed candidates from all over the state, principal B. L. Hale was unable to find applicants who had four years of college training and five years of teaching experience and who were willing to work for only $149 a month. Eventually new instructors were found for all subjects except science, which he was forced to teach himself.

the goal of school integration still remained elusive, with southern representatives blocking a 1949 attempt to desegregate the schools of Washington, D.C., Jim Crow would, clearly, soon fall in southern schools.

Resistance and Precedent. Jim Crow politicians and educators responded to the civil rights developments of 1948 by offering African Americans half a loaf: segregated educational facilities that they promised to bring to par with those of white schools. Since many of the civil rights suits demanded access for blacks to white graduate and professional schools (as there were no comparable black institutions), in 1948 fourteen southern governors met in Savannah, Georgia, to form a nonprofit group known as the Board of Control for Southern Regional Education. The board's goal was to establish separate but equal black educational facilities wherever possible. The impossibility as well as the absurdity of this goal were soon apparent. In 1949 the board revealed that to bring southern black schools up to white standards would require $545 million — and that was for facilities alone. They furthermore went to extraordinary lengths simply to avoid black students taking classes with whites. In 1948, when Ada Lois Sipuel applied for admission to the University of Oklahoma Law School, the university responded by creating a segregated law school —at enormous expense — for her and two other blacks. A similar situation occurred that same year when Oklahoma accepted an African American candidate, G. W. McLaurin, for a doctorate of education. Rather than create a separate school for McLaurin, they allowed him to attend classes

Radcliffe College promotional photo showing a graduate geologist doing petroleum research in the late 1940s

Particular Problems with the Job. At this time teachers were usually women; only 15 percent of all elementary- and high-school teachers were male. This gender inequity and the shortage of teachers in general were caused by the same things that created shortages after World War I and the Depression: low salaries, poor working conditions, and meager benefits. As a result, teachers often went on strike trying to force local governments to increase funding. During the 1946–1947 school year there were twelve major teachers' strikes in school systems across the country. Initially the general populace seemed to have sympathy for the teachers. A Gallup poll in 1946 showed that most Americans sympathized with the teachers, yet little if anything could be done to alleviate the problem.

The "Red Scare." The growing movement to purge Communists from society spilled into the education field. Across the country near-hysteria raged concerning the "Red menace" of communism. Teachers were forced to sign loyalty oaths and vow that they were not Communists; those suspected of Communist sympathies were fired. Of course, this panic meant that anyone perceived

as being a troublemaker was a Communist, so teachers began shying away from their demands for better working conditions and pay. When William Goslin, the superintendent of public schools in Pasadena, California, proposed a tax increase to help pay for schools and teachers, he was accused by conservatives of being a Communist and was forced to resign. Thus the teachers' demands were effectively quelled.

Sources:

William Henry Chafe, *The American Woman* (New York: Oxford University Press, 1972);

Edgar W. Knight, *Education in the United States* (New York: Macmillan, 1951).

WOMEN IN EDUCATION

Wartime Changes. World War II opened up many new possibilities for women. Expanded opportunities and better-paying jobs meant that they no longer would be forced into the stereotypical roles of teachers, secretaries, or housewives — while men were in the military, at least. War industry allowed them to be blue-collar workers, such as welders and taxi drivers, as well as business employees. Given the opportunity, women left education in droves. Colleges were quick to understand the implications of having more women on career tracks, and many developed curricula tailored for women.

Changing Curricula. Before the war, women's colleges prepared their graduates for marriage and for home. Courses developed included child development, hygiene, home economics, and decorating. In 1924 Vassar College instituted a curriculum specially designed to educate women along the lines of what were supposed to be their chief interests and responsibilities: motherhood and the home. In contrast, with the American entrance into the war Rensselaer Polytechnic Institute enrolled its first female student; the Curtiss-Wright Company sent eight hundred women to college to learn engineering; and other companies began hiring female chemists, lawyers, and brokers.

Harvard Sets the Pace. Separation of the sexes had been the norm in institutions of higher learning in the United States during the first half of the twentieth century, but women's responses to the opportunities provided by the war established that they were capable workers, and many wanted the option of entering or remaining in the workforce after the fighting ceased and the men returned home. In the late 1940s Harvard University became the first Ivy League coeducational school when it allowed female juniors, seniors, and graduate students from Radcliffe College to attend classes. In 1947 the arrangement with Radcliffe was made permanent. Other colleges and universities around the country followed, although initially there were some problems.

Resistance to the Plan. There was much resistance to the coeducational trend. The belief that fraternization between students of different genders would hamper ed-

---

POOR PENMANSHIP

By 1947 most schools no longer taught separate classes in traditional penmanship. Students were taught to print but not to write in cursive. There were no more flourishes, curlicues, or arm exercises. In Seattle, for instance, a new penmanship supervisor was not appointed after the old one died in 1945. In Los Angeles applicants for teaching positions were no longer required to pass a handwriting test.

---

ucation caused protests. Students and professors alike did not want to have professors act as chaperons. Surprisingly, most progress for women in higher education was made in the southern states at schools such as Florida State University. Most degrees earned by women were in education, English, home economics, and business.

Success. As women and men adjusted to coeducation, states realized that there was little need for separate institutions for them, especially since coeducational universities reduced the need for duplicate programs when colleges were segregated by sex. Thus, with the growth of women's earning potential came the beginnings of the demise of most state-supported schools for single-gender education.

Sources:

William Henry Chafe, *The American Woman* (New York: Oxford University Press, 1972);

John D. Pulliam, *History of Education in America* (Columbus, Ohio: Merrill, 1982).

HEADLINE MAKERS

CARL WILLIAM ACKERMAN

1890-1970

DEAN OF COLUMBIA GRADUATE SCHOOL OF JOURNALISM

Freedom of the Press. One of the first systematic instructors of journalism in the United States, Carl William Ackerman was moved by the belief that if the press does not police itself, it will be policed from outside. Therefore, he saw a great need for journalistic education to enhance potential journalists' understanding of press etiquette and standards. Influenced by his days as a war correspondent, he perceived that an unsystematic presentation of the news leads democracies to horrible wars.

Early Work. Ackerman's work as a journalist began in 1915 when, during World War I, he was a correspondent for the United Press. In 1917 he became a special writer for *The New York Tribune,* reporting on France, Spain, Switzerland, and Mexico. In 1917 he also began writing for the *Saturday Evening Post.* By 1919 he was in Siberia with the Allied forces as a correspondent for *The New York Times.* He became director for the Foreign News Service for the *Philadelphia Ledger* in 1919 when he returned to the United States. From 1921 to 1931 he worked in public relations, first as president of his own company and then as assistant to the president of General Motors.

Academic Work. Ackerman was appointed dean of Columbia University's School of Journalism, from which he had graduated eighteen years earlier, in 1931. It was turned into a graduate school within a year after his arrival. In October 1943 the graduate school of journalism in Chung-ching, affiliated with the Central Political Institute of China, was organized by Ackerman, who assisted in procuring two anonymous financial gifts.

Ideas on the Press. Both in his work as a teacher and as a journalist, Ackerman's major concern was maintaining the freedom of the press. In his many speeches and articles dealing with the subject he frequently underscored what he expressed in 1936, that he was "dedicated to the study of the daily newspaper and government. We need scientific studies of the press, by the press, and for the press, which will contribute to the progress of journalism as the great educational foundations have advanced medicine." He also made many statements against censorship, as in his open letter to Otto Dietrich, Nazi press chief in Germany: "No nation has ever been able to create confidence in its money by government decree. The same conditions apply to the printed and the spoken word as a medium of exchange between nations. Good news, meaning truthful information, always has and always will drive bad news, meaning false information, out of circulation."

The Fight against Censorship. Although various government agencies, including those in the United States, attempted to silence the press during World War II under the guise of preserving national security, Ackerman saw this sort of activity as censorship. He spoke often about how traditional democracy relied upon freedom of speech, firmly supporting the Bill of Rights. He also felt that American journalists must challenge any attempts by the government to regulate salaries or working hours of newspaper employees.

Other Activities. During the war Ackerman visited Trinidad, Buenos Aires, Uruguay, and Brazil, promoting freedom of the press and pointing out that adequate supplies were not being delivered to these countries. To promote freedom of the press during the war Ackerman, along with a committee appointed by the American Society of Newspaper Editors, visited England, the Netherlands, Norway, Czechoslovakia, France, Italy, Greece, Egypt, Palestine, and the Philippines. During this world tour he discovered that the bulk of the populace knew little of the war activities; thus Ackerman and the rest of the committee proposed a postwar world conference on freedom of the press. His continued work in such endeavors contributed much to the cultural understanding between nations.

Source:
Richard Terrill Baker, *A History of the Graduate School of Journalism, Columbia University* (New York: Columbia University Press, 1954).

MORTIMER ADLER

1902-

EDUCATOR, PHILOSOPHER, AND AUTHOR

Great Books Pioneer. Mortimer Adler became well known during the 1940s when he, Robert M. Hutchins, and others challenged the academic world by attempting to establish a Great Books curriculum for undergraduates beginning in 1946. Taking up writer and educator John Erskine's proposal of 52 books — reading one per week — and expanding it initially to 176 books before revising it to 76, Adler felt that the reading and understanding of these classics would provide all of the background an undergraduate would require. He convinced Hutchins, president of the University of Chicago, to implement his plan. While its success was limited on the larger scale, it did receive some acceptance at extension campuses, where the Great Books idea became something of a fad; courses, seminars, and lectures became popular among aspiring weekend scholars.

Early Scholarly Success. Adler was a brilliant student whose scholarship was second only to a self-described "anal-erotic compulsion — the need to order and arrange things and keep them rigidly fixed in the order I have imposed on them." His personality won him few friends and many detractors, and in 1923 he was denied his baccalaureate degree from Columbia University, where he was first in his class after finishing his degree work in three years, because he refused to take a compulsory swimming test. Five years later he received his Ph.D. in psychology from Columbia, and he began teaching at the University of Chicago in 1930. He believed that the dominant influence on the educational thought of his time — John Dewey, one of his Columbia professors — was a disaster, opting to believe in the existence of absolute and universal truths and values as opposed to Dewey's pragmatic rejection of fixed ends and his espousal of experimentation. Adler believed that values concerning a "good education for all men at all times" could be taught and tried to include them in his Great Books ideal. He felt that the implementation of these universals should replace the elective systems of higher education, which he believed only added to the aimlessness and superficiality of students. He expressed these views in his many articles, books, and lectures, especially in his best-known work, *How to Read a Book: The Art of Getting a Liberal Education* (1940). This volume topped the best-seller lists and made him a household name.

Curriculum Failure. However, his Great Books curriculum never became integrated within academe. Critics attacked the program for the works it included (they wondered about the universal value of Michael Faraday's *Experimental Researches in Electricity*) and those it omitted. An expanded version of the Great Books texts, the fifty-four-volume *Encyclopaedia Britannica* set (1952) including 442 works, had no introductions or commentary, forcing the readers to depend either upon discussion leaders to provide background and contextual information or upon the two-volume *The Great Ideas: A Synopticon of Great Books of the Western World* (1952), a comprehensive index he edited that one critic compared to "a footnote that went berserk for two thousand pages." Although Adler continued to promote his educational ideas and was involved with a 1990 revision of both publications, the Great Books idea gradually fell by the wayside.

Sources:

Mortimer J. Adler, *Philosopher At Large: An Intellectual Autobiography* (New York: Macmillan, 1977);

Russell Jacoby, *Dogmatic Wisdom* (New York: Doubleday, 1994).

SARAH G. BLANDING

1898-1985

COLLEGE PRESIDENT, CHAIR OF EDUCATION COMMITTEE OF NEW YORK STATE WOMEN'S COUNCIL

From Social Scientist to Home Economist. Sarah Gibson Blanding began her career as an assistant professor of political science at the University of Kentucky in 1937. Her credentials included a year of study at the London School of Economics (1928–1929). She remained at the University of Kentucky, later becoming the dean of women, until 1941, when she became director of the New York State College of Home Economics at Cornell University. During her tenure there wartime demands for home-economics services quadrupled. She expedited requests for help by promoting food and nutrition education, childcare techniques, conservation and preservation of war materials in short supply, mass feeding, and maintenance of equipment.

Dewey Calls. Blanding's efforts at Cornell did not go unnoticed. During the last years of World War II Gov. Thomas Dewey of New York appointed Blanding to several state government posts, including director of the Human Nutrition Division of the State Emergency Food Commission and consultant to the State Defense Council's Division of Volunteer Participation. But her work was not limited to the local or state levels. As the war progressed, she was selected as the only female member of several national committees, which enhanced her reputation as an administrator.

The Presidency of Vassar. In February 1946 Blanding sought and obtained the post of president of Vassar College, succeeding Henry MacCracken, who had been president since 1915. She was selected because she was "the best possible person, man or woman." *The New York Herald Tribune* noted that Blanding "was a fresh, vigorous, and resourceful person with a mind of proved capacity, and, most of all, balanced judgment." She believed that her main mission was to maintain Vassar's high quality of education for women; ironically, this came at a time when the college, to help alleviate the overcrowding of men's colleges, began accepting male war veterans on the GI Bill as students working toward Vassar degrees.

National Honors. Blanding received national recognition for her efforts on behalf of women's education at Vassar. She toured often, lecturing that the balance of good and evil was so precarious that the scales could be tipped in either direction, so democracy was in a perilous position. In the process she received honorary doctorates from several colleges, including the University of Kentucky. She was appointed by President Harry S Truman to the National Commission on Higher Education, whose aim was to reexamine the system of education in the United States; later Governor Dewey appointed her to a committee to study the need for a state university system in New York. At her inauguration to the National Commission on Higher Education in October 1946, Blanding was given the War Department's Civilian Service Award for her service to the secretary of war. Cited during the ceremony were her exceptional efforts in developing activities for the Women's Army Corps and her leadership as a member of the army and navy committees on welfare and recreation. She was then appointed to the War Department Civilian Advisory Council and to the Chief of Staff's Advisory Committee for the Women's Army Corps.

Source:
Jean Nowell, "New President Greets 1,440 at Vassar Opening," *New York Herald Tribune*, 8 September 1946, p. 33.

ANDREW DAVID HOLT

1904-1972

NEA PRESIDENT

The Last NEA President of the Decade. As the president of the National Education Association (NEA), the world's largest teachers' organization, Andrew David Holt took control of the organization in 1949 at a point when education in America was at a crossroads. By the time of his inauguration the organization boasted a membership of eight hundred thousand. One significant event of his election year was the adoption of a resolution by the

NEA called "Preservation of Democracy," which facilitated the purging of Communists from the ranks of the NEA and from the schools. The doctrine became part of the McCarthyism of the 1950s.

Early Preparation. Holt reached the presidency of the NEA after serving for twelve years in the Tennessee Education Association (TEA) while he worked as principal of the training school and director of teacher training at West Tennessee State College. In 1937 he completed his Ph.D. from Columbia University, was elected secretary-treasurer of the TEA, and was named editor of *The Tennessee Teacher*. He also joined the board of directors of the Tennessee Congress of Parents and Teachers, spending a great deal of time traveling around Tennessee and the rest of the country talking to teachers, students, and civic organizations. Among his greatest accomplishments during this period was his successful lobbying of the Tennessee legislature for laws establishing many benefits for teachers — including sick leave, continuing contracts, retirement pay and insurance, and guaranteed nine-month contracts. During World War II Holt was commissioned as a captain in the army. His main task was to visit schools and lecture to students and faculty about what they could do for the war effort. Holt was promoted to the rank of major and visited all forty-eight states.

Legislative Bulldog. Holt's greatest achievement came with his election as president of the NEA. He had served the organization as chairman of the NEA–American Legion Committee in 1946 and as first vice-president of the NEA in 1948. He was proud that during his twelve years of service in Tennessee he had been responsible for legislation directing that each teacher with a bachelor's degree would receive a $470 raise. Holt stated that he was "gratified over this . . . but at the same time I see it only as one more incident in a nation-wide move to show teachers in a tangible way the public is behind them."

NEA President. Holt's experience paved the way for his election in 1949, the year in which the "Preservation of Democracy" resolution was passed. Ironically, he had witnessed firsthand the purging of teachers because of their beliefs, suspected or otherwise. A portion of the resolution's draft read, "The whole spirit of free American education will be subverted unless teachers are free to speak for themselves. It is because members of the Communist party are required to surrender this right as a consequence of becoming part of a movement characterized by conspiracy and deceit, that they shall be excluded from employment as teachers and from membership in the National Education Association." The resolution also stated that "as a measure of defense . . . American schools should teach about communism and all forms of totalitarianism." While ostensibly protesting the suppression of free speech under communism, the resolution did the same thing within American education.

Source:
David Caute, *The Great Fear: The Anti-Communist Purge under Truman and Eisenhower* (New York: Simon & Schuster, 1978).

SIDNEY HOOK

1902-1989

PHILOSOPHER, EDUCATOR

Prominent Intellectual. A well-known college professor who expressed views on virtually all the major political and social issues of his times, Sidney Hook was among the notable American intellectuals whose political thinking underwent a major shift between the 1920s and the late 1940s, as he and other leftists became increasingly disillusioned with the Soviet Union. Hook embraced Marxist theory in the 1920s, but by the beginning of the Cold War in the late 1940s, he had turned to a conservative defense of democracy.

Early Years. Hook was born and raised in Brooklyn, New York, and began studying philosophy as an undergraduate at the City College of New York. After receiving a B.S. in 1923, he began teaching in New York City public schools and enrolled in graduate studies in philosophy at Columbia University. Hook got a master's degree in 1926 and won a university fellowship to continue his doctoral studies with philosopher John Dewey, who had a profound influence on Hook's thinking. He completed his doctorate in 1927. His dissertation, *The Metaphysics of Pragmatism* (1927), displays Dewey's influence and includes a preface by Dewey in the published version. Hook began as an instructor in philosophy at New York University in 1927 and continued to teach philosophy there until his retirement in 1970. In 1929, as a Guggenheim Fellow, he studied in Berlin, Munich, and Moscow, where at the Marx-Engels Institute he pursued what he called his "active interest in the theory and practice of the working class movement." After his return to New York the following year, he began lecturing at the New School for Social Research while continuing to teach at New York University and writing *Towards the Understanding of Karl Marx: A Revolutionary Interpretation* (1933). One reviewer called this book "the best presentation of the social philosophy of Karl Marx in the English language."

A Shifting Away from Marxism. Hook was expelled from the Communist Party in 1932 for expressing his philosophical differences with party ideology and defending Leon Trotsky after he fell out of favor with Joseph Stalin. While Hook continued to espouse revolutionary Marxism — helping to launch a new communist party, the American Workers Party, in 1933 — a shift in his thinking became evident in his 1940 book, *Reason, Social Myths and Democracy,* in which he pointed to the propaganda of Adolf Hitler, Benito Mussolini, and Joseph Stalin as threats to democracy. Hook warned that "those who believe in democracy must distinguish intelligently . . . between honest opposition *within* the framework of the democratic process [and an opposition dictated from without, which] must be swiftly dealt with if democracy is to survive." A review in the *Nation* described Hook's attitude toward Marxism as "moving from heresy to apostasy."

Cold War Anti-Communist. By the late 1940s Hook became a solid defender of democracy against communism. In 1949 he organized Americans for Intellectual Freedom, a group of two hundred intellectuals, cultural leaders, and artists, to protest the allegedly Communist-controlled Cultural and Scientific Conference for World Peace then convening in New York. In April of that year Hook went to Paris as a representative of Americans for Intellectual Freedom, in opposition to the Communist-backed Congress of Partisans for Peace, which was meeting at the same time. Hook's group then created the American Committee for Cultural Freedom, with Hook as its chairman, speaking out against "the distortion of words in Communist practice."

The McCarthy Era. During the 1950s Hook increased his anti-Communist activities among scholars abroad, associating with the group that published the CIA-funded *Encounter* magazine. Hook especially attacked "ritualistic liberals" — progressives with good intentions who, Hook believed, confused the political situation and paved the way for authoritarian Communists. Alarmed at the growing right-wing attack on American education, however, Hook tried to distinguish between legitimate academic freedom and illegitimate Communist indoctrination — a distinction ignored by the right-wing "witch hunters" trying to purge American classrooms of all left-of-center teachers.

Later Years. In the 1960s and 1970s Hook remained consistently anti-Marxist in voicing his opposition to the New Left, but fewer and fewer people listened. As Irving Howe once commented, "It was Hook's fate as an ever-poised polemicist, that almost anyone could find something to disagree with . . . in his writings and therefore dismiss his genuine contributions." Hook once told a philosophy class: "I've always been out of step: A premature Marxist. A premature anti-Fascist. A premature anti-Communist."

Sources:
Alexander Bloom, *Prodigal Sons: The New York Intellectuals and Their World* (New York: Oxford University Press, 1986);

Sidney Hook, *Out of Step: An Unquiet Life in the Twentieth Century* (New York: Harper & Row, 1987);

Alan Wald, *The New York Intellectuals* (Chapel Hill: University of North Carolina Press, 1987).

ROBERT M. HUTCHINS

1899-1977

UNIVERSITY PRESIDENT, EDUCATIONAL INNOVATOR

"The Tradition of the West." President of the University of Chicago by the age of thirty, Robert M. Hutchins's sudden rise to prominence in education was due to his ability to put educational philosophy into an accessible public form. An arresting speaker, Hutchins gave over one hundred speeches a year, most of them deploring the state of American education. Hutchins condemned egalitarianism and progressive education. Something of an elitist, he also feared that the increasing specialization of society was undermining its civilized foundation. His solution was to advocate a classics-based education designed to familiarize all citizens with "the tradition of the West." In the 1940s such an educational philosophy had enormous appeal, especially after the barbarism of the Nazis. It also appealed to those who feared the communism of the East and those who were anxious over the increasingly amoral use of technology. Hutchins's attitudes toward education offered Americans certainty after the unsettling developments of the Holocaust, the Cold War, and the atom bomb.

Background. Son of a minister at Union Theological Seminary in New York, Hutchins came from a family that on both sides traced their ancestry to the original New England colonists. At age eight Hutchins relocated with his family to Oberlin, Ohio, where his father had accepted a teaching position. Hutchins himself went on to Oberlin College, adopting deeply its Calvinistic strictures regarding personal restraint and moral certitude. World War I interrupted his college career, and Hutchins served in the ambulance corps in Italy long enough to absorb a host of European languages and to become disillusioned about the romance of war. With the end of the conflict he enrolled in Yale, completed his studies, and went on to graduate from the law school. He passed the Connecticut bar, but rather than practice law he began an astonishing career with the Yale Corporation as a fundraiser and administrator as well as a faculty member of the law school.

Yale. By 1927 Hutchins was dean of the law school, earning a public reputation as a boy wonder for the speed with which he earned the prestigious post. Much of the credit for Hutchins's success, however, must go to Yale president James Angell. Like Hutchins, Angell saw the curriculum at Yale as outdated and unscientific; he sought to modernize the university by providing more interdisciplinary courses and giving students more autonomy on campus, in a manner similar to that pioneered by Harvard and Columbia. Hutchins was Angell's choice to

shake up the law school. Hutchins did just that, bringing men such as William O. Douglas to Yale. Both Douglas and Hutchins were proponents of legal realism and sociological jurisprudence, philosophies which integrated social science and legal precedent. Angell and Hutchins also expanded their interdisciplinary study of the law by establishing the Institute of Human Relations, which brought the law faculty and the medical faculty together to explore the psychological roots of crime and justice. His reputation as a scholar and academic administrator was such that in 1929 he was offered the post of president of the University of Chicago. Only thirty years old at the time, he served in this position until 1945, when he was named chancellor of the university, a position he held until 1951.

In Loco Parentis. At Chicago Hutchins continued his efforts to modernize the university. One of the most irritating traditions in higher education for modernizers such as Hutchins were the in loco parentis (in the place of parents) rules. In loco parentis referred to the nineteenth-century tradition that colleges should act in place of the absent parent and monitor the social and moral behavior of the students. Curfews and complex rules regarding drinking, dancing, and dating were common on most campuses. Hutchins believed the students were adults by college age and could monitor their own behavior, and he dispensed with in loco parentis. He also believed students could successfully plan their own educations. The freedom with which students could plan general and elective courses at Chicago was unprecedented and became the model for American universities generally.

Salary Equality. At Chicago Hutchins also equalized the pay scales of university professors. He was troubled by the disparity in pay between older, established scholars and younger, struggling academics. Older professors not only enjoyed higher salaries as a result of their seniority but often earned hefty incomes from outside publishing contracts. Hutchins, arguing that it was the younger scholars, often raising families, who needed the greater income (an observation somewhat obvious during the Depression), initiated a voluntary program whereby senior scholars turned over outside income to the university and the university raised the pay scales for all professors, young and old alike. An in-demand speaker, Hutchins himself led the way by turning over his considerable income from lectures to the university.

Neo-Thomism. Despite his modernizing efforts, Hutchins was most widely known for his advocacy of a classics-based humanities curriculum, which he first proposed in a 1936 book, *Higher Learning in America.* Hutchins was profoundly influenced by his friend, philosophy professor Mortimer Adler. Adler was an acerbic, antagonistic personality believing absolutely that pragmatism — the philosophical foundation of progressive education — was leading American civilization into decline. So indelicate was Adler in his opinions that when Hutchins appointed him to the Chicago faculty in 1930, it led to several resignations and continual tension between Hutchins and the faculty. In part, sustained ill will was also a function of Adler's increasing influence with Hutchins. Where at Yale Hutchins was determined to make education more scientific, modern, and plural, at Chicago he substantially abandoned these goals. Adler was developing into the leading practitioner of a school of philosophy based on the medieval scholasticism of Saint Thomas Aquinas. Hutchins became something of a medievalist himself and found in the university of the Middle Ages a model for the present. By the 1940s Hutchins advocated a unified liberal arts/humanist curriculum for Chicago not unlike that found in the great universities of the premodern period. This Thomistic education, oriented around a curriculum of "Great Books" and a "hierarchy of truths," supposedly would provide an antidote to the overwhelming emphasis on science and technology in modern education. The Thomistic model would become the basis of Hutchins's educational philosophy, and he would spend much of the 1940s defending the idea.

Opponents Respond. Opponents of Thomistic education charged that Hutchins was attempting to roll back the modernization of American universities. The debate between Hutchins, Adler, and associates such as John Nef and Stringfellow Barr, and opponents led by John Dewey, Sidney Hook, and University of Wisconsin president Glenn Frank became quite heated. Adler and Hutchins charged that absent a Thomistic education, society disintegrated into fascism or communism. Hutchins in fact argued that the type of progressive education and pragmatic philosophy embodied in the work of John Dewey undermined eternal truths and led to authoritarianism. When schools adopt progressive education, he argued, "the journey from the man of good will to Hitler is complete." Hutchins's opponents replied that it was the Thomistic concept itself that was authoritarian. "As far as I can see," noted Dewey, "President Hutchins has completely evaded the problem of who is to determine the definite truths that constitute the hierarchy." Despite his position, Hutchins could not convince the faculty at Chicago to reconstruct itself on a Thomistic basis. Nonetheless, the idea remained at the center of educational controversies during the 1940s and into the next decade.

Politics, Science, Humanities. To some extent the debate over Thomistic education during the 1940s unfairly stigmatized Hutchins as an educational and political conservative. In fact he was a political liberal and lifelong Democrat. An engaging speaker, Hutchins was often proposed as a political candidate, Supreme Court justice, and head of New Deal agencies such as the National Recovery Administration. None of these

appointments came to pass, but Hutchins, along with Vannevar Bush and James B. Conant, became one of the key academic administrators of joint government/industrial/university research ventures during the war, setting an important precedent for such ventures during the Cold War. Under his superintendence the world's first controlled nuclear reaction was sustained by a Chicago research team. The wartime emphasis on university science, however, jibed uncomfortably with Hutchins's humanistic bias. As a result, during the war the university began a humanist, interdisciplinary study group that achieved postwar acclaim: the Committee on Social Thought. An interdisciplinary graduate program, the Committee on Social Thought benefited from the participation of leading expatriate European intellectuals such as Paul Tillich, Jacques Maritain, Arnold Schoenberg, John Von Neumann, Friedrich von Hayek, and Hannah Arendt. Oriented around a curriculum Hutchins's associate John Nef called "the fundamentals," the Committee on Social Thought offered a humanist antidote to the reigning wartime emphasis on science and technology. To Hutchins such high-minded intellectual work was all the more important in a postwar environment dominated by the presence of the atomic bomb — a technology to which Hutchins had partially contributed.

Later Work. The anti-Communist hysteria of the late 1940s raised Hutchins's hackles and led him toward his later work in political and philanthropic organization. When, in 1949, the Illinois legislature sent the Seditious Activities Investigating Commission to assess the loyalty of the Chicago faculty, Hutchins ably defended his teachers and denounced such inquests as "the greatest menace to the United States since Hitler." He followed this defense by becoming, in 1954, president of the Fund for the Republic, a Ford Foundation group dedicated to combating the civil liberties abuses of the McCarthy era. The fund also attacked racial discrimination and sponsored academic studies of civil rights. For his efforts Hutchins was pilloried by the Right and investigated by the House Un-American Activities Committee, but he continued his activities, directing the fund to create the Center for the Study of Democratic Institutions, a think tank, in 1959. In the 1960s the center became one of the leading liberal study centers in the United States, attempting to lessen Cold War tension between the United States and Russia through cultural exchanges, even during the tumult of Vietnam. Hutchins retired as head of the center in 1974 but returned as president in 1975. He maintained this position until he died on 14 May 1977.

Sources:

Harry S. Ashmore, *Unseasonable Truths: The Life of Robert Maynard Hutchins* (Boston: Little, Brown, 1989);

Edward A. Purcell, Jr., *The Crisis of Democratic Theory: Scientific Naturalism and the Problem of Value* (Lexington: University Press of Kentucky, 1973).

OWEN LATTIMORE

1900-1989

ASIAN SCHOLAR

Asian Expertise. Owen Lattimore, who served from 1938 to 1941 as director of the Walter Himes Page School of International Relations at Johns Hopkins University, was a noted Asian scholar whose expertise was put to use by the United States government during World War II and the subsequent reconstruction of Asia. In 1941 he was appointed by President Franklin D. Roosevelt as political adviser to Chiang Kai-shek of China, an appointment based mainly on his understanding of China, Manchuria, and Inner Mongolia.

More Overseas Posts and Recall to Duty. In late 1942 Lattimore became the deputy director of the overseas branch of the United States government and was in charge of the Pacific operations with the Office of War Information. He remained in this post until June 1944, when he was asked to return to China as a member of the vice-president's diplomatic party. He resigned in 1945 so that he could return to his initial love, teaching. However, his return to academic life was short-lived. In October 1945 President Harry S Truman asked him to become the special economic adviser to Edwin W. Pauley, whom Truman had named as the head of an economic mission to Japan. This request was due in part to the impression that Lattimore during his diplomatic career and in his writings had consistently supported democracy in Asia.

Major Works. As a writer Lattimore is best remembered for three groundbreaking works. His *Inner Asian Frontiers* (1940), a history of China's northern and western frontiers, was followed by *Mongol Journeys* (1941), a work described by *The New York Times* as "an easily and sometimes beautifully written book." But perhaps his most noted work was *Solution in Asia* (1945), supposedly one of only two books on the president's desk when he announced the surrender of Japan. This work, which was greeted enthusiastically by reviewers, discussed the future of Asian countries after the war and called for the Allies to develop an understanding of the Asian need for self-identity. He noted that Asians "may be illiterate, but they know the kind of world they want to live in." This work became one of the three books selected by the Recommended Book Committee of the Council of Books in Wartime.

Witch Hunt Victim. All of the good that Lattimore did for American education and foreign policy was forgotten when he was accused by Sen. Joseph McCarthy in 1950 of being the top Soviet espionage agent operating in the United States. Evidence against Lattimore was scarce, and the testimony against him was almost comical. When he appeared before the McCarran Subcommittee in February 1953 he was charged with being a Communist sympathizer; two and a half years later the government dropped the case. However, his academic career was destroyed, for few students dared to study under him. He left the United States to teach at Leeds University in England before he returned to China in 1972, where in 1974 he was accused of being an international spy but was exonerated.

Source:
Andrew Caute, *The Great Fear: The Anti-Communist Purge under Truman and Eisenhower* (New York: Simon & Schuster, 1978)

FREDERICK DOUGLAS PATTERSON

1901-1988

COLLEGE PRESIDENT, FOUNDER OF THE UNITED NEGRO COLLEGE FUND

President at Tuskegee. In 1935 Frederick Douglas Patterson became president of Tuskegee Normal and Industrial Institute, one of the foremost African American institutions of higher education in the country. His stated purpose at the time of his inauguration was not only to increase the vocational training of his students but also to raise them to higher levels of academic competency and thus make them more qualified wage earners. He is also remembered for his creation in 1943 of the United Negro College Fund, an organization dedicated to raising and distributing scholarships to deserving minority students.

School Lunches. After adding courses on the principles of nutrition and dietetics to the curriculum of Tuskegee, Patterson oversaw the adoption and growth of the federally sponsored school-lunch program. He felt that this program must be expanded because academic achievement rested on a strong nutritional base, which many underprivileged children lacked. He firmly believed that for Tuskegee to thrive, the school had to reach its potential students before they fell victim to poverty.

The Carver Foundation. In the early 1940s Patterson's administration also established the George Washington Carver Foundation, which provided grants and monies to qualified students. Begun in 1940 by Carver himself, the foundation nearly doubled its assets in six years, rising from thirty-three thousand dollars to sixty thousand dollars. The fund expanded its base by undertaking research from commercial firms, and by 1947 eleven students working under grants were researching in paper, ink, foods, and animal nutrition.

Creation of the United Negro College Fund. In 1943 Patterson called a meeting of the heads of all of the major predominantly black institutions of higher education to plan a joint fund-raising venture. The result was the organization of the United Negro College Fund, of which he was elected president. Originally twenty-seven institutions joined the organization, which was incorporated in New York. By 1945 the group had grown to thirty-two members, and by 1947 the organization was raising more than a million dollars annually.

National Committees. As a member of President Harry S Truman's Commission on Higher Education, Patterson helped file a 1947 report calling for the reorganization of higher education in the United States. The commission listed as its main priority doubling the number of students attending college. It also called for more types of scholarships, fellowships, and grants and called for the end of segregation — not because of ethical questions but because of the duplication of separate but comparable black and white programs. The commission also called for free education for all through the junior college level and a lowering of tuition and fees at colleges, graduate schools, and professional schools. Most of these suggestions were not enacted.

Construction. In 1946 Patterson's plan to improve the housing of farmers earning substandard incomes was reported and discussed in *The New York Times*. He felt that these lower-class tenants could create building blocks and erect fireproof structures inexpensively. This report attracted several potential investors, models were built on the Tuskegee campus, and the students constructed a four-room house for a neighboring farmer. As in other ventures, Patterson was in housing a man of vision and versatility.

Source:
Frederick D. Patterson, *Chronicles of Faith: The Autobiography of Frederick D. Patterson* (Tuscaloosa: University of Alabama Press, 1991).

MABEL STUDEBAKER

1901-1983

EDUCATOR, PRESIDENT OF THE NATIONAL EDUCATION ASSOCIATION

Early Activities. In 1925 Mabel Studebaker became a teacher in the Erie, Pennsylvania, public-school system, where she taught science at various levels for many years. During this time she gradually became active in local, state, and national teaching organizations. She eventually became a champion for the rights of educators, whom she felt were underpaid and overworked. She wrote many articles for various publications about the general need for improvement of educational standards in the United States. She felt that teachers needed to unite nationally in order to improve conditions and standardize salaries. She believed that improved conditions for teachers would have a beneficial effect upon democracy in general.

Tour of the United Kingdom. In the fall of 1945 Studebaker was asked by the British government to visit eighty-five primary schools in Great Britain in order to encourage greater understanding between elementary teachers in Great Britain and the United States. She and three other American teachers met with their British counterparts to discuss how best to educate children. The result was a pamphlet, written by Studebaker and the three teachers, called "Boys and Girls of the United Kingdom."

NEA President. At the annual National Education Association (NEA) meeting in 1948 Studebaker was elected president. At the time the organization included approximately 450,000 members. Under her leadership the NEA became more organized in an attempt to remedy the deplorable conditions of teaching, including an adoption of a minimal salary schedule. This action created a schism in the organization, whose membership was then dominated by school administrators opposed to Studebaker's attempts to reform compensation for teachers. This idea became so unpopular that Studebaker was replaced in 1949 by Andrew David Holt, a move that represented a considerable defeat for Studebaker and her supporters.

Source:
Wayne Urban, *Why Teachers Organized* (Detroit: Wayne State University Press, 1982).

PEOPLE IN THE NEWS

Professor **Jacques Barzun** suggested in *The Teacher in America* (1945) that the United States does not possess the best of all possible educational systems.

Myrtle Hooper Dahl, president of the National Education Association in 1941, led its annual convention in planning a national teaching employment service, a teaching program to educate ten million illiterate people, and a plan to train teachers of other subjects in math and science.

In 1940 **Clarence A. Dykstra** was granted an indefinite leave of absence as president of the University of Wisconsin to serve as the U.S. director of the Selective Service.

In March 1949 **Albert Einstein** published a portion of his autobiography. In the excerpt he discussed his own education and his repugnance for learning only to pass examinations: "It is, in fact, nothing short of a miracle that the modern methods of instruction have not yet entirely strangled the holy curiosity of inquiry."

In 1949 New York State Senate majority leader **Benjamin Feinberg** proposed a bill to purge Communist teachers from the state public school systems. The bill passed, giving the New York Board of Regents the right to weed out "subversive" teachers.

A twelve-part series by Pulitzer Prize–winning author **Benjamin Fine** on problems in American education was published in 1947 in *The New York Times.*

In April 1943 **Hugh Russell Fraser** and twotime Pulitzer Prize–winner **Allan Nevins** created a test to determine the amount of American history high-school graduates retain from secondary education.

In an article in the January 1946 *Harper's* **George Henry,** principal of a high school in Dover, Delaware, contended that one-third of all high-school students are unable to read well enough to understand textbooks.

Maj. Gen. **Campbell B. Hodges,** the highest-ranking military officer in Louisiana, assumed the presidency of Louisiana State University in July 1941.

In 1944 Fisk University president **Thomas Elsa Jones** kicked off the campaign to raise $1.5 million for the United Negro College Fund, to be shared among twenty-seven predominantly black colleges and universities.

In 1949 the first student to enroll in the Langston University Law School for Negroes, **Theophilus Roberts,** finished his examinations with above-average scores. Since he was the only student, the school then closed.

Yale University president **Charles Seymour** announced in 1944 that war veterans would not attend Yale University under the GI Bill; instead they would attend the Institute of Collegiate Study to become acclimated to the rigors of academia.

After a successful tenure as an assistant professor at the University of Minnesota, in 1945 **B. F. Skinner** became a professor at Indiana University. In 1948 he published *Walden Two,* a fictionalized account of a utopian society.

Guy Everett Snavely, executive director of the Association of American Colleges, estimated in 1941 that some 250,000 students would enroll in special three-year, degree-earning courses of study.

John Ward Studebaker, U.S. commissioner of education, noted in December 1947 that it was a waste of time for most high-school students to read such classic works of literature as Sir Walter Scott's *Ivanhoe* and George Eliot's *Silas Marner,* saying that "sufficient competence in reading to comprehend newspapers and magazines" was all the average person needed. Further, he claimed that only a few gifted individuals could ever achieve a true comprehension of algebra or geometry.

DEATHS

James Rowland Angell, 79, psychology professor and president of Yale University (1921–1937), 4 March 1949.

Leonard Porter Ayres, 67, author of monographs on education, 29 October 1946.

William Chandler Bagley, 72, education periodicals editor and opponent of progressive education, 1 July 1946.

Charles A. Beard, 74, historian and director of the Training School for Public Service in New York (1917–1922), 1 September 1948.

Isaiah Bowman, 71, former president of Johns Hopkins University, 6 January 1950.

Percy Holmes Boynton, 70, University of Chicago English professor whose textbooks were widely used, 8 July 1946.

William Brandenburg, 71, president of the American Association of Teachers Colleges, 29 October 1940.

Nicholas Murray Butler, 83, president of Columbia College, Chicago (1902–1945), 7 December 1947.

Morris R. Cohen, 67, widely acclaimed author and professor of philosophy at City College of New York, 28 January 1947.

James W. Crabtree, 81, secretary of the National Education Association (1917–1935), 9 June 1945.

Wilber Lucius Cross, 86, Yale University English professor and governor of Connecticut from 1930 to 1938, 5 October 1948.

Walter E. Dandy, 60, associate professor at Johns Hopkins University and a renowned brain surgeon, 14 April 1946.

Robert E. Doherty, 65, president of Carnegie Institute of Technology (1909–1931) and known for his extensions of theory in alternating current, 19 October 1950.

Harriet Wiseman Elliott, 63, professor at the University of North Carolina and the only female member of the National Defense Commission, 6 August 1947.

William Preston Few, 72, president and cofounder of Duke University, 16 October 1940.

Thomas Sovereign Gates, 75, financier and president of the University of Pennsylvania (1930–1944), 8 April 1948.

Ernest R. Groves, 69, sociologist and founder of the University of North Carolina conference on the conservation of marriage and the family in 1934, 28 August 1946.

George McLean Harper, 83, Princeton University professor of Romance languages, 14 July 1947.

Samuel Northrup Harper, 61, noted Russian scholar, 18 January 1943.

Emily Hickman, 66, history teacher and chair of the 1944 Committee on the Cause and Cure of War, 12 June 1947.

Rufus Jones, 82, professor of philosophy at Haverford College (1904–1934) and founder in 1917 of the American Friends Service Committee, 16 June 1945.

Raymond Asa Kent, 59, president of the University of Louisville and education consultant to the federal government, 26 February 1943.

George Lyman Kittridge, 81, English professor at Harvard University (1894–1936), 23 July 1941.

Joshua L. Liebman, 41, teacher of Jewish philosophy at Boston University and author of the best-seller *Piece of Mind*, 9 June 1949.

Abbot Lawrence Lowell, 86, president of Harvard University (1909–1933) and education author, 6 January 1943.

Harley F. MacNair, 55, noted China scholar and professor at the University of Chicago, 22 June 1947.

John Benjamin Magee, 55, educator and theologian, president of Cornell College, 6 April 1943.

James Lukens McConaughty, 60, president of Wesleyan University (1925–1943) and governor of Connecticut (1946–1948), 7 March 1948.

Roland Morris, 71, professor of law at the University of Pennsylvania and former ambassador to Japan, 23 November 1946.

Jesse Homer Newlon, 59, former Denver superintendent and president of the National Education Association, 1 September 1941.

George C. Odell, 82, professor emeritus at Columbia University and author of many works on American theater, 17 October 1949.

Albert Ten Eyck Olmstead, 65, renowned professor of oriental history at the University of Chicago, 11 April 1945.

Frederick Bayley Pratt, 80, president of the Pratt Institute from 1923 to 1935, 3 May 1945.

Aurelia Henry Reinhardt, 70, president of Mills College who served as the first female moderator of the Unitarian churches of the United States, 28 January 1948.

L. S. Rowe, 75, professor of political science and director of the Pan American Union from 1920 to 1946, 5 December 1946.

Wiley Blount Rutledge, Jr., 55, professor and dean of the College of Law, State University of Iowa, and former Supreme Court justice, 10 September 1949.

Olga Samaroff, 65, music teacher at The Juilliard School and cofounder of the Musicians' Emergency Fund, 17 May 1948.

Edward Reilly Stettinius, Jr., 49, former rector of the University of Virginia, 31 October 1949.

Donald Bertrand Tresidder, 53, physician and former president of Stanford University, 28 January 1948.

William Thomas Walsh, 57, biographer and educator, head of Roxbury School (1933–1947), 22 February 1949.

Mary E. Wooley, 84, first woman to receive a degree from Brown University (1884) and president of Mount Holyoke College for thirty-seven years, 5 September 1947.

Hugh Young, 74, professor of urology at Johns Hopkins University, 23 August 1945.

PUBLICATIONS

R. K. Bent and H. H. Kronenberg, *Principles of Secondary Education* (New York: McGraw-Hill, 1949);

Paul Blanshard, *American Freedom and Catholic Power* (Boston: Beacon, 1949);

F. J. Brown, *Educational Sociology* (London: Technical Press, 1948);

James Conant Bryant, *Education in a World Divided* (Cambridge, Mass.: Harvard University Press, 1948);

Oliver C. Carmichael, *The Changing Role of Higher Education* (New York: Macmillan, 1949);

F. Clarke, *Freedom in an Educative Society* (London: University of London Press, 1948);

Committee on Work Conference on Higher Education of the Southern Association of Colleges and Secondary Schools, *Higher Education in the South* (Chapel Hill: University of North Carolina Press, 1947);

A. Davis, *Social Class Influences upon Learning* (Cambridge, Mass.: Harvard University Press, 1948);

John Dewey, *Problems of Men* (New York: Philosophical Library, 1946);

Newton Edwards and Herman G. Richey, *The School in American Social Order: The Dynamics of American Education* (Boston: Houghton Mifflin, 1947);

Henry Holmes, ed., *Fundamental Education* (New York: Macmillan, 1947);

Charles S. Johnson, *The Negro College Graduate* (Chapel Hill: University of North Carolina Press, 1947);

I. L. Kandel, *The Impact of the War upon American Education* (Chapel Hill: University of North Carolina Press, 1948);

R. C. Lodge, *Plato's Theory of Education* (New York: Harcourt, 1947);

Paul Monroe, *Founding of the American School System* (New York: Macmillan, 1940);

J. M. O'Neil, *Religion and Education under the Constitution* (New York: Harper, 1949);

President and Fellows of Harvard College, *General Education in a Free Society* (Cambridge, Mass.: Harvard University Press, 1945);

President's Commission on Higher Education, *Higher Education for American Democracy* (Washington, D.C.: United States Printing Office, 1947);

H. Rivlin, *Teaching Adolescents in Secondary Schools* (New York: Appleton-Century-Crofts, 1948);

Mortimer Smith, *And Madly Teach: A Layman Looks at Public School Education* (Chicago: Regnery, 1949);

W. L. Warner, R. J. Havighurst, and M. B. Loeb, *Who Shall Be Educated?* (New York: Routledge, 1946);

Thomas Woody, *Life and Education in Early Societies* (New York: Macmillan, 1949).

FASHION

by JANE GERHARD

CONTENTS

Sidebars and tables are listed in italics

1940

- Automaker Henry Ford and other high-profile Americans join the America First committee to pressure President Franklin D. Roosevelt to avoid United States involvement in World War II.

- Automobile manufacturers install a better quality of glass in windshields, improving visibility by 62 percent.

- Architect Frank Lloyd Wright completes the People's Church in Kansas City, bringing modernism to church architecture.

- Colorfast textiles are improved, allowing prints to be more durable through many washings.

- New automobiles and trucks numbering 4,476,000 are produced in the United States, a 25 percent increase over 1939. Americans own 69 percent of the world's cars.

- Japanese silk supplies to the United States continue to dwindle under the trade embargo between the two countries.

Fall   With the fall of Paris to the Nazis in June, the United States experiences its first fashion season without French designers.

1941

- Charles Eames and Eero Saarinen win first prize in the Museum of Modern Art competition for functional furniture.

- Architects Walter Gropius and Marcel Breuer are commissioned by the U.S. government to design a 250-unit defense housing project called Aluminum City in New Kensington, Pennsylvania.

- College women and debutantes go hatless, a trend that alarms the millinery industry.

- The fashion industry grows across the country, with Saint Louis, Los Angeles, Boston, Philadelphia, and Chicago challenging New York as America's fashion production center.

- New York mayor Fiorello H. La Guardia, acting as national director of civil defense, appoints a committee of stylists to submit designs for women's uniforms.

- Plywood paneling, treated with resin and buffed into a shine, becomes popular in interior design.

- Ludwig Mies van der Rohe's master plan for the Illinois Institute of Technology applies his distinctive design to low buildings.

Jan.   Mayor La Guardia sponsors a press event, "New York Fashion Futures," in an attempt to secure New York as the fashion center of the world.

24 Nov.   *Life* magazine publishes an article on movie star Veronica Lake's hair, claiming that it is "comparable in value, fame and world influence to Deanna Durbin's voice, Fred Astaire's feet or Marlene Dietrich's legs."

7 Dec.   Japan bombs Pearl Harbor, Hawaii. The next day President Roosevelt signs the declaration of war against Japan, signaling U.S. entry into World War II.

1942

- With restrictions on metal, U.S. designers start producing dresses that fasten without any of the traditional devices such as hooks, snaps, buttons, or zippers.

- By midyear automobile production falls to 39 percent of the previous year's figures as the auto industry converts to building planes, anti-aircraft guns, ambulances, and tanks for the military.

- Prefabricated buildings are put into military service, and the United States ships a demountable hospital of twenty-two buildings to England.

- The U.S. government establishes the National War Board, the War Production Board, and the Supply Priorities and Allocations Board to oversee domestic consumption and production.

- Claire McCardell's "popover" dress wins a *Harper's Bazaar* competition for the most attractive and practical housedress.

- Henry Russell Hitchcock publishes his monograph on Frank Lloyd Wright, *In the Nature of Materials,* and identifies what he calls a uniquely American kind of architecture.

- President Roosevelt sets defense goals of sixty thousand planes, forty-five thousand tanks, and eight million tons of ships to be built by 1942, and U.S. manufacturers strive to meet the challenge.

- With government metal restrictions in place, a range of household goods is produced for the first time in glass and plastic, including the glass kettle, ceramic ware, and a plastic juicer.

- Mid-nineteenth-century ironwork decorating buildings throughout the country is claimed for the war effort and melted down for munitions, resulting in the disappearance of cast-iron lacework and metallic horse troughs as urban architectural embellishments.

- The nave of the great Cathedral of Saint John the Divine in New York, begun in 1892, is completed.

Feb. The War Production Board commandeers all of Du Pont's supply of nylon for parachutes, tires, netting, and tents.

22 Feb. The manufacture of motor vehicles for the civilian market ceases as the auto industry aids in the war effort.

Apr. Order L-41 is issued, prohibiting all but essential war construction.

June The American Institute of Architects, with the Producers' Council, issues a bulletin, *The Conservation of Critical Materials in Construction,* to serve as a guideline for building construction during the war.

25 June The American Institute of Architects announces at its Detroit convention that it has created a division of Pan-American affairs, headed by Dean Leopold Arnaud of the Columbia University School of Architecture. It will sponsor exhibitions and exchange scholarships with Latin American countries.

July The War Production Board limits the manufacture of beauty supplies because of the need to conserve the metal used in cosmetic packaging. The ban lasts only four months, as women across the country protest.

1943

- The U.S. Army uses 519.1 million pairs of socks and 229.4 million pairs of pants.

- Wright begins designing the circular, spiral-ramp interior for the Guggenheim Museum in New York; his innovative, ambitious design takes a decade to complete.

- In response to shortages in housing, manufacturers develop a fold-up "suitcase" house. The house is completely fabricated on an assembly line, can be assembled in twenty minutes, and weighs less than twenty-five hundred pounds. The government plans to ship the "suitcase" to Europe to house the military and the growing numbers of refugees.

- The U.S. government averts a wool shortage by releasing millions of pounds of wool and ending restrictions on its use.

- Designers introduce glitter into their evening wear, with sequins, beads, and embroidery appearing on wools, crepes, sheer fabrics, and sweaters.

- Designer Norman Norell wins the first Coty American Fashion Critics' Award.

- The total number of motor vehicles manufactured in the United States is less than in any year since 1914, as the auto industry continues to build tanks and jeeps instead of civilian cars.

- A rumored shortage of black fabric triggers a run on women's black dresses.

25 Jan. The world's largest office building, the thirty-four-acre Pentagon, is completed in Arlington, Virginia.

Mar. New war-housing family units numbering 123,000 are completed, and another 147,000 are placed under construction. Most of the publicly financed housing is destined for dismantling after the war.

13 Apr. In Washington, D.C., President Roosevelt dedicates the Jefferson Memorial on the two-hundredth anniversary of Thomas Jefferson's birth.

17 May *Life* magazine declares the "safe and stylish" wardrobe designed for Boeing's new female workforce a new fashion fad on the West Coast.

1944

- The Servicemen's Readjustment Act becomes law, offering returning servicemen and servicewomen a range of low-interest housing and educational loans, helping to propel millions of Americans into the middle class.

- Saarinen shares first prize with Oliver Lundquist in a contest to design small, affordable postwar houses. The design helps to introduce prefabricated houses as a solution to the problem of postwar housing.

- Air conditioning is introduced in motor vehicles.

Mar. A "prefab" housing exhibit in New York dismisses the threat of prefabricated housing to traditional builders, claiming that the rumored prefab housing boom originated with prefab builders themselves.

25 Aug. Paris is liberated by Allied troops, allowing French clothing designers to return to the fashion stage.

1945

- The United States Foreign Economic Administration promises England thirty thousand prefabricated houses to be used in bombed areas. The homes are twenty-four by twenty-four feet, with a living room, two bedrooms, a kitchen, a bathroom, and a four-foot porch, and are set up on four-inch concrete slabs.

- As the war ends, U.S. cities report a growing housing crisis: 98 percent of cities report shortages of houses, and more than 90 percent report shortages of apartments.

12 Apr. President Roosevelt dies at the "little White House" in Warm Springs, Georgia. A few hours later Vice-president Harry S Truman becomes the thirty-third president of the United States.

16 July Movie star Rita Hayworth wins the title of "Number One Back Home Glamour Girl" in an overseas poll of U.S. enlisted men.

6 Aug. The U.S. military drops a hydrogen bomb with a photo of Rita Hayworth on the Bikini Islands. Four days later a skimpy bathing suit is named after the islands.

Sept. Paris designers hold their first fashion show since the outbreak of World War II.

1 Oct. The U.S. government lifts the ban on housing construction to permit the building of thirty-two thousand units for citizens not involved in the war effort.

29 Oct. War Production Board chairman J. A. Krug revokes Ration Order 2-B, which limited the sale of automobiles to civilians with special government-issued certificates.

1946

- *Life* magazine reports a frenzy of consumer buying by a public weary of rationing and shortages.

- Eames exhibits his designs in the first one-man furniture show by the Museum of Modern Art.

- Gropius publishes *Rebuilding Our Communities*, in which he gives details of his city-planning and urban-decentralization projects.

- Breuer completes the Robinson House in Williamstown, Massachusetts, and it becomes the model for the popular split-level house.

- The Franklin D. Roosevelt dime goes into circulation.

1947

- Designer Christian Dior single-handedly restores the supremacy of French couture with his controversial New Look. Small waistlines, padded hips, longer hems, and full skirts revive the feminine silhouette and set the dominant look for the postwar United States.

- A comprehensive exhibit of Mies van der Rohe's work is held at the Museum of Modern Art in New York.

- The 1947 Studebaker Starlight surprises and delights consumers and car experts. Its great sweep of glass in the wraparound rear window inspires countless jokes about whether the car is coming or going.

- Architect Philip Johnson's monograph *Mies van der Rohe* is published.

- *Vogue* magazine compares the new Oldsmobile, the "dynamic design of the Future," to the architecture of Wright.

15 Sept. *Time* magazine reports a fashion counterrevolution, as some American women reject Dior's New Look as expensive and faddish.

1948

- American architects post record employment levels, as the nation's construction volume for the first half of the year runs 25 percent above 1947 levels.

- Architect Eleanor Raymond completes the Sun House, the last of three houses in which she explores the new potentials of plywood, paneling, and prefabrication.

- Independent automakers Hudson and Studebaker capture a record-breaking 18 percent of the domestic automobile market, up from their 10 percent market share in 1941.

- Architect Alvar Aalto challenges the dominance of the International Style with the completion of the Baker House dormitory at the Massachusetts Institute of Technology, foreshadowing the postmodern experimentation of the 1970s.

- Ludwig Mies van der Rohe's first executed tall buildings, the Promontory Apartments, are completed in Chicago.

- U.S. auto producers emphasize durability, claiming they have successfully doubled the average life span of the car from 6.5 years in 1925 to 13.4 years in 1948.

- Preston Tucker announces that the Tucker Torpedo is the new American dream car.

- Universal adoption of automatic transmissions is nearly complete in U.S. cars.

- General Motors produces a new high-compression engine, the V-8, able to offer more horsepower than any previous automobile engine. The V-8 is efficient enough to power new frills such as power brakes, power steering, power seats, and air conditioning.

- U.S. designers again consider Paris the fashion capital of the world.

1 Mar. Saarinen wins first prize in the competition for a Saint Louis memorial to Thomas Jefferson and the western expansion of the frontier. The *New York Herald Tribune* declares that his design will "rank among the nation's great monuments."

Sept. Designer Adrian opens the Adrian Room in New York's Gunthers.

28 Sept. New York house builders Levitt and Sons build a sample Levittown on Long Island and sell fifty-three houses at a total of $1.1 million, breaking the world record for house selling. By the end of the week forty-seven more have been sold, and hundreds of customers have been put on a waiting list.

Fall Christian Dior announces the opening of the U.S. branch of his design house, consolidating his influence on U.S. fashion. He starts mass-producing a line of about ninety dresses for wholesale in the United States at $59.75 and up. His first American collection debuts in November, making him the first French designer to be successful in designing and producing in the United States.

1949

- The Gunnison Homes division of U.S. Steel Corporation announces a twenty-four by twenty-eight foot, two-bedroom, steel and plywood house to sell for six thousand dollars. The firm's factories produce a house every twenty minutes.

- Architect Philip Johnson incorporates the design principles of Mies van der Rohe in his New Canaan, Connecticut, residence, the Glass House.

- The continued postwar demand for new cars and a more plentiful steel supply make 1949 a record year for automobile production.

- The rubber industry unveils its tubeless tire, which does away with the inner tube. The tubeless tire is resistant to blowouts and is expected to make motorists' travels safer and more trouble free.

- Fashion designer Adele Simpson opens her medium-priced line of clothing in New York.

- The Cadillac receives a new V-8, 160-horsepower engine, which can move the car from zero to sixty miles per hour in thirty seconds and is fifteen percent more fuel efficient than the 1948 model.

- The Architects Collaborative, proponents of the International Style, complete one of their first designs, the Harvard University Graduate Center.

- In Pacific Palisades, California, Eames designs one of the first stylish and expensive prefabricated houses. That year he is also given the first annual award of the American Institute of Decorators.

- Chrysler breaks the one-million-dollar sales mark for the first time since 1927.

July   After prolonged debate Congress passes President Truman's public-housing bill, the largest public-housing program in U.S. history. The act calls for the construction of 810,000 units of low-rent housing.

OVERVIEW

Watching, Waiting, and Joining. As the decade opened, Americans watched uneasily as the war in Europe and the Pacific rim escalated. The Axis countries of Germany, Italy, and Japan seemed to be gaining strength, and many feared that America's allies were being overwhelmed. Yet in 1940, with the war taking place on two fronts, the United States was still ambivalent about entering the hostilities. Henry Ford, the inventor of the automobile, joined with other concerned Americans to form the America First committee in an effort to discourage President Franklin D. Roosevelt from entering the war. It was not until the Japanese bombed Pearl Harbor, Hawaii, on 7 December 1941 that Americans rallied to defend "freedom, liberty, and democracy" at home and abroad.

War Limits and Restrictions. In fashion and design — clothing, architecture, furniture, interior design, and automobiles — the war affected not only the production of goods but their style and design. For fashion designers, interior designers, automobile designers, and architects, the war restricted access to certain materials and set guidelines for domestic production and consumption. Raw materials such as silk, metal, rubber, nylon, and wool were in short supply. Steel once used by the auto industry now went to build tanks and ships; cloth that once went to designers now dressed soldiers. Such restrictions on supplies directly affected designs. Clothes were tighter, rooms were more functional and versatile, and buildings were more efficient and simple.

No More Business as Usual. Once the United States entered the war, the entire country began a period of intense social and economic transformation. The imperative to produce goods necessary for the war galvanized the entire country. Women, minorities, and teenagers flocked to urban centers to work in high-paying war-industry jobs. Many Americans at home finally had money to buy new products, new clothes, and new homes after years of economic hardship. Ironically, however, most of these desired items were in short supply. The dearth of goods created a desire for them that fueled a period of intense consumerism later in the decade as Americans eagerly stocked their homes with new products, filled their closets with the latest fashions, and parked their new cars in their suburban garages.

The Automobile Industry. The war produced both unprecedented restrictions and opportunities for industries. The interruption of business as usual rejuvenated some businesses while forcing others to close. In the case of the automobile industry, the war temporarily suspended the development of new designs and models as manufacturers shifted to supplying defense needs. Overnight, it seemed, automobile plants churned out thousands of tanks, airplanes, and anti-aircraft weapons. Detroit essentially stopped making cars, and sales plummeted. Yet in converting to defense work, companies benefited from an influx of new income, new technology, and new ideas. This helped American car manufacturers dominate the postwar global market.

Fashion. The war kept the feminine silhouette at its 1939 look: padded square shoulders in suits and dresses that narrowed at the waist and fell straight down to midcalf. The government limited the amount of fabric that could be used in dresses, coats, and suits in an effort to save every yard of cloth and to discourage the cycle of discarding the unfashionable for the latest new look. The classic dresses of the 1940s were tailored and elegant in their formfitting lines yet were unadorned by buttons, pockets, or other extras. Rather than these embellishments, women dressed up their suits with accessories such as eye-catching hats; long, flat, leather handbags; high heels; and red lipstick.

Menswear. Men's fashions in the 1940s were also static and restricted. Men stopped wearing double-breasted suits and the classic vest-jacket-slacks combination and instead dressed in simple two-piece suits in gray, brown, or black. Pants had smaller cuffs, shirts had fewer pockets, and jackets were squared with shoulder padding. Yet unlike women's wear in the 1940s, men's fashion design almost completely ceased, as more and more men joined the war. The producers of men's clothes stopped making suits and started making uniforms, creating a domestic shortage in clothing for men.

Modernist Architects. The war changed Western architecture by driving many famous European architects to the United States. These prestigious émigrés took posts in U.S. universities and firms and trained a generation of students in the modernist International Style. Notables such as Walter Gropius, Marcel Breuer, Eliel and Eero Saarinen, and Ludwig Mies van der Rohe transformed the look of U.S. cities with their tall skyscrapers sheathed in glass and chrome. American architect Frank Lloyd Wright, who began a surprising second career in the mid 1930s with his naturalistic designs, was the lone voice against the Internationalist aesthetic coming to dominate American architecture.

Prefabricated Houses. The war also spawned new developments in prefabrication. Because of the great need for military housing and for temporary accommodations for defense workers, American architects experimented with factory made housing. Military bases at home and abroad relied on these inexpensive and efficient new units, which were typically long, low buildings built on a slab of cement with few internal walls. Innovators created a range of unique solutions to these housing problems, and many observers believed that such revolutions in prefabricated housing would permanently change U.S. cities. While many of these utopian expectations never materialized, the war nonetheless expanded the use of prefabrication and the development of inexpensive housing. Abraham Levitt capitalized on these developments to build the largest suburbs in the world at that time. Levittowns, communities of new suburbanites living in nearly identical houses for less than ten thousand dollars, appeared rapidly by the late 1940s. The growth of such suburban communities both depended on the automobile to transport people to urban work centers and helped to fuel America's postwar romance with the car.

New Materials at Home. American homes were also affected by war shortages. Household goods switched from metal to plastic or glass. Pipes, light fixtures, blenders, juicers, and pots and pans were made in ceramic or plastic instead of metal. Linoleum for floors became popular, as did the use of plywood paneling. The new wonder fiber, nylon, produced by Du Pont, promised to increase the durability of carpets and furniture materials, improve screens, and contribute to many other household products, but the government commandeered Du Pont's supplies for the duration of the war.

The Beginning of the Postwar Period. With the end of the war in 1945, Americans found much had changed. The Depression of the 1930s had long passed, and more Americans had more money in their pockets and in their savings accounts than they had in a generation. Likewise, as industries converted back to domestic production, they introduced a new range of moderately priced, technologically improved products, including better cars, refrigerators, radios, televisions, washing machines, and vacuum cleaners. While some women left wartime jobs to have children, others held on to their jobs so they could buy new products. Americans were eager to put the war behind them, and they did so by turning their energies to home and family and by building a new sense of security.

Fashion Reconversion. With the home at the center of many Americans' attention, fashion and design also reconverted to emphasize maternal femininity, corporate masculinity, and the growing size of the American postwar family. Automobile manufacturers produced large, streamlined, powerful cars that resembled America's victorious aircraft bombers. The Sunday drive became a ritual as Americans proudly displayed their new cars and enjoyed watching and being watched by their neighbors. Women's fashions emphasized soft curves and full skirts as the New Look displaced the angular, narrow wartime look. Men's fashions adopted the corporate look of gray and brown suits, crisp white shirts, and narrow ties. After work, men dressed in sporty leisure wear comfortable enough to wear when barbecuing or playing with children.

The Age of Affluence. With more things to buy and with more Americans in a buying mood, the country entered an unprecedented period of economic expansion. The affluence of the 1950s had its roots in the technological advances of the war years as well as wartime restrictions on the production of goods, which left a backlog of appliances, carpets, clothes, and cars unbought. As the decade ended, clothes were luxurious, cars were covered with shiny chrome, and corporate America glittered with metal and glass. Americans retreated to suburbia and enjoyed the spoils of a hard-won victory.

TOPICS IN THE NEWS

AMERICAN FASHION GOES TO WAR

Americans Watch and Worry. Even before the United States entered World War II, American life had been transformed by the fighting in Europe. While terrified at the prospect of war, Americans nonetheless felt relief at the first stirrings of economic recovery from what had seemed like the endless Depression of the 1930s. U.S. factories worked hard trying to meet the civilian and defense needs of European allies, which improved employment in the United States. But as much as Americans enjoyed the new prosperity generated by the war, the security for which they longed was threatened by the increasing pressure for the United States to enter the hostilities. In December 1941 President Franklin D. Roosevelt declared war on Japan, and Americans soberly prepared for battle.

Domestic Preparations. As with many industries, the war presented the American fashion world with both unprecedented restrictions and unique opportunities. The war affected fashion through the newly developed War Production Board (WPB), through which Roosevelt exercised "general responsibility" over the nation's economy. The WPB allocated scarce materials and adjusted domestic production and consumption to war needs. Through the Supply Priorities and Allocations Board (SPAB), the government set price limits on consumer goods and directed existing supplies to war-related industries. For fashion, this translated into restrictions on fabric for clothes, metals for zippers and buttons, silk for stockings, and leather for shoes.

Wartime Domestic Restrictions. The WPB touched nearly every aspect of the consumer economy, including the fashion industry. Domestic supplies of wool, cotton, linen, rayon, silk, and nylon were commandeered by the government for military uniforms and supplies. So great was the military's need for fabric that it depleted stocks of clothes, coats, linens, and shoes available on the home front. The board even went so far as to tell people what to knit (wool socks, for example) and to whom to send it (the Red Cross). Volunteer groups gathered and recycled tin, aluminum, brass, and rubber to supply the need for war materials.

L-85. Order L-85, first announced in 1943, affected every kind of clothing produced in America except for wedding gowns, maternity clothes, infant wear, and religious vestments. The guidelines outlined by the government dictated that only one and three-fourths yards of fabric be used per dress. The purpose of Order L-85 was to discourage any change in fashion that would necessitate adjustment of machinery, technique, extra labor, or changed consumer expectations. The government wanted all its resources directed at winning the war, which meant that every yard of cloth, every button, and every silk stocking was seen as crucial to victory. Yet the government did not have to define strict guidelines for every aspect of fashion. The market did much of that, as fabrics and supplies dwindled.

Goodbye to the Double-Breasted Suit. The war's effect on women's fashions was to freeze them at 1939 looks, but government fabric restrictions more directly changed what men wore. Instead of three-piece suits, men now wore single-breasted, two-piece suits with pants without pleats or cuffs. "Fancy-back" jackets, which had a long pleat down the back and gathered slightly at the waist and which were popularized by Clark Gable, were banned, as were double-breasted dinner suits. Beyond these restrictions, the most important force limiting menswear was the marketplace itself. Men's clothing manufacturers turned all their energy to producing uniforms rather than civilian clothes. In some regions of the country men had difficulty even finding a suit to buy. Stocks emptied and were not replaced until the war ended. Such shortages were felt most acutely after the war when men returned from overseas to find that stores had little to offer them, no matter the price.

Narrow Silhouette for Women. Order L-85 shortened women's hemlines and popularized hip-length jackets and narrow pants. To save cloth, blouses were pared of cuffs, double yokes, and sashes and were adorned with only one pocket. Scarves and hoods were also restricted.

Due to limits on wool, women were encouraged to dress in wool blends and rayon variations such as rayon gabardine, which became the most prevalent wool substitute for both men's and women's wear.

Limits on Leather. Leather was also highly prized by the government. Since foot soldiers used up to a pair of boots a month, Order L-217 restricted the amount of leather available for civilian shoes. Shoe manufacturers turned to cork, rope, and plastic as alternatives to leather soles. Order L-217 went so far as to dictate six colors of leather permitted for women's shoes and specified that no more than two colors could be used in each shoe. Fabrics filled in for leather wherever possible in pocketbooks, belts, and shoes such as the espadrille. Despite the fact that the military replaced the leather Sam Browne belt in its uniform in 1943, leather remained a luxury item well into the postwar years.

Dyes, Makeup, and Soap. Restrictions were also placed on colored fabrics, makeup, and soap. Artificial dyes were made from the same raw material needed in dynamite manufacturing, and during the war those substances were available in limited quantities for fabric producers. While American women continued to enjoy a range of colored fabrics throughout the war, they were urged to wear undyed materials as much as possible. Alcohol and glycerine, components in makeup, perfume, and soaps, were also needed for the war effort. Plastic makeup containers and other domestic applications for plastic such as aspirin bottles were also in short supply, as was rubber for girdles, brassieres, and rain boots.

Revolution in Hosiery. Women's silk stockings were one of the first items to be affected by the war. Japan, long the largest source of silk in the world, raised the price of silk throughout the late 1930s. Women complained in 1939 about the high cost of silk stockings — up from $.69 to $1.89 per pair — and their fragility. Women wanted a stronger stocking that could withstand many washings without tearing or running. On 19 February 1940 Du Pont announced the development of a new synthetic fiber that had the strength of elastic but the sheerness of silk, promising that its new fiber, nylon, would soon replace silk in stockings. Yet in 1940 nylon stockings were hard to get and no less expensive than silk. Despite these obstacles many American women sought out the new stockings.

Silk Versus Nylon. With the outbreak of war between Japan and the United States in December 1941, Japan ended all shipments of silk, which sent the price of silk stockings skyrocketing and consumers into a frenzy of buying and hoarding. The military restrictions on the civilian use of nylon came months after Du Pont released its first shipment. The government commandeered all nylon for use in parachutes, airplane tires, netting, and tents. American women would have to wait for the revolution in hosiery until after the war. Until then they tried to find the few stockings available, and a brisk black

POSTWAR SERVICE FOR NYLON

During World War II, Du Pont, the Delaware producer of nylon, discovered a wide array of applications for its famous new fiber. Nylon was invented in the 1930s and initially used in women's stockings, but it soon proved useful in such products as toothbrushes, parachutes, aircraft tires, cords, and surgical sutures. Anticipating the postwar market, Du Pont began wartime experiments with nylon as a solid plastic designed to be as versatile as glass. Du Pont hoped that nylon would be used after the war in outdoor furniture; seats for subways, trolleys, and buses; drapery and upholstery fabrics, show curtains, slipcovers, and window screens; tennis and badminton racket strings and fishing lines; paint brushes; and shoes, handbags, and luggage.

Source: "Nylon for Everything," *Time*, 42 (16 August 1943): 38–39.

market developed to meet the demand. Many women began painting seams on their legs in the summer to give them the appearance of wearing stockings when they were not.

Accessories. Jewelry was also affected by wartime restrictions. Platinum was reserved for military uses, and much jewelry was made from yellow, pink, and white gold and set with large, shiny stones such as topaz, aquamarine, and amethyst. Mexican jewelry, with its bold designs and bright colors, became popular in the 1940s. With scarves as limited as stockings, these large pieces often were the only adornment in the stylized, trim look of the war years.

Sources:
Caroline Rennolds Milbank, *Couture: The Great Fashion Designers* (London: Thames & Hudson, 1985);

Milbank, *New York Fashion: The Evolution of American Style* (New York: Abrams, 1989).

CLOTHES FOR WOMEN

Shoulder Pads and Hats. The dominant silhouette of the early 1940s featured broad shoulders that gracefully tapered into a tailored waist over a narrow skirt that fell just below the knees. Shoulder pads were found in nearly every dress, suit, and jacket. The padded, broad shoulders lent women an air of strength and authority, traits valued in women in the 1940s and seen as crucial to surviving the war. Most outfits were topped with a hat, which aided in the popularity of American milliners such as Lily Daché, John Frederics, and Sally Victor. Hat designers added tall brims that gave the appearance of height or wide ones that gave a sense of summertime grace. Others trimmed the crown to the bare minimum, topping it with

Scene at the Boston Store in Chicago in February 1942, when nylon stockings were offered for seventy-nine cents a pair

wiry fabric curls, veils, bows, jewelry, or fur. When wool was scarce, Daché used yarn, specifically mop yarn and twine, and even made caps from the gold epaulets of uniforms.

Popular Looks. Despite government regulations and restrictions, women in the 1940s had a variety of looks from which to choose. One of the most dominant included a padded, broad-shouldered jacket and pencil skirt worn with platform-soled shoes and a high-crowned hat, large jewelry, long pocketbook, and bold red lipstick. A variation was a short jacket worn over a slightly flared skirt, a string of pearls, and pumps. Many women tucked a small piece of lace in the pocket or collar of these outfits as a feminine contrast to the military look popular in this period. Women often wore their hair in two contrasting looks. The first, popularized by Joan Crawford, included soft, partially curled pageboy bangs with long hair pulled back off the face and neck. The second, made popular by Veronica Lake, was a much looser look, with long hair worn to the shoulders, parted on the side, and falling dramatically across the face.

Casual and Practical. Many women spent the war years in gabardine tailored shirtwaist dresses that were

comfortable as well as fashionable and came in a variety of fabrics and colors. The "town and country" look had a casual feel without imitating men's traditional sportswear. The peasant look — drawstring neckline, small puffed sleeves, and gathered, narrow skirt — was also popular. Dinner wear was scaled back for the average woman during the war. Claire McCardell designed evening wear that came with a matching apron for hostesses who did their own cooking. High-style evening wear was columnar in design, with added drapery to give it an elegant, almost Greek, feel. Other classic evening dresses were designed to resemble a Renaissance-period costume.

Youth Fashions. The word *teenager* entered standard usage in the 1940s and was distinctively American. Along with the new title came new social rituals, new looks, and new behaviors generated by and for teenagers. In fashion this translated into sweater sets for girls worn over narrow skirts that flared at the knee, bobby socks, and loafers or saddle shoes. Boys wore V-necked sweaters, short cotton jackets, and loafers. Blue jeans, associated with manual labor and thus unacceptable for

BOOTLEGS AND BLACK MARKETS

In 1946 *Newsweek* reported that women were finding stockings in the oddest places. In New York a butcher boy could deliver a pair of nylons for $3, nearly double the cost at a store. A cigar store just off Broadway had them for $3.50 if the customer said, "Charlie sent me." In other American cities the story was the same. Why? By the end of February 1946 the nation's manufacturers had turned out 76,872,912 pairs of nylons, almost two pairs for every American woman old enough to wear them, but millions of them were disappearing. Or rather, they were moving through the booming black market that had begun during the war. American women, *Newsweek* reported, were tired of standing in line for hours to get one pair of stockings of undetermined color and often of inferior quality at "ceiling prices." They resented being gouged by black marketeers, yet their need for stockings made them depend on them just the same. Beauty parlors buzzed with rumors: "Where have all the nylons gone? To Mexico?" No, government officials explained. The black market was the big hole down which the nylons were vanishing. Finally, in mid April the attorney general ordered the Justice Department to shut down the secret commerce and crack down on the marketeers.

Source: "Stockings: Leg Bootleg," *Newsweek*, 27 (29 April 1946): 66.

---

school, were worn by boys playing or doing chores around the house.

Off to School. College-bound women preferred skirts, sweaters, and jumpers to the suited look of Hollywood. Particularly popular were the clothes of the B. H. Wragge Company. Its collections of separates — jackets, skirts, vests, blouses, jumpers, shirtwaist dresses, and coats — were designed to mix and match in a variety of combinations. Many college women collected as many Wragge pieces as they could. This concept of mix-and-match separates became one of the most important elements of American ready-to-wear fashion. Many male undergraduates enlisted in the military, but those who stayed home wore white shirts with ties along with sweaters or jackets. Pants and blue jeans were worn to relax in the dormitory or outside. College-age women made going hatless a new fashion, preferring longer hairstyles and curls similar to the style of Veronica Lake to the extravagant hat favored by women a few years their senior.

Source:
Caroline Rennolds Milbank, *New York Fashion: The Evolution of American Style* (New York: Abrams, 1989).

ENLISTED WEAR ABROAD AND AT HOME: MEN AND WOMEN IN UNIFORM

Men in Uniform. When American men enlisted in the army in 1941 they were issued a uniform that was the final product of hard-won battle experience, design savvy, and mass production. Overriding concerns in designing military uniforms were fabric durability and the ability of the fabric to dry quickly. The most immediate effect of the war on traditional uniform design was the use of new fabrics. With soldiers in the tropics, uniforms were made of cotton, shirts were looser and more comfortable, and new fibers such as nylon helped create a barrier against insects. Pants also changed. Replacing the tight leggings used in World War I, pants narrowed around the ankle. Uniforms also came in a range of colors to help soldiers blend into the diverse areas in which they fought. Officers' shirts ranged from yellowish-drab to dark green. Nonregulation gray or forest-green shirts, trousers, and caps appeared, and the yellowish chino khaki fabric became popular.

What Soldiers Wore. A U.S. infantryman in the European theater in 1944 would typically be dressed in an olive-drab wool service shirt and trousers, a greenish water-repellent M43 field jacket, and a supply of pile liners and woolen sweaters to be worn under the basic field uniform depending on weather conditions. Knitted woolen stocking caps were worn under the helmet. The soldier would also be issued a high-laced combat boot with a buckled ankle flap that acted as a built-in gaiter. In the summer, or for those men fighting in the Pacific, soldiers wore pale, lightweight twill shirts and trousers, a light cap, and boots.

The Versatile Helmet. In 1942 the British-styled helmet was replaced by the versatile M1 helmet, which consisted of a steel outer shell with a chin strap and a plastic-fiber inner shell or liner. The light liner could be worn alone away from the front rather than the heavy and more tiring steel shell. The outer shell was crucial protection from shell fragments and bullets, yet it could also be used as a seat, a washbasin, a soup kettle, or an entrenching tool in emergencies. Because of the inner lining, the steel shell could be worn immediately without thorough cleaning. A light webbing typically covered the helmet.

Women in the Military. World War II presented women with new opportunities to join the military. More than 350,000 women served in the war as nurses, clerical workers, and service pilots and in the Coast Guard. In 1942 the Women's Auxiliary Corps (Wac) was created, and in 1943 women's divisions of the U.S. Navy and the Marines were formed. New images of women in uniform filled the nation's newspapers, magazines, and newsreels. Women working for volunteer agencies at home, such as the Women's Voluntary Services, often wore uniforms as well. New York mayor Fiorello La Guardia, acting in his new capacity as national director of civilian defense, appointed a committee of New York designers to submit

Women's fashion, 1943

ideas for civilian uniforms. Mainbocher, an American designer just back from Paris in 1940, designed uniforms for the Women Accepted for Volunteer Emergency Service (Waves), the women's division of the U.S. Navy; the Marine Women's Corps; the American Red Cross; and the Girl Scouts.

Defense Work Shortages. As men left to fight the war, they created a labor shortage at home. The tremendous demand for tanks, bombers, ships, and munitions required thousands of new workers to produce the necessary war goods to defeat the Axis powers. To meet the need for workers, industry turned to women and minorities — workers formerly shut out of the high-paying skilled jobs. More than six million women, including wives and mothers of all racial and ethnic groups, went to work outside the home for the first time during the war.

Women's Work Clothes. Most of these women found work in clerical and factory jobs in war-related industries.

But the most newsworthy jobs women held during the war were in shipbuilding and armaments factories, predominantly in the West. These women frequently wore the same clothing on the job as men: sturdy overalls or trousers, hard hats, tool belts, and thick-soled shoes. Yet many new female workers resisted looking too much like their male counterparts and continued to wear skirts and dresses, which had the potential to get caught in the heavy machinery many women used. Boeing solved the problem of what women should wear to work. In May 1943 *Life* reported a West Coast fashion fad caused by the new work clothes designed by Muriel King for Boeing's new female workers. Boeing liked the new uniforms because they were pared of unnecessary fabrics; neither sleeves, flaps, nor cuffs would catch in machinery. The workers liked the uniforms because of their flattering cuts (*Life* described them as having "slimming waistlines, high-cut bosom lines, and trim trousers").

VERONICA LAKE'S HAIR

In November 1941 *Life* declared that "the 49th minute of the movie *I Wanted Wings* is already marked as one of the historic moments of the cinema. It was the moment when an unknown young actress named Veronica Lake walked into camera range and waggled a head of long blonde hair at a suddenly enchanted public." Not since the blonde locks of Jean Harlow in the 1930s had Hollywood produced such hair mania. Lake's hair, *Life* reported, had been "acclaimed by men, copied by girls, cursed by mothers, and viewed with alarm by moralists." Alternately called "the strip-tease style," the "sheep-dog style," and the "bad-girl style" by fans and foes, Lake's hair had propelled her into the center of a fashion controversy: could "good girls" let their hair dangle across the forehead and swankily cover an eye? Were Lake's locks bad for morals or good for morale? *Life* said, "Miss Lake thus finds herself . . . the owner and custodian of a personal property comparable in value, fame and world influence to . . . Fred Astaire's feet, or Marlene Dietrich's legs."

Source: "Veronica Lake's Hair Is Cinema Property of World Influence," *Life*, 11 (24 November 1941): 58–62.

Emphasizing the Feminine. While women enjoyed the new opportunities war work presented them, many were concerned about maintaining their femininity while doing so-called men's work. Many war workers wore fancy hairstyles and heavy makeup to work. Rosie the Riveter, the image of the female welder with her hair pulled back, with lipstick and pink-painted fingernails, became a national icon. After punching their factory time cards, most women made a point of returning to the more traditional feminine look. Popular leisure wear emphasized the feminine with belted or tailored dresses that pinched in the waist and were made of soft colored and printed fabrics.

Sources:

Barbara Clark and Kathy Peiss, *Men and Women: A History of Costume, Gender, and Power* (Washington, D.C.: Smithsonian Institution, 1989);

John Elting and Michael McAfee, eds., *Military Uniforms in America: The Modern Era — From 1868* (Westbrook, Conn.: Presidio, 1988);

Martin Windrow and Gerry Embleton, *Military Dress of North America, 1665–1970* (New York: Scribners, 1973).

FASHION DESIGNERS

Cutting the French Apron Strings. As was true for many industries, the war had an unexpected effect on the American fashion industry. With the fall of Paris to the Nazis in 1940, the city was effectively cut off from the world of international fashion shows, fashion journalism, and fashion manufacturing. Without the French as a guide, American fashion was forced inward. This gave American designers the opportunity to make a name for themselves with the American public.

A Boom to the Industry. Under the encouragement of Mayor Fiorello La Guardia, New York made a bid to be the next fashion capital of the Western world. La Guardia worked with designers and the press to organize new shows and new press coverage of New York designers. Yet the dominance in fashion of New York was challenged almost immediately by Los Angeles, Philadelphia, and Boston, as designers across the country enjoyed their own liberation from French influence. The American fashion industry boomed during the war years, demonstrating that American designers had style and ingenuity. The clothes Americans produced in large quantities were stylish and well made.

Hollywood's Influence. With Paris silent, Hollywood became a dominant influence in setting trends. Adrian, Hollywood's premier costume designer, introduced high fashion to millions of American moviegoers. His imposing square-shouldered fashions, designed originally to camouflage Joan Crawford's large shoulders, soon became trademarks for them both. In 1941 he established his own line of women's clothes, Adrian, Ltd., in Beverly Hills and offered fashionable ready-to-wear and custom-designed clothes. While New York–based fashion magazines jealously ignored him whenever they could, many women embraced his look and made Adrian designs the most prevalent look of the 1940s.

Innovations and Imagination. American designers were innovative in the face of limited supplies and government restrictions on fabrics. Metal for zippers and buttons was needed by the military and became a luxury item. Designers adjusted their patterns to reduce the need for metallic fastening devices. Corsets returned to laces instead of zippers, while designer Claire McCardell used buttons and made dresses from surplus cotton balloon cloth. B. H. Wragge, a separates designer for the college set, showed wrap dresses that fastened with giant safety pins. At the opposite economic extreme, Karen Stark designed dresses that used sterling silver zippers, a metal too costly for the military. Others cut dresses that draped so that they needed only two buttons. Wholesale designer Joset Walker launched a drawstring-waisted dress that was easy to wash and iron and did not use any fastening devices.

Patriotic Designs. American designers made staying within the government limits on clothes a patriotic duty, and many took pride in using even less fabric than was allotted. Vera Maxwell, known for her elegant tweeds, designed a coat using only two and one-quarter yards of fabric. The coat had no collar or revers, had no overlap at the front, and was perfectly straight. Connie Adams designed a coat made of the best-quality mattress ticking

WACS, in light colored uniforms, and WAVES, in navy blue

instead of compromising with inferior wool or other materials. The trim, striped, tailored coat with its military line of eight brass buttons perfectly symbolized the ingenuity of American designers during the war. In the same spirit, Adrian designed the stylish Victory suit. It had a long, narrow jacket that fastened at the waist with a fabric tie of the same material. The shirt was made with a yoke of nonmatching, recycled material that did not show under the jacket.

Solving the Supply Problem. American designers invented a range of solutions to the problem of dwindling supplies. Tom Brigance came up with the "sleeveless sleeve," made of folds of fabric that gently cupped the shoulder. Other designers relied on cap sleeves, which saved a full yard of cloth. Fira Benson put "income tax" pockets on jackets, so named because they felt bottomless to the wearer because they ended at the hem rather than at the typical five-inch length. Because the pockets were cut in the jacket itself, they required less fabric. In the interests of saving fabric, Harvey Berin came out with a ready-to-wear dress in 1942 that looked like a suit. The sleeves and skirt were made of crepe, the more valuable wool fabric reserved for a vestlike effect. Rhinestone buttons made the dress versatile for evening or day wear. For women whose houses were cold due to a shortage of heating oil, designer Mainbocher provided evening sweaters and cardigans with embroidered glitter and beads. Other designers came up with elegant versions of the jumpsuit and coveralls worn by many workers at defense-related industries.

What Would Follow? With the end of the war in 1945, many Americans speculated about new postwar looks. With no significant change in the silhouette since the late 1930s, fashion editors in newspaper columns across the country speculated over materials and designs. By 1946 fabrics were returning to prewar levels of avail-ability, and American designers began experimenting with more frivolous and feminine fashions. Skirts became fuller and longer and were dropped from a hip yoke. Coats were cut with much more cloth, and dresses featured leg-of-mutton sleeves. Tunics and bustles returned, as did high heels and sheer hose. As many Americans started moving from the city to the suburbs, American fashion designers pioneered a new style whose quiet feminine elegance was suitable for the home, not just the public world of the theater, the opera, and restaurants.

Nylon. One of the most significant influences in postwar fashion was the introduction of nylon to a range of fabrics and household items. Nylon soon displaced silk in hosiery and rubber in corsets and appeared in lingerie, negligees, blouses, scarves, gloves, and sweaters. It also appeared in dress fabrics as blends because it washed easily and required little, if any, ironing. Manufacturers of luxury items initially looked down on nylon, but its advantages in terms of care and shape soon won over most of the American public despite criticism from the world of high couture.

The New Look. In 1947 French designer Christian Dior unveiled his New Look, which consisted of a tiny wasp waistline, longer and fuller skirts, sloping shoulders, and soft, full collars and sleeves. Avoiding the padded shoulders that characterized wartime women's fashion, the style introduced padded bras and skirts in their place. While the so-called New Look had been popular throughout the war, Dior added a fuller and more curved feminine style, a dramatic departure from the classic 1939 silhouette. American designers followed suit. Ceil Chapman introduced a bouffant evening dress that emphasized a woman's curves and delicacy. Similarly, Anne Fogarty introduced a crinoline underskirt to be worn under full-cut skirts that was particularly popular with petite and college-age women.

Sixth Army officer in M1 steel helmet, New Guinea, 1944

For most men not in uniform during the war years the dominant look was short hair, shoulder-padded jackets that narrowed at the waist, and pants that tapered with little if any cuffing. But a small group of American men adopted an appearance that expressed dissension against the idea of clean-cut, patriotic manhood. Excluded by age, ethnic background, race, or poverty from mainstream society, some young Mexican Americans and some young African American men wore zoot suits. In defiance of the clothing restrictions, the zoot suit consisted of a oversized jacket with shoulder pads and exaggerated lapels which fell to knee level. The pants were baggy at the knee and narrowed at the ankle. Zoot-suiters finished off the look with a pocket watch on a long chain and a large, floppy hat. Women put together their own version, consisting of a long jacket; a short, tight black skirt with fishnet stockings; and a pompadour hairdo and heavy makeup. A dramatic contrast to the military uniforms of the day, the zoot suit symbolized a rejection of mainstream culture by young Mexican Americans and African Americans. On the night of 4 June 1943 two hundred cars and taxis filled with white sailors roamed the streets of east Los Angeles in search of young Mexican Americans dressed in zoot suits. The sailors assaulted their victims at random, and riots broke out that lasted for days. To contain the chaos on the streets the Los Angeles City Council passed legislation making the wearing of a zoot suit in public a criminal offense. A federal judge issued a restraining order against a clothing store that specialized in the suits.

Sources: Thomas J. McCarthy, "Report from Los Angeles," *Commonweal,* 38 (25 June 1943): 243–244;

Ruth D. Tuck, "Behind the Zoot Suit Riots," *Survey Graphic,* 32 (August 1943): 313–316.

Celebrating Femininity. Dior's New Look marked not just a new postwar silhouette but a new celebration of the differences between men and women. Curves attained through corsets, seen in the 1920s and 1930s as things only old ladies wore, were now essential accessories for the fashion-conscious woman. Women's silhouettes were no longer angular — as seen in Adrian's designs for Joan Crawford, with her padded shoulders and narrow skirt — but were soft, busty, and molded like Marilyn Monroe's hourglass figure. While Adrian's designs dressed women for their expanded roles in the wartime home front, Dior's fashions dressed women for their traditional roles as wives and girlfriends. The country was largely in step with the New Look emphasis on femininity and the home. Dior's statement "I know very well the women" seemed in 1947 to be absolutely correct.

Fashion Turmoil. However, the New Look was not embraced by all American women. In fact, the New Look so angered some women that they organized to protest it. In Dallas, Bobbie Woodward, a twenty-four-year-old housewife and mother of two, saw no reason why she should hide her legs under long skirts and why her draftsman husband should buy her a new wardrobe. In August 1947 she founded the Little Below the Knee (LBK) Club to encourage a small drop in hems rather than a wholesale return to long skirts. By September *Time* had declared that a counterrevolution against the New Look was under way, as branches of the LBK Club opened across the country. San Antonio LBK members picketed downtown stores with the cry, "The Alamo fell, but our hemlines will not." Husbands who disliked the prices for New Look fashions formed the League of Broke Husbands and picketed in Valdosta, Georgia. *Time* went so far as to suggest that the New Look was merely a ploy to boost the fashion industry. Despite such protests, the New Look remained popular and dominated American fashions until the 1960s.

Prices. High prices placed the New Look out of the reach of many consumers, and many deemed it an insult to tempt women with what they could not afford — or

Mattress-ticking coat by Connie Adams, 1946. It cost about $17.

even afford to copy. But Dior's were not the only clothes to be out of reach financially to many women. A simple daytime dress by a well-known designer in 1949 cost $110 to $135; a designer suit or coat cost anywhere from $195 to $450. Alterations were costly as well. Such high prices helped the ready-to-wear industry as women turned their sights on what they could afford rather than to the luxuries of Paris.

The Gray Flannel Corporate Look. With men home from the war, men's fashions also changed in order to emphasize their return to the role of breadwinner. The look that dominated men's fashions was the gray flannel suit: a three-button, single-breasted, dark-gray flannel suit with narrow shoulders, small lapels, flaps on the pockets, and pleatless pants. A variation came in dark blue. Men wore simple, crisp cotton shirts with slim striped ties. The Chesterfield beige raincoat with a black velvet collar or the single-breasted, straight-lined tweed overcoat were popular. Narrow-brimmed hats with pinched crowns completed the look. When relaxing at home, men donned relaxed, casual sportswear. Jeans or cotton pants and cotton sneakers were worn with sweaters, cardigans, or tweed jackets.

Sources:

Elaine Tyler May, *Homeward Bound: American Families in the Cold War* (New York: Basic Books, 1988);

Caroline Rennolds Milbank, *Couture: The Great Fashion Designers* (London: Thames & Hudson, 1985);

Milbank, *New York Fashion: The Evolution of American Style* (New York: Abrams, 1989).

IMPORTING THE INTERNATIONAL STYLE: ARCHITECTURE IN THE UNITED STATES

The Look. World War II indirectly brought modern architecture to the United States. Modern architecture emphasized function over form and simplicity over elaboration and embraced new materials and metals. The cool surfaces of glass and metal characteristic of what Philip Johnson and Henry Russell Hitchcock called the International Style captured the modern fascination with technology and applied it to big and small structures alike. One center of modernist architecture was the Bauhaus in Germany, which gained notoriety in the 1930s through its principle designers Peter Bejrems, Walter Gropius, and Marcel Breuer. Their "monuments to modernism" owed nothing outwardly to traditional and local architectural vocabularies but instead emphasized the inseparability of structure (materials used and the foundations of the structure) and form (style).

New Arrivals. One important and immediate effect of the war on American architecture came in the years before the United States entered the conflict. Many European architects fled to the United States in the late 1930s to escape the political oppression of the Nazis and an increasingly less favorable economic environment. The transplanting of such talent to American cities, particularly Chicago, shifted the center of architecture from Europe to America and American design schools. Gropius was appointed chairman of the architecture department at Harvard University, where he hired longtime partner Breuer; Eero Saarinen taught at Cranbrook Academy of Art in Bloomfield Hills, Michigan; László Moholy-Nagy, a former colleague of Gropius, taught at the Institute of Design in Chicago; Alvar Aalto worked at the Massachusetts Institute of Technology (MIT); and Eric Mendelson taught at the University of Southern California.

Adapting Modernism to America. These émigré architects helped to establish modernist architecture in the United States. In doing so, they introduced the International Style to their students while adapting its modernist vision to their new country. Gropius's first American works were detached houses done in collaboration with Breuer. The houses, such as Gropius's own house (1937) in Lincoln, Massachusetts, and the Robinson House (1947) in Williamstown, Massachusetts, combined classic New England vernacular architecture with modernist elements. The Lincoln House was constructed from a wood frame with vertical board siding along with glass block, low walls of irregular stones, and a prefabricated cast-iron spiral stair, giving the New England shingle house an entirely new and modern appearance. Similarly,

Aalto's design for the Baker House dormitory (1948) at MIT altered the smooth, rectilinear slab of the International Style by erecting a six-story serpentine building, textured in red brick, that curved along the Charles River.

The Glass Wall. A typical feature of the International Style was the use of large glass panes for walls. The so-called glass curtain brought natural light deep into the building while functioning as a wall. Thus the glass wall or curtain perfectly captured the modernist joining of function and form by blurring the line between outside and inside, giving the appearance that the interior space reached continuously outward. Johnson's residence in New Canaan, Connecticut, the Glass House (1949), became the model for modern architecture's application in home design. The Glass House was just that: a small, geometric house, with walls almost entirely of glass, that blended into the landscape despite its use of modern materials.

Ludwig Mies van der Rohe. Ludwig Mies van der Rohe established the recognizable style of the 1940s by providing a working vernacular for modernist American design. His earlier work in Germany focused on transforming the skyscraper from a uniform stone block to a more fluid and technically advanced structure. He was one of the first architects to use the glass wall or curtain as a thin "skin" over the "skeleton" of the building's structure. His first executed buildings in the United States were in Chicago — the Promontory Apartments (1948–1949) and the pair of apartment towers for 860–880 Lake Shore Drive (1948–1951). Both relied heavily on steel grids framing long ribbons of glass.

New Applications for Modernism. Mies van der Rohe also designed the campus of the Illinois Institute of Technology (IIT, 1939–1941), where he headed the architecture faculty from 1938 to 1958. The low buildings were predominantly rectilinear in shape and were made of simple materials, such as black-painted steel, buff-colored brick, and aluminum-framed windows. The IIT project, together with his glass-curtain walls, became a foundation for postwar architecture. IIT was also the first modern campus to be designed by one architect.

Miesian Architecture. His glass wall became the most visible sign of Miesian architecture and a popular expression of an increasingly technological culture. Pietro Bellushci's Equitable Savings and Loan (1948) in Portland, Oregon, used a polished sheet-aluminum skin to cover the building's reinforced concrete frame. Darker, cast-aluminum spandrels and tinted glass gave the effect of a single, smooth reflective plane more machinelike than any building by Mies van der Rohe. The firm Skidmore, Owings and Merrill made Miesian architecture a symbol of financial muscle, as in the Lever House in New York (1952). Saarinen's early work also drew heavily on the IIT campus plan, most notably in Saarinen's General Motors Technical Center in Warren, Michigan (1948–1965). Johnson also utilized Miesian designs, specifically in his Glass House. Its visible steel framing and open plan, separating rooms by limited partitions or the placement of furniture, emphasized Mies van der Rohe's concentration on structure as expressive form.

The War and the Profession. World War II affected American architecture on many fronts. While the economic depression of the 1930s had slowed construction and kept many architects underemployed, the war presented its own set of limits on the profession. Civilian housing construction was put on hold, as existing supplies were needed for the construction of military bases and temporary housing units. After the war, the need for new buildings burgeoned. The devastation of European cities created a pressing need for new buildings, city streets, factories, and housing. At home, the postwar economic boom generated an unprecedented market for new homes. Architects after the war had plenty of work to do; as a result, the ranks of the profession swelled.

Functionalism Goes to War. Once the United States had entered the war the government took control of all domestic construction. In April 1942 the War Production Board (WPB) issued Order L-41, prohibiting all but essential war construction. With resources for all construction requiring approval from the Supply Priorities and Allocations Board (SPAB), architects turned their attention to large, federally sponsored low-cost housing projects and military bases. With their modular framing, prefabrication, and simple, functional planning, both

Metallurgy and Chemical Engineering Building at the Illinois Institute of Technology designed by Mies van der Rohe and built between 1942 and 1946

demonstrated the very qualities modern architecture espoused. Such housing projects designed by modernists included Channel Heights in San Pedro, California (1943), by Richard Neutra, and Aluminum City Terrace housing in New Kensingson, Pennsylvania (1941), by Gropius and Breuer. Stringent cost limits proved beneficial in these spartan, but distinguished, examples of modern wartime architecture.

Materials and Construction. Plastic became increasingly popular as a building material, as metals were commandeered for defense purposes. Plastics were used in light fixtures, furniture, floor coverings, paints, varnishes, and laminated boards. Low-cost housing for military troops abroad, housing of displaced Europeans, temporary housing for American workers, detention camps for interned Japanese Americans, and other projects stimulated innovative construction techniques. Prefabricated wooden houses were assembled from small units on-site or built in the shop and delivered to the site in sections. Structures were secured by screws, bolts, and glue.

New Ideas. The need for fast, inexpensive housing generated unique designs from American architects. One house designer based his ideas on the circular, galvanized, sheet-steel grain bin, which made single-room structures by stamping insulated steel panels into a dome shape. Popularly known as "igloos," these structures divided the interior space with curtains, were easily transported, and resisted earthquakes, fires, hurricanes, air raids, and in-

sects. Many commentators believed that such houses would transform American cities.

Industrial Architecture. Architects also found work in heavy industry. As business geared up for war by converting to defense-related work, the need for new buildings increased. Albert Kahn's design for the Ford aircraft plant at Willow Run, Michigan, epitomized the wartime need for technical efficiency, quality control, and productivity in industrial buildings. Other noteworthy industrial designs were the North American Aviation plant at Grand Prairie, Texas, the Buick airplane engine plant near Chicago, the Hudson Motor naval gun plant at Detroit, and the Packard Motor Company's Rolls-Royce aircraft motor plant in Detroit.

Postwar Projections. With defense plants and the major part of war housing completed by 1945, architects and engineers began anticipating postwar construction needs. The National Housing Agency, established in 1942 to regulate domestic construction, expected that four hundred thousand houses at a cost of $5,000 each would be needed immediately after the war and predicted that the demand would rise to one million a year. The 1944 Servicemen's Readjustment Act, also known as the GI Bill of Rights, provided servicemen and servicewomen homes costing up to $10,000 without any form of down payment. By 1947 the GI Bill had underwritten mortgages for more than one million veterans. Home owner-

In February 1943 *Newsweek* reported the opening of the largest office building in the world in Arlington, Virginia: the $70 million, five-sided, five-tiered Pentagon, which had no less than sixteen and a half miles of corridors. Housing thirty thousand War Department personnel, the Pentagon was the new nerve center of the nation's war and defense effort. However, the enormous size of the building posed its own set of problems, particularly navigation. Visitors and employees were frequently getting lost in its miles of hallways. One woman, late for an appointment, spent more than two hours searching for her destination. It took the War Department another hour to extricate her from the labyrinth. *Newsweek* reported that visitors were handed a guide card with colored squares denoting the floors and numerals and letters telling the floor, ring, corridor, and bay of the office sought. Guides were provided for the faint of heart. Some employees complained of feeling suffocated in offices that felt more like "a fortress without windows" than a place of employment. Others developed a fear of being in the Pentagon's large open spaces as they wandered through its endless lobbies and corridors. Still others complained that the soundproofing of the new building was so effective that they were unable to work without the din from the street. Relieved Navy Department employees, who were supposed to move into the Pentagon but did not, wrote a little jingle which *Newsweek* published: "Carry me back to the Pentagon Building — Five sides instead of the four that make a square; Carry me back to Old Virginny, 'Cause that's the only way you'll ever get me there!"

Source: "Race between Claustrophobia and Agorophobia for Those Pent Up in Washington's Pentagon," *Newsweek*, 21 (15 February 1943): 64–65.

ship rose from 43.6 percent in 1940 to 55 percent in 1950.

Prefabricated Houses. Several surveys predicted that the postwar house would have one story — including three bedrooms or a room convertible to a third bedroom, the equivalent of two bathrooms, a pitched rather than flat roof, no basement, and fewer but larger windows — and would be mass-produced but not standardized. In 1945 the architecture firm Kump, Wurster and Bernardi introduced a design for postwar housing based on advances in prefabrication during the war. Their design dictated that interior walls would bear no weight, thus allowing complete freedom in arranging rooms. Also in

1945 architect George Fred Keck introduced his Solar Home, in which solar orientation and panel heating were combined to ensure maximum heat efficiency. A gas furnace was used to heat the house through floor-laid clay tile ducts.

The Birth of Levittown and Suburbia. In 1948 Levitt and Sons, the country's largest house builders, transformed a fifteen-hundred-acre Long Island potato field into Levittown, the fastest-growing community in the nation — ten thousand homes by 1950. Their four-room houses — with panel heating, two-room fireplaces, electric kitchens, automatic laundries, and expansion attics — sold for $6,999 to $7,999. Veterans and an eager population waited to purchase a Levitt home. The firm cut its own lumber in its own forests, bought most of its other materials directly from the manufacturers, and hired nonunion labor to keep costs low. The Levitts reversed typical assembly-line techniques to keep up with demand: the unit was stationary, and the laborers moved around it, performed their jobs, and then moved on to the next unit. With such techniques a Levitt house was finished every twenty-four minutes, complete with trees and shrubs. With Levittown, prefabrication and the postwar demand for affordable housing formed a comfortable relationship and helped the growth of suburbia.

Sources:

William Dudley Hunt, Jr., *Encyclopedia of American Architecture* (New York: McGraw-Hill, 1980);

John Jacobus, *Twentieth Century Architecture: The Middle Years, 1940–1965* (New York: Praeger, 1966);

Marcus Whiffen and Frederick Koeper, *American Architecture, 1607–1976* (Cambridge, Mass.: MIT Press, 1981).

MODERN HOMES

A Postwar Housing Boom. In the second half of the decade the United States began to experience what would become the largest housing boom in its history. The economic expansion stimulated by the war translated into more money in the pockets of many people who dreamed of owning a house. Thanks to the GI Bill, veterans enjoyed access to low-interest housing loans and assistance with down payments. These factors meant that after 1945 many Americans were buying houses, often in the newly developed suburbs. The housing options facing American home buyers were eclectic, ranging from the utilitarian to the elegant.

Choices of Styles. The great need for houses in the postwar years was met with an explosion of construction, a refinement of mass production, and a broad mix of styles. In southern California architects revived the Stick style, first introduced at the turn of the century, which was characterized by its use of the wall surface as a decorative element rather than as a functional support. Its other notable features were its gable roof, overhanging eaves, and porches decorated with diagonal or curved braces. The mission style was also revived in California in the postwar years. Like the Stick style, mission-style

In late February 1949 Abraham Levitt and his son Alfred sent replies to the thousands of veterans who had previously applied for inexpensive Levitt houses. The first 350 in line on Monday, 7 March, the Levitts wrote, would get houses in a new group under construction; other applicants, if any, would get slips entitling them to houses as they went up. The price: $7,999 — $90 down and $58 a month. The Levitts anticipated that the line would start forming Sunday night. But at 11 P.M. Friday night, *Newsweek* reported, former GIs began showing up with chairs, sleeping bags, cushions, and food. The GIs organized guards to ward off claim jumpers and made sure that some could go eat without losing their places. By Sunday the line was longer than anyone had imagined, with applicants far outnumbering available houses. The Levitts gave out numbers for 350 houses, took names and addresses for the next batch, and called the police. The police were given the job of explaining to the teeming crowd that the Levitts were sold out. "We could have sold over two thousand homes," commented Levitt.

Source: "The Line at Levitt's," *Newsweek*, 33 (21 March 1949): 66–67.

Equitable Savings and Loan Association Building, Portland, Oregon, designed by Pietro Belluschi and completed in 1948

houses had deep eaves, overhanging roofs, and open porches. The mission style expressed the Hispanic roots of California and that of the Christian missions of the nineteenth century. It incorporated such features as arches, open courtyards, and low, often red, tile roofs. Other styles that appeared in suburbs across the country included the ranch house, a one-story structure with a low-pitched roof, wide, overhanging eaves, a big picture window, and decorative shutters and iron porch supports. The split-level house modified the ranch design by adding a second story to one section of the structure. The colonial-style house, with its classical Greek columns and shuttered windows, continued to dominate American tastes in the East. For consumers interested in architectural purity, the International Style house was also available, characterized by smooth external surfaces curtaining the structure of the building much like skyscrapers of the International Style.

Functionalism. American interior design in the 1940s mirrored architectural concerns with structure and form. Functionalism, as it was called, held that the art of design should be utilitarian. Functionalist designs were dominated by efficiency and economy of production rather than visual appeal, and beauty was considered intrinsically linked to the purity of function. Visual ornamentation, or eye appeal, had no legitimate existence independent of use, thus inverting the traditional preoccupations of interior design.

Functionalist Floor Plans. Functionalism brought about a new sense of interior spatial planning. Functionalists thought that a room should be planned from the center outward; doors, windows, partitions, and other fixed elements should be placed to enhance the convenient use of the room. The ornamental details of traditional design were eliminated. Sobriety and simplicity were dominant characteristics, and the functionalist room was painted in neutral hues. The fascination with utility and the efficient use of space translated into a growth in multipurpose rooms. The living room that also served as a dining room was a common example of such a dual-purpose room, as was the office that served as a third bedroom.

Lighting. Interior designers of the 1940s were also more concerned with lighting than they had been in earlier decades. No longer was lighting added to the room design; rather, it was built into the planning. Large windows made greater use of daylight and became popular. Track lighting and indirect and semidirect lighting by bulbs hidden in coves were also common.

Furniture. Functionalism in furniture design developed partially in response to the new range of materials and fibers available for use and partially from changes in room design. The Victorian style, with its ornate, cluttered interiors, had been popular in America since the turn of the century. By the 1930s designers tended to

Philip Johnson's Glass House in New Canaan, Connecticut, 1949

reject cushioned and textured period pieces and opted instead for spare, simple forms. Chromium alloys and aluminum replaced wood for bracing or supports in chairs, while cushions were replaced by smooth, shaped laminated wood panels. Textile manufacturers experimented to create fabrics of rougher or thicker textures for the spare lines of sofas and chairs. Most important, modern furniture was mass-produced. Its comparatively simple contours and surfaces allowed for large numbers to be produced easily, with none of the handwork of engravings, carving, or special cushions that marked earlier styles of furniture.

The Eames Chair. Charles Eames did more than any other designer to establish the look of modern furniture as spare, formfitting, and uncushioned. His well-known chairs of molded plywood, tubular steel, and wire mesh broke new ground while introducing the potential of modern materials to furniture designers. His simple, functional chairs and tables were considered revolutionary because they were made almost wholly by machine. He used rubber shock mounts to join the back and seat to the chair frame, which gave the chair a flexibility that wood chairs lacked. Virtually indestructible, the Eames chair was, as a *New York Herald Tribune* reviewer commented, "extraordinarily comfortable, built low and responsive to the body."

Colors. By 1949 Americans had a much broader range of decorating options than at the start of the decade. Most strikingly, Americans rushed to bolder colors in textiles, wallpaper, painted walls, and general room schemes. Bright red, citron or mustard yellow, lavender,

and chocolate were popular in 1949. Wallpapers became more reflective of modern art and murals. The trend toward spaciousness continued, and consumers had a greater choice of furniture. Most of it was compact, nonobtrusive, and unadorned by extraneous decoration. Built-in shelves, corner cupboards, and settees, often with storage drawers beneath, became common features of American homes.

Sources:
Virginia McAlester and Lee McAlester, *A Field Guide to American Homes* (New York: Knopf, 1984);

Meyric R. Rogers, *American Interior Design: The Traditions and Development of Domestic Design from Colonial Times to the Present* (New York: Norton, 1947).

REDESIGNING THE AMERICAN CAR: CONVERSION AND BACK AGAIN

Interruption and Conversion. Throughout the 1930s American automobile producers had been moving toward a longer, sleeker, and lower design for cars. But such developments were interrupted in 1941 when the U.S. automobile industry was assigned a leading role in the American war effort. As a result, factory production of civilian cars virtually stopped. The automobile industry converted from manufacturing cars to producing tanks, jeeps, trucks, aircraft parts, marine engines, radios, refrigerators, torpedo parts, and anti-aircraft guns to arm the United States and its allies.

A Reluctant Ford. Henry Ford, designer of the Model T and founder of one of the country's biggest automobile companies, opposed U.S. involvement in European hos-

Living-room furniture designed by Charles Eames, 1948, and exhibited at the Museum of Modern Art

tilities from their outbreak in the late 1930s. Ford, who had grown more and more suspicious of his rival automakers over the years, wanted nothing to do with war preparations. Thus, when President Franklin D. Roosevelt appointed General Motors president William Knudsen to head the new National Advisory Defense Committee in May 1940, Ford believed that the president was attempting a takeover of his company. With cajoling and pressure from friends and family, Ford finally agreed to produce airplane engines in November and soon became a vital force in arming the Allies and the United States. In 1942 Ford opened the Willow Run plant at Ypsilanti, Michigan, and started producing B-24 bombers.

Seizing New Opportunities. The new president of General Motors (GM), Charles "Engine Charlie" Erwin, adopted an entirely different approach to the war than Ford. GM had maintained contacts with the War and Navy Departments throughout the 1930s, and when the war broke out GM received $1.3 million in Allied defense contracts. In the five years of war production GM expanded by 50 percent. The company produced $12.3 billion worth of military supplies, only one-third of which was at all related to its civilian products. Such defense work made GM the largest and most powerful automaker in the United States.

European GM. Ironically, at the same time that GM was supplying the United States and the Allies with military equipment, a subsidiary of GM in Europe, Opel, was providing the Nazis with vital military machinery. In 1929 GM bought controlling shares in Adam Opel AG, a German automaker, as a way to avoid high tariffs on American imports. By the mid 1930s Opel constituted GM's wedge into the European market and accounted for 27 percent of German automobile sales. Soon the combined sales of Opel and Vauxhall, another auto company in which GM invested, exceeded those of GM's imports.

"Enemy Property." However, with the outbreak of war in the late 1930s the commander of the German army, field marshal Hermann Göring, announced that the army needed one hundred thousand trucks and that he expected Opel and European Ford producers to supply them. When Germany declared war on the United States on 11 December 1941 Adolf Hitler seized GM and Ford plants as "enemy property." Ford and GM soon became the chief suppliers of trucks, other vehicles, and aircraft engines for the Axis powers. Between 1939 and 1945 GM and Ford German subsidiaries built nearly 90 percent of their armored three-ton half-trucks and more than 70 percent of the Reich's medium- and heavy-duty

1947 Chrysler Town and Country convertible

trucks. According to U.S. intelligence these vehicles served as "the backbone of the German Army's transport system."

The General Purpose Vehicle. One of the longest-lasting innovations to come from the war was the jeep. A condensation of General Purpose Vehicle (GPV), the jeep was considered by many to be one of the best products of the war. Its design was inspired by a U.S. Army-sponsored competition for a strong, fast, sturdy vehicle. The "plunky little machine," as one observer noted, "seemed willing to go anywhere, do anything, and [was] regarded with great affection by the troops." After the war an independent automobile manufacturer, Willys, concentrated on a peacetime version of the jeep as an off-road workhorse and recreation vehicle.

A Job Well Done. The major U.S. automakers successfully overcame the many challenges the war posed, developing skills and machinery that would help them in the postwar years. By the war's end, the U.S. auto industry had produced 4,131,000 engines, including 450,000 aircraft and 170,000 marine engines; 5,947,000 guns; and 27,000 complete aircraft. These materials constituted one-fifth of the entire war production of the United States. American superiority in mass-production techniques, developed in the auto industry, was a key factor in the Allied victory.

A Stronger Engine. Although the war drastically interrupted the automobile industry, factories that converted to airplane and tank production were fitted with new machinery and new technology that revolutionized automobile manufacturing after the war. The development of a more powerful engine, the V-8, was one of the important technical improvements of the war years. The engine, originally developed by GM, increased the horsepower of motor vehicles and gave cars much more speed and control than prewar models. The V-8 also generated enough extra power to operate a new line of frills that soon became standard in many American cars, including power brakes and steering, power windows, and air conditioning. Another improvement was the creation of the automatic transmission, which was adopted by most manufacturers. Spurred by wartime shortages, auto manufacturers also increased the fuel efficiencies of their vehicles.

Postwar Automania. Even before the war had ended, Detroit was looking ahead to when the soldiers would return and automakers could turn their attention once again to the domestic market. As one Buick advertisement in 1946 put it, "We aim to make those Buicks all the returning warriors have dreamed about — cars that from go-treadle to stop light will fit the stirring pattern of the lively, exciting, forward-moving new world so many millions have fought for. . . ." Automakers confi-

The "custom touch" adds luxury to the 1949 Lincoln Cosmopolitan!

"Custom" Comfort!
—that's the Lincoln Idea

NATURALLY, you expect to enjoy comfort and luxury in a fine automobile. But the very *special* luxurious comfort of the 1949 Lincoln Cosmopolitan will exceed your fondest expectations!

No other fine car offers you a wider "custom" choice of rich upholstery... or such elegant interior refinements. (Even electrically operated windows are "standard" on this car!)

And the interior is more spacious than ever, with broad, foam-rubber cushioned seats. Visibility, too, is on the same generous scale. The Lincoln Cosmopolitan windshield is a glistening one-piece arc of safety glass almost five feet wide.

And never have you driven such a thoroughly comfortable car. It rides as smoothly as a drifting cloud...handles lightly. Its engine—the great new Lincoln

V-type "Eight"—has no equal for all-round durability, low operating cost and efficiency. Its powerful new brakes are unsurpassed for safe, gentle stops.

Nothing has been spared to make this Lincoln Cosmopolitan the most comfortable car of all. *Ask your dealer for a demonstration ride tomorrow—and discover this yourself!*

LINCOLN-MERCURY DIVISION OF FORD MOTOR CO.

White side-wall tires, rear lamps (and rear wheel shields on the Lincoln) are optional.

The most beautiful car in the whole wide world—the 1949 Lincoln Cosmopolitan—Lincoln's style and luxury leader. Shown, the Sport Sedan.

The powerful 1949 Lincoln—performance star of the fine-car field.

Lincoln
Builder of the Lincoln and the Lincoln Cosmopolitan

Advertisement for the 1949 Lincoln

AMERICA'S FAVORITE BOMBSHELL

On 16 July 1945 *Life* magazine crowned movie star Rita Hayworth "The Great American Love Goddess." Lovely, sexy, and slightly exotic in her looks, Hayworth found a unique place in American military history through her photographs. GIs plastered their living quarters, tanks, and aircraft with her image. She was, as *Life* reported, the "Oscar winner" of American pin-up girls during the war. Her picture was even plastered on the atomic bomb that was dropped on the Bikini Islands in 1946. When asked to comment about her literal status as a bombshell, she was reported to have burst into tears of joy. "Why should I mind?" she said. "I like having my picture taken and being a glamorous person." Hayworth's fame grew throughout the 1940s and 1950s. She appeared in several motion pictures, costarring with Hollywood's most famous leading men, including Cary Grant in *Only Angels Have Wings* (1939) and Fred Astaire in *You'll Never Get Rich* (1941) and *You Were Never Lovelier* (1942). Astaire claimed she was his favorite dancing partner. She also made headlines with her marriages to director Orson Welles, producer James Hill, and Prince Aly Khan.

Sources: "Rita Hayworth Wins GI Oscar," *Life* (16 July 1945): 30.

---

dently anticipated a postwar seller's market unmatched since the first Model T. After fifteen years of economic deprivation and wartime austerity, the public was ready to buy. At the war's end *Fortune* magazine reported that 25.8 million cars were registered in the United States, half of them more than ten years old. Forecasters predicted a potential five-year new-car market of at least 20 million, and they were right. Car sales between 1946 and 1950 added up to 21.4 million.

Buyers Beware. The postwar automobile market was a tough place for buyers. Cars that had been nursed through the Depression were junkers when the war finally ended. With money in many consumers' pockets and a shortage of cars, prices soared. A government attempt to hold down prices to 1942 levels failed, as automakers insisted that they could not hold down costs with demand outrunning supply. Bribery and dealer markups were commonplace. One Oklahoma dealer was prepared to offer immediate delivery only on the condition that the customer also purchase his dog for four hundred dollars; the dog "strayed" back to the showroom after each sale. Another car-hungry customer bet his dealer seven hundred dollars that he could hold his breath for three minutes; after pocketing the bet, the dealer

suddenly discovered that he had a new car in stock after all.

Styling. The postwar car was wider and lower than its 1939 precursor and had greater visibility with its improved glass and its newly curved windshield; the new windshield design increased driver visibility by 40 percent. Fenders became part of the body of the car itself rather than appendages. Passengers sat lower in the car, shifting the car's center of gravity and enhancing the driver's control. The new auto bodies provided a more comfortable ride. The dashboards of the new cars grouped the instruments into one spot where drivers could see them without taking their attention off the road. The new instrument panels used significantly less chrome, as designers worked to remove distracting reflections from the dashboard and windshield.

What Was Offered. The hardtop convertible was extremely popular with the postwar public. Not a convertible in the usual sense, it had a regular convertible frame and body on which a low, detachable steel top was fitted. Another new design, the utility sedan, was a combination station wagon and sedan, with the back divided into three sections that could be opened for loading from the rear. Following the pattern established by GM, manufacturers also developed a price range of cars, each designed to fit a

1948 Ford

specific rung on the socio-economic ladder. Ford, for example, built Lincolns for the working, middle, and upper classes, with prices ranging from $2,500 to $4,800 for the custom-built Lincoln Continental. Ford also offered a new Mercury that it hoped would challenge family cars such as De Sotos, Pontiacs, Oldsmobiles, and Buicks.

Independents Challenge the Major Automakers. The postwar demand for automobiles fueled the most successful period for independent automobile manufacturers in U.S. history. While the major automakers still dominated the domestic market, Hudson, Studebaker, Tucker, and Kaiser-Frazer captured a record-breaking 18 percent of the market in 1948 and 14 percent in 1949, the industry's biggest year to date. Independents strove to offer the American car-buying public distinctive alternatives.

Opportunities and Winners. The conversion to defense production helped some floundering independent automobile companies to survive. The Hudson Motor Company lost more than $1.5 million in 1940, but throughout the war the company averaged nearly $2 million a year in profits making aircraft guns, invasion-barge engines, and aircraft parts. By the war's end Hudson president A. Edward Barit was determined to recapture the company's former place as a leader in independent automaking and was one of the first to reconvert. In 1946

Hudson turned out 93,000 cars, nearly 6,000 more than its 1940 total. At the same time, Barit pushed his designers to come up with something new. The 1948 Hudson was so low that passengers stepped over the frame and down into it from the curb, yet it had more headroom and width than other cars. Hudson succeeded in seizing the opportunity the war presented to the industry: by 1947 it had doubled its profits to $5.7 million.

"The Most Amazing American Car." The Tucker Torpedo was the postwar epitome of the dream car. Preston Tucker, founder of the Tucker Company, aspired to create an automobile entirely free from what he considered Detroit's stodgy designs and worn-out ideas. Labeled the "Car of Tomorrow," the Torpedo included a dazzling array of features, the most daring of which was its rear-mounted engine. It had a third headlight that turned with the wheels, a padded dashboard, a pop-out windshield, and a host of new safety features. At the war's end Tucker leased a huge Chicago aircraft engine plant and set out to raise money to fund his venture by selling dealer franchises and stocks. While skeptics called the Tucker Torpedo a pipe dream, journalist Tom McCahill claimed, "The car is real dynamite! . . . I want to go on record here and now as saying that it is the most amazing American car I have ever seen to date." Tucker's dreams, however, soon ran aground when the Securities and Ex-

Advertisement for the 1949 Nash Airflyte

change Commission investigated him for fraud and theft in the promotion and financing of the Torpedo. A jury found him innocent, but not before newspaper headlines had tried and convicted him. Tucker claimed Detroit set out to destroy him, saying, "We were jobbed." By the 1950s the independents' challenge to Detroit faded, as many consumers came to see them as too high-priced an alternative to Ford, GM, and Chrysler.

Foreign Imports. By the late 1940s European automakers once again began sending autos to the United States. Though smaller, more fuel-efficient, and cheaper, these cars did not constitute a serious threat to the dominance of American automakers. However, the French Renault (priced at $1,265), the British Austin ($1,660), and the British Ford ($1,570) successfully undercut the price of the large American cars. Desperate for dollars, British and French manufacturers sent up to 75 percent of their production to the United States. Some U.S. consumers, tired of paying high prices for unwanted accessories, leaped at the opportunity to buy a cheaper car.

Sources:

E. Edson Armi, *The Art of American Car Design: The Profession and Personalities* (University Park: Pennsylvania State University Press, 1990);

James Flink, *The Automobile Age* (Cambridge, Mass.: MIT Press, 1988);

Stephen W. Sears, *The American Heritage History of the Automobile in America* (New York: American Heritage/Simon & Schuster, 1977).

HEADLINE MAKERS

ADRIAN

1903-1959

HOLLYWOOD DRESS DESIGNER

Designer of the Stars. Adrian, described as "Hollywood's highest-priced couturier," designed the look that dominated American fashion in the first half of the 1940s. Gilbert Adrian studied at the Parsons School of Design in New York and at its Paris campus before becoming a costume designer for revues in New York. Adrian then moved to Hollywood and designed clothes for M-G-M through the 1930s. In 1942, with American designers cut off from Paris, Adrian opened his own fashion house in Beverly Hills, showing both ready-to-wear and custom-made clothes and hats. In 1944 he won a Coty American Fashion Critics' Award, and in 1946 he brought out two perfumes, Sinner and Saint, with accompanying lipsticks.

The Look. The look Adrian made famous in the 1940s consisted of a long jacket with little or no collar or lapel, a single-button front closure at the waist, wide shoulders with long fitted sleeves sporting two darts at each elbow, and a straight skirt with a kick pleat. Made famous by Joan Crawford, the designer's fashions fit perfectly with wartime fabric restrictions. Adrian also enjoyed using large, dramatic prints — incorporating his favorite animals, gigantic playing cards, palm leaves, or Etruscan figures — for his long dinner dresses. These dresses were usually made in fluid fabrics and characterized by asymmetric drapery. He also designed long dresses composed of abstract patchwork of solid colors known as "Picasso" or "Braque" dresses. More-formal evening wear included his full-skirted ball gowns of watercolor taffetas. Adrian had only been in business for himself ten years when in 1952 he suffered a heart attack. He closed his business and moved with his wife to Brazil, where he designed men's shirts and ties as well as theater costumes until his death in 1959.

Source:
Caroline Rennolds Milbank, *Couture: The Great Fashion Designers* (London: Thames & Hudson, 1985).

MARCEL BREUER

1902-1981

ARCHITECT

Modernist Architect. Hungarian American architect Marcel Breuer had been a student and a faculty member at the Bauhaus in Germany before arriving in the United States in 1937 to join Walter Gropius on the faculty of Harvard University. Breuer's work embodied many elements of fine architecture. He combined traditional wood and brick with newer materials such as concrete and metal. A modernist, Breuer emphasized in his designs the structure and form characteristic of the International Style and played an important role in establishing the style in the United States.

From Germany to America. Breuer was born in Pécs, Hungary, in 1902. After graduating from secondary school in 1920, he enrolled in the Bauhaus, which was founded by Gropius in Dessau, Germany. In 1924 Breuer received his degree and joined the faculty as a master of carpentry, remaining there until 1928. While at the Bauhaus, Breuer designed several modern chairs and other furniture employing bent, tubular steel frames. In 1928 Breuer and Gropius left the Bauhaus to form their own practice, which survived the international depression of the 1930s and the rising cultural control of the Nazi regime. In 1935 they left Germany for London; two years later they moved to the United States. Breuer kept his post at Harvard University until 1941. The following year he organized his own practice in Cambridge, Massachusetts, then moved to New York in 1946.

On His Own. Breuer designed houses and other residential buildings throughout the 1940s. Among his most notable houses are the Aluminum City Terrace Housing buildings (1942) in New Kensington, Pennsylvania, the

Geller House (1945) in Lawrence, New York, and the Robinson House (1947) in Williamstown, Massachusetts. In 1946 he designed and constructed a house in the garden of the Museum of Modern Art in New York, which brought him to the attention of architects and the general public. He soon received commissions for other houses and for larger buildings.

Later Career. Notable buildings by Breuer include the Ferry Cooperative dormitory at Vassar College, in Poughkeepsie, New York (1951); the UNESCO headquarters in Paris (1958), designed in association with Pier Luigi Nervi and Bernard Zehrfuss; the IBM building in La Gaude, France (1962); the Whitney Museum of American Art in New York (1966); and the U.S. Department of Housing and Urban Development building in Washington, D.C. (1967). In 1968 he received the highest award of the American Institute of Architects, the Gold Medal. He retired in 1977 and died in 1981.

Sources:

Peter Blake, *Marcel Breuer: Architect and Designer* (New York: Museum of Modern Art/Architectural Record, 1949);

Christopher Wilk, *Marcel Breuer, Furniture and Interiors* (New York: Museum of Modern Art, 1981).

CLAIRE MCCARDELL

1905-1958

FASHION DESIGNER

Queen of the Casual Separates. With her first collection in 1941, Claire McCardell became a significant figure in the fashion world. Unlike many of the designs of her contemporaries, which she considered "strident," her dresses were soft in style. She was the first designer to take sportswear and make it for every possible need. Golf skirts and bathing suits were as important to her as evening dresses. Her designs shared a set of characteristic features. Bathing suits were made with the same halter necklines and out of the same fabrics as her dresses. Wrapped or peasant-inspired tops appeared in bathing suits and dresses alike. Jersey, denim, chambray, and taffeta were equally topstitched, spaghetti ties were wrapped around the waists of leisure and dress clothes, and wool was used for leotards as well as wedding dresses.

The "Popover." McCardell was born in Frederick, Maryland, in 1905. She attended the Parsons School of Design starting in 1925 and two years later went to the Paris division of Parsons to study fashion design. She graduated in 1928 and spent five years working in various fashion houses. In 1932 she went to Townley Frocks as a design assistant; after the first showing of her dress designs she was promoted to designer. In 1942 she conceived the idea for her popular "Popover" wraparound

housedress for women whose maids were leaving them for factory and defense work. The Popover dress, which sold for $6.95, was designed in response to a request from *Harper's Bazaar* for an all-purpose housework dress. With its topstitched denim with a wrap front, large patch pockets, and attached oven mitt, it sold in the tens of thousands.

The "Diaper" Bathing Suit. McCardell introduced many details from men's clothes to women's clothes, such as large pockets, shirtsleeve shoulders, stitching on blue jeans, and trouser pleats. She also introduced ballet slippers as dress accessories as a way for women to deal with restricted amounts of shoe leather. In 1943 she brought out her well-known "diaper" bathing suit, with brass fishing-boot hooks up the side. In the winter of 1946 she showed her Empire collar and in the fall of 1949 her "bandanna" neckline.

Successes and Prizes. Even when working within the guidelines set by the government, McCardell managed to achieve a flowing look. She used colorful patches for dress sleeves and pockets in order to conserve materials. Her use of natural shoulders and generous skirts predated Christian Dior's 1947 New Look. She also designed civil-defense uniforms. She received the Mademoiselle Merit Award (1943), the Coty American Fashion Critics' Award (1944), and the Women's National Press Club Award (1950). In April 1953 she held a retrospective exhibition of her designs from 1933 to 1953 at the Frank Perls Gallery in Beverly Hills.

Source:

Caroline Rennolds Milbank, *Couture: The Great Fashion Designers* (London: Thames & Hudson, 1985).

JOHN MERRILL

1896-1975

ARCHITECT

Founder of SOM. In 1939 John Ogden Merrill joined architects Louis Skidmore and Nathaniel Owings to found Skidmore, Owings and Merrill (SOM), one of America's foremost architectural firms. Best known for designing large office buildings, the firm was noted for its sophisticated, artful handling of big buildings for big institutions and businesses and for its use of glass- and metal-curtain walls.

Training. Merrill was born in Saint Paul, Minnesota, in 1896. He attended the University of Wisconsin from 1915 to 1917, when service in World War I interrupted his studies; he served as an officer in the army until 1919. After the war he transferred to the architecture school at the Massachusetts Institute of Technology and graduated in 1921. He worked in various offices and a short time for the Federal Housing Authority. In 1939 he joined Skidmore and Owings in their partnership.

Architect of the Manhattan Project. In 1942 Merrill moved to Tennessee to take charge of designing the secret buildings at Oak Ridge. The firm designed a town for 75,000 people who worked on and supported the Manhattan Project, which produced the first atomic bomb. He supervised the work on the buildings at Oak Ridge until 1945, when he moved to the firm's Chicago offices. Having become an expert in the technology of buildings and building codes, he directed a major revision of the building code for Chicago from 1947 to 1949.

SOM and Corporate America. While Merrill retired from the firm in 1948, SOM continued to build its reputation for high-quality construction using innovative designs. SOM perfected the artistry of soaring skyscrapers. The Sears Roebuck Tower (1974), the world's highest building, is considered SOM's finest work to date. SOM is also known for other corporate and institutional designs, including the entire campus of the U.S. Air Force Academy (1962) in Colorado Springs.

Source:
SOM: Architecture of Skidmore, Owings and Merrill, 1963–1973 (New York: Architectural Book Publishers, 1974).

EERO SAARINEN

1910-1961

ARCHITECT AND FURNITURE DESIGNER

From a Family of Architects. Born in Kirkkunummi, Finland, in 1910, Eero Saarinen was the youngest child of the famous architect Eliel Saarinen, who explained that his son was "born practically on the drafting board." Saarinen's uncle, aunt, and grandfather were also architects. When he was thirteen the family moved to the United States, and his father became director of the Cranbrook Academy of Art in Bloomfield Hills, Michigan. Saarinen graduated from high school in 1929 and went to Paris to study sculpture. Upon his return to the United States he worked in his father's office on furniture designs. In 1931 he entered the Yale School of Architecture. From 1939 to 1947 he worked for his father's firm of Saarinen, Swanson, and Saarinen, afterward called Saarinen, Saarinen and Associates. His work was interrupted by three years of wartime service in the Office of Strategic Services in Washington, D.C.

Functional Furniture. In 1941 Saarinen won two prizes in the New York Museum of Modern Art competition for functional furniture design for pieces on which he and Charles Eames had collaborated. The winning designs were molded living-room chairs and sectional living-room furniture. The 15 November 1948 issue of *Life* included photographs of a fabric-covered plastic-shell chair designed by Saarinen and manufactured by Knoll Associates and commented that designers such as Saarinen "used industrial materials like foam rubber, steel tubing, plywood and plastic to produce strange and unfamiliar shapes which are nonetheless comfortable and which . . . could lead to a whole new kind of really cheap, modern furniture."

More Innovation. Saarinen continued to design innovative chairs. After winning the functional furniture design contest he began working on "organic" chair designs, resulting in the "womb" chair, which eased the sitter into a fetal position and was considered by many to be the most comfortable chair ever made. In the late 1950s he designed what was called the pedestal group, in which the body of the chair and its base were a unified structure. Both the womb chair and the pedestal group sold well throughout the 1950s.

Architect. Saarinen was an accomplished architect as well. His achievements include his designs for the Smithsonian Art Gallery in Washington, D.C., and the master plan for the University of Michigan campus in Ann Arbor. He also designed the Massachusetts Institute of Technology's Kresge Auditorium (1955) and chapel (1955) in Cambridge, Massachusetts; the TWA Terminal at John F. Kennedy International Airport in New York (1960); and the famous Gateway Arch in Saint Louis (1965). He died in 1961 at age fifty-one.

Source:
Allan Temko, *Eero Saarinen* (New York: Braziller, 1962).

ADELE SIMPSON

1903-

FASHION DESIGNER

Quintessential New York Designer. Adele Simpson exemplified the finest in American fashion design for nearly five decades, turning out collections of flattering, tasteful, and functional clothing for women. She was best known for her matching ensembles of coats and dresses. She served her apprenticeship in a New York ready-to-wear house and studied at the Pratt Institute of Design in Brooklyn before becoming a top-paid designer in the 1920s. Throughout the 1930s and 1940s she had her own label as designer for Mary Lee Fashions. In 1949 she established her own firm.

Natural-Born Talent. The youngest of five daughters, Simpson became interested in sewing at an early age, designing and making the outfits she and her sisters wore to school. After graduating from the Pratt Institute of Design, she became the head designer of a New York ready-to-wear clothes house at age nineteen. After she moved to Mary Lee Fashions her designs won the industry's top prizes, including the Coty American Fashion Critics' Award in 1947.

New Applications for Cotton. Simpson's reputation during the war was as a pioneer of inexpensive sportswear in an expensive age. In 1946 she was one of the first designers to use cotton for both day and evening wear. Most clothing manufacturers considered cotton suitable only for work clothes, but she disagreed. In using cotton in a variety of clothes she opened the fashion world to its versatility, which won her the acclaim of the cotton industry. Other firsts for which she was credited include couturier raincoats, day and evening boots, matching coats and skirts, and dresses that can be stepped into rather than pulled over the head. Simpson also outfitted first ladies Mamie Eisenhower, Lady Bird Johnson, and Pat Nixon.

Source:
Caroline Rennolds Milbank, *New York Fashion: The Evolution of American Style* (New York: Abrams, 1989).

PAULINE TRIGERE

1912-1961

FASHION DESIGNER

Starting from Scratch. In 1942 Pauline Trigere started to design clothes in a New York loft and produced a small, yet eye-catching collection of a dozen dresses. She then invited buyers to her loft to see her designs, which she hung from rafters and light fixtures. In 1944, due largely to her persistence and good taste, her ready-to-wear clothes won notice from the press. In 1949 she won the first of her three Coty American Fashion Critics' Awards. Although her creations tended to be conservative, she pioneered many fashions, including reversible coats and wool evening dresses, collars that moved and folded, black dresses with sheer tops, sleeveless coats, and cape-collared coats and tunics.

Early Life. Trigere was born in Paris in 1912 to a tailor and a dressmaker. At age ten she could operate the Singer sewing machine and help her mother with custom tailoring. At fourteen she made her own clothes, which were the envy of her friends. While in college she was an apprentice in the salon of Martial et Armand, where she claimed she learned the subtleties of bias cuts and fabrics. In 1937 she moved to New York, where she worked with designer Hattie Carnegie. In 1942 Trigere started her own business, with her brother in charge of the business end of the company. He took her first collection of outfits cross-country by bus to sell to department stores. They soon were selling more than they could produce.

Unusual Techniques. Trigere designed her clothes in an unusual way, cutting material directly on a live model, which resulted in clothes characterized by imaginative tailoring. Her clothes stood out in the 1940s because she did not rely on traditional techniques to give interest or movement to a narrow dress but instead let the cut stand on its own. Her fortes were coats, wool dresses, cocktail dresses, and evening dresses that were dramatic without being fussy. Her price range in the 1940s started at ninety dollars. She was inducted into the Fashion Hall of Fame in 1959.

Source:
Caroline Rennolds Milbank, *New York Fashion: The Evolution of American Style* (New York: Abrams, 1989).

SALLY VICTOR

1905-1977

MILLINER

The Dean of Hats. The creator of many hat fashions, Sally Victor has been called "the dean of American millinery design." Among the best known of her designs are the baby bonnet, the collapsible straw hat, the Flemish sailor hat, the war worker's turban, the Grecian pillbox, and the airwave hat. She received the Fashion Critics Millinery Award in 1943. She was also an ardent advocate of establishing American designers in the fashion world and did much to promote New York as a fashion center.

Getting Started. Born in 1905 in Scranton, Pennsylvania, Victor was one of eight children. When she was two her family moved to New York, where as a teenager she learned to sew her own clothes. In 1926 she took a job as head millinery buyer at Bamberger's, a large New Jersey department store. The following year she married Sergiu F. Victor, head of the wholesale millinery house of Serge, where she soon became the chief designer. In 1934 she opened her own retail millinery salon. The Sally Victor salon prospered through the Depression due to her originality and shrewd business sense, which helped propel her to the headlines during World War II. When materials were in short supply during the war she refused to depend on textile manufacturers, instead experimenting with any fabrics she could acquire, often dying and weaving them in her salon to get the effects she desired.

Establishing American Designs. With the fall of Paris in 1940 Victor saw an opportunity to strengthen the position of American fashion design. Toward that end, in 1942 she and two other prominent hat designers, Lily Daché and John Frederics, worked together at the request of the millinery industry to create fall and winter trends in hats. Their hats were labeled "Millinery Fashion Inspiration, Inc.," and were very successful. Victor also designed a beret for the U.S. Cadet Nurse Corps and a denim work hat for General Electric that had an adjustable hood of fabric that confined the long hair of women workers, preventing accidents.

Source:
Caroline Rennolds Milbank, *New York Fashion: The Evolution of American Style* (New York: Abrams, 1989).

PEOPLE IN THE NEWS

In 1940 **Elizabeth Arden,** the cosmetics and skin cream mogul, branched out into clothing with the assistance of designer Charles James.

In the fall of 1945 **Julia Coburn,** former director of the Tobe-Coburn School of Fashion Design, articulated the postwar dilemma facing designers: what will women want to wear after years of wartime restrictions?

Movie star **Rita Hayworth** set off a controversy in her title role in *Gilda* (1946) for the scene in which she strips off her arm-length gloves. While the sexy scene dazzled thousands of her male fans, it upset many critics and conservatives who deemed it inappropriate for the viewing public.

During World War II Hollywood designer **Edith Head** visited Manhattan and expressed nostalgia in *The New York Times* for the lushness of Hollywood costumes before the war: "How well I remember the day when we would swirl fox skins around the hem of a secretary's dress or put a white satin uniform on a trained nurse. Now we hold to stark realism."

On 28 May 1940 **William S. Knudsen,** president of General Motors, resigned to assume the chairmanship of President Franklin D. Roosevelt's newly formed National Advisory Defense Committee, a group composed of business leaders to help ready America to enter the war.

In 1943 **Eleanor Lambert,** a fashion publicist who helped establish New York as a world fashion center, founded the Costume Institute, which later became part of the Metropolitan Museum of Art, and helped start the annual fashion awards sponsored by Coty.

During World War II designer **Mainbocher** designed uniforms for the Women Accepted for Volunteer Emergency Service (Waves), the Women's Marines, the American Red Cross, and the Girl Scouts.

In 1940 designer **Vera Maxwell** showed her "reefer suit," a daytime suit consisting of a reed-slim coat with matching skirt and a simple blouse.

Germaine Monteil, a New York fashion designer who later founded a cosmetics firm, debuted a Renaissance-inspired evening dress at a special fashion exhibit held at the Metropolitan Museum of Art in 1942. The exhibit featured mannequins wearing contemporary clothes by New York designers scattered throughout the galleries.

In 1947 critic **Lewis Mumford** pointed out the limits of the International Style in domestic architecture when he praised the Bay Region style for its "native and humane form of modernism." These architects, he wrote, "took care that their houses did not resemble factories or museums."

In 1941 architect **Wallace Neff** unveiled his "igloo" design for a house made by depositing concrete on an inflated canvas balloon in order to create a circular structure.

Women's Wear Daily fashion editor **Winifred Ovite** complained in August 1944 of the abandonment of American-made designs in the rush to "salute a liberated Paris."

In 1942 **Virginia Pope,** fashion editor of *The New York Times,* started the annual "Fashion of the Times" show.

In 1947 **Sophie of Saks** became the first designer to be featured on the cover of *Time.*

In 1948 Hudson automobile designer **Frank Spring** unveiled an entirely new look for postwar American cars. His "step down" design dropped the car's floor, enabling the roof to be lowered without a loss of headroom.

On 27 January 1945 fashion heiress **Gloria Vanderbilt di Cicco,** who stood to inherit $4.5 million on her twenty-first birthday on 20 February, announced that she and her husband, Pasquale di Cicco, had separated and would seek a divorce. On 21 April Vanderbilt married orchestra conductor Leopold Stokowski in Mexico.

In 1942 **Sydney Wragge** of the B. H. Wragge Company helped popularize women's separates by offering stores and editors brochures about how the clothes worked together and guidelines for how to promote and display them.

Architect **Frank Lloyd Wright** was awarded the Gold Medal of the American Institute of Architects in 1949 despite his never having joined the association.

AWARDS

COTY AMERICAN FASHION CRITICS' AWARD

(The "Winnie" — to an individual selected as the leading designer of American women's fashions)

1943 — Norman Norell

1944 — Claire McCardell

1945 — Gilbert Adrian

      Tina Leser

      Emily Wilkens

1946 — Omar Kiam of Ben Reig

      Vincent Monte-San

      Claire Potter

1947 — Jacob Horwitz

      Mark Mooring

      Nettie Rosenstein

      Adele Simpson

1948 — Hattie Carnegie

1949 — Pauline Trigere

SPECIAL AWARDS

1943 — Lily Daché

      John Frederics

      Sally Victor

1944 — Phelps Associates

1945 — No Award

1946 — No Award

1947 — No Award

1948 — Joseph De Leo

      Maximilian

1949 — David Evins

      Toni Owen

THOMAS B. CLARKE PRIZE

(Given by the National Academy of Design for interior design)

1940 — Hugo Ballin

1941 — Dan Lutz

1942 — Douglas W. Gorsline

1943 — No Award

1944 — Robert Philipp

1945 — Eugene Higgins

      Raphael Soyer

1946 — No Award

1947 — Louis DiValentin

1948 — Raphael Soyer

1949 — Eugene Berman

AMERICAN INSTITUTE OF ARCHITECTS (AIA)

AIA Gold Medal (Awarded to an individual for distinguished service to the architectural profession or to the institute. It is the institute's highest honor.)

1940 — No Award

1941 — No Award

1942 — No Award

1943 — No Award

1944 — Louis Henri Sullivan

1945 — No Award

1946 — No Award

1947 — Eliel Saarinen

1948 — Charles D. Maginnis

1949 — Frank Lloyd Wright

DEATHS

Charles Sumner Beach, 94, inventor of the industrial knitting machine, 19 March 1947.

David Beecroft, 68, pioneer in the automobile industry and former president of the Society of Automobile Engineers, 5 November 1943.

Elmer Jared Bliss, 78, founder of the Regal Shoe Company, a well-known manufacturer of women's shoes, 1 July 1945.

William Starling Burgess, 68, naval architect and pioneering airplane designer, 19 March 1947.

George Cary, 86, nationally known architect, 5 May 1945.

Frederick C. Chandler, 71, one of the founders of the Chandler Motor Car Company, 18 February 1945.

Ralph A. Cram, 78, internationally famous architect who redesigned the Cathedral of Saint John the Divine in New York, 22 September 1942.

Paul Philippe Cret, 68, well-known architect, 8 September 1945.

V. Chapin Daggett, 84, founder and director of Daggett and Ramdell, a cosmetics manufacturer, 9 December 1943.

M. Max Dunning, 72, architectural adviser to the Public Buildings Administration commissioner, 19 April 1945.

Ernest Flagg, 90, designer of the U.S. Naval Academy in Annapolis, 10 April 1947.

Edsel Bryant Ford, 49, president of the Ford Motor Company and son and sole heir of Henry Ford, 26 May 1943.

Henry Ford, 83, inventor of the Model T and creator of the modern automobile factory production system, 7 April 1947.

Joseph B. Gembering, 75, executive builder of New York's Triborough Bridge, 3 October 1943.

John Byron Goldsborough, 79, engineer in charge of the construction of several subways in New York and the Croton Dam, 26 March 1943.

Thomas P. Henry, 67, former president of the American Automobile Association, 8 September 1945.

S. Rae Hickok, 61, president of Hickok Manufacturing Company, the largest maker of men's belts and buckles, 19 December 1945.

Francis Jaques, 62, architect who designed Pershing Hall, the American Legion headquarters in Paris, 3 August 1943.

Elizabeth Jordan, 79, author and former editor of *Harper's Bazaar,* 24 February 1947.

Albert Kahn, 73, architect and engineer who revolutionized the construction of industrial plants and designed the Ford aircraft plant at Willow Run, 8 December 1942.

William S. Knudsen, 69, president of the General Motors Corporation, who served as the production coordinator for the United States during World War II, 27 April 1948.

Howard C. Marmon, 66, designer of the Marmon Car and former vice-president and chief designer of the Marmon Motor Company, 4 April 1943.

Harry A. Miller, 68, designer and builder of race cars, boats, and airplane engines, 3 May 1943.

Howard Myers, 52, publisher of *Architectural Forum* and innovator in housing design, 18 September 1947.

Charles W. Nash, former president of General Motors and later head of the Nash Motor Company, 6 June 1948.

Patrick M. O'Meara, 55, nationally known architect of Catholic institutions, 26 October 1945.

Raymond M. Owen, 70, designer of the Owen-Magnetic, an early electric automobile, 29 April 1943.

Charles Alonzo Rich, 88, architect known for his designs for college buildings and opera houses, 3 December 1943.

Holton D. Robinson, 82, noted bridge engineer and designer of the George Washington Bridge over the Hudson River in New York, 7 May 1945.

Harry Sussman, 54, chief naval architect of the U.S. Naval Yard in Brooklyn, 13 December 1945.

Egerton Swartwout, 72, architect of the Missouri capitol, 18 February 1943.

PUBLICATIONS

Elizabeth Burris-Meyer, *This Is Fashion* (New York: Harper, 1943);

Le Corbusier, *When the Cathedrals Were White: A Journey to the Country of Timid People* (New York: Reynal & Hitchcock, 1947);

Thomas Hawk Creighton, ed., *Building for Modern Man; A Symposium* (Princeton: Princeton University Press, 1949);

John Peebles Deem, *The Book of Houses* (New York: Crown, 1946);

Beryl Williams Epstein, *Fashion Is Our Business* (Philadelphia: Lippincott, 1945);

James Marston Fitch, *American Building: the Forces That Shaped It* (Boston: Houghton Mifflin, 1948);

S. Giedion, *Space, Time, and Architecture: The Growth of a New Tradition* (Cambridge, Mass.: Harvard University Press, 1947);

Raymond K. Graff, *The Prefabricated House, A Practical Guide for the Prospective Buyer* (Garden City, N.Y.: Doubleday, 1947);

Talbot Hamlin, *Architecture: An Art for All Men* (New York: Columbia University Press, 1947);

Hamlin, *Architecture Through the Ages* (New York: Putnam, 1940);

Elizabeth Hawes, *Fashion is Spinach* (New York: Grossett & Dunlap, 1940);

Joseph Hudnut, *Architecture and the Spirit of Man* (Cambridge, Mass.: Harvard University Press, 1949);

Clarence John Laughlin, *Ghosts Along the Mississippi, An Essay on the Poetic Interpretation of Louisiana's Plantation Architecture* (New York: Scribners, 1948);

George Nelson, *Tomorrow's House* (New York: Simon & Schuster, 1945);

Meyric R. Rogers, *American Interior Design: The Traditions and Development of Domestic Design from Colonial Times to the Present* (New York: Norton, 1947);

Christopher George Sinsabaugh, *Who Me? Forty Years of Automobile History* (Detroit: Arnold-Powers, 1940);

Walter Darwin Teague, *Design This Day: The Technique of Order in the Machine Age* (New York: Harcourt, Brace, 1940);

Arthur Kissam Train, *The Story of Everyday Things* (New York: Harper, 1941);

Michael Vertes, *Art and Fashion* (New York & London: Studio, 1944);

Royal Barry Wills, *Houses for Good Living* (New York: Architectual Book Company, 1946);

Wills, *Houses for Homemakers* (New York: Watts, 1945);

Frank Lloyd Wright, *Frank Lloyd Wright on Architecture; Selected Writings 1894–1940* (New York: Duell, Sloan & Pearce, 1941);

Wright, *When Democracy Builds* (Chicago: University of Chicago Press, 1945);

Architectural Digest, periodical;

Architectural Forum, periodical;

Architectural Record, periodical;

Glamour, periodical;

Harper's Bazaar, periodical;

House and Garden, periodical;

Ladies' Home Journal, periodical;

Motor Trend, periodical;

Vogue, periodical.

C H A P T E R   S I X

GOVERNMENT AND POLITICS

by PAUL ATWOOD

CONTENTS

1940

3 Jan. In his State of the Union Address, President Franklin D. Roosevelt asks Congress for $1.8 billion for defense, an unprecedented sum that alarms isolationists.

26 Jan. The 1911 U.S.-Japan Treaty of Commerce expires, and Secretary of State Cordell Hull informs the Japanese government that trade will continue only on a day-to-day basis.

17 Apr. Secretary of State Hull responds to the Japanese warning against any change in the status of the Dutch East Indies, saying intervention would prejudice the peace and security of the Pacific.

25 May President Roosevelt establishes the Office of Emergency Management.

3 June The War Department agrees to sell Britain millions of dollars' worth of outdated munitions and aircraft.

10 June President Roosevelt declares that U.S. policy is changing from "neutrality" to "non-belligerency." Isolationists predict that this shift will lead to America's entrance into the war.

11–13 June Congress passes both the Naval Supply Act and the Military Supply Act, authorizing $3.3 billion for defense projects.

20 June President Roosevelt nominates two prominent Republicans for his cabinet in a move toward bipartisanship on war preparations: Henry L. Stimson, formerly secretary of state under Herbert Hoover, as war secretary and retired U.S. Army Col. Frank Knox as secretary of the navy.

28 June Republicans nominate Wendell L. Willkie as their presidential candidate; Charles McNary is nominated as his running mate two days later.

28 June Congress passes the Alien Registration Act (Smith Act), which requires registration and fingerprinting of all foreigners in the United States and makes it illegal to advocate the overthrow of the U.S. government.

15–19 July The Democratic National Convention nominates Roosevelt for an unprecedented third term. Henry A. Wallace is chosen as his running mate.

20 July Congress authorizes a "two-ocean" navy, appropriating $4 billion to build up its number of warships.

3 Sept. The United States agrees to give fifty destroyers in exchange for rights to construct naval and air bases on British territories in the Western Hemisphere.

12 Sept. U.S. ambassador to Japan Joseph Grew warns that imposition of an embargo on Japan will be interpreted as an act tantamount to war in Tokyo.

16 Sept. President Roosevelt signs the Selective Service Act, requiring men ages twenty-one to thirty-five to register for military training.

26 Sept. President Roosevelt announces an embargo on exporting scrap iron and steel except to Britain and the Western Hemisphere, cutting off Japan from vital raw materials.

27 Sept. The Tripartite Pact, a ten-year military and economic alliance among Germany, Italy, and Japan, is formalized. The three Axis powers pledge mutual assistance to one another in case of attack by any nation not already at war with another member. Observers see this pact as a clear warning to the United States.

29 Oct. Secretary of War Stimson draws the first number in Selective Service lottery, initiating the first peacetime draft in American history.

5 Nov.	President Roosevelt is reelected in an electoral-college landslide but wins the popular vote by only 5 million ballots.
29 Dec.	President Roosevelt makes his "arsenal of democracy" speech, pledging to become the chief munitions supplier of the Allies.

1941

6 Jan.	In his State of the Union Address President Roosevelt asks Congress to support the Lend-Lease program. He also outlines the "four essential freedoms" for which the Allies are fighting: freedom of speech, freedom of worship, freedom from want, and freedom from fear.
7 Jan.	President Roosevelt sets up the Office of Production Management, appointing William S. Knudsen director.
20 Jan.	Roosevelt and Wallace are inaugurated as president and vice-president.
3 Feb.	The U.S. Supreme Court rules in *United States* v. *Darby Lumber Co.* that the Fair Labor Standards Act of 1938 is constitutional.
11 Mar.	Congress passes the Lend-Lease Act, extending credit or arms to Britain in exchange for items or services of equal value. The initial appropriation is $7.8 billion.
11 Apr.	President Roosevelt establishes the Office of Price Administration (OPA) to control wages and prices for the duration of the war. Roosevelt informs Winston Churchill that the United States will extend its "security zone" to 26° longitude — the middle of the Atlantic — and will commit American security patrols to these waters.
27 May	President Roosevelt declares that an "unlimited national emergency" faces the United States.
9 June	A Brazilian ship reports that the U.S. freighter *Robin Moor* was sunk in the Atlantic by a German submarine on 21 May. President Roosevelt orders troops to seize the North American Aviation Company after striking workers interfere with defense production.
16 June	President Roosevelt closes all German consulates in the United States, followed by closure of Italian consulates on 20 June.
22 June	Germany declares war on the Soviet Union, betraying the Hitler-Stalin Pact. President Roosevelt promises Joseph Stalin Lend-Lease assistance to aid the Soviets.
25 June	The Fair Employment Practices Committee is established by President Roosevelt's executive order to prevent discrimination on the basis of race or creed in defense plants.
28 June	The Office of Scientific Research and Development (OSRD) is set up by executive order, with Dr. Vannevar Bush as chairman. The OSRD will coordinate the development of radar, sonar, and the first stages of the atomic bomb.
7 July	U.S. Marines land in Iceland as part of an agreement with its government to protect the island from German occupation.
25 July	In response to the Japanese invasion of Indochina on 24 June the United States freezes all Japanese assets.

26 July	Gen. Douglas MacArthur is named commander in chief of all U.S. forces in the Far East, including the National Guard of the Philippines, which is brought under U.S. control.
14 Aug.	President Roosevelt and British prime minister Winston Churchill meet to discuss the Atlantic Charter, which becomes the blueprint for the United Nations.
18 Aug.	President Roosevelt signs a bill requiring eighteen months of active duty for Selective Service draftees.
11 Sept.	After the 4 September German attack on the U.S.S. *Greer*, President Roosevelt orders a "shoot on sight" policy against all Axis ships within the U.S. sea frontier, beginning an undeclared naval war in the North Atlantic.
17 Oct.	The U.S.S. *Kearny* is torpedoed, with a loss of eleven sailors.
30 Oct.	The U.S.S. *Reuben James* is sunk. Though this act is a grave provocation, much of the American public is still reluctant to go to war.
17 Nov.	In Washington, D.C., Japanese ambassador Nomura Kichisaburo and special envoy Kurusu Saburo suggest that war could result if the United States does not remove its economic embargo and refrain from interfering with Japanese activities in China and the Pacific.
26 Nov.	U.S. secretary of state Cordell Hull demands Japan's withdrawal from China and Indochina in exchange for any removal of trade restrictions.
30 Nov.	Japanese prime minister Tojo Hideki publicly asserts that all American and British influence in East Asia must be eliminated.
2 Dec.	The United States demands to know why Japan is reinforcing troops in Indochina.
6 Dec.	President Roosevelt appeals directly to Emperor Hirohito to preserve peace between Japan and the United States.
7 Dec.	Japan attacks Pearl Harbor, Hawaii, as well as U.S. bases in Thailand, Malaya, Singapore, the Philippines, Guam, Wake Island, and Hong Kong.
8 Dec.	Calling the Japanese attack "a date which will live in infamy," President Roosevelt asks Congress for a declaration of war against Japan. Only one member fails to vote for the declaration: Rep. Jeannette Rankin of Montana, a committed pacifist who also voted against American involvement in World War I.
11 Dec.	Germany declares war on the United States, with Italy following suit.
16 Dec.	President Roosevelt appoints a special commission to investigate events at Pearl Harbor.
17 Dec.	Adm. Chester Nimitz takes command of Pacific Fleet, replacing Adm. Husband Kimmel.
22 Dec.	President Roosevelt signs a new draft act requiring all males ages eighteen to sixty-five to register for military service and all males twenty to forty-four to be prepared to enter active duty.

1942

1 Jan.	With twenty-five other nations, the United States signs the Declaration of United Nations. All of the countries affirm their alliance against the Axis and pledge not to make a separate peace with Germany.

2 Jan.	Japan takes Manila, capital of the Philippines, and General MacArthur retreats to the Bataan Peninsula.
6 Jan.	In his State of the Union Address President Roosevelt asks for $56 billion for the war.
12 Jan.	The National War Labor Board is established to settle labor disputes.
24 Jan.	The special commission established to investigate the Pearl Harbor debacle finds Gen. Walter C. Short and Adm. Husband Kimmel guilty of dereliction of duty.
30 Jan.	The Emergency Price Control Act takes effect, placing ceilings on prices and rents.
6 Feb.	The U.S. War Department announces that Britain and the United States have combined their chiefs of staff to coordinate war efforts.
19 Feb.	President Roosevelt issues Executive Order 9066, authorizing the removal of Japanese Americans on the West Coast from their homes and their internment in concentration camps.
23 Feb.	An oil refinery near Santa Barbara, California, is shelled by a Japanese submarine — one of the few instances in which U.S. continental territory is attacked.
27 Feb.	Battle of the Java Sea begins. By 1 March the Allies have suffered a major defeat, with most ships sunk or disabled.
11 Mar.	General MacArthur issues his famous declaration "I shall return!," leaving seventy-five thousand troops behind and turning command of the Philippines over to Gen. Jonathan Wainright.
9 Apr.	The Bataan Peninsula falls to the Japanese; tens of thousands of American and Philippine troops and civilians are forced on an eighty-five-mile "death march."
18 Apr.	Sixteen carrier-based U.S. bombers led by Brig. Gen. James H. Doolittle bomb Tokyo and other Japanese cities, forcing Japan to alter its defense program and boosting American morale.
4–9 May	In the Battle of the Coral Sea, the first sea battle in which ships do not confront each other but dispatch aircraft to attack the other's fleet, the United States wins its first significant victory and thwarts Japan's advance southward to Australia.
6 May	All U.S. forces in the Philippines surrender after the fall of Corregidor.
4–6 June	In the turning point of the Pacific naval war the Japanese lose the Battle of Midway, which stops their advance across the Pacific. After this crucial battle the Japanese will fight a defensive war.
13 June	The Office of Strategic Services (OSS), the forerunner of the Central Intelligence Agency, is established with Maj. Gen. William "Wild Bill" Donovan as director.
18 June	Prime Minister Churchill arrives in Washington, D.C., for a conference with President Roosevelt.
21 June	Japan completes its occupation of Attu and Kiska Islands in the Aleutians.
25 June	Maj. Gen. Dwight D. Eisenhower is appointed commander of U.S. forces in Europe.

15 July	In what becomes known as the "Little Steel" formula, the War Labor Board allows a 15 percent wage increase to thousands of steelworkers in the smaller steel firms, pegging increases for most unionized workers to cost-of-living increases.
7 Aug.	The Battle of Guadalcanal, the first amphibious offensive operation carried out by the U.S. Navy and Marine Corps, begins in the Pacific Solomon Islands.
17 Aug.	The U.S. Eighth Air Force conducts the first raids against German positions in Rouen, France.
7 Oct.	President Roosevelt announces his intention to promote the United Nations Commission to Investigate War Crimes, letting the Axis powers know that certain actions will not be permitted as acts of war.
3 Nov.	In midterm elections the Republicans gain significantly. Though Congress is still run by Democrats, a loose coalition of conservatives from both parties dominates. In New York, Thomas E. Dewey is elected governor and immediately becomes the Republican presidential front-runner for 1944.
8 Nov.	Operation Torch begins with four hundred thousand Allied troops landing in Algeria and Morocco in northern Africa. Under the command of General Eisenhower, the invasion is intended to secure the Suez Canal and oil reserves of the Levant, to aid in the assault on Italy, to relieve pressure on the Red Army, and to support the British offensive in Egypt.
13 Nov.	The Selective Service Act is amended to draft males as young as eighteen. Lt. Gen. Lewis Hershey estimates that the U.S. Armed Forces will number 10 million within a year.
4 Dec.	Giving it what he calls an "honorable discharge," President Roosevelt terminates the Works Projects Administration. In June the Civilian Conservation Corps had also been disbanded. With millions of men overseas and with women taking jobs in defense plants, unemployment has completely vanished.

1943

11 Jan.	President Roosevelt asks Congress for more than $100 billion to continue the war, nearly double the request of the previous year.
14 Jan.	The Casablanca Conference begins. By 24 January President Roosevelt and Prime Minister Churchill will decide to demand unconditional surrender from the Axis.
9 Feb.	Japanese troops evacuate Guadalcanal, signaling the success of the U.S. Solomon campaign.
8 Apr.	President Roosevelt freezes all wages, prices, and salaries in an effort to curb inflation.
1 May	In the name of "national security," President Roosevelt seizes all bituminous-coal mines in the eastern United States in response to wildcat strikes that threaten war production.
7–9 May	Axis troops surrender in North Africa, with five hundred thousand men as casualties or taken prisoner.
11 May	U.S. troops begin to retake Attu in the Aleutians.

27 May	President Roosevelt creates the Office of War Mobilization to coordinate the nation's total war effort. He also issues an executive order requiring anti-discrimination clauses in all government/industry war contracts.
10 June	The Current Tax Payment Act takes effect, requiring the withholding of federal income taxes from individual paychecks on a regular basis. This act revolutionizes the collecting of taxes and gives government more power to spend than before.
14 June	The U.S. Supreme Court rules that it is unconstitutional to expel schoolchildren for not saluting the flag.
22 June	Following dozens of deaths and the deployment of federal troops, the nation's worst race riot ends in Detroit.
25 June	Over President Roosevelt's veto, Congress passes the Smith-Connally Act, making it illegal to strike in war industries and enabling the government to take over industries striking illegally.
10 July	The Allied invasion of Sicily begins.
19 July	The Allies bomb selected targets in and around Rome in an effort to induce Italy to surrender.
25 July	After twenty-one years in power Benito Mussolini is forced to resign. His successor, Marshal Pietro Badoglio, immediately begins to make plans to remove Italy from the war.
2 Aug.	A rumor that a black serviceman has been murdered by whites sparks a riot in Harlem that results in five deaths and causes $5 million worth of damage.
17 Aug.	Axis troops surrender in Sicily.
3 Sept.	The Allies launch an invasion of Italy. On 8 September Marshal Badoglio signs a surrender, which Germany views as betrayal and which leads that country to treat Italy as an enemy.
13 Oct.	Italy declares war on Germany.
26 Nov.	At the conclusion of the Cairo Conference, Roosevelt, Churchill, and Chiang Kai-shek of China agree that all Chinese territories seized by Japan will be returned and that Korea will be granted independence.
28 Nov.–1 Dec.	In the first meeting with all three Allied leaders present, Roosevelt, Churchill, and Stalin meet at Tehran to plan the Allied invasion of Europe.
17 Dec.	Congress repeals all Chinese Exclusion Acts enacted throughout the century.
24 Dec.	General Eisenhower is named commander of all Allied forces in Europe.
27 Dec.	The federal government seizes all the nation's railroads after illegal strikes.

1944

13 Jan.	President Roosevelt submits to Congress a budget of more than $30 billion less than that of the previous year, signaling his optimism about a favorable outcome of the war.
19 Jan.	The federal government returns seized railroads to private owners.

22 Jan. President Roosevelt creates the War Refugee Board to help resettle millions of refugees after the war.

4 Mar. After months of bombing other German cities, nearly fifteen hundred Allied aircraft begin bombing Berlin, Germany's capital.

29 Mar. Congress authorizes $1.35 billion to seed the United Nations Relief and Rehabilitation Fund, initiating a massive program to aid Europe's displaced millions.

3 Apr. In *Smith* v. *Allwright* the U.S. Supreme Court rules that blacks cannot be denied the right to vote in the Texas Democratic primary.

22 Apr. The Allies launch a surprise offensive in Dutch New Guinea, quickly defeating the Japanese forces.

26 Apr. U.S. Army troops seize Montgomery Ward after it defies an order from the National Labor Relations Board to extend a contract with its union employees. Sewell Avery, the chairman, is physically carried from the firm's headquarters.

3 May Meat rationing ends in the United States with the exception of choice cuts of beef and steak.

18 May After months of intense fighting in Italy, the Allies take Monte Cassino and force the Germans to retreat.

23 May Allied forces break out of the German encirclement on the beaches at Anzio and move toward Rome to link up with forces victorious in the mountains.

4 June Rome falls to Allied forces after the Germans evacuate.

6 June The long-planned "Operation Overlord," the invasion of Nazi-occupied France, begins on D-Day on the beaches of Normandy in northern France. By day's end 150,000 troops successfully land, catching the Germans off guard. Within a week more than 350,000 troops are moving toward Germany.

20 June The Battle of the Philippine Sea ends with the decisive defeat of Japanese forces.

22 June President Roosevelt signs the Serviceman's Readjustment Act, better known as the GI Bill of Rights. Providing low-interest loans for postwar housing and funds for education, the act will change the demographic map of the United States by fostering suburbanization and will open up higher education to many working-class Americans for the first time.

28 June Meeting in Chicago, the Republican Party nominates Thomas E. Dewey as its presidential candidate, with Gov. John Bricker of Ohio nominated for vice-president.

21 July The Democratic Party nominates Roosevelt for an unprecedented fourth term as president. Sen. Harry S Truman of Missouri is nominated to replace Henry Wallace as vice-president.

22 July The Bretton Woods Conference in New Hampshire, begun 1 July, ends. Representatives of forty-four nations, not including the Soviet Union, establish the International Monetary Fund (IMF) and the International Bank for Reconstruction and Development (the World Bank). The United States provides 25 percent of the capital for the IMF and 35 percent for the World Bank, giving it effective leadership of the postwar economy.

9 Aug. The island of Guam, one of the first American-held territories to fall to the Japanese in 1941, is retaken.

14 Aug. The War Production Board allows the production of various domestic appliances, such as electric ranges and vacuum cleaners, to resume.

25 Aug.	Paris is liberated by Allied forces.
11 Sept.	American forces enter Germany for the first time, taking up positions a few miles beyond the border.
16 Sept.	At the second Quebec Conference, Roosevelt and Churchill agree on the division of Germany into occupied zones. Although previously open to U.S. secretary of the treasury Henry Morgenthau's plan to deindustrialize Germany after the war, Roosevelt insists that the productivity of Germany's Ruhr Valley is key to re-creating a postwar global economy.
7 Oct.	The Dumbarton Oaks Conference in Washington, D.C., ends, with the United States, Britain, the Soviet Union, and China agreeing on the basis for the United Nations Charter and the structure of the organization.
20 Oct.	U.S. forces invade Leyte Island in the Philippines under the leadership of General MacArthur.
21 Oct.	U.S. forces capture Aachen, the first large German city to fall.
7 Nov.	President Roosevelt wins an unprecedented fourth term.
15 Dec.	Congress passes an act creating new military ranks. Three five-star generals are named, including Dwight D. Eisenhower and Douglas MacArthur, as well as three five-star admirals, including Chester Nimitz.
16 Dec.	German forces launch a surprise counteroffensive, seeking to thwart the Allied invasion. Succeeding at first in throwing back Allied troops, the Germans push deep into the Ardennes Forest of Belgium, creating a bulge in the Allied lines. Within a month the Germans have lost the Battle of the Bulge.
22 Dec.	Gen. Anthony McAuliffe issues his often-quoted reply to a German demand that he surrender his 101st Airborne Division, surrounded at Bastogne in the Ardennes: "Nuts!"

1945

20 Jan.	Roosevelt is inaugurated for his fourth term as president.
3 Feb.	A force of one thousand U.S. bombers raids Berlin.
11 Feb.	The Yalta Conference ends with Roosevelt, Churchill, and Stalin agreeing on the postwar division of Europe and Asia, on the treatment of war criminals, and on holding the first meeting of the United Nations to discuss further issues.
24 Feb.	Manila, capital of the Philippines, is retaken by U.S. forces.
7 Mar.	The first units of the U.S. Army cross the Rhine River at Remagen.
16 Mar.	The Battle of Iwo Jima ends in Allied victory.
25 Mar.	All German troops have been driven east of the Rhine River.
12 Apr.	President Roosevelt dies of a cerebral hemorrhage. Truman is sworn in as president.
25 Apr.	American and Russian troops meet at the Elbe River in a great show of camaraderie and fraternity.
30 Apr.	Hitler commits suicide in his underground bunker in Berlin.

8 May	Germany surrenders, ending the European war. Victory in Europe (V-E) Day is declared in the United States as massive celebrations erupt.
11 May	The U.S. aircraft carrier *Bunker Hill* is attacked by Japanese kamikaze aircraft, exacting a death toll of 373.
5 June	The United States, Britain, France, and the Soviet Union agree to the division and occupation of Germany and to a similar division of Berlin. Future failure to agree on terms for the reunification of Germany will lead to tensions between the West and the Soviets.
21 June	After the bloodiest battle of the Pacific war Japanese troops surrender at Okinawa.
5 July	After the loss of nearly twelve thousand Americans, U.S. forces recapture the Philippines.
16 July	The first atomic bomb is detonated at Alamogordo, New Mexico.
17 July	President Truman attends the first session of the final wartime conference between the Allies at Potsdam, Germany, and issues an ultimatum to Japan.
28 July	The Senate ratifies the United Nations Charter by a vote of 89–2.
6 Aug.	The United States drops an atomic bomb on Hiroshima, Japan. The resulting devastation amazes even the scientists who created it. More than fifty thousand people perish in seconds, and four square miles of the city are reduced to rubble.
8 Aug.	In keeping with previous agreements, the Soviet Union enters the war in the Far East.
9 Aug.	An atomic bomb is dropped, on Nagasaki in southern Japan, killing forty thousand Japanese civilians immediately. Tokyo announces its intention to surrender.
14 Aug.	The War Manpower Commission lifts all manpower controls.
27 Aug.	The Allies begin to divide Korea, with the Soviets occupying territory north of the thirty-eighth parallel, the Americans the southern half of the peninsula.
29 Aug.	General MacArthur is named supreme Allied commander of Japan.
2 Sept.	Japan signs a formal surrender onboard the U.S.S. *Missouri* in Tokyo Bay. Ho Chi Minh declares Vietnam independent of French rule. American OSS officers are on the platform, as is the American flag.
6 Sept.	President Truman announces his economic recovery plan to Congress. Later known as the "Fair Deal," the program promises full employment, a substantial raise in the minimum wage, the extension of Social Security, national health insurance, federal aid to education, and government-sponsored housing for the poor.
2 Oct.	The London Conference ends with the failure of Soviets and Western Allies to reach agreement about peace treaties to be signed with Germany and her allies.
19 Nov.	President Truman asks Congress to establish a compulsory universal health-insurance program.
20 Nov.	General Eisenhower replaces Gen. George C. Marshall as army chief of staff. In Nuremberg, Germany, the trials of Nazis charged with war crimes begin.

21 Nov.	In the first postwar demonstration of labor unrest, the members of the United Auto Workers (UAW) go on strike against General Motors in Detroit.
14 Dec.	General Marshall is named special ambassador to China to make peace between the Communist forces of Mao Tse-tung and the Nationalist forces of Chiang Kai-shek.
31 Dec.	President Truman dismantles the War Labor Board, replacing it with the Wage Stabilization Board in an effort to slow the pace of rapidly growing labor unrest.

1946

9 Jan.	In forty-four states nearly eight thousand Western Electric employees go out on strike, demanding hourly wage increases of five to seven cents.
10 Jan.	The first General Assembly of the United Nations meets in London. Heading the American delegation are Secretary of State James F. Byrnes and Eleanor Roosevelt.
15 Jan.	United Electrical, Radio and Machine Workers members go on strike in sixteen states.
20 Jan.	President Truman establishes the Control Intelligence Group, which becomes the Central Intelligence Agency (CIA).
21 Jan.	The United Steelworkers close down the nation's steel plants over wage contracts.
24 Jan.	The United Nations sets up an Atomic Energy Commission and proclaims its intention to restrict atomic energy to peaceful uses.
20 Feb.	Under the Employment Act of 1946 the Council of Economic Advisers is established to make an annual economic report to the nation.
21 Feb.	President Truman establishes the Office of Economic Stabilization to deal with conversion to a peacetime economy.
5 Mar.	Former prime minister Churchill delivers his "Iron Curtain" speech at Westminster College in Fulton, Missouri, with President Truman in attendance.
13 Mar.	Some 175,000 UAW workers end their 113-day strike against General Motors.
1 Apr.	More than four hundred thousand United Mine Workers (UMW) members strike the nation's mines over wages and health care.
29 Apr.	The U.S. Department of Agriculture reports that farm prices, and hence the cost of food, are at record highs, underscoring the need for higher wages among workers.
23 May	The nation's rail-transportation network is shut down by the Railroad Trainmen and Locomotive Engineers Brotherhoods.
30 May	The UMW end their fifty-nine-day walkout with substantial wage increases and a welfare-retirement fund paid for by mining companies.
3 June	The U.S. Supreme Court rules in *Morgan* v. *Commonwealth of Virginia* that segregated seating on interstate buses is unconstitutional.
14 June	The Baruch Plan, calling for control of atomic energy, is presented to the United Nations. The plan calls for the destruction of the U.S. stockpile of A-bombs and UN-monitored on-site inspections of the atomic-research facilities of all member nations.

20 June   The Senate confirms the nomination of Frederick Moore Vinson as chief justice of the U.S. Supreme Court.

1 July   As debate proceeds in the UN about the Baruch Plan, the United States detonates its fourth atomic bomb, on the Bikini Atoll in the Marshall Islands. The Soviet Union says that it cannot accept a monopoly of atomic power in the hands of the United States with only a vague promise to surrender authority to the UN.

4 July   The United States grants political independence to the Philippines, though maintaining the right to station ships and planes on Philippine territory at Subic Bay and Clark Air Base.

25 July   Reacting to the concerns of consumers and labor, President Truman signs a bill extending wartime price controls for one more year.

Aug.   The Fulbright Act is passed, providing scholarships for American students to study abroad and for foreign students to study in the United States.

1 Aug.   Under the McMahon Act, the U.S. Atomic Energy Commission (AEC) is established to provide civilian control over military and nonmilitary atomic-energy development.

2 Aug.   Congress passes the Legislative Reorganization Act, which requires registration of political lobbyists and the reporting of expenses.

20 Sept.   U.S. secretary of commerce Henry A. Wallace is forced to resign after publicly criticizing President Truman's conduct of U.S.-Soviet relations. Wallace proclaims that American actions are promoting a dangerous arms race, advocating instead "friendly, peaceful competition" with the Soviets.

1 Oct.   Acting secretary of state Dean Acheson states unequivocally that the United States intends to remain in Korea to see that it is reunited under a free government.

5 Nov.   Republicans gain control of both the House of Representatives and the Senate.

9 Nov.   Responding to pressures from business and conservatives, President Truman lifts price controls on most consumer goods even though recently enacted legislation is supposed to safeguard against this for six more months.

5 Dec.   Despite conservative opposition, especially in the South, President Truman issues Executive Order 9809, creating the Committee on Civil Rights to investigate the treatment of blacks in the United States — the first time in American history that a president focuses on civil liberties for racial minorities.

31 Dec.   President Truman issues a proclamation declaring a formal cessation of World War II hostilities.

1947

7 Jan.   President Truman names George C. Marshall as U.S. secretary of state.

12 Mar.   Announcing his "containment policy," President Truman declares that the United States will provide $400 million to Greece and Turkey to fight communism. This "Truman Doctrine" will commit the United States to becoming a global anticommunist policeman.

21 Mar.	Reflecting concern about the growing power of the presidency, Congress approves the Twenty-second Amendment to the U.S. Constitution, which would limit the president to two four-year terms or to ten years in office. The proposed amendment then goes to the states for ratification.
22 Mar.	Both reflecting the rising tide of anticommunism and spurring it, President Truman announces a program to investigate the loyalty of government employees.
2 Apr.	The UN grants the United States trusteeship over the three-million-square-mile territory of Micronesia in the Pacific.
5 June	At Harvard University commencement exercises, Secretary of State Marshall announces the European Recovery Plan that will bear his name. Ultimately the nations of Western Europe will receive more than $12 billion in aid for reconstruction.
23 June	Over President Truman's veto, Congress passes the Taft-Hartley Act (Labor Management Relations Act), which bans the closed shop by which only union members may be hired and which permits employers to sue unions for damages incurred in strikes. The act also allows the government to enforce an eighty-day cooling-off period, forbids political contributions by unions, and requires union leaders to swear they are not Communists.
July	In an article published in *Foreign Affairs,* George F. Kennan proposes a policy of "containment" toward the Soviet Union.
18 July	The Presidential Succession Act is passed, making the Speaker of the House of Representatives next in line for the presidency after the vice-president.
26 July	The National Security Act abolishes the old Department of War, replacing it with a new Defense Department, which integrates the army, navy, and newly created air force under the command of the new cabinet position of secretary of defense. James V. Forrestal is named to be the first secretary of defense. The act also creates the National Security Council and the Central Intelligence Agency.
2 Sept.	President Truman flies to Brazil to sign the Inter-American Treaty of Reciprocal Assistance (Rio Pact), in which nineteen American nations commit themselves to "collective defense against aggression."
19 Sept.	Gen. Albert C. Wedemeyer returns from China to propose a military-aid program to the Nationalist regime under Chiang Kai-shek.
5 Oct.	For the first time in the nation's history the president uses the new medium of television to speak to the American public.
9 Oct.	President Truman ignores advice from most of his advisers, instead heeding presidential counsel Clark Clifford in supporting autonomous Arab and Jewish states in Palestine.
18 Oct.	The House Un-American Activities Committee (HUAC) launches an extensive investigation into Communist activities in the movie industry.
29 Oct.	President Truman endorses the report of his Committee on Civil Rights calling for an end to segregation in every aspect of American life, urging that steps be taken to implement social, political, and economic equality.
29 Dec.	Henry A. Wallace announces that he will run for president as a third-party candidate.

1948

12 Jan. The U.S. Supreme Court in *Sipuel* v. *Oklahoma Board of Regents* rules that no state can discriminate against law-school applicants on the basis of race.

23 Jan. The UN Korean Commission, responsible for conducting elections throughout the peninsula, is informed by the Soviet Union that it cannot enter North Korea.

2 Feb. President Truman sends a civil rights proposal to Congress, calling for an end to segregation in education and employment, but it is turned down. The American Federation of Labor declines to endorse Wallace for president.

7 Feb. Dwight D. Eisenhower retires from the army to become president of Columbia University. Both the Democrats and Republicans attempt to interest him in the presidency.

8 Mar. The U.S. Supreme Court rules in *McCollum* v. *Board of Education* that religious training in public schools is unconstitutional.

15 Mar. More than two hundred thousand coal miners strike for better pension plans.

20 Apr. Even though UMW president John L. Lewis has called off the coal strike, a federal court levies a $1.4 million fine against the union and a $20,000 fine against Lewis for contempt of court in the wake of the strike.

30 Apr. The International Conference of American States, with twenty-one members in attendance at Bogotá, Colombia, establishes the Organization of American States (OAS).

1 May The Democratic People's Republic of Korea (North Korea) is established. The nation claims the right to rule over all of Korea.

10 May Faced with a nationwide railroad strike, President Truman orders the army to seize and run the railways. Elections are held in southern Korea after Soviet-occupied North Korea refuses to cooperate.

14 May Israel declares its independence from Britain as a sovereign state. The United States becomes the first nation to recognize the new country.

25 May The UAW and General Motors sign the first contract pegged to cost-of-living increases.

7 June The United States and its Western European allies formulate a plan to create West Germany.

11 June The Vandenberg Resolution passes in the Senate, allowing the United States to enter into collective security alliances outside the Western Hemisphere.

24 June President Truman signs a new Selective Service Act requiring all males eighteen to twenty-five to register for military service. Republicans nominate Thomas E. Dewey as their presidential candidate. The next day Earl Warren is named as his running mate.

25 June Congress passes the Displaced Persons Act, which allows 205,000 refugees from Soviet-controlled Eastern Europe to enter the United States.

26 June In response to the Soviet shutdown of all traffic from the West into Berlin on 24 June, the United States initiates the Berlin airlift. For the next year nearly 275,000 flights will provide Berliners with 2.3 million tons of food and fuel.

15 July	The Democratic National Convention nominates Truman for reelection, with Sen. Alben Barkley of Kentucky as his running mate.
17 July	Having walked out of the Democratic convention two days earlier, Southern Democrats form the States Rights Party ("Dixiecrats") and nominate Gov. Strom Thurmond of South Carolina for president. Their platform stresses states' rights and segregation.
22 July	In Philadelphia other dissident Democrats form a fourth party, the Progressive Party, and nominate Henry A. Wallace for president.
26 July	President Truman ends racial segregation in the armed forces and federal civil service by executive orders.
3 Aug.	Former Communist Whittaker Chambers accuses Alger Hiss, a high-ranking State Department diplomat, of membership in the Communist Party, lending credence to right-wing charges that subversives have infiltrated the government.
15 Aug.	The Republic of South Korea is established, with Syngman Rhee as its president. Rhee immediately initiates covert military actions designed to reunify the peninsula.
2 Nov.	Defying the polls and the political pundits, President Truman is reelected by a margin of 2.2 million popular and 114 electoral votes.
6 Dec.	Richard M. Nixon, member of the House Un-American Activities Committee, accuses the Truman administration of covering up evidence of Communist infiltration into the federal government.

1949

3 Jan.	The U.S. Supreme Court rules that the provision of the Taft-Hartley Act banning the closed shop is constitutional.
7 Jan.	U.S. secretary of state George C. Marshall says that for health reasons he will resign on 20 January, the date of the presidential inauguration.
14 Jan.	In the first major antitrust suit brought by the government since before World War II, the Justice Department proposes to break up the American Telephone and Telegraph Company (AT&T) and separate its production subsidiary, Western Electric.
19 Jan.	Congress increases the president's salary to $100,000 per year, also providing him with $50,000 for expenses.
20 Jan.	President Truman is inaugurated for his second term. In his speech he emphasizes foreign aid.
2 Mar.	Proving that the United States possesses intercontinental air-strike capabilities, the U.S. Air Force's B-50 bomber circumnavigates the globe.
4 Apr.	The North Atlantic Treaty Organization (NATO) is founded as a mutual defense pact among the Western Allies.
12 May	The Soviet Union lifts the Berlin blockade.
23 May	The Federal Republic of Germany (West Germany) is formally established.
29 June	The United States removes the last of its combat troops from South Korea.

15 July   President Truman signs the Housing Act, providing federal funds for the construction of public housing to alleviate the shortage remaining from the Depression.

21 July   The Senate ratifies the NATO treaty.

5 Aug.   In a white paper the U.S. State Department declares that the corruption and incompetence of Chiang Kai-shek in China has made possible its takeover by Communists. Anticommunists in Congress immediately accuse the Truman administration of losing China.

10 Aug.   President Truman signs the National Security Act, placing defense secretaries under the authority of the Department of Defense.

11 Aug.   Gen. Omar Bradley is named chairman of the Joint Chiefs of Staff.

24 Aug.   Tom Clark is sworn in as an associate justice of the U.S. Supreme Court.

21 Sept.   President Truman signs the Mutual Defense Assistance Act, providing military aid to NATO allies.

23 Sept.   President Truman announces that the Soviets have detonated their first atomic bomb.

1 Oct.   Mao Tse-tung announces the creation of the People's Republic of China. The United States does not recognize the new government.

4 Oct.   The Senate confirms Sherman Minton's nomination to the U.S. Supreme Court.

14 Oct.   Having been tried under the Smith Act for conspiracy to overthrow the United States government, eleven Communists are found guilty and sentenced to prison.

24 Oct.   The United Nations headquarters in New York City is dedicated.

26 Oct.   The Fair Labor Standards Act is amended to raise the minimum wage from forty cents to seventy-five cents an hour.

31 Oct.   Walter Reuther, president of the Congress of Industrial Organizations (CIO), begins to purge the organization of Communists, who have long been allowed to operate within CIO unions.

9 Dec.   HUAC chairman J. Parnell Thomas is found guilty of payroll padding and is sentenced to six to eighteen months in prison.

OVERVIEW

At The Crossroads. The years 1940–1949 proved to be one of the most momentous decades in the history of the United States — indeed, in the history of the world. The ordeal of total war engulfed most of the European continent, as well as East Asia and North Africa. Naval engagements took place on all the oceans, and for the first time modern air forces obliterated entire cities. The term *genocide* entered the mainstream of the English language with Adolf Hitler's attempt to exterminate the Jews. Many nations that sought to avoid direct warfare nonetheless endured the clash of armies on their soil, while others were indirectly drawn into the war when they provided vital resources for combatants. No nation remained entirely neutral. Exceedingly rapid technological advances in the art of mass killing proved strikingly that the human race had arrived at a crossroads. By 1949 the United States and the Soviet Union possessed the atomic bomb and other nations were sure to follow. Humanity now had a sure means by which to make itself extinct.

A Nation Transformed. The United States emerged from the war changed forever. More than 16 million men and women were mobilized for wartime service, and nearly half of them served in the theaters of combat. More than 300,000 Americans lost their lives. Domestically, wartime decisions created a social and economic revolution. An American who slept from 1939 to 1949 would not have recognized the nation on awaking, so deep and extensive were the changes wrought. The war had ended the Great Depression, healing the ravages of mass unemployment. Millions of poor and working-class Americans were elevated by wartime wages and government policies into the ranks of the middle class. Americans began a demographic boom that promised to alter radically the political landscape. Giant corporations and an enlarged federal bureaucracy amassed unprecedented wealth and power. Most startling of all the changes was the expanded presence of the military in American life. Before World War II the United States possessed a small military and no tradition of a large-scale professional army. After the war millions of Americans remained under arms, and the fastest growing industries were those that produced weapons. In the late 1940s the government was reorganized to create the Department of Defense,

the Central Intelligence Agency, and the National Security Council — signaling a new and potentially ominous preoccupation with national security. So militarized did the United States become after 1945 that in his departing remarks, as he left office in 1961, President Dwight D. Eisenhower decried the unwarranted ability of a "military-industrial complex" to set the national agenda. Echoing the concerns of George Washington's farewell address, the man who had served as supreme Allied commander in Europe during World War II said that "Every gun that is made, every warship launched, every rocket fired signifies, in the final sense, a theft from those who hunger and are not fed. . . ."

The Arsenal of Democracy. As the 1940s began, Europe and East Asia were already at war. Though President Franklin Delano Roosevelt had promised the nation's mothers during the election of 1940 that their sons would not be called to fight in a foreign war, he knew that American support for Britain, France, and China would almost certainly require direct military intervention by the United States. The majority of the American public, however, was opposed to intervention. Their position, known as "isolationism," was that America should attend to its domestic affairs, buffered from foreign strife by two oceans. Many American citizens considered their nation's involvement in World War I to have been a mistake. In 1940, though they broadly supported the victims of German and Japanese aggression, most urged that the United States avoid foreign entanglements. President Roosevelt found himself walking a tightrope between those who adamantly maintained that the United States should avoid involvement in Europe or Asia, and those influential "interventionists" who argued that American interests demanded direct military action. In spirit Roosevelt sided with the latter, but he was also a pragmatist who knew enough not to oppose public opinion, especially during an election year. While proclaiming neutrality and making campaign promises not to send American boys overseas, Roosevelt nevertheless called up the National Guard and implemented conscription into the armed forces. After his reelection was safely secured, Roosevelt declared that the United States would become the "arsenal of democracy," providing arms to Britain. By spring 1941, well before the Japanese attack on Pearl

Harbor, the United States was conducting naval warfare against German submarines in the North Atlantic. Following Hitler's attack on Russia, Roosevelt extended Lend-Lease aid to the Soviet Union. Knowing that Germany would not allow the United States to provide inexhaustible supplies to Britain and Russia, Roosevelt reasoned that Germany would commit some act that would overcome isolationist opposition at home. Instead, Japan committed the act necessary to inflame public opinion and ensure that the United States would enter World War II, attacking American naval and army bases in Hawaii on 7 December 1941. Four days later, believing that de facto sea battles between Germany and the United States signaled American intentions to engage the Germans, Hitler declared war on the United States. Congress reciprocated, and America was at war around the globe.

The Politics of War. Though Americans were enraged at the Japanese sneak attack at Pearl Harbor, and millions of young men instantly volunteered for military service, the public had no sense, as Roosevelt and his advisers did, of how long and costly the war would be. Roosevelt minimized the political consequences of the war by focusing on armaments production and leaving the bulk of the fighting and dying to the British and Russians. Had U.S. casualties been significantly higher it is probable that public support for the war — and for the policies of accepting nothing but unconditional surrender from Germany and Japan — would have been compromised. Roosevelt understood the limits of public support and stayed within them. At the same time he assumed unprecedented wartime powers, which had the potential to provoke public wrath, especially in an age of dictators. Yet, as long as victory seemed credible and none too costly, the president remained one of the most popular chief executives in U.S. history — and remained in office longer than any president before or since.

The War and the New Deal. In the 1930s Roosevelt crafted a Democratic coalition, enabling his administration to pass sweeping legislation that altered the relationship of government to the national economy. For the first time in American history the power of government was used to enhance the economic security of working-class Americans. Governmental intervention in the economy had previously favored wealthy Americans and powerful corporations. The New Deal fostered a new "welfare state," resulting in socially beneficial programs such as social security, unemployment insurance, and public housing. Continued support for such government intervention on behalf of the poor rested on a political coalition of labor, urban ethnic groups, women, blacks, and middle-class liberals. Laissez-faire conservatives maintained that relief subsidies for the poor fostered dependency and eroded the work ethic. Meanwhile, they added, the economy remained depressed. As World War II approached, and military spending began to increase dramatically, however, public spending presented opportunities for those whom Roosevelt had labeled "economic royalists." Big businesses would accept subsidies for the impoverished if government would guarantee profits for those industries engaged in war production. The welfare state was wedded to a new "warfare state." In the process businessmen were catapulted to positions of influence in government well beyond their previous status. After the war — successful in their efforts to retain and enlarge the military-industrial complex by focusing on the dangers of Communist expansion overseas — the new conservatives increased their power. Meanwhile, the domestic anticommunist hysteria that accompanied the Cold War helped to weaken the New Deal coalition. Moreover, social-welfare programs and increased militancy among black Americans for civil rights alienated Southern traditional conservatives, who increasingly challenged the liberalism of the Democratic Party.

The Failure of GOP Economics. In the 1940s conservative Republicans opposed the New Deal with decreasing force. Their strategy in the 1936 election had emphasized classical conservative laissez-faire theories and condemned the welfare state. By 1940 that wing of the Republican Party had little credibility, as liberal Republicans such as Wendell Willkie and Thomas E. Dewey gained ascendancy in the party. In response to the Democratic realignment, the Republican Party split in two. On the increasingly less influential side were the classical conservatives wedded to "trickle-down" economics; on the other were those industrialists and financiers who came to agree with Roosevelt that government "pump priming" and the expansion of international trade were crucial to the future of the American economy.

GOP Isolationism Discredited. While there were isolationists in both parties, the Republicans were associated with those who sought to maintain "Fortress America" behind the moats of the Atlantic and Pacific. Some more-progressive Republicans hearkened back to traditional warnings to avoid foreign entanglements; others seemed to flirt with fascism in their "hands-off America" proposals, arguing that a strong authoritarian central government at home, like those abroad, could restore economic and political order. Both variants of Republican isolationism attacked Roosevelt's policies as leading to war. After Pearl Harbor such isolationists were eclipsed, though some continued to hold forth. While old-line isolationists were among those Republicans to recapture control of Congress briefly in the mid 1940s, they were out of touch with a public increasingly wary of Communism.

The Emergence of the Anticommunist Republicans. Though Republicans recaptured Congress in the midterm elections of 1946, many knew that traditional appeals to the electorate were no longer viable. Many younger conservatives deeply distrusted the new Republican liberals who had embraced the welfare state, calling it "creeping socialism." When Cold War tensions surfaced after World War II, opportunists such as Sen. Joseph R.

McCarthy of Wisconsin and Congressman Richard M. Nixon of California seized on public anxiety over Communism to attack the administration of President Harry S Truman for not being vigilant enough against the new menace. Though the new Republican politicians knew little about international Communism, they understood how to capitalize on the public mood. McCarthy eventually went so far as to accuse members of the Truman Administration of being Communist sympathizers.

A World Leader. Public esteem for President Roosevelt was enhanced by his careful development of American war goals that advanced the position of the United States as the greatest world power. While Prime Minister Winston Churchill wanted American troops to save the British Empire, Roosevelt knew that the war would break the backbone of British power, and he steadfastly positioned the United States to take Britain's place in global affairs. Simultaneously, Roosevelt forced the Soviet Union to bear the brunt of the fight against the Nazis. In the end it was the Red Army that crushed Hitler — at a cost so great that Soviet victory could only be called Pyrrhic. With 25 million dead, with its major cities in ruins, and with its infrastructure obliterated, Russia was in no real position to challenge the newly won power of the United States. To some, however, the fact that the Communist giant existed at all, with the largest (though poorly equipped) army on earth, threatened the postwar agenda of creating a new world order of democratic regimes and free-market economies. Though President Roosevelt had conducted the war with the minimum possible number of casualties, he was nevertheless faulted by his successors for "giving away" Eastern Europe to the Soviets at the 1945 Yalta Conference. Thereafter, his enemies cultivated the myth that Roosevelt had "sold out" to the Communists during the last months of his presidency. Though he had led the nation through its most difficult days, Roosevelt's reputation suffered after his death, as those who believed that the mere presence of the Soviet Union after the war placed the United States in grave danger faulted Roosevelt for making America's victory less than absolute.

The National Security State and the Affluent Society. Necessity dictated the structure of the American economy during the war. It also put Roosevelt's New Deal administration in partnership with the very "economic royalists" the president had accused of having brought on the Great Depression. Throughout the 1930 infusions of federal tax dollars into the economy failed to end mass unemployment or to increase industrial or agricultural production substantially. Ultimately, only the investment of government revenues in new military and related industries ended the Great Depression. Yet production for war had to be calibrated carefully to manpower and resource availability, while simultaneously avoiding price inflation. To ensure the expertise and loyalty of big business, Roosevelt created new civilian bureaucracies to oversee corporate production and put corporate chief executives in charge. The War Production Board guaranteed profits for military contractors, while deferring or reducing taxes, and saw to it that the government paid for the costs of new plants and factories. By the end of the war many new corporations, some of which had not even existed before the war, dominated the American economy. Public approval of this unprecedented partnership between government and big business ran high because it had ended unemployment and dramatically raised living standards. Yet highly placed decision makers feared a return to economic depression at war's end. Industrialist Charles E. Wilson suggested that the government create a "permanent war economy." Although most of the military was demobilized after World War II, an unprecedented 2 million men remained under arms, and by 1947 enormous military expenditures resumed. By decade's end a symbiotic relationship between the largest corporations and the new defense agencies had been created. Public prosperity had become tied to permanent production for permanent war. The logic of such preparations seemed to many to lead inevitably to future armed conflict and to a chilling arms race.

AMERICA AT WAR: BACKGROUND TO INVOLVEMENT

The Imbalance of Power. In American popular mythology World War II began on 7 December 1941, the "day of infamy" when the Japanese attacked U.S. naval and army bases at Pearl Harbor without warning. The Japanese attack, however, did not occur in a vacuum; nor did Hitler's subsequent declaration of war on the United States on 11 December. World War II was caused by World War I — or, more accurately, by the failure of that war and the subsequent Treaty of Versailles to resolve important issues among the major powers, including comparative advantages in markets and financial resources, in military and naval strength, and in national prestige.

Versailles Discarded. The Treaty of Versailles was imposed by the victorious Allies on a defeated Germany. Vindictive and harsh, the treaty was intended to punish Germany by compelling her to surrender territory to France, Poland, and Czechoslovakia; to suffer an Allied occupation army in the Rhineland; to pay heavy reparations for damages caused to the Allies; and to submit to a clause in the treaty admitting "guilt" for initiating the war. Alone among the Allies, the United States wanted to restore Germany's economic strength so that it could serve as the anchor of America's European trade. When the treaty was signed in June 1919, the German economy had collapsed, and a state of near civil war existed between German leftist and rightist elements. The German people easily came to believe that they had been stabbed in the back by the harshness of the Allies and the perfidy of Communists. Between 1920 and 1935 provisions of the treaty were systematically discarded or weakened, with the result that Adolf Hitler finally repudiated it altogether, intending to restore Germany to the first rank of powerful nations.

German and Japanese Expansionism. Germany and Japan were latecomers to the game of empire. Both countries became modern nation-states only in the late nineteenth century, and each felt threatened by the power and wealth of the great European empires. To guarantee their security and economic interests, both believed they would have to acquire empires of their own. Germany was lim-

Franklin Delano Roosevelt and Winston Churchill at the Atlantic Charter Conference in Argentia, Newfoundland, in August 1941. Gen. George C. Marshall is in uniform behind Churchill.

ited largely to European acquisitions, and during World War I it sought to dominate central Europe. Hitler's war aims during the late 1930s essentially replicated those of Kaiser Wilhelm II before him. Japan, meanwhile, followed the model of England, another small island with limited resources. The only field for Japanese expansion lay on the East Asian mainland. Japan annexed Taiwan in 1895, and in 1910 it formally annexed Korea, a country in which it had wielded heavy influence for several decades. In 1931 Japan invaded Manchuria. By the late 1930s Japan's warlords had decided to expand to the south, thus directly threatening the American-dominated Philippines, as well as British, French, and Dutch possessions.

Appeasement Before and After Munich. In 1935 Hitler publicly repudiated the Treaty of Versailles and sent into the Rhineland the army he had created for three years in violation of the treaty. In 1938 Hitler invaded Austria and incorporated it into the German Reich. Badly frightened, France and Britain agreed that year at the Munich Conference to the German annexation of the Sudetenland area of Czechoslovakia, home to three million Germans. Calling the agreement appeasement, Winston Churchill predicted correctly that it would encourage Hitler to seize even more land. On 3 September 1939 German troops

World War II army recruiting billboard

marched into Poland. Britain and France declared war immediately, hoping to contain German power. The world would quickly learn that the Germans had secretly and rapidly developed strategies that would enable them to overrun much of eastern and western Europe. Hitler was aided in these plans by a secret 1940 treaty with Joseph Stalin of the Soviet Union, whereby the Soviets tolerated the German invasion of western Poland while Soviets occupied the eastern portion of that nation, as well as Finland, and annexed the Baltic states of Latvia, Lithuania, and Estonia.

An End to Appeasement. Until the invasion of Poland on 3 September 1939 Germany had declared that its territorial ambitions were restricted to the areas where sizable numbers of Germans dwelled, such as the Sudetenland and Austria. Its Axis alliance partner Japan had insisted that its conflict with China was intended to preserve Japanese access to that nation's vital natural resources. Yet Japan's announcement of its intention to create a Greater East Asian Co-Prosperity Sphere was seen by many as a code for imperial expansion at the expense of the established empires. By 1940 it was clear that Germany and Japan were bent on imperial conquest. American officials, already appalled by the militarism and authoritarianism of the Axis, feared that their national expansion would eclipse American ability to secure markets and raw materials

in those same regions. A Germany in control of the European core and a Japanese empire effectively sealing off East Asia, coupled with the preexisting Soviet Socialist bloc, would leave few outlets for American goods, thus limiting the capacity of the United States to emerge from the Depression. As the influential *Fortune Roundtable* put matters: "What interests us primarily is the longer-range question of whether the American capitalist system could continue to function if most of Europe and Asia should abolish free enterprise." American strategy until 1940 had been limited essentially to moral arguments urging both Germany and Japan to accept a world of open doors, globally integrated markets, and disarmament as the only rational choices for all the powerful nations. Axis intransigence led American officials to initiatives which presupposed war as the only means of achieving peace.

Isolationism. The predominant mood in the United States at this time was deeply isolationist. Many citizens believed that the nation's losses during World War I far outweighed any gains. During the early 1930s public hearings chaired by congressman Gerald Nye had done much to convince the public that World War I had resulted from the machinations of Wall Street cliques who benefited from arms sales and loans to the belligerents. The notion that "merchants of death" were responsible for manipulating America into war was widespread, and

Page from a Japanese code book showing the five-digit diplomatic cable cipher used during World War II

influential men such as Charles Lindbergh and retired U.S. Marine Corps Maj. Gen. Smedley D. Butler promoted the idea of "Fortress America" ensconced safely between the moats of the Atlantic and the Pacific, armed for defense but not for intervention into the corrupt affairs of Europe.

Interventionism. Interventionists, by contrast, insisted that the future of America lay in establishing peace and stability abroad for the sake of trade and commerce. A world divided into closed and self-contained trading blocs was a world in which America would not prosper. Interventionists anticipated that renewed American trade abroad might end the Depression. The United States thus had a vital stake in ensuring that the outcome of the war in Europe and Asia favored liberal democracies and market economic systems. Not all interventionists advocated direct military involvement toward this end. Many argued that economic assistance, as in the case of the Lend-Lease Plan, would be enough to ensure the survival of the western democracies. Others, however, insisted that liberal democracy and free enterprise would perish in a world dominated by authoritarian regimes. Such interventionists saw no alternative to military engagement. Even Wendell Willkie, the unsuccessful Republican contender for president in 1940, went on to write a best-seller titled *One World* (1943), arguing that peace was possible only in a world shaped by America. Roosevelt and his administration were sympathetic to interventionist arguments. As the German armies slashed across Europe, Roosevelt hoped that he might sway public opinion in favor of intervention by helping the British on the high seas and provoking German retaliation.

The Nazi Occupation of Western Europe. After the German invasion of Poland there was a lull in the German blitzkrieg, or lightning war. On the western front little happened, and many isolationists argued that Hitler had fulfilled his ambitions for German "living space" (lebensraum) in the east and would negotiate a peace with France and Britain. The Nazi spring offensive rendered those hopes vain. In April and May Germany quickly subdued Denmark, Norway, Belgium, and Holland. By mid June Paris had fallen to the German juggernaut, and at the infamous debacle of Dunkirk the British were forced to evacuate what few troops they had on the European mainland. In response Roosevelt increased the U.S. defense budget to nearly $2 billion and announced that the United States was changing from a policy of neutrality to one of "nonbelligerency," which in practice meant open support of the Allies short of war. The isolationists charged, correctly, that this act would lead inevitably to real combat.

The Battle of Britain. In midsummer Congress appropriated $4 billion more for naval construction. Simultaneously, Hitler was launching Operation Sea Lion, a planned invasion of the British Isles. The cross-channel attack began with a colossal assault by the German air force, intended to destroy British air capabilities. Believing that the bombing of civilians would destroy British morale, Hitler also launched the infamous blitz of London and other cities, causing widespread civilian casualties. The blitz, however, sidetracked German forces from their original objective and diminished their effectiveness against the Royal Air Force (RAF). The RAF fought valiantly, suffering enormous losses, and by November they had prevented a German invasion.

The Rattlesnakes of the Sea. In conjunction with the air war against Britain — hoping to deny Britain vital materials, many of which were accessible only from the United States — Hitler initiated a sea war, employing his dreaded submarines to frightening effect. These same "rattlesnakes of the sea," as Roosevelt labeled them, had prompted an American declaration of war in 1917. In August 1940 Roosevelt announced, over some congressional opposition, that he would give fifty American destroyers to Britain in exchange for U.S. naval access to British possessions. The exchange constituted an overt act of war, but Hitler was as yet unwilling to confront the United States. As was the case in World War I, the British navy effectively blockaded German ports while German submarines sank British cargo ships. While officially observing neutrality provisions that forbade them to aid British warships protecting convoys of British merchant vessels, the U.S. Navy secretly attempted to convey information about the movements of German vessels to the British. On a few occasions American ships actually dropped depth charges against German submarines that were threatening American cargoes on British ships. These acts resulted in steadily escalating violence between the American and German navies. By depicting German attacks as naked aggression against innocent American ships, Roosevelt inflamed public opinion, thereby eroding the isolationist base.

Isolationism and Domestic Politics. In Asia, meanwhile, Japanese expansion mirrored Hitler's activities in Europe. By summer 1940 the Japanese had crossed into French Indochina, within striking distance of the Dutch East Indies and the American Philippines. In July the United States announced an embargo on the export of scrap steel and iron outside the Western Hemisphere. Ostensibly a neutral act, the embargo was in fact directed against Japan, for that nation alone was dependent upon such imports from the United States. The apprehension of the public mounted. In 1937, 64 percent of Americans were deeply isolationist; by 1940 only 39 percent were. In his reelection campaign Roosevelt's rhetoric remained isolationist. On 16 September, however, he signed the Selective Training and Service Act, requiring the registration of men between the ages of twenty-one and thirty-five for military training. In October the president told concerned mothers at a Boston rally that "your boys are not going to be sent into any foreign wars." By the end of this eventful year he would announce that the United States would become the "arsenal of democracy," stipulating that henceforth the United States would manufacture and provide all the armaments necessary for the Allies to defeat the Axis. By 1941 America had implicitly sided with the Allies.

The Battle of the Atlantic. In his 1941 State of the Union Address, Roosevelt asked Congress to pass a bill to allow easy acquisition of arms and matériel by the British. In contrast to his modest budget proposals of the previous year, Roosevelt also asked Congress for nearly $11 billion for defense. Unknown to any but a few within the U.S. government, highly secret discussions were underway with Britain to coordinate military operations against the Axis. War planners agreed to concentrate first on the defeat of Germany, as the more serious of the two opponents, then on Japan. By early February 1941 the Battle of the Atlantic between Germany and Britain had escalated, and in response Roosevelt extended the American "sea frontier," and American naval protection, into the middle of that ocean. Desperate to deny Britain her supply lines, Germany ignored this warning. In March Congress passed the Lend-Lease Act, appropriating $7 billion for Britain. In that same month Roosevelt used broad powers assigned to him by Congress to freeze German and Italian assets in the United States and to close their consulates. In July U.S. Marines landed in Iceland to preempt any use of that territory for German naval vessels, and later that month Roosevelt froze all Japanese assets in response to the Japanese incursion into Indochina. Meeting secretly aboard warships in the North Atlantic, Prime Minister Winston Churchill and President Roosevelt announced the Atlantic Charter. Later endorsed by the Soviet Union, this charter became the basis for establishing the United Nations. In September, responding to an attack by a German submarine on the USS *Greer,* Roosevelt ordered the arming of American merchant vessels and a "shoot on sight" mandate against all German warships in the mid Atlantic. On Navy Day, 27 October 1941 — ten days after the Germans torpedoed and damaged the American destroyer *Kearny* off the coast of Greenland — the president declared: "America has been attacked, the shooting has started." Three days later, the Germans torpedoed the U.S.S *Reuben James,* which sank with the loss of more than one hundred seamen.

Hitler Invades the Soviet Union. The Hitler-Stalin Pact of 1939 had stunned Stalin's friends and enemies alike. Western opponents of the Soviets had always hoped that Hitler's territorial ambitions would lead him into the east; while western Communists had believed Stalin to be implacably opposed to fascism. In fact both forms of authoritarianism were utterly incompatible, and the mutual alliance was merely temporary — an armed truce. Hitler took advantage of the respite from hostilities with Stalin to enlarge and train his forces and focus his attention on the West. The Soviet Union overran Finland during this period, but the tiny Finnish forces were able to exact a surprisingly heavy toll on Soviet troops. Observers, including Hitler, took notice of the poor condition of the Red Army. Stalin had neglected the military and had executed thousands of high-ranking army officers during the political purges of the late 1930s, leaving Soviet forces virtually leaderless. Seizing on this advantage, Hitler launched a sudden attack on his erstwhile ally on 22 June 1941, quickly overwhelming Russian resistance and moving to the gates of Moscow by winter. If Russia fell, then German troops could be redeployed to the West and perhaps launch another attack on Britain. Despite traditional animosity to communism in the United States and widespread revulsion against Stalin's pact with the Nazis, Roosevelt immediately extended Lend-Lease aid to the Soviet Union. This assistance helped the Russians hold their lines. More significant, however, in blunting the German offensive was the scorched-earth policy of the retreating Red Army, which denied the Germans supplies. Hitler had, moreover, waited too long. An earlier diversion of the *Wehrmacht* to save Mussolini's failed invasion of Greece had postponed Operation Barbarossa, the invasion of Russia, by nearly three months. At the moment his troops were poised to capture the Soviet capital, the Russian winter intervened, and Hitler was forced to halt his operations. With American aid flowing through the Far Eastern port of Vladivostok the Soviet Union was able to withstand the initial onslaught and ultimately to turn the tide. At the crucial

It was no mystery that the Japanese were preparing for war with the United States. By the 1920s each nation had recognized the other as its most serious rival for domination of the western Pacific. Almost as soon as the catastrophe in Hawaii occurred, some historians and political analysts began speaking of a conspiracy of highly placed officials in Washington, D.C. The "Back Door to War" theorists — whose name derives from the title of the book in which historian Charles C. Tansill put forth one of the chief statements of this theory — believed that by issuing Japan an ultimatum to withdraw from East Asia or face Allied military action, Roosevelt and his advisers were inviting the Japanese to attack. The conspiracy theorists believed that the president left U.S. Pacific forces vulnerable on purpose, so that any Japanese attack would be so destructive as to eradicate any domestic opposition to entering the war. Given the undeclared naval war between the United States and Germany in the North Atlantic, the outbreak of war with Japan would also open the way for war against Japan's Axis ally Germany. According to revisionist historians, Roosevelt's primary aim was in fact war with Germany.

Many of these conspiracy theorists were isolationists who believed that the United States had no reason to enter World War II. These revisionists said that neither Japan nor Germany wanted war with the United States, and they pointed to a November 1941 statement in which Secretary of War Henry L. Stimson said that the problem of U.S.-Japanese relations was "how we should maneuver them into the position of firing the first shot." Since the United States knew the Japanese fleet was moving, conspiracy theorists asked, why did Roosevelt not send the American fleet to meet them and thus avert the attack at Pearl Harbor? They also asked why the U.S. carriers were out to sea that fateful morning, charging that Roosevelt had sacrificed the battleships, knowing their destruction would be sufficient provocation to make the public prowar, while reserving the carriers intact, knowing that they would be necessary to defeat the Japanese.

Historians who discount the Back Door to War theory argue that the case for a conspiracy is purely circumstantial; no documentation exists to prove it. These antirevisionists note that the Axis alliance was defensive and did not require Germany to declare war on the United States. Thus, there was no guarantee that a backdoor strategy to get the United States into a war with Germany would work. Furthermore, Japanese naval and troop concentrations were in Southeast Asia, so it was logical for military authorities to believe that a Japanese attack would come there, probably in the Philippines, rather than in Hawaii, where army and navy commanders had been told to relax their preparations for war. While the United States knew the Japanese fleet was moving, no one knew where it was, so American ships could not be dispatched to intercept it. Finally, the carriers at Pearl Harbor were out on routine maneuvers; their absence during the attack was not planned.

While there is no proof that Roosevelt and his advisers conspired to bring the United States into the war, it is clear that two men were forced unfairly to bear the brunt of the blame for the lack of military preparedness for Pearl Harbor — Adm. Husband Kimmel and Gen. Walter C. Short, the navy and army commanders on Hawaii. Joseph Grew, U.S. ambassador to Japan, had warned that the Japanese might try to attack Pearl Harbor, but navy authorities called such a move logistically improbable. They said Hawaii was too far from Japan, and Kimmel's superiors had told him the attack would come elsewhere. While he and Short were not court-martialed, they underwent a full congressional inquiry and were forced to retire early and sit out the war in disgrace.

Sources: Charles A. Beard, *President Roosevelt and the Coming of the War, 1941* (New Haven: Yale University Press, 1948);

Charles C. Tansill, *Back Door to War: Roosevelt Foreign Policy, 1933–1941* (Chicago: University of Chicago Press, 1952).

Battle of Stalingrad in 1943 Soviet troops inflicted enormous losses on their enemies and began the long process of pushing them back to Germany.

The Empire of the Rising Sun. In the Far East war began in 1931 with the Japanese invasion of Manchuria. Tokyo had also chafed at the outcome of the Treaty of Versailles and felt excluded from the club of great powers. Japanese leaders felt especially that they should have been accorded dominant status in East Asia. Instead it was clear that both the United States and Britain intended the region for themselves. Since 1899 the United States had promoted an "Open Door Policy" by which the western powers and Japan ostensibly could have equal access to the resources and markets in China. The industrial advantages that the United States had over its competitors, however, virtually ensured American predominance.

```
NAVAL MESSAGE          )        NAVY DE:  )TMENT
PHONE EXTENSION NUMBER                          MESSAGE
                                               PRECEDENCE
FROM    OPNAV              ADDRESSEES
                        CINCAF  CINCPAC    PRIBRIORITY
RELEASED BY  INGERSOLL                       ROUTINE
DATE    NOV 27 1981                          DEFERRED
TOR CODEROOM                CINCLANT  SPENAVO  PRIORITY
DECODED BY                                   ROUTINE
                                             DEFERRED
PARAPHRASED BY   SHALL                        4544

INDICATE BY ASTERISK ADDRESSEES FOR WHICH MAIL DELIVERY IS SATISFACTORY
                272337 CR  0921
UNLESS OTHERWISE DESIGNATED THIS DISPATCH WILL BE TRANSMITTED WITH DEFERRED PRECEDENCE
ORIGINATOR FILL IN DATE AND TIME FOR DEFERRED AND MAIL DELIVERY
                                DATE          TIME       GCT
TEXT                      NG
THIS DISPATCH IS TO BE CONSIDERED A WAR WARNING. NEGOTIATIONS
WITH JAPAN LOOKING TOWARD STABILIZATION OF CONDITIONS IN
THE PACIFIC HAVE CEASED AND AN AGGRESSIVE MOVE BY JAPAN IS EX-
PECTED WITHIN THE NEXT FEW DAYS.  THE NUMBER AND EQUIPMENT OF
JAP TROOPS AND THE ORGANIZATION OF NAVAL TASK FORCES INDICATES
AN AMPHIBIOUS EXPEDITION AGAINST EITHER THE PHILIPPINES OR KRA
PENINSULA OR POSSIBLY BORNEO.  EXECUTE AN APPROPRIATE DEFENSIVE
DEPLOYMENT PREPARATORY TO CARRYING OUT THE TASKS ASSIGNED IN
WPL46X INFORM DISTRICT AND ARMY AUTHORITIES. A SIMILAR WARNING
IS BEING SENT BY WAR DEPARTMENT.  SPENAVO INFORM BRITISH. CON-
TINENTAL DISTRICT GUAM SAMOA DIRECTED TAKE APPROPRIATE MEASURES
AGAINST SABOTAGE.

12....ORIGINATOR   RECORD COPY TO WPD WARDEPT...        CNO
NOV 28 '41 PM      FILE(88)
4544-16

S E C R E T                          SEE ART 76(4)
                                     NAV REGS
WPD WDGS
MAKE ORIGINAL ONLY, DELIVER TO COMMUNICATION WATCH OFFICER IN PERSON
```

Navy "war warning" sent to Adm. Husband Kimmel and Gen.
Walter Short at Pearl Harbor eleven days before
the Japanese attack

Facing a growing population, diminishing food reserves, and inadequate raw materials for its industrial production, Tokyo expanded its colonial rule by extending "Greater Japan" to the mainland of China. Colluding with its Axis alliance partners Nazi Germany and Fascist Italy, Japan forced the United States, Britain, and France to be vigilant on two fronts. As Hitler occupied attention in Europe, Japan seized European colonies in Asia. The United States sought to preserve the Open Door Policy and to extract peace guarantees from Tokyo, but throughout the decade Japan moved steadily down the coast of China, seizing French Indochina in 1940, and threatening the oil reserves of the Dutch East Indies, British dominions in Malaya and India, and the American bases in the Philippines.

Head to Head with Japan. Prior to 1940 the Japanese government had attempted to compromise with the United States within the limits of what it judged to be Japanese national interest. In July of that year hard-line militarists took over the government of Japan, even threatening Emperor Hirohito with assassination should he try to block the appointment of a new government. As late as summer 1941, however, the new prime minister, Prince Konoye Fumimaro, sought ways to avoid war. In January 1941, ostensibly at his insistence, a "peace" proposal was floated, promising the withdrawal of Japanese troops from China in return for American economic as-

sistance to Japan. Given the position of Japanese militarists, Washington doubted the Konoye government could deliver on such promises. Yet in February Japan sent a new ambassador to the United States, Adm. Nomura Kichisaburo, to begin talks with Secretary of State Cordell Hull, who demanded that Japan withdraw from the Asian mainland to its home islands.

Embargo. Meanwhile, the American oil embargo prompted Japan to pressure the Dutch for access to supplies in the East Indies. Japan began to stockpile oil and aviation gasoline. American officials wondered if this move was intended to meet the challenge of the embargo or to prepare for war. Oil was the lifeblood of Japan's military capacity, and the American embargo became the most crucial event in the entire sequence of events leading to war. Japan was faced with a critical choice: abandon its decade-long effort to control China and return to its home islands, or go to war with the most industrially productive, technologically advanced nation on earth. Faced with a "Hobson's choice" between acceding to American demands or going to war against the United States, Japanese leaders chose a lightning strike at the bulk of the American fleet in Hawaii, hoping to cause enough damage to deter a powerful American response. Desiring to use this strike as the basis for a negotiated compromise over the disposition of East Asian riches, Japan instead provoked the United States to total war, the consequences of which ultimately reduced much of Japan to rubble.

Last Attempts at Compromise. American cryptographers, using a system code named "Magic," had broken the top-secret Japanese diplomatic cable cipher and were thus privy to Japan's plans. American officials knew as early as July 1941 that Japan had decided to continue expanding south through Indochina and Siam (modern Thailand), whence they would put pressure on British Malaya and the Dutch East Indies. American strategists also knew that the United States did not have the capacity to carry on naval warfare in both oceans. Given the "Germany first" strategy, the problem became how to delay armed confrontation with Japan as long as possible. American diplomats stalled the Japanese while the British reinforced their garrison in Singapore, and the United States fortified Guam and took long-range bombers to the Philippines. To many Japanese these actions foreshadowed an Anglo-American surprise attack on Japan, so Japanese militants demanded that Japan attack first. When it became clear that Konoye's government could achieve no diplomatic breakthrough, the prime minister resigned, to be replaced by the hard-line Gen. Tojo Hideki. Even so, to appease the emperor, on 5 November, a little more than a month before Pearl Harbor, the Tojo government allowed a few more weeks for diplomacy, but it warned that unless a negotiated settlement favorable to Japan was reached by 25 November, Japan would go to war.

On 6 December 1941, a full fifteen hours before the Japanese attacked Pearl Harbor, President Franklin D. Roosevelt was handed a translation of a decrypted telegram sent by the Japanese foreign ministry in Tokyo to the Japanese ambassador to the United States, Adm. Nomura Kichisaburo. After studying the document carefully, Roosevelt turned to his most trusted adviser, Harry L. Hopkins, and said: "This means war!" Although he did not know where the Japanese would strike, the president now knew that an attack was imminent. In 1940 the U.S. military had devised a remarkable new electronic deciphering machine that enabled the U.S. Army Special Intelligence Service (SIS) and the Office of Naval Operations (ONI) to read Japan's top-secret diplomatic transmissions, which the Japanese thought were undecipherable. Code-named "Magic," the decipherment of the Japanese diplomatic code stands as one of the most important achievements in the history of intelligence operations.

For a time the ONI could also decipher Japanese naval codes, but they were changed shortly after Magic was perfected, and the Americans were never again able to decrypt them. Nevertheless, the decrypted diplomatic messages alone provided enough information to give fair warning of Japanese military intentions. Yet military intelligence officials were reluctant to share information with the White House for fear that "amateurs" in the administration would inadvertently betray Magic's existence. Roosevelt himself was not authorized to read Magic transcripts until 23 January 1941 — 140 days after the first top-level Japanese dispatches had been decoded. Even then many transcriptions never reached his desk. Intelligence specialists did not place a high priority on reading deciphered foreign-ministry cables because they knew diplomats would not be privy to the battle plans of the Imperial Navy. Focusing primarily on naval dispatches, they failed to interpret correctly information provided by Magic. Many transcripts that could have told them Pearl Harbor was the target were disregarded or remained unread on 7 December 1941.

Magic provided remarkable information. It told Washington that on 27 September 1940 Germany, Italy, and Japan had secretly signed the Tripartite Pact promising to aid each other in case of attack. Magic signaled the invasion of Indochina by the Japanese Imperial Army, and by deciphering messages between Germany and Japan it informed the United States that Adolf Hitler intended to attack the Soviet Union in June 1941.

In Magic's "finest hour," on 4 August 1941, it revealed Japan's decision not to attack the Soviet Union but to advance to the south and to begin to "arm for an all-out war against Britain and the United States" in order to break "the British-American encirclement" of Japan.

The Japanese overtly signaled their military intentions on 1 November 1941, when they suddenly changed all radio call signals for the Imperial Navy and began maneuvers intended to hide the positions of key carrier task forces. On 19 November Magic intercepted the "winds" code, by which Tokyo signaled its embassies of its intention to attack throughout Southeast Asia. ONI and SIS commanders realized "It meant war — and we knew it meant war." On 25 November Secretary of State Cordell Hull informed a cabinet meeting, "They are poised for attack — they might attack at any time." Two days later President Roosevelt and the War Department issued a "final alert" ordering all Pacific commanders to prepare for attack. On 2 December Tokyo ordered all embassies to "destroy all codes except one . . . and all confidential documents," a clear indication of impending war. As intelligence analysts contemplated where the attack would take place, Col. Rufus Bratton, commander of SIS, asked his counterpart at ONI, Comdr. Arthur McCollum, whether the attack might come at Pearl Harbor. "Out of the question," said McCollum.

When the Magic transcript Roosevelt read on 6 December was sent to U.S. Army Chief of Staff Gen. George C. Marshall, he was out riding his horse. It was nearly 1 P.M. in Washington, the time the Japanese had set to break off diplomatic relations, and nearly 6 A.M. at Pearl Harbor. Immediate warnings went to American forces in the Philippines and the Canal Zone, as well as to the Presidio Army Base in San Francisco. Afraid of compromising Magic by sending a message by military channels that the Japanese were likely to be monitoring, Marshall decided to send a warning to Pearl Harbor via Western Union. Bearing no special indication that it was urgent, the message was given to a bicycle messenger who reached army headquarters at 11:45, nearly four hours after the Japanese attack began. A sergeant put the message in a hopper with other messages, and it arrived on the desk of Gen. Walter C. Short at 4 o'clock in the afternoon.

Source: Ladislas Farago, *The Broken Seal: "Operation Magic" and the Secret Road to Pearl Harbor* (New York: Random House, 1967).

Pearl Harbor, 7 December 1941

To Pearl Harbor. In fall of 1941 all Japanese army and navy units were secretly warned: "war with Netherlands, America, England inevitable, general operational preparations to be completed by early December." The United States knew about this decision because it had used "Magic" to crack the Japanese diplomatic code. In November Tokyo sent special envoy Kurusu Saburo to join Ambassador Nomura in Washington for direct talks. The United States rejected "Plan A" submitted by the Japanese diplomats for lack of ironclad guarantees of a Japanese withdrawal from China. Acting on his own, Kurusu proposed a cooling-off period in which neither side would take action, but he was rebuked by his own government for making this offer. Another initiative, "Plan B," was subsequently rejected by Washington because it insisted on removal of support for the Chinese leader, Chiang Kai-shek, a proposal tantamount to abandonment of China. According to Herbert Feis, a diplomat involved in these discussions, this last demand constituted an "insistence on war." American newspapers printed stories that the United States was about to "sell out" China, and the government dropped all efforts to reach a last-minute accord. On 27 November the State Department declared that matters were now in the hands of the Department of War. That same day an alert went out to all commanders in the Pacific, including Adm. Husband Kimmel and Gen. Walter Short at Pearl Har-

bor, reading: "This dispatch is to be considered a war warning."

The Day of Infamy. Washington knew that Japan had decided to go to war after 25 November and that a Japanese carrier task force had been launched. The most likely targets appeared to be in Southeast Asia or the Philippines because the main American Pacific forces were at Hawaii, more than three thousand miles away. Washington judged an attack against Pearl Harbor to be all but logistically impossible. Nevertheless, in a carefully orchestrated refueling tactic, the Japanese fleet slipped past Guam and Midway, bringing nearly two hundred Mitsubishi-manufactured Zero aircraft within striking distance of most of the American Pacific fleet. Japanese fliers "zeroing" in on Battleship Row at Pearl Harbor were amazed at meeting no resistance. Despite the war alert Pearl Harbor was asleep. Many Japanese pilots wondered whether the American high command had remembered that the Russo-Japanese War of 1904–1905 had begun with a surprise attack at the Russian base at Port Arthur. Though Chief of Staff George Marshall had tried to send a warning via Western Union, it arrived too late. The messenger set out on bicycle from downtown Honolulu in time to witness the first wave of Japanese attacks. He arrived at army headquarters nearly two hours after the attack ended.

The End of Isolation. The strike by Japan killed 2,335 military personnel and wounded 1,178. Nineteen capital ships of the American fleet were sunk or damaged, and 150 aircraft were destroyed in the worst military disaster in the nation's history. Shock waves reverberated throughout the United States, immediately extinguishing most antiwar sentiment. So emotionally devastating was the news of Pearl Harbor that members of an entire generation of Americans can remember exactly where they were on 7 December 1941, when they first heard of the attack. Roosevelt appeared before Congress the next day and received an almost unanimous declaration of war. In the Senate every member voted for war; only one member of the House of Representatives — Jeannette Rankin, who had also opposed World War I — cast a vote in opposition. That morning army, navy, and marine recruiting offices were overrun with volunteers. The United States had finally entered the most titanic war in history.

Germany Declares War. The Tripartite Pact did not require any members of the Axis alliance to come to the aid of the others unless a member nation was attacked. Because Japan was the aggressor at Pearl Harbor, Hitler was not required to declare war on the United States. For this reason it is often argued that his decision to do so was the act of extreme irrationality that sealed his fate; had Hitler not announced overt war against the United States, Roosevelt's hands would have been tied by the isolationists, and Germany would have been free to wage war in Europe without interference from America. This interpretation ignores the extent to which American interventionists were alarmed by Hitler's goal of estab-

American prisoners of war, Bataan Peninsula in the Philippines, 9 April 1942

lishing economic control of Europe, inhibiting American free trade and thwarting the ability of the United States to emerge from the Great Depression. The United States was already battling Germany in the North Atlantic, and Hitler believed that the United States would directly intervene in Europe just as it had in 1917. Thinking that Japan had delivered a more devastating blow to American military power than in fact it had, and that forcing the United States to fight a two-front war was to his advantage, Hitler declared war on 11 December 1941. Two days later, Congress responded in kind.

Sources:

Robert A. Dallek, *Franklin D. Roosevelt and American Foreign Policy, 1932–1945* (New York: Oxford University Press, 1981);

Herbert Feis, *The Road To Pearl Harbor* (Princeton, N.J.: Princeton University Press, 1971);

Arnold A. Offner, *American Appeasement: United States Foreign Policy and Germany, 1933–1938* (New York: Norton, 1976);

John E. Wiltz, *From Isolation to War, 1931–1941* (Arlington Heights, Ill.: AHM Publishing, 1968).

AMERICA AT WAR: FROM HUMILIATION TO HEGEMONY IN THE PACIFIC

Setbacks in the Pacific. Three days after Pearl Harbor the Japanese Imperial Army invaded the American-controlled Philippines. Despite the war alert and the debacle at Hawaii, the entire American air fleet at Clark Field remained uncamouflaged and lined up on runways wingtip to wingtip. It was thus destroyed on the ground. Had it remained intact it might have thwarted, or delayed, the invasion. Meanwhile, the Japanese continued their drive into Thailand, Malaya, and Singapore. In quick order the American territories of Guam and Wake Island fell before Christmas. The new year witnessed Japan's takeover of the Dutch East Indies, and on 26–28 February a major defeat for Allied naval forces in the Battle of the Java Sea, where American forces were all but wiped out. By then the American garrison in the Philippines had withdrawn to the Bataan Peninsula, where it was overwhelmed and forced to surrender on 9 April. More than seventy-five thousand Americans and Filipinos would be forced on a "Death March" to Japanese prison camps. A majority of those taken prisoner died of maltreatment, hunger, and disease. All was not loss and defeat, however. In mid April Gen. James Doolittle led a force of bombers in the first American air raid on Tokyo. Most of the aircraft were either shot down or crash-landed in China for lack of fuel. The raids were not

Five bombers from the USS *Hornet* attacking a Japanese
heavy cruiser during the Battle of Midway

intended to have strategic impact but rather to boost the American public's morale.

Turning Point. Though the first six months of the Pacific War bore bitter tidings for Americans, in spring 1942 the fortunes of Japan began to change. The master plan drawn up by Adm. Yamamoto Isoruku — to inflict maximum damage on the American navy in order to buy precious time to negotiate — was thwarted by the unpredictable. On the morning of 7 December 1941 the aircraft carriers at Pearl Harbor, the heart of the American fleet, were at sea. Their destruction had been the most important aspect of the Japanese war aims because without them American military operations in the Pacific would have no air support. With its carriers intact the United States could strike back much more quickly than Yamamoto desired. He had told his superiors that he could "run wild" for the first six months or year of war, but he had no confidence for the second and third years. In May 1942 his prediction began to prove true. When a Japanese carrier force threatened the Allied air base at Port Moresby, New Guinea, the Battle of the Coral Sea became the first naval engagement in history in which ships did not fire on each other. Rather, the entire battle took place between planes based on the carriers of each fleet. The result was a decisive U.S. victory, made possible by the presence of the American carriers not destroyed at Pearl Harbor. Though the U.S.S. *Lexington* was destroyed, it and the *Yorktown* put three Japanese carriers out of commission and prevented any further Japanese expansion southward to Australia. The following month, at the Battle of Midway, with Japan's capital carriers missing, the United States broke the entire Japanese naval initiative. From then on Tokyo would fight a completely defensive war.

Guadalcanal. Eight months to the day after Pearl Harbor the United States launched the amphibious operations that eventually would push Japanese forces all the way back to the home islands. At an inconspicuous dot in the Pacific, the 1st Marine Division waded ashore under withering fire to establish its beachhead. Guadalcanal, a small island in the Solomon archipelago, was the scene of fighting more savage and brutal than anything in the annals of American warfare. Marines had been warned that the Japanese took no prisoners, and propaganda photos of captured fliers being beheaded were circulated before the invasion. The initial landings brought heavy casualties to marines struggling off landing craft, stimulating rage among the assaulting troops. Americans used flame throwers for the first time, and Japanese attempting to surrender were incinerated instead. Marines decapitated their enemies, displaying their heads atop tanks as trophies, while in jungle outposts severed heads of Japanese were impaled on stakes around the perimeters of the camps as grisly warning to enemy infiltrators. So frightened were both sides in the ferocious fighting that each came to believe they were fighting beasts, not men. As a result, fears based upon presumed racial traits of the other side began to preoccupy soldiers of both nations. Propaganda on each side depicted the other as pitiless subhumans, and combat degenerated into a "war without mercy." Japanese soldiers were ordered not to surrender, and American marines were told to take no prisoners. Expecting no compassion, neither side gave any. Racial stereotypes would predominate for the duration of the war, making combat for each toehold of territory in the Pacific a nightmare. Each battle became more horrific and costly than the last, culminating in the appallingly savage spring 1945 battles of Iwo Jima and Okinawa, where 130,000 Japanese and nearly 15,000 Americans lost their lives. At Okinawa 25,000 U.S. soldiers were evacuated after becoming psychologically disabled by combat fatigue, another measure of the ferocity of the fighting.

Winning the Pacific War. On 9 February 1943, six months after the American landings on Guadalcanal, the island was liberated from Japanese control. From then on American strategy involved an "island-hopping" campaign designed to defeat key Japanese forces and isolate others from resupply. Over the next few years small islands such as Bougainville, Tarawa, and Peleliu loomed large on the landscape of history as increasingly bloody battles were fought to wrest them from Japanese occupation. In April, in a symbolically important event, American fighter planes ambushed a plane carrying Admiral Yamamoto, shooting it down and killing him after a message decrypted by "Magic" had revealed Yamamoto's

Gen. Dwight D. Eisenhower with two aides just before the launch of Operation Torch, an amphibious landing on the shores of Morocco and Algeria

itinerary. In late 1943 U.S. forces moved from the Solomon Islands to the Gilberts. The new year witnessed a rapid movement through the Admiralty, Marshall, and Caroline chains, and then on to New Guinea. By mid July Saipan was captured, providing the United States with an air base from which to direct a long-range bombing campaign against Japan itself. On 10 August Guam was recaptured. In late October — a few days after American forces led by Gen. Douglas MacArthur returned to the Philippines — the U.S. Navy inflicted calamitous losses on the Japanese fleet in the Battle of Leyte Gulf. After this disaster Japanese military tactics became increasingly suicidal. The term *kamikaze* entered the American lexicon. Desperate to protect the home islands, the Japanese trained teenage boys to get aircraft airborne but not to land. They were expected to crash their planes into enemy ships, sacrificing their lives for the homeland. Though Americans saw the suicide runs as evidence of Japanese fanaticism, they were also proof of desperation.

Sources:

Harry Elmer Barnes, *Perpetual War For Perpetual Peace: A Critical Examination of the Foreign Policy of Franklin Delano Roosevelt* (New York: Greenwood Press, 1969);

Robert A. Dallek, *Franklin D. Roosevelt and American Foreign Policy, 1932–1945* (New York: Oxford University Press, 1981);

Robert A. Divine, *Roosevelt and World War II* (Baltimore: Johns Hopkins Press, 1969);

Bruce M. Russett, *No Clear and Present Danger* (New York: Harper & Row, 1972);

C. L. Sulzberger, *The American Heritage Picture History of World War II* (New York: American Heritage Publishing House, 1966).

AMERICA AT WAR: THE CAMPAIGNS IN NORTH AFRICA AND ITALY

The Battle for Oil Reserves. The Mediterranean Sea and the Suez Canal, which allowed passage into the Indian Ocean, had been the lifeline linking Britain and France to their African and Asian colonies and to the oil reserves of Iraq, Iran, and the Arabian Peninsula. Hitler wanted to deny these resources to his enemies and acquire them himself, but he was unwilling to commit troops to take them by force because such actions would

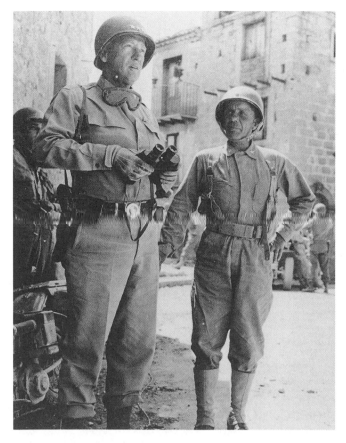

Gen. George S. Patton, left, in Sicily, July 1943

mand of the Afrika Korps in February 1941. Using speed, surprise, and deceit, Rommel routed British forces in some of the most inglorious days in British military history. (Rommel once mounted cardboard "tanks" on Volkswagens to trick the British into believing his forces were more numerous than they were.) The fall of Tobruk, Libya, in June 1942 enabled the Germans to advance into Egypt, where the British retreated to El Alamein, within sixty miles of the port of Alexandria. This dire situation resulted in a change of British commanders. Gen. Bernard Montgomery took over with orders to defeat Rommel. Single-mindedly, Montgomery ordered his forces to clear more than 500,000 mines planted by the Germans to stop British armor, with ghastly losses of nearly 14,000 men. Rommel's casualties were even higher. In October, after four bloody days at El Alamein, the Desert Fox's forces had been decisively defeated, and they were unaware as they retreated westward that a new blow was yet to come.

Operation Torch: A Dress Rehearsal For D-Day. The British victory in the crucial Battle of El Alamein caused a long, slow westward retreat of the German tank corps and made possible the American-led Operation Torch on 8 November 1942. An amphibious landing on the shores of Morocco and Algeria, Operation Torch was the largest such undertaking ever attempted, and it served as the dress rehearsal for the even larger Operation Overlord on D-Day 1944. The success of Operation Torch catapulted its planner, Lt. Gen. Dwight D. Eisenhower, into the front ranks of American strategists and led to his later appointment as supreme Allied commander in Europe. As Eisenhower said: "No government had ever attempted to carry out an overseas expedition involving a journey of thousands of miles from its bases. . . ." Because it worked, Operation Torch made Operation Overlord seem possible. At the same time, however, the landing in North Africa resulted in the first American casualties outside the Pacific and naval campaigns. Because Algeria, Tunisia, and Morocco were governed by the Vichy government of France, these casualties had come at the hands of French troops. President Roosevelt regarded French collaboration with the Nazis as evidence of perfidy, and he never trusted the French again. Yet Allied success in North Africa made possible a viable Free French Resistance under Gen. Charles de Gaulle.

American Armor Enters the Desert War. In February General Rommel nearly broke the back of Operation Torch at the Battle of the Kasserine Pass, but he was forced to halt for lack of food and fuel. Subsequently, he was relieved of duty, and his replacement found himself facing American armored divisions under the command of Maj. Gen. George Patton. Soldiers had never before faced warfare in a place like the deserts of North Africa, an area as vast and as featureless as the sea. Commanders took to navigating by the stars as sailors did. Keeping armies supplied with water, and machinery with fuel, was a constant and major concern. Soldiers lived constantly

have weakened his position in Europe. Instead he exploited anti-British sentiment to obtain from the Persians a treaty guaranteeing Germany access to oil and another from the Turks assuring German entry to the Black Sea and the Mediterranean. Benito Mussolini complicated these plans, however. Like its Axis ally Germany, Italy had chafed at its lack of an overseas empire and had invaded Ethiopia in 1935. In September 1940, when Hitler's western blitzkrieg seemed about to achieve early victory, Mussolini sent troops to threaten British-held Egypt. Simultaneously he invaded Greece, thus jeopardizing British control over the Mediterranean. Italian maneuvers proved inept, however, and German armored divisions had to be sent to the rescue. Because German divisions were diverted to Greece and North Africa, Hitler had to postpone Operation Barbarossa, the invasion of Russia. Gen. George C. Marshall, U.S. Army chief of staff, later said that Hitler's overextension in North Africa "subsequently became one of the principal factors in Germany's defeat."

El Alamein. In September 1940 Italian forces in their colony Libya launched a drive against the British in Egypt. Mussolini harbored dreams of expanding the Italian empire into areas once held by ancient Rome, but Italian forces were humiliated in North Africa, as they were in the Balkans. Hoping to drive the British from the Suez Canal and to rescue his Italian allies, Hitler sent Gen. Erwin Rommel, the "Desert Fox," to take com-

Franklin Delano Roosevelt, Winston Churchill, and Joseph Stalin at the Tehran Conference, 30 November 1943

encased in dust. Many on both sides could see little purpose in fighting and dying over what seemed like worthless sand. Nevertheless, in combination with Montgomery's forces, Patton and his men decisively defeated Hitler's Afrika Korps and set the stage for the subsequent invasion of Sicily and mainland Italy. Though the war in North Africa seemed a sideshow, especially to Stalin, who was facing 90 percent of the Nazi legions, it was extremely important in demonstrating that large-scale amphibious operations were possible and that an invasion of the European mainland could succeed.

The Soft Underbelly of Europe. The military value of the Italian campaign remains in question among historians to this day. It seemed logical to put one of Hitler's allies out of commission, and planners argued that an Anglo-American army landing in Italy would draw German divisions away from the Russian front. American strategic planners believed an invasion of Italy would be relatively easy and provide an avenue of approach into the core of Europe. Yet the Apennines, the bony spine of Italy, combined with a harsh winter and the grim determination of the Nazis to hold northern Italy, made this phase of the war much more costly than the Allies expected. Hitler's commanders had long been aware of the vulnerability of the long Italian coastline and had taken care to place effective defenses at strategic sites. While only a small part of the *Wehrmacht* was stationed in Italy, these forces were highly trained and determined to prevent an Allied breakthrough to Germany from the south.

The Invasion of Sicily. After successfully deceiving the Germans about the site of the planned invasion, the Allied armada began landing troops on the south coast of

Sicily in July 1943. As with the later Normandy landing, rough weather almost created a disaster, but by midday Eisenhower was reporting success. Most Italian soldiers offered only token resistance and surrendered quickly, while Italian civilians brought flowers and wine to the invading troops. German troops, however, mounted a stiff defense. General Patton moved quickly to seize Palermo, the capital of Sicily, and then vied with Montgomery to be first to take Messina, across the narrow channel from the "toe" of the Italian peninsula. "This is a horse race in which the prestige of the U.S. Army is at stake," said Patton. Patton won the race, and American troops entered a deserted city. The Nazis had evacuated to the mainland. In Italy the psychological effect of rapid defeat in Sicily broke the back of Mussolini's government. On 25 July he resigned, and the new government, led by Pietro Badoglio, began peace negotiations with the Allies. The announcement of Italian surrender, coupled with their easy victories, led to wild celebrations among British and American troops, but their excitement was premature. Convinced that the Italian campaign was won, they were completely unprepared for the hardships ahead. Seeing Badoglio's quick surrender as betrayal by an ally, the Germans quickly reinforced their troops in Italy to prevent an Allied movement northward to threaten Austria and Germany.

Anzio. The Allied invasion of Italy began on 9 September 1943 at the sandy beaches near Salerno, where soldiers met withering fire from German coastal defenses. Later that month, when American and British troops entered Naples, German demolition teams destroyed the port facilities. As the invasion continued, Allied troops were forced to fight for every inch of moun-

The Japanese ruling elite had been divided about relations with the United States since Commodore Matthew Perry opened Japanese ports to American trade in 1854. Most agreed that their nation should adopt Western technology and military organization, and Japan rapidly modernized to become a first-rate military power. Yet she was still at a disadvantage. Because Japan had been backward and powerless throughout the period of Western empire building, the resources of Asia were largely controlled by foreigners. Though Europeans had expanded into Asia by conquest, they condemned the Japanese invasions of Korea and Manchuria, prompting a prominent Japanese diplomat to exclaim that Europe had taught Japan the game of poker, only to condemn the game as immoral after winning most of the chips. Japanese militarists believed that the only solution to their overpopulation and lack of natural resources was expansion, to gain not only much-needed space and sources of raw materials but also markets for finished goods. Japanese officials chafed at the attempts of the United States and the League of Nations to restrict their annexation of new territory, fearing that the Western powers were pursuing a racist agenda bent on making Japan a subordinate satellite in a world system managed by others. Believing Japan to be a great nation, they insisted that they were as entitled to control East Asia as Britain was to rule India or as the United States was to dominate the Western Hemisphere.

Japanese military actions since the turn of the century had in fact provided an outlet on the Asian mainland for surplus population, where Japanese farmed, mined natural resources, and produced industrial goods for the benefit of the home islands. In effect Japan had already integrated the economy of eastern China into her own. To withdraw from China entirely, as the United States demanded, would have necessitated moving millions of Japanese from mainland Asia back to Japan itself, with little but promises to feed them. Withdrawal from China would have caused more than social and economic upheaval, however, as the Japanese army was firmly opposed to such action and would almost certainly overthrow any government that attempted it. The alternative to meeting American and British demands was an attack on British and American interests in the East, hoping to get a bargaining chip that would lead to maintaining the status quo. A major attack that could disrupt the ability of the American military to retaliate rapidly might also buy Japan time to bolster its defenses and create a series of impregnable fortresses across the Pacific. Japanese leaders hoped that the next step would be a negotiated settlement in Japan's favor. Japan might have opted to attack its archenemy Russia and attempt to annex Siberia. The development of natural resources in northern Asia was a long way off, however, whereas successful seizure of Southeast Asia meant rapid economic and strategic gains. More important, Japanese leaders saw the United States becoming the most militarily powerful nation and knew that time was short for building their empire. When the United States cut off Japanese supplies of steel and oil in 1940–1941 and then issued an ultimatum demanding that Japan withdraw from China and Indochina or face war, Tokyo believed it was faced with the proverbial "Hobson's choice," that is, no choice at all, but to attack Pearl Harbor.

Source: Bruce M. Russett, *No Clear and Present Danger: A Skeptical View of U.S. Entry Into World War II* (New York: Harper & Row, 1972).

tainous territory. Even in the valleys they had to cross rivers at flood stage, under constant fire. The commander of the American Sixth Corps, Maj. Gen. John P. Lucas, wrote in his diary: "I hope I never have to see another mountain again as long as I live." In January 1944 the attempt to cross the Rapido River and establish a bridgehead north of Cassino failed, as soldiers of the Thirty-Sixth Army Division panicked, many refusing to board boats. Of those who managed to cross, all were either killed or taken prisoner. German mountain defenses made the capture of Rome seem nearly impossible. That same month Eisenhower, who reasoned that the Italian capital could be taken only by drawing German troops down from the mountains, ordered an amphibious attack at Anzio, south of Rome on a broad coastal plain. He hoped that this two-pronged strategy would enable troops in the mountains to break through the German defenses, but the Germans dug in at the monastery of Monte Cassino, overlooking a strategic pass into a valley leading to Rome. There the campaign bogged down. Success at Anzio depended on taking Monte Cassino. Even as Allied planes dropped more than a thousand tons of bombs on the monastery, reducing it to rubble, the Germans continued to hold on until 18 May. In the final week of fighting alone Allied casualties were reported at more than four thousand fatalities with an equal number missing and presumed dead. Allied forces at Anzio, hemmed in since January, broke out of German encirclement on 23–24 May, as enemy forces retreated. Seeing a chance to capture Rome before the British, American general Mark Clark led his troops into the Eternal City on 4 June. By doing so he allowed the bulk of the German army to escape to fight another day. His superior officers were outraged, but the capture of Rome made Clark a popular hero, with Italian and American civilians alike.

The Last Days of Mussolini. After Mussolini was forced to resign in July 1943, he was held under house arrest by his successor, Badoglio. The following September German commandos rescued Mussolini in a daring raid. Following Hitler's orders, Mussolini set up a puppet government for German-controlled areas of northern Italy. On 28 April 1945, while British and American troops were forcing the last Germans out of Italy, Italian Communist partisans executed Mussolini. As the Germans signed an unconditional surrender of all their troops in Italy, the partisans took Mussolini's body to Milan, where they hanged it upside down in the public square.

Hiroshima before it was bombed

Sources:

Harry Elmer Barnes, *Perpetual War For Perpetual Peace: A Critical Examination of the Foreign Policy of Franklin Delano Roosevelt* (New York: Greenwood Press, 1969);

Robert A. Dallek, *Franklin D. Roosevelt and American Foreign Policy, 1932–1945* (New York: Oxford University Press, 1981);

Robert A. Divine, *Roosevelt and World War II* (Baltimore: Johns Hopkins Press, 1969);

Bruce M. Russett, *No Clear and Present Danger* (New York: Harper & Row, 1972);

C. L. Sulzberger, *The American Heritage Picture History of World War II* (New York: American Heritage Publishing House, 1966).

AMERICA AT WAR: THE FINAL PUSH IN EUROPE

Planning the D-Day Invasion. President Franklin D. Roosevelt and Prime Minister Winston Churchill had met regularly since the United States entered the war. Since the inclusion of Russia in the alliance came about essentially as a marriage of convenience, it is not surprising that Russia was not included in strategic planning until midway through the war. Both the United States and Britain had been hostile to the Communist state since its birth in 1917. Some politicians in England and America even believed that their nations should have allied themselves with Germany against Russia. As a senator in 1940, Harry S Truman had declared, "If we see that Germany is winning then we should help Russia and if Russia is winning we ought to help Germany, . . . and let them kill as many as possible." At the Casablanca Conference in January 1943, Roosevelt and Churchill announced demands for the unconditional surrender of Germany and Japan, ensuring their other allies that an armistice like the one which ended World War I would not endanger future peace and reassuring Stalin that they would not conclude a separate peace with Hitler. They also planned the invasion of Sicily and Italy while considering a plan to invade France by crossing the English Channel. Though not present, Stalin made clear his desire for the establishment of a significant second front somewhere in western Europe to draw off the bulk of the German forces then concentrated on the Russian front. At the Quebec Conference in August 1943, again not attended by Stalin, final agreement was reached on the cross-channel invasion of Europe, which was set for 1 May 1944. Since Soviet troops were engaging the *Wehrmacht* virtually alone at the time of the conference, Stalin could easily believe that the United States and Great Britain were deliberately biding their time to ensure that Russian forces would absorb most of the Allied casualties. Even the invasion of Italy that September did not draw many German troops away from the Russian front. Logistically, though, it was not yet possible for the United States to ferry enough troops and equipment across the Atlantic to enter the European theater of operation in a meaningful way. Moreover, even if Britain and America had been able to open a second European front at that time, they would have incurred the same sort of heavy casualties the Russians were enduring. Roosevelt would never have been able to promote his policy of unconditional surrender to the American public in the face of such losses. In late 1943, at the Tehran Conference, Roosevelt and Churchill came face to face with Stalin. Then they had to tell him that until such time as the difficulties of crossing the English Channel with a formidable armada could be solved, the Russians would have to bear the brunt of the fighting and dying.

The Liberation of Europe. After a year and a half of preparations the greatest amphibious force ever assembled was ready to cross the English Channel. In a single day, 6 June 1944, Operation Overlord successfully moved 150,000 men onto the European continent. Within days of D-Day two armies, landing at separate beachheads —

Hiroshima after the atomic bomb was dropped on
8 August 1945

code named Omaha and Utah — in Normandy, converged to present a solid line against the Germans. Hitler believed the Normandy invasions to be a diversion for a larger incursion to the south, and despite pleas from his commanders he allowed the northern French coast to remain relatively undefended. That mistake was one of the reasons that high-level members of the German officer corps made an attempt on Hitler's life on 20 July 1944. Despite a few setbacks, notably the infamous Battle of the Bulge in the dense Ardennes Forest of Belgium, the Allied armies moved inexorably toward the German heartland. By winter 1945, as American air power devastated German airfields, factories, and oil depots, civilian populations were targeted in hopes of breaking German morale. In February 1945 the city of Dresden was firebombed, killing 135,000 civilians. Heavy bombing of other German cities followed. By spring the capital, Berlin, lay in ruins, a "city of the dead" and a grim symbol of the failed Third Reich. On 30 April 1945 Adolf Hitler put a gun to his head and pulled the trigger. On 7 May the remnants of the German army surrendered unconditionally. Raucous crowds in the Allied capitals demonstrated their happiness on V-E (Victory in Europe) Day, but joy quickly turned to somber reflection as thoughts turned to battle left to be fought in the Pacific.

The Yalta Conference. During 4–11 February 1945 — with the defeat of the Axis imminent — Roosevelt, Churchill, and Stalin met at Yalta, in Crimea, to discuss the shape of the postwar world. On the agenda were issues raised but not resolved in previous meetings: Soviet entry into the war against Japan; the government and borders of Poland; the fate of Germany and Eastern Europe; and the number of seats to be accorded the Soviet Union in the new United Nations. Complicating matters was the rapid advance of the Red Army toward Berlin. When the D-Day invasion had begun, Stalin had staged a coordinating Russian offensive in the east. Fearing Russians more than the Americans and British, two-thirds of the German forces were fighting desperately and in vain to keep the Red Army at bay.

The Soviets and Eastern Europe. It was clear to Roosevelt that by the time of the inevitable German surrender Soviet forces would occupy Berlin, as well as all of Eastern Europe. Roosevelt was realistic and pragmatic, and he understood that nothing could be done to dislodge the Red Army from positions that had cost it so many lives. Germany would be divided into four occupation zones to be controlled by the United States, Great Britain, France, and the Soviet Union. Eastern Europe would become a Soviet sphere of influence. Stalin viewed Soviet control of Eastern Europe as a "matter of life and death." Twice in the twentieth century German troops had invaded Russia by marching through Poland. Some Eastern European countries had assisted the Germans in their Russian campaign. During World War II the Soviets lost more than 25 million people, and Stalin sought to ensure that no government on his borders could pose any future threat. He agreed to free elections in Poland, which his troops had under firm control, but he later reneged on his promise. Roosevelt believed that his personal relationship with Stalin could ensure adequate treatment for the peoples under Soviet control and that he could ease American concerns about democratic governments and open markets in the region. Furthermore, the Soviet leader wanted something in return for entering the war against Japan; at the very least he wanted the territories Russia had lost to Japan in the Russo-Japanese War of 1904–1905. In return for Stalin's agreement to invade Japanese-occupied Manchuria within two or three months after the defeat of Germany, Roosevelt agreed to these territorial demands. At the same time, Stalin agreed to accept three UN seats for the Soviet Union, instead of one for each of the sixteen republics in the Soviet Union, as he had first proposed. Presuming that Stalin never bargained in good faith, some critics called such notions naive; many condemned the Yalta accords as a sellout of American interests. American officials opposed to Roosevelt's agreements at Yalta feared that Russia would seek to occupy Japanese territory, thereby jeopardizing plans for the postwar reconstruction of that nation. Roosevelt's conciliatory views died with him on 12 April 1945, and men hostile to his conception of the postwar world gained ascendancy in American politics.

Sources:

Harry Elmer Barnes, *Perpetual War For Perpetual Peace: A Critical Examination of the Foreign Policy of Franklin Delano Roosevelt* (New York: Greenwood Press, 1969);

Robert A. Dallek, *Franklin D. Roosevelt and American Foreign Policy, 1932–1945* (New York: Oxford University Press, 1981);

Robert A. Divine, *Roosevelt and World War II* (Baltimore: Johns Hopkins Press, 1969);

Bruce M. Russett, *No Clear and Present Danger* (New York: Harper & Row, 1972);

C. L. Sulzberger, *The American Heritage Picture History of World War II* (New York: American Heritage Publishing House, 1966).

AMERICA AT WAR: THE WAR ENDS IN THE PACIFIC

Bombing Japan. Shortly after the success of American troops in Normandy, U.S. long-range bombers began to pummel the Japanese mainland. In October MacArthur returned to the Philippines as he had promised, and in March U.S. Marines completed the capture of Iwo Jima in the bloodiest fighting in the Pacific up to that time. The raising of the flag on Mount Suribachi after the Iwo Jima campaign became the symbol of American triumph. Yet even worse fighting took place in June on Okinawa, the gateway to the Japanese home islands, where some 13,000 Americans and 100,000 Japanese lost their lives. So savage was the fighting in the last months of the Pacific War that troops in the field came to fear that a presumed invasion of Japan proper would cost the United States a million casualties, dwarfing the losses at Normandy the year before. The need to avoid such shocking losses became the overriding concern in the official rationale for what happened next.

Hiroshima and Nagasaki. On 16 July 1945 the United States detonated the world's first atomic bomb at Alamogordo, New Mexico. On 6 August a single American bomber flying over Hiroshima, the eighth largest city in Japan, dropped one bomb, code-named "Little Boy." The resulting explosion, astounding even the scientists who created it, leveled more than four square miles of the city, instantly killing more than 50,000 people. As Stalin had agreed, Soviet troops entered the war in Asia on 8 August, as American demands for the unconditional surrender of Japan went unanswered. The Japanese government was confused at first, unable to verify the dimensions of the damage in Hiroshima because of destroyed communications lines. By the time Tokyo realized the catastrophic power of the Americans' unprecedented new weapon, the deadline for surrender had passed. Thus, on 9 August a second bomb, "Fat Man," was dropped on Nagasaki, essentially destroying that city as well. The next day the Japanese Supreme Council voted to surrender unconditionally. On the fifteenth, V-J Day, the Allies accepted it. The most horrific war in human history had finally ended. The victors' effort to pick up the pieces would soon lead to new strife and a bipolar world tense with the possibility of nuclear war.

Sources:
Harry Elmer Barnes, *Perpetual War For Perpetual Peace: A Critical Examination of the Foreign Policy of Franklin Delano Roosevelt* (New York: Greenwood Press, 1969);

Robert A. Dallek, *Franklin D. Roosevelt and American Foreign Policy, 1932–1945* (New York: Oxford University Press, 1981);

Robert A. Divine, *Roosevelt and World War II* (Baltimore: Johns Hopkins Press, 1969);

Bruce M. Russett, *No Clear and Present Danger* (New York: Harper & Row, 1972);

C. L. Sulzberger, *The American Heritage Picture History of World War II* (New York: American Heritage Publishing House, 1966).

AMERICA AT WAR: THE WAR AT HOME

The Public Prepares. Though the Japanese attack at Pearl Harbor virtually wiped out isolationist sentiment and unified the United States for war, there was little public romanticism or glorification of war, as there was when the country entered World War I. The American public understood that the war would be costly and disruptive of everyday life. To meet the challenge the American people were encouraged by wartime propaganda to expect and accept the intrusion of government into daily affairs. Though somewhat conditioned to government intervention by federal programs during the Great Depression, the scale on which the government ran the war economy and invested in it caused many in public life to worry about a possible long-term alteration in American traditions. They feared that the defeat of the totalitarian Axis powers might well require the United States to adopt some their enemies' methods of social and economic organization.

Mobilization. Alone of all the Allies, the United States had the manpower and resources to supply the entire war effort — and to win the war. Organizing this task properly would make or break the cause. No political leader was better placed than President Franklin D. Roosevelt to head this endeavor, and most Americans followed his lead with deep loyalty. Lauded as the architect of the New Deal, the president was believed by much of the public to have vanquished the Depression by force of his personality alone. The reality was different: despite success at alleviating the worst rigors of unemployment, hunger, and homelessness, government welfare programs had not cured the Depression. Ultimately, only mobilization for total war overcame the malaise. Before Pearl Harbor the Lend-Lease program and military preparedness required stepped-up production. The Selective Service Act of 1940 initiated the process of drafting young men for military service. Roosevelt's closest adviser, Harry Hopkins, announced total mobilization and streamlining of the economy. Labor would be allocated, goods rationed, and nonessentials — right down to college courses — eliminated. Hopkins was quoted as saying, "I see no reason for wasting time on . . . nonessentials, such as Chaucer or Latin. . . . A diploma can only be framed and hung on the wall, a shell that a boy or girl helps to make can kill a lot of Japs."

Economic Conversion. Between 1940 and 1946 the federal government spent $370 billion to prosecute the war, compared with the $46 billion it spent under the New Deal. No one worried any longer about overproduction, a much-feared weakness in American capitalism and one of the major causes of the Depression. War expenditures included items such as servicemen's wages, veterans' benefits, investment in synthetic-rubber development, and the building of bomber and tank factories. Costs associated with conversion from civilian production to war production were paid almost entirely by the federal government — that is, the American taxpayer.

President Harry S Truman at first had profound misgivings about using atomic bombs against civilians, and he explained his decision to drop atomic bombs on the Japanese cities of Hiroshima and Nagasaki by stressing that the bombings were necessary to end the war, thereby saving the lives of many Americans and Japanese alike. Almost immediately after Hiroshima and Nagasaki, public doubts about the military necessity of the atomic bombings emerged. It was well known in the highest circles of the American government that Japan was using back-channel diplomatic means to seek an end of the war. The Office of Strategic Services (OSS) and the Strategic Bombing Survey stressed the near-total collapse of the Japanese economy and military. Allied bombing raids had badly damaged or reduced to rubble all but eight Japanese cities. Japanese factories had been obliterated. Most Japanese troops were in China, cut off from and unable to defend the home islands. The Japanese navy had ceased to exist. Many of Truman's military advisers — including Navy Secretary James Forrestal, Gen. Dwight D. Eisenhower, and Admiral of the Fleet William D. Leahy — were adamantly opposed to the bombings, believing that continued conventional bombing, a naval blockade, and the entry of the Soviet Union into the Asian war would end the war quickly. American policy had always called for unconditional surrender by all the Axis powers. Truman and some of his advisers were loath to accept a negotiated settlement to the Pacific war, particularly since Japan was all but prostrate. At the same time, Japanese kamikazes, while evidence of growing Japanese desperation, were taking a toll on the U.S. Navy. The cost of the Manhattan Project to build the atomic bomb was more than $2 billion, and some administration officials, including Gen. George C. Marshall, believed that failure to use the fruits of this expensive project while American servicemen were still dying would subject President Truman to severe public criticism.

Most historical questions about the use of the atomic bombs have focused on the worsening relations between the United States and the Soviet Union. Under terms specified at Yalta the Red Army was to enter the Far Eastern war on 8 August 1945. Before the first successful atomic test at Alamogordo, New Mexico, on 16 July 1945, American officials believed Soviet participation to be essential to Japanese defeat. After the successful atomic test, however, the United States had the power to force a quick surrender before Soviet troops could occupy Japanese territory. Truman did not want the same sort of quarrels over Asian territories that the Allies were having over Eastern Europe. A joint Soviet-American occupation of defeated Japan would have wrecked American strategies for the postwar reconstruction of Asian markets. As Secretary of War Henry Stimson had written in his diary, the United States "held all the cards . . . and we mustn't be a fool about the way we play them." The distance between American and Soviet national interests was already evident, and some of Truman's advisers warned of future conflict. The United States had to display some counterweight to the combat-toughened Red Army. The fireballs over Hiroshima and Nagasaki announced America's power and the willingness to use it.

Sources: Gar Alperovitz, *Atomic Diplomacy: Hiroshima and Potsdam* (New York: Simon & Schuster, 1965);

Martin Sherwin, *A World Destroyed: The Atomic Bomb and the Grand Alliance* (New York: Knopf, 1975).

For the first time income taxes were levied on the working and middle classes. To ensure revenues the government used the unprecedented means of payroll deduction. Bond drives were also an important means of financing defense output. To control inflation Uncle Sam was forced to impose wage and price controls, an outrage to free-market advocates, but these critics were somewhat mollified by the simultaneous suspension of the antitrust laws, which were supposed to prevent the emergence of monopolies in the marketplace. To win the cooperation of big business even further, the government instituted the "cost-plus-a-fixed-fee contract," which spelled out a guaranteed profit for all government contractors. By the early war years Wall Street financiers, who had until recently denounced the Roosevelt Administration as a "pack of semi-communist wolves," were demanding the predominant share of government contracts for the industrial corporations they represented. As Secretary of War Henry L. Stimson put it: "If you are going to go to war, or prepare for war, in a capitalist country, you have got to let business make money out of the process or business won't work." By the end of the war, corporate giants would dominate the American economy as never before. In 1940 about 175,000 firms accounted for 70 percent of the nation's manufacturing output, while 100 other companies provided the remaining 30 percent. Three years later, with production doubled, the ratio was exactly reversed.

Japanese-American soldiers in the American army in Italy

Subduing Labor. Though Roosevelt called for voluntary cooperation from all parties in the war effort, it was clear that corporate energies would best be mobilized by economic enticements. For labor, however, coercion was the rule. The crisis of the Depression had made labor unruly to say the least and had spurred the creation of new, powerful, industrial unions in the Congress of Industrial Organizations (CIO). The 1930s had witnessed strikes and pitched violence between labor, police, and national guardsmen. The expansion in the number of wartime jobs put a damper on labor militancy; yet absenteeism and turnover were rife throughout most industries, primarily because of poor working conditions and low pay. Consequently, the government and business wanted to regulate the labor force. First the power to draft men into the military was transferred to a new agency, the War Manpower Commission, headed by Paul V. McNutt, a former governor of Indiana. In January 1943 he issued his infamous "work or fight" order, which ended all military deferments to people in jobs deemed unessential. Thus, many laborers were forced to leave their current occupations and go to work in defense industries. Labor leaders were outraged at the double standard of incentives for business and compulsion for labor. Only one labor representative sat on the War Production Board, and nearly two-thirds of the War Labor Board had no union affiliation or were known to be suspicious of the union movement. Wages were removed from the realm of collective bargaining. Strict wage controls would be the order of the day. If an ordinary worker wanted or needed more money, he — or increasingly she — would have to work overtime. Labor leaders expressed alarm at these developments. Philip Murray of the CIO said that "if anyone . . . is foolish enough to believe that national regimentation . . . will not give us a complete Fascist control over American workers during this war, then I say they are perfectly crazy."

Rationing. Perhaps no form of government intervention in the economy rankled Americans as much as rationing. Government price-control plans nonetheless hinged on it. By early 1943 consumers needed ration coupons to buy gasoline, meat, coffee, butter, sugar, shoes, and other items. Each family was allocated coupons on the basis of size, and theoretically, no one could get more than a fair share. Yet every interest group in the country scrambled to get preferential treatment, putting political pressure on the Office of Price Administration. Corruption was inevitable given the temptation by many to profit by selling goods to individuals without coupons or to sell extra coupons to people who were not entitled to them. Those able to pay a premium price were able to acquire scarce goods without difficulty, while the less privileged often went without. Prices inevitably crept upward, ahead of wage increases. The rationing program seemed almost designed to set citizens against each other, and it was with great relief that all such controls were lifted at the end of the war. Then, however, prices exploded uncontrollably, rapidly increasing in great disproportion to wages.

Labor During the War. Shortly after Pearl Harbor both labor and business promised to refrain from strikes and lockouts for the duration of the war. Nevertheless, nearly 1 million workers took part in work stoppages in 1942, while 3.1 million did so the following year. The American industrial workplace, despite rhetoric about the patriotic duty of Americans to be fair to each other, remained a dangerous and often dehumanizing place. As late as 1944 more Americans were being killed or maimed on the job than in battle overseas. Coal mining was by far the most dangerous occupation in the nation, and despite the high profits enjoyed by the industry, wages for coal miners failed to keep up with price increases. In spring 1943 John L. Lewis of the United Mine Workers union called the rank and file out of the pits. Given the patriotism of wartime, the public response was overwhelmingly negative, and Lewis may well have become the most unpopular man in America. Even the Communist Party lashed out at Lewis, claiming that he had forced the miners to strike and given Adolf Hitler a major victory. In response to the strike President Roosevelt ordered Secretary of the Interior Harold Ickes to take over all anthracite and bituminous coal mines on 1 May. A few days later the president announced that since the nationalization had made coal miners government employees, they had no right to strike, but the dispute continued. The War Labor Board (WLB) insisted that the strike posed "a serious threat to the maintenance of Government by law and order" and urged prison for union officials. Secretary Ickes countered, "There are not enough jails in the country to hold these men, and if there were, I must point out that a jailed miner produces no more coal than a striking miner." Nevertheless, in June Congress responded by passing the Smith-Connally Bill, which expanded the president's powers to nationalize industrial workshops and made it a crime to encourage strikes in such plants. Roosevelt tried and failed to veto the bill, and its passage did not bring peace to the coalfields or any other industrial sector. Ultimately, the coal strike was solved only by going to the root of the problem. In November wages were raised by using a technicality that did not violate the no-pay-increase provision of the WLB. (By mid October all the mines had been returned to their owners.) For the first time in American history mine wages reached parity with the rest of the industrial workforce. Despite the victory, the strike nonetheless provoked labor's enemies to increase their attacks on the movement and set the stage for postwar labor/management confrontations.

Rosie the Riveter. The loss of millions of men to the armed forces, coupled with massive industrial expansion, created a severe labor shortage and opened unprecedented job opportunities for women. Between 1940 and

RAISING THE FLAG ON MOUNT SURIBACHI

The image of U.S. Marines raising the flag on the battlefield of Iwo Jima on 23 February 1945 has become one of the central icons of American military virtue. Joe Rosenthal's photograph of this striking tableau immediately struck the popular imagination and won the Associated Press photographer a Pulitzer Prize as well as inspiring a John Wayne movie, *The Sands of Iwo Jima*, and the colossal U.S. Marine Corps Memorial at Arlington National Cemetery. This vision of heroic infantrymen raising Old Glory as the battle raged around them has come to symbolize American strength, purpose, and character. Yet Rosenthal's famous photograph is not a picture of the original flag raising, which took place earlier the same day and was documented by a more prosaic photograph than Rosenthal's. Later, after more combat photographers gravitated to Mount Suribachi, the highest point on the island, there was an impromptu ceremony in which the first flag was replaced by a larger one. Photographers had time to consider the aesthetics of the shot, and many different angles of the event were shot and distributed to the press, with Rosenthal's photo becoming by far the best known. No dishonesty was intended. Raising the second flag was also dangerous since it provided a target for enemy snipers. Yet the heroism of those responsible for the first flag raising — photographed by Louis Lowery for the Marine Corps magazine, *Leatherneck*, under extreme conditions — has been all but forgotten. Those men were part of the first company of marines that had made their way up the mountain under heavy fire, and many of them died in combat later the same day or in the savage fighting that continued for another month. Nevertheless, the U.S. Marine Corps views the image in Rosenthal's photograph as emblematic of the bravery and devotion expected of all marines, and the flag in that photo is kept at U.S. Marine Corps Headquarters in Washington, D.C.

Source: Karal Ann Marling and John Wetenhall, *Iwo Jima: Monuments, Memories and the American Hero* (Cambridge, Mass.: Harvard University Press, 1991).

1945 the number of employed women increased by 50 percent, up by some 6 million. At war's end nearly one-third of the workforce was women. In aircraft production the number of women employed in 1941 was 143. At the end of 1942 the number stood at 65,000. The entrance of women into the industrial workforce ran counter to assumptions about the traditional place of women. Often men voiced fears that femininity would be undermined and women "masculinized." The columnist Max Lerner said the war was developing a "new Amazon" who "could outdrink, outswear, and outswagger the men." Such expressions hid the real fear: who would do the menial tasks of housecleaning, cooking, washing, and child rearing? Certainly not men. Said one woman: "My husband wants a wife, not a career woman." To overcome popular prejudices against working women, the Office of War Information produced propaganda films intended to show that wartime work for women was highly patriotic. The War Manpower Commission stepped up its efforts to recruit women. Yet the government did little to promote job equality for them. There was no legislation mandating child-care centers, and the few that existed had far too few places to accommodate all the children of working mothers, making it difficult for women to juggle home and work. Women's pay, furthermore, averaged around two-thirds that of men, meaning that income lost because a male provider was overseas was not replaced. Inevitably, as child truancy and juvenile delinquency rates rose, women were blamed for failing to maintain the integrity of the family. By 1944 films and women's magazines were reversing gears and encouraging women to remain at home. At the end of the war women were laid off first. Some 4 million women lost jobs between 1944 and 1946. Issues that showed some promise of being addressed during the war — especially equal pay and child care — vanished. A bill to provide equal pay for men and women in private employment died in Congress in July 1946.

Sources:

John Morton Blum, *V Was For Victory: Politics and American Culture During World War II* (New York: Harcourt Brace Jovanovich, 1976);

Frank Freidel, *FDR: Launching the New Deal* (Boston: Little, Brown, 1973);

Eric F. Goldman, *A Rendezvous With Destiny: A History of Modern American Reform* (New York: Knopf, 1952; revised and abridged edition, New York: Vintage, 1956);

Doris Kearns Goodwin, *No Ordinary Time: Franklin and Eleanor Roosevelt: The Homefront in World War II* (New York: Simon & Schuster, 1994);

William Graebner, *The Age of Doubt: American Thought and Culture in the 1940s* (Boston: Twayne, 1990);

Richard Lingeman, *Don't You Know There's a War on? The American Home Front, 1941–1945* (New York: Putnam, 1970);

Geoffrey Perrett, *Days of Sadness, Years of Triumph: The American People, 1939–1945* (Madison: University of Wisconsin Press, 1985);

Richard Polenberg, *War and Society: The United States, 1941–1945* (Philadelphia: Lippincott, 1972);

Allan M. Winkler, *Home Front U.S.A.: America During World War II* (Arlington Heights, Ill.: Harlan-Davidson, 1986).

AMERICA AT WAR: THE INTERNMENT OF JAPANESE AMERICANS

Denial of Civil Rights. The imprisonment of Japanese Americans during World War II was one of the gravest violations of constitutional liberties in the history of the United States. Although their internment was a direct result of animosities raised by the attack on Pearl Harbor, the wartime treatment of Japanese Americans is also symptomatic of the anti-Asian sentiment present in the western United States since the arrival of Chinese as laborers on the construction of the Central Pacific Railroad in the 1860s. When overcrowding in Japan also sent waves of immigrants eastward in search of opportunity, West Coast states and cities passed laws discriminating against foreign-born Japanese and established segregated schools. In 1924 the U.S. government passed the Alien Restriction Act, which prevented recent Asian — but not European — immigrants from owning property and obtaining citizenship. Clannish and facing discrimination from most of their neighbors, the Japanese kept to themselves along the western seaboard. Possessed of a strong work ethic, they prospered, but numbering only 110,000 they were a tiny minority, politically powerless.

Executive Order 9066. Anti-Japanese sentiment intensified rapidly after Pearl Harbor. Rumors were rife that Japanese Americans were engaging in sabotage for Tokyo. As a result, race hatred became overt and vicious. Barbershops offered "free shaves for Japs, not responsible for accidents." Gov. Chase Clark of Idaho said that "Japs live like rats, breed like rats, and act like rats." Lt. Gen. John DeWitt, head of the Western Defense Command, was quoted as saying, "A Jap's a Jap.... It makes no difference whether he is an American citizen or not." The army insisted that all Japanese and Japanese Americans living on the West Coast were security risks. On 19 February 1942 President Roosevelt signed Executive Order 9066, providing for the roundup and evacuation to internment camps of all Japanese, citizens and aliens alike, from the West Coast states of California, Oregon, and Washington. Though the order also applied to German and Italian aliens, the only American citizens affected were those of Japanese descent. Civil libertarians were outraged and noted that such actions were unconstitutional, but the internment continued. State officials assisted the federal government in the evacuations, and California State Attorney General Earl Warren played a prominent role. He would later support civil rights for blacks as chief justice of the Supreme Court, but in 1942 he was swept up in the anti-Japanese fervor. Milton Eisenhower, Gen. Dwight D. Eisenhower's brother, served as first head of the War Relocation Authority, which removed all Japanese Americans to ten campsites in seven states, all in remote, desolate areas. In the process of relocation Japanese Americans became subject to illegal search and seizures of property. Accused of no specific crimes, they were nevertheless arrested by authorities and removed to what amounted to jail. Under the terms of relocation, Japanese Americans had to liquidate assets hurriedly, at below-market prices. Many who failed to sell properties before the deadline lost them entirely. As the years of internment passed, deeds and titles disappeared. When internees returned to their former homes after the war, many found their houses occupied by others; their possessions had vanished.

HELP RESCUE THROUGH EMIGRATION HELP

שפּאַן מיט נעראַטעװעטע דורך האַיאַס
קומען צו אונזערע ברענגען!

העלפֿט זיי קומען

װײזט אײער דערבאַרמונג הײַנט

העלפֿט האַיאַס העלפֿט
אין דער הײליגער רעטונגס אַרבעט

שנדר׳ט פֿאַר האַיאַס

CONTRIBUTE TO HIAS

HEBREW SHELTERING and IMMIGRANT AID SOCIETY
10 TREMONT STREET, BOSTON, MASS.

Poster in Hebrew appealing for money to support HIAS, an
immigration agency that aided Jewish refugees during
the Holocaust

The Constitution at Bay. Neither Secretary of War
Henry L. Stimson nor Attorney General Francis Biddle
believed that Japanese Americans constituted any more
of a military threat than Americans of Italian or German
descent. Yet neither was willing to make a strong case to
the president. Roosevelt succumbed to political pressures
placed on Washington by West Coast state officials,
who, in turn, were responding to constituents — some of
whom saw the evacuations as a way to eliminate their
successful competition and took advantage of the opportunity to seize Japanese American properties. Few
Americans condemned the internment. A noted syndicated columnist, Westbrook Pegler, wrote openly, "I hate
the Japanese." A few voices, such as *The Christian Century*, warned that "This whole policy of resort to concentration camps is headed toward destruction of constitutional rights." Yet most of the American press contributed little to the defense of constitutional rights. Nor did
Congress behave with principle. West Coast delegates to
the House of Representatives, along with other members,
introduced a bill to deprive Japanese born in America of

their citizenship, a measure which controverted the Fourteenth Amendment. In *Hirabayashi* v. *United States* the
U.S. Supreme Court ruled on 21 June 1942 that General
DeWitt had the authority to ban Japanese from their own
houses, claiming that "residents having ethnic affiliations
with an invading enemy may be a greater source of danger
than those of different ancestry." On 18 December 1944,
in *Korematsu* v. *United States*, the court upheld the exclusion of Japanese Americans from the West Coast, arguing that in times of war the court ought not to impinge
on military authorities unless proof existed that their
fears were groundless. Justice Frank Murphy dissented
from the majority opinion, saying that the ruling constituted a "legalization of racism." While the FBI and the
Office of Naval Investigation both concluded that Japanese Americans had not engaged in acts of sabotage, their
findings were withheld from the court.

The Patriotism of Japanese Americans. The federal
government required all inmates of the internment camps
to sign oaths of loyalty to the United States. Though
doing so did not result in release, the majority of detain-
ees did sign. Most of those who refused had been born in
Japan or were Nisei (American-born children of Japanese
immigrants) embittered by their treatment in the camps.
About eight thousand Japanese were deported. Those
who remained were determined, in the words of Sen.
Daniel Inouye, to show the nation that they "were just as
good Americans" as any. Japanese Americans in the internment camps made American flags to promote the war
effort, and in every camp, every morning, inmates rose at
dawn to salute the flag. In 1943 the War Department
announced that it would begin screening male internees
for conscription into the U.S. Army. Two all–Japanese
American units were created, one from internees in the
camps and one from Hawaii, where Japanese were not
subject to detention. Both these units, and many individuals as well (including Senator Inouye), were decorated
for heroism. The all-Japanese 442nd Regimental Combat
Team remains one of the most highly honored American
military units in American history. Despite this record of
patriotism, many Nisei war veterans were refused service
in restaurants and barbershops. Some of them were even
lynched. After the war whites in communities where Japanese had once lived turned out to say "stay away." By the
end of the war Japanese Americans had lost more than
$400 million in property and income, with little redress
available.

Sources:
John Morton Blum, *V Was For Victory: Politics and American Culture
During World War II* (New York: Harcourt Brace Jovanovich,
1976);

Eric F. Goldman, *A Rendezvous With Destiny: A History of Modern
American Reform* (New York: Knopf, 1952; revised and abridged
edition, New York: Vintage, 1956);

Jeanne Wakatsuki Houston and James D. Houston, *Farewell to
Manzanar: A True Story of Japanese-American Experience During and
After the World War II Internment* (Boston: Houghton Mifflin,
1973);

Richard Lingeman, *Don't You Know There's a War On? The American Home Front, 1941–1945* (New York: Putnam, 1970);

Richard Polenberg, *War and Society: The United States, 1941–1945* (Philadelphia: Lippincott, 1972);

Edward H. Spicer, Asael T. Hansen, Katherine Luomala, and Marvin K. Opler, *Impounded People: Japanese-Americans in the Relocation Centers* (Tucson: University of Arizona Press, 1969).

AMERICA'S RESPONSE TO THE HOLOCAUST

The Jews in America. Jews were among the first European settlers in America and have played a role in the development of the United States since colonial times. Anti-Semitism, the hatred of Jews based partly upon long-standing myths about their role in Christ's crucifixion, accompanied their arrival in America. Serious incidents of discrimination against them, however, did not erupt until the great wave of Jewish immigration from Russia and Eastern Europe began around the turn of the twentieth century. In the 1920s the Ku Klux Klan began to direct its venom at Jews as well as blacks and Catholics. The Immigration Act of 1924, by locking in immigration quotas from 1890, intentionally limited the number of Jews allowed into the United States. By the 1930s Hitler's terror campaign against the Jews of Germany was underway and well known. As huge numbers of Jewish refugees sought entry into the United States, American anti-Semitism increased in response. To some extent the unemployment engendered by the Great Depression fed anti-immigrant sentiment, but the real problem was the widespread dislike, if not hatred, of Jews. The well-known sociologist David Rieseman declared in 1939 that anti-Semitism in America "was just below the boiling point." Public-opinion polls confirmed the fact. In some circles the Roosevelt Administration's social and economic program was known as the "Jew Deal," because the president had appointed Jews such as Treasury Secretary Henry Morgenthau and U.S. Supreme Court Justice Felix Frankfurter and because many American Jews were vocal in the appeal for social and economic justice throughout the Depression.

The Holocaust in Europe. In Germany large-scale persecution of the Jews was underway by 1933. Before his rise to power in that year, Adolf Hitler had published a book titled *Mein Kampf* (1924; *My Struggle*), which described his plans to rid eastern and central Europe of the "Jewish problem." By 1938 Jews in Germany had been deprived of citizenship and property and confined to segregated areas. Once the Nazis invaded Poland a massive roundup of Jews throughout German-occupied territories began, and concentration camps were opened to house them and exploit their labor. By July 1941 Hitler had issued his infamous order to find "a complete solution to the Jewish question in the German sphere of influence." The following January Hitler's subordinates met at the infamous Wansee Conference, where they developed "the Final Solution of the Jewish Question," a plan to murder all the Jews of Europe. Implementation

began immediately. The slave-labor camps, such as Auschwitz and Buchenwald, became "factories for death." So irrational was this program of extermination that the Nazis were willing to murder millions of Jews at the very moment when they needed their labor to win the war. The attempted genocide of the Jews forced the Germans to rely on others for necessary labor, and the administration of the "death camps" required the diversion of troops and vital resources that otherwise might have been directed to the German war effort. Yet to Hitler and his followers the Jews were the enemy, and Hitler's war against the Jews stands as one of the greatest crimes against humanity.

What Did Americans Know, and When Did They Know It? By late 1941 influential Jewish newspapers in the United States were publishing refugees' reports that a German program to exterminate the Jews was underway in Europe. In August 1942 the U.S. Department of State received word from a German industrialist that essentially confirmed American Jewish leaders' worst fears. The State Department put up roadblocks against the ever-increasing number of Jewish refugees, claiming that it could gain no other confirmation that such an incredible event was taking place. Yet by November 1942 many newspapers were reporting the systematic extermination of more than 2 million Jews in Nazi-occupied Europe. The previous July twenty thousand people, including Mayor Fiorello La Guardia and Gov. Herbert Lehman, attended a rally at Madison Square Garden in New York to protest Hitler's atrocities. President Roosevelt sent a message promising that the Nazis responsible for crimes against the Jews would be punished when the war was won, but Jewish organizations felt they could not wait that long. They began to pressure the Roosevelt Administration to find a way to intervene, either by paying Hitler to release Jews or by bombing the death camps set up across Eastern Europe. Officials were convinced that any ransom paid to Hitler would be used to build his armed forces and that bombing would merely divert precious airpower from winning the war. Yet air campaigns were diverted to aid Poles holed up in Warsaw, and bombing runs were directed at oil installations only minutes from the infamous "factory for death" at Auschwitz.

Roosevelt's Political Dilemma. Roosevelt was in a political quandary. The midterm elections of 1942 had resulted in Republican control of both the House and Senate. Conservatives were adamant in their refusal to admit refugees to the United States. Roosevelt was sensitive to the fact that his administration had been labeled the "Jew Deal," and noting the conservative shift in the mood of the electorate, he worried about his chances in the presidential election of 1944. While Congress had also issued a condemnation of Hitler's pogrom, many Congressmen were notorious for their racism and anti-Semitism. Some even used the word *kike* on the floor of the House of Representatives. M. Michael Edelstein, a Jewish congressman from New York, died of a heart attack while rising to oppose the use of such epithets. Meanwhile, the State Department argued that accepting refugees from Germany and the occupied countries "would take the burden and curse off Hitler." In response the liberal journal *The Nation* (3 March 1943) published a biting editorial declaring that "you and I and the President, and the Congress, and the State Department are accessories to the crime and share Hitler's guilt." Mass-circulation magazines such as *Time* and *Life,* which could have had a major impact on public opinion, ignored the problem completely. Finally, owing to the efforts of Treasury Secretary Henry Morgenthau and Eleanor Roosevelt, President Roosevelt was persuaded to set up a War Refugee Board in late 1944. This agency was responsible for not only the Jews but other ethnic groups, including Greeks and Poles, as well. At the end of the war only twenty-one thousand European Jews, out of a population of millions, had been admitted to the United States. Public response to the Holocaust and the refugee problem was astonishingly insensitive. In a letter to the White House one woman said, "They are the reason for Hitler," and that therefore America owed Jews nothing. In a letter to Jewish congressman Samuel Dickstein of New York, another person wrote: "We fought to preserve America for Americans and our children, not for a bunch of refujews." In 1946, when Nazi atrocities were well known, a Gallup poll showed that 72 percent of Americans were still opposed to admitting Jews or other refugees.

Sources:

Henry L. Feingold, *The Politics of Rescue: The Roosevelt Administration and the Holocaust, 1938–1945,* expanded and updated edition (New York: Holocaust Library, 1980);

Haskell Lookstein, *Were We Our Brothers Keepers?: The Public Response of American Jews to the Holocaust, 1938–1944* (New York: Hartmore House, 1985);

David Wyman, *The Abandonment of the Jews: America and the Holocaust, 1941–1945* (New York: Pantheon, 1984).

CIVIL RIGHTS

The March On Washington Movement. The modern civil rights movement has its origins in the early 1940s, as civil rights organizers used the Roosevelt administration's condemnation of the Nazis' racist ideology as an opportunity to accuse Roosevelt of being all too tolerant of racism in America. In January 1941, nearly a year before Pearl Harbor, A. Philip Randolph called for a massive 1 July March On Washington to shake up white America. As head of the all-black Brotherhood of Sleeping Car Porters, Randolph was a powerful labor leader who could mobilize the black masses in ways that middle-class organizations such as the National Association for the Advancement of Colored People (NAACP) could not. The NAACP stressed legal action; Randolph urged direct action. The NAACP welcomed whites, while the March On Washington Movement (MOWM) excluded them, though not for racist reasons. While separatist in structure, the MOWM had integration as its goal. According to Randolph, "Negroes are the only people who are the

Line of voters in the first Georgia primary in which blacks were allowed to participate, 17 July 1946

victims of Jim Crow, and it is they who must . . . assume the responsibility to abolish it." If the administration wanted the support of blacks, said Randolph, it would have to offer blacks something other than maintenance of the status quo. The two principal demands put forward by the MOWM were withholding of defense contracts from industries that practiced discrimination and the desegregation of the armed forces and federal employment. On 25 June, facing political embarrassment as well as potential violence in the southern city of Washington, Roosevelt issued Executive Order 8802, which required that all government agencies, job-training programs, and defense contractors cease discrimination, while also creating a Fair Employment Practices Committee to investigate violations. Although the MOWM did not achieve all its goals, Randolph called off the march but announced that the nationwide MOWM committees would continue to function. Integration of the armed forces would have to wait. Many white Americans considered black Americans inferior to whites, and it was widely believed that whites would not fight alongside fellow citizens with darker skins than theirs. Both Secretary of War Stimson and Gen. George C. Marshall, U.S. Army chief of staff, insisted that segregation had to remain in force for the sake of military morale. Nevertheless, a precedent had been established. The MOWM had proved that the threat of mass action, coupled with organizational unity, could get results. Most important, the success of the movement legitimized black leaders who insisted that the loyalty of black Americans rested on the nation's commitment to equality. Nothing less than the end of second-class citizenship would do. As one African American newspaper put it, "Only a fool would fight for continued enslavement, starvation, humiliation and lynching."

The Congress of Racial Equality. The NAACP was the oldest and best-known civil rights organization in the United States. Its methods centered on exposing problems, propagandizing about them, applying political pressure to elected officials, and using the courts. Many black organizers and their white allies felt these methods were too slow and ineffective. Emboldened by Randolph's direct-action approach, a group of pacifists founded the Congress of Racial Equality (CORE) in 1943. Hoping to promote acts of civil disobedience against discriminatory laws, they drew their inspiration from Mohandas Gandhi in India. Linking direct action to economic issues, CORE favored the tactic of the peaceful but disruptive sit-in, and in the 1940s it was able to desegregate theaters and restaurants in key northern cities such as Chicago and Detroit even though their demonstrations often promoted racial tension. CORE's philosophy and tactics would greatly influence Martin Luther King, Jr., in the 1950s and 1960s.

The Fair Employment Practices Committee. Critics adamantly denounced the FEPC, charging that it kowtowed to the "special interests" of blacks. In the overtly racist tone of the day, one Southern newspaper labeled it "dat cummittee fer de perteksun of Rastas and Sambo," while Sen. John Rankin of Mississippi said the FEPC heralded the beginning of a communist dictatorship. Major businesses refused to hire blacks or train them in skilled jobs. For example, the North American Aviation Corporation stated: "The Negro will be considered only as janitors and in other similar capacities. . . . Regardless of their training as aircraft workers we will not employ them." In the labor movement AFL unions continued to segregate black workers into the least-skilled jobs (when they could not exclude them from membership altogether). CIO leaders took up the cause of full job equality, but they had to overcome some rank-and-file opposition. Even FEPC Chairman Mark Ethridge stated that investigation of discrimination — not segregation per se — was the purpose of his committee. Thus, in the Deep South and in border cities such as Baltimore the committee accepted arrangements whereby blacks and whites remained at separate ends of plant facilities.

The Philadelphia Transit Strike. Yet, the FEPC scored a major victory for equal rights in dealing with the Philadelphia transit strike of 1944. In that city the Transport Workers Union had traditionally opposed training blacks as streetcar operators, but in March 1944 — acting on instructions from the FEPC to cease discriminatory practices — new union leadership negotiated contracts that left out the usual discriminatory language. Many union members stated that a vote for the contract was "a vote to give your job to a nigger," and on 1 August they staged a walkout. The federal government sent the army to run the transit system, placing armed regular-army troops on the streetcars, while announcing that striking workers would either be drafted or denied unemployment benefits. The strike collapsed within forty-eight hours. A few blacks were trained almost immediately, and by mid August they were operating streetcars. Despite its moderation the FEPC made many political enemies. In summer 1945 Congress ordered the dissolution of the committee within the year, and President Truman failed in his efforts to make it a permanent federal commission.

Segregation and Prejudice Resurgent. The growing activism of black Americans alarmed both Southern Democrats, who opposed any concessions to blacks, and Northern liberals, who thought events were moving too quickly. Oswald Garrison Villard, one of the white founders of the NAACP, said: "I would not go too fast in enforcing social rights . . . age-long conditions of prejudice and of deliberate white supremacy cannot be cured by legislation or government fiat." The *Memphis Cotton-Trade Journal* denied that any problems existed: "the Southern Negro is not mistreated. He has a care-free, child-like mentality, and looks to the white man to solve his problems and to take care of him." Rumors flew in the South, where it was believed that when white men were drafted, blacks would seize control of the region. In August 1942 Sen. John Bankhead of Alabama requested that blacks drafted from the North be trained only in northern army camps lest they infect Southern black soldiers with irreverent racial attitudes. Because Southerners played a central role in the Democratic coalition (as did blacks), one congressman reminded Roosevelt that the race issue could destroy the Democratic Party. In the midst of such acrimony race riots broke out in several northern cities during the war. The worst, in Detroit in 1943, was the outcome of a volatile mixture of Southern whites drawn to jobs in the automotive-defense industry and blacks recruited under directives from the FEPC.

Voting Rights. In the midst of this unrest the U.S. Supreme Court ruled in 1944 against all-white party primaries in the South. In eight Southern states such primaries had been designed to get around the Fourteenth Amendment guarantee of voting rights. Earlier court decisions had maintained that political parties were private organizations, not subject to the amendment, but in *Smith* v. *Allwright* the court reversed itself (to severe denunciation in the South) and enfranchised about seventy-five thousand middle-class blacks below the Mason-Dixon Line. Many barriers to complete enfranchisement for blacks remained, however, including literacy tests and the poll tax, which effectively excluded impoverished blacks. Nevertheless, the wall of de jure segregation had been breached, however slightly.

The Segregated Armed Forces. Black Americans fought in all the nation's wars, though usually under segregated conditions. After World War I, however, a resurgence of Social Darwinism and Ku Klux Klan activity resulted in a virtually all-white military. Military authorities claimed that black troops had performed poorly in World War I, often justifying their conclusions by pointing to "the inherent psychology of the colored race and their need for leadership." Civil rights leaders countered that Jim Crow training facilities and discriminatory provisioning had left black soldiers at a deliberate disadvantage. In 1940 only ninety-seven thousand blacks were in uniform. Blacks were not allowed to join either the U.S. Army Air Corps or the U.S. Marine Corps. In the navy African Americans could serve only as mess men, while in the army segregated service units, called "plantation battalions" by black troops, were commanded by white officers. The handful of black officers were never assigned to white units. The army was a microcosm of the greater society, and calls for desegregation were decried by officials. As Secretary of War Stimson put matters: "What these foolish leaders of the colored race are seeking is at the bottom social equality."

The Impact of World War II on Race Relations. The greatest influence on the future of the civil rights movement was the service overseas of millions of black Americans. Although not expected to perform combat roles, most black army troops were given some infantry training, and the demand for manpower, coupled with the pressure of civil rights leaders, eventually led to the creation of all-black combat regiments. General Patton personally supervised the training of blacks in his tank corps. In the Battle of the Bulge, the critical winter campaign of 1944–1945 when the German counteroffensive almost stopped the American advance into Germany, black troops were called up en masse to plug the gaps. They played an important role during this battle, proving beyond any doubt that they were the equal of any other units. Black troops were also among the first to liberate some of the Nazi death camps. Yet despite these achievements, there was little effort made to recognize them. Indeed, segregation remained the rule even to the extent that blood plasma supplies were divided by race. White soldiers could not be transfused with "black blood" or vice versa, resulting in needless casualties. Nevertheless, African Americans returned to the United States infused with pride in their service. More important, they believed they were owed a debt. Having risked their lives for democracy, few would any longer accept second-class status and ride at the back of the bus. Around the country, black veterans organized local civil rights groups. A new generation of young blacks, tempered in the furnace of war, demanded that the Democratic Party make its promises of social justice meaningful to them.

Truman and Civil Rights. Though he came from Missouri, traditionally a segregationist state, President Truman was a Democrat who understood the importance of the black vote in the North. Black pluralities in major cities enabled him to carry key states in the election of 1948. He also understood that America's reputation on race did not carry well in the emerging states of Africa and Asia. In December 1946, after Congress refused to extend the FEPC as a permanent federal commission, he issued Executive Order 9809, setting up the President's Committee on Civil Rights, which called for an end to segregation in every aspect of American life. Unwilling to go that far, Truman nonetheless proposed major civil rights legislation in early 1948, asking Congress to pass federal laws protecting voting rights, punishing lynching severely, and abolishing the hated poll taxes, as well as creating a new FEPC and establishing a Civil Rights Division in the Justice Department with wide latitude to enforce the new laws. The program was ultimately eviscerated by powerful Southern Democrats in Congress. Archsegregationists, known as Dixiecrats, controlled key committee chairmanships in both houses of Congress. Sen. James Eastland of Mississippi claimed that Truman's bill proved "that organized mongrel minorities control the government." Ultimately, Southerners offered compromises that Truman could not accept. Their measures would have given antilynching jurisdiction to the states. Dixiecrats also offered to put the issue of the poll taxes to a constitutional amendment, knowing that since three-quarters of the states would have to approve, the issue was dead before it got started. Truman found himself thwarted at every turn, but he was able to bypass Congress to some extent in July 1948, when he issued executive orders eliminating discrimination in federal hiring and ending segregation in the armed forces, though it would take the Korean War to force the army to cooperate. The U.S. Supreme Court also began to make a few inroads for racial justice, opening avenues taken even more frequently in the 1950s. In 1948 the court ruled by a vote of six to zero in favor of the NAACP contention that state courts could not uphold discrimination in housing. The stage was being set for a full-scale reversal of the legal bases of racial separation.

Sources:

A. Russell Buchanan, *Black Americans in World War II* (Santa Barbara, Cal. & Oxford, U.K.: Clio, 1977);

Eric F. Goldman, *A Rendezvous With Destiny: A History of Modern American Reform* (New York: Knopf, 1952; revised and abridged edition, New York: Vintage, 1956);

Ulysses Lee, *The Employment of Negro Troops,* United States Army in World War II, Special Studies, no. 8 (Washington, D.C.: Office of the Chief of Military History, United States Army, 1966);

Howard Zinn, *Postwar America, 1945–1971* (Indianapolis: Bobbs-Merrill, 1973).

THE COLD WAR: PRELUDE IN WARTIME

The Origins of the Cold War. The United States and Great Britain accepted the Soviet Union as an ally during World War II out of necessity. Prime Minister Winston Churchill said that the German threat was such that if "Hitler had invaded hell, I would have made a pact with

Triumphant General Dwight D. Eisenhower in a New York City ticker-tape parade on 18 June 1945

the devil," and many Allied leaders characterized the Soviets in demonic terms. The roots of such attitudes were decades deep. From the moment the Bolsheviks took power in Russia in 1917, they were at odds with the Western powers. First, the Russians signed a separate peace treaty with the Germans in World War I, enabling Kaiser Wilhelm II to transfer troops to the western front, thereby increasing pressure on the Allies. The Bolsheviks expropriated many Western properties without compensating their owners, and then the new Russian leaders began to stir up revolutionary activity against Western governments. Britain, France, and the United States found the new Russia so intolerable that in 1920 a coalition of the Western powers and Japan landed troops throughout the Soviet Union in an effort to kill the Communist revolution in its infancy. From the Soviet perspective such intervention in their internal affairs constituted an act of war, and hostility between the Soviet Union and the West continued until Hitler invaded Russia in 1941. The United States had taken the lead in thawing relations with the Russians in 1934, when President Franklin D. Roosevelt normalized relations with the Soviet Union. But distrust remained on both sides. The American people and their representatives continued to be deeply anticommunist.

American Anticommunism. Anticommunism was an important part of the long and often violent history of organized labor in the United States. Although communists played a virtually insignificant role in setting up American unions, opponents of labor unions and industrial reform were quick to label reformers communists. The situation became worse after the Bolshevik Revolu-

tion. At the end of World War I investigations, raids, arrests, and prosecutions by the U.S. Justice Department and the new Federal Bureau of Investigation (FBI) touched off a "Red Scare," which led to a series of attacks on dissident immigrants and some American citizens accused of being Bolshevik agents. A wave of intolerance followed throughout the United States, during which political ideas imported with new immigrants were condemned as alien and "un-American." By 1934 Congress had set up a new committee, the House Un-American Activities Committee (HUAC), to guard the political purity of the United States. Though ostensibly initiated to thwart Nazi propaganda, HUAC focused its attention on those who criticized the system from the Left, devoting most of its hearings to rooting out "communist" subversion.

The Spider and the Scorpion. By the time Germany invaded the Soviet Union in 1941, most Americans distrusted both nations. Comparing the two dictatorships to a tarantula and a scorpion locked in a bottle, Sen. Harry S Truman urged that the United States should take care to aid whichever side was losing and hope that both Hitler and Stalin would destroy one another. Though glad of any assistance he could get, through Lend-Lease or direct military aid, Soviet leader Joseph Stalin nevertheless did not believe in the altruism of his new allies. Nor did Roosevelt and Churchill believe that the Soviets would be friendly to the Western system. All parties understood that the alliance was a marriage of convenience that would probably come unraveled once the mutual threat ended. Indeed, all three sides of the alliance had markedly different war aims that were bound to con-

Front page of *The New York Times,* 13 April 1945

some in the Soviet elite came to believe that Truman's suggestion was the secret strategy of the Western allies. Logistical problems, however, were the main reason for American inability to mobilize rapidly to enter the European war. Though the initial U.S. strategy was to deal with Germany first and then Japan, the military unpreparedness of the United States precluded this approach. In 1938 the United States had an army of fewer than 300,000 men. In terms of numbers and equipment the Czech army was better prepared than the Americans, and the Czechs were crushed in days by the German *Wehrmacht.* Drafting, training, equipping, and transporting hundreds of thousands of American troops to mainland Europe took years of preparation, remaining impossible until mid 1944. To mollify Stalin, Churchill and Roosevelt planned an invasion of the Italian peninsula, which successfully knocked Italy out of the war by 1943. But this military success created serious political problems between the United States and the Soviets and helped to polarize relations later.

The Problem of Italy. The American and British invasion of Italy was intended in part to draw off some German divisions from Russia, but a negligible number of troops was diverted. The Italian campaign was not planned as an immediate prelude to a direct attack on Germany. Invasion of the European heartland from Italy would be too difficult to accomplish because of the barrier provided by the Alps. Strategically, therefore, the Italian invasion accomplished little. Politically, however, it presaged the Cold War. The rapidity of the Allied victory over Italy left the issue of how to reorganize the Italian government. Throughout the years of Fascism in Italy the only real opposition to Benito Mussolini's rule came from the Communists. Fascism was a militantly anticommunist political philosophy, and the Communists were the first of the European political parties to go underground. During the Italian campaign, Communist partisans provided valuable intelligence and guerrilla assistance to invading Allied armies. The Italian Communists wanted Fascism defeated even more than the Allies, and they hoped to be in a position to take over the reins of government. They reasoned that their long opposition to Mussolini, and their assistance to the Allies, assured them that. Yet because of the traditional anticommunism of the United States and Britain, neither wanted to see the Italian Communists in power, even though links between the Italian Communists and Stalin were tenuous. The Soviet leader nonetheless insisted that Italian Communists should have at least a share in the new government. Britain and the United States refused, arguing that Soviet troops had not participated in the assault on Italy; therefore, Stalin could have no say in the administration of Italy. Those powers engaged in the liberation and occupation of particular territories would decide their future forms of government. The United States and Britain thus established a precedent that would have serious

flict as World War II came to a close. The British wanted to preserve their empire. The Soviets aimed to nullify all threats to themselves and to guarantee the loyalty or pacification of all states on their borders. The United States hoped to guarantee economic expansion by establishing open markets and democratic governments.

The Problem of the Second Front. Conflicting war goals inevitably made for a conflict over the peace. Throughout the war the alliance was unbalanced by the close cooperation between the United States and Britain and their hesitant, almost reluctant, inclusion of the Soviet Union in strategy sessions. Stalin's foremost objective in the early stage of the war was for his two allies to set up a second front in Europe to take the pressure off the Soviet Union. For most of the war fully 80 percent of German divisions were concentrated on the Russian front, and the Soviets were bearing the brunt of the slaughter. In the end the Soviet Union would suffer more than 25 million war dead, compared with 2 million British and 400,000 American deaths. In addition more than seventy thousand cities and towns in Soviet territory were reduced to rubble by the Germans; most roads and rail lines were destroyed, as well as crops and herds of livestock. Russia suffered more than any other single nation in World War II, and the way in which the United States and Britain fought the war seemed to Stalin to indicate an unwillingness to share the burden equally. Indeed,

Potsdam, July 1945. Seated: Clement R. Attlee, Harry S Truman, and Joseph Stalin; standing: Adm. William D. Leahy, Ernest Bevin, James Byrnes, and Vyacheslav M. Molotov

ramifications later, when the whole of Eastern Europe was liberated by Russian troops.

The Question of Germany and Japan. Throughout the war Roosevelt and Churchill met regularly to determine the disposition of territories taken in battle, to plan the establishment of a new international peacekeeping organization, and to discuss the reordering of the postwar global economy. To some extent their ability to meet was the result of their relative proximity, while Stalin remained bottled up in a distant nation under siege. It was not until 1943 that all three leaders met face to face. For the most part Stalin agreed to the plans the others made in his absence, reasoning that most of them did not impinge on his essential goals. Once he began meeting with Roosevelt and Churchill, however, Stalin began to play hardball. At Tehran in late 1943 the Soviet leader approved the cross-channel invasion of Europe and agreed to participate in the war against Japan once Hitler was defeated. In return for assistance in the Asian theater, the Soviet Union would get territorial concessions in the Far East — chiefly territories taken from Russia by Japan in 1905 and

Outer Mongolia. With respect to Germany both Roosevelt and Stalin were agreed: it should be disarmed and divided among the Allies. As for the nations bordering the Soviet Union, Roosevelt agreed that the United States would not demand "self-determination" in these areas. All these provisions put Roosevelt at odds with career diplomats and with those interventionists who believed that the overarching goal of U.S. policy in the war should be to reshape the world to assure American economic dominance. While Roosevelt was not deaf to such arguments, he also knew that there was little he could do to get Soviet troops out of Eastern Europe once they were there.

Yalta: Realpolitik or Sellout? Roosevelt was criticized bitterly throughout his presidency, but nothing enraged his conservative enemies, and even some of his allies, more than the Yalta agreements of February 1945. His critics charged that Roosevelt had given away Eastern Europe to the Communist tyrant Stalin, enhancing the possibility of Soviet domination of Western Europe. The Yalta agreements were the result of no such conspiracy but rather of political and military realities. Suffering a

President Truman reading the Japanese surrender to reporters

serious illness that would shortly result in his death, Roosevelt was a far-seeing pragmatist. He understood that the defeat of Germany had been rendered possible by the fighting on the Russian front, however heroic the Normandy invasion had been. The Red Army, the largest and most combat-experienced on earth, was sweeping through Romania, Poland, Czechoslovakia, and Hungary. American and British troops were still two hundred miles from Berlin. Soviet casualties incurred as a necessary cost of Soviet military success on the Eastern front ensured that many fewer American casualties would be suffered. Roosevelt had to acknowledge the Russians' major sacrifices. While interventionists envisioned American dominance in Eastern Europe after World War II, the United States could not impose its will there without going to war with Russia, an impossibility given the American public's expectations of imminent peace. Stalin pointed out that the nations of Eastern Europe had allied themselves with Hitler and had provided troops to help in the German invasion of Russia. Thus, these Eastern European countries were subject to the rules of war and liable to punishment by the victor, just as the United States and Great Britain had imposed their will in Italy. The language of the Yalta agreements was thus vague, and the provision for "free" elections in Eastern Europe after the war turned out to be unworkable. In fact, given the preponderance of Soviet power, if

those elections had been held, they would have been no "freer" than the elections held in Italy, from which the Communists were excluded. The central issue, however, was the fate of Germany. Though Roosevelt had entertained suggestions to dismember Germany, the postwar economic ambitions of the United States required Germany to be revitalized so that it could serve as the anchor for profitable trade between the United States and Europe. This goal conflicted with the Soviet desire to see Germany deindustrialized and demilitarized. Both sides agreed that Germany would be temporarily divided into four separate zones and reunified later on terms acceptable to the four occupying nations of Great Britain, France, the United States, and the Soviet Union. The reunification provision also proved unworkable.

The Impact of Roosevelt's Death. When Roosevelt died on 12 April 1945, an entire generation of Americans had known no other president. The longest-serving chief executive in U.S. history, Roosevelt had dominated domestic politics and had become a towering international figure. Many Americans looked to him to solve the nation's problems by himself. In fact, President Roosevelt had governed by balancing opposing forces while using his political skills and sheer will to reshape the United States and the world. His relations with his two allies had always been informed by practical realities, and he believed profoundly that his personal relations with world leaders, especially Stalin, would ensure that wartime agreements and postwar amity would prevail. With Roosevelt's death a change took place in American foreign policy. In retrospect one of Roosevelt's chief failings as chief executive may have been the way in which he kept his vice presidents uninformed about his conduct of the war and his personal diplomacy. Though Vice President Harry S Truman's relations with the Soviets have been lauded as expert, in fact Truman came into the White House ill-prepared and badly educated about world affairs. As he once put it himself, "They never tell me anything around here." Given Roosevelt's awareness of his failing health, it remains a mystery why he did not better prepare his possible successors.

"Give 'em Hell, Harry!" No one was more surprised at his elevation to the presidency than Harry S Truman. Nominated in 1944 as Roosevelt's running mate, Truman was a compromise candidate chosen to head off a conservative insurgency against the president. Although well versed in domestic issues, Truman knew virtually nothing of foreign affairs. Only on the day he was sworn in as president was Truman informed by Secretary of War Henry L. Stimson of the top-secret atomic-bomb project. As he took up office, American and British troops were defeating Hitler's armies in western Germany, while in eastern Germany the Red Army was overrunning Berlin. In the Far East, Japan was fighting a desperate, last-ditch effort to protect her home islands. Truman would preside over the end of the war and would be the champion of American interests expected to exact the spoils of war. To that end Truman came out swinging, upending his predecessor's politics of compromise and pragmatism in favor of hard-nosed confrontation.

The Confrontation Begins: Potsdam. On 17–26 July 1945 in the Berlin suburb of Potsdam, one of the few German cities not reduced to rubble, the leaders of the Big Three — Truman, Stalin, and the new British prime minister Clement Atlee (who replaced Churchill at mid-conference owing to Churchill's defeat in British elections) — met to work out the loose ends of reconstructing a war-ravaged world. The particulars of Soviet entry into the war against Japan were on the agenda, as were the nature of the peace treaties to be signed and the critical issue of German reparations. Unlike Roosevelt, Truman had little regard for Stalin. The day before the conference began, the United States had successfully tested its first atomic bomb. Truman's knowledge of this event changed the entire tenor of discussions with the Soviets. As Stimson stated, it was clear "that we held all the cards." The military advantages of the Red Army — its sheer size and experience — now seemed more than balanced by atomic weapons. Subsequently, the United States became less and less accommodating to the Russians. Although the Soviet entry into the war against Japan was still technically an issue, U.S. officials realized that there was no longer any real need for such intervention. Moreover, American fears of what might happen if

Soviet troops invaded the Japanese home islands were eased by the knowledge that use of the new weapon could force the Japanese to surrender well before Russian troops could occupy any part of Japan itself. While American plans for the reconstruction of postwar Germany had been thwarted because Russians occupied nearly half of that territory, the same problem would not arise in Japan. The accords signed at Potsdam allowed each occupying power to extract reparations from its zone in Germany, but this agreement limited the Soviets' ability to acquire the money necessary to rebuild Russia because most of the valuable industrial capital was in the western zones. The issue of Poland, an unsolved problem at Yalta, arose anew in Potsdam. When the British insisted on free elections in Poland, Stalin asked if the British planned on allowing Communists to vote in Greece, which British troops occupied. A seemingly minor issue of waterway traffic in central Europe signaled future tensions. In line with American open-market goals, Truman insisted on international control of the eighteen-hundred-mile-long Danube River, which traversed Soviet-held territories. Stalin asked if an international authority would be set up to govern traffic in the Panama and Suez canals, controlled by the United States and Britain. Truman claimed that Stalin's attitude "showed how his mind worked and what he was after. . . . The Russians were planning world conquest." But the Soviets thought Truman and Atlee were trying to impose a political double standard and concluded that global domination was what the West desired.

Sources:

Gar Alperovitz, *Atomic Diplomacy: Hiroshima and Potsdam* (New York: Simon & Schuster, 1965);

John Lewis Gaddis, *The United States and the Origins of the Cold War, 1941–1947* (New York: Columbia University Press, 1972);

Thomas McCormick, *America's Half-Century: United States Foreign Policy in the Cold War* (Baltimore: Johns Hopkins University Press, 1989);

Daniel Yergin, *Shattered Peace: The Origins of the Cold War and the National Security State* (Boston: Houghton Mifflin, 1977).

THE COLD WAR: POSTWAR TENSIONS

The Factor of the Third World. Alone of all the belligerent nations, the United States emerged from the war with its home soil unscathed and richer for having developed its wartime economy. Roosevelt and the internationalists knew that the other great powers of Europe were going to be severely weakened by the war, that the collapse of the European world empires was virtually inevitable, and that the United States alone was in the position to take economic advantage of this situation, especially in the Third World colonies of European nations. Even as the Japanese were signing the formal documents of surrender on 2 September 1945, the Vietnamese in Southeast Asia were declaring their independence from France. Before long Great Britain, once the largest empire in the history of the world, was forced to grant independence to many of its colonies — including India,

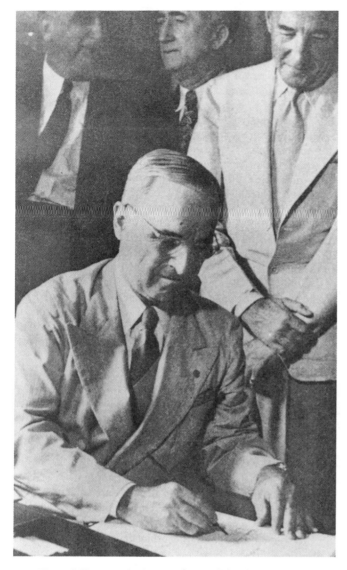

Harry S Truman signing the $3.75 billion loan to Great Britain, 15 July 1946

raw materials and resources — a situation made more extreme after Eastern Europe, long the source of raw materials for Western industries, went Communist. American officials feared that such economic destabilization was a prelude to Russian domination of Western Europe. Thus, the Third World became the crucial arena of Soviet confrontation. While the majority of new nations to emerge from the collapse of the old empires did gravitate into the orbit of the Western system, during the early years of the Cold War the deep hostility of these countries to the West suggested that the opposite might occur. Competition for influence in these countries would ultimately produce several bloody "proxy" wars, as in Korea, Vietnam, Angola, and Afghanistan, fought between belligerents armed and funded by the United States on one side and by the Soviet Union on the other.

Atomic Diplomacy. It was impossible to keep atomic technology secret. The basic theories behind the release of atomic energy had been known before World War II among physicists worldwide. Once the United States detonated its atomic bomb, demonstrating the accuracy of those theories, it became inevitable that other nations would build their own atomic bombs. Given the mounting tensions between the two superpowers, it was clear that an atomic-arms race would develop. Within the American decision-making elite, opinion was split as to whether the atomic research and weapons development should be handed over to an international control agency under the United Nations or whether the United States should seek to keep its monopoly. Physicist J. Robert Oppenheimer — the director of the research laboratory in Los Alamos, New Mexico, where the bomb was developed — and many other scientists who had worked on the bomb hoped for international control, but they were outmaneuvered easily by those whose intention it was to keep the United States the sole atomic power. On 14 June 1946, Bernard Baruch, the U.S. representative to the United Nations Atomic Energy Committee, presented a plan for the control of nuclear energy to the committee. The Baruch Plan, as it became known, proposed an international authority that would promote peaceful uses of atomic energy, would have authority to enter any nation to inspect atomic-energy facilities, and would destroy existing nuclear weapons. The Baruch Plan was unprecedented in its seeming concession of an American military advantage to the cause of peace. Since the United States was the sole manufacturer of atomic weapons, however, they were the only authority capable of dismantling them. To the Russians the Baruch Plan suggested that while they would be required to submit their military sites to American inspection, the dismantling of American weapons would be overseen by Americans. Furthermore, American officials refused to share atomic secrets with the Soviets until after a system of inspections began. Soviet officials believed that the Baruch Plan would require them to sacrifice the entirety of their atomic program for vague American promises

Burma, Malaya — and mandates such as Palestine. France, the Netherlands, Belgium, and other European nations also began, willingly or unwillingly, to lose their colonies. By the mid 1950s Africa and Asia were ablaze with the fires of decolonization. U.S. officials hoped to establish American economic dominance in these areas. Because the Europeans had imposed Western-style capitalism on their colonies by force and had exploited them, however, communist and socialist political movements had developed in many of these regions, including Vietnam. Should this so-called Third World of Asia and Africa align itself with the Communist bloc, plans for American domination of formerly colonial economies would be seriously jeopardized. While the Soviet Union did not have the resources to rule the decolonized world, it could, and did, promote national independence for European colonies in the hopes that new nations would cement ties to the Soviet Union. Communist nationalism in the Third World, furthermore, threatened European economies, already in perilous condition, with a loss of that the United States would do the same. The Russians therefore rejected the plan, and an atomic-arms race began in earnest, culminating with the development of the Soviet atomic bomb in 1949.

The Postwar Global Economy. Well before World War II, New York had replaced London as the financial center of the Western economic system. In the aftermath of the most destructive war in history, the position of Wall Street was even stronger. Possessing the only major economy undamaged by the war, the United States was able to impose economic requirements on other nations. American policy makers envisioned enhanced material rewards for Americans — and secondarily for the world at large. Achieving this goal required the repair of damaged economies in Europe and Asia and the imposition of free markets where they had not previously existed. The international monetary system would have to be rationalized and made compatible with the American dollar. The July 1944 conference of Allied financial planners at Bretton Woods, New Hampshire, created the machinery of the modern global economy by creating the World Bank and the International Monetary Fund (IMF). One-third of the capital and directorships of the World Bank were to be held by the United States, enabling it to set the world financial agenda. The World Bank would provide reconstruction loans to nations that opened their accounting methods to American control and formulated their economic practices according to American requirements. The IMF was created to ensure that all national currencies would be convertible to U.S. dollars in a fixed ratio, which benefited American trade balances. Although this system would ultimately collapse in the 1970s, it served for three decades as the master plan for the reorganization of the global economy according to American designs.

Loans to the Soviet Union. Soviet leaders were primarily concerned with rebuilding the shattered infrastructure of their nation. In 1945 they requested $6 billion in reconstruction loans from the United States. After American officials ignored this request, the Soviets formally asked for a loan of the much-reduced sum of $1 billion, again with no success. The Americans' refusal to assist the Soviet Union soured relations between the two allies. As the Russians were well aware, at the same time the United States was turning down Russian requests, the Americans were working out the details of reconstruction loans and other aid to Britain and France, as well as to Germany and other former Axis enemies, including nations that had joined in the German invasion of the Soviet Union during the war. Anti-American officials within the Kremlin viewed such actions as confirmation of a Western plot to destroy the Soviet Union. Yet from the American perspective, loans to the Soviets made little economic sense. Most American economists believed the state-controlled Soviet economy was virtually impenetrable by American business. American political leaders also feared that the Soviet Union might well become an economic powerhouse, better situated than the United States to dominate the lucrative European market, which officials viewed as vital to American trade. Grand strategists of the global economy, such as Dean Acheson — who would become a chief architect of both the Truman Doctrine and the Marshall Plan — also feared that Soviet economic resurgence would re-create a Eurasian trading bloc similar to that almost created by Germany and Japan. Many American officials were determined to prevent the formation of such a bloc and equally determined to enforce an open door to trade worldwide. Even in 1944, two years before the Cold War political policy of "containment" was formulated, American officials were adamant about containing Soviet economic power.

Crisis in the Mediterranean. Several events in the late 1940s also increased Cold War tensions. The first postwar showdown was a dispute over the Dardanelles, the narrow strait connecting the Aegean Sea to the Sea of Mamara, which in turn is connected to the Black Sea by the Bosporus. Thus whoever controls the Dardanelles, which separate the Gallipoli Peninsula of European Turkey from Asian Turkey, controls the only outlet from the Black Sea. Because the Dardanelles gave Russia warm-water access to the Atlantic Ocean, Western leaders considered that strategic waterway an object of Soviet expansionist ambition. Turkey was a traditional enemy of Russia, and although it had claimed neutrality during the war, it had allowed the Germans free passage through the Dardanelles during their invasion of the Soviet Union. With Turkey in control of the Dardanelles, the Soviets feared that their access to the Mediterranean could be blocked. Truman proposed internationalization of the waterway, but in March 1945 Stalin insisted on joint Russo-Turkish control. Backed by the United States, the Turks refused this option. When Stalin asked what the United States might do if some South American country demanded the right to shut it out of the Panama Canal, Truman responded that Russia had a secret ambition to conquer Turkey (an unlikely event given the postwar condition of the Soviet infrastructure and economy). No sooner had this situation been resolved in the favor of the Turks than tensions mounted over Iran. To deny its strategic oil reserves to the Nazis, the British and Soviets had occupied Iran early in August 1941, with the British stationing its troops in southern Iran while the Soviets controlled the north. In the Anglo-Russian Treaty of January 1942 both Allied nations had promised to withdraw their troops from Iran within six months after the end of the war. The Nazi occupation of Eastern Europe and Russia, however, had resulted in the near-total destruction of Soviet oil production. Consequently, in March 1946 — with all British troops out of Iran — the Soviets announced that they would not withdraw until they received guarantees of access to Iranian oil. At that time the United States was moving to replace the British in domination of Iranian oil operations, and it looked on the Soviet occupation as threatening to its long-range

During World War II the federal tax collector would reach into nearly every American pocket. To finance the gargantuan costs of the war the government had to find new sources of revenue beyond the traditional tariff and excise taxes on consumption of luxuries. In 1942 Congress took the unprecedented move of taxing virtually every American wage earner. Though a federal income tax had been levied during the Civil War, the enormously unpopular measure had been struck down by the U.S. Supreme Court. It took until 1913 for enough states to ratify a constitutional amendment enabling Congress to assess a tax on personal income. At first the tax was levied on only the wealthy, and even then it was not collected efficiently. Taking the recently enacted Social Security tax as a model, the U.S. Treasury Department initiated income-tax collection by payroll deduction in 1943. Though there was deep opposition to the new tax codes, they were passed in deference to the wartime emergency. Few expected that the income taxes would continue after the war, but Treasury Secretary Henry Morgenthau and others argued that continued taxation would enlarge the government's ability to extend the social safety net created by the New Deal.

The tax rate was progressive — meaning that high incomes were taxed at higher rates than low incomes. At one point President Roosevelt had even called for a 100 percent tax on all income over $25,000, a piece of political rhetoric designed to win acceptance for the new tax law from the low-paid wage earner, whose tax rate in 1943 ranged between 4 and 6 percent. Opponents labeled the new income tax "expropriation" of property.

Conservative opposition to the income tax waned rapidly, however, as the war progressed, and big business saw how much of the new revenue was being funneled to the corporations. Fiscal conservatives agreed to spend government dollars to assist the unemployed, widows, and orphans so long as federal funds could also be allocated to the defense industries. The Cold War provided reason enough for expanded military spending, and that, in turn, required a permanent income tax. Beginning in 1949, costs for defense steadily mounted, and so did tax rates on low incomes. The lowest income-tax rate rose from 4 percent in 1943 to 28 percent in 1993.

Federal borrowing during World War II reached previously unparalleled heights, primarily by selling Treasury Bonds guaranteed by the U.S. taxpayer, a practice which continues to this day. Redeemable after the war, many war bonds were sold in small denominations to citizens whose savings were actually offset by the taxes they paid to guarantee them. Large-denomination bonds were purchased by the wealthy — Americans and foreigners alike — which contributed to the national debt and the need for even higher taxes in the future. Critics of the way the nation financed the war were already warning in 1943 that the United States was hitching its future to a permanent deficit budget, the burden of which would have to be borne by new taxpayers. They also prophesied that the redirection of funds from social programs to military purposes would drive the political agenda to the right, away from pressing social needs.

Sources: Seymour Melman, *The Permanent War Economy: American Capitalism in Decline* (New York: Simon & Schuster, 1974);

John F. Witte, *The Politics and Development of the Federal Income Tax* (Madison: University of Wisconsin Press, 1985).

---

economic interests. Moving to defuse the situation the U.S. government announced that it had convinced Iran to give the Soviet Union a 40 percent share of the Iranian oil market if the Soviets withdrew their troops. Stalin ordered the troops home. In May, immediately after the last Soviet soldiers were gone, the Iranian parliament reneged on the deal. Although the Truman administration continued to claim that the Soviets were aiming at global conquest, Soviet troops did not reenter Iran. Scarcely accommodating by nature, Stalin nonetheless understood that the Soviet Union was in a precarious position which required careful diplomacy on his part.

The Permanent War Economy. In January 1944 Charles E. Wilson, formerly chairman of the General Electric corporation, called for a "permanent war economy" to safeguard postwar America from a return to depression. As a member of the War Production Board, Wilson spoke for many industrialists and financiers, as well as government officials, who feared that the drop in war production — accompanied by the infusion into the job market of millions of veterans seeking employment — would precipitate a new economic crisis which would sap the international strength and position of the United States. Wilson called for long-term arrangements under which the largest corporations would maintain permanent liaisons with the military. Continued war production would be preparation for future emergencies. After the nation's lack of readiness for Pearl Harbor such logic seemed unassailable. Moreover, one of the primary war aims of the internationalists had been to prevent the

Nearly 16 million men and women served in the armed forces during World War II. While this service ended Depression-era unemployment for many, it also constituted sacrifice "above and beyond the call of duty." Consequently, organizations such as the Veterans of Foreign Wars and the American Legion persuaded President Roosevelt to sponsor a bill that would provide added compensation for military service during World War II, as well as educational and housing opportunities to the nation's veterans. The money provided to veterans would serve to stimulate consumer spending and economic development, and educational provisions would cushion the impact of returning vets on the job market. Ultimately, the GI Bill of Rights, or Serviceman's Readjustment Act of 1944, revolutionized higher education and initiated the suburbanization of America. (*GI*, the label soldiers had given themselves, stands for "Government Issued.")

The act provided veterans preferences in hiring, up to four years of higher education or vocational training, one year of unemployment benefits, and home loans provided at no interest and guaranteed by the Veterans Administration. Prior to the Great Depression, veterans benefits had been paid only to the disabled or indigent. The lessons of deficit spending during the 1930s and wartime had taught that such tax-supported measures could stimulate construction and economic expansion.

More than 10 million GIs collected benefits. Most were in the form of housing loans, which made the dream of home ownership possible for an entire generation. Owing to the decline of construction during the Depression, the nation's housing stock was depleted. The increased availability of mortgage loans created an enormous construction boom across America, particularly in the suburbs of major cities, and had the ripple effect of promoting employment for construction workers and stimulating new housing-construction technologies. Since the overwhelming majority of the beneficiaries of the GI Bill were white, however, so-called white flight to the suburbs portended future demographic shifts and economic disruptions in the nation's inner cities.

As a result of the GI Bill, the American higher education system was radically altered. Before the war, access to college was virtually limited to the affluent. Now American colleges and universities competed for the educational funds provided to soldiers, most of whom had never expected to acquire much more than a high-school education. The GI Bill provided tuition, housing, and dependent benefits, and institutions were hard-pressed to accommodate the newcomers. Soon the federal government began to award grants to universities for expansion and for new programs to help GIs succeed. Public universities, especially, were awarded grants that caused exponential growth in their sizes and budgets. In 1946–1947 alone more than 2.5 million veterans attended institutions of higher education or vocational training. Suddenly, middle-class economic status seemed within reach of a generation raised in poverty. For black veterans opportunities for higher education seemed especially providential, and many used their education as leaders of the civil rights movement.

creation of a world divided into economic blocs, each sealed off from the others. The internationalists envisioned a postwar global economy guided and controlled by the United States. The permanent war economy proposed by Wilson would provide the United States with the means to confront the military power of the Soviets, and, since a globally integrated economy would require worldwide allies who also needed to be armed, the military-industrial complex would meet their needs while ensuring profitability for itself. Critics, such as Vice President Henry Wallace, warned that such arrangements would create or exacerbate confrontation as well as create a national economic dependency on war production. A permanent war economy would require enemies whose existence could justify perpetual preparation for war.

The "Iron Curtain." At the moment of his greatest triumph Prime Minister Winston Churchill of Great Britain was voted out of office during the Potsdam Conference. At loose ends after the war, Churchill was determined to regain a place at the center of world events. On 5 March 1946, at the invitation of President Truman, Churchill made one of his most famous speeches before an audience at Westminster College in Fulton, Missouri. Denouncing Soviet control of Eastern Europe, he declared that "From Stettin in the Baltic to Trieste in the Adriatic, an iron curtain has descended across the continent." Claiming that the Soviets aimed at "the indefinite expansion of their power and doctrines," he also asserted that they constituted "a growing challenge and peril to Christian civilization." According to Churchill, the only salvation lay in the "fraternal association of the English-speaking peoples" and a military alliance founded on a monopoly of the atomic bomb. Churchill knew he was overstating his case. His eloquent and vehement words were intended to galvanize the American and British people for a new round of military confrontation, and they helped to polarize American-Soviet relations further. The speech also contributed an important new term — *iron curtain* — to the emerging vocabulary of the Cold War. Ironically, in secret meetings with Stalin in 1944 — resulting in what historians term the "Percentage Deal" — Churchill had himself helped to craft agreements that had resulted in the Soviet domination of Eastern Europe.

Containment. Another Cold War term was coined in 1947 — *containment.* In July a little-known American diplomat named George F. Kennan, one of the few members of the American foreign service who had lived in the Soviet Union and spoke Russian, published an article that had a major influence on American policy toward the Soviet Union. Basing his views on twenty years of observations, he argued that while Soviet ideology was aggressive and while the Russians sought to export the doctrines of Soviet-style Communism, Stalin's actual foreign-policy actions would be focused upon the defense of Soviet territory. In "The Sources of Soviet Conduct," published in *Foreign Affairs,* the journal of the foreign policy establishment, Kennan argued that the United States should seek to contain the spread of Soviet ideology by political means, essentially by seeking to prove that the American system was superior to the Soviets'. President Truman seized upon the term *containment,* making it the watchword of a policy that differed from Kennan's assessment in claiming the Soviets were territorially and militaristically expansionist. Henceforth the United States would focus its foreign-policy efforts on halting the spread of Communism. Speaking much later, Kennan concluded that American political and military planners had "exaggerated Soviet behavior" to create an "image of the totally inhuman and totally malevolent adversary." Kennan reflected that such characterizations created a political atmosphere in the United States such that "any attempt on anyone's part to deny its reality appears as an act of treason or frivolity."

The Truman Doctrine. Early in 1947 the British government informed President Truman that it could no longer afford to maintain control in Greece, where a Communist takeover was feared. The situation in Greece resembled that of Italy in many ways. During the war Communist partisans had opposed the Germans and their Greek Fascist allies. Under the terms of Churchill and Stalin's "Percentage Deal" of 1944, the Soviets accorded the British control of Greece, which they were in the process of liberating from the Germans. The British not only kept in power many of the same Greeks who had collaborated with Hitler, but they also reimposed the monarchy. Outraged Greek Communists initiated a civil war. Because of his agreement with Churchill, Stalin did not come to the aid of this indigenous Communist movement, but the British position within Greece was weak. The British-installed monarchy had little popular support, and the Communists enjoyed the backing of the

peasantry as well as Communists throughout the Balkan Peninsula. While Stalin did not send troops, the Greek civil war was blamed on Soviet expansionism, as was an indigenous Communist insurgency in Turkey that took place at the same time. Undersecretary of State Dean Acheson told Congress that "like apples in a barrel infected by one rotten one, the corruption of Greece would affect Iran and all to the east." In response to pleas from Great Britain, President Truman announced that the United States would provide $400 million to arm "free peoples who are resisting attempted subjugation by armed minorities or by outside pressure." The Truman Doctrine succeeded in alarming the American people, and it signaled a change in American foreign policy. Henceforth the United States would confront Communism wherever it arose and attempt to police the globe in accordance with that agenda.

The Marshall Plan. Indigenous Communist parties also enjoyed considerable popular support in Western Europe, based in large part on the Communists' wartime resistance to the Nazis. Postwar elections in Italy, France, and the Low Countries resulted in substantial gains for the Communists, alarming American officials. Policy makers argued that American economic assistance in European reconstruction would minimize Communist political influence, just as American military assistance blunted Communist guerrilla offensives in Greece and Turkey. To Truman military assistance to Greece and Turkey and economic assistance to Western Europe would be "two halves of the same walnut." Although the United States had already granted loans for European reconstruction, a more sweeping program would accomplish several objectives. First, Americans would grant assistance only to those countries that purged their governments of Communist participation. Second, sweeping assistance would be closely supervised by American administrators careful to maintain American economic advantages. Third, assistance would provide badly needed humanitarian relief, undercutting popular support for political radicalism and restoring the prewar status quo. In a speech delivered at Harvard University on 5 June 1947, U.S. Secretary of State George Marshall proposed the sweeping program of economic aid to Europe that soon became known as the Marshall Plan. The Truman administration sold the unprecedented $17-billion program by stressing its anticommunist components to congressional conservatives and by emphasizing its humanitarian elements to liberals. By 1948 the governments of France and Italy had rid themselves of Communist participation, and Communists were losing popular support, owing in part to covert operations by the newly created Central Intelligence Agency (CIA). Although the Soviets were offered Marshall Plan assistance, American officials understood that the stipulations attached to the aid would assure Russian repudiation of the plan. As predicted, they rejected the Marshall Plan at the 1947 meeting of Allied foreign ministers in Paris. By fall Moscow had revived its agency of international revolution, the Comintern, and announced that "the Truman-Marshall Plan is a constituent part, the European section of the general plan of world expansionist policy carried on by the United States." Russia began to tighten its grip on the East. The military and political subjugation the Soviet Union had previously exercised against Poland and Romania was directed against Bulgaria, Hungary, and Czechoslovakia. By 1948 an iron curtain had indeed been drawn across Eastern Europe.

The Berlin Blockade. The Marshall Plan brought the unresolved issue of Germany to a crisis point. Marshall Plan reconstruction of Germany presumed a stable economic and political base, but Germany remained politically divided and economically disordered. At the end of World War II the Allies had separated Germany into four occupation zones: the United States, with Britain and France, supervised western and southern Germany, while the Soviets held the east. Complicating this scheme was a parallel situation in Berlin. While the city was also divided into four separate zones, it was located entirely within the Soviet sector of Germany. Although occupation of Germany was intended to be a temporary measure, the Allies were unable to agree on terms for reunification, and troops remained on station. Having suffered invasion by Germany twice since 1914, the Soviets were understandably afraid that a reunited and reindustrialized Germany would again become a threat. Russia also wanted war reparations from Germany, but the United States and Britain were unwilling to agree to such terms. The bulk of the German industrial base was located in the western zones, and the Soviets hoped their Allies would transfer reparations from these areas to them. American internationalists, however, sought a rapid reconstruction of the German economy as the basis for renewed European trade; they feared that heavy reparations would destabilize the German economy and lead to political upheaval — as they had after World War I. The Marshall Plan ended efforts to find a compromise between American and Soviet approaches to the German question. Western German officials accepted Marshall Plan funds; eastern German officials, following the Soviets, rejected the aid. By mid June 1948 the United States, Great Britain, and France had unified the western occupation zones and established a standard currency, the deutsche mark, creating West Germany as a unified political and economic entity. On 24 June the Soviets responded by closing all traffic between its occupation zone and West Germany and blockaded Berlin in an attempt to force the Americans, British, and French out of eastern Germany. Cut off from overland supplies, the Western powers began virtually nonstop airlifting of cargo to Berlin to reinforce their position. The United States sent one hundred B-29 bombers to bases in England, within striking distance of the Soviet Union. The world braced for war, but fearing atomic bombardment, Stalin backed down on 12 May 1949 and reopened over-land transport. He also stepped up research and development on the Soviet atomic bomb. Meanwhile, the division of Germany into separate western and eastern states became permanent. In the west the Federal Republic of Germany held elections on 14 August; in the east the German Democratic Republic — a Soviet-dominated, one-party state — was declared on 7 October. Like Germany, all of Europe was soon divided into two hostile camps.

The National-Security State. Confrontation in Europe led inevitably to militarization. In July 1947 Congress passed the landmark National Security Act. Under its provisions the military services were streamlined and brought under the command of the newly established U.S. Department of Defense. The National Security Council was created to advise the president on relations with the Communist world. The Central Intelligence Agency was established and given a mandate to engage in covert operations against individuals and governments that U.S. officials considered threatening to American interests. The National Security Act destabilized the constitutional balance of federal authority, giving the presidency enormous powers to meet the demands of the Cold War. Over the next thirty years Congress would gradually become marginalized in the conduct of foreign policy. Critics argued that the Cold War had altered American government into an aggressive national-security state.

NATO. Establishment of the North Atlantic Treaty Organization (NATO) on 4 April 1949 united the nations of Western Europe into an integrated military alliance against the Soviet Union. There were twelve charter members: Belgium, Canada, Denmark, France, Great Britain, Iceland, Italy, Luxembourg, the Netherlands, Norway, Portugal, and the United States. (Greece and Turkey joined in 1952, and West Germany entered the alliance in 1955.) The United States benefited from this alliance because other NATO countries were dependent on U.S. aid to maintain their defenses. As Marshall Plan aid helped their economies to recover, NATO members would be purchasing U.S. armaments for their security, a benefit redounding to the American military-industrial complex. The very existence of this "entangling alliance," so contrary to American isolationist tradition, also enlarged Americans' fears about the Soviet threat, contributing to the rise of the anticommunist witch hunts of 1947–1954.

The Origins of McCarthyism. The Republicans won control of both houses of Congress in the midterm elections of 1946 with a new generation of conservative Republicans determined to undermine the New Deal and Truman's prospects for reelection. Among the newcomers was freshman senator Joseph R. McCarthy of Wisconsin, whose name would shortly enter the American political lexicon. The term *McCarthyism* came to stand for militant anticommunism, a willingness to force consensus by political repression, and intolerance of dissent.

It is often forgotten that Roosevelt suffered from the debilitating effects of polio. He was such a strong leader, at exactly the moment when his country needed such a president, that his personal struggles with his physical paralysis are overlooked. Yet the president was constantly aware of his physical limitations and of the psychological strength he needed to overcome them. He often sought to lend inspiration to others in similar predicaments. Most of the time his aides and the press conspired never to show the president using his crutches or wheelchair. Yet shortly after Pearl Harbor, when he visited military hospitals in Hawaii, he expressly ordered that he be pushed in his wheelchair through the amputee and paralysis wards so that these severely wounded soldiers could see that their commander in chief had suffered grievous injuries but had overcome them. Many of the soldiers and sailors the president visited that day had been unaware of Roosevelt's condition, and some wept openly (as did his aides) as the president made his rounds.

Throughout World War II, one of the most dismal chapters in American history, President Roosevelt tried often to lift the nation's spirits, even when discussing serious subjects. During the 1944 campaign Roosevelt used a personal attack by his Republican opponent, Thomas E. Dewey. Speaking in a tone of mock severity, Roosevelt said:

> These Republican leaders have not been content with attacks on me, or my wife, or on my sons. No, not content with that, they now include my little dog, Fala. Well, of course, I don't resent attacks, and my family doesn't resent attacks, but Fala *does* resent them. You know . . . Fala's . . . a scottie, ... as soon as he learned that the Republican fiction writers in Congress had concocted a story that I had left him behind on an Aleutian Island and had sent a destroyer back to find him — at a cost to the taxpayers of two or three, or eight, or twenty million dollars — his Scotch soul was furious. He has not been the same dog since.

The president's remarks caused uproarious laughter, helping to lift the wartime mood of his audience, but he scored political points as well, all at Dewey's expense.

Source: Joseph Alsop, *FDR, 1882–1945: A Centenary Remembrance* (New York: Viking, 1982).

At the same time it masqueraded as patriotism of the highest sort. During the McCarthyite Communist witch hunt of 1947–1954 tens of thousands of American citizens were denied the right to hold dissenting political beliefs and often suffered imprisonment or loss of employment. Persistent attacks by McCarthy's followers finally undermined the New Deal political coalition in the election of 1952, resulting in a Republican landslide. Ironically, the stage for McCarthyism was set by Truman himself. In order to persuade the public and Congress that military and foreign-aid expenditures were necessary, Truman had called the Communists a threat to the peace and security of the globe. At the same time he also planted the seed that became the flower of McCarthyite dogma — that international Communism had set its sights on subverting the United States from within. The Truman administration assisted the House Un-American Activities Committee (HUAC) in its efforts to condemn the political activities of homegrown Communists, and in 1947 Truman ordered all federal employees to sign oaths of loyalty to the U.S. government, a move that suggested to much of the public that Communists must have already infiltrated the federal government. McCarthy alleged in 1950 that not only were there Communists at the very core of American government, but this infiltration had occurred on Truman's watch. Truman and the Democrats were defeated by the charge that they had not been watchful enough to prevent this subversion.

The Soviet A-Bomb. The United States had initiated the Manhattan Project in response to warnings from Albert Einstein and Leo Szilard that the Germans were capable of making an atomic bomb. Fearful of becoming vulnerable, Roosevelt ordered the largest secret technological undertaking in history to develop atomic weaponry first. Yet the basic discoveries that made the bomb possible had been made before the war and publicized throughout the world scientific community. Consequently, the Soviets had begun their own atomic bomb project in the early part of World War II. Though not nearly as extensive as the Manhattan Project, the Soviet atomic enterprise took advantage of the same theoretical breakthroughs as the American project. The use of atomic bombs at Hiroshima and Nagasaki demonstrated that key ideas about nuclear fission worked. These demonstrations of the bomb actually helped Soviet atomic scientists. As Philip Morrison, a Manhattan Project physicist, put it: "The only secret about atomic bombs was that there was no secret." Sooner or later the Soviets would develop their own atomic weapons, and the state of tension between the United States and the Soviet Union spurred the Soviets to mount their own crash development program. The CIA estimated that the Soviets would achieve success in the mid 1950s. When President Truman announced on 23 September 1949 that the Soviet Union had detonated its first atomic bomb, many believed that Communist spies and traitors must have delivered atomic secrets to the enemy. Soviet spies were undoubtedly at work in the United States, just as American spies operated in the Soviet Union. The degree to which Soviets had penetrated the well-guarded atomic projects scattered across the United States was unclear, however. In 1950 two American citizens with Communist ties, Julius and Ethel Rosenberg, were charged with conspiracy to commit espionage for allegedly giving plans for the atomic bomb to the Soviet Union. Evidence against them was flimsy and circumstantial, which kept them from being tried for the more serious crime of treason, but they were convicted and sentenced to death, a penalty usually reserved for treason cases. Despite a global campaign to spare them, they were electrocuted in 1953. The anticommunist crusade had become a witch hunt.

China Goes Communist. Shortly after the Soviets exploded their bomb, a Communist revolutionary army led by Mao Tse-tung overthrew the U.S.-backed government in China. One of the main issues in the American disagreements with Japan that led to Pearl Harbor was Japanese occupation of China. A civil war between Mao's Communists and anticommunist warlords led by Chiang Kai-shek had been raging since the late 1920s, decreasing only slightly during the Chinese war with Japan that began in 1937. During World War II China experts such as Gen. Joseph "Vinegar Joe" Stilwell had warned that support of General Chiang was a waste of American time and resources and argued that the United States could make friends of the Chinese Communists because there was no love between Mao and the Soviets. But in the anticommunist atmosphere of the late 1940s no politician could embrace such ideas. Instead, the right wing of the Republican Party, led by McCarthy and Congressman Richard M. Nixon of California, began to attack Truman for having "lost China." Although England, France, and other American allies quickly accepted reality and recognized Mao's government, the United States refused to acknowledge the legitimacy of Communist China. Undersecretary of State Dean Rusk, later to head the State Department under Presidents John F. Kennedy and Lyndon B. Johnson, asserted that Mao was a Soviet puppet and declared that the Chinese Communist Party "is not the government of China. It does not pass the first test. It is not Chinese." Even then the Sino-Soviet animosity was evident, yet members of the American foreign-policy establishment feared for their careers unless they adopted hard-line anticommunist positions. The United States officially recognized the government of Chiang Kai-shek, which had fled to the island of Taiwan, as the government of all China, implacably setting itself against the new mainland Chinese regime.

The American Century. In 1941 Henry Luce, the publisher of *Time*, *Life*, and *Fortune* magazines, declared that the next one hundred years would be the "American Century." As Luce put it, the United States could exert unprecedented influence "for such purposes as we see fit and by such means as we see fit." Indeed, at the close of World War II the United States possessed the greatest might and prestige of any nation in history. American internationalists such as Luce had triumphed, and they stood poised to reorder the world. Yet, another power had also emerged from the dust of war. Unlike the United States, the Soviet Union was economically and socially devastated by the war, but it possessed formidable economic potential and the largest, most battle-hardened army on earth. The Soviets reasoned that their sacrifices had entitled them to a share in postwar decision making. But just as differing wartime objectives had divided the United States and Soviet Union, so differing national interests separated them in peacetime. Inability to compromise led to hardening of positions on both sides and finally to confrontation. In the process the citizens of both nations watched the growth of potentially devastating nuclear stockpiles with mounting anxiety.

Legacies of the Cold War. For Americans the Cold War stimulated a mentality that divided the world into "them" and "us." The public came to understand the Cold War in black-and-white terms, even when gray reality prevailed. The Cold War mentality became dogmatic and inflexible, forcing reality to conform to a preexistent set of principles. As Sen. J. William Fulbright once commented, "Like medieval theologians we had a philosophy that explained everything in advance." Open public debate became a casualty of the Cold War. Critics of Cold War foreign policy or of anticommunist hysteria were labeled "fellow travelers" of the Communists, or traitors. As the political climate became more ideological, the United States was led into "hot" wars in Korea and Vietnam. To sustain the military capacity to confront communism, the American economy became wedded to permanent production for war, while former enemies such as Germany and Japan devoted their resources to economic competition and by the 1970s began to eclipse the United States in many areas of production. The pursuit of victory in the Cold War threatened the American domination of the global marketplace so hard-won in World War II.

Sources:

Richard M. Freeland, *The Truman Doctrine and the Origins of McCarthyism: Foreign Policy, Domestic Politics, and Internal Security, 1946–1948* (New York: Schocken, 1974);

John Lewis Gaddis, *The United States and the Origins of the Cold War, 1941–1947* (New York: Columbia University Press, 1972);

Melvyn P. Leffler, *A Preponderance of Power: National Security, the Truman Administration, and the Cold War* (Stanford, Cal.: Stanford University Press, 1992);

Thomas McCormick, *America's Half-Century: United States Foreign Policy in the Cold War* (Baltimore: Johns Hopkins University Press, 1989).

THE DEVELOPMENT OF THE AFFLUENT SOCIETY

Wartime Prosperity. As World War II drew to a close many Americans wondered if it would be followed by a return to depression and massive job losses. Huge government outlays for the defense production ended unemployment, made the American worker the best paid in the world, and raised the financial expectations of the American public. Government spending for goods and services soared from $11 billion in 1939 to $117 billion in 1945. The gross national product (GNP) went from $100 billion in 1940 to $200 billion in 1945. With 6 percent of the world's population, the United States was producing 50 percent of the world's goods. As a result the personal consumption of civilians rose by 25 percent, reaching the highest level in U.S. history. In 1939 about 15 percent of Americans were unemployed; by 1945 that rate had been reduced virtually to zero. Before the great stock market crash of 1929, fewer than one-third of Americans had earnings that put them in the economic middle class. After the war two-thirds qualified. At the same time, about 14 million soldiers and sailors were poised to return to the labor market.

The End of Laissez-Faire. The initial New Deal spending programs of Franklin Roosevelt had been harshly attacked by laissez-faire economists and businessmen, who believed that the economy would right itself if business were left to look out for its own interests with a minimum of government regulation. For three-quarters of a century American business had built a consensus that government intervention in the free-market economy was detrimental to economic health. "That government which governs least, governs best" was their motto. Yet government provided lands, canals, railways, tax exemptions, and other forms of aid to large corporations without providing comparable benefits for the poor ordinary working people. Many businesspeople feared that governmental intervention would undermine the work ethic and create dependency. They saw periods of high unemployment as beneficial because they lowered wages and forced the "lazy" to work. In previous depressions their advice had been to "wait it out" while the economy eventually balanced itself. The Great Depression, however, was so destructive that the Roosevelt administration believed government intervention was a necessity, not only to ward off political upheaval but to stave off massive starvation in some areas.

The New Deal Primes the Economic Pump. In 1932, when Roosevelt was running for his first term as president, the unemployment rate stood at 25 percent nationwide, while in some areas it was half the working population. In heavily industrialized cities such as Toledo, Ohio, more than 75 percent of working men were unemployed. There was no unemployment insurance, no welfare, and no public housing. Private charities such as the Salvation Army were expected to pick up the pieces, but they were quickly overwhelmed. To increase employment and consumer spending the New Deal invested in public works, public jobs programs, and Social Security as a way to prime the pump of economic recovery. The idea was originated by John Maynard Keynes, a British economist, who argued that government spending could stimulate consumer purchases, which in turn would encourage production to meet increased demand. Yet, the funds injected into the economy by Roosevelt's New Deal programs were insufficient to overcome the Depression. The

massive amounts of money required for war production, however, not only returned the nation to full employment but catapulted the entire economy into overdrive. Economists concluded that Keynesianism worked, and, based on that conclusion, they planned for the future.

The Permanent War Economy. Roosevelt had looked upon the opponents of the New Deal as antiquated and out of touch with reality. He blamed "economic royalists" for having mismanaged the economy and condemned their heartlessness toward the unemployed. The old-line laissez-faire businessmen equated Roosevelt's programs with communism. Yet by the end of World War II many of Roosevelt's harshest critics had come to see government economic intervention and planning as beneficial to them. In 1940 about 175,000 firms accounted for 70 percent of the nation's manufacturing output, while the 100 largest corporations provided the other 30 percent. By war's end this ratio was exactly reversed. Control of the U.S. economy had been concentrated in the hands of a tiny minority. Fundamentally, government expenditures had returned business and government to the cozy relationship they enjoyed in the days of laissez-faire. With every other major industrial economy in the world in disarray, the American economy boomed. Some of this largesse was distributed to working people through New Deal programs or in wages. Such prosperity meant that for the first time in American history, government intervention into the economy benefited the wealthy and the poor.

The Welfare/Warfare State. Because the social welfare programs of the New Deal had meant the difference between disaster and survival for millions of Americans during the Depression, it became politically dangerous to cut spending on them, though extreme right-wing politicians called for ending various programs from time to time. By the end of World War II most Republicans who had previously opposed the welfare state embraced it. Both of Thomas Dewey's presidential bids featured rhetorical support for the New Deal. The flip side of providing a safety net beneath the unemployed and underprivileged was that industrial and financial profits could also be maintained by government spending. New Dealers and conservative businessmen implicitly struck a bargain: if corporations wanted to benefit from U.S. tax dollars, they would have to approve government revenues for unemployment compensation, veterans benefits, public housing, and public-health programs. Previously seen as tax giveaways to the undeserving poor, social-welfare measures were now perceived as boons to business as well. For example, public works such as highway and hospital construction ensured that federal revenues went to construction firms, which in turn would hire some of the very taxpayers whose money was paying for the building projects. Social Security and unemployment checks would be spent, thus stimulating the consumer economy. Spending for the military-industrial complex would provide such economic benefits on an even grander scale. By the early 1950s such diverse groups as businessmen, union leaders and workers, engineers, government bureaucrats, and liberal and conservative intellectuals reached a consensus that continued government spending for welfare and warfare was economically and politically necessary.

Benefits of the Welfare/Warfare State. At first the benefits of a permanent war economy linked with social-welfare spending seem unassailable. During the war the government had invested approximately $20 billion in new factories, virtually ending unemployment and giving workers considerable disposable income. Because of wartime rationing, there were few goods to purchase, so they put their money into bank accounts, resulting in a $140 billion savings pool available for banks to invest in new industrial and service sectors of the economy. During the war American productivity rose at about 7 percent annually, but between 1945–1960 shot up to 10 percent per year. Defense expenditures dropped between 1946 and 1948, but federal spending on education, health, and highways doubled. After the Korean War, defense spending more than doubled from $70 billion in 1950 to $151 billion in 1960. With such rates of profit, increasing funds were available for investment in new technologies and new industries. Agricultural income rocketed from $4 billion in 1940 to $12.3 billion in 1960, but acreage cultivated rose only by 4 percent. Farm-machinery improvements and chemical fertilizers, developed as offshoots of war production, made the difference. During the war a synthetic-rubber industry had been created by the government; after the war the petrochemical industry took it over. The Marshall Plan provided more than $12 billion in aid to Europe; much of this money was used to purchase goods from the United States. Even after the plan ended in 1952, continued foreign aid became a mainstay of government spending. Profiting at record levels, U.S. corporations invested overseas. Ten giant oil companies opened up Middle East oil and sunk new wells in Venezuela. Coca-Cola spread everywhere, provoking somewhat humorous fears about the "coca-colonization" of the globe. American exports rose from $20 billion in 1944 to $125 billion in 1970. By 1950 American steel companies were working at 98 percent of capacity; back orders for refrigerators — virtually unattainable during the war — were the largest on record. Sales of automobiles were so rapid that the Big Three auto companies actually lowered prices. As the decade of the 1940s ended, the Christmas buying season of 1949 was the most profitable in retail history. Many believed that the new partnership of business and government would avert future depressions, end poverty, and usher in the golden age of affluence.

Sources:
Richard J. Barnet, *The Roots of War* (New York: Atheneum, 1972);

John Kenneth Galbraith, *The Affluent Society* (Boston: Houghton Mifflin, 1960);

Seymour Melman, *Pentagon Capitalism: The Political Economy of War* (New York: McGraw-Hill, 1970);

Franklin D. Roosevelt and Henry Wallace during the 1940 presidential campaign

Melman, *The Permanent War Economy: American Capitalism in Decline* (New York: Simon & Schuster, 1974).

NATIONAL POLITICS: DEMOCRATIC PRIMARIES AND CONVENTION 1940

Roosevelt's Bid for a Third Term. In 1940 President Franklin D. Roosevelt sought a third term as president. Following in a tradition established by George Washington, no previous president had ever run for a third term, even though the Constitution did not yet forbid it. Roosevelt had claimed to close associates that he had no intention of seeking another term, yet he controlled the Democratic Party and knew that popular opinion would support him if he ran again. Foreign affairs, moreover, were bringing the war ever closer to America. Few Democrats could imagine any other man at the helm of the U.S. government in such perilous times. Roosevelt and his advisers shaped a careful strategy to make it appear that the president was not seeking the nomination but that the Democratic Party and the American people were drafting him. Other Democrats tried their hands in state primaries. John Nance Garner, Roosevelt's vice president since 1932, had broken with the president over the "court packing" plan of 1937 — through which Roosevelt had hoped to appoint new, sympathetic justices to U.S. Supreme Court. Opposing much of the later New Deal, "Cactus Jack" Garner announced in December 1939 that he would seek the nomination. Although Roosevelt did not declare himself a candidate, state Democratic Parties ran his name on ballots, and in state primaries he easily defeated Garner. Meanwhile James A. "Big Jim" Farley, the postmaster general and chairman of the Democratic National Committee, became convinced that Roosevelt would not run again and declared his own candidacy. He won a slate of delegates in the Massachusetts primary, but in his home state of New York the press criticized his candidacy on the grounds that as a Catholic he could not win the election. City bosses, moreover, were convinced that only Roosevelt could carry the Democratic Party to victory. One week before the convention Roosevelt informed his longtime friend Farley that he would accept a draft from the party. Philosophically against a third term for president, Farley refused to stand aside and resigned both his cabinet position and his party chairmanship, severing a long and mutually beneficial relationship.

"Drafting" Roosevelt. Shortly before the Democratic National Convention opened in Chicago on 15 July, Roosevelt arranged for his closest associate, Harry Hopkins, to deliver a message to the delegates that Roosevelt had "no wish" to be nominated and that they should feel free to vote for any candidate. This ploy to stampede the convention into demanding Roosevelt's candidacy was successful. On 17 July the president broke the logjam of debate over the platform by revising the foreign-policy plank. To the statement that the United States would not participate in any foreign wars, or send Americans to fight overseas, Roosevelt added the words "except in case of attack." Mayor Edward J. Kelly of Chicago, one of the most powerful big-city bosses, gave a rousing endorsement of the president, saying, "The salvation of the nation rests in one man. . . . We must overrule his comfort and convenience and draft Roosevelt." On the first ballot the president received 946 votes to 72 for Farley and 61 for Garner. All that remained was to find a running mate.

Wallace for Vice President. Roosevelt was adamant that his own choice for vice president be nominated. He had considered Secretary of State Cordell Hull but decided Hull was too old, too conservative, and too unenthusiastic about the New Deal. Sen. James F. Byrnes of South Carolina had two liabilities: he was a former Catholic and a southerner who might cost the ticket votes in the North and West. Secretary of Agriculture Henry A. Wallace had liabilities as well. He was not trusted by party stalwarts because he had been a Republican until 1928, and he had never run for office before. Yet he had moved into the most liberal wing of the party and was an ardent supporter of Roosevelt's deficit-spending program and foreign policy. Those delegates who knew Wallace considered him an able administrator, but most had never heard of him. Opposition to Wallace was intense, as party bosses supported favorite sons. Yet the president's insistence, a speech by Eleanor Roosevelt, and the endorsement of the disappointed Byrnes won Wallace the nomination.

NATIONAL POLITICS: REPUBLICAN PRIMARIES AND CONVENTION 1940

Republican Challengers. In early 1940 there appeared to be three serious candidates for the Republican nomination. A Gallup poll indicated that Thomas E. Dewey, former district attorney of New York, was the leading contender, favored by 43 percent of party members. Sen. Robert A. Taft of Ohio was the choice of 17 percent of Republicans, while 22 percent liked Sen. Arthur H. Vandenberg of Michigan. Though Dewey was the front-runner, he was young — only thirty-seven — and had never held an important office. Secretary of the Interior Harold Ickes quipped that Dewey "had thrown his diaper into the ring." Taft, son of former president William Howard Taft, was lacking in personal appeal, and many party leaders did not think Vandenberg was ambitious enough. In 1940 concern over the sudden escalation of the war in Europe turned public focus on the Republican candidates' lack of foreign-policy experience. Outflanked by Roosevelt on foreign policy, the Republicans searched for a new candidate. They turned to a man who had only recently switched to their party and who had never held any elective or appointive government office. Reasoning that the party could not unseat Roosevelt by waging a conservative campaign against him, party leaders turned to Wendell L. Willkie, a liberal Republican, who lambasted the Democrats for the failure of the New Deal to end the Depression.

A Most Untypical Candidate. The Luce publishing empire, together with the *New York Herald Tribune* and influential Madison Avenue advertising executives, had already mounted an intensive campaign to bring Willkie to public attention. By late 1939 and early 1940 the *Reader's Digest* and *The New Republic* had also run favorable articles emphasizing Willkie's support of much New Deal legislation, his qualified support for Keynesian government economics, and his anti-isolationism. Willkie's liabilities included having been a Wall Street lawyer and chief executive of a privately owned utility company. His political inexperience worried some, as did his lack of Republican credentials. As one senator told him: "Well Wendell, you know that back in Indiana it's all right for the town whore to join the church, but they don't let her lead the choir the first night."

Convention Maneuvers. The other Republican candidates were bewildered by the Willkie phenomenon. Both folksy and cosmopolitan, Willkie had a natural charm that attracted many — especially after his buildup in the Republican press. Willkie clubs had sprung up across the country, and voters who ordinarily avoided politics sent thousands of telegrams to the national convention in Philadelphia. Needing only a simple majority to win the nomination, Willkie's forces waited out each ballot. Their strategy was to begin with a small but respectable showing and add to it from ballot to ballot, as more and more delegates were freed from their obligations to favorite sons. To those who questioned his Republican pedigree Willkie's floor managers replied: "Is the Republican Party a closed corporation? Do you have to be born into it?" Dewey led the first ballot with about one-third of the vote, but support for him went steadily downhill thereafter. On 28 June Willkie won on the sixth ballot. To counter the perception that Willkie was a tool of private utilities, the convention nominated Sen. Charles L. McNary of Oregon, a proponent of public power and reclamation projects, as Willkie's running mate.

NATIONAL POLITICS: ELECTION 1940

Domestic Issues. Roosevelt was vulnerable on economic issues. Despite New Deal efforts such as social security, a fair-labor act, unemployment insurance, and public housing, government spending had not adequately "primed" the economic pump. The economic slump of the late 1930s was dubbed the "Roosevelt recession." Though unemployment was down from the catastrophic 25 percent rate of the year Roosevelt took office, it had edged up to nearly 15 percent by 1938. Members of Roosevelt's own party thought the New Deal went too far in redistributing wealth, and many disapproved of his efforts to stack the Supreme Court to win approval of his programs. Roosevelt's attempted purge of conservative Democrats in 1938 left his right flank exposed.

A Foreign Policy Coup. Roosevelt had already begun to undercut Republican challenges when he appointed Republican stalwarts Henry L. Stimson as secretary of war and Frank Knox as secretary of the navy only four days before the Republican National Convention, ostensibly in a gesture toward bipartisanship in foreign policy. Though Republicans tended to be isolationist, they constantly criticized what they called Roosevelt's negligence of national defense. Stimson had been secretary of state under President Herbert Hoover, and Knox was a retired army colonel. Better appointments than these could not have been found by any Republican candidate. The Republican National Committee was so angry at Stimson and Knox that its chairman sought to banish them from the party. As usual, the president was being shrewd, sending a message that he, better than any other politician, could judge talent and exercise leadership. As he emphasized in his nationally broadcast nomination speech, the nation needed his experience more than ever: "If our Government should pass to other hands next January — untried hands, inexperienced hands — we can merely hope and pray that they will not substitute appeasement and compromise with those who seek to destroy all democracies everywhere, including here."

The Republicans Attempt To Play the Labor Card. Emphasizing the failure of the New Deal to create jobs, Willkie made a play for backing from labor. He reiterated his support for all the gains labor had made throughout the turbulent 1930s, upholding the right of collective bargaining and promising to strengthen Social Security. Roosevelt's old rival, John L. Lewis of the CIO, endorsed Willkie. Yet Willkie seriously alienated potential allies in the labor movement when he promised that his new secretary of labor "won't be a woman." This slap at Roosevelt's labor secretary, Frances Perkins, enraged labor and women alike. Roosevelt's rank-and-file support was immense. He continued to attack business monopoly and point to American poverty, promising that government would guarantee labor "a fair share of the national income."

House	76th Congress	77th Congress	Gain/Loss
Democrats	261	268	+7
Republicans	164	162	-2
Independents	4	5	+1

Senate	76th Congress	77th Congress	Gain/Loss
Democrats	69	66	-3
Republicans	23	28	+5
Independents	4	2	-2

Willkie Outgunned. Promising an even newer New Deal, Willkie was running as the candidate of an essentially conservative party. Many Republicans saw him as an interloper and an amateur. But his main weakness was that he could not compete with the commander in chief. Roosevelt declined to debate Willkie but allowed his associates to attack him freely. The irrepressible Ickes lampooned Willkie's Hoosier and legal background by calling him "a simple barefoot Wall Street lawyer." Meanwhile, the president acted presidential, seeking and obtaining an unprecedented $11.5-billion defense budget from Congress. When Roosevelt sought Willkie's support for his Selective Service bill, he did not get it. (Willkie's running mate voted for it, though Taft and Vandenberg did not.) In September, when the president announced the destroyers-for-bases deal with England, Willkie called it "the most arbitrary and dictatorial action ever taken by any president in the history of the United States." Though Gallup poll numbers had been promising for Willkie in August, by September the new figures indicated he was heading for defeat. Willkie had attacked what he termed a slow defense buildup; yet unemployment was decreasing as weapons production increased. Labeling Roosevelt the candidate of the pro-Nazi elements, Willkie called the president an isolationist and said that he had "telephoned Mussolini and Hitler and urged them to sell Czechoslovakia down the river at Munich." While his press secretary quickly asserted that the Republican had "misspoken," the damage was done. Willkie then contradicted himself and called Roosevelt a warmonger. Willkie promised that if he were elected, "our boys shall stay out of European wars." The mood of the electorate warranted such talk, and Roosevelt said essentially the same thing. Yet as election day approached, and war seemed more and more imminent, the voters seemed to agree with Mayor Fiorello La Guardia of New York, who said he preferred "Roosevelt with his known faults to Willkie with his unknown virtues." Though Willkie lost by nearly 5 million votes, and won only 82 electoral votes to Roosevelt's 449, he made a considerably better showing against Roosevelt than any other Republican and pointed up where the Democrats were vulnerable.

Sources:

Arthur M. Schlesinger, Jr., *The Age of Roosevelt*, 3 volumes (Boston: Houghton Mifflin, 1956–1960);

Schlesinger, ed., *The History of American Presidential Elections, 1789–1968* (New York: Chelsea House, 1971);

Schlesinger, ed., *History of U.S. Political Parties* (New York: Chelsea House, 1973).

House	77th Congress	78th Congress	Gain/ Loss
Democrats	268	218	-50
Republicans	162	208	+46
Independents	5	4	-1

Senate	77th Congress	78th Congress	Gain/ Loss
Democrats	66	58	-8
Republicans	28	37	+9
Independents	2	1	-1

NATIONAL POLITICS: ELECTION 1942

Roosevelt Vacillates. Roosevelt's liberal advisers insisted that the war was a crusade against fascism and political tyranny abroad and against elitist economic rule and racism at home. Roosevelt was aware, however, that to struggle against the Right at home would alienate those business leaders whose expertise in production was necessary for victory. Somehow class conflict would have to be ameliorated, and a sense of national unity fostered. The president, moreover, needed to act as commander in chief, emphasizing foreign relations. Roosevelt thus veered from one style of leadership to another. When he joined Winston Churchill in issuing the Atlantic Charter on 12 August 1941, he stressed social commitments as a major basis for Allied cooperation. Yet, by the congressional elections of 1942 the president was calling for "an end to politics" and took virtually no interest in the selection of his crucial wartime Congress. The normal midterm swing away from the party in power was intensified in 1942 by military reversals and inflation. Labor was unhappy with wage controls, farmers with price limits, consumers with inflation, and rationing. Wartime mobility of the workforce and the absence of millions of men overseas combined with popular disgruntlement to result in a low turnout for the midterm elections.

Republican Gains. Republicans made strong gains in both houses of Congress and won several important governorships. In New York Thomas E. Dewey broke a twenty-year Democratic hold on the governorship and was catapulted into national prominence. The congressional elections strengthened the hands of the conservatives, who went on the offensive after 1942, capturing the Republican National Committee from the Willkie forces and positioning Sen. Robert A. Taft of Ohio as leading spokesman for the Republican Party.

NATIONAL POLITICS: DEMOCRATIC PRIMARIES AND CONVENTION 1944

Vulnerable Democrats. If Roosevelt's third term was unprecedented, his running for a fourth term seemed almost unimaginable. Roosevelt had grown visibly older under the strain of war, and Republican gains in the midterm elections of 1942 had weakened the Roosevelt Democratic coalition. Though the darkest days of the war had passed, victory was by no means assured. Some polls indicated that many who had previously voted for Roosevelt would not do so again if the war ended, and perhaps as many as 50 percent would vote for a Republican if the president did not run. Labor's gains during the Depression had been weakened by passage of the Smith-Connally Act, restricting labor's right to strike and its political activities. Though the president had vetoed the bill, a Democratic but newly conservative Congress had overridden the veto. Roosevelt was vulnerable on taxes too. Congress cut his requests for higher taxes to support the war. Instead, the House and Senate passed a bill which reduced revenues but included the entirely new provision of payroll withholding. The bill also granted concessions to airlines, lumber, and oil interests. Calling the bill a program of relief "not for the needy but for the greedy," Roosevelt vetoed it as well, but it too was overridden, signaling that the president's control of his own party might be incomplete.

The "Good Soldier." Roosevelt's most compelling strength lay in his role as commander in chief of the military, the title he preferred throughout the war. Although he had clearly changed hats — becoming "Dr. Win-the-War" after being "Dr. New Deal" — he renewed his commitment to social justice during the period leading up to his fourth nomination. In late 1943 he championed, and Congress passed, the GI Bill of Rights, providing college tuition, home loans, and other sorts of aid to returning veterans. On 11 January 1944, in his eleventh State of the Union Address, Roosevelt gave what was probably the most "radical speech of his life." Calling for an "economic Bill of Rights," the president insisted that all Americans were owed the rights to jobs, decent housing, and education, as well as protection from sickness, unemployment, and the anxieties of old age. To accomplish these goals, said Roosevelt, the United States must first win the war. By hitching social justice to military victory, Roosevelt renewed the sources of his political strength. Though a feeble anti-Roosevelt faction formed within the Democratic Party, it fizzled before the convention opened. One week before that event Roosevelt released a statement that as a "good soldier" he would accept renomination.

Franklin Delano Roosevelt delivering his fourth inaugural address, 20 January 1945. His son James is in uniform directly behind him.

The "Dump Wallace" Movement. Wallace was more liberal than the president himself and as such was opposed by the Democratic Party bosses. Many of them felt he was too independent, too prolabor, and too outspoken in his support for racial equality, and they did not want him to became president should their worst fears about Roosevelt's failing health prove true. Though Wallace was the president's own choice for a running mate, Roosevelt knew he was facing open rebellion within the Democratic Party and told his advisers that he would inform Wallace of his decision to choose a new running mate. Yet when Wallace offered to step down, Roosevelt urged him to remain in the running. At the same time, however, the president also seemed to encourage James F. Byrnes to run for nomination. After party leaders once again objected to Byrnes's having been a Roman Catholic and to his lack of appeal to labor and blacks, Roosevelt released a letter indicating his preference for Wallace. On 18 July at the Democratic National Convention in Chicago, Wallace seconded Roosevelt's nomination and was greeted by thunderous applause. Shouts of "We Want Wallace" continued until the chairman of the convention adjourned the session. The fol-

lowing night police were used to keep Wallace supporters out of the galleries. Meanwhile, party leaders told the delegates that Sen. Harry S Truman of Missouri was Roosevelt's choice.

Truman Nominated. Truman's name had come up as part of the routine process of looking over the field of potential vice-presidential candidates. As one party leader put it, Truman "was the only one who fitted." He had a good record in the Senate, his labor votes were good, and as a senator from a border state, he was believed to be a conservative on racial issues. Roosevelt knew that he could not win with Wallace and that any effort to do so would dangerously split the party, so he acquiesced to those who wanted Truman. Roosevelt was then persuaded to draft another letter, this time expressing a preference for either Truman or Supreme Court Justice William O. Douglas, a man who had no chance of winning the nomination. After the first ballot showed that Wallace led Truman by only 110 votes, state delegations abandoned their favorite-son candidates and shifted to Truman, who won decisively on the second ballot.

Thomas E. Dewey accepting the Republican presidential nomination in 1948

NATIONAL POLITICS: REPUBLICAN PRIMARIES AND CONVENTION 1944

Targeting Roosevelt's Health. The Republicans tried gingerly to draw attention to Roosevelt's health. He had been hospitalized from late 1943 to early 1944 and had been diagnosed with arteriosclerosis and hypertensive heart disease. Doctors prescribed rest, and his closest aides were alarmed by his deteriorating physical condition. Photographers generally tried not to take unflattering pictures of the president, and often he appeared hale and hardy. Yet occasionally a published photograph would reveal how frail he had become. Republican newspapers especially emphasized Roosevelt's poor health.

The Communist Bogey Appears. Meanwhile, Republican strategists attacked the system of wartime controls, arguing they would lead to an administrative "dictatorship" tinged by communism. The president and Congress were then at odds over the Communist Party. Roosevelt had enlisted Communist support for the war, primarily because Stalin was now an ally. American Communists, for their part, had agreed to disband the party in favor of a more loosely organized "Communist Political Association," and they endorsed Roosevelt's wartime measures. The House Un-American Activities Committee (HUAC) was holding hearings in an attempt to document the perfidy of Communists, looking into the pasts of many officials in the Roosevelt Administration and condemning the president for his pardon in 1941 of American Communist Party chief Earl Browder, who had been serving time for perjury. Republican contender Thomas E. Dewey said Roosevelt had so weakened the Democratic Party that "the forces of communism are, in fact, now capturing it." Though these tactics had little

effect in 1944, they presaged the turmoil the issue would arouse in the next presidential election — and beyond.

Willkie Rejected. At the beginning of 1944 Willkie was a front-runner for the Republican nomination. His best-selling book *One World* (1943) had kept him in the limelight, but he was out of touch with the isolationist, virulently anti-Roosevelt, Republican Old Guard, which had regained control of party machinery after the 1942 elections. Willkie had not built himself a base in the GOP. In the 1944 New Hampshire primary Willkie won six out of eleven delegates, but in the very next state, Wisconsin, he failed to secure a single one. He promptly withdrew from the race. Some party regulars tried to push the candidacy of Gen. Douglas MacArthur, who had been absent from the country for nearly ten years. MacArthur, who was basking in the light of his Pacific victories, seemed an attractive candidate, but when he inadvertently let it be known that he agreed with conservative assessments that the Roosevelt Administration was composed of "left-wingers" and "monarchists," his prospects among moderate Republicans collapsed.

Dewey Is Nominated. Once the GOP ruled out MacArthur there was no doubt that Thomas E. Dewey would be the Republican candidate. Dewey was governor of New York, the same position from which Roosevelt had ascended to the presidency. While he had the support of more than half the party, especially moderates, Dewey was disliked by many Republicans and by the press. He seemed stiff, lacking the common touch. Harold Ickes likened him to the "bridegroom on the wedding cake." Though Dewey claimed to oppose the New Deal, the party platform endorsed the National Labor Relations Act, the Social Security Act, unemployment insurance, farm supports, and other New Deal measures. After the convention *The New York Times* editorialized that Dewey was running on the "domestic program of the New Deal." Not only were Dewey and the party pledging to keep the "welfare state," but they were placing it beyond the range of partisan dispute, making it unlikely that the United States would return to the laissez-faire conditions of the past. With no other candidate before the convention, Dewey won on the first ballot 1,056 to 1. (One lone delegate cast a vote for MacArthur.) No other Republican candidate who was not a sitting president had ever won such a lopsided victory.

NATIONAL POLITICS: ELECTION 1944

Dewey's Offensive. Though Dewey resisted the temptation to attack the president for the American military's unpreparedness at Pearl Harbor, he maintained that the Republicans could manage the war better. He focused on the issue of taxes and on the anti-Roosevelt passions of the Irish, Italian, and German Americans. He charged Roosevelt with a secret plan to keep men in the military after the war rather than risking widespread unemployment again. Other Republicans kept red-baiting the Democrats, and in the South Roosevelt was attacked for drafting blacks who challenged segregation. Seizing the race issue, the Republicans began an alliance with conservative Democrats that would eventually break the Democratic lock on the "solid South."

Political Action Committees. During the last six weeks of the campaign, the Political Action Committee (PAC) of the Congress of Industrial Organization (CIO) registered nearly 7 million additional voters — important because of the millions of men serving overseas and because in general the larger the voter turnout the more likely Democrats to win. The PAC had been organized in 1943 by CIO official Sidney Hillman and Philip Murray of the United Auto Workers as a way of getting around the prohibition on union politicking in the Smith-Connally Act. The committee was organized to accept "voluntary" contributions from union members to be used as the committee saw fit. Thus, no union funds would be donated to candidates. The activities of the PAC involved a fundamental reordering of priorities for labor — away from concerns limited to the workplace and toward engagement in the national priorities of the Democratic Party. In the process it became one of the primary financial pillars of the party. Labor PACs contributed more than $2 million — more than 30 percent of the total Democratic campaign fund — in the election of 1944. The PAC also served as a target for the enemies of labor, who charged that Hillman was a Communist stooge. (Eventually, conservative opponents of the welfare state would organize their own PACs.) Republicans such as Clare Boothe Luce used thinly disguised anti-Semitism in attempts to discredit Hillman and the many Jews who were prominent in the CIO. Dewey charged that the CIO was dominated by Communists, insisting that the

House	78th Congress	79th Congress	Gain/Loss
Democrats	218	242	+24
Republicans	208	190	-18
Independents	4	2	-2

Senate	78th Congress	79th Congress	Gain/Loss
Democrats	58	56	-2
Republicans	37	38	+1
Independents	1	1	0

Democratic Party had been "taken over by Earl Browder and Sidney Hillman."

The Emergence of the Public-Opinion Poll. Although Gallup had been conducting interviews for some time, new methods of gathering information about voter preferences had been developed by 1944 and had led to the entry of other polling organizations into the field. Gallup found that by substituting "secret ballots" for personal interviews, where the individual was identified, poll takers could get more-honest responses. As a result of the guarantee of anonymity, the Gallup, Cantrill, and Roper polls began to reveal information that had previously gone unreported. For example, as much as 10 percent of lower-income voters were against Roosevelt because of the payroll withholding of income taxes. The Irish, Italian, and German communities blamed him for the war. The typical voter appeared to select candidates on the basis of only one or two particular issues. Using information provided by such opinion polls, the Roosevelt Administration discovered that it had to have a large turnout, one of the reasons the CIO-PAC was organized. The age of the pollsters had arrived.

Roosevelt's Slimmest Victory. The president began to campaign in earnest only at the end of September. Addressing the International Brotherhood of Teamsters, Roosevelt ridiculed GOP claims that he mismanaged the war effort by saying that the Republicans were the very people who had opposed Lend-Lease and blocked every attempt to arm the United States. He praised labor for its contributions to manufacturing weapons, noting that all labor leaders, save John L. Lewis of the United Mine Workers, had condemned war-industry strikes. He hit his opponents hard for failing to pass a bill enabling soldiers overseas to vote by absentee ballot (a measure that clearly would have favored him), and he promised that the Roosevelt administration had a plan to discharge veterans as rapidly as possible after the war. In October Roosevelt lambasted "labor-baiters and bigots" who stuck the label "communist" on all progressives and foreign-born citizens with whom they disagreed. Events overseas helped Roosevelt as well. Operation Overlord, launched on 6 June 1944, had proved successful, and Allied armies were racing toward Germany. MacArthur made his famous return to the Philippines on 20 October, and a few days later the Battle of Leyte Gulf all but destroyed the Japanese navy. Roosevelt's appeal to the electorate not "to switch horses in the middle of the stream" was based on his able war record. On the eve of the election he promised a postwar economy that would provide "close to" 60 million jobs (a figure actually reached in 1947). Roosevelt's margin of victory — 3.6 million votes — was his closest ever, probably because of the absence of millions of voting soldiers — and his electoral-vote margin was slim. Yet the Democrats made significant gains in both the House and Senate, and among the freshman legislators were Wayne Morse, J. William Fulbright, Helen Gahagan Douglas, and Adam Clayton Powell — all of whom would later play crucial roles in the Democratic Party.

The Urbanization of the Democratic Party. The key to Roosevelt's fourth-term victory was the urban vote. Residence had become a major determinant of voter preference. Roosevelt had taken the states with the largest numbers of electoral votes by winning in the biggest cities. War production had caused a tremendous, in some cases exponential, growth of cities, as new industries sprang up overnight and attracted millions of workers from rural areas to new urban megalopolises. Migration of workers to San Diego, Los Angeles, and San Francisco had made California one of the most important states to win. The urban voter, overwhelmingly working class and newly dependent on the social safety net created by the New Deal, would become a mainstay of the Democratic Party for the next four decades, except in the Deep South, where white alienation from the growing civil rights agenda of the Democrats would lead increasingly to abandonment of the party and to national political realignment.

Sources:

Arthur M. Schlesinger, Jr., *The Age of Roosevelt*, 3 volumes (Boston: Houghton Mifflin, 1956–1960);

Schlesinger, ed., *The History of American Presidential Elections, 1789–1968* (New York: Chelsea House, 1971);

Schlesinger, ed., *History of U.S. Political Parties* (New York: Chelsea House, 1973).

NATIONAL POLITICS: ELECTION 1946

The Republicans Gain Control of Congress. Public irritation with the Democrats' handling of reconversion to a peacetime economy and worries over tension with the Soviets spurred a sudden shift in voting behavior in 1946, resulting in Republican control of both the House and the Senate for the first time since 1928. Truman, who had become president on Roosevelt's death in April 1945, had alienated Southern Democrats by calling for a Fair Employment Practices Commission (FEPC) to prevent job discrimination against blacks, and Truman's

House	79th Congress	80th Congress	Gain/ Loss
Democrats	242	188	-54
Republicans	190	245	+55
Independents	2	1	-1

Senate	79th Congress	80th Congress	Gain/ Loss
Democrats	56	45	-11
Republicans	38	51	+13
Independents	1	0	-1

brief nationalization of the nation's railroads to halt a strike by railway workers in spring 1946 almost split the Democrats. Meanwhile, the president's lifting of wartime price controls angered liberals, labor, and consumers. Running on the slogan "Had Enough? Vote Republican," the GOP profited from the mood of the electorate. After its victories in the congressional elections, the GOP was able to obstruct Truman Administration programs, and older conservatives spoke of dismantling the New Deal. Moderate Republicans reined in these laissez-faire diehards, however, reminding them that recipients of Depression-era subsidies had become powerful pressure groups that could not be ignored or alienated. Though the GOP attempted to revive its long-lost reputation as the champion of African Americans, Republican efforts amounted to little more than rhetoric, and they stopped short of endorsing civil rights. The Republicans sacrificed nothing in this respect because they could blame racial intransigence on Democratic white supremacists in the South. The winners in off-year elections customarily won the next presidential contest, and the GOP sought to capitalize on public impatience with a wave of postwar strikes, reasoning that few groups would object to legislation curtailing the power of the unions. While fiscal conservatives were alarmed at spending for proposed foreign-aid programs, a crop of freshman Republican legislators, including Sen. Joseph R. McCarthy of Wisconsin, sensed that the Democrats were vulnerable on their handling of postwar relations with the Soviet Union.

Truman's Popularity Slides. It was inevitable that Truman would be compared unfavorably with his popular predecessor. His unsteady leadership on postwar economic concerns angered consumers: while allowing prices to rise he had attempted to keep labor's wage demands in check. Liberal Democrats believed he favored business interests in his attempt to appoint Democratic Party Chairman Edwin W. Pauley to the post of assistant navy secretary. Secretary of the Interior Harold Ickes charged that Pauley, an independent oil producer, would exert undue influence on federal oil policy. Such internal squabbles damaged party unity; the most serious involved

Alben Barkley and Harry S Truman after winning the 1948 vice-presidential and presidential election

the firing of Henry A. Wallace from his post as commerce secretary. Wallace had publicly criticized Truman's handling of foreign policy, arguing that the president's increasingly harsh responses to the Soviets pushed them to fulfill his advisers' prophecies. Initially Truman acknowledged Wallace's remarks approvingly; later he denounced them. As a result, liberals began to back away from Truman. Meanwhile, Republican right-wingers lambasted Truman for vacillating on the Soviets and the threat of domestic communism. Anticommunist Democrats — particularly in the South and within the labor movement — began to threaten the stability of the New Deal coalition. The election results jolted the Democrats, who lost twelve seats in the Senate and fifty-eight in the House. Damage to the liberal-labor faction was particularly acute. Liberal Democrats lost seven out of eight seats in the Senate and thirty-seven of sixty-nine in the House. Many in the party considered Truman an embarrassment. Arkansas Democrat J. William Fulbright even remarked sardonically that Truman ought to appoint a Republican secretary of state (who, since there was no vice president, was next in succession for the presidency) and then resign, giving the voters the Republican president they wanted. Democratic prospects for 1948 seemed dismal.

NATIONAL POLITICS: DEMOCRATIC PRIMARIES AND CONVENTION 1948

Truman's Weakness. The most obvious sign of weakness in Truman and the Democrats was the Republicans'

success in the 1946 elections, which resulted in their control of both houses of Congress. The once-powerful Democratic coalition had developed fissures. Black war veterans were in no mood to accept the humiliation of segregationist "Jim Crow" laws. Labor had been clashing with the administration since the end of wartime price controls. Liberals were angry at the president's firing of Henry A. Wallace from his cabinet post in 1946. Where Democrats had been elected in 1946 they were conservatives rather than New Dealers. To many Democrats and much of the public in general the president seemed weak, vacillating, inexperienced, and too reliant on his advisers. As yet there was no consensus on the developing Cold War, and the liberal wing of the party saw Truman as bellicose, uncompromising, and betraying Roosevelt's vision of the possibilities for global peace and security. Simultaneously, conservative Democrats criticized civil rights efforts and condemned him for not being anticommunist enough. Even so, the party had retained much of its Roosevelt base, particularly blue-collar voters and farmers. *Fortune* magazine reported that 39 percent of the electorate was still Democratic while 33 percent was Republican. Moreover, independents were leaning toward the Democrats. The race was Truman's to win, and he had a record as a dogged campaigner.

The Politics of Anticommunism. The liberal wing of the Democratic Party, led by Wallace, saw Truman's get-tough policy toward the Soviets as a betrayal of his predecessor's vision. In their view Truman's confrontational style was leading toward a terrifying arms race and the possibility of global war. They also felt that paranoia at home was leading to rigid political conformity and repression of dissent. The loyalty-oath program fed public fears that Communists had infiltrated the government in preparation for its violent overthrow. Such thinking reinforced the red-baiting tactics of GOP right-wingers such as Richard Nixon and Joseph McCarthy. Truman's anticommunist policies abroad and at home alienated his support on the left and right margins of the American polity.

Wallace's Progressive Party Candidacy. Believing that he was the true heir to Roosevelt's liberalism and foreign policy, Henry A. Wallace thought that he had enough support among Democrats to gain the presidency but that party bosses would deny him the nomination. In 1947 he decided to revitalize the moribund Progressive Party and run as its presidential candidate. Discontent with Truman's foreign policy was the basis of the Wallace movement. Wallace argued that the continuation and extension of the New Deal depended on peace and on a United Nations capable of fostering cooperation among nations. In Wallace's view the growing Cold War was driven by the big armaments businesses. His platform was not anticapitalist, however. He was convinced that a world of free enterprise, open markets, and democratic governments was the only way to ensure American — and global — prosperity. He also felt that the arms race diverted the nation's productive resources and cost Americans trade in worldwide nonmilitary markets, leading inevitably to closed and competitive zones throughout the world. The permanent war economy that the government supported was a poor substitute for devoting American efforts to manufacturing, foreign trade, and amicable relations with other powerful nations.

Truman Plays the Anticommunist Card. It was clear that if Wallace received support from the liberals and labor within the Democratic Party, Truman would lose the election. Clark Clifford, Truman's general counsel and most important adviser, masterminded an effort to identify Wallace with the Communists. Inside the CIO there was a power struggle going on between the Communists, who had played a major role in the creation of the CIO, and anticommunists such as Philip Murray, who had become president of the organization, declared that Wallace's new party was controlled by Communists. The CIO, moreover, announced support of the Marshall Plan because of its provision that reconstruction funds delivered to devastated Europe would have to be spent in the United States, thus stimulating investment and jobs at home. Almost all major labor leaders, including Walter Reuther of the United Auto Workers and William Green of the AFL, condemned Communist political activity and denied Wallace support from labor. Soviet actions abroad also helped Truman. Fearing that Marshall Plan aid might go to nations on their borders and thus draw them into the Western orbit, the Soviets staged a coup against the government of Czechoslovakia, and in June

1947 Stalin initiated the blockade of Berlin. Wallace, hinting that Truman's actions provoked Stalin, bungled badly in his efforts to explain away developments. Truman responded by attacking Wallace for his naïveté and for his "pro-communism." Although such charges were unfounded, Wallace's effort to maintain balance and compromise in foreign affairs was out of step with a newly anticommunist electorate — itself a product of the Cold War.

The Politics of Race. The 1944 U.S. Supreme Court decision outlawing all-white primaries increased the number of African American voters, strengthening the voice of black war veterans who had risked their lives for democracy overseas and leading to erosion of Jim Crow in the South. Truman's 1948 civil rights message to Congress, the first ever delivered by a president, was seen as a betrayal by Southern politicians who had helped to engineer Truman's vice-presidential nomination in 1944, and Southern Democrats began to bolt the party. In February 1948 Gov. J. Strom Thurmond of South Carolina protested against "all Federal legislation dealing with the separation of the races." Thurmond warned that the South was "aroused" and that it was "no longer in the bag" for the Democrats. Truman's advisers, especially Clifford, argued that the increase in black voters more than compensated for the party's loss of disgruntled Southerners, especially in the far West, where defense industries had created an enormous population of enfranchised blacks. Nevertheless, most Democratic leaders were astonished at what happened when Truman won the nomination at Philadelphia in July.

Truman Renominated. Party leaders were pessimistic about Truman's chances. They hoped to recruit Gen. Dwight D. Eisenhower, who had expressed no party preference. Failing that, some tried Justice William O. Douglas, but he was too liberal for those supporting Eisenhower. Sen. Claude Pepper of Florida announced his candidacy but received little support. The convention almost reluctantly endorsed Truman. Because of his weak position, the president had little say about the party platform or about the choice of his running mate. Worried about the rebellion on the Left, Truman wanted Douglas to run with him, but Douglas refused, and party stalwarts insisted on Senate Minority Leader Alben W. Barkley of Kentucky, a man of Truman's age, from a border state, and representing the Democratic center. In many ways like Truman, Barkley was seen as the counterweight to the revolt of the Southern delegates.

The Bolt of the Dixiecrats. Party bosses wanted a moderate plank on civil rights, but Americans For Democratic Action (ADA), a new party caucus led by Hubert Humphrey of Minnesota, insisted on affirming Truman's earlier civil rights message. Inflamed by this turn of events, Southern Democrats repudiated the civil rights plank and all recent racial initiatives. ADA leaders concluded that a fight over civil rights was "what we need to stir up this convention and win the election." The ADA plank was voted in, and the Southerners stalked out of the convention. Declaring that "principle was above any party," they reconvened in Birmingham, Alabama, later that month to nominate Thurmond as the candidate of "States Rights Democrats." Not intending to create what would be a fourth party, the "Dixiecrats" were nonetheless forced by some state laws to do just that. Dixiecrat strategy was to win all the South's 127 electoral votes, thereby denying either Truman or his opponent a majority in the electoral college and throwing the contest into the House of Representatives. There each state would have one vote, and the South might get its candidates elected or at least serve notice that outsiders could not decide its way of life.

House	80th Congress	81st Congress	Gain/Loss
Democrats	188	263	+75
Republicans	245	171	-74
Independents	0	1	+1

Senate	80th Congress	81st Congress	Gain/Loss
Democrats	45	54	+9
Republicans	51	42	-9
Independents	0	0	0

NATIONAL POLITICS: REPUBLICAN PRIMARIES AND CONVENTION 1948

A Mixed Bag of Candidates. At the beginning of 1948, polls showed Dewey in the lead for the Republican nomination, but he was closely followed by Harold Stassen, Robert A. Taft, Arthur Vandenberg, Douglas MacArthur, and Earl Warren. Stassen was popular with the voters; Taft was believed to be incapable of defeating Truman; Warren was not widely known outside of his home state of California; MacArthur was out of the country, serving as commander of the Allied occupation forces in Japan. The battle in the primaries seesawed between Dewey and Stassen. As the Republican convention drew near, Dewey was more than ten percentage points farther ahead of Truman than Stassen, while Taft had strong support from the party leadership. When the Republicans met in Philadelphia in June, they appealed to the South by taking a call for a permanent Fair Employment Practices Commission out of the platform. The efficiency of the Dewey organization and the ineptitude of Taft's followers ultimately led to Dewey's nomination on the third ballot. Earl Warren was nominated as Dewey's running mate without opposition. The GOP ticket immediately led in the polls. As the convention ended, even Democratic newspapers were predicting Truman's defeat in November.

NATIONAL POLITICS: ELECTION 1948

Pessimism Among the Democrats. Truman was in an unusual and difficult position. Both the left and right wings of his party had bolted to form separate parties. His popularity was low. The Republicans were stronger than they had been since 1932, and Dewey was expected to win easily. But both renegade movements had serious problems. Though his advisers urged him to repudiate the Communists in his movement, Wallace refused to do so, arguing that he would be guilty of the very red-baiting of which he accused Truman. When Wallace allowed the Progressive Party to be endorsed by the Communist Party U.S.A., his popular support declined dramatically. As much as 51 percent of the public believed that

Wallace's party was run by the Communists. Harold Ickes said that the Progressive Party had broken with Roosevelt's policies and represented "the most serious attempt in the history of our nation by a totalitarian group to capture and destroy American liberalism." In the developing atmosphere of the Cold War the caricature of Wallace as a Communist sympathizer destroyed him politically. The Dixiecrats, too, were limited by their emphasis on the politics of race in the South, where poverty and the need for rural electrification and flood control were also important issues. Barnstorming across the nation, Truman aimed his campaign at the "three key groups" of workers, veterans, and blacks. Believing that black voter registration in the North would more than make up for losses to the Dixiecrats, Truman issued a presidential order desegregating the armed forces and the federal civil service. He promised a strong defense and continued military spending and called for repeal of the Taft-Hartley Law, passed by the Republican Congress in 1947 to limit the unions' right to strike and dilute their political power. Dewey, however, languished in the belief that he had already won. He did not even campaign in the South, missing an opportunity to profit from the Dixiecrat revolt.

Truman Beats the Oddsmakers. So certain were the pundits of Truman's impending political demise that before the vote count was complete one newspaper even published a banner headline declaring Dewey the winner. One of the most famous political photographs depicts a beaming Truman displaying the headline while celebrating his victory. Legend now has it that Truman was the only one not surprised by his win. Clearly the election results demonstrated problems in the evolving science of pollsterism. Truman had waged a strenuous and carefully calibrated campaign, relying on party loyalties in the South, the black vote, and labor. Winning 49.5 percent of the popular vote to Dewey's 45 percent, Truman lost only 2.3 million votes to both Wallace and Thurmond. In the electoral college Truman received 303 electoral votes to Dewey's 189, while Thurmond garnered all others. Truman won by running on the accomplishments of the New

Deal and by keeping the Roosevelt coalition relatively intact. He was also assisted by an extraordinarily low voter turnout. Despite a population growth of 20 million, fewer citizens voted than in the election of 1940.

Presentiments of Southern Realignment. While the Democrats' efforts to check the Southern revolt were successful, the Dixiecrats won the four states with the heaviest concentrations of largely disenfranchised blacks — Alabama, Mississippi, Louisiana, and South Carolina. Roosevelt had won these states every time he had run for president. Truman's losing them in 1948 signaled the breakup of the "solid South" as a bulwark of the Democratic Party. Traditional supporters of states' rights, the South resented growing federal centralization, and the politics of racial fear was clearly a potent force. In the "rim" South, the Republicans made striking gains in the large cities of Texas, Florida, Georgia, and Virginia, anticipating the Republican landslide in the election of 1952.

Sources:

Robert J. Donovan, *Conflict and Crisis: The Presidency of Harry S Truman, 1945–1948* (New York: Norton, 1977);

Alonzo L. Hamby, *Beyond the New Deal: Harry S Truman and American Liberalism* (New York: Columbia University Press, 1973);

Arthur M. Schlesinger, Jr., *The Age of Roosevelt,* 3 volumes (Boston: Houghton Mifflin, 1956–1960);

Schlesinger, ed., *The History of American Presidential Elections, 1789–1968* (New York: Chelsea House, 1971);

Schlesinger, ed., *History of U.S. Political Parties* (New York: Chelsea House, 1973).

HEADLINE MAKERS

RALPH BUNCHE

1904-1971

DIPLOMAT, UNDERSECRETARY-GENERAL OF THE UNITED NATIONS

Prominent Figure. In 1950 Ralph Bunche became the first black person awarded the Nobel Peace Prize for his role in fostering an armistice between warring Arabs and Israelis. The award brought to public attention a long record of public service. Bunche was a central figure among blacks, and although less well known during the 1940s than W. E. B. Du Bois or A. Philip Randolph, like them he prepared the way for the civil rights revolution of the 1950s and 1960s. An early leader in forming American policy in Africa, Bunche played a major intellectual role in the decolonization movement after World War II.

Respected Scholar. The grandson of slaves, Bunche was born on 7 August 1904 in Detroit. Showing intellectual promise early, he excelled academically and graduated with honors from the University of California, Los Angeles. He attended graduate school at Harvard University and became a faculty member at Howard University in Washington, D.C., the "Black Athens" of America. He then returned to Harvard to complete his Ph.D. in government and international relations in 1934. Widely considered one of the foremost students of race relations, he became the chief assistant to the Swedish sociologist Gunnar Myrdal, contributing to his groundbreaking study *An American Dilemma: The Negro Problem and Modern Democracy* (1944). Joining the Office of Strategic Services (OSS) in World War II as an analyst, Bunche quickly became the intelligence agency's expert on Africa and the Far East and wrote the handbook given to every GI entering the North African combat theater.

Skillful Diplomat. In 1944 Bunche joined the State Department's Division of Dependent Area Affairs, then in 1947 was appointed to the United Nations to deal with territories under UN trusteeship. In that capacity he was assigned to Palestine at the moment when many surviving European Jews were flocking to their ancestral homeland to seek a nation of their own. Britain had indicated its willingness to grant independence to Palestine, but monarchs in neighboring states insisted that it become an Arab nation. The partition of Palestine into Jewish and Arab states precipitated the first Arab-Israeli War. When the UN mediator in the conflict, Count Folke Bernadotte of Sweden, was assassinated by Jewish terrorists, Bunche replaced him and used his extraordinary diplomatic skills to craft a cease-fire acceptable to both sides. His diplomacy led him to be considered by President Harry S Truman for the post of undersecretary of state, but the nomination was abandoned as too provocative a challenge to the prevailing color line. The Swedish government noticed Bunche's talents, however, and awarded him the Nobel Peace Prize. In 1955 he was appointed Undersecretary of the United Nations, the highest position held by an American in the organization at the time, and he continued to mediate conflicts throughout the world. He became undersecretary-general in 1967.

Under Attack. As a black intellectual deeply concerned about segregation in America, Bunche was drawn to radical critiques of Western imperialism and colonialism, especially to class-based economic analyses of exploitation. Like many intellectuals during the 1930s, he was involved in Marxist study groups and radical organizations. He inevitably became the focus of McCarthyite witch hunts in the 1950s, resulting in FBI and Senate investigations into his past. His relationship with Alger Hiss, when the two were State Department colleagues, was criticized, and his writings and his memberships in the National Negro League and teachers' unions were scrutinized. The fact that he had associated with Communists was presented as evidence that he was a secret Communist. Responding to these attacks, he defended his intellectual freedom to read and write as he pleased under the First Amendment and to associate with anyone of his choosing, but he denied ever having been a member of the Communist Party, and his work in the OSS, the State Department, and the UN indicated a deep antipathy to Soviet policies. The attack on Bunche was part of an orchestrated campaign to characterize the civil rights struggle as a Communist plot. Later, despite endorsements by W. Averell Harriman, David Rockefeller, and other pillars of the establishment, Bunche was not offered the post of ambassador to the Soviet Union by President John F. Kennedy because of the lingering effect of these attacks.

Civil Rights Advocate. Ironically, because he became part of the American political establishment, Bunche was also attacked by Du Bois and others on the left wing of the African American community. Yet in his writings on race Bunche condemned the American system of segregation, advocating nothing less than full equality for blacks. He especially stressed the importance of economic justice and became a trusted adviser of Martin Luther King, Jr., advocating peaceful means for fundamental change. He condemned the war in Vietnam as a misappropriation of valuable resources for destructive purposes and urged, with King, a redirection of military spending to domestic purposes to curb poverty. Though he is little remembered today, Bunche was renowned as one of the most intelligent and humane diplomats the United States has ever produced.

Source:
Brian Urquhart, *Ralph Bunche: An American Life* (New York: Norton, 1993).

THOMAS E. DEWEY

1902-1971

GOVERNOR OF NEW YORK (1943-1955), REPUBLICAN PRESIDENTIAL CANDIDATE (1944, 1948)

Famous Defeat. In one of the most famous photographs in American political history, a beaming President Harry S Truman is shown displaying the headline of the first edition of the *Chicago Daily Tribune* following the 1948 presidential election. In a banner headline the newspaper trumpets Thomas E. Dewey's win over the incumbent Truman. The *Tribune* got it wrong, of course: Truman won by 2.2 million popular votes and 114 electoral votes. Dewey's defeat disappointed his formidable constituency in the Republican Party and set him politically adrift for much of the 1950s. In the 1940s, however, Dewey — along with Robert Taft and Arthur Vandenberg — was a politician whose name was synonymous with the Grand Old Party.

Successful Prosecutor. Born in Owosso, Michigan, on 24 March 1902 to a middle-class family, Dewey was educated in public schools and attended the University of Michigan and Columbia University Law School. Admitted to the New York bar, he made Manhattan his home and involved himself in local politics. In 1931 he was appointed assistant U.S. attorney for the Southern District of New York and began successfully prosecuting the racketeers and bootleggers of the Prohibition era. Named full U.S. attorney in 1933, Dewey earned a considerable reputation as a racketbuster in a New York plagued by organized crime. His probes of garment district racketeers and of the Murder, Inc., gang organized by Salvatore "Lucky" Luciano and Louis Lepke led to federal imprisonment for Lepke and deportation for Luciano. As a result of his high visibility in these investigations, Dewey was able to launch his campaigns for the governorship of New York.

Successful Governor. After failing in his first bid in 1938, Dewey was elected to three successive terms beginning in 1942. He was an unorthodox Republican, fiscally conservative but socially liberal. Both of his presidential campaign platforms endorsed New Deal measures and promised to protect such programs as Social Security and unemployment insurance. As governor he pushed through the first law in any state against racial discrimination in employment, took measures to ensure that the labor mediation board was fair, improved state unemployment and disability benefits for workers, and undertook a massive highway-construction program. Largely due to wartime federal spending bounties, between 1943 and 1948 he was able to reduce New York State tax rates by 50 percent and still achieve a $600-million state surplus and reduce New York's debt. State aid to public education and public assistance doubled during his administration, more than fourteen thousand hospital beds were added throughout the state, thirty thousand units of public housing were built, and state workers received hefty raises. Dewey seemed to be a Republican who could match President Franklin D. Roosevelt's largesse to the poor while reining in spending, but this fiscal illusion was made possible by massive federal outlays.

Presidential Candidate. Dewey easily won the 1944 Republican nomination but had to run against President Roosevelt in the midst of World War II. Though the Republicans attempted to criticize the administration's handling of the war, by 1944 it seemed that victory was in sight, and the nation was unwilling to make a change in leadership in midstream. The election of 1948 was another matter. The Republicans had gained control of both houses of Congress in 1946, and President Truman's popularity had declined precipitously. Cold War tensions were beginning to mount, and conservatives were meeting with success by accusing the Democrats of weakness toward the Soviets. Conservative Republicans had also mounted an attack on labor that resulted in passage of the Taft-Hartley Act, which restricted labor's powers. Encouraged by these developments, Dewey failed to campaign with intensity. In contrast, Truman barnstormed the country with his famous whistle-stop campaign. Speaking to ordinary Americans from the back of his train, Truman managed to revive the faltering Democratic coalition. Accepting defeat with dignity,

Dewey later declined to head the Republican ticket in 1952 but played a role in nominating Dwight D. Eisenhower and Richard Nixon. Nixon later sought to repay this political favor and Dewey's efforts against John F. Kennedy in 1960 by nominating him to be chief justice of the Supreme Court. Dewey instead urged that Warren Burger be named. His health declined over the next few years, and Dewey succumbed to cancer and heart disease on 16 March 1971.

Source:
Richard Norton Smith, *Thomas E. Dewey and His Times* (New York: Simon & Schuster, 1982).

DWIGHT D. EISENHOWER

1890-1969

SUPREME ALLIED MILITARY COMMANDER (1943-1945)

Second Act. Dwight D. Eisenhower's military career in World War II belies F. Scott Fitzgerald's observation that there are no second acts in American life. By 1938 Eisenhower's career was by any objective standard over, and his ambitions were thwarted. By 1950 he was the most recognizable figure in the United States and a shoo-in to the presidency in 1952. Between those two dates he served as supreme Allied military commander in World War II and president of Columbia University. As it did for so many Americans, World War II gave him a second chance, and he used his talent for organization and administration to lead the United States to victory and himself to the pinnacle of power and success.

Early Career. Eisenhower, or "Ike," as he was often called, grew up in modest means in the farming community of Abilene, Kansas. An athlete and a good student with a penchant for history and math, he won an appointment to West Point in 1910. His early military career was unexceptional; for a man of his high ambitions, his rise in the ranks was painfully slow. Although he earned a Distinguished Service Medal for his organization of the Tank Corps, he missed service in World War I. He earned a reputation as a competent administrator; compared to more flamboyant soldiers, such as George S. Patton or Douglas MacArthur, he was overshadowed. He served in unglamorous postings in Panama and the Philippines. By 1938, forty-eight years old and still a lieutenant colonel, he contemplated retirement. It seemed his career was over.

War. The outbreak of World War II presented Eisenhower with an opportunity he quickly seized. He argued that this war, more than previous conflicts, would require careful planning and logistical precision — skills at which he excelled. He also possessed a keen political sense and a shrewd judgment of personal character, traits honed during his labors under MacArthur in the Philippines. Both abilities served him well during the war. Better than most American officers during the conflict, he understood the intertwined political and military character of the war. Unique among the high-ranking staff of the Allies, he possessed the temperament and focus necessary to juggle the competing imperatives of often mercurial generals, such as Patton and British general Bernard Montgomery. Eisenhower's talents were noted and prized early on by Army Chief of Staff George C. Marshall, who assigned him to the War Plans Division of the General Staff after the Japanese attack on Pearl Harbor on 7 December 1941. By February 1942 Eisenhower headed the division; by summer he was on his way to England as head of U.S. forces in Europe. In November 1941 he supervised Operation Torch, the Allied invasion of North Africa, and went on to lead the invasion of Italy. On 15 January 1943 he traveled to Casablanca, Morocco, to apprise British prime minister Winston Churchill and President Franklin D. Roosevelt on European theater operations. On 10 February 1943 he became a four-star general, the highest rank in the army at the time. He was also appointed supreme commander of the Allied Expeditionary Force, the combined military agency responsible for liberating Europe from the Nazis. At fifty-two, Eisenhower had arrived.

Operation Overlord. Eisenhower's place in world history was set by nightfall, 6 June 1944. On that date, D-Day, he successfully began Operation Overlord, the Allied invasion of France that within a year would end the war in Europe. A monumental seaborne assault across the English Channel, Operation Overlord had been nearly two years in the making, and he had been responsible for it from the start. It was a task that would overwhelm most men. As part of the assault force and in supporting positions, he had to coordinate the activities of 2.8 million personnel; 5,000 ships and landing craft would be needed to cross the channel; 14,000 land vehicles were to be transported for use in France; 14,500 tons of supplies were to be landed on the first day of the invasion; 7,000 aircraft would support the assault; and in preparation for the landing Allied air corps would drop 76,000 tons of bombs and 23,000 airborne troops on Normandy, the area of France where the invasion would take place. The logistical problem involved in a cross-channel invasion was akin to moving a city the size of Madison, Wisconsin — including its vehicles and buildings — sixty to one hundred miles in one night. Against the troops, moreover, would be arrayed the hardened defenses of Hitler's Fortress Europa, the troops of Erwin Rommel, and German numerical superiority. Yet by 12 June the Normandy invasion had been so successful that Eisenhower and Marshall crossed the channel to inspect the beachhead. What Churchill had called "the most difficult and complicated operation that has ever taken place" had been accomplished. Eleven months later Eisenhower accepted the unconditional surrender of Germany in a school in Rheims, France.

President. Eisenhower's low-key, confident approach to victory in war made him a folk hero in America. He was an immediate postwar political prospect, but he opted for a slightly less pressured vocation as army chief of staff under President Harry S Truman from 1945 to 1948. In 1948 he accepted the presidency of Columbia University in New York. No academic, however, he quickly returned to public life. In 1950 he assumed command of the new North Atlantic Treaty Organization (NATO). In 1952, as a result of continuous prompting by friends and associates, he ran for president. Enormously popular with the public, he won easily and was reelected in 1956. Although during the presidential campaign of 1960 Eisenhower's administration was portrayed as vapid, almost geriatric — a portrayal reinforced by his 1955 heart attack — Eisenhower proved a solid, cautious president. Through diplomacy he ended the Korean War; through sound management he sustained a prosperous economy; by statesmanship he avoided war at a time when the Cold War threatened to escalate into nuclear combat. In light of subsequent events, perhaps his greatest accomplishment was to avoid engaging U.S. military forces in combat in Vietnam, as was proposed in 1954. When he died in 1969, his presidency was widely considered the most successful of the postwar administrations, and his sober leadership remains his legacy.

Source:
Stephen Ambrose, *Eisenhower: Soldier and President* (New York: Simon & Schuster, 1990).

JAMES V. FORRESTAL

1892-1949

FIRST U.S. SECRETARY OF DEFENSE

A Tragic Story. The story of James Vincent Forrestal is a tragic one. A man of humble birth raised high by his own ambition, he was brought low by his doubts about his worthiness to possess his exalted status. He entered the upper reaches of patrician power and was accepted as one among equals, but he seems never to have accepted himself as such. As secretary of the navy during World War II, he reinvented the U.S. fleet, enabling it to conduct the sea operations and marine landings that brought victory in both the Atlantic and Pacific. Rewarded by being named the first secretary of defense, he sought vainly to bring unity and central control to competing services. One of the most anti-Communist members of the foreign policy elite, he was convinced that war with the Soviet Union was inevitable; he tried desperately to convince President Harry S Truman to increase military spending but was dismissed as too hawkish. Convinced that both his political enemies and Communists were conspiring to kill him, and expressing despondency at his own failures, Forrestal was hospitalized in a psychiatric unit at Bethesda Naval Hospital, where he committed suicide by jumping from a sixteenth-floor window. Though honored at his funeral in Arlington National Cemetery as the most patriotic of public servants, he died believing he had betrayed his past and his country.

Humble Origins. Born in Dutchess County, New York, not far from the birthplace of his political patron, Franklin D. Roosevelt, Forrestal came from a background a world apart from aristocratic Hyde Park. Despite his working-class, immigrant Irish roots, Forrestal worked his way to Princeton University, yet he always carried himself, as one of his friends said, "like Jimmy Cagney," proud of his boxer's spring and a nose broken twice in the ring. He was admired by his privileged classmates, but he chafed at the humiliation of being one of the few students forced to work while living in the town's poorest neighborhood. The ambivalence he felt about the world he left and the world he entered left him at home in neither, and the resulting psychological tension was channeled into a relentless work ethic.

From Wall Street to the White House. After college Forrestal obtained a position on Wall Street at William A. Read and Company (later Dillon, Read and Company), eventually one of the most powerful investment houses in the world. Serving in the navy during World War I, first as a seaman and then as an aviator, implanted in him a near religious attachment to it. Returning to Wall Street after the war, Forrestal became a multimillionaire and escaped the worst of the stock market crash of 1929. Although he sheltered nearly a million dollars from taxes in Canada during the Depression, he became a participant in the reform of the Securities and Exchange Commission under President Roosevelt, which led to his appointment in June 1940 as one of the president's advisers.

Military Secretary. Forrestal's managerial expertise and prior military service led to his appointment two months later as undersecretary of the navy. He became secretary of the navy on 19 May 1944. During World War II Forrestal linked the navy's procurement system to the civilian production sector, quickly turning the fleet into the largest, most powerful in the world. The navy became his life. He toured the Normandy beachheads with Gen. Dwight D. Eisenhower and was on the shore at Iwo Jima on the fourth day of the battle. Forrestal's success with the navy led to his appointment as the nation's first secretary of defense in 1947 when the military cabinet positions were combined. His job was to stop interservice rivalries and to centralize the management of the war machine.

Actions and Ideas. Perhaps as a result of his deprived background, Forrestal was a proponent of social equality. While on Wall Street he had been a member of the Urban League, and while secretary of the navy he was instrumental in upgrading the status of black sailors from messmen to full combat seamen. He also insisted that the newly formed Women Accepted for Volunteer Emergency Service (Waves) be integrated as well. Despite his vaunted pugnacity, he opposed the use of atomic bombs at the close of World War II, though not from any squeamishness about targeting civilians. As a student of military affairs he agreed with Generals Eisenhower and Curtis LeMay and others that the Japanese were already defeated and prepared to surrender. Atomic devastation of Japan would create such bad feelings, he believed, that the reintegration of Japan into the American-led global economy would be compromised. He believed that a generously reconstructed Japan, minus atomic destruction, would enable the defeated nation to become a linchpin of containment against the Soviet Union. Forrestal advised President Truman to retain Emperor Hirohito, even though this violated the previously declared policy of unconditional surrender.

Cold Warrior. With a hatred of communism lodged deeply in his Catholic background, Forrestal became one of the key proponents of a postwar military buildup against the Soviet Union, which he viewed as having replaced Germany as America's foremost enemy. He played a major role in shaping George F. Kennan's ideas about containment, transforming them from political goals to military ones. Exaggerating the Soviet military threat to paranoid levels, Forrestal set the pace for the establishment of Pacific bases and Mediterranean patrols. As a member of the inner circle of policy makers he also urged the creation of a secret intelligence network to conduct covert operations.

Breakup. The causes of Forrestal's postwar psychological disintegration are not known. He appears to have suffered considerable guilt about an early renunciation of his family and his Catholic faith. He never felt fully accepted by those he believed had been born to power, though most of them thought highly of him. His inability to unify the military services in anything but name may have led him to question the value of his earlier successes. In any case, he became increasingly irrational, believing for example that the Soviets were intent on fighting a war over Berlin in 1949 despite assurances to the contrary by overseas intelligence services. When he opposed recognition of Israel on the grounds that it would imperil American access to Middle East oil he was labeled an anti-Semite. Public attacks by journalists against his personal integrity unhinged him completely. When Secretary of State George C. Marshall declined to endorse his demands for increased deficit spending for the military, Forrestal began to see conspiracies to oust him and started behaving in ways that made his replacement inevitable. He refused to resign, even though his public opposition to Truman's defense budget was embarrassing the president. When Truman named Louis Johnson to replace him as secretary of defense, Forrestal came apart completely. Believing that Communists and Jews were conspiring against his life, he had to be hospi-

talized at Bethesda, where despite precautions he was able to take his own life.

Source:

Townsend Hoopes and Douglas Brinkley, *Driven Patriot: The Life of James Forrestal* (New York: Knopf, 1992).

OVETA CULP HOBBY

1905-

DIRECTOR OF WOMEN'S ARMY CORPS

Administrator. An unusually energetic and talented woman, Oveta Culp Hobby presided over the formation of America's first female military corps during World War II. The Women's Army Corps (WAC) was to a great extent her invention. She labored against many bureaucratic dismissals of female soldiering and struggled to prevent the WACs from devolving into menial assistants to the male corps. She also held the WACs to high moral standards to offset suggestions that the WACs were glorified camp followers and prostitutes. She forged the WAC into a disciplined unit that earned the respect of male and female commentators.

Prodigy. Born Oveta Culp on 5 January 1905 in Killeen, Texas, she was a gifted student who followed her father into law. A graduate of the University of Texas Law School, by age twenty she was not only Houston's assistant city attorney but also parliamentarian of the Texas legislature and codifier of Texas banking laws. At twenty-six she married William Hobby, a former governor and publisher of the *Houston Post*, and worked her way up in the ranks of the newspaper from book editor to executive vice-president. Seemingly inexhaustible, from 1933 to 1941 she remained Texas parliamentarian, helped manage the *Post*, bore two children, wrote a textbook on parliamentary practice called *Mr. Chairman* (1936), was president of the Texas League of Women Voters, and was director of a radio station and a bank.

WAC. In 1941 Hobby went to Washington to head the newly formed women's division of the War Department's Bureau of Public Relations. At the request of Army Chief of Staff George C. Marshall she drafted plans for the formation of a women's auxiliary to the male army, which ultimately resulted in the formation of the WAC. While many of the auxiliary positions were in jobs traditionally open to women, such as secretaries and executive assistants, Hobby struggled to get the WACs involved in male-dominated fields such as war planning, cartography, and cryptography. She also initiated a program of recruiting black women for the officer corps, an unusual idea at the time. By 1943 she oversaw the activities of more than one hundred thousand WACs in a variety of noncombat positions. That year she was made a colonel in the army, but male opposition blocked her from the rank of general. She received the Distinguished Service Medal in honor of her work. Following the war she resigned her commission and returned to Houston. She was only forty years old.

HEW. In 1953 Hobby was re-called by Dwight D. Eisenhower to Washington. Now president, Eisenhower appointed her the first secretary of the Department of Health, Education, and Welfare (HEW), making her the second female cabinet member. She took the appointment at a controversial moment, when many remained convinced that the federal government had no role in the nation's health or education. She nonetheless ably oversaw the administration of the Public Health Service, the Food and Drug Administration, the Office of Education, and the Bureau of Old Age and Survivors Insurance — all departments of HEW. She also supervised the distribution of Jonas Salk's polio vaccine in 1955. At fifty she resigned her position, returning to Houston to help her ailing husband, who died in 1964. She proved as able in business as in administration, by 1983 building up the *Houston Post* into a $100-million enterprise and being listed by *Texas Business* as the only woman among the twenty most powerful Texans.

Source:
"Hobby's Army," *Time*, 43 (17 January 1944): 57–62.

GEORGE C. MARSHALL

1880-1959

ARMY GENERAL, CHIEF OF STAFF, U.S. SECRETARY OF STATE (1947-1949), U.S. SECRETARY OF DEFENSE (1950-1951)

Important General and Statesman. Gen. George C. Marshall's bureaucratic career soared as America evolved from a largely isolated economic powerhouse to the world's military superpower and global policeman. Though he never came under fire himself, Marshall planned key offensives during World War I and trained the leading generals of World War II. As army chief of staff during the World War II, he shaped and managed all elements of global strategy and in the armed peace that followed shaped critical aspects of the postwar global economy in line with the goals of American internationalists. As the civilian secretary of state and later secretary of defense, Marshall served as one of the principal strategists of the Cold War. He became the only military man ever awarded the Nobel Peace Prize for his organization of the postwar reconstruction of Europe, a program termed the Marshall Plan in his honor.

Rising in the Ranks. Marshall came of age at a time when the United States began to assume a prominent part on the world stage. Entering the Virginia Military Institute in 1897, he was commissioned as a second lieutenant in 1902. From the beginning of his military career he showed outstanding talent and aptitude for strategy and command. During World War I he served as chief tactical officer under Gen. John J. Pershing, helping to plan the first American offensives in France and other important campaigns. As a result of his skills he was promoted to chief of operations of the First Army by the end of the war. He served as the executive officer of the Fifteenth Infantry Regiment in China, then became the chief of the Infantry School at Fort Benning, Georgia. There he deeply influenced army doctrine and trained Omar Bradley, J. Lawton Collins, Joseph W. Stilwell, Matthew Ridgway, and Walter Bedell Smith — all of whom later were key commanders and planners in World War II.

War Strategist. War loomed on the horizon in the late 1930s, and in 1938 Marshall was called to Washington to help the nation prepare for its possibility. In April 1939 Marshall was named army chief of staff by President Franklin D. Roosevelt, becoming a four-star general in the process. He officially took office on 1 September 1939, the day Germany invaded Poland. At that time army forces included only 175,000 men, making it the nineteenth largest in the world. By 1943, under Marshall's command, the army numbered more than 8 million men and was the best-equipped and best-trained in the world. But his role was not confined only to strictly military matters. President Roosevelt quickly learned to appreciate Marshall's organizational skill and made him a key participant in strategic planning by including him at the major wartime conferences at Washington, Casablanca, Quebec, Tehran, Cairo, Malta, and Yalta. At the end of the war he accompanied President Truman at Potsdam. Marshall was the one who pushed for and won approval for the cross-channel invasion of France, and he appointed Dwight D. Eisenhower to command it.

Criticism. Marshall's career was not without controversy. His judgment was questioned after the 7 December 1941 Japanese attack on Pearl Harbor, and the 1944 Normandy expedition seemed impossible to many on the general staff. His role in the decision to use the atomic bomb against Japan in 1945 was also criticized, as was his central position in the developing Cold War. But he was widely seen as a man of such unquestioned integrity and intelligence, with deep respect among his peers and subordinates, that he was able to weather such criticism.

The Truman Doctrine and the Marshall Plan. Stepping down as chief of staff on 20 November 1945, Marshall immediately was sent by President Truman on a special mission to China to broker peace between the Chinese Nationalists and Communists. His efforts were unsuccessful, primarily because he failed to recognize that the Communists' political and military strength gave them little reason to compromise with the American military client Chiang Kai-shek. Communist suspicions of American intentions were in fact exacerbated, contributing to later Cold War animosity between the United States and China. In January 1947 President Truman re-called Marshall from China and appointed him secretary of state. He advised Truman to get tougher with Soviet premier Joseph Stalin and to militarize George F. Kennan's diplomatic containment policy. The Truman Doctrine, by which the United States took its first steps as global policeman, resulted from such advice. Along with other American geostrategists, Marshall worried about political instability in war-ravaged Europe, which could serve as a breeding ground for communism. Marshall believed that European industries had to be rebuilt in order to provide an alternative to Communist or Socialist reconstruction and create a market for American goods. Consequently, in June 1947 Marshall announced the European Recovery Plan, by which the United States would provide loans and grants to any nation in Europe. Marshall anticipated that recovery funds would be used to promote an American political and economic agenda in Europe. Most reconstruction monies were to be spent on American products and used to hire American firms. Europe was thus tied, if not integrated, into the American-dominated global economic system. As the arrangement rebuilt Western Europe, it also benefited many U.S. corporations. All Marshall Plan participants, moreover, were required to open their economies to inspection by U.S. experts and to accept American economic practices. American officials, for example, forbade the nationalization of key German and British industries and pressured the French and Italian governments to remove Communists from their ministries. Soviet-bloc countries refused these arrangements. The Soviets, moreover, were alarmed that aid was to be provided to Germany. The Marshall Plan thus also contributed to Cold War tensions.

Late Career. Marshall resigned in 1949 due to illness but was called out of retirement the following year to deal with the crisis of the Korean War as secretary of defense. He retired again in 1951 following attacks by Sen. Joseph R. McCarthy, but he remained an active-duty general available for consultation by the government. In 1953 he became the only soldier ever awarded the Nobel Peace Prize, which he received for the European Recovery Program. He died in Washington, D.C., on 16 October 1959 and was buried in Arlington National Cemetery.

Source:
Ed Craig, *General of the Army: George C. Marshall, Soldier and Statesman* (New York: Norton, 1990).

GEORGE S. PATTON

1885-1945

MAJOR GENERAL, U.S. ARMY TANK CORPS

Idiosyncratic Leader. Perhaps no other military figure in American history, with the exception of George Armstrong Custer, was more impetuous, flamboyant, or controversial than Maj. Gen. George S. Patton, nicknamed "Old Blood and Guts." A swashbuckler wearing ivory-handled six-guns, he was a great deal more successful in battle than Custer and contributed to the Allied victory at the crucial Battle of the Bulge in 1945. A man consumed by military history and tradition, Patton could nevertheless disregard classic military rules, demonstrating a fearless initiative that often pulled victory from the edge of catastrophe. Considered arrogant by fellow officers and ruthless by his troops, Patton was instrumental in transforming the obsolete U.S. Cavalry into a modern armored corps that defeated some of the best German panzer divisions. Patton sometimes claimed to be the reincarnation of Julius Caesar and often cited Caesar's campaigns against the barbarians during his own operations against the Germans. Believing himself a man of destiny, Patton was ever certain of victory, and his confidence was infectious to his troops.

Military Man. Born to an old Virginia military family, Patton was destined for an army career. He attended the Virginia Military Institute and graduated from West Point in 1909. He served as an aide to Gen. John J. Pershing during the Mexican expedition of 1916 and followed him to Europe the next year, assigned the task of organizing the first tank brigades in World War I. He won a battlefield promotion during the Meuse-Argonne offensive, for which he also received the Distinguished Service Cross and the Distinguished Service Medal. His men initially thought him mad because he seemed oblivious to danger, but eventually Patton's troops considered him blessed by good fortune.

World War II Hero. After World War I Patton shuffled between a series of training posts, where he struggled to maintain his visibility. In 1942 he was finally given command of the First Armored Corps in California, and he trained his men relentlessly in the sand and desert near Death Valley. This practice proved of critical importance in the extremely harsh conditions these men later faced in the Sahara Desert as Patton led Allied armored units to victory over the "Desert Fox," German general Erwin Rommel. After this success Patton joined British tank forces and swept the Nazis from Sicily in thirty-eight days. In 1944, after the Normandy landings had opened breaches in German defenses, Patton's Third Army swept into Brittany and onward toward Paris, helping to create a hopeless situation for the German commander, who soon surrendered. When the Battle of the Bulge began, Patton, anticipating the counteroffensive, turned his forces around and contained the German initiative.

Integration. Despite Patton's reputation as a racist, during the Battle of the Bulge he called up black troops, who, though trained as carefully as white tankers, had always been held in reserve owing to traditional racist doubts about their abilities. The presence of black troops in the armored corps and elsewhere helped to plug the critical gap made by the Germans. After the Battle of the Bulge, Patton kept his black troops with his main force, and many of them were among the first to liberate the Nazi death camps in the west.

Controversial Leader. Patton was sometimes a martinet when his mood was foul, and his temper was legendary. His irascibility more than once got him in trouble with his superiors. He came close to losing his command in 1943 when, while visiting two separate military hospitals in Italy, he struck two soldiers who appeared to be uninjured, accusing them of cowardice. The first man was later shown to be suffering from malaria and dysentery. A week after the first incident Patton confronted another young man who was suffering from shell shock. In the presence of members of the press Patton called the soldier a "yellow son of a bitch" and drew his revolver, threatening to execute the boy on the spot. Only the intervention of the colonel in charge of the hospital stopped Patton, who was severely reprimanded by Gen. Dwight D. Eisenhower and threatened with the loss of his command unless he issued a public apology, which he did under protest. As his tank corps entered Germany, Patton publicly stated that he should be given free rein to race toward the distant capital of Berlin and beat the Soviets, engaging them in battle if necessary; his remarks strained relations with America's Soviet allies. Reprimanded once again by Eisenhower, Patton was warned that another breach would prove damaging to his career. Nevertheless, Patton was soon publicly admiring the fighting qualities of the Germans while disparaging the Soviets. He went hunting with a captured German commander and told anyone who would listen that the United States had fought the "wrong enemy" and should be fostering an alliance with the Germans before it was too late to spare Europe from the Russians. Openly contemptuous of the Jews languishing in the squalid death camps, Patton declared that the Allied "de-Nazification" of Germany would deplete Europe of the very people necessary to preserve Western civilization from the "barbarians" of the East. As a result of these statements he was relieved of command and reassigned to a unit drawing up a history of the European campaign — a position to his liking, since he was a first-rate military historian. Shortly after, however, he was injured in a car accident near Mannheim, Germany. Though his injuries did not appear life-threatening, his condition worsened sud-

denly, and he died in a military hospital on 21 December 1945.

Source:
Ladislaw Farago, *The Last Days of Patton* (New York: McGraw-Hill, 1981).

FRANCES PERKINS

1882-1965

U.S. SECRETARY OF LABOR 1933-1945

Advocate of Workers. Frances Perkins was the first woman ever appointed to a cabinet position in the United States. As secretary of labor during all of President Franklin D. Roosevelt's administrations she was instrumental in shaping government recognition of the American labor movement. By rebuilding a nearly defunct department she was able to enforce the sweeping legislation that emerged from the New Deal, which aimed to impart rights and dignity ordinary working people never before enjoyed. As an expert on the health and safety of workers, especially women and children, Perkins left an indelible stamp upon the Labor Department and contributed to widespread public support for fair and safe workplaces.

Social Reformer. Born in Boston on 10 April 1882 to a prosperous upper-middle-class family, in 1902 Perkins graduated from Mount Holyoke College, where she adopted the social activism characteristic of privileged educated women during the era. A few years after graduation she began working closely with Jane Addams of Chicago's Hull House, where she observed firsthand the tremendous problems of poverty and social isolation endured by the many immigrants flowing into America at the turn of the century. Perceiving that America was becoming increasingly polarized into a nation of "haves" and "have-nots," she became a reform leader seeking legislation to protect children and improve unsafe working conditions. After moving to New York to earn a master's degree in social economics from Columbia University, she was profoundly moved in 1911 when she witnessed the tragic Triangle Shirtwaist Company fire, in which locked doors in an eighth-floor garment sweatshop led to the deaths of 146 workers, mostly women and children. Over the next two decades Perkins committed herself to reforming the horrendous conditions under which the working poor of New York labored.

To the Cabinet. From 1912 to 1917 Perkins served as a member of the Committee on Safety of the City of New York, where she met Roosevelt. After World War I she worked on and became chair of the New York State Industrial Commission and in 1929 was appointed the state's industrial commissioner by then-governor Roosevelt. When the Depression struck in 1929, Perkins was among the first to call for unemployment compensation, then a rarely considered remedy for joblessness. Hers was a prominent voice arguing for direct government intervention in the workings of the private economy to ensure justice and equity for the unemployed. She was opposed by many industrialists for her reformism and by many labor organizers for her gender, but her competence, integrity, and commitment made her Roosevelt's first choice for labor secretary when he was elected president in 1932. Perkins immediately went to work to revive a virtually moribund department to meet the challenge of the Depression, and she was the guiding force behind the Social Security Act, the National Labor Relations Act, minimum-wage laws, welfare, and public works. As labor secretary she was responsible for enforcing the Fair Labor Standards Act and became a scourge of those in private industry who sought to circumvent the law. Once the New Deal legislation was safely passed, Perkins devoted her energies to bolstering the power of the Labor Department to oversee fair labor practices and made the Bureau of Labor Statistics one of the most vital sources of information to economists and political scientists while ensuring that the bureau also gauged the economic health of the American worker.

Controversy. Perkins's tenure as labor secretary was fraught with controversy. Because she took labor's side in its struggle with management she was sometimes labeled a Communist, foreshadowing the anticommunist hysteria of the late 1940s and the 1950s. In 1934 she refused to initiate proceedings to deport Harry Bridges, the Australian-born leader of the West Coast Longshoremen's Union. An alleged Communist, Bridges led a long and costly general strike in San Francisco. Her critics were further outraged in 1937 when she refused to condemn the sit-down strikers in Flint, Michigan, for their takeover of General Motors auto plants, and she argued against sending in troops to oust the workers. One of her enemies, Rep. J. Parnell Thomas, offered a bill of impeachment against her in 1939. In hearings held before the House Judiciary Committee she defended her record, stating that she had refused to initiate procedures to deport Bridges because he had rights of due process no committee of Congress could override. Her impeachment was halted.

Friend to Labor. Labor has seldom had a better friend in government than Perkins. Two months after Roosevelt's death she resigned from the Labor Department, believing that President Harry S Truman should have his own cabinet, and she published her memoir *The Roosevelt I Knew* (1946). President Truman appointed her to the U.S. Civil Service Commission, where she served until 1953. She lectured widely on the problems of working people, continuing to champion progressive social legislation until her death in New York on 14 May 1965.

Source:
George Martin, *Madam Secretary: Frances Perkins* (Boston: Houghton Mifflin, 1976).

JEANNETTE RANKIN

1880-1973

FIRST WOMAN ELECTED TO CONGRESS

Lifelong Pacifist. Because she was the only member of Congress to cast her vote against war with Japan on 8 December 1941, Jeannette Rankin is associated by some with appeasement or even disloyalty. However, her vote was entirely consistent with the views she had championed since she had voted against American entry into World War I in 1917, and she had run for Congress in 1940 as an overtly antiwar candidate. A lifelong pacifist, she was also a leader in movements for women's suffrage and social justice. In 1968, at age 87, she led five thousand women in a march against the war in Vietnam, remaining true to her principles until the very end.

The First Congresswoman. Born on the western frontier in Montana on 11 June 1880, Rankin became active in the women's suffrage movement early and became legislative secretary of the National American Woman Suffrage Association in 1913. Many western states adopted suffrage amendments before the federal government did, and Rankin was able to win election to Congress — the first woman ever to do so — from Montana in 1916. She introduced the first bill calling for full citizenship for women independent of their husbands. An early isolationist, she cast her vote against President Woodrow Wilson's call for war in 1917 along with forty-eight other members of Congress.

Standing Alone. Rankin's antiwar stand cost her the Republican nomination for the U.S. Senate in 1918, and she left the House to become a lobbyist for suffrage and to return to social work. As war again approached in the 1930s, she renewed her commitment to pacifism and successfully ran an explicitly isolationist, antiwar campaign for Congress once again. She created a national furor by casting her lone dissenting vote against entering the war in 1941, thereby destroying her political career forever. After leaving Congress she continued to lecture on feminism, becoming a model to the more radical feminists who emerged in the 1960s. Ending her life as she began it, she remained a staunch opponent of the Vietnam War, dying only months after the Paris Peace Accords were signed in 1973. Despite the unpopularity of her views and votes, she remained a symbol of political conviction and courage.

Source:
Hannah Josephson, *Jeannette Rankin: First Lady in Congress* (Indianapolis: Bobbs-Merrill, 1974).

FRANKLIN D. ROOSEVELT

1882-1945

PRESIDENT OF THE UNITED STATES, 1933-1945

Influential President. Franklin Delano Roosevelt is the only person to have been elected president of the United States four times. This fact alone testifies to his influence and popularity, at least among much of the American population. Among the most intelligent and complex of presidents, Roosevelt almost certainly left the greatest legacy of any in this century. He virtually created a proactive, socially responsible government, initiating several programs that today are taken for granted. He led the nation through most of World War II, leaving the United States the wealthiest and most powerful nation on earth. He helped to lay the foundation of the United Nations, hoping that the institution would serve the interest of peace and cooperation among the remaining global powers.

Upper-Class Origins. The thirty-second president was born to a wealthy patrician family in the Hudson Valley of New York in 1882. A descendant of early Dutch settlers, Roosevelt was the son of a Wall Street lawyer and of a society mother whose own father had won a great fortune through trading in China. His early years were full of the ease and self-indulgence characteristic of the upper class of that era. A graduate of the elite preparatory school Groton, he then attended Harvard College and later Harvard Law School, becoming a Wall Street lawyer himself and astonishing his colleagues repeatedly by asserting his intention of becoming president of the United States.

Entering Politics. In 1910 Roosevelt won a seat in the New York state senate. Two years later his support for Woodrow Wilson led to his appointment as assistant secretary of the navy, a post he held throughout Wilson's presidency. Profoundly affected by the carnage in Europe during World War I, he wished to avoid sending Americans into war but was a lifelong proponent of military preparedness — one of the great ironies of his life, considering the debacle at Pearl Harbor.

Adversity. In the 1920 elections Roosevelt was chosen as the Democratic vice-presidential candidate and gained national recognition despite the Democrats' defeat. He returned to Wall Street but in 1921 was stricken with polio and paralyzed from the waist down. Prior to this shattering event he had been self-absorbed in the manner of those born to comfort and entitlement. His paralysis led to introspection, and he found strength and courage he had not known existed. He also developed an awareness of and compassion for the suffering of others, which helped him to see, more clearly than others of his class, the suffering of the unemployed during the Depression.

From Governor to President. Roosevelt won the governorship of New York in 1928 when Al Smith left the post to seek the Democratic nomination for president. Shaken by the enormity of the Depression, Roosevelt became the first governor to state publicly that government had an obligation to the jobless — a new approach to a perennial problem in American life. The traditional attitude was that government had no business interfering with the workings of the free market. Most businessmen and politicians advocated a laissez-faire attitude, arguing that the economy would eventually right itself and that hardships, however tragic, had to be endured. Such was the rhetoric of President Herbert Hoover, whom Roosevelt defeated in the 1932 presidential election by promising a "New Deal" for the average American.

The New Deal. President Roosevelt began his New Deal by offering to put government at the service of the ordinary American. He condemned the concentration of ownership in business, warning of "economic oligarchy." Calling for a "reappraisal of values," he insisted that government must develop "an economic declaration of rights, an economic constitutional order." He attacked the Depression cautiously, however, employing measures approved by conservatives. He strengthened government control over the banking system and initiated agricultural price supports. His National Recovery Act (NRA), later declared unconstitutional by the Supreme Court, was developed largely with the assistance of businessmen and industrialists. More radically, he began programs of direct relief to working people. Though opposed by those he called "economic royalists," Roosevelt did succeed in establishing the Works Progress Administration (WPA, later the Works Projects Administration), a publicly funded jobs program for the unemployed, and in getting Congress to pass the Social Security Act. In his second term, with his popular support waning, he succeeded in passing the National Labor Relations Act, which gave labor the right to strike and to bargain collectively for wages and better working conditions. Providing for a National Labor Relations Board to arbitrate between business and labor, the Wagner Act became the heart of the second phase of the New Deal by cementing the loyalties of labor to his policies.

Uphill Battle. Government intervention on behalf of the destitute required deficit spending and higher taxes. Many advisers in Roosevelt's brain trust were influenced by the theories of British economist John Maynard Keynes, who argued for government spending to stimulate both production and consumption. Such measures were deeply opposed by conservatives, who felt they would be forced to foot the tax burden. By 1937 Roosevelt understood that even continued government spending would not be enough to pull the country out of depression. By 1938 unemployment had climbed back up to 15 percent of the labor force. His failure to purge conservative Democrats in the election of 1938 meant that the New Deal measures were all but dead; the Democratic Party had spent itself as the agency of reform. Ultimately, the New Deal failed to end the Depression. The "processes of recovery," said the president, came only with war.

War and the Economy. Critics have accused Roosevelt of manipulating the United States into war in order to use "military Keynesianism" to cure the Depression. This view holds that he clearly understood that government investment in war-making industries would overcome mass unemployment, just as similar Axis spending had done for the economies in those countries. According to this view, events in Europe and Asia had led him to conclude that future U.S. prosperity depended on the ability of the United States to shape the postwar order in accordance with its trade imperatives. If the war could be fought with minimal American casualties and with great profit to the economy as a whole, the United States would emerge from the war by far the most powerful nation on earth, able to set the international agenda. Believing himself better positioned than Wilson had been after World War I, some scholars maintain, Roosevelt had faith in his own ability to foster a "new world order" of functioning democracies and open markets. At the end of hostilities the prosperity induced by the war economy would be replaced by increased overseas trade with America's allies and its former enemies. This vision depended upon the willingness of Britain to accept a secondary role and on Soviet premier Joseph Stalin's cooperation. Above all, it depended on the presence of Roosevelt himself.

Winning the War. To be sure, Roosevelt was a pivotal figure during World War II. Before the United States even entered the war, he pushed for assistance to Britain (and later to the Soviet Union) through the Lend-Lease Act in 1940, in which nations that would later become U.S. allies received war materials in exchange for their return, replacement, or reimbursement later. After the United States entered the war following the Japanese attack on Pearl Harbor on 7 December 1941, he pushed for rapid mobilization and was a central figure, along with British prime minister Winston Churchill and Stalin, in establishing strategies to win the war and plans for recovery afterward.

Legacy. Roosevelt died of a cerebral hemorrhage, related to his circulatory problems, on 12 April 1945 at Warm Springs, Georgia. Virtually all Americans of the time can remember exactly where they were when they heard of his death. Many soldiers overseas could remember no other president. He was simultaneously perhaps the most loved and hated of all presidents, seen as devious, deceitful, and dictatorial by his enemies and as the savior of the economy and defender of democracy by his friends. He was certainly the author of the idea that government ought to provide moral leadership on behalf of the powerless.

Sources:

Doris Kearns Goodwin, *No Ordinary Time: Franklin and Eleanor Roosevelt, The Home Front in World War II* (New York: Simon & Schuster, 1994);

Richard Hofstadter, *The American Political Tradition* (New York: Random House, 1948).

HARRY S TRUMAN

1884-1972

PRESIDENT OF THE UNITED STATES, 1945-1953

Burdened President. Harry S Truman became the thirty-third president of the United States upon the death of President Franklin D. Roosevelt in 1945. Compared inevitably to his predecessor at first, Truman seemed poorly suited to the office. Unlike many national politicians, he had never been ambitious for the presidency. A politician specializing in domestic issues, he found himself overwhelmed by foreign affairs. Beginning his presidency with the terrible burden of having to decide whether to use the atomic bomb, he ended it embroiled in war in Korea. He was a New Dealer through and through, committed to social and racial justice at home. While his own "Fair Deal" went largely unimplemented, it nevertheless set the agenda for the "Great Society" reforms of a later generation.

Soldier and Politician. The son of farmers, Truman was born on 8 May 1884 and grew up in rural Missouri. A serious, bookish, sheltered youth, he harbored ambitions to attend West Point but was denied admission due to poor eyesight. Nonetheless, he enlisted and became an artillery captain in the trenches of Europe during World War I. His combat experience changed him profoundly, toughening him physically and emotionally and giving him a deep appreciation for military strength. At the end of the war he joined veterans' organizations and became a colonel in the U.S. Army Reserve. As an army officer he was required to command soldiers from different ethnic and religious backgrounds from his own. As a result, he developed social and personal skills that earned him the respect of his men and later benefited him in politics. After briefly owning a small business, he entered the rough-and-tumble world of Kansas City politics during the 1920s.

Judge, Senator, President. Joining the Democratic political machine of "Boss" Jim Pendergast, Truman became a county judge, and in 1934 he was the Pendergast choice for the U.S. Senate. Though elected under a cloud of suspicion about the honesty of the polling, as senator Truman developed a reputation for scrupulous honesty and became a loyal New Dealer. In his second Senate term he headed the Special Committee to Investigate the National Defense Program. This

"Truman Committee" exposed fraud and waste in government contracting and reputedly saved taxpayers more than $15 billion. Catapulted into prominence by his leadership of the committee, in 1942 he appeared on the cover of *Time* magazine. In 1944 he was chosen to replace Henry A. Wallace as the Democratic vice-presidential candidate as a concession to conservatives. Though he never sought the presidency, Truman found himself in the highest office of the land after only fifty-one days as vice-president. Consequently, the decision whether to use the newly developed atomic bomb to end the war with Japan was his.

Foreign Policy. Lacking foreign policy expertise, Truman had to rely on Roosevelt's advisers, many of whom had grown disillusioned and frustrated with Roosevelt's personal style of diplomacy and with his willingness to cooperate with Soviet premier Joseph Stalin. A staunch anticommunist, Truman found the advice to get tough with the Soviets easy to take, and the development of the atomic bomb bolstered confidence. He considered the events of the prewar years as proof that appeasement was dangerous, and he soon saw Stalin as the equivalent of Adolf Hitler. Unable to free Eastern Europe from Soviet domination, however, he sought to contain communism within the regions it occupied after World War II. The Soviets never attempted to go beyond their security zone; indeed, they withdrew from Iran and eventually Austria. Nevertheless, Truman insisted on seeing Soviet moves as evidence of their militant expansionism and committed his administration to the creation of the "National Security State," which ultimately tripled defense spending and drove taxes to unprecedented levels. In 1947 he issued the Truman Doctrine, promising to fund anticommunist movements in Europe. He also won passage of the Marshall Plan, providing $17 billion for the reconstruction of ravaged Europe — a measure designed to thwart Soviet influence and to stimulate the American economy. Also in 1947 Truman created what would become the Central Intelligence Agency, ostensibly to collect data, but the agency soon became involved in attempts to overthrow foreign governments — both Communist and non-Communist.

Domestic Policy. Having fostered the idea that the Soviets were out to conquer the world and jeopardize America, Truman in his domestic policies became hostage to his foreign policy and thus aided the advance of highly conservative politicians. His loyalty program implied that disloyal Americans, perhaps Communists, had penetrated the government itself. His surprising support for civil rights led many racists to conclude that this was part of an international Communist conspiracy to weaken the American way of life. Truman favored the poor, submitting an "Economic Bill of Rights" to Congress in September 1945, a signal of his intention to deepen the New Deal. But the 1946 elections resulted in Democratic defeat. His efforts to restrain wages while allowing prices to rise frustrated organized labor, but he won them back

in the 1948 elections by vetoing (albeit unsuccessfully) the Taft-Hartley Act, which placed restrictions on the power of labor. Even before his 1948 reelection bid he enraged Southern Democrats by sending the first civil rights measure to Congress, vowing to end second-class status for black Americans. Though he was often accused of cynically promoting civil rights to win the black vote, it took great political courage on the part of a politician from a former slave state to challenge the Jim Crow system. Truman succeeded in desegregating the armed forces over great opposition from the military and in 1949 won passage of the Housing Act, which cleared some slums and provided decent housing for some of the nation's poor. He failed, owing to the rise of Southern Democrats known as Dixiecrats, to end lynchings, poll taxes, discrimination in public transportation, and other forms of racial segregation but succeeded in raising public consciousness about these issues for future attempts at resolving them.

Foreign Problems. Commentators predicted Truman's defeat to Republican candidate Thomas Dewey, but two other parties were in the race, and he won reelection with less than half the popular vote. In his second term he continued to be dogged by foreign affairs. The crucial year 1949 saw the detonation of the first Soviet atomic bomb and the Chinese Revolution, in which the most populous nation on earth went Communist. Republicans attributed both of these events to the president's shortcomings. Some accused Truman of losing China to the Communists, while the House Un-American Activities Committee claimed that spies and traitors had sold atomic secrets to America's enemies. In 1950 a long-simmering tension between North and South Korea broke out into full-scale war, and Truman worked through the United Nations to send an American army to drive the Communists back to the North. Allowing his advisers to convince him that North Korea could be liberated from Communist rule, he then changed the military's mission. He authorized American forces to penetrate to the Chinese border, prompting the Chinese to dispatch a million soldiers to meet the threat. The results were battlefield setbacks for America and a protracted stalemate, which further undermined Truman's popularity. Truman did show his capability as a wartime leader by firing Gen. Douglas MacArthur as commander of forces in Korea. MacArthur had publicly criticized Truman's decision not to widen the war by using atomic weapons against the Chinese. Truman saw clearly that an attack against Chinese territory would precipitate World War III, and he returned to his original policy of containing Communism on the Korean peninsula.

Bowing Out. Though Truman could legally have run again in 1952, he had served for virtually eight years, and his and the Democrats' popularity was low. McCarthyite foes had succeeded in portraying him as softer on Communism than required, and the costs of the Korean War had fueled inflation. The discovery of corruption among some members of his administration sealed his desire not to run for reelection. His handpicked candidate, Adlai F. Stevenson, was roundly defeated by Dwight D. Eisenhower in 1952, which gave Republicans control of both Congress and the White House. Truman retired to become the Democratic Party's elder statesman, lecturing extensively, writing his memoirs, and overseeing the construction of the Truman Library in Independence, Missouri. In one of his last efforts at public service he refused to endorse Lyndon Johnson's prosecution of the war in Vietnam. The man who had refused to recognize Vietnamese independence in 1945 and had subsequently financed the French effort to recolonize Indochina had learned valuable lessons in Korea. Truman died the day after Christmas 1972. His obituary in *The New York Times* ran for seven pages.

Source:
David McCullough, *Truman* (New York: Simon & Schuster, 1992).

HENRY A. WALLACE

1888-1965

VICE PRESIDENT OF THE UNITED STATES, 1941-1945, PROGRESSIVE PARTY PRESIDENTIAL CANDIDATE, 1948

Spokesman for the Common Man. Henry A. Wallace began his political career as secretary of agriculture under President Franklin D. Roosevelt and served as Roosevelt's vice-president from 1941 to 1945, only to be replaced by Harry S Truman in Roosevelt's reelection bid due to his increasing belief that compromise and cooperation could be achieved with the Soviet Union. Perhaps more than any other Democrat of his day, with the exception of Roosevelt, Wallace represented the socially conscious and compassionate wing of the New Deal. Had he remained vice-president he would have been president upon Roosevelt's death in 1945; though he would have been pressured by the same advisers as Truman, his approach to the issues of postwar global reconstruction would undoubtedly have been different. Wallace hoped to make government responsive to the needs of America's weakest, its farmers and laborers, by committing it to the goal of rational economic planning and the regulation of industry. He looked forward to a "century of the common man." Possessing a religious faith in the inherent goodness of humanity, he believed that a global New Deal might be effected after World War II, with the United States as its leader. Though his faith in the capacity of Soviet leaders to accept such a vision now seems naive, his critique of the "get tough" policies of Truman toward Stalin as inherently destabilizing and dangerous to the national security and economic well-being of the United States proved prophetic.

Editor and Secretary. Wallace was born on 7 October 1888 in rural Iowa and raised in the conservative, Protestant, Republican agricultural tradition of the late nineteenth century. After graduating from Iowa State College with a degree in agricultural science, he began to edit *Wallace's Farmer,* one of the most important agricultural periodicals of his day, which had been founded by his father. The young Wallace was also an agricultural scientist and developed significant advances in plant genetics, especially in hybrid corn, which made him independently wealthy. Yet he never lost touch with his roots. The human tragedy associated with the Depression actually hit farmers earlier in the 1920s, and his sense of the human and economic waste involved in unfettered capitalism led him to join the Democratic Party. Through his editorials he was greatly responsible for winning conservative Iowa to the New Deal and was rewarded by President Roosevelt with the post of secretary of agriculture from 1933 to 1941, where he was charged with implementing the New Deal's Agricultural Adjustment Act. Wallace raised farm prices by limiting production and subsidized farmers not to grow certain crops. This benefited large corporate farmers much more than small growers, with the result that small landholders were often forced to sell their land to richer neighbors and become laborers or sharecroppers themselves. This led Wallace to support sharecroppers' unions, a move which embittered agricultural businesses and landholding interests. To increase demand for food products and to help overcome malnutrition among the urban poor, Wallace implemented food stamps. Sometimes credited with successfully saving agriculture from disaster, his reform measures helped to lighten the burden, but American agriculture was also helped substantially by the same event that renewed industrial production — World War II.

Vice President. When Roosevelt chose Wallace as his vice-presidential candidate in 1940 he told Secretary of Labor Frances Perkins that he "would be a good man if something happened to the President." Political virtues, however, dictated Roosevelt's choice. Wallace came from the most famous farm family in the nation and was vital to winning the farm vote; also, he was no isolationist. After winning office again Roosevelt appointed Wallace to the secret policy group to study the possibility of developing an atomic bomb. Wallace argued then that civilization could be defended "by the power of the atom bomb." Yet after Hiroshima and Nagasaki he changed his mind, and bucking prevailing ideology he condemned atomic-weapons production for the dangerous arms race it created.

Secretary and Editor. Many Democratic Party stalwarts had deeply opposed Wallace's nomination in 1940, but Roosevelt threatened to withdraw his own name if the convention failed to endorse him. In 1944, however, the party threatened open revolt if Wallace were not bumped from the Democratic ticket in favor of a more conservative candidate. Despite personal reservations, Roosevelt caved in for the sake of party unity and accepted the nomination of Harry S Truman. Wallace was deeply disappointed but remained loyal to Roosevelt, accepting the post of secretary of commerce, where he performed ably until early 1946. When Truman became president upon Roosevelt's death in 1945, Wallace became unhappy with the growing rift between the United States and the Soviet Union, worrying that antagonisms might result in conflict. He publicly criticized Truman's hard-line policies toward the Soviets, and the president demanded his resignation. From 1946 to 1947 he served as the editor of the liberal periodical *The New Republic,* a position he used to promote his ideas about U.S. cooperation with the Soviets.

Candidate. In 1948 Wallace announced his Progressive Party candidacy for president. Mocked as a "communist dupe" and "Stalinoid" by some fellow liberals and noncommunist leftists and as a "Stalinist stooge" by the Right, he faced an uphill battle. He nevertheless represented a potentially huge constituency which feared the consequences of Cold War, the atomic arms race, and their effect upon American democracy. In a gesture reminiscent of the wartime Popular Front, Wallace allowed Communists to participate in his campaign, and the press declared him coopted by Stalin. He received nearly a million popular votes but not a single electoral vote. In hindsight, it seems politically blind for Wallace to have so misread the public's rising anticommunist mood. On the other hand, he knew that the minuscule American Communist Party had not the remotest chance of sub-verting the government. Nor did he believe that the threat to democracy came from the Left. Instead, he continued to believe that the greatest threat to American democracy came from right-wing conservatives who used anticommunist rhetoric to cover their own attack on American society.

Later Observations. Wallace later regretted his 1948 campaign, especially as he saw how ruthless and mendacious the Soviets could be. Yet he had predicted that very behavior as the logical outcome of confrontational policies. He broke with the Progressive Party he had created because it refused to support the Korean War. As if to prove his anticommunist credentials, he began to condemn the Soviets and Chinese in speeches and in print. He endorsed the rhetoric of the Eisenhower years, even publicly supporting the president against Democratic candidate Adlai Stevenson, who had once worked for Wallace in the Agriculture Department. As he aged he seemed to return to verities he had promoted in his youth, arguing that labor had become too selfish and bemoaning the mechanized society that had lost the values of a rural civilization. Before his death on 18 November 1965 he demonstrated his knack for prophecy had not been lost. Noting that President Lyndon Johnson's Great Society was in trouble, he foresaw the Republican victory of 1968.

Sources:

Dwight MacDonald, *Henry Wallace: The Man and the Myth* (New York: Vanguard, 1948);

Norman D. Markowitz, *The Rise and Fall of the People's Century: Henry A. Wallace and American Liberalism, 1941–48* (New York: Free Press, 1973).

PEOPLE IN THE NEWS

Attorney General **Francis Biddle** declared on 12 October 1942 that 600,000 Italian citizens residing in the United States were no longer "enemy aliens." American citizens of Japanese descent, meanwhile, were interned in concentration camps.

Returning to Mississippi to run for reelection in November 1946, Sen. **Theodore Gilmore Bilbo** answered northern critics of his white-supremacist speeches by saying, "We tell our Negro-loving Yankee friends to go straight to hell."

In July 1944 Republican vice-presidential candidate **John Bricker** made the first public statement of the Dewey-Bricker team about the Democrats' choice for vice-president, saying, "Truman — that's his name, isn't it? I can never remember that name."

On 27 October 1942 **James F. Byrnes,** director of the Office of Economic Stabilization and former associate justice of the Supreme Court, issued regulations limiting individual salaries at twenty-five thousand dollars (before taxes, charitable contributions, and fixed obligations), including President Franklin D. Roosevelt's. This meant that all salaries more than this amount were to be taxed at a rate of 100 percent. The measure was rescinded by Roosevelt under pressure from conservatives in Congress.

On 3 August 1948 **Whittaker Chambers,** an admitted Communist, accused State Department official **Alger Hiss** of stealing and disseminating top-secret government documents to the Soviet Union.

On 31 May 1945 **William J. ("Wild Bill") Donovan,** director of the Office of Strategic Services (OSS), reported to President Harry S Truman that the Japanese were ready to cease hostilities provided that they could maintain possession of their home islands.

Army air forces under the command of Brig. Gen. **James Doolittle** initiated the first air raids over Tokyo on 18 April 1942.

On 22 March 1945 **William Green,** president of the American Federation of Labor (AFL), urged that Congress approve the Bretton Woods Agreements creating the World Bank and the International Monetary Fund in order to provide jobs for American workers in the reconstruction of the postwar world.

On 12 September 1940 U.S. ambassador to Japan **Joseph J. Grew** warned that Japan would interpret the embargo imposed by the United States as a hostile act.

On 27 September 1943 **W. Averell Harriman,** a leading railroad industrialist and Wall Street financier, was named ambassador to the Soviet Union. He became one of the principal architects of the Cold War.

Former president **Herbert Hoover** told the Senate Foreign Relations Committee on 3 November 1943 that the United States has a "moral obligation" to feed the "stricken peoples" of Europe who have been overrun by the Nazis.

On 3 January 1941 Federal Bureau of Investigation Director **J. Edgar Hoover** said that, compared to a similar period during World War I, there had been a "negligible amount of sabotage" conducted against the United States. Hoover later issued a report, kept top-secret throughout World War II, that Japanese Americans performed no acts of sabotage and did not pose a threat to the internal security of the United States.

On 14 April 1944 Secretary of the Interior **Harold J. Ickes** proposed that all government-owned war-production plants be turned over to United States veterans by issuing them stock certificates so that the plants could compete with existing private industry after the war.

Having volunteered for active duty immediately after voting for war on 8 December 1941, Congressman **Lyndon B. Johnson** of Texas returned to the United States to report to President Franklin D. Roosevelt on conditions in the Pacific. Entering naval service as a lieutenant commander, Johnson was released after slightly more than one year of service, but not before being awarded the Silver Star by Roosevelt for air action in which he was a passenger.

On 28 June 1943 Gov. **Harry F. Kelly** of Michigan called out the National Guard to quell racial riots in Detroit. State forces were inadequate, and President Roosevelt was forced to order army troops into the city.

On 18 November 1940 U.S. ambassador to Great Britain **Joseph P. Kennedy** said, "Democracy is finished in England." He added that Britain was not fighting for democracy: "That's bunk — she's fighting for self-preservation."

On 25 June 1941 navy secretary **Frank Knox** announced that work on modernizing the fleet had been completed and that the navy "is now ready for action."

On 20 August 1941 **William S. Knudsen,** director of the Office of Production Management, declared that the country was not showing the "proper spirit" in the defense production program, "probably because no one has dropped any bombs on us yet."

In order to draw public attention to the Nazi genocide of Jews and others in Europe, Mayor **Fiorello La Guardia** of New York urged citizens to observe a day of mourning and prayer for the victims on 2 December 1943.

On 3 May 1949 Gen. **Douglas MacArthur,** as de facto ruler of Japan, imposed his new constitution upon the Japanese. The document provided for the creation of political parties, the recognition of labor unions and women's suffrage, land reform, and the destruction of the *zaibatsu,* Japan's military-industrial complex.

On 15 January 1944 Secretary of the Treasury **Henry R. Morgenthau,** citing a study undertaken by his staff, accused the State Department of covering up the Holocaust in Europe and met with President Franklin D. Roosevelt to urge him to create the War Refugee Board to save as many Nazi victims as possible in the time remaining.

On 3 June 1942 **Philip Murray,** president of the Congress of Industrial Organizations (CIO), condemned **John L. Lewis,** head of the United Mine Workers (UMW), as a "grave danger to the security of our nation" who is "hell bent on creating national confusion and national disunity."

On 6 December 1948 Congressman **Richard M. Nixon** of California, a member of the House Un-American Activities Committee (HUAC), accused the White House of "concealing facts" about Communist penetration of the State Department.

Because he advocated conscription, Sen. **Claude Pepper** of Florida was hanged in effigy on Capitol Hill by women calling themselves "The Congress of American Mothers" on 2 September 1940. Afterward Pepper said, "Their hanging me in effigy is a splendid example of what we all desire — freedom of speech and freedom of action."

According to a Gallup poll of 21 December 1942, **Eleanor Roosevelt,** wife of the president, was the target of more criticism and praise than any other woman in American history.

Speaking before the Senate Military Affairs Committee on 15 July 1940, Secretary of War **Henry L. Stimson** declared that in the aftermath of Germany's blitzkrieg in Europe, "We may be next."

On 26 March 1942 Sen. **Harry S Truman,** chairman of the Special Committee Investigating War Contracts, said that the Standard Oil Company was guilty of treason for sharing its formula for synthetic rubber with the German firm of I.G. Farbenindustrie and not with the U.S. Navy during 1939–1940.

In an article for *Collier's* in January 1944, Sen. **Arthur H. Vandenberg** said that Franklin D. Roosevelt intended to run for reelection based on his record of managing the war effort. He offered Gen. **Douglas MacArthur** as a Republican alternative, asking, "Shall we not offer the people a better commander in chief?"

William Allen White, newspaper editor and leading internationalist, resigned his leadership of the Committee to Defend America by Aiding the Allies on 2 January 1941.

Charged with the responsibility of feeding the United States and Great Britain during the "defense emergency," Secretary of Agriculture **Claude Wickard** said, "Food will win the war and write the peace."

In April 1943 **Wendell Willkie,** Republican candidate for president in 1940, published his book *One World,* in which he argued that America must extend its political and economic freedoms to the entire world and be prepared to defend the peace.

On 2 September 1942 Rabbi **Stephen S. Wise,** president of the American Jewish Congress, sent a letter to Undersecretary of State **Sumner Welles** informing him of documented evidence that the Nazis were conducting mass murders of Jews in Europe. Though the State Department was already in possession of this evidence, it declared for the next fourteen months that it could not confirm Wise's claims.

DEATHS

Charles A. Beard, 73, leading historian who believed that President Franklin D. Roosevelt actively sought to lead the United States into World War II, 1 September 1948.

Theodore G. Bilbo, 69, senator from Mississippi (1935–1947), leader of conservative opposition to racial progress in both the New Deal and World War II, 21 August 1947.

William E. Borah, 74, progressive senator from Idaho (1907–1940), leading isolationist before World War II and part of the opposition that defeated President Woodrow Wilson's League of Nations Treaty, 19 January 1940.

Louis D. Brandeis, 84, associate justice of the U.S. Supreme Court (1916–1939) and the first Jew appointed to the highest court, opponent of trusts and monopolies known for his devotion to free speech, 5 October 1941.

Philippe-Jean Bunau-Varilla, 81, French engineer engaged in secret machinations with the Theodore Roosevelt administration to sever Panama from Colombia in order to build and operate the Panama Canal under U.S. control, 18 May 1940.

Smedley Darlington Butler, 58, Marine Corps major general, winner of two Congressional Medals of Honor, leading opponent of U.S. entry into World War II who promoted a national defense system through which "a rat couldn't crawl," 21 June 1940.

Josephus Daniels, 85, U.S. secretary of the navy (1913–1921) who in 1914 ordered naval operations against Mexico in the aftermath of the Mexican Revolution of 1911, 15 January 1948.

Jean Darlan, 61, foreign minister and minister of defense of France (1941–1942) under the Nazi-controlled Vichy government who concluded an armistice with the United States and Great Britain after the Allied invasion of North Africa in November 1942, assassinated by an anti-Vichy extremist, 24 December 1942.

William E. Dodd, 70, U.S. ambassador to Germany (1933–1937) whose warnings about Adolf Hitler awakened President Franklin D. Roosevelt to the Nazi menace, 9 February 1940.

Marcus M. Garvey, 60, Jamaican-born black-nationalist leader who founded the Universal Negro Improvement Association (UNIA) branches in New York City and instituted a "Back-to-Africa" movement among African Americans during the 1920s, 10 June 1940.

Emma Goldman, 70, noted anarchist known as "Red Emma" who, as an émigré from Lithuania, opposed the Soviet government and whose political ideas led to a jail term (1917–1919) and deportation (1919) from the United States during the post–World War I "Red Scare," 14 May 1940.

Willis C. Hawley, 77, representative from Oregon (1907–1933) and coauthor of the Smoot-Hawley Tariff Act (1930) for contracting international trade, which many scholars consider one of the underlying causes of World War II, 24 July 1941.

Sidney Hillman, 59, prominent American labor leader, president of Amalgamated Clothing Workers of America (from 1914), principal founder of the Congress of Industrial Organizations (CIO), head of the labor division for the War Production Board (1942), and vice-chairman of the World Federation of Trade Unions (1945–1946), 10 July 1946.

Harry L. Hopkins, 55, President Franklin D. Roosevelt's closest adviser who, as head of the Works Progress (later Projects) Administration (1935–1938), oversaw the distribution of $8.5 billion in unemployment relief and thus personified the ideology of government social responsibility outlined in the New Deal, 29 January 1946.

Charles Evans Hughes, 86, chief justice of the U.S. Supreme Court (1930–1941), U.S. secretary of state (1921–1925), and Republican candidate for president in 1916 whose attempts to block many New Deal measures led to President Franklin D. Roosevelt's 1937 attempt to "pack" the Supreme Court, 27 August 1948.

John Maynard Keynes, 63, British economist whose theories on the causes and remedies of prolonged unemployment and recession revolutionized the field of economics and led New Deal advocates to adopt government spending as a remedy for the Depression, 21 April 1946.

Frank Knox, 70, army colonel who served in the Spanish-American War and World War I, Republican nominee for vice-president (1936), and secretary of the navy (1940–1944) who was appointed to the post to deflect partisan charges that U.S. defense needs were going unmet by the Democrats, 28 April 1944.

Fiorello La Guardia, 64, populist representative from New York (1917–1921, 1923–1933), outspoken mayor of New York City (1934–1945) who was a leading spokesman for the poor during the Depression and head of the United Nations Relief and Rehabilitation Administration (1946) aiding refugees of World War II, 20 September 1947.

William G. McAdoo, 77, secretary of the treasury (1913–1918) under President Woodrow Wilson, among the key advisers arguing that American prosperity required ties with England and France during World War I, 1 February 1941.

George S. Patton, 60, army general known as "Old Blood and Guts," the first man detailed to the U.S. Army Tank Corps (1917), led U.S. armed forces to victory over German panzers (1944–1945), 21 December 1945.

John J. Pershing, 87, army general and commander in chief of the American Expeditionary Force (1917–1919) whose 1918 offensive destroyed German resistance during World War I, 15 July 1948.

Max Planck, 89, German physicist and 1918 Nobel Prize winner, one of the originators of quantum theory whose studies helped lay the groundwork for the development of the atomic bomb, 3 October 1947.

Franklin D. Roosevelt, 63, president of the United States (1933–1945) and only president to be elected for third and fourth terms, instituted legislative and administrative reforms known as the New Deal, declared war on Japan (8 December 1941) and conferred on war strategy with Allied heads of state during World War II, 12 April 1945.

Theodore Roosevelt, Jr., 56, army brigadier general, son of President Theodore Roosevelt and an organizer of the American Legion who served in both world wars and died in Normandy, 12 July 1944.

Alfred E. Smith, 70, governor of New York (1919–1920, 1923–1928), Democratic presidential candidate (1928) and first Roman Catholic to run for that office, 4 October 1944.

Reed Smoot, 79, senator from Utah (1903–1933) and coauthor of the Smoot-Hawley Tariff Act (1930) for contracting international trade, which many scholars consider one of the underlying causes of World War II, 9 February 1941.

Joseph W. Stilwell, 63, army general who commanded U.S. forces in China, Burma, and India (1942–1944) and who warned that American support for Chiang Kai-shek in China would lead to disaster, 12 October 1946.

Harlan F. Stone, 73, U.S. Supreme Court chief justice (1941–1946) whose influence helped uphold the constitutionality of Japanese American internments, 22 April 1946.

Charles W. Taussig, 51, leading industrialist who was a principal member of President Franklin D. Roosevelt's brain trust, the inner circle of advisers who helped shape the New Deal, 10 May 1948.

Tojo Hideki, 57, prime minister of Japan (1941–1944), architect of Japanese aggressive strategy in Asia who approved the sneak attack on Pearl Harbor, Hawaii, executed as a war criminal, 23 December 1948.

Martha E. Truman, 94, mother of President Harry S Truman, 26 July 1947.

William Allen White, 75, noted Republican newspaper editor and columnist who headed the Committee to Defend America by Aiding the Allies, the interventionist opposition to the isolationists prior to World War II, 29 January 1944.

Wendell L. Willkie, 52, Republican presidential candidate (1940) and author of the highly influential book *One World* (1943), which helped shape America's postwar internationalist perspective, 8 October 1944.

PUBLICATIONS

Saul Alinsky, *John L. Lewis: An Unauthorized Biography* (New York: Putnam, 1949);

Hanson W. Baldwin, *Strategy for Victory* (New York: Norton, 1942);

Baldwin, *United We Stand: Defense of the Western Hemisphere* (London: Whittlesey House / New York: McGraw-Hill, 1941);

Stephen Vincent Benét, *Zero Hour: A Summons to the Free* (New York & Toronto: Farrar & Rinehart, 1940);

Eduard Bernays, *Speak Up for Democracy: What You Can Do — Practical Plan of Action for Every American Citizen* (New York: Viking, 1940);

Leonard Broom and Ruth Riemer, *Removal and Return: The Socio-Economic Effects of the War on Japanese-Americans* (Berkeley & Los Angeles: University of California Press, 1949);

James Burnham, *The Managerial Revolution: What is Happening in the World* (New York: Day, 1941);

Vannevar Bush, *Science, The Endless Frontier: A Report to the President* (Washington, D.C.: U.S. Government Printing Office, 1945);

Bruce Catton, *The Warlords of Washington* (New York: Harcourt Brace, 1948);

Peter Drucker, *The Future of Industrial Man: A Conservative Approach* (New York: Farrar & Rinehart, 1941);

Ethel Gorham, *So Your Husband's Gone To War* (Garden City, N.Y.: Doubleday, Doran, 1942);

Morton Grodzins, *Americans Betrayed: Politics and the Japanese Evacuation* (Chicago: University of Chicago Press, 1949);

Friedrich Hayek, *The Road to Serfdom* (Chicago: University of Chicago Press, 1944);

John Hersey, *Hiroshima* (New York: Knopf, 1946);

Harold J. Laski, *The Strategy of Freedom: An Open Letter to American Youth* (New York & London: Harper, 1941);

Alfred McClung Lee and Norman D. Humphrey, *Race Riot* (New York: Dryden, 1943);

Max Lerner, *Ideas For the Ice Age: Studies in a Revolutionary Era* (New York: Viking, 1941);

Anne Morrow Lindbergh, *The Wave of the Future: A Confession of Faith* (New York: Harcourt Brace, 1940);

Walter Lippmann, *U.S. Foreign Policy: Shield of the Republic* (Boston: Little, Brown, 1943);

Lippmann, *U.S. War Aims* (Boston: Little, Brown, 1944);

Henry Luce, *The American Century* (New York: Farrar & Rinehart, 1941);

Archibald MacLeish, *The American Cause* (New York: Duell, Sloan & Pearce, 1942);

Carey McWilliams, *Prejudice, Japanese-Americans: Symbols of Racial Intolerance* (Boston: Little, Brown, 1944);

Margaret Mead, *And Keep Your Powder Dry: An Anthropologist Looks at America* (New York: Morrow, 1942);

Samuel Eliot Morison, *The Rising Sun in the Pacific* (Boston: Little, Brown, 1948);

Lewis Mumford, *Faith for Living* (New York: Harcourt Brace, 1940);

Gunnar Myrdal, *An American Dilemma: The Negro Problem and Modern Democracy* (New York: Harper, 1944);

Donald M. Nelson, *Arsenal of Democracy: The Story of American War Production* (New York: Harcourt Brace, 1946);

James Reston, *Prelude to Victory* (New York: Knopf, 1942);

Carl Sandburg, *Home Front Memo* (New York: Harcourt Brace, 1943);

Arthur M. Schlesinger, *Political and Social Growth of the United States 1865–1940* (New York: Macmillan, 1942);

Pitirim Sorokin, *The Crisis of Our Age* (New York: Dutton, 1942);

I. F. Stone, *Business As Usual: The First Year of Defense* (New York: Modern Age, 1942);

Henry A. Wallace, *The Century of the Common Man* (New York: Reynal & Hitchcock, 1943);

Summer Welles, *The Time for Decision* (New York: Harper, 1944);

Wendell L. Willkie, *One World* (New York: Simon & Schuster, 1943).

LAW AND JUSTICE

by MICHAEL L. PIERCE

CONTENTS

Sidebars and tables are listed in italics.

1940

28 June The Alien Registration Act (Smith Act) is passed. This law makes it unlawful for any individual to call for the overthrow of any government in the United States by force. It also makes it unlawful to join or found any group which teaches such a doctrine.

16 Sept. Passage of the Selective Training and Service Act is secured. This bill calls for the first peacetime draft program in U.S. history.

1941

31 Jan. Justice James Clark McReynolds retires from the Supreme Court after serving for twenty-six years.

12 June Sen. James F. Byrnes is nominated and confirmed on the same day to an appointment as an associate justice of the Supreme Court.

25 June The Fair Employment Practices Committee (FEPC) is established to halt discrimination in war production industries and government employment.

27 June Justice Harlan Fiske Stone is confirmed by the Senate to replace Charles Evans Hughes as chief justice upon Hughes's retirement.

1 July Chief Justice Hughes retires after serving as chief justice for eleven years.

11 July Robert H. Jackson is sworn in as an associate justice of the Supreme Court.

1942

1 Jan. The United Nations Declaration is signed in Washington, D.C. Twenty-six nations, including the United States, the Soviet Union, Great Britain, and China, pledge to utilize all of their economic and military strength against the Axis powers.

19 Feb. Per executive order of the president, the secretary of war is authorized to prescribe areas on the West Coast from which persons might be excluded. By 29 March over 110,000 Japanese Americans from California, Arizona, Oregon, and Washington have been moved to relocation camps.

3 Oct. After serving only sixteen months, Justice James Byrnes resigns to accept appointment as the director of the Office of Economic Stabilization.

1943

- The Withholding Tax Act is passed by Congress. Its dual purpose is to generate more tax money for the war effort and to reduce inflationary pressure on domestic prices by lowering the take-home pay of workers.

11 Jan. U.S. Court of Appeals judge Wiley B. Rutledge is nominated as an associate justice of the Supreme Court.

9 Feb. To deal with the labor shortage, President Franklin D. Roosevelt issues an executive order mandating a minimum workweek of forty-eight hours, with overtime to be paid for any work over forty hours.

10 May The U.S. Supreme Court rules (8–2) that the Federal Communications Commission (FCC) has the legitimate authority to regulate the major broadcasting chains on behalf of the public.

1944

17 May — The Supreme Court refuses to review a lower court decision that held that Japanese who are born in this country are American citizens and are therefore entitled to vote. A challenger, John T. Regan, had argued unsuccessfully that "dishonesty, deceit and hypocrisy are racial characteristics of the Japanese," thus making them unfit for American citizenship.

25 June — The Labor Disputes Act (Smith-Connally Anti-Strike Act) is passed, broadening the president's power to seize industrial plants where labor disturbances threaten to interfere with war production.

27 Dec. — President Roosevelt orders the U.S. Army to take possession of all U.S. railroads to head off a threatened strike by railroad workers. The railroads are returned to private control on 18 January 1944.

22 June — President Roosevelt approves the GI Bill of Rights, to assist returning World War II veterans in obtaining educational and housing benefits.

1–22 July — The United Nations Monetary and Financial Conference (the Bretton Woods Conference) is held at Bretton Woods, New Hampshire. The conference establishes the International Monetary Fund in order to help stabilize national currencies in the hopes of increasing world trade.

21 Aug.– 7 Oct. — The Dumbarton Oaks Conference is held near Washington, D.C. The initial proposals to which the participants (the United States, the Soviet Union, Great Britain, and China) agree serve as the guidelines for the charter of the United Nations.

17 Dec. — The U.S. Army announces that effective 2 January 1945 it will end the mass exclusion of Japanese Americans from the West Coast.

1945

25 Apr.– 26 June — The United Nations Conference on International Organization is held in San Francisco. Over the course of two months a charter is worked out; it is unanimously approved on 25 June. The UN Charter is signed on 26 June.

10 July — Five prisoners of war, formerly members of Rommel's Afrika Korps, are hanged at Fort Leavenworth for the murder of a fellow prisoner. These executions are the first ever conducted of foreign prisoners of war in the United States.

28 July — The U.S. Senate ratifies the United Nations Charter by a vote of 89 to 2.

31 July — Justice Owen J. Roberts, who supervised an inquiry into the attack on Pearl Harbor and who headed a commission that traced art objects stolen by the Germans during World War II, resigns from the Supreme Court after serving since 1930.

8 Aug. — President Harry S Truman signs the UN Charter.

1 Oct. — Sen. Harold H. Burton takes the oath of office as an associate justice of the Supreme Court.

20 Nov. — War-crime trials of Nazis begin in Nuremburg, Germany.

1946

14 Dec.	Josef Kramer, "the Beast of Belsen"; three of his female guards; and seven other Nazis are hanged in Hameln, Germany, after a British military court convicted them for atrocities.

1947

10 Jan.	The first session of the United Nations General Assembly is held in London.
19 Jan.	The International Military Tribunal for the Far East is established to try Japanese leaders on war-crime charges.
21 Mar.	President Truman issues Executive Order 9835, which requires the investigation of all government employees or applicants for government positions.
24 June	Fred M. Vinson, former secretary of the treasury, takes the oath of office as new chief justice of the Supreme Court.
26 July	The National Security Act unifies the army, navy, marines, and air force into a new military structure accountable to a secretary of defense with cabinet status. The act also establishes the National Security Council and the Central Intelligence Agency (CIA).
24 Mar.	The Twenty-second Amendment to the U.S. Constitution is proposed. This amendment prohibits any person from holding more than two full terms as president of the United States or two full terms and more than two years in addition as acting president (for a theoretical total of ten years). This amendment is subsequently ratified on 26 February 1951.
18 July	President Truman signs the Presidential Succession Act , rewriting the law passed in 1886 regarding presidential succession. The new law makes the Speaker of the House next in the line of succession, followed by the president pro tempore of the Senate, the secretary of state, and the cabinet members according to rank.

1948

•	The Economic Cooperation Act (also known as the Marshall Plan, after former general and then secretary of state George C. Marshall) passes. The plan calls for financing the economic recovery of Western Europe following the devastation of World War II. The U.S. Congress appropriates $13 billion to fund the plan, and all involved call it a "smashing success."
22 June	The Selective Service Act is passed after the earlier version expires. The new version provides for registration of all men between the ages of eighteen and twenty-five, with active draft service to be limited to twenty-one months.
30 July	President Truman orders equality in the armed services. Four days earlier Truman banned by executive order discrimination in the hiring of federal employees.
3 Aug.	The House Un-American Activities Committee hears testimony from admitted Communist courier Whittaker Chambers that a State Department official, Alger Hiss, had been a member of a Communist organization prior to World War II. Hiss is later indicted for perjury and, after a first trial ending in a hung jury, is found guilty and sentenced to five years in prison.

1949

- The North Atlantic Treaty creates the North Atlantic Treaty Organization (NATO), a mutual-defense treaty between the United States and most of the countries of Western Europe. Its purpose is to defend against possible Soviet aggression.

17 June   Gov. James E. Folsom of Alabama, following raids by hooded men who whipped several people, signs a bill forbidding the wearing of masks.

2 Aug.   Attorney General Tom C. Clark is nominated as an associate justice of the Supreme Court by President Truman.

15 Sept.   U.S. Court of Appeals judge Sherman Minton is nominated as an associate justice to the Supreme Court.

14 Oct.   Eleven leaders of the U.S. Communist Party are convicted of violation of the Smith Act of 1940. Their convictions are subsequently affirmed by the U.S. Supreme Court in 1951.

OVERVIEW

A Changing Society. With the advent of the 1940s came an increased prosperity as well as the higher risk of conflict with other nations. Both possibilities had effects on the law. The efforts of President Franklin D. Roosevelt, first elected in 1932, to fight the Great Depression with his New Deal program led to great changes in society and government and brought challenges in the legal realm from both advocates and opponents. Roosevelt's almost dictatorial attitude toward bending the courts to his way of thinking, the most obvious example being his thwarted attempt to pack the Supreme Court in 1937 with additional associate justices of his own choosing, affected the Supreme Court well into the 1940s. Although the court-packing plan failed, Roosevelt appointed eight supreme court justices during his term in office, and they frequently reflected his liberal social perspective. The entry of the United States into World War II brought new legal questions, which brought to the law questions of world morality and politics.

The Worst . . . and the Best. During the first half of the decade, events affecting national security led many in the United States either to propose actively or acquiesce in actions that today would be unthinkable. A U.S. Army general misled government officials into believing that Japanese American citizens living on the West Coast might be a threat to national security. All Japanese Americans living on the West Coast, a number approaching 110,000, were forcibly removed from their homes and placed in internment camps. But the war also brought out the best in many other Americans. A Japanese American combat unit made up of many of these same displaced citizens became the most heavily decorated combat regiment in American history. And despite the widespread belief that Japanese Americans were a potential threat to national security, many Americans spoke out against the injustice of the suspension of constitutional rights for these citizens. Famed American nature photographer Ansel Adams documented the unity and strength of the internees at the Manzanar camp, the only time he ever photographed people. And Supreme Court justice Robert Jackson later called the internment "the legalization of racism."

Crime in the 1940s. Despite the focus of the populace on the war effort, crime continued unabated. Public interest in the more spectacular crimes grew with the increasing reliance upon national media such as radio and newpapers. The emergence of television later in the decade promised an even greater public interest in crime during the 1950s. Americans were able to learn of the mass murders committed by Howard Unruh only minutes after they occurred; they could follow the prison riot that came to be known as the battle for Alcatraz — over the three days that it happened. Las Vegas, Nevada, a small, undistinguished town of which few had heard, began its climb into the minds of Americans as the gambling mecca of the world. Unsurprisingly, along with that reputation for gambling went the realities of crime: loan sharking, prostitution, and the burgeoning drug trade.

War and Justice. As distressing rumors of genocide and widespread ethnic slaughter began to filter out of Europe and the Far East midway through World War II, the people in the United States began to think of legal responses to the carnage. Americans knew that war by its very nature was a brutal and bloody affair. Certainly, no city or town in the United States escaped having one or more of its citizens wounded or killed in the war. In war, soldiers are expected to fight and die, and, occasionally, innocent civilians are injured or killed as well. But ever since the mid nineteenth century the law of war had developed certain rules, and most nations gave medical treatment to wounded enemy soldiers who had been taken prisoner and avoided, when possible, the killing of civilians. However, as the rumors grew of thousands, and later millions, of Jewish and Slavic civilians being rounded up by Nazi Germany and shipped to concentration camps, concern in the Allied countries that wholesale genocide might be occurring led to calls for international war tribunals to prosecute those found responsible for war crimes. As the Allied armies liberated camps with names like Auschwitz, Bergen-Belsen, and Dachau, the enormity of the slaughter became apparent. For the first time in the history of modern war, systematic attacks on unarmed civilians by armed forces had occurred in Europe. Similar crimes had occurred during the Japanese occupation of Asian nations as well, and war-crime trials began in both Japan and Germany. While the trials could do nothing to punish war crimes adequately, the trials were an affirmation by the international community, led by the United States, that the rule of law had prevailed.

The Beginnings of the Global Community. The late 1940s also witnessed the finalization of an organization founded in the hope that it would help all nations avoid future wars like the one just fought. The League of Nations, founded with much the same hope after World War I, had faltered and eventually failed due in large part to the refusal of the United States to join and abide by its dictates. As a result of the emergence of the United States as a leader among nations in World War II and an acknowledgment of its self-interest in a peaceful, increasingly interdependent world, the United States was a leader in the formation of the United Nations. One of its chief duties was set as the regulation of international law among member nations, providing a way to help settle disputes short of armed conflict.

The Changing Face of a People. Prior to World War II, the United States and its people tended to have an isolationist view of the world. The result of the world-wide action of World War II was that many Americans, including the foot soldier but especially those in the government, became more worldly and cosmopolitan in their views. The law, interpreted by an increasingly younger and more liberal Supreme Court, began to reflect Americans' more expansive view of their society and the U.S. Constitution. The Supreme Court rendered more and more decisions defining and outlining specific rights that Americans possessed. These decisions concerned such topics as the freedom of speech, which now included the freedom not to salute the flag; the right to own property was now extended to all, regardless of their color or the shape of their eyes. Americans had the right to a trial by a jury of their peers, which now could include members of all races.

The Cold War. The increasing tension between the United States and the Soviet Union led to restrictive laws, such as the Smith Act. Some U.S. senators and representatives took actions that bordered on the unconstitutional. Individuals or groups held to be Communist or pro-Soviet were subject to official or informal sanctions by individuals, businesses, or the government. The dynamic generated by the conflict between those claiming emerging rights and those seeking to restrict individual rights led to an increasingly activist Supreme Court and paved the way for introspective interpretation of American law for decades to follow.

TOPICS IN THE NEWS

CIVIL LIBERTIES AND PATRIOTISM

The Challenge of War. Historically, civil liberties and war have proved incompatible. Abraham Lincoln suspended the constitutional requirement that defendants be charged with crimes before imprisonment during the Civil War; Woodrow Wilson restricted free speech and open political activity during the First World War. Civil liberties during World War II were also restricted. While the government did significantly restrict freedom of speech, freedom of movement, and freedom of political association during the decade, federal officials were reluctant to engage in wholesale suspension of civil liberties. Such a suspension would evoke political opposition contrary to the efficiency of the war effort and would make the distinction between the United States and its enemies — a distinction crucial to the propaganda war — too blurry. Two Supreme Court cases regarding the individual's ability to refrain from overt displays of patriotism addressed this limit on wartime coercion. In the *Minersville School District* v. *Gobitis* case of 1940 the Supreme Court held that the government could demand individual participation in civic ritual designed to instill patriotism and a sense of unity; in the *West Virginia State Board of Education* v. *Barnette* case of 1943 the Supreme Court set limits to the degree to which the government could demand such participation.

A Wartime Ritual. The Pledge of Allegiance, first published in 1893, was widely adopted during and after World War I to evoke a spirit of national unity. Most Americans complied with the recitation of the pledge, some enthusiastically, many without feeling one way or another. By the 1920s it had become a simple school ritual (albeit enforced in many states by law) for most Americans. For Jehovah's Witnesses, however, the pledge presented a violation of their religious faith.

False Idols. Jehovah's Witnesses were an evangelical sect that numbered about 115,000 in 1942. They believed that this world was under the domination of Satan and that churches, governments, and other social institutions were under his control. They asserted that the Bible, in Exod. 20: 3–5, forbade them from saluting any flag since this would be a violation of the law of God. The particular passage upon which the Jehovah's Witnesses relied

states that "You shall not have other gods beside me. You shall not carve idols for yourselves in the shape of anything in the sky above or on the earth below or in the waters beneath the earth; you shall not bow down before them or worship them." For Jehovah's Witnesses, school requirements that their children participate in pledge requirements violated their right to freedom of religion.

Not Saying the Pledge. In 1935 the Minersville, Pennsylvania, public school expelled twelve-year-old Lillian Gobitis and her ten-year-old brother, William, for failure to participate in the state-mandated Pledge of Allegiance to the United States flag. The children were not disruptive in class but stood in silence while their classmates recited the pledge. Both were the children of Jehovah's Witnesses.

Appeal. When the children were expelled from school, their parents were forced to enroll them in private schools at their own expense. Their father, on their behalf and on behalf of others similarly situated, brought suit challenging the expulsion. Both the U.S. District Court in Pennsylvania and the Circuit Court of Appeals ruled against the school district and upheld the children's right to refuse to engage in the flag-salute ceremony. Since these decisions ran counter to several cases previously ruled on by the Supreme Court, the court agreed to hear the case and to reconsider the entire situation.

The Constitutional Issue. The Supreme Court quickly dispensed with the Jehovah's Witnesses' argument that the expulsions violated their freedom of religion, agreeing with Justice Felix Frankfurter that there was no "absolute" claim to this right. Instead, the Court considered the degree of coercion necessary to advance national unity and to safeguard individual rights. They began, in other words, by assuming that a certain amount of public ritual, backed by coercion, was necessary for the smooth running of society — in peace or wartime. As Frankfurter put it, the precise issue for the court to decide was "whether the legislatures of the various states and the authorities in a thousand counties and school districts of this country are barred from determining the appropriateness of various means to evoke that unifying sentiment without which there can ultimately be no liberties, civil or religious."

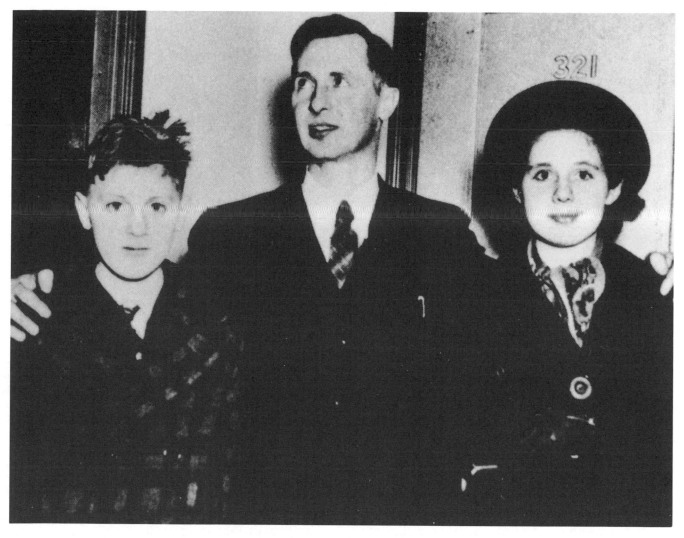

Jehovah's Witness Henry Gobitis, with his children William and Lillian, who were expelled from school in Minersville, Pennsylvania, for refusing to salute the flag

Brainwashing. Complicating the *Gobitis* decision was the argument of the school district that the Jehovah's Witnesses, via their near absolute rejection of society, were fundamentally brainwashing their children. The school district argued that it was the obligation of education to liberate children from such tyranny, an argument loaded with the heated politics of the era, a time when Germany was training its Hitler Youth for war. The school district argued that the pledge was part of a larger program of civic education for the children, one vital in maintaining social cohesion. The Court substantially agreed, remarking in their final decision that what the school authorities were really asserting in forcing the Gobitis children to say the pledge was a right to "awaken in the child's mind considerations as to the significance of the flag contrary to those implanted by the parent."

The Interest of the State. On 3 June 1940 the Court reversed the rulings of the lower federal courts and held that the Pennsylvania legislature had the right to include the Pledge of Allegiance as part of its overall introduction of the young to patriotic principles. The Court felt that the legitimate interests of the state legislature in mandating the Pledge of Allegiance outweighed an absolute right of a child in such a situation to refuse. The Court stated that "But for us to insist that, though the ceremony may be required, exceptional immunity must be given to dissidents, is to maintain that there is no basis for a legislative judgment that such an exemption might introduce elements of difficulty into the school discipline, might cast doubts in the minds of other children which would themselves weaken the effect of the exercise."

Results. In essence the court was refusing to pass judgment on the content of school education, opening up the possibility, all too real at a time when Nazi ideology was forced on German students, that the schools might become an agency for ideological instruction. The Court, however, felt that parents exercised greater influence over their children than did the state. As long as the parents' right to contradict the instruction their children received by the state remained inviolate, mass public indoctrination of students was unlikely. By agreeing with the state of Pennsylvania that some sort of civic education was

Students saluting the American flag, a practice that could not be required by schools after the 1943 Supreme Court decision in *West Virginia State Board of Education* v. *Barnette*

necessary to form a cohesive society and at the same time refusing to specify the content of that instruction, the Court set an important precedent for wartime legislation designed to secure the general good — sometimes at individual expense.

Spirit of Americanism. The Court's confidence that ideological indoctrination would be unlikely in American schools was soon tested. Despite the *Gobitis* decision, Jehovah's Witnesses continued to refuse to pledge allegiance to the flag. Physical attacks on Jehovah's Witnesses for suspected disloyalty escalated, especially after Pearl Harbor. Hard on the heels of the *Gobitis* decision, the West Virginia legislature changed its laws to require that all schools conduct courses of instruction in history and civics. The purpose of the course of instruction was for "teaching, fostering and perpetuating the ideals, principles and spirit of Americanism, and increasing the knowledge of the organization and machinery of government." On 9 January 1942 the West Virginia Board of Education also adopted a resolution which contained portions of the Supreme Court's *Gobitis* decision and which ordered that the salute to the flag would become "a regular part of the program of activities in the public schools," in that all teachers and pupils would be "required to participate in the salute honoring

the nation represented by the flag; provided, however, that refusal to salute the flag be regarded as an act of insubordination, and shall be dealt with accordingly."

Punishment. The West Virginia legislature provided that children who refused to salute the flag in the prescribed manner would be expelled and that the expulsions would continue until compliance was achieved. In the meantime the child was to be held unlawfully absent from school, and proceedings could be instituted against the child in court to label him or her a delinquent. Furthermore, the parents were liable to be prosecuted for the delinquency, and, if convicted, they could be subject to a fine of up to fifty dollars and/or a jail term not to exceed thirty days.

The Witnesses Challenge. Once again the Jehovah's Witnesses challenged the law. Their argument repeated that they considered the flag to be an "image" which they were forbidden by God to worship or salute. They argued that their children were unduly punished by the legislation, noting that officials threatened to send expelled children to reformatories constructed to house juveniles convicted of serious crimes. The Federal District Court in West Virginia refused to restrain the West Virginia Board of Education from punishing the children of Walter Barnette, and on that basis he appealed to the U.S. Supreme Court and asked them to overrule their 1940 *Gobitis* decision.

Protected Speech. Less than three years after *Gobitis*, the Supreme Court thus once again considered the relationship between civil rights and the government's capacity to inculcate a sense of national unity. Even the American Legion averred that the pledge should be voluntary. This time the Supreme Court agreed, overturning *Gobitis* and invalidating the West Virginia law. Once again, however, they did not rule on the issue of whether the pledge violated the right of the individual to practice religion freely. Instead, the Court considered the *Barnette* case from the standpoint of freedom of speech, arguing that the refusal to participate in flag pledges constituted a form of protected speech.

Reversal. Perhaps benefiting from the sharp wartime contrast between democracy and fascism, the Supreme Court saw in the refusal to participate in mandated civic ritual a fundamental component of democracy. "We set up government by consent of the governed," reasoned the Court, "and the Bill of Rights denies those in power any legal opportunity to coerce that consent. Authority here is to be controlled by public opinion, not public opinion by authority." The Court found the mandated pledge inverted the reason for free speech, twisting the "individual's right to speak his own mind" into something that would "compel him to utter what was not in his mind." The Court did not reverse its position that public rituals were important in cultivating social unity, but it acknowledged that not all local, state, and federal authorities would scrupulously respect individuals who did not care to participate in such rituals: "We think the action of the local authorities in compelling the flag salute and pledge transcends constitutional limitations on their power and invades the sphere of intellect and spirit which is the purpose of the First Amendment to our Constitution to reserve from all official control." In the midst of a war that saw civil liberties compromised by the Smith Act and the internments of Japanese Americans, the Supreme Court was setting limits to coercive authority and upholding the right of dissent.

Sources:

Kermit L. Hall, ed., *The Oxford Companion to the Supreme Court* (New York: Oxford University Press, 1992);

Merlin Owen Newton, *Armed With the Constitution: Jehovah's Witnesses in Alabama and the U.S. Supreme Court* (Tuscaloosa: University of Alabama Press, 1994).

CIVIL RIGHTS CASES

Jim Crow. Since before the turn of the century in the South, black Americans had been relegated to the status of second-class citizens, denied by law and legal subterfuge fundamental civil rights such as the right to vote, the right to free assembly, the right to freedom of speech, and the right to due legal process. The system, known commonly as Jim Crow, had a dubious standing in the law.

Since the passage of the Thirteenth, Fourteenth, and Fifteenth Amendments to the Constitution after the Civil War, blacks were entitled to the same legal protections as white citizens. A series of late–nineteenth century Supreme Court interpretations of these amendments, however, reduced the scope of protections. The most important of these decisions was *Plessy* v. *Ferguson* (1896), which interpreted the Fourteenth Amendment in such a manner that it established the legal foundation for Jim Crow.

Segregation. In *Plessy* v. *Ferguson* the Court established the legal pattern for the erection of two societies in the South, one white and one black. The men who drafted the Fourteenth Amendment had intended it to prevent state governments from denying black Americans rights guaranteed by the Constitution. In *Plessy*, however, the Court maintained that so long as state governments provided due legal process and legal freedoms equal to those of white citizens, they could maintain separate institutions to administer these rights. The interpretation opened the way to a segregated society in the South. Southern state governments passed laws forbidding blacks and whites from social and institutional association. Blacks and whites rode on different train cars and on different parts of buses, and they waited in separate areas of bus and train stations. Entrances and exits to buildings were segregated, as were public bathrooms and water fountains. There were separate prisons for blacks and whites, separate hospitals, separate churches, even separate homes for the blind. In 1905 Georgia set up separate parks for blacks and whites; in 1935 Oklahoma forbade blacks and whites from boating together; in 1930 Birmingham, Alabama, made it illegal for blacks and whites to play dominoes and checkers together. Most important, state governments set up separate education systems. Nowhere in the South did white and black children attend school together.

Subterfuge. According to *Plessy*, segregated education was constitutional, so long as the black schools were equal to those of whites. But black and white schools were not equal. Because most blacks were denied the right to vote in most southern states, school boards were comprised of whites. On average they funded white schools at rates twice that of black schools, and white teachers' salaries were on average 30 percent higher than those of black teachers. School boards provided inadequate buildings, textbooks, and buses to black students, and there was almost no graduate education provided for black Americans in most states in the South. The second-class status of black education symbolized the reality of Jim Crow in almost every southern institution: black public restrooms were rare and poorly maintained, black water fountains rusty, and black train cars old and uncomfortable. Separate was not equal in the Jim Crow South. Separate was second-rate. *Plessy* was used by southern governments as an excuse to neglect their obligations to black citizens.

Violence. Jim Crow used more than *Plessy* to relegate black Americans to a second-class status. A variety of legal subterfuges, buttressed by popular political assent (in both the North and South) sustained the system. The right to vote was denied blacks through tactics such as the white primary (restricting voting in primaries or membership in the Democratic Party to whites), grandfather clauses (laws that restricted the right to vote to blacks whose ancestors had voted before the Civil War — when blacks were legally denied the right to vote), or through poll taxes (fees ostensibly charged to both black and white voters before they could vote but which actually were assessed against poor blacks, effectively preventing them from voting). Such subterfuges successfully squelched black participation in southern politics. In the election of 1940, for example, only 2.5 percent of southern blacks voted. Such laws were unconstitutional but unchallenged, in part because white public opinion sustained such laws, but also because white violence and political pressure against blacks were constant features in southern life. Blacks who pressed their constitutional rights in the courts risked losing their homes, their jobs, and often their lives. Lynching, the unpunished murder of blacks by white mobs, repeatedly occurred in the South, even into the 1940s. The legal system was often incapable of dealing with lynching and violence against blacks, as all-white juries almost never convicted whites of violence against blacks. Many states reinforced the inability of the law to stop lynching by barring blacks from serving on juries. And the Jim Crow system often implicitly depended upon violence to prevent black challenges to its constitutional legitimacy. Thus, a cycle of unjust application of the law and unpunished violence outside the law effectively denied southern blacks their constitutional rights.

Challenges. In 1935 a northern-based civil rights organization, the National Association for the Advancement of Colored People (NAACP), began legal challenges to the Jim Crow system in the South. Led by Howard University law professor Charles Houston, teams of NAACP lawyers including William Hastie, Thurgood Marshall, Leon A. Ransom, Oliver W. Hill, and James M. Nebrit, Jr., challenged state Jim Crow laws concerning voting, criminal rights, and segregation in housing, education, and transportation. They focused their campaign on the upper South, where the risk of violence to black plaintiffs was less than in the Deep South, and amassed a legal-defense fund with assistance from the American Fund for Public Service. They anticipated first challenging the equality of the segregated facilities in the South, setting a precedent for a later challenge to the very notion of segregation itself. Although the NAACP was not the sole civil rights organization challenging Jim Crow in the courts, its program was the best financed and the best planned.

Transportation. As the segregated railcars of Louisiana had occasioned the *Plessy* case of 1896, civil rights reformers naturally took aim at Jim Crow in transportation. One of the most important of the cases in the 1940s began in 1936, when a black congressman, Arthur Mitchell, took a train from Chicago to Hot Springs, Arkansas. As he entered the South, the Rock Island Railroad forced him to move out of a comfortable, air-conditioned railroad car into a dirty, uncomfortable car reserved for blacks and baggage. When Mitchell returned to Washington, he filed a complaint with the Interstate Commerce Commission, which replied that the railroad was only complying with the Jim Crow laws. Mitchell filed suit in the courts to challenge the constitutionality of the Jim Crow segregation laws. The 28 April 1941 decision in *Mitchell* v. *United States* represented a mixed victory for civil rights reformers. The court required that the accommodations for blacks on interstate trains be equal to those of whites but left in place the *Plessy* approval of segregated transportation. Less ambiguous was the June 1946 Supreme Court decision in *Morgan* v. *Virginia*, wherein the Supreme Court outlawed Jim Crow laws requiring the segregation of passengers in interstate transportation. The transportation companies, however, did nothing to comply with the new law, and when several activists from the Congress of Racial Equality (CORE) challenged the continuing segregation in interstate transportation in 1947, they were arrested. When their legal funding ran out, they abandoned further challenges, and segregation in interstate transportation continued to be practiced in the South until the Freedom Rides of the early 1960s.

Voting and Criminal Rights. Jim Crow stripped black Americans of two fundamental rights of American citizenship: the right to vote and the right to be tried before a jury of one's peers. Court challenges in the 1940s returned some of these rights, although they would not be successfully recovered until after the passage of the Voting Rights Act of 1965. *Lane* v. *Wilson* (1939) struck down Oklahoma's grandfather clause. Two cases, *United States* v. *Classic* (1941) and *Smith* v. *Allwright* (1944), invalidated the white primary. A series of Supreme Court decisions, beginning in 1935 and culminating in *Smith* v. *Texas* (1940), overturned convictions of black defendants in the South on the basis that blacks were legally prevented from serving on juries. Another Supreme Court ruling, *Chambers* v. *Florida* (1940), halted the common police practice of rounding up blacks and "sweating out" — through the use of force, deprivation, and torture — confessions to crimes they did not commit. The *Chambers* case began in 1936 in a small Florida town where a white man had been murdered. Town police rounded up twenty-five to forty black men, arrested them without warrants, and confined them to jail for six days. Police grilled them incessantly, finally extracting a confession from one man. On the basis of the confession, four men were convicted of murder and sentenced to death. When Florida appellate courts upheld the judgment, the NAACP appealed the case to the Supreme Court.

On Abraham Lincoln's birthday in 1940, the Court invalidated the confession and the process of using the "third degree" against black Americans. Writing for the Court, Justice Hugo Black offered this opinion: "No higher duty, no more solemn responsibility, rests upon this Court, than that of translating into living law and maintaining this constitutional shield deliberately planned and inscribed for the benefit of every human being subject to our Constitution — of whatever race, creed, or persuasion."

Housing. In 1926 the Supreme Court had upheld the right of landowners and real estate agents to bind buyers of property to restrictive covenants. Such covenants obligated the purchaser of land or property not to sell the land at a future date to any member of the "Negro or Mongolian" races. In 1938 a challenge to restrictive covenants before the Illinois Supreme Court by African American homebuyers in Chicago resulted in the partial overturn of the Illinois decision; a follow-up case, *Shelley* v. *Kraemer* (1948), abolished restrictive covenants as an infringement of the Fourteenth Amendment right to equal protection of the laws — an interpretation of the Fourteenth Amendment that returned to its original intent.

Education. The NAACP campaign against segregated schools was the most successful of its anti–Jim Crow efforts. The NAACP first challenged Jim Crow in education by pointing out the unequal quality of black education in the South. The plan was to force southern schools to own up to the obligation in *Plessy* that black education be equal to white, hoping that the extraordinary expense involved in bringing black schools up to standard would lead southern states simply to abandon segregated schools. When that failed to occur, the NAACP argued that segregated schools inherently disadvantaged students, limiting their ability to gain the skills necessary to be competitive with white students and imparting a debilitating psychological stigma on the student. In a 1939 Missouri case, for example, the NAACP petitioned the state either to integrate its law school or to provide a separate law school for a single black student. It chose to do the latter but only after the Supreme Court ordered it to do so. The NAACP took a similar approach in *Sweatt* v. *Painter* (1949), a Texas case where the Court abolished a separate black law school on the basis that it was inferior to the state's white law school. In *McLaurin* v. *Oklahoma* the Court went further, agreeing with the NAACP that the University of Oklahoma graduate school was acting illegally in segregating a black student within the classroom (by use of a curtain which prevented him from being seen), as well as isolating him in the cafeteria and library. "Such restrictions," ruled the Court, "impair and inhibit his ability to study, engage in discussions and exchange views with other students, and, in general, to learn his profession." *McLaurin* set the precedent for the ground-breaking *Brown* v. *Board of Education of Topeka, Kansas* ruling of 1954. Holding that "Separate

educational facilities are inherently unequal," the Court finally reversed *Plessy* v. *Ferguson*. The long NAACP struggle to abolish the legal foundation of Jim Crow had been won.

Sources:

Harvard Sitkoff, *A New Deal for Blacks: The Emergence of Civil Rights as a National Issue* (New York: Oxford University Press, 1978);

C. Vann Woodward, *The Strange Career of Jim Crow*, third edition (New York: Oxford University Press, 1974).

HOUSE UN-AMERICAN ACTIVITIES COMMITTEE

House Un-American Activities Committee. The House of Representatives began its work investigating subversive activity by U.S. citizens in 1930 as the Fish Committee and in 1934 as the McCormack Committee. In 1938 the committee was revived as the Dies Committee (after the name of its chairman, Martin Dies, Jr., D–Texas) to investigate the activities of communist and fascist organizations on the home front. Despite the strong anticommunism of Chairman Dies, before and during World War II the committee concentrated on fascist organizations.

The Permanent Committee. In January 1945 the special committee was transformed into a permanent standing committee of the House. In Public Law 601, the seventy-ninth Congress authorized HUAC to investigate the following:

(1) the extent, character and objects of un-American propaganda activities in the United States, (2) the diffusion within the United States of subversive and un-American propaganda that is instigated from foreign countries or of a domestic origin and attacks the principal form of government as guaranteed by our Constitution, and (3) all other questions in relation thereto that would aid Congress in any remedial legislation.

Such a vague and wide-ranging authorization opened the door to mischief by ambitious congressmen.

Communists in Hollywood. It has been estimated that from the middle 1930s to the middle 1950s as many as three hundred Hollywood actors, writers, directors, and designers joined the Communist Party. The former secretary of the Southern California Communist Party estimated that membership in the party reached a wartime high of four thousand. When the Soviet Union was allied with the United States during World War II, ultra-patriotic organizations, such as the Hollywood Writers' Mobilization and the Hollywood Anti-Nazi League, attracted people from the leftist extreme of the political spectrum. In addition, the emerging leftist theatrical unions in Hollywood, and their calls for higher wages for screenwriters and actors, had a large part in recruiting Hollywood movie people into the Communist Party.

Backlash. In 1947 the United States adopted a policy of containment toward the Soviet Union, proposing to stop further Soviet territorial expansion. The change in policy soured U.S.-U.S.S.R. relations and raised wariness about Communists in the United States. In March 1947 Rep. John Rankin, a member of HUAC, called for a cleansing of the film industry. Some HUAC members, such as chairman J. Parnell Thomas, were concerned with possible "Communist propaganda" being injected into Hollywood movies.

Witch–Hunt. At hearings before HUAC on 28–30 October 1947, actors, directors, and writers were "investigated" to determine their political leanings in an effort to purge Hollywood of Communists. The list of witnesses included forty-one names, nineteen of whom were classified as unfriendly. The list of witnesses was filled with stars and industry bigwigs: Walt Disney, Gary Cooper, Rod Taylor, and Ronald Reagan, among others. The one question the committee eventually asked each witness was "Are you now or have you ever been a member of the Communist Party of the United States?"

The Hollywood Ten. Ten individuals, including Dalton Trumbo, Ring Lardner, Jr., Lester Cole, and Albert Maltz, refused to answer the question during the hearings. In November 1947 they were cited for contempt of Congress for invoking either their Fifth Amendment right to be free from self-incrimination or their First Amendment right to freedom of speech and assembly. They were indicted by a grand jury in December and were found guilty of contempt in April 1948. The convictions were upheld on appeal, and the Supreme Court, following the deaths of two liberal justices (Frank Murphy and Wiley Blount Rutledge were replaced by Tom Clark and Sherman Minton, who both supported the government in Cold War cases), declined to hear the appeal in April 1950. The Hollywood Ten went to federal prison, where they were incarcerated with committee chairman J. Parnell Thomas, who had been convicted of padding the payrolls of his congressional staff.

Hiss-Chambers Case. After the war the permanent committee turned its attention almost entirely to the perceived Communist threat. On 31 July 1948 HUAC began to hear evidence from two former Communists, Elizabeth Bentley and Whittaker Chambers, the latter a writer for Henry Luce's *Time* magazine. During his testimony Chambers accused former State Department official Alger Hiss of being a Communist agent. When Hiss heard of Chambers's testimony he demanded to be heard in rebuttal. He appeared on 25 August 1948. This testimony, Chambers's subsequent appearance in front of a New York grand jury, Hiss's libel suit against Chambers, and Hiss's two trials for perjury took the case out of the realm of HUAC and into the regular court system. The conviction of Hiss for perjury in 1950 justified for many the techniques of HUAC.

The Shape of Things to Come. The work of HUAC in the 1940s, while not as wide-ranging as that under the Senate Permanent Investigations Committee under the chairmanship of Joseph McCarthy, was the beginning of

Japanese Americans digging potatoes at the Tule-Lake, California, relocation center

the great search for Communists in American life that dominated the early part of the 1950s. These congressional investigations concentrated attention on the great questions about individual rights and national security that remained for the courts to answer.

Sources:

Mari Jo Buhle, Paul Buhle, and Dan Georgekas, eds., *Encyclopedia of the American Left* (New York: Garland, 1990);

David Caute, *The Great Fear: The Anti-Communist Purge Under Truman and Eisenhower* (New York: Simon & Schuster, 1978);

Bernard F. Dick, *Radical Innocence: A Critical Study of the Hollywood Ten* (Lexington: University of Kentucky Press, 1989);

Kermit L. Hall, *The Oxford Companion to the Supreme Court of the United States* (New York: Oxford University Press, 1992);

Stefan Kanfer, *A Journal of the Plague Years* (New York: Atheneum, 1973).

THE INTERNMENT OF JAPANESE AMERICANS

Japanese Americans to Internment Camps. On 31 March 1942 Japanese American residents along the West Coast of the United States were directed to report to control stations and register the names of all family members. They were then told when and where to report with their families for relocation to an assembly area and then an internment camp. The times for evacuation varied from four days to as much as two weeks. The Japanese Americans were forced under the circumstances to liquidate some or all of their property within that period. Many white Americans took advantage of the situation and offered pennies on the dollar to purchase possessions from those soon to be interned.

Personal Losses. Many Japanese Americans lost their land to foreclosure or were forced to sell at cut-rate prices. Even the U.S. government was not above taking

Entrance to the Manzanar Relocation Center

advantage of the situation. Nearly two thousand internees were assured that their cars would be safely stored by the Federal Reserve Bank. The army soon offered to purchase the vehicles at vastly undervalued prices. Those internees who chose not to sell were notified in late 1942 that their vehicles had been "requisitioned" by the army for use in the war effort.

Relocation Centers. This evacuation and internment came about as the result of Executive Order 9066, which was signed by President Franklin Roosevelt on 19 February 1942. The order provided that "the successful prosecution of the war requires every possible protection against espionage and against sabotage to national defense material, national defense premises, and national defense utilities. . . ." The army orders enforcing Roosevelt's edict mandated a curfew for Japanese Americans living in the area of internment. For the two months following the attack on Pearl Harbor, the president had been under increasing pressure from Gen. John L. DeWitt of the Western Defense Command and various state politicians from California, Oregon, and Washington to "do something about the Japs" living in these areas. When President Roosevelt issued the order, it was partly because of the anxiety over Pearl Harbor. Asian Americans, not just Japanese, also faced racism on the West Coast.

Manzanar. The first operational internment camp was named Manzanar, and it was located in southern California. The name has come to be identified with all internment camps operated by the government from 1942 to 1945. Over these three years, ten camps opened and eventually held approximately 120,000 people for varying periods in California, Arizona, Wyoming, Colorado, Utah, and Arkansas. The evacuees were only allowed to bring with them what they could carry. The final report of the 1983 Commission on Wartime Relocation and Internment of Citizens found property lost to the Japanese Americans through arson, theft, or vandalism was valued between $810 million and $2 billion (in 1983 dollars). The report further placed the total loss of property and income during that period as high as $6.2 billion.

Legal Battles. Not unexpectedly, the roundup and interning of American citizens in camps led to legal fights. The first case to rise to the Supreme Court was *Hirabayashi* v. *United States*. Gordon Hirabayashi, an American-born citizen of Japanese ancestry and a senior at the University of Washington, intentionally violated both the curfew and the order to relocate, saying that to follow the orders would abdicate his rights as a U.S. citizen. He was arrested, convicted, and sentenced to two concurrent three-month sentences. The Supreme Court, which published its decision in the *Hirabayashi* case on 21 June 1943, ruled only on the constitutionality of the curfew and its restriction to those citizens of Japanese ancestry. Writing for a unanimous court, Justice Harlan F. Stone held that Congress and the president could take into account the relative lack of assimilation of Japanese Americans into U.S. society in judging the military risk in allowing freedom of movement for a group whose loyalty "could not be precisely and quickly ascertained." The narrow ruling did not address the larger questions of the legality of the internment.

Korematsu v. United States. The most important case was that of Fred Toyoosaburo Korematsu, a U.S. citizen of Japanese descent. Korematsu was also a worker in a defense-industry job. When the internment began, Korematsu moved to another town, changed his name, and claimed he was of Spanish and Hawaiian descent. He was later arrested, convicted, and sentenced to five years in prison. He was paroled and then interned to a camp in Topaz, Utah. Korematsu's case made it quickly to the Supreme Court, where it was argued in October 1944.

Contradictory Orders. Korematsu argued that the executive order and the Civilian Exclusion Orders issued by the army were conflicting, that, as a defense worker and a Japanese American, he was both forbidden from leaving the exclusion area and forbidden from remaining there. The Court decided on 18 December 1944 that a person cannot be convicted for doing the very thing which it is a crime to fail to do. But it also found, in a decision written by Justice Hugo Black, that the outstanding orders here did not contain such contradictory terms. On 27 March 1942 an order was issued which prohibited Korematsu and all others of Japanese ancestry from leaving the area in which they lived, but that order was only in effect until such time that a future order should permit those individuals to leave the area. The future order was issued on 3 May 1942, and it is for this reason that Korematsu was convicted, since he had not followed the 3 May order to leave the area and report to "assembly areas" prior to transportation to "detention centers."

Racism versus Military Necessity. In Black's opinion, the U.S. Supreme Court found that military need made the actions of the government legal:

> Our task would be simple, our duty clear, were this a case involving the imprisonment of a loyal citizen in a concentration camp because of racial prejudice. Regardless of the true nature of the assembly and relocation areas . . . and we deem it unjustifiable to call them concentration camps with all the ugly connotations that term applies . . . we are dealing specifically with nothing but an exclusion order. To cast this case into outlines of racial prejudice, without reference to the real military dangers which were presented, merely confuses the issue. Korematsu was not excluded from a military area because of hostility to him and his race. He *was* excluded because we are at war with the Japanese empire, because the properly constituted military authorities feared an invasion on our west coast and felt constrained to take proper security measures. . . . We cannot — by availing our-

selves of the calm perspective of hindsight — now say that at that time these actions weren't justified.

Jackson's Dissent. Justice Robert Jackson, who later led the American presence at the Nuremburg war-crime trials, led the dissent:

> Korematsu was born on our soil, of parents born in Japan. The Constitution makes him a citizen of the United States by nativity and a citizen of California by residence. No claim is made that he is not loyal to this country. There is no suggestion that apart from the matter involved here, he is not law abiding and well disposed. Korematsu, however, has been convicted of an act not commonly a crime. It consists merely of being present in the state whereof he is a citizen, near the place where he was born, and where all his life he has lived.

Justice Jackson further noted that the way in which the military orders were written, in his opinion, gave Korematsu only one choice, that being to submit himself to the authorities and undergo examination, custody, and transportation out of the area to be followed by an indeterminate confinement period in detention camps. Jackson also noted that had Korematsu been a German alien enemy, an Italian alien enemy, or a citizen of American-born ancestors convicted of treason, but out on parole, he would not have been subject to the order. Only Korematsu's presence as a person of Japanese ancestry violated the military order. "His conviction for this act, rests solely on the orders of General DeWitt [the military commander of the West Coast] . . . I cannot say, from any evidence before me, that the orders of General DeWitt were not reasonably expedient military precautions, nor could I say that they were. But, even if they were permissible military procedures, I deny that it follows that they are constitutional. If, as the Court holds, it does follow, then we may as well say that any military order will be constitutional and have done with it."

Certified as Loyal. Despite the finding of the orders as legal, the Japanese American interns were able to be "certified" as loyal. They were then allowed to leave the various camps, usually to jobs in the Midwest or the East. Many of the Manzanar emigrants left to work as temporary migrant laborers. During the summer of 1942 thousands of Japanese Americans who volunteered to work as seasonal laborers were credited with saving the sugar beet crop of several western states. On 18 December 1944 it was announced that all relocation centers would be closed before the end of 1945 and the War Relocation Act program would be ended by 30 June 1946.

Belated Apology. In 1988 the U.S. Congress passed a bill formally apologizing to Japanese Americans for their internment in American detention camps. The bill provided that Japanese Americans who had been interned and who were still living would receive a onetime payment of twenty thousand dollars to compensate them in some part for the ordeal through which they had suffered.

Sources:

Camp and Community: Manzanar and the Owens Valley (Fullerton: California State University, Japanese American Oral History Project, 1977);

Peter H. Irons, *Justice at War* (New York: Oxford University Press, 1983).

MILITARY JUSTICE REFORMS

The Brink of Collapse. One of the most controversial areas of the law in the 1940s concerned the administration of military justice. The system of courts-martial that existed prior to the war was set up for a small military, comprising less than 300,000 servicemen. As many as 16.5 million people served in World War II; the existent system of military justice failed to accommodate them. During World War II social scientists, using data from the 1940 census, determined that the armed forces held nearly 30 percent of the nation's potential criminals. They pushed the system to the brink of collapse. Approximately 2 million court-martial convictions were handed down during the war, an average of sixty convictions a day every day. Many of these convictions were arbitrary and punitive. Military law is different than conventional criminal law, and the rights of suspects are more limited. By the end of the war sensational abuses of civil rights by military courts were being publicized in the press, and a public outcry ensued. By the end of the decade the system of military justice in the United States had been radically reformed and more ably met the needs of the large, professional Cold War military.

Abuses. Military justice was a key component in maintaining discipline during World War II. Military tribunals and punishments, for example, were designed to prevent desertions from the battlefront or dereliction of duty that might result in the death or injury of other soldiers. They punished infractions of the rule of war, such as plundering and the rape and massacre of civilians, as well as acts which would be criminal in any environment, such as robbery or narcotics peddling. Military courts were often convened in the field, under the pressure of war. Many abuses resulted. Sentences were harsh and inconsistent. Presiding officers in courts-martial were often untrained in legal procedure and the review of evidence; sometimes they were senior officers pursuing personal vendettas; enlisted men complained of prejudicial treatment by officers. The accused rarely enjoyed adequate counsel or understood clearly the nature of the proceedings; there were almost no opportunities for appealing a sentence. Complaints about brutal treatment in military stockades were common.

Reform. By the end of the war the military responded to such complaints, recognizing that abuses in the system diverted manpower and retarded organizational efficiency. Several committees were established to investigate the military justice system and recommend reforms, including the Ballantine Committee (1943, 1946), the Vanderbilt Committee (1946), and the Doolittle Board (1946). Furthermore, among the millions of servicemen in World War II, many were trained lawyers astonished at the system of military justice. Ernest W. Gibson, after the war the governor of Vermont, was shocked by the abuse of the rights of the accused he had witnessed in the Pacific theater. Franklin Riter, a brigadier general who served in Europe, returned to lead the American Legion campaign for the revision of military justice. Many veterans who returned to law practice after the war made their local bar associations advocates of reform. Such civilians put pressure on the military to speed up the reconstruction of military justice. Their efforts paid off. A systematic army review of cases resulted in the invalidation or reduction of almost 85 percent of sentences. In 1947 and 1948 Congress debated various proposals for reform; the newly created Defense Department organized a committee, headed by Harvard law professor Edmund N. Morgan, to propose revisions to the military code of justice. They framed a new Uniform Code of Military Justice. Among its provisions the code provided for enlisted representation on tribunals where an enlisted man was being judged; counsel was provided during pretrial investigations; a judge advocate general, specially trained in rules of evidence and procedure, was assigned to tribunals; and a Court of Military Appeals was created to hear appeals. Congress debated the code throughout 1949 and passed it in 1950. It became effective 31 May 1951.

Source:

William T. Generous, Jr., *Swords and Scales: The Development of the Uniform Code of Military Justice* (Port Washington, N.Y.: Kennikat Press, 1973).

THE NUREMBERG WAR CRIMES TRIAL

Judgment Day. Following the end of World War II, the Allies (United States, France, Great Britain, and the Union of Soviet Socialist Republics) established a military court to try Axis leaders for war crimes. The most famous of these trials were held at Nuremberg, Germany, from November 1945 through October 1946.

Origins of the Tribunal. On 8 August 1945 representatives from the provisional government of France, the United States, Great Britain, and the Soviet Union met in London and signed an agreement that included a charter to set up an international military tribunal to try major Axis leaders for crimes against peace (such as planning war); crimes against humanity (genocide); war crimes (murder or ill-treatment of civilians or prisoners of war); and conspiracy to commit crimes listed in the first three groups. The tribunal consisted of one member, plus an alternate, from each of the four countries who had signed the London agreement. Eventually, nineteen other countries accepted the terms of the agreement.

The Twenty-Four. At the first trial of Nazi leaders, twenty-four individuals were initially scheduled to be prosecuted. One committed suicide in prison prior to trial (Robert Ley), and one other was found to be physically and mentally unfit to be tried (Gustav Krupp von Bohlen und Halbuch). The remaining twenty-two defendants appeared in court through 216 court sessions, heard

Courtroom during the Nuremberg trials

evidence presented against them, and were allowed to call witnesses or cross-examine witnesses brought against them. Eleven months after the trial began, verdicts were entered. Twelve of the Nazis were sentenced to death, including Alfred Rosenberg, Joachim von Ribbentrop, Wilhelm Keitel, Martin Bormann (tried in absentia), and Hermann Goering. Three were acquitted; four were sentenced to up to twenty years in prison; and three, including Rudolf Hess, were sentenced to life imprisonment.

The Nazi Defense. The major defenses offered by the Nazis were that they were only following the orders of their superiors and that the trial was an exercise in adjudication ex post facto (trial for a crime that was not a crime when committed). The tribunal rejected these defenses, holding that the crimes committed were crimes under international law before World War II and holding further that men commit crimes and that only by punishing the men who actually commit the crimes could the provisions of international law be enforced against nations.

Aftermath. After the initial trial of the Nazi leaders, thousands of other lesser soldiers and Nazi officials were prosecuted by different military courts run by different Allied governments. The Americans held 809 trials in Germany and Japan, involving over 1,600 defendants. The French tried over 2,100 people, and the British tried nearly 1,000.

Source:
Joseph E. Persico, *Nuremberg: Infamy on Trial* (New York: Viking, 1994).

THE SMITH ACT

Concern Over Subversives. Enacted by the U.S. Congress and signed by President Franklin D. Roosevelt in 1940, the Alien Registration Act, best known as the Smith Act, was one of the most controversial laws passed in response to concerns over possibly subversive groups operating in the United States. A product of prewar anx-

ieties, the Smith Act was proposed by Rep. Howard W. Smith of Virginia. The controversial aspects of the law were the sections that made it illegal to hold certain public opinions and that outlawed certain kinds of speech. Section I stipulated a ten-thousand-dollar fine and ten years in prison for attempting to undermine the morale of the armed forces. Sections II and III — the heart of the act and the sections which gave pause to so many civil libertarians — outlined the same penalties for anyone convicted who "advocates, abets, advises, or teaches" the violent overthrow of the U.S. government. It also outlawed the publication or distribution of any material advocating revolution and the organization or membership in any group advocating subversion. The act also had prohibitions against conspiracy to violate any provisions of the law.

The First Convictions. The act was first invoked in 1941 against twenty-eight members of Trotskyite factions of the Socialist Workers Party in Minnesota and the Minneapolis, Minnesota, Teamsters Local 544. The Trotskyites were accused of denouncing what they called the imperialist war aims of the U.S. government. Their arrest and trial under the Smith Act was supported by the Communist Party U.S.A., which bitterly opposed the Trotskyite opposition to the war. Eighteen of those arrested actually faced trial in 1943. All eighteen were convicted and sentenced in 1944 to terms ranging from twelve to eighteen months in prison.

Reluctance to Prosecute. After the entrance of the United States into the war in December 1941 as an ally of the Soviet Union, prosecutors were reluctant to use the Smith Act against domestic Communists. This reluctance folded after the war. In 1948 the Smith Act was repealed, but it was revised immediately and reenacted, effective on 1 September 1948, though with a significant difference. The reconstituted Smith Act required a showing of overt acts made in furtherance of an attempt to advocate or actually attempt to overthrow the government by force. Thinking subversive thoughts was not prohibited by the new Smith Act.

The 1948 Trials. In 1948 eleven Communist Party members were arrested under the new provisions of the Smith Act. Under intense pressure from Republicans to prove he was not soft on communism, President Harry S Truman directed the Justice Department to prepare indictments for the National Board of the Communist Party U.S.A. In 1949 the group was tried and convicted. The eleven were released on bail of $260,000 provided by the Civil Rights Congress, a front organization operated in the interests of the Communist Party. They immediately appealed to the Second District Court of Appeals, where the convictions were upheld under an opinion by Judge Learned Hand. The case was appealed to the U.S. Supreme Court, which affirmed the ruling of the Second Court of Appeals. The 1951 Supreme Court case, *Dennis* v. *United States,* upheld the constitutionality of the Smith Act and modified its speech provisions, lessen-

TWO VIEWS ON THE SMITH ACT

"If Government is aware that a group aiming at its overthrow is attempting to indoctrinate its members and to commit them to a course whereby they will strike when the leaders feel the circumstances permit, action by the Government is required. . . . Certainly an attempt to overthrow the Government by force, even though doomed from the outset because of inadequate numbers or powers of the revolutionists, is a sufficient evil for Congress to prevent."

Fred M. Vinson, chief justice, U.S. Supreme Court

"It is a commonplace that there may be a grain of truth in the most uncouth doctrine, however false and repellent the balance may be. Suppressing advocates of overthrow inevitably will also silence critics who do not advocate overthrow but fear that their criticism may be so construed."

Felix Frankfurter, associate justice, U.S. Supreme Court

ing the protection of free speech. Writing for the court, Chief Justice Fred Vinson wrote that in each case the court "must ask whether the gravity of the 'evil' discounted by its improbability, justifies such invasion of free speech as is necessary to avoid the danger." With the Smith Act upheld, four of the eleven, including future Communist Party chairman Gus Hall, jumped bail. All were eventually recaptured, one not until 1957.

The Smith Act Legacy. During the 1940s and the 1950s, 141 individuals were charged with violations of the Smith Act. Because of appeals and later Supreme Court decisions (*Smith* v. *United States* [1957] and *Scales* v. *United States*), only twenty-nine actually served time. Despite the low number of those actually incarcerated, the Smith Act posed a serious impediment to free speech and political activity by the political Left. Although its tenets have been softened over the years, the basic principles of the balance between individual liberties after government action have yet to be abandoned by the Court.

Sources:

Mari Jo Buhle, Paul Buhle, and Dan Georgekas, eds., *Encyclopedia of the American Left* (New York: Garland, 1990);

David Caute, *The Great Fear: The Anti-Communist Purge Under Truman and Eisenhower* (New York: Simon & Schuster, 1978);

Kermit L. Hall, *The Oxford Companion to the Supreme Court of the United States* (New York: Oxford University Press, 1992);

The Smith Act and the Supreme Court (New York: American Civil Liberties Union, 1952).

SPECTACULAR CRIMES OF THE 1940S

The Black Dahlia Case. The 1947 murder of Elizabeth Short is notable in that it garnered the greatest number of spurious confessions in California history. Short, who had become known as the Black Dahlia for her propensity always to dress in black, was born in 1925. By the age of twenty-two she had achieved a reputation as an aspiring actress who would go to bed with anyone who could possibly offer her a part in a movie. On 15 January 1947 her naked body was found cut in half and eviscerated in a vacant lot in a Los Angeles suburb. On her thigh were carved the initials "BD," presumably for Black Dahlia. Her murder seemed to bring out the worst among the psychologically disturbed in the Los Angeles area. The police were overwhelmed with the number of people who confessed to the murder. However, at least two tantalizing leads developed. A letter writer sent Short's social security card, birth certificate, and address book (with one page missing) to the police but never followed up with a promised letter. Another and possibly the most promising confession involved a twenty-nine-year-old army corporal who seemed to possess many facts related to her death. He was later determined to be psychologically unbalanced and was eventually dismissed as a suspect.

The Lonely Hearts Killers. Martha Beck, along with her lover Raymond Fernandez, may have been responsible for twenty murders in the 1940s, although they were only charged and convicted in three. Beck and Fernandez were known as the Lonely Hearts Killers, as they teamed up to swindle lonely women who advertised for companionship in the "lonely hearts" sections of local newspapers. Although Beck and Fernandez seemed almost normal, the testimony at their trial showed them to be anything but. Fernandez proposed to Janet Fay, an Albany, New York, widow. Fay sold her house in Albany and traveled to Valley Stream, Long Island, to meet her fiancé Fernandez and his "sister" Beck. After gaining control of Fay's money, Beck and Fernandez beat her to death with a hammer. A few weeks later Beck and Fernandez killed Delphine Downing, a Grand Rapids, Michigan, widow. A few days after Downing was shot, Beck drowned Downing's twenty-month-old child in a bathtub. They buried the corpses in cement in the cellar and went to see a movie. Upon their return the police had arrived, having been tipped off by suspicious neighbors who had not seen Downing for some time. They were arrested and subsequently convicted for murder and sentenced to death. The Lonely Hearts Murders led to restrictions on these types of clubs, but little could be done to establish safeguards against murderous predators.

Caryl Chessman. Caryl Chessman was born in 1921 and was put to death in 1960. What occurred in the intervening years led to four books, one of which was a best-seller and was made into a movie. In January 1948 Chessman had been on parole for six weeks when he was arrested as a possible suspect in the Red Light Bandit attacks in Los Angeles. The attacks occurred in secluded areas — local lovers' lanes — where the bandit would rob victims. He tricked and confused them, using a flashing

In the critical World War II year of 1944 a huge "I Am an American Day" ceremony was held in Central Park, New York City, on 21 May. Many thousands of people were present, including many new citizens. The speaker was Learned Hand, whose long tenure on the Second Circuit Court of Appeals had made him the best known judge who was not sitting on the Supreme Court. His brief address was so eloquent and so moving that the text immediately became the object of wide demand. It was quickly printed and reprinted and also put into anthologies. The impact was so great that Judge Hand was invited to address a similar gathering the next year. The address went as follows:

> We have gathered here to affirm a faith, a faith in a common purpose, a common conviction, a common devotion. Some of us have chosen America as the land of our adoption; the rest have come from those who did the same. For this reason we have some right to consider ourselves a picked group, a group of those who had the courage to break from the past and brave the dangers and the loneliness of a strange land. What was the object that nerved us, or those who went before us, to this choice? We sought liberty; freedom from oppression, freedom from want, freedom to be ourselves. This we then sought; this we now believe that we are by way of winning. What do we mean when we say that first of all we seek liberty? I often wonder whether we do not rest our hopes too much upon constitutions, upon laws and upon courts. These are false hopes; believe me, these are false hopes. Liberty lies in the hearts of men and women; when it dies there, no constitution, no law, no court can save it; no constitution, no law, no court can even do much to help it. While it lies there it needs no constitution, no law, no court to save it. And what is this liberty which must lie in the hearts of men and women? It is not the ruthless, the unbridled will; it is not freedom to do as one likes. That is the denial of liberty, and leads straight to its overthrow. A society in which men recognize no check upon their freedom soon becomes a society where freedom is the possession of only a savage few; as we have learned to our sorrow.
>
> What then is the spirit of liberty? I cannot define it; I can only tell you my own faith. The spirit of liberty is the spirit which is not too sure that it is right; the spirit of liberty is the spirit which seeks to understand the minds of other men and women; the spirit of liberty is the spirit which weighs their interests alongside its own without bias; the spirit of liberty remembers that not even a sparrow falls to earth unheeded; the spirit of liberty is the spirit of Him who, near two thousand years ago, taught mankind that lesson it has never learned, but has never quite forgotten; that there may be a kingdom where the least shall be heard and considered side by side with the greatest. And now in that spirit, that spirit of an America which has never been, and which may never be; nay, which never will be except as the conscience and courage of Americans create it; yet in the spirit of that America which lies hidden in some form in the aspirations of us all; in the spirit of that America for which our young men are at this moment fighting and dying; in that spirit of liberty and of America I ask you to rise and with me pledge our faith in the glorious destiny of our beloved country.

Source: Learned Hand, *The Spirit of Liberty: Papers and Addresses of Learned Hand*, collected by Irving Dilliard (New York: Knopf, 1952).

---

red light similar to that found on police cars. On several occasions he forced a female victim into his car, left the scene, and raped her. Although Chessman confessed to the crimes, he claimed that his confession had been tortured out of him by police. Nonetheless, Chessman was found guilty under the "Little Lindbergh" law of California, which made it a crime to kidnap someone and cause bodily harm to that person. Although he had not killed or held anyone for ransom, he was sentenced to death. Eight years of appeals followed, and eight scheduled dates of execution were postponed. During his legal fight he became famous, and millions of people wrote letters or signed petitions on his behalf. Included in the list of notable persons who opposed his death were the queen of Belgium, Norman Mailer, Eleanor Roosevelt, Billy Graham, and Robert Frost. On 2 May 1960 Chessman lost his fight. Although a stay of execution had been issued by federal judge Louis Goodman, his secretary, relaying the notice of the stay, misdialed the number to the prison. By the time she finally got through, the cyanide pellets had been dropped. Caryl Chessman was dead.

Who Killed Carlo Tresca? The answer to that question is, most likely, the Mafia. Carlo Tresca was born the son of a wealthy landowning family in Sulmona, Italy, in 1879. By the middle of the 1890s, however, the family had lost its land and privileged status due to a series of bad investments and a poor economy. He was deeply disappointed by these events, and his disenchantment with the status quo led him to turn to anarchism as a political philosophy. He found employment as the editor of the Socialist Party newspaper in Italy but was forced to flee to America when his diatribes earned him too many enemies. It was in America that he eventually became well known as an anti-Communist and an anti-Fascist. In that role he used much of his energy to rage against Benito Mussolini in the Italian-language newspaper that he published, *Il Martello*. Mussolini had his name placed on a death list in 1931, but it was not until 1943 that the sentence was actually carried out. Vito Genovese, a leader of the New York Mafia, had been forced to leave the United States in the 1930s in order to escape a murder indictment. He managed to ingratiate himself with Mussolini and the Fascist cause. After Mussolini complained to him about Tresca's anti-Fascist activities in America, Genovese informed Mussolini that he would take care of the problem. On 11 January 1943, as Carlo Tresca crossed Fifteenth Street in New York with his friend, Giuseppe Calabi, they paused under a streetlamp. Another man stepped from the darkness and shot Tresca once in the back and once in the head, killing him instantly. For several years the crime was listed as an unsolved political assassination; however, it is now commonly believed that Vito Genovese ordered the killing to ingratiate himself further with Mussolini. It is believed that the hit was carried out by Carmine Galante (later a top Mafia leader who was himself killed in 1979).

The Alcatraz Prison Rebellion and Escape. On 2 May 1945 inmates at the Alcatraz federal prison in San Francisco Bay staged a riot and, securing weapons, fought a gun battle with prison guards in an effort to shoot their way out. Notable was the fact that for the first time in the history of Alcatraz, inmates were able to obtain firearms during their attempt to escape. The escape plan began to take shape when three inmates, Bernie Coy, Joseph "Dutch" Cretzer, and Miran "Buddy" Thompson, joined forces at Alcatraz. Coy had designed and built a bar spreader and had figured out a way to gain access to the prison armory. The three ringleaders and three other inmates staged an uprising in a cellblock and took nine guards as hostages. U.S. Marines were ordered to the island prison to reinforce the officers. On the second day of the riot, sporadic fighting continued between the guards and convicts. The inmate leaders attempted to negotiate a deal with prison officials, but this was rebuffed with a demand for total surrender. On the third day of the uprising, when it became apparent that the inmates would not prevail, Thompson ordered Cretzer to kill the hostages since they were the only ones who could identify Thompson as being involved in the escape attempt. Against Coy's orders not to kill any hostages, Cretzer shot all nine. During the last stages of the battle, Coy and Cretzer were killed. Secure in the belief that his involvement in the uprising would remain unknown, Thompson returned to his cell. Ironically, only one of the guards shot by Cretzer had actually been killed, and Thompson was later convicted of murder and sentenced to death. Thompson became the first person put to death in the California gas chamber on 3 December 1948.

The Lynching of Willie Earle. Willie Earle had the dubious distinction of being an example of not only one of the most vicious lynchings in American history but also being the subject of one of the most shameful examples of justice denied as well. Earle was taken into custody for questioning in the stabbing death of a taxi driver near Liberty, South Carolina. Although he was not charged with the murder, word spread of his arrest and a lynch mob, armed with guns and knives, broke into the Pickens County Jail and forced the jailer to turn Earle over to them. He was taken to Saluda Dam, "ques-

tioned," and forced to "confess" by the mob. Earle was then driven to Greenville County, where he was beaten, stabbed, and finally shot. During the lynching, the mob reportedly cut large chunks of flesh from his still-living body. The viciousness of the murder shocked the nation. The FBI investigated and identified twenty-eight persons who were part of the mob, twenty-six of whom eventually confessed their involvement. Despite the confessions and a minimal defense, the all-white jury found all of the defendants not guilty.

Howard Unruh, Mass Murderer. On 5 September 1949 Howard Unruh entered the annals of American crime history as one of its most bizarre and vicious mass murderers. On that day he began his killing spree at 9:20 A.M. when he entered a shoe repair shop in Camden, New Jersey, and shot the proprietor Joe Pilkarchik to death with a 9-mm Luger. He then entered the barbershop next door and shot six-year-old Orvis Smith to death, followed immediately by shooting the barber who had been cutting the boy's hair. He then sought out druggist Maurice Cohen, killing him too before going back outside and indiscriminately shooting pedestrians, car drivers, and a three-year-old boy who was looking out a window. He only stopped when he ran out of ammunition and calmly returned to his home. In twelve minutes he had killed thirteen people. The police surrounded his house and exchanged gunfire with him. During the firefight an assistant editor from the *Camden Courier-Post* called the Unruh home and, much to his surprise, found him at the other end. The editor had a short conversation with Unruh during the gunfight and asked the murderer how many he had killed, to which Unruh reportedly replied, "I don't know yet. I haven't counted them, but it looks like a pretty good score." Shortly thereafter, tear gas forced him out of the house, whereupon he informed police, "I'm no psycho, I have a good mind." The authorities did not agree. He was judged insane and committed to a mental institution.

Terry Almodovar, Murderer. On 2 November 1942 the body of Louisa Almodovar was found on a hill in Central Park in New York City. The police immediately listed the husband, Terry Almodovar, as a possible suspect but did not discount the possibility that Louisa was killed by an unknown park criminal. Terry Almodovar seemed to have an airtight alibi. At the time of Louisa's death, her husband had been at a dance hall and had twenty-two girls who supported his story as having been there the whole time. At the time the science of forensics was rapidly progressing. The police delivered Terry's suit to the medical examiner, who made a spectrogram of the dirt from the trousers. The dirt matched that taken from the scene where the body was found. Terry still insisted that he had not been to Central Park on the night of the murder. The medical examiner, Dr. Alexander Gettler, also found grass spikelets in the cuff of Terry's pants, and these matched those found at the scene of the murder as well. Dr. Gettler turned for assistance to a botany professor at the City College of New York, Joseph Copeland. Professor Copeland identified the spikelets as *Pancium dicoth milleflorium,* a rare species in the New York area. It only grew in one area of the city, the small hill where the murder had been committed. When informed of this Terry Almodovar suddenly remembered that he had gone through Central Park in September of 1942. Professor Copeland informed the authorities that the spikelets were at a stage of development that could not have occurred before 10 or 15 October but could certainly have been at that stage of blooming on 1 November, the night of the murder. On 9 March 1943 Terry Almodovar went to the electric chair . . . done in by a blade of grass.

Source:
Carl Sifakis, *The Encyclopedia of American Crime* (New York: Facts On File, 1982).

THE SUPREME COURT IN THE 1940S

Blows to Stare Decisis. In law the doctrine of stare decisis (to stand by decided matters) is the policy of making contemporary judgments according to previous judgments and decisions. The doctrine is fundamentally conservative, binding the law to the past, regardless of current circumstances. In the twentieth century it was often challenged by the judicial philosophies of sociological jurisprudence and legal realism, which integrate contemporary concerns and social science into legal decisions. Beginning in the late 1930s and early 1940s, the Supreme Court began to undergo a dramatic change from stare decisis to legal realism. The effect of the Great Depression on law set these changes into motion. The Supreme Court refused to alter contractual and constitutional law to meet the economic emergency and invalidated one New Deal program after another. The Supreme Court also affirmed segregation statutes at a time when civil rights activists inside and outside of the Roosevelt administration were pressing for the dismantling of Jim Crow laws. After 1936 the Roosevelt administration and much of the public viewed the Supreme Court as obstructing progress, stifling reform through its rigid adherence to stare decisis. Roosevelt's court-packing plan of 1937 was a heavy-handed attempt to shift the Court's rulings. It failed, but as Roosevelt appointees Hugo Black (1937), Stanley Reed (1938), Felix Frankfurter (1939), Frank Murphy (1940), and Robert Jackson (1941) took their place on the bench, they brought with them legal realism and a penchant for championing the underdog that shifted the court away from stare decisis and toward liberalism.

The Preferred Freedoms Doctrine. Harlan Stone gave a hint of things to come in the opinion he wrote as an associate justice in the case of *United States* v. *Carolene Products* (1938). In a footnote he argued that the Court was justified in taking a tolerant view of governmental economic policies, but it should give "more exacting judicial scrutiny" to any policy that restricted political processes or was hostile to "discrete or insular minorities."

During his subsequent tenure as chief justice, from 1941 to 1946, the Supreme Court did in fact adopt this position, eventually leading to a string of significant decisions in civil rights cases, and ultimately to one of the most important civil rights cases up to that point, the 1954 *Brown* v. *Board of Education* case on school desegregation.

Support for Civil Liberties and Civil Rights. During the 1940s, the Court began to establish its support of civil liberties through a series of decisions, including the famous Jehovah's Witnesses cases. The Jehovah's Witnesses religious sect became one of the most important litigants to appear before the Supreme Court. In the ten years between 1938 and 1948, they brought roughly twenty cases before the Court. The first case in which the Court ever fused the words of the First Amendment regarding free exercise of religion into the meaning of the Fourteenth Amendment was a Jehovah's Witnesses case (*Cantwell* v. *Connecticut* [1940]). The Jehovah's Witnesses believe that the Second Coming of Jesus Christ is imminent, and in order to reach as many as possible before this event, they utilized an aggressive approach to door-to-door evangelism. The aggressive nature of the efforts and the content of the literature that was distributed (much of it was anti-Catholic) upset many and led to efforts by local communities to restrict the activities of the Witnesses. The Court struck down many of these ordinances as infringing on the right of freedom of religion. However, the Court did support laws which regulated the time, place, and manner of evangelical efforts. For example, the Court held that the states could regulate child labor or require the sect to obtain a license to hold a parade on public streets.

New Constitutional Doctrine. Perhaps the most significant new doctrine to develop from the 1940s was the Court's broadened interpretation of the due process clause of the Fourteenth Amendment. This amendment essentially states that no state shall deprive any person of life, liberty, or property without due process of law. The privileges and immunities clause guarantees that no state shall make any law which abridges the rights of a citizen of another state. Almost all of the rights of criminal defendants that are protected by the Bill of Rights have been applied to the states through the Fourteenth Amendment, including the right to a public trial (*In re Oliver,* 1948).

Other Significant Decisions. In *Avery* v. *Alabama* (1940) the Court held that the right to counsel must include the opportunity to consult with a lawyer and prepare a defense. That same year the Court held that a confession obtained by force violated the due process clause of the Fourteenth Amendment and reversed the death sentences of four blacks (*Chambers* v. *Florida*). In *Smith* v. *Texas* (1940) the Court held that an indictment by a grand jury from which blacks were excluded must be struck down. In 1942 the Court declared Georgia's "peonage law" (a form of involuntary servitude), in which a debtor was forced to work off his debt on the creditor's

THE TRIAL OF THE NAZI SABOTEURS

Although there were few reports of war sabotage on the home front during World War II, one case was so spectacular as to generate much press attention. On 13 and 17 June 1942 German submarines landed two specially trained groups of Nazi saboteurs on Long Island and in Florida. They intended to destroy several aluminum plants. All the saboteurs had lived in the United States before the war, were fluent in English, and knew American customs. They were nonetheless promptly arrested. The New York saboteurs, landing less than a mile from a Coast Guard station, had their cache of explosives discovered and were caught in Manhattan within hours. They eventually revealed to the FBI the existence of the Florida team, the members of which were also arrested. President Roosevelt, determined to make an example of the saboteurs, convened a seven-man military tribunal to judge the saboteurs and execute them. The saboteurs appealed their case to the Supreme Court, arguing the president had no right to convene the military commission. The Supreme Court disagreed, citing the president's constitutional war emergency powers. On 8 August 1942 President Roosevelt announced that two of the saboteurs had been given lengthy jail terms. The other six of the saboteurs were executed in the electric chair.

land, to be unconstitutional under the Thirteenth Amendment, which abolished slavery. In the 1943 case of *McNabb* v. *United States,* the Court found that an accused person must be taken before a judicial representative without delay after his arrest. In *Smith* v. *Allwright* (1943), exclusion of blacks from a political party convention was held unconstitutional. In *Bob-Lo Excursion Co.* v. *Michigan* (1948) the Court ruled that the Michigan Civil Rights Act guaranteeing equal accommodations on public carriers is legal.

Time of Transition. During the 1940s the Supreme Court began the transition from a jurisprudence based on the rights of and limits on government to one more interested in the constitutional rights of individuals. The terms of Harlan Stone (1941–1946) and Fred Vinson (1946–1953) as chief justice brought the development of legal principles and habits of reasoning that had revolutionary effects on American society in the Supreme Court under Earl Warren in the 1950s and 1960s.

Source:
Kermit L. Hall, ed., *Oxford Companion to the Supreme Court* (New York: Oxford University Press, 1992).

THE UNITED NATIONS

Legacy of Violence and Disorder. The push for world government, or at least a code of international law, reached unprecedented heights during World War II and its aftermath. With the memory of the destruction and disillusion of World War I still widely held and the failure of the League of Nations, the outbreak of World War II gave impetus to the need for some structure which could rectify the situations which gave rise to worldwide violence.

The Atlantic Charter. The most far-reaching attempt to codify international law began in August 1941 with a meeting between British prime minister Winston Churchill and U.S. president Franklin D. Roosevelt. The two agreed to a declaration of principles of fighting and ending World War II, of which the United States was not yet officially a participant. Called the Atlantic Charter by Churchill and Roosevelt, the declaration contained many of the ideas later used in the United Nations Charter, including the following provisions: no territorial change would occur after the war without the agreement of the people of the lands concerned; all people had the right to choose their form of government; all states would be guaranteed access to raw materials and world trade; all states could adopt the goal of abandoning the use of force. On 1 January 1942 the twenty-six nations allied in the war against the Axis powers agreed to the Atlantic Charter and promised not to make a "separate peace or armistice" with the Axis powers.

Dumbarton Oaks. As the war progressed seemingly inexorably toward victory, work continued on a structure of world security. The conference held at Dumbarton Oaks, a private estate near Washington, D.C., from 21 August to 7 October 1944 worked to set up for an international security organization to be founded after the war. The participating nations were the United States, China, the Soviet Union, and Great Britain. Agreement was reached on 90 percent of the proposals which concerned the United Nations, as the security organization was to be called; the General Assembly; the International Court of Justice; and the Economic and Social Council.

The Yalta Conference. At the Yalta Conference of 4–11 February 1945, the leaders of the Soviet Union, the United States, and Great Britain reviewed, completed, and approved the work of the Dumbarton Oaks conference and called for a conference to be held in San Francisco, California, beginning 25 April 1945 in order to prepare the United Nations Charter. For the next few months the nations of the world studied the proposals made at Dumbarton Oaks and Yalta in order to prepare amendments and their own positions at the San Francisco conference.

The San Francisco Conference. The San Francisco conference, known officially as the United Nations Conference on International Organization, began on schedule and ran until 25 June 1945. Delegates from fifty

The dedication of the United Nations Headquarters in New York, New York, 24 October 1949

nations approved the United Nations Charter on the final day. It came into force when the United States, the Soviet Union, France, Great Britain, and China and a majority of the other fifty countries deposited their instruments of ratification. This occurred on 24 October 1945, which is now known as United Nations Day.

Goals and Limits. The goal of preventing war and torture has not met with overwhelming success. The United Nations, however, at least provides a venue for discussing the problems which start wars, in addition to providing an outlet for discussing world problems.

HEADLINE MAKERS

FELIX FRANKFURTER

1882-1965

ASSOCIATE JUSTICE OF THE U.S. SUPREME COURT

Roosevelt and Frankfurter. Felix Frankfurter joined the Supreme Court at a critical juncture in its history. Only a few years before, the conservative justices of the Court had barely survived an attempt by President Roosevelt to "pack the Court" with younger, more liberal members who Roosevelt hoped would sanction the president's New Deal policies. Roosevelt lost the battle, but he succeeded in pushing the court into a more liberal direction and gained several appointments in subsequent years. Frankfurter was one of the first new justices appointed by Roosevelt. He joined the Court when it began a shift toward approving greater civil rights for individuals and a broader, more liberal interpretation of the Constitution.

Background. Felix Frankfurter was born in Vienna, Austria, on 15 November 1882. His father, Leopold, brought the family to New York City in 1894, where he set up shop as a linen merchant. Felix became a U.S. citizen when his father was naturalized in 1898. Felix received a B.A. from the College of the City of New York in 1902 and entered Harvard Law School the following year. Upon his graduation from Harvard in 1906, he became an associate in a New York law firm and a year later joined the staff of the U.S. Attorney. While working in this office under the tutelege of Henry L. Stimson, he was first exposed to public service and developed a lifelong interest in federal law. Frankfurter later worked as a legal adviser to Stimson when Stimson was appointed secretary of war under President William Howard Taft. In 1914 he accepted an appointment to teach at Harvard Law School, where he taught until his appointment as an associate justice on 30 January 1939.

Radical Advocate. During Frankfurter's early years as a lawyer, he developed an abiding sense of history and tradition, upon which he drew to become an expert in areas of law that relied heavily on procedure. This attention to following proper procedure in the law led him to side with those people who during the early part of the twentieth century were often the victims of judicial errors brought on more by hysteria than attention to the law. After World War I he was one of the original founders of the American Civil Liberties Union and became identified with several radical causes and cases of the time, including that of Sacco and Vanzetti, two Italian anarchists convicted of murder under suspicious circumstances. Frankfurter lost his attempt to save their lives, but by pointing out the flaws in the government case, he drew attention to the bias against his clients due to their political beliefs and made Sacco and Vanzetti a cause célèbre.

New Dealer. In 1928 Frankfurter was asked by Gov. Franklin D. Roosevelt of New York for help concerning the regulation of public utilities. When Roosevelt was elected president in 1932, he offered Frankfurter the post of solicitor general of the United States, which Frankfurter declined. Despite this, Roosevelt often turned to him for advice in establishing his New Deal programs, especially in areas like the regulation of stocks and bonds. Frankfurter privately disagreed with President Roosevelt's court-packing plan of 1937; nonetheless, he provided the president with verbal and written ammunition used in criticizing the Supreme Court's obstructionist record on New Deal legislation.

Rights of the Individual. Frankfurter was appointed to fill the seat vacated by Justice Benjamin Cardozo's death in 1938. He sat on the Supreme Court during a time when civil rights and liberties were beginning to come to the forefront of public debate. During the 1940s he led the Court in defending the rights to equal protection and guarantees of due process. In *McNabb* v. *United States* (1947) he led the Court in forbidding the use of confessions obtained during lengthy preliminary detentions of suspected criminals. He dissented in *Harris* v. *United States* (1947), disagreeing with the majority's approval of a warrantless search.

The Public Good. Although a defender of individual rights, Justice Frankfurter did not believe in an absolute individualism superseding the rule of law. While often leading the fight for protection of individual rights, he nonetheless wrote several decisions favoring the general good over individual liberties, most notably in *Minersville School District* v. *Gobitis.* Justice Frankfurter suffered a stroke in April 1962 and retired from the Supreme Court in August of that year. He was awarded the Presidential Medal of Freedom (America's highest civilian award) in 1963. He died in 1965.

Source:
Melvin I. Vrovsky, *Felix Frankfurter, Judicial Restraint, and Individual Liberties* (Boston: Twayne, 1991).

ALGER HISS

1904-

LAWYER, DIPLOMAT, CONVICTED PERJURER

Victim or Spy? To some, Alger Hiss was a person who was in the wrong place at the wrong time. To others, he was a Communist sympathizer and spy. But whether he was unjustly accused of a crime he did not commit or whether he was a spy who escaped justice may never be truly known. What is certain is that his presence on the national scene at a critical point in American history serves to highlight the antisubversive feelings in America during the 1940s and the period leading up to the McCarthy "Red Scare" of the 1950s.

Quick Rise to the Top. Alger Hiss was born in Baltimore, Maryland, on 11 November 1904. After graduating from Harvard Law School in 1929, he was a law clerk for Supreme Court justice Oliver Wendell Holmes between 1929 and 1930. He entered the service of the federal government in 1933 and in 1936 went to work in the State Department. By 1945 he had risen far enough in the State Department ranks to act as an adviser to President Roosevelt at the Yalta Conference in 1945. Subsequently, he briefly served as temporary secretary-general of the United Nations at the San Francisco conference in the late spring of 1945. In 1946 he was elected president of the Carnegie Endowment for International Peace, which he held until 1949.

The Pumpkin Papers. In August 1948 Whittaker Chambers, an editor at *Time* magazine, appeared before the House Un-American Activities Committee and accused Hiss of belonging to the same underground Communist organization that Chambers had been a member

of prior to World War II. Chambers claimed to have received secret State Department documents from Hiss for delivery to the Soviets. An investigation led by Congressman Richard M. Nixon included a trip to Chambers's farm where he produced microfilm of documents allegedly produced by Hiss, from their hiding place in a hollowed-out pumpkin. The unusual nature of the so-called "Pumpkin Papers" and the high level of government in which Hiss circulated helped thrust Congressman Nixon to the forefront of public interest and helped fuel the fire of those who believed that Communists were infiltrating the U.S. government.

Lucky Break? By the time the espionage charge had been leveled by Chambers, the statute of limitations to charge Hiss with spying had run out. However, Hiss was eventually tried on perjury charges related to his testimony before Congress that he had never met Chambers before. His first trial in 1949 ended in a hung jury. Retried in 1950, he was convicted and served three years of a five-year sentence. He was disbarred in 1951.

Vindication Denied. Over the years since, Hiss and his supporters have put forth compelling arguments that "evidence" was mishandled and possibly invented. He made several attempts to reopen his case after the Freedom of Information Act was passed in 1975, on the grounds that evidence which would have exonerated him was withheld from the courts. To date, his attempts have not met with success. He was readmitted to the Massachusetts bar on 5 August 1975. He has reconciled himself to the probability that the ultimate judges of his guilt or innocence will be historians of the future.

Sources:
Alger Hiss, *Recollections of a Life* (New York: Holt, 1988);
Allen Weinstein, *Perjury: The Hiss-Chambers Case* (New York: Knopf, 1978).

CHARLES HOUSTON

1895-1950

LAWYER AND CIVIL RIGHTS LEADER

Mr. Civil Rights. While some may say that Martin Luther King, Jr., or Thurgood Marshall led the fight for civil rights in the twentieth century, most historians would agree that the real trailblazer was Charles Houston. In fact, his successor as NAACP legal counsel, Thurgood Marshall (a Supreme Court justice from 1967 to 1991), stated at the opening of the new Howard University Law School building in 1958 that Charles Houston was the rightful holder of the title "The First Mr. Civil Rights."

Artillery. Charles Hamilton Houston was born in

Washington, D.C., on 3 September 1895. He graduated from high school at the age of fifteen and enrolled in Amherst College, where he received his B.A. degree in 1915. During World War I, after completing the Negro officers' training camp, he was commissioned a first lieutenant in the infantry and subsequently attended the army's field artillery school. Houston entered the field artillery precisely because the prevailing "wisdom" of the time was that African Americans were unable to complete the requirements for this branch of the service since it involved complex mathematics, and Houston's intent was to disprove this belief. After successfully completing the training, he was assigned overseas until 1919.

Lawyer. Upon his return from the war, Houston chose to follow in the footsteps of his father, William, and become a lawyer. He enrolled in Harvard Law School in 1919 and received the bachelor of laws degree, cum laude, in 1922. He stayed on for another year and earned the S.J.D. degree as well. From 1924 through 1929 he was a partner with his father in the Washington, D.C., firm of Houston and Houston. In 1929 he accepted the position of vice-dean of Howard Law School and became its dean from 1932 to 1935. He also became very involved in and, some would say, founded the civil rights movement. In 1932 he assisted in the preparation of the court brief in the case of *Nixon* v. *Condon,* in which the Supreme Court ruled that a Texas "whites only election primary" was unconstitutional.

NAACP. Between 1935 and 1940 he served as special counsel to the National Association for the Advancement of Colored People before returning to the private practice of law. He later served as chairman of the NAACP national legal committee from 1948 to 1950. He remained a member of the legal committee for the rest of his life. He worked on or argued several civil rights cases in the 1930s and 1940s, including *Norris* v. *Alabama* in 1935. In this case the Supreme Court set aside the convictions of nine young black men who had been charged with rape. The Court found, with the help of the brief that Houston had written, that Alabama's organized exclusion of blacks from juries was a violation of the U.S. Constitution.

Houston was known for his strength in preparing briefs and in oral arguments before the Court. Whether he was presenting cold, hard facts in a brief or speaking strongly and passionately during argument, he pushed himself to excel. While maintaining a law practice, he also served as a vice president of the American Council on Race Relations. President Roosevelt appointed him to the Fair Employment Practices Committee in 1944, but he resigned in 1945 after a dispute with President Truman and in protest of discriminatory hiring practices of the Washington, D.C., transit authority. He died of coronary occlusion in 1950.

Source:
Genna Rae McNeil, *Groundwork: Charles H. Houston and the Struggle for Civil Rights* (Philadelphia: University of Pennsylvania Press, 1983).

ROBERT JACKSON

1892-1954

ASSOCIATE JUSTICE OF U.S. SUPREME COURT, U.S. REPRESENTATIVE AND CHIEF COUNSEL TO THE NUREMBERG WAR CRIME TRIALS

Small-Town Lawyer. Robert Houghwout Jackson was born on 13 February 1892 in Spring Creek, Pennsylvania. He graduated from high school in 1910 and entered Albany Law School in 1911 but was forced to leave after one year due to a lack of funds and never obtained a law degree. He had previously clerked in the law office of Frank Mott, his mother's cousin, and resumed his clerkship after leaving law school. He was admitted to the New York bar in 1913, during an era when one could "read for the bar" after working for a period as a clerk to a lawyer or judge. During the next twenty years, as he ran a typical small-town law practice, he became well known as a leading trial lawyer.

New Dealer. In 1930 Gov. Franklin D. Roosevelt appointed Jackson to a commission to study the state's judicial system. In 1932 Jackson crisscrossed the state of New York in support of Roosevelt's campaign for president. Two years later, President Roosevelt appointed him general counsel to the Internal Revenue Service. Jackson subsequently served as special counsel and as assistant attorney general in the Department of the Treasury, Department of Justice, and the Securities and Exchange Commission until 1938. In that year Roosevelt appointed Jackson solicitor general of the United States, and in 1940 he was appointed attorney general. In June of 1941 Jackson was nominated to become an associate justice to the Supreme Court and was promptly confirmed.

Study in Contrasts. Justice Jackson served on the Supreme Court from 1941 until his death in 1954. During that period he was a study in contrasts. On one hand his decisions were often liberal, when, for example, he rejected a California law forbidding citizens who had no means of support from moving into that state, by declaring that the right of entry into any state was "a privilege of citizenship of the United States." On the other hand he wrote a uniquely conservative dissent in *Korematsu* v. *United States* (1944). While the majority upheld the Japanese relocation policy, Jackson argued that the government should not even be required to defend its policy since it was made during wartime, as the emergency justified governmental authorities to act outside the realm of the Constitution. Despite this opinion Justice Jackson was sometimes a firm defender of the First Amendment and its guarantees of freedom of speech, religion, and the press. He wrote the majority decision in *West Virginia* v. *Barnette* (1943) and declared a "right of silence" under the First Amendment, where the Court declared as unconstitutional a state law that prescribed mandatory saluting of the flag by schoolchildren.

Nuremberg. In May 1945 Justice Jackson accepted an appointment from President Truman as U.S. representative and chief counsel to the Nuremberg war-crime trials of Nazi officials. He was instrumental in convincing the Allies (especially the Soviets, who simply wished to shoot the Nazi officials) of the need to hold fair trials in part to formalize a new rule of international law, establishing that officials of another nation could be held liable for crimes against humanity. Although Jackson had no previous experience as a prosecutor, his organized building of the case and a forceful closing argument are generally credited with tightening the noose around the necks of the Nazi officials. Justice Jackson suffered a major heart attack in March 1954 but participated in the decision of *Brown* v. *Board of Education* on 17 May 1954. He subsequently disregarded the advice of his physician and returned to a full schedule in October of 1954. He suffered a fatal heart attack only days later and died in Washington, D.C., on 9 October 1954.

FRED TOYOSABURO KOREMATSU

1919-

KOREMATSU V. UNITED STATES (1944)

Horrible Wrong. Fred Korematsu never wanted to be famous, and he never wanted to be convicted of a crime. But he was convicted of a crime, and his name will be forever associated in the annals of American justice with the wrong that can be done when basic safeguards of the Constitution are nullified for reasons of political or, as in Korematsu's case, military expediency.

Nisei. Toyosaburo Korematsu was born in Oakland, California, in 1919. He was a Nisei, or first generation Japanese American, born in the United States. He picked up the name "Fred" one year in school when a teacher who had trouble pronouncing his name called him Fred. He liked the name and it stuck. Korematsu graduated from high school in 1938 and worked in the family flower nursery. In June 1941 Korematsu and five friends went to the local post office to volunteer for service in the armed forces. Although his friends were given applications, Korematsu was turned away and was informed that the officer had orders not to accept Japanese Americans.

Executive Order 9066. During the months leading up to the Japanese attack on Pearl Harbor, Korematsu had

been dating an Italian American girl named Ida Boitano. Her parents disapproved of the mixed-race dating, but she continued to date him nonetheless. Just months after the attack on Pearl Harbor, President Roosevelt signed Executive Order 9066, which authorized the military to relocate any persons it wished from certain areas due to reasons of military security. On 2 May 1942 the army posted notices on local telephone poles ordering all persons of Japanese ancestry to report to military authorities only one week later, prepared to move into "assembly areas." Since the order only applied to Japanese Americans living in Pacific Coast states, Korematsu decided to ask Ida to move with him to Nevada where they could get married. She had second thoughts about leaving her family, so Korematsu assumed an identity as a person of Spanish Hawaiian descent while he continued to live in a boarding house in Oakland. On 30 May 1942 he was spotted by someone who knew him and was arrested for violating Order 9066. Korematsu and Boitano eventually ended their relationship.

Arrest and Trial. His arrest made headlines, and a lawyer named Ernest Besig with the American Civil Liberties Union offered to represent him in a battle over the constitutionality of Executive Order 9066. Although Korematsu was freed on bail, he was almost immediately picked up by military police and sent to the Tanforan Assembly Center, where his family had been moved. Korematsu was tried on 8 September 1942. Although the trial judge was impressed with his testimony concerning the racial aspect of the evacuation order (no other racial group was evacuated), he still found Korematsu guilty of violating the military order to evacuate. Rather than send him to prison, however, the judge sentenced him to five years of probation. The conviction was upheld by the court of appeals in late 1943. The case was appealed to the Supreme Court. In a split decision the Court ruled against Korematsu on 18 December 1944. One of the three dissenting justices, Frank Murphy, called the evacuation order a "legalization of racism."

New Trial. For the next thirty-eight years, Korematsu led an average American life. He married and had two children. Then, in January 1982, he was contacted by a law professor named Peter Irons. Irons told Korematsu that he had uncovered some government documents that had never been given to Korematsu's defense team or provided to any of the courts that had heard his case. Had the documents been presented to the courts, Korematsu would probably have prevailed. Fred Korematsu sought a new trial in U.S. District Court, and, with the help of Irons and another lawyer, Dale Minami (whose parents had been evacuated to the Heart Mountain camp in Wyoming), a new trial was granted. The main thrust of Korematsu's argument was that he had lost his case because lawyers for the government had lied or concealed important documents. Judge Marilyn Patel ruled in Korematsu's favor, forty years after the original trial. In 1983 Fred Toyosaburo Korematsu received the prestigious Earl Warren Human Rights Award from the American Civil Liberties Union.

Source:

Peter H. Irons, *Justice at War* (New York: Oxford University Press, 1983).

LOUIS LEPKE

1897-1944

GANGSTER; HEAD OF "MURDER, INC."

Gangster. Louis Lepke had the dubious distinction of being executed as the indirect result of founding and building a very successful, though illegal, business. A famous gangster of the 1930s and 1940s, he is perhaps best known by the name of his business, Murder, Incorporated.

Criminal Education. Louis Lepke, as he was popularly known, was born Louis Bookhouse in Manhattan, New York. His only known occupation was as a criminal. He graduated from simple pushcart robberies at the age of sixteen to organizing protection rackets at the age of seventeen. Too short at five feet seven and one-half inches to intimidate successfully those he sought to "protect," he joined forces with Jacob Shapiro, a huge man whom he met on the day that they both attempted to rob the same pushcart. They joined the Lower East Side gang and worked in establishing control over the city's garment industry.

Murder, Inc. On 15 October 1926 Lepke machine-gunned Jacob "Little Augie" Orgen to death and succeeded to the position of undisputed leader of the city's garment and business rackets. Often described as the "brains of the operation" and "shrewd," Lepke began recruiting mainly Jewish criminals from other gangs to establish his own hit teams and continued to intimidate unions. At one point his organization controlled the 400,000-member Clothing Workers Union as well as trucking and motion-picture operators unions. By 1932 Lepke had helped establish a national crime syndicate with other notable gangsters like "Bugsy" Siegel, Meyer Lansky, "Lucky" Luciano, Frank Costello, and Albert Anastasia. In 1933 he proposed the establishment of a national enforcement division of the syndicate made up of hired killers who would go anywhere to assassinate those who opposed the syndicate. Murder, Incorporated, was born.

"The Fix Is In." By the end of the 1930s, Lepke's crime operation was so large that he was having trouble controlling all of it. Murder, Inc., employed so many hired killers that it was only a matter of time before some of them began to crack and provide information to the authorities when they themselves were caught for murdering someone. One of the killers, Max Rubin, eventu-

ally implicated Lepke in the killing of Joseph Rosen. In 1939 Moey Wolinsky had advised Lepke that the syndicate board had decided that he should turn himself in to be tried on narcotics charges. Wolinsky also told him that, as part of the deal, "the fix was in" and Lepke would not be turned over to the New York authorities to be tried for Rosen's murder.

Execution. While Lepke was serving a fourteen-year sentence on narcotics charges, he was in fact tried and found guilty of the murder of Joseph Rosen and sentenced to die in the electric chair. As it turned out, there was no deal to keep Lepke from being turned over to the New York authorities. He had been double-crossed. He fought the sentence for four years, and, during that period he continued to issue orders through Murder, Inc., to kill those who had betrayed him — including Abe "Kid Twist" Reles, one of the first to implicate him for murder and who subsequently fell from a hotel window while under police protection. Lepke also ordered the murder of Moey Wolinsky, who was shot to death in 1943. Louis Lepke was electrocuted in Sing Sing prison in New York on 4 March 1944 and was the only highly placed member of the national crime syndicate ever to be executed.

BENJAMIN "BUGSY" SIEGEL

1906-1947

GANGSTER; GAMBLING PIONEER

Visionary. Bugsy Siegel believed that in order to get ahead, you had to have class. As a gangster who ran gambling rackets, he was something of a visionary. As part of an expansion of gambling activities in the West, he is credited with putting the small Nevada town of Las Vegas on the map as the king of the world gambling capitals.

Fiery Youth. Benjamin Siegel was born on 28 February 1906 in Brooklyn, New York. In a manner similiar to fellow gangster Louis Lepke, Siegel began his criminal career by preying upon pushcart vendors with a sidekick named Morris Sedway. Unlike Lepke, Siegel did not usually beat the vendors he was trying to convince to buy protection from him. Rather he would simply have Sedway pour kerosene over the vendors' merchandise and then light it on fire. It usually only took a vendor one lesson to decide to pay the "insurance."

Gambling Rackets. During the 1920s and 1930s Siegel continued his climb up the underworld ladder until he became involved in a killing in the early part of the 1930s. As a result of this murder, several attempts were made on his life. With the heat turned up, he reportedly approached syndicate leaders regarding a plan to consolidate criminal undertakings in California with Jack Dragna, who at the time controlled the underworld in that state. Siegel contacted an old friend with whom he had grown up in New York, the film actor George Raft, who reportedly liked Siegel and was happy to introduce him to various Hollywood actors and studio directors. With the help of Dragna, Siegel operated various gambling establishments, including a floating casino. Siegel was reportedly involved in the murder of a gangster named Harry Greenberg after it was rumored that Greenberg had become a police informant. He was later acquitted of the murder and turned more of his attention to increasing gambling revenue for the syndicate.

The Flamingo. In 1945 Siegel decided to establish a gambling hotel in a small town called Las Vegas, Nevada. According to reports, he borrowed $3 million from the syndicate and eventually spent $6 million total in building the Flamingo Hotel. As the first legalized gambling casino in the United States, the Flamingo became famous nationwide, and Bugsy drew enormous profits from it. At some point in 1946 or 1947, he apparently had a disagreement with the syndicate regarding its claim to the $3 million it had put up to help finance the hotel.

A Bad Roll of the Dice. On behalf of the syndicate, Lucky Luciano contacted Bugsy and instructed him to meet with syndicate members in Havana, Cuba, which was then one of the gambling centers of the world, often frequented by American gangsters. Siegel apparently refused to return the $3 million, perhaps thinking that as a gambling crime czar he had little to fear from the syndicate. He was wrong. On 20 June 1947, as Siegel sat in the living room of his girlfriend, syndicate prostitute Virginia Hill, he was shot three times in the head and killed instantly. At about the same time, his longtime friend and companion Moey Sedway, accompanied by several syndicate members, appeared at the Flamingo Hotel and informed the manager that they were taking over.

PEOPLE IN THE NEWS

In April 1941 **John Arena,** the editor of "La Tribuna," was shot to death in Chicago. Arena had been an American citizen for only six months at the time of his death. He had testified before Congress regarding spying activities of Ovra, the Fascist Italian secret police, who had been obtaining national defense secrets from industrial workers.

In October 1942 Associate Justice **James F. Byrnes** resigned from the U.S. Supreme Court to accept an appointment from President **Franklin D. Roosevelt** to be director of the Economic Stabilization Board, a new authority created to attempt to contain wartime inflation.

In March 1949 **Frank Costello,** alleged New York City gangster, was described by the California Commission on Organized Crime as the "reputed head" of a nationwide $2 billion slot machine racket that invested millions in bribing public officials. His response was to deny that he was the "boss of New York," and he stated that "I couldn't square a traffic ticket myself."

In April 1945 the Supreme Court reversed the conviction of **Anthony Cramer,** a German-born American citizen, for giving aid and comfort to two of eight Nazi saboteurs who landed in New York in 1942. In this first test of the treason laws of the United States, the Court held (5–4) that the federal government had not proved the charges by the definitions of the treason law of 1790.

In June 1947 Mayor **James M. Curley** of Boston began his six-to-eighteen-month sentence for mail fraud at the Federal Correctional Institution at Danbury, Connecticut.

In May 1948 World War II veteran **Garry Davis** renounced his U.S. citizenship and petitioned the United Nations to make him the first "citizen of the world." When the United Nations ignored his request, he became a "stateless person" and moved to France.

In June 1947 a federal court jury convicted **Eugene Dennis,** who was general secretary of the Communist Party, of contempt of Congress for his refusal to testify before the House Un-American Activities Committee.

On 28 March 1940 the Reverend **Walter Dworecki,** former pastor of the Camden, New Jersey, Polish Baptist Church, was executed for his involvement in the murder of his daughter. His daughter, Wanda, was only eighteen when she was murdered in April of 1939, shortly after her father had insured her life for $6,000.

In June 1947 **Gerhart Eisler** was convicted in federal court for contempt of Congress for his refusal to testify before the House Un-American Activities Committee. It was alleged that he was the principal Kremlin spy in the United States.

In April 1949 Metropolitan Opera tenor **"Mignon" John Garris,** thirty-six, was found shot to death in an alleyway in Atlanta, Georgia.

In March 1949 **Mildred E. Gillars,** nicknamed "Axis Sally" and charged with treason for her wartime Nazi propaganda broadcasts to American troops in Europe, was convicted and sentenced to prison for ten to thirty years and fined $10,000.

In February 1942 the U.S. District Court in Brooklyn, New York, ruled that **Beatrice Goldstein** must be paid the $12,000 proceeds on her husband's life, even though he was electrocuted for murder.

In February 1946 **Green H. Hackworth,** former legal adviser to Secretary of State **James F. Byrnes,** was elected on the first ballot as one of fifteen judges to be appointed to the International Court of Justice by joint vote of the United Nations General Assembly and Security Council.

In January 1945 Minneapolis, Minnesota, newspaper publisher and antivice crusader **Arthur Kasherman** was shot to death from a passing motor vehicle. His was the third death of this type in the previous eleven years in the city.

In February 1941 Gen. **Walter G. Krivitsky** was found shot to death in a room where he lived under the name of **Walter Poref.** He had claimed to have been a former leader of Soviet army intelligence under **Joseph Stalin.** The police listed the death as a suicide, but friends believed he may have been assassinated.

In October 1942 two black men, **Charlie Land** and Ernest Green, were found lynched and hanging from a bridge after a mob had removed them from the Quitman, Mississippi, jail. They had previously pleaded guilty to attacking a twelve-year-old white girl.

In August 1949 Dade County, Georgia, sheriff **John Lynch,** three deputy sheriffs, and eight others were indicted by a federal grand jury for the masked whipping of seven black men in Hooker, Georgia, on 12 April.

In July 1949 **William Mason,** a radio commentator with a reputation as a crusader, was shot and killed in Alice, Texas. Deputy Sheriff **Sam Smithwick,** whom Mason had mentioned on his program, later surrendered and was charged with murder.

In March 1943 alleged gangster **Frank Nitti,** who had recently been indicted in New York City in connection with a labor union racket, was found shot to death in a suburb of Chicago.

In April 1947 **Alvin J. Paris,** whose arrest led to the uncovering of a plan to fix the National Football League championship game on 15 December 1946, was sentenced to one year in prison. Two other cohorts were sentenced as well.

On 7 December 1941 the governor of Hawaii, **J. B. Poindexter,** turned over government of the Hawaiian Islands to military authorities. The islands were ruled by martial law until 24 October 1944.

On 28 December 1944, evoking his war powers, President **Franklin Roosevelt** and the federal government took possession of nine Montgomery Ward and Company manufacturing plants in order to settle labor disputes. Montgomery Ward chairman **Sewell Avery** had to be bodily removed from his offices and filed suit to have the seizure invalidated. Appealed to the Supreme Court, the case was dismissed as moot after the plants were returned to Avery on 18 October 1945.

On 31 January 1945 Pvt. **Eddie Slovik** was executed for desertion. He was the first American to be executed for desertion since the Civil War.

In November 1941 Mrs. **Ethel Leta Juanita Spinelli** became the first woman to die in the California gas chamber. She was convicted of murder for her involvement in the slaying of one of her own gang members.

In April 1946 **Tojo Hideki,** the premier of Japan during World War II, and seven others were indicted on fifty-five counts of war crimes, including murder, for the deaths at Pearl Harbor, Shanghai, Hong Kong, and the Philippines.

In June 1949 **Eddie Waitkus,** first baseman with the Philadelphia Phillies, was shot and seriously wounded in Chicago by nineteen-year-old **Ruth Ann Steinhagen.** After her statement to police that "I had to shoot someone," she was committed to the Kankakee State Hospital for the criminally insane.

In June 1941 **Robert White,** a black man charged with attacking a white woman, was shot to death in the Conroe, Texas, courtroom where a jury was being selected for his trial. Two prior convictions for the crime had been overturned. The woman's husband was released on $500 bail and was later acquitted of White's murder.

In June 1941 **Charles "The Bug" Workman,** who had been charged with the murder of **Arthur "Dutch Schultz" Flegenheimer,** pleaded "no defense" and was sentenced to life imprisonment for the 1935 murder.

In February 1946 the Supreme Court (6-2) upheld the conviction of Gen. **Tomoyuki Yamashita,** former commander of Japanese forces in the Philippines, on atrocity charges. He was hanged on 23 February.

In April 1940 the body of **Hyman Yuran** was found in a shallow grave near Loch Sheldrake, New York. Police, acting on a tip, found the body of the New York City dress manufacturer who disappeared in 1938, shortly after being indicted as an alleged collector for **Louis Lepke** in the New York garment district.

DEATHS

Louis Brandeis, 84, retired associate justice of the U.S. Supreme Court, 5 October 1941.

Col. G. W. Burleigh, 69, soldier, church leader, and lawyer, 15 March 1940.

Al(phonse) Capone, 48, Italian American former gangster, 25 January 1947.

John H. Clarke, 87, former associate justice of the U.S. Supreme Court who resigned in 1922 to promote American participation in the League of Nations, 22 March 1945.

P. D. Cravath, 78, president of the Metropolitan Opera Association and lawyer, 1 July 1940.

Mrs. M. P. Falconer, 79, prison reformer, 26 November 1941.

I. F. Fischer, 81, U.S. customs judge in New York City, 16 March 1940.

J. S. Fisher, 73, former governor of Pennsylvania and lawyer, 25 June 1940.

E. W. Graser, 32, lawyer and radio actor who portrayed the Lone Ranger, 8 April 1941.

Grafton Green, 74, chief justice of the Tennessee Supreme Court and judge at the Scopes "Monkey" trial (creationism versus evolution), 27 January 1947.

Arthur D. Hill, 78, one of the attorneys in the Sacco and Vanzetti case, 29 November 1947.

Henry Horner, 61, governor of Illinois, lawyer and former judge, 6 October 1940.

A. J. Houston, 87, U.S. senator from Texas, lawyer, and last surviving son of Texas patriot Sam Houston, 26 June 1941.

Charles Evans Hughes, 86, retired chief justice of the U.S. Supreme Court, former governor of New York, U.S. secretary of state, and Republican nominee for president in 1916, 27 August 1948.

George Washington Kirchwey, 87, criminologist, warden of Sing Sing Prison, lawyer, and dean of Columbia University Law School, 3 March 1942.

James McReynolds, 84, retired associate justice of the Supreme Court, 24 August 1946.

John Bassett Moore, 86, former member of the Permanent Court of International Justice and noted authority on international law, 12 November 1947.

Frank W. Murphy, 59, former mayor of Detroit, governor general of the Philippines, governor of Michigan, U.S. attorney general, and associate justice of the Supreme Court, 19 July 1949.

Bradley Palmer, 80, retired Boston lawyer and former member of the U.S. peace delegation in 1919, 9 November 1946.

S. H. Piles, 81, diplomat, lawyer, and former U.S. senator from Washington, 11 March 1940.

Heartsill Ragon, 55, U.S. judge and former congressman, 15 September 1940.

Prof. J. S. Reeves, 70, authority on international law, 7 July 1942.

Edward J. Reilly, 64, criminal lawyer and defense counsel in the Lindbergh kidnapping case, 25 December 1946.

Henry Ridgely, 71, blind lawyer and banker, 13 July 1940.

T. L. Robinson, 60, New York attorney and member of the Dawes German Reparations board, 20 February 1940.

Wiley Rutledge, 55, former professor of law and dean at several law schools, associate justice of the Supreme Court, 10 September 1949.

F. M. Sackett, 72, former ambassador to Germany, former U.S. senator from Kentucky and lawyer, 18 May 1941.

Arthur H. Sapp, 63, lawyer and former president of Rotary International, 9 June 1946.

Harlan Fiske Stone, 73, chief justice of the U.S. Supreme Court, former dean of Columbia Law School, and U.S. attorney general, 22 April 1946.

S. M. Stroock, 67, president of the American Jewish Committee and lawyer, 11 September 1941.

George Sutherland, 80, retired associate justice of the U.S. Supreme Court and former U.S. senator from Utah, 18 July 1942.

Willis Van Devanter, 81, retired associate justice of the U.S. Supreme Court, 8 February 1941.

Wendell L. Willkie, 52, lawyer and Republican presidential candidate in 1940, 8 October 1944.

Maj. Gen. Blanton Winship, 77, former governor of Puerto Rico and former judge advocate general, 9 October 1947.

PUBLICATIONS

Catherine D. Bowen, *Yankee From Olympus: Justice Holmes and his Family* (Boston: Little, Brown, 1944);

Esther Lucile Brown, *Lawyers, Law Schools and the Public Service* (New York: Russell Sage Foundation, 1948);

Charles H. Butler, *A Century at the Bar of the Supreme Court of the United States* (New York: Putnam, 1942);

Edmond Nathaniel Cahn, *The Sense of Injustice, a Anthropocentric View of Law* (New York: New York University Press, 1949);

Robert K. Carr, *Federal Protection of Civil Rights: Quest For A Sword* (Ithaca, N.Y.: Cornell University Press, 1949);

Edmond Samuel Corwin, *Understanding the Constitution* (New York: Sloane, 1949);

Charles P. Curtis, *Lions Under the Throne: A Study of the Supreme Court* (Boston: Houghton Mifflin, 1947);

Erik Erikson, *The Supreme Court and the New Deal* (Rosemead, Cal.: Rosemead Review Press, 1940);

Osmond K. Fraenkel, *Our Civil Liberties* (New York: Viking, 1944);

Jerome Frank, *Courts on Trial: Myth and Reality in American Justice* (Princeton: Princeton University Press, 1949);

Fritz Grob, *The Relativity of War and Peace, a Study in Law, History, and Politics* (New Haven: Yale University Press, 1949);

Dick Hyman, *It's Against the Law* (New York: A & S, 1949);

Philip C. Jessup, *A Modern Law of Nations, An Introduction* (New York: Macmillan, 1948);

Vincent A. Kleinfeld, *Federal Food, Drug, and Cosmetic Act; Judicial and Administrative Record, 1938–1949* (Chicago: Commerce Clearing House, 1949);

Samuel J. Konefsky, *Chief Justice Stone and the Supreme Court* (New York: Macmillan, 1946);

Wesley McCune, *The Nine Young Men* (New York: Harper, 1947);

George Frederick Miller, *Absentee Voters and Suffrage Laws* (Washington, D.C.: Daylion, 1949);

Francis Walter Moshall, *Popular Guide to Legal Principles* (New York: W. H. Wise, 1949);

Frederick Arthur Philbrick, *Language and the Law: The Semantics of Forensic English* (New York: Macmillan, 1949);

Henry Rottschaefer, *The Constitution and Socio-Economic Change* (Ann Arbor: University of Michigan Law School, 1948);

Alva Tisdale Southworth, *The Common Sense of the Constitution and Leading Supreme Court Decisions* (Boston: Allyn & Bacon, 1949);

Arthur T. Vanderbilt, *Men and Measures in the Law* (New York: Knopf, 1949).

LIFESTYLES AND SOCIAL TRENDS

by MARGO HORN

CONTENTS

Sidebars and tables are listed in italics.

1940

- Fifty-one percent of women between the ages of twenty and twenty-four are married.

- The National Association for the Advancement of Colored People (NAACP) denounces the military's policy of segregating blacks.

- Nickel jukeboxes appear in restaurants, taverns, tearooms, variety stores, and gas stations. Sixteen records play for fifty cents.

- Annual attendance at baseball games is estimated at ten million.

- Weekly movie attendance is estimated at eighty million.

9 Apr. The governor of New York State signs a bill permitting children to be absent from school for religious observances and education.

1941

- The median age at first marriage is 24 for men and 21.5 for women.

- A national committee is formed to work for abolition of the poll tax, which prevents many blacks from voting in southern states.

- "Rosie the Riveter," named for Rosina Bonavita, becomes the emblem of the American woman working in the defense industries.

- With the improvement of the economy, car sales soar. Alcohol consumption also rises.

15 Jan. A. Philip Randolph calls for a 1 July March on Washington to demand an end to discrimination in defense-industry employment.

25 June President Franklin D. Roosevelt signs Executive Order 8802, banning racial discrimination in the defense industries and creating the Fair Employment Practices Committee.

15 Dec. Because of the war Harvard, Yale, Princeton, and other American universities announce that they are cutting the undergraduate program from four to three years by offering year-round sessions. Seventy-six medical schools also cut their programs from four years to three.

27 Dec. Rationing of automobile tires begins.

1942

- The Congress of Racial Equality (CORE) is founded by James Farmer, Bayard Rustin, and A. J. Muste, Christian pacifists who plan to use the nonviolent-resistance tactics of Mohandas Gandhi to fight racial discrimination and segregation.

- The Committee on Women in World Affairs is founded.

- Single men ages eighteen to thirty-five and married men ages eighteen to twenty-six are eligible for the draft.

- Willow Run, outside Detroit, becomes the fastest-growing city in the United States, as thousands move there to work in the B-24 bomber plant.

- Forty percent of the vegetables consumed in the United States are grown in victory gardens.

1943

2 Jan.	The Office of Civilian Supply announces that all civilian car and truck production will cease for the duration of the war.
19 Feb.	President Roosevelt signs Executive Order 9066, ordering the removal of all Japanese Americans on the West Coast to internment camps for the duration of the war.
27 Apr.	The Office of Price Administration (OPA) halts sugar sales for about a week while consumers register for sugar-rationing coupon books.
1 Dec.	Nationwide gasoline and fuel-oil rationing begins.

- Sales of Bibles increase 25 percent, and religious books are popular.

- A scarcity of goods and improved individual income combine to create long lines at grocery stores, movies, bars, and restaurants.

- Cabs must take as many passengers as they can carry.

- Long-distance telephone calls are limited to five minutes.

- The government orders a minimum forty-eight-hour workweek in key defense plants. Labor shortages result in new practices that "pamper" employees. Awards, fringe benefits, piped-in music, coffee breaks, and suggestion boxes are all introduced in the workplace.

- Teenage fads include slumber parties, pep rallies, beach parties, and Saturday nights at soda shops with jukeboxes and meeting dates at hamburger "joints." Boys wear army boots while girls favor baggy, rolled-up blue jeans and sloppy shirttails.

1 Jan.	Meat is rationed to twenty-eight ounces per person per week, butter is rationed at four ounces per week, the sale of sliced bread is banned, and flour and canned goods are also rationed. Shoes are rationed to three pairs a year; new sneakers are not available because of a rubber shortage.
7 Jan.	Opera singer Marian Anderson is the first African American to perform in Constitution Hall, Washington, D.C. The Daughters of the American Revolution (DAR), who own the hall, gained considerable notoriety when they refused Anderson's request to rent the hall in 1939.
20 June	Rioting between blacks and whites breaks out in Detroit and lasts forty-eight hours.
1 Aug.	During race riots in Harlem, New York, five blacks are killed and five hundred are injured. Damages are estimated at $5 million.
2 Aug.	The federal government begins the Emergency Maternity and Infant Care Program (EMIC), under which the government pays the entire cost of medical care for wives and infant children of enlisted men in the four lowest pay grades.
30 Dec.	U.S. Post Office officials charge *Esquire* magazine with being "lewd" and "lascivious," suspending its second-class mailing privileges as of 28 February 1944.

1944

- Fifty-eight percent of women between the ages of twenty and twenty-four are married.

- The United Negro College Fund is established.

- Thirty percent of the 19 million workingwomen in the United States are employed in factory jobs; 3.27 million women are employed in defense industries. The U.S. Census Bureau estimates that 2.75 million employed women have 4.5 million children under the age of fourteen.

- Slacks become popular with workingwomen.

- Sales of baking powder fall because workingwomen are baking less often.

17 Feb. The Southern Regional Council is founded to improve educational, economic, and racial conditions in the South.

3 Apr. In its decision on *Smith* v. *Allwright* the U.S. Supreme Court rules that blacks cannot be barred from voting in political party primaries.

29 May A New York judge finds *The First Lady Chatterley,* the first version of D. H. Lawrence's *Lady Chatterley's Lover,* obscene and orders that Dial Press, the American publisher, stand trial. A higher court reverses the decision on 1 November.

1 Nov. • Quadruplets are delivered by caesarean section for the first time.

1945

- The birthrate stands at 2.4 births per woman.

- One abortion occurs for every 150 live births.

- 18,610,000 women are employed outside their homes. The Women's Bureau reports that 80 percent of them want to continue working after the war.

- Children buy Defense Stamps weekly; schools have air-raid drills.

- Toys are scarce; stores have no bicycles, skates, sleds, or electric trains.

- Laid off because their jobs have been given to returning veterans, women autoworkers stage a protest march with posters reading "Stop Discrimination Because of Sex."

- The U.S. Supreme Court affirms the right of states to recognize or reject Nevada divorce decrees.

4 June A U.S. Appeals Court revokes the suspension of *Esquire* magazine's second-class mailing privileges.

Aug. Gasoline rationing ends.

Nov. All previously rationed items except sugar are available.

Dec. Many families take their first vacations since the bombing of Pearl Harbor. Cabaret shows open in many cities. They are by-products of the army's USO shows for the troops.

1946

- The Baby Boom begins: the birthrate is up 20 percent over 1945. Seventy-four percent of couples have their first child during their first year of marriage.

- Two hundred thousand couples are involved in divorce proceedings.

- The cost of living is up 33 percent over 1941. Consumers who have been forced to save because of rationing during the war are unhappy with continuing shortages of goods as their buying power declines. A *New York Daily News* headline declares, "Prices soar, buyers sore. . . ."

- Bread consumption drops as flour and wheat are shipped to Europe. Flour whiteners are added for Americans who dislike dark bread.

- Advancements in car design include the Nash 600, made with a single unit of welded steel; the Studebaker Champion, with aircraft-style "no-glare" dials on the instrument panel; and the Chrysler Town and Country, a luxury station wagon.

- An RCA ten-inch television set sells for $374.

- Dr. Benjamin Spock's *The Commonsense Book of Baby and Child Care* is published.

6 Apr. Oklahoma City public-health officials are the first to use penicillin to treat venereal disease among civilians.

2 July For the first time since Reconstruction blacks vote in the Mississippi Democratic primary.

5 Dec. President Harry S Truman's Executive Order 9809 establishes the President's Committee on Civil Rights.

1947

- The birthrate reaches 2.8 births per woman.

- Housing shortages cause six million families to double up with friends or relatives.

- Women lose one million factory jobs, half a million clerical positions, three hundred thousand jobs in commercial services, and one hundred thousand jobs in sales as companies hire returning veterans.

- College enrollment rises to an all-time high of 6.1 million students as 4 million returning veterans use the opportunities for education, housing, and business provided by the GI Bill of Rights.

- The Georgia Supreme Court revokes the charter of the Ku Klux Klan.

- Bernard Baruch coins the expression "Cold War." Journalist Walter Lippmann popularizes the phrase.

Jan. The number of veterans in college peaks at 1.2 million, or 8.9 percent of all demobilized male World War II veterans.

Apr. All but 3 percent of male veteran heads of households are employed.

10 Apr. Jackie Robinson signs with the Brooklyn Dodgers, becoming the first black in major league baseball.

11 June Sugar rationing ends, sparking an enormous increase in ice-cream consumption.

July In an article signed "X" in *Foreign Affairs,* George Kennan proposes the policy of "containment" toward the Soviet Union, which becomes the basis of American foreign policy.

3 Dec. The U.S. Motion Picture Association votes to regulate against glorification of crime on the screen. The Screen Directors Guild bars members of the Communist Party from holding office. A Hollywood blacklist compiled by studio executives includes three hundred writers, directors, and actors who are alleged to be Communist sympathizers.

1948

- Inflation rises. A house that cost $4,440 in 1939 now costs $9,060. Clothing prices are up 93 percent, food 129 percent, home furnishings 93.3 percent, and rent 12.2 percent. Gas and electricity are down 4.8 percent.

- In North Carolina a government-supported program provides children with a well-balanced lunch of black-eyed peas, eggs, cheese, potatoes, a biscuit, milk, and a tangerine — all for five cents.

- Chlorophyll gum, candies, and toothpaste are a nationwide fad. Frozen foods have become popular.

- The Baskin-Robbins chain of ice-cream shops opens.

- The bikini bathing suit, named for the Bikini Atoll nuclear test site, arrives on American beaches.

- Fifty cities ban books dealing with crime or sex.

2 Feb. President Truman asks Congress to pass strong civil rights legislation. Passage is blocked by powerful Southern Democrats.

9 July A Nevada court declares prostitution legal in Reno.

26 July President Truman signs executive orders integrating the armed forces and the federal civil service.

13 Sept. Margaret Chase Smith of Maine becomes the first woman to be elected to the U.S. Senate.

1949

- Abraham Levitt and his sons William and Alfred convert a Long Island potato field into a prefabricated "carbon copy" suburban community called "Levittown." For $7,990 ($60 per month and no down payment) the consumer can purchase a four-room house with attic, outdoor barbecue, washing machine, and 12 1/2-inch built-in television set.

- The Baby Boom levels off at 3.58 million live births.

- Antibiotics and immunization bring infant deaths down to 31.3 per thousand, from 47 per thousand in 1940.

- Maternal mortality plunges from 37.6 per ten thousand live births in 1940 to 8.3 per ten thousand in 1949.

- Ninety percent of boys and 74 percent of girls questioned in a national poll of high-school-age young people think it is "all right for young people to pet or 'neck' when they are out on dates."

Jan. For the first time blacks are invited to events surrounding a presidential inauguration and stay in the same Washington, D.C., hotels as whites.

OVERVIEW

The Great Depression and World War II. The Great Depression and World War II cast long shadows over American life in the 1940s. During the 1930s President Franklin D. Roosevelt's New Deal created a sense of economic optimism and eased the suffering of many, but it did not eradicate poverty or solve the economic crisis. In 1941 as many as 40 percent of all American families lived below poverty level. Nearly eight million workers earned less than the legal minimum wage. Another eight million Americans were unemployed, and the median income was only $2,000 per year. While the economic picture improved during the 1940s, the sense of crisis created by the Depression permanently altered lifestyles and attitudes. The so-called depression mentality of fear and economic caution marked an entire generation, even as the economy boomed after World War II.

America at War. World War II presented a new series of demands and dislocations that further reconfigured personal life. Most immediately, the armed forces conscripted ten million men, including fathers, after 1943. The war effort demanded stepped-up production at home to equip the military and maintain civilian needs. The Gross National Product and manufacturing output doubled in the war, as American industry limited or suspended production of consumer goods to devote its efforts to making weapons and war materiel. No civilian automobiles and trucks were manufactured from 1942 until after the war. Other steel, rubber, or electrical consumer goods were scarce or unavailable. Government entered people's daily lives, raising taxes, rationing scarce commodities, controlling prices, and allocating labor for military and civilian production, even restricting where individuals lived or worked.

Wartime Prosperity. Most Americans tolerated government restrictions as temporary necessities, and stepped-up industrial production improved the material lives of many people. The labor force expanded from 56,180,000 in 1940 to 65,290,000 in 1945. Average yearly earnings rose from $754 in 1940 to $1,289 in 1944. While more than half of all Americans lived in poverty during the Depression, by the end of the war just over one-third were poor. Another third earned wages that gave them significant disposable income for the first time.

The Postwar Years. When the war came to an end in 1945, many Americans wondered if the higher standard of living brought about by a wartime economy could be sustained in peacetime. Having experienced the Depression, they feared yet another crisis once millions of soldiers reentered the civilian workplace in an economy no longer stimulated by massive wartime production. Yet in spite of major dislocations caused by the reconversion to peacetime business and manufacturing, no new crisis occurred. Several factors cushioned the economy after the war. Demobilization occurred slowly, and military expenditures remained high. During the war Americans had saved billions of dollars, which they spent on new homes and newly available cars and appliances once the war ended. Wartime profits gave businesses money to invest in plants and equipment for civilian production. The United States was the only major industrial nation to emerge unscathed from World War II, and American loans to war-torn European nations gave these countries funds to purchase American-made goods. The Servicemen's Readjustment Act of 1944 gave veterans one year of unemployment compensation, financial assistance for job training and education, and low-interest loans to buy homes, farms, and businesses. This aid to veterans and their families, known as the GI Bill of Rights, helped nearly one-quarter of the population and further stimulated the economy.

Inflation. While many Americans benefited from the immediate prosperity of the postwar years, complete economic recovery proved elusive. By the end of the decade inflation became the new economic woe. With one-third of the population still below the poverty line in 1949, it was unclear if the United States had developed an economy capable of providing an adequate livelihood to all its citizens.

Containment and the Cold War. The late 1940s marked the beginning of the Cold War. Fear of communism manifested itself in the Red-baiting that began in 1946 and in a policy of containment directed at the Soviet Union. Postwar politics generated serious concerns about global security. Once the United States dropped atomic bombs on Hiroshima and Nagasaki, the world entered the nuclear age. The United States and the Soviet Union stared at one another with fear and hostility. The Cold War began to chill the nation, creating profound insecurity about the future. As Dean Acheson said in 1947, "the nation must be on permanent alert."

Containment and Conformity. Political containment translated into expectations of strict behavioral conformity. During the war years Americans saved and delayed gratification. This postponement created pent-up desires to spend and create, and many feared that this stored energy might not be channeled properly. Security and behavioral conformity came to be valued above personal risk and experimentation. Parents were urged to rear their children properly, lest they be vulnerable to Communist subversion.

Ethnicity and Race in the 1940s. The war years encouraged the assimilation of white ethnics from European backgrounds into American society. Americans' revulsion at the Nazi ideology of racial purity led them to reject assertions of Anglo-Saxon supremacy in the United States. The Alien Registration Act of 1940 encouraged aliens to become American citizens, and between 1943 and 1944 nearly one million people — mostly from Italian and Eastern European backgrounds — were naturalized. Wartime propaganda patriotically stressed that though we are from different backgrounds, "We Are All American." Yet the 1940s version of pluralism emphasized the blending of ethnic differences into the "melting pot" of American society. The distinctive ethnic identities of these new citizens were not valued, and nonwhites were not welcomed into the melting pot.

Wartime Discrimination against Mexican Americans. When Mexican Americans managed to get jobs in the defense industry, they were given the most-menial and lowest-paid positions. White Americans' deep animosity toward them became apparent in the "Zoot Suit" Riots of June 1943. Named for a distinctive style of suit that was popular among young Mexican Americans and African Americans, these riots erupted in Los Angeles after white soldiers heard false reports that a Mexican American youth had beaten a sailor.

Internment of Japanese Americans. The U.S. government's treatment of Japanese Americans during World War II is a shameful example of institutionalized racism. After Japanese forces attacked Pearl Harbor on 7 December 1941, first- and second-generation Japanese Americans living on the West Coast were judged to be threats to national security. In February 1942, 120,000 West Coast residents of Japanese origin were ordered to leave their homes, jobs, and property and were taken to inland internment camps, where they were held for the duration of the war. Few of those interned represented any actual security threat. Two-thirds of them were American citizens by birth.

Discrimination against African Americans. While they continued to suffer from segregation and discrimination, African Americans managed to make modest gains during the military crisis. In 1941 they succeeded in pressuring President Roosevelt to ban racial discrimination in defense production. Although his executive order was difficult to enforce, the number of African American skilled workers more than doubled during the war, and their presence in semiskilled jobs increased by an even larger measure. While the 1939 average income of a nonwhite male worker was only 41 percent of a white man's, by 1950 the percentage had increased to 61. The war also accelerated the migration of African Americans from the rural South to northern and western cities, a movement that improved their economic prospects and their political strength. These improvements in the status of African Americans set the stage for the civil rights movement of the 1950s and 1960s.

Women in the Workplace. The successive crises of the Depression and the war created a greater egalitarianism in Americans' concepts of gender roles. The economic hard times of the Depression and the demands of wartime production pushed women into the workforce. The Depression forced many wives and mothers to find ways to supplement their reduced family incomes, but government pronouncements and policies reinforced the ideology of the traditional family. The inability to provide for his family eroded an unemployed man's sense of masculinity, and married women who worked outside the home were often perceived as taking jobs away from men. As a result women faced job discrimination. This situation changed dramatically with the employment opportunities presented by World War II.

Workingwomen in Wartime. Two years after the United States entered the war, the unemployment rate had dropped from 14 percent to zero. Men were not the only ones to don military uniforms. Some women joined the WACS, the WAVES, or the SPARS — the women's branches of the U.S. Army, Navy, and Coast Guard. Wartime industrial mobilization required the labor of those men and women not in the military. Suddenly the government and the media affirmed the importance of workingwomen and welcomed them to the workforce, particularly to jobs in the defense industry.

Postwar Reversion to Tradition. The success of women in the wartime workforce briefly challenged traditional gender roles. Women's economic gains in the wartime boom raised their expectations for sustained equality of opportunity after the war, but the shift in attitude toward the workingwoman was only temporary. After 1945, as returning veterans reclaimed jobs women had held in wartime, the image of the full-time wife and mother was reintroduced as "modern" and necessary to meet the new psychological stresses of life in the age of atomic insecurity.

The Family. The economic hardships of the Depression created strain in marriages and family life and caused a decline in marriage and birthrates. Those who did marry in the 1930s postponed childbearing or had fewer children. The war accelerated the process of family formation. The marriage rate went up between 1940 and 1946, as many couples rushed into matrimony, often just before the husband's departure to the war overseas. During the same period the birthrate rose as well, from 19.4 to 24.1 births per thousand women. Absent husbands and fathers, wartime rations, and working mothers characterized family life in the early 1940s.

The Baby Boom. Marriage rates continued to soar after the war, and there was a sharp rise in the birthrate that has become known as the Baby Boom. The Baby Boom generation reshaped the American family and American culture for decades to come. American society celebrated domesticity after the war. The average family had a ranch or split-level house, a car, and 2.5 children. The ideal of the good life was represented by a full-time wife and mother who had shiny new appliances in her kitchen, and a husband and father who was the sole breadwinner.

The Birth of Suburbia. This idealized good life was set in one of the new suburban communities that suddenly sprawled across the American landscape after World War II. Postwar prosperity and government subsidies made home ownership accessible to large numbers of middle-class Americans for the first time. Pent-up consumer demand resulted in a huge postwar buying spree as young families spent their wartime savings to furnish their new homes, clothe their babies, and put cars in their new garages. In each of the four years following the war Americans moved into more than a million new houses and bought 21.4 million cars, 20 million refrigerators, and 5.5 million stoves.

The Cold War and Suburbia. Fear of atomic war also contributed to the rise of suburbia. Atomic scientists advised the depopulation of urban centers to avoid a concentration of industries and homes in potential target areas. New roads provided quick escape routes from cities to the suburbs. As President Dwight D. Eisenhower explained in 1956, "the road net must permit quick evacuation of target areas" in the event of a nuclear attack.

MEET THE FOLKS

On 1 September 1947 *Time* magazine offered a portrait of the American public compiled by the famous Gallup polling company. The average U.S. man, it reported, was 5 feet 9 inches tall and weighed 158 pounds. The average woman was 5 feet 4 inches tall and weighed 132 pounds. Women believed that three children constituted the ideal family and wanted no babies until the second year of marriage. Most of the quarrels between "Mr. and Mrs. America" were prompted by money, jealousy, and children — in that order. Seven out of ten U.S. adults believed in spanking their offspring. Less than a third of U.S. families said grace at meals. Seven out of ten preferred dogs to cats, and no one wanted his or her son to go into politics.

Source: "Manners and Morals," *Time*, 50 (1 September 1947): 14–15.

TOPICS IN THE NEWS

THE AMERICAN WOMAN AT WORK

Rosie the Riveter. One popular image of the American woman in the 1940s was that of "Rosie the Riveter" — the strong, independent woman defense worker, wearing overalls and doing her part to help the United States win the war. Government posters featured women rolling up their sleeves and affirming that "We Can Do It." Newspapers and magazines were filled with photographs and drawings of women building bombers, tanks, and ships. Radio stations sponsored contests for "Working Women Win Wars Week." The woman wielding an acetylene torch became as common a media image as the soft and feminine girl in the Palmolive soap ad. American women followed Rosie the Riveter out of the kitchen and onto the shop floor. The number of workingwomen rose from 11,970,000 in 1940 to 18,610,000 in 1945. By the end of the war one in every four wives was employed. Women comprised 36.1 percent of the civilian workforce and were enjoying the increases in income created by the wartime economy.

Opportunity. In the mid 1930s, 80 percent of Americans objected to wives working outside the home, but by 1942 only 40 percent still disapproved. The labor shortage in American industry was responsible for this shift in opinion. As more men were drafted into military service, women took their places on the assembly lines. Once women's employment became vital to the war effort, it was applauded as patriotic. Between 1940 and 1945 women's presence in the labor force grew by more than 50 percent.

Tradition. While the war made new opportunities available for many women, and most Americans approved of women in the labor force as a patriotic necessity, traditional gender assumptions retained their hold. In the workplace the workingwoman was still the exception, tolerated because of the wartime emergency. Twenty percent of working wives reported that they went to work over their husbands' objections. The government position was that "now, as in peacetime, a mother's primary duty is to her home and children." Although some 1.5 million mothers with small children worked, child care remained inadequate. The government financed only 3,102 child-care centers to serve working mothers, providing for only

Government poster urging women to take over jobs left vacant by men who entered military service

a small fraction of the children in need of care. Most working mothers left their children with family members or left them to fend for themselves. The scarcity of institutional assistance for these women implied that while society approved of workingwomen, it still expected them to take care of their children themselves. Furthermore, most considered women in the workplace a temporary phenomenon. Though women proved themselves the equal of men in many jobs, they were paid less. Since most of these workingwomen had been trained primarily to be homemakers, they lacked the education and skills necessary to enter career paths leading to good pay, advancement, and security. They were placed in low-level jobs defined as acceptable for women, increasing the seg-

Workingwomen during World War II

regation of women into a narrow, devalued sector of the workplace.

Raised Expectations. Despite discrimination against them, three out of four employed women — including 69 percent of the working wives — wanted to continue working after the war. They were disappointed. Government, private sector, and union policies made it nearly impossible for women to avoid economic dependence on men, even if they continued to hold jobs. After the war a woman's average weekly pay fell from $50 to $37, a decline of 26 percent that contrasts sharply to an overall postwar decrease of 4 percent. Although three-quarters of women employed in war industries were still employed in 1946, 90 percent of them were earning less than they earned during the war. Faced with a postwar decrease in the already inadequate number of child-care facilities, many working mothers withdrew from the workforce. While the actual number of women in paid employment rose, they tended to be older women with no children to care for at home, and they were employed in an increasingly narrow range of jobs.

Realities. The policies that guided the reconversion to a peacetime economy cost many women their jobs. By law male veterans were rewarded for their service with priority in the competition for their old jobs. Unions had rarely granted women seniority, and as the last hired they were the first fired. In the first two months after the war the aircraft industry laid off eight hundred thousand workers, the majority of them women.

Women and the Peacetime Military. Women were also squeezed out of the armed forces after the war. Such work was considered "unfeminine," and peacetime employers did not offer them jobs that used the skills they had acquired in the military. Worse still, female veterans were defined as dependents rather than providers in their homes, and therefore they were not eligible for the veterans' benefits that so advantaged their male counterparts.

Return to Tradition. After the war, woman's proper place was again defined as the home. In 1946 Frieda Miller, chief of the Women's Bureau in the U.S. Labor Department, noted a change in public attitude from "excessive admiration for women's capacity to do anything, over to the idea . . . that women ought to be delighted to give up any job and return to their proper sphere — the kitchen." Experts such as anthropologist Margaret Mead and sociologist Willard Waller suggested that the independent woman had gotten "out of hand." Fears that the absence of mothers from home would lead to a rise in juvenile delinquency were increasingly voiced in newspapers and magazines. Psychologists stressed that the anxieties of returning veterans and the uncertainties created by the Cold War were best eased by full-time wives and mothers. Despite the success of Rosie the Riveter, the domestic ideal reasserted itself. While some married women remained in the workforce, they were chiefly in low-paying jobs, kept that way by the prevailing notion that the husband was the primary breadwinner and the wife's earnings were supplemental income, "pin money" to spend on luxuries.

Sources:

William Chafe, *The American Woman: Her Changing Social, Economic, and Political Roles, 1920–1970* (New York: Oxford University Press, 1972);

Susan M. Hartmann, *The Home Front and Beyond: American Women in the 1940s* (Boston: Twayne, 1982);

Rosalind Rosenberg, *Divided Lives: American Women in the Twentieth Century* (New York: Hill & Wang, 1992).

THE TIME MAGAZINE MAN OF THE YEAR
1940 Winston Churchill
1941 Franklin D. Roosevelt
1942 Joseph Stalin
1943 George C. Marshall
1944 Dwight D. Eisenhower
1945 Harry S Truman
1946 James F. Byrnes
1947 George C. Marshall
1948 Harry S Truman
1949 Winston Churchill

MALE EXPERIENCE

Manhood and Service. For most American men the 1940s began with military service: putting on uniforms and risking their lives overseas. World War II lasted three years longer than World War I, and six times as many young American males were drafted to serve in it. The entrance of the United States into World War I was accompanied by an outburst of proclamations about patriotism, courage, and glory, but soldiers who went overseas with visions of proving their valor in the ultimate test of manhood discovered instead the horrors of modern warfare and came home questioning the ideals for which they had fought. Americans in the military during World War II had learned from their predecessors' experience and were far less likely to view war as a measure of masculinity or a patriotic crusade. They accepted military service as a necessity and served loyally, but they had few expectations of personal glory.

The Rush to the Altar. Faced with separation from their loved ones, many newly drafted men — mostly those who had already planned to marry — hastened to do so before leaving for the army. There was a deluge of marriage licenses issued in the month following the Japanese bombing of Pearl Harbor on 7 December 1941. A man's military service came to stand for the protection of the American family. In a conversation on a 1942 radio program a young soldier explained the meaning of the war to his girlfriend: "This war's . . . about *all* young people like us. About love and gettin' hitched, and havin' a home and some kids, and breathin' fresh air out in the suburbs . . . about livin' and workin' *decent*, like free people."

The Military Family. Government policy reinforced the stability of the serviceman's family. Excluding married men from the draft proved impossible after 1941, and fathers were no longer deferred after 1943, but beginning in 1942 the government provided servicemen a family allotment, part of which was prorated according to family size and structure. These allotments provided servicemen substantial incentive to marry, especially when their wives could supplement this income by taking readily available semiskilled jobs at good pay in the defense industry. As one historian of the period has noted: "Men were everywhere and able to get married, subsidized by a government with a nest egg of pay. And because work for women was everywhere available and the girl could add to the man's government allowance, the couple was able to marry when they wanted to, young and ardent."

Separation. The separation of families became a major theme of popular culture during wartime, both reflecting and reinforcing the desire for a secure domestic life. Films such as *Since You Went Away* (1943) and *Tender Comrade* (1943) connected the home front to the battlefront and focused on the anxiety and grief involved in losing a loved one to war. Popular songs also expressed such themes, usually in the form of sentimental ballads: "I'll Be Seeing You" (1944), "Together" (1944), "It's Been a Long, Long Time" (1945), and "Sentimental Journey" (1945). Even children's tales echoed the theme of separation. *Make Way for Ducklings*, Robert McCloskey's 1941 storybook about ducks in Boston, became tremendously popular during the war owing in great part to its theme of a female-led family that must avoid hazardous situations until they are reunited with the father duck. Such cultural artifacts emphasized to servicemen that they were above all fighting to return home.

Annual Increase or Decrease of Numbers of First Marriages in New York State (apart from New York City), by Sex and Age, 1940–1946 (in percentages)

	Males			Females		
	20	24	28	17	21	25
1939 to 1940	30.7	21.0	24.8	25.9	17.7	31.1
1940 to 1941	56.5	12.0	2.1	18.4	24.7	4.9
1941 to 1942	26.8	−17.5	−13.9	8.9	−7.4	−16.0
1942 to 1943	−40.7	−29.2	−26.4	−31.0	−61.8	−61.9
1943 to 1944	−6.3	−12.1	−19.3	−11.0	63.5	53.2
1944 to 1945	7.6	22.0	41.5	−52.4	15.1	75.5
1945 to 1946	56.3	87.9	77.0	43.1	71.0	74.9

SOURCE: Calculated from New York State, Department of Health, Division of Vital Statistics, *Annual Report,* annual.

Wartime Trauma. While fighting to protect hearth and home, servicemen suffered psychological as well as physical wounds. Of the thirty-seven thousand veterans admitted to Veterans Administration (VA) hospitals as inpatients in 1946, more than half were treated for neuropsychiatric problems. Knowledge of the trauma they had suffered fueled widespread public anxiety over the ability of returning soldiers to resume their roles as citizens, husbands, and fathers.

Postwar Expectations. Once they returned home veterans wanted above all to live "the good life." To these men who had lived through the Depression as well as the war, this way of life meant security above all else. Though white middle-class men faced few obstacles in the pursuit of educational and career goals, the jobs they entered brought little opportunity for self-fulfillment. The American workplace had changed during the war years, even for businessmen and professionals. Veterans found jobs in large, impersonal organizations that demanded conformity in return for job security and advancement. While the experience of service in the large, impersonal wartime armed forces had prepared them for this sort of postwar employment, veterans' peacetime work no longer provided them an arena for the exercise of "manly" aggressiveness, authority, or individualism. Giving up autonomy for security and good benefits in the workplace, American men turned to their families for fulfillment and happiness.

Family Life. For many veterans who returned home uncertain about their ability to function in postwar society, male authority was secure only in the family and only if the wife remained subordinate. In the prosperous postwar economy of the late 1940s, many men succeeded in providing for their families in great abundance. Middle-class women affirmed their husbands' perception of "family breadwinner" as the most important masculine role.

Sources:
Elaine Tyler May, *Homeward Bound: American Families in the Cold War Era* (New York: Basic Books, 1988);

Steven Mintz and Susan Kellogg, *Domestic Revolutions: A Social History of American Family Life* (New York: Free Press, 1988);

John Modell, *Into One's Own: From Youth to Adulthood in the United States, 1920–1975* (Berkeley: University of California Press, 1989).

ON THE HOME FRONT

The Family in Wartime. World War II spurred enormous changes in family life. First, wartime industry and the military draft caused massive migration: more than fifteen million people moved, searching for defense jobs or following family members to the next military base. Americans poured into major defense centers, especially cities such as San Diego, Los Angeles, San Francisco, Mobile, and Wichita. The war and the booming economy that accompanied it also impacted patterns of marriage and childbearing. Couples had delayed marriage and childbearing during the Depression; men and women rushed to the altar after 1941 and had record numbers of children.

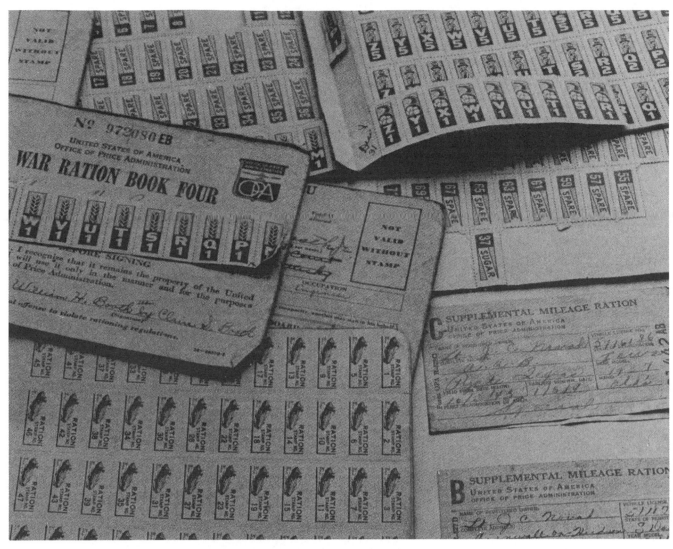

Food-ration stamps and gas-ration cards (lower right)

Marriage and Babies. While these marriages typically followed long engagements, many others were more spontaneous. When actor Mickey Rooney was a private stationed at Camp Siebert, Alabama, he proposed to a seventeen-year-old girl on their first date, and they were married seven days later. As Rooney later explained, "I married Betty Jane because I was determined to marry someone. I'd had some drinks, was hurt and lonely, reached and grabbed." Other young soldiers married in haste to have a secure image of a sweetheart to hold on to in the midst of battle. If marriage rates had continued at 1930s levels, there would have been three million fewer marriages than actually took place in the United States between 1940 and 1946. Many of these newlyweds had a "goodbye baby" before the husband went overseas. Others quickly conceived the babies they postponed during the Depression. By 1943 the birthrate had risen to a sixteen-year peak, and it remained high throughout the postwar Baby Boom of 1946–1964.

Prosperity and Shortages. The war years brought prosperity to all segments of the population: indeed, the income of the poorest one-fifth rose 68 percent, the greatest increase for any group. Yet the war also brought higher prices and shortages of housing, food, clothing, electricity, and transportation that eroded the standard of living of most families. Homemakers made up for these shortages by growing vegetables in backyard victory gardens, by cooking meatless casseroles, and by conserving everything for the war effort, including kitchen fat for lubricating machinery.

Wartime Rationing. To an American public unused to any kind of wartime deprivation, wartime rationing of food and gasoline came as a great shock. The Emergency Price Control Act, signed by President Roosevelt on 30 January 1942, established the Office of Price Administration (OPA), which had the authority to ration and fix price ceilings on goods and commodities sold on the retail market. A rubber shortage had already caused the rationing of tires on 27 December 1941, and soon everything Americans liked to eat most was strictly rationed as well. Ration-coupon books for sugar and coffee were issued in early 1942. In early 1943 the OPA began a

THE NATIONAL GO-TO-SCHOOL DRIVE

With so many teenagers employed in wartime jobs, educators began to worry about getting young people to attend school. The U.S. Office of Education launched a "National Go-to-School Drive" for the 1944–1945 academic year, calling on communities to stress the value of education:

Hats off to American boys and girls! They have shown superb readiness and eagerness to share in the work of the war. . . . Millions of youngsters have taken full-time jobs. Others have added jobs on top of school work. Now the time has come when all of us must scrutinize far more carefully than we have in the first 3 years of the war the use that is being made of the capacities, energies and time of our teenage young people. . . . Some work experience may have significant educational value for some young people. For the vast majority of them, however, school provides the greatest opportunity for development, and adults should help to give school PRIORITY NUMBER ONE now.

Source: U.S. Department of Labor, U.S. Office of Education, *National Go-to-School Drive 1944–1945: A Handbook for Communities* (Washington, D.C.: U.S. Government Printing Office, 1944).

point-ration plan that applied to meat, fats and oils, cheese, and processed foods. Shoes were later rationed under the point system as well. The OPA issued books of ration stamps with numbers of points printed on them and then assigned specific point values to rationed items. To replenish their stock grocers sent the stamps to the wholesaler. The wholesaler then turned the stamps in at the local bank and got credit to buy more food. The system proved to be complicated and impractical. The average grocer had to handle some 3.5 billion tiny stamps each month. Sometimes they ran out of the gummed sheets on which they were supposed to stick the stamps. One wholesaler had to haul loose stamps to the bank in bushel baskets. In spite of rationing, however, Americans ate better during the war than before. In 1943, despite the rationing of meat, meat consumption rose to 128.9 pounds per person per year. The Department of Agriculture reported that in 1945, Americans ate more food than at any other time in history. By the end of 1945 rationing of everything except sugar had ended. Sugar rationing continued until 11 June 1947.

Gasoline Rationing. Gasoline rationing, instituted along with fuel-oil rationing on 1 December 1942, was particularly unpopular. A sticker-and-coupon system established gasoline allotments for civilian vehicles in four categories: "A" for cars used only for pleasure, "B" for those driven to work, "C" for those driven at work, and "E" for emergency vehicles. Many drivers who received "A" stickers, which limited them to only three gallons of gas per week, managed to get extra coupons, and some stations were willing to sell gas at higher prices to drivers without coupons. Cheating on gas rationing became a national scandal by late 1942.

Absentee Husbands. World War II also separated husbands and wives, fathers and children. Sixteen million men were separated from their families by the military, and nearly one family in five lost at least one or more relative to the war. Servicemen's wives endured loneliness and the stress of raising their children without their husbands. One wrote, "I try not to worry and if I can't sleep at night I just take a sleeping pill. Life seems more like existing to me than living." The federal allotment check of fifty dollars a month with twenty dollars extra per child was inadequate for many families, forcing wives to move in with their parents or other relatives. This doubling up created its own stresses, even in the best circumstances. As one woman wrote, "I get along well with my mother, but I had my own home long enough to develop my own methods of keeping house, so Mother and I have altogether different ideas of how a house should be run."

Children in Wartime. Young children also felt the pains of the wartime dislocations. Too young to remember fathers long absent overseas and raised by grandparents or neighbors while their mothers worked, these children coped with instability and uncertainty. One mother noted the difficulty in disciplining her children alone: "The kids don't seem to mind as much as they did when he was home." The demands of the war relaxed school-attendance requirements as well as child labor laws, and children shared both wartime excitement and anxiety. Though adult observers expressed characteristic alarm over the lack of supervision and authority figures in their lives, many children adjusted well.

Youth. Many teenagers deferred or left school to enter the labor force during the war. By 1943 legislators had reacted to the military state of emergency by relaxing child-labor laws. Sixty-two acts relating to the employment of minors were passed in twenty-seven states. Most of these laws were in force for the duration of the war only. According to a U.S. Census Bureau survey in April 1944, one in five schoolboys aged fourteen and fifteen, and more than two in five boys aged sixteen and seventeen, were gainfully employed. Though fewer teenage girls worked, by 1944 a third of sixteen- to eighteen-year-old girls surveyed had jobs. By that date 35 percent of teenagers in these age groups had left school altogether and gone to work. This wartime employment briefly reversed the overall twentieth-century trend toward the prolonged economic dependence of young people on their parents because of longer time in school and lack of opportunity for employment.

Teenagers in Factories. Most of the wartime jobs for young people were in manufacturing. The nature of such production jobs had important implications for the way

One of 2.5 million victory gardens in the United States in 1943

they grew up. A manufacturing job made strict demands on a youth's time and offered little opportunity for continued academic training. While some boys dropped out of school at fifteen or sixteen to take these jobs, most chose to stay in school and endured the long combined hours of employment and school. Working teens surveyed at three Michigan high schools in the spring of 1944 said they enjoyed their jobs and found them educational and added that work did not interfere with their schooling. Moreover, families with more than one worker enjoyed greater prosperity.

The Temptations of Prosperity. Wartime employment for young people may have been patriotic, but as in any disruption of the typical pattern of adolescent development, it provoked adult fears of increased juvenile delinquency. Some adults blamed teenagers' increased prosperity for creating greater temptations. A U.S. Department of Education pamphlet, *Guidance Problems in Wartime* (1942), claimed that it was "obvious that there was an unfortunate effect of young people's sudden prosperity: their opportunity to have a good time; to enjoy elaborate food, clothing, automobiles." School guidance counselors encouraged prudence and frugality among "suddenly prosperous" young people, urging them to buy war bonds and save for the future, lest they develop ex-

pensive tastes they would be unable to meet in the future.

Juvenile Delinquency. A perceived rise in juvenile crime paralleled an actual increase in youthful autonomy in the war years; many aspects of adolescents' lives were free from adult scrutiny for the first time. As the demands of the war brought teenagers into the labor force, they also weakened the influence of family and community over their behavior. Juvenile delinquency supposedly increased sharply during the war, particularly sexual promiscuity among young girls who sometimes confused sex with patriotism. According to a young man facing the draft in 1942, "a guy ought to have something to remember when he's facing submarines and death. Something more than a few hugs and kisses." The U.S. Children's Bureau denied any moral decay among youth and explained away the increase in girls' cases in juvenile courts as the result of greater legal vigilance. But some moral reformers in the war years noted the appearance of girls known as "khaki-wackies": "The new type is the young girl in her late teens and early twenties, the young woman in every field of life who is determined to have one fling or better." The problem was not prostitution but sexual excess. Charges of disorderly conduct increased almost two hundred percent in the war years, and charges for

WHAT TO TALK ABOUT ON A DATE

A 1948 manual for teenagers offered the following advice:

A smart Teen-Ager thinks about how to start a conversation with Jimmy long before she closes the front door behind her. This does not mean planned sentences — copying Susie's lines, popping out with the newest slang phrase every other minute. It means figuring out subjects of mutual interest that make good conversation easy. Look over these conversation starters:

Tell Jimmy you remember the first time you ever laid eyes on him: "It was the first day of school three years ago in Latin class and you were wearing a red tie."

Talk about animals. "My dog has fleas — what'll I do?"

Talk about foreign languages: "Are you taking French?" "Have you ever traveled?"

Source: Edith Heal, *The Teen-Age Manual: A Guide to Popularity and Success* (New York: Simon & Schuster, 1948).

---

so-called moral offenses increased markedly as well. Observers explained that these young people were "channeling" their youthful emotions "into a burning feeling of patriotism" that had no legitimate or immediate outlet. Wartime young people were simply more agitated than the typical youth in peacetime. There were reports of increasing restlessness, emotional instability, and hostility to adult authority figures among teenagers everywhere. Yet wartime peer culture oriented most young people toward social involvement, loyalty, and individual achievement.

Sources:
Steven Mintz and Susan Kellogg, *Domestic Revolutions: A Social History of American Family Life* (New York: Free Press, 1988);

This Fabulous Century: 1940–1950 (New York: Time-Life Books, 1969).

THE POSTWAR YOUTH CULTURE

Reemergence of the Youth Culture. An American youth culture based on adolescent leisure activities had emerged in the prosperous 1920s, but it was sharply curtailed by the financial stringency of the Depression. During the prosperous years that followed World War II it blossomed once again. Middle-class and many working-class teenagers had money to spend on recreation and dating, and they did so with exuberance. The practice of adolescent dating, which also began in the 1920s, grew after the war. Teenagers in this postwar generation were given more autonomy by their parents than adolescents of earlier generations, but the extent of their newfound freedom, especially in regard to experimentation with sex,

varied with social and economic class. In general, poor black teenagers growing up in the South had more freedom to engage in premarital sex than black adolescents with wealthier parents. Young, urban working-class men and women who dropped out of high school met in dance halls, bowling alleys, and skating rinks and were less restricted in their sexual activity than high-school students.

High-School Dating. High-school attendance rose dramatically after the war, and student culture defined dating rituals for the great majority of teenagers. High-school cliques regulated dating by defining the proper choice of partners and proper behavior on dates. The high-school social order differed by gender: boys who were star athletes were most admired, while a girl's prestige was measured by her popularity with boys. With adolescents heading eagerly toward marriage at younger ages, dating was a delicate dance orchestrated by the girl. A girl tried to attract boys subtly. Her cardinal rule was never to let a boy know she was chasing him, but to let him think he had "caught" her. Membership in a clique of popular teenagers enhanced a girl's value on the dating market, since nothing impressed boys more than a girl who was known as part of a "leading crowd" of students who were well dressed and self-confident. High-school dating provided opportunities for intimacy and sexual exploration, but it usually stopped at petting.

Sources:
Beth Bailey, *From Front Porch to Back Seat: Courtship in Twentieth-Century America* (Baltimore: Johns Hopkins University Press, 1988);

Elaine Tyler May, *Homeward Bound: American Families in the Cold War Era* (New York: Basic Books, 1988);

John Modell, *Into One's Own: From Youth to Adulthood in the United States, 1920–1975* (Berkeley: University of California Press, 1989).

RACE RELATIONS

"A Jap's a Jap" (Lt. Gen. John L. DeWitt, commander of Western Defense, 1941). In the aftermath of the Japanese attack on Pearl Harbor waves of racism and hatred directed at Japanese and Japanese Americans swept the West Coast. On 19 February 1942 President Roosevelt signed Executive Order 9066, ordering Japanese and Japanese Americans living in California, Oregon, and Washington to be relocated to internment camps for the duration of the war. Some of these people were "Issei," Japanese immigrants still tied to Japanese tradition, and a small number were "Kibei," American-born Japanese who studied in Japan, but most were "Nisei," American-born children of Issei parents, citizens of the United States by birthright and assimilated into American culture. The U.S. government made little distinction among these groups, denying many the legal rights that were theirs by virtue of their citizenship. One cost of the internment to the already tight American economy was the loss of two-thirds of the U.S. vegetable crop, previously grown by Japanese American farmers on the West Coast.

Barbershop in Parker, Arizona, 1944

Loss of Rights and Property. Within days of the attack on Pearl Harbor, Japanese Americans on the West Coast were fired from civil service jobs, their licenses to practice medicine and law were revoked, their businesses were boycotted, and their insurance policies were canceled. By spring 1942 their constitutional rights to due process were suspended. "The only good Jap is a dead Jap," a congressman from California shouted from the floor of the House of Representatives. Overt racism was mixed with fears that Japanese Americans were threats to military security and public safety. As California's attorney general Earl Warren — a Republican who was considered liberal on most issues — said in 1942, "When we are dealing with the Caucasian race we have methods that will test . . . loyalty. But when we deal with the Japanese, we are in an entirely different field." Yet security concerns quickly proved unfounded, as J. Edgar Hoover, director of the Federal Bureau of Investigation (FBI), acknowledged that Japanese Americans were not signaling Japanese submarines with laundry hanging on their clotheslines or taking photographs of the Golden Gate Bridge to help Japanese troops attacking San Francisco. Yet officials remained convinced that Japanese Americans might

resort to mob violence if there were another bombing of Hawaii or a submarine attack on the West Coast. This fear was a primary motive for the roundup and relocation of Japanese and Japanese Americans to what one California congressman called "inland concentration camps." Among the Japanese Americans who protested their internment at congressional hearings in 1942 was Miki Masoka, who asked, "Has the Gestapo come to America? Have we not risen in righteous anger at Hitler's mistreatment of the Jews? Then is it not incongruous that [American] citizens of Japanese descent should be similarly mistreated and persecuted?"

Internment. Japanese Americans were treated like prisoners. Young children who did not know English were tagged and herded with their families onto trucks. Families were housed in horse stalls before being moved to makeshift camps in remote and barren areas of Arizona, Arkansas, inland California, Colorado, Idaho, Utah, and Wyoming. Innocent and respectable people lived for years in one-room barracks without privacy, their farms, homes, businesses, and bank accounts confiscated. Mothers and fathers endured the indignity in silent

F Street in the Heart Mountain Relocation Center, one of the camps where Japanese Americans were held during World War II

apathy and depression, while their Nisei children often exploded in anger, some refusing to sign a loyalty oath and renouncing their American citizenship. Others volunteered to serve in the U.S. Army and were part of the elite, but segregated, 442nd Division, the most decorated combat division in the army. On 2 January 1945 the order excluding Japanese Americans from the West Coast was terminated, and in 1959 citizenship was restored to those Japanese Americans who had renounced their citizenship in the camps. In 1989 President George Bush signed the Internment Compensation Act awarding twenty thousand dollars to each surviving victim of the relocation order. Further reparations were paid in 1993, when a successful class-action suit brought a ruling that the constitutional rights of the internees had been violated.

Rising Black Expectations. African Americans lost patience with segregation and discrimination during World War II. On 15 January 1941 black labor leader A. Philip Randolph, known as the "Gandhi of the Negroes" for his use of passive resistance to protest racial discrimination, called for an orderly demonstration of blacks on 1 July in Washington, D.C., to protest their exclusion from employment in the defense industries. On 25 June, after meeting with Randolph and other black leaders a week

earlier, President Roosevelt preempted the demonstration by issuing Executive Order 8802, banning racial discrimination in defense industries and government and establishing a Fair Employment Practices Committee (FEPC) to investigate discrimination. The order did help many blacks find work in defense plants, though generally in nonskilled, low-paying jobs. Still, the number of blacks in skilled positions more than doubled, and those in semiskilled positions increased by an even larger percentage. The availability of defense-industry jobs lured blacks from the South to northern and western cities. Away from southern states, where poll taxes and unequally administered literacy tests prevented most African Americans from registering to vote, these blacks not only increased their incomes but also found a greater voice in politics. During the war years blacks overall saw a modest improvement in their standard of living and laid the groundwork for the civil rights movement of the 1950s.

Blacks in the Military. An executive order could not end long-standing prejudice, nor did it change conditions in the armed forces, where African Americans were accepted into the military far less often than whites, served in segregated units, were given inferior assignments, and

Detroit, June 1943, where thirty-five people were killed in race riots

advanced in the ranks slower than whites. In 1940 there were five black officers in the regular army and none in the navy. During the war opportunities for blacks in the military increased greatly. At the same time, military bases — particularly in the South and the West — were hotbeds of racial tension, fueled by resentment over the inferiority of recreational facilities for blacks to those enjoyed by whites, as well as whites' prejudice toward blacks. Among the first of several riots to arise from such situations was the one that followed the alleged lynching of a black soldier at Fort Benning, Georgia, in 1941. Another, at Camp Stewart, Georgia, in summer 1943 arose when military police clashed with black soldiers protesting segregation of post facilities and racial discrimination in a nearby town.

Race Riots in the Cities. Yet military-post riots paled in comparison to the explosions of black anger in Detroit and New York in summer 1943. One hot June day in Detroit black and white youths became involved in a small fight at a crowded beach. Within an hour and a half about five thousand people were rioting, their anger fueled by rumors. One such report, that a black woman and her baby had been thrown off a bridge, brought white sailors and inner-city blacks rushing to the scene with clubs and chains. The riot raged out of control for three days over large parts of the city until President Roosevelt declared a state of emergency and called in six thousand national guard troops. Twenty-five blacks and nine whites were killed, and more than seven hundred people were injured. The Detroit riot of 1943 remains one of the worst race riots in American history. After it was over Edward Jeffries, the white mayor of Detroit, prompted further racial tension with the warning "We'll know what to do next time."

The Harlem Riot. In August a riot erupted in the Harlem section of New York City after a fight between a black military policeman (in the presence of his mother) and a white policeman. The two scuffled, and after the

BREAKING THE COLOR BARRIER

President Franklin D. Roosevelt's Executive Order 8802, issued on 25 June 1941, banned racial discrimination in the defense industry and government. The order, an important early step in improving economic opportunities for African Americans, read in part:

Whereas it is the policy of the United States to encourage full participation in the national defense program by all citizens of the United States, regardless of race, creed, color, or national origin, in the firm belief that the democratic way of life within the Nation can be defended successfully only with the help and support of all groups within its borders. . . .

Now, therefore . . . as a prerequisite to the successful conduct of our national defense production effort, I do hereby reaffirm the policy of the United States that there shall be no discrimination in the employment of workers in defense industries or government because of race, creed, color, or national origin. . . .

MP started to run off with the policeman's nightstick, the policeman shot him in the shoulder. The rumor spread through black Harlem that a black soldier had been shot in the back and killed. The ensuing riot left 5 dead, 367 injured, and damages amounting to more than $5 million.

Racism Discredited. Black frustration mounted after the war, as blacks got less than their share of jobs and income in the booming postwar economy. Public acceptance of racism began to change, however. Various academic organizations, responding to Nazi claims of Aryan superiority, spoke out against racism. The American Anthropological Association, for example, argued that there was no scientific proof of psychological or cultural differences based on race. Psychologists made similar arguments, ascribing Nazi claims of the inferiority of non-Aryans to the desire to find scapegoats. Gunnar Myrdal's groundbreaking study *An American Dilemma* (1944) addressed racism, distinguishing whites' perceptions of blacks' demands from their actual needs and interests.

Governmental Response. Having failed to convince Congress to make President Roosevelt's wartime FEPC a permanent commission, President Harry S Truman established the President's Committee on Civil Rights on 5 December 1946 to advise him on issues related to discrimination. On 2 February 1948, acting on many of their recommendations, President Truman delivered the first ever presidential civil rights address to Congress, proposing legislation to ban poll taxes, a federal anti-

lynching law, and the establishment of a permanent federal Fair Employment Practices Commission. Passage was blocked by powerful Southern Democrats. Change came more quickly in the military. The navy ended segregation in 1946, and on 26 July 1948 President Truman signed Executive Order 9981, banning segregation in all branches of the military. On the same day he also ordered the desegregation of the federal civil service.

Sources:

Michael Barone, *Our Country: The Shaping of America from Roosevelt to Reagan* (New York: Free Press, 1990);

A. Russell Buchanan, *Black Americans in World War II* (Santa Barbara & London: Clio, 1977);

John P. Diggins, *The Proud Decades: America in War and in Peace, 1941–1960* (New York: Norton, 1988);

John Hope Franklin and Isidore Starr, *The Negro in Twentieth Century America* (New York: Random House, 1967);

Ulysses Lee, *The Employment of Negro Troops*, United States Army in World War II, Special Studies, no. 8 (Washington, D.C.: Office of the Chief of Military History, United States Army, 1966).

SEX AND SEXUALITY

The Pursuit of Sexual Pleasure. By the 1940s many Americans had adopted liberal attitudes toward heterosexual activity. They affirmed heterosexual pleasure as a good in itself, defined sexual satisfaction as a basic component of personal happiness and successful marriage, and accepted youthful sexual experimentation as preparation for adulthood. This new liberalism was solidified by the growing availability in the 1930s and 1940s of reliable contraceptives that separated sex from reproduction, allowing uninhibited pursuit of sexual pleasure. Sexual content appeared in movies and magazines with greater frequency as an emerging youth culture celebrated heterosexual expression, and husbands and wives came to view continuing erotic pleasure as a major component of marriage.

Sex and War. The war also contributed to liberalized attitudes toward sex. Lonely soldiers away from home engaged in sexual experimentation, and concerns over the spread of venereal disease in the military resulted in frank discussions of sex. Pictures of "pinup" girls appeared in servicemen's barracks, and flight crews were allowed to decorate the fronts of their planes with sexually explicit pictures of women. Like the pinups, this "nose art" was thought to boost morale.

Contraception. By the 1940s Margaret Sanger, who had led the birth-control movement since the 1910s, had succeeded in making effective contraception available to large numbers of American women. As a result of Sanger's tireless activism, there were more than eight hundred birth-control clinics across the country by 1942. These clinics were necessary because the diaphragm, then the most effective method of contraception, had to be fitted to each woman individually by trained medical personnel. A survey of contraceptive usage in the 1940s compared white married women born in the late nineteenth century with those born in the second decade of

An example of "nose art" that appeared on the front of American bombers during World War II

the twentieth century. In the older group two-fifths reported extensive use of condoms by their husbands, and 31 percent said they used diaphragms. By contrast 61 percent of the respondents in the younger group said they used diaphragms frequently. Contraceptive use outside the white middle class spread more slowly, but by the 1940s the rates for African American women went up markedly. This increased contraceptive use among black women reflected racial prejudice as much as changing attitudes toward sex among blacks. White fears of black population growth led to the availability of birth-control devices and education in southern public-health clinics.

Postwar Repression. Although the war contributed to a general liberalization of attitudes toward sex within marriage, the postwar baby boom years were characterized by an ethos of strict moral condemnation of sex outside marriage. The strict sexual mores of American culture after 1945 were often linked to the Cold War security concerns. A range of high-level officials and influential thinkers linked communism with sexual depravity. As Republican Party chairman Guy Gabrielson explained, "sexual perverts . . . have infiltrated our Government in recent years, . . . [and are] perhaps as dangerous as the actual Communists." According to this logic, sexual excess or degeneracy made individuals easy prey for Communist tactics. It was feared that Communist agents would use evidence of homosexuality or extramarital affairs to blackmail government officials into handing over top-secret information. For Americans in the late 1940s

"normal" heterosexual behavior leading to marriage represented "maturity" and "responsibility." Those who "deviated" from this course were viewed as irresponsible, immature, and weak.

Homosexuality. The relatively relaxed sexual attitudes of the war years tolerated the establishment of same-sex communities and the increasing visibility of gay men and lesbians, but the postwar years brought on a wave of publicly sanctioned homophobia. The label *pervert* was loosely applied to individuals who engaged in behavior ranging from same-sex relationships between consenting adults to violent criminals who raped and murdered. Persecution of homosexual men and women became intense. Gay-baiting was as fierce as Red-baiting, and it created stigmas, encouraged harassment, and destroyed careers.

Sexual Paranoia. The persecution of homosexuals that began in the late 1940s and continued in the early 1950s was the most blatant form of sexual paranoia that linked so-called perversion to national weakness. Public fear also turned to "sexual psychopaths" who, like homosexuals and Communists, were supposedly lurking everywhere. Women who did not fulfill the prescribed roles of wife and mother were also threatening: untraditional mothers might disrupt the masculine development of their sons; prostitutes and promiscuous women tempted men with their seductiveness. Sexual energy channeled exclusively into marriage was thought crucial to national security. Faithful husbands and fathers wore the label "family man" as a symbol of virility and patriotism.

With titles such as "What You Can Do to Help the Returning Veteran" and "Will He Be Changed?," many postwar articles in women's magazines expressed the widely held belief that veterans would have trouble readjusting to civilian life. An article in *Good Housekeeping* advised, "After two or three weeks he should be finished with talking, with oppressive remembering. If he still goes over the same stories, reveals the same emotions, you had best consult a psychiatrist. This condition is neurotic." *House Beautiful* published photographs of a living room designed for a general's house and suggested, "Home must be the greatest rehabilitation center of them all." Female veterans were met with a reassertion of traditional notions of femininity. *House Beautiful* said WACS and WAVES would be starved for feminine frills and would expect their bedrooms to be redecorated: "G.I. Jane will retool with ruffles."

Source: *This Fabulous Century: 1940–1950* (New York: Time-Life Books: 1969).

Sources:

Estelle B. Freeman and John D. Emilio, *Intimate Matters: A History of Sexuality in America* (New York: Harper & Row, 1988);

Elaine Tyler May, *Homeward Bound: American Families in the Cold War Era* (New York: Basic Books, 1988).

SUBURBANIZATION

The Fad of the Forties. The suburban building craze of the 1940s transformed American society. The war created an enormous housing shortage, which prompted the postwar construction boom that built suburbia. Housing starts went from 114,000 in 1944 to an all-time high of 1,692,000 in 1950. This massive construction of single-family suburban houses was largely subsidized by the federal government. The 1944 GI Bill of Rights created a program that provided federally insured loans to veterans and encouraged private investment in the housing mortgage market. Tax benefits also favored homeowners in the 1940s. Government-insured mortgages subsidized the building of single houses on large suburban tracts such as Levittown on Long Island. A veteran could buy a house in this suburb of New York City with no down payment and a thirty-year mortgage with payments of fifty-six dollars per month, far less than the rent for the average apartment in many cities. By 1946 for the first time the majority of American families lived in houses they owned.

The Exclusion of Blacks from Suburbia. Suburban life was not available to all Americans. During the 1940s blacks were excluded by de facto segregation as well as by the Federal Housing Authority (FHA) practice of encouraging covenants in deeds that forbade the sale of FHA-financed homes to blacks. In 1948 these covenants were declared unconstitutional by the U.S. Supreme Court in *Shelly* v. *Kraemer*. The FHA also had a policy of "redlining" inner-city neighborhoods: on city maps it drew red lines around predominantly black inner-city neighborhoods and refused to insure loans for houses in those areas on the grounds that they lacked "economic stability" or "protection from adverse conditions." Such practices fostered the decay of inner cities and further separated blacks and whites.

The Suburban Good Life. Yet for middle-class whites life in suburbia embodied the American dream of the good life. Suburbia offered protection from urban unrest and class conflict. Cold War ideology also spurred the move to suburbia. In 1947 newsman George Putnam described suburban shopping centers as "concrete expressions of the practical idealism that built America . . . plenty of free parking for all those cars that we capitalists seem to acquire. Who can help but contrast [them] with what you'd find under communism." A journal published by atomic scientists devoted an issue to "defense through decentralization," urging depopulation of the urban core to "avoid a concentration of residences or industries in a potential target area for a nuclear attack."

Families in Suburbia. Suburban homes reinforced a specific vision of family life. Houses were designed to accommodate a married couple and their standard "2.3" children. Builders assumed that housewives would be at home full-time and that men would be away at work all day. Home designs facilitated a mother's supervision of her children: kitchens were near the front so mothers could cook while they watched the children outside, and living rooms had picture windows that also enabled a mother to see her children playing. The suburban home was designed to be a self-contained universe: new appliances made housework efficient and easy while televisions, home games, and backyards provided opportunities for recreation, amusement, family togetherness, and fun.

Barbecues in Levittown. Young suburban families went on spending sprees to "keep up with the Joneses," to have the same new appliances and toys as the family next door. A 1960 study of the psychology of spending noted: "The impact of suburbia on consumer behavior can hardly be overstated. . . . Young people choose to marry early, to have several children in the early years of marriage, to live in nice neighborhoods, and to have cars, washing machines, refrigerators, television sets, and several other appliances at the same time." The suburban good life revolved around home and children, with families gathering at a neighbor's house for Sunday barbecues or at Little League games. Family-centered consumption was viewed as an investment in the strength and stability of family life, rather than a conspicuous display of affluence. In the climate of the Cold War suburban domesticity was considered proof of the superiority of the American way of life.

Sources:

George Katona, *The Powerful Consumer: Psychological Studies of the American Economy* (New York: McGraw-Hill, 1960);

Elaine Tyler May, *Homeward Bound: American Families in the Cold War Era* (New York: Basic Books, 1988).

HEADLINE MAKERS

HANNAH ARENDT

1906-1975

PHILOSOPHER, POLITICAL THEORIST

A Philosopher of Her Times. Hannah Arendt is best known for her groundbreaking book *The Origins of Totalitarianism* (1951), an influential study of anti-Semitism, imperialism, and authoritarianism. Her historical analysis of Nazism, the Holocaust, and the nature of evil established her reputation as an important philosopher and political thinker.

Early Years. Born to middle-class Jewish parents in Hannover, Germany, Arendt grew up in Königsberg and Berlin and began her university studies in Marburg in 1924. There she studied philosophy with Martin Heidegger, who became a close friend. She also studied at Freiburg with Edmund Husserl and went on to Heidelberg, where she received her doctorate in philosophy in 1929, having written her dissertation under the supervision of Karl Jaspers. Jaspers and Heidegger profoundly influenced Arendt's later philosophical work.

Life in Nazi Germany. Arendt married writer Gunther Stern in 1929 and began writing *Rachel Varnhagen: The Life of a Jewess* (1957), a biography of an eighteenth-century Berlin salon hostess. Her work on the book was interrupted in 1933, afer the Nazis imprisoned her briefly for Zionist activities. Released a week later, Arendt escaped with Stern to Paris. There she worked for various Jewish organizations. Her marriage to Stern ended in 1936, when she met Heinrich Blücher, a working-class, gentile Jewish Berliner who was a Communist until 1939. Arendt and Blücher were married in 1940, and soon thereafter they managed to escape during the German invasion of France and made their way to New York in the spring of 1941.

The War Years in New York. In New York Arendt wrote columns on Jewish history. Other European expatriates, including philosopher Paul Tillich, helped Arendt place her articles in journals such as *Jewish Social Studies, Jewish Frontier,* and *Review of Politics.* As Arendt and Blücher learned English, they became friends with American intellectuals including Alfred Kazin, Mary McCarthy, and Philip Rahv.

The Origins of Totalitarianism. In the late 1940s Arendt worked as a director of research at the Conference on Jewish Relations (1944–1946), taught history part-time at Brooklyn College, and was senior editor at Schocken Books (1946–1948). During those years she published articles on political philosophy in *Partisan Review, Review of Politics,* and *The Nation.* She also worked on locating Jewish survivors of the Holocaust and retrieving Jewish property taken by the Nazis and served on a campaign supporting the establishment of a binational Arab-Jewish state in Palestine. She also began developing her published essays into *The Origins of Totalitarianism* (1951). The work was the first major study to examine authoritarianism in the light of the Holocaust, and it received immediate acclaim.

The "Banality of Evil." Arendt became a U.S. citizen in 1951. In spring 1961, as a reporter for *The New Yorker* magazine, she attended the trial of Nazi Adolf Eichmann, who was on trial in Jerusalem for his role in planning and overseeing the deportation and execution of Jews in Nazi death camps. Her account, published in book form as *Eichmann in Jerusalem: A Report on the Banality of Evil* (1964), portrayed Eichmann not as a psychopath or innately evil but as banal and thoughtless. According to Arendt's radical reformulation, Eichmann was not unlike the rest of humankind, and all people are capable of such evil. Arendt spent her later years writing and teaching about the evils of authoritarianism and bureaucracy.

Sources:

Derwent May, *Hannah Arendt* (Harmondsworth, U.K. & New York: Penguin, 1986);

Elisabeth Young-Bruehl, Entry on Arendt, in *Notable American Women: The Modern Period, A Biographical Dictionary,* edited by Barbara Sicherman and Carol Hurd Green with Ilene Kantrov and Harriette Walker (Cambridge, Mass. & London: Harvard University Press, 1980), pp. 33–37;

Young-Bruehl, *Hannah Arendt, For Love of the World* (New Haven: Yale University Press, 1982).

MARY McLEOD BETHUNE

1875-1955

EDUCATOR, CIVIL RIGHTS LEADER

Crusader for Racial Equality. For more than three decades (1920–1935) Mary McLeod Bethune was known as the "most influential black woman in the United States." For all blacks, but especially for black women, she emphasized the need for education and for the opportunity to break free from oppressive social and political boundaries. She urged blacks to unite in one political movement and believed that the government could be used to improve the black race. She once summarized her beliefs as "self-control, self-respect, self-reliance, and race pride."

Early Years. Born near Mayesville, South Carolina, Mary McLeod was the fifteenth of the seventeen children of Sam and Patsy McLeod, slaves freed after the Civil War. Beginning her education at a black mission school near Mayesville, McLeod quickly learned all its teachers could offer her, and in 1888 she won a scholarship to attend Scotia Seminary, a Presbyterian school for black girls in Concord, New Hampshire. At that school, which emphasized religion and industrial education and had both whites and blacks on its faculty, she enrolled in the normal and scientific course, which prepared her to teach. After graduating in July 1894, she received a scholarship to the Bible Institute for Home and Foreign Missions in Chicago, where she spent a year preparing for missionary work in Africa.

Teaching Career. When she learned there were no missionary openings for blacks in Africa, McLeod went to teach at the Haines Normal and Industrial Institute in Augusta, Georgia. There she met the dynamic founder and principal of the school, Lucy Laney, whose service to others made her an important role model for McLeod. After a year at Haines, McLeod went on to teach at the Kindell Institute in Sumter, South Carolina. There she met Albertus Bethune, whom she married in 1898. Not long after the birth of their only child, Albert McLeod Bethune, in 1899, the family moved to Palatka, Florida, where Mary Bethune opened a Presbyterian mission

school. Albertus Bethune did not share his wife's commitment to missionary work, and the couple separated.

Origins of Bethune-Cookman College. In 1904 Bethune went to Daytona Beach, Florida, where she established the Daytona Normal and Industrial Institute, a girls' school modeled on Scotia Seminary. Because of Bethune's administrative abilities, the school grew rapidly. Like other black schools at the time, it stressed religious and industrial education, but Bethune also sought to expand educational opportunities for blacks. After World War I she urged ambitious students to attend college. In 1923 the school was merged with the all-male Cookman Institute of Jacksonville, Florida, and became a coeducational college. In 1929 it was officially renamed Bethune-Cookman College, and three years later it earned regional accreditation as a junior college. In 1943 its first four-year students graduated with degrees in teacher education. Bethune served as president of Bethune-Cookman until December 1942.

Civil Rights Leader. In December 1935 Bethune created the National Council of Negro Women, serving as its president until 1949. In August 1935, on the recommendation of Eleanor Roosevelt, Bethune was appointed to the thirty-five member National Advisory Committee to the National Youth Administration (NYA), and in June 1936 she was put in charge of Negro Affairs within the NYA. Two and a half years later she became director of the Division of Negro Affairs, responsible for ensuring that a fair share of the agency budget went to programs for blacks. In 1942 she persuaded the agency to employ regional Negro Affairs representatives and guided the creation of school-aid programs and funding for black colleges and graduate students. During the war she also effectively lobbied for the employment of black youths in the defense industries, which had discriminated against African Americans until President Franklin D. Roosevelt's 1941 executive order demanding equal treatment for blacks in hiring for those factories. Bethune represented the interests of blacks to the Roosevelt administration, urging the president to advance civil rights and appealing directly to Eleanor Roosevelt to promote the cause of blacks.

Retirement. Mary Bethune left Washington, D.C., and retired in Daytona in 1944, when the NYA closed. She resigned as president of the National Council of Negro Women in 1949, at the age of seventy-four. She continued to fight for racial equality until her death in 1955.

Sources:

Rackham Holt, *Mary McLeod Bethune* (Garden City, N.Y.: Doubleday, 1964);

Elaine M. Smith, Entry on Bethune, in *Notable American Women: The Modern Period, A Biographical Dictionary,* edited by Barbara Sicherman and Carol Hurd Green with Ilene Kantrov and Harriette Walker (Cambridge, Mass. & London: Harvard University Press, 1980), pp. 76–80;

Emma Gelders Sterne, *Mary McLeod Bethune* (New York: Knopf, 1957).

James Farmer

1920-

Civil Rights Leader

A Founder of CORE. From the time he helped to found the Congress of Racial Equality (CORE) in 1942, James Farmer was one of the most effective and widely recognized African American leaders in the United States, serving as national director of CORE until 1966. He brought to the American civil rights movement the nonviolent methods of public protest that were responsible for many of the movement's greatest achievements.

Early Life. Farmer was born in Marshall, Texas, where his father, the first black man in Texas to earn a Ph.D., taught at the all-black Wiley College. As the son of a college professor, Farmer had a fairly sheltered childhood. He first learned he was "colored" when he was a small boy and his mother explained to him why he could not drink from a whites-only water fountain at a local drugstore. After receiving a B.S. in chemistry from Wiley College, Farmer enrolled in the School of Religion at Howard University, intending to become a Methodist minister. He earned a bachelor of divinity degree in 1941 but refused ordination because the Methodist Church was segregated. As he explained later, "I didn't see how I could honestly preach the Gospel of Christ in a church that practiced discrimination." Instead he took a job as race-relations secretary to the pacifist Fellowship of Reconciliation, and in 1942, at age twenty-two, he joined with two other Christian pacifists — Bayard Rustin and A. J. Muste — to found CORE, an interracial organization dedicated to the use of Gandhian methods of nonviolent protest as a direct challenge to American racism.

Civil Rights Leader. In 1943 CORE staged its first successful sit-in at a segregated restaurant in Chicago — inventing a tactic that was employed throughout the South in the 1960s. It also pioneered another tactic widely used in the 1960s: the Freedom Ride. Following the U.S. Supreme Court decision in *Morgan* v. *Virginia* (1946) — which invalidated segregation on interstate buses — integrated teams of CORE members rode buses throughout the upper South, purposely violating the segregation laws to test the effect of the ruling. When the NAACP withdrew its funding of legal fees for arrested Freedom Riders, the project fell apart, amid some recrimination. Despite its failure the project set the precedent for the successful CORE Freedom Rides of the 1960s.

CORE Strategy. In his 1965 book, *Freedom — When?*, Farmer called for direct political action on the part of blacks: "This means much more than endorsing candidates on a national level. . . . More crucially, it means . . . *running our own people* on the local and state

level. . . . It means placing the right people in decision-making and planning positions at the local, state, and federal agencies, and 'infiltrating' party politics on a ward and precinct level." Farmer believed in changing political and social systems from within, calling attention to inequity through peaceful demonstrations. During the 1960s CORE had broad impact nationwide. Farmer increased the number of local branches and stepped up direct-action protests. He received national attention with CORE black-voter registration drives and anti-discrimination protests, including a demonstration at the 1964 New York World's Fair.

New Directions. In 1966, as younger leaders at CORE began espousing black separatism, Farmer left the organization. In 1969 he was criticized by some African Americans for taking the position of assistant secretary of health, education, and welfare (HEW) in the Republican administration of President Richard M. Nixon. Farmer accepted the appointment because he believed he could use it to further the interests of African Americans. He did succeed in increasing the number of blacks employed by the agency, but he resigned not long after beginning the job because he came to feel that he could accomplish little at HEW. Until 1981 he was active as a lecturer and as director of the Council on Minority Planning and Strategy, a black think tank in Washington, D.C.

Sources:
James Farmer, *Freedom — When?* (New York: Random House, 1965);

Farmer, *Lay Bare the Heart: An Autobiography of the Civil Rights Movement* (New York: Arbor House, 1985);

Charles D. Lowery and John F. Marszalek, eds. *Encyclopedia of African-American Civil Rights: From Emancipation to the Present* (Westport, Conn.: Greenwood Press, 1992).

Alfred Kinsey

1894-1956

Zoologist, Sex Researcher

Controversial Sex Researcher. In the repressive social climate of the late 1940s and early 1950s Alfred Kinsey's *Sexual Behavior in the Human Male* (1948) and *Sexual Behavior in the Human Female* (1953) were widely criticized, and he was subject to personal attacks. In 1953, for example, the *Chicago Tribune* called him a "real menace to society." Yet his extensive research into Americans' sexual habits transformed the way they think about their sexuality.

Early Years. Kinsey was born in Hoboken, New Jersey, where his father taught at Stevens Institute of Technology. He graduated from Bowdoin College in 1916 and received an Sc.D. (doctor of science) degree in zoology at Harvard University in 1920. Later that year he went to teach zoology at Indiana University, where he remained for most of his life.

Research on Gall Wasps. During the 1930s Kinsey published a series of papers reporting the results of his groundbreaking research on the habits of the gall wasp, for which he traveled some eighty thousand miles in Mexico and Central America. As *Time* magazine explained, "he measured, catalogued and preserved 3,500,000 specimens to demonstrate their individual variations. . . . He took and recorded 28 different [microscopic] measurements on each wasp."

Examining Human Sexuality. Kinsey noted the lack of scientific information on human sexual behavior when he taught courses on marriage problems. In the late 1930s he made this subject his new research topic, bringing to it the passion for minute detail that had served him so well in his study of gall wasps as well as a lifelong interest in people. As he explained later, "I was struck by the fact that a large area of living had not been studied on a broad, objective basis, and started out to do so."

Beginning Research. Kinsey began by interviewing his friends on their sexual experiences and worked out statistical methods to calculate his findings. Indiana University endorsed his project, and after funding his early work himself, Kinsey received a grant from the National Research Council in 1940. Soon the Rockefeller Foundation was providing forty thousand dollars annually for the research. With his assistants and co-authors Wardell B. Pomeroy and Clyde E. Martin, Kinsey conducted a massive survey, interviewing thousands of men and women all over the United States.

Kinsey's Methods. *Sexual Behavior in the Human Male* is a statistical analysis based on 5,300 case histories, and *Sexual Behavior in the Human Female* is based on interviews with 5,940 women. Kinsey's studies are the most elaborate descriptions ever assembled of the sexual habits of white, mostly middle-class Americans. He catalogued in great detail the frequency and incidence of masturbation, premarital petting and intercourse, marital intercourse, extramarital sex, and homosexuality. The large numbers of cases in his samples allowed him to capture a wide range of behavioral variations.

Controversial Findings. *Sexual Behavior in the Human Male* sold almost 250,000 copies. Both studies shocked traditional moralists. Kinsey's research on men revealed that masturbation and heterosexual petting were nearly universal and that more than a third of adult males had had some homosexual experience. While the range and frequency of women's experiences were narrower than males, his findings also changed the conventional view of women's sexual behavior. More than three-fifths of women surveyed engaged in masturbation; 90 percent participated in petting; half engaged in premarital intercourse; and a quarter had had extramarital sexual relations. Kinsey's findings were sharply at odds with the American public's ideas about their fellow citizens' sexual mores, and his dispassionate statistical presentation challenged Americans to revise their sexual values to match

their sexual behavior. All of the royalties from Kinsey's studies went to fund the Institute for Sex Research in Bloomington, Indiana, which Kinsey founded in 1942 and directed until his death at age sixty-two in 1956.

Sources:
Cornelia V. Christenson, *Kinsey: A Biography* (Bloomington: Indiana University Press, 1971);

Wardell Baxter Pomeroy, *Dr. Kinsey and the Institute for Sex Research* (New York: Harper & Row, 1972).

ROBERT MOSES

1888-1981

URBAN PLANNER AND ADMINISTRATOR

Master Builder. Robert Moses did more than anyone else in the twentieth century to shape the landscape of New York City. He built parks, playgrounds, and swimming pools all over the city and linked the five boroughs with a system of highways, bridges, and tunnels. He also planned a statewide system of parks for New York State.

Early Years. Robert Moses was born in New Haven, Connecticut, and raised in Manhattan. After earning bachelor's degrees from Yale University (1909) and Oxford University (1911), he did graduate work at Oxford (M.A., 1913) and Columbia University (Ph.D., 1914).

Administrative Reform. Moses's first position was in the New York City Bureau of Municipal Research, where he took on the task of administrative reform. He worked there from 1913 until the United States entered World War I in 1918, when he went to work with the U.S. Shipping Board. In 1919 Moses worked for the National Federation of Employees, preparing a plan to regulate the salaries of government employees that was later adopted by Congress. That same year New York governor Alfred E. Smith appointed Moses chief of staff for the New York State Reconstruction Commission, charged with streamlining the state government.

Parks. Moses began what was to be his life's work in 1920, when he submitted to Governor Smith a plan for statewide improvement of parks and highways. In 1924 Moses was named chairman of the New York State Council of Parks and president of the Long Island Park Commission. He held both posts until 1963. In the 1920s and 1930s he created a system of parks across the state of New York from Buffalo to Long Island. Accessible only by car, these parks earned Moses the reputation for designing open-space areas for use by people with automobiles.

For Cars and Recreation. When he became New York City parks commissioner in 1934, Moses brought his ideas about parks to the city. Remaining in this position until 1960, Moses transformed the New York City parks system. In the 1930s alone, he built more than three hundred playgrounds, fifteen swimming pools, and seven golf courses. During his long career he increased the number of New York City playgrounds from 119 to 777. He also added eight thousand acres of new parkland to the park system, democratizing it by bringing parks and recreation facilities to many neighborhoods. There were limits to his vision. Black neighborhoods were underserved in his plans.

Highways. In the 1930s Moses linked the five boroughs of New York City with a network of highways, bridges, and tunnels. He directed the construction of the Henry Hudson Parkway leading from Manhattan to the Bronx, and the Belt Parkway around Brooklyn. In 1936 he became chairman of the Triborough Bridge Authority, which oversaw the construction of a bridge connecting Manhattan, Queens, and the Bronx. Moses also improved the waterfront around the city and created Jones Beach and the parkways on Long Island. Between 1946 and 1953 no public improvement in New York City was made without Moses's involvement and approval. Immediately after World War II, Moses began to implement plans for the six elevated expressways that eventually crisscrossed the city. These new roads eased traffic problems for middle-class commuters from the suburbs, but at the same time they adversely affected the lives of many city dwellers, particularly the urban poor. Thousands of people were evicted from their homes as neighborhoods were demolished or cut in two by highway construction. Whether forced into sterile new housing projects or in vastly altered surroundings, people lost the sense of community and shared experience they had had in their old neighborhoods.

Political Candidate. After his defeat as Republican candidate for governor of New York in 1934, Moses declined several bids to run as the Republican candidate for mayor of New York City in the late 1940s and early 1950s. Controversial because of his autocratic style of management, Moses retired from the last of his important positions, chairman of the consolidated Triborough Bridge and New York City Tunnel Authority, in 1968. He had held the post since 1946 and continued even after retirement to work as a planning consultant.

Sources:

Robert A. Caro, *The Power Broker: Robert Moses and the Fall of New York* (New York: Knopf, 1974);

Roy Rosenzweig and Elizabeth Blackmar, "Urban Parks," in *Encyclopedia of American Social History*, 3 volumes, edited by Mary Kupiec Cayton, Elliott J. Gorn, and Peter T. Williams (New York: Scribners, 1993), III: 1694;

Joel Schwartz, *The New York Approach: Robert Moses, Urban Liberals and Redevelopment of the Inner City* (Columbus: Ohio State University Press, 1993).

PEOPLE IN THE NEWS

On 28 February 1943 **Carrie Chapman Catt,** honorary president of the League of Women Voters, issued a statement opposing an Equal Rights Amendment before Congress.

On 11 April 1947 **Stanley B. Cofall,** director of liquor control for the state of Ohio, announced the abolishment of the rationing of liquor, in effect since May 1943.

In July 1949 **Dr. Samuel J. Green,** of Georgia, Grand Dragon of the Ku Klux Klan was interviewed for the *Nation* magazine. Responding to the question of why the KKK always wore disguises, Green replied that "So many people are prejudiced against the Klan these days."

In 1942 **Mary Halleren** entered the Officer Candidate School of the newly formed Women's Army Auxiliary Corps. A year later she commanded the first Women's Army Corps (WAC) unit sent overseas, and in 1945 she was appointed director of all women's overseas units. She became director of the WAC in 1946, and in 1948, when the WAC was officially integrated into the army, Halleren, by then a colonel, became the first woman to receive a U.S. Army commission.

In 1943, responding to public concerns over reports of immorality in the ranks of the Women's Army Corps, director of the WACs **Oveta Culp Hobby** announced that contraceptives would no longer be issued to women in the corps.

On 15 July 1941 Judge **John S. McClelland** of the Great Atlantic and Pacific Tea Company grocery store chain announced that the company would adopt the five-day, forty-eight-hour workweek.

On 16 July 1941 two doctors, **Morris J. Renner** and **Nathaniel Collins,** and four assistants were arrested in New York City for operating what was termed a "wholesale abortion mill."

On 4 September 1949 black singer **Paul Robeson** gave a concert in Peekskill, New York. Because Robeson was widely criticized for his leftist politics, mobs of anti-Communists attacked concertgoers, leading to the arrests of six people. A grand jury refused to indict the attackers on the grounds that the concert abetted Communists — "the shock troops of a revolutionary force which is controlled by a foreign power."

On 11 April 1947 **Jackie Robinson** became the first black to appear in a major-league-baseball uniform when he took the field for the Brooklyn Dodgers against the New York Yankees.

In June 1949 Mr. and Mrs. **Clark Seabloom** returned to their Tacoma, Washington, home to find it ransacked.

The only thing missing was the cream skimmed from the tops of four bottles of milk.

In March 1947 British historian **Arnold J. Toynbee** delivered a series of sold-out lectures at Bryn Mawr College. Toynbee was in the midst of a triumphant tour celebrating his bestselling multivolume series *A Study of History.*

On 28 February 1943 **Steve Vassilakos,** a peanut vendor who occupied a corner outside the White House for thirty-eight years, died.

On 16 July 1941, at a meeting in Cambridge, Massachusetts, Professor **Carle C. Zimmerman** called on Americans to have more children, preferably three or four, and at a younger age. At the same meeting **Eleanor Roosevelt** endorsed the call for more children. A later speaker, Lt. Col. **Donald F. Currier,** reported that only 34.8 percent of draftees passed the physical examination.

DEATHS

Hendrik Christian Andersen, 68, sculptor and painter who advocated peace by promoting the erection of a "Universal City," 19 December 1940.

William Banks, 100, commander in chief of United Confederate Veterans, 6 January 1946.

Matilda G. Bausch, 85, philanthropist and wife of Edward Bausch, chairman of the board of Bausch and Lomb Optical Company, 14 July 1940.

Theodore Bear, 76, creator of the teddy bear, 19 November 1940.

Maude Potter Bennett, 80?, social leader and widow of noted sportsman, financier, and eccentric James Gordon Bennett, 4 February 1946.

Rose Ann Billington, 83, noted suffragist and member of the National Democratic Committee, 12 October 1942.

Emily P. Bissell, 86, writer and social worker who originated the Christmas Seal drive to fight tuberculosis, 8 March 1947.

Harriet Stanton Blatch, 84, leader in the fight for woman suffrage leader, daughter of Henry Brewster Stanton and suffrage leader Elizabeth Cady Stanton, 20 November 1940.

Gen. Ballington Booth, 81, founder of the Volunteers of America (1896), 5 October 1940.

Helen Varick Boswell, 78, suffrage leader; founder and thirty-year president of the Women's Forum of New York, 5 January 1942.

Edward Riley Bradley, 86, philanthropist and four-time Kentucky Derby winner, 15 August 1946.

Sophonisba Preston Breckinridge, 82, pioneer social worker, educator, lawyer, and author, 30 July 1948.

Abraham Arden Brill, 74, psychiatrist whose translations introduced the writings of Sigmund Freud to the English-speaking world, 2 March 1948.

Emerson Brooks, founder of the Boy Rangers of America and pioneer automobile body manufacturer, 23 July 1948.

Miss Anne Brown, 86, a principal of the Brown School, fashionable New York institution for girls in the 1880s and 1890s, 2 February 1940.

Mrs. William Adams Brown, 75, national president of the Women's Land Army in World War I and founder of the Cosmopolitan Club, 12 December 1942.

Jacques Bustanoby, 62, one of four brothers who founded several famous restaurants in New York City including Café des Beaux Arts, 23 March 1942.

Peter V. Cacchione, 50, New York City councilman from Brooklyn after 1941 and first self-declared Communist ever to hold elective public office in New York State, 6 October 1947.

Louise Whitfield Carnegie, 89, widow of Andrew Carnegie, steel magnate and philanthropist, 24 June 1946.

Earl Carroll, 54, Hollywood nightclub impresario and Broadway producer of lavish and gaudy revues, *Earl Carroll Vanities* (1923–1935), 17 June 1948.

Carrie Chapman Catt, 88, suffragist and peace leader chosen by Susan B. Anthony as her successor as president of the National American Woman Suffrage Association, 9 March 1947.

Emmanuel Chapman, 43, psychologist, philosopher, and chairman of the Committee of Catholics for Human Rights, 17 April 1948.

Starling Winston Childs, 76, investment banker and codonor of ten million dollars for the Jane Coffin Childs Memorial Fund for cancer research at Yale University, 20 December 1946.

Walter P. Chrysler, 65, automobile manufacturer who introduced the Chrysler, De Soto, and Plymouth automobiles and built the world's then-tallest building, the Chrysler Building in New York City, 18 August 1940.

S. Kent Costikyan, 82, well-known connoisseur and importer of Oriental rugs, 3 July 1949.

Dwight F. Davis, 66, public official who in 1900 donated the Davis Cup for the world team-tennis championship, 28 November 1945.

William Morgan "Billy" De Beck, 52, American comic artist and creator of Barney Google, Spark Plug, and other characters, 11 November 1942.

Edward Thomas Devine, 80, social-welfare worker, author, and editor, 27 February 1948.

Thomas Dixon, 82, Baptist minister and author of pro–Ku Klux Klan novel *The Clansman* (1905), which was the basis of D. W. Griffith's film *Birth of a Nation* (1915), 3 April 1946.

James M. Doran, 57, commissioner of prohibition (1927–1930) and administrator of Distilled Spirits Institute after 1933, 8 September 1942.

Bessie Clarke Drouet, 61, author of psychic works, 27 August 1940.

Mrs. Birdsall Otis Edey, 67, national commissioner and former president of Girl Scouts of America, 17 March 1940.

John Lovejoy Elliott, 73, leader of Society for Ethical Culture; founder of the Hudson Guild Neighborhood House, 12 April 1942.

Dorothy Harrison Eustis, 60, founder and former president of The Seeing Eye, Inc., philanthropic institution, 8 September 1946.

Beatrice Fairfax (Marie Manning Gasch), 70, famous newspaper columnist who gave advice to dejected lovers, 28 November 1945.

Marcus Feder, 89, tobacconist known as the "father of the American cigarette," 25 July 1942.

Msgr. Edward Joseph Flanagan, 61, founder of Boys Town, Nebraska (1922), 15 May 1948.

Robert Garland, 86, known as the "father of daylight savings time," 19 April 1949.

Mrs. John M. Glenn, 70, internationally known welfare worker and wife of the general director of the Russell Sage Foundation, 3 November 1940.

Emma Goldman, 70, famous anarchist who emigrated from Lithuania (1885) and was deported in 1919 after several arrests and a jail term (1917–1919) for agitation, 14 May 1940.

Samuel Green, 59, imperial wizard of Associated Klans of Georgia, 18 August 1949.

Paul Percy Harris, 78, founder of the Rotary Club (1905), 27 January 1947.

T. Arnold Hill, 58, leader in social work for African Americans; associated with the National Urban League (1914–1940), 1 August 1947.

Charles H. Ingersoll, 82, codeveloped (1892) the Ingersoll one-dollar watch, "the watch that made the dollar famous," 21 September 1948.

Frank J. Irwin, 48, founder of Disabled American Veterans, 3 August 1942.

Anna M. Jarvis, 84, founder of Mother's Day, 24 November 1948.

William E. "Pussyfoot" Johnson, 82, prohibition crusader who acquired his nickname through his methods of pursuing lawbreakers in Indian Territory, 2 February 1945.

Sarah H. Joslyn, 89, Nevada's wealthiest woman and donor of $4.6 million to establish the Joslyn Memorial in memory of her husband, George A. Joslyn, founder of Western Newspaper Union, 28 February 1940.

Susan Myra Kingsbury, 78, sociologist and champion of equal rights for women, 28 November 1949.

Harriet Burton Laidlaw, 75, suffragist and worker for peace, 25 January 1949.

Huddie "Leadbelly" Ledbetter, 60, known as one of the greatest American folk and blues singers, 6 December 1949.

Blanche Le Rallec, 87, acclaimed designer of fancy, high-priced wedding and anniversary cakes, 18 March 1940.

John Avery Lomax, 80, collector of American folk songs who recorded more than ten thousand songs for the Library of Congress, 26 January 1948.

Carole Lombard, 32, motion-picture star and wife of Clark Gable, 16 January 1942.

Jimmie Lunceford, 45, African American jazz band leader, 13 July 1947.

Col. Albert K. Lyman, 57, first Hawaiian to attain the rank of brigadier general in the United States Army, 13 August 1942.

Alexander James McGavick, 85, founder of the Catholic Youth Organization and sponsor of the Big Brother Movement, 25 August 1948.

Joseph W. Molyneaux, 76, retired U.S. district judge who was noted for his strict sentences imposed on convicted bootleggers during prohibition, 24 January 1940.

"Hamburger Mary" Morris, 52, owner of the famous "Hamburger Mary" restaurant in New York City where thousands of aspiring yet unsuccessful theater actors were fed, 26 February 1940.

Dan O'Brien, 90, widely known as "the king of the hoboes" in New York City, 29 October 1949.

Lucy Parsons, 83, noted anarchist whose first husband, Albert R. Parsons, was hanged for complicity in the Chicago Haymarket Riot of 1886, 7 March 1942.

Jessie Reed, 43, noted for her beauty and one of the highest paid showgirls in history, 18 September 1940.

Maj. Philip Rhinelander, 74, member of one of the oldest families in New York City and owner of large amounts of city real estate, 18 March 1940.

Robert LeRoy Ripley, 55, author who featured odd facts in his *Believe It or Not* cartoons, 27 May 1949.

Abby Greene Rockefeller, 73, wife of John D. Rockefeller, Jr., a founder of the Museum of Modern Art in New York, and supporter of many philanthropies, 5 April 1948.

Rt. Rev. Msgr. John A. Ryan, 76, nationally recognized labor expert and pioneer of minimum-wage legislation, 16 September 1945.

Alice Salomon, 76, German-American sociologist, educator, and internationally prominent feminist, 30 August 1948.

Emil Seidel, 82, first Socialist ever to be mayor of a large U.S. city (Milwaukee, 1910–1912), 24 June 1947.

Alice L. Seligsberg, 67, Jewish welfare worker and former president of the Women's Zionist Organization of America, 27 August 1940.

Hannah McCormick Simms, 64, congresswoman and political leader who worked on behalf of woman suffrage and labor, 31 December 1944.

Philip Hal Sims, 62, bridge expert and onetime world champion, 26 February 1949.

Thomas O'Conor Sloane, 88, scientist and author, editor of *Amazing Stories* magazine, and associate editor of *Science and Invention*, 7 August 1940.

Eva Tanguay, 68, Canadian American vaudeville star who shocked audiences with scanty costumes and risqué songs and was billed as the "Girl Who Made Vaudeville Famous," 11 January 1947.

Marion Sayle Taylor, 53, famous radio personality known as the "Voice of Experience," 1 February 1942.

John Evans Terwilliger, 61, manager of the Tiffany Foundation, 20 August 1940.

Henry Kendall Thaw, 76, playboy who shot and killed the famous architect Stanford White in 1906, 22 February 1947.

Edward Thorndike, 75, psychologist at Columbia University Teacher's College who developed intelligence tests for use by the U.S. Army in World War I, 9 August 1949.

Frank Tinney, 53, blackface comedian, 27 November 1940.

Charles B. Towns, 85, pioneer in the treatment of drug addiction and founder of the Charles B. Towns Hospital in New York City, 20 February 1947.

Leonard Tufts, 75, founder and developer of the North Carolina resort of Pinehurst, 19 February 1945.

Andrew J. Volstead, 87, author of the Volstead Act (1919), which instituted the prohibition of alcohol, 20 January 1947.

Evander Berry Wall, 80, well-known New York dandy, 5 May 1940.

Max M. Warburg, 79, German American international banker and philanthropist who aided Jews emigrating from Nazi Germany, 26 December 1946.

Alexander Stewart Webb, 77, banker and president after 1937 of the American Society for the Prevention of Cruelty to Animals, 22 January 1948.

James E. West, 71, chief executive of the Boy Scouts of America (1911–1943), 15 May 1948.

George Joseph Whelan, 80, one of three brothers who founded United Cigar Stores Company, 29 December 1945.

Peter A. B. Widener II, 53, Philadelphia businessman, philanthropist, and art patron, 20 April 1948.

Charles Sumner Woolworth, 90, cofounder of five-and-ten-cent stores and chairman of F. W. Woolworth Company (1919–1944), 7 January 1947.

PUBLICATIONS

James Agee and Walker Evans, *Let Us Now Praise Famous Men: Three Tenant Families* (Boston: Houghton Mifflin, 1941);

Ernest W. Burgess and Harvey J. Locke, *The Family: From Institution to Companionship* (New York & Cincinnati: American Book Company, 1945);

St. Clair Drake and Horace J. Cayton, *Black Metropolis: A Study of Negro Life in a Northern City* (New York: Harcourt, Brace, 1945);

Max Eastman, *Heroes I Have Known* (New York: Simon & Schuster, 1942);

Josephine Gerth, *Highways to Jobs for Women: How to Pick College Courses for Your Career* (New York: Woman's Press, 1948);

Katherine Glover, *Women at Work in Wartime* (New York: Public Affairs Committee, 1943);

Sidonie Matsner Gruenberg, ed., *The Family in a World at War* (New York & London: Harper, 1942);

Steven Hart and Lucy Brown, *How to Get Your Man and Hold Him* (New York, 1944);

Reuben Hill and Howard Becker, eds., *Marriage and the Family* (Boston: D. C. Heath, 1942);

Sidney Hook, *The Hero in History: A Study in Limitation and Possibility* (New York: John Day, 1943);

Eric Johnston, *American Unlimited* (Garden City, N.Y.: Doubleday, Doran, 1944);

Alfred Kinsey, Wardell B. Pomeroy, and Clyde E. Martin, *Sexual Behavior in the Human Male* (Philadelphia: W. B. Saunders, 1949);

Ferdinand Lundberg and Marynia F. Farnham, *Modern Woman: The Lost Sex* (New York: Harper, 1947);

Margaret Mead, *And Keep Your Powder Dry: An Anthropologist Looks at America* (New York: Morrow, 1942);

Mead, *Male and Female: A Study of the Sexes in a Changing World* (New York: Morrow, 1949);

Francis Merrill, *Social Problems on the Home Front: A Study of War-Time Influences* (New York: Harper, 1948);

Gunnar Myrdal, with the assistance of Richard Sterner and Arnold Rose, *An American Dilemma: The Negro Problem and Modern Democracy* (New York & London: Harper, 1944);

Ruth Shallcross, *Should Married Women Work?* (New York: Public Affairs Committee, 1940);

Edmund Wilson, *To the Finland Station: A Study in the Writing and Acting of History* (New York: Harcourt, Brace, 1940);

Harper's, periodical;

Ladies' Home Journal, periodical;

The Nation, periodical;

New Republic, periodical;

The New Yorker, periodical;

Partisan Review, periodical.

CHAPTER NINE

MEDIA

by VICTOR BONDI, JAMES W. HIPP, and DARREN HARRIS-FAIN

CONTENTS

Sidebars and tables are listed in italics.

1940

- Election returns are telecast for the first time.

- *Truth or Consequences* debuts on radio.

- The radio show *Superman* begins, providing the source for such lines as "Up, up, and away!" and "This looks like a job for Superman!"

1 Jan.   W6XAO in Los Angeles telecasts the Rose Bowl Parade for the first time.

5 Jan.   Edwin H. Armstrong demonstrates high-fidelity radio, broadcast in frequency modulation (FM), over station WIMOJ in Worcester, Massachusetts.

Feb.   *Whiz Comics*, introducing C. C. Beck's Captain Marvel, is published.

Spring   The first issue of *Batman* is published.

20 Mar.   Radio Corporation of America (RCA) begins a publicity campaign for broadcasts of the visual technology, television, which it hopes to begin 1 September 1940.

Apr.   Batman's sidekick, Robin, is introduced in *Detective Comics*.

8 Apr.   The Federal Communications Commission (FCC) begins hearings to determine whether RCA has a monopoly on television technology and manufacturing. On 28 May it condemns RCA's monopolistic practices.

20 May   The FCC authorizes commercial FM radio stations to begin 1 January 1941.

June   Will Eisner's *The Spirit* debuts as a weekly comic book distributed in newspapers.

4 Sept.   The Columbia Broadcasting System (CBS) demonstrates color television transmission over its New York station, W2XAB.

1941

- Amateur radio stations are shut down for the duration of World War II.

- *Ellery Queen's Mystery* magazine appears on the newsstands.

- Captain America is created by Joe Simon and Jack Kirby for Timely Comics.

- Charles Moulton's Wonder Woman debuts.

16 Jan.   In an important licensing decision, the FCC forbids partisan political activities by broadcasters, asserting that "the broadcaster cannot be an advocate."

26 Feb.   The Justice Department drops its antitrust suit against the American Society of Composers, Authors and Publishers (ASCAP) following the signing of a consent decree that opens the field of royalty collections to a new company, Broadcast Music Incorporated (BMI).

Apr.   Blondie and Dagwood Bumstead become parents for a second time in Chic Young's *Blondie*. The baby girl is named Cookie by one of the 431,275 readers who submit names in a contest.

Parents Magazine Institute, concerned about the amount of fantasy in comic books, offers the first issue of *True Comics*, with stories about historic events and real-life heroes. It is the first educational comic book.

2 May   The FCC issues a study, *Report on Chain Broadcasting*, calling for sweeping changes to combat monopolies in the ownership of radio stations and networks.

3 May	The FCC establishes industrywide standards for television manufacturing and broadcasting.
25 June	RCA introduces the Orthicon Television Camera, a vast improvement over previous television cameras.
Fall	Archie makes his comic-book debut.
Oct.	Gilberton Comics introduces comic-book adaptations of literary works in *Classic Comics; the name is later changed to Classics Illustrated.*
Dec.	Walt Kelly's Pogo is introduced in *Animal Comics*.

1942

- The A. C. Nielsen company introduces a mechanical box attached to radios to determine which programs have the most listeners. The device becomes the basis of the radio ratings (and later television ratings) system.
- *Negro Digest* debuts.
- *Business Week* estimates that the comic-book industry is enjoying sales of $15 million a year.

15 Jan.	The National Association of Broadcasters (NAB) issues its "Code of Wartime Practices for American Broadcasters," guidelines for stations regarding the reporting of war news and information.
23 Feb.	The FCC announces that no new radio or television station permits will be issued for the duration of the war in order to channel construction and electronic equipment toward military purposes.
Spring	Crockett Johnson's comic strip *Barnaby* debuts.

1943

- Wire recording devices, the predecessor of the magnetic tape recorder, are used by journalists reporting the invasion of Italy.
- Ed Sullivan begins his own radio show.

10 May	In *NBC* v. *the United States* the U.S. Supreme Court upholds the right of the FCC to regulate broadcasting.

1944

- *The Paul Harvey News* debuts on radio.
- *Seventeen* magazine first appears.

28 Sept.	The Radio Technical Planning Board (RTPB) of the FCC begins hearings with the leaders of the electronic, broadcast, and defense industries to determine postwar allocation of the electromagnetic spectrum and to determine how to introduce new broadcast technologies to the public.

1945

- *Ozzie and Harriet* begins on radio.
- *Ebony* magazine is founded by John H. Johnson.

- Arnold Gingrich leaves *Esquire* due to a conflict with the magazine's publisher. He is asked to return to its editorship four years later, and in 1952 he will become publisher and vice-president of the magazine.

12 Apr. The death of Franklin D. Roosevelt, who used radio effectively in his "fireside chats," is the first of a U.S. president to receive extensive broadcast coverage.

27 June The RTPB issues its final report on the division of the electromagnetic spectrum, assigning television spectrum bandwidths in the very high and ultrahigh frequency ranges, from 44 to 216 MHz.

1946

- The first coaxial television cable, linking New York, Philadelphia, and Washington, is laid.

- The National Cartoonists Society initiates the Billy DeBeck Award for outstanding cartoonist of the year. Recipients in the 1940s include Milton Caniff for *Steve Canyon*, Al Capp for *L'il Abner*, Chic Young for *Blondie*, and Alex Raymond for *Rip Kirby*. In 1954 the award is renamed the Reuben in honor of Rube Goldberg.

7 Mar. The FCC issues its report, *Public Service Responsibility of Broadcast Licensees*, defining the parameters of public conduct for broadcasters, including limits to advertising, local obligations, and political fairness.

16 Apr. President Harry S Truman signs the Lea Act, limiting the legal power of labor unions in the broadcasting industry.

1947

- The kinescope, a film camera capable of recording television broadcasts, is introduced.

- Peter C. Goldmark of CBS Records develops the long-playing microgroove 33 1/3 rpm record.

- The International Telecommunications Union meets in Atlantic City to discuss issues of international channel allocation and interference.

- American Business Consultants, a for-profit anti-Communist group, begins publication of its *Counterattack* newsletter, which will aid in widespread blacklisting.

Jan. Milton Caniff begins a new comic strip, *Steve Canyon*, two weeks after his last work on *Terry and the Pirates*, which he created.

1948

- Both Democratic and Republican Party conventions are televised.

July In response to criticism over the growing number of crime comics and over scantily clad women in comics, a handful of comic-book publishers form the Association of Comics Magazine Publishers and establishes a code of standards in order to encourage self-regulation in the face of possible censorship. The effort is ignored by most comic-book publishers.

29 Sept. Due to increased television interference, the FCC suspends licensing of new television stations. The "temporary" freeze on television lasts nearly four years.

1949

- Walt Kelly's *Pogo* first appears in newspapers.

20 Jan. President Truman's inauguration is telecast.

1 June The FCC issues guidelines regarding the presentation of news and editorializing to broadcasters, asserting that editorializing can occur only after broadcasters have presented "all reasonable viewpoints" to the public.

Fall The *Magazine of Fantasy and Science Fiction* appears for the first time.

OVERVIEW

World War II Dominates. The 1940s were dominated by World War II. This was as true for the media as it was for other areas of American life. From 1941 until the majority of the troops returned home in 1946, newspapers and radio concentrated their coverage on the war. From small-town newspapers reporting the content of letters received from hometown soldiers to reports on the latest battle, the war was the overwhelming event of the decade. The newspaper war correspondent, epitomized by Ernie Pyle, became the lifeline for citizens who could not experience the valor and horror of war. Margaret Bourke-White, as a photographer for *Life* magazine, brought images of the war and the world to Americans and became a celebrity herself.

Military Media. Thirty-seven American newspeople, among them Pyle, lost their lives in World War II. At the scenes of conflict, the men and women in uniform were kept informed by thousands of military newspapers, the most important being *Stars and Stripes*. More important for the postwar world were the thousands of military people who worked on miltary newspapers and improved the quality of U.S. newspapers after the war.

Radio in the 1940s. Radio showed its importance in the nearly instant reporting of major events, such as the Battle of Britain and the bombing of Pearl Harbor. Edward R. Murrow and William Shirer, among many others, set the news standard for the Columbia Broadcasting System (CBS) network, a standard that would follow into the new dominant format, television, and last for decades after the war. But radio was not just a purveyor of news during the war. Radio meant entertainment, and the 1940s was the last decade in which radio was dominant. Music had long been a staple of radio, much of it performed live. Musicians had been unhappy for many years with what radio paid them for their talents. In the 1914 the American Society of Composers, Authors and Publishers (ASCAP) was formed to collect royalties. Musicians and composers remained unhappy with the situation in the early 1940s, especially with the increased use of records on radio. Boycotts by ASCAP led radio broadcasters to form Broadcast Music Incorpoarated (BMI) as an alternative liscencing group in 1939. Legal battles erupted in the 1940s that remained unsettled decades later.

Beginnings of Television. Television had become a viable technology in the late 1930s, but legal delays, and then the war, halted widespread introduction until the late 1940s. After the war the broadcast companies put large amounts of money into television, starving radio, which had been their focus for twenty years. Most of the radio programs were transferred to television by the early 1950s, leaving the radio with music. As quickly as radio had transformed American life in the 1920s, television began a new revolution in the 1940s and 1950s. Federal rules mandated more competition in the television world, causing the National Broadcasting Company (NBC) to divest itself of one of its radio networks; that network became the American Broadcasting Company (ABC).

Comic Books. The stultifying years of the Depression and the war were leveling influences on American society. Most everyone suffered through those two events, and the resulting sense of unity was an opportunity for business to sell to a mass market of everyday Americans. Two examples of this trend are the comic book and the paperback book. Comic books were successful in the 1940s, as they provided cheap, exciting entertainment. Superheroes flourished during a time in which evil was all too real in the world. Captain Marvel, Captain America, Batman, and other heroes like them did battle with evil and fed the imagination of the youth of the United States. On a slightly higher plane, at least sometimes, was the paperback book. The first American paperback imprint was Pocket Books, created in 1939. Many other imprints followed over the next decade, reprinting both literary classics and entertaining genre stories such as Westerns and detective fiction.

McCarthyism. But the end of the war and the rise of the Soviet Union as a European and world power brought new problems that erupted in unlikely spots, such as the media. The first rumbling of institutional anticommunism led to the blacklist, whereby motion picture, television, and radio artists and writers were denied the freedom to work under their own names. During the 1950s the darkness of McCarthyism intensified before the pain of these victims eased.

Transition. War can bring about revolutions, both in the countries that are defeated militarily and the countries of the victors. The media revolution in the United States did not occur immediately after the war. During and after the war, indeed even during the Depression of the 1930s, revolutionary seeds were sown in the media that did not fully bear fruit until the 1950s, a truly revolutionary decade.

TOPICS IN THE NEWS

ASCAP VERSUS BMI

Performance and Payment. By the 1940s, years of dispute had divided broadcasters and American songwriters. At the heart of their controversy was compensation for music played over the radio. Most radio broadcasts were live, and the musicians and composers were paid for a single performance, but to musicians and composers payment for a single performance alone did not seem fair when that one performance was being received by millions of listeners. Had those millions been packed into one concert hall, the musicians's share of the receipts would presumably have been huge. Broadcasters argued that it was impossible to pay licensing fees based on how many listeners tuned in, because no one knew what that number was. Besides, it was the technology of radio that made such enormous audiences possible. From the broadcasters' standpoint, it was enough to pay the musician and the songwriter for the single performance. In the 1930s, broadcasters, organized into the National Association of Broadcasters (NAB), compromised with composers and songwriters, who had been organized since 1914 into the American Society of Composers, Authors and Publishers (ASCAP). Radio stations paid ASCAP a variable royalty of between 3 and 5 percent of the station's gross revenue from advertising sales. This compromise satisfied no one. Broadcasters turned to drama, news, and special events to avoid paying the songwriters, and in 1937 ASCAP suggested they would demand greater royalties when the current contract between musicians and broadcasters expired in 1940.

Records. Complicating the argument between ASCAP and NAB was the increasing use by radio stations of recorded music. Recording technology was still imperfect, and fidelity was low, but stations nonetheless began to play records, introduced by a studio announcer known as a disc jockey. Once again the problem of compensating the musicians and composers on the records presented itself. Before 1940 many musicians, such as Bing Crosby or Fred Waring, sold records stamped with

RADIO REPORTS THE DEATH OF ROOSEVELT

Following many wartime improvements in the reporting of news by radio, American broadcasting succeeded in uniting the nation as never before on 12 April 1945, the day President Franklin Roosevelt died. First reports in the early evening were confused, sometimes erroneously reporting the deaths of other public figures. By late that night, however, radio listeners coast-to-coast were united in national mourning over the president's passing. Radios broadcast repeated summaries of FDR's career, prospects for the war without his leadership, and somber music. The networks and some local stations suspended advertising from the day of FDR's death until his burial in Hyde Park four days later. CBS reporter Arthur Godfrey, describing Roosevelt's funeral procession down Pennsylvania Avenue, broke down in tears and had to turn the broadcast over to a studio announcer. Much of the nation shared his sentiments. Radio provided an unprecedented outlet for the nation's collective grief — just as, four months later, radio became the mechanism for the national celebration of the end of the war.

"NOT LICENSED FOR RADIO BROADCAST." In 1940, however, the Supreme Court ruled that radio stations, having purchased the record, could play it. By 1941 disc-jockey programs such as WNEW's *Make Believe Ballroom* were restructuring the nature of music broadcasts. Far cheaper for a broadcaster than live performances, disc jockeys and recorded music were taking over the airwaves.

Boycott and BMI. ASCAP, as well as the American Federation of Musicians, responded to these developments by boycotting the airwaves. Lacking a new royalty contract with increased rates, ASCAP pulled music it licensed from the air in 1941. In 1942 the American Federation of Musicians followed suit. By a unanimous vote at its annual convention, these musicians agreed to halt the making of new recordings. Radio was left with meager fare: recordings of unlicensed songs such as Stephen Foster's "Jeannie With the Light Brown Hair." But broadcasters were not without resources. They had organized their own royalty agency, Broadcast Music Incorporated (BMI), in 1939. The upstart BMI quickly became a magnet for regional musicians, such as rhythm-and-blues or country-and-western artists, who were traditionally neglected by the New York–based ASCAP. ASCAP's boycott was broken, and they settled for a less advantageous royalty rate than they had originally earned. In 1943 and 1944 record companies compromised with the American Federation of Musicians and created a welfare fund to facilitate payments to musicians. The record industry returned to full production, now for the new disc jockey–dominated broadcast industry. Although ASCAP and BMI received equal royalty rates from broadcasters, musicians could now choose which of the two agencies collected royalty payments, a situation unacceptable to ASCAP. In the 1950s and 1960s ASCAP would initiate a series of unsuccessful lawsuits to recover the position they lost during the boycott of 1941.

Sources:
Steve Chapple and Reebee Garofalo, *Rock 'n' Roll is Here to Pay: The History and Politics of the Music Industry* (Chicago: Nelson-Hall, 1977);

John Ryan, *The Production of Culture in the Music Industry: The ASCAP-BMI Controversy* (Lanham, Md.: University Press of America, 1985).

THE BLACKLIST

Suspicion. Blacklisting was the practice whereby broadcasters agreed not to hire someone whose political opinions were "controversial." The blacklist was a destructive social phenomenon that swept through the broadcasting industry in the late 1940s and continued until the early 1960s. Often associated with the more directly political phenomenon of McCarthyism, blacklisting meant economic devastation to thousands whose political sympathies were left of center. The broadcasting industry, like many other sectors in American society, was seized by an anti-Communist hysteria. Unable to find work in film, radio, or television, many actors, screenwriters, and directors saw their careers ruined; some left the country in order to find work abroad; a despairing few committed suicide. In most cases little more than the mere suspicion of associating with Communists landed an individual on the blacklist, which included an estimated seventeen hundred individuals during its term of influence. Leftist political activities (especially during World War II when the Soviet Union was a U.S. ally) landed one on the blacklist automatically. The blacklist had a chilling effect on political activism among members of the broadcasting industry; more important, it

RECORDS AND THE JUKEBOX

When the 1940s began, phonograph records were limited to albums that played at 78 rpm (revolutions per minute). Besides the fact that these records could hold only four minutes of music per side, they were made of shellac and thus scratched and broke easily. By the end of the decade, however, phonograph technology had improved dramatically. In 1948 Columbia Records introduced the vinyl long-playing record (LP), which was more durable, provided better sound reproduction, and could hold nearly twenty-five minutes of music per side. On the heels of the 33 1/3 rpm LP came the 45 rpm record, introduced by RCA Victor, which could record only as much music as a 78 rpm record but shared the improvements offered by the LP. Such developments were a boon to the jukebox, which had first gained popularity in the 1930s. With the use of 45 rpm records, its survival was ensured into the 1950s and beyond.

Source: Lawrence G. Goldsmith, "War in Three Speeds," *Nation*, 168 (7 May 1949): 523–525.

robbed the industry of many talented people unwilling to cut their opinions to fit anti-Communist models.

Origins. The origins of the blacklist are found in broad anti-Communist sentiment that began to mount after World War I and, more directly, the post–World War II fear of subversion in a time when the broadcast industry was highly visible. Red-baiting was a favorite tactic of many groups even before the war ended. Conservatives discontented with government regulation charged that the New Deal was Communistic; business leaders characterized strikes as Communist-inspired; labor leaders gained advantages within their own unions by claiming their opponents were Communists. For the most part the public dismissed such charges as unfounded or partisan. As the Cold War heated up after World War II, however, foreign events seemed to verify suspicion at home, and the Truman administration, in announcing the Truman doctrine and the Marshall Plan, perceived a Communist ideological offensive against the United States. In 1947 the administration itself began a loyalty program among government employees, and the Federal Bureau of Investigation (FBI) uncovered several minor spy rings, which suggested Communist infiltration of the government. The entertainment industry was also suspect. Many remained anxious over the ease with which the Nazis had used the media to propagandize the German people. Many Americans felt uncomfortable with the media power concentrated in Los Angeles and New York — and with the often prominent role Jews played in the entertainment industry. By 1947 many citizens were receptive to the suggestion that Communist agents in

Hollywood and New York were attempting to use the media to subvert U.S. institutions.

HUAC. While there were members of the entertainment industry, especially writers, who had been Communists or supported Communist causes, film, radio, and television were firmly in the hands of conservative businessmen fundamentally more interested in profits than politics. But they answered to advertisers, and advertisers answered to consumers, and via the threat of a consumer boycott anti-Communist activists were able to establish the blacklist. A consumer boycott was first suggested in the wake of the October 1947 hearings investigating Hollywood conducted by the House Un-American Activities Committee (HUAC). While uncovering no Communist conspiracy, HUAC did send ten prominent screenwriters, who refused to answer questions regarding their political beliefs, to prison for contempt of Congress. Public response to the hearings was generally apathetic, but the studio chiefs in Hollywood, afraid of the rumblings of a consumer boycott suggested by groups such as the American Legion, decided to ensure that they would suffer no political backlash by employing controversial persons. Hollywood was entering a difficult period. The government was charging many Hollywood studios with antitrust violations (resulting in a significant breakup of the studio system in 1948); many stars were forming their own production companies independent of the studios; and television promised to be a ruthless competitor to the movie industry. Following a 24–25 November 1947 meeting by studio heads at New York's Waldorf-Astoria hotel, Hollywood chiefs announced that they would screen potential employees for political activism or Communist sympathies. The blacklist had begun.

Businessmen. Businessmen in New York quickly moved in to establish a for-profit screening service to prevent advertisers as well as motion picture, radio, and television producers from hiring suspect personnel. American Business Consultants (ABC) was a group of three former FBI men who published *Counterattack*, a newsletter that listed the political affiliation and history of performers and writers. Funded by the militantly anti-Communist businessman Alfred Kohlberg, ABC would screen a potential employee for a five-dollar fee to determine whether he or she had a subversive background. ABC and *Counterattack* rarely accused an individual of Communist membership and subversion, lest they be sued for libel; they merely suggested a questionable background — enough for most employers to avoid hiring the individual. Their innuendo was buttressed by the efforts of anti-Communist fanatics who mounted letter-writing campaigns and boycotts against employers foolish enough to challenge the blacklist. The most famous of these fanatics was a Syracuse, New York, supermarket proprietor named Laurence "Larry" Johnson. When Block Drug Company, the makers of Amm-i-dent, a chlorophyll toothpaste, sponsored a television series using actors on the blacklist, Johnson threatened to dis-

Theodore Kirkpatrick, editor of the anti-Communist periodical *Counterattack*

play their toothpaste in his stores alongside that of a competitor with a sign indicating that the competitor shunned "Stalin's little creatures," while Block tolerated Communists; Johnson added that he would sponsor a national boycott of the product. Block capitulated and stopped sponsoring the series. Such tactics reinforced the power of ABC and the blacklist over broadcasters. Within two years ABC was earning two hundred thousand dollars per year from its services.

Effects. In 1950 ABC published a 215-page booklet entitled *Red Channels*, listing such celebrities as Leonard Bernstein, Lee J. Cobb, Aaron Copland, Langston Hughes, and Burl Ives as suspect. *Red Channels* became the semiofficial guide of the blacklist. The more famous on the blacklist could weather the slander, but for the less well known, the effect was devastating. Millard Lampell, a writer, was told by a sympathetic producer that his career was "dead . . I couldn't touch you with a barge pole." Dancer Paul Draper moved to Europe, unable to earn a living in the United States. Jean Muir, of the television series *The Goldbergs,* found her career crushed; Philip Loeb, who had starred in the same program, was shut out of performing and committed suicide. Actors abandoned participation in civil rights movements and hid their dust-covered copies of Marx. Eventually, ABC and a spin-off company, Aware, realized the profits that could be made charging actors and writers fees to strike their names from the lists of the suspected. Actress Kim

Members of the House Un-American Activities Committee, from left to right: Rep. Richard Vail (R.–Ill.); Chairman J. Parnell Thomas (R.–N.J.); Rep. John McDowell (R.–Pa.); Robert Stripling, chief counsel; Rep. Richard Nixon (R.–Calif.)

Hunter paid two hundred dollars to have her name removed from the blacklist. Eventually, the blacklist self-destructed from such tactics, when in 1963 a feisty Texan, John Henry Faulk, won a lawsuit for conspiracy and extortion against Aware and Laurence Johnson. Until then American broadcasting was subject to a political filtering process that removed some of its most free-spirited and creative talent.

Sources:

David Caute, *The Great Fear: The Anti-Communist Purge Under Truman and Eisenhower* (New York: Simon & Schuster, 1978);

Richard M. Fried, *Nightmare in Red: The McCarthy Era in Perspective* (New York: Oxford University Press, 1990);

Stephen J. Whitfield, *The Culture of the Cold War* (Baltimore: Johns Hopkins University Press, 1991).

COMIC STRIPS

Part of American Culture. The growth of an American middle class with leisure time and money to spend, starting in the late nineteenth century, culminated in the development of a commercial popular culture in the early twentieth century that was unparalleled in its inventiveness and success. By 1940 these media included radio shows, pulp magazines, and comic books, as well as the forerunner of the comic book, comic strips, which had existed since the 1890s.

Continuing Success. As in radio the comic strips of the 1940s were largely a continuation of the successes of the previous decade. While there were many humor strips that gave the funnies their name — among them Al Capp's *L'il Abner* and Crockett Johnson's *Barnaby* — both decades saw a proliferation of narrative strips with continuing characters. Two types dominated: adventure strips such as Milton Caniff's *Terry and the Pirates* and *Steve Canyon*, Will Eisner's *The Spirit*, Lee Falk's *The Phantom* and *Mandrake the Magician*, Harold Foster's *Prince Valiant*, Chester Gould's *Dick Tracy*, and Alex Raymond's *Flash Gordon;* and soap-opera strips such as Allen Saunders and Dale Connor's *Mary Worth*, Dale Messick's *Brenda Starr,* and Nicholas Dallis's *Rex Morgan, M.D..* Many of these continued for decades.

World War II absorbed America's attention for the four years in which it fought, from December 1941 to August 1945. It is natural, then, that American popular culture was also preoccupied with the conflict. In comic books and strips, movies, animated cartoons, and many other media, patriotism and propaganda were rampant. For instance, Timely Comics launched Captain America early in 1941, while National Periodical Publications introduced Wonder Woman later that year. Like National Periodical's Superman, introduced in 1938, both superheroes fought for truth, justice, and the American way. Both also wore patriotic costumes, and along with many other superheroes of the period their enemies included Axis foes. The cover of the first issue of *Captain America*, for instance, showed the hero dealing a blow to Adolf Hitler.

While the comics dealt with the Axis threat seriously (though with a strong fantasy element), there were also humorous treatments. The Three Stooges and Charlie Chaplin produced anti-Hitler movies within months of each other in 1940, while Warner Bros. and Walt Disney Studios created several animated cartoons mocking the Axis powers and their leaders. A Disney cartoon commissioned by the U.S. Treasury Department about the need to pay taxes, for instance, turned into *Der Fuehrer's Face* (1943), featuring Donald Duck in a Nazi-ruled country. Warner Bros. also pro-

duced cartoons for the government, a series of shorts featuring a Private Snafu to be shown at military bases. For the American public, Bugs Bunny fought the good fight in such movies as *Bugs Bunny Nips the Nips* (1944), *Hare Force* (1944), and *Herr Meets Hare* (1945), in which Bugs pops up in Germany and impersonates Adolf Hitler (fooling Hermann Göring).

Sometimes the passions stirred by the war had the unfortunate effect of leading to hateful, racist propaganda, particularly where Japan was concerned. In the 1943 Batman movie serial, for instance, is a reference to "the shifty-eyed Japs" relocated by a "wise government," while in *Bugs Bunny Nips the Nips* the popular cartoon character, in aiding the Allied war effort, uses such slurs as "monkey face" and "slant-eyes" in referring to the Japanese. In reissuing period movies in recent years companies have sometimes dubbed over the offensive terms. The Bugs Bunny cartoon was released with other cartoons in its original form on videotape but then withdrawn due to protests. Both practices raise the problem of how to deal with offensive material that is part of America's cultural and historical past.

Sources: Robert Sklar, *Film: An International History of the Medium* (New York: Abrams, 1993);

James Van Hise, *Batmania* (Las Vegas: Pioneer, 1989).

Sources:

Ron Goulart, ed., *The Encyclopedia of American Comics* (New York & Oxford: Facts On File, 1990);

M. Thomas Inge, "Comic Strips," in *Handbook of American Popular Culture*, edited by Inge, second edition (New York: Greenwood Press, 1989), pp. 205–228.

EDUCATIONAL BROADCASTING RETURNS

A Neglected Idea. Since the establishment of nationwide commercial broadcasting in the 1920s, media critics had argued that the full potential of mass-communications technology such as radio was not being realized. They found the absence of educational broadcasting especially troubling. Commercial radio, driven by advertising dollars, focused on entertainment and rarely presented the public with in-depth news analysis, fine arts, or complex informational programming. Critics argued that radio could become a formidable tool for in-depth information and education and pressured the networks and the government to require such broadcasting. They were ineffective before World War II, but during the war

the Federal Communications Commission (FCC), which supervised American broadcasting, began a sweeping reconsideration of broadcasting's public responsibility. Because the new technologies of frequency modulation (FM) radio and television promised to open new broadcasting horizons, the FCC revised established restrictions. For the first time, they set aside certain bandwidths of the electromagnetic spectrum for educational broadcasting. Educational television and educational radio were born.

A Shaky Start. Ardently opposed by commercial interests, educational broadcasting got off to a difficult start. The FCC, responding to commercial pressure, rarely granted educational broadcasters AM radio licenses. FM licenses were readily granted, because most American radios only received AM signals, and thus the FM market was unattractive to the networks and advertisers. Similar economic considerations also governed the development of educational television. Commercial broadcasters vehemently opposed FCC licenses for educational broadcasting on the commercially lucrative very-high-frequency

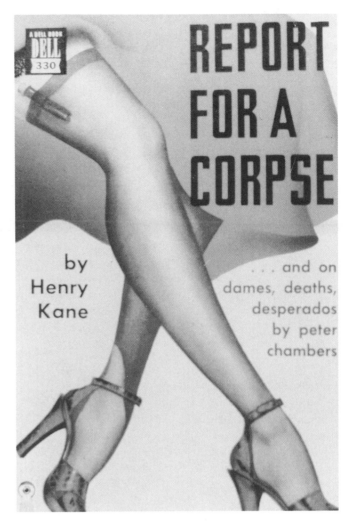

1949 Dell paperback cover

(VHF) wavelengths. Most American television receivers carried the VHF signal, and commercial broadcasters wanted the FCC to reserve VHF channels for their transmissions. Educational programming was thus shunted to the ultrahigh frequency (UHF) wavelengths, effectively blocking its development.

Precedent for the Future. Despite commercial opposition, educational broadcasting did begin in the 1940s. Small-scale educational programming on FM radio was such a success that by 1948 the FCC revised its broadcast rules and permitted educational programming by radio stations limited to 10 watts of power — enough for a two- to five-mile transmission radius. The FCC normally limited licenses to stations with 250 watts of power or more, but the 10-watt stations, usually located on college campuses, effectively met the needs of the local community and provided on-site training for broadcasting students. By 1952 there were ninety-two educational FM stations operating. Similarly, educational television was located on college campuses, servicing local communities and providing valuable experience for broadcasting students. By 1948 five universities in the United States operated their own television stations. Given the enormous expenses involved in television production, however, educational television would not become a significant force in broadcasting until the federal government began to underwrite the costs of educational television in the 1960s.

Source:
Christopher H. Sterling and John M. Kittross, *Stay Tuned: A Concise History of American Broadcasting* (Belmont, Cal.: Wadsworth, 1978).

FROM THE PULPS TO THE PAPERBACKS

The End of an Era. Few periods in history are static, but the 1940s was particularly a period of transition for the United States, with its victory in World War II and its emergence from the conflict as a world economic and military superpower. Changes were also evident in American popular culture: radio enjoyed the last years of its heyday as the most successful broadcast medium before television claimed dominance, and one medium that had enjoyed extreme popularity since the 1920s, the pulp magazine, succumbed to the dual challenge of comic books for younger readers and paperback books for adults. In addition the magazines and radio often shared the same audience and even characters, such as the Shadow, but like radio the magazines lost potential readers to the exciting new medium of television.

The Heyday of the Pulps. With roots in the late nineteenth century, the pulps — sensational magazines ranging widely in quality, with gaudy covers and cheap pulpwood pages — were looked down upon by the guardians of high culture but were extremely popular, their extravagant tales encompassing such popular genres as adventure, romance, crime, horror, science fiction, and the Western. Characters such as the Shadow and Doc Savage were among the popular heroes of the age; writers such as H. P. Lovecraft and Robert E. Howard (the creator of Conan) gained cult followings; and magazines such as

Black Mask, Weird Tales, and *Astounding Science-Fiction* dominated their respective genres. Throughout the 1920s and 1930s, though many magazines came and went, sales of pulp magazines skyrocketed.

The Beginning of the End. While the pulps were at their height in the 1930s, however, the seeds of their decline were also present. Popular writers such as Lovecraft and Howard died, magazines such as *Black Mask* lost its best writers to the book publishers, and comic books, which were heavily influenced by the pulps and shared many similarities with them, began to encroach on their market. Also, the pulps generally had a bad reputation with much of the American public, and editors such as John W. Campbell, Jr., of *Astounding Science-Fiction* changed the format of their magazines to avoid being associated with them. The final blow, however, was the paperback.

The Origins of the American Paperback. Though books with paper covers had been published in the United States since the nineteenth century, paperbacks as they are now known did not appear until the late 1930s as inexpensive reprints of best-selling or literary works. The trend began in Britain with the success of Penguin Books, introduced in 1936. In 1939 Robert Fair de Graff founded Pocket Books, which was soon successful due to the books' low cost; their colorful, eye-catching covers; and their availability at newsstands as well as bookstores. Pocket Books soon found itself competing with imitators, including Avon Books (founded in 1941), Dell Books (founded in 1943), and Popular Library (also founded in 1943). Although paper was in short supply during World War II, the paperbacks prospered, with more publishers entering the market: Bantam Books, created by Ian Ballantine, in 1945; the New American Library (NAL), with its fiction Signet Books and nonfiction Mentor Books, in 1948; and Gold Medal Books in 1949.

Sex and Violence. The commercial success of paperbacks was directly related to their content, which often took up where the pulps left off. In particular, after the war, book covers and the books themselves became increasingly provocative and sensationalistic, promising readers straightforward tales of sex, violence, and depravity. A telling example is Mickey Spillane's *I, the Jury:* it enjoyed a small success in 1947 when published in hardcover, but after Signet published it the following year it sold more than 2 million copies within two years. Featuring Spillane's hard-boiled detective Mike Hammer, the novel had all the major elements that made paperbacks popular.

The End of the Pulps. Like the pulps, and to a lesser extent comic books, paperbacks could titillate readers as other media — including radio, television, and movies — could not. The last of the pulps was published in the 1950s, with only detective and science fiction and fantasy magazines carrying on their legacy.

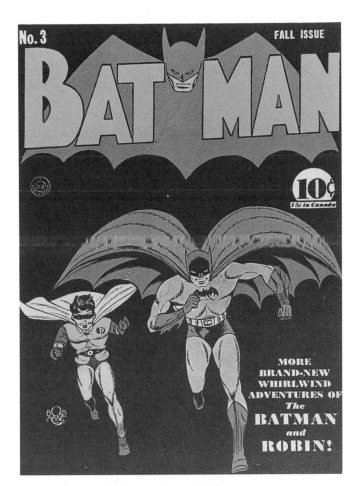

Fall 1940 comic-book cover

Sources:

Thomas L. Bonn, *Under Cover: An Illustrated History of American Mass Market Paperbacks* (Harmondsworth, U.K.: Penguin, 1982);

Piet Schreuders, *Paperbacks, U.S.A.: A Graphic History, 1939–1959,* translated by Josh Pachter (San Diego: Blue Dolphin, 1981);

Lee Server, *Danger Is My Business: An Illustrated History of the Fabulous Pulp Magazines* (San Francisco: Chronicle, 1993);

Server, *Over My Dead Body: The Sensational Age of the American Paperback — 1945–1955* (San Francisco: Chronicle, 1994).

THE GOLDEN AGE OF COMIC BOOKS

The Golden Decade. By 1940 the comic book, a medium created in the United States, had existed for exactly seven years. The first comic books were reprintings of newspaper comic strips, but they quickly turned to publishing original stories considerably longer than the strips. Historians have labeled the 1930s and 1940s, the first two decades of U.S. comic books, the golden age, and the comic book was at its height during the 1940s, which established the medium as part of American culture.

Something for Everyone. The first few years were a period of experimenting with what readers, mostly children and adolescents but also adults, appreciated. In imitation of the popular pulp magazines, which influenced most comic-book writers and artists along with movies and radio shows, stories in different genres soon became the norm, including adventure, crime, fantasy and science fiction, horror, romance, war, and Westerns. Another popular subgenre was about *teenagers,* a term that gained widespread use starting in the 1940s, and chief among these humor comics were those featuring Archie and his friends. Created by Bob Montana, the Archie characters first appeared in 1941 and soon became the most popular nonheroic characters in comic-book history. Comic books also developed a few genres of their own, including "funny animal" stories (no doubt influenced by animated cartoons such as those created by Walt Disney Studios) and, most notably, with another nod to the pulps, the superhero. Costumed crime fighters were popular in the mid 1930s, but their dominance over the field was assured with the overwhelming popularity of two characters introduced by National Periodical Publications in 1938 and 1939: Superman, created by Jerry Siegel and Joe Shuster, and Batman, created by Bob Kane.

The Reign of the Superheroes. By 1940, the best year for comic books to that time in terms of sales, there were more than 150 titles in publication. National Periodical Publications introduced a whole series of new costumed heroes, including the golden age versions of Flash, Hawkman, and Green Lantern (all would be reinterpreted later), as well as Batman's sidekick, Robin. Other heroes — including Timely's Captain America and National's Wonder Woman, both introduced in 1941 — fit in with the growing patriotism of the country as it silently prepared for war. Another popular superhero was C. C. Beck's Captain Marvel, introduced in Fawcett's *Whiz Comics* in 1940. More humorous than most other costumed heroes, Captain Marvel nonetheless succeeded with fans and, like many other heroes, acquired a youthful sidekick with whom fans could further identify. Another humorous superhero was Jack Cole's Plastic Man, introduced in 1941.

From Crime Fighters to Crime. Though a wide range of comics was available, superheroes dominated most of the decade. After World War II, however, tastes began to shift. Westerns and romance comics became extremely popular, as did crime comics such as *Crime Does Not Pay,* which had begun in 1942. Crime comics remained successful into the next decade; along with horror comics and the frequent depiction of sexy, scantily clad women, they were singled out as a bad influence on children, which led to concern about the content of comic books and a widespread self-censorship of the comics in the mid 1950s.

A Rare Legacy. The freedom that comic-book creators enjoyed, for better or worse, during the 1940s accounts for much of the comic book's appeal, as does the energy evident in the new industry. Besides nostalgia the value of comic books from the 1940s as collectors' items today has much to do with how little they were valued during the period. Some were lost to bonfires protesting their content, many were discarded by parents when they

thought their children were too old for them, and many were lost to wartime paper drives.

Sources:

Mike Benton, *The Comic Book in America: An Illustrated History,* revised edition (Dallas: Taylor, 1993);

Ron Goulart, *Great History of Comic Books* (Chicago & New York: Contemporary Books, 1986);

M. Thomas Inge, "Comic Books," in *Handbook of American Popular Culture,* edited by Inge (New York: Greenwood Press, 1988), pp. 75–99;

Paul Sassiene, *The Comic Book: The One Essential Guide for Comic Book Fans Everywhere* (Edison, N.J.: Chartwell, 1994).

MILITARY MEDIA

Peak of Influence. The military press reached its historic high in numbers and influence during World War II. From the beginning of U.S. involvement in the war, thousands of publications sprang up in training camps, battlefronts, and strategic locations around the world to report the news of home and the war, keep up morale, and propagandize the war effort.

Hammett. Many newspapers were printed in small, out of the way places. Many of these were mimeographed. The *Adakian* was one of these small papers, edited and printed at the army base in Adak, Alaska, under the leadership of Cpl. Dashiell Hammett. Hammett, a novelist well known for his detective stories, saw the first issue published on 19 January 1944. Among the staff members who worked on the paper during its nearly two-year run was Bernard Kalb, who later became a well-known print and television journalist.

Stars and Stripes. The biggest and best-known of the miltary newspapers was *Stars and Stripes,* a paper which first appeared in several forms during the Civil War.

The 25 April 1945 issue of the most successful military newspaper

azine was first published in New York City, but by the end of the war there were twenty-three separate editions and a paid subscription of more than 2 million people.

Building Morale and Purpose. The service newspapers and magazines were staffed by military personnel, which no doubt helped the rising quality of small-town newspapers after the war. But more important, the military print media did much to maintain the morale of the troops in the field. Gen. George Marshall was quoted in *Stars and Stripes* on 18 April 1942 on the importance of the military newspaper:

> A soldier's newpaper, in these grave times, is more than a morsel of news. It is a symbol of the things we are fighting to preserve and spread in this threatened world. It represents the free thought and free expression of a free people.

Questions of Loyalty. But after the war those symbols came under attack. In 1946 the War Department ordered the screening of all information and education personnel "to establish complete loyalty to the United States." The Tokyo edition of *Stars and Stripes* was especially hard hit. Two staff members were fired for failing the loyalty test; some accused the Tokyo *Stars and Stripes* of writing pro-Communist editorials and censoring news that showed the Soviet Union in a bad light. In addition to helping bring about victory in World War II, the military media showed the types of problems arising from victory and the first arguments of the Cold War.

Sources:

Michael Anglo, *Service Newspapers of the Second World War* (London: Jupiter, 1977);

Alfred Emile Cornebise, *Ranks and Columns: Armed Forces Newspapers in American Wars* (Westport, Conn.: Greenwood Press, 1993).

MONOPOLY INVESTIGATIONS

Monopoly and the Airwaves. Since the introduction of mass-communication technologies, U.S. politicians and businessmen had been concerned about the relationship between communication and business monopoly. Most mass-communication technologies were naturally monopolistic: telephone and telegraph signals, in order to be effective, travel over a single set of lines and cables; radio broadcasts must be assigned specific frequencies on the electromagnetic spectrum in order to be heard clearly. Politicians, responding to public concerns (and to the concerns of businessmen dependent upon mass communications), monitored and regulated mass communications to ensure equality in fees charged to the public and to maintain fair political use of the airwaves. Government oversight of mass communications was increased following the creation of the FCC in 1934. Empowered to license and oversee broadcast activities, during the 1930s the FCC focused its attention primarily on investigating activities it felt violated the public trust — false radio advertising, for example. In 1938, transferring the investigation of ad claims to the Federal Trade Commission (FTC), the FCC established a commission to investigate

During World War I only one edition of the paper, datelined Paris, was published; in World War II nearly thirty editions appeared at one time or another. The first World War II edition was published 18 April 1942 in London, and the weekly was designated volume two, as opposed to the volume one of World War I. The first daily edition of World War II, designated volume three, appeared on 2 November 1942 and was headquartered in the offices of the London *Times*.

News From All Over. The news carried in *Stars and Stripes* and the myriad of other military newspapers was provided by military reporters; the Army News Service, a wire service run by the military; and civilian magazines such as *Time* and *Newsweek*. An average issue of the paper included news of the war, especially about events on other fronts; news from the United States, such as the latest song hits; book reviews; cartoons, featuring such cartoonists as Bill Mauldin; and, always, photographs of beautiful women.

Yank Magazine. Another important media venue was *Yank* magazine, a monthly that made its first appearance on 17 June 1942. A historical and entertainment magazine, *Yank* was most famous for two cartoon characters that made their debuts there: G.I. Joe, drawn by David Breger, and Sad Sack, drawn by George Baker. The mag-

"chain broadcasting" — the practice whereby the major broadcasting networks, such as CBS and NBC, owned and operated chains of radio stations (affiliates) around the country. On 2 May 1941 the FCC issued *Report on Chain Broadcasting*, a summary of the commission's findings.

Findings and Recommendations. The FCC report concluded that chain broadcasting was fundamentally monopolistic. They were especially concerned about the political implications involved in a communications corporation owning two or more networks or two or more broadcast stations in a single market. The Roosevelt administration, smarting under criticism from Republican-dominated media outlets, argued that if one person or group of persons owned the majority of media outlets in a given area, they would be capable of unduly influencing public opinion. The FCC proposed to forbid chain broadcasting and single ownership of multiple media outlets. They established new rules regarding multiple ownership and forced local stations to be more responsive to the needs of their immediate communities. In October 1941 NBC and CBS took the FCC to court, arguing the new rules violated their rights of trade. They also attacked the FCC through supporters in Congress, under the leadership of Congressman Eugene E. Cox of Georgia, who launched a brief and ineffective investigation of the FCC.

Diversity. In 1943 the Supreme Court upheld the FCC rules, forever altering the character of American broadcasting. Although the large networks announced that the decision spelled doom for broadcasting, the effects of the judgment were limited. The Radio Corporation of America (RCA), the parent company of NBC, was forced to divest itself of one of its two networks. Bought by Edward J. Noble, a candy manufacturer who had made a fortune with Life Savers, the network became the basis of the American Broadcasting Company (ABC) in 1945. Smaller networks such as the Mutual and Keystone thrived in the new environment of independent, unaffiliated local stations. With the postwar lifting of the ban on radio manufacture and station construction, returning veterans with radio experience opened hundreds of new stations. The broadcasters built revenues by increasingly focusing on specialized programming, such as swing or classical music, which helped erode the power of the old radio networks. Radio network advertising revenue fell from $23 million to $11 million in the seven years following the end of the war. By 1952 the networks had lost half of all their affiliates, but NBC and CBS continued to be profitable, as they shifted their resources to a new, less-regulated sector of the communications business: television.

Sources:

Erik Barnouw, *The Golden Web: A History of Broadcasting in the United States,* Volume II — 1933–1953 (New York: Oxford University Press, 1968);

Lewis J. Paper, *Empire: William S. Paley and the Making of CBS* (New York: St. Martin's Press, 1987).

VOICE OF THE ENEMY

During World War II the U.S. government began the Voice of America, propaganda broadcasts to occupied and enemy nations designed to demoralize the enemy. Enemies of the United States, of course, did the same, especially via broadcasts aimed at advancing U.S. troops. Axis broadcasts drew many listeners among the troops because they often played American popular music between propaganda sermons and misinformation. The nicknames of enemy broadcast announcers became household names by the end of the war: "Tokyo Rose" (Iva Ikuko Toguri), who told the troops their wives and girlfriends were having affairs with other men while they fought; "Axis Sally" (Mildred Gillars), an Ohio woman imprisoned after the war (1949–1956); "Lord Haw Haw" (William Joyce), who broadcast Nazi propaganda in English with an upper-class British accent and was hanged for treason by the British after the war. The most famous announcer of all was American poet Ezra Pound, broadcasting from Fascist Italy. Pound was arrested following the war for his activities but was judged unfit to stand trial. He was confined in St. Elizabeths mental hospital in Washington, D.C., from 1946 until 1958, when he was released.

PROPAGANDA AND THE NEWS

Propaganda. When, in 1934, Nazis seized the government of Austria, their first act was to occupy not a government building but a radio station. The act symbolized the new importance the control and dissemination of information had in modern political life. News control and propaganda were central to the success of authoritarian states. By 1940 many members of the U.S. media were expressing deep concern about the control of the news and the effectiveness of propaganda, which was commonly defined as the manipulation of news and information for political purposes. Stalinist Russia and Nazi Germany used the new technology of cinema to rally the masses; the Fascist governments of Italy and Germany used the even newer technology of radio to garner broad support for their policies; everywhere in war-torn Europe censors imposed themselves on journalism. How propaganda worked was the subject of great discussion, and media analysts argued pointedly about the relationship between propaganda and unbiased news. It was not an abstract debate. Radio rabble-rousers, such as conservative commentator Fr. Charles Coughlin, already enjoyed large audiences in the Midwest; critics of the Roosevelt administration hinted that FDR's successful fireside chats over radio, as well as the industry regulation of the FCC, were signs of impending dictatorship.

Edward R. Murrow broadcasting news of the Allied invasion of France. Beside him is the military censor, his hand on the switch that would interrupt the transmission if he felt it necessary.

A well-orchestrated media campaign, filled with bald distortions, had destroyed Upton Sinclair's 1934 run for governor of California. Reporting from Europe, journalists and broadcasters found it difficult to adhere to an unbiased and objective presentation of the news. During the Spanish civil war of 1936–1939, H. V. Kaltenborn waxed indignant over Fascist atrocities in his radio broadcasts for CBS; the Hearst press, distorting events in Spain, cast Francisco Franco's Fascists as "insurgents" and the Republican government as "reds." Eric Sevareid, witnessing the fall of France, felt a complacent press was much to blame and urged CBS to abandon neutrality in reporting European events. Other European correspondents, who repeatedly saw their reporting lost to censors, were all too aware of how the objective press could be turned to partisan ends. For journalists and broadcasters in the late 1930s, the boundaries between news and propaganda were indistinct.

The CBS Style. Some in the U.S. media were not troubled by the blurry distinction between news and propaganda. The Hearst press was famous for its sensationalism and distortion; the Luce publishing empire readily acknowledged that its presentation of the news reflected the bias of its publisher. Luce argued that the mere selection of one news item over another reflected bias and that an objective presentation of the news was impossible. Most industry insiders agreed with Luce but nonetheless strove for balance and fairness in the presentation of the news. In part this struggle represented a philosophical commitment to fairness, but it also reflected commercial and political realities. Overt editorializing sometimes cost a network commercial sponsors and carried the risk of intervention by offended politicians. CBS was the first of the major networks to institutionalize fairness as part of its broadcasts. It often sponsored a roundtable of opposing viewpoints following the broadcast of important events, and it demanded low-key, dispassionate reporting of its journalists. ("We must not display a tenth of the emotion that a broadcaster does when describing a prize fight," explained Sevareid.) Edward R. Murrow's broadcasts from besieged London made the style famous. Murrow's reports were not exactly objective, and he himself sought to sway the sentiment of Americans toward intervention in the war on the side of the British. But the CBS style was subtly understated and enormously effective.

THE BOYS IN THE BASEMENT

Often criticized and sometimes grudgingly admired, Franklin Roosevelt's innovative use of radio was a persistent thorn in the side of his political opponents. This was never more the case than at the Democratic National Convention in Chicago in 1940. Roosevelt's strategy for running for an unprecedented third term as president was to appear reluctant, suggesting that it was grassroots support, rather than ambition, which led him to the hustings. FDR did enjoy considerable support among the delegates, much of it, however, halfhearted — and that made for a moribund convention. Listeners, however, heard the convention enthusiastically draft Roosevelt. Mayor Kelly of Chicago, a partisan of FDR, packed loyal supporters into the basement of the convention hall. Their cheers at the mention of Roosevelt's name, picked up by strategically placed microphones, were broadcast over loudspeakers and over the radio — generating a sense that the convention's endorsement of Roosevelt was spontaneous and wholehearted.

The other broadcast networks followed suit. In 1940 NBC and the Mutual network issued a joint statement forbidding their war correspondents from efforts "to influence action or opinion of others one way or another." In 1941 such a position became law, as the FCC, ruling on a licensing request from a Boston station, declared, "A truly free radio cannot be used to advocate the causes of the licensee. . . ."

Censorship and the War. The relationship between news and propaganda became more complex after Pearl Harbor. Although some suggested that the U.S. media should be nationalized and controlled by the government for the duration of the war, government intervention in the media was limited. It did create several agencies to monitor the press. The Office of Facts and Figures, under Archibald MacLeish, had been created before the war to combat the distortion of news in the media. The Office of War Information had a similar function after its creation in 1942 and additionally monitored shortwave broadcasts to ensure that important military secrets were not revealed. The War Department refused to permit the publication of photographs showing dead U.S. soldiers. The Office of Censorship under Byron Price closed amateur radio stations for fear of espionage broadcasts and forbade the transmission of weather news or the announcement of troop, ship, or plane movements. It also abolished man-on-the-street interviews, fearing that spies would send coded information in ad-lib form.

Dangers of Censorship. Aside from these measures, however, the Office of Censorship relied on voluntary censorship by the media. Government officials feared that heavy-handed censorship would be viewed as a Fascist attempt to manipulate opinion, obscuring the differences between democracy and authoritarian rule. More important, policy makers feared a political backlash against the war effort if heavy censorship was invoked. While enemies of the nation's black press, for example, sought to use the war emergency to shut it down, Attorney General Francis Biddle feared the consequences of such an act on the morale of African Americans, who were making vital contributions to the war effort. Government officials, moreover, trusted that the prowar consensus that swept the public with Pearl Harbor would be reflected in the press.

Voluntary Censorship. They were not disappointed. Editors and broadcasters took seriously the Office of Censorship guidelines not to betray military movements or undermine morale. Newspapers and radio stations regularly submitted stories to the Office of Censorship for approval and tightened journalistic standards to ensure that information was safe for publication. Censorship had the effect of making the distinction between propaganda and news sharper because it demanded greater accuracy in reporting. No longer would lazy reporters cite "informed sources" or "reliable informants" in their news stories without verifying the information. The war made the U.S. press fairer and more judicious.

Propaganda Efforts. At the same time the press was codifying a new set of journalistic ethics, the government was refining its propaganda efforts, learning much from foreign propaganda broadcasts. In 1941 the FCC established the Foreign Broadcast Intelligence Service to monitor and transcribe German and Japanese propaganda aimed at the United States. In turn the War Department directed propaganda broadcasts at Germany and Japan. Transmitted from British Broadcasting Corporation (BBC) equipment in England, and on mobile units operated by the military in the Pacific, U.S. propaganda broadcasts were under the supervision of the Psychological Warfare Branch (PWB) of the Office of War Information. PWB specialized in two types of broadcasts: the first, "white" broadcasts, were aimed to demoralize the enemy and undermine their morale; the second, "black" broadcasts, imitated Axis transmissions, and sought to confuse the enemy during military operations. PWB's most successful white broadcast was a daily series entitled *Briefe die sie nicht erreichten* (Letters That Didn't Reach You), wherein announcers read letters by demoralized German soldiers to the Nazi homeland. Their most famous black radio project was a 1944 broadcast from Radio Luxembourg that purported to be an official German station. During the invasion of the German heartland, this station broadcast misinformation regarding the offensive and created widespread panic in cities far from the actual military operations.

The Debate Continues. Following the war, the debate over fairness and objectivity in the news continued. During the war, labor unions repeatedly complained that radio stations denied them access to air and advertising time on the grounds that their perspectives were partisan. Broadcasters also routinely denied air and ad time to Communist groups, arguing that the Smith Act of 1940 made Communists an illegal partisan group. Right-wingers, on the other hand, continued to slant the news in ways that were frankly propagandistic. The most notorious example was that of the radio network owned by Detroit businessman George Richards. A virulent anti-Semite, who derided President Roosevelt as a Communistic "Jew-lover," Richards demanded his station managers twist the news to accord his particular sensibility. His activities were so authoritarian that in 1948 a group of journalists formerly in the employ of Richards protested to the FCC about his tactics. The FCC began hearings to consider suspending Richards's radio licenses, taking testimony from scores of witnesses that he forced them to slant and falsify news. Richards spent over $2 million to maintain his stations before, at the height of the controversy, he died. His widow pledged not to interfere in the presentation of the news, and the Richards family was allowed to retain its radio stations.

Editorials. The FCC indulged Richards because it had concluded that unbiased presentation of the news was impossible. By 1946 it had begun to roll back its 1941 decision prohibiting journalistic advocacy. Issuing a blue-covered report entitled *Public Service Responsibility of Broadcast Licensees,* it established new guidelines for programming acceptable to the FCC. Taking note of the de facto censorship of labor from the airwaves, it obliged broadcasters to present a balanced presentation of the news rather than maintaining strict neutrality (often violated in practice). More important, it required broadcasters to meet their public obligations by being increasingly responsive to local needs, by limiting commercial advertising, and by increasing public-affairs programming. Although many broadcasters protested the guidelines found in the FCC's "blue book," many media leaders, including William S. Paley of CBS, had suggested similar ideas. Paley, who had often insisted that news be unbiased, concluded during the war that commentary and editorial opinion were permissible so long as they were clearly presented as distinct from the news. His solution became that of the FCC. In 1949 it thoroughly reversed the 1941 decision and permitted explicit editorial commentaries by journalists, so long as opposing viewpoints were presented. This ruling became the basis of the later "fairness doctrine," which sought to maintain political diversity by forcing broadcasters to present all sides. News, in other words, should strive to be objective, but it could be propagandistic so long as a plurality of opinion was presented.

Father Charles Coughlin

Sources:

Erik Barnouw, *The Golden Web: A History of Broadcasting in the United States, Volume II — 1933 to 1953* (New York: Oxford University Press, 1968);

Theodore F. Koop, *Weapon of Silence* (Chicago: University of Chicago, 1946);

Eric Sevareid, *Not So Wild A Dream* (New York: Knopf, 1946);

Patrick S. Washburn, *A Question of Sedition: The Federal Government's Investigation of the Black Press During World War II* (New York: Oxford University Press, 1986).

RADIO: THE END OF THE GOLDEN AGE

The Once and Former King. After a "pioneer period" from the first successful experiments in the 1890s to the 1920s, radio entered a golden age in the 1930s. Before the first truly successful television broadcasts early in the 1940s, radio was the only broadcast medium, and its popularity in the United States during the time rivaled that of television since the late 1940s. For two decades radio was king.

Little Change. The nature of the golden age of radio was established in the 1930s, and radio programming remained basically unchanged during the 1940s. Comedy-variety shows featuring popular actors and musicians, soap operas, adventure programs such as *The Shadow* and *The Lone Ranger,* and news dominated the airwaves. The only substantial difference between the decades was the amount of news on the radio, which

ONE OF THE TRULY GREAT

THE GREAT NEW
1950 PHILCOS
cost as much as
$200⁰⁰ LESS
than last year..and now
the advertised price
is the final price...
nothing else to buy

Advertisement, late 1949

increased substantially when the United States entered World War II in 1941.

In Television's Shadow. Ironically, the successes of radio provided the foundations for its own decline in the face of television. Its successive improvements in broadcast technology provided the nuts and bolts for television, and its evolution from local broadcasting to national networks such as NBC, CBS, and ABC created corporate entities that would employ this technology for greater potential profits in television, essentially abandoning radio in the process. In addition, many of the first stars of television got their starts in radio. When the networks and the stars shifted their energies to the new medium after the end of World War II enabled them to do so, the local stations who had broadcast their offerings were left behind. These stations for the most part became local broadcasters once again, perhaps relying on a network for news but focusing their energies on music and local advertising.

Source:
Erik Barnouw, *The Golden Web: A History of Broadcasting in the United States, Volume II — 1933 to 1953* (New York: Oxford University Press, 1968).

TELEVISION IS BORN

Slow Development. Although the basic components of television were developed as early as the 1870s, the technology was not sophisticated enough to broadcast an image until the 1920s. Even then television was too crude for widespread use. There were eighteen experimental television stations in the United States in 1931, but opposition to the new medium by radio broadcasters and a lack of funding during the Depression left these promising starts wanting. Nonetheless, technical innovations by inventors such as Vladimir Zworykin and Philo Farnsworth refined and improved television, and RCA was ready to introduce widespread commercial manufacture of television sets by 1938. RCA's competitors opposed the deployment of a national broadcast system based on RCA technology and moved to block the licensing of commercial broadcasting by the FCC. In 1940 a government panel concluded that RCA was attempting to establish industry broadcasting standards on terms disadvantageous to its competitors, and it reviewed and revised television broadcasting standards. On 3 May 1941 the FCC established guidelines more equitable for a variety of television manufacturers, opening the way for widespread commercial television broadcasting in the United States. On 1 July 1941 CBS and NBC switched their New York stations from experimental to commercial status, broadcasting about fifteen hours of programming a week. Television sets, extremely expensive at the time, limited the expansion of the technology. By the time of Pearl Harbor, there were only ten thousand to twenty thousand receivers in use in the United States, and broadcasting was limited to a few urban centers. The war put a hold on the expansion of television. The FCC forbade building new television stations in order to conserve materials for the war. For the moment television's potential remained unrealized.

Postwar Boom. The hiatus in television growth during World War II gave television manufacturers an opportunity to improve existing technology using electronic innovations developed during the war. The image orthicon, a sensitive television camera developed by RCA in 1945, was an important advance. Postwar introduction of television nonetheless took place slowly at first, then developed in a rush. The sheer expense involved in building a television station — at a time when profits were unproven — retarded investor support. Television costs generally ran ten times higher than those of radio, and few stations posted profits before 1952. Most stations were thus owned by business concerns that could sustain long-term losses. Television manufacturers bought stations, hoping to spark sales of their products. Allen B. Dumont, a television-set maker, bought several East Coast stations after the war, hoping to build a network to support his manufacturing. Newspapers also bought local stations, anticipating that television's immediacy would be a boon to the news business. Most important, however, the old radio networks and large independent radio stations moved into television. NBC was the most powerful of these networks, with over twenty-five national affiliates by 1948. CBS quickly developed a reputation for outstanding news broadcasting. Noble's ABC struggled until 1951, when it absorbed and was revitalized by a powerful entertainment company, United Paramount

Milton Berle, in striped shirt, after having been hit in the face with a pie on the *Texaco Star Theater* in 1948

Theaters. Concerned about the potential of the new industry, radio networks moved into television to control their losses. But the networks also moved into television broadcasting because it was less regulated by the FCC than was radio. Despite the ban on monopolies, NBC, CBS, and ABC exercised enormous control over affiliate stations in major markets, and by the early 1960s the "big three" networks had a virtual monopoly on U.S. television broadcasting.

Programming. As radio networks moved to dominate television broadcasting, they brought many of the popular radio shows and personalities to television. *Life of Riley,* a popular program dealing with a blue-collar worker, made the transition, as did comedies such as *Our Miss Brooks,* starring Eve Arden, *The Goldbergs, Ozzie and Harriet,* and *Amos and Andy.* Radio format staples, such as the talent shows *Original Amateur Hour* and Arthur Godfrey's *Talent Scouts,* relocated to the small screen. *Your Hit Parade* had run for fifteen years on radio before it moved to television in 1950. The program featured contemporary best-selling pop tunes. Crime-detective dramas, such as *Dragnet,* jumped from radio to television, as did the "thriller" programs aimed at school-age children, such as *Sky King* and *Superman.* Sports broadcasting was, of course, immensely popular, as were original children's programs such as *Super Circus, Howdy Doody,* and *Kukla, Fran, and Ollie.* Television also borrowed

radio newsmen and formats. Reporters made famous by World War II, such as Edward R. Murrow, extended their celebrity to television. Network public-affairs programming, such as *Meet the Press* and *Hear It Now* (which became *See It Now*), also made the transition to television. A staple of early television, the variety show, was borrowed from vaudeville theater. The imperturbable Ed Sullivan hosted the long-running *Toast of the Town,* while Sid Caesar and Imogene Coca made *Your Show of Shows* an audience favorite.

Uncle Miltie. By far the most popular program in television's early years was a similar variety program, *Texaco Star Theater,* starring Milton Berle, a forty-year-old comedian when NBC hired him for the program in 1948. A Borscht Belt vaudevillian, he specialized in slapstick humor and manic, unflagging energy. By the fall of 1948 Berle's program had earned a 94.7 rating in the television markets — meaning that when he was on television, 94.7 percent of the viewers in the United States tuned into his program. The next year "Uncle Miltie," as he was affectionately called, graced the cover of *Time* and *Newsweek.* His name was synonymous with television when the medium served urban, ethnic audiences — 35 percent of viewers lived in New York. As television expanded into the heartland, Berle's humor seemed less vital, and his jokes about New York and its ethnic groups fell flat. His fortunes declined, and by 1955 television's first superstar was dropped from *Texaco Star Theater*.

The Television Freeze. Uncle Miltie was not the only casualty of television's expansion. By 1948 the growth of television in the Northeast was so great that the FCC's original channel allocation plan, drafted only three years earlier, had to be revised. Because there were only thirteen channels available for VHF television broadcasts, the FCC had the unenviable task of making sure that stations were assigned broadcast frequencies fairly and competitively. With channel one assigned to emergency broadcasting, the FCC had to balance carefully the assignment of twelve channels in major metropolitan areas such as New York City. Geography was an important factor: New York could easily sustain twelve commercial channels, but other communities within two hundred broadcast miles of New York (including Philadelphia and Hartford) also needed channels; if the same channel were assigned to stations in close broadcast proximity, the signals would interfere with one another. In 1948 interference and channel assignment were overwhelming problems. The FCC responded by freezing the licensing of new stations, ostensibly for a six- to nine-month period. In fact, the freeze lasted until 14 April 1952. Although it retarded the construction of new stations, the freeze lessened competitive pressures on existing stations, allowing them to standardize production and broadcast practices. The freeze also gave the FCC time to adjudicate a terrific battle between RCA and CBS over the technological standard to be adopted in color-television transmissions, an issue resolved in RCA's favor in 1953. The freeze was resolved by a careful geographic allocation of VHF channels and by opening up the ultrahigh frequency (UHF) bands to commercial television. By the end of the freeze, all the technological, commercial, and licensing elements of the television industry were in place. In the 1950s television would undergo explosive growth and transform the character of American culture irrevocably.

Source:
Erik Barnouw, *The Golden Web: A History of Broadcasting in the United States, Volume II — 1933–1953* (New York: Oxford University Press, 1968).

HEADLINE MAKERS

MARGARET BOURKE-WHITE

1906-1971

PHOTOJOURNALIST

War Journalist. In an era which acclaimed the war journalist, none was more renowned than Margaret Bourke-White. Her photographs for *Life* magazine brought World War II home with clarity and sensitivity for millions of Americans; her courage on the battlefront became legendary. Bourke-White set many firsts for women during the war — the first woman to fly on bombing missions, for instance — and her work was superior to that of most U.S. photographers, male or female. When U.S. troops liberated the Nazi death camps, Bourke-White was there, documenting the tragedy of the camps and relaying unforgettable images of the atrocities to the public.

Background. Daughter of an engineer-inventor and a strong-willed, independent housewife, Bourke-White was raised in a household that embraced female equality and ambition. Her father, holding several machine patents, instilled in Bourke-White a fascination and awe for machines that would later advance her career considerably. He was also an amateur photographer, although Bourke-White claimed she did not begin photographing until after his death in 1922. When she enrolled at Columbia University in 1921, it was with the intention of becoming a biologist. (She ultimately received a B.A. in biology from Cornell.) A series of art photography classes with Clarence H. White, associated with the innovative Photo-Secession school of Alfred Stieglitz, cinched photography as a vocation, but Bourke-White had a difficult time getting started. She switched universities several times due to money problems and suffered through a brief, failed marriage. By 1927 she had steeled her resolve to make a living as an independent photographer, and she relocated to Cleveland to make her mark.

Photojournalist. Cleveland was in the midst of the industrial boom of the 1920s, and Bourke-White established her reputation in the new field of industrial photography. She was drawn to the symmetry and power of big industry, and her photos, with their overtones of art, made an impression — not only among Cleveland's industrialists, busy hiring her to photograph steel furnaces and assembly lines, but among magazine publishers such as Henry R. Luce, owner of *Time*. Luce had planned a new magazine, *Fortune*, to cater to American business, and Bourke-White's photographs fit his format well. She contributed the photographs for the lead article in the first issue, and thereafter the magazine was to a great extent dependent upon her bold, iconographic photographs. She took what she termed "symbolic" photographs: single images that would come to represent entire ideas and concepts. She pioneered photojournalism in *Fortune*, which built entire articles around her images. By the early 1930s she was the most famous photojournalist in the United States.

Icons and Politics. Bourke-White's skill with the camera was such that she had her choice of assignments. In the early 1930s she traveled to the Soviet Union, before the United States had established diplomatic relations with that nation. Her photographs of Soviet industry became some of the first images of the Soviet Union seen by Americans, and she became an in-demand lecturer on the Soviet Union. In 1935 she was called upon to photograph President Franklin D. Roosevelt and began documenting New Deal public-works projects. In 1936 one such photograph, of the Fort Peck dam in Montana, became the cover of the first issue of Luce's new photo magazine, *Life*. *Life* became an important forum for Bourke-White's work, especially for photographs of the dust bowl or the Depression, such as the 1937 picture of Louisville flood victims lined up for assistance before a billboard proclaiming that the United States maintained the world's highest standard of living. She dropped her earlier awe of machines and became fascinated by human drama. She joined progressive political organizations, such as the American Artists' Congress, dedicated to using art to publicize the plight of the disadvantaged, and stopped taking photographs for major advertisers. She even, for a time, broke with Luce to work in a more liberal journal, *PM,* but ultimately returned to *Life.* In 1937 she published *You Have Seen Their Faces,* a photo-essay on sharecropping, with text by the man who would become her second husband, Erskine Caldwell. It was a popular success and paved the way for subsequent protest photo-essays, such as James Agee and Walter Evans's *Let Us Now Praise Famous Men* (1941) or those of Robert Frank. In 1938 Bourke-White and Caldwell decided to apply a similar formula to a book on Europe. They arrived in time for the Munich crisis.

War and Liberation. As the political crisis in Europe disintegrated into war, Bourke-White was there, capturing the drama of the experience. She traveled from London to Libya and from Syria to Siberia during the conflict. The first woman accredited as a war correspondent, she survived the sinking of the SS *Strath-Allan* off North Africa and flew on B-17 bombing runs over Tunis. Trusted by the Soviets for her previous work on the Soviet Union, Bourke-White scooped her fellow photojournalists by being the only American at work in the U.S.S.R. when the Germans invaded. She also accompanied U.S. troops during the invasion of Italy, developing an almost mythological reputation for her willingness to hazard enemy fire to get dangerous aerial shots. In 1945 she was with Gen. George Patton's forces as they liberated Buchenwald and took classic photographs that highlighted the spectral gazes of the prisoners of the concentration camp; she reached the Erla work camp and took appalling photos of the massacre hours after SS troops incinerated over three hundred inmates. Following the war, Bourke-White published many photographs of Europe in ruins, bringing the cost of war home to many Americans via the pages of *Life.* She also traveled to India, becoming one of the first American photographers to cover the burgeoning nationalist movements of the third world. She shot photos of Mohandas K. Gandhi at his spinning wheel, the slaughter in the Punjab, and Pakistani refugees, and she published the photographs in a well-received book, *Halfway to Freedom* (1949).

Last Battle. By the 1950s Bourke-White had traveled to thirty-six countries and taken hundreds of thousands of photographs. In 1952 she returned to war, this time in Korea. Rather than photograph the battles, she published a photo-essay in *Life* that focused on the trauma of civil war for one Korean family. It was to be her last major assignment. In the early 1950s she was diagnosed as having Parkinson's disease. Bourke-White's worldwide adventurism ground to a halt, and her work ended as she devoted her attention to fighting the illness. She publi-

cized her struggle through a 1960 television dramatization of her life and through the publication of her autobiography, *Portrait of Myself,* in 1963. After twenty years of fighting Parkinson's, Bourke-White died on 27 August 1971.

Sources:
Vicki Goldberg, *Margaret Bourke-White: A Biography* (New York: Harper & Row, 1986);

Robert E. Hood, *Twelve at War: Great Photographers Under Fire* (New York: Putnam, 1967).

JOHN W. CAMPBELL, JR.

1910-1971

SCIENCE-FICTION WRITER AND MAGAZINE EDITOR

Influential Editor. The term *golden age* is used with great frequency to refer to popular culture of the 1930s and 1940s, whether referring to radio, comic books, or science fiction. Rarely, however, can such a golden age be as closely identified with the work of one person as the science-fiction golden age can with John W. Campbell, Jr. During the late 1930s and throughout the 1940s he was the most influential editor in the field, discovering impressive new talents and pushing the genre to a level more sophisticated than that of most previous American science fiction, which relied heavily on adventure formulas and gadgetry.

From Writer to Editor. Campbell began writing science fiction while in his teens and published his first stories before completing his studies in physics at the Massachusetts Institute of Technology and Duke University. He built a name for himself as a writer during the 1930s, at first with space opera, then under the pseudonym Don A. Stuart, with moody, atmospheric stories such as "Twilight" (1934) and "Who Goes There?" (1938). In the second half of the decade he became increasingly associated with *Astounding Science-Fiction,* edited by F. Orlin Tremaine. In 1937 he became its next editor, a position he retained until his death.

New Writers, New Ideas. Campbell wrote little fiction after assuming the editorship of *Astounding Science-Fiction,* devoting his energies instead to making his the best science-fiction magazine in the United States. He succeeded, bringing his knowledge of good writing as an author to bear on the writings of others. He was supportive of new writers, offering them extremely detailed feedback on their work and even giving them ideas of his own to improve their stories. Within two years he had discovered a stable of writers who have since been recognized as major figures in the field, including Isaac Asimov, Lester del Rey, Robert A. Heinlein, Theodore Sturgeon, and A. E. Van Vogt. He also attracted more-established writers into his fold, among them L. Sprague de Camp, L. Ron Hubbard, Henry Kuttner, C. L. Moore, Clifford D. Simak, and Jack Williamson. In the pages of *Astounding Science-Fiction* Campbell published many science-fiction classics by these authors and others. Though it published several fantasy classics, he was less successful with the fantasy magazine *Unknown,* which he began in 1939 and ended four years later.

Future Realism. Campbell, like his counterparts, stressed good storytelling, but he also strove for realism — psychological and sociological as well as scientific — within the conventions of the genre. His goal, he stated, was to publish stories about the future that would seem like journalism to a reader from that future. Sometimes this resulted in writers predicting things before they came to pass. *Astounding Science-Fiction* was publishing stories about moon landings and atomic-plant meltdowns long before such events became reality, and one story — Cleve Cartmill's "Deadline" (1944) — brought Campbell a visit from U.S. intelligence agents demanding to know how the magazine had acquired the "secret" of how to build an atomic bomb, which had been published as part of the story, from the Manhattan Project.

After the Golden Age. Campbell remained an important figure in science fiction until his death, but the influence he exercised in the 1940s waned for various reasons after the decade had passed. First, the dominance of *Astounding Science-Fiction* was effectively challenged in the 1950s by new magazines such as the *Magazine of Fantasy and Science Fiction* (founded 1949) and *Galaxy* (founded 1950) — both of which were as innovative in publishing new writers and ideas as Campbell had been more than a decade earlier. In contrast Campbell became more conservative, both artistically and politically, and some of the new ideas he entertained — most notably Hubbard's new "science" of dianetics, first explained in an article in the May 1950 issue of *Astounding Science-Fiction* — earned him more ridicule than respect. In addition, he was losing authors to the changing science-fiction market: writers such as Heinlein and Asimov realized they could reach more people and make more money by writing for mainstream magazines with wider circulations and by fulfilling the new demand for science-fiction books (most American science fiction before World War II had been published in magazines). Nevertheless, *Astounding Science Fiction* (renamed *Analog Science Fact — Science Fiction* in 1960) continued to remain one of the most popular magazines in the field, and Campbell was widely mourned when he died in 1971.

Sources:
Brian W. Aldiss and David Wingrove, *Trillion Year Spree: The History of Science Fiction* (New York: Atheneum, 1986);

Thomas D. Clareson, *Understanding Contemporary American Science Fiction: The Formative Period (1926–1970)* (Columbia: University of South Carolina Press, 1990).

WILL EISNER

1917-

COMIC-BOOK WRITER AND ARTIST

A Man of Many Talents. Will Eisner was one of the most innovative and talented comic-book writers, artists, and editors of the late 1930s and the 1940s. Best known for writing and drawing *The Spirit,* he was also prominent in the industry for creating several memorable characters, among them Blackhawk and Sheena, Queen of the Jungle. In the case of *The Spirit,* he was also one of the few comic-book figures from this period to retain control over his creation.

An Early Start. Born in Brooklyn, Eisner entered the new field of comic books in 1936 while still a teenager. With Jerry Iger he formed a company that produced comics for different publishers, including Fiction House, Fox, and Quality. (One artist for the Eisner-Iger partnership, Bob Kane, soon went on to create Batman.) During this period he and Iger created Sheena, drawn by Mort Meskin, and Dollman, drawn by Lou Fine. The company prospered, but Eisner wanted to do more than mass-produce formulaic comic books for kids. Consequently, when the *Chicago Tribune* decided to create a comic-book magazine in the spring of 1940 in order to compete with the wildly successful comic-book industry, Eisner jumped at the offer to write and draw a weekly, sixteen-page comic that would be distributed in a newspaper rather than on the newsstands. The result was *The Spirit.*

The Spirit. The conception of Eisner's new character, a crimefighter with a secret identity, owed much to the popular superhero comic books, but everything else about the comic was entirely original. Rather than a colorful costume, Denny Colt wore a blue business suit with matching mask and fedora to fight crime as the Spirit. He possessed no superpowers — merely a powerful physique, above-average intelligence, and the capacity to get hit a lot and still stand up. *The Spirit* was also noteworthy for its inclusion of the Spirit's friend Ebony, the first African American character to appear on a continuing basis in an American comic book. Though a humorous character drawn as a caricature in line with popular-culture stereotypes of the day, Ebony was also a three-dimensional character and sometimes the focus of serious subplots within the book.

Art and Business. *The Spirit* was significant for other reasons as well. For one thing, many comic-book writers and artists toiled anonymously, churning out books on a work-for-hire basis; Eisner, in contrast, received prominent billing in each issue and added to his profits from his company by retaining all rights to the character. A shrewd businessman, he was also a consummate artist.

He combined comedy and drama in skillfully told stories, created believable characters, and set them in gritty, yet evocatively drawn, settings.

Successes. *The Spirit* was published through newspaper syndication for twelve years and was then reprinted in different comics on various occasions. While Eisner remained active with this comic and others, he also turned his attention to promoting the form through book-length graphic novels and his study *Comics and Sequential Art* (1985), illustrated with many examples from his own work.

Sources:

Mike Benton, *The Comic Book in America: An Illustrated History,* revised edition (Dallas: Taylor, 1993);

Ron Goulart, *Great History of Comic Books* (Chicago & New York: Contemporary Books, 1986).

JOHN H. JOHNSON

1918-

MAGAZINE PUBLISHER

Success Story. John H. Johnson entered publishing at age twenty-four, when, after white bankers refused to loan him money, he used his mother's furniture as collateral for a five-hundred-dollar loan in order to send out twenty thousand letters promoting a new magazine, to be called *Negro Digest.* By the 1990s Johnson, a multimillionaire, was the most influential and prosperous African American businessman in the country. In the intervening fifty years his magazines, particularly *Ebony,* had become an integral part of American culture.

Aspiration. Johnson was born to a poor family in Arkansas City, Arkansas. When he was six his father died in a sawmill accident. Because Arkansas City had no high school for blacks, he and his mother moved to Chicago when he was in his teens on money she earned as a cook. The move paid off: Johnson excelled in high school in academics and leadership, and he edited the school newspaper and served as business manager of its yearbook. Influenced by his mother, he saw hard work and determination as essential to succeeding in a society in which blacks were afforded little opportunity for success. He graduated from high school with honors and received a tuition-only scholarship to the University of Chicago; he was able to accept it thanks to Harry H. Pace, president of the black-owned Supreme Life Insurance Company of America, who offered him a part-time office job. Working with African American professionals was another powerful influence on him, and he stopped attending the University of Chicago after two years to focus on his office work. (In 1938–1940 he resumed his studies at the Northwestern School of Commerce.)

Inspiration. Johnson's first job for the company was to read articles from contemporary publications and select those of interest to blacks for the company newsletter sent to clients. This task, along with the success of *Reader's Digest,* gave him the idea of creating a magazine that would reprint articles and publish feature articles for a black audience. Through his initial letter promoting *Negro Digest* he convinced three thousand people to contribute two dollars each toward charter subscriptions; with the six thousand dollars he received he published the first issue of the magazine in November 1942.

In Leaps and Bounds. Johnson had difficulties at first in getting his magazine to readers. It was declined by distributors at the time, who said it lacked an audience. In response he encouraged thirty Supreme Life employees to ask for the magazine at newsstands and buy it to prod dealers to request it from distributors. It worked in Chicago (he then bought back and resold the magazines), and then he tried it in other large cities. Within a year *Negro Digest* had a circulation of fifty thousand. Circulation tripled when Eleanor Roosevelt contributed to an ongoing feature, "If I Were a Negro." Another feature of the magazine was called "My Most Humiliating Jim Crow Experience." Throughout the 1940s *Negro Digest* offered what Johnson promised with the first issue: "a complete survey of current Negro life and thought . . . dedicated to the development of interracial understanding and the promotion of national unity. It stands unqualifiedly for . . . the integration of all citizens into the democratic process." In 1951 *Negro Digest* was discontinued when Johnson introduced *Jet,* a weekly news magazine, but it was reintroduced in 1961. In 1970 it was renamed *Black World* and under editor Hoyt W. Fuller became the most militant of his publications. It ceased publication in 1976.

Ebony. Johnson's best-known magazine, *Ebony,* premiered in November 1945. Modeled after popular magazines featuring pictures and short articles such as *Life* and *Look,* the magazine aimed "to mirror the happier side of Negro life — the positive, everyday achievements from Harlem to Hollywood." However, Johnson added, it would address racial problems seriously. Supporters have consistently praised *Ebony* for its positive depictions of African American life and its encouraging messages to its many readers. By 1985, forty years after its initial publication, its circulation had risen from a press run of 25,000, with an estimated 125,000 readers, to a press run of 2.3 million, with an estimated 9 million readers.

Continuing Success. On the successes of *Negro Digest* and *Ebony* Johnson built a publishing and financial empire. He introduced other magazines, most notably *Jet,* and pursued other business interests, among them radio, television, and cosmetics. He is also the chief executive officer of the Supreme Life Insurance Company. His many awards include the Spingarn Medal from the National Association for the Advancement of Colored People (NAACP) in 1966 and the Publisher of the Year

Award from the Magazine Publishers Association in 1972.

Sources:

"*Ebony's* Johnson," *Newsweek*, 34 (7 November 1949): 60;

John H. Johnson, *Succeeding Against the Odds* (New York: Warner, 1989);

A. James Reichley, "How John Johnson Made It," *Fortune* (January 1968): 152–180.

HENRY R. LUCE

1898-1967

PUBLISHER, TIME, LIFE, AND FORTUNE MAGAZINES

The American Publisher. Henry R. Luce was one of the most influential magazine publishers in the United States in the twentieth century. The magazines he began, *Time, Life,* and *Fortune,* had a profound impact on U.S. publishing and American public opinion. *Time* defined the modern newsmagazine, and *Life* established photo-documentary journalism. Moreover, the phenomenal success of these magazines gave Luce a platform from which to promote deeply held political and social ambitions. Wendell Willkie's internationalism was to some extent a product of Luce's influence, and the 1940 Republican candidate for president owed much of his popularity to Luce and his magazines. Luce championed U.S. assistance to China, intervention in World War II, and the escalation of the Cold War long before these issues became popular. His instincts both anticipated and seemed perfectly keyed to public interests. In a highly influential editorial of 1941 he argued that the United States should take advantage of World War II to subordinate economic competitors and restructure the world's political economy "for such purposes as we see fit and by such means as we see fit." According to Luce, an "American Century" had dawned; after the war the public, heady with success and enjoying unprecedented prosperity, agreed. Luce seemed prophetic, and he was widely acknowledged as one of the foremost proponents of internationalism — the American publisher of the new American century.

Young Expansionist. The acclaim Luce enjoyed as a publicist for U.S. internationalism in the 1940s was the fulfillment of a lifetime's ambition. Son of a Presbyterian missionary to China, Luce adopted much of his father's crusading faith in the manifest destiny of the United States. Arriving with the first U.S. diplomatic and business missions, the elder Luce saw his task as not only involving the conversion of the Chinese to Christianity but also the expansion of U.S. political and economic institutions into Asia. It was a goal his son would never abandon, pursuing it, like his father, with an almost jingoistic zeal. Educated in China, England, and the United States, young Luce entered Yale in 1916, making a name for himself as a tireless and humorless journalist. Joining the staff of the Yale *Daily News,* Luce used the occasion of the entry of the United States into World War I to propagate his nationalism, advocating much the same international role for the United States as he would in World War II. Given his religious background, Luce found atheistic communism repugnant and also published the first of many anti-Communist broadsides in the wake of the Bolshevik Revolution.

Making Time. Following graduation in 1920, Luce took a series of editorial jobs, eventually relocating to New York. With a fellow *Daily News* alumnus, Britton Hadden, he set out to launch a newsweekly magazine, tentatively entitled "Facts." Unlike newsmagazines of the day, Luce and Hadden's glossy would be written secondhand, with the editors summarizing material appearing originally in newspapers and magazines around the globe. The new magazine, now titled *Time,* would also specialize in breezy, accessible prose, which became known among journalists as "Timestyle." Dropped articles and adjectives, inverted sentence structure, and a staccato punctuation that compressed the material for an intended audience of "busy men" were the main elements of Timestyle. *Time* also announced, in its 3 March 1923 first issue, that "complete neutrality on public questions and important news is probably as undesirable as it is impossible." From that moment forward, *Time* was not only a magazine intended to inform; it was a magazine intended as Luce's platform.

Advocate. *Time,* as well as later Luce developments *Fortune* (begun in 1929) and *Life* (begun in 1936), routinely championed the interests of eastern, Republican businessmen — a solid core of subscribers who weathered the Depression well. Luce advocated a laissez-faire policy as a solution to the Depression, backed Hoover in 1932, and opposed the New Deal. Luce also expanded his activities into new media, beginning a topical radio series, "March of Time," which featured sensational dramatizations of the week's events, complete with sound effects such as gunshots. Later he introduced a newsreel series with the same title. As the Luce empire grew, it became an important organ for international news, tilting the public toward Luce's particular conception of American internationalism by its presentation of events. Until the middle 1930s Luce and *Time* promoted fascism, especially that espoused by Mussolini, as a solution to the dangers of communism. As Hitler's regime spiraled to new depths of brutality, however, Luce followed his readership into Fascist opposition. Luce and *Time* were irate at the normalization of diplomatic relations with the Soviet Union in 1933 and continued to portray the Communist state negatively. China, in the midst of a civil war between Communists and Nationalists (as well as at war against the Japanese), in the mid 1930s earned repeated exposure in the pages of *Time* and *Life*, especially in the form of sympathetic articles on the Nationalist leader Chiang Kai-shek.

Internationalist. After the Munich crisis of 1938, the Luce publications began to advocate U.S. intervention to oppose Hitler in Europe. In this Luce was bucking the tide of isolationist sentiment, especially within the Republican Party. He had strengthened his ties with the Republicans, backing Alf Landon in 1936. In 1940 Luce actively promoted a political outsider, Wendell Willkie, as the Republican nominee for president. Willkie, like Luce, was an internationalist, convinced that only the United States could impose order on a chaotic world. Luce was a trusted adviser, hoping to become secretary of state after a Willkie victory. His ambitions dashed with Willkie's defeat, Luce turned toward his second wife, Clare Boothe Luce, giving her the publicity she needed to win a seat in Congress in 1942. He also continued to press for a more expansive U.S. role in the world. Pearl Harbor greatly simplified his efforts. After the declaration of war he turned his publications toward the task of achieving victory, although he was unsettled that events had cast the United States and the Soviet Union as allies against Germany. By 1943 a *Fortune* poll found that 81 percent of Americans approved of the coalition with the Soviet Union and hoped to continue to pursue the alliance after the war. Luce, loathing Stalin and communism, was determined to prevent this.

Cold Warrior. Luce and his magazines were instrumental in promoting the Cold War by molding American public opinion against the Soviets. *Time* and *Life* accomplished this by subtle — and not so subtle — use of analogies and metaphors. For example, *Life*, in an essay on the devil, suggested he resided in Moscow. Both magazines were among the first press voices to suggest that communism and fascism — polar opposites in ideology — were politically equivalent and to make analogies between Hitler and Stalin. They consistently suggested that Soviet actions were filled with evil intent and advocated large-scale military build-up. They promoted domestic anti-Communists such as Richard Nixon and Joseph McCarthy (although later Luce would deny being a McCarthy supporter) and repeatedly attacked leading Democrats, such as Harry S Truman and Secretary of State Dean Acheson, for being soft on communism. Some of this zealous anticommunism was due to Whittaker Chambers, a *Time* senior editor who would become famous for accusing a State Department official, Alger Hiss, of spying for the Soviet Union. Luce, however, was the main general of the anti-Communist crusade. His speeches to civic groups during this period are full sermons on the dangers of the Soviets and on God's choice of the United States as "a principal instrument of His will on earth." Luce was also the leader of the China Lobby, a group of conservative organizations that funneled millions of dollars in U.S. assistance to Chiang Kai-shek in China. Luce featured the Chinese generalissimo repeatedly on the cover of *Time*, giving the public the impres-

sion that he enjoyed widespread Chinese popularity. This was not the case, and Chiang's corrupt and inept Nationalists fell to Mao's Communists in 1949. Luce was livid, and his magazines were among the first to echo the Republican charge that the Democrats had "lost" China. The charge, coming after the Soviet explosion of the atomic bomb and right before the Korean War, was fatal to the political prospects of the Democrats. They were crushed in the 1952 election. Luce was no doubt a political force.

Establishment. In the 1950s and 1960s Luce's influence and power were substantial, and his magazines became, more or less, organs of the American *establishment* — a term often used to describe the elite of conservative, corporate, anti-Communist internationalists centered in Washington, D.C., and New York City. Winston Churchill labeled him one of the seven most powerful men in the United States. His magazines, including a new recreational title, *Sports Illustrated,* were read by nearly 50 million people weekly, and his company had branched out into book publication, recordings, and entertainment. The 1963 fortieth anniversary of *Time* was the social event of the season, featuring over three hundred distinguished guests who had graced the cover of *Time.* With age his militant anticommunism mellowed, but he retained a keen interest in Asian affairs and was foremost among those advocating U.S. military intervention in Vietnam. In 1964 he turned over the management of the Time publications to Hedley Donovan, but he never really retired, continuing to applaud U.S. intervention in Vietnam and U.S. confrontation with Communist China. He died of a coronary occlusion on 28 February 1967.

Sources:

John Kobler, *Luce: His Time, Life and Fortune* (London: Macdonald, 1968);

W. A. Swanberg, *Luce and His Empire* (New York: Scribners, 1972).

BILL MAULDIN

1921-

CARTOONIST

Army Cartoonist. Bill Mauldin became one of the best-known cartoonists of the 1940s on the strength of his World War II series *Up Front.* Syndicated in addition to their publication in his division newspaper and later the *Stars and Stripes,* his cartoons about army life were a favorite of enlisted men and civilians alike. In 1945 he received the Pulitzer Prize, at age twenty-four the youngest person to do so.

Civilian Life. Mauldin was born in Mountain Park, New Mexico, and by the time he was a teenager he was drawing posters for local merchants. At his Phoenix high school he worked on the school newspaper. He studied at the Chicago Academy of Fine Arts with money borrowed from his grandparents. He had no trouble securing work as a freelance cartoonist, but during the Depression he found it difficult to support himself, so in 1940 he joined the National Guard. Almost immediately his unit was activated as part of the U.S. army, with Mauldin serving first in a truck unit and then in the infantry. He began submitting cartoons to his division's newspaper, in the process creating his two most memorable characters.

An Unsentimental View of War. Willie and Joe, Mauldin's everyman GIs, allowed him to explore the humorous as well as darker aspects of war; they also allowed him to poke fun at the military brass, some of whom would have kept his cartoons from publication were they not so popular with the enlisted men. Their popularity with the American public also helped to ensure their continued publication, and they moved to *Stars and Stripes* in 1944.

Postwar Career. After the war ended Mauldin received a lucrative contract to continue *Up Front* as *Willie and Joe*, which dealt with the characters' return to civilian life. Though his collections *Up Front* (1945) and *Back Home* (1947) sold well, the newspaper cartoons did not prosper, and in 1949 he left cartooning for nine years in order to pursue other interests, including acting and aviation. In 1958 he became an editorial cartoonist for the *St. Louis Post-Dispatch*; the following year he won his second Pulitzer Prize. In 1962 he moved to the *Chicago Sun-Times*, where he has spent the remainder of his career as a respected editorial cartoonist.

Source:
Dennis Wepman, "Bill Mauldin," in *The Encyclopedia of American Comics*, edited by Ron Goulart (New York & Oxford: Facts On File, 1990), pp. 253–254.

DREW PEARSON

1896-1969

JOURNALIST

Muckraking Journalist. Drew Pearson served as one of Washington's premier muckraking journalists for over thirty years, writing the syndicated column "Washington Merry-Go-Round," first with Robert S. Allen and later with Jack Anderson.

World Journey. Pearson was born in Evanston, Illinois, to a Quaker professor who served as governor of the Virgin Islands. After graduating from Swarthmore College in 1919, Pearson traveled to post–World War I Europe to learn about diplomacy but instead became the director of relief in the Balkans for the British Red Cross. In 1921 he returned to the United States. In 1922 he began a self-financed world journey, signing on as seaman on the merchant vessel S.S. *President Madison* for a journey to the Far East. He jumped ship in Yokohama, Japan, and traveled for two years in Japan, the Soviet Union, China, the Phillipines, Australia, New Zealand, and India.

Newspaper Beginnings. During his travels Pearson began publishing his impressions in Australian newspapers. In 1923 he continued his travels into Europe and gained a newspaper syndicate contract. His most important work from this period was his interview series Europe's Twelve Greatest Men. In 1925, after a trip to Japan and China, he married, and the next year he took a job on the staff of the *United States Daily* newspaper. With this position Pearson began his rise in the world of Washington journalism. In 1928 he traveled with Secretary of State Clark Kellogg on trips to Paris and Dublin and with President Calvin Coolidge to Havana.

Washington Merry-Go-Round. In 1929 he joined the staff of the *Baltimore Sun* and continued his work as a diplomatic and foreign-affairs reporter. During the presidency of Herbert Hoover and the first years of what became the Great Depression, Pearson became friends with Robert Allen, the Washington bureau chief of the *Christian Science Monitor*. The two often met and discussed ways to print inside stories of Washington politics that their respective papers refused to publish. In 1931 they wrote and published anonymously *Washington Merry-Go-Round*, a compilation of rumor and gossip that caused an uproar in official Washington circles. A sequel, *More Washington Merry-Go-Round*, was published in 1932, but the identity of the authors was revealed, and both Pearson and Allen were dismissed from their jobs.

Daily Column and Radio. Faced with unemployment Pearson and Allen signed with United Features Syndicate to produce a daily "Washington Merry-Go-Round" column. By 1941 it was printed in 350 papers around the world. In February 1941 they began a weekly radio broadcast on NBC that Pearson claimed was a safeguard against censorship efforts by the syndicate or by individual papers. A liberal with a controversialist edge, Pearson campaigned for internationalism abroad and civil rights at home. During the war he had impeccable sources within the War Department and the intelligence groups. In April 1941 he predicted the breakdown of the Nazi-Soviet pact and the German invasion two months before these events happened. In 1943 Pearson broke the story of Gen. George S. Patton striking a soldier who was suffering from battle fatigue.

Nobel Prize Nomination. In 1947 Pearson organized a public movement to donate food for the war survivors in Europe. His talent for publicity and self-promotion was so successful that seven hundred train-car loads of food were distributed in Italy and France through his efforts. He received most of the credit and was nominated for the 1947 Nobel Peace Prize. But he was best known after the war for his attacks on the House Un-American Activities Committee (HUAC), on which he was relentless from the beginning. Pearson was such a thorn in the side of Sen. Joseph McCarthy that in December 1950 McCarthy attacked him physically.

Continuing Influence. Pearson's career continued into the late 1960s; where his influence waned in one degree, it continued in another. After Allen quit the "Washington Merry-Go-Round" during the war, Pearson continued the column on his own. In the late 1940s he recruited a young newspaperman, Jack Anderson, to work with him on it. Anderson, who ended up on President Richard Nixon's enemies list in the early 1970s, was a muckraker in Pearson's image. He was not, however, nearly as principled. It is in his tactics and his doggedness that Pearson's influence lives.

Source:
Oliver Pilat, *Drew Pearson: An Unauthorized Biography* (New York: Harper's Magazine Press, 1973).

ERNIE PYLE

1900-1945

WAR CORRESPONDENT

The Regular American. Ernie Pyle was the most famous war correspondent the United States ever produced. A Midwesterner who quit college after three years, Pyle was the eyes and voice of the regular American, able to describe the experience of individuals at war in the language of the readers at home.

First Newspaper Job. Pyle missed World War I when his parents ordered him to graduate from high school and refused to allow him to enlist. As a senior at Indiana University in January 1923, Pyle quit to accept a job as a reporter on the *LaPorte* (Ind.) *Herald.* In just a few months he was offered a job as a reporter on the *Washington Daily News.*

Traveling the Country. In July 1925 he married Geraldine "Jerry" Seibolds, an intelligent but troubled civil-service worker. Calling themselves bohemians, the couple did not allow their friends to know of their marriage for many years. In summer 1926 the Pyles quit their jobs and traveled around the United States. After nine thousand miles in ten weeks, the Pyles ended up in New York, where Ernie took a job on the copy desk at the *Evening World.* In December 1927 Pyle returned to Washington, D.C., and the *Washington Daily News,* where he began the first aviation column in the United States.

Roving Columnist. In 1932 he was promoted to managing editor, a position he did not enjoy but which he kept for three years. In 1934 a long automobile trip taken

to convalesce from a nasty case of influenza suggested his ultimate talent. After his return to Washington he wrote a series of well-received columns about his vacation trip. He convinced Scripps-Howard, the owner of the *Washington Daily News,* to employ him as a roving columnist. He began writing six columns per week to be printed in the twenty-six Scripps-Howard papers. For five years Pyle traveled throughout the United States, writing his six columns per week, the whole week's worth often completed in one day.

The Battle of Britain. In November 1940 Pyle sailed for Great Britain to report on the Battle of Britain. One of his first stories shows his talent for writing and for reporting:

> Someday when peace has returned to this odd world I want to come to London again and stand on a certain balcony on a moonlit night and look down upon the peaceful silver curve of the Thames with its dark bridges.

> And standing there I want to tell somebody who has never seen it how London looked on a certain night in the holiday season of the year 1940.

> For on that night this old, old city — even though I must bite my tongue in shame for saying it — was the most beautiful sight I have ever seen.

> It was a night when London was ringed and stabbed with fire.

The Costs of War. Over the next four years Pyle traveled through the war zones, both Atlantic and Pacific — Great Britain, Ireland, North Africa, Sicily, Italy, France, and the islands of the Pacific theater. As he watched the youth of the United States march across Europe and the Pacific Islands, he became fascinated at what war was doing to these young men. They were becoming killers, he realized; he told, indeed warned, the people back home that if and when their brothers, sons, and husbands returned home they would be extremely different from the way they had been when they left.

Okinawa. Pyle left for his last trip at the end of 1944. From Hawaii he traveled with units of the First Marine Division to Okinawa for the invasion that began on 1 April 1945. He went ashore five hours after the first landing and spent two days on the island. He then returned to the ship in order to write. He made several more trips to the island to accompany the Marines. On 17 April 1945 the Marines landed on Ie Shima, a ten-square-mile island west of Okinawa. Pyle did not go ashore on the landing day, as was his normal procedure, but instead waited until the following day. On 18 April 1945 he was killed by a Japanese sniper. There was a great outpouring of grief for the man who had made the life of a soldier and the experience of war available to so many. Gen. Omar Bradley commented that "I have known no finer man, no finer soldier than he."

Source:
Ernie's War: The Best of Ernie Pyle's World War II Dispatches, edited, with a biographical essay, by David Nichols (New York: Random House, 1986).

PEOPLE IN THE NEWS

In February 1940 American Society of Composers, Authors, and Publishers (ASCAP) president **Gene Buck** was arrested in Phoenix, Arizona, on extortion charges. The charges, stemming from a licensing dispute between ASCAP and a radio station, were dropped when Arizona governor R. T. Jones refused extradition to New York.

Early in 1942 Rep. **Eugene E. Cox** of Georgia began a House investigation of FCC chairman Lawrence Fly and the FCC, which was dropped when it was revealed that Cox had taken kickbacks from a Georgia radio station.

On 6 June 1945 six people connected to the foreign-policy journal *Amerasia,* including publisher **Philip Jaffe,** were arrested and charged with espionage when they were found to have had substantial classified State Department files passed to them by disgruntled officials critical of U.S. support for Chiang Kai-shek's Chinese Nationalists. There was little evidence to support the charge, and the cases against the six were dropped, fueling suspicions on the far Right that a Communist conspiracy was at work within the State Department.

In June 1940 **James Caesar Petrillo** was elected president of the American Federation of Musicians. During the next few years, he would lead a struggle for royalty payments to musicians from radio broadcasters.

In 1942 former newsman **Byron Price** became head of the U.S. Office of Censorship, a wartime agency set up to monitor overseas communications within the United States and American broadcasting.

On 10 March 1944 Col. **David S. Sarnoff** of the reserve officer's corps reported for duty in the Army Signal Corps. Sarnoff, the president of RCA, was placed in charge of allocation of materials and communications for D-Day.

Published by Pocket Books, **Benjamin Spock**'s *Baby and Child Care* quickly became the best-selling paperback book of the 1940s and 1950s.

When **Joe Shuster** and **Jerry Siegel** sold their comic-book character Superman to National Periodical Publications (later DC Comics) in 1938, they signed away all rights to the character but continued to draw and write the strip. When they took the company to court in 1947 to increase their royalties they lost the case and their jobs writing and drawing Superman. In 1975, in response to public outrage that DC had made millions from Superman while his creators received nothing, DC established an annual stipend for each.

One of the more stunning radio programs aired in the summer of 1943 was *Open Letter on Race Hatred,* a CBS dramatization of the June race riots in Detroit. The program, advocating racial tolerance, concluded with a piece read by former Republican presidential candidate, **Wendell Willkie.**

AWARDS

PULITZER PRIZES FOR JOURNALISM

1940

Public Service: *Waterbury* (Conn.) *Republican-American*

Reporting (General): S. Burton Heath, *New York World-Telegram*

Correspondence: Otto D. Tolischus, *The New York Times*

Editorial Writing: Bart Howard, *St. Louis Post-Dispatch*

Editorial Cartoons: Edmund Duffy, *Baltimore Sun*

1941

Public Service: *St. Louis Post-Dispatch*

Reporting (General): Westbrook Pegler, *New York World-Telegram*

Correspondence: Group award to American war correspondents

Editorial Writing: Reuben Maury, *New York Daily News*

Editorial Cartoons: Jacob Burck, *Chicago Times*

Special Citation: *The New York Times* foreign news report

1942

Public Service: *Los Angeles Times*

Reporting (General): Stanton Delaplane, *San Francisco Chronicle*

Telegraphic Reporting (National): Louis Stark, *The New York Times*

Telegraphic Reporting (International): Laurence Edmund Allen, Associated Press Correspondence, and Carlos P. Romulo, *Philippines Herald*

Editorial Writing: Geoffrey Parsons, *New York Herald Tribune*

Editorial Cartoons: Herbert Lawrence Block (Herblock), NEA Service

Photography: Milton Brooks, *Detroit News*

1943

Public Service: *Omaha World-Herald*

Reporting (General): George Weller, *Chicago Daily News*

Telegraphic Reporting (National): No award

Telegraphic Reporting (International): Ira Wolfert, North American Newspaper Alliance

Correspondence: Hanson W. Baldwin, *The New York Times*

Editorial Writing: Forrest W. Seymour, *Des Moines Register & Tribune*

Editorial Cartoons: Jay N. Darling, *New York Herald Tribune*

Photography: Frank Noel, Associated Press

1944

Public Service: *The New York Times*

Reporting (General): Paul Schoenstein and Associates, *New York Journal-American*

Telegraphic Reporting (National): Dewey L. Fleming, *Baltimore Sun*

Telegraphic Reporting (International): Daniel de Luce, Associated Press

Correspondence: Ernest Taylor Pyle, Scripps-Howard Newspapers

Editorial Writing: Henry J. Haskell, *Kansas City Star*

Editorial Cartoons: Clifford K. Berryman, *Washington Evening Star*

Photography: Frank Filan, Associated Press, and Earle L. Bunker, *Omaha World-Herald*

Special Citation: Byron Price, director of Office of Censorship, and William Allen White

1945

Public Service: *Detroit Free Press*

Reporting (General): Jack S. McDowell, *San Francisco Call-Bulletin*

Telegraphic Reporting (National): James Reston, *The New York Times*

Telegraphic Reporting (International): Mark S. Watson, *Baltimore Sun*

Correspondence: Harold V. Boyle, Associated Press

Editorial Writing: George W. Potter, *Providence Journal-Bulletin*

Editorial Cartoons: Sgt. Bill Mauldin, United Features Syndicate

Photography: Joe Rosenthal, Associated Press

Special Citation: American press cartographers

1946

Public Service: *Scranton* (Pa.) *Times*

Reporting (General): William L. Laurence, *The New York Times*

Telegraphic Reporting (National): Edward A. Harris, *St. Louis Post-Dispatch*

Telegraphic Reporting (International): Homer William Bigart, *New York Herald Tribune*

Correspondence: Arnaldo Cortesi, *The New York Times*

Editorial Writing: Hodding Carter, *Delta Democrat-Times* (Greenville, Mississippi)

Editorial Cartoons: Bruce A. Russell, *Los Angeles Times*

Photography: No award

1947

Public Service: *Baltimore Sun*

Reporting (General): Frederick Woltman, *New York World-Telegram*

Telegraphic Reporting (National): Edward T. Folliard, *Washington Post*

Telegraphic Reporting (International): Eddy Gilmore, Associated Press

Correspondence: Brooks Atkinson, *The New York Times*

Editorial Writing: William H. Grimes, *Wall Street Journal*

Editorial Cartoons: Vaughn Shoemaker, *Chicago Daily News*

Photography: Arnold Hardy, Atlanta, Georgia

Special Citation: Columbia University, its Graduate School of Journalism, and the *St. Louis Post-Dispatch*, marking the centennial of Joseph Pulitzer's birth

1948

Public Service: *St. Louis Post-Dispatch*

Reporting (General): George E. Goodwin, *Atlanta Journal*

National Reporting: Bert Andrews, *New York Herald Tribune*, and Nat S. Finney, *Minneapolis Tribune*

International Reporting: Paul W. Ward, *Baltimore Sun*

Editorial Writing: Virginius Dabney, *Richmond Times Dispatch*

Editorial Cartoons: Reuben L. Goldberg, *New York Sun*

Photography: Frank Cushing, *Boston Traveler*

Special Citation: Dr. Frank Diehl Fackenthal

1949

Public Service: *Nebraska State Journal*

Reporting (General): Malcolm Johnson, *New York Sun*

National Reporting: C. P. Trussell, *The New York Times*

International Reporting: Price Day, *Baltimore Sun*

Editorial Writing: John H. Crider, *Boston Herald*, and Herbert Elliston, *Washington Post*

Editorial Cartoons: Lute Pease, *Newark Evening News*

Photography: Nathaniel Fein, *New York Herald Tribune*

DEATHS

Nicholas Afonsky, 51, artist for Sunday *Little Orphan Annie* strip, 16 June 1943.

Carl Anderson, 83, creator of the *Henry* comic strip, 4 November 1948.

Harold MacDonald Anderson, 64, editorial writer on the staff of the *New York Sun;* author of the famous editorial "Lindbergh Flies Alone," which appeared when Charles A. Lindbergh was making his solo flight to France in 1927, 26 December 1940.

Millard V. Atwood, 55, newspaper editor, 3 November 1941.

Ray Stanard Baker, 76, prolific author and magazine editor, awarded the 1940 Pulitzer Prize for his biography of Woodrow Wilson, 12 July 1946.

Stuart Ballantine, 47, radio engineer, 7 May 1944.

Ralph W. Barnes, 41, foreign correspondent of the *New York Herald Tribune,* 19 November 1940.

Nat A. Barrows, 44, journalist and correspondent for the *Boston Globe,* famous for his series on submarines, 12 July 1949.

George Barton, 74, journalist and writer of mystery stories, 17 March 1940.

Edward Price Bell, 74, newspaperman, 23 September 1943.

James O'Donnell Bennett, 69, retired member of the staff of the *Chicago Tribune* and one of the best-known American newspapermen, 27 February 1940.

May Birkhead, 55, correspondent and fashion writer, 27 October 1941.

Alexander Black, 81, author, newspaper editor, and expert on photography, 8 May 1940.

Paul Block, 63, newspaper publisher, 22 June 1941.

Stephen Bolles, congressman and newspaperman, 8 July 1941.

George G. Booth, 84, publisher of both the Scripps and Booth newspaper chains, 11 April 1949.

Edward Bowes, 71, radio producer and showman who inaugurated the "amateur hour" radio format, 13 June 1946.

Tom Breneman, 45, radio performer and showman, famous for his daytime program *Breakfast at Sardi's,* 28 April 1948.

Frank E. Butler, 71, radio engineer who assisted Lee De Forest in his early experiments with radio, 6 January 1948.

Victor F. Calverton, 40, founder and editor of the *Modern Quarterly,* 20 November 1940.

Joseph J. Canavan, 53, former newspaper editor and chairman of the New York State Board of Parole, 10 October 1940.

Clifton B. Carberry, managing editor of the *Boston Post* since 1907 and widely known as the author of its "John Bantry" articles, 8 June 1940.

Frank Wesley Carson, 60, newspaper editor, 19 March 1941.

James Mckeen Cattell, 83, psychologist whose dismissal from Columbia University for criticizing the draft during World War I was controversial, editor of *Science* (1894–1944), 20 January 1944.

Owen Cattell, 42, assistant to the editor of *Science,* official weekly journal of the American Association for the Advancement of Science; business manager of Science Press, 26 March 1940.

Harry Chandler, 80, newspaper publisher, 23 September 1944.

Raymond Clapper, 52, journalist and columnist, 3 February 1944.

Negley Dakin Cochran, 77, newspaper editor, 13 April 1941.

Franklin Coe, 68, former publisher of *Town and Country,* 20 February 1940.

William Haskell Coffin, 63, magazine illustrator and portrait painter, 12 May 1941.

Frank Condon, 58, sports writer for magazines and author of short stories, 19 December 1940.

Frank Conrad, 67, engineer and radio expert, 11 December 1941.

Al Copland, 75, turf editor of the *New York Daily News,* 29 June 1940.

Frank Crowninshield, 75, editor of *Vanity Fair* (1914–1935) credited with introducing the French modernist painters to the United States through reproductions in his magazine, 28 December 1947.

John Trevor Custis, 68, newspaper editor, 3 December 1944.

Josephus Daniels, 85, editor of the *Raleigh* (N.C.) *News and Observer,* secretary of the navy under President Woodrow Wilson, ambassador to Mexico under President Franklin Roosevelt, 15 January 1940.

William Morgan "Billy" De Beck, 52, creator of the comic strip *Barney Google,* 11 November 1942.

Charles Henry Dennis, 83, reporter, editor, and columnist for the *Chicago Daily News,* 25 September 1943.

William Thompson Dewart, 68, newspaper publisher, 27 January 1944.

Nelson Doubleday, 59, chairman of the board of Doubleday Publishing, one of the largest publishing houses in the world, 11 January 1949.

Walter Jack Duncan, 60, artist and magazine illustrator, 11 April 1941.

J. Allan Dunn, 69, author, journalist, and explorer, 25 March 1941.

William Atherton Du Puy, 65, journalist and author, 11 August 1941.

James N. Durkin, 54, widely known New Jersey police reporter, 23 June 1940.

Richard M. Fairbanks, 60, newspaper publisher, 26 July 1944.

Alvin Irwin Findley, 81, editor in chief and director of the Iron Age Publishing Company of New York for twenty-one years, 12 December 1940.

G. Selmer Fougner, 56, newspaperman, 2 April 1941.

M. C. Gaines, 51, comic-book pioneer, 20 August 1947.

Charles Dana Gibson, 77, artist and illustrator of the famous "Gibson Girl," who appeared in many magazines, 23 December 1944.

Walter Samuel Goodland, 83, small-town Wisconsin newspaperman elected governor in 1945, 12 March 1947.

Frederic William Goudy, 82, type designer whose typefaces are widely used in publishing, 11 May 1947.

Charles Gratke, 47, newspaperman, foreign editor of the *Christian Science Monitor,* 12 July 1949.

Clarence Clark Hamlin, 72, newspaper publisher, political leader, and well-known attorney, 30 September 1940.

Nelson Harding, 65, cartoonist, 7 August 1944.

Henry S. Harper, 77, publisher, 1 March 1944.

Lee Foster Hartman, 61, magazine editor, 23 September 1941.

Rev. Francis J. Healy, 57, editor in chief of the *Tablet* Roman Catholic weekly, 10 December 1940.

Burton J. Hendrick, 77, muckraking journalist at *McClure's Magazine* and Pulitzer Prize–winning author, 24 March 1949.

George Herriman, 66, creator of *Krazy Kat* and other comic strips, 25 April 1944.

Benjamin Franklin Irvine, 77, noted blind editor of the *Oregon Journal,* 1 May 1940.

George Sibley Johns, 83, newspaper editor, 16 July 1941.

Billy Jones, 51, pioneer radio singer and comedian, with partner Ernie Hare formed the Happiness Boys, 23 November 1940.

Theodore Goldsmith Joslin, 54, newspaperman, 12 April 1944.

Edward Leggett Keen, 73, newspaperman, 7 October 1943.

Frederick W. Kellogg, 73, publisher and founder of many newspapers in the Midwest and Far West, 5 September 1940.

Albert R. Kessinger, 74, newspaper editor and publisher, 24 February 1941.

Edwin John Kiest, 79, newspaper publisher, 11 August 1941.

Willis Sharpe Kilmer, 71, newspaper publisher and patent medicine manufacturer, 12 July 1940.

Herbert R. Knickerbocker, 51, foreign correspondent for the International News Service, winner of the Pulitzer Prize in 1931, 12 July 1949.

Dr. Henry McElderry Knower, 71, managing editor of the *American Journal of Anatomy* for twenty-one years, 10 January 1940.

W. Franklin Knox, 70, conservative publisher of the *Chicago Daily News,* GOP vice-presidential candidate in 1936, secretary of the navy from 1940 to 1944, 28 April 1944.

Rex Lardner, 59, magazine editor, 23 June 1941.

Bruno Lessing (Rudolph Block), 69, newspaper columnist, 29 April 1940.

Lloyd Downs Lewis, 57, author and managing editor of the *Chicago Daily News,* 21 April 1949.

Philip Littell, 75, writer and journalist, 31 October (?) 1943.

John Avery Lomax, 80, recorder and collector of folk songs, 26 January 1948.

W. E. MacFarlane, 60, newspaper executive, 9 October 1944.

Jacob Magidoff, 74, editor and journalist, 26 August 1943.

Joseph Warren Teets Mason, 62, columnist and editor, 13 May 1941.

Samuel S. McClure, 92, founder and publisher of *McClure's Magazine*, perhaps the most famous muckraking journal of the Progressive era, 21 March 1949.

John Tinney McCutcheon, 79, Pulitzer Prize–winning political cartoonist, 10 June 1949.

James H. McGraw, 87, cofounder of the McGraw-Hill publishing firm, one of the largest publishers of technical journals and books, 21 February 1948.

Marvin Hunter McIntyre, 65, editor of the *Washington* (D.C.) *Times*, secretary to Franklin Delano Roosevelt, 13 December 1943.

Neysa McMein, 59, fashion illustrator whose works appeared in the *Saturday Evening Post, McCall's,* and *Collier's,* among other magazines, credited for the beauty vogue associated with the "McMein girl," 12 May 1949.

James Jackson Montague, 68, newspaperman, 16 December 1941.

William Emmet Moore, 63, newspaper editor, 27 December 1941.

Truman Spencer Morgan, 72, president of F. W. Dodge Corporation, publishers of trade journals and catalogues, 21 December 1940.

Charles Moulton (William Moulton Marston), 53, creator of Wonder Woman, 2 May 1947.

Frederick E. Murphey, 67, publisher of the *Minneapolis Times Tribune*, 14 February 1940.

J. Edwin Murphy, 66, journalist, 29 March 1943.

Frank B. Noyes, 85, president of the *Washington* (D.C.) *Star,* one of the founders of the Associated Press, 1 December 1948.

Frank Michael O'Brien, 68, Pulitzer Prize–winning author and editor for the *New York Sun*, 22 September 1943.

Howard V. O'Brien, 59, columnist with the *Chicago Daily News*, 30 September 1947.

Joseph Jefferson O'Neill, 61, widely known New York newspaperman, later a publicity expert in Hollywood, 17 April 1940.

Chase Salmon Osborn, 88, owner and publisher of the *Milwaukee Sentinel,* governor of Michigan (1911–1913), 11 April 1949.

George B. Parker, 63, editor in chief of the Scripps-Howard newspaper chain, winner of the Pulitzer Prize for editorials in 1936, 10 October 1949.

Eleanor Medill Patterson, 63, granddaughter of Joseph Medill (founder of the *Chicago Tribune*), added the *Washington* (D.C.) *Times-Herald* to the *Tribune* newspapers in 1939; also noted for her outspoken opposition to the presidency of Franklin Roosevelt, 24 July 1948.

Joseph Medill Patterson, 67, newspaper editor and publisher of the *New York Daily News* who promoted such comics strips as *Dick Tracy, Gasoline Alley, Little Orphan Annie,* and *Terry and the Pirates,* 26 May 1946.

John Sanburn Phillips, 87, publisher, along with Samuel S. McClure organized one of the first newspaper feature syndicates, 28 February 1949.

Ernest T. Pyle, 44, famed war correspondent, killed during the Okinawa operation, 18 April 1945.

Ogden M. Reid, 64, editor and president of the *New York Herald Tribune*, 3 January 1947.

Robert LeRoy Ripley, 57, illustrator famous for his *Believe It or Not* cartoons, 27 May 1949.

William Carman Roberts, 64, magazine editor, 21 November 1941.

Victor Rosewater, 69, editor, publisher, and politician, 12 July 1940.

Damon Runyon, 51, author and journalist, reporter for the Hearst press, later famous for short stories set on Broadway, 10 December 1946.

John Pitts Sanborn, 62, newspaperman and music critic, 7 March 1941.

Frederick William Saward, 70, editor and publisher of *Saward's Journal,* a coal-trade weekly, 23 April 1940.

James Schermerhorn, 76, newspaper publisher, 2 December 1941.

Otto Schmidt, newspaper and magazine artist, 20 May 1940.

Alexander R. Sharton, 63, newspaper publisher, 30 January 1943.

Edwin Llewellyn Shuman, 78, magazine editor, 13 December 1941.

Thomas O'Conor Sloane, 88, scientist and author, former editor of *Amazing Stories* magazine, and associate editor of *Science and Invention*, 7 August 1940.

Col. Clarence James Smith, 66, journalist, part owner of the *Allentown* (Pa.) *Morning Call*, 28 August 1940.

Renée Stern, 65, author and newspaperwoman, 19 May 1940.

John Leighton Stewart, 63, founder of the Pennsylvania Publishers Association, 31 May 1940.

Frank Parker Stockbridge, 70, author and journalist, former managing editor of the old *New York Evening Mail,* the *New York Globe,* and the *New York Herald,* 7 December 1940.

Allison Stone, 67, publisher of the *Providence Journal,* 11 September 1940.

Edward Howard Suydam, 55, artist and magazine illustrator, 23 December 1940.

Ida Tarbell, 86, muckraking journalist famous for her study of the Standard Oil Company, 6 January 1944.

Charles Henry Taylor, 73, journalist, 18 August 1941.

Samuel Emory Thomason, 61, newspaper publisher, 20 March 1944.

Paul Thompson, 62, pioneer news photographer who got his start by taking pictures of Mark Twain, 20 November 1940.

Charles Hanson Towne, 72, author and editor of *Harper's Bazaar* (1926–1931), 28 February 1949.

Grenville Vernon, 58, author and journalist, 30 November 1941.

Oswald Garrison Villard, 77, publisher of the *New York Evening Post* and the *Nation* magazine, 1 October 1949.

John Thompson Whitaker, 40, foreign correspondent for the *Chicago Daily News*, 11 September 1946.

Matthew White, Jr., 83, for twenty-eight years dramatic editor of *Munsey's Magazine*, 17 September 1940.

Trumbull White, 73, magazine editor, author, and explorer, 13 December 1941.

William Allen White, 75, journalist and editor who elevated the *Emporia* (Kans.) *Gazette* to international prominence based on the strength of his editorials, 29 January 1944.

Frederic William Wile, 67, newspaperman and author, 7 April 1941.

Casper Salathiel Yost, 76, newspaper editor, 30 May 1941.

Arthur Henry Young, 77, illustrator, cartoonist, and social activist, best known for his work in the *Masses* and *New Masses* magazines, 29 December 1943.

PUBLICATIONS

Francis Chase, Jr., *Sound and Fury: An Informal History of Broadcasting* (New York: Harper, 1942);

Federal Communications Commission, *Report on Chain Broadcasting* (Washington: Federal Communications Commission, 1941);

Thomas H. Hutchinson, *Here is Television: Your Window on the World* (New York: Hastings House, 1946);

Theodore F. Koop, *Weapon of Silence* (Chicago: University of Chicago, 1946);

Paul F. Lazarsfeld and Harry Field, *The People Look at Radio* (Chapel Hill: University of North Carolina Press, 1946);

Lazarsfeld and Patricia L. Kendall, *Radio Listening in America: The People Look at Radio — Again* (Englewood Cliffs, N.J.: Prentice-Hall, 1948);

Edward R. Murrow, *This is London* (New York: Simon & Schuster, 1941);

Office of War Information, *When Radio Writes for War: A Digest of Practical Suggestions on Wartime Radio Scripts* (Washington: Office of War Information, 1943);

Wilber Schramm, *Communications in Modern Society* (Urbana: University of Illinois Press, 1948);

Eric Sevareid, *Not So Wild A Dream* (New York: Knopf, 1946);

Martin Sheridan, *Comics and Their Creators* (Boston: Hale, Cushman & Flint, 1942);

E. P. J. Shurick, *The First Quarter Century of American Broadcasting* (Kansas City: Midland, 1946);

Charles A. Siepmann, *Radio's Second Chance* (Boston: Little, Brown, 1946);

Coulton Waugh, *The Comics* (New York: Macmillan, 1947);

Llewellyn White, *The American Radio: A report on the broadcasting industry in the United States from the Commission on Freedom of the Press* (Chicago: University of Chicago, 1947);

Broadcasting, periodical;

Counterattack, monthly newsletter;

FCC Reports, annual reports;

Radio Annual, periodical;

Radio Daily, periodical;

TV Guide, periodical;

Variety, periodical.

MEDICINE AND HEALTH

by JOAN D. LAXSON

CONTENTS

Sidebars and tables are listed in italics.

1940

- The Rh factor is described.

- Sister Elizabeth Kenny brings her controversial massage treatment for polio to Minneapolis.

8 Mar. The American Association for the Advancement of Science reports the discovery of pantothenic acid, an essential vitamin for normal growth in plant and animal life.

11 Mar. Doctors at Montefiore Hospital in New York report the development of a hormone to prevent surgical shock.

22 May The American Social Hygiene Association reports that tests performed over a five-year period indicate that 3 percent of U.S. adults have syphilis.

The Council of Foods of the American Medical Association (AMA) gives its first seal of approval to the Bird's Eye Corporation for its quick-frozen foods.

20 July Eli Lilly and Company announces the development of a simple test to determine if an overdose of sulfa drugs has been given to a patient.

26 Aug. Three southern West Virginia counties close schools due to a polio epidemic that has already claimed ten lives.

28 Aug. The National Foundation for Infantile Paralysis rushes aid to Indiana to help combat an outbreak of polio.

10 Oct. The medical faculty at Stockholm University announces it will not award the Nobel Prize for medicine in 1940 because of the ongoing war.

21 Oct. The Clinical College of the American College of Surgeons recommends a detailed plan for having doctors serve in the military without causing hardships at home.

The Rockefeller Foundation announces it will make a recently developed vaccine available to Britain to fight influenza in the war zone.

31 Oct. Sulfaguanidine is announced as a cure for bacterial dysentery, a common disease among troops in the tropics.

28 Nov. The American Chemical Society reports the wartime shortage of Indian monkeys may hamper medical research in human diseases.

3 Dec. Health officials estimate fifty thousand cases of influenza in Los Angeles in a California epidemic.

5 Dec. The influenza epidemic spreads to Oregon, Washington, New Mexico, Arizona, and Idaho.

1941

- Clinical use of oral anticoagulants is initiated.

- Clinical trials of penicillin are initiated.

Jan. Medical researchers report progress in the fight against pneumonia and infantile paralysis.

5 Feb. A federal antitrust suit against the American Medical Association, the Medical Society of Washington, the Washington Academy of Surgery, and the Harris County (Texas) Medical Society begins in Washington.

16 Feb. U.S. Indian Health Service physicians report trachoma, a common sight-destroying disease among Native Americans, is a virus and can be successfully treated in three weeks with sulfanilamide.

25 Mar. The U.S. Public Health Service reports the most serious measles outbreak in seven years along the Eastern Seaboard and spreading westward.

27 Mar. Group Health Association, Inc., a nonprofit organization chartered by New York State, offers preventive medical care as well as treatment to state residents for twenty-four dollars or less a year.

4 Apr. A federal jury convicts the AMA and the Medical Society of Washington of Sherman Antitrust Act violations but acquits eighteen individual defendants.

5 May News of the new drug penicillin is announced to the public.

Sept. The polio epidemic kills eighty-seven people.

4 Dec. The National Foundation for Infantile Paralysis announces its approval of the massage polio treatment developed by Elizabeth Kenny; other medical professionals debate the value of this treatment.

1942

- Red Cross collects blood for treating battle casualties.

- Kenny method of treatment of infantile paralysis causes disputes.

June Medical researchers report progress in the immunization of infants against whooping cough.

15 June The Federal Court of Appeals upholds conviction of the AMA and the Medical Society of the District of Columbia on charges of conspiring to violate the Sherman Antitrust Law.

16 Oct. Georgia health officials order the quarantine of all venereal-disease cases and the detention and treatment of all victims of veneral diseases not receiving medical care after incidence grows to epidemic proportions in the state.

26 Oct. Six New York hospitals announce they will teach the Kenny treatment for infantile paralysis of hot applications, massage, and exercise.

7 Nov. The AMA council on foods and nutrition suggests consumption of sugar in candy and soft drinks, which are low in nutritional value, be limited.

28 Nov. The *Journal of the American Medical Association* (*JAMA*) reports albumin in human blood can be injected or transfused in a highly concentrated form to relieve shock.

1943

- Streptomycin is discovered.

- Adrenocorticotropic hormone (ACTH) is isolated from the anterior pituitary gland.

- Sulfa drugs are credited with saving numerous lives in army hospitals.

28 Jan. An international meeting of sixty-eight physicians is held in New York to study combat fatigue.

15 Apr. The American Chemical Society announces that a chemical compound known as 2, 3, 5 tri-iode-benzoic acid checks the growth of the tuberculosis bacilli.

29 Apr.   Six Parke, Davis and Company scientists announce the isolation of a fourteenth type of vitamin B in crystalline form from liver.

14 May   Merck and Company Labs in New Jersey develops biotin, a vitamin essential to life function.

13 July   The U.S. Navy announces the development of a "mist-like" inhalable serum, 90 percent effective in preventing influenza.

30 July   An infantile paralysis epidemic spreads through Texas, California, Washington, Kansas, and New York.

25 Aug.   The National Research Council reports penicillin is a potential antibacterial agent when injected or applied locally but is ineffective taken orally.

8 Sept.   The American Chemical Society announces the development of "penicillin B," which is ten times more powerful than existing penicillin.

27 Oct.   *JAMA* reports that a new sulfa drug, desoxyephedronium sulfathiazole, brings prompt relief from colds and seems to shorten their duration.

3 Nov.   The U.S. Census Bureau reports U.S. cancer deaths totaled 163,400 in 1942.

25 Nov.   Schenley Distillers Corporation announces it has developed a new method of manufacturing penicillin.

1944

- The transforming factor in pneumococci is identified as DNA.

- The first blue-baby operation is performed.

- Early ambulation after surgery and childbirth is introduced.

3 Mar.   The magazine *Air Force* reports the drug benzedrene has been used to help pilots fight off sleepiness and fatigue on return trips of combat missions.

16 Mar.   Representatives of twenty-one penicillin producers meet to work out agreements for exchange of technical information to increase the output of the drug.

10 Apr.   The annual report of the National Foundation for Infantile Paralysis expresses regret at the publicity given the Kenny method for treating the disease.

15 June   An AMA committee of orthopedic physicians files a report criticizing the Kenny method.

20 June   The National Foundation for Infantile Paralysis announces grants of $1.12 million will be made to twenty-seven universities and other institutes to aid studies of the disease.

29 June   The American Red Cross announces development of a serum to prevent measles.

13 July   Mayo Clinic physicians say cigarettes may harm wounded men by constricting blood vessels.

7 Aug.   The U.S. Public Health Service says gonorrhea can be cured in seven and one-half hours with penicillin.

17 Aug.   An infantile paralysis outbreak reaches epidemic proportions in New York, North Carolina, Kentucky, Pennsylvania, and Virginia.

24 Aug.   *Science* magazine reports that a mold of the penicillin group inhibits the growth of tuberculosis bacilli.

26 Aug.	The New York State Hospital Commission reports insulin shock treatment has enabled 55 percent of those treated for dementia praecox to become useful members of society.
9 Sept.	Harvard Medical School reports the development of a synthetic skin from blood plasma to heal burns.
23 Nov.	*JAMA* claims Americans with a normal diet do not benefit from vitamins.

1945

- Promin therapy is proven effective against leprosy.
- The American Cancer Society is incorporated.

14 Jan.	U.S. Army research reveals that jaundice is transferred via flies, polluted water, and other means in much the same way as dysentery.
Feb.	Oral penicillin is introduced.
23 Mar.	The Census Bureau reports the death rate from cancer in the United States has more than doubled since 1900.
23 May	*JAMA* reveals five typhoid patients treated successfully with a new drug called streptomycin.
24 May	Several new drugs, including streptomycin, corticin, and pleurotin, enter the market.
11 July	Cheplin Laboratories says penicillin will be released to the public as tablets, ointment, and eyedrops on 1 August.
18 July	The AMA offers a fourteen-point program to provide medical care for all people without increased taxation.
7 Aug.	Planning for the Sloan-Kettering Cancer Research Center begins in New York.
14 Nov.	*JAMA* reports successful treatment of scarlet fever by injecting penicillin into the muscles every three hours for seven days.
24 Nov.	The navy reports a cure for cholera using blood plasma and sulfadiazine and saline solution.
Dec.	An influenza epidemic grips the nation.
16 Dec.	The American Chemical Society reports the discovery of a new sulfa drug, metachloride, which may surpass Atabrine and quinine in treating malaria.

1946

- The American Academy of Dental Medicine is founded.
- Penicillin is produced synthetically.
- The Hospital Survey and Construction (Hill-Burton) Act is passed by Congress.
- The National Mental Health Act is passed by Congress.
- The Communicable Disease Center is established at Atlanta.

3 Jan.	The U.S. Office of Scientific Research and Development reports the discovery of a new synthetic drug, SN 7618, which relieves malarial attacks more quickly than Atabrine or quinine.

31 Mar.   The American Geographic Society announces plans for an atlas of diseases to aid in the study of the relationship between environment and health.

6 Apr.   Oklahoma City residents turn out for tests in the nation's first citywide rapid-treatment drive against venereal disease.

12 Apr.   Evidence is presented to an American Chemical Society meeting that submicroscopic, viruslike substances are among the causes of cancer.

17 Apr.   The American Cancer Society reveals a proposed $3-million cancer research program using radioactive isotopes produced in atom-bomb research.

9 May   The U.S. Army Commission on Neurotropic Diseases announces the development of a vaccine against dengue.

2 Aug.   The U.S. nuclear plant at Oak Ridge, Tennessee, makes the first sale of a radioactive isotope to a private institution when it sells one millicurie of carbon 14 to the Barnard Free Skin and Cancer Hospital in Saint Louis for use in cancer research.

8 Aug.   Temple University Medical School announces the development of a device to allow doctors to detect heart disease in early stages.

9 Aug.   The U.S. Public Health Service reports the worst infantile paralysis epidemic since 1916.

2 Oct.   The Association for the Advancement of Research on Multiple Sclerosis is formed in New York.

6 Oct.   A group of University of Chicago scientists reports isolating a hormone called enterogastrone, which may be a permanent chemical cure for peptic ulcers.

27 Oct.   The American Social Hygiene Association announces that reported cases of syphilis increased 42 percent in the twelve months ending 30 June.

12 Nov.   *JAMA* reports that three doctors at Chicago Children's Memorial Hospital have successfully operated on blue babies whose malformed hearts cannot pump enough blood to their lungs.

1947

- Remissions in acute leukemia with the antifolates are induced.

- Work on the artificial kidney begins at Peter Bent Brigham Hospital in Boston.

Jan.   Medical researchers report progress in finding causes of infantile paralysis.

7 Jan.   Spring Grove Street Hospital in Maryland announces the release of several "incurable" psychiatric patients who had undergone prefrontal lobotomies, separating the emotional and action centers of the brain.

10 Feb.   The Planned Parenthood Federation of America announces that a recent poll of U.S. doctors shows 97.8 percent in favor of birth control.

18 Mar.   The Atomic Bomb Casualty Commission reports some abnormalities among children recently born to atomic-bomb victims in Hiroshima and Nagasaki.

11 Apr.   University of Chicago researchers report a commercial dye, toludine blue, that counteracts destruction of blood corpuscles resulting from exposure to radioactivity.

6 May	Outbreak of infant diarrhea in Philadelphia is checked after causing twenty-seven deaths.
21 June	The War Department announces plans to build the world's largest medical research center at Forest Glen, Maryland.
19 July	The University of Illinois announces plans to begin the first large-scale manufacture of a tuberculosis vaccine, known as BCG.
17 Sept.	The Warm Springs Foundation ends a three-day conference on infantile paralysis after hearing reports emphasizing the lack of current medical knowledge on polio's diagnosis and treatment.
3 Oct.	The American Association of Science Workers urges the United Nations to study bacteriological warfare, which it calls the world's "pre-eminent terror weapon."
24 Nov.	The Southern Medical Association, meeting in Baltimore, drops its ban on attendance of African American physicians at its scientific sessions.

1948

•	The Kinsey report on sexual behavior of the human male is published.
8 Jan.	The National Foundation for Infantile Paralysis announces the allocation of $1.18 million to U.S. and Canadian universities for polio research and training.
6 Mar.	The U.S. Atomic Energy Commission announces free distribution of certain radioactive isotopes for use in cancer treatment.
21 Apr.	The U.S. Atomic Energy Commission reports the successful use of irradiated cobalt in cancer treatment.
3 May	The University of Minnesota announces isolation of human poliomyelitis virus in concentrated form for the first time.
18 May	The Medical Society of the State of New York adopts a resolution urging elimination of racial discrimination in admission to the American Medical Association.
20 May	The American Psychiatric Association meeting hears reports on the prevention of epilepsy seizures through the use of dilantin and mesantoin.
19 June	The American Heart Association meeting hears experts advise anti-blood-clotting drugs significantly reduce deaths from coronary thrombosis.
27 June	Army researchers report that chloromycetin, a new drug, can cure typhoid fever within three days.
17 July	The first international poliomyelitis conference ends in New York after voting to set up a permanent World Congress on Polio.
4 Aug.	The Public Health Service reports new polio outbreaks in North Carolina, Texas, and California.
10 Aug.	The American Cancer Society announces an expanded program of $3.5 million in cancer-research awards for the coming year.
25 Aug.	The World Health Organization announces development of a chemical dehydration process for extracting insulin, simplifying production of the drug and raising hopes of alleviating the world insulin shortage.
	Lederle Laboratories in New York announces discovery of APF (animal protein factor), a vitamin that builds red corpuscles in pernicious-anemia sufferers.

8 Sept.   Yale Medical School reports development of a rubberized nylon respirator to replace the iron lung for polio victims.

15 Oct.   The U.S. Public Health Service announces that a five-minute test to detect diabetes will be used in a nationwide effort to find an estimated one million hidden diabetes cases.

18 Oct.   New York City begins a fluoridation program by coating the teeth of fifty thousand children with sodium fluoride to prevent decay.

3 Dec.   The AMA ends a four-day meeting in Saint Louis after making plans to raise $3.5 million to fight President Truman's national health-insurance program.

6 Dec.   The American Dental Association announces its opposition to Truman's proposed national health insurance.

20 Dec.   Researchers at nuclear laboratories in the United States report five scientists are going blind as a result of their work with cyclotrons.

1949

- The first molecular disease — sickle-cell anemia — is described.
- The antihypertensive effect of rauwolfia is reported.
- G. D. Searle & Company introduces Dramamine as a motion-sickness remedy.
- The National Institute of Mental Health is established.
- Lithium is first used in the treatment of psychiatric disease.

2 Feb.   The AMA presents an alternative to Truman's compulsory medical-insurance plan, stressing expansion of voluntary medical plans and greater state aid to the indigent.

18 Feb.   The Food and Drug Administration orders lithium chloride, a salt substitute, withdrawn from the market after four deaths are traced to its use.

27 Feb.   The American Cancer Society and National Cancer Institute meeting hears a report linking increased cigarette smoking to the rapid rise in incidence of lung cancer during the last twenty-five years.

28 Feb.   The New York County Medical Society, the largest member of the AMA, refuses to support the AMA's fight against Truman's compulsory medical-insurance proposal.

6 Apr.   Seventy-four patients die in a fire at St. Anthony's Hospital in Effingham, Illinois, the second worst hospital fire in U.S. history.

20 Apr.   Mayo Clinic researchers report isolation of an adrenal gland hormone that is effective in relieving rheumatoid arthritis.

16 May   Johns Hopkins University doctors report the motion-sickness drug Dramamine relieves morning sickness in many pregnant women.

20 May   The Regional Council for Education, charged with carrying through the southern plan for a segregated higher-education system, begins signing contracts with universities in Virginia, Louisiana, Georgia, and Tennessee for medical and dental training.

5 July   The William Warner Company in New York announces development of a new method for synthesizing vitamin A on a commercial scale.

27 July Armour Laboratories in Chicago announces development of a method for commercial production of ACTH, a pituitary extract used in the treatment of arthritis, rheumatic fever, and gout.

12 Aug. The African American–dominated National Medical Association refuses to take a position on the issue of national health insurance at its Detroit convention, despite a request from the AMA to oppose the plan.

16 Aug. The U.S. Public Health Service reports the average life span of an American is 66.0 years, up from the prewar average of 63.

Yale researchers report the isolation of a "false polio" virus which produces symptoms similar to those of poliomyelitis.

29 Aug. A 22-million-volt betatron is used to treat two cancer patients at the University of Illinois at Chicago hospital, the first application of a nuclear device in cancer therapy.

5 Sept. The American Veterans of World War II passes a resolution against a national health-insurance system.

23 Sept. The Senate approves a five-year, $280-million program for the construction of medical schools and other health-professional training facilities.

8 Dec. The House of Delegates of the AMA unanimously approves a twenty-five-dollar levy on all AMA members to fight Truman's proposed national health-insurance plan.

OVERVIEW

A New Age of American Medicine. The year 1940 marked the beginning of a new period in American medicine. The demands of the impending world war brought about a great coordination of financing and teamwork in medical research and development. The biomedical sciences had developed rapidly during the first four decades of the twentieth century. The war effort combined these medical advances with new technical and research capabilities. During World War II research efforts produced the miracle drugs penicillin and the sulfonamides, the insecticide DDT, new medical technology based on radioactive by-products of the atomic bomb, better vaccines, and improved hygienic measures. Disability from venereal disease was dramatically altered by new methods of treatment with the new drugs. The increased availability of blood and plasma for transfusions led to dramatic progress in surgery during the decade. Wartime attention to mental-health issues in the military brought about an enhanced public image of psychiatry. During the decade psychiatry made a marked shift away from rural-based institutions warehousing the mentally disabled to a more proactive treatment of mental illness.

Medicine and the Federal Government. The year 1940 also marked the beginning of a new era in the relationship of the federal government to medical research and development. Government involvement in medicine took the form of increased support for medical research and the development of new federal agencies, including such groups as the National Heart Institute, the National Institute of Mental Health, and the Center for Disease Control, headquartered in Atlanta, Georgia. The American Medical Association and many politicians serving in Congress were not willing to go so far as to support President Franklin D. Roosevelt's or President Harry S Truman's calls for a national health-insurance program. Their opponents called these programs socialized medicine. But Congress could and did promote the nation's health by focusing on such legislation as the 1946 Hospital Survey and Construction Act (the Hill-Burton Act). Under this act the federal government provided badly needed dollars for new hospital construction but was barred from any federal regulation of hospitals. By decade's end there were 6,572 hospitals in the country, an increase of 281 from 1940. The average length of time an American stayed in the hospital decreased from 13.7 days in 1940 to 10.6 days in 1950. While research and hospital building was the primary focus in the nation, medical education went through a period of relative neglect. The decision to expand hospitals without expanding medical-school enrollments led to an acute shortage of interns and residents in the nation's hospitals.

Shortages. Physicians and hospitals both were in short supply at the beginning of the decade. The war further complicated the situation. In 1940 there were 133 physicians for every 100,000 Americans — about one doctor for every 752 people. By 1944, with so many physicians in active military service, civilian doctors saw on average 1,700 people per year. By decade's end the country began to awaken to the seriousness of the doctor shortage. Between 1925 and 1950 the population of the United States increased from 115 million to 151 million, but only six new medical schools were established. In 1949 eighteen states still had no medical schools.

Physicians' Salaries. Physicians' salaries increased dramatically over the decade, beginning with an average gross income of $7,632 in 1940 and ending in 1949 at $19,710. This increase paralleled an equally dramatic rise in total medical-care expenses in the nation: from $3.018 billion in 1940 to $8.11 billion in 1949.

Public Health. The effective methods developed to reduce infant mortality and to prevent or cure infectious diseases continued to cause a rise in the average age of the population. From 1940 to 1950 the percentage of the population over age 64 increased from 6.9 percent to 8.2 percent. The diseases of the elderly — cancer, heart disease, and stroke — rose proportionately. Deaths from these diseases increased during the decade because there were more elderly people. Americans in 1940 viewed syphilis as their most serious public-health problem. Arsenic compounds were still the preferred treatment until the stepped-up research of World War II made penicillin the major weapon against syphilis. By 1949 the incidence of syphilis was still high, but sufferers no longer needed to fear its ravages. Nationwide public-health programs brought the new treatments to the attention of the public through public-relations campaigns designed to get venereal-disease victims to come forth for treatment.

Polio. While tuberculosis hospitals and sanatoriums closed by the dozens because of the powers of newly discovered antibiotics, one scourge of humankind still resisted a cure. Throughout the decade the United States saw some of the worst infantile paralysis (also known as poliomyelitis or polio) epidemics in the nation's history, ending with the widespread epidemic of 1949, which claimed over thirty thousand victims. During the war the army was disturbed to discover that polio — thought of primarily as a children's disease — was a problem suffered by its troops. Polio vaccines were still several years away, and the decade was marked by quarantines and colorful and controversial figures such as Sister Elizabeth Kenny, who advocated new means of treatment for paralyzed patients.

Medical Costs. In 1944 the median income for an American family was $2,378. On average this typical family paid $148 a year for their medical expenses, about 6 percent of their income. Poor families, with a yearly income of $500 after taxes, spent about $62 (or 12 percent of their net income) on medical care; the wealthiest (those averaging over $5,000 after taxes) spent $265 (5 percent of their net income) a year on medical expenses.

Medicine as a Metaphor for Progress. The groundwork was laid in the 1940s for many changes in medical practice because of the expansion of knowledge and the improvement of equipment. Hospitals began to become the center of practice, leading to a proliferating number of specialists, a staggering increase in costs, and a decrease in the number of family doctors. The increase in the government's expenditures and the success of medical scientific research during the decade left Americans with the impression that adequate financing could speed up the conquest of disease. In the 1940s medicine became a metaphor for progress in the minds of Americans.

James Bordley III and A. McGehee Harvey, *Two Centuries of American Medicine* (Philadelphia: Saunders, 1976);

Historical Statistics of the United States, Colonial Times to 1970, Bicentennial Edition, Part 2 (Washington, D.C.: U.S. Bureau of the Census, 1975), pp. 303, 318;

Paul Starr, *The Social Transformation of American Medicine* (New York: Basic Books, 1982);

Statistical Abstract of the United States: 1952 (Washington, D.C.: U.S. Bureau of the Census), p. 262;

Statistical Abstract of the United States: 1955 (Washington, D.C.: U.S. Bureau of the Census), pp. 78, 79, 301;

Statistical Abstract of the United States: 1960 (Washington, D.C.: U.S. Bureau of the Census), p. 75.

TOPICS IN THE NEWS

ALLERGY RELIEF: THE ANTIHISTAMINES

Allergy Miseries. Sneezing, sniffling, weeping, itching, gasping. In 1946 an estimated 10–15 percent of the population, some 13–20 million, suffered a vast gallery of allergic symptoms. In the Minnesota winters a strapping young man bundled himself so thoroughly against his allergy to the cold that his wife had to lead him down the street. Even the exposure of the skin around his eyes to the cold swelled him up as though he had been stung by dozens of wasps. Some sufferers dreaded spring, with its tree-pollen-induced sneezing and itchy eyes, while others dreaded the ragweed season in late summer. Allergies were a source of misery to millions.

Histamine. Until the discovery of a new treatment, allergy sufferers had to avoid cats, eggs, feathers, pollen — whatever caused their reaction — or take frequent desensitizing injections. More convenient relief came in 1946 with the discovery of something new — histamine — the chemical catalyst in the allergic reaction. Although histamine was known for many years, its normal place in the body's complex chemistry was still not well understood until the 1940s.

Antihistamine. In the allergic individual, histamine becomes an irritant itself. It creates leaks in the capillaries, causing fluid to escape into the tissues, producing congestion, runny noses, and skin blisters. It can also constrict small bronchial tubes in asthmatics, bringing about a fall in blood pressure and even death. Researchers in the 1940s searched for antihistamine compounds which would turn off the histamine faucet to relieve suffering. In 1946 they finally developed an effective antihistamine with a fifty-letter name, *beta dimethylaminoethyl benzhydryl ether hydrochloride*, later known as *Benadryl*.

A Potato-Lover's Delight. Benadryl was the outcome of a research project begun in 1941 at the University of Cincinnati by a twenty-six-year-old assistant professor of chemistry, George Rieveschl, Jr. Originally developed as an antispasmodic drug for colicky babies, Rieveschl's drug also turned out to be potent as an antihistamine. It became the focus for an exhaustive two-year series of pharmacological tests and clinical trials on more than two thousand patients. In Detroit one young chemist refused to wait for outside reports from the trials. He loved pota-

toes but was miserably allergic to them. Would Benadryl let him enjoy his favorite dish? He took two capsules, devoured a double order of french fries, and waited for his eyes to smart, his nose to run, his sneezing to start, and his stuffy head to throb. It did not happen.

A Symptomatic Treatment. Benadryl was not, however, a cure for allergies; instead, it merely acted as a treatment for the symptoms. Clinical trials reported it to be beneficial in 85 percent of the hay-fever cases and about 50 percent of allergic asthmas. Driving away hives was its most spectacular achievement. It also cleared up some cases of "penicillin rash," an allergic reaction seen increasingly as the new miracle drug became more widely used. Like many new drugs, it did have side effects, but

---

THE "GUINEA PIGS" OF ATOMIC WARFARE

In April 1947, nearly two years after the dropping of atomic bombs on Hiroshima and Nagasaki, a U.S. mission of physicians who examined the survivors reported on the "first guinea pigs" of atomic warfare.

U.S. and Japanese doctors found that mysterious scars continued months after victims' burns from the atomic bombs' heat and ultraviolet radiation healed. The doctors feared these ugly keloid scars might foretell cancer. Sterility was found in blast victims who had been up to three miles from the target center. One-third of the men were sterile, and fully two-thirds of the women suffered menstrual disturbances and miscarriages. The doctors received reports of malformed babies and feared for the generations yet to come. Atomic radiation was known to change genetic material. The report said, "There is good reason to believe that reproductive disturbances, malignancies of one form or another, shortened life span, altered genetic pattern, etc., will in time appear in greater or lesser degrees."

Source: "Generations Yet Unborn," *Time* (7 April 1947): 57–58.

---

hay-fever sufferers and other allergics were more than willing to put up with sleepiness, dizziness, dryness of the mouth, and occasional nervousness to gain relief from their allergy symptoms. Researchers continued to look to develop other antihistamine chemicals, but Benadryl was among the first and the most versatile of the new antihistamine drugs.

Source:
Steven M. Spencer, "New Hope for the Allergic," *Saturday Evening Post* (20 April 1946): 21+.

ATOMIC MEDICINE

Benefits from the Atomic Bomb. An elderly man crushes his leg in an accident. A severe infection forces a decision to amputate. But where should the surgeon cut? Above the knee or below the knee? If the man's knee joint can be saved, he will learn to walk again more easily. To make the correct decision, the surgeon must know how far up the patient's leg his blood circulation is impaired. A nurse injects a solution of radioactive salt into his arm. A Geiger counter near the patient's injured kneecap registers the information. The radioactive salt, now part of his blood, is carried by his veins from his arm into his knee joint. The circulation up to that point still functions. His knee can be saved. The same Manhattan Project that developed atomic weapons to destroy human life also developed by-products in the form of radioisotopes, such as those referred to in the example above, to use in saving lives. After the end of World War II these isotopes — by-products of atomic energy — were put to work in hospitals and laboratories to treat diseases and study the human body.

Tracers for the Study of Diseases. These radioactive materials were used as tracers to search for the cause of a disease, map blood circulation, or research the basic nature of bodily processes in disease and health. A scientist could chemically compound the radioactive atoms with ordinary atoms to build a "marked molecule." Radiation, registering on the Geiger counter, showed what happened to the molecule, whose identity otherwise disappeared after entering into the human body. Radioactive salt allowed the scientist to trace the circulation of the blood. A marked molecule of sugar could unravel the complicated series of steps it takes to convert food energy calories into muscle work. Mass spectrography — an atom-weighing machine — used a stable isotope, heavy hydrogen, to prove parts of the body that once were considered stable were actually being destroyed and simultaneously rebuilt with new atoms. Scientists learned half the blood plasma in a person's body is replaced in this way every twelve days; half the protein of the liver, in six days. Old secrets were being solved.

Treatment of Cancer. Radioisotopes gave doctors an important tool with which to treat certain diseases. Earlier radiation therapies, such as X-ray machines, aimed cell-killing radiation at diseased organs from outside the

body and could damage healthy tissues as well as diseased ones. Radioisotopes could work from within. The new materials became a powerful and highly selective weapon for the destruction of certain types of cancer. Radioiodine, absorbed by the thyroid gland, was given to people suffering from cancer of the thyroid. In this way a source of radiation, more effective than the scarce and expensive radium, arrived directly in the malignant cells of the thyroid. Acute leukemia cases that no longer responded to X-ray treatment were temporarily controlled with radiophosphorus.

New Hopes. Cost to the institutions receiving the shipments of radioisotopes was small, but scientists needed special equipment to handle the new and often dangerous materials. The government's atom-bomb production plant at Oak Ridge, Tennessee, soon adapted uranium piles to the mass production of radioactive by-product material. Scientists believed a longer and healthier life for millions would come from the deadly material that rained down on Hiroshima and Nagasaki in 1945.

Sources:
Harry M. Davis, "The Atom Goes to Work for Medicine," *New York Times Magazine* (22 September 1946): 15+;

"Lifesaving Role of the Atom. Wider Use of Its By-Products in Medicine," *U.S. News & World Report* (7 May 1948): 26–27.

THE CENTER FOR DISEASE CONTROL

Epidemics and the War Effort. Every fall, as Americans begin sneezing and coughing by the thousands, U.S. public-health officials brace themselves for one of nature's most dependable epidemics — influenza. In the 1940s there were other epidemics to fear — polio, malaria, typhus, dengue, and yellow fever, to name a few. Epidemics are caused by highly contagious and rapidly spreading diseases. Many disease carriers were found throughout the country when military personnel and former prisoners of war returned during the war, bringing with them typhus and malaria. These diseases threatened

Turbine blower spraying DDT on trees to control gypsy-moth caterpillars and other defoliating insects in July 1946

citizens living near military establishments and people working in essential war industries. The federal government felt it had to act.

The Office of Malaria Control in War Areas. An emergency World War II organization called the Office of Malaria Control in War Areas (MCWA) reduced the danger of malaria transmission in the country. Teams of specially trained and equipped specialists worked efficiently on the problem under the new organization. Atlanta, Georgia, a central point of endemic malaria, became its home base. MCWA was originally set up to solve the problem of malaria alone. In 1943 it expanded its focus to attack dengue in Hawaii and yellow fever in the southeastern United States. The availability of the new insecticide DDT revolutionized its efforts. In 1945 MCWA's responsibilities broadened again, as typhus control became part of the program and as rodent control specialists also joined the organization.

The Center for Disease Control. During its short life span MCWA demonstrated the wisdom and efficiency of solving health problems by using teams of specially trained scientists whose activities were coordinated under one organization. This experience directly influenced the U.S. Public Health Service (USPHS) to convert the MCWA personnel and facilities to peacetime operations. On 1 July 1946 Dr. Thomas Parran, surgeon general of the USPHS, redesignated MCWA as the Communicable Disease Center (later known as the Center for Disease Control [CDC]), with headquarters in Atlanta. It was the first federal health organization ever set up to coordinate a national control program against diseases spread from person to person, from animals, or from the environment to humans. Working relationships with state health departments were established through MCWA, and these were maintained.

Improving the Health of Americans. Substantial laboratory and research information was developed by the CDC and provided to the states. The Epidemiology Division was established to analyze epidemics using statistics and other descriptive methods; it also created a training program. The CDC began to assume a major role in national health emergencies and explored potential global health activities. The 1940s marked a time of great expansion of federal expenditures and support of health and medical research.

Source:
James Bordley III and A. McGehee Harvey, *Two Centuries of American Medicine* (Philadelphia: Saunders, 1976), pp. 440–444.

DDT – BEFORE SILENT SPRING

An Extraordinary Insecticide. In early June 1944 wartime censorship was lifted from one of the great scientific discoveries of World War II. "DDT will be to preventive medicine what Lister's discovery of antiseptics was to surgery," said Lt. Col. A. L. Ahnfeldt of the U.S. surgeon general's office. DDT stopped a typhus epidemic in Naples and promised to wipe out mosquitos and malaria; to eradicate the household fly, cockroach, and bedbug; and to control some of the most damaging insects that prey on the world's crops.

Amazing Properties. DDT (dichlorodiphenyltrichloroethane) was first synthesized in 1874 from chlorine, alcohol, and sulfuric acid. Its insecticidal powers were discovered in the middle 1930s. It remained active for weeks or even months, and it eliminated the need for repeated respraying. In 1944 the use of DDT as a delousing agent was publicly known for several months, when the army and the manufacturers of the insecticide joined in announcing some of its other amazing properties:

• Sprayed on a wall, it killed any fly that touched the wall, for as long as three months.

• A bed sprayed with DDT remained deadly to bedbugs for three hundred days.

• Clothing dusted with it was safe from typhus-bearing lice for a month, even after eight launderings.

• A few ounces dropped in a swamp killed all mosquito larvae.

• It was deadly to such common household pests as moths, roaches, termites, and fleas.

• As a crop protector, it was effective against potato beetles, cabbage worms, apple-codling moths, Japanese beetles, aphids, fruit worms, and even corn borers.

Control of Typhus. Effective control of typhus required eliminating lice as a carrier of the disease. During World War II DDT was made up into a powder known as AL63, used to spray soldiers' clothing at regular intervals. The insecticide impregnated all underclothing to provide individual protection against typhus. So great was DDT's potential that seven U.S. laboratories and hundreds of biochemists concentrated on refining it. Manufacturers turned out about 350,000 pounds a month — all for the army. The pure chemical itself had little effect; it was good only in an oil solution or when mixed with an inert powder. According to scientists, concentrated DDT was toxic to men and animals when swallowed, but in the weak dilutions used for sprays and dusts, "it has been found harmless to the skin." When the war ended other uses for the chemical were quickly found, especially in the agricultural industry. In the 1940s the public looked at DDT as a great scientific gift. But with the publication of marine biologist Rachel Carson's 1962 study, *Silent Spring,* the public and the scientific community became alarmed by DDT's devastating effects on the natural environment, and use of the chemical within the United States was gradually curtailed.

Sources:

"DDT," *Time* (12 June 1944): 66+;

Roderick E. McGrew, *Encyclopedia of Medical History* (New York: McGraw-Hill, 1985), pp. 171–172, 351.

DISCRIMINATION IN MEDICAL SCHOOLS

The proportion of "minority-group" students admitted to medical schools in a normal prewar year (1940) varied widely depending on the school:

Percent admitted:

School	Catholics	Italians	Blacks	Jews
Yale University	14	4	4	12
Tufts College Medical School	50	10	0	15
University of Illinois	20	5	1.5	41.8
University of Rochester	13	2	0.6	6
Bowman Gray School of Medicine of Wake Forest College	1.5	0	0	1.5
Hahnemann Medical College	31	9	0	9
Case Western Reserve University	21	8	1	15.5
Creighton University	54	18	0	4
University of Buffalo	36.97	10.9	0	10.9
Women's Medical College of Pennsylvania	15	3	0.9	31
Syracuse University College of Medicine	17.8	4.5	0	12.7
Queens University at Kingston	13.67	2.16	0	5.4
Georgetown University School of Medicine	85	19	0	8
Boston University	50	15	0.3	20
University of Virginia	3	1	0	10

Source: Frank Kingdon, "Discrimination in Medical Colleges," *American Mercury* (October 1945): 397.

Students on the steps of Howard University Medical School, one of only two black medical schools in the country, in 1944

DISCRIMINATION IN MEDICAL COLLEGES

Anti-Semitism. "Leo," a bright and personable young man, dreamed of becoming a physician. After graduating from Thomas Jefferson High School in New York City, he took a premed course at Ohio University. He had an excellent scholastic record and a distinguished athletic history when he filed his first application for admission to medical school. With his record he had no doubts about being accepted. But his application was turned down. After receiving rejections from eighty-seven other schools, he took an M.A. at Yale with top honors. One of his professors made a personal effort to enroll him in a medical school, but without success. Leo was excluded because he was Jewish.

Quota Systems. Medical schools in the 1940s were badly overcrowded, and prejudice and discrimination against certain groups were both subtle and overt factors in admission decisions. For every vacant place in the freshman class, seven or eight individuals applied. Medical officials estimated that 35–50 percent of the applicants were Jewish. Only one out of every thirteen Jewish applicants got in. From 1925 to 1945, before Nazi racism shamed many Americans into reconsidering their own anti-Semitic behavior and attitudes, the number of Jew-

ish students in medical schools was reduced by roughly 50 percent. The situation for African Americans was even worse. Of the seventy-eight approved medical schools, one-third were in southern and border states. All twenty-six of these institutions were closed to black students. By the 1940s there were only two black medical schools in the United States — Howard and Meharry. Women were limited to about 5 percent of medical-school admissions, and hidden quota systems existed for other groups, including Catholics and Italians.

The European Alternative. Before the war the minority student who wanted to become a physician and could not get admitted to an American medical school could go abroad to study. In one class in a Scottish medical school there were seventeen American men — sixteen Jews and one African American. After the war the National Board of Medical Examiners decided that it would no longer admit graduates of foreign medical schools to its examinations. Exceptions were granted to individuals with degrees from English universities, but not Scottish ones.

Roadblocks. Even if an individual gained entrance to a medical school, he might not be able to get an appointment to a hospital staff. African Americans and foreign-born doctors, particularly Italians and Slavs, were almost

Obituary notices in the *Journal of the American Medical Association* routinely include physicians' achievements. These notices range in length according to an individual's accomplishments. The printer puts the notices in order by length, with longer ones preceding shorter ones. In 1942 a Brooklyn doctor analyzed thirty of the weekly lists and found the doctors with the longest notices died at an average age of 64.6 years. The last ten doctors on the list — those who had not gained prominence and thereby a longer obituary — lived on to 69.3 years. The price of success seemed to be about five years of a doctor's life.

Source: "50 and 100 Years Age," *Scientific American* (November 1992): 14.

written, continued to keep certain Americans from practicing medicine.

Sources:

Bruce Bliven, "For 'Nordics' Only," *New Republic* (8 December 1947): 18–20;

Oswald Hall, "The Stages of a Medical Career," *American Journal of Sociology* (March 1948): 331;

Frank Kingdon, "Discrimination in Medical Colleges," *The American Mercury* (October 1945): 391–398;

Paul Starr, *The Social Transformation of American Medicine* (New York: Basic Books, 1982).

completely unrepresented on hospital staffs. When they did get positions, they tended to be at the lower levels of the system. A 1940 study of the informal organization of medical practice in Providence, Rhode Island, found appointment decisions depended largely on nontechnical considerations, such as personality and social background. "In the earlier days," said a hospital administrator, "we had competitive examinations [to select interns], but we had to discontinue those. The person who did best on an examination might not show up well in the intern situation. He might lack tact; he might not show presence of mind in crises; or he might not be able to take orders. And more than likely the persons who did best on the written examinations would be Jewish." Membership in the local medical society was an informal prerequisite for membership on the staff of most local hospitals. The American Medical Society required all hospitals accredited for internship training to appoint only members of the local medical society. This was another way to keep blacks out because they were excluded from the local societies, especially in the South.

Certain Americans Need Not Apply. Realizing the grave shortage of doctors at the time, many medical associations began to question these practices in the 1940s. Medical colleges denied the facts revealed by studies of the quota systems, each saying its admission system was based on geographic distribution rather than on race or religion. However, other Americans accused the quota system of perpetuating the type of racism commonly associated with Nazism. Critics charged that quotas maintained "racism at the very moment when Americans of every race, creed and color are fighting together to safeguard our democratic way of life." On 24 November 1947 the Southern Medical Association, meeting in Baltimore, dropped its ban on African American physicians at its scientific sessions. But quota systems, written and un-

ELECTROCONVULSIVE THERAPY

A Treatment for Mental Illness. In the 1940s there were few treatments available for mental illnesses. One regimen, called shock therapy, involved the use of drugs or electricity to treat severe mental disorders by inducing coma or convulsions. Early shock treatments used such chemicals as insulin, camphor, or metrazol. Injections of increasing levels of insulin deoxygenated the blood and induced a deep coma. Metrazol was used to produce convulsions. The therapeutic benefit of the drug shock therapies seemed to be greatest with schizophrenics. In 1938 Ugo Cerletti of Italy first developed an electric-shock therapy technique. It proved to be less dangerous, more controlled, and less expensive than the drug treatments. It rapidly became the primary medical treatment for the mentally ill, since there was little else available. At a meeting of the New York Academy of Medicine in February 1944, physicians concluded that the benefits of electroconvulsive therapy far outweighed the dangers involved. Physicians considered electric-shock therapy especially beneficial in cases of severe depression or "melancholia," as an alternative to months or years in a mental hospital. In these cases treatments were used about three times a week for two to eight weeks or more. In cases of extreme psychosis psychiatrists gave as many as three treatments a day over a period of several weeks.

Shocked into Sanity. The victim of dementia praecox (schizophrenia) lay strapped to a hospital table. Electrode paste was rubbed on one or perhaps both temples. A felt gag was carefully placed into his mouth, and he was given curare, a South American drug used by Native Americans on their blowgun darts, to paralyze nerves and to soften the coming spasm. Electrodes were placed on the paste, and a current of seventy to one hundred volts was applied for one-tenth of a second. Unconsciousness followed immediately, as the shock caused an electrical storm that obliterated the normal electrical patterns of the brain. The patient convulsed, like someone having an epileptic seizure. The patient revived in a few minutes and could not remember what had happened. The electric shock going directly through his brain disabled his mind, and the memory loss, confusion, and disorientation may have jolted him out of his dementia and literally shocked him into sanity.

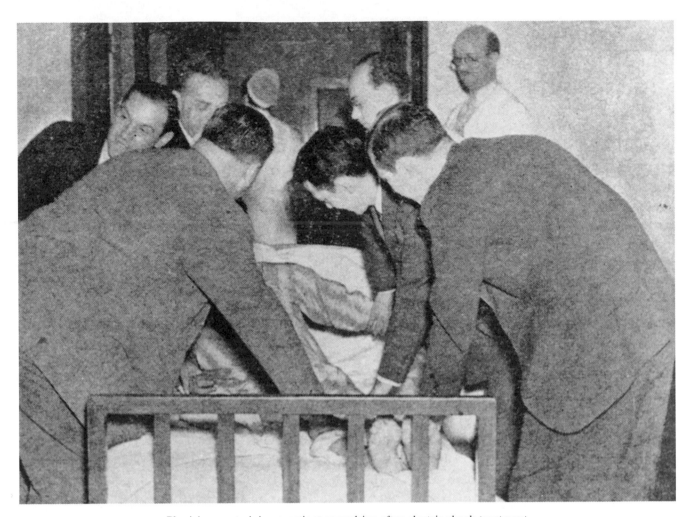

Physicians restraining a patient convulsing after electric shock treatment

Electrical Amnesia. Doctors believed electric-shock treatment did not greatly endanger patients, except for individuals with severe arterial weakness or with rheumatic hearts. They even reported successful shock therapy with two pregnant women, one in the fourth and the other in the fifth month of gestation. Some patients complained afterward of cramps and soreness in the back and calves of the legs from the convulsions during the seizures. Injuries were greatly reduced after the introduction of nerve-paralyzing drugs and improved hospital techniques. The memory defects lasted from a few weeks after treatment to a few months. "The shock does not destroy memory," reported the doctors. "It merely disorganizes it. . . ." Psychiatrists noted some of the best results when the mental patient was shocked into amnesia and temporarily freed from painful anxieties and depression. But its success in treating depressive diseases led to excessive and sometimes abusive use to treat a wide range of mental illnesses for which it was not effective. It began to fall out of favor as stimulants, tranquilizers, and other psychotropic drugs became available in the 1950s and 1960s. Drug therapy, however, did not entirely replace the use of electroconvulsive therapy. In recent years shock therapy has regained mainstream medical community approval, and its usage is rising in hospitals, although the treatment is still considered controversial.

Sources:

Eric Berne, *A Layman's Guide to Psychiatry and Psychoanalysis,* third edition (New York: Simon & Schuster, 1968), pp. 328–330;

Peter R. Breggin, *Toxic Psychiatry* (New York: St. Martin's Press, 1991), pp. 189, 195, 198;

"Shocked to Sanity," *Newsweek* (21 February 1944): 74–75.

HARRY S TRUMAN AND THE AMA

National Health Insurance and the AMA. In the 1940s, if an American president wanted to stir up a hornet's nest with the American Medical Association (AMA), all he had to do was propose some form of national health insurance. National health insurance already existed in many European nations, including Germany, which had established the first national system of compulsory sickness insurance in 1883. The first attempts to secure some form of national health insurance for the United States began in 1915 with an early proposal from the American Association for Labor Legislation to give medical coverage to workers and their dependents. Since reformers saw health insurance as a way to subordinate medical practice to public health and to change the method of payment from fee-for-service to salary or capitation (a single fee for each patient during each year), tensions arose when physicians saw this potential attack on their income and autonomy. After the 1938 elections President Franklin D. Roosevelt sent a national health-care program to Congress, but the bill was not passed. Toward the end of his life he indicated he would press for health insurance once the war was over. In 1944 he asked Congress to agree to an "economic bill of rights," including a right to adequate medical care. Three months after the end of the war his successor, Harry S Truman, called upon Congress to pass a national program to assure citizens the right to adequate medical care and protection from the "economic fears" of illness. By the time President Truman brought a health-care bill to Congress on 19 November 1945, the AMA saw it as a full-fledged government attempt to regiment medicine and to control the freedom which the association's members had enjoyed for the ninety-eight years of its existence. "No socialized medicine!" buzzed the doctors.

The Truman Plan. Truman's plan was similar to Roosevelt's New Deal health program of 1938, but he emphasized different aspects. He was strongly committed to health insurance, and his five-point plan suggested

1) increased federal aid for constructing needed hospitals and other facilities;

2) expansion of public-health, maternal-health, and child-health services;

3) increased education and research for the medical profession;

4) compulsory health insurance; and

5) disability insurance.

His recommendations reversed the order of the 1938 program. Unlike Roosevelt's earlier program, which proposed a separate system of medical care for the needy, Truman proposed a single health-insurance system that would include all classes of society. It was this point that angered the AMA.

Reaction. Public reaction to Truman's plan was initially favorable, but Congress's reception was mixed. Sen. Robert Taft of Ohio, the senior Republican, called the plan socialist. "It is to my mind the most socialistic measure this Congress has ever had before it," complained Taft. The AMA was furious. Ever since 1933, when its president had warned members to agree with the policy of the association, the *AMA* had fought against anything that sounded like "socialized medicine." "By this measure," said 170 AMA delegates of the policy-making group of the association, "the medical profession and the sick whom they treat will be directly under political control . . . and doctors in America will become clock watchers and slaves of a system. Now, if ever, those who believe in the American democracy must make their belief

MEDICAL "FADS" OF THE 1940S

Dr. Harry Bakwin, associate professor of pediatrics at New York University College of Medicine, stated his case against medicine's modern "fads" for children in the *New England Journal of Medicine* in 1945:

• In New York 61 percent of New York eleven-year-olds studied already had their tonsils removed, and doctors advised that one-half of the remaining 39 percent needed theirs out. Bakwin called the craze for tonsil removal "a useless expenditure of time, effort, and money."

•Most doctors advocated separating newborn babies from their mothers and putting them on a clock-ruled feeding schedule. Bakwin maintained that the practice is inhumane and almost bound to produce anxiety in parents and loss of appetite in children.

•Doctors diagnosed flatfeet, large tonsils, malocclusion (crooked teeth), heart murmurs, and poor posture as serious ailments. According to Bakwin, these are only normal childhood variations better left alone.

Source: "Doctor, Spare the Scalpel!," *Time* (9 July 1945): 46–47.

known to their representatives so that the attempt to enslave medicine as first among the professions, industries, or trades to be socialized will meet the ignominious defeat it deserves."

Defeat. When the Republicans took control of Congress in 1946, they had no interest in passing national health insurance. The president focused more attention on the issue as the 1948 election approached. After Truman's surprise victory, the AMA thought the end of the world as they knew it had come. It assessed each of its members an additional $25 solely for the purpose of fighting national health insurance. Its battle in 1949 cost $1.5 million, at that time the most expensive lobbying effort in American history. "Would socialized medicine lead to socialization of other phases of American life?" demanded one pamphlet. It answered, "Lenin thought so. He declared: 'Socialized medicine is the keystone to the arch of the Socialist State.'" (The Library of Congress was not able to locate this quotation in Lenin's writings.) Even though the administration insisted that national health insurance was not "socialized medicine," the AMA campaign was so successful that even supporters of the bill identified it as socialization and therefore tantamount to communism. Public support dropped rapidly, and as anti-Communist sentiment rose later in the decade, national health insurance all but disappeared

Advertisement urging Americans to be considerate of overworked physicians

from sight, defeated by the AMA's considerable wealth, prestige, and publicity and by support from businesses that did not want the additional costs of health insurance. From that time public policy on health care fragmented, and each government health agency pursued its own special agenda. A unifying national health-insurance proposal was down, but not out, and would appear again from time to time in the decades to come.

Sources:
"It's Socialized Medicine, All Right, Says AMA of the Truman Proposal," *Newsweek* (17 December 1945): 84+;

Paul Starr, *The Social Transformation of American Medicine* (New York: Basic Books, 1982), pp. 237–286.

HOSPITALS AND THE HILL-BURTON ACT

The Hospital Shortage. In the early 1940s, if you needed to go to the hospital, you might have had to travel quite a distance to find one. During the Great Depression of the 1930s little building of new hospitals occurred, and many of the existing hospitals deteriorated. More than one thousand counties in the nation had no hospital facilities of any type. During the war emergency, communities crowded with workers in the munitions and other wartime plants encouraged the building of many small hospitals, often of flimsy construction. After the war the hospital industry was desperate for aid. Its needs had been deferred for a decade and a half of depression and war. Conservatives in Congress were finally induced to build new hospitals as an alternative to national health insurance.

The Hill-Burton Act. Two hospital-construction programs were adopted immediately after the war, one to expand the Veterans Administration hospitals for the millions of returning veterans who would need medical attention, the other to aid the nation's community hospitals. In 1942 the Commission on Hospital Care was formed by joint action of the American Hospital Association and the U.S. Public Health Service. In 1946 Con-

gress enacted the Hospital Survey and Construction Act (the Hill-Burton Act, named after its Senate sponsors, Lister Hill and Harold H. Burton), based on the recommendations of the federally appointed Commission on Hospital Care. The purpose of the act was to provide funds to the states for the planning and construction of hospitals. Proposals for national health insurance made by President Truman favored financing more-comprehensive medical services. But the measures adopted via the Hill-Burton Act put the power of public finance behind hospitals alone.

No Government Control of Medicine. The Hill-Burton Act expressly forbade governmental interference in the operation of the hospitals. Federal administrators had no say about the amount of funding any state or individual hospital would receive. The states were to estimate regional hospital needs; when an applicant from an area received a grant, the area would go to the bottom of the list and had to wait to apply for further grants. Advocates of the Hill-Burton Act argued that the program would help provide access to hospital care for poor families and impoverished communities that otherwise could not afford to build hospitals. Funding provisions of the act itself, however, gave most federal assistance to middle-income communities. Initially the act required two-thirds of the construction cost to be supplied from local funding sources, meaning the poorest communities —

A PRESCRIPTION FOR LONGEVITY

In 1944 a German refugee physician, Dr. Martin Gumpert, published a book, *You Are Younger Than You Think,* suggesting that it is possible for most people to live to be at least one hundred. To get to that ripe-old age Gumpert suggested the following:

•Moderate indulgence in drinking and smoking.

•Do not retire: "Idleness is [a] ticket to death."

•An active (but not too active) sex life: Gumpert advised against December-May marriages; they often killed the older partner.

•Eat fewer calories but more vitamins and minerals. Breakfast in bed is good for the elderly, along with a hearty lunch and light supper. One should consume a diet of mild cheeses, milk, butter, scrambled eggs, lean meat, macaroni, well-cooked vegetables, bananas, and stewed fruit. Oldsters should avoid raw or smoked meat, raw vegetables, and rich cheeses.

•Avoid extremely hot or cold baths or long soaks. For elders the best routine is a daily sponging with warm water.

Source: "Life Begins at 60," *Time* (14 April 1944): 56+.

---

the very ones that needed help the most — rarely were able to raise the initial capital. Many hospitals in the South, moreover, refused to treat black people, who were among the poorest of American citizens. The law itself prohibited racial discrimination by any federally assisted hospital, though it accepted the construction of separate but equal facilities. The Supreme Court ruled these provisions of the Hill-Burton Act unconstitutional in 1963. In the Hill-Burton program states' rights and community autonomy limited federal intervention. Despite the growth of government aid to medicine in the 1940s, American culture and constitutional heritage once again worked against government control of medicine.

Sources:

James Bordley III and A. McGehee Harvey, *Two Centuries of American Medicine* (Philadelphia: Saunders, 1976), pp. 434–435;

Paul Starr, *The Social Transformation of American Medicine* (New York: Basic Books, 1982), pp. 347–351.

IT'S PATRIOTIC TO STAY HEALTHY!

Patriotism and Public Health. During World War II most Americans felt patriotism demanded eating less meat and sugar, driving fewer miles, conserving tin cans, and generally doing without normal consumer items.

While few thought of patriotism in terms of keeping their families healthy, the government gave it considerable thought. With ten thousand physicians already in uniform and sixteen thousand more needed by the army before December 1942, government and health officials felt civilians would have to "curtail their aches and pains for the duration." To this end, federal programs for better nutrition and physical fitness were developed and publicized for schools, colleges, industry, and the home. Their purpose was to develop a strong, vigorous, and healthy population with courage enough to endure a long war.

How to Be Healthy. Public-health authorities told Americans they had many ways to promote their health and prevent disease. Eating a well-balanced diet could prevent deficiency diseases such as pellagra, scurvy, and rickets. Inoculations protected against many diseases. Improved sanitation of water, milk, and food supplies and isolation and quarantine of infected persons as well as disinfection could check communicable diseases. Good health habits and proper diet were weapons against many disorders such as dental cavities, eyestrain, obesity, low body weight, flatfeet, indigestion, constipation, acne, and poor posture. "Let's be patriotic, then," said *Parents' Magazine,* "and have at least as much respect for the human organism as we now have for our winter overcoats, our rubber tires, our electric refrigerators and radios."

Preventive Medicine. "This is an era of preventive medicine," the *Parents' Magazine* article announced. It recommended annual physical exams for adults and exams twice a year for children. "Father is usually an offender in this respect," warned the author. "He cannot see the sense of a visit to the doctor when he feels fit." An appeal to his patriotism, advised *Parents' Magazine,* should do the trick. A dental checkup was also considered essential, not only for proper dental functioning, but also to prevent disease from spreading to other parts of the body from infections in the mouth. Immunization was still an issue. Even with absolute protection in the form of vaccination against diphtheria and smallpox, cases of these illnesses often occurred, especially in states which did not require vaccination.

Health in the Home. During the war Americans were called upon to assess their living conditions. Public-health authorities recommended three factors important in a healthy home environment: a temperature between 66 and 70 degrees Fahrenheit, humidity from 40 to 60 percent, and most important, "a reasonable amount of movement of air." Lighting should be improved where needed, to prevent ruining eyesight. Patriotic citizens were cautioned about the thirty-two thousand fatalities and 3.5 million disabling injuries a year caused by accidents such as falls, burns and scalds, and cuts and scratches. The American Red Cross provided first-aid training in the belief that this would make citizens accident-prevention conscious. Good nutrition was the most important factor in good health, especially after Dr. Nor-

PSYCHOSOMATIC AILMENTS

During World War II army physicians discovered that one-quarter of the cardiac patients in army hospitals had conditions traceable to emotional turmoil rather than physical defects. According to Brig. Gen. William C. Menninger, head of the Army Psychiatric Division, one-fifth to one-third of officers and men ailing with gastrointestinal disorders were ill for the same reasons. Sick civilians also suffered from their emotions. Leading specialists estimated that over 50 percent of common medical complaints were psychogenic, or linked to the mind.

There were not enough trained psychiatrists to handle these psychosomatic ailments. In 1946, of the nation's 160,000 accredited medical doctors, only 3,500 were psychiatrists. To aid the general practitioner in treating his patients' emotional problems, a neuropsychiatrist from Chicago recommended the "narcosynthesis" technique used widely during the war for combat fatigue. A patient given the truth serum sodium amytal would speak openly, and the doctor could quickly find the underlying psychological disturbance leading to the bodily complaint.

Source: "Mind Over Matter," *Newsweek* (27 May 1946): 60.

man Jolliffe of Bellevue Hospital referred to the high rate of malnutrition throughout the country as "a national disgrace in peacetime and a national danger in wartime." With studies indicating that only one-fifth of urban dwellers and one-half of country families were well nourished, the government launched campaigns to educate Americans about proper diet. Mothers were encouraged by Paul V. McNutt, federal security administrator, to feed their families for "health, for strength, and for the courage to win through against all obstacles," rather than to go out to get a war job.

Win the War with Health. "These are unusual times of stress," authorities warned families, "and we must all realize that a complacent attitude toward health can no longer be tolerated." Public awareness of the recent innovations in medicine encouraged health consciousness. Good nutrition and physical fitness were as essential to winning the war as tanks and guns. Patriotic health programs were for everyone.

Source:
Stella B. Applebaum, "Keep Your Family Up to Par: Patriotic Health Programs for Everyone," *Parents' Magazine* (August 1942): 21+.

MEDICINE AND WORLD WAR II

A Medical Success. For medical science World War II was a spur to startling advances. Newly discovered antibiotics such as penicillin and other drugs were rapidly made available by government sponsorship for research, manufacture, and distribution. The war demonstrated the effectiveness of preventive psychiatry. Men who were kept near the front lines and treated could often return to active duty. New techniques for treating and storing blood plasma resulted in the saving of lives. Many of these discoveries were later adapted for peacetime usage.

Medical Education. Medical education in the United States accelerated during the war years. The training of wartime doctors consisted of three intense years of twelve months each instead of the usual four years of nine months each. U.S. medical schools geared up to produce physicians needed for the war effort more quickly, but this system was not adopted by any other of the countries at war. Some medical professionals feared the potential of a calamitous impact from this new system of training. A. N. Richards, the chairman of the Committee on Medical Research of the Office of Scientific Research and Development, claimed at least 30 percent of the physicians under forty-five years of age were men whose training resulted in superficial learning, poor discipline, and "a minimum of that contemplation and discussion from which spring habits of independent thought." Richards called for added training for them, fearing a postwar "serious loss" in the ranks of qualified physicians.

Physicians in the Military. In peacetime the Army Medical Corps personnel numbered about 1,200. To provide medical service for a wartime army of 8 million, the Corps increased to 46,000, including 52 general hospital units, and 20 evacuation hospital units. During their service in the battlefields, many physicians experienced group practice for the first time and came home interested in a reorganization of medical practice to minimize the ineffectiveness of the traditional individual practice. Psychiatrists and psychologists also joined the ranks. Over 1 million men were rejected from military service because of psychological and neurological disorders, and another 850,000 soldiers were hospitalized for mental problems during the war. In 1940 there were 25 medical officers assigned to psychiatry in the army, but during the war it had to assign 2,400 more. Psychiatrists and others later presented these statistics to show the United States had a great unmet need for psychiatric services and promoted the expansion of psychiatry as a medical specialization.

Medical Research. World War II, more than President Roosevelt's New Deal, began the great expansion of the federal government's support of medicine. The war gave a priority to medical research to protect military personnel against injuries, disease, exposure, and fatigue. Among the many problems were protection against influenza, pneumonia, dysentery, and gangrene; prophylaxis

MORE DEADLY THAN WAR

During World War II diseases of the heart and blood vessels were the United States' number one public-health enemy. They killed more people than the next five leading causes of death combined (excluding accidents). Although 325,000 American men died in battle, during the same period two million Americans died from heart disease. Despite the dimensions of the problem, at that time there were only 374 physicians specializing in cardiology in the United States.

The U.S. Census Bureau reported in 1945 that nearly twice as many U.S. citizens died of cancer during 1942–1944 as were killed by enemy action in World War II.

Sources: "Killer No. 1," *Time* (9 February 1948): 71–72;

"Medicine," *Time* (31 December 1945): 71.

Eleanor Roosevelt with polio victims at Children's Hospital in Washington, D.C., 1940

and treatment of streptococcus infections and venereal disease; discovery of a substitute for quinine in the treatment of malaria; acceleration of convalescence; prevention and control of bacterial infections of wounds and burns; avoidance and treatment of shock; methods of restoring blood volume after hemorrhage and preservation of whole blood for transport from the United States to combat theaters; procedures for nerve regeneration and nerve repair following injury; protection of aviators against lack of oxygen and cold and from blackout; means for better adaptation of men to extremes of heat, cold, and humidity; protection against poison gases; and development of insecticides and repellents to guard against insect-borne tropical diseases.

Medical Accomplishments and the War. By the war's end many medical advances became available for civilian as well as military use. Vaccines were created to lessen the incidence of typhus, cholera, and forms of influenza. A little-known drug, Atabrine, reduced the menace of malaria more effectively than earlier drugs. Treatments for measles and infectious jaundice were developed from human blood plasma. The German-made insecticide DDT, brought as a sample from Switzerland in 1942, was used during the war to battle insect-borne diseases such as typhus. Penicillin and other powerful antibiotics were researched, developed, and produced. In many of these cases the war effort transformed difficult laboratory experiments into major postwar medical industries. It took less than three years for huge supplies of penicillin to be developed by pharmaceutical companies and made available to troops as a weapon against infection. Ironically, however, even as the war accelerated recognition of the benefits of government support for medicine, it also generated demands for the postwar autonomy of the majority of physicians. Unlike Europe, which developed ad-

ditional government-controlled national health systems after the war, American doctors more often than not resented their subordination in the ranks of the military and resisted efforts to establish a civilian national health system after the war. As Richards put it, for doctors, military service had spurred a "recognition that [government] regimentation in any restrictive sense is abhorrent."

Sources:

A. N. Richards, "The Impact of the War on Medicine," *Science* (10 May 1946): 575–578;

Paul Starr, *The Social Transformation of American Medicine* (New York: Basic Books, 1982), pp. 344–345.

POLIO

Polio Epidemics and Public Health. In the 1940s poliomyelitis (also known as infantile paralysis or polio) epidemics continued to be a scourge. Young children were the most susceptible to this virus-borne disease. Parents were terrified when their youngsters complained of headaches, sore throats, and fever, fearing these symptoms foretold the onset of the dreaded disease. Most instances of contact with the viruses resulted in only mild symptoms and complete recovery in one to three days. But if polio invaded the nervous system, about 25 percent of the patients suffered mild disabilities, and another 25 percent sustained severe permanent disability, such as

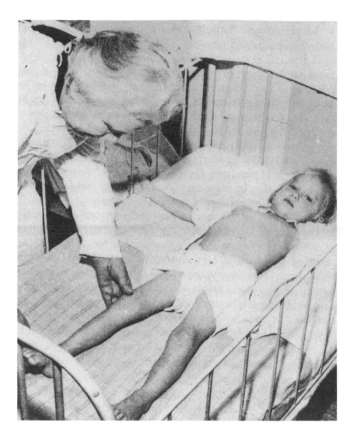

Sister Kenny treating a polio victim with her hot-pack method

paralysis of the arms and legs. If paralysis developed in the muscles of their throats, death from polio became a terrifying possibility.

Summer Epidemics. In addition to being the most susceptible, children were also the most effective spreaders of this highly communicable disease. Summer epidemics caused the closing of swimming pools and playgrounds and the virtual imprisonment of restless children indoors as the nation came under siege from polioviruses. Polio was not the most prevalent disease at the time, but it was deeply feared as the leading crippler of children, and more children died of polio than of any other infectious disease.

The Cost of Sanitation. Ironically, some scientists now believe that the public-health and sanitation movements contributed to these terrible epidemics. Before the advent of better sanitary conditions, children became infected with polio at an early age, when the disease tended to be nearly harmless and invisible, and they would then have lifelong immunity to it. Better sanitary conditions meant polio now struck many more children and adults later in their lives. Even Franklin D. Roosevelt, the U.S. president at the beginning of the decade, had been a polio sufferer. He had contracted the disease as a young adult, and although he kept it successfully hidden from most of his countrymen, Roosevelt needed iron braces and crutches to lock his paralyzed legs in place. During the 1940s the problem of adult infection grew. In 1949 the

U.S. Public Health Service published figures showing the shift: in 1916, 95 percent of the cases were children nine or under; in 1947 the figure fell to 52 percent. But the distribution of victims in the age group ten to nineteen rose from 3 percent in 1916 to 38 percent in 1947.

Military Significance. Before the outbreak of World War II polio did not seem to be a disease that would be significant for the military. The shifting of the age distribution of cases, however, caused a totally unsuspected problem for the troops. Polio swept through the ranks of the military, especially those stationed in tropical areas. Age specific immunity existed among the indigenous populations in tropical areas, but they passed the disease to the unprotected troops. Poliomyelitis was added to the list of dysentery, hepatitis, and other acute viral and parasitic infections creating problems for the armed forces.

Medical Treatment. The total number of polio cases in the country continued to grow after the war. By decade's end case incidence in the United States was over thirty thousand per year. In 1943 studies with monkeys indicated gamma globulin, a blood derivative, protected them against an experimental inoculation of poliovirus. Because of the war, no field trial could be conducted to test whether gamma globulin would have the same protective effect against polio in humans. The only preventive measures lay in the realm of public health — sanitation, isolation, and quarantine. No cure was known. Treatment consisted of mechanical devices such as the iron lung to aid respiration and orthopedic and rehabilitative measures. Such figures as Sister Elizabeth Kenny, who successfully challenged the medical orthodoxy in its theories of the aftercare of paralytic polio, became notorious during the decade.

Poliovirus in Tissue Culture. The names Jonas Salk and Albert Sabin, developers in the 1950s of the vaccines used today, are the ones most often associated with the battle and conquest over polio. But in the 1940s Dr. John F. Enders, a Harvard virologist, managed to produce the poliovirus in test tubes, which meant that the incredibly expensive and relatively unproductive method of producing it in monkey spinal columns could now be bypassed. An enormous amount of virus in some form, either dead or greatly weakened, was needed before widespread production of a vaccine could begin. For his development of the test-tube technique that would lead to the manufacture of poliovirus Enders was awarded a Nobel Prize in 1954.

Sources:
Roderick E. McGrew, *Encyclopedia of Medical History* (New York: McGraw-Hill, 1985), p. 275;

John R. Paul, *A History of Poliomyelitis* (New Haven: Yale University Press, 1971), pp. 346–356;

Rick Smolan, Phillip Moffit, Robert Coles, and Richard Flaste, *Medicine's Great Journey. One Hundred Years of Healing* (Boston: Little, Brown, 1992), pp. 29–30.

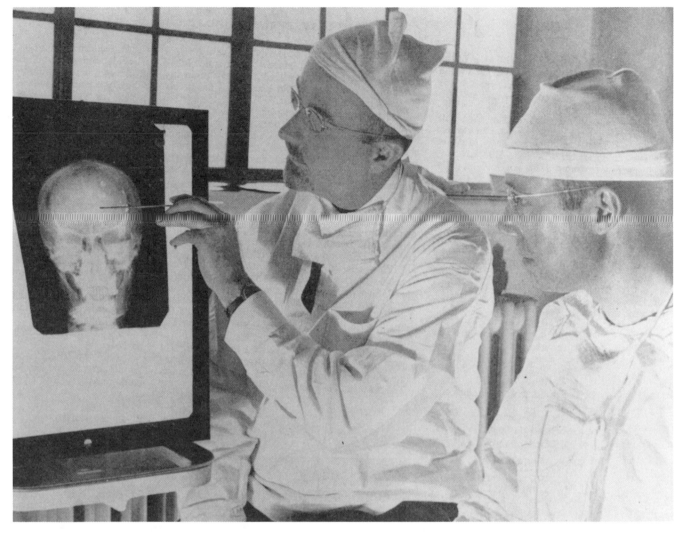

Drs. Walter Freeman and James W. Watts planning a frontal lobotomy

PSYCHIATRY AFTER WORLD WAR II

Psychiatry and the War. Psychiatry came to the attention of the government and the public during World War II, when more than a million men were rejected from military service because of mental or neurological disorders. Of those inducted into the army and later given medical discharges, 40 percent were dismissed for psychiatric reasons. During the war 850,000 soldiers were hospitalized for psychiatric disorders. Many conscientious objectors were assigned to serve in mental hospitals during the war years and brought back with them tales of neglect, overcrowding, and brutal treatment in the public mental hospitals. Psychiatrists and others blamed these problems on a great, unmet need for psychiatric services.

The Scandal of Neglect. At the end of the war the scandal of public mental hospitals became the subject of Mary Jane Ward's best-selling novel in 1946, *The Snake Pit*. In another widely read book, *The Shame of the States* (1948), the historian and journalist Albert Deutsch compared scenes in American mental hospitals to the horrors of Nazi concentration camps. Deutsch and many others called for closer medical oversight of mental hospitals.

A Shift in Orientation. Many European refugee psychiatrists contributed to postwar psychiatry. Before the war American psychiatry was centered around rural-based institutional "retreats," where physicians specialized in a variety of unsystematic treatments for "nervous disorders." European refugees brought a more urban, psychoanalytically oriented profession to America's middle class, specializing in the treatment of neurosis and anxiety.

Government Action. Because of the state-hospital scandal and the unexpected success in the treatment of psychiatric patients by the military's psychiatric services during the war, Congress was persuaded to pass the National Mental Health Act in 1946. With the federal assistance authorized by this act thousands of psychiatrists, psychologists, social workers, and nurses were educated. In 1949 the government created the National Institute of Mental Health (NIMH), a division of the National Institutes of Health (NIH). With government support psychiatry shifted toward proactive prevention of mental illness and away from the after-the-fall institutional warehousing of the mentally disabled that created such a scandal after World War II.

Sources:

James Bordley III and A. McGehee Harvey, *Two Centuries of American Medicine* (Philadelphia: Saunders, 1976), pp. 740–743;

William Menninger, *Psychiatry in a Troubled World: Yesterday's War and Today's Challenge* (New York: Macmillan, 1948);

Paul Starr, *The Social Transformation of American Medicine* (New York: Basic Books, 1982), pp. 344–346.

PSYCHOSURGERY

A New Operation on the Brain. In 1941 the word *psychosurgery* was not yet in the dictionary. Nevertheless, that year some two hundred Americans had their worries, persecution complexes, suicidal tendencies, obsessions, indecisiveness, or nervous tensions literally cut out of their brains. Many of these patients, surgeons claimed, were transformed into "useful members of society." Psychosurgery severed the connections between the prefrontal lobes and the thalamus in the brain and seemed a viable solution for those desperate cases unsuccessfully treated by drugs, shock therapy, or psychoanalysis. Physicians thought psychosurgery, also popularly known as lobotomy, gave intractable patients a chance of "being restored to the world with a more flexible personality" rather than living out a life of mental insanity.

Cutting Out Cares. The psychosurgical technique was first developed in 1935 by a Portuguese surgeon, Egas Moniz. For his surgery Moniz developed an instrument similar to an apple corer. When psychosurgery entered the United States in 1936, American physicians Walter Freeman and James W. Watts of George Washington University replaced his tool with a long needle with a hollow shaft to probe the brain. Instead of boring through the top of the skull, they bored through the temples. The patient, given only a local anesthetic, was encouraged to sing and pray. When he gave disoriented replies to questions, the doctors knew their cut was deep enough. After a long period of recovery the doctors reported a patient's emotional responses still existed, but the patients were more manageable and less likely to have violent, psychotic episodes. Patients were, however, indifferent to social amenities and sometimes embarrassed their family and friends. Their foresight was also impaired, but the doctors believed the psychopathic or psychotic personality was a worse alternative.

Public Reaction. Psychosurgery enjoyed a brief popularity in the 1940s. Toward the end of the decade public opinion reacted against the treatment when sources such as the Washington, D.C., Psychiatric Society publicized the treatment. Lobotomies were criticized for being used indiscriminately by many doctors who did not report their failures. Surgeons operated all too often on a patient without even a preliminary psychiatric examination, and there was not enough follow-up evidence to support pro-

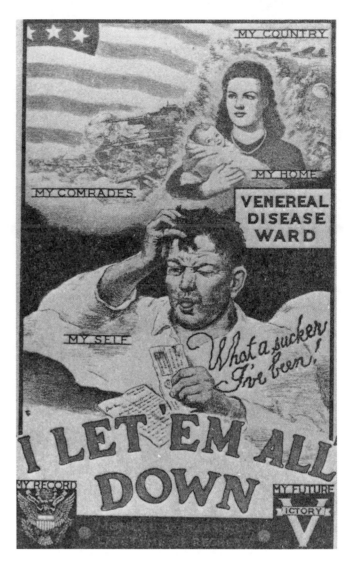

Poster urging servicemen to act responsibly to avoid venereal disease

lobotomy claims. Opinion against the treatment claimed the "cure" was as bad as the mental disease. Intractable patients were easier to handle, but "even when they are improved, they are still nothing to brag about." The operation itself was irreversible. But psychosurgery did not disappear. It has returned to favor in recent years accompanied by review boards to oversee the selection of cases for surgery better.

Sources:

Waldemar Kaempffert, "Turning the Mind Inside Out," *Saturday Evening Post* (24 May 1941): 18–19+;

"Lobotomy Disappointment," *Newsweek* (12 December 1949): 51;

Roderick E. McGrew, *Encyclopedia of Medical History* (New York: McGraw-Hill, 1985), p. 283;

"Psychosurgery," *Time* (30 November 1942): 48.

VENEREAL DISEASE

Public-Health Concerns. In 1940, 46 percent of Americans polled listed syphilis as their number one pub-

SINGING AGAINST SYPHILIS

In 1949 a nickel in a jukebox could get you a tune by balladeer Tom Glazer called "An Ignorant Cowboy." Its last verse twanged:

A ranch on the range isn't likely to find
Much use for a cowboy who's dead, lame or blind,
So if you've known Katey,
Please listen to this:
Only a doctor can cure syphilis!

The tune was part of a national health campaign against venereal disease sponsored by the United States Public Health Service which hoped to reach the estimated two million unreported syphilis victims in the United States. The objective was to get them to come forth and accept penicillin treatment. Each year saw 220,000 new cases — 373,296 cases were reported and treated in 1947, and 338,141 in 1948. Gonorrhea required one day of penicillin treatment. Syphilis took eight days.

Source: "Knock-Out Campaign," *Time* (11 July 1949): 47–48.

---

lic-health concern. Of the major venereal diseases gonorrhea is the oldest and most common. In males it is self-limiting and tends to subside in four to six days. Women appear to be at least three times more susceptible than men, and ninety percent of them show no symptoms. In women the disease can persist for a long time and render them infertile. For both men and women the gonococci can enter the bloodstream and attack joints, the endocardium, or the eyes. Children born to mothers with gonorrhea often become blind, although washing the eyes of the newborn with silver nitrate helps reduce this risk. Gonorrhea is neither a killing disease nor a major crippler, but it severely reduces the health of its victims. Syphilis, another form of venereal disease, is, on the other hand, a crippler and a killer. It can be a long-term, insidious, degenerative disease that can lead to insanity and severe damage to the cardiovascular system and nervous system. It is estimated that 66 percent of those infected with the disease who go untreated may suffer few effects, but a full 30 percent may expect to develop serious problems later in their lives. Before antibiotic treatment became widely available in the 1940s, insanity caused by syphilis may have accounted for as much as 10 percent of admissions to insane asylums. Before the age of antibiotics Americans had much to fear from these diseases.

A Social Problem. Before the Great Depression venereal disease was viewed as the outcome of personal lack of control and immorality. By 1940, however, many physicians, including Surgeon General Thomas Parran, viewed the illness as a social problem worthy of government intervention. As World War II loomed, the American military developed an antidisease regime emphasizing a combination of education, control of prostitution, medical treatment of the infected with arsenic compounds, and extensive case finding and contact tracing. Sulfonamides were available for treating gonorrhea, but penicillin did not become widely available until 1944.

Just Say, "No." Venereal education in the military tried to create "syphilophobia" among the men, but with little success. "It may surprise you, indeed, to know what little importance the average enlisted man attaches to venereal infections," noted Lt. Commander Leo Shifrin. "Most of them think as little of a gonorrheal infection as they do of the ordinary common cold." With the introduction of antibiotics in late 1943, the very nature and meaning of venereal infection changed. Now that venereal diseases were more treatable, fear and "syphilophobia" were no longer effective as preventatives. Instead the army inaugurated a program to ensure that troops were provided with both condoms and drug treatments.

VD and "Victory Girls." The war also revised the classic American debates about the military and prostitution and the sexual double standard: should prostitution be regulated or outlawed? The army attempted complete repression of prostitution, but many physicians argued that prostitution was best dealt with by regulation and medical inspection. It was, they argued, a lesser evil, an outlet for uncontrollable sexual drives, and would protect society against the greater evils of homosexuality, seduction, and rape. Military officials arrested thousands of prostitutes, but army physicians reported these women were only a minority of the soldiers' sexual contacts. So the military turned its attention to the "promiscuous" girl next door. "Victory girls" were the young women of "loose morals," eager to support the war effort and "to have one fling or better" with soldiers. Unable to control the activities of such women, the army redoubled its protection efforts, implicitly sanctioning the sexual activities of men, even as authorities lambasted the sexual activities of the "victory girl." Some physicians suggested that the whole situation might be better handled by a "stern father and a good doctor."

A "Magic Bullet?" The discovery of the effectiveness of penicillin changed the approach to the control of venereal diseases both during the war and afterward. As penicillin became widely available, disease rates began to fall. The demands of the war dramatically shortened the time for testing, research, production, and distribution. The rapid deployment of penicillin may have prevented a major venereal-disease epidemic that public-health officials feared would occur during demobilization. After the war public-health officials shifted their attention to identifying and treating preexisting cases of venereal disease. The U.S. Public Health Service sponsored nationwide health campaigns in an attempt to seek out and treat

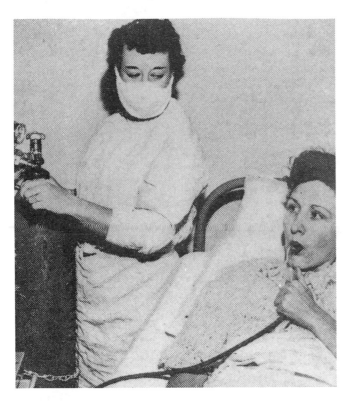

TB patient inhaling streptomycin, the postwar wonder drug that effectively eradicated tuberculosis

sufferers. Rates of venereal disease quickly dropped. However, the new cures were short-lived. Sulfa-resistant strains of gonococci appeared, and syphilis and gonorrhea developed resistance to penicillin. Both diseases today are rapidly increasing worldwide.

Source:
Allan M. Brandt, *No Magic Bullet. A Social History of Venereal Disease in the United States Since 1880* (New York: Oxford University Press, 1985).

THE WONDER DRUGS: "MAGIC BULLETS" AGAINST DISEASE

Serendipity and Science. New medical drugs are discovered in a variety of ways. Many of the most useful drugs are found by serendipity — fortunate and unexpected discovery by accident. Scientists testing sulfonamide drugs, for example, discovered that these compounds are useful as diuretics. Other drugs take years of painstaking research. This was the case with some antibiotics, such as streptomycin. Long years of experimentation and extensive clinical trials usually precede the widespread introduction of a new drug. The medical demands of World War II accelerated the development of drugs in the 1940s.

The Sulfa Drugs. The major killers of the nineteenth and early twentieth centuries were infectious diseases. The groundwork to eradicate the killer diseases began in the laboratories of the dye industry rather than in medical labs. The first real breakthrough came in 1932, when scientists discovered that the red azo dye, Prontosil, pro-

tected experimental mice against streptococcal infections. German physicist and chemist Gerhard Domagk won a Nobel Prize in medicine in 1939 for this discovery, but the Nazis forced him to decline the award. The modern era of antibacterial chemotherapy truly began in 1936, when workers at the Pasteur Institute in Paris discovered sulfanilamide, the active component of the dye. Many derivatives of sulfanilamide were soon created and tested, and U.S. scientists made many important contributions to sulfonamide research. Sulfapyridine, sulfathiazole, and sulfadiazine came in rapid succession, each more effective than the other.

Battles Fought with Drugs and Bullets. The outbreak of World War II brought the sulfa drugs to public attention. They were used in the war effort, most notably in New Guinea, where U.S. and Australian troops used sulfaguanidine against dysentery. The Japanese had only old and ineffective remedies. The sulfa drug helped the Allied troops remain healthy and defeat the debilitated Japanese. These compounds are bacteriostatic; that is, they affect the bacteria's metabolism and prevent them from multiplying in the host. This allows natural body defenses to take over against the invader. The new sulfa drugs were also used to treat streptococcus infection, pneumonia, gonorrhea, meningitis, and many other diseases. Their discovery gave physicians many more options for treating bacterial infections and gave chemotherapy a critical role in medical practice.

The Antibiotics. A French bacteriologist named Paul Vuillemin coined the word *antibiosis* in 1889 to describe the condition in nature when "one creature destroys the life of another to preserve his own." Vuillemin compared the lion attacking its prey with the behavior of antagonistic microorganisms. In the 1940s scientists discovered a host of bacterial agents that attacked other bacteria harmful to human life. These antibiotics — penicillin, streptomycin, and isoniazid — further enlarged the chemotherapeutic arsenal.

Penicillin. Sir Alexander Fleming, a British bacteriologist, first identified penicillin in 1928. Until World War II penicillin, produced in old whiskey and milk bottles, was a biological curiosity of dubious value. Although studies indicated it could destroy staphylococcus organisms, it was too difficult to produce to be of practical use. Scientists from Oxford University nonetheless came to the United States in 1941 and interested American scientists in its production. Scientists soon discovered an improved, highly productive form of penicillin on a rotting cantaloupe in a Peoria, Illinois, market, and American pharmaceutical manufacturers began mass production of the drug. The U.S. government sped up production when it took control of the entire penicillin output during the war. In 1942 there was hardly enough penicillin to treat a hundred patients; by late 1943 the United States produced enough for its military needs and those of its allies. By 1945 manufacturers produced enough penicillin for civilian needs.

Streptomycin. In the mid 1940s Selman A. Waksman, a soil microbiologist who studied fungi, introduced another weapon against disease by isolating actinomycin. Unfortunately, this antibiotic had dangerous toxic effects and was useless for medical therapy. But in 1944 he cultivated another species of fungus and isolated streptomycin. Streptomycin is an antibacterial agent effective against a large number of pathogenic bacteria not affected by penicillin, especially the tubercle bacillus. The introduction of streptomycin eradicated tuberculosis as a major public-health threat and closed tuberculosis sanatoriums around the world.

Broad-Spectrum Antibiotics. Antibiotics able to cure a wide range of infectious diseases are known as broad-spectrum drugs. Chloromycetin, a powerful drug against typhus, originated in a moonlight walk of two scientists at a Chemical Society meeting on the Chesapeake Bay in 1943. Paul R. Burkholder, a microbiologist at Yale University, and Oliver Kamm, research director of Parke, Davis and Company and widely known for his development of earlier antibiotics, chatted about soil microorganisms. Kamm interested Burkholder in the search for other, more effective antibiotics from the soil. Burkholder began to collect soil samples and examine their organisms for antibiotic activity. Of seven thousand soil samples sent from people in many parts of the world, four produced organisms that appeared to be unusually effective against virulent bacteria. One of these, grown from a sample from Venezuela, was named *Streptomyces venezuelae*. Parke, Davis and Company researchers ultimately produced chloromycetin from it. Chloromycetin became available for general use in 1949 and successfully treated typhoid fever and other diseases.

A Revolutionary Disease Therapy. After World War II, with the increasing development of the pharmaceutical industry and proof of chemotherapy's treatment effectiveness, an intensive search for effective agents for particular diseases continued. Other antibiotics, such as bacitracin, chloramphenicol, tetracycline, erythromycin, and Aureomycin, have been identified. Apart from some of the problems of their toxic effects, the sulfonamides and the antibiotics, including penicillin, have lost effectiveness because bacterial strains have developed which are immune to the drugs' actions. Since 1940 the development of antibiotics has revolutionized disease therapy and enormously increased the expectation of successful treatment for formerly intractable diseases.

Source:
James Bordley III and A. McGehee Harvey, *Two Centuries of American Medicine* (Philadelphia: Saunders, 1976), pp. 445–470.

HEADLINE MAKERS

DR. ALFRED BLALOCK

1899-1964

CODEVELOPER OF THE OPERATION THAT SAVED
BLUE BABIES

A Pioneering Operation. On 9 November 1944 Johns Hopkins surgeon Alfred Blalock carefully made a long incision and exposed a child's beating heart. Then, for three hours, he performed an operation no one had ever done before. The baby was slightly more than a year old but only weighed ten pounds and was not expected to live. Blalock believed that he and Dr. Helen Taussig had discovered how to increase blood flow to the lungs in "blue babies" suffering from anoxemia, or an inadequate oxygen supply. With the baby's heart exposed, Blalock could select a medium-sized artery, clamp it, cut it through, and tie off the useless upper end. He stitched the lower end into a hole he had made in the side of the pulmonary artery, thus bypassing the pulmonary artery's narrow entrance. All the time the operation was going on, one of the baby's lungs was collapsed. When he removed the clamps to let the blood flow, it flowed around and down into the pulmonary artery and to the lungs. The baby began to breathe more freely.

Blue Babies. A blue baby is an infant with cyanosis, a bluish coloration of the skin resulting from incomplete oxygenation of the blood in the arteries. Bright red, oxygenated blood gives the skin a pinkish tint. Unoxygenated blood is bluish-purple, producing the skin color which is characteristic of blue babies. Cyanosis commonly occurs as a result of a congenital heart defect. In the fetus a duct carries venous blood away from the nonfunctioning lungs to the aorta and eventually into the placental circulation, where a gas exchange occurs between fetal and maternal blood. After birth the shunt normally closes, allowing venous blood to be carried through the baby's pulmonary artery to the lungs for gas exchange. In some babies, however, the duct fails to close. The result is a chronic deficiency of oxygen in the blood. Cyanosis is also seen in a congenital condition when a hole in the wall between the right and left ventricles of the heart allows venous and arterial blood to mix. Without treatment, the average blue baby only lived for twelve years.

Vascular Surgery. Alfred Blalock was born in Culloden, Georgia, in 1899. He saw service in the U.S. Army in World War I and was awarded his M.D. by Johns Hopkins School of Medicine in Baltimore in 1922. He became interested in surgery during his internship at the Johns Hopkins Hospital. In 1925 the young doctor became a resident surgeon and instructor in surgery at Vanderbilt University Hospital in Nashville, Tennessee. Blalock achieved national prominence in the field of vascular surgery during his thirteen years at Vanderbilt. He became a pioneer in tracing the causes of shock, from either injury or surgery, to the loss of blood or body fluids. He was among the first to use large amounts of blood and plasma against shock, a technique which allowed new procedures in surgery in World War II.

A Medical Partnership. In 1941 Blalock became professor of surgery and chief surgeon at his alma mater, Johns Hopkins Hospital, where he met Helen B. Taussig. Dr. Taussig's interest in the physiology of the heart came during her work at the Boston University Medical School when a dean told her, "It won't do you any harm to be interested in one of the larger organs of the body." By the time Blalock arrived at Johns Hopkins, Taussig was well established as a pediatrician who believed that blue babies could be cured by an operation similar to the one she knew Blalock had performed on dogs while he was at Vanderbilt Hospital. The two physicians discussed the possibility of a surgical treatment for cyanotic heart disease. When Taussig suggested increasing the blood flow to the lungs by hooking up the subclavian artery with the pulmonary artery, Blalock said it might be possible. In order to prove cyanosis was due to the lack of oxygen in the blood caused by narrowness or closure of an artery, Blalock created artificial cyanosis in dogs and then operated, widening the artificially closed artery. After two years of experiments with two hundred procedures on dogs, he told Taussig he was ready to attempt to save a baby, and in 1944 he performed his first reoxygenation surgery on a blue baby.

The Hero of Blue Babies. Though the infant improved at first and began to gain weight, he died nine months later. But this pioneering surgery did prove that the pulmonary artery could be bypassed. In 1945, after Blalock had done sixty-five blue-baby operations, he suddenly became a hero in the press when reporters discovered he had saved 80 percent of his "doomed" patients. Patients came from all over the world; Blalock operated on suitable children after they had been thoroughly evaluated by Taussig. Before each operation the surgeons told the parents the risks were great. Fathers, they found, were the timid ones. Mothers usually said to go ahead. From 1945 to 1950 surgery was performed on more than one thousand cyanotic patients. With improvements in surgical technique and better selection of cases, operative mortality fell from 20.3 percent in 1945 to 4.7 percent in 1950. Blalock's operation was a great pioneering achievement that gave many ill children a relatively normal existence. It did not, however, cure the underlying cause of the birth defect; it relieved the cyanosis only partially and left behind the basic defects in the heart.

Sources:

"Blue Babies," *Time* (31 December 1945): 71;

James Bordley III and A. McGehee Harvey, *Two Centuries of American Medicine* (Philadelphia: Saunders, 1976), pp. 505–507;

L. Drake, "Gift of Life; Today Blue Babies Live and Thrive," *Collier's* (6 April 1946): 20+.

DR. CHARLES R. DREW

1904-1950

BLOOD RESEARCHER WHOSE WORK SAVED LIVES IN WORLD WAR II

Blood-Transfusion Specialist. The story of the career of the African American surgeon Charles R. Drew illustrates the tragic loss of human potential in a society afflicted with racism. While his pioneering work in blood research was responsible for saving countless lives during World War II, he was unheralded in his day and died unnoticed.

A Medical Pioneer. Charles Drew was born 3 June 1904 in his grandmother's house in Washington, D.C. His father was a carpet layer, the only African American in the Carpet and Tile Layers Union. His mother, a graduate of Howard University's Miner Normal School in Washington, was a homemaker. His parents encouraged their five children to aim high and to take their studies seriously. Drew grew up in a comfortable home filled with books and classical music in the ethnically mixed neighborhood known as Foggy Bottom. After his graduation from Amherst College in 1926, he entered McGill Medical College in Montreal, Canada. At the age of twenty-nine he received his M.D. and Master of Surgery degrees from McGill and was honored with the Williams Prize, given annually to the top five men in the class. In 1939, Drew joined the faculty of Howard University Medical School, one of the two black medical schools in the United States. Awarded a General Education Board fellowship to Columbia University Medical School, he worked in blood research. As a second world war loomed in Europe, Drew was aware of how crucial blood would be to treat the wounded, but in most cases blood was transfused from one person to another. Drew studied plasma, the yellowish liquid in blood, and solved the problem of storage and transfusion through blood-bank programs. In recognition of his contribution Columbia University awarded him the degree of Doctor of Medical Science. Drew was the first African American doctor to earn this degree.

Director of the American Red Cross Blood Bank. At the outbreak of World War II Drew received a stunning call from his former professor of anatomy at McGill. Dr. John Beattie, director of the research laboratories of the Royal College of Surgeons, requested "five thousand ampules of dried plasma for transfusion." Drew knew this amount of dried blood did not exist, but he set to work to produce it. By September 1940 he headed the "Blood for Britain" project. The following year he became the director of the American Red Cross Blood Bank and the assistant director of blood procurement for the National Research Council. At the time, government officials segregated the blood of black and white donors. Drew refused to honor the practice and took his stand against the army, maintaining that all human blood was the same. The U.S. Army turned against him, and he was criticized by white doctors. In October 1941 Drew lost his fight with the army when his enemies forced him out of his Red Cross job. He was "let go" and "permitted" to return to a professorship in surgery at Howard University Medical School at a time when most doctors were serving in the armed forces. His enemies suggested the position he had held in the blood bank was too high a post for a black man.

High Honors. Drew's research in blood plasma won him honors, including the Spingarn Medal of the National Association for the Advancement of Colored People "for the highest and noblest achievement by an American negro." Both Virginia State College and Amherst College awarded him honorary degrees. But he never became a member of the American Medical Association, because his local chapter in Washington, D.C., was segregated. Drew died in an automobile accident in North Carolina in 1950.

Sources:

Roland Bertol, *Charles Drew* (New York: Crowell, 1970);

Herbert M. Morais, *The History of the Negro in Medicine,* third edition (New York: Publishers Company, 1970), pp. 107–109;

Obituary, *New York Times* (2 April 1950): 76;

Rinna Evelyn Wolfe, *Charles Richard Drew, M.D.* (New York: Watts, 1991).

SISTER ELIZABETH KENNY

1886-1952

A NEW TREATMENT FOR POLIO VICTIMS

"Use Your Best Observation and Judgment." For most of this century standard treatment for polio included immobilizing the limbs of paralyzed victims in a variety of braces, casts, and forms for months. Physicians believed this prevented strong, normal muscles from pulling weak muscles out of position. An Australian bush nurse named Elizabeth Kenny rejected this standard approach and ultimately reformed therapeutic treatments of paralytic poliomyelitis. In 1910 Sister Kenny (Australian chief nurses are commissioned as "sister") first confronted a small epidemic of infantile paralysis in the Australian bush country. "Use your best observation and judgment," said the nearest physician, forty miles away. Knowing nothing about the disease and thrown on her own resources, Sister Kenny decided to treat polio's symptomatic muscle spasms. She used hot water, massage, and exercise, and her patients seemed to respond to the treatment. Claiming to have brought polio victims "back to normalcy," Sister Kenny was both encouraged by some doctors to keep it up and rebuked by other physicians as a quack.

A Message of Hope. Elizabeth Kenny hoped to revolutionize the treatment of poliomyelitis in its early stages. Doctors believed the affected muscles were limp and needed to be supported. Sister Kenny was convinced that the flaccid muscles were actually the ones that had not been affected by polio but were disabled by the neighboring muscles in spasm. When limbs were bound in casts, the nerve paths to healthy muscles stopped working, and these muscles, too, became paralyzed. Her message of hope came when public opinion was sensitive to polio issues. When the nurse from Queensland made her way via London to Minneapolis in 1940, she received an enthusiastic reception. At first her theories were positively received by both the *Journal of the American Medical Association* and the National Foundation for Infantile Paralysis. Sister Kenny maintained that 90 percent of polio patients could be restored to normal health if given her treatment at the onset of the disease. By contrast, physicians claimed a recovery rate from 20 to 40 percent.

A Controversial Figure. The road to acceptance by the medical profession was neither easy nor permanent. Australian physicians called her refusal to use splints, "a grievous error . . . fraught with great danger." In her eagerness to impress investigating doctors, she sometimes exaggerated her successes. Her critics were many, and their number multiplied as she became involved in a bruising battle with the medical-research establishment. By 1944 both the National Foundation for Infantile Pa-

ralysis and orthopedic physicians expressed their doubts over her method of treatment, calling it a "fad of the moment." For her part Sister Kenny was determined not to fall under the control of the foundation, and it, in turn, refused to make a major grant to her program. She was a controversial figure who inspired an almost fanatic devotion in some followers. She was not a salaried employee at Minneapolis General Hospital, and she did not accept money from patients' families. If someone sent money, she turned it over for research. Her supporters established the Sister Kenny Foundation in 1945, which made research grants and, with the University of Minnesota and the Minnesota Health Department, supported work on live-virus oral polio vaccine.

A Step Forward. In time the medical world came to recognize her treatment as an important step forward in preventing some of the terrible deformities that occurred, but her last years were still filled with bitter conflict. In 1950 she returned to Australia, saying her mission in America was completed. "Through storm and stress, frustration, false accusations and misunderstandings, I have diligently served the people of the world," she said, leaving behind clinics in Minnesota, New York, New Jersey, Michigan, and California. The United States acknowledged her when in 1950 Congress passed a bill giving her free entry into the United States, a privilege given only once before, to the Marquis de Lafayette. She is considered by many to be the mother of modern physical rehabilitation. Less than two years after her death, her dream of a vaccine to prevent polio was realized. Developed by Dr. Jonas Edward Salk, it was widely distributed in 1954.

Sources:

Emily Crofford, *Healing Warrior. A Story about Sister Elizabeth Kenny* (Minneapolis: Carolrhoda Books, 1989);

"Sister Kenny Dies in Her Sleep at 66," *New York Times* (30 November 1952): 1+;

Robert M. Yoder, "Healer from the Outback," *Saturday Evening Post* (17 January 1942): 18–19+.

MRS. ALBERT D. LASKER

1900-1994

THE "NOBLE CONSPIRACY" AND THE PRIVATE LOBBY FOR MEDICAL RESEARCH

Public Investment in Medical Science. Between 1900 and 1940 major sources of financing for medical research were nongovernmental, with private foundations and universities the principal sponsors and hosts of basic research. Before World War II most American scientists opposed large-scale federal financing or coordination of research.

The war changed such attitudes by increasing government sponsorship of medicine and making research a priority. Following the war the emergence of a private, lay lobby for medical research greatly expanded government support. Henceforth the U.S. government and its tax dollars would become an important part of the U.S. medical establishment.

"Mary and Her Little Lambs." The chief architect of the lobby was Mrs. Albert D. Lasker, wife of a prominent and wealthy citizen who had made a fortune in advertising. Mary Lasker had worked with voluntary organizations and took a major role in reorganizing the American Cancer Society. She knew of the National Health Survey of 1936, which emphasized the poor state of health among American people. The fact that four million of fourteen million men examined for military service before June 1944 had been rejected as mentally or physically unfit convinced her and others that American public health had to be improved. Her experience with private sector health-oriented organizations proved to her that public funding support was required in the fight against disease. Lasker had a friend, Florence Mahoney, who had experience campaigning for improvement of health programs; and through her family's connections with the Cox newspaper chain, Mahoney had the power to help on the political front in the battle for expanded medical-research support. This "noble conspiracy," also known as "Mary and her little lambs," believed the doctors and research scientists were too used to thinking small. Lasker, as a result of her background, was used to thinking big, and she had the conviction something could and should be done about increasing the government's sponsorship of medical research.

Medical Research as a Popular Cause. The public was accustomed to mass medical fund-raising by such organizations as the March of Dimes. Public-opinion polls showed support for more expansive government assistance to medicine. The Lasker lobby cultivated key figures in Congress, many of whom were opponents of national health insurance. Many covered their political opposition to national health insurance by voting generous appropriations for medical research instead. Lasker's money and Mahoney's editorials pressured politicians to support government funding for medical research. Lasker encouraged doctors and research scientists to ask for more money from Congress than ever before, and Congress approved it. Lasker's "noble conspiracy" helped to create governmental support of medical research and education.

Sources:

James Bordley III and A. McGehee Harvey, *Two Centuries of American Medicine* (Philadelphia: Saunders, 1976), pp. 358–361;

Paul Starr, *The Social Transformation of American Medicine* (New York: Basic Books, 1982), pp. 338–344.

WILLIAM CLAIRE MENNINGER

1899-1966

ADVOCATE FOR MENTAL- HEALTH TREATMENT

Contributions to Psychiatry. Psychiatry was a field few American medical practitioners knew much about in the 1940s. There was a widespread notion that psychiatry was either hilariously funny or sacrilegious or maybe even subversive. The popularization of Freudian psychoanalysis in the United States contributed to this perception. William Claire Menninger greatly contributed to a new perspective on psychiatry in the United States and to the rapid development of the field. Because of the large number of psychiatric problems and casualties in the U.S. Army during World War II, Surgeon General Norman T. Kirk declared psychiatry equal to medicine and surgery, and in December 1943 he appointed Brig. Gen. William Menninger as director of the Neuropsychiatry Consultants Division. As Menninger directed the expansion of the army's psychiatric work, his good-humored personality and professional ability helped him break down many of the walls of suspicion and hostility against psychiatry and improved the military's handling of soldiers with mental problems. He greatly expanded the United States Army's Neuropsychiatric Division and publicized the need for greater mental-health treatment to the American public.

The "Mayo Clinic of Psychiatry." Menninger received his M.D. from Cornell University in 1924, then interned at Bellevue Hospital in New York City. He, his father, Charles Frederick Menninger, and brother, Karl Augustus Menninger, cofounded the famed Menninger Clinic in Topeka, Kansas, in 1920. After his internship he joined his father and brother at their clinic. Known to many as the "Mayo Clinic of Psychiatry," the Menninger Clinic greatly influenced psychiatric practice in America. At the time of its founding it was the largest training center for psychiatrists in the world.

Improving Army Psychiatry in World War II. When World War II broke out, Menninger joined the army as a neuropsychiatric consultant. Alarmed at the high percentage (39 percent) of men rejected for military service because of personality disorders and the high rate of neuropsychiatric discharges, Menninger markedly improved army psychiatry during the war. As chief of the Neuropsychiatric Consultants Division in the Office of the Surgeon General, Menninger broke down "many walls of hostility and suspicion against psychiatry that impeded proper treatment of mental cases in military service." To make up for the shortage of trained psychiatrists during the war, Menninger's division created special intensive three-month courses for young army doctors.

Recognizing the Importance of Treatment. One of Menninger's greatest contributions to mental health and psychiatry called for the recognition of the importance of mental hygiene. "Many Army misfits could have been prevented," wrote Menninger, "if there had been greater use of psychiatric and mental hygiene services in the educational system of the country." He once summed up his attitude toward psychiatry and mental illness: "The problem is to convince people that emotional disturbances do exist, that they are a kind of sickness and that they can be helped by psychiatry. Too often people can't understand the nature of their problem. . . . It never occurs to them they have an emotional disease." His work with the military and his publicity of the importance of psychiatry and mental hygiene helped lead to changes in public perceptions of mental health and psychiatry. In recognition of his "outstanding service in the field of mental hygiene," he was awarded an Albert Lasker Award in 1944. Many regard the Lasker Award as the American equivalent of a Nobel Prize. Menninger was an active author whose books published during the 1940s were *Psychiatry in a Troubled World: Yesterday's War and Today's Challenge* (Macmillan, 1948) and *Psychiatry, Its Evolution and Present Status* (Cornell University Press, 1948).

Sources:

"Dr. William Claire Menninger Dies; President of Psychiatric Clinic," *New York Times* (7 September 1966): 1+;

William Claire Menninger, "The Mentally or Emotionally Handicapped Veteran," *Annals of the American Academy of Political and Social Science* (May 1945).

B. F. SKINNER

1904-1990

AMERICA'S PREEMINENT BEHAVIORAL PSYCHOLOGIST

Literature's Loss Is Psychology's Gain. B. F. Skinner, the foremost behavioral psychologist in the United States, first imagined a career for himself as an author of fiction and poetry. In his senior year at Hamilton College in Clinton, New York, he sent some short stories to the poet Robert Frost. Frost's response, "I ought to say you have the touch of art," encouraged the young Skinner to spend the year following his graduation writing short stories at his parents' home in Scranton, Pennsylvania. His discovery of "the unhappy fact that I had nothing to say" led him to go on to graduate school in psychology, "hoping to remedy that shortcoming." During his undergraduate days at Hamilton, Skinner had read an English translation of Ivan Pavlov's *Conditioned Reflexes* and the philosopher Bertrand Russell's articles on behaviorism. Also inspired by John B. Watson's work on the relatively new theory of behaviorism, Skinner decided to attend Harvard University for his graduate work in psychology, receiving his Ph.D. in 1931.

The Theory of Operant Conditioning. Skinner founded radical behaviorism and the experimental analysis of behavior. Earlier psychologists, such as Freud, explained behavior by referring to unconscious, purely mental states. Behavioral psychology explains learning and human behavior as a response to environmental stimuli. Learning is believed to take place through association once an individual makes the connection between his or her behavior and the consequences of that behavior. Skinner believed the scientific method of studying behavior was the best approach to understanding human nature. Since he only believed in what he could empirically observe, he dismissed the "mysterious world of the mind," including free will. His experiments with animals led him to formulate his theory of operant conditioning. He believed that all behavioral patterns, including human behavior, were the result of external factors such as positive or negative reinforcements — rewards or punishments — rather than the individual's internal interpretation of a situation. For Skinner, behavior was controlled by the environment, not by internal forces.

Project Pigeon. World War II contributed to the development of modern science and psychology in many unusual ways. It gave Skinner the opportunity for the practical use of his theory of operant conditioning. In 1940 he began experimenting with pigeons, which he believed could be trained to guide armed missiles to intercept and destroy enemy aircraft. Skinner received support from the Office of Scientific Research and Development, and Project Pigeon was underway. The plan was to train the birds to peck at the center of a target image and to place them in the nose of a missile behind a ground-glass plate carrying electricity. The missile's guidance system was to be controlled by impulses generated by the pecking of the pigeons. The plan was never actually put into practice, although tests proved its feasibility.

The Social Inventor. B. F. Skinner first came to public attention in 1945 when the October issue of the *Ladies' Home Journal* published an article describing the "air-crib," or "baby tender," as he called it, he had built for his second daughter, Deborah, who spent most of her first two years of life in it. A big, air-conditioned, soundproof, germ-free box, it was designed to provide a healthy environment for the baby to sleep and play without blankets or clothing. The device generated much interest and controversy, especially from several well-known pediatricians and child psychologists who criticized its usefulness.

A Design for Living. But Skinner was no stranger to controversy. Some of his detractors dismissed him as a "rat psychologist" because of his psychological experimentation using animals. He extended his ideas to education by developing teaching machines to reinforce students' correct responses immediately. He also extended the possible use of this kind of conditioning to create a utopian community founded on behaviorist principles. Under the appropriate conditions, Skinner argued, human behavior could be regulated by behaviorist principles in such a way that the perfect society could develop. Combining his love of writing and psychology, he published his controversial utopian novel, *Walden Two*, in 1948 to a mixed critical reception. Several communes, including Twin Oaks in Virginia and East Wind in Missouri, organized themselves according to the outline of *Walden Two*.

Contributions. His critics were concerned that control of behavior violated a person's free will, but Skinner countered, claiming he was scientifically analyzing the behavioral controls of parents, teachers, and the environment. "I am not trying to change people," he insisted. "All I want to do is change the world in which they live." His ideas of operant conditioning have been successfully used in education, behavior therapy, and in many weight-control and smoking clinics.

Sources:

Daniel W. Bjork, *B. F. Skinner. A Life* (New York: Basic Books, 1993);

Obituary, *New York Times* (20 August 1990): 1+.

HARRY STACK SULLIVAN

1892-1949

THE "INTERPERSONAL" THEORY OF PSYCHIATRY

A "National Resource." A federal government official called Harry Stack Sullivan "one of our important, largely unutilized national resources" when he served as a psychiatric consultant to the director of the Selective Service System during World War II. Sullivan himself believed his chief contribution to modern psychiatry was to define its meaning as "the scientific study of personality and of interpersonal relations."

The Importance of Social Factors. Isolated as a boy on a New York farm, the young Sullivan was fascinated with people and their relationships. He toyed with the idea of becoming a physicist, but by the time he graduated from high school he had decided to study medicine and psychiatry. In order to pay his Chicago College of Medicine and Surgery debts, Sullivan began his medical career as an internist. His career in psychiatry officially began when the federal government hired him as U.S. veterans' liaison officer at St. Elizabeths Hospital for the Insane in Washington, D.C., where he made his reputation as a humane and creative therapist with schizophrenic patients. From there he went to the Sheppard and Enoch Pratt Hospital in Baltimore, where his studies on schizophrenic patients convinced him of the importance of so-

cial factors in explaining mental health or illness. He began to focus his attention on the social sciences and encouraged the American Psychiatric Association to set up a standing committee on the relations of psychiatry and the social sciences. During World War II Sullivan applied his psychiatric theories to the Selective Service System and was medical adviser to the War Department general staff.

Treating Schizophrenia. Sullivan believed personality and personality disturbance were a function of interpersonal relations. Unlike Freud, he insisted later periods, especially adolescence, were as critical as the first five years for personality development. Since he believed mental illnesses were a "problem-solving" reaction to an unbearable situation, Sullivan insisted schizophrenia, no matter how bizarre, could be treated. He is recognized as the psychiatrist who removed schizophrenia from the class of incurable disorders, unlike Freud, who believed schizophrenia was untreatable because his "talking therapy" was useless with people who could not communicate rationally. Sullivan's contributions to the technique of clinical interviewing pioneered efforts to understand and help the severely disturbed. Sullivan was also the first to suggest that the therapist could be a greater participant in helping the patient cope with his behavior, instead of merely striving to understand it. His orientation deemphasized biology and sexuality in explaining human behavior, and his new theory of the importance of interpersonal relations revolutionized psychiatry by broadening its relevance to social problems and helped to bring it into the modern age.

Source:

Helen Swick Perry, *Psychiatrist of America, the Life of Harry Stack Sullivan* (Cambridge, Mass.: Belknap Press, 1982).

SELMAN A. WAKSMAN

1888-1973

THE DISCOVERER OF STREPTOMYCIN

Painstaking Research. Sometimes medical discoveries are dramatic accidents. In other cases they are the result of years of painstaking research. Selman A. Waksman, a microbiologist, and his small group of assistants worked for years to unearth the new antibiotic, streptomycin, which comes from the soil. Their discovery set into motion a chain of events that led to the closing of many tuberculosis sanatoriums because there were no longer enough patients to keep them open.

Antibiotics from the Earth. Waksman was born in Russia and at the age of twenty-two came to the United States. He graduated from Rutgers University and began his career in the field of science as a research assistant at the New Jersey Agricultural Experiment Station. He received his Ph.D. in biochemistry from the University of California. Studying the microbial inhabitants of the soil for thirty-nine years, he observed that actinomycetes (a genus of fungi) won out against other microorganisms and even killed tubercle bacilli. For four years Waksman and his associates investigated the huge family of actinomycetes, trying to find an antibiotic that would destroy the germs surviving penicillin's attack (the gram-negative bacteria) but not harm the human body. The first antibiotic to be isolated by his team at Rutgers in 1940 came from this fungi genus and was named actinomycin. It successfully affected *M. tuberculosis* (the tubercle bacillus) but was extremely toxic. At last in 1943 Waksman and his staff isolated streptomycin. It appeared to affect tuberculosis bacilli and had a comparatively low level of toxicity.

Clinical Experimentation. In wartime it was difficult to get supplies of any drugs, let alone unproven ones, to use in experiments. After Waksman's meeting with the pharmaceutical firm Merck and Company, Merck agreed to make streptomycin available in enough quantities to experiment successfully with tuberculous infection in guinea pigs. Clinical trials in human patients indicated streptomycin had a highly favorable effect upon pulmonary tuberculosis. Its effect on tuberculous meningitis and miliary tuberculosis, which were almost always fatal, was even more dramatic. Streptomycin even proved to have a more extensive antibacterial action against a large number of pathogenic bacteria, many of which are not influenced by penicillin.

Nobel Prize Winner. The production of streptomycin grew into a great industry. For his ingenious, systematic, and successful study of microorganisms of the soil, which resulted in the discovery of one of the wonder-drug antibiotics, Waksman was awarded a Nobel Prize for medicine or physiology in 1952.

Sources:
James Bordley III and A. McGehee Harvey, *Two Centuries of American Medicine* (Philadelphia: Saunders, 1976), pp. 456–460;

Selman A. Waksman, *My Life with the Microbes* (New York: Simon & Schuster, 1954).

PEOPLE IN THE NEWS

On 30 March 1941 **Dr. Frank E. Adair,** chairman of the executive committee of the American Society for the Control of Cancer, reported a 30 percent increase in cures of operable breast cancer from 1920 to 1935.

Drs. Herbert D. Adams and **Leo V. Hand** of Boston announced on 6 January 1942 the revival of a man whose heart had stopped beating for twenty minutes during a lung operation.

University of Illinois professor **Dr. H. W. Anderson** announced on 15 August 1945 that the drug streptomycin might surpass penicillin in effectiveness.

Dr. George C. Andrews of New York Presbyterian Hospital said on 7 April 1941 that "smoker's cancer" of the lower lip was not from smoking but was a result of a chronic inflammation of the lower lip from habitual sunburn.

On 5 May 1949 **Dr. Oswald Avery** of Nashville received the Passano Prize for isolating pneumonia germs and classifying the disease into four types.

Temple University Medical School announced on 8 August 1946 the development of the electrocardiograph by **Dr. Bert Boone,** allowing doctors to detect heart disease in the early stages by photographing heart motion.

Dr. R. C. Brock reported on 10 June 1948 the first successful operation within the human heart to relieve pulmonary stenosis.

W. G. Campbell, U.S. commissioner of food and drugs, reported on 6 February 1941 that there was no known reliable substance to cure the common cold.

Senator **Arthur Capper** (R–Kansas) urged the adoption of federal and state health-insurance laws on 18 January 1941.

Pittsburgh immunologist **Bettina Carter** announced on 5 October 1948 the development of a blood extract, Rh hapten, to save the lives of Rh babies whose blood type differed from the mother's.

On 13 July 1940 **Charles H. Cartwright** and **Arthur F. Turner** announced the invention of nonreflecting glass for use in microscopes and other optical devices.

On 22 November 1941 **Dr. Leslie A. Chambers** and **Werner Henlie** of the University of Pennsylvania showed the first electron-microscope photographs made of the influenza virus type A.

On 1 November 1944 quadruplets, three girls and a boy, were born in Philadelphia to **Kathleen Cirminello** by a cesarean section, the first time the procedure was used for such a multiple birth.

Dr. Albert Claude of the Rockefeller Institute for Medical Research said on 19 April 1941 that the mitochondria of the cell may be the cause of cancer.

On 1 April 1942 **Dr. David R. Climenko** of Winthrop Chemical Company reported that a synthetic, non-habit-forming substitute for morphine named Demerol had been successfully tested on eight hundred persons.

On 10 June 1942 doctors **Philip Cohen** and **Samuel J. Scadron** reported to the American Medical Association that they apparently had immunized infants against whooping cough by vaccinating the mothers three months before giving birth.

Col. **James Cooney,** the head of the army surgeon general's special-projects division, claimed on 12 November 1948 that the atomic bomb leaves little radiation and kills primarily with its blast.

Dr. H. J. Corper of the National Jewish Hospital in Denver announced the isolation of a tuberculosis vaccine on 26 February 1940.

On 22 April 1940 Professor **E. A. Doisy** of Saint Louis University reported the synthetic re-creation of vitamin K, essential for the prevention of hemorrhaging.

Massachusetts Institute of Technology radiologist **Richard Dresser** announced on 5 December 1947 that a three-million-volt X-ray machine had been successfully used in treating cancer.

On 5 June 1941 **Dr. Louis I. Dublin,** statistician of the Metropolitan Life Insurance Company, said that infant mortality in the United States had declined by 45 percent in the last twenty years.

Biochemist **Rene Dubos** announced on 11 July 1947 the development of a method for laboratory cultivation of the tuberculosis bacilli, speeding efforts to find a cure.

On 12 April 1940 **Dr. Paul Ehrlich** of Mount Sinai Hospital in New York reported on his finding a five-day chemical treatment for syphilis.

On 12 August 1941 **Drs. Clyde K. Emery, S. R. Baker,** and **Melville Jacobs** of the California Institute of Technology announced completion of the world's most powerful X-ray tube, expected to generate two to three million volts, for cancer treatment and research.

Dr. John Enders reported on 2 April 1946 the isolation of the mumps virus, making serums and vaccines possible.

On 23 March 1945 **Dr. Norbert Fell** of Parke, Davis and Company secured a patent on a method to control hay fever, asthma, and similar allergies by use of an antigen for building resistance to allergic reactions.

American Medical Association executive director **Dr. Morris Fishbein** said on 10 October 1943 that U.S. Army hospitals were saving 99 percent of the wounded and credited the use of sulfa drugs.

Sir Alexander Fleming, discoverer of penicillin, dedicated the new $3-million Oklahoma Medical Research Foundation in Oklahoma City on 3 July 1949.

On 8 May 1941 **Drs. H. L. Friedell** and **L. M. Rosenthal** of the Chicago Tumor Institute reported in the *Journal of the American Medical Association* that chewing tobacco is a factor causing cancer of the mouth.

On 20 April 1944 **Dr. James L. Gamble** reported that experiments showed glucose prevented excretions of body water and could be useful in keeping castaways at sea alive.

Drs. Phyllis Harroun and **F. E. Beckert** of the University of California Medical School reported on 18 March 1946 that a combination of nitrous oxide and curare made possible the use of electric-knife operations without the danger of sparks causing explosions in the patients' lungs.

The *Journal of the American Medical Association* reported on 20 January 1943 that **Drs. Robert A. Hingson** and **Waldo B. Edwards** had created a new painless childbirth technique called "continuous caudal analgesia."

On 12 June 1946 Mayo Clinic doctors **H. Corwin Hinshaw** and **William Feldman** reported that streptomycin seemed to check tuberculosis but was too toxic for wide use.

On 10 February 1943 **Dr. William A. Holla** reported that mice were probably carriers of poliomyelitis and spread it by contaminating food.

Dr. Bayard T. Horton of the Mayo Clinic reported on 12 June 1940 that the compound histamine was effective in combating severe headaches.

On 19 May 1943 the National Academy of Sciences gave the first Charles L. Mayer Award to **Dr. Charles Huggins** of the University of Chicago for his cancer research.

Col. **Paul Keller** reported in the 8 June 1946 *Journal of the American Medical Association* that the primary results of the radiation disease suffered by Hiroshima and Nagasaki survivors were the suppression of the blood-formation system and a disturbed liver function.

On 24 January 1942 **Dr. John M. Kenny** of New York reported progress against certain types of cancer using phosphorus made radioactive by a giant atom-smashing cyclotron.

The army surgeon general, Maj. Gen. **Norman Kirk,** said on 3 November 1944 that the incidence of malaria had been reduced by one-fourth since the early part of the war.

On 13 June 1944 the newly elected president of the American Medical Association, **Dr. Herman Kretschmer,** condemned the widespread use of vitamins as extravagant and useless.

Dr. Ernest O. Lawrence, University of California physicist, said on 10 October 1941 that the element strontium can be made artificially radioactive and then used like radium to destroy cancer cells.

On 6 January 1942 **Drs. Harold H. Lefft** and **J. Arthur MacLean** reported a new method of X-raying the brain involving replacing serous fluid with di-iodo-tyrosine mixed with gelatine.

On 7 February 1940 **Drs. Sidney O. Levinson, Frank Neuwelt,** and **Heinrich Nichols** announced that blood serum, the colorless liquid component of blood, could be used as the basis of a blood substitute.

On 15 February 1945 **Dr. Raymond Libby** of the American Cyanamide Company developed a method for administering penicillin by mouth by suspending the medicine in cottonseed oil and placing it in a gelatin capsule.

Dr. Dorman Lichty of Ann Arbor, Michigan, demonstrated on 6 August 1948 a new, lightweight respirator for polio victims.

Dr. Clarence Cook Little of the Roscoe B. Jackson Memorial Laboratory for Cancer Research said on 24 September 1944 that cancer is acquired by humans through a combination of hereditary and environmental conditions.

On 9 October 1946 **Dr. R. F. Loeb** revealed the development of pentaquine, a drug which can cure malaria instead of suppressing it.

On 6 June 1946 a German refugee, **Dr. Walter Loewe,** developed a drug called anthallan, which relieved hay fever and other allergies.

Drs. **Hubert Loring** and **C. E. Schwerdt** of Stanford University announced on 10 January 1947 that they had isolated the polio virus, opening the way to work on prevention of the disease.

Dr. **Bertram Lou-Beer** of the University of California reported on 28 June 1946 the successful use of a by-product of atomic research, radioactive phosphorus, in the treatment of superficial skin cancers.

Capt. **James Loveless** and Col. **William Denton** of the U.S. Army Medical Corps reported on 13 March 1943 that sulfathiazole may be a gonorrhea preventive.

On 27 August 1949 biochemist **Russell Marker** reported the isolation, from the tropical yam, of the hormone cortisone, important in the treatment of arthritis.

On 30 October 1942 **Dr. Henry R. McCarroll** told the American Public Health Association that the Kenny method of treating infantile paralysis with hot applications, massage, and exercise was hopeless for controlling the aftereffects of the disease.

William Cardinal O'Connell, archbishop of Boston, said on 21 October 1942 that the Catholic Church opposed birth control and regarded it as "the decadence of pagan license."

Drs. **Kurt A. Oster** and **Harry Sobotka** of Mount Sinai Hospital, New York, reported on 10 September 1942 that injections of adrenocrome, an adrenalin derivative, had successfully reduced high blood pressure to normal in experiments on rats and dogs.

U.S. Public Health Service Director **Thomas Parran** said on 9 October 1947 that the nation needed 50 percent more doctors than had graduated from medical school.

On 25 May 1949 **Dr. Benjamin Pasamanik** of Kings County Hospital in Brooklyn received the $1,500 Lester Hofheimer Research Award for a study showing Negroes have the same mental capacity as other races.

Drs. **John R. Paul** and **James D. Trask** of the Yale University School of Medicine announced on 16 October 1941 the discovery of flies carrying the virus of infantile paralysis after feeding in sewage systems.

Drs. **Raymond Pearl** and **W. Edwin Moffett** of Johns Hopkins University reported on 7 January 1940 that the length of a person's life was probably linked to his heart rate.

On 3 January 1941 **Dr. Norman Plummer** of Cornell University Medical College reported on a decrease in the death rate of pneumonia victims using sulfanilamide drugs.

On 8 October 1941 **Dr. Norman Plummer** said sulfadiazine cured a case of subacute bacterial endocarditis, a previously 100 percent fatal infectious heart disease.

On 8 May 1940 Drs. **Philip Polatin, Hyman Spotnitz,** and **Benjamin Wiesel** of New York State Psychiatric Institute reported the successful use of insulin in the shock treatment of mental patients.

Dr. **Henry G. Poncher** of the University of Illinois reported on 15 May 1941 that the recently discovered vitamin K was valuable in preventing hemorrhages in newborn infants.

On 29 May 1941 federal judge **James M. Proctor** fined the American Medical Association $2,500 and the Medical Society of Washington $1,500 for antitrust-law violations.

Dr. **I. M. Rabinowitch** reported on 19 February 1946 that a fifteen-year test of a high-carbohydrate diet on five thousand diabetics showed they may eat an ordinary amount of sweets and starches but must avoid fats.

Drs. **Charles H. Rammelkamp** and **Chester S. Keefer** of the Boston University School of Medicine reported on 5 November 1941 on a new substance, tyrothrycin, or gramicidin, which may be used in healing local infections without harming the tissues.

On 18 December 1941 **Dr. Willard C. Rappleye** of the Association of American Medical Colleges announced that seventy-six medical schools were planning to operate year-round to reduce the four-year curriculum to three years because of war needs for doctors.

Ollie W. Reed of the Agriculture Department said on 8 February 1943 that the process of extracting riboflavin (vitamin B_2) from milk was being perfected so that it could be used in bread and other foods.

Dr. **Garwood Richardson** of Northwestern University reported on 22 April 1949 the development of an accurate urine test for pregnancy.

On 24 May 1945 **Dr. William Robbins** revealed his discovery of six new antibiotic drugs: pleurotin, grisic acid, pleurin, irpexin, obtusin, and cortisin.

John D. Rockefeller, Jr., donated $2 million to the New York Memorial Cancer Center on 12 December 1949.

As he dedicated the $4 million National Health Institute in Bethesda, Maryland, on 31 October 1940, President **Franklin D. Roosevelt** said the government did not intend to socialize medical practice.

Dr. **Simon Ruskin** told the American Chemical Society meeting on 11 April 1940 that vitamin C was useful in combating allergies.

Dr. **Murray Sanders** of Columbia University announced on 1 September 1948 the first successful use of the drug phenosulfazole to cure infantile paralysis in mice.

On 10 January 1941 Drs. **Edwin W. Schultz** and **Hubert Loring** of Stanford University announced an extraction of the infantile paralysis virus almost free of impurities and ready for scientific examination.

On 15 March 1940 Drs. **Richard Steckal** and **John Murlin** of Rochester University reported successful attempts to make cancer cells normal by treating them with insulin.

On 2 September 1948 President **Harry S Truman** revealed details of a proposed ten-year public-health program, committing $4.3 billion in federal, state, and local funds to medical insurance, research, and education.

Biologist **F. L. Vanderplank** announced on 23 July 1946 a method of preventing African sleeping sickness by disturbing the African tsetse fly's reproductive system and rendering its bite innocuous.

Dr. Carl Voegtlin, director of the National Cancer Institute, and **Dr. C. P. Rhoads** of the Memorial Hospital in New York reported on 4 November 1941 their discovery of major respiratory differences between cancer cells and normal cells that might lead to a new chemical approach in the fight against cancer.

On 1 February 1940 Senators **Robert F. Wagner** (D–New York) and **Walter George** (D–Georgia) introduced legislation seeking $10 million in federal funds for rural hospital construction.

Dr. Selman Waksman, discoverer of streptomycin, reported on 24 March 1949 in *Science* magazine that neomycin, a new antibiotic, was as effective in treating tuberculosis as streptomycin.

On 23 April 1941 Professor **Russell M. Wilder** of the Mayo Foundation reported that two-thirds of the nation suffered from serious malnutrition because of improper diet.

On 29 April 1941 **Dr. Ernest Witebsky** of the University of Buffalo Medical School reported a new test for diagnosing trichinosis in humans.

Dr. E. R. Witner said on 1 December 1941 that the formation of cancer in brain cells can be detected in its earliest stages with a petrographic microscope.

On 3 May 1944 **Drs. Robert Woodward** and **William Doering** produced synthetic quinine from coal-tar products.

On 13 January 1940 Professor **Hans Zinsser** of Harvard Medical School announced the development of a method to mass-produce a vaccine to combat European typhus.

AWARDS

NOBEL PRIZE WINNERS IN MEDICINE OR PHYSIOLOGY

1940

No award.

1941

No award.

1942

No award.

1943

Henrik C. P. Dam (Denmark) for his discovery of vitamin K.

Edward A. Doisy (United States) for his work in the chemistry of vitamin K.

1944

Joseph Erlanger (United States) and **Herbert S. Gasser** (United States) for their discoveries on the differentiated functions of single nerve fibers.

1945

Sir Alexander Fleming, Ernst B. Chain, and **Sir Howard W. Florey** (Great Britain) for their discovery of penicillin and its effect on curing certain infectious diseases.

1946

Herman J. Muller (United States) for discovering mutations by the use of X rays.

1947

Carl F. Cori (United States) and **Gerty T. Cori** (United States, born in Czechoslovakia) for their research on the catalytic conversion of glycogen.

1948

Paul H. Muller (Switzerland) for his discovery of DDT as an efficient insecticide.

1949

Walter R. Hess (Switzerland) for his discovery of the role of the interbrain as a "coordinator" of internal-organ activity.

Antonio Moniz (Portugal) for his work on the treatment of some psychoses by prefrontal lobotomy.

AMERICAN MEDICAL ASSOCIATION DISTINGUISHED SERVICE AWARD RECIPIENTS

The AMA Distinguished Service Award honors a member of the association for general meritorious service.

1940

Chevalier Jackson, Philadelphia, Pennsylvania

1941

James Ewing, New York, New York

1942

Ludvig Hektoen, Chicago, Illinois

1943

Elliott P. Joslin, Boston, Massachusetts

1944

George Dock, Pasadena, California

1945

George R. Minot, Boston, Massachusetts

1946

Anton J. Carlson, Chicago, Illinois

1947

Henry A. Christian, Boston, Massachusetts

1948

Isaac A. Abt, Chicago, Illinois

1949

Seale Harris, Birmingham, Alabama

ALBERT LASKER AWARDS

The Albert Lasker Awards are given in honor of medical research of a pioneering nature. The Lasker Awards were initially given by various medical and health organizations in appropriate fields rather than through the foundation which funds them.

ALBERT LASKER AWARDS GIVEN THROUGH THE AMERICAN PUBLIC HEALTH ASSOCIATION

Basic Research Awards

1946

Carl Ferdinand Cori for work in carbohydrate metabolism and clarifying the action of insulin in diabetes.

1947

Oswald T. Avery for studies on the chemical construction of bacteria.

Thomas Francis, Jr., for research on influenza and development of a vaccine against types A and B.

Homer Smith for cardiovascular and renal physiology research.

1948

Vincent Du Vigneaud for basic studies of transmethylation and contributions to structure and synthesis of biotin and penicillin.

Selman A. Waksman and Rene J. Dubos jointly for studies of antibiotic properties of soil bacteria. Waksman was also cited for the discovery of streptomycin.

1949

Andre Cournand for work on the physiology of circulation and the diagnosis and treatment of heart disease.

William S. Tillett and L. S. Christensen for the discovery and purification of streptokinase and streptodornase enzymes.

Clinical Research Awards

1946

John Friend Mahoney, pioneer in treatment of syphilis with penicillin.

1947

No award.

1948

No award.

1949

Max Theiler for experiments leading to the production of two effective vaccines against yellow fever.

Basic and Clinical Research Awards

1946

Karl Landsteiner, Alexander Wiener, and Philip Levine for their discovery of the Rh factor in blood and its significance in blood transfusions and as a cause of sickness and death of infants before and after birth.

1947

No award.

1948

No award.

1949

Edward C. Kendall and Philip S. Hench for chemical, physiological, and clinical studies of adrenal hormones culminating in the use of cortisone in rheumatic-disease therapy.

Special Awards

1947

Thomas Parran for his leadership in public-health administration as surgeon general of the United States and as the president of International Health Conference and for his contributions to the control of venereal diseases.

1949

Haven Emerson for his development of a national program of rural community-health services.

Public-Service Awards

1946

Alfred Newton Richards for his organization and administration of the Committee on Medical Research of the Office of Scientific Research and Development. Richards supervised the wartime mass production of penicillin, the search for an antimalarial drug, and preparation of blood plasma.

1947

Alice Hamilton, a leader in toxicology and contributor to the prevention of occupational diseases and betterment of workers' health.

1948

R. E. Dyer for his microbiological research and service as director of the National Institutes of Health during the war and postwar years.

Martha M. Eliot for her organization and operation of the Emergency Maternal and Infant Care Program of the Children's Bureau.

1949

Marion W. Sheahan for leadership in nursing and public health.

ALBERT LASKER AWARDS GIVEN THROUGH PLANNED PARENTHOOD— WORLD POPULATION

1945

John McLeod for research on the metabolism and mobility of human sperm cells.

1946

Robert Latou Dickinson for work on human fertility and its control — as gynecologist, anatomist, educator, scholar, and artist.

Irl Cephas Reggin for making Planned Parenthood available as part of Virginia's state public-health program.

1947

Alan F. Guttmacher for leadership in marriage counseling.

Abraham Stone for leadership in marriage counseling.

1948

John Rock for treatment of childless couples and help to parents in planning their families.

Richard N. Pierson, who mobilized the medical profession on behalf of family planning.

1949

George M. Cooper for services in maternal and child health.

Carl G. Hartman for his work on the physiology of the human reproductive system.

ALBERT LASKER AWARDS GIVEN THROUGH THE NATIONAL COMMITTEE AGAINST MENTAL ILLNESS

1944

Brig. Gen. William Claire Menninger for his advancement of mental health in the field of war psychiatry.

1945

Maj. Gen. G. Brock Chisholm for advancement of mental health in rehabilitation.

Brig. Gen. John Rawlings Rees for advancement of mental health in rehabilitation.

1946

W. Horsley Gantt for experimental modification and analysis of behavior.

Jules H. Masserman for his investigations into neurotic behavior.

Walter Lerch and D. P. Sharpe, who aroused the people of Ohio to start major improvements in hospital care of mental patients.

1947

Lawrence K. Frank for contributions through adult education, particularly through parent/child relationships and child-development programs.

Catherine MacKenzie, a reporter and columnist who provided a campaign of education on the care and emotional development of children.

1948

C. Anderson Aldrich, who educated physicians in psychological aspects of pediatrics.

Mike Gorman, a reporter whose contributions resulted in new mental-health legislation and increased appropriations in the field.

Al Ostrow, a reporter who helped give public and legislative support for programs for the mentally ill in California.

1949

Mildred C. Scoville for the integration of mental-health concepts in medical education and practice.

Albert Deutsch for the advancement of mental health through books and magazine and newspaper articles.

PASSANO FOUNDATION AWARDS

Passano Foundation Awards honor distinguished work done in the United States in medical research.

1945

Edwin Joseph Cohn, Harvard Medical School, Cambridge, Mass.

1946

Ernest William Goodpasture, Vanderbilt University, Nashville, Tenn.

1947

Selman A. Waksman, New Jersey Agricultural Experiment Station, Princeton, N.J.

1948

Alfred Blalock, Johns Hopkins University School of Medicine, Baltimore.

Helen Brooke Taussig, Johns Hopkins University School of Medicine, Baltimore.

1949

Oswald Theodore Avery, Rockefeller Institute for Medical Research, New York.

NURSING AWARDS

The **Florence Nightingale Award** of the International Committee of the Red Cross is given every two years to not more than thirty-six nurses and voluntary aides, honoring exceptional devotion to the sick and wounded in situations of war, epidemics, or natural disaster. It is an international award with recipients from all over the world. Those listed below represent the United States.

1941

No awards

1943

No awards

1945

No awards

1947

Lt. Col. Ida W. Danielson

Mrs. Walter Lippmann

1949

Alta Elizabeth Dines

Mary M. Roberts

The **Mary Adelaide Nutting Award** is given every two years to honor outstanding leadership and achievement in nursing education or nursing service.

1944

Mary Adelaide Nutting

1947

International Council of Nurses

Isabel Maitland Stewart

1949

Annie Warburton Goodrich

Mary M. Roberts

DEATHS

Dr. Fred H. Albee, 68, world-famous orthopedic surgeon, 15 February 1945.

Lewis Allen, 75, nationally known radiologist and teacher at the University of Kansas medical school, 28 May 1948.

Dr. William Seaman Bainbridge, 77, New York City cancer authority, 22 Sept 1947.

Dr. Edward Robinson Baldwin, 82, tuberculosis authority, 6 May 1947.

Sir Frederick Grant Banting, 49, codiscoverer of insulin and Nobel Prize winner killed in a military plane crash, 21 February 1941.

Dr. Rupert Blue, 80, former U.S. surgeon general, 12 April 1948.

Col. Earle Booth, 66, former Broadway producer who organized the Blood Donor Service, 12 September 1949.

Dr. Abraham Brill, 73, psychiatrist who first translated Sigmund Freud's work into English, 1 March 1948.

Dr. Harvey J. Burkhart, 85, director of Eastman Dental Foundation, 22 September 1946.

Sister Leopoldina Burns, 85, the last surviving aide to Father Damien in leper nursing, 3 June 1942.

Dr. Eben Carey, 57, famous anatomist and dean of Marquette University medical school, 5 June 1947.

Dr. C. V. Chapin, 85, public-health expert and authority on sanitation and methods of infection, 31 January 1941.

Captain Robert Dexter Conrad, ?, assistant director of the Brookhaven National Laboratory and a leading organizer of cancer research, died of leukemia, 26 July 1949.

Dr. William Cramer, 67, cancer specialist, 10 August 1945.

Capt. Orrin Crankshaw, 34, medical officer, former Yale teacher, 23 February 1945.

Dr. George W. Crile, 78, clinical research specialist and surgeon who performed the first direct blood transfusion in 1905 and developed the nerve-block system of anesthesia, 7 January 1943.

Dr. Hugh Scott Cumming, 79, former U.S. surgeon general, 20 December 1948.

Dr. Walter Dandy, 60, known as the foremost neurosurgeon of his time, 19 April 1946.

Dr. Annie Surgis Daniel, 85, one of America's first women doctors, 10 August 1944.

Dr. Christian Deetjan, 77, a pioneer in X-ray treatment who lost his fingers and forearm in 1930 as a result of his work, died from research-related burns, 28 December 1940.

Dr. James Ewing, 76, authority and pioneer in cancer radium treatments, 16 May 1943.

Dr. Leroy Upson Gardner, 57, silicosis authority, 24 October 1946.

Paul Goedrich, 61, Austrian-born chemist and developer of sulfa drugs, 15 March 1948.

Dr. Menas Gregory, 64, psychiatrist who directed the psychiatric department at Bellevue Hospital and was chiefly responsible for its development, 2 November 1941.

Dr. Don Gudakunst, 51, director of the National Foundation for Infantile Paralysis, 20 January 1946.

Dr. Henry E. Hale, 76, pneumonia expert, 5 November 1946.

Dr. Eugene Hurd, 59, World War I army surgeon and American newspaper correspondent, 19 May 1941.

Dr. Smith Ely Jelliffe, 78, neurologist and psychiatrist, 25 September 1945.

Dr. John Harvey Kellogg, 91, health expert, inventor of medical and surgical instruments, founder of the Battle Creek Sanitarium, and cofounder, with his brother, of the W. K. Kellogg Cereal Company, 14 December 1943.

Maj. Albert Bond Lambert, 70, former head of Lambert Pharmaceutical Company, aviation enthusiast, 12 November 1946.

Karl Landsteiner, 75, Austrian-American physician who assisted in discovery of Rh factor in blood and whose work in typing blood led to safe blood transfusions; winner of 1930 Nobel Prize for medicine, 26 June 1943.

Dr. Veador Leonard, 59, discoverer of a new antiseptic, 11 September 1947.

Dr. John Long, 75, U.S. health expert who ended plagues throughout Latin America, 18 September 1949.

William H. Luden, 90, originator of mentholated cough drops, 8 May 1949.

Dr. Frank Barr Mallory, 78, pathologist who discovered and isolated the scarlet-fever bacillus and also discovered the cause of cirrhosis of the liver, 27 September 1941.

Dr. William Moulton Marston, 53, psychologist, originator of the lie-detector test, 2 May 1947.

Dr. John H. Outland, 75, surgeon and former football star, 24 March 1947.

Dr. Ralph Parker, 61, discoverer of the vaccine for Rocky Mountain spotted fever, 4 September 1949.

Dr. Richard Pearson, 76, expert on tropical diseases and epidemics, 4 July 1948.

Dr. Ralph Pemberton, 71, authority on arthritis and rheumatism, 17 June 1949.

Dr. Max Pinner, 56, authority on tuberculosis, 7 January 1948.

Harry Plotz, 55, a bacteriologist who discovered the typhus bacillus and the measles virus, 6 January 1947.

Dr. Hanns Sachs, 66, psychoanalyst and one of Freud's earliest students, 10 January 1947.

Dr. Milicent W. Shinn, 82, child-psychology authority and first woman to receive a Ph.D. from the University of California, 4 August 1940.

Dr. C. W. Stiles, 73, discoverer of hookworm, 24 January 1941.

Dr. William Stone, 79, pioneer in the use of radium in cancer treatment, 27 June 1946.

Dr. Frederic A. Washburn, 80, former head of Massachusetts General Hospital, 20 August 1949.

Dr. William C. White, 72, a leading tuberculosis researcher, 11 August 1947.

Philip Winnek, 40, biochemist who pioneered the development of sulfa drugs, 18 December 1948.

Dr. Hans Zinsser, 61, world's leading authority on typhus, 4 September 1940.

PUBLICATIONS

Kenneth F.Albrecht, *Modern Management in Clinical Medicine* (New York: McBride, 1946);

Raymond B. Allen, *Medical Education and the Changing Order* (New York: Commonwealth Fund, 1946);

George William Bachman, *The Issue of Compulsory Health Insurance* (Washington, D.C.: Brookings Institution, 1948);

L. F. Barker, *Time and the Physician* (New York: Putnam, 1942);

Louis H. Bauer, *Private Enterprise or Government in Medicine* (Springfield, Ill.: Thomas, 1948);

F. C. Bishop, "Insect Problems in World War II with Special References to the Insecticide DDT," *American Journal of Public Health* (April 1945): 373–378;

Ernst Philip Boas, *Treatment of the Patient Past Fifty* (Chicago: Year Book Publishing, 1944);

Amy Francis Brown, *Medical Nursing* (Philadelphia: Saunders, 1945);

F. A. Bryan, "Radioactive Isotopes in Medicine," *Hygeia* (April 1947): 286–287+;

E. Chain, H. W. Florey, and others, "Penicillin as a Chemotherapeutic Agent," *Lancet*, 2 (1940): 226;

Alfred Einstein Cohn, *No Retreat from Reason, and Other Essays* (New York: Harcourt Brace, 1948);

E. H. L. Corwin, *The American Hospital* (New York: Commonwealth Fund, 1946);

Albert Deutsch, *The Mentally Ill in America* (New York: Columbia University Press, 1944);

B. M. Duggar, "Aureomycin: A Product of Continuing Search for New Antibiotics," *Annals of the New York Academy of Science*, 51 (1948): 177;

Helen Flanders Dunbar, *Mind and Body: Psychosomatic Medicine* (New York: Random House, 1947);

Oscar Ross Ewing, *How Shall We Pay For Health Care* (New York: Public Administration, 1949);

Nathaniel Wales Faxon, *The Hospital in Contemporary Life* (Cambridge, Mass.: Harvard University Press, 1949);

Morris Fishbein, ed., *Common Ailments of Man* (Garden City, N.Y.: Garden City Publishing, 1945);

Fishbein, ed., *Doctors at War* (New York: Dutton, 1945);

Fishbein, *The History of the American Medical Association* (New York: Saunders, 1947);

J. F. Fulton, "Peacetime Implications of Wartime Medical Discoveries," *American Scholar* (October 1946): 506–515;

Iago Galdston, *Behind the Sulfa Drugs* (New York: Knopf, 1940);

Joseph Garland, *The Story of Medicine* (Boston: Houghton Mifflin, 1949);

A. D. Gordon, "Keeping Up with the Allergy Sleuths," *Science Digest* (October 1945): 7–10;

G. W. Gray, "The Antibiotics," *Scientific American*, 181 (1949): 26;

Alexander R. Griffin, *Out of Carnage* (New York: Howell, Soskin, 1945);

Douglas Guthrie, *A History of Medicine* (Philadelphia: Lippincott, 1946);

C. D. Haagensen, *A Hundred Years of Medicine* (New York: Sheridan, 1943);

Oswald Hall, "The Stages of a Medical Career," *American Journal of Sociology* (March 1948): 331;

James Corimer Halliday, *Psychological Medicine, A Study of the Sick Society* (New York: Norton, 1948);

Noel Gordon Harris, ed., *Modern Trends in Psychological Medicine, 1948* (New York: Hoeben, 1948);

Ruth Fox Hume, *Great Men of Medicine* (New York: Random House, 1947);

Institute on Medical Education, *Trends in Medical Education* (New York: Commonwealth Fund, 1949);

Institute on Public Medicine, *Social Medicine: Its Derivations and Objectives* (New York: Commonwealth Fund, 1949);

Morton Charles Kahn, *Public Health and Preventive Medicine* (New York: Oxford University Prtess, 1943);

Emerson Crosby Kelly, *Encyclopedia of Medical Sources* (Baltimore, Md.: Williams & Wilkins, 1948);

R. A. Kocher, "Doctors, War, and Medicine," *New Republic* (14 May 1945): 670–672;

Abraham Levinson, *Pioneers of Pediatrics* (New York: Froben, 1943);

T. Mahony, *The Merchants of Life: An Account of the American Pharmaceutical Industry* (Freeport, N.Y.: Books for Library Press, 1949);

Albert Q. Maisel, *Miracles of Military Medicine* (New York: Duell, Sloan & Pearce, 1943);

Carl Malmberg, *140 Million Patients* (New York: Reynal & Hitchcock, 1947);

De Witt McKenzie, *Men Without Guns* (Philadelphia: Blackiston, 1945);

William Menninger, *Psychiatry in a Troubled World: Yesterday's War and Today's Challenge* (New York: Macmillan, 1948);

Benjamin Frank Miller, *You and Your Doctor* (New York: Whittelsey, 1948);

J. Solon Mordell, *The Prescription Study of the Pharmaceutical Survey* (Washington, D.C.: American Council on Education, 1949);

Frederick Dodge Mott, *Rural Health and Medical Care* (New York: McGraw-Hill, 1948);

National Health Assembly, *America's Health: A Report to the Nation* (New York: Harper, 1949);

New York Academy of Medicine, *Medicine in the Changing Order* (New York: Commonwealth Fund, 1947);

Charles Malden Oman, *Doctors Aweigh: The Story of the United States Navy Medical Corps in Action* (New York: Doubleday, Doran, 1943);

Nathaniel Palyi, *Compulsory Medical Care and the Welfare State* (Chicago: National Institute of Professional Services, 1949);

Thomas Parran and Raymond Vonderlehr, *Plain Words About Venereal Disease* (New York: Reynal & Hitchcock, 1941);

J. R. Paul, "Poliomyelitis Attack Rates in American Troops (1940–1948)," *American Journal of Hygiene*, 50 (1949): 57–62.

"Prostitution is an Axis Partner," *American Journal of Public Health* (January 1942): 85–86;

R. H. Shryock, *American Medical Research: Past and Present* (New York: Commonwealth Fund, 1947);

Shryock, *The Development of Modern Medicine* (New York: Knopf, 1947);

Henry Louis Sigerist, *Civilization and Disease* (Ithica, N.Y.: Cornell University Press, 1943);

Sigerist, *Medicine and Human Welfare* (New Haven: Yale University Press, 1941);

John A. Silver, *Manufacture of Compressed Tablets* (Philadelphia: Stokes, 1944);

Wilson George Smillie, *Preventive Medicine and Public Health* (New York: Macmillan, 1946);

Bernhard Joseph Stern, *Medical Services by Government, Local, State, and Federal* (New York: Commonwealth Fund, 1946);

Edward Julius Stieglitz, *A Future for Preventive Medicine* (New York: Commomwealth Fund, 1945);

Harry Stack Sullivan, "Remobilization for Enduring Peace and Social Progress," *Psychiatry* (August 1947): 239–252;

Ludwig Teleky, *History of Factory and Mine Hygiene* (New York: Columbia University Press, 1948);

Philip Van Ingen, *The New York Academy of Medicine, the First Hundred Years* (New York: Columbia University Press, 1949);

Selman Waksman, *My Life with the Microbes* (New York: Simon & Schuster, 1954).

C. M. Wheeler, "Control of Typhus in Italy 1943–1944 by Use of DDT," *American Journal of Public Health* (February 1946): 119–129.

Charles Edward Amory Winslow, *The Conquest of Epidemic Disease: A Chapter in the History of Ideas* (Princeton: Princeton University Press, 1944);

Maxwell Meyer Wintrobe, *The March of Medicine* (Salt Lake City: University of Utah, 1945);

William Henry Woglom, *Discoverers for Medicine* (New Haven: Yale University Press, 1949);

Charles Oscar Young, *The Doctor Recommends* (Los Angeles: Wetzel, 1946);

G. Zilboorg, ed., *One Hundred Years of American Psychiatry* (New York: Columbia University Press, 1944).

"Keeping up with Medicine," in *Good Housekeeping;*

"Medical Newsnotes," in *Science Illustrated;*

"Medicine," in *Time;*

"What's New in Medicine," in *Science Digest* (continued as "Progress in Medicine" in the early 1940s).

CHAPTER ELEVEN

RELIGION

by VICTOR BONDI and DONALD L. JONES

CONTENTS

Sidebars and tables listed in italics.

1940

- Protestant missionary E. Stanley Jones's book *Is the Kingdom of God Realism?* is published.

- The United States establishes a diplomatic counsel at the Vatican for the first time since 1868.

- The Conference on Science, Philosophy, and Religion in Their Relation to the Democratic Way of Life is organized by Lyman Bryson and Louis Finkelstein.

- Rabbi Abraham J. Heschel arrives in the United States insisting humanity must make a distinction between good and evil.

- Roland H. Bainton's book on the life of Martin Luther, *Here I Stand,* is published.

- The United Jewish Appeal is founded.

- Catherine Clarke founds the Saint Benedict Center, a gathering place for Catholic students at Harvard University.

- William E. Hocking's book *Living Religions and a World Faith* is published.

1941

- Catholic leaders reform and reissue the Baltimore Catechism, the basis of Catholic educational instruction.

- Federations, welfare bodies, or community councils function in 266 urban centers, embracing 97 percent of the U.S. Jewish population.

19 Jan. The Institute for Propaganda Analysis estimates there are 450,000 Christian pacifists in the United States.

20 May President Franklin Roosevelt moves Thanksgiving to the last Thursday of November from earlier in the month.

22 May Pope Pius XII warns four thousand Catholic girls against wearing "daring" dresses that may "prove dangerous for the soul."

24 May German authorities issue a decree banning all Catholic periodicals and newspapers after 1 June.

1 June The Soviet government announces there are 8,338 churches, mosques, and synagogues in the Soviet Union.

6 Sept. The Presbyterian Church in the United States reports a membership decrease of 8,654 to a new total of 2,013,247.

30 Nov. An anonymous book published in Berlin titled *Gott und Volk* (God and People) states that "we Germans have been called by fate to be the first to break with Christianity."

30 Nov. More than sixteen thousand attend the opening of the entire interior length of the Cathedral of Saint John the Divine in New York, the longest Gothic cathedral in the world (601 feet).

1942

- The Buddhist Mission of North America is sufficiently established to change its name to the Buddhist Churches of America.

- A symposium on the body and soul set up by *Fortune* magazine includes Jacques Maritain, Julian Huxley, William E. Hocking, William P. Montagu, and Willard L. Sperry.

14 Apr. The *Saturday Evening Post* disclaims any anti-Semitic bias in an article by Milton Mayer titled "The Case Against the Jew."

30 Apr. The official Catholic Directory reports there are 22,556,242 Catholics in the United States.

June An interracial group dedicated to nonviolent action forms the Congress of Racial Equality.

11 Aug. The Inter-Allied Information Commission charges that the Gestapo has killed eight hundred Polish priests and imprisoned three thousand more in a drive to abolish Christianity.

14 Aug. The National Lutheran Council announces combined membership of 5,052,000 in 1941.

1943

- Pope Pius XII issues an encyclical called *Mystici Corporis* that equates the Roman Catholic Church with the "mystical body of Christ."

- Trude Weiss-Rosmarin's book *Judaism and Christianity: The Differences* is critical of a called-for partnership between Judaism and Christianity.

6 Jan. The Selective Service System reports that of the more than 5 million men called in the draft only 6,277 (0.1 percent) are conscientious objectors.

26 Mar. The National Jewish Welfare Board reports that Rabbi Alexander Goode is the first Jewish chaplain killed in the war.

26 Apr. U.S. Jews begin a six-week period of "mourning and intercession" on behalf of European Jews "exterminated by Hitler."

7 June Membership in the Methodist Church is reported at 6,640,424.

19 July The American Bible Society announces plans to distribute 1.8 million Bibles during the year.

22 July British officials report 4,100 churches destroyed or damaged in Nazi raids.

7 Oct. The Episcopal Church, while meeting in Cleveland, retains its ban on divorce.

1944

- A Gallup poll reveals that 58 percent of adult Americans attended a religious service in the past four weeks.

- Msgr. Fulton J. Sheen, professor of philosophy at Catholic University of America, stresses praying daily for Joseph Stalin.

- Bass-baritone George Beverly Shea becomes the first member of Billy Graham's evangelistic team.

- Kathryn Kuhlman, well-known faith healer and evangelist, is credited with rekindling interest in the Holy Spirit. She says she experienced her baptism of the Holy Spirit "on a dead-end street in Los Angeles" when she and the Holy Spirit "made each other promises."

2 Jan.   The Federal Council of Churches announces that 256 religious bodies in the United States report a membership of 68,501,186 in 1942.

3 May   The General Conference of Methodism rejects a resolution to admit women to full rights as ministers.

18 May   The official Catholic Directory reports the U.S. Catholic population at 23,419,701 — an increase of 474,564 over 1943.

22 Sept.   The Presbyterian Church in the United States reports membership at 2,098,091 — an increase of 46,222 from the previous year.

1945

- The National Opinion Research Center reports that only 6 percent of those identifying themselves as Catholics said they seldom or never attended worship, in comparison with 19 percent of Protestants, 32 percent of Jews.

- Mordecai M. Kaplan revises Americanized Jewish prayer books by excising all references to gender differences, including giving thanks to God for "not having made me a woman."

- A Jesuit named Leonard Feeney is named director of Saint Benedict Center at Harvard. His staunch anti-Jewish, anti-Protestant position later leads to his being dismissed from the Society of Jesus.

4 Feb.   Alexei, metropolitan of Leningrad, is crowned patriarch of the Russian Orthodox Church in Moscow.

9 Apr.   German pastor and theologian Dietrich Bonhoeffer is hanged in a Gestapo prison at Flossenburg.

12 Apr.   Following President Roosevelt's sudden death, Harry S Truman, a Baptist and Mason, takes the oath of office, saying to reporters, "Pray for me!"

16 May   The Reverend Dr. Henry Sloane Coffin retires as president of Union Theological Seminary in New York and is succeeded by the Reverend Dr. Henry P. Van Dusen.

23 Dec.   Pope Pius XII names thirty-two cardinals, including Francis J. Spellman of New York.

1946

- Rabbi Morris Silverman edits the first authoritative prayer book in the Conservative movement.

1 Jan.   The Japanese emperor, Hirohito, announces that he is no longer divine.

11 Feb.   A new translation of the New Testament, the Revised Standard Version, is published by the International Council of Religious Education.

20 Feb.   Representatives from one hundred Protestant and Orthodox churches from thirty-two countries meet in Geneva to plan a 1948 general assembly in the Netherlands to establish the World Council of Churches on a permanent basis.

5 Mar.   The Federal Council of Churches of Christ in America, representing 27 million church members, condemns the atomic bombing of Japan in August 1945.

6 Mar.   President Truman tells the Federal Council of Churches of Christ in America that only a moral and spiritual awakening can save the world from disaster.

21 Apr.	In New York City Easter crowds throng churches, and a record one million people parade on Fifth Avenue.
14 June	The official Catholic Directory announces there are 24,402,124 Catholics in the United States.
25 Aug.	The National Stewardship Institute reports that contributions to U.S. churches dropped $1,055,345,483 in the thirteen-year period from 1933 through 1945.

1947

- The fundamentalist Bob Jones University moves from Cleveland, Tennessee, to Greenville, South Carolina.

- Two Bedouin boys discover the first of the Dead Sea Scrolls in a cave at Qumran, in British-occupied Palestine.

- The Reverend Dr. Harold A. Bosley — lecturer, author, and liberal Methodist preacher, whose ministry has spanned fifty years — is appointed dean of the Divinity School at Duke University.

28 Jan.	A copy of *The Bay Psalm Book* (1640), the first book printed in the English colonies in North America, sells for $151,000 at a New York auction.
23 July	A Southern Methodist women's conference condemns race discrimination and the recent Greenville, South Carolina, lynching acquittals.
8 Aug.	The American Jewish Congress reports that Jewish communal property destroyed by the Nazis in Germany totals $100 million.
23 Oct.	The National Catholic Education Association reveals that a record three million students attend Catholic schools.
10 Nov.	The Protestant Film Commission presents *Beyond Our Own*, the first full-length film ever sponsored by a church group.

1948

- Martin Luther King, Jr., graduates from Morehouse College and is ordained at Ebenezer Baptist Church in Atlanta.

10 Jan.	A Gallup poll shows that 94 percent of Americans believe in God and 68 percent believe in life after death.
11 Jan.	The Reverend Dr. G. Bromley Oxnam, Methodist bishop of Washington, D.C., helps found Protestants and Others Organized for the Separation of Church and State, an organization designed to limit Roman Catholic influence in American politics.
1 May	The Southern Baptist handbook reports a membership of 27,804,047.
1 July	The official Catholic Directory reports 26,075,697 Catholics in the United States at the end of 1947.
1 Aug.	The *Christian Herald* reports that a record 77,386,188 Americans are church members — a gain of 3,713,000 over 1946.
19 Aug.	The International Council of Christian Churches, a fundamentalist organization of forty-five Protestant churches from eighteen countries, assails the World Council of Churches as antibiblical.

1949

22 Aug.	The first assembly of the World Council of Churches opens in Amsterdam, with 450 delegates and 1,000 other officials of 150 Protestant and Orthodox churches from 42 nations present. The Vatican forbids Catholics to attend even as observers.

- Episcopal bishop James Pike is named chaplain of Columbia University with a mandate from its new president, Dwight D. Eisenhower, to turn the religion department into a going concern.

- Walter A. Maier, Missouri Synod Lutheran minister and founder of *The Lutheran Hour* (and its preacher for the first seventeen years), writes seventeen books in the 1940s.

22 Jan.	Athenagoras, Greek Orthodox archbishop of North and South America, is enthroned patriarch of Constantinople. President Truman provides his own plane to assist the patriarch's move to Turkey.
21 Apr.	A new U.S. Catholic catechism is issued, the first revision in sixty years. It maintains that "outside the Church there is no salvation."
9 May	Methodist Church membership has grown from 7,856,060 in 1939 to 8,651,062.
9 June	Vatican Radio announces there are 338,250,000 Catholics in the world.
25 June	The Vatican announces that ten years of excavation at the Basilica of Saint Peter in Rome confirms the tradition that Saint Peter is buried there.
30 June	The official Catholic Directory reports U.S. Catholic membership at 26,718,343.
11 Aug.	Fragments of the oldest known Bible manuscripts (fourth–third century B.C.) are taken from a Palestinian cave near the Dead Sea.
9 Sept.	A U.S. expedition abandons its search for Noah's Ark after twelve days of futile hunting on Mount Ararat in Turkey.
25 Sept.	Thirty-one-year-old evangelical minister Billy Graham begins a revival in Los Angeles, attended by over 350,000 people.

OVERVIEW

Return to the Churches. After a long period of decline during the Depression, American churches experienced a revival — unique among the belligerents — following World War II. Church membership skyrocketed, and thousands of new congregations were formed. About 43 percent of the public attended church before the war; by 1950 more than 55 percent were members of religious groups, a figure that would increase to 69 percent by the end of the 1950s. Pollsters in 1947 revealed that the public held religious leaders in greater esteem than political figures and businessmen. By 1950 Americans spent an astonishing $409 million to fund church construction. Three hundred thousand new members joined the Southern Baptists from 1945 to 1949, and Catholics baptized 1 million infants a year. This amazing return to the churches was in part due to the experience of war, but it was also a function of the social pressures present in the age of affluence that arose from the war. It was the dominant characteristic of American religion during the decade.

Protestant Membership. The largest faith in the United States, Protestantism was represented by more than 250 denominations. The largest Protestant body was the Methodist Church, with 8 million members and 40,000 churches. With an annual budget of nearly $200 million, the Methodists operated 77 colleges and universities, 70 hospitals, and 10 seminaries. The Southern Baptist Convention was the next largest denomination in the United States, with 6 million members and 27,000 congregations. Active in mission work, the Southern Baptists maintained more than 300 missions in 22 foreign countries. The Presbyterian Church remained divided into Northern and Southern branches in this period (they would reunite in 1983), but combined they represented 2.7 million members in 12,000 local churches. Many other Protestant denominations had more than a million members each, including the Episcopal Church, the United Lutheran Church in America, the Christian Church (Disciples of Christ), the Northern Baptist Convention, the Congregational Christian Churches, and the Evangelical Lutheran Synod. There were also many small Protestant denominations, especially among evangelical and holiness churches, that would significantly increase their memberships after the 1940s. Finally, many believ-ers practiced in unorthodox sects far outside mainline Protestant denominations. In the 1940s there were approximately 1 million Mormons, 300,000 Jehovah's Witnesses, 225,000 Christian Scientists, and 70,000 Buddhists in the United States.

Catholics and Jews. Catholicism and Judaism were the predominant religions of immigrant groups who came to the United States by the millions at the turn of the century. With 25 million communicants, Catholicism was the largest religious body in the United States. Centered in northeastern cities, Catholicism was organized into 15,000 parishes and serviced by 25,000 priests. The Catholic Church in the United States administered an educational system with more than 10,000 elementary and secondary schools, 225 colleges and universities, and 388 seminaries. Catholics also provided many charitable services, including 800 hospitals, 367 nursing schools, 254 homes for the aged, and 352 orphanages and asylums. The nation's 5 million Jews were divided into Orthodox, Conservative, and Reform branches and were represented by 600 local community councils and more than 200 periodicals. Many synagogues also operated schools; by 1944 there were 238 Jewish schools in New York City alone.

City and Suburb. Both Catholicism and Judaism were predominantly urban entities; Protestantism was almost the exclusive faith of rural America. The difference in location between these two groups before World War II often exacerbated interfaith animosity, but as the character of the cities changed during the war, with rural protestants migrating to urban centers to work in defense industries and urban Catholics and Jews taking their basic training in rural America, these distinctions became blurred. As the cities changed after the war, with Catholics and Jews moving to the suburbs and black protestants moving to the cities, established patterns of religious and ethnic practices were disrupted. The Catholic Church began to minister to urban blacks, and Protestant ritual influenced services in suburban Catholic and Jewish houses of worship. The war set these changes into motion; it also affected the churches in other ways.

The War Church. American religious leaders labored mightily to come to grips with the war. Like any other institution, for the most part the churches were simply absorbed into the larger military effort. Nearly eight thousand clergy enrolled in the ranks of the service as chaplains, and churches provided Bibles and devotional literature to the troops. As America's moral conscience, however, the churches had unique responsibilities during the war. American churches redoubled their efforts on the home front, providing aid and comfort to separated families and monitoring the war's effect on the nation's morality. American religious leaders, such as Archbishop Francis Spellman of New York, traveled to the front and conducted services for the troops. Spellman, along with other religious leaders such as Rabbi Stephen Wise and theologian Reinhold Niebuhr, helped political leaders clarify the moral consequences of the war and attempted to direct war goals to ethical and positive ends. Other religious leaders, such as A. J. Muste, unable to accept the brutality of war for whatever end, advised conscientious objectors and kept a small but vocal pacifist movement alive. Military chaplains added to their regular ministerial functions the role of psychological counselor to the shell-shocked. Many took courses in modern psychology to meet the need for counseling and, fusing this training to their religious background, created pastoral psychology. All religious leaders struggled with the grieving of families and the destructiveness of war. Their counsel of faith — at a time when it sometimes seemed God had abandoned humanity — was vital to maintaining courage in the face of adversity.

Liberalism. War was not the only phenomenon that transformed American religion in the 1940s. Longer-term trends in theology and religious practice coalesced and reshaped the landscape of American faith. In general, religion was unmistakably more liberal. Interdenominational rivalry gave way to a spirit of ecumenical cooperation; interfaith animosity was replaced by religious tolerance. All three main American faiths — Protestantism, Catholicism, and Judaism — went through radical theological reconstruction in the 1930s and 1940s, harmonizing the essence of their doctrines with the innovative intellectual concepts and mores of modern society. The events of the early 1940s reinforced and supported these theological reconstructions. The Nazis and the Holocaust discredited religious intolerance; the human potential for evil central to the reconstructed theologies of the 1940s was obvious in the violence of war; the need for humility and charity was all the more pressing after the development of the atomic bomb. Legacies of older, conservative theologies were nonetheless evident during the 1940s. Anti-Semitism remained an issue in the early

years of the decade and returned encoded in anti-communism by the end of the 1940s. Tensions between Catholics and Protestants were manifest in disputes over educational funding for schools and confrontations over avant-garde art. Protestant fundamentalism and conservatism surfaced in storefront churches and Billy Graham's 1949 revival. Yet even these manifestations of older religious traditions were different. Graham's revival, for example, owed much to the anticommunism of the time, and he went out of his way to counsel religious tolerance and personal humility. Protestant anti-Catholicism focused on issues rather than being generalized as a sweeping hate. Jewish fundamentalism was transformed by Zionism. Even the most determinedly otherworldly theologies of the time were changed by the press of events.

Perils of Prosperity. In many ways the most challenging force for change in American religion was its success. After World War II the economic prosperity of the period supported unprecedented growth in the churches. American congregations became affluent and suburban. Churchgoing became part of the suburban lifestyle, a sign of community, protection against suspicions of Communist sympathies, and a badge of conformity. For the immigrant faiths of Catholicism and Judaism the homogenizing force of the suburbs tended to bleach out the distinctive ethnic character of the faith. In the late 1940s Catholic and Jewish conservatives complained that their faiths were becoming more Protestant, but the opposite was also true: few Protestants objected any longer to Catholic pageantry or Judaic ritual, at least with the violence that had at one time dominated interfaith relations. The suburbs made different faiths neighbors and blurred the distinctions between them. All were to a great degree leveled by a common consumer culture, and there was a growing tendency for religion itself to be just one more commodity. Partisans of "mind cure" and positive thought, such as Norman Vincent Peale, offered an instant, therapeutic equivalent to liturgy and faith. As the decade closed, many churches combined their piety with sermons that were more entertaining than enlightening and planned more church socials than church services. Many serious theologians such H. Richard Niebuhr, while favoring the growing tolerance between faiths and the generally liberal thrust of religion, worried that American faith was being ruined by success, blended into a spiritually unpalatable stew. Niebuhr and others argued that the spectacular growth of churches was irrelevant if faith became as shallow as it was broad. Their criticisms would only escalate in subsequent decades.

TOPICS IN THE NEWS

CATHOLICISM AND MODERNISM

Transition. The 1940s were a decade of momentous change for Catholicism in the United States. Traditional Catholicism was challenged on every front: liturgical, philosophical, and organizational. The Catholic Church in general became more worldly, liberal, and egalitarian. Modernism, a catchall term that signified the multiple and diverse forces arrayed against tradition, confronted and transformed American Catholicism. This confrontation was long delayed. Unlike other churches, the Catholic Church failed to come to adequate terms with concepts and ideas that had transformed other theologies in the nineteenth century. Evolutionary theory, for example, restructured American Protestantism at the turn of the century. When Father John A. Zahm of Notre Dame University attempted a synthesis of Darwinism and Catholicism in 1896, the Vatican had him silenced. After World War II a reckoning with modernism could no longer be avoided. This confrontation made the 1940s one of the most dynamic decades in the history of American Catholicism.

Tradition. By tradition, American Catholicism was a religion of immigrants, connected to the turn-of-the-century migration of Irish, Germans, Italians, Poles, French Canadians, east Europeans, and later immigrations of Latin Americans. For all of these groups Catholicism was tied to the immigration and acculturation experience, usually as a bulwark against a complete abandonment of the immigrant's previous identity. The situation was complicated by a great degree of anticlericalism among many immigrants, especially Italians, and the experience of labor activism, which forced the American Catholic Church into a series of compromises with European tradition long before the 1940s. But for the most part the Catholic Church was for these immigrants what it had been in Europe: the church of the poor, the stern overseer of community life and personal morality, a conservative force, and a fixture of the status quo. Catholic Church organization tended to be rigidly hierarchical, with much of its liturgical practice conducted in Latin. Catholic education was often doctrinaire and authoritarian. According to church rules, Catholic children were forbidden from attending school with non-Catholic chil-dren, but bishops almost never enforced this order. Many American Catholic leaders ardently denounced modern life, especially condemning birth control, divorce, and morally suspect entertainment. Cardinal Dennis Dougherty of Philadelphia went so far as to advocate a Catholic boycott of all movies. As the condition of these immigrant groups changed, however, so did American Catholicism. The most significant change in the life of immigrants during the 1940s was the great nationalizing force of the war and then the unprecedented economic prosperity that followed. The American immigrant became upwardly mobile, middle class, more distinctly American. So too did American Catholicism.

Unionism. Upward mobility for American immigrants was connected to the ability of trade unions to force businesses to grant higher wages and benefits to workers. American Catholicism was tied to the labor movement (two-thirds of all unionized workers were Catholics) and became integral in forming the political base of the New Deal. Competing with Socialists and Communists for the heart and soul of the labor movement, Catholicism made labor more conservative, while labor made Catholicism more liberal. Catholic trade-union organizers such as John J. Burke, John A. Ryan, Raymond A. McGowan, Francis J. Haas, Charles O. Rice, and the Association of Catholic Trade Unionists (ACTU) forced church fathers to abandon their status quo conservatism and actively take up the plight of the poor. More radical was the trade unionism of Dorothy Day and the Catholic Worker Movement, which opened houses of hospitality where the poor and unemployed could find food and shelter. By 1942 thirty-two houses were operating, as well as several rural communes where Catholics practiced simple living. Day and her associates not only advocated more equitable distribution of wealth but challenged the philosophical basis of church hierarchy. The result of these pressures was a Vatican encyclical, *Mystici Corporis* (1943), which significantly restructured the church's organization as a collective entity. Catholicism became less hierarchical and granted a new recognition to the efforts of the laity within the church.

Commonweal. Also important in the liberalization of American Catholicism were the efforts of both Catholic and non-Catholic intellectuals associated with the journal *Commonweal*, founded in 1924. *Commonweal* became the locus for intellectual fusions of traditional Catholicism and the innovations of modernism, including Darwinian evolution, psychoanalysis, pragmatism, and Keynesian economics. The work of the Catholic paleontologist Pierre Teilhard de Chardin provided a viable synthesis of Catholicism and evolution, and biblical scholars such as Edwin V. O'Hara of Kansas City and Martin Hellreigel of Saint Louis pioneered more-modern interpretations of the gospels.

Neo-Thomism. Another intellectual trend with profound consequences for American Catholicism was neo-Thomism. Originally a Continental movement led by the great Christian scholar Étienne Gilson and the philosopher Jacques Maritain, neo-Thomism renewed attention to the work of medieval theologian Thomas Aquinas, who synthesized the Catholic practice and science of his day. Neo-Thomism attempted something similar for the 1940s: a fusion of faith, humanistic philosophy, and modern science. Its most ardent champions in the United States were Fulton J. Sheen, who propagated the concept on his popular radio program; University of Chicago president Robert M. Hutchins; and his associate, philosopher Mortimer Adler.

Liturgical Transformation. The combination of trade unionism, *Commonweal* Catholicism, and neo-Thomism set into motion a revolution in Catholicism that would culminate in the Second Vatican Council of the 1960s. In many ways the reforms of the Second Vatican Council began with Pope Pius XII's encyclical *Mediator Dei* (1947), itself the outcome of modernizing and liberalizing forces, as well as the singular efforts of Virgil Michel, a Benedictine monk from Minnesota whose publishing enterprise, Liturgical Press, was instrumental in prompting liturgical renewal. *Mediator Dei* transformed Catholic liturgical service, providing for vernacular translations of the missal, wider use of vernacular language in preaching and worship, the encouragement of congregational participation, and a renewed emphasis on Holy Communion. Bilingual Catholic education also declined, especially in Polish-speaking schools, as English became the sole language of instruction. These reforms increased popular participation in the church in the late 1940s and sparked a return to the church in the 1950s. From 1940 to 1960 the ranks of Catholic practitioners doubled, from 21 million to 42 million. The relatively liberal, mainstream attitudes of these new communicants would be instrumental in developing support for the increased cooperation among the different American faiths evident in the ecumenical movement, as well as for the reforms of the Second Vatican Council.

Sources:

Sydney E. Ahlstrom, *A Religious History of the American People* (New Haven & London: Yale University Press, 1972);

Jay P. Dolan, *The American Catholic Experience: A History from Colonial Times to the Present* (Garden City, N.Y.: Doubleday, 1985).

AN INTERFAITH SACRIFICE

One of the most frequently told stories of World War II concerned the 1942 sinking of an American troop carrier, the *Dorchester*, by German submarines in the North Atlantic. As the troops scrambled to escape the sinking ship, it was discovered that the complement was four life jackets short. The four chaplains aboard gave their vests to four enlisted men. As retold by survivors, the four chaplains — two Protestant ministers, a rabbi, and a Catholic priest — were last seen praying together on the deck of the doomed ship. The *Dorchester* tale was often repeated during and after the war as an example of the interfaith cooperation possible in the United States.

Source: Arthur Hertzberg, *The Jews in America: Four Centuries of an Uneasy Encounter — A History* (New York: Simon & Schuster, 1989).

THE CHURCHES AND WORLD WAR II

Activism. Like every other institution in American life, the churches of the United States were deeply involved in World War II. Churches provided moral guidance, spiritual advice, and comfort to millions of soldiers in the battlefield and millions of families on the home front. Many members of the clergy enlisted in the military as chaplains, and churches provided Bibles and other religious items to the troops. Churches were often the location of bond rallies and scrap drives. Some clerics advised pacifism during the war and coordinated small opposition groups. Most, however, were engaged in the struggle against Germany and Japan and afterward became important agents in postwar reconstruction. Significant clergymen, such as Reinhold Niebuhr and Francis Spellman, were instrumental in framing American policy during and after the war, and churches and religious periodicals acted as shapers of public opinion throughout the period.

Toward War. The developments of the late 1930s and early 1940s that propelled the world toward war had a different impact on different churches. American Catholics were troubled and divided by events in Europe. Rome was deeply opposed to atheistic communism, and many Catholics in Europe and the United States therefore supported or remained sympathetic to the anti-Communist philosophy of fascism. This was especially the case after Francisco Franco's Fascists attacked Republican Spain in 1936. Franco's claim that he was acting for Spanish Catholicism and rescuing Spain from communism was persuasive among many American Catholics, who raised funds for the Fascist troops. Catholic labor unions and the Catholic Worker movement supported Republican Spain, but the American Catholic leadership was for the most part united behind Franco. After 1940 many in the pro-Franco leadership became advocates of isolationism,

Archbishop Francis Spellman administering communion to American troops in Italy, 1944

especially after the United States extended Lend-Lease aid to Russia in 1941. Catholics closely tied to the Roosevelt administration, however, backed intervention. Catholic leaders such as John A. Ryan, Edwin V. O'Hara, Joseph P. Hurley, James A. Ryan, Bernard Sheil, and New York archbishop Spellman were exceptional in their backing of the administration. Isolationism split the Catholic Worker movement, as prounion leaders followed President Franklin D. Roosevelt's lead and advocated American intervention in the war, while committed pacifists such as Dorothy Day sought to prevent American involvement. Protestant leaders were similarly divided in their sympathies. Robert Calhoun, C. C. Morrison, and Morrison's periodical *Christian Century* were opposed to intervention and advocated Christian pacifism. By contrast, a periodical founded in 1941, *Christianity and Crisis,* mobilized the talents of interventionist Protestants such as John Bennett, Henry Van Dusen, and Francis Miller to attack isolationism. Jews held the greatest unanimity of opinion. With millions of fellow Jews being persecuted by the Nazis, almost all Jewish religious leaders favored intervention.

After Pearl Harbor. As it did with American public opinion generally, the Japanese attack on Pearl Harbor on 7 December 1941 rallied church opinion behind American involvement in the war. Almost every church and denomination backed the war; the "army" of pacifists

so often cited by isolationists dwindled to about 1 percent of draftees. Nearly eight thousand clergymen of every denomination served as chaplains during the war, and home-front churches raised money for the troops and supplied the military with Bibles, prayer books, and devotional literature. Nonetheless, American church leaders remained deeply troubled by the wholesale slaughter of humanity and were stunned by the Holocaust. They attempted to turn the calamity of war to good effect by focusing public opinion on war goals and postwar reconstruction. American Catholic bishops, in a 1943 letter, "The Essentials of a Good Peace," hoped that the war against the Nazis would put to an end racist ideologies that obscured the unity of humanity; a 1944 letter reinforced the war aims articulated in the Atlantic Charter; and in 1945 the bishops pleaded for mercy for the defeated enemies. Spellman, along with John F. O'Hara and William McCarty, helped organize the work of chaplains during the war and coordinated the activities of other humanitarian war organizations such as the War Relief and Emergency Committee and the War Relief Services. Spellman also toured various war fronts, reassuring the troops that "in serving your country and in a just cause, you are also serving God." Other Catholics were less certain about the divine mandate accompanying American troops. In 1944 Catholic theologian John C. Ford objected to the indiscriminate bombing campaigns of the air corps, and the leading Catholic journals of

U.S. postage stamp depicting four chaplains who died on the USS *Dorchester* in February 1943

opinion protested the atomic bombings of Hiroshima and Nagasaki. Even Spellman had his doubts about the Allies' demand that the Axis surrender unconditionally, fearing the demand would prolong an already bloody conflict and result in a vengeful peace.

The Home Front. American religious leaders were also troubled by the war's impact on the home front. Many worried over a rise in ruthlessness and brutality that would be difficult to extinguish after the war. Many also expressed anxiety over the separation of families and feared a rise in juvenile delinquency and sexual promiscuity as a result of absentee fathers and mothers burdened by service in the defense industry. Church boards discussed methods for curbing "traffic in drink," a rising divorce rate, and sensational reports of gambling, prostitution, and teenage gang activity. Their congregants shared these concerns, as one national poll revealed that a majority felt the war was contributing to a rise in general immorality.

War, Faith, and Nationalism. The impact of the war experience on American religion is complex and varied. Undoubtedly, the war turned many Americans toward the church as a source of solace in uncertain times; as was commonly said, "there are no atheists in foxholes." The sheer magnitude of the devastation was humbling, as were calamities such as the Holocaust. Neo-orthodox Protestant theologians especially emphasized that the eruption of war proved the inability of humanity to guide itself without divine assistance, a point they reiterated after Hiroshima. Millions, overwhelmed by the war experience, turned to their churches. Victory in the war, however, convinced many that the United States was God's chosen nation and that American piety was the key to success on the battlefield. Such an attitude led to a kind of cultural arrogance, often underscoring American intervention in foreign affairs or affirming extreme anticommunism. It also led to anxiety over the spiritual condition of American society. If the United States were God's chosen nation, widespread immorality could be a sign of the withdraw of his favor. To prevent this, close policing of the nation's morals might be necessary, and

religion could well become almost compulsory. Dwight D. Eisenhower made this connection between nationalism and piety explicit in a 1946 address. "Without God there could be no American form of government, nor an American way of life," he said. "Recognition of the Supreme Being is the first — and most basic — expression of Americanism."

Source:
Robert Wuthnow, *The Restructuring of American Religion: Society and Faith Since World War II* (Princeton: Princeton University Press, 1988).

COMMUNISM AND THE FAITHFUL

Red Churches. By the end of the 1940s, among anti-Communist crusaders it had become almost axiomatic that communism had infiltrated American churches and was using the pulpit as a base from which to subvert American society. Such beliefs were common among many church leaders, congressional investigators, and policy makers, as seen in the National Security Council Memorandum 68 (1950), which listed the churches as one of the institutions that worldwide communism "sought to stultify and turn against our purposes." As American churches in the 1930s and 1940s had been instrumental in pursuing progressive political causes, anti-Communists suspicious of anything left of center interpreted church advocacy of causes such as civil rights as proof of a Communist conspiracy among the congregations. If anything, however, American churches in the 1940s were foremost among institutions opposing communism and contributing to the McCarthyism of the period. When it came to communism, American churches were first among its opponents.

Catholic Anticommunism. Perhaps the most militantly anti-Communist church in the United States was the Catholic Church. The Vatican had denounced communism following the publication of Karl Marx and Friedrich Engels's *The Communist Manifesto* in 1848. Echoing Rome, American Catholic leaders objected to the atheism and materialism of communism and were suspicious of Communist activity in American trade unions as well as distrusting of Soviet activities abroad. Even during the wartime alliance with the Soviet Union, Catholic leaders criticized Russian activities in Catholic publications. As the Red Army liberated Eastern Europe, American Catholics feared for the fate of East European Catholic churches. The situation was complicated by the fact that some Catholic officials in Eastern Europe had been active or passive collaborators with the Fascists, but Americans viewed the situation unambiguously. For them suppression of Catholicism in the East was symptomatic of Communist authoritarianism. While Pope Pius XII failed to excommunicate any Nazis, even after the Holocaust, he excommunicated Catholics who embraced communism in 1949. Responding to the suppression of Catholicism in the East, archbishop Francis Spellman of New York announced that "Communism is

No better example of the penetration of the Cold War into American theology can be found than in the cult of Fátima. Fátima was the Portuguese location of a purported visit of the Virgin Mary in 1917 — the same year of the Bolshevik Revolution and an aborted radical attack in Portugal. A shepherd child, Lucia dos Santos, claimed to have witnessed the Marian visitation and later connected the event to a prophecy that the Communist regime in Russia would be overthrown and the Soviet Union reclaimed for Christianity. Thereafter, Fátima became central to Cold War Catholicism, and praying to Fátima was claimed to assist the heavenly forces struggling against the Communists.

Unamerican" in February 1946. Archbishop Richard J. Cushing of Boston argued that same year that Catholicism was one of America's "greatest bulwarks" against communism. In 1948 the Catechetical Guild of Saint Paul produced a comic book, *Is This Tomorrow?*, that featured Communists storming Saint Patrick's Cathedral in New York and nailing Archbishop Spellman to the door. The Catholic War Veterans and the Knights of Columbus acted as active anti-Communist groups in the late 1940s, and Fulton J. Sheen used his radio pulpit and books such as *Communism and the Conscience of the West* and *Philosophy of Religion* (both 1948) to espouse the anti-Communist cause. Catholics who had long contended with Communists for leadership in many unions were instrumental in purging the labor unions of Communist influence in 1948 and 1949. And lay Catholics — such as former Communist informants Louis Budenz and Elizabeth Bentley and senators Joseph McCarthy of Wisconsin, Pat McCarran of Nevada, and Brian McMahon of Connecticut — were among the foremost anti-Communist leaders in America.

Protestant Anticommunism. The Catholic Church was not alone in its religious opposition to communism. Many mainline Protestant churches and evangelical church leaders also opposed communism in principle and the Soviet Union in practice. Billy Graham, the evangelical preacher who became a media sensation in the late 1940s, preached an unabashed anti-Communist doctrine during a 1949 Los Angeles revival:

> God is giving us a desperate choice, a choice of either revival or judgment. There is no alternative! . . . The world is divided into two camps! On one side we see Communism . . . [which] has declared war against God, against Christ, against the Bible, and against all religion! . . . Unless the Western world has an old-fashioned revival, we cannot last!

Graham's black-and-white worldview was echoed by many and led many church leaders to advocate anti-Communist political positions. Graham himself backed McCarthy's investigations of the State Department and seconded Republican criticisms of the Truman administration's Asian policy. Anti-Communist Protestants echoed Graham's equation of communism and evil. To the Presbyterian director of the Federal Bureau of Investigation, J. Edgar Hoover, communism was "the moral foe of Christianity." For the most part, however, mainline Protestant church leaders were ambivalent about the anti-Communist crusade, judging it likely to damage progressive political causes in its sweeping attack on communism. Reinhold Niebuhr, the foremost Protestant theologian in the United States, deplored McCarthyism both for its blind assault on progressive political causes and because he believed McCarthy's sweeping charges limited the effectiveness of a genuine anti-Communist crusade. His 1944 book, *The Children of Light and the Children of Darkness,* was often cited by anti-Communists who glossed over the book's subtle anti-authoritarian arguments in their rush to use it to disparage Russia. Their zeal helps to explain the ambivalence many mainline Protestant leaders felt toward anti-communism.

Jews and Anticommunism. The response of American Jews to the anti-Communist crusade of the late 1940s was even more ambiguous than that of Protestant leaders. While many secular Jews had participated in Communist activities in the 1930s, some were soured on communism by the 1939 Nazi-Soviet pact. Many Jews nonetheless remained favorably disposed to left-wing activity because of the tradition of Jewish trade unionism in America and because the Soviet Union had outlawed anti-Semitism. Such Jews became targets of anti-Communist wrath in the late 1940s, which was heavily tinged with anti-Semitism. In a sense much of the Red Scare of the 1940s was a continuation of the anti-Semitism of the 1930s by other means. With the Holocaust repudiating overt displays of anti-Semitism in the United States, American anti-Semites attacked Jews through the vehicle of anti-communism. The Dies committee, militantly anti-Semitic in the 1930s, was better known as the anti-Communist House Un-American Activities Committee (HUAC) in the 1940s. HUAC focused its investigations on education and the motion-picture and television industries, in part because of the influence of Jews in these fields; Jews within the defense establishment — including the father of the atomic bomb, J. Robert Oppenheimer — were the focus of anti-Communist suspicions. At the same time, Jews were becoming increasingly a part of the American mainstream, and some Jews adopted an anti-Communist perspective as part of their general ascent into the mainstream. Some Jews, including Joseph McCarthy's counsels Roy Cohn and David Schine, even became leading anti-Communists, but the anti-Semitic tinges of the crusade limited its appeal to most Jews.

John Foster Dulles, sitting at center, with Reinhold Niebuhr, at his left, and other members of the American delegation at the world Christian conference in Cambridge, England, 1946

Sources:

James Hennesey, *American Catholics: A History of the Roman Catholic Community in the United States* (New York: Oxford University Press, 1981);

Stephen Whitfield, *The Culture of the Cold War* (Baltimore: Johns Hopkins University Press, 1991).

ECUMENISM AND THE WORLD COUNCIL OF CHURCHES

The Ecumenical Spirit. The 1940s brought an unprecedented lessening of tensions between faiths and cooperation between denominations. A spirit of ecumenism, or cooperation between churches, dominated. This new spirit had a variety of sources, including the impact of the Holocaust, the development of Catholic modernism, wartime cooperation between British and American churches, and the suburbanization of churches. At the popular level the new spirit sought to do away with long-standing religious animosities, especially between Catholics and Jews and between Protestants and Catholics. The ecumenical spirit also created new organizational cooperation between denominations, especially in charity work, missionary activities, and political programs. These activities found expression in the creation of the World Council of Churches in 1948 and would result in the creation of a formal ecumenical body, the National Council of Churches, in 1950. By the end of the decade the ecumenical movement had thus become a worldwide phenomenon that was led by many American clergymen, including Henry Van Dusen, John Bennett, and Reinhold Niebuhr.

Wartime Cooperation. Before World War II differing Protestant denominations routinely cooperated with one another in charity work or social reform. In the 1940s these informal experiences became formalized and organized. The Depression led the way, forcing fragmented denominations, such as the Methodists or the Lutherans, to unify for the sake of economic efficiency. World War II especially advanced cooperation. Protestant denominations set aside their theological and liturgical differences to assist one another in ministering to the spiritual needs of soldiers and their families. Coming from diverse backgrounds and often ministering to a broad spectrum of denominations and faiths, army chaplains specialized in harmonizing various elements of different faiths and received an education in the theologies of other faiths in the process. Servicemen themselves set aside religious differences to work with one another during the conflict and were instrumental in eliminating a pervasive anti-Catholicism present in American culture.

Tolerance. Ecumenism and interfaith tolerance had strong intellectual foundations in the 1940s. The Holo-

May 1942 hearing to determine whether Father Charles Coughlin's *Social Justice* should lose its second-class mailing privileges

caust thoroughly discredited anti-Semitic cultural tendencies, especially among intellectuals, and demonstrated to all but the most insensitive the dangerous possibilities of vitriolic religious intolerance. Among theologians of the three great American faiths, the war and the Holocaust engendered a sense of humility and sparked a restructuring of the theological roots of all three faiths in order to reassert their humanist core. Catholic theologian Jacques Maritain, Jewish intellectual Martin Buber, and Protestant thinkers Reinhold Niebuhr and Paul Tillich borrowed liberally from one another and created rigorous, humanist theologies for their respective faiths.

World Council of Churches. The World Council of Churches was the ultimate expression of Christian ecumenism. A federation of Protestant and Eastern Orthodox churches, the World Council of Churches sponsored cooperative mission work, theological study, and humanitarian assistance. The first steps toward the World Council of Churches were taken at a World Missionary Conference in Edinburgh, Scotland, in 1910. An attempt to coordinate the missionary activities among various denominations, the conference established a basis for broader interdenominational cooperation. Thereafter, British theologians especially sought reconciliation between various Christian denominations. In the United States similar goals were pursued by the Federal Council of the Churches of Christ, an interdenominational group that coordinated peace activities with funding from Andrew Carnegie. World War I also advanced ecumenical tendencies, thanks in part to the ardent participation of Eastern Orthodox clergy. Various conferences continued to pursue the ecumenical ideal throughout the 1920s and 1930s, especially in response to Nazi attacks upon German Jews and churches. In 1937 the second World Conference on Life and Work convened in Oxford, England,

and drafted the organizational foundations for a World Council of Churches. World War II interrupted this work but at the same time greatly advanced it. The World Council, not yet formally convened, nonetheless acted as an administrative agency to coordinate church activities in occupied Europe; it also abetted the flight of refugees and provided services for prisoners of war. The American Bible Society donated a constant stream of devotional literature, distributed through the World Council. When war ended in Europe, the World Council was preoccupied with reconstruction assistance, working with the United Nations Relief and Rehabilitation Association (UNRRA) and the International Refugee Organization (IRO). World Council members were especially instrumental in rebuilding a denazified German church. In 1948 the World Council convened its first conference as an official body in Amsterdam. Ecumenism had been institutionalized in American Christian life.

Sources:

G. K. A. Bell, *The Kingship of Christ* (Harmondsworth, U.K. & Baltimore: Penguin, 1954);

Darril Hudson, *The Ecumenical Movement in World Affairs* (London: Weidenfeld & Nicolson, 1969).

FUNDAMENTALISM AND LIBERAL PROTESTANTISM

Toward Liberalism. Since the Civil War the mainline Protestant denominations proved surprisingly capable of adapting intellectual challenges such as Darwinian evolution, biblical research, artistic modernism, and philosophical naturalism into their theologies and practices. There was a general trend toward liberalism, which meant that mainline Protestantism attempted to remain broadly and optimistically humanistic and began treating the Bible less as a book of literal truth than as a book of symbolic and metaphoric wisdom. Not all Protestants followed the trend, however. One important group of Protestants rejected almost all of the philosophical innovations of the modern era and attempted a return to the "fundamentals" of Protestantism. At the Niagara Bible Conference of 1895 fundamentalists set forth five essential articles of faith: the inerrancy of Scripture, the divinity and virgin birth of Christ, the idea of "substitutionary atonement" (Christ taking the place of sinners on the cross), the physical Resurrection, and the bodily return of Christ to earth. These fundamentals, amended and supplemented, were widely publicized in a series of tracts published between 1910 and 1915 called *The Fundamentals*. They became the basis of modern fundamentalism.

Controversy. Before the 1940s fundamentalists often clashed with liberals, especially at Protestant seminaries and other sites of religious instruction. Well-known liberals such as Harry Emerson Fosdick often clashed in Protestant periodicals with fundamentalists such as J. Gresham Machen. In the 1920s differences of opinion regarding the literal truth of the Bible became heated, culminating in the famous Scopes trial of 1925 and the denunciations of liberalism by flamboyant evangelist Billy Sunday. The Scopes trial and Sunday did fundamentalism more harm than good. By the end of World War II fundamentalists were generally in retreat, their theology associated by the public with ignorance and intolerance. American Protestantism seemed to have moved definitively into the liberal camp.

Realignment. The victory of liberal Protestantism was less than complete, however. Increasingly suburban and socially oriented, liberal Protestantism tended to lack both intellectual rigor and spiritual fulfillment. Liberal ministers struggled to come to grips with the blow that Nazism and the Holocaust gave to their optimistic assessments of human nature. Liberal Protestantism seemed to drift theologically and spiritually, although the intervention of neo-orthodox theology revitalized the theological premises of liberal Protestantism. At the same time, fundamentalists were mobilizing. Harold J. Ockenga, pastor of the historic Park Street Church in Boston, believed he could recruit new congregants from among the ranks of demoralized adherents of liberal Protestantism. He helped found the National Association of Evangelicals (NAE) in 1942. The next year fundamentalists organized Youth for Christ, an agency of teen recruitment. A broad coalition of Protestant conservatives, the NAE attempted to foster interfundamentalist unity. By 1947 it had grown to include thirty denominations and more than 1.3 million members. Ockenga was a leading spokesman for "the new evangelicals," a phrase he coined in 1947. Another champion of this movement was Carl F. H. Henry, who in 1956 would found and edit *Christianity Today.* By 1967 this evangelical journal had 150,000 paid subscribers. In 1947 Henry wrote *The Uneasy Conscience of Modern Fundamentalism,* in which he issued a call for American conservatives to combine social responsibility and biblical fidelity. The year 1947 saw the founding of the Fuller Theological Seminary in Pasadena, California, one of the most respected evangelical schools and a center for scholarly fundamentalism. During the closing years of the 1940s there was a renewal of evangelical scholarship, led by the publication of E. J. Carnell's *Introduction to Christian Apologetics* (1948). This work established Carnell as the new intellectual spokesman for conservatism, and he became president of Fuller. In 1949 the Evangelical Theological Society was formed as a professional organization committed to the inerrancy of Scripture and the promotion of evangelical scholarship. That year also brought a dynamic evangelist, Billy Graham, to public attention. Graham conducted a highly publicized revival and crusade in the fall that attracted thousands of participants. With church attendance rising for both liberals and fundamentalists, theological controversies between the two groups would soon resume.

Sources:
Winthrop S. Hudson, *Religion in America: A Historical Account of the Development of American Religious Life* (New York: Scribners, 1981);

Gerald L. K. Smith, Father Charles E. Coughlin, and Francis E. Townsend, right-wing political commentators

William R. Hutchison, *The Modernist Impulse in American Protestantism* (Cambridge, Mass.: Harvard University Press, 1976).

Judaism and Assimilation

Drift. Like Catholicism, Judaism in America was largely a religion of immigrants. By 1937 nearly 5 million Jews lived in the United States, nearly all of them recent immigrants or children of immigrants, with half of them living in New York City. Like Catholicism, therefore, Judaism in America was tied to the assimilation process. Jews who were determined to maintain a preexistent cultural identity clung to Judaism in its Old World, orthodox form. Many spoke Yiddish, a language unique to east European ghettos, and attempted a degree of isolation from American culture in tightly knit urban neighborhoods. By the 1930s, however, most Jews were drifting away from their faith, especially those determined to assimilate into American society. Many first-generation Jews were repelled by the orthodox religious practices of their parents, burdened as it was with the taint of "foreignness." A 1935 survey in New York City revealed that almost 75 percent of young Jews failed to attend synagogue in the past year. The majority of Jews in the Depression identified themselves more as an ethnic group than a religious faith, and many abandoned any sense of Jewish identity whatsoever. The 1940s were different. Inspired by the anti-Semitism of the Nazis and others, by the rise of Zionism and the establishment of the state of Israel, and by the invigoration of American variants of Judaism, many Jews returned to their faith.

Pre–World War II anti-Semitic political cartoon

Anti-Semitism. Nothing was more instrumental in sparking a resurgence of Jewish consciousness than the anti-Semitism of the interwar years. Adolf Hitler and the Nazis were not alone in scapegoating Jews for the economic dislocations of the era. Anti-Semites in the United States, such as Charles Coughlin, Gerald L. K. Smith, and Henry Ford, offered elaborate conspiracy theories blaming the Depression and communism on Jews. Although such anti-Semitism was fundamentally rhetorical in the United States, in combination with the oppression of Jews in Europe such pronouncements reunified a Jewish community that had begun to fragment. The Holocaust, of course, advanced this process, unifying the community in collective grief. As important as the Holocaust was in subsequently contributing to a sense of Jewish identity, however, in the 1940s Jews cited the Holocaust more often as a phenomenon unlikely to occur in the United States. The postwar environment, with its suburbs and upward mobility, moreover, tended to mold Judaism into less of a distinctive ethnic philosophy and more into a American faith akin to Catholicism and Protestantism — one with regular family services and social activities. When combined with a common pride many Jews felt about their World War II service, the Holocaust and the suburbs actually served to knit Jewish identity more closely to American nationalism.

Zionism. The establishment of the state of Israel, coming soon after the Holocaust in Europe, also returned many Jews to their religious roots. Zionism, a movement to return the Jews to Palestine, was connected both to the anti-Semitism of the Nazis and to that of American bigots. In the 1930s organizations such as the American Jewish Committee and the American Jewish Congress raised funds to facilitate the creation of Israel in Palestine, arguing that only a Jewish state could protect Jews from anti-Semitism. After World War II, American Jewish groups such as United Jewish Appeal financed the transportation of Jewish Holocaust survivors from Europe to Palestine. In 1947 United Jewish Appeal raised $117 million for the Zionists. Even American Jews who were not active Zionists sympathized with the Zionist movement; after Israel was established in 1948, it enjoyed widespread Jewish support.

Conservative and Reform Judaism. While anti-Semitism and Zionism were important in aiding the postwar return to Judaism, neither was specifically religious. Conservative and Reform Judaism, however, were sets of religious practices instrumental in returning Jews to their faith. By the 1940s Judaism in America was divided into three fundamental branches: Orthodox Judaism, rooted in Old World ritual, was declining, but slowly; Reform Judaism, incorporating many Protestant concepts and modern scientific ideas, enjoyed steady popularity; and Conservative Judaism, a fusion of Orthodox and Reform practice, was gaining adherents. After World War II both Conservative and Reform Judaism led a renewal in the faith. Reform theologians, such as Leo S. Baeck, rethought the universalism that was a part of the Reform tradition before World War II. He singled out Judaism as a faith of moral dedication, oriented toward reform in this world. In the wake of the war Conservative rabbis, especially at the Jewish Theological Seminary in New York, rejected many of the more optimistic assessments of human nature present in liberal humanism and embraced the existentialist theologies of thinkers such as Martin Buber and Abraham Heschel. Their work was similar to that of neo-orthodox Protestant theologians in that they renewed Judaism as a serious moral philosophy and appealed to many lapsed congregants. Conservative and Reform Judaism became distinctly modern American versions of the faith, capable of being embraced at the same time that Jews assimilated into American society.

Revival. By the mid 1950s observers were discussing the Jewish "revival," and new Jewish congregations in the suburbs were developing. Five times as many Jews attended Reform synagogues in 1956 as had in 1936, and the growth among Conservative congregations was nearly as great. As Jews moved out of insular urban neighborhoods to affluent and predominantly Protestant suburban neighborhoods, increased Jewish religious practice helped maintain a sense of distinctive culture, and the combination of Reform Judaism's restatement of ideals and Conservative Judaism's moral seriousness fired a new Jewish imagination in America — ironically at the very moment when Jewish assimilation into American society became complete.

Sources:

Sydney E. Ahlstrom, *A Religious History of the American People* (New Haven & London: Yale University Press, 1972);

Winthrop S. Hudson, *Religion in America: A Historical Account of American Religious Life*, third edition (New York: Scribners, 1981).

NEO-ORTHODOXY

Modernization. The most important development in theology in the 1940s was neo-orthodoxy, a significant reformulation of the Calvinist core of Protestantism. Guided by Protestant theologians such as Reinhold Niebuhr and his brother H. Richard Niebuhr, as well as Swiss theologian Karl Barth and German exile Paul Tillich, neo-orthodoxy harmonized liberal Protestantism with a host of modern concepts — including existentialism, psychoanalysis, and Marxism — to revitalize the Calvinist emphasis on sin and individual free will. Like Catholic modernism and the reconstruction of Conservative and Reform Judaism, the neo-orthodox intellectual movement began during the Depression but became most important in the 1940s. During the decade, events such as World War II, the Holocaust, and the atomic bombing of Hiroshima and Nagasaki seemed to sanction the neo-orthodox worldview, which was based on the insufficiency of human reason and good will. Disseminated in hundreds of seminaries in the 1940s and 1950s, neo-orthodox theology was profoundly influential with Protestant clergy.

Sin. Perhaps the most important aspect of neo-orthodoxy was its reformulation of the concept of sin. Orthodox Calvinism insisted that sin was innate in individuals; only the redeeming power of God could overcome it. Neo-orthodox theologians argued much the same by use of modern concepts. To Reinhold Niebuhr, sin was the human capacity for solipsism, for making oneself the center of the world. Like Sigmund Freud he postulated a fundamentally unconscious and wicked side to human decency, a side against which the penitent Christian must endlessly strive. Such a notion sat uncomfortably with the more optimistic mainline Protestantism of the era. After the calamities of World War II, however, many believers began to embrace Niebuhr's reformulation of human sin.

Paradox. Calvinist orthodoxy considered human beings both potentially divine and actually depraved; neo-orthodoxy also considered human nature as fundamentally paradoxical. To Niebuhr, human advance was inevitably plagued by backsliding moments of shattering barbarism, and societies, because they compounded the paradoxical essence of individuals, were inevitably rocked by bloodletting and civil war. He favored the parable of the Tower of Babel, a stunning technological achievement whose foundations were hopelessly flawed. Niebuhr's insight was almost prophetic: his allusion to the Tower of Babel was often cited after the development of the atomic bomb. For Niebuhr, humanity's essential paradox meant that the greater the achievement of civilization, the greater civilization's potential for evil. Such a theology explained to many how Germany, one of the world's great cultures, could have disintegrated into Nazism.

Loneliness. The neo-orthodox theologians were deeply influenced by the existentialist philosophy prominent in Europe during the interwar period, seeing in it a more modern expression of the orthodox Calvinist notion of loneliness and dread. The philosophy of Danish thinker Søren Kierkegaard was particularly appealing, because he argued that existential dread was derived from human sin. Such dread was also a function of the isolation and loneliness of the individual, whom the neo-orthodox theologians argued would remain desperate and lonely without God's saving grace. The neo-orthodox emphasis on the loneliness of the human condition appealed to many who faced the traumas of the war experience without assistance.

Hope and Faith. In order to resolve the sinfulness, paradox, and loneliness that plagued the human condition, neo-orthodox theologians recommended religious conversion and pious behavior. "Man does not know himself truly except as he knows himself confronted by

God," wrote Niebuhr in the manifesto of neo-orthodoxy, his two-volume *The Nature and Destiny of Man* (1941, 1943). "Only in that confrontation does he become aware of his full stature and freedom and of the evil in him." For neo-orthodox theologians, only acceptance of God's salvation can mediate human tragedy, granting finite humans a sense of infinite possibility, making possible progress despite human destructiveness, and perfecting moral behavior in light of innate depravity. The neo-orthodox sense of human limits and humility had enormous appeal after the upheavals of the war and the Holocaust and offered a powerful corrective to the more utopian estimates of human nature characteristic among many Protestants during the Depression. As such, neo-orthodoxy became an important component of postwar Protestantism and perhaps the best restatement of the Protestant tradition in the twentieth century.

Sources:

Sydney E. Ahlstrom, *A Religious History of the American People* (New Haven & London: Yale University Press, 1972);

Richard Wightman Fox, *Reinhold Niebuhr: A Biography* (New York: Pantheon, 1985).

POSTWAR PROSPERITY AND THE RETURN TO THE CHURCHES

Revival. The most distinguishing feature of American religion in the 1940s was its revival. Church membership, in decline before the war, skyrocketed in the latter half of the decade. Postwar prosperity renewed the economic base of many American churches, which expanded rapidly. New churches were built in the burgeoning postwar suburbs; established urban ministries were renewed. Most importantly, the economic prosperity of the postwar years made churchgoing into something of a status symbol, a badge of upward mobility. While there were theological and spiritual reasons for the return to the churches, most notably the impact of World War II, millions of prosperous working-class families aspiring to the ranks of the middle class saw churchgoing as a definitively all-American activity. Church membership in the late 1940s was both a product and a symbol of American affluence.

Decline. Most American denominations had declined in membership and revenues during the Depression. The stock-market crash of 1929 had wiped out the investments and holdings of many churches. As churches reduced services to cut expenses, they lost members. Total church expenditures from 1926 to 1936 declined 36 percent. Although some churches (especially evangelical churches) increased their memberships during the 1930s, the majority lost members or entered into a period of slow growth. By 1940 less than half the population of the United States maintained any church affiliation.

Recovery. Wartime economic recovery prefaced the postwar return to the churches. After World War II churches had the revenues to extend their services and activities, and they attracted new members. By 1950, 55 percent of Americans cited a church affiliation. According to a National Opinion Research Center poll in 1946, two out of every three Americans claimed to attend religious services at least once a month. The return to the churches was so great that many denominations complained of a shortage of clergy. The Southern Baptists found that only ten thousand of its twenty-seven thousand churches were ministered to by full-time pastors; the Methodists discovered only fifteen thousand of its forty thousand pulpits were occupied by trained, full-time clergy. Lay leadership covered the shortage of clergy but did so inadequately, and seminaries around the country began active recruitment campaigns. By 1950 Protestant and Jewish seminaries had doubled their enrollments; Catholics increased theirs 30 percent. The shortage of clergy was a sign of the robust health of American religion after World War II. Drawn back to the churches and synagogues by the trauma of the war experience, the shock of the Holocaust, and the social conformity of the newly emergent suburbs, Americans of every background and denomination renewed their association with religion.

Boom. The booming expansion in postwar church building represents the revival of postwar religion well. During the Depression declining revenues had for the most part suspended church building. Though church revenues increased during the war — growing from $1.06 billion to $1.74 billion, an increase of 64 percent — wartime material shortages prevented church construction. By V-J Day in August 1945, most congregations had done little or no physical expansion for fifteen years. They quickly made up for lost time. In Decatur, Illinois, for example, sixteen new Methodist churches were built from 1945 to 1960; San Diego added eleven new Baptist churches during the same period. The Southern Baptist Convention alone built five hundred new churches between 1946 and 1949; Catholics added 3,000 new parishes, opened 1,000 new elementary schools, and erected 125 new hospitals. By 1950, $336 million was being spent on religious construction in order to house the millions of new congregants and schoolchildren returning to the church. Like the newly constructed suburbs and superhighways, the recently built churches (usually modern in style) became a fixture of the postwar landscape.

Anxiety. While religion as an institution was revived by the postwar prosperity, many theologians expressed anxiety concerning the motives behind the revival. Many feared that religion had become another consumable commodity in American life akin to new cars, homes, and televisions. Clergy advised their congregations not to become too comfortable with worldly possessions. As John Mackay, president of Princeton Theological Seminary, cautioned in 1948, "Lovely things . . . will come to you, many things that you will cherish, that you will be proud to have. Remember this. Do not use them for ostentation but only for inspiration." Privately, many clergy expressed disdain for religious fervor that went no deeper than

RELIGION IN THE COURTS

Although there had been many cases involving the establishment clause of the First Amendment prior to 1947, the case of *Everson* v. *Board of Education of Ewing Township* that year has endured as one of the most significant cases on the establishment of religion in the history of the U.S. Supreme Court *Everson* was a case in which the Court held that the New Jersey statute providing state support for bus transportation to parochial schools was constitutional. Arch Everson contended that the state had no business reimbursing parents whose children were bused to schools owned and operated by the Catholic Church. But the court ruled, by a five-to-four vote, against Everson, stating that money is given to parents of students who are sent to acceptable schools; no money is given to the schools themselves.

In 1948 another major case involving church/state relations was decided, *McCollum* v. *Board of Education.* In an eight-to-one decision the U.S. Supreme Court nullified a released-time program in Illinois that made it possible for students to receive sectarian instruction on school time and on school property. A time set aside by public-school districts at the start of each school day for prayer, the court held, violates the Constitution.

Sources: John C. Bennett, *Christians and the State* (New York: Scribners, 1958);

Robert F. Drinan, *Religion, the Courts, and Public Policy* (New York: McGraw-Hill, 1963);

Leo Pfeffer, *Church, State, and Freedom,* second edition (Boston: Beacon, 1967);

Joseph Tussman, ed., *The Supreme Court on Church and State* (New York: Oxford University Press, 1962).

weekly church attendance for the purposes of "keeping up with the Joneses." As the 1940s gave way to 1950s developments such as drive-in churches, mail-order ministry, and televangelists, mainline church leaders became increasingly uncomfortable with the combination of commerce and faith. So too were the baby boomers, growing up in staid churches of the 1950s. Both groups would experiment with countercultural expressions of religiosity in the 1960s in an attempt to revitalize the spiritual poverty endemic in the prosperous postwar congregations of the late 1940s.

Source:
Robert Wuthnow, *The Restructuring of American Religion: Society and Faith Since World War II* (Princeton: Princeton University Press, 1988).

RELIGIOUS BEST-SELLERS

Growth. As a natural consequence of increased interest in religion during the 1940s, along with growing prosperity, sales of books dealing with religious matters prospered during the decade. Religious best-sellers ranged from popular self-help books and humorous reflections on religious life to novels with religious characters or situations to studies by or about well-known religious figures.

Bible Characters. In 1940 Alan Watts published *The Meaning of Happiness,* which dealt not with a future reward for the good but with a present reality for those living in harmony with nature. Two best-selling novels appeared in 1942: *The Robe,* by Lloyd C. Douglas, and Franz Werfel's *The Song of Bernadette.* Also that year, the pastor for forty-four years of New York's Madison Avenue Methodist Church, Ralph W. Sockman, published *The Highway of God,* his Lyman Beecher Lectures on Preaching from the previous year at Yale University. Best-sellers for 1943 included Sholem Asch's *The Apostle,* a life of Paul, and *On Being a Real Person,* by an eloquent preacher and preeminent apologist for liberal Christianity, Harry Emerson Fosdick. That same year saw the release of *David,* a life of the biblical king by Duff Cooper; Col. Robert L. Scott's *God Is My Co-Pilot;* and *Clerical Errors,* the recollections of a minister named Louis Tucker.

Quakers and Mormons. *Caesar and Christ* by Will Durant appeared in 1944, along with *Papa Was a Preacher* by Alyene Porter, a humorous account by a Texas parson's daughter. That same year saw the release of *Chaim Weizmann,* edited by Meyer W. Weisgal, Camille M. Cianfarra's *The Vatican and the War,* and *Heaven Below* by E. H. Clayton, the story of thirty years as a missionary teacher in China. In 1945 *The Friendly Persuasion* by Jessamyn West featured a Quaker family in nineteenth-century Indiana, and *The Human Life of Jesus* by John Erskine appeared. Two additional books with religious themes were published that year: *Children of the Covenant* by Richard Scowcroft, the story of the Mormons; and *The World, The Flesh, and Father Smith* by Bruce Marshall, about a Catholic priest in a Scottish town.

Healing and Peace of Mind. In 1946 Rabbi Joshua Loth Liebman's best-selling book of spiritual self-help, *Peace of Mind,* was published, as were Russell Janney's *The Miracle of the Bells* and Gladys Schmitt's *David the King.* The following year saw the publication of Arnold Toynbee's best-seller, *An Outline to History,* an updated abridgment of the first six volumes of Toynbee's *A Study of History.* The West would survive, he said, only if westerners turn to God. The year 1947 also saw the publication of Agnes Sligh Turnbull's *The Bishop's Mantle* and Pentecostal faith healer Oral Roberts's book *If You Need Healing — Do These Things.*

On 25 September 1949 a thirty-one-year-old preacher from North Carolina, Billy Graham, began what was to be a three-week revival under a Ringling Brothers circus tent in Los Angeles. Crowds were impressive but not at capacity until press magnate William Randolph Hearst catapulted Graham into the national spotlight with a two-word memo to his associates: "Puff Graham." Now the hottest ticket in town, 350,000 came to hear him, including Gene Autry and Jane Russell. Cecil B. DeMille offered him a screen test. Three weeks stretched into eight, and the postwar revival of religion in America had found its champion.

Source: William Martin, *A Prophet with Honor: The Billy Graham Story* (New York: Morrow, 1991).

Merton and Gandhi. The year 1948 saw the release of two huge best-sellers: Lloyd C. Douglas's novel about Peter, *The Big Fisherman,* and Trappist monk Thomas Merton's spiritual autobiography, *The Seven Storey Mountain.* Also appearing were Jean-Paul Sartre's *Anti-Semite and Jew;* Blanche Cannon's *Nothing Ever Happens Sunday Morning,* about the effects of a minister's self-righteousness; and *Nehru on Gandhi,* by Jawaharlal Nehru.

Banner Year. The year 1949 was the most notable year in the decade for best-sellers; no fewer than seven appeared. Peter Marshall's sermons and prayers *Mr. Jones, Meet the Master* was published by his wife, Catherine. It stayed on the best-seller list for almost a year. Fulton Oursler's best-known work, *The Greatest Story Ever Told,* was a landmark in American popular piety. Paul Blanshard criticized Roman Catholic hierarchy in *American Freedom and Catholic Power.* Norman Vincent Peale published *A Guide to Confident Living,* and Sholem Asch's *Mary,* the story of the mother of Jesus, appeared. Vincent J. Sheean's *Lead, Kindly Light: Gandhi and the Way to Peace* was released, as was Fulton J. Sheen's best-selling book on conversion, *Peace of Soul.* That same year Perry Miller published *Jonathan Edwards,* and Ann Carnahan's *The Vatican* appeared. Fosdick released *The Man from Nazareth as His Companions Saw Him,* and Sinclair Lewis published his twenty-first novel, *The God-Seeker,* about a Christian missionary who seeks God amid the Sioux in the mid nineteenth century.

Source:
Donald B. Meyer, *The Positive Thinkers: A Study of the Quest for Health, Wealth, and Personal Power from Mary Baker Eddy to Norman Vincent Peale* (Garden City, N.Y.: Doubleday, 1965).

THE RELIGIOUS RESPONSE TO THE ATOMIC BOMB

"I Am Become Death." "I am become Death, the shatterer of worlds," a line from the Bhagavad Gita, was J. Robert Oppenheimer's only thought after the blinding flash of the first atomic bomb test at Alamogordo, New Mexico, on 16 July 1945. The August bombing of the Japanese cities of Hiroshima and Nagasaki had a less literary relation to death: hundreds of thousands died in the blasts or from the radiation sickness that followed. Such devastation and the technology that made it possible naturally evoked much commentary from theologians and the clergy. Despite the fact that the public overwhelmingly approved of the atomic bomb, America's religious leaders responded to the bomb less unanimously. Their doubts and misgivings about living in an atomic world soon became part of American popular culture.

Protests. Most Americans agreed with theologian Reinhold Niebuhr that the bombings of Hiroshima and Nagasaki were justified, because it was "used to save the lives of thousands of American soldiers who would otherwise have perished on the beaches of Japan." The vast majority of Protestant and Catholic clergy deplored the presence of atomic weapons but maintained that their use to end the war was justified — and perhaps would be justified in the future. Protestant layman Arthur H. Compton went further, seeing in the American development of the bomb a sign of God's providence. "Atomic power is ours," Compton told an Episcopal Church conference, "and who can deny it was God's will that we should have it?" Some clergy, however, dissented from such thinking. Immediately after the bombing a group of thirty-four clergy denounced the bomb as "an atrocity of a new magnitude," stating that its "reckless and irresponsible employment against an already virtually beaten foe will have to receive judgment before God and the conscience of humankind." Niebuhr was sufficiently ambivalent about the use of the bomb to sign a 1946 report by the Federal Council of Churches, which condemned the bombing as "morally indefensible." "As the power that first used the atomic bomb under these circumstances," the report stated, "we have sinned grievously against the law of God and against the people of Japan."

Apocalypse. Some religious observers interpreted the development of the atomic bomb as presaging the end of the world. To them, the destructive power of the weapon made possible the apocalypse prophesied in the Bible. One Manhattan Project scientist wrote that "humanity stands on a tiny ledge above the abyss of annihilation." A 1948 fundamentalist periodical argued, "The hands of the clock of Bible prophecy appear to be moving onward and upward to the time when it must strike — the midnight hour." In 1949 Baptist evangelist Billy Graham, conducting a revival in Los Angeles at the same time President Harry S Truman revealed that the Soviet Union also possessed the atomic bomb, urged people to

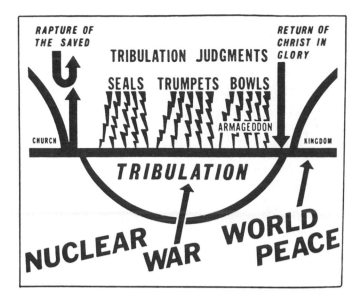

Post–WW II prophecy chart distributed by the Bible Believers' Evangelistic Association predicting the end of the world

repent their sins immediately because, he said, "An arms race unprecedented in the history of the world is driving us madly toward destruction!"

Humility. Most religious interpreters viewed the development of the atomic bomb as an occasion for increased humility on the part of individuals. Niebuhr stressed the paradox of the bomb's development, that the greatest technological achievement of humanity quite possibly could lead to its extinction. As such, an increased sense of Christian humility was necessary to prevent the irresponsible use of such weaponry. The *Christian Century* in a 15 August 1945 editorial said that instead of indulging in self-congratulation, Americans "should now be standing in penitence before the Creator of the power which the atom has hitherto kept inviolate." Jewish theologians argued much the same. In 1945 Rabbi Beryl D. Cohon of Temple Sinai in Brookline, Massachusetts, said, "We have drawn from the infinite storehouse of God's world enormous powers, and have converted them into instruments of destruction. . . . Unless we discipline the revelation of atomic power by the revelation of Mount Sinai, making it subservient to the Moral Law, we shall . . . reduce our earth to a dead cinder spinning in space in infinite futility."

Activism. A corollary to the argument that the atomic bomb occasioned increased humility was the demand that moral individuals work harder to achieve a harmonious, peaceful world where atomic war was impossible. "We must recognize that a desperate struggle is on for the soul of the world," one Methodist minister maintained, a struggle that "requires . . . a great godly company of men and women with no axe to grind, desiring only to save, serve, help and heal." A 1946 *American Scholar* symposium on the bomb called for a "moral transformation" to eliminate war. A Michigan rabbi demanded that human-

ity enter its "adulthood" in order to control the bomb. Lewis Mumford in his book *Program for Survival* (1946) called for the mobilization of religion to instruct men and women in the art of self-control. All the great religions, he said, had sought to curb destructive impulses and foster love. In a nuclear age, he argued, religion must go further and reduce conceit, complacency, and pride. Richard M. Fagley, a member of the Federal Council of Churches Commission on a Just and Durable Peace, wrote just two months after the bombs were dropped on Japan that the only alternative to total world disaster was "repentance and regeneration." The fate of the world, he said, "depends upon the ability of the moral and religious forces . . . to call men effectively to repentance, worship, service." Such advocacy led religious practitioners in two directions: toward moral judgment of the self and regeneration and toward the social activism necessary to prevent war in the future. Both responses would be important in the coming decades, becoming a permanent part of American culture and contributing to the social conformity of the 1950s, the civil rights and antiwar movements of the 1960s, the neoconservatism of the 1970s and 1980s, and the antinuclear movement of the early 1980s.

Sources:

Paul S. Boyer, *By The Bomb's Early Light: American Thought and Culture at the Dawn of the Atomic Age* (New York: Pantheon, 1985);

Richard W. Fox, *Reinhold Niebuhr: A Biography* (New York: Harper & Row, 1985);

Edward L. Long, *The Christian Response to the Atomic Crisis* (Philadelphia: Westminster, 1950);

Mark Silk, *Spiritual Politics: Religion and America Since World War II* (New York: Simon & Schuster, 1988);

Robert Wuthnow, *The Restructuring of American Religion: Society and Faith Since World War II* (Princeton: Princeton University Press, 1988).

RELIGIOUS RESPONSE TO THE HOLOCAUST

A Muted Memory. As horrific as was the Holocaust in retrospect, it is surprising how muted the response to the calamity was in the 1940s. For non-Jews the Holocaust tended to be discussed in the context of German barbarism, a manifestation of the moral bankruptcy of war, or a sign of deep-seated human depravity. Many associated it with the other catastrophes of the period — with Japanese brutality toward prisoners of war, Japanese medical experimentation in Manchuria, and the Bataan death march in the Philippines; with the Lidice massacre and the murders in Katyn Forest; with scorched-earth warfare in Russia; with carpet bombing of European cities; and with V-2 rockets and the atom bombing of Hiroshima and Nagasaki.

Refugee Policy. As terrible as these events were, to a great extent they paled before the intentional, systematic extermination of 9 million innocent human beings (6 million of them Jewish) in the Nazi death factories. Placing the Holocaust in context perhaps assuaged more than

Former inmate, in striped uniform, providing verification for an Allied observer that the oven at Nordhausen had been used as a crematorium

a few guilty consciences: although the Nazis established the death camps, many nationalities were complicit in the Holocaust, especially in eastern Europe. Western governments, including that of the United States, continually downplayed the Nazi oppression of Jews before World War II, and none of the democracies liberalized their immigration policies during the Depression to provide German and east European Jews with refuge. In 1938, in fact, after the Nazis had begun wholesale appropriation of Jewish businesses, public-opinion polls showed that 83 percent of Americans favored increasing immigration restrictions. In 1939 only 10 percent of the legal quota of Jewish immigrants to the United States was filled. In 1939, moreover, a proposal to admit twenty thousand Jewish children to the United States was killed in Congress. Despite press reports of Nazi oppression, there remained considerable anti-Semitism within the United States. During the Depression anti-Semites such as Charles Coughlin, Gerald L. K. Smith, and Henry Ford had reinforced popular anti-Semitic stereotypes. As late as 1944, polls revealed that 65 percent of the public believed that Jews held too much American wealth and power. Popular opposition to refugee immigration remained high. The 1939 tragedy of the *St. Louis*, a German ship filled with nearly nine hundred Jews, illustrates the point. When the ship attempted to dock in the United States they were turned away and ultimately forced to return to Hamburg, after which the majority met their deaths later in the camps. While after the outbreak of war the U.S. State Department approved the admission of thirty-two hundred prominent Jewish intellectuals, academics, artists, and scientists, in June 1941 it cut off the migration, arguing that spies had infiltrated the immigrant stream. The Nazis initiated their "final solution" soon after.

War Refugee Board. By fall 1942 news of the Holocaust had reached American Jewish leaders, who pleaded in vain for some type of rescue attempt from the government. The government rejected proposals to bomb the rail lines to the death camps or to bomb the camps directly on the grounds that it would involve too great a reordering of war priorities. Not until 22 January 1944 did the Roosevelt administration establish a War Refugee Board, which restructured immigration policy and actively attempted to rescue east European Jews. The board did have some success rescuing Hungarian Jews, paying ransoms to Nazi officials in return for Jewish lives, but for the majority of Jews in Europe it was too late. By the end of the war fewer than 111,000 Jews had been rescued and provided refuge by the United States. However, there was little the American government could do. The Nazis were so determined to exterminate the Jews that they compromised their war effort badly and raced to murder as many Jews as possible, even in the closing days of the war. Even in Hungary more than half a million Jews died in the gas chambers.

Jewish Response. While American Jewish leaders unanimously condemned Nazi policies toward Jews even before the Holocaust, they were by no means united in recommending a response to the crisis. Boycotts of German goods, financial assistance to relatives, and proposals to ransom German Jews were forwarded; due to wrangling within the American Jewish community and slim support from non-Jews, all floundered. These proposals were complicated by Zionist resistance to British rule in Palestine and Jewish support for British resistance to the Nazis. Zionists argued that the laggard response of the Western democracies to Nazi oppression was proof the Jews must establish an independent Hebrew state; others continued to seek the help of Gentiles. The wrangling continued, no unified program developed, and no real rescue was made. Given the anti-Semitism within the United States, the chaos of war, and the sheer physical inability to move into eastern Europe, there was perhaps little for American Jews to do but wrangle. Such ineffectuality, however, wore heavily after the war.

Liberation. In 1945 Allied armies began to liberate the death camps of Europe. As graphic photographs and journalistic reports of the camps returned to the United States, the disbelief many Americans expressed at reports of the Holocaust in 1942 became horribly ironic. Still, the Holocaust was an unprecedented event that stunned many and boggled the imagination. Jews sank into despair, especially troubled by the ineffectiveness of their rescue efforts during the war. Liberal Protestants fell into silence, their optimistic assessments of human nature hopelessly compromised. The Catholic Church offered few insights beyond truisms, plagued by the overt collaboration of many east European clergy with the Nazis. With little public discussion, the response to the Holocaust became a private affair, especially among Jewish families who lost relatives. In a sense American public religion was perhaps too stunned to offer a clear assessment, and the 1940s passed with remarkably little reflection on the Holocaust, although in subsequent decades the witness of writers such as Anne Frank, Elie Wiesel, Primo Levi, and others would ensure a most terrible place for the Holocaust in the memory of Western society.

Sources:

Henry L. Feingold, *A Time for Searching: Entering the Mainstream, 1920–1945* (Baltimore: Johns Hopkins University Press, 1992);

Arthur Hertzberg, *The Jews in America: Four Centuries of an Uneasy Encounter — A History* (New York: Simon & Schuster, 1989).

URBANIZATION AND THE BLACK CHURCH

Segregation. American churches in the 1940s were almost entirely segregated. A 1946 estimate suggested that no more than one-half of 1 percent of blacks attended church with whites. Instead, African Americans actively promoted and supported their own churches. There were thirty-four predominately black denominations, the largest of which, the National Baptist Convention of America, possessed 4.4 million members. The heart of black church strength was in the Baptist and Methodist churches of the South. Led by a segregated middle class of black professionals, they unified community life, mitigated the difficulties of poverty, and provided a distinct culture and identity for African Americans. Black congregations were far more engaged in services than their white counterparts, and black spirituals and gospel music bound the churches together. In the 1940s southern black churches remained important, but as more and more African Americans migrated from the rural South to the industrialized North to take jobs in defense industries, the character of black religion began to change.

Secularization and Differentiation. The new black churches of the urban North were different from those in the South, being more secularized and cosmopolitan. Northern black churches were divided according to social class in a way similar to the social divisions of white churches. Wealthy blacks formed Episcopal, Presbyterian, or Congregational churches; middle-class blacks formed African Methodist or Baptist congregations. Both groups were usually ministered to by well-educated, professionally trained clergy. New and poor black migrants to the city, however, congregated in small, intimate storefront churches of often diverse practices, usually ministered to by untrained but enthusiastic laity. Often connected to Pentecostal, Holiness, New Thought, and other evangelical churches, the storefronts specialized in the types of services typical among white and black evangelists and circuit riders in the rural South: enthusiastic, dramatic services designed to inspire sudden conversions. More than a few of these churches were dismissed by journalists and observers such as Ira Reid as cults and frauds, but they held an undeniable attraction to displaced, poor black migrants and were often successful in providing order and structure to disorganized lives.

Divine and Grace. The most popular of the storefront preachers in the 1940s was Father Divine. George Baker was a former Baptist minister who set up a "Peace Mission" in Harlem in 1931; by 1941, as "Father Divine," Baker was famous in New York and expanded his operations to Philadelphia. Divine claimed to be the incarnation of God and became known for his bountiful chicken dinners and his egalitarian church. The Peace Mission urged communicants to abstain from crime, liquor, gambling, and race hatred; exhorted them to "peace" in all things; and promised health and well-being if one lived exactly according to the teachings of Father Divine. Similar to Father Divine was "Sweet Daddy" Grace. An immigrant from Portugal or the Azores, Bishop Charles Emmanuel Grace also claimed the powers of God and toured from city to city demonstrating his gifts, including healings, blessings, ceremonial honors, and ecstasies of the spirit. Sweet Daddy Grace's Houses of Prayer of All Nations specialized in lively services featuring monarchical pomp, propulsive music, and frenzied dancing. Like Father Divine, Grace demanded absolute obedience, preached racial tolerance, and required his adherents to deposit their wages with him, since their spirits were so filled they did not need money.

Nation of Islam. In contrast to the black cults of Father Divine and Sweet Daddy Grace, the storefront ministry of the Nation of Islam (or Black Muslims, as they were commonly known) was far less individualistic and had a distinct social agenda. A powerful combination of Islam and militant black nationalism, in the 1940s the Nation of Islam was a small movement centered in Detroit and Chicago. Led by Elijah Muhammad — born Robert Poole, the son of a Baptist minister from Georgia — the Black Muslims reversed the reigning race stereotypes of the day, asserting that whites were an inferior, demonic race. The Nation of Islam claimed that white Christianity was on the verge of being overthrown by God; they advocated black separatism and a strict moral, ritual, and economic self-determination in anticipation of that event. Because Muhammad refused to kill on any order save that given by Allah, he was incarcerated for draft resistance during World War II, but he turned this to his advantage, and in the 1950s the Nation of Islam would become known for the prison recruitment methods he pioneered. One charismatic prison convert — Malcolm Little, who took the name Malcolm X — would garner worldwide attention to the movement in the early 1960s.

Catholic Recruitment. After World War II, as more and more white ethnic groups moved toward the suburbs, more and more blacks and Hispanics moved into the cities. This migration greatly challenged the Catholic Church, the traditional church of white ethnic city dwellers. Some Catholic churches picked up and moved to the suburbs, but the majority remained at the center of urban neighborhoods, even as the ethnic composition of those neighborhoods changed. Approximately 365,000 blacks belonged to the Catholic Church, occupying 408 local churches, 306 elementary schools, and 30 high schools. Adapting church attitudes and services for a radically different population proved difficult; nonetheless, by the end of the decade many urban dioceses had begun actively to solicit African American converts.

Churches and Civil Rights. In the South the postwar black church became a magnet for African American protest. African Americans had many grievances, including Jim Crow laws in the South that denied them fundamental rights, such as the vote, disrespect for and denigration of their war service; and an unequal wage structure that prevented blacks from enjoying many of the benefits of postwar prosperity. The black church, as the voice of the community, protested these conditions, in the 1940s for the most part in vain. There were religiously based civil rights organizations in the 1940s: the Fellowship of Reconciliation (FOR) and the Congress of Racial Equality (CORE), for example. Neither was distinctly southern or denominational. Congressman Adam Clayton Powell, Jr., from his base in Harlem's Abyssinian Baptist Church, also organized small-scale civil rights protests in New York City. The next generation of civil rights leaders spent the 1940s for the most part in integrated seminaries, where they gained invaluable training and experience. For the most part, however, civil rights activism had yet to begin. Instead, the southern black church nurtured the movement until the 1950s, when organizations such as the Southern Christian Leadership Conference, a group of black ministers, would lead the first successful campaigns to abolish Jim Crow.

Sources:

Sydney E. Ahlstrom, *A Religious History of the American People* (New Haven & London: Yale University Press, 1972);

Robert Wuthnow, *The Restructuring of American Religion: Society and Faith Since World War II* (Princeton: Princeton University Press, 1988).

HEADLINE MAKERS

A. J. MUSTE

1885-1967

PACIFIST, FOUNDER OF CORE

Out of Step. In the 1940s few Americans were more out of step with public opinion than Abraham Johannes Muste. After the Japanese attack on Pearl Harbor on 7 December 1941, the country rallied behind the war effort; Muste, one of the most ardent pacifists in American history, counseled those resisting the war. After World War II the nation slowly but certainly closed ranks around the struggle against the Soviet Union; Muste dissented, propagating the Cold War "third camp" position — opposing both Communist political tyranny and capitalist economic oppression. And while many Americans in the postwar years came to support black equality, few did so with the fervor of Muste, who helped form the trailblazing civil rights organization Congress of Racial Equality (CORE). He also popularized Mohandas K. Gandhi's philosophy of peace in the United States, teaching nonviolence to a generation of civil rights leaders. Muste was out of step with his countrymen, but out in front of most on the path to social justice.

Background. Born in the Dutch shipping port of Zierikzee on 8 January 1885, Muste was the son of a poor but pious coachman who brought his family to the New World in 1891 in search of opportunity. Settling in Grand Rapids, Michigan, the Mustes continued to struggle economically but were able to pay for his education at the Hope Preparatory School and Hope College in Holland, Michigan, in the hope that he would become a Dutch Reformed minister. Valedictorian of his class of 1905, he taught Greek and English for a time, married, and enrolled at New Brunswick Theological Seminary in New Jersey to complete his religious training. He supple-mented his rigorous and conservative Bible study with courses at Columbia University in New York, where he was most impressed with the tolerant ethics of philosophy professor Frederick Woodbridge.

Social Gospel and Pacifism. From his earliest ministry in New York City, Muste was struck by the contrast between the abject poverty of the immigrants and the affluence of New York's elite. His own Washington Heights congregation was wealthy, and for Muste, continuing his education at the liberal Union Theological Seminary, the contrast between the complacency of the haves and desperation of the have-nots was too much to bear. Plagued by a spiritual crisis, he resigned from his church in 1914. He resolved to devote himself to the reformism of the social gospel, a religious movement based upon social service. He moved to Massachusetts and began to read works by Christian mystics and pacifists. As he did, the world spiraled toward war. With the outbreak of World War I, Muste joined the Fellowship of Reconciliation (FOR), a pacifist group seeking to create a new "world order based on Love." He soon had a falling-out with FOR, but he later returned to the organization. His pacifist stand after the United States entered the conflict cost him his pulpit, and he joined the Quakers.

Labor Organizing. Following the war Muste extended his social activism, participating in many of the labor strikes sweeping the Northeast. In 1921 his labor organizing led to a position with the Brookwood Labor College in Katonah, New York, where he would organize labor, teach, and raise a family for the next twelve years. He proved a tenacious labor-organizing infighter, upbraiding the American Federation of Labor (AFL) for its complacency and condemning Communist Party organizing as "remote and irrelevant." Impatient with both groups, he helped organize the Conference for Progressive Labor Action (CPLA) in 1929. The CPLA quickly proved itself a labor-organizing force, especially in the South. By the early 1930s the CPLA was also engaged in several sensational civil liberties trials, including that of the Scottsboro Nine — nine black youths on trial for supposedly raping a white woman in Alabama. Muste became more involved in left-wing politics in this period than before, migrating among various leftist organizations, abandoning his earlier religious outlook, living in utter destitution, and becoming an advocate of violent revolution among the American working class. Political struggle, however, took its toll. When friends, concerned about his health, raised money for a European vacation in 1936, he was again on the verge of spiritual crisis.

Revelation. Europe was ablaze with portents of world war. In 1936 Benito Mussolini's Fascists attacked Ethiopia; Francisco Franco's Fascists attacked the Republican government of Spain; Nazis were beginning to rise to power in Eastern Europe; and Soviet premier Joseph Stalin had begun his purges. Against this backdrop Muste wrestled with fifteen years of ineffectual political activism. In Paris, at the church of Saint Sulpice, he reported that an inner voice assured him, "This is where you belong, in the church, not outside it." He immediately decided to rededicate his life to Christianity. He repudiated Marxism but remained committed to social justice and pacifism. To him, they were of a piece with Christianity. In lectures and sermons he stressed that the Judeo-Christian tradition was the tradition of democratic workers and that pacifism was the only possible course for a follower of Christ. He returned to the impoverished neighborhoods of New York; rejoined the FOR; assumed the directorship of the Labor Temple, a Presbyterian outreach center in New York; and focused on the revolutionary possibilities of earnest Christianity.

Nonviolence. As World War II approached, Muste was one of the few observers who saw American policies and actions as inadvertently promoting German fascism and Japanese militarism. In *Nonviolence in an Aggressive World* (1940) he pointed to the injustice of the Versailles settlement and American war-debt collection as some of the causes of war; he also saw America's competition with Japan in the Pacific as economically motivated. Although he harbored no illusions about the brutality of the Nazis, fascism's barbarism for Muste presented a theological challenge, a test of his Christian forgiveness. "If I can't love Hitler," Muste remarked, "I can't love at all." Such an attitude set him far outside the American mainstream; he was not, however, out of step with the few thousand Americans objecting to military service on religious grounds. He became their aide and confidant, shepherding conscientious-objection cases through military tribunals and civilian courts. Muste himself violated a 1942 presidential order requiring all males between forty-five and sixty-five to register with the Selective Service, but he was not prosecuted. He also worked with conscientious objectors in jail, encouraging inmate strikes in the South to end the segregation of prisons. The war brought vocal protests from Muste, who particularly objected to the carpet bombing of cities. He believed the war to be ushering in a new dark age, filled with militarism and

inhumanity. He interpreted the atomic bombing of Japan as confirmation of his fears that the United States would take on the worst characteristics of its enemies, and the bombings compelled him to increase his pacifist activities after the war ended. For him Christian pacifism was vitally important to the survival of humanity in a nuclear world. He thus became the foremost practitioner of what he called "Holy Disobedience."

Peacemakers. After the war Muste served as chairman of the FOR's Committee for Amnesty, petitioning the government to grant amnesties to conscientious objectors, a crusade waged for the most part in vain. In 1948 he founded Peacemakers, a grass roots organization dedicated to Christian pacifism and nonviolence. Peacemakers organized the Tax Refusal Committee to help people who refused to pay taxes on the grounds that the revenues were used to pay for the American military. Muste himself refused to file a tax return from 1948 to 1952 because of his opposition to atomic weapons research. The government won a judgment against him for back taxes in 1960, but as he lived at a subsistence level and his income was for the most part in the form of charitable gifts, the judgment scarcely affected him. Nonetheless, his tax refusal became a model for many Christian pacifists, especially those who joined Peacemakers. Until the end of his life Muste continued to be central to pacifist activism, participating in civil disobedience by protesting the building of nuclear weapons and organizing draft resistance during the Vietnam War.

Gandhi and CORE. During World War II Muste also profoundly influenced a group of young Christian activists within FOR who dedicated themselves to Gandhi's philosophy of nonviolence known as satyagraha. Gandhi's philosophy was one of "active nonviolence." To Gandhi, passive acceptance of immoral political practices made one complicit with evil; instead, the moral individual must actively oppose evil, using the weapons of civil disobedience — love and forgiveness. This philosophy appealed to the FOR activists who had already committed themselves to the Christian forgiveness central to the Sermon on the Mount. They were also drawn to Gandhi's emphasis on the liberation of racially oppressed minorities. Muste had independently arrived at many of these same positions. In 1943 he published a book opposed to the Jim Crow system in the South, advocating nonviolent direct action to attack it. *What the Bible Teaches about Freedom: A Message to the Negro Churches* drew the young pacifists of FOR, especially Bayard Rustin, James Farmer, and George Houser, to Muste. They organized CORE to oppose Jim Crow, and Muste gave them FOR funding for their projects — the most important of which was the Journey of Reconciliation, a 1947 attempt to desegregate interstate buses in the South. Later in the 1940s and in the 1950s, Muste's lectures on pacifism and nonviolence inspired many civil rights leaders, such as Martin Luther King, Jr., and James Lawson. In the 1960s he broadened his efforts to found the World

Peace Brigade, a nonviolent organization promoting Third World liberation. He also helped organize later civil rights actions, such as the 1963 Albany Movement.

Success. Most hallmarks of personal success eluded Muste. He remained impoverished his entire life; he was not famous outside antiwar circles; and aside from receiving the Gandhi Peace Award, which he treasured, he received few honors. Yet by the time of his death in 1967 he was revered by many in the antiwar and civil rights movements. Perhaps the best assessment of his life was offered by King on the occasion of Muste's eightieth birthday: "You have climbed the mountain and have seen the great and abiding truth to which you have dedicated your life. Throughout the world you are honored as our most effective exponent of pacifism. You have been a great friend and inspiration to me and the whole nonviolent movement. Without you the American Negro might never have caught the meaning of true love for humanity."

Sources:
August Meier and Elliott Rudwick, *CORE: A Study in the Civil Rights Movement, 1942–1968* (New York: Oxford University Press, 1973);

Jo Ann Ooiman Robinson, *Abraham Went Out: A Biography of A. J. Muste* (Philadelphia: Temple University Press, 1981).

REINHOLD NIEBUHR

1892-1971

PROTESTANT THEOLOGIAN

Number One Theologian. America's preeminent religious intellectual in the middle third of the twentieth century, Reinhold Niebuhr was also an important figure in social and political affairs. His picture graced the cover of *Time* magazine's twenty-fifth anniversary issue in 1948, and two years later the same publication called him "the number one theologian of United States Protestantism." His professional reputation was the equal of his public acclaim. The foremost philosopher of Protestant neo-orthodoxy, Niebuhr in his reconstruction of the faith was highly influential among theologians. He is perhaps best known for his "Serenity Prayer," first published in 1951:

> God, give us the serenity to accept what cannot be changed;
> give us the courage to change what should be changed;
> give us the wisdom to distinguish one from the other."

Background. Born on 21 June 1892, Niebuhr was of German descent. His father was a minister in the German Evangelical Synod, a small, conservative, midwestern denomination. His father preached a combination of liberal ecumenism and conservative piety, oppositions his son would become famous for reconciling. Early on, Nie-

buhr decided to follow his father into the ministry. Like his father, he studied at the Eden Theological Seminary in Wellston, Missouri. When his father died in 1913, Niebuhr took his place at his father's pulpit in Lincoln, Illinois, but with a grant to study at the Yale Divinity School in hand, he soon made his way east to New Haven, Connecticut. He was graduated in 1915 and assumed the pulpit of the Bethel Evangelical Church in Detroit. There he was immediately occupied with the effect of World War I on the German American congregation. Viewing the Prussian monarchy as authoritarian and corrupt, he tied to mobilize opinion in favor of American intervention against Germany and sought to quell German nationalism among his congregants. His efforts set a precedent for the future, and he would spend his career as engaged in political and social issues as he was concerned with spiritual questions, especially after he took a position at the Union Theological Seminary in New York in 1928.

First Major Work. Niebuhr's first major work of theology, *Moral Man and Immoral Society* (1932), evidenced his unique fusion of spiritual and temporal concerns. In the 1920s Bethel had been at the center of public discussions of the social changes sweeping through Detroit during the automobile age. Niebuhr liked liberal Protestantism's emphasis on the social gospel and social reform but disliked the moderation with which so many liberal clergy advocated reform. He was at the forefront of a group of Protestant intellectuals calling for the Christianization of industry and lending assistance to union organizing. With the Depression he moved Left, joining the Socialist Party and pressing his advocacy of labor more forcefully. In *Moral Man and Immoral Society* he tried to reconcile the need for possible labor violence with Christian morality. Attacking by turns liberal Protestantism, Christian pacifism, and dogmatic Marxism, he sought to demonstrate that the ethical imperative of Christian reformers sometimes required violence. He also deployed a host of intellectual arguments to which he would later return, the most important of which postulated that the innate depravity of individuals more often than not led to thoroughly depraved social institutions.

Neo-orthodoxy. His book's deft arguments came at a moment in American intellectual life when many progressive thinkers, such as Edmund Wilson and John Chamberlain, were shifting left. As perhaps the most studied exposition of the problem of Marxism and reform, Niebuhr's book was acclaimed. It had its detractors, however, especially Niebuhr's younger brother, H. Richard Niebuhr, a theologian at the Yale Divinity School. Richard criticized his brother for excessive politicizing and for abandoning more purely theological concerns. H. Richard Niebuhr was at the forefront of American intellectuals rethinking the fundamental premises of liberal Protestantism and constructing a new, more rigorous Protestant theology, neo-orthodoxy, and he brought his brother into this endeavor. Constantly sharpening his ideas off Richard, Reinhold became the foremost public exponent of the new theology, producing a classic two-volume neo-orthodox study, *The Nature and Destiny of Man,* in 1941 and 1943.

Humanity's Sinful Nature. In *The Nature and Destiny of Man* Niebuhr expounded the most systematic discussion of neo-orthodoxy. In contrast to the liberal Protestant theologians of the day, he insisted on humanity's imperfection, depravity, sinful nature, and distance from God. He advised readers to maintain a sharp sense of their own humility and to accept Christian faith as the only means by which the existential sufferings of life can be alleviated. Although neo-orthodoxy remained socially progressive, Niebuhr expressed an understanding of the complexity of political action missing in his earlier work and counseled patience, stoicism, and limited expectations — concepts perfectly keyed to the disillusionment of liberals who witnessed the massacre of the Jews or to radicals shaken by the Stalinist purges. Niebuhr himself moved toward the political center, and in his next book, *The Children of Light and the Children of Darkness* (1944), he defended democratic principles in an age that could no longer sustain utopian optimism.

Activism, Paradox, Protest. As part of his centrism, Niebuhr joined several political groups, such as the Union for Democratic Action and the Americans for Democratic Action (which opposed Henry Wallace's 1948 presidential campaign). He became for a time something of a cold warrior (although never a red-baiter), especially after the 1949 publication of his *Faith and History: A Comparison of Christian and Modern Views of History.* In this book he argued that the Christian conception of history was a better basis for understanding politics than more recent models of history such as Marxism. The book solidified his public stature as an establishment theologian and led to a close association with the U.S. State Department. He followed it with a well-received meditation on American culture, *The Irony of American History* (1951), which viewed the nation and the Cold War as fraught with paradox. In the 1960s Niebuhr's own actions were sometimes viewed paradoxically by critics. A figurehead of the establishment, he nonetheless supported the civil rights movement and opposed the Vietnam War. In 1969, at age seventy-six, he was enough of a critic of the establishment that President Richard M. Nixon had him investigated by the FBI. He died 1 June 1971.

Sources:

Charles C. Brown, *Niebuhr and His Age: Reinhold Niebuhr's Prophetic Role in the Twentieth Century* (Philadelphia: Trinity, 1992);

Kenneth Durkin, *Reinhold Niebuhr* (Harrisburg, Pa.: Morehouse, 1990);

Richard Wightman Fox, *Reinhold Niebuhr: A Biography* (New York: Pantheon, 1986);

Ronald H. Stone, *Reinhold Niebuhr: Prophet to Politicians* (Nashville: Abingdon, 1972).

NORMAN VINCENT PEALE

1898-1993

AUTHOR AND MINISTER

Simple Style. A country boy from Ohio, Norman Vincent Peale trained at Boston University Seminary and began his full-time ministry at a church in Brooklyn in 1924. He married Ruth Stafford on 20 June 1930 and two years later accepted a call to the Dutch Reformed Marble Collegiate Church in New York, where he was soon attracting large crowds with his simple preaching style. He appealed to middle- and upper-middle-class Americans struggling to survive a Depression and two world wars.

Mid 1940s. Before World War II Peale wrote *The Art of Living* (1937), which sold poorly but which announced the theme to which he would return in later books: "applied Christianity helps people to tap [the] reservoir of power within themselves." In the mid 1940s Peale began a newsletter called *Guideposts,* which offered anecdotes and inspirational accounts of faith in action. It soon achieved a circulation of more than 800,000. With New York psychiatrist Smiley Blanton he established the Blanton-Peale Institute of Religion and Health, which focused on the relationship of faith and mental health. In 1940 Peale and Blanton had published *Faith Is the Answer,* an interesting mix of religious truisms and distorted psychoanalysis. They argued that religious faith unlocked the unconscious mind, a position exactly opposite to what Sigmund Freud had argued in *Civilization and Its Discontents* (1930). In 1948 Peale published *A Guide to Confident Living,* which established his anecdotal style for inspirational messages. Its how-to messages — such as "How to Get Rid of Your Inferiority Complex" and "How to Think Your Way to Success" — proved popular, as did the repetitious feel-good "Spirit Lifter" phrases studding his 1950 *Inspiring Messages for Daily Living.*

Positive Thinking. Peale became the country's leading apostle of "mind cure" and self-confidence, or, as he called his next book, *The Power of Positive Thinking* (1952). It opened with the advice "Believe in yourself!" It remained on the best-seller lists for more than two years and sold more than one million copies during that period. Peale also was a regular guest on radio and television. According to him, spiritual difficulties derive primarily from mental attitudes. He recommended healthy doses of prayer to improve mental attitudes and energize the individual.

Last Years. Often criticized by some for distorting Christianity into a gospel of success and belief in oneself rather than in God, Peale was named one of the "Twelve Best U.S. Salesmen" in 1954. He published an autobiography, *The True Joy of Positive Living*, in 1984. He died on Christmas Eve 1993 at age ninety-five.

Sources:

Allan R. Broadhurst, *He Speaks the Word of God: A Study of the Sermons of Norman Vincent Peale* (Englewood Cliffs, N.J.: Prentice-Hall, 1963);

Carol V. R. George, *God's Salesman: Norman Vincent Peale and the Power of Positive Thinking* (New York: Oxford University Press, 1993);

Arthur Gordon, *Norman Vincent Peale: Minister to Millions — A Biography* (Englewood Cliffs, N.J.: Prentice-Hall, 1958);

Donald B. Meyer, *The Positive Thinkers: A Study of the Quest for Health, Wealth, and Personal Power from Mary Baker Eddy to Norman Vincent Peale* (Garden City, N.Y.: Doubleday, 1965).

FRANCIS J. SPELLMAN

1889-1967

ARCHBISHOP OF NEW YORK

The American Pope. On 23 December 1945 Francis J. Spellman, archbishop of New York, was named cardinal by Pope Pius XII. The appointment represented the culmination of an extraordinary career within the Catholic Church and within American society. By 1945 Spellman was the leading Roman Catholic clergyman in the United States, the confidant of powerful political and business figures, and the spiritual leader of the largest Catholic archdiocese in America. His influence on American political affairs, both domestic and foreign, was considerable, leading critics to dub him "the American Pope."

Background. Spellman was born in Whitman, Massachusetts, on 4 May 1889 to an upper-middle-class grocer. An indifferent and unexceptional student, he nonetheless went to Fordham University in 1907, determined to make his mark in the priesthood. After graduating he attended the North American College in Rome, where he ingratiated himself with several powerful bishops. Already Spellman evidenced a knack for cultivating relationships with the powerful and well-placed, although it was not through charm, as Spellman was noted throughout his life for his brusque and unmannered treatment of others. He was accepted into the priesthood on 14 May 1916 and assigned as a chaplain at Saint Clement's Home, an institution for elderly women in Boston. He was soon reassigned to the Catholic newspaper *Pilot* as a subscription manager and editor.

Rise in the Church. Spellman's thinly veiled ambition soon ran afoul of Boston's archbishop, William O'Connell, and hurt his reputation in church circles. His contacts in Rome nonetheless returned him to the Vatican in 1925. As a church administrator Spellman proved adept at money management and at negotiating church affairs with businessmen and political figures. In 1927 he met papal diplomat Eugenio Pacelli, who had been the Vatican's ambassador to Germany, and embraced his militant anticommunism. The two men began a long and close association, which was especially beneficial to Spellman after Pacelli became Pope Pius XII in 1939. Spellman soon became the leading American at the Vatican, acting as a de facto emissary to the United States and as a de facto American ambassador to Rome. In 1932 he was named auxiliary archbishop to Boston and returned home. In Boston he quickly made allies of powerful political figures, especially Irish Catholic politicians such as Joseph P. Kennedy, Sr., and Boston mayor James Michael Curley. He also continued his climb in the Roman Catholic hierarchy. In 1939 he became archbishop of the New York archdiocese, the largest and most powerful in the United States. He used the position to make himself even more powerful, eventually earning the archdiocese in New York the nickname of "the Powerhouse."

Interventionist. Spellman's activities before and during World War II made him a nationally recognized figure. As archbishop of the nation's most powerful archdiocese, with nearly 2 million Catholic voters, he was a magnet for political figures. He sought them out as well, eager to associate the church more closely with national endeavors. He strengthened his ties to the presidency of Franklin D. Roosevelt, combating the isolationism prevalent in the Catholic hierarchy before World War II. At the National Eucharistic Congress in June 1941 he connected Roosevelt's Atlantic Charter to the church, arguing that the real peace program of the Allies had ten points — the Ten Commandments. In the fall of 1941 Spellman had even drafted an official statement on world interventionism that Roosevelt read at the first drawing of the draft. "We really can no longer afford to be moles who cannot see or ostriches who will not see," wrote Spellman. "We Americans want peace and we shall be prepared for a peace, but not a peace whose definition is slavery or death."

Wartime Activities. With the outbreak of war Spellman's political duties increased. He acted as Roosevelt's secret emissary to foreign governments, such as that of Spain, when such communications proved too politically volatile for official channels. He also made a habit of visiting the front lines, conducting masses for the troops and bolstering morale. On 13 March 1943 he said mass over the grave of Rev. Clement Falter, a Catholic chaplain who was the first chaplain killed in the war.

The Chaplain of the Cold War. Spellman was a militant anti-Communist, constantly ferreting out red activities. He contributed to the fear and suspicion between the United States and the Soviet Union that followed the wartime alliance. In 1944 he had a Polish-American priest, Stanislaus Orelemanski, banished to a monastery after the priest encouraged closer American relations with the Soviets. Spellman denounced communism from the pulpit routinely, in 1948 asserting, "We stand at a crossroads of civilization, a civilization threatened with the crucifixion of Communism." He was a prominent radio figure, urging Americans to "weed out and counteract" Communist subversives within the United States. When grave-diggers at the church-owned Calvary Cemetery went on strike for higher wages in 1949, he automatically condemned them as Communists. Naturally enough, he was among Sen. Joseph McCarthy's most ardent champions, endorsing him at a 1953 mass in Saint Patrick's Cathedral in New York. When Jesuit leader Robert Harnett denounced McCarthy in the pages of the Jesuit journal *America,* Spellman had the Vatican silence him. The senator saw it as officious meddling, but the FBI in an attempt to purge communism from the labor unions.

Public Aid to Schools. During World War II the success of federal assistance in abetting American higher education set a precedent for proposals for federal aid for all American education. Spellman was instrumental in attempting to get this assistance extended to parochial schools. However, many Americans, anxious over the separation of church and state, favored assistance to public schools alone. When Spellman denounced a 1949 congressional bill that limited assistance to public schools, he was admonished by Eleanor Roosevelt concerning the separation of church and state. He replied by accusing her of anti-Catholicism, a common tactic for him with non-Catholic enemies. His response to the affair (the bill ultimately died), as well as his thin-skinned tendency to heap abuse on detractors, did much to harm the ecumenical spirit dominant in the postwar era, as did his stands on several moral issues.

Morals and the Public Good. Like many other Catholic leaders, Spellman was concerned with the impact of mass media on social morals and consistently reacted to movies he considered morally offensive. In November 1941 he denounced Greta Garbo's movie *Two-Faced Woman* as "dangerous to public morals." He actively condemned two movies in the 1950s, Roberto Rossellini's *The Miracle* (1950) for its "sacrilegious" nature and *Baby Doll* (1956) for its "corrupting influence." His attack on such films was not limited to speeches. In New York a theater in which *The Miracle* played was closed due to fire violations, as Spellman applied political pressure to city leaders. After two academics, Frank Getlein of Fairfield University and William P. Clancy of Notre Dame University, expressed support for the movie, they were fired from their posts. Spellman's campaign backfired, however, as *The Miracle* became a liberal cause célèbre, leading in part to the U.S. Supreme Court decision striking blasphemy from the criminal code in 1952. Nevertheless, Spellman sent priests into the lobbies of theaters showing *Baby Doll* to take down the names of any parishioner attending the film.

Later Activities. Spellman's anticommunism and patriotism only gained strength in the 1950s, and he continued his trips to military camps abroad, especially during the Korean War. The election of John F. Kennedy to the presidency, however, marked the beginning of Spellman's decline in power. Kennedy favored the cardinal of Boston, Richard Cushing, to Spellman. Spellman, moreover, opposed the liberalization of Catholicism that occurred after the Second Vatican Council (1962–1964) and fell out of favor in Rome. His vocal advocacy of American military involvement and bombing in Vietnam, moreover, strained his relations with the more pacific Vatican to the breaking point. His power waned considerably, and he was no longer a political force to be feared when he died on 2 December 1967.

Source:
John Cooney, *The American Pope: The Life and Times of Francis Cardinal Spellman* (New York: Times Books, 1984).

PAUL TILLICH

1886-1965

THEOLOGIAN

Religion and Culture. Along with Reinhold Niebuhr, Paul Tillich was the most influential Protestant theologian in the United States in the middle of the twentieth century. Tillich was adept at linking religion with all aspects of culture, including science, art, philosophy, psychology, and ethics.

Integrating Modernism. Born in Starzeddel, Germany, in 1886, Tillich was the son of a Lutheran pastor who instilled in him what he recalled as a "heightened consciousness of duty and sin." By age twenty-four Tillich had received his doctorate in philosophy from the University of Breslau. Drawn to the Romantic philosophy of Friedrich Schelling, Tillich was also preoccupied with resolving the challenges modern philosophy and science presented to traditional Protestantism. Under the influence of one of his teachers, Martin Kähler, he sought to integrate modernism into Protestant theology without compromising the distinctive message of Christianity, which he interpreted as being a "self-transcending realism."

Religious Socialism. By age twenty-six Tillich had been ordained by the Evangelical Church of the Prussian Union and had taken a church in Berlin. Personally shattered by his experience as a chaplain in World War I, he drifted into the bohemian artistic milieu of postwar Berlin, developing a type of religious socialism that offended the Nazis. Because of his defense of left-wing and Jewish students, he was suspended from a position at the University of Frankfurt in 1933, and with Niebuhr's assistance later that year immigrated to the United States to assume a teaching post at Union Theological Seminary in New York. He became an American citizen in 1940. Following a twenty-two-year teaching career at Union, he taught for six years beginning in 1954 at Harvard Divinity School. He published two important books in 1948: *The Protestant Era* and *The Shaking of the Foundations*.

Systematic Theology. Thirty years in the making, Tillich published his three-volume *Systematic Theology* (1951, 1957, 1963) over a twelve-year period. His work represents the last great American effort to explicate the whole of Christian thought for the modern world. Tillich relied on categories borrowed from classical metaphysics, and throughout one observes what he referred to as the Protestant principle: "the protesting voice of the prophet outside the temple calling the people back to God."

Sources:

James Luther Adams, *Paul Tillich's Philosophy of Culture, Science, and Religion* (Washington, D.C.: University Press of America, 1982);

Wilhelm Pauck, *Paul Tillich: His Life and Thought* (New York: Harper & Row, 1976);

Ronald H. Stone, *Paul Tillich's Radical Social Thought* (Atlanta: John Knox, 1980);

Mark Kline Taylor, *Paul Tillich: Theologian of the Boundaries* (San Francisco: Collins, 1987).

D. ELTON TRUEBLOOD

1900-1994

THEOLOGIAN AND AUTHOR

Popular Theologian. D. Elton Trueblood, whose Quaker ancestors settled in America in 1682, was one of the most prominent theologians in the United States during the 1940s. Educated at the Harvard School of Theology and Johns Hopkins University, he was less an intellectual than a popularizer of religious thought. His studies of religion were widely read in the 1940s and contributed to the revival of religion during the decade.

Author. Trueblood was the author of thirty-three books, five of them published in the 1940s: *The Logic of Belief* (1942), *The Predicament of Modern Man* (1944), *Foundations for Reconstruction* (1946), *Alternative to Futility* (1948), and *The Common Ventures of Life: Marriage, Birth, Work, and Death* (1949). In his work he sought to enlighten the "literate secular reader" rather than the professional theologian. He hoped his works would inspire people to work toward a "redemptive" society based upon Christian principles. In 1944, concerned that the war had resulted in a "cut flower" civilization — one cut off from its roots — he sought to reassure readers that the moral and religious bases of Western civilization remained intact. This idea was also central to his acclaimed book *The Life We Prize* (1951), which also argued that the Christian ideal of society was more revolutionary than any fascist or Marxist doctrine.

Presidential Advisor. Trueblood's work lent itself to Cold War applications, and in 1954 he assumed a post as chief of religious policy for the United States Information Agency (USIA), overseeing broadcasts for the Voice of America. A registered Republican, he also drafted several presidential proclamations dealing with religion during the Eisenhower administration.

Philosophy Professor. Originally a professor of philosophy at the Quaker-sponsored Haverford College in Pennsylvania, Trueblood became chaplain and professor of philosophy at Stanford University in 1936. From 1946 until his retirement in 1966 he served as professor of philosophy at Earlham College and School of Religion, a Quaker institution in Richmond, Indiana. He developed many curriculum innovations designed to advance a ministry of the laity. He died on 20 December 1994 at age ninety-four.

Source:

Elton Trueblood, *The Best of Elton Trueblood: An Anthology* (Nashville: Impact, 1979).

PEOPLE IN THE NEWS

On 8 October 1947 **Herbert W. Armstrong,** founder of the Worldwide Church of God, established Ambassador College in Pasadena, California.

Archbishop Athenagoras I was enthroned as patriarch of the Greek Orthodox Church on 22 January 1949.

On 7 July 1946 Pope Pius XII canonized **Mother Frances Xavier Cabrini** of Chicago as the first American saint for having established convents and orphanages in several cities around the world. She died in 1917.

Under the Espionage Act of 1917, the U.S. government on 14 April 1942 banned the anti-Semitic weekly *Social Justice,* published by **Father Charles E. Coughlin** of Detroit.

On 8 November 1944 the **Most Reverend Richard J. Cushing** was installed as archbishop of Boston, making him, at forty-nine, the world's youngest archbishop. On 13 October 1947 Cushing opened the ninth annual convention of the Congress of Industrial Organizations (CIO) by noting that members of the Catholic hierarchy in the United States are, without exception, sons of workingmen.

Dr. Louis Finkelstein, a Jew; **Dr. William Adams Brown,** a Protestant; and **Rev. Elliot Ross,** a Catholic, collaborated on a 1941 book, *Religions of Democracy,* published by the National Conference of Christians and Jews.

The **Reverend Dr. Harry Emerson Fosdick,** dean of liberal Protestant ministers, on 26 May 1946 preached his last sermon in Riverside Church, New York, before his retirement.

On 8 October 1942 the **Reverend Dr. Frederick Brown Harris** was elected chaplain of the U.S. Senate.

On 26 May 1949 **Thomas Merton** was ordained a Trappist monk at Our Lady of Gethsemani Monastery near Bardstown, Kentucky.

On 13 November 1949 the American Jewish Congress elected **Rabbi Irving Miller** to succeed the late **Rabbi Stephen S. Wise** as president.

William Cardinal O'Connell, archbishop of Boston, said on 21 October 1942 that "unequivocally and absolutely the Catholic Church condemns and denounces birth control."

The **Reverend Dr. G. Bromley Oxnam,** Methodist bishop of the New York area, was elected president of the Federal Council of Churches of Christ in America on 29 November 1944. He served until 1946, when he was elected president of the World Council of Churches, a position he held until 1952.

On 6 January 1941 **President Franklin D. Roosevelt** outlined for Congress the "Four Freedoms," including "the freedom of every person to worship God in his own way — everywhere in the world."

In April 1943 **Francis J. Spellman,** Archbishop of New York, led thousands in a Good Friday procession along the Via Dolorosa in Jerusalem and celebrated mass in the Basilica of the Holy Sepulcher.

Margaret Woodrow Wilson, daughter of the former president, announced on 28 January 1943 that she had been a follower of Sri Aurobindo, India's most prominent mystic, for the past four years.

Rabbi Stephen S. Wise, president of the American Jewish Congress, urged American Jews to abandon all ideas of isolationism on 16 May 1942.

DEATHS

Rev. George Aaron Barton, 83, Episcopal clergyman and expert on biblical literature and Semitic languages, 28 June 1942.

Rev. Warren Akin Candler, 84, bishop of the Methodist Episcopal Church, South, and chancellor of Emory University, 25 September 1941.

Rev. James Cannon, Jr., 79, bishop of the Methodist Episcopal Church, South, and aggressive advocate of Prohibition, 6 September 1944.

Rev. William Chalmers Covert, 77, moderator of the General Assembly of the Presbyterian Church in the United States, 4 February 1942.

Rev. William Horace Day, 75, moderator of the National Council of Congregational Churches, 16 March 1942.

Marcus Garvey, 52, Jamaican black nationalist and advocate of a future black homeland in an "Africa for Africans," 10 June 1940.

Dr. Jesse Herman Holmes, 78, Quaker who founded the organization that became the American Friends Service Committee, 27 May 1942.

Rev. Methodios Kourkoulis, 79, leader in the Greek Orthodox Church, 9 April 1941.

Rev. Peter Marshall, 46, former pastor of the New York Avenue Presbyterian Church and chaplain of the U.S. Senate, 25 January 1949.

Rev. Shailer Mathews, 78, theologian, author, and dean emeritus of the University of Chicago Divinity School, 23 October 1941.

Rev. Cleland Boyd McAfee, 77, moderator of the General Assembly of the Presbyterian Church, 4 February 1944.

Aimee Semple McPherson, 53, controversial Pentecostal evangelist and founder of the International Church of the Foursquare Gospel in Los Angeles, 27 September 1944.

Rev. James Moffatt, 73, professor emeritus of church history at Union Theological Seminary in New York, 27 June 1944.

Rev. Ze Barney Thorne Phillips, 67, dean of Washington Cathedral and chaplain of the U.S. Senate, 10 May 1942.

Judge Joseph Franklin Rutherford, 72, founder of the Jehovah's Witnesses, 9 January 1942.

Monsignor John A. Ryan, 76, prominent American Catholic spokesman in areas of social reform and economic rights, 16 September 1945.

Dr. Don Odell Shelton, 73, founder of the National Bible Institute to train foreign missionaries, 29 January 1941.

Rev. Joseph Stolz, 79, Jewish philanthropist and dean of Reform rabbis in America, 7 February 1941.

Rev. Ernest Fremont Tittle, 63, internationally respected Methodist leader, 3 August 1949.

Rev. Francis B. Upham, 78, pastor of the John Street Church in New York, the oldest Methodist Church in the United States, 19 March 1941.

Stephen Wise, 75, New York rabbi who mobilized the American Jewish Congress to resist Nazism and helped found the World Jewish Congress, 19 April 1949.

PUBLICATIONS

Aaron Ignatius Abell, *The Urban Impact on American Protestantism, 1865–1900* (Cambridge, Mass.: Harvard University Press, 1943);

Gustaf Aulén, *Church, Law, and Society* (New York: Scribners, 1948);

Donald M. Baillie, *God Was in Christ* (New York: Scribners, 1948);

Salo Wittmayer Baron, *Modern Nationalism and Religion* (New York: Harper, 1947);

Sufi M. R. Bengale, *Life of Muhammad* (Chicago: Moslem Sunrise, 1942);

John C. Bennett, *Christian Ethics and Social Policy* (New York: Scribners, 1946);

Bennett, *Christianity and Communism* (New York: Association, 1948);

Andrew Blackwood, *Pastoral Leadership* (New York: Abingdon-Cokesbury, 1949);

Dietrich Bonhoeffer, *The Cost of Discipleship* (New York: Macmillan, 1949);

Harold A. Bosley, *Main Issues Confronting Christendom* (New York: Harper, 1948);

Bosley, *The Philosophical Heritage of the Christian Faith* (Chicago: Willett, Clark, 1944);

John Wick Bowman, *The Religion of Maturity* (New York: Abingdon-Cokesbury, 1948);

Charles S. Braden, *Man's Quest for Salvation* (Chicago: Willett, Clark, 1941);

Braden, *These Also Believe* (New York: Macmillan, 1949);

Marion J. Bradshaw, *Philosophical Foundations of Faith* (New York: Columbia University Press, 1941);

William Adams Brown, *A Creed for Free Men* (New York: Scribners, 1941);

Emil Brunner, *Christianity and Civilization* (Philadelphia: Westminster, 1949);

Brunner, *The Divine-Human Encounter* (Philadelphia: Westminster, 1943);

Brunner, *Revelation and Reason* (Philadelphia: Westminster, 1946);

Martin Buber, *The Prophetic Faith* (New York: Macmillan, 1949);

Shirley Jackson Case, *Christianity in a Changing World* (New York: Harper, 1941);

Elmer T. Clark, *Small Sects in America* (New York: Abingdon-Cokesbury, 1949);

Charles Norris Cochrane, *Christianity and Classical Culture* (New York: Oxford University Press, 1944);

Henry Sloane Coffin, *God Confronts Man in History* (New York: Scribners, 1947);

D. R. Davies, *Reinhold Niebuhr: Prophet from America* (New York: Macmillan, 1948);

L. Harold DeWolf, *The Religious Revolt Against Reason* (New York: Harper, 1949);

Sherwood Eddy, *Man Discovers God* (New York: Harper, 1942);

Harrison Elliott, *Can Religious Education Be Christian?* (New York: Macmillan, 1940);

Arthur H. Fauset, *Black Gods of the Metropolis* (Philadelphia: University of Pennsylvania Press, 1944);

Nels F. S. Ferré, *Faith and Reason* (New York: Harper, 1946);

Louis Finkelstein, ed., *The Jews: Their History, Culture, and Religion* (Philadelphia: Jewish Publication Society, 1949);

Albert I. Gordon, *Jews in Transition* (Minneapolis: University of Minnesota Press, 1949);

Georgia Harkness, *Prayer and the Common Life* (New York: Abingdon-Cokesbury, 1948);

Charles Hartshorne, *Man's Vision of God* (Chicago: Willett, Clark, 1941);

Charles H. Hopkins, *The Rise of the Social Gospel in American Protestantism* (New Haven: Yale University Press, 1940);

Walter M. Horton, *Theology in Transition* (New York: Harper, 1943);

Philip Hughes, *A Popular History of the Catholic Church* (New York: Macmillan, 1949);

Neal Hughley, *Trends in Protestant Social Idealism* (New York: King's Crown, 1948);

Howard B. Jefferson, *Experience and the Christian Faith* (New York: Abingdon-Cokesbury, 1942);

Mordecai M. Kaplan, *The Future of the American Jew* (New York: Macmillan, 1948);

Richard Kroner, *The Primacy of Faith* (New York: Macmillan, 1943);

Frank Loescher, *The Protestant Church and the Negro* (New York: Association, 1948);

Henry F. May, *Protestant Churches and Industrial America* (New York: Harper, 1949);

Theodore Maynard, *The Story of American Catholicism* (New York: Macmillan, 1941);

Randolph C. Miller, *What Can We Believe?* (New York: Scribners, 1941);

Conrad Moehlman, *School and Church* (New York: Harper, 1944);

Charles C. Morrison, *Can Protestantism Win America?* (New York: Harper, 1948);

John R. Mott, *The Larger Evangelism* (New York: Abingdon-Cokesbury, 1944);

A. J. Muste, *Not By Might* (New York: Harpers, 1947);

John Oman, *Honest Religion* (New York: Macmillan, 1941);

G. Bromley Oxnam, *Preaching in a Revolutionary Age* (New York: Abingdon-Cokesbury, 1944);

James Parkes, *Judaism and Christianity* (Chicago: University of Chicago Press, 1948);

John A. Ryan, *Social Doctrine in Action* (New York: Harper, 1941);

Fulton J. Sheen, *Philosophy of Religion* (New York: Appleton Century Crofts, 1948);

H. Shelton Smith, *Faith and Nurture* (New York: Scribners, 1941);

Willard L. Sperry, *Religion in America* (New York: Macmillan, 1946);

Herbert H. Stroup, *The Jehovah's Witnesses* (New York: Columbia University Press, 1945);

William W. Sweet, *The American Churches* (New York: Abingdon-Cokesbury, 1948);

Howard Thurman, *The Negro Spiritual Speaks of Life and Death* (New York: Harper, 1947);

Henry P. Van Dusen, *World Christianity* (New York: Abingdon-Cokesbury, 1947);

Walter van Kirk, *Religion and the World of Tomorrow* (Chicago: Willett, Clark, 1941);

Meyer Waxman, *A Handbook of Judaism* (New York: Bloch, 1947);

J. W. Whale, *Christian Doctrine* (New York: Macmillan, 1941);

J. Milton Yinger, *Religion in the Struggle for Power* (Durham, N.C.: Duke University Press, 1946);

American Jewish Year Book, periodical;

Christian Century, periodical;

Christianity and Crisis, periodical;

Commentary, periodical;

Jewish Review, periodical;

Theology Today, periodical.

CHAPTER TWELVE

SCIENCE AND TECHNOLOGY

by MARGO HORN

CONTENTS

Sidebars and tables listed in italics.

1940

- One of the first antibiotics developed in the United States — actinomycin, created by Selman Waksman of Rutgers University — proves too poisonous for use in humans.

12 Feb. The first color television broadcast in America by RCA is accomplished, but development of the new technology is hampered by the need for special equipment.

15 May The Vought-Sikorsky corporation conducts the first completely successful helicopter flight.

15 June President Franklin D. Roosevelt establishes the National Defense Research Committee (NDRC), a new federal agency headed by Vannevar Bush to mobilize science for military purposes.

July Physicist James Hillier of RCA completes construction of the first high-resolution electron microscope.

8 July TWA introduces commercial flights with pressurized cabins.

Oct. The Radiation Laboratory, a microwave-radiation lab nicknamed "Rad Lab," is established at the Massachusetts Institute of Technology to develop an airborne radar-intercept system.

1941

- John Vincent Atanasoff and Clifford Berry complete the Atanasoff Berry Computer (ABC), an unworkable prototype of the programmable digital computer.

- Industrial applications of fluorescent lighting increase to such an extent that three times as many fluorescent bulbs are manufactured by the end of 1941 as in 1940.

- Plutonium is isolated by Edwin M. McMillan and Glenn Theodore Seaborg.

Mar. Nylon is first used to string tennis rackets.

Apr. Under the direction of Lee DuBridge, Rad Lab physicists develop a workable prototype of the microwave AI-10 aircraft radar to detect both aircraft and submarines.

28 June An executive order by President Roosevelt establishes the Office of Scientific Research and Development (OSRD), a larger federal agency that includes the NDRC, to oversee and coordinate all wartime research and development.

Aug. The Rad Lab ASV (air-to-surface-vessel radar) detects ships twenty to thirty miles away and surfaced submarines two to five miles away.

1942

- Biologist Konrad E. Bloch and colleagues describe the biosynthesis of cholesterol.

- Industrialist Henry J. Kaiser perfects prefabrication and mass production techniques in shipbuilding. His Vancouver, Washington, ship works constructs a 10,500-ton Liberty ship in a record-setting seven and a half days.

- Napalm is developed by Harvard scientist Louis F. Fieser for use in U.S. Army flamethrowers.

Jan. Physicists working on nuclear fission unite to form the Metallurgical Laboratory at the University of Chicago.

June President Roosevelt gives Vannevar Bush approval for the Manhattan Project, a secret, large-scale effort to build an atomic bomb.

Summer Tests begin on the first American jet aircraft, the P-59A, at Muroc Army Base, California.

Dec. President Roosevelt approves $400 million for the Manhattan Project.

2 Dec. Physicist Enrico Fermi achieves the first controlled release of nuclear energy in a chain reaction.

1943

- Biologists Salvador Luria and Max Delbruck demonstrate spontaneous mutation in bacteria.

- Biophysicist Britton Chance provides experimental evidence for the formation of an enzyme, substrate complex.

- Physicist Luis Alvarez guides a distant plane to a landing using radar.

Dec. Howard Aiken completes the Harvard-IBM Mark I Automatic Sequence-Controlled Calculator (ASCC).

1944

- An artificially produced plant species, *Ehrharta erecta*, is established in a natural environment.

- Biologists Colin MacCleod, Oswald Avery, and Maclyn McCarty provide evidence that DNA and not protein in chromosomes is responsible for heredity.

- The U.S. military uses the insecticide DDT to eradicate body lice among troops and civilians.

- Ralph Wyckoff and Robley Williams develop the metal-shadowing technique, permitting three-dimensional photographs with the electron microscope.

1 Mar. The Manhattan Project laboratory at Oak Ridge, Tennessee, produces the first milligrams of plutonium.

Nov. Grote Reber publishes the first radio-contour maps of the universe.

1945

- Geneticist George Beadle and biochemist Edward Tatum formulate the one gene–one enzyme hypothesis.

- Engineers J. Presper Eckert, Jr., and John W. Mauchly complete the ENIAC (Electronic Numerical Integrator and Calculator), the first successful automatic electronic digital computer.

16 July In the Trinity Test, the first atomic bomb is tested at Alamogordo, New Mexico.

6 Aug.   The first atomic bomb used in warfare, an American uranium bomb, is dropped on Hiroshima, Japan, killing more than fifty thousand.

9 Aug.   Americans drop a plutonium atomic bomb on Nagasaki, Japan, killing more than forty thousand.

1946

- Biochemist Seymour Stanley Cohen pioneers the use of radioactive labeling of microorganisms.

- Physicists Felix Bloch and Edward Purcell independently introduce the technique of nuclear magnetic resonance.

- Anthropologist Ruth Benedict publishes *The Chrysanthemum and the Sword*, an effort to explain Japanese culture to the West; her study was financed by the U.S. government during World War II.

12 July   Vincent Schaefer performs cloud seeding using dry ice.

1 Aug.   The U.S. Atomic Energy Commission is established.

1947

- Chemist Willard Libby develops a radiocarbon-dating technique using the decay rate of carbon-14 atoms.

21 Feb.   Edwin Land invents a camera-and-film system, later sold as the Polaroid Land Camera, that develops pictures inside the camera in about one minute.

June   Pan American Airways' *America*, a Lockheed Constellation airplane, takes off from New York's La Guardia Airport en route to becoming the world's first globe-circling passenger airplane.

14 Oct.   The Bell X-1, piloted by Capt. Charles E. Yeager, becomes the world's first airplane to fly faster than the speed of sound.

1948

- John Bardeen, W. H. Brattain, and William Shockley invent the point-contact transistor.

- Alfred Kinsey's *Sexual Behavior in the Human Male* is published.

- Chemist Karl Folkers isolates vitamin B$_{12}$.

- Peter Goldmark develops the first long-playing record.

3 June   The largest existing telescope, the two-hundred-inch Hale telescope, is completed at Mount Palomar Observatory at the California Institute of Technology.

20 Nov.   The U.S. Army Signal Corps sets a new balloon altitude record of 26.5 miles.

1949

- Anthropologist Margaret Mead publishes *Male and Female: A Study of the Sexes in a Changing World*, claiming that many aspects of Western culture result from child-rearing practices in the West.

- Biologists John Enders, Thomas Weller, and Frederick Robbins cultivate the poliovirus in vitro on human embryonic tissue.

- General Mills and Pillsbury market the first prepared cake mixes.

- Maurice Wilkes builds EDSAC, the first working computer with a stored program.

- Richard Feynman delivers a paper, "Space-Time Approach in Quantum Electrodynamics," in which he introduces "Feynman diagrams" to calculate the probable path integrals for electromagnetic scattering of atomic particles.

Feb. Edwin M. McMillan announces the first artificially produced mesons.

24 Feb. The first rocket with more than one stage is successfully launched.

25 Feb. The U.S. Navy sets a new rocketry altitude record at White Sands, New Mexico, when the WAC Corporal rocket reaches a height of 250 miles.

2 Mar. U.S. Air Force Superfortress B-50, *Lucky Lady II,* completes the first nonstop flight around the world.

OVERVIEW

Wartime Science. During World War II most scientific research served military imperatives as the U.S. government harnessed science and technology to win the war. The demands of wartime served to speed up scientific innovations — including not only new arms but also new intelligence and transportation technology — which in turn transformed the way the military waged war. World War II transformed science as well, linking science and politics. National-security interests required secrecy of scientists, contradicting the American ideal of free scientific exchange. The Cold War ideology of the postwar period involved science in the arms race and the race into space. With the development of the first atom bomb, American scientists ushered in the atomic age, as the public expressed a mixture of admiration and fear at this tremendous scientific achievement.

Government and Science. Helped by government subsidy and coordination of the private and public sectors, technological advancement in the 1940s proceeded at a pace paralleled only by the rapid rate of change during the industrial revolution of the mid nineteenth century. In 1941, the federal government established the Office of Scientific Research and Development (OSRD) to oversee all wartime scientific and technical research. The OSRD brought together scientists, industrialists, engineers, and military personnel to develop new technology to serve the war effort. War-related research resulted in scientific innovations that were widely put to civilian use immediately after the war, resulting in enormous changes in the way most Americans lived: synthetic rubber, radar, DDT, penicillin, jet-powered aircraft, helicopters, atomic energy, and the electronic computer were all wartime innovations.

Physicists Make the Atomic Bomb. Developments in nuclear physics in the late 1930s set the stage for the development of the atomic bomb in the early 1940s. German physicists Lise Meitner and Otto Hahn coined the term *nuclear fission* in 1939 to describe the new nuclear reactions they observed in their experiments with uranium: they discovered that the U-235 isotope of uranium could be split into smaller atoms when its nucleus was bombarded with slow-speed neutrons, making possible a chain reaction in which huge amounts of energy

were produced. American scientists soon applied this discovery to their own research. By 1940 physicists in the United States had some twenty cyclotrons and at least a dozen other types of nuclear accelerators of different types. Many accelerators were employed for medical purposes, especially for the production of radioactive isotopes, but almost all were used some of the time for nuclear research related to the bomb. When the United States entered World War II in December 1941 many politically liberal scientists were pacifists and opposed the war on moral grounds. As Nazi atrocities became widely known, however, most of these scientists changed their positions on the war.

The European Brain Drain. The rise and spread of fascism and anti-Semitism during the 1930s triggered a massive wave of emigration among European intellectuals. Many came to the United States, where they made a major impact on all aspects of American life, especially science and technology. Among the twenty-two thousand to twenty-six thousand professional people who emigrated from Europe to the United States between 1933 and 1944 were some of the best European scientists and mathematicians. The largest number of émigré scientists came from Germany, but among the first were scientists from Hungary, where fascist dictator Miklós Horthy had enacted anti-Semitic laws in the 1920s. Others came from Austria, Czechoslovakia, Poland, the Low Countries, and France as Hitler's armies swept through those nations in 1938–1940. Still others fled from Stalinism in the Soviet Union. The general brilliance of the émigré scientists is suggested by the number of Nobel Prize winners in their midst. Physicists Albert Einstein of Germany, Enrico Fermi of Italy, and Victor Hess of Austria — as well as physical chemist Peter Joseph Debye of the Netherlands, physiologist Otto Loewi of Germany, and biochemist Otto Meyerhof of Germany — had all won Nobel Prizes before they immigrated to the United States. An equally impressive number of European-born scientists became Nobel laureates after settling in this country; they include physicists Hans Bethe, Felix Bloch, Maria Goeppert Mayer, and Otto Stern — all from Germany — as well as Emilio Segrè from Italy and Eugene Wigner from Hungary; biochemists Konrad Bloch and Fritz Lipmann from Germany and Severo Ochoa from

Spain; and biophysicist Georg von Békésy from Hungary.

Contributions to American Science. The émigrés' most important contribution to wartime science was their work on the Manhattan Project. Among the physicists and physical chemists involved in various aspects of this project to develop the atomic bomb were Hans Bethe, Felix Bloch, and James Franck from Germany; Enrico Fermi, Sergio de Benedetti, and Bruno Rossi from Italy; Eugene Rabinowitch from Russia; Marcel Schein from Czechoslovakia; Leo Szilard, Edward Teller, and Eugene Wigner from Hungary; Stanislaw Ulam from Poland; and Victor Weisskopf from Austria. Mathematician John Von Neumann from Hungary, a colleague of Einstein at the Princeton Institute for Advanced Study, also worked on the Manhattan Project, as well as making important contributions to the development of modern computers and game theory, now widely used to analyze economic and political situations. During the same decade German astronomers Walter Baade and Rudolph Minkowski did important work at the Mount Wilson and Mount Palomar Observatories in California, while Russian émigré George Gamow at Columbia formulated his "Big Bang" theory to explain the origin of the universe. In genetics Erwin Chargaff from Austria, Max Delbrück and Heinz Fraenkel-Conrat from Germany, Salvador Luria from Italy, and Severo Ochoa from Spain did research on nucleic acids that contributed to James Watson and Francis Crick's discovery of the structure of DNA in the early 1950s. After the war the United States and the Soviet Union began competing for the German rocket scientists who had developed the V-2. Some twenty — including Wernher von Braun, Walter Dornberger, Herbert Axter, and Hans Lindenberg — came to the United States, where they made important contributions to the American missile and space programs.

The Case of Albert Einstein. German physicist Albert Einstein was a socialist and pacifist who urged scientists to refuse their expertise to the military. Yet in 1933, after fleeing Nazi Germany and settling in the United States, he publicly declared that he "saw no alternative to the rearmament of the western democracies." In 1939, at the request of physicists Leo Szilard, Edward Teller, and Eugene Wigner, Einstein wrote a letter to President Franklin D. Roosevelt pointing out the dangerous military potential presented by nuclear fission but also warning Roosevelt that Germany might be developing atomic weaponry. The letter helped initiate American efforts to build an atomic bomb. Einstein neither participated in nor had any knowledge of that secret project until the results became public knowledge. Roosevelt authorized the secret research effort known as the Manhattan Project, in late December 1941. After the war Einstein campaigned for the establishment of a world government and the abolition of war.

Pure and Applied Scientific Research in Wartime. So-called pure science involves the pursuit of fundamental answers to theoretical questions without regard to the practical or moral implications of the outcome. Discoveries made in pure scientific research may later be applied to solve practical problems, as in the development of new medical treatments. Wartime imperatives in the 1940s forged an unusually tight link between pure scientific research and its applications, as major discoveries in theoretical physics were pressed into use in developing the atomic bomb. Innovations in engineering and chemistry, such as radar technology or synthetic rubber, were also directed primarily toward application in the war effort.

Biological Research. Unlike scientists in many other fields, most biologists managed to carry on their own theoretical agenda in the 1940s as they pursued the answers to basic questions relating to metabolism, neurophysiology, and, perhaps most significant, genetic processes. Scientific researchers rest on each other's shoulders: they function as a community, building on each new discovery to reach the next. An excellent illustration of this building process is the 1944 discovery by biologists Colin MacCleod, Oswald Avery, and Maclyn McCarty that nucleic acids and not proteins are responsible for the transfer of hereditary traits. This discovery was a major building block for Watson and Crick, who mapped the structure of the nucleic acid DNA in the early 1950s, one of the most phenomenal breakthroughs in twentieth-century science.

TOPICS IN THE NEWS

ANTHROPOLOGY

Culture and Personality. During the 1940s anthropologists, who study human beings in relation to their physical and social environments, focused on the ways in which culture influences personality. In her *Coming of Age in Samoa* (1928), a classic example of a culture and personality study, anthropologist Margaret Mead found none of the internal psychological conflict and rebellion characteristic of adolescents in the West among Samoan girls, demonstrating the relativity of Western concepts of psychological development and arguing that psychology cannot be understood without taking culture into account. Mead had become well known by the 1940s, and this influential study was republished for the armed forces in 1945. During World War II Mead engaged in war work for the National Research Council and the Office of War Information (OWI) and wrote *And Keep Your Powder Dry* (1942), in which she explored the large, complex culture of the United States, employing research methods developed to examine small, premodern societies. Faced with the rise of fascism abroad, she told her readers, "Every social institution which teaches human beings to cringe to those above and step on those below must be replaced by institutions which teach people to look each other in the eye."

Understanding Japan. Sponsored by the OWI, Mead's friend and colleague Ruth Benedict, a pacifist, did research on the Japanese character. In *The Chrysanthemum and the Sword: Patterns of Japanese Culture* (1946) she explained that the wartime behavior of the Japanese was the result of cultural expectations that individuals suppress their emotions and personal desires for the good of the family and the nation. She argued that Japanese culture required enormous self-discipline and that this repression made the Japanese overly submissive to higher, particularly military, authority. She interpreted the Japanese to the American public with great sensitivity, humanizing behavior that Americans had regarded as barbaric. Benedict's study influenced both the American public's perception of the Japanese and the design of postwar U.S. policies toward Japan. Benedict argued persuasively that it would be fruitless for the U.S. government to attempt "to create by fiat a free, democratic

Japan" but that Japan "will seek her place within a world at peace if circumstances permit."

Sources:

Margaret M. Caffrey, *Ruth Benedict: Stranger in This Land* (Austin: University of Texas Press, 1989);

Jane Howard, *Margaret Mead: A Life* (New York: Simon & Schuster, 1984).

ARCHAEOLOGY

The Function of Artifacts. During the 1940s American archaeology moved from a concern with chronological ordering of artifacts to an interest in the function of an object and the context in which it was used. Archaeologists began to look at artifacts as the material relics of social and cultural behavior. The function of a specific object was determined by paying careful attention to where it was found. For example, in a 1943 study of copper and shell artifacts uncovered in the southeastern United States, archaeologist John W. Bennett concluded on the basis of their appearence and context that they were ritual paraphernalia. After almost identical pieces were found in distant sites such as Georgia and Oklahoma, Bennett concluded that he was dealing with the material remains of a widespread religious cult. Bennett's interpretation was a major step in archaeological methodology because it employed both the immediate "microcontext" in which the artifacts were found and the "macrocontext," comparing his findings to those at geographically distant sites.

Settlement Patterns. Examinations of settlement patterns were often the focus of contextual-functional archaeological studies in the 1940s. It was believed that the way people arranged themselves in the landscape, where they settled in relation to natural features and to other people, held important clues to the archaeologist's understanding of social organization. Most of the research on settlement patterns in the 1940s occurred outside the United States. For example, American archaeologist Gordon R. Willey's 1946 study of the Viru Valley in Peru argued that settlement patterns reflect the natural environment and are directly shaped by widely held cultural needs. This work ushered in a new appreciation for the social dimension in archaeological study.

Culture and Natural Environment. Archaeologists in the 1940s also explored the relationships between culture and the natural environment, which related closely to the understanding of context, function, and settlement patterns. Archaeologists embarked on this reasearch in part as a reaction to American anthropologists' lack of interest in the environment as an explanatory factor in the development of culture. One such study, completed in 1939 by archaeologists R. Heizer and S. Cook, examined California shell mounds, waste heaps left behind by ancient peoples. Heizer and Cook were able to reconstruct the diet of the people who made the mounds, and then — using creative formulae based on the weight of the debris they estimated the size of the population that had lived at each site.

Unearthing the Dead Sea Scrolls. The major discovery in classical archaeology during the 1940s was the unearthing of the Dead Sea Scrolls in 1947, during the political turmoil that resulted in the establishment of the independent state of Israel. One member of the team of four archaeologists who initially acquired the Dead Sea Scrolls was an American, John Strugnell, a professor at the Harvard University Divinity School who later became the chief editor of the published texts of the scrolls. The first of the Dead Sea Scrolls were discovered by young Bedouin shepherds in a cave near the village of Qumran, on the northwestern shore of the Dead Sea, in what is now Israel. The Bedouins took the scrolls to a Muslim clergyman in Bethlehem, who in turn took them to Jerusalem, where Eleizer Sukenik, professor of archaeology at Hebrew University, verified their authenticity. When he first traveled to Qumran in 1948, risking physical danger because of the political unrest, Sukenik wrote in his diary that "this was one of the greatest finds ever made in Palestine." Seven scrolls were unearthed in the cave by 1948, and by 1956 eight hundred scrolls were uncovered in a second, nearby cave of Murabbaat. The Dead Sea Scrolls include the biblical book of Isaiah, a narrative called *Genesis Apocryphon*, a book of thanksgiving psalms, and a work titled *The War of the Sons of Light Against the Sons of Darkness*. The unearthing of the scrolls enhanced scholars' understanding of the Old Testament, the early growth of the Christian church, and the nature of Judaism.

Source:

Thurman L. Coss, *Secrets from the Caves: A Layman's Guide to the Dead Sea Scrolls* (New York: Abingdon Press, 1963);

A. Douglas Tushingham, "The Men Who Hid the Dead Sea Scrolls," *National Geographic*, 64 (December 1958): 784–808;

Gordon R. Willey and Jeremy Sabloff, *A History of American Archaeology* (San Francisco: Freeman, 1974).

ASTRONOMY

The Big Bang Theory. During the first decades of the twentieth century cosmologists, physicists, and astronomers proposed various theories about the formation of the universe, debating whether the universe was static or dynamic and expanding. In the 1940s astronomer George Gamow and his colleagues at George Washington University proposed a model of the universe developed from Albert Einstein's 1916 theory of relativity and Edwin Hubble's first measurements of distances in galaxies in 1929. Gamow's Big Bang theory hypothesizes that the universe began with the explosion of primeval matter in a state of extreme heat and high density, beginning the ongoing dynamic expansion of the universe. Gamow theorized that primordial matter consisted of neutrons and their decay products — protons and electrons mixed together — in a sea of high-energy radiation. This matter provided the basic ingredients for the formation of heavier and heavier elements as the universe continued to expand. Gamow had formulated these ideas by 1940 and spent most of the 1940s working with physicists Ralph Asher Alpher and Robert Herman on mathematical calculations of heavy-element formation. Gamow presented the Big Bang theory publicly in 1948, and it was accepted by many astronomers as a valid interpretation of the astronomical evidence. In the decades since 1948, evidence to support parts of the theory has emerged, and it has for the most part been accepted as the best explanation for the origin of the universe.

Radio Astronomy. During the late 1930s and early 1940s Grote Reber made major advancements in radio astronomy. A young radio engineer at the Stewart-Warner Company in Chicago, Reber had read about Karl Jansky's 1931 discovery of naturally occurring radio waves coming from the sky. Reber planned how he could map the stars by measuring the distribution of the radiation intensity throughout the sky at different wavelengths. In 1937 — in the yard of his Wheaton, Illinois, home — he built a radio telescope with a 9.5-meter parabolic reflecting dish that replaced the mirrors in a conventional telescope. Until 1947 he was the only active radio astronomer in the world. In November 1944 he published a complete sky survey, after collecting more than two hundred chart recordings. These radio maps revealed that the peak radiation intensity came from hot, bright stars at the center of our galaxy, located in the constellation Sagittarius. Reber also discovered that radio waves could penetrate the interstellar dust that obscures much of the Milky Way when it is viewed with conventional telescopes. His observations from 1945 to 1947 resulted in maps of the Milky Way with nearly three times better resolution of details than in previous charts. Reber's work led to widespread use of the radio telescope as an important astronomical tool, as scientists developed radio telescopes of increasing size and sophistication.

Galactic Astronomy. Walter Baade, working at the Mount Wilson and Mount Palomar Observatories in California, was able because of his access to these large telescopes to photograph stars in portions of remote galaxies — a technically difficult and theoretically important achievement that led to his division of stars into two stellar populations according to age. In population I are

Wartime aircraft plant

young stars, the most luminous of which are blue. Population II stars are older stars, the brightest of which are red. Population I stars are formed from the interstellar dust created by the explosion of population II stars and are particularly concentrated in areas of interstellar dust, as in the arms of spiral galaxies. Population II stars are located in dust-free regions, as at the centers of spiral galaxies, where star formation has long ago ceased. This classification of star populations represents a milestone in the history of stellar astronomy.

Sources:

George Gamow, *The Creation of the Universe* (New York: Viking, 1952);

John Gribbin, *In Search of the Big Bang* (New York: Bantam, 1986);

J. S. Hey, *The Evolution of Radio Astronomy* (New York: Science History Publications, 1973);

Albrecht Unsöld and Bodo Baschek, *The New Cosmos*, translated by William D. Brewer, fourth edition, revised (Berlin: Springer, 1991).

AVIATION

Military Aircraft. Aircraft played an important role in World War II, with the military using them for purposes such as long-range bombing missions, protection of land and sea convoys, diversion of enemy fire, provision of cover for ground and naval assaults, and transportation of troops, munitions, and supplies. The wartime needs of the military spurred advancements in aviation. By the late 1930s improvements had taken propeller aircraft with piston engines to their farthest limits of speed and power, and wartime aeronautic research was directed toward solving the aerodynamic problems of developing jet aircraft. Innovations in aviation during the war included not only jet-propelled aircraft but also the helicopter, the winged pilotless missile, and the long-range rocket.

NACA. Responsibility for the development of military aviation rested with the National Advisory Committee for Aeronautics (NACA), which served both the army and the navy. The committee, led by physicist Joseph S. Ames of Johns Hopkins University, sponsored studies of the fundamental principles of flight. The results of such research included the development of a streamlined engine covering that permitted greater speed without increased engine power or fuel consumption, as well as leakproof fuel tanks and aluminum air frames. The industrial buildup necessary for the United States to produce some 296,000 military aircraft in the early 1940s dramatically stimulated the domestic economy.

Strategic Aircraft. During the war the United States developed bombers with increasing strategic capability. The Boeing B-17 Flying Fortress, first tested in 1936, had a range of 1,864 miles and carried a bomb load of 4,400 pounds. The B-29 Super Fortress, developed in the late 1930s but not used by the military until late 1944, had a range of more than 4,000 miles with up to 10 tons of bombs, allowing the United States to bomb Japan from bases in Iwo Jima. An even greater improvement was the B-36, introduced into service in 1947. The first intercontinental strategic bomber, it could carry 38 tons of bombs up to 3,700 miles or 4.5 tons up to 9,950 miles.

Jets. Wartime competition hastened the development of jet aircraft. The first American jet fighter was the P-59A Airacomet, designed by Bell Aircraft Company. Initially tested in summer 1942, it was never used in combat because it lacked power and consumed too much fuel. On 28 July 1944 the German Messerschmitt Me-262 became the first jet flown in combat. The first American jet put into service by the military was the Lockheed F-80 Shooting Star, successfully tested in January 1944. In February 1945 the U.S. Army Air Corps announced that the F-80 had been perfected for use in combat, but the planes did not reach air force units in time for use in the war. (They later saw combat in the Korean War.) At the close of World War II, Jerome C. Hunsaker, then chairman of NACA, declared that the end of the war also meant the "end to the development of the airplane as conceived by Wilbur and Orville Wright." The propeller-driven airplane used during the war had power that would have seemed impossible to the Wright brothers. The end of the war marked the beginning of the age of jet propulsion and supersonic flight.

Supersonic Flight. Propeller planes and early jets were not powerful enough to break the sound barrier. When an aircraft reaches the speed of sound, which is about 741 miles per hour at sea level and less at higher altitudes, air particles cannot flow around the plane, and they are compressed into a barrier in front of the plane. As the nose of an aircraft penetrates this wall of air, it creates a shock wave that makes a sound resembling an explosion when it reaches the ground. In 1943 forward-looking engineers John Stack of NACA and Robert Woods of Bell Aircraft recognized that the future of aviation lay in breaking the sonic barrier. They convinced NACA, the U.S. Army Air Corps, and the U.S. Navy to undertake a program exploring supersonic travel. The first aircraft developed as part of this program was the Bell X-1, powered by a rocket that developed six thousand pounds of thrust. On 14 October 1947 the X-1, piloted by Capt. Charles E. Yeager, became the first aircraft to break the sound barrier. Since the speed of sound varies at different altitudes, supersonic flight required a new system of measuring speed. Ernst Mach of Austria developed the new scale: Mach 1 represents the speed of sound regardless of altitude; Mach 2 is twice the speed of sound. Speeds from Mach 1 through Mach 4 are termed supersonic, and

those above Mach 5 are called hypersonic. (Yeager's pioneering flight, for example, exceeded Mach 1 but did not reach Mach 2.)

Civilian Air Transport. After the war military aircraft were converted for civilian use. Civilian air travel rose dramatically from 2.5 million passengers transported in 1937 to 21 million in 1947. As more and more people traveled by air, the aeronautic industry improved the speed and passenger capacity of commercial airliners. For example, the DC-4, in use in 1947, carried forty-two passengers and reached a maximum speed of 211 miles per hour, while the DC-6, introduced in 1950, could carry sixty-six people at speeds of up to 261 miles per hour.

Sources:

Joseph J. Corn, *The Winged Gospel: America's Romance with Aviation, 1900–1950* (New York: Oxford University Press, 1983);

C. H. Hildreth and Bernard C. Nalty, *1001 Questions Answered About Aviation History* (New York: Dodd, Mead, 1969);

Jane's Encyclopedia of Aviation (London: Jane's, 1980).

BIOLOGY: GENETICS

How Traits Are Inherited. In the early 1940s researchers made a major breakthrough in genetics, the branch of biology that deals with inherited characteristics in all forms of life. They established how hereditary information is carried by chromosomes, threadlike structures composed of nucleic acids and proteins that exist within the nucleus of the cell. Each chromosome is made up of individual genes that determine specific hereditary factors (color of hair and eyes, for example). The major question for geneticists in the 1940s was what gives these strands of proteins and nucleic acids the special ability to transmit information about an organism's traits. This question would not be answered entirely until the early 1950s, but important strides were made in the 1940s, as geneticists made discoveries that lay behind James Watson and Francis Crick's groundbreaking discovery in 1952 of the double-helix structure of DNA (deoxyribonucleic acid).

Nucleic Acids. The first step toward this discovery came in 1944, when Colin MacCleod, Oswald Avery, and Maclyn McCarty at the Rockefeller Institute showed that nucleic acids, not the proteins that surround them in chromosomes, determine genetic traits in pneumococcal bacteria. The next research task was determining how nucleic acids work. Geneticist Barbara McClintock, who received the Nobel Prize for medicine or physiology in 1983, provided another piece of this puzzle late in the 1940s. McClintock formulated the concept of "transposable elements," explaining that genes can shift their positions on chromosomes from one generation to the next and exert control over the expression of other genes. McClintock's discovery of transposable elements, or "jumping genes," was dismissed by many other scientists at first but was verified by research conducted in the 1960s.

Sources:

Rene J. Dubos, *The Professor, The Institute, and DNA* (New York: Rockefeller University Press, 1976);

Nina Fedoroff and David Botstein, eds., *The Dynamic Genome: Barbara McClintock's Ideas in the Century of Genetics* (Plainview, N.Y.: Cold Spring Harbor Laboratory Press, 1992);

Horace Freeland Judson, *The Eighth Day of Creation: Makers of the Revolution in Biology* (New York: Simon & Schuster, 1979);

G. Kass-Simon and Patricia Farnes, eds., with the assistance of Deborah Nash, *Women of Science: Righting the Record* (Bloomington: Indiana University Press, 1990);

Evelyn Fox Keller, *A Feeling for the Organism: The Life and Works of Barbara McClintock* (New York: Freeman, 1983);

Daniel Kevles, *In the Name of Eugenics: Genetics and the Uses of Human Heredity* (New York: Knopf, 1985).

BIOLOGY: THE EVOLUTIONARY SYNTHESIS

A Single Theory of Evolution. A major breakthrough for biological science came in 1947, when — after two decades of noncommunication — two branches of evolutionary biology, experimental geneticists and population biologists, fused their opposing theories of evolution into a single model known as the evolutionary synthesis. This synthesis involved reconciling Charles Darwin's mid–nineteenth century idea of natural selection with the early–twentieth century genetic understanding of the transmission of inherited characteristics. This agreement was reached because new scientific discoveries had broken down the barriers that had seemed to separate the two theories.

The Princeton Conference. The extraordinary degree of consensus reached among evolutionists was confirmed at a conference organized by the National Research Council and held in Princeton, New Jersey, on 2–4 January 1947. Conference organizers brought together representatives of the most divergent fields, including paleontologists, morphologists, ecologists, ethologists, systematists, and geneticists. Fifteen years earlier such a gathering would have been the scene of bitter, irreconcilable arguments. No such thing happened at Princeton; indeed, it was difficult to spark any controversy at all.

Source:

Ernst Mayr and William B. Provine, *The Evolutionary Synthesis: Perspectives on the Unification of Biology* (Cambridge, Mass.: Harvard University Press, 1980).

COMPUTER SCIENCE AND INFORMATION TECHNOLOGY

Collaborative Efforts. Early computers are examples of the scientific innovations that resulted from the collaboration of the military, academia, and private industry. Unlike future generations of digital computers, early computers were bulky systems that slowly and clumsily combined various tasks — including gathering, storing, and processing data.

The Mark I. As early as 1937 IBM and Harvard University agreed to cooperate on producing "an automatically operated assembly of calculating machines," primarily for the "use of scientists." IBM envisioned the project as a contribution to science, not as a commercial venture, and expected favorable publicity in the scientific community as its reward for its expenditure of money, time, and parts. In 1943 Howard Aiken at Harvard invented the IBM Automatic Sequence Controlled Calculator (ASCC), soon known as Harvard Mark I. The new computer was first demonstrated to the Harvard faculty in December 1943. The Mark I showed that a complex calculating machine could work automatically, performing operations in sequence, and it could follow a preset program from the entry of the data to the production of the final results. In 1944 the Mark I was turned over to the navy for wartime use. After the war Aiken established the nation's first master's and doctoral degree programs in computer science at Harvard University to provide mathematically trained programmers for the new computers being planned and built.

The Colossus and the ENIAC. The Mark I was an electromechanical and decimal machine that performed calculations using a decimal, or base ten, number system. During the war British and American scientists working independently and secretly developed the first electronic analog computers. These machines make their calculations by analogy, using some quantity or relationship, such as current or displacement, to represent real-world phenomena and solve a problem. A typical use of analog computers is in navigation. Though slow by contemporary standards, they were faster and more sophisticated than the Mark I. British scientist Alan Turing invented the digital Colossus computer, first used in 1944 to break the Germans' Enigma code for sending top-secret wartime messages, giving the Allies an enormous intelligence advantage. Turing's digital compiling process operated by calculating problems using number-based logic. The theory of digital logic he devised was used by American engineers J. Presper Eckert, Jr., and John Mauchly at the University of Pennsylvania, who developed the ENIAC (Electronic Numerical Integrator and Computer), the first general-purpose electronic digital computer. Completed in 1946, the ENIAC was enormous, as large as a boxcar. It weighed thirty tons and had eighteen thousand vacuum tubes; it was programmed by plugging cables from one part to another, like a telephone switchboard.

Sources:

Glen Fleck, ed., *A Computer Perspective* (Cambridge, Mass.: Harvard University Press, 1973);

N. Metropolis, J. Howlett, and Gian Carolo Rota, eds., *A History of Computing in the Twentieth Century* (New York: Academic Press, 1980);

Michael R. Williams, *A History of Computing Technology* (Englewood Cliffs, N.J.: Prentice-Hall, 1985).

CYBERNETICS

Computers and the Human Mind. By 1948, with computation science freed from wartime demands, a new

ENIAC, the first general-purpose electronic digital computer, 1946

area of scientific research had emerged. *Cybernetics,* a word coined by mathematician Norbert Wiener, attempts to find common elements in the functioning of automatic machines and that of the human nervous system. He chose the name *cybernetics,* taken from the Greek word meaning "steersman," because of the importance in the nervous system of control or feedback mechanisms, which he likened to the steering engine of a ship. Cybernetics brought together collaborators from diverse fields, including John Von Neumann, a mathematician at the Institute for Advanced Study at Princeton; physiologist Warren McCulloch of the University of Pennsylvania; Kurt Lewin, a psychologist from Massachusetts Institute of Technology; and husband and wife anthropologists Gregory Bateson and Margaret Mead. In studying the workings of the new computers, these researchers found an enormous similarity between the functioning of the brain and the machine. They demonstrated that computers are capable of complex brain functions such as memory, association, and choice. They also asserted that the human brain behaves much like a machine. Wiener, a leading popularizer of this theory, predicted the application of cybernetics to everything from the design of con-

trol mechanisms for artificial limbs, to psychiatry, to the complete mechanization of industry.

Cybernetics and Psychology. Anthropologist Gregory Bateson soon creatively applied cybernetic theory to psychopathology in families. He theorized that all families, like cybernetic machines, have feedback mechanisms such as communication patterns to bring them back to steady-state equilibrium. Later Bateson applied this analogy to the families of schizophrenics. After listening to talk in schizophrenic families, he learned that it was not chaotic. It had meaning when it was interpreted in the context of family communication patterns. He also noticed that when a schizophrenic family member got well, someone else in the family got worse. Applying cybernetics, Bateson explained that the family was regulating itself through feedback mechanisms that enabled it to return to a steady state in the face of change.

Sources:

Clark A. Elliott and Margaret W. Rossiter, *Science at Harvard: Historical Perspectives* (Bethlehem, Pa.: Lehigh University Press, 1992);

Steve J. Heimes, *John Von Neumann and Norbert Weiner: From Mathematics to the Technologies of Life and Death* (Cambridge, Mass.: MIT Press, 1980);

Creators of the first nuclear chain reaction on the steps of Eckhart Hall, University of Chicago. Back row (left to right): Norman Hilberry, Samuel Allison, Thomas Brill, Robert G. Nobles, Warren Nyer, and Marvin Wilkening. Middle row: Harold Agnew, William Sturm, Harold Lichtenberger, Leona Woods Marshall, and Leo Szilard. Front row: Enrico Fermi, Walter Zinn, Albert Wattenberg, and Herbert Anderson.

Nobert Wiener, *Cybernetics; or, Control and Communication in the Animal and the Machine* (New York: Wiley, 1948).

EARTH SCIENCE: RAINMAKERS

Changing the Weather. In 1943 earth scientists began to investigate the possibility of weather modification. Working at the General Electric Research Laboratory, Irving Langmuir and Vincent Joseph Schaefer began collaborating in a study of how cold temperature and humidity combine to form rime, a thin coating of ice, on all objects exposed to the weather. After observing the way ice forms on airplanes as they pass through cold clouds, Langmuir and Schaefer moved to broader research on clouds and the causes of precipitation.

Human-Made Rainfall. After months of experimentation, Schaefer determined that precipitation is caused in supercooled clouds — clouds at or below freezing in which ice crystals and water drops both exist; the ice crystals grow bigger as the water droplets become smaller, until all the moisture is gone or the ice crystals are heavy enough to fall from the cloud. If the temperature at some point above the ground is above freezing, it rains; if not, it snows. After several unsuccessful attempts to create precipitation on a deep-freeze unit in his laboratory, Schaefer one day tossed in a handful of dry ice and was rewarded with a miniature snowfall. He and Langmuir then reproduced the experiment in nature. On 13 November 1946 Schaefer flew over Mount Greylock in Massachusetts and sprinkled several pounds of dry ice into a supercooled cloud. He then asked the pilot to fly under the cloud, where he saw a flurry of snow. By the time this precipitation reached the ground, where Langmuir was waiting, it had become rain.

"Little Boy" and "Fat Man," the bombs dropped, respectively,
on Hiroshima and Nagasaki

Sources:

Louis J. Battan, *Harvesting the Clouds: Advances in Weather Modification* (Garden City, N.Y.: Doubleday, 1969);

Clark C. Spence, *The Rainmakers: American "Pluviculture" to World War II* (Lincoln: University of Nebraska Press, 1980).

MATHEMATICS: GAME THEORY

The Minimax Theorem. A major innovation in applied mathematics during the 1940s was the use of game theory to create models of economic and social behavior. Game theory analyzes conflicts by creating mathematical models of them. Mathematician John Von Neumann presented the minimax theorem, an initial contribution to the theory, in 1929. The minimax theorem applies to "zero-sum," or no-win games, pure rivalries in which one side's gain is the other's loss. Von Neumann and economist Oskar Morgenstern, both of Princeton University, explained their methods of creating mathematical models of conflicts in their 1944 book, *Theory of Games and Economic Behavior*.

"Non-Zero-Sum" Games. Another game theorist at Princeton in the late 1940s was John Nash, whose dissertation (1950) elaborated on Von Neumann's theory. Focusing on "non-zero-sum" games, Nash described "win-win" rivalries, in which mutual gain is possible, "lose-lose" contests, in which both sides could lose, and games in which win-lose, win-win, and lose-lose situations all exist together. Nash turned game theory into a powerful tool for analyzing economic situations such as trade negotiations and business competition as well as political situations related to the Cold War and nuclear arms negotiations.

Sources:

Sylvia Nasar, "The Lost Years of a Nobel Laureate," *New York Times*, 14 November 1994, III: 1, 8;

William Poundstone, *Prisoner's Dilemma* (New York: Doubleday, 1992).

NUCLEAR RESEARCH

Fermi Achieves the First Chain Reaction. In late 1942 — in a squash court under the stands of Stagg Field, the unused University of Chicago football stadium — a group of physicists led by Enrico Fermi, who had received the 1938 Nobel Prize in physics for his work with radioactivity, constructed a chain-reacting nuclear pile with six tons of uranium metal and fifty tons of uranium oxide encased in four hundred tons of graphite. On 2 December Fermi slowly withdrew the reaction-control rods. As the clicks of neutron counters increased steadily, reminding those present of "a mounting frenzy of crickets," Fermi announced that the pile had reached critical mass, that is, enough material in the pile had become radioactive to create a chain reaction by means of nuclear fission (the splitting of the atomic nucleus). Thus, he achieved the first controlled release of nuclear energy.

Nuclear Physics and the War Effort. The Japanese bombing of Pearl Harbor on 7 December 1941 and the subsequent entrance of the United States into World War II had added a sense of urgency to nuclear research. Amid fears that the Germans might be building an atomic bomb, President Franklin D. Roosevelt authorized the Manhattan Project, a top-secret, large-scale effort to build an atomic bomb within three years.

The Manhattan Project. This huge project was sponsored by the Office of Scientific Research and Development (OSRD), a government agency formed in June 1941 to oversee and coordinate wartime scientific research under the direction of electrical engineer and physicist Vannevar Bush. By late December 1942 Roosevelt had authorized $400 million for the Manhattan Project, headed by Gen. Leslie R. Groves. Involving a huge team of scientists from many disciplines and the U.S. Army Corps of Engineers, the Manhattan Project secretly constructed a plutonium-generating reactor at Hanford, Washington; a gas-diffusion facility at Oak Ridge, Tennessee; and a physics research laboratory at Los Alamos, New Mexico. Under the direction of Berkeley physicist J. Robert Oppenheimer, the Los Alamos team set out to design and build bombs from the materials produced by Hanford and Oak Ridge. They faced the technical problem of how to amass fissionable material and shape it into a workable bomb. By March 1944 the Oak Ridge experiments yielded the first milligrams of plutonium, and by early 1945 the Hanford facilities began turning out pure plutonium.

After the atomic bombings of Hiroshima and Nagasaki, Americans entered into a love affair with the atom. Magazines such as *Science Illustrated* and *Popular Mechanics* predicted that atomic power would be the energy source of the future. They speculated that "Nuclear-8 sedans" would replace gasoline-powered cars and nuclear aircraft would make fuel-powered airplanes obsolete. Nuclear excavation would revolutionize mining, they said, and atomic farming would eliminate poverty. Some prognosticators looked forward to the day when artificial nuclear-powered suns mounted on towers would control the weather.

The term *atomic* was used in equally fanciful ways. Within hours of the Hiroshima blast the bartender at the Washington Press Club had invented the "Atomic Cocktail" (Pernod and gin), and within days stores were advertising "Atomic Sales." Before long, shoppers could buy "Atomic jewelry." (One piece was a pearl "bomb" exploding with various mock gemstones.) In 1946 kids could get an "Atomic Bomb Ring" for fifteen cents and a Kix cereal box top. A Louisville collection agency advertised that it would use its "Atomic Force" to wipe out delinquent accounts. By 1947 the Manhattan telephone directory listed forty-five businesses with "atomic" in their names, including the Atomic Undergarment Company. The previous fall Hollywood starlet Linda Christians was labeled "The Anatomic Bomb." Other terms associated with the bomb also began to seem "sexy." In July 1946, after the United States conducted an atomic-bomb test at the Pacific atoll of Bikini, a fashion designer named a new abbreviated two-piece bathing suit the bikini.

Country music also got a good bit of mileage from the bomb. One of the first songs it inspired was Karl Davis and Harry Taylor's "When the Atomic Bomb Fell," recorded in December 1945. The song claimed that the bomb gave the Japanese just what they deserved:

> Smoke and fire it did flow
> Through the land of Tokyo
> There was brimstone and dust everywhere.
> When it all cleared away,
> There the cruel Jap did lay,
> The answer to our fighting boy's prayer.

In the same month the Slim Gaillard Quartet recorded "Atomic Cocktail," and in early 1946 the Buchanan Brothers had a major hit with "Atomic Power." Other popular songs of 1946 and 1947 included "Atom Buster," "Atom Polka," and "Atom Bomb Baby."

Source: Paul Boyer, *By the Bomb's Early Light: American Thought and Culture at the Dawn of the Atomic Age* (New York: Pantheon, 1985).

To Build the Bomb. The Los Alamos scientists had to understand critical-mass behavior in order to design a workable bomb. That is, they had to find out how a critical mass of uranium 235 or plutonium would behave in the split second between the start of the chain reaction and the resulting explosion. They also had to avoid the predetonation of the plutonium. Solving these problems represented a formidable challenge. The solution was an implosion bomb: they surrounded a mass of subcritical plutonium with high explosives that, when detonated, produced a spherically symmetrical shock wave traveling toward the center of the bomb. The shock wave compressed the plutonium into a critical mass and kept it compressed while a rapid chain reaction occurred, maximizing energy release while avoiding predetonation.

The Trinity Test. On 16 July 1945 at Alamogordo, two hundred miles from the Los Alamos weapons lab, scientists tried out the first plutonium device. The explosion lit the predawn desert sky and shook the earth with the power of twenty thousand tons of dynamite. The atomic age had begun.

Hiroshima and Nagasaki. On 6 August 1945 the American Superfortress bomber *Enola Gay* dropped a uranium bomb called "Little Boy" on Hiroshima, Japan, killing more than fifty thousand people and totally destroying four square miles of the city. Three days later another American bomber dropped "Fat Man," a plutonium bomb, on Nagasaki, killing more than forty thousand and destroying a third of the city. The Japanese surrendered the next day.

Scientific Responsibility. Many scientists were deeply troubled by their role in creating the atomic bomb and led efforts to persuade Congress of the importance of arms control. Physicist Eugene Rabinowitch committed himself to "fight to prevent science from becoming an executioner of mankind." Many liberal scientists also wanted the United States to share atomic-energy secrets with the rest of the world and establish a system of United Nations control. Yet, according to a September 1945 survey, 75 percent of the American people wanted the United States to retain control of the bomb. Efforts at international control failed in the late 1940s, as the

Nagasaki, August 1945

expressed awareness that if ethical rules were adopted "then obviously a great deal of our present human tracer studies must be discontinued." The minutes reported that there were "ethical and medico-legal objections to the administration of radioactive materials without the patients' knowledge or consent," and they expressed the concern that there would be even greater government culpability "if a Federal agency condones human guinea pig experimentation." Yet the U.S. Defense Department circumvented the objections of the AEC, and hundreds of people were irradiated — most often in the thyroid gland — in medical experiments conducted during the late 1940s and 1950s.

The Hydrogen Bomb. Despite the objections of scientists and public fears, government policy makers pressed for the development of further nuclear weapons and prevailed. Physicist Edward Teller, who had been involved in the Manhattan Project, passionately supported the development of a hydrogen bomb, a device that works by fusion — the creation of an atomic nucleus by the union of two lighter nuclei. Deriving its power from the same process that creates the heat and light of the sun, a hydrogen or thermonuclear bomb is a superbomb a thousand times more powerful than the bombs dropped on Hiroshima and Nagasaki. The question of developing the hydrogen bomb rested with the general advisory committee of the AEC, established by the 1946 Atomic Energy Act. Many top scientists, led by Fermi and Oppenheimer, opposed developing the hydrogen bomb, arguing that scientists had not always behaved responsibly in nuclear research. Five of six scientists on the AEC advisory board felt that developing the superbomb could spark an uncontrollable arms race and that the only hope for world peace lay in refusing to allow development of the bomb. Yet President Harry S Truman was concerned that the Russians were developing nuclear weapons (they exploded an atomic bomb in 1949), and in 1950 he authorized a crash program to build the hydrogen bomb.

Creation of the National Science Foundation. It was clear that in the atomic age it had just entered, the United States needed to establish national policies to govern scientific, especially nuclear, research. Scientists, academic leaders, and policy makers were concerned that the freedom of pure scientific research would be compromised by financial ties to industry and the military. Scientists, congressional leaders, and many in the Truman administration believed that the best way to halt the military's increasing role in academic science was for Congress to create the National Science Foundation (NSF). Under the direction of scientists, the NSF would plan a federally mandated scientific research program. Truman vetoed the original 1947 legislation because he wanted the agency to be controlled directly by the president, not by a board of scientists. After compromise legislation, which allowed for shared presidential and scientific control, the act establishing the NSF was passed

United States adopted a defensive Cold War outlook toward the Soviet Union and other Communist nations.

A Shift in Public Opinion. The atomic bombings of Japan were denounced in liberal religious circles as cause for "American shame." Most people were ambivalent, relieved that war had ended but fearful that perhaps science had finally gone too far. Early polls revealed that the public overwhelmingly backed the use of atomic bombs against Japan because it brought the war to a speedy end. In a September 1945 Gallup poll 65 percent of respondents agreed with the statement that the development of the atomic bomb was "a good thing." Yet public response changed dramatically as time passed. By October 1947 only 55 percent continued to affirm that it was a good thing, while those who considered the bomb "a bad thing" more than doubled, from 17 percent in 1945 to 36 percent in 1947.

Health Hazards. As early as 1947 there were concerns about the health hazards of radiation research. Military researchers pressed for radiation experiments on humans, while physicians and biologists warned of the possible dangers. Dr. Shield Warren, chief medical officer of the Atomic Energy Commission (AEC), said in July 1949 that he was "taking an increasingly dim view of human experimentation." Later that year the Joint Panel on the Medical Aspects of Atomic Warfare was established to monitor atomic research in the U.S. Defense Department. Minutes of one panel meeting made public in 1994 by Congress and signed by President Truman in March 1950. The NSF provided federal support for basic scientific training and research that was largely insulated from political interests and dedicated to the advancement of science.

Sources:

Barton J. Bernstein, "Roosevelt, Truman, and the Atomic Bomb: A Reinterpretation," *Political Science Quarterly*, 90 (Spring 1975): 23–69;

Paul Boyer, *By the Bomb's Early Light: American Thought and Culture at the Dawn of the Nuclear Age* (New York: Pantheon, 1985);

Arthur Holly Compton, *Atomic Quest: A Personal Narrative* (New York: Oxford University Press, 1956);

Leslie R. Groves, *Now It Can Be Told: The Story of the Manhattan Project* (New York: Harper, 1962);

Daniel Kevles, *The Physicists: The History of a Scientific Community in Modern America* (New York: Knopf, 1978);

Martin J. Sherwin, *A World Destroyed: The Atomic Bomb and the Grand Alliance* (New York: Knopf, 1975).

ORGANIC CHEMISTRY

"Your Servant the Molecule" (Monsanto slogan, 1944). During the 1940s advances in organic chemistry, the study of carbon compounds, led to the development of synthetic chemicals and a tremendous growth in the American chemical industry. Advances in the understanding of the arrangement of atoms in molecules and the nature of chemical reactions paved the way for the development of synthetics, such as saccharin and plastic, that had a wide-ranging effect on consumer products, transforming everything from fabrics to food production to home appliances. Ten chemical corporations built on the new synthetic chemistry — including Celanese and Monsanto, as well as old-line, giant chemical companies such as Du Pont, Allied Chemical, and Union Carbide — accounted for nearly 9 percent of the total assets of the top one hundred industrials in 1948, signifying the "chemicalization" of American industry.

New Synthetics. While chemistry remained a mystery to most Americans, its applications changed their lives. The new plastic polyethylene, introduced in 1944 by Du Pont, is a tough thermoplastic able to withstand a wide temperature range. Its diverse uses include collapsible tubes for food and cosmetics, as well as medical equipment, lighting fixtures, and furniture. Also introduced in 1944, polysiloxane polymer (silicone) was produced by the Corning Company. By the end of the decade Shell, Dow, and Ciba had introduced epoxide resins for electrical use, laminates, paints, and varnishes. Research at the Shell Corporation from 1939 to 1942 made it possible to increase the octane rating of gasoline. Synthetic rubber was made from the petroleum derivative butadiene. By 1945 the ESSO Company (Standard Oil of New Jersey) had produced five hundred thousand tons of butadiene, almost all of which went into the production of synthetic rubber.

JAMES B. CONANT: ACADEMIC AT WAR

James Bryant Conant (1893–1978) gave up research in chemistry when he became president of Harvard University in 1933, but he continued to influence the course of American science, especially during World War II. In 1940 Vannevar Bush, head of the National Defense Research Committee (NDRC), appointed Conant to this new group, which was intended to coordinate scientific efforts on wartime projects. The following year Conant established an NDRC office in London and began an information-exchange program between British and American scientists. One of the most significant results of this exchange was the improvement of American radar installations. In 1941 — when Bush became head of the Office of Scientific Research and Development (OSRD), which included the NDRC — Conant became head of the NDRC and held the post for the remainder of the war. During that time he was responsible for important projects such as microwave radar and synthetic rubber. He also worked closely with Bush in obtaining the funds for the Manhattan Project to build the atomic bomb, and then he designed and organized the research program. In fall 1942, after the military draft had created a severe shortage of trained scientists, Conant urged the Roosevelt administration to send students to college at federal expense and argued that well-trained scientists should not be drafted.

Source: James Hershberg, *James B. Conant: Harvard to Hiroshima and the Making of the Nuclear Age* (New York: Knopf, 1993).

Source:

Arnold Thrackray, Jeffrey Sturchio, P. Thomas Carroll, and Robert Bush, *Chemistry in America, 1876–1976* (Dordrecht, The Netherlands: Reidel, 1985).

RADAR

Discovery of Radar. Though the principles of radar — an acronym for *radio detection and ranging* — were understood in the early 1930s, its application in the United States was slow to develop. In 1930 Lawrence Hyland of the Naval Research Laboratory observed that radio signals transmitted from the ground were reflected back by passing airplanes and showed up on a radio-wave detection screen. This discovery opened up the possibility of developing a system to detect and locate aircraft. The U.S. Army did not recognize the importance of radar until 1936, when it established a radar research unit at the U.S. Army Signal Corps laboratory in Fort Monmouth, New Jersey. Research moved slowly because the navy classified pulse-radar research as secret, preventing the navy and army from exchanging information.

Radarscope, 1945

The Tizard Mission. After the outbreak of World War II Great Britain helped to strengthen U.S. radar operations. In summer 1940 Prime Minister Winston Churchill sent a technical mission to the United States. Its director, Sir Henry Tizard, a defense scientist who believed in the full exchange of technical information, brought Britain's most vital secrets of military technology. Led by Alfred Loomis, head of the radar section of the National Defense Research Committee (NDRC), American scientists were in the throes of developing microwave radar, which had the advantages of using small antennae, accurately locating low-flying aircraft, and discriminating between adjacent targets. The Tizard Mission brought to the United States the resonant cavity magnetron, which emitted radiation at an intensity thousands of times greater than the most advanced American tube. Loomis claimed that the British magnetron advanced the U.S. radar program by two years. The British desperately needed an airborne radar-intercept system to help them cope with German night bombing. Loomis agreed to develop the magnetron into an airborne-intercept system and established a project code-named AI-10.

The Rad Lab. Under contract from the NDRC, project AI-10 was established at the Massachusetts Institute of Technology, where the MIT Radiation Laboratory, known as the "Rad Lab," was created especially for the project. Physicist Lee DuBridge from the University of Rochester directed the Rad Lab and recruited a staff of nearly forty young nuclear physicists. Quickly building a microwave lab of wood and tar paper on the roof of one of MIT's tall buildings, they succeeded by April 1941 in developing a workable prototype of the microwave AI-10 that detected both aircraft and submarines.

Robert Watson-Watt Reinforces U.S. Radar. In 1941 British radar expert Robert Watson-Watt inspected U.S. aerial defenses and found the American radar barrier filled with holes. Watson-Watt made a series of suggestions — including relocating stations and providing ground control of aerial interceptions — to provide the United States with effective coverage.

The ASV. Following British innovations, Rad Lab scientists made building an airborne submarine-detection unit their top priority, and by August 1941 they had designed the Rad Lab ASV (air-to-surface vessel) radar, which detected ships twenty to thirty miles away and submarines at the surface two to five miles away. In December flight trials of the ASV so impressed the U.S. Army that by January 1942, with the United States at war, the U.S. Army Air Corps requested ten Rad Lab ASV radar units to equip B-18 aircraft for patrol along critical American coastal sea lanes.

Loran. By March 1942, B-18 bombers and naval destroyers equipped with long-wave ASV search radar were able to keep enemy submarines three hundred miles from the coast. During 1942 Rad Lab physicists also developed loran (long-range navigation) radar for in-flight navigation. By the end of 1942 the Rad Lab budget had reached $1,150,000 a month, and by 1945 it employed nearly five hundred physicists. Wartime innovation in radar technology led to the development of the civilian radar systems installed at U.S. airports after the war.

Source:
Henry Guerlac, *Radar in World War II* (Los Angeles: Tomash / New York: American Institute of Physics, 1987).

ROCKETRY

The German V-2. Rocket technology was first developed by the Germans in 1929 as a way to enhance its artillery power. The first V-2 rocket, developed by Wernher von Braun, was successfully tested on 3 October 1942. The V-2 was a huge, fast missile. When it reached a speed of 5,577 feet per second, the engine shut off and the missile continued to climb on a ballistic trajectory that had a maximum altitude of fifty miles, almost entirely above the atmosphere. More than three thousand German V-2s caused enormous devastation in England and Europe in 1944 and 1945. At the end of World War II American military scientists aggressively seized the technology behind the V-2 and brought German rocket scientists, including von Braun, to the United States. The V-2, considered a masterpiece of technology, differed little from the rockets later designed for the American space program, for which von Braun laid the foundations.

Project Hermes. The first phase of the U.S. rocketry program was Project Hermes, the "Ordnance Guided Missile and Rocket Programs," initiated by the U.S. government in November 1944. Charged with the development of long-range guided missiles for use against ground targets and high-altitude aircraft, project engineers investigated all aspects of rocketry, including missile structures, transonic and supersonic aerodynamics and ramjet engines, missile guidance and control, ground launch equipment and handling, instrumentation, fuels and propellants, and rocket engines. In the first phase of Hermes, U.S. scientists studied German missiles used in the war, and by using military intelligence they identified confiscated hardware and collected important pieces for shipment to the United States. The result of this operation was three hundred train-car loads of V-2 missile parts, which were unloaded at Las Cruces, New Mexico, in July 1945.

Operation Paperclip. The second phase of Hermes was Operation Paperclip, the acquisition of top German rocket scientists. After the war four hundred German scientists surrendered to the United States. One hundred of them were chosen to be sent to the United States to perform scientific research. The name "Operation Paperclip" comes from the placing of a paperclip on the folder of each scientist selected. Twenty of these German scientists went to the White Sands Missile Range in New Mexico, where, under contract from General Electric, they deciphered specifications and drawings necessary to build V-2s. By the time the General Electric contract expired on 30 June 1951, sixty-seven V-2 rockets had been built and fired.

Project Bumper. In October 1946 Project Bumper was instituted to investigate the separation problems of two-stage liquid rockets and to pursue the goal of launching a rocket beyond the earth's gravitational field. Project Bumper combined the V-2 with the WAC Corporal rocket. (WAC is an acronym for *without altitude control.*) The WAC Corporal was placed as deeply as possible into the V-2 booster, with enough space in the instrument compartment for the necessary guidance equipment. The design of Bumper involved a two-year collaboration among General Electric, the Jet Propulsion Laboratory (JPL), and the Douglas Aircraft Company. On 24 February 1949 *Bumper Five* reached 410 kilometers above the earth, becoming the first true space vehicle. Then, in July 1950, another two-stage rocket based on the V-2, with a WAC Corporal rocket mounted on its nose, was launched from Cape Canaveral, Florida.

BALLOON BOMBS

Innovative technology was commonly used for military purposes in World War II, most spectacularly when Germany launched the high-tech V-2 rocket against England. Japan used a low-tech, but no less dangerous, weapon against the United States. Taking advantage of prevailing westerly wind currents across the Pacific, Japan launched thousands of high-altitude balloons armed with bombs to float across the ocean and explode in the United States. Nearly 300 made it to the West Coast, some landing as far east as Iowa and Kansas. Most failed to detonate, but a few did spark wildfires, and six people were killed by a bomb explosion in Oregon. Government authorities kept the balloons a secret because they were afraid the Japanese would be inspired to launch more balloons if they knew some had reached their target. The secrecy was effective, and the Japanese soon abandoned the project, a decision that was lucky for the United States. Recently recovered documents suggest that in 1944 Japanese military officials seriously considered using the balloons to carry serious diseases such as anthrax and plague to the United States.

Sources:
Walter R. Dornberger, *V-2,* translated by James Cleugh and Geoffrey Halliday (New York: Viking, 1954);

Eugene M. Emme, ed., *The History of Rocket Technology* (Detroit: Wayne State University Press, 1964);

Gregory P. Kennedy, *Vengeance Weapon 2: The V-2 Guided Missile* (Washington, D.C.: Smithsonian Institution Press, 1983);

Frederick J. Ordway and Mitchell R. Sharpe, *The Rocket Team* (Cambridge, Mass.: MIT Press, 1982).

TELEVISION

Television Technology. Television was introduced to Americans at the 1939 New York World's Fair, but World War II interrupted its commercial development. The first color television broadcast was a private demonstration by RCA at its New Jersey Laboratories on 12 February 1940. On 1 September 1940 CBS entered the competition by demonstrating to the public a superior sequential color system based on the research of engineer Peter Carl Goldmark, who was inspired to develop a color-television system when he saw the spectacular Technicolor movie *Gone With the Wind,* released in 1939.

The Television Boom. After the Federal Communications Commission (FCC) adopted standards for black-and-white television in 1941, RCA gave NBC leadership in the development of black-and-white technology. Because of the war, television was still a novelty, confined to a few thousand urban homes, as late as 1946. The television boom did not begin until 1949. CBS and NBC competed fiercely to create a workable color system. CBS and RCA began manufacturing color television sets in the early 1950s, but networks did not begin televising all prime-time shows in color until the mid 1960s.

Sources:

Erik Barnouw, *A History of Broadcasting in the United States,* 3 volumes (New York: Oxford University Press, 1966–1970);

Kenneth Bilby, *The General: David Sarnoff and the Rise of the Communications Industry* (New York: Harper & Row, 1986);

Donald G. Fink and David M. Lutyens, *The Physics of Television* (Garden City, N.Y.: Doubleday, 1960);

Sally Bedell Smith, *In All His Glory: The Life of William S. Paley* (New York: Simon & Schuster, 1990).

THE TRANSISTOR

Limitations of Vacuum Tubes. Before 1948 electrical engineers used vacuum tubes in radios, televisions, computers, and other electrical devices. These bulky tubes, usually encased in glass, typically performed one function each, such as amplifying electronic signals. A complex electrical circuit required several tubes, a lot of space, and good ventilation, since the tubes emitted heat and failed when they got too hot. Moreover, vacuum tubes were inefficient; large amounts of electricity had to be input into the electrical circuit to make a set of tubes work.

The Transistor. At the end of 1947 William Shockley, John Bardeen, and Walter H. Brattain, working at the Bell Telephone Laboratories, developed the transistor as an efficient alternative to vacuum tubes. The Bell physicists found that by introducing impurities into semiconductors, normally either silicon or germanium, and attaching the semiconductors to a metallic base, they could amplify electronic signals. The transistor could be composed of microscopic parts, and it operated at much cooler temperatures than vacuum tubes. Transistors were also sturdy, lending themselves well to use in portable appliances. Most significant, though, transistors could operate an electrical circuit with as little as one-twentieth of the initial power required by vacuum tubes.

Everyday Uses of Transistors. When the discovery was announced in 1948, scientists recognized its importance immediately, but it took half a decade before engineers adapted the transistor to everyday use. By the mid 1950s transistors were used in practically every electronic product available, and by the end of the decade they had virtually displaced the vacuum tube. Shockley, Bardeen, and Brattain won the Nobel Prize in 1956 for their discovery of the transistor.

Source:

Jeremy Bernstein, *Three Degrees Above Zero: Bell Labs in the Information Age* (New York: Scribners, 1984);

Prescott C. Mabon, *Mission Communications: The Story of Bell Laboratories* (Murray Hill, N.J.: Bell Telephone Laboratories, 1975);

Frank H. Rockett, "The Transistor," *Scientific American,* 179 (December 1948): 53–54;

F. M. Smits, ed., *A History of Engineering and Science in the Bell System: Electronics Technology (1925–1975)* (Indianapolis: AT&T Customer Information Center, 1985).

HEADLINE MAKERS

JOHN VINCENT ATANASOFF

1904-1982

ELECTRICAL ENGINEER, MATHEMATICIAN, PHYSICIST

Computer Pioneer. John Vincent Atanasoff invented the first automatic digital computer, but before he perfected his design, others had developed computers that were more sophisticated than his, and his contribution to computer technology was nearly forgotten.

Early Years. Atanasoff became interested in calculating at the age of nine, when his father, an electrical engineer, gave him a slide rule. After receiving a B.S. in electrical engineering at the University of Florida in 1925, Atanasoff earned an M.A. in mathematics at Iowa State University (1926) and a Ph.D. in physics from the University of Wisconsin (1930).

Inventing a Computer. Atanasoff encountered the limits of existing calculating instruments as he worked on the extensive calculations for his doctoral dissertation on the electrical properties of helium. As a professor of mathematics and physics at Iowa State, he began to work on an improved calculating machine during the 1930s. In 1937 he developed the idea for an electronic digital machine that would use binary numbers (base two) instead of the traditional decimal (base ten) of existing calculating machines; it would have memory, and unlike existing analog calculators it would operate by direct logic rather than by analogy. In 1939 Atanasoff and his assistant, Clifford Berry, built a prototype of the Atanasoff Berry Computer (ABC) that impressed Iowa State enough to earn them a university grant of $850 to build a fully operating machine.

Problems. Completed in late 1941, the ABC was too slow. It could not be programmed, and it contained systematic errors. While Atanasoff could have improved the machine, the outbreak of World War II took him away from the project. He spent the war years working for the Naval Ordnance Laboratory in Washington, D.C., and stayed on after the war. In 1946 he was asked to build a computer for the navy, but the project was canceled after a few months, when the army revealed the existence of the ENIAC computer, developed for them by J. Presper Eckert, Jr., and John Mauchly. Although Mauchly had examined the ABC and talked to Atanasoff about his invention, the ENIAC — which was in fact more sophisticated and efficient than the ABC — was also said to be different from the ABC. Eckert and Mauchly were widely credited with inventing the first automatic digital computer.

Recognition. Amid the confusion of Atanasoff's leaving Iowa State for war work, the university had never completed the patent application for the ABC, and Atanasoff's contribution to computer history was largely ignored or forgotten until the 1970s. The Sperry Rand Corporation, which had bought the patent to the ENIAC, was charging royalties to other computer manufacturers. Honeywell refused to pay, claiming that the Sperry Rand patent was not valid, since ENIAC was not an original invention but was derived from the ABC and from information Atanasoff passed to John Mauchly in the early 1940s. Sperry Rand sued Honeywell. On 17 October 1973, after six years of litigation, a U.S. District Court judge ruled, "Eckert and Mauchly did not themselves first invent the automatic electronic digital computer, but instead derived that subject matter from one Dr. John V. Atanasoff."

Sources:

Alice R. Burks and Arthur W. Burks, *The First Electronic Computer: The Atanasoff Story* (Ann Arbor: University of Michigan Press, 1988);

Clark R. Mollenhoff, *Atanasoff: Forgotten Father of the Computer* (Ames: Iowa State University Press, 1988).

VANNEVAR BUSH

1890-1974

ELECTRICAL ENGINEER, ADMINISTRATOR

Directing Wartime Research. "I'm no scientist, I'm an engineer," Vannevar Bush claimed late in his life. Yet as head of the U.S. Office of Scientific Research and Development (OSRD) during World War II, he presided over the development of the atomic bomb and made a major impact on the course of scientific research in the United States both during and after the war.

Education. Born in Boston to a Universalist minister and his wife, Bush put himself through Tufts University by tutoring football stars in mathematics. Bush earned B.S. and M.S. degrees in engineering from Tufts in 1913, and in 1916 the Massachusetts Institute of Technology (MIT) and Harvard University jointly awarded him a doctorate in electrical engineering.

Early Career. Bush returned to the faculty at Tufts, where he had taught before pursuing his doctorate. In 1917, when the United States entered World War I, Bush was selected to work at the U.S. Navy antisubmarine laboratory in New London, Connecticut. He developed a submarine detector that was never used and drew the conclusion that lack of communication between scientists and government leaders and lack of coordination of scientists' efforts had led to the underuse of scientists' talents in the war effort. In 1919 Bush joined the MIT faculty as associate professor of electrical-power transmission. By 1923 he was a full professor, and in 1932 he became first vice-president and dean of engineering.

Research at MIT. At MIT Bush's research resulted in improvements in the designs of vacuum tubes and four-engine bombers and inventions such as the justifying typewriter, the cinema integraph, and especially the differential analyzer, which has been called the most important calculator of its time. Designed to solve lengthy equations and capable of calculating the answers to as many as twenty-five sets of data in a few minutes, it was used during World War II for purposes such as calculating ballistics tables and the curvature of radar antennas.

Carnegie Institution. In 1939 Bush became president of the Carnegie Institution in Washington, D.C. At the same time, he became chairman of the National Advisory Committee for Aeronautics.

Organizing Government Science. With the outbreak of World War II, Bush became concerned about the need to mobilize American scientists and coordinate their efforts for national defense. Deeply troubled by the prospect that the Germans might be making an atomic bomb, he sought the establishment of a federal agency to ensure that scientists, not politicians or military technicians, would direct wartime science. Bush joined with President Karl Compton of MIT, President James B. Conant of Harvard, and Frank B. Jewitt, president of the National Academy of Sciences, to devise the National Defense Research Committee (NDRC), which President Franklin D. Roosevelt established in June 1940 with Bush as chairman. A year later President Roosevelt created the larger OSRD — including the NDRC, a newly created Advisory Council and Committee on Medical Research, and other groups — appointing Bush to head the OSRD.

The OSRD. Bush's greatest challenge and major achievement at the OSRD was to maintain the confidence of the military, which distrusted civilian compliance with security regulations, while fighting the drafting of bright young scientists into the armed forces. Bush also had to get adequate funds for research and make certain that projects were fairly distributed between government, academic, and industrial facilities. The OSRD oversaw the development of new technologies and many new weapons (including the atomic bomb), as well as production of the antibiotic penicillin and improved blood substitutes and antimalarial drugs. Bush showed exceptional ability in administering the huge numbers of individuals and facilities involved in work for the OSRD.

Postwar Work. In September 1947, after the OSRD had been dissolved, Bush was appointed director of the Joint Research and Development Board, responsible for resolving "differences among the several departments and agencies of the military establishments." He was also instrumental in creating the National Science Foundation (NSF) in 1950. He also backed the formation of the Atomic Energy Commission (AEC) in 1946, which many scientists felt would lead to the military domination of atomic research but which Bush considered a necessary control to ensure responsible experimentation. Bush's view of science has been called elitist, but he has been justifiably praised for his often successful attempts to protect what he considered the "best science" from fleeting political interests. After the war Bush stayed close to the Truman administration, but in the 1950s he found his power considerably diminished. He tried unsuccessfully to delay the testing of the hydrogen bomb in 1952, and in 1954 he stood behind J. Robert Oppenheimer when his loyalty was questioned for opposing the development of that weapon. Bush retired as president of Carnegie Institution in 1955 but remained active on the boards of MIT and various corporations until his death in 1974.

Sources:

Colin B. Burke, *Information and Secrecy: Vannevar Bush, Ultra, and the Other Memex* (Metuchen, N.J.: Scarecrow Press, 1993);

Vannevar Bush, *Pieces of the Action* (New York: Morrow, 1970);

Daniel J. Kevles, *The Physicists: The History of a Scientific Community in Modern America* (New York: Knopf, 1978);

James M. Nyce and Paul Kahn, eds., *From Memex to Hypertext: Vannevar Bush and the Mind's Machine* (Boston: Academic Press, 1991).

Sources:

Martha J. Bailey, Entry on Cori, in her *American Women in Science: A Biographical Dictionary* (Denver, Santa Barbara & Oxford, U.K.: ABC-CLIO, 1994), pp. 70–71;

John Parascandola, Entry on Cori, in *Notable American Women: The Modern Period,* edited by Barbara Sicherman and Carol Hurd Green with Ilene Kantrov and Harriette Walker (Cambridge, Mass. & London: Harvard University Press, 1980), pp. 165–167.

GERTY THERESA CORI

1896-1957

BIOCHEMIST, PHYSICIAN

Nobel Prize Winner. Gerty Theresa Cori was the first American to receive the Nobel Prize for medicine or physiology. She shared the 1947 prize with her husband, Carl Cori, and with Argentinian Bernardo Houssay.

Early Years. Born Gerty Theresa Radnitz in Prague, then part of the Austro-Hungarian Empire, Cori entered the medical school of the German University of Prague in 1914 and graduated in 1920, the same year she married Carl Cori, a fellow student with whom she shared an interest in laboratory research. They collaborated on their first project, a study of the immune bodies in blood, in the first year they were married.

Research in the United States. The Coris immigrated to the United States in 1922 and worked at the New York Institute for the Study of Malignant Diseases (later Roswell Park Memorial Institute) in Buffalo. They continued to work together on research projects even after Carl Cori was advised by colleagues and employers that such collaboration would be detrimental to his career. In 1931 they moved to the medical school at Washington University in Saint Louis, where Carl Cori became chair of the department of pharmacology. Because university nepotism rules forbade the appointment to the faculty of two members of the same family, Gerty Cori was hired as a research associate at a low, token salary. She was finally given a regular faculty appointment as professor of biochemistry in 1947, when she and her husband won the Nobel Prize. The Coris were given the prize for the elucidation of the metabolism of the essential carbohydrate glycogen, which consists of large numbers of glucose molecules bound together and which breaks down into glucose as the body requires it for energy. By identifying the metabolic processes and the enzymes involved, the Coris established how glycogen was synthesized and broken down and under what conditions. Gerty Cori also developed the conceptual classification of glycogen-storage diseases, becoming the first scientist to demonstrate that a defect in an enzyme was the cause of a human genetic disease. This discovery was described in 1958 as "an unmatched scientific achievement." In 1948 the American Chemical Society gave her the Garvan Medal, awarded to a woman chemist for excellence.

ENRICO FERMI

1901-1954

PHYSICIST

Nobel Prize Winner. The winner of the Nobel Prize for physics in 1938, Enrico Fermi played a prominent role in the harnessing of nuclear energy and the development of the atomic bomb.

Early Years. Born in Rome, Italy, Fermi earned a doctorate at the University of Pisa in 1922 and spent the next two years abroad on a fellowship that allowed him to study with physicists Max Born in Göttingen and Paul Ehrenfest in Leiden. Returning to Italy in 1924, he became a lecturer in Florence, and by 1927 he had earned a reputation as a leader in the international community of theoretical physics. In that year he was appointed to the first Italian chair of theoretical physics, established at the University of Rome. During the 1930s he experimented with initiating nuclear reactions by bombarding atomic nuclei with neutrons, the work for which he won a Nobel Prize in 1938. Earlier that year the passage of Fascist anti-Jewish laws in Italy deeply troubled Fermi and his wife, who was Jewish. Fermi and his family went to Stockholm for the Nobel Prize ceremony and sailed from there directly to the United States, where he had already accepted a job at Columbia University.

Building the Bomb. Fermi continued his research at Columbia University until 1942, when he joined the team of Manhattan Project physicists who worked at the University of Chicago Metallurgical Laboratory. The purpose of the Manhattan Project was to build an atomic bomb, and the Chicago group set out to produce a controlled nuclear chain reaction to test the feasibility of producing plutonium in an atomic pile. Fermi's achievement of this goal on 2 December 1942 led to the development of a workable atomic bomb, which was successfully tested in July 1945 and dropped on the Japanese cities of Hiroshima and Nagasaki the following month. Fermi — with fellow scientists J. Robert Oppenheimer, Arthur Compton, and Ernest Lawrence — was part of a four-man panel that advised U.S. secretary of war Henry Stimson, "We can propose no technical demonstration likely to bring an end to the war; we can see no acceptable alternative to military use." After the war Fermi became a professor at the University of Chicago Institute for Nuclear Studies and continued to advise the government on nuclear weapons by serving on the general advisory committee of the Atomic Energy Commission. He died in 1954 at the age of fifty-three.

Sources:

Laura Fermi, *Atoms in the Family: My Life with Enrico Fermi* (Chicago: University of Chicago Press, 1954);

Daniel J. Kevles, *The Physicists: The History of a Scientific Community in Modern America* (New York: Knopf, 1978);

Emilio Segre, *Enrico Fermi: Physicist* (Chicago: University of Chicago Press, 1970).

J. ROBERT OPPENHEIMER

1904-1967

PHYSICIST

Young Genius. Born in New York City, J. Robert Oppenheimer completed the four-year undergraduate program at Harvard University in three years, studying classical languages as well as chemistry and physics and graduating summa cum laude in 1925. He spent the next four years traveling in Europe and studying at Cambridge University and then at the University of Göttingen, where he worked with physicist Max Born and earned a Ph.D. in 1927. Oppenheimer also spent time with physicists Paul Ehrenfest in Leiden and Wolfgang Pauli in Zurich.

Berkeley. When Oppenheimer returned to the United States in 1929, he was twenty-five and had already published sixteen papers on various aspects of theoretical physics. He received a joint appointment at the University of California, Berkeley, and California Institute of Technology, leading centers of physics research in the country. Within just a few years Oppenheimer earned a reputation as a dynamic and revered teacher of theoretical physics while devoting his research work to some of the most important questions in physics of the times. In 1942, when President Franklin D. Roosevelt approved the formation of the Manhattan Project to build an atomic bomb, Oppenheimer was asked to be in charge of work on theoretical problems connected to the production, and he assembled a team of physicists, including Edward Teller.

Los Alamos. Because experimental data had to come to Oppenheimer's group from laboratories all over the country, progress was slow. In March 1943, at Oppenheimer's suggestion, Gen. Leslie Groves, director of the Manhattan Project, established one central special-weapons laboratory at Los Alamos, New Mexico, and made Oppenheimer the director. Many eminent physicists converged at the remote desert site. In mid 1944, under tremendous military pressure to produce an atomic bomb, Oppenheimer reorganized the lab, forming a team called the Cowpuncher Committee to design a workable bomb. By early March 1945 the Cowpunchers had formulated plans for a plutonium implosion bomb and were rushing to make a prototype that could be tested in the New Mexico desert.

Testing the Bomb. Before dawn on 16 July 1945, in the desert near Alamogordo, New Mexico, Oppenheimer stood in the doorway of a bunker and watched the explosion of the bomb. As a spot of light exploded in the darkness and burst into a rainbow of fire that colored the surrounding mountains and desert, the literary Oppenheimer thought of a line from the Hindu holy book the Bhagavad Gita, referring to the "radiance of a thousand suns." Within seconds a shock wave blasted with the power of twenty thousand tons of TNT, and Oppenheimer thought of another passage from the same book, in which the god Vishnu takes on a fiery, multifaced form and declares: "Now I am become Death, the Destroyer of worlds."

Bombing Japan. Within weeks the United States dropped atomic bombs on Hiroshima and Nagasaki. Oppenheimer and Enrico Fermi were part of a panel of four scientists who supported the bombings as the best means to end the war quickly. When Oppenheimer was asked about the future of nuclear weapons, he responded: "If you ask: 'Can we make them more terrible?' the answer is yes. If you ask : 'Can we make a lot of them?' the answer is yes. If you ask: 'Can we make them terribly more terrible?' the answer is probably."

The Hydrogen Bomb and the Cold War. In 1946 Oppenheimer was made chairman of the general advisory committee to the newly created Atomic Energy Commission (AEC), and in October 1947 he became director of the Institute for Advanced Study at Princeton University. He opposed the building of the hydrogen bomb, a thermonuclear bomb that works by atomic fusion and is a thousand times more powerful than the bombs dropped on Japan. Like his fellow physicists Fermi and Isidore Rabi, Oppenheimer believed that by not developing this weapon of mass destruction the United States had "a unique opportunity of providing by example some limitation on the totality of war and thus of eliminating the fear and arousing the hope of mankind." Yet as the postwar political climate disintegrated into the Cold War with the Soviet Union and an anti-Communist "red scare" at home, the liberal Oppenheimer was caught in the midst of controversy. In December 1953 the AEC withdrew Oppenheimer's security clearance, blocking his access to secret scientific information because of questions about his loyalty to the United States government. Oppenheimer demanded a hearing and went before the AEC Personnel Security Board, where he was charged with having had Communist and left-wing associations in the 1930s and early 1940s and criticized for his opposition to building the hydrogen bomb. These accusations deeply pained Oppenheimer and struck at the heart of the physics community. Eminent physicists and policy makers testified on Oppenheimer's behalf, but his greatest opponent was his former associate Edward Teller, who had enthusiastically supported building the hydrogen bomb and called Oppenheimer a "Communist and advocate of Soviet appeasement." Unwilling to go so far as to accuse Oppenheimer of disloyalty, Teller testified that "his actions frankly appeared to me confused and complicated. I would like to see the vital interests of this country in hands which I understand better and therefore trust more. . . ." The three-man board concluded that Oppenheimer was a loyal citizen but voted two to one to censure Oppenheimer for opposing the H-bomb. The AEC declined to censure him but concluded that he had exhibited "willful disregard of the normal and proper obligations of security" and upheld the suspension of his security clearance. Many in the scientific community were outraged.

Recognition. Oppenheimer continued to head the Institute for Advanced Study at Princeton, where his lectures were frequently followed by enthusiastic, supportive applauses. It was not until 1963 that a step was taken toward reconciliation of old differences. President John F. Kennedy, who respected and celebrated pure science, decided to present Oppenheimer the coveted Fermi Award of the AEC. Kennedy did not live to confer the award, which was presented on 2 December 1963 by President Lyndon B. Johnson, in the presence of Teller. In accepting the award, Oppenheimer commented, "In his later years, Jefferson often wrote of the 'brotherly spirit of science which unites into a family all of its votaries. . . .' We have not, I know, always given evidence of that brotherly spirit of science. This . . . is in part because . . . we are engaged in this great enterprise of our time, testing whether men can . . . live without war as the great arbiter of history. . . . I think it is just possible, Mr. President, that it has taken some charity and some courage for you to make this award today."

Sources:

Peter Goodchild, *J. Robert Oppenheimer: Shatterer of Worlds* (Boston: Houghton Mifflin, 1981);

Daniel J. Kevles, *The Physicists: The History of a Scientific Community in Modern America* (New York: Knopf, 1978);

Herbert F. York, *The Advisors: Oppenheimer, Teller, and the Superbomb* (San Francisco: Freeman, 1976).

EDWARD TELLER

1908-

PHYSICIST

Father of the Hydrogen Bomb. Edward Teller played an important role in the Manhattan Project, which developed the first atomic bomb during World War II. After the war, when many other scientists were calling for caution in research on further nuclear weapons, Teller was an outspoken advocate for building the powerful hydrogen bomb and other thermonuclear weapons.

Early Years. Born in Budapest, Hungary, then part of the crumbling Austro-Hungarian Empire, Teller was born into a middle-class Jewish family. He studied briefly at the University of Budapest (1925) before entering the Institute of Technology in Karlsruhe, Germany, in January 1926 to study chemical engineering. In 1928 he went on to the University of Munich to study physics. That summer his right foot was severed in a streetcar accident, and after several months of convalescence at home in Budapest, he enrolled at the University of Leipzig later that year. There Teller studied with physicist Werner Heisenberg and became increasingly aware of the growing threat of Nazism. After earning his Ph.D. in 1930, Teller accepted an assistantship for postgraduate work in physics at the University of Göttingen, a sign of his growing reputation among German physicists. Yet with the rise of Adolf Hitler in 1933, Teller realized that, as a Jew, he had no future in Germany. After living in Denmark and London, he immigrated to the United States in 1935 and became a professor of physics at George Washington University.

The Manhattan Project. In 1940, after the National Defense Research Committee (NDRC) was formed to coordinate wartime research, committee head Vannevar Bush made Teller a consultant to the Uranium Committee, a group created in response to warnings that Germany was preparing to make an atomic bomb. Two years later, after President Franklin D. Roosevelt approved the Manhattan Project to build an atomic bomb, J. Robert Oppenheimer brought Teller, who had become a U.S. citizen in 1941, to Berkeley as part of a group of theoretical physicists to work on problems related to developing the bomb. When Oppenheimer became head of a centralized nuclear-research laboratory in Los Alamos, New Mexico, Teller played an important role on the research team that developed the plutonium bomb that was dropped on the Japanese cities of Hiroshima and Nagasaki in August 1945. Yet while other scientists were working on the details of this bomb, which was based on the principles of nuclear fission, Teller insisted on working on a far more powerful thermonuclear weapon — the hydrogen bomb — which was based on nuclear fusion.

Anti-Communist. In the late 1940s Teller, whose childhood had been scarred by the imminent Russian invasion of Hungary during World War I and whose native country came under Communist control after World War II, emerged as a militant anti-Communist and pursued his research on the hydrogen bomb with mathematician Stanislaw Ulam. When the Soviet Union tested an atomic bomb in 1949, Teller urged President Harry S Truman to support a crash program to build thermonuclear weapons. Many other scientists, including Oppenheimer, James B. Conant, Enrico Fermi, and I. I. Rabi — who served as the general advisory committee to the Atomic Energy Commission (AEC) — opposed development of this H-bomb, but early in 1950 Truman ordered its speedy development. By 1951 Teller and Ulam had designed an ingenious, militarily practical hydrogen bomb. Even Oppenheimer later described it as "technically so sweet" one could hardly argue against building it. When it was tested in 1954, it exploded with the force of fifteen million tons of TNT.

Controversy. After the successful explosion of the hydrogen bomb, Teller moved to Livermore Laboratories at the University of California, Berkeley, to do research for the AEC. In 1954 he was ostracized by many in the scientific community for testifying against Oppenheimer when Oppenheimer's security clearance was revoked. He retired from Berkeley in 1975 but continued to express his Cold War philosophy by supporting the Strategic Defense Initiative (SDI), better known as Star Wars, during the administration of President Ronald Reagan.

Sources:

Stanley A. Blumberg and Gwinn Owens, *Energy in Conflict: The Life and Times of Edward Teller* (New York: Putnam, 1976);

Blumberg and Louis G. Panos, *Edward Teller: Giant of the Golden Age of Physics* (New York: Scribners, 1990);

Herbert F. York, *The Advisors: Oppenheimer, Teller, and the Superbomb* (San Francisco: Freeman, 1976),

PEOPLE IN THE NEWS

In 1940 physical chemist **Philip Abelson** and physicist **Edwin McMillan** discovered neptunium, the first transuranic (heavier than uranium) element.

During the 1940s physicist **Arthur Compton,** winner of the 1927 Nobel Prize for physics for his discovery of the dual nature of electromagnetic radiation, directed research for the Manhattan Project, setting up the Metallurgical Laboratory at the University of Chicago in 1942.

Molecular biologists **Max Delbruck** and **Salvador Luria** collaborated in 1940 to show the dynamics of bacterial mutations. In 1945 Delbruck demonstrated that the bacteriophage (a virus that infects and sometimes destroys bacteria) can reproduce sexually.

In 1949 biologists **John Enders, Thomas Weller,** and **Frederick Robbins** cultivated poliovirus in vitro (that is, outside the human body) on human embryonic tissue.

In 1940 physicists **Richard Feyman, Julian Schwinger,** and **Sin-Itiro Tomonaga** began development of the modern theory of quantum electrodynamics; their work continued until 1950.

In 1947 physiologists **Ralph Gerard, Judith Graham,** and **Gilbert Ling** produced a microelectrode that permitted precise study of the chemical and physical properties of muscle and nerve cells.

In June 1942 **Gen. Leslie R. Groves,** the U.S. Army engineer who built the Pentagon, was given command of the Manhattan Project to build an atomic bomb.

In 1945 biologist **Alfred Day Hershey** — a founder, with Delbruck and Luria, of the so-called phage group of researchers — showed that spontaneous mutations can occur in bacterial viruses. The next year, at the same time as Delbruck, he demonstrated that genetic recombination takes places between bacteriophages present in the same cell. These fundamental contributions to molecular biology were building blocks in developing an understanding of the form and function of DNA.

In 1947 biochemist **Fritz Lipmann** explained the mechanism through which cells obtain energy. He discovered that the purpose of metabolism was to deliver energy into cells and identified a molecule, adenosine triphosphate (ATP), as the source of muscular energy.

In 1944 geneticist **Barbara McClintock** — whose 1931 paper "A Correlation of Cytological and Genetical Crossing-Over in *Zea Mays*" became a classic work on chromosomal behavior — was elected to the National Academy of Sciences.

A theory formulated by Berkeley physicist **Edwin Mattison McMillan** led to the invention of the synchrocyclotron, which became operational in November 1946. A powerful subatomic particle accelerator, the synchrocyclotron overcame the slowing of particle acceleration created in earlier cyclotrons by the increasing the mass of particles relative to the speed of light. In February 1949 McMillan used the synchrocyclotron to produce the first synthetically created mesons, charged subatomic particles with a mass in excess of two hundred times that of the electron.

In 1949 physicist **Lise Meitner** became the first woman to receive the Max Planck Medal for outstanding achievement in theoretical physics. She received the Planck Medal with Otto Hahn for their work on radioactivity and their 1939 explanation of fission of the uranium nucleus, which was quickly applied by physicists in the Manhattan Project.

In 1946 chemist **Linus Pauling** formulated the valence-bond theory, suggesting how enzymes work as catalysts in chemical reactions.

In 1943 **Carl Seyfert** discovered a class of galaxies with bright, small nuclei emitting radio energy. Named Seyfert Galaxies in his honor, they are thought to be related to quasars (quasi-stellar radio sources), discovered by astronomers in the 1960s.

In 1941 **Robert Woodworth** published his report *Heredity and Environment,* which summarized research on twins and foster children that, according to Woodworth, demonstrated that intelligence is largely dependent on heredity. Finding that children in families living on a low socio-economic level performed much better on intelligence tests than anticipated, Woodworth said, "instead of saying that these children have made good in spite of poor heredity, we must conclude that their heredity was good or fair in spite of the low status and unsatisfactory behavior of their own parents."

AWARDS

NOBEL PRIZES

1940

No award.

1941

No award.

1942

No award.

1943

German American chemist **Otto Stern** wins the Nobel Prize for physics for outstanding achievements including development of the molecular-beam method, co-discovery of the quantization of space, measurement of atomic magnetic moments, demonstration of the wave nature of atoms and molecules, and discovery of the magnetic moment of the proton.

1944

Isidor Isaac Rabi of the United States wins the Nobel Prize for physics for his discovery and measurement of the radio-frequency spectra of atomic nuclei by using the resonance method.

1945

Austrian American physicist **Wolfgang Pauli** wins the Nobel Prize for physics for his 1925 discovery of the Pauli Exclusion Principle in quantum mechanics, in which no two electrons in an atom may be in the same quantum state.

1946

James B. Sumner, John H. Northrop, and **Wendell M. Stanley,** all of the United States, share the Nobel Prize for chemistry — Sumner for his research in the crystallization of enzymes, Northrop and Stanley for their research in preparing enzymes and virus proteins in pure form.

Percy Williams Bridgman of the United States wins the Nobel Prize for physics for his invention of a device to produce extremely high pressures and resulting discoveries in high-pressure physics.

1949

William F. Giauque of the United States wins the Nobel Prize for chemistry for his research in thermodynamics, especially on the behavior of substances at extremely low temperatures.

DEATHS

Florence Bascom, 83, geologist who built the geology department at Bryn Mawr College to prominence, 18 June 1945.

Franz Boaz, 87, anthropologist who established the discipline of anthropology in the United States and built Columbia University into a center for anthropological research and training, 22 December 1942.

Annie Jump Cannon, 78, astronomer who worked on the classification of bright southern stars, 13 April 1941.

George Washington Carver, 79, agricultural chemist who introduced the lucrative peanut crop to the South and developed many by-products, such as peanut oil, and who received the Roosevelt Medal in 1939, 5 January 1943.

Charles B. Davenport, 78, geneticist who emphasized hereditarian explanation and eugenics in the early decades of the twentieth century, 18 February 1944.

Robert Hutchings Goddard, 63, physicist who designed the first successful liquid-fuel rockets (1926), which by 1935 reached supersonic speeds, 10 August 1945.

Ida Hyde, 91, neurobiologist, first woman to do research at Harvard Medical School, and inventor of the first microelectrode for use in intracellular work, 22 August 1945.

Thomas Midgley, Jr., 55, chemist who introduced the antiknock lead additive (1921) to solve the violent automobile-engine knock problem caused by fuels and who discovered freon (dichlorodefluoromethane), a nonflammable, cheap, nontoxic refrigerant, 2 November 1944.

T. H. Morgan, 79, geneticist who introduced the chromosome theory of inheritance, 4 December 1945.

Nikola Tesla, 87, electrical engineer who developed the first alternating current (AC) motor (1887), which, with transformers, was an easier and cheaper way to transmit high voltages long distances and which in 1891 became the standard electric current, 7 January 1943.

Orville Wright, 76, aviation pioneer who with his brother Wilbur built and flew the first airplane (1903) at Kitty Hawk, North Carolina, 30 January 1948.

PUBLICATIONS

Ruth Benedict, *The Chrysanthemum and the Sword: Patterns of Japanese Culture* (Boston: Houghton Mifflin, 1946);

Benedict, *Race, Science and Politics* (New York: Modern Age Books, 1940);

Joseph C. Boyce, ed., *New Weapons for Air Warfare* (Boston: Little, Brown, 1947);

Lyman Bryson and Louis Finkelstein, eds., *Science, Philosophy and Religion*, Conference on Science, Philosophy and Religion in Their Relation to the Democratic Way of Life (New York: Columbia University, 1942);

John E. Burchard, ed., *Rockets, Guns and Targets* (Boston: Little, Brown, 1948);

James B. Conant, *On Understanding Science* (New Haven, Conn.: Yale University Press, 1947);

Ladislas Farago and Gordon Allport, *German Psychological Warfare* (New York: Putnam, 1942);

R. Goldschmidt, *The Material Basis of Evolution* (New Haven: Yale University Press, 1940);

Julian Huxley, *Evolution: The Modern Synthesis* (London: Allen & Unwin, 1942);

Huxley, ed., *The New Systematics* (Oxford: Clarendon Press, 1940);

William L. Laurence, *Dawn over Zero: The Story of the Atomic Bomb* (New York: Knopf, 1946; enlarged, 1947);

Ralph Linton, *Acculturation in Seven American Indian Tribes* (New York: Appleton-Century, 1940);

Malcolm MacLaren, *The Rise of the Electrical Industry in the Nineteenth Century* (Princeton, N.J.: Princeton University Press, 1943);

W. Rupert Maclaurin, *Invention and Innovation in the Radio Industry* (New York: Macmillan, 1949);

Ernst Mayr, *Systematics and the Origin of the Species* (New York: Columbia University Press, 1942);

Margaret Mead, *Environment and Education* (Chicago: University of Chicago, Committee on Human Development, 1942);

Mead, *Male and Female* (New York: Morrow, 1949);

Mead, *The Maoris and Their Arts* (New York: American Museum of Natural History, 1945);

Mead and Gregory Bateson, *Balinese Character: A Photographic Analysis* (New York: New York Academy of Sciences, 1942);

Science and the War: A Symposium Presented at the Seventy-fifth Anniversary Meeting of the Kansas Academy of Science (Lawrence: Kansas Academy of Science, 1943);

G. G. Simpson, *Tempo and Mode in Evolution* (New York: Columbia University Press, 1944);

Irvin Stewart, *Organizing Scientific Research for the War: The Administrative History of the Office of Scientific Research and Development* (Boston: Little, Brown, 1948);

Albert Vorseller, "Science and the Battle of the Atlantic," *Yale Review*, 35 (June 1946): 671–674;

Norbert Weiner, *Cybernetics; or, Control and Communication in the Animal and the Machine* (New York: Wiley, 1948);

Leonard D. White, *Civil Service in Wartime* (Chicago: University of Chicago Press, 1945);

R. S. Woodworth, *Heredity and Environment: A Critical Study of Recently Published Materials on Twins and Foster Children* (New York: Social Science Research Council, 1941);

Science, periodical;

Scientific American, periodical.

SPORTS

by SCOTT DERKS and MARGO HORN

CONTENTS

Sidebars and tables are listed in italics.

1940

12 Jan.	The University of Chicago announces the elimination of its football program, saying the sport is a handicap to education.
17 Feb.	New world records in the shot put by John Blozis and the sixty-yard high hurdles by Allan Tolmich are established in the Melrose Games in New York.
28 Feb.	WXBS broadcasts the first televised college basketball games, featuring Pittsburgh–Fordham and New York University–Georgetown from Madison Square Garden.
2 Mar.	Bobby Riggs wins the national indoor tennis title in Chicago.
1 Apr.	The Track Writers' Association names Greg Rice as the outstanding athlete of the 1940 indoor season.
3 Apr.	The Finnish education minister says Finland cannot host the Olympic Games in 1940; the games are canceled because of war and do not resume until 1948.
21 Apr.	George A. Heitzler is elected president of the American Professional Football League. On 13 July the new American Professional Football League forms with six teams.
27 Apr.	Cyclist Raymond "Slug" Bryan establishes an Amateur Bicycle League of America record, riding from New York to San Francisco in twenty-seven days, eleven hours, and reaching the West Coast on 24 May.
30 Apr.	The American Football Coaches Association gives the first Amos Alonzo Stagg Award to Donald Grant Herring, Jr.
4 May	A 35–1 long shot, Gallahadion wins the Kentucky Derby.
24 May	The first night baseball game in the Polo Grounds, New York, is witnessed by 22,260 people.
27 May	New York Yankee outfielder Joe DiMaggio receives the Golden Laurel as the outstanding U.S. athlete of 1939.
10 July	Golfer Patty Berg signs a six-year pro contract.
19 July	Tony Zale captures the National Boxing Association (NBA) middleweight championship by knocking out Al Hostak in ten rounds.
28 Aug.	Reuben Fine defeats J. C. Thompson in fifteen moves to win the U.S. Chess Federation's open championship at Dallas, Texas.
8 Sept.	The Baltimore Elite Giants defeat the New York Cubans 3–0 to win the Ruppert Memorial Cup, the highest achievement in Negro baseball.
8 Oct.	The Cincinnati Reds defeat the Detroit Tigers 2–1 in the seventh game of the World Series.
29 Oct.	The American Olympic Commission officially disbands with $110,000 in its treasury.
1 Nov.	Ken Overlin retains the New York Commission middleweight boxing championship in a fifteen-round decision over Steve Belloise.
5 Nov.	Baseball writers choose Hank Greenberg of Detroit as the American League player of the year. Greenberg's statistics include a .340 batting average, a league-leading 41 home runs, and 150 RBIs (runs batted in).

1941

- The Brooklyn Dodgers begin wearing batting helmets on orders from general manager Larry MacPhail.

- The Chicago Bears score 396 points in eleven games, a record not broken until 1950.

1 Jan. Morris Brown College of Atlanta defeats Wilberforce University 19–3 in the first annual Steel Bowl (also called the Vulcan Bowl) at Birmingham, Alabama, before 8,000 fans to determine the national Negro college football title.

17 Jan. Welterweight boxing champion Fritzie Zivic defeats former champ Henry Armstrong, from whom he won the championship on 4 October 1940.

19 Jan. Bob Feller signs a record $30,000 contract with the Cleveland Indians. Just twenty-two years old, Feller already has 82 wins.

15 Feb. Greg Rice sets a world record of 8:53.4 in winning the 2-mile run in the New York Athletic Club games.

16 Feb. Joe Louis knocks out Gus Dorazio in his fourteenth defense of his world heavyweight crown.

21 Feb. Tony Zale successfully defends his middleweight title by knocking out Steve Mamakos.

22 Feb. Greg Rice sets a new world indoor record of 13:51 in the 3-mile run in the National Amateur Athletic Union (AAU) Championships.

25 Feb. The New York Rangers defeat the Boston Bruins 2–0, ending the Bruins' winning streak of twenty-three games, a league record.

6 Mar. New York Yankee Joe DiMaggio ends his holdout by signing a $35,000 contract, a $2,500 raise for the 1941 season.

13 Mar. The Boston Bruins win their third straight National Hockey League (NHL) championship, defeating the New York Americans.

21 Mar. Heavyweight boxing champion Joe Louis knocks out Abe Simon in the first round, the fifteenth "Bum of the Month" Louis has dispatched since winning the boxing title in 1937.

29 Mar. The University of Wisconsin beats Washington State 39–34 to win the National Collegiate Athletic Association (NCAA) basketball championship.

3 Apr. All eleven first-string players on the Boston University football team volunteer for service in the U.S. Naval Air Corps.

6 Apr. Craig Wood wins the Masters golf tournament.

8 Apr. In his sixteenth world heavyweight title defense, Joe Louis defeats Tony Musto.

9 Apr. Bobby Jones, Francis Ouimet, Walter Hagen, and Gene Sarazen are the first inductees into the Golf Hall of Fame.

12 Apr. The Boston Bruins beat the Detroit Red Wings 3–2 to win the Stanley Cup in four straight games.

27 Apr. Stockholders of the Boston Bees change the National League (NL) baseball team's name to the Boston Braves.

3 May   Whirlaway, ridden by Eddie Arcaro, sets a new Kentucky Derby course record of 2:01 for the 1 1/4-mile track.

7 May   Detroit Tigers star outfielder Hank Greenberg is inducted into the army.

15 May   Twenty-six-year-old Joe DiMaggio of the New York Yankees begins his fifty-six-game hitting streak.

23 May   Joe Louis defends his heavyweight crown for the seventeenth time, defeating Buddy Baer.

2 June   Baseball great Lou Gehrig, known as the Iron Horse, dies of amyotrophic lateral sclerosis (ALS), which forced him out of the lineup on 2 May 1939 after 2,130 consecutive games.

7 June   Whirlaway wins the Belmont Stakes, becoming the first Triple Crown winner since War Admiral in 1937.

11 June   The Cleveland Rams of the National Football League (NFL) are sold to Dan Reeves and Fred Levy, Jr., for a reported $140,000.

16 June   Lou Salica wins a fifteen-round decision over Tommy Forte to retain his bantamweight title.

18 June   Joe Louis knocks out light-heavyweight champion Billy Conn in the thirteenth round in a close fight to retain the heavyweight championship and win his eighteenth defense of the title.

17 July   Joe DiMaggio's fifty-six-game hitting streak ends before 67,468 fans in Cleveland.

25 July   Red Sox pitcher Lefty Grove earns his three-hundredth career victory.

29 July   Freddie Cochrane beats Fritzie Zivic to win the world welterweight boxing title.

26 Aug.   Gus Lesnevich defends the light-heavyweight boxing title against Tami Mauriello.

31 Aug.   Ben Hogan shoots a seventy-two-hole total of 275, seventeen under par and five under Henry Picard's 1937 record, to win the $5,000 Open Golf Championship in Hershey, Pennsylvania.

4 Sept.   The New York Yankees win their twelfth American League (AL) pennant, their fifth in the last six years. This date is the earliest a pennant has ever been won in the American League.

7 Sept.   Bobby Riggs beats Frank Kovacs in Forest Hills, New York, to regain the national tennis singles championship; Sarah Palfrey Cooke, runner-up in 1934 and 1935, defeats Pauline Betz for the women's title.

21 Sept.   The Homestead (Pennsylvania) Grays defeat the New York Cuban Stars 20–0 and 5–0 in a doubleheader at Yankee Stadium to win the Negro National Baseball League championship.

25 Sept.   The Brooklyn Dodgers win their first pennant since 1920.

28 Sept.   Ted Williams of the Boston Red Sox goes two for three against the Philadelphia Athletics to end the season with a batting average of .4057; he wins the American League batting crown.

29 Sept.	Joe Louis successfully defends his world heavyweight championship title for nineteenth time, scoring a technical knockout over Lou Nova.
6 Oct.	The New York Yankees win their ninth World Series, defeating the Dodgers four games to one.
11 Nov.	New York Yankee center fielder Joe DiMaggio is chosen as the most valuable American League player of 1941 by the Baseball Writers' Association.
19 Nov.	Jackie Wilson captures the NBA featherweight title, defeating Richie Lemos in a twelve-round fight in Los Angeles.
28 Nov.	Bruce Smith of the University of Minnesota wins the Heisman Trophy as the most outstanding college player of the year. Tony Zale wins the undisputed world middleweight championship, beating Georgie Abrams in a fifteen-round bout in New York.
30 Nov.	Green Bay Packers end Don Hutson scores 29 points, breaking six league records and tying two in an NFL game with the Washington Redskins.
1 Dec.	The University of Minnesota is selected as the country's leading college team for the second consecutive year by an Associated Press poll of football experts; Duke University is second, Notre Dame University third.
14 Dec.	The Green Bay Packers and the Chicago Bears play in the first divisional playoff in the history of the league; the Bears win 33–14.
15 Dec.	Following the Japanese bombing of Pearl Harbor on 7 December, the Rose Bowl is transferred to Durham, North Carolina, from Pasadena, California, to eliminate the chance of a Japanese bombing of the annual West Coast football classic.
19 Dec.	Sammy Angott gains a fifteen-round decision over Lew Jenkins to win the lightweight title.
21 Dec.	The Chicago Bears win the NFL championship for the second successive year, winning 37–9 over the New York Giants.

1942

•	Twelve of the forty-one minor-league baseball leagues fold, two when seacoast dimout regulations prevent night games. Sixty American colleges abandon football; 76 percent of football-playing colleges waive the rule barring freshmen from varsity teams.
9 Jan.	Heavyweight champion Joe Louis knocks out Buddy Baer in the first round of a rematch, winning his twentieth title defense. He donates his purse to the Navy Relief Fund.
10 Jan.	The U.S. Golf Association cancels the open, the amateur, the women's amateur, and the amateur public championships for one year due to the war.
20 Jan.	Former Saint Louis Cardinal second baseman Roger Hornsby is named to the Baseball Hall of Fame.
31 Jan.	Leo Durocher signs a contract to manage the Brooklyn Dodgers.
12 Feb.	Leslie MacMitchell of New York University runs the mile in 4:08, the fastest time ever in college competition.

28 Feb.   Greg Rice sets a new world indoor 3-mile record of 13:45.7 at the National AAU meet in New York; on 9 March he will also set a new world record in the 2 1/2-mile run.

25 Mar.   Six world indoors records are set at a Bronx track meet: in the 2-mile relay by Seton Hall; the 1-mile relay by Georgetown University; the 880-yard run and the 800-meter run by John Borican; and the 440-yard run and the 400-meter run by Ray Cochran.

27 Mar.   Army private and heavyweight champion Joe Louis knocks out Abe Simon in the sixth round in Madison Square Garden.

28 Mar.   Stanford routs Dartmouth 53–38 in Kansas City to win the NCAA basketball title.

4 Apr.   Yale wins the National AAU swimming championship in New Haven, Connecticut.

18 Apr.   The Toronto Maple Leafs defeat the Detroit Red Wings 3–1 in Toronto to win the NHL championship and the Stanley Cup, four games to three.

9 May   Alsab wins the Preakness Stakes with a record time of 1:57 for the 1 3/16-mile race.

15 May   Sammy Angott wins a split decision over Allie Stolz to retain his light-heavyweight title.

18 May   The New York police commissioner ends night baseball in the city for the war's duration because the glow from lights endangers shipping.

21 May   Boston Red Sox great Ted Williams joins the military.

30 May   Penn State University captures the IC 4-A track title to become the first team ever to capture both indoor and outdoor titles in same year.

1 June   The Chicago Cubs buy Jimmie Foxx, thirty-four years old, from the Boston Red Sox. Foxx has been named the American League's Most Valuable Player (MVP) three times.

6 June   Kentucky Derby winner Shut Out captures the $53,020 Belmont Stakes.

13 June   The University of Southern California wins its eighth consecutive NCAA track and field championship.

19 June   Thirty-nine-year-old Paul "Big Poison" Waner of the Boston Braves singles to center field against the Pittsburgh Pirates for his three-thousandth hit.

21 June   Ben Hogan scores a record low of 271 to win the Hale America golf tournament.

July   A series of three all-star baseball games, which include players currently in the service, nets $171,000 for the Army and Navy Relief Funds and baseball's Bat and Ball Fund.

4 July   Don Budge beats Bobby Riggs in the final round of the professional national tennis championship in Forest Hills, New York.

15 July   Whirlaway passes Seabiscuit as the top money-winning racehorse, capturing the Massachusetts Handicap at Suffolk Downs, setting a new track record of 1:48 1/5. The horse's lifetime earnings now top $454,336.

31 July   Sugar Ray Robinson wins his thirty-third straight fight by unanimous decision in a nontitle match against lightweight champion Sammy Angott.

9 Aug.   The national AAU men's outdoor swimming championships end with three world records: in the 1-mile freestyle by Keo Nakama of Ohio State University, 20:29.0; the 440-yard freestyle by William Smith, 4:39.6; and the 880-yard freestyle by William Smith, 9:54.6.

Sept.   All-army all-star teams challenge professional football teams in an eight-game exhibition designed to raise $1 million for Army Relief.

6 Sept.   Pauline Betz defeats nineteen-year-old U.S. girls' tennis champion Louise Brough in the national women's singles tennis championship in Forest Hills, New York.

7 Sept.   Ted Schroeder defeats Frank Parker to win the men's national singles tennis title in Forest Hills, New York.

29 Sept.   The Kansas City Monarchs defeat the Homestead Grays to win the Negro World Series.

5 Oct.   The Saint Louis Cardinals defeat the Yankees before 69,052 fans in Yankee Stadium to win the World Series in five games.

12 Oct.   A planned rematch between Sgt. Joe Louis, world heavyweight champion, and Pvt. Billy Conn is canceled.

29 Oct.   Branch Rickey becomes president and general manager of the Brooklyn Dodgers, replacing Larry MacPhail, who has entered the army.

2–9 Nov.   New York Yankee Joe Gordon is named MVP for the American League; Saint Louis Cardinal pitcher Morton Cooper is named MVP in the National League by baseball writers for his twenty-two wins, including ten shutouts.

6 Nov.   Sugar Ray Robinson scores his thirty-eighth straight professional boxing victory with a win over Victor Dellicurti.

20 Nov.   Twenty-year-old Willie Pep dethrones Chalky Wright in fifteen rounds to capture the world featherweight boxing championship.

Dec.   Connie Schwoegler of Madison, Wisconsin, is the upset winner of the All Star Bowling tournament, defeating national champion Ned Day, who has held the title since 1938.

5 Dec.   Willie Mosconi regains the pocket billiard championship by winning nine of ten matches in national tournament play.

9 Dec.   Green Bay Packer back Cecil Isbell is the NFL forward passing champion with 146 completions out of 268 attempts for 2,021 yards and 24 touchdowns.

13 Dec.   The Washington Redskins upset the Chicago Bears 14–6 to win the NFL championship.

18 Dec.   The Associated Press selects Frank Sinkwich, University of Georgia football player, as outstanding male athlete of the year; swimmer Gloria Callen as best woman athlete; and the Saint Louis Cardinals as outstanding team. Lightweight champion Beau Jack (Sidney Walker) knocks out top contender Tippy Larkin in the third round to win the New York Boxing Commission title.

1943

17 Jan. New York baseball writers name Boston Red Sox outfielder Ted Williams player of the year. Williams earns the 1942 "triple crown" with a .356 batting average, 36 home runs, and 137 RBIs.

26 Jan. Baseball great Vernon "Left" Gomez, pitcher with the New York Yankees since 1931, is sold to the Boston Braves.

5 Feb. Sugar Ray Robinson's 40-bout winning streak ends when Jake La Motta takes a ten-round decision in Olympia Stadium, Detroit.

20 Feb. New York sportsman William D. Cox and a syndicate of ten associates purchase the Philadelphia Phillies for $230,000.

27 Feb. New York University wins the team title at the fifty-fifth AAU indoor track championships.

10 Mar. World bantamweight champion Manuel Ortiz retains his title with an eleventh-round technical knockout of Lou Salica. Dartmouth wins its sixth consecutive Eastern Intercollegiate League basketball championship, defeating Penn 70–34.

11 Mar. The Detroit Red Wings defeat the Toronto Maple Leafs to clinch their fourth NHL title in ten years.

20 Mar. Ensign Cornelius Warmerdam pole-vaults 15 feet, 8 1/2 inches at the Chicago Relays, beating his own world record.

25 Mar. Pauline Betz wins the national indoors singles, doubles, and mixed doubles titles in a Chestnut Hill, Massachusetts, tournament.

26 Mar. Greg Rice breaks his own world record for the 2-mile run with a time of 8:51.

27 Mar. The Ohio State University swim team wins the NCAA title; in April the team wins the National AAU swimming championship.

6 Apr. The Cleveland Rams withdraw from the NFL for the remainder of the war.

8 Apr. The Detroit Red Wings defeat the Boston Bruins 2–0 to win the NHL Stanley Cup in four straight games.

19 May Bob Montgomery outpoints Beau Jack in fifteen rounds at Madison Square Garden to win the lightweight championship; Beau Jack regains the title in a fifteen-rounder on 19 November.

26 May Manuel Ortiz outpoints Joe Robelto to retain the world bantamweight title.

5 June Ensign Hugh S. Cannon sets a world record for the discus throw with a distance of 174 feet, 10 1/8 inches in the Metropolitan AAU senior championships. Count Fleet wins the Belmont Stakes by 30 lengths, earning $35,340.

8 June World featherweight champion Willie Pep retains his title with a win over Sal Bartolo.

20 June The NFL grants Ted Collins a Boston football franchise for the 1944 season.

28 June Thoroughbred champion Whirlaway retires after winning thirty-two races and a record $561,161.

July Still recovering from a serious automobile accident, golfer Patty Berg wins the Western Open medal, then enlists in the marines.

24 July	Swedish runner Gunder Hagg sets a new American record in the mile in 4:05.3 during a U.S. tour; on 7 August he will set a new American outdoor mark of 8:51.3 for two miles.
5 Sept.	Yale University wins the team National AAU swimming championship.
6 Sept.	Lt. Joe Hunt, on temporary leave from the navy, beats Coast Guardsman Jack Kramer to win the National Tennis Championships at Forest Hills; Pauline Betz wins her second straight women's title, defeating Louise Brough.
8 Sept.	New York Giants pitcher Ace Adams plays in his sixty-second game and sets a new major-league record for games worked by a pitcher in one year.
Oct.	Brooklyn Dodgers player-manager Leo Durocher is fired and rehired by Branch Rickey within a two-week period.
2 Oct.	The army cancels a tour by major-league baseball teams of Pacific war areas because of transportation shortages.
11 Oct.	The New York Yankees win the World Series, defeating the Saint Louis Cardinals four games to one.
2 Nov.	Saint Louis Cardinal outfielder Stan Musial is named MVP of the National League by the Baseball Writers' Association; Spud Chandler, New York Yankees pitcher, is named MVP for the American League on 9 November.
14 Nov.	Chicago Bears football quarterback Sid Luckman becomes the first pro to throw seven touchdown passes in one game.
23 Nov.	Philadelphia Phillies owner William Cox is banned from baseball for betting on his own team.
28 Nov.	Notre Dame quarterback Angelo Bertelli wins the Heisman Trophy as the outstanding college football player of the year.
10 Dec.	A *New York World Telegram* annual poll names eighty-one-year-old coach Amos Alonzo Stagg, College of the Pacific, as coach of the year.
26 Dec.	The Chicago Bears beat the Washington Redskins 41–12 to win the NFL championship.

1944

17 Jan.	Byron Nelson wins the $10,000 San Francisco Open golf tournament with a 13-under-par 275.
21 Jan.	The Boston Braves are sold to Joseph Maney, Guido Rugo, and Louis Perini.
6 Feb.	A baseball postwar committee recommends that major- and minor-league players in the service be allowed to return to their previous clubs at the same salary as when they left.
3 Mar.	Bob Montgomery regains the lightweight boxing title from Beau Jack in a fifteen-round bout.
15 Mar.	World bantamweight champion Manuel Ortiz outpoints Ernesto Aguilar in a fifteen-round bout.

28 Mar.   The University of Utah defeats Dartmouth 42–40 to win the NCAA basketball title.

13 Apr.   The Montreal Canadiens defeat the Chicago Black Hawks for the fourth successive time in the Stanley Cup playoffs to win the NHL title.

27 Apr.   Boston Braves pitcher Jim Tobin pitches the first major-league no-hitter since 1941, defeating the Brooklyn Dodgers.

6 May   Pensive wins the Kentucky Derby at Churchill Downs; a week later Pensive wins the Preakness and $60,075.

23 May   The University of Chicago notifies the Big Ten that it is withdrawing from all athletic competition.

26 May   The first circular boxing ring in the United States, made of aluminum tubing and covered with heavy velvet cloth, is used in a San Francisco shipyard exhibition bout between Vic Grupico and former middleweight champion Fred Apostoli.

3 June   Bounding Home spoils Pensive's run for the Triple Crown by winning the Belmont Stakes.

10 June   The University of Illinois wins the NCAA track and field championships in Milwaukee.

24 June   Olympic champion Babe Didrikson Zaharias wins the Women's Western Golf Open in Chicago.

30 July   Ann Curtis sets a new world record for the women's 880-yard freestyle swim with a mark of 11:08.6.

3 Sept.   Pauline Betz wins the women's national tennis title, defeating Margaret Osborne at Forest Hills, New York; Frank Parker wins the men's title the next day, defeating William Talbert.

21 Sept.   The Saint Louis Cardinals capture their third NL pennant in a row and their eighth overall.

29 Sept.   Willie Pep retains his world featherweight title in a rematch with Chalky Wright.

1 Oct.   The Saint Louis Browns beat the New York Yankees 5–2 to win the AL pennant on the last day of the season, thus setting up a crosstown World Series with the Saint Louis Cardinals.

9 Oct.   The Saint Louis Cardinals win the sixth game of the World Series 3–1 to defeat the Saint Louis Browns.

10 Oct.   Martin Marion of the Saint Louis Cardinals and Bobby Doerr of the Boston Red Sox are named NL and AL players of the year by *The Sporting News*.

1 Nov.   Branch Rickey, Walter O'Malley, and Andrew Schmitz purchase 25 percent of the Brooklyn Dodgers stock.

21 Nov.   Saint Louis Cardinal shortstop Martin Marion named NL MVP by baseball writers; Detroit pitcher Hal Newhouser is named AL MVP a week later.

25 Nov.   Baseball commissioner Kenesaw Mountain Landis dies at age seventy-eight; he is named to the Baseball Hall of Fame on 10 December.

27 Nov.   Plans for the new U.S. Football League, featuring eight teams in 1945, are announced, with Red Grange as president.

1 Dec.   The Heisman Trophy presented to Leslie Horvath of Ohio State.

18 Dec.   Swimmer Ann Curtis and golfer Byron Nelson are named outstanding athletes of 1944 by an Associated Press poll. Curtis also wins the James E. Sullivan award as outstanding athlete of 1944 on 4 January 1945.

23 Dec.   War Mobilization and Reconversion Director James F. Byrnes bans all horse racing effective 3 January to save labor and critical materials.

1945

16 Jan.   President Franklin D. Roosevelt says he favors the continuation of the baseball season if it does not interfere with war production.

20 Jan.   Gil Dodds retires from track to devote his time and energy to religious work. The 1948 Olympics will lure him out of retirement.

26 Jan.   A syndicate consisting of Larry MacPhail, Dan Topping, and Del Webb buys 96.88 percent of the New York Yankees and its minor-league properties for $2.8 million from the heirs of the late Col. Jacob Ruppert.

30 Jan.   William Alexander, Georgia Tech football coach since 1920, resigns; Bobby Dodd is named his successor.

31 Jan.   Five Brooklyn College basketball players admit accepting a $1,000 bribe to throw a game with the University of Akron.

8 Feb.   Lt. Paul Brown agrees to coach the newly created Cleveland team of the All-American Football Conference, effective when he leaves the service.

19 Feb.   Willie Pep successfully defends his featherweight title with a fifteen-round decision over Phil Terranova.

21 Feb.   The 1945 All-Star baseball game is canceled as a travel-conservation measure.

29 Mar.   Oklahoma A&M upsets DePaul University 52–44 to win the NCAA basketball championship.

2 Apr.   Frank Sinkwich of the Detroit Lions wins the Joe F. Carr Trophy for the NFL's MVP.

8 Apr.   Byron Nelson sets a new Professional Golfers' Association (PGA) record for 72 holes, winning the Iron Lung Open Golf Tournament in Atlanta with a 263 score.

22 Apr.   The Toronto Maple Leafs win the NHL Stanley Cup, defeating the Detroit Red Wings four games to three.

24 Apr.   U.S. senator A. B. "Happy" Chandler is named baseball commissioner, receiving a seven-year, $50,000-per-year contract.

7 May   Branch Rickey announces the formation of the United Negro Baseball League with six teams.

9 May   The ban on horse racing is lifted. Santa Anita in Arcadia, California, and Jamaica in New York resume races within days.

23 June Babe Didrikson Zaharias takes her third Western Women's Open Golf title with a victory over Dorothy Germain in Indianapolis.

1 July Welby Van Horn wins the national professional tennis championship over John Nogrady in New York.

6 July Boston Braves outfielder Tommy Holmes hits safely in his thirty-fourth consecutive game, a new NL record.

10 Aug. Richard Muckerman becomes president of the Saint Louis Browns baseball team with the purchase of stock from Donald Barnes.

12 Aug. Michigan State University captures the national AAU swimming team title in Akron, Ohio.

13 Aug. Branch Rickey and two associates increase holdings in the Brooklyn Dodgers to 75 percent.

15 Aug. AL umpire Ernest Stewart is fired for asking for higher salaries for umpires.

17 Aug. The defense transportation director ends curbs on travel to professional and amateur sporting events.

2–3 Sept. Sarah Palfrey Cooke beats Pauline Betz to win the women's national tennis title. Frank Parker defeats Bill Talbert for the men's title.

9 Sept. Dick Fowler of the Philadelphia Athletics pitches a 1–0 no-hitter over the Saint Louis Browns.

29–30 Sept. The Chicago Cubs win their sixteenth NL pennant. The Detroit Tigers beat the Saint Louis Browns to capture the AL pennant.

10 Oct. The Detroit Tigers win the World Series over the Chicago Cubs four games to three.

14 Oct. Byron Nelson breaks his own world record for a par-70 golf course by shooting 66 to win the Seattle Open.

23 Oct. Jackie Robinson becomes the first black player admitted to organized professional baseball as he signs with Montreal of the International League, a Brooklyn Dodgers farm team.

12 Nov. The American League announces a record paid attendance for the 1945 season of 5,580,420.

14 Nov. Chicago Cubs first baseman Phil Cavarretta is named the NL MVP by baseball writers; Detroit Tigers pitcher Hal Newhouser is named AL MVP a week later.

Dec. The baseball commissioner and the National League owners vote to hold night games in 1946; the American League votes no.

16 Dec. The Cleveland Rams defeat the Washington Redskins 15–14 in Cleveland to win the NFL championship.

21 Dec.	Golfers Byron Nelson and Babe Didrikson Zaharias are named male and female athletes of the year by an Associated Press poll.
26 Dec.	*Ring* magazine selects featherweight champion Willie Pep as fighter of the year.

1946

Jan.	The NFL grants the Cleveland Rams a franchise in Los Angeles, one of the eight cities the All-American Football Conference has selected.
4 Jan.	The professional All-American Football Conference votes to start the 1946 season with an eight-club league.
10 Jan.	The AAU and the NCAA enter into a formal partnership, agreeing for the first time to respect each other's rights, rules, and territories.
11 Jan.	Bert Bell succeeds Elmer Layden as NFL commissioner.
15 Jan.	Army fullback Felix "Doc" Blanchard is named the James E. Sullivan winner for 1945 as the year's outstanding amateur athlete.
23 Jan.	Bobby Riggs retains his world professional tennis title by defeating Don Budge in Los Angeles.
21 Mar.	Kenny Washington becomes the first black in the NFL since 1933, signing with the Los Angeles Rams.
26 Mar.	Oklahoma A&M takes the NCAA basketball title with a 43–40 victory over the University of North Carolina.
30 Mar.	Ohio State University wins the NCAA swimming title in New Haven, Connecticut.
1 Apr.	The eight-team Mexican Baseball League is formed and signs some American players, including Dodger catcher Mickey Owens. On 16 April baseball commissioner Albert Chandler rules that players who jump to foreign leagues are automatically suspended for five years.
7 Apr.	Joseph Vendeur of Philadelphia sets two new world records in swimming: 2:19.5 for the 200-hundred-yard breaststroke and 2:35.6 for the 200-meter breaststroke.
9 Apr.	The Montreal Canadiens defeat the Boston Bruins to capture the NHL Stanley Cup four games to one.
23 Apr.	The Baseball Hall of Fame announces its inductees: Joseph Tinker, Johnny Evers, Frank Chance, Jack Chesbro, Clark Griffith, Joseph McGinnity, Edward Waddell, Eddie Plank, Ed Walsh, Jesse Burkett, and Tom McCarthy.
30 Apr.	Bob Feller of the Cleveland Indians pitches a no-hitter in a 1–0 victory over the New York Yankees.
6 May	The New York Yankees become the first baseball team to travel entirely by air. They sign a contract with United Air Lines for the 1946 season.
14 May	Gus Lesnevich is declared undisputed world light-heavyweight champion by knocking out British Empire champion Freddie Mills in ten rounds.

1 June   Assault, ridden by Warren Mehrtens, wins the $100,000 Belmont Stakes, becoming the seventh horse in history to win the Triple Crown.

16 June   Byron Nelson loses the U.S. Open golf title when his caddie accidentally kicks his ball.

19 June   Joe Louis knocks out Billy Conn in eight rounds in a heavyweight rematch. Ringside seats sell for $100 for the first time. This is the first heavyweight fight ever televised.

23 June   The University of Illinois wins the NCAA track and field championship.

25 June   A chartered bus carrying Spokane's International League baseball team plunges down a five-hundred-foot mountainside in the Cascades, killing eight.

9 July   Ted Williams hits three home runs in the thirteenth annual All-Star Game to power the AL to a 12–0 victory over the NL.

9 Aug.   All eight American and National League baseball games are played at night for the first time in history.

20 Aug.   Pittsburgh Pirates players reject the American Baseball Guild in baseball's first collective-bargaining election.

28 Aug.   A meeting of American and National League owners results in an agreement to give players representation in creating rules and policies, to set a minimum salary, and to establish a pension fund.

8 Sept.   Jack Kramer defeats Tom Brown to win the national singles amateur tennis title at Forest Hills, New York; Pauline Betz beats Doris Hart for the women's title.

11 Sept.   The Brooklyn Dodgers and the Cincinnati Reds battle nineteen scoreless innings to the longest 0–0 tie in baseball history.

18 Sept.   Heavyweight champion Joe Louis defends his title for the twenty-third time, winning a first-round knockout over Tami Mauriello.

27 Sept.   Middleweight champion Tony Zale knocks out Rocky Graziano in the sixth round to retain his title.

29 Sept.   Cleveland Indians pitcher Bob Feller sets a new strike mark of 348 for the season.

3 Oct.   The Saint Louis Cardinals capture a first-ever league championship playoff against Brooklyn when the season ends in a tie.

13 Oct.   The Saint Louis Cardinals defeat the Boston Red Sox four games to three to win the World Series.

1 Nov.   The professional Basketball Association of America starts its first season.

22 Nov.   Saint Louis Cardinal Stan Musial is named the NL MVP by the Baseball Writers' Association.

3 Dec.   Notre Dame is named the best college football team by an Associated Press sportswriters poll.

15 Dec.   An attempted fix of the NFL title game between the Chicago Bears and the New York Giants is exposed. Alvin Paris is arrested on charges that he tried to bribe New York Giants players Merle Hapes and Frank Filchock.

19 Dec.	Sugar Ray Robinson outpoints Tom Bell in fifteen rounds to earn the welterweight boxing crown.
23 Dec.	Babe Didrikson Zaharias, winner of the 1946 women's golf championship, is chosen outstanding woman athlete of the year by an Associated Press poll of sportswriters.
27 Dec.	Davis Cup tennis competition resumes after six years. The United States team wins the Cup for the first time since 1938, defeating Australia 5–0 in Melbourne.

1947

1 Jan.	A college football boom spawns a proliferation of New Year's Day bowl games, such as the Raisin Bowl, won by San Jose State 20–0 over Utah State. Claude "Buddy" Young of Illinois is the first black player to score a touchdown in Rose Bowl history. Illinois wins 45–14 over UCLA.
7 Jan.	Harold Dade takes the world bantamweight boxing title from Manuel Ortiz in fifteen rounds in San Francisco. Ortiz will retake the title from Dade on 12 March in a fifteen-round decision.
8 Jan.	After fifty-one years as a baseball executive, New York Yankees chairman Edward Barrow announces his retirement.
31 Jan.	The War Department rejects the requests of Felix "Doc" Blanchard, Glenn Davis, and Barney Poole for leave from the armed forces to play professional football.
26 Feb.	Retired admiral Jonas Ingram is named commissioner of the All-American Football Conference.
13 Mar.	Pittsburgh Steelers halfback Bill Dudley is named the NFL MVP of 1946.
25 Mar.	Holy Cross defeats Oklahoma A&M 58–47 to win the NCAA basketball tournament.
30 Mar.	The Washington Capitols and the Chicago Bruins win the Eastern and Western Division titles of the Basketball Association of America (BAA).
9 Apr.	Leo Durocher, manager of the Brooklyn Dodgers, is suspended for "unpleasant incidents detrimental to baseball" — associating with gamblers. Burt Shotton is named to succeed Durocher on 17 April.
10 Apr.	Jackie Robinson becomes the first black player to play major-league baseball in the twentieth century after the Dodgers purchase his Montreal contract.
19 Apr.	The Toronto Maple Leafs win the NHL Stanley Cup playoffs over Montreal four games to two.
22 Apr.	The Basketball Association of America first playoff championship is won by the Philadelphia Warriors over the Chicago Stags four games to one.
17 May	The United States regains the Walker Cup in golf competition in St. Andrews, Scotland.
27 May	Montreal Canadien right wing Maurice Richard wins the NHL MVP award.
30 May	Mauri Rose wins the thirty-first annual Indianapolis 500 racing classic in 4:17:52.17.

25 June	Boxer Jimmy Doyle dies of a cerebral hemorrhage in Cleveland after losing a fight to welterweight champion Sugar Ray Robinson.
5 July	First baseman Larry Doby becomes first black player in the American League, signing a contract with the Cleveland Indians.
16 July	Rocky Graziano wins the world middleweight championship by a technical knockout over Tony Zale in the sixth round.
4 Aug.	Ike Williams takes the world lightweight boxing title from Bob Montgomery with a sixth-round knockout.
14 Aug.	Babe Didrikson Zaharias relinquishes her amateur status to accept $300,000 for a series of golf movies.
24 Aug.	The Crystal Plunge swim team of San Francisco wins the AAU outdoor championships in Chicago.
12 Sept.	Pittsburgh Pirates outfielder Ralph Kiner sets a major-league record, hitting eight home runs in four games.
12 Sept.	Dodgers infielder Jackie Robinson is named baseball's rookie of the year by *The Sporting News*.
14 Sept.	Jack Kramer and Louise Brough take the national men's and women's tennis titles at Forest Hills, New York.
3 Oct.	Yankee Bill Bevens pitches a no-hitter for 8 2/3 innings in the fourth World Series game against Brooklyn. The Yankees lose the game 3–2 in the ninth inning.
30 Sept.– 6 Oct.	The World Series is televised for the first time, with Gillette Safety Razor and Ford Motors paying $65,000 for joint sponsorship. The Yankees take their eleventh World Series title over the Brooklyn Dodgers four games to three. Major-league baseball draws a record attendance of 19.9 million fans for the season.
7 Oct.	Larry MacPhail sells his shares of the world-champion New York Yankees to partners Dan Topping and Del Webb for an estimated $2 million dollars.
1 Nov.	Thoroughbred racehorse champion Man O' War dies of a heart attack.
20 Nov.	Boston Braves third baseman Bob Elliott is named the NL MVP; New York Yankees center fielder Joe DiMaggio wins MVP for the AL on 27 November.
25 Nov.	A Saint Louis syndicate headed by Postmaster General Robert E. Hannegan buys Sam Breadon's 75 percent interest in the Cardinals and its sixteen-team minor-league farm system. The price is estimated at $3 million dollars.
1 Dec.	Notre Dame quarterback Johnny Lujack is named winner of the Heisman Trophy as the best college football player of 1947.
5 Dec.	Heavyweight boxing champion Joe Louis survives two knockdowns against "Jersey" Joe Walcott to win a fifteen-round split decision, his twenty-fourth consecutive victory.
6 Dec.	Leo Durocher is reinstated as manager of the Brooklyn Dodgers, ending a one-year suspension.

13 Dec.	The Missouri Valley Conference votes to ban all racial bias in athletics by September 1950.
19 Dec.	Sugar Ray Robinson retains his world welterweight boxing title with a technical knockout of Chuck Taylor in the sixth round.
31 Dec.	The AAU presents the James E. Sullivan Trophy for the year's outstanding amateur athlete to sculls champion John Kelly, Jr.

1948

3 Jan.	Jimmy Demaret wins the 1947 Vardon Trophy as the best American tournament golfer from the PGA.
15 Jan.	The Lions football team is purchased by a Detroit syndicate headed by Lyle Fife for $200,000 hundred thousand dollars.
17 Jan.	Black professional golfers Bill Spiller, Ted Rhodes, and Madison Gunter sue the Richmond (Virginia) Golf Club and the PGA for $105,000, charging they were barred from a Richmond golf tournament on racial grounds.
30 Jan.	The fifth Winter Olympiad opens in Saint Moritz, Switzerland, with twenty-seven nations participating. They are the first Olympic games since 1936.
Feb.	Dick Button becomes the first American to win a figure-skating championship in the Olympics.
24 Feb.	World featherweight boxing champion Willie Pep retains his title with a knockout of Humberto Sierra.
5 Mar.	Gus Lesnevich retains his world light-heavyweight title by knocking out Billy Fox in the first round.
20 Mar.	Billy Talbert and Pat Todd win the men's and women's singles tennis championships in New York.
23 Mar.	The University of Kentucky defeats Baylor 58–42 to win the NCAA basketball championship.
4 Apr.	Dick Button and Gretchen Merrill retain their national figure-skating championship titles in competition at Colorado Springs, Colorado.
6 Apr.	The U.S. Golf Association bars Babe Didrikson Zaharias from the National Golf Open, ruling that the tournament is restricted to men.
14 Apr.	The Toronto Maple Leafs defeat the Detroit Red Wings in four straight games to win the NHL Stanley Cup.
17 Apr.	The Minneapolis Lakers defeat the Rochester Royals to win the National Basketball League championship.
21 Apr.	The Baltimore Bullets defeat the Philadelphia Warriors to capture the Basketball Association of America title.
1 May	Eddie Arcaro rides Citation to victory in the seventy-fourth Kentucky Derby, winning $83,400.
10 May	The Basketball Association of America expands to twelve teams when four teams jump from the National Basketball League.

15 May	Mel Patton runs the 100-yard dash in 9.3 seconds, a world record that remains unmatched for six years.
25 May	Ben Hogan captures the PGA title in Saint Louis.
31 May	Mauri Rose wins his second straight Indianapolis 500 with an record average speed of 119.813 miles per hour, earning $28,000.
10 June	Tony Zale regains the world middleweight boxing title by knocking out Rocky Graziano in third round.
12 June	Citation wins the $117,300 Belmont Stakes to become eighth horse to win racing's Triple Crown.
20 June	Jack Kramer defeats Bobby Riggs for the U.S. professional tennis singles title in Forest Hills, New York.
25 June	Heavyweight champion Joe Louis knocks out Joe Walcott in eleventh round for Louis's twenty-fifth and last title defense. He announces his retirement from boxing following the fight.
28 June	Sugar Ray Robinson successfully defends his welterweight title with a fifteen-round decision over Bernard Docusen.
7 July	The Cleveland Indians sign Negro American League pitching star Satchel Paige, who started his career in 1925.
16 July	Leo Durocher replaces Mel Ott as manager of the New York Giants; Burt Shotton succeeds Durocher at Brooklyn.
26 July	Freddie Mills captures the world light-heavyweight title by defeating Gus Lesnevich in a fifteen-round decision in London.
July–Aug.	The 1948 Olympics, held in London, without the Soviet Union, draws 1.5 million spectators. The United States leads in gold medals with thirty-eight.
6 Aug.	Bob Mathias wins his first Olympic decathlon at age seventeen with 7,139 points.
16 Aug.	Home-run king George Herman "Babe" Ruth — the New York Yankees out-fielder who tied or set seventy-six baseball hitting records, including most home runs in one season — dies at age fifty-three of throat cancer.
18 Sept.	*The Sporting News* names Saint Louis Cardinal Stan Musial and Cleveland Indian manager-shortstop Lou Boudreau as outstanding baseball players of 1948.
19 Sept.	Pancho Gonzales and Margaret Osborne duPont win the men's and women's amateur singles titles at Forest Hills, New York.
21 Sept.	Marcel Cerdan defeats Tony Zale to gain the world middleweight boxing title.
23 Sept.	World lightweight champion Ike Williams retains his title by knocking out Jesse Flores in the tenth round.
11 Oct.	The Cleveland Indians win the World Series four games to two with a 4–3 victory over the Boston Braves.
	Casey Stengel is named manager of New York Yankees.
16 Oct.	Citation raises his career winnings to $820,000, winning the $111,700 International Gold Cup at Belmont Park.

28 Oct.   Sandy Saddler takes the featherweight boxing championship from Willie Pep with a fourth-round knockout.

29 Nov.   University of Pennsylvania center Chuck Bednarik wins the Maxwell Club Trophy as the top college football player.

30 Nov.   The Negro National League dissolves, leaving the ten-team Negro American League the only segregated baseball association. Southern Methodist University halfback Doak Walker wins the Heisman Trophy.

2 Dec.   Saint Louis Cardinals star Stan Musial is named the NL MVP for the second straight year.

19 Dec.   The Philadelphia Eagles win the NFL playoff; the Cleveland Browns win the All-American Conference title.

20 Dec.   Officials of the NFL and the All-American Football Conference discuss a possible merger of their organizations, but no agreement is reached.

1949

6 Jan.   Lou Boudreau is named best male athlete of 1948 by an Associated Press poll of sportswriters.

16 Jan.   Marshall Teague wins the National Stock Car championship in a 100-mile race at Daytona Beach, Florida.

2 Feb.   Bill and Charles DeWitt acquire control of the Saint Louis Browns baseball team from Richard Muckerman for an estimated $1 million dollars.

7 Feb.   New York Yankee outfielder Joe DiMaggio signs for $90,000.

10 Feb.   Joe Fulks scores 63 points for the Philadelphia Warriors, setting a Basketball Association of America individual-game scoring record.

11 Feb.   Willie Pep regains his featherweight crown, winning a fifteen-round decision over Sandy Saddler.

26 Feb.   West Point cadet James Sholtz sets a world shot put record of 60 feet, 7 3/4 inches.

1 Mar.   Ezzard Charles and Joe Walcott are selected to fight for the right to succeed Joe Louis as world heavyweight champion.

7 Mar.   Boston Red Sox outfielder and AL batting champion Ted Williams signs for $100,000 dollars a year, becoming the highest-paid player in baseball.

15 Mar.   West Virginia State defeats North Carolina College 60–53 to win the black intercollegiate basketball title.

26 Mar.   The University of Kentucky beats Oklahoma A&M 46–36 to win the NCAA basketball title.

10 Apr.   Sam Snead wins the $10,000 Masters golf tournament in Augusta, Georgia.

16 Apr.   The Toronto Maple Leafs beat the Boston Bruins in four straight games to win the NHL Stanley Cup.

26 Apr.   Former middleweight champion Tony Zale retires from boxing at age thirty-five.

3 May   New York Giants manager Leo Durocher is reinstated after a five-day suspension for assaulting a spectator at the New York Polo Grounds.

7 May   At 16–1 odds Ponder wins the seventy-fifth running of the Kentucky Derby; Ponder finishes fifth at the Preakness a week later.

30 May   Bill Holland wins the Indianapolis 500, averaging 121.327 miles per hour.

5 June   Baseball Commissioner Chandler reinstates eighteen baseball players suspended from American baseball for jumping to the now-defunct Mexican League.

11 June   Capot wins the $91,500 Belmont Stakes, having previously won the Preakness.

16 June   Jake La Motta knocks out Marcel Cerdan in the ninth round to become middleweight titleholder.

22 June   Ezzard Charles wins the world heavyweight title left vacant by the retirement of Joe Louis in a fifteen-round decision over "Jersey" Joe Walcott; he later beats Gus Lesnevich, Pat Valentino, and Freddie Beshore to become the undisputed heavyweight champion.

26 June   Bobby Riggs captures the U.S. professional tennis singles title in New York; Don Budge and Frank Kovacs take the doubles title.

July   The Soviet Union charges that American sports programs actually train youth for war making.

5 July   The New York Giants sign their first black players, outfielder Monte Irvin and infielder Hank Thompson, from Jersey City.

11 July   Sugar Ray Robinson retains his world welterweight boxing crown with a fifteenth-round decision over Kid Gavilan.

12 July   Major-league club owners agree to establish safety warning tracks in outfields beginning in the 1950 season.

26 July   Joey Maxim wins the light-heavyweight boxing title in a fifteen-round decision over Freddie Mills.

3 Aug.   The Basketball Association of America and the National Basketball League merge to form the new National Basketball Association (NBA).

6 Aug.   Chicago White Sox shortstop Luke Appling sets a new major-league record by playing his 2,154th game in nineteen years.

5 Sept.   Pancho Gonzales and Margaret Osborne duPont win the men's and women's singles titles at the U.S. tennis championships at Forest Hills, New York.

2 Oct.   The New York Yankees and the Brooklyn Dodgers win pennants in the American and National Leagues on the final day of the season.

9 Oct.   The New York Yankees win the World Series, defeating the Brooklyn Dodgers four games to one.

23 Oct.	Brooklyn Dodgers pitcher Don Newcombe and Saint Louis Browns outfielder Roy Seivers are named rookies of the year by *Sporting News*.
19 Nov.	Jackie Robinson is named NL MVP for 1949 by the Baseball Writers Association, the first black player to receive this honor.
21 Nov.	A Cleveland syndicate headed by businessman Ellis Ryan buys the Cleveland Indians from Bill Veeck for $2.2 million.
24 Nov.	Boston Red Sox outfielder Ted Williams is named AL MVP by the Baseball Writers Association.
5 Dec.	Ike Williams retains his lightweight boxing title with a fifteen-round decision over Freddie Dawson.
9 Dec.	The NFL and the All-American Conference end their four-year rivalry as they merge into a single National-American Football League.
10 Dec.	An American Football Coaches Association poll names Bud Wilkinson of Oklahoma as coach of the year. Notre Dame coach Frank Leahy is named Football Man of the Year by the Football Writers Association on 20 December.

OVERVIEW

Sports and War. World War II shaped sports in the 1940s, as it did all of American culture. The sports world did its best to maintain business as usual, but all organized games and contests were disrupted after 7 December 1941, when the Japanese bombed Pearl Harbor, and the disruption continued until well after the end of the war in August 1945. Able-bodied men were expected to serve in the military, and most qualified professional athletes answered the call. Early in 1941 sports stars inducted into the armed forces included baseball player Hank Greenberg and football players Dave Smulker and Chuck Gelatka. By 1945, 509 active major league baseball players had served, some two hundred colleges had disbanded their football teams because players went to war, and four thousand boxers, including five world champions, had joined the military. With the affirmation of President Roosevelt's "green light," urging baseball to continue during wartime as long as eligible players did not avoid the draft, organized sports carried on but with tight budgets and a shortage of players. Still, sports events provided a welcome diversion that boosted the morale of the nation.

Race. No event in the sports world of the 1940s was as important as the breaking of the color barrier in major league baseball in April 1947. When Jackie Robinson played for the Brooklyn Dodgers, the long process of integrating professional sports was begun. Even though Joe Louis had been heavyweight boxing champion since 1937 and Sugar Ray Robinson had won the welterweight title in 1946 — both of them regarded as the best fighters of the day if not of the century — boxing did not carry the social significance baseball did. By the end of the 1940s, a handful of blacks played in the major leagues, and they were among the sport's finest players. In football and basketball, college teams integrated before the pros. When Chuck Cooper from Duquesne University joined the Boston Celtics in 1950 to become the first black professional basketball player, games were canceled in protest. College football teams that included blacks were forced to call off games in mid-decade, especially in the South. Charles Pierce was the first black to play against a southern team, when Harvard, Pierce's team, played the University of Virginia in 1947.

Gender. Just as the wartime labor shortage gave women opportunities to work at traditional men's jobs in defense plants, the shortage of men on the playing fields briefly gave women athletes a chance to play in the spotlight. With the threat of canceling the 1943 baseball season looming before the major league owners, Philip Wrigley of the Chicago Cubs and Branch Rickey, the managerial genius of the Brooklyn Dodgers, created the All-American Girls Baseball League, which enjoyed surprising, though brief, success. Women made lasting gains in the world of golf, due to the achievements of two spectacular stars, Mildred "Babe" Didrikson and Patty Berg, and women's tennis began to attract attention at the end of the decade when Gussie Moran brought sex appeal to the courts.

Money. Professional sports took the first steps toward becoming big business after World War II. In the early 1940s professional sports were still reeling financially from the Depression. Professional basketball was unorganized, and players averaged only about $50 per week, playing 150 games a season. While attendance at baseball games dropped during the war, only 1943 was a disastrous year, and even then twelve of the sixteen major league teams reported profits. In 1947 players negotiated a minimum salary for the first time ($5,500 per year), and the owners agreed to establish the first players' pension fund. In the postwar years, as it became possible for teams to travel more and as television began providing revenue to teams, salaries soared. Saint Louis Cardinal star Stan Musial was making $50,000 per year by 1950, and he got a 70 percent raise the next year. Before the war professional football players earned an average of $150 per game; by 1949 their salaries had increased to an average of $5,000 per season. In the individual sports the best athletes were paid well, and those who did not quite measure up struggled. Joe Louis routinely earned six-figure purses for his fights, and champions in the lower weight classes earned $30,000 or more for championship matches, depending on the draw. Jockeys Eddie Arcaro, Johnny Longden, and Ted Atkinson earned upward of $70,000 per year. Professional golf was bolstered by Fred Corcoran and his management of the Professional Golfers' Association tour that in 1946 included thirty tournaments with total prizes of $750,000, the winner getting about $12,000 per tournament. Professional tennis became a lucrative business for the handful of players who toured with Jack Kramer, Bobby Riggs, and other champions. Kramer was guaranteed $50,000 against a share of ticket sales in 1947 for an eighty-nine-match international tour that brought revenues of $383,000.

Postwar Sports. Big-time sports changed rapidly with the prosperity that followed World War II. Major sports formed new professional organizations; new money and talent poured into the sports world; television transformed sports from organized games into organized entertainment. Auto racing, football, basketball, and golf established players' organizations after the war. Oversight commissions regulated each sport, setting standards of equipment, rules of play, and business practices, with the authority to negotiate labor contracts and enter into other business agreements for concessions and the licensing of rights. After the war, television changed the face of American sports. In 1946 broadcast revenues to major league baseball from television were $1 million. Six years later broadcast income had jumped to $5 million, and it was only beginning. With television came the merchandising of sports to attract revenue from sources other than ticket sales. Sports was quickly becoming a business of making heroes who could be used to sell goods to their fans. The idealists' voices were lost in the din of hustlers hawking products, and yet, despite all obstacles, sports continued to produce great athletes whose achievements awed and delighted fans. It was still a grand time.

AUTOMOBILE RACING: INDIANAPOLIS

Wilbur Shaw. Wilbur Shaw was the top name in Indianapolis-type car racing in 1940 and 1941. In 1940 Shaw, driving a Maserati, won his third Indianapolis 500 and became the first driver to win the race two years in a row. He was a favorite to repeat in 1941, and with sixty-two laps to go he pulled in for a pit stop more than two minutes ahead of the second-place car. As he exited the pit, the race began to slip away. During his stop, he had damaged the spokes on his right rear wheel, and the tire began to tear loose. Before he could return to the pit, he lost control of the car, bounced off the wall, and came to rest against a concrete barrier, with a fuel-tank brace wedged against his spine. His career as a race driver was over. The race was won by the man who inherited Shaw's mantle as the track's premier driver — Mauri Rose, driving in relief for Floyd Davis.

War Casualty. Indianapolis was idle from 1942 to 1945, and it seemed, briefly, that it might be shut down. The legendary track needed repair, an infusion of capital, and expert management if it was to survive. Racing fan Tony Hulman, a businessman from Terre Haute, Indiana, had the resources to revive the track and the Indianapolis 500, held annually on Memorial Day. He bought the track in 1945 and hired Wilbur Shaw as general manager. Shaw did his job admirably. In 1946 he staged a 500 that was a financial success, despite inferior racing equipment owing to wartime shortages. Twenty-four cars dropped out of the race due to wrecks and mechanical difficulties, including Rose, who hit the wall. The race was won that year by George Robson.

Rose and Holland. The rest of the decade at Indianapolis belonged to the Blue Crown Special team owned by Lou Moore. The two team cars were driven by Mauri Rose, a veteran of ten Indianapolis 500 races, and rookie Bill Holland. In 1947 Holland was leading the race a minute ahead of Rose with forty laps to go. Apparently because of misunderstood instructions from the pit, Holland slowed down to reduce wear on his car, while Rose raced full out. Thinking he was two laps ahead, Holland let Rose pass him on the 193rd lap of the 200-lap race, and Rose took the winner's purse. The drivers for that race split a $137,425 purse, and Shaw saw to it that the

Bill France, 1948

purse increased each year. Rose set a new track record in 1948, with Holland a lap behind in second. In 1949 the same duel developed again, this time with Rose fifty-one seconds behind Holland with 100 miles to go. Rose's car failed in the 192nd lap, and Holland won his first Indianapolis 500, setting a new record, finishing four hours, ten minutes, and twenty-three seconds after he had begun. By 1949 the Indianapolis 500, thanks in large part to the management of Wilbur Shaw, was reestablished as the most important automobile race in America.

Stock car racers on a dirt track

Source:
Wilbur Shaw, *Gentlemen, Start Your Engines* (London: Bodley Head, 1956).

AUTOMOBILE RACING: STOCK CARS

White Lightning. A competitive Indianapolis-type racer cost about $30,000 after the war. That was too much for a band of southerners who liked to build and drive race cars. They knew how to buy a heap at a junkyard and turn it into a race car for about $2,500. Their racers were called stock cars because they looked like passenger vehicles, and their competitions were originally called pasture races, because in the early days the drivers would gather in a farmer's pasture on Sunday afternoons to race. Most of the stock car tracks of the late 1940s were made of compacted clay, and many of the drivers had served their apprenticeship running moonshine liquor, 120 gallons at a time, from the stills where it was illegally made, to thirsty customers. Outrunning the law became a mark of honor among the moonshine drivers, and their outlaw attitude shaped stock car racing. The moonshiners were so prominent among drivers in the early stock car races that Atlanta passed a local ordinance prohibiting moonshiners from participating in automobile racing. One of the sport's treasured anecdotes was the story of moonshiner/driver Bob Flock, who was waiting to start a race in Atlanta in the late 1940s when he was spotted by a police captain who knew he hauled liquor. The captain ordered two motorcycle patrolmen to come at Flock from different directions on the track to trap him. Realizing his predicament, Flock sped off and gained enough speed on the third turn to jump the cyclone fence around the track and land in the parking lot. There he made his successful getaway, and two days later he turned himself in.

NASCAR. There were several stock car racing clubs after the war, the most successful of which was the National Association for Stock Car Auto Racing (NASCAR), owned by entrepreneur Bill France. He promoted late-model automobile racing, which employed cars that were no more than three years old and were supposed to be the same as cars purchasable in dealer showrooms. In fact, the cars of the time were not made well enough to race, and modifications were necessary for the track, but to spectators late-model racing offered the excitement of seeing competition among the car models they saw every day on the street and maybe even owned. Ford Motor Company saw the promotional opportunities NASCAR offered and became an avid early sponsor. France called his stock car races Grand Nationals, and he staged the first at the Charlotte Speedway on 19 June 1949. It was won by Glen Dunway, but when his car was inspected after the race, officials found that Dunway had attached brackets to the springs to make the car handle better in turns. He was disqualified, and second-place finisher Jim Roper was declared the winner.

Source:
Kim Chapin, *Fast As White Lightning: The Story of Stock Car Racing* (New York: Dial, 1981).

BASEBALL

Old-Time Baseball. The 1940s rank as one of the most spectacular decades in baseball history, despite the disruption of war. At the beginning of the 1940s, games were played in the daytime by white players and watched by fans who normally lived fairly close to the park. When the decade ended, night games were an accepted and crucial part of professional baseball; black players were not only participating, they were reshaping the game; and radio, television, and modern-style marketing promotions were captivating fans in every part of the county.

The Two-Team Monopoly. During most of the decade the Saint Louis Cardinals and Brooklyn Dodgers turned the National League into an exclusive, two-team monopoly. From 1941 through 1949, the Cardinals and Dodgers won seven pennants. Only the Chicago Cubs, in 1945, and Boston Red Sox, in 1948, disrupted the two-team battle for supremacy. In 1941 and 1942 the Dodgers and Cardinals went to the final day of the season before the National League champion was determined. In 1946 they were tied at season's end, forcing the first National League playoff in modern times. The teams also shared something other than success — a general manager. Branch Rickey, who had established the farm system that eventually provided the Cardinals with nine pennants, went to Brooklyn in 1942, and within a short time the "Bums of Brooklyn" had something to cheer about.

Heroes Galore. Some of the greatest legends of baseball played during the 1940s. Saint Louis outfielder Stan Musial boasted a .346 batting average and 302 doubles during the decade to lead the National League, while Ted Williams was champion of the decade in the American League, with a .356 batting average, 234 home runs, and 893 runs batted in. In pitching, Detroit's Hal Newhouser of the American League collected the most wins, 190; the lowest earned-run average; 2.83, and most strikeouts; 1,579. In 1944 and 1945 he was also the first player since Jimmie Foxx to win back-to-back Most Valuable Player awards for his performance. Only Babe Ruth had homered more than Ralph Kiner, who led the National

Pete Gray, one-armed outfielder for the Saint Louis Browns, 1945

League seven straight times, collecting 369 home runs in ten years, or one every fourteen times at bat. Cleveland shortstop-manager Lou Boudreau's 1948 season, when he won the Most Valuable Player award, included a .355 batting average, 106 runs batted in, and 116 runs scored.

Memorable Beginnings. The decade began with plenty of baseball excitement. The American League Detroit Tigers beat the Cleveland Indians and their future Hall of Famer Bob Feller — winner of twenty-seven games that year — on the final day of the season for the right to meet the Cincinnati Reds in the World Series. The Reds, on the other hand, had to activate their forty-year-old coach Jimmy Wilson for service behind the plate because one catcher was injured and the other committed suicide as the season drew to a close. The Reds went on to win their first world championship in twenty-one years in 1940. But it was the following year, the 1941 season, that captured the attention of America. For sports fans even the war in Europe did not overshadow Ted Williams's .406 hitting display or Joe DiMaggio's record-breaking fifty-six-game hitting streak. It was a baseball connoisseur's year. On the last day of the season Williams approached a doubleheader batting .3996, which would have been rounded off to the magic average of .400 and made him the first player since 1931 to crack the .400 barrier. Yet, Williams declined to sit out the game to preserve his record. In a magnificent display of confi-

Joe DiMaggio, on 29 June 1941, hitting in his forty-first consecutive game, breaking George Sisler's American League record

dence and skill, Williams went six for eight against Philadelphia to finish with a .406 batting average.

DiMaggio. Despite the consistency and skill of Williams's season-long march toward the history books, it was DiMaggio's quest for baseball's longest hitting streak that captured the most attention in 1941. Once he hit safely in thirty-eight games and streaked for the record of forty-four, set in 1897, fans followed his every turn at bat. The consecutive hitting streak ran from 15 May to 17 July; DiMaggio won the American League Most Valuable Player award; and the Yankees won the pennant and the right to play against the Brooklyn Dodgers in the World Series. In the fourth game of the series with the Yankees behind 3–4 in the ninth inning, Dodger catcher Mickey Owen dropped a game-ending strike three and allowed Yankee outfielder Tommy Henrich to make it safely to first base. The Yankees rallied to win the game 7–4 and build a 3–1 lead in the series. That same year, Lou Gehrig, one of the most popular Yankees ever, died at age thirty-eight, two years after he missed the first game of his career due to a mysterious debilitating disease. He bid farewell to his fans at Yankee Stadium on 4 July 1939, designated Lou Gehrig Day, and died on 2 June 1941. Amyotrophic lateral sclerosis was thereafter referred to as Lou Gehrig's disease.

Baseball Goes to War. Nineteen games into the 1941 season, Detroit slugger Hank Greenberg was inducted into the army, symbolizing the changes ahead for baseball. He was not the first major leaguer to be drafted; that distinction fell to Philadelphia pitcher Hugh Malcahy, but because he was a highly paid star, Greenberg's induction made headlines and set off considerable debate about the role of baseball during wartime. At first the impact of the draft was manageable. In 1942, for example, 328 out of 607 major league ballplayers were in uniform. But that quickly changed. In May 1942 Joe DiMaggio was sworn in as a U.S. Army Air Force aviation cadet; by 1943 pitcher Bob Feller was the navy captain of a 40-mm gun crew, and hundreds of other healthy young men followed. In 1945, 565 players of 607 were fighting the war. For many older players the interruption for military service meant the end of their baseball careers, but 1941 stars Hank Greenberg, Joe DiMaggio, Bob Feller, Stan Musial, and Ted Williams all resumed their careers following the war. On the baseball field the Saint Louis Cardinals won the first of three consecutive pennants in 1942 and then went on to defeat the New York Yankees in the World Series; the Boston Red Sox's Ted Williams won the triple crown with a .356 batting average, 36 home runs, and 137 RBIs. As the 1943 season approached and

Jackie Robinson and Branch Rickey

the ranks of the able-bodied disappeared from the baseball diamond, owners turned to veterans whose age kept them out of the service. Players such as Spud Chandler, Joe Kuhel, Dutch Leonard, and Johnny Niggeling extended their careers, sometimes into their forties, because of the war. Marginal players also got their chance. Nick Etten, who had been in the majors since 1938 but could boast of only one good season, led the American League in homers with 22 in 1944 and led the league in RBIs with 111 in 1946. The most notable indication of the lack of players was one-armed outfielder Pete Gray, signed by the Saint Louis Browns in 1945. Gray played seventy-seven games for the Browns, hitting .218. When he caught the ball in the outfield, he would throw the ball up in the air, throw the glove off his left hand, catch the ball, and throw it into play.

Roosevelt's "Green Light" Letter. As the war effort demanded more and more professional players, the baseball executives, the press, and the public began to wonder whether the sport should continue during the war years. In response President Franklin D. Roosevelt wrote a letter to Baseball Commissioner Kenesaw Mountain Landis on 15 January 1942, urging him to keep baseball alive during the war and forming an unusual pact between two powerful men. Roosevelt's "green light" letter affirmed the importance of baseball as a recreation for hardworking Americans. But in return for allowing baseball to continue, Roosevelt stipulated that all players of military age should, without question, enter the armed forces. The president trusted Landis to ensure that all players

eligible for the draft would enter the service. When J. G. Taylor Spink, owner of *The Sporting News,* asked Roosevelt in 1944 for special draft exemptions for baseball players, Landis intervened. Landis wrote the director of the Selective Service, saying that baseball did not want special treatment in the draft since this would break his agreement with Roosevelt and cause "bitter public resentment" that would damage the integrity of the game. Keeping baseball alive during the war years was financially crucial to the game's future. It kept fan interest alive and franchises operating to set the stage for full resumption after the war. As the president pointed out, baseball also did, indeed, provide an important diversion and morale booster to both workers in defense plants and soldiers overseas, who followed the major leagues closely. Recognizing the role of baseball in America, the Japanese took extraordinary steps to jam broadcasts of the World Series. For the soldier, whether his team was winning or losing, the continuity of baseball represented business as usual on the home front in a time of crisis.

Breaking the Color Barrier. Many factors throughout American culture set the stage for the integration of major league baseball in 1947. Thousands of black Americans migrated to northern National League cities from the rural South before and during World War II. In the 1940s, for the first time urban blacks formed an identifiable voting bloc and consumer market to be reckoned with by politicians and businessmen alike. The war itself caused a reassessment of American racial attitudes, as the Nazi ideology of racial supremacy discredited American ideas of white superiority. World War II also raised the aspirations of blacks, eager to take their place in the American dream.

Branch Rickey and the Brooklyn Dodgers. Branch Rickey, the general manager of the Brooklyn Dodgers, knew how to seize a moment. Rickey was known in the sports world as the "Mahatma," since he combined "God, your father, and Tammany Hall leader." He was moved by postwar agitation over baseball's segregation, and in 1945 he took it upon himself to integrate major league baseball. A pious Methodist, Rickey remembers, "I couldn't face my God much longer knowing that His black creatures are held separate and distinct from His white creations in the game that has given me all I own." Rickey planned his moves carefully. He consulted historians and sociologists on race relations in order to anticipate reactions to the great experiment he planned. These consultants convinced him, idealistically, that if Americans were brought together in the common goal of integration, they would be able to overcome their racial prejudices. But because of the opposition to blacks in baseball, Rickey had to act deviously. He announced that he was going to establish a new all-black league, financed and run by the Dodgers. Everyone knew Rickey's fondness for the dollar, so the announcement was accepted at face value by the baseball world. One of the teams in the proposed league was to be in Brooklyn. Under that cover

MR. RICKEY

Baseball innovator Branch Rickey was instrumental in shaping the modern game, forming farm teams, recruiting black players and introducing solid business practices. In 1913, Rickey helped introduce Ladies' Days with the Saint Louis Brown and took the idea across town in 1917 to the Saint Louis Cardinals, raising the caliber of fans and earning his salary of $15,000 a year. In spring training, he introduced innovations such as batting cages, blackboard drills, and sliding pits. In 1927, he authorized the first radio broadcasts of major league baseball games. By far his most important contribution to Saint Louis and later the Brooklyn Dodgers was the development of the farm system. By establishing a chain of teams to feed players to the major leagues, the Cardinals became competitive with the wealthier teams of the era. Rickey moved to Brooklyn in 1942 to become president and general manager of the Dodgers, a team best known for their bonehead plays and mediocre record. There he created a sound farm system and won pennants in 1947 and 1949. He eventually purchased the club with Walter O'Malley and John L. Smith. Brilliant and quotable, Rickey's name will always be linked to the signing of Jackie Robinson in 1947 that integrated the major leagues. In later years, he sold his Dodger stock for $1 million, attempted to organize a third major league that inspired the established league to create the New York Mets, Los Angeles Angels, Houston Colt 45s and the new Washington Senators.

Rickey interviewed Jackie Robinson in August 1945. Robinson was an outstanding athlete. He had been the first man to letter in four varsity sports at UCLA, including baseball, basketball, football, and track and field, and he had been a good shortstop for the Monarchs in 1945, his first year in the Negro Leagues.

The Deal. Robinson went to his interview with Rickey believing the cover story about a new league. Rickey, on the other hand, wanted to be sure that Robinson was the right player for his bold plan. He needed to find a man with superlative skills as a ballplayer who also had sufficient self-control to endure with dignity the torment and abuse he would suffer. The most famous players in the Negro Leagues — Josh Gibson, Satchel Paige, Buck Leonard, and Cool Papa Bell — were past their prime. Robinson, at twenty-six, was coming into his best years, and he seemed to possess the character for which Rickey was looking. Rickey interviewed Robinson for three hours. During that time he challenged Robinson to say how he would react, for instance, if he were spiked by an opposing player and then called racial names. Robinson remembered saying, "Are you looking for a Negro who is afraid to fight back?" Rickey answered, "I'm looking for a ballplayer with guts enough not to fight back." Robinson's first step toward the major leagues was a season for the Montreal Royals in 1946. He was paid a $3,000 signing bonus and $600 a month, more than his Negro League contract called for and enough to allow him to get married. He opened the season with a home run his first time at bat and finished the day with four hits in four trips to the plate and two stolen bases. That year he led the International League in hitting with a .349 average. A year later, on 15 April 1947, Robinson played first base for the Brooklyn Dodgers against the Boston Braves at Ebbets Field, becoming the first black player in major league baseball.

The Reaction. Although Rickey took great pains to ensure the success of the experiment, it created enormous controversy. His own team threatened a mutiny; his fellow owners worried that black fans would drive away white fans and destroy the game of baseball. Some teams said they would refuse to play against Robinson. Members of the Saint Louis Cardinals secretly planned to strike. National League president Ford Frick moved quickly. He told the players involved that they would be suspended if they went through with their proposed action. "You will find that the friends you think you have in the press box will not support you, that you will be outcasts," Frick said. "I do not care if half the league strikes. Those who do it will encounter quick retribution. They will be suspended, and I don't care if it wrecks the National League for five years. This is the United States of America, and one citizen has as much right to play as another." Once Robinson played for the Dodgers, black attendance reportedly increased as much as 50 percent in some cities, causing owners to fear that too much black attendance would "threaten the value of Major League franchises." The nation watched, fascinated. In a patronizing address to middle-class black leaders in 1947, Rickey appealed to the black community not to call too much attention to Robinson's presence. "The biggest threat to (Robinson's) success is the Negro people themselves. . . . You'll strut. You'll wear badges, you'll hold Jack Robinson Days. . . . You'll get drunk. You'll fight. You'll be arrested. . . . You'll symbolize his importance into a national comedy . . . and an ultimate tragedy." The *Chicago Defender* warned, "Let's not make him a race problem; he's just a ballplayer." Through it all Robinson kept quiet, just doing his job on the field. He had a good year, batting .297 and winning the Rookie of the Year award. When there were enough blacks in the league for Robinson to shed his role as pioneer, he became a highly vocal player. Throughout his career Robinson hit .311 over ten years. His best season was his third, 1949, when he led the league with a .342 average and thirty-seven stolen bases, winning the Most Valuable Player award.

The Result. In 1948 Rickey signed black catcher Roy

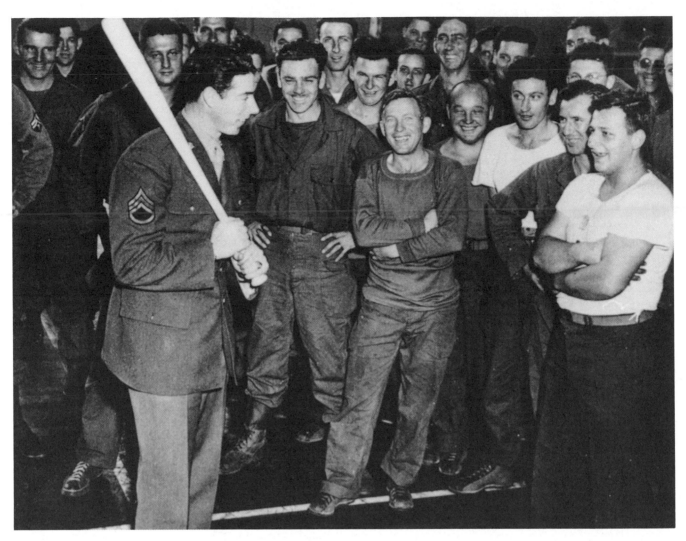

Joe DiMaggio after he joined the army in 1941

Campanella, and the preseason exhibition tour that year was easy for the Brooklyn Dodgers, and lucrative. Everyone, it seemed, wanted a look at Branch Rickey's Negro sensations. In Fort Worth, Texas, the Dodgers drew 7,563 customers, then more than doubled that total the next day with 15,507 fans — an all-time park record. In Dallas the turnout was 11,379, including 6,800 blacks. In Oklahoma City, 10,137 people showed up to gawk — half black, half white. In seven games, from Fort Worth to Asheville, North Carolina, the Brooklyn Dodgers played before 63,398 people.

Slow Progress. Integration was a bumpy road, but Jackie Robinson's pioneering step paved the way for more black players in the major leagues in the 1940s. Pitcher Don Newcombe joined the Dodgers in 1949. The New York Giants signed Hank Thompson and Monte Irvin in 1948. Much of the excitement of the National League in the 1950s and 1960s revolved around players such as Willie Mays, Hank Aaron, Willie McCovy, Bob Gibson, and Maury Wills — all black. But racial progress was far slower in the American League. Only three blacks were signed in the American League in the 1940s: Larry Doby,

Satchel Paige, and Luke Easter, all of whom played for the Cleveland Indians under the leadership of Bill Veeck. It took twelve years after Robinson's first game with the Dodgers for the Boston Red Sox to integrate; they were the last all-white team. Between 1947 and 1959 blacks made up only a small percentage of the major league. But the black players were outstanding performers, winning nine of the National League's Most Valuable Player awards, with Campanella winning three times and Ernie Banks winning twice. Black players also won nine Rookie of the Year awards during that period.

Changing of the Guard. The death of Kenesaw Mountain Landis in 1945 ushered in a new era in baseball, as control shifted from the baseball commissioner to the team owners for the first time since 1919. Following the disgrace of the Black Sox scandal during the World Series of 1919, the sixteen major league baseball club owners cringed under the iron-handed rule of their self-appointed commissioner and employee, Judge Landis. The scandal had allowed Landis to exercise near-dictatorial powers, and he used them to restore the image of the national pastime. His death marked major changes to the

After the war, James "Cool Papa" Bell, one of the Negro Leagues' fastest and most exciting players, was offered an opportunity to play for the Major League's St. Louis Browns, when his skills were declining and opportunities for black baseball players were improving. Instead, he took a job a professional scout, helping to pave the way for other black players to make the major leagues. Bell took credit for promoting the career of Dodger great Jackie Robinson, Chicago Cubs star Ernie Banks, and Yankee Elston Howard. Once known as the "black Ty Cobb," Bell was elected to the Hall of Fame on 13 February 1974 at the age of 70.

rules the major leagues lived by, from the disposition of his successor, former Kentucky governor Albert B. "Happy" Chandler. The commissioner would no longer be allowed personal interpretation of the rules and spontaneous introduction of his own laws; the commissioner's decisions could be taken to court; and rules and joint actions of the major leagues could no longer be vetoed because the commissioner held them to be "detrimental to baseball." Happy Chandler signed a seven-year contract that paid him $50,000 annually. With the owners back in charge, he earned every dime, wrestling with the problems, financial and otherwise, associated with an America returning from the war: the role of blacks in baseball, the creation of new teams, the challenge of a rival Mexican Baseball League, the pooling of revenues, the emergence of player unions, and the rising cost of doing business in that transitional era.

Baseball after the War. Played before an enthusiastic and appreciative postwar crowd, baseball in the closing years of the decade rarely lacked excitement. Baseball's best players were back from the war, and America was ready for anything. In 1946 Bob Feller returned from four years in the navy to reestablish himself as one of the game's finest pitchers, winning twenty-six games for the Cleveland Indians, ten by shutout. Led by Stan Musial, the Cardinals beat the Dodgers in the first pennant playoff since 1908, then edged the Red Sox in a tense seven-game World Series. In 1947 Ted Williams excited the American League with his hitting, winning the triple crown (leading the league in batting average, home runs, and runs batted in) for the second time, but lost the Most Valuable Player award to the "Yankee Clipper," Joe DiMaggio. The New York Yankees returned to baseball dominance that year, beating the Dodgers in a World Series considered to be the best of the decade. After losing the first two games the Dodgers came back to tie the series. In the fourth game Yankee Bill Bevens was

one out away from a World Series no-hitter with a 2–1 lead when he put two men on and then allowed Cookie Lavagetto to double, losing his no-hitter and the game to the Dodgers. Fittingly, 1947 was the first year of televised baseball games.

1948 and 1949. In 1948 the Cleveland Indians, featuring pitchers Bob Feller and Satchel Paige, won their first pennant since 1920, and the Boston Braves captured their first National League title since 1914 in a year known for power hitting. Ralph Kiner and Johnny Mize each hit forty home runs. Stan Musial had one of his best seasons, batting .376 with thirty-nine homers. The Indians won the 1948 World Series as baseball's popularity boomed. The fifth game of the World Series was played before 86,288 in Cleveland Stadium. In 1948 two traditional rivals, the New York Yankees and the Brooklyn Dodgers, both reasserted themselves. For the Yankees it was the beginning of the Casey Stengel era. He led the Yankees to the world championship in 1949, a year in which more than 20 million fans paid to see major league and minor league games.

Sources:

Martin Appel and Burt Goldblatt, *Baseball's Best: The Hall of Fame Gallery* (New York: McGraw-Hill, 1977);

Glenn Dickey, *The History of American League Baseball Since 1901* (New York: Stein & Day, 1980);

Dickey, *The History of National League Baseball Since 1876* (New York: Stein & Day, 1979);

Jim Kaplan, *Golden Years of Baseball* (New York: Crescent, 1992);

Milton J. Shapiro, *The Year They Won the Most Valuable Player Award* (New York: Messner, 1966).

BASEBALL, WOMEN'S STYLE

AAGBL. In 1943 with half of the players on the sixteen major league baseball teams in the armed forces, the All-American Girls Baseball League (AAGBL) was formed. The AAGBL was the idea of Philip Wrigley, owner of the Chicago Cubs, and Branch Rickey, general manager of the Brooklyn Dodgers. Wrigley, who was based in Chicago, chose midwestern home cities for the four teams in the league. There were the Racine (Wisconsin) Belles; the Kenosha (Wisconsin) Comets; the South Bend (Indiana) Blue Sox; and the Rockford (Illinois) Peaches. City leaders paid $22,500 for each franchise in support of the belief that women's professional baseball was a patriotic effort to provide diversion for wartime workers laboring under extraordinary pressure. The league recruited players and assigned them to one of the four teams on the basis of ability, with a view toward forming a competitive league. Recruits came from amateur softball leagues nationwide, and the chosen players were rewarded well, though their salaries were not comparable to those of major league men. At a time when women in the workplace made perhaps $10 or $20 a week, AAGBL players made between $45 and $85 per week during the four-month regular season. They played

Dorothy Kamenshek, first baseman for the Rockford Peaches

most days, with doubleheaders on weekends, and traveled from city to city on team buses.

Charm School. The Wrigley organization expected AAGBL players to be superior athletes, but it also expected them to display feminine qualities. Rigid rules of dress and deportment were enforced. The players' hair had to show under their baseball caps, and their uniforms were one-piece tunic dresses with skirts above the knee. Tomboy behavior was strictly limited. Early recruits attended finishing schools and charm schools, one of which was conducted by Helena Rubenstein.

The Game. Future Hall of Fame players Max Carey and Jimmie Foxx were recruited to coach the teams, which played initially with a ball that was 12 inches in circumference, the size of a softball, and later with a ball more like a hardball, 10 3/8 inches around. By 1948 the base path distances and the distances between home plate and the pitcher's mound were lengthened so the game resembled that played by male major leaguers. The qual-

ity of play in the AAGBL was excellent. Of the last game of the 1946 season, a fourteen-inning contest between the Racine Belles and the Rockford Peaches, Max Carey said "barring none, even the majors, it's the best game I've ever seen." The AAGBL had performance averages that matched those of the men. The best single-season batting average was .429 by Joanne Weaver, who holds the distinction of being the last top-level professional baseball player to hit over .400 on the season. The all-around league leader in batting, runs scored, and fewest strikeouts was Dottie Kamenshek, who hit .316 in 1946 and .306 in 1947.

Performances. The AAGBL lasted until 1954, though the return of veteran major leaguers after the war drained the league of its commercial promise. League management was disorganized, and the attention of fans was directed toward the return to normal after the war. The AABGL faded slowly, but memories of the league's glory days remained vivid for those experienced them.

Bob Kurland, seven-foot center for Oklahoma A&M, shaking hands with his coach, Hank Iba, in 1946 after their team won its second consecutive NCAA championship

Source:
Susan E. Johnson, *When Women Played Hardball* (Seattle: Seal Press, 1994).

BASKETBALL, COLLEGE

Before the War. A revolutionary rule change in 1938 unshackled college basketball from the cumbersome, mandatory jump ball at the center of the court after every basket. The decision brought speed and nonstop action to the game and opened up new styles of play, including the jump shot. Washington State coach Jack Friel said, "Ironically, I didn't believe in the shot at first. I simply couldn't conceive of a kid jumping off the floor and shooting accurately from the distance they do. I was soon converted, however, and the jump shot is the big weapon now. I think the present teams score more by accident, with their excellent jump shooters, than our old teams did by design."

NCAA. The National Collegiate Athletic Association (NCAA) tournament was in its infancy as the decade opened. The first NCAA tournament, staged in 1939, was won by Oregon in a small gym on the campus of Northwestern University in Evanston, Illinois. Critics insisted, though, that the older National Invitational Tournament (NIT), played at Madison Square Garden, attracted better teams and determined the real national champion. The Indiana Hoosiers swept the second

NCAA tournament 60–42 over the University of Kansas. At the beginning of the 1940s, coaches were experimenting with substitutions. During the 1941 NCAA tournament final, Washington State employed a fast-breaking offense with a two-platoon substitution system to tire their opponent, but the strategy failed, as Wisconsin won 39–34. Washington State coach Jack Friel explained, "I substituted a lot. In fact, I think I was one of the first to use the two-platoon system. Basketball was developing into a racehorse game. I finally came to the conclusion that players really couldn't stay in there and pitch on defense; to play good defense, they needed some rest. So by 1941 I was substituting a lot, and after that I platooned all the time." The Pitt-Fordham and NYU-Georgetown doubleheader games on 28 February 1940 were the first college basketball games broadcast on television; they appeared on experimental station W2XMS, forerunner to New York's WNBC. One year later, in another landmark for sports broadcasting, the 1941 NCAA tournament final between Wisconsin and Washington State was broadcast by Mutual Broadcasting Network on national radio for the first time.

The War Years. The 1941–1942 season had just begun when the Japanese attacked Pearl Harbor in December 1941. Entire teams were wiped out by the ensuing draft. Many schools dropped the sport for the duration of the war, and the teams that remained were kept alive by a rule change allowing freshmen to compete as varsity players. Basketball was affected less than other sports by the wartime shortage of men, because the players' height often made them ineligible for military service. College basketball teams got taller in the war years. West Texas State boasted a 6-foot-10-inch center and a front line that averaged 6 feet, 6 inches. College basketball during the war was also a game for young athletes, because the draft took older players. Four of the starting five players on Illinois's exciting 1943 team, which compiled a record of 17–1, were named All–Big Ten, but the team was unable to play in either the NCAA or NIT tournament because the heart of the team was drafted by tournament time. A year later, Utah's NCAA-championship team, which practiced all year in church gyms because their field house had been appropriated by the army, was composed of players whose average age was 18 1/2 years. In an effort to do its part for the war effort, the NCAA staged its championship games in Madison Square Garden from 1943 to 1945 and then played the NIT champion as a benefit for the Red Cross.

The College Big Man. College basketball took another leap toward the modern game in the mid 1940s with the introduction of big, agile players who could freely roam the court. In 1945 coach Hank Iba of Oklahoma A&M led the way, building his NCAA-championship team around seven-footer Bob "Foothills" Kurland, the core of a squad billed as the "tallest team on earth." Kurland's defensive skill under the basket led directly to new goaltending rules following his sophomore year.

That same year NIT champion DePaul was led by 6-foot, 10-inch George Mikan. His coach, Ray Meyer, instituted a rigorous program of rope skipping, shadow boxing, and running to increase the agility of his big man. The hype was so great that when the two teams finally met in the Red Cross final at Madison Square Garden, 18,148 fans showed up for what was billed as the "battle of the goons." The showdown of the NCAA and NIT winners proved to be a lackluster game, won by Oklahoma A&M 52–44, in part because Mikan fouled out after fourteen minutes, but the contest clearly helped establish the role of the quick, agile centers in college basketball. Both centers were also significant in the establishment of professional basketball. Mikan, who averaged 23.1 points his senior year, signed with the Chicago American Gears in 1946. His contract was the largest paid to that time to a basketball pro — twelve thousand dollars a season for five years.

College Basketball after the War. As soldiers came back from duty and reenrolled in college, college basketball progressed to a new level of sports entertainment. Oklahoma A&M won the NCAA championship two years in a row, in 1945–1946 and 1946–1947, the first team to win two NCAA titles, consecutive or otherwise. But the postwar era belonged to Adolph Rupp, whose Kentucky Wildcats won four NCAA titles from 1945 to 1954. In the decade after World War II no one coached so many championship teams, produced so many All-Americans, or won so many games as Rupp. In 1947–1948 Kentucky went 36–3, won the Southeastern Conference title for the fifth time in a row, then routed Baylor 58–42 in the NCAA finals. One year later, Kentucky established twenty-two NCAA team and individual records in winning its second national championship in a row, defeating Oklahoma A&M 46–36. The Wildcats were led by Alex Groza, who was named the tournament's Most Valuable Player for the second year in a row. The end of the decade was noteworthy for the appearance of a remarkable player — 6 foot, 1 inch Bob Cousy of Holy Cross. His passing, dribbling, quickness, and sound technique made him the prototype of the imaginative, wide-open-style players who excelled in the 1950s. Just as the decade began with one defining rule change, it ended with another: coaches could talk to their team during a time-out without a penalty. Basketball was a national game by 1949, as reflected by the national ranking that the Associated Press began publishing that year. Kentucky, which finished 36–1, was the first AP national champion.

Black Collegians after the War. When black servicemen returned from the war and attended college on the GI Bill of Rights, more black players appeared on the courts of white colleges and universities. Tennessee coach John Mauer refused to allow his team to play Duquesne University if there was even a remote possibility of Charles "Chuck" Cooper participating in the game. Several weeks later, on 15 January 1947, the

University of Miami canceled the Orange Bowl against Duquesne, citing a city ordinance prohibiting blacks and whites from playing in the same event. In 1948 all the teams in the National Association of Intercollegiate Athletics (NAIA) basketball tournament were expected to sign a contract prohibiting blacks from playing. Several schools protested, including Manhattan College, which, though it did not have any black players, announced it would resign unless the ban was lifted. The tournament organizers backed down, but the issue did not go away.

Blacks in Basketball. Blacks began slowly to assert themselves as superior basketball players during the 1940s, and one team boldly led the way. The Harlem Globetrotters walked off with the world professional basketball championship in 1940, the second year in a row that the designation went to an all-black team; the Renaissance Big-Five won in 1939. Called the "greatest Negro team of all time," the Globetrotters were organized in 1927 by Abe Saperstein, a Jewish social worker on Chicago's North Side. By 1940 the Globetrotters were one of the few financially successful professional basketball teams in the country, and they displayed extraordinary skill. There was not an organized national league then, so professional teams were barnstormers; they traveled the country playing college teams and pickup games where they could find them. Good players made fifty dollars a week, and, if they played for the Globetrotters, they traveled about 35,000 miles per year, playing about 150 games and enduring accommodations that most people would consider unsuitable. Because they were so good and so entertaining, the Globetrotters found games and audiences. They played for about 350,000 people in 1940. The Globetrotters were so formidable that Saperstein

"Jumpin' " Joe Fulks in the 1947 championship game, won by the Philadelphia Warriors

instructed them to play hard for only the first ten minutes of a game, and then to slow things down and amuse the crowd by clowning. Known more as entertainers than athletes, the Globetrotters were invited to the world professional basketball tournament by promoters who anticipated that they would put on a good show and be gone after the first round. They were wrong. In the 1940s the Globetrotters became international entertainers, playing before Pope Pius XII and to a white-tie audience at London's Wimbledon Stadium. Six-foot-three Reese "Goose" Tatum, nicknamed the "Clown Prince of Basketball," developed many of the moves, no-look passes, and fakes that became standard among top basketball athletes in later years. In 1946 Marques Haynes joined the team, contributing his remarkable dribbling skills. He was without equal as a ball handler.

Professional Basketball. Struggling financially in the early 1940s, professional basketball was able to begin establishing itself as a big-league sport after the war. Riding the crest of college basketball popularity, pro basketball captured a paying audience thanks to a group of arena owners led by Walter Brown, president of the Boston Garden, who met in New York on 6 June 1946 to form a new professional league. Maurice Podoloff was named president of the newly formed Basketball Associ-

ation of America (BAA). A talented attorney, Podoloff pioneered an offense-oriented league designed to attract fans. To create the most exciting game possible, zone defenses were prohibited, man-to-man contests were promoted, and a format for championship playoffs was created. Teams were organized in eleven cities, all east of the Mississippi River. These new franchises competed with the smaller National Basketball League (NBL) teams operating mostly in small midwestern cities. Immediately a bidding battle for the outstanding players of the day ensued. The National Basketball League captured the first prize when it signed college great George Mikan from DePaul. The BAA fought back the next year by adding four midwestern franchises, including Minneapolis, Mikan's team. In 1949 the two leagues merged into the National Basketball Association (NBA) with seventeen teams, with Podoloff still at the helm. In the first NBA championship game that year, Minneapolis, led by Mikan, who averaged 27.4 points a game, defeated Anderson, Indiana, in a hotly contested six-game series. The Globetrotters proved themselves again as legitimate professional players in 1948 and 1949, when they beat the world champion Lakers twice.

Creating Stars. During the early days when the Basketball Association of America was struggling for survival, one player helped the league capture attention. The association's first star was the Philadelphia Warriors' Joe Fulks. In the 1940s, when it was still considered a major feat to score twenty points in a single game, the 6-foot, 5-inch former marine stunned the basketball world by averaging more than twenty points per game in 1946–1947. Playing a sixty-game schedule, he boosted fan appeal by scoring more than thirty points on twelve occasions, with a single-game high of forty-one points. Fulks's high-scoring efforts helped transform the deliberate, low-scoring game so many fans knew as basketball. Known for his exciting, twisting, two-handed pivot shots, the forerunner of the modern jump shot, Fulks won the scoring championship in 1946, the league's first year. His nearest rival averaged 16.8 points per game. "Jumpin' " Joe Fulks's most celebrated achievement was his career-high sixty-three points against the Indiana Jets in 1949, a time when most teams did not score that many points in an entire game. Fulks retired in 1954, having scored 8,003 points for a 16.4 points-per-game average. Only towering George Mikan of Minneapolis had scored more at that time.

George Mikan. The 6-foot, 10-inch George Mikan first captured national attention while playing for DePaul University in Chicago in 1944. A star throughout his college career, Mikan was a key figure in making professional basketball a popular, profitable sport. Playing for the Minneapolis Lakers for six years, Mikan led the league in scoring three times, averaging 22.4 points during his career, leading the Lakers to five championships. Mikan was so dominating and popular that on one occasion the marquee of Madison Square Garden announced

Jake La Motta after winning the middleweight championship from Marcel Cerdan on 16 June 1949. Joe Louis is standing behind La Motta.

the evening game: "Tonight George Mikan vs. Knicks." His control inside caused the NBA to widen the lanes under the basket from six to twelve feet to make the game more competitive. In 1950 the Associated Press named Mikan the outstanding player of the first half of the twentieth century, and he was elected to the NBA's all-star team each of his six playing years. He retired at the end of the 1954 season to attend law school but returned for a short time in the middle of the 1955–1956 season.

Sources:

Zander Hollander, ed., *The Modern Encyclopedia of Basketball,* revised edition (New York: Four Winds Press, 1973);

John D. McCallum, *College Basketball, U.S.A., Since 1892* (New York: Stein & Day, 1978);

Douglas A. Noverr and Lawrence E. Ziewacz, *The Games They Played: Sports in American History, 1865–1980* (Chicago: Nelson-Hall, 1983);

Art Rust, Jr., and Edna Rust, *Art Rust's Illustrated History of the Black Athlete* (Garden City, N.Y.: Doubleday, 1985).

Boxing

The Heyday of Boxing. The 1940s were the heyday of American boxing. Champions included featherweight Willie Pep, who won sixty-two fights in a row before he was beaten by lightweight Sammy Angott and then seventy-one more (with one draw) before Sandy Saddler took his title on 28 October 1948. When the decade closed, Pep was champion again, having defeated Saddler in the rematch. Among the lightweights, there was Beau Jack, the popular "Georgia Shoe Shine Boy," who fought a series of championship fights with another southerner, Bob Montgomery. After the war Ike Williams won the championship and ruled the division for the rest of the decade. Among the welterweights, there were Henry Armstrong, who had moved up in weight, Fritzie Zivic, Red Cochrane, and Marty Servo. All except Cochrane were beaten by the best fighter in the division, Sugar Ray Robinson. Jake La Motta had similar problems in the middleweight division, which included champions Tony Zale and Rocky Graziano, who knocked Zale out in the sixth round on 16 July 1947 to win the title in all states but New York, which had suspended Graziano's license to box. Impressive Frenchman Marcel Cerdan held the championship for one fight before he lost to La Motta on

Sugar Ray Robinson falling through the ropes after being hit by Jake La Motta on 5 February 1943. La Motta won a ten-round decision, Robinson's first loss in forty fights.

16 June 1949 and then had his career cut short by a plane crash. Billy Conn was the best of the light heavyweights before the war, but he gave up his title to fight for bigger purses as a heavyweight. He left the division in the hands of Gus Lesnevich, who lost the title to Englishman Freddie Mills, who was, in turn, stopped in his first defense by the champion who dominated the division into the next decade, Joey Maxim. Among the heavyweights there was only one memorable champion — Joe Louis. He held the title from 1937 until he retired in 1948. Ezzard Charles won the vacated title on 29 June 1949 in a contest with "Jersey" Joe Walcott, the other top contender.

The Bum of the Month Club. Throughout the term of his championship Louis was a popular fighter with an untainted reputation. A Louis fight was guaranteed to generate interest, partly because he was so admired among blacks and partly because boxing aficionados admired his skill. Even when Louis was fighting what Jack Miley of the *New York Post* called members of the "Bum of the Month Club," he reliably attracted boxing fans and press coverage. A major factor in the popularity of Louis

and boxing in general was radio and, late in the decade, television broadcasts. It was claimed that only President Roosevelt, in the most successful of his "fireside chats," attracted more radio listeners than a Joe Louis fight. "The fists of Joe Louis are the megaphones and microphones of his race on the nights that he defends his championship," Ed Sullivan observed in his "Little Old New York" column in the *New York Daily News*. Surveys showed that about two-thirds of radio listeners tuned in to Louis's fights. That meant an audience of as many as 50 million in the early 1940s, and such an audience meant advertising revenue and a healthy income to the promoter.

The Kingmaker. Joe Louis had been the undisputed heavyweight champion of the world for two and a half years by the beginning of 1940. He had defended his title eight times, and he had provided the foundation for one of the most powerful sports empires in history. Louis's fights were promoted by Mike Jacobs, owner of the Twentieth Century Sporting Club. Jacobs had begun his career as a ticket scalper and a protégé of the famed Tex

AN EYE FOR AN EYE

Light-heavyweight boxer Sam Baroudi won twenty-three of his forty-five fights by knockout, including one in 1947 from which killed his opponent, Glen Smith, in the ring. Baroudi's forty-sixth fight was in 1948 against heavyweight contender Ezzard Charles. In the last round of that bout, Baroudi suffered the only knockdown of his career; Charles's head punches caused a hemorrhage in Baroudi's brain, which killed him.

Rickard, promoter for boxing events at Madison Square Garden. When Rickard died in 1929 and Jacobs was denied the opportunity to promote fights at the Garden, he entered into a silent partnership (because their professions prevented boxing promotions) with newsman and short-story writer Damon Runyon; Edward Frayne, sports editor of the *New York American;* and Bill Farnsworth, sports editor of the *New York Journal,* to promote Louis and compete with the Garden for top fights. By 1940 Jacobs, who had promoted Louis since the mid 1930s, had squeezed out his partners and used his control of the champion's fights to force binding promotions contracts with most of the good fighters of the day. To fight Louis, boxers had to sign with Jacobs. By 1940 Jacobs had also secured the right to promote all fights at Madison Square Garden; to fight at any of the other major arenas in New York, including Saint Nicholas Arena and Yankee Stadium, where Jacobs had exclusive leases for boxing events, a fighter had to sign with the Twentieth Century Sporting Club. He got at least 10 percent of the fighter's purse and some percentage of the gate, in addition to whatever subsidiary deals he was able to make. He often lent fighters money while they were training, for example, and he exacted a fee and frequently a percentage of the boxer's future earnings in exchange. When fight revenues were unexpectedly low, Jacobs reduced the fighters' guarantees, leaving them without recourse, except to voice cautious complaints on Jacobs Beach, as the sidewalks outside his Broadway ticket office and headquarters were called. In 1940 Jacobs controlled the championship fighters of every major weight class in boxing, and his domination was unchallenged by other promoters.

Frankie Carbo, the Superintendent. Criminal interests were attracted to boxing from its beginnings. People bet on boxing matches, and gamblers figured out early on that there was money to be made by controlling fighters and fixing fights. With Louis's popularity and the huge revenue boxing matches produced, organized criminals paid increased attention. During the 1940s boxing was ruled by a gangland boxing czar, a cohort of Jacobs in control of the boxing commissions and virtually every fight held on the East Coast. He was Frankie Carbo, a professional killer whose first arrest for murder was in 1924 when he was twenty. In 1939 Carbo was alleged to be the triggerman in the Hollywood killing of Harry Schacter (also know as Harry Greenberg), which led to his indictment for murder, along with Bugsy Siegel and Louis Lepke, and to the breakup of Murder, Incorporated. Carbo was released when the star defense witness, Abe Reles, fell to his death from the window of the hotel where he was being held under protective custody. His guards said he jumped; knowledgeable observers thought otherwise. Carbo bragged — even testified under oath — that he controlled Jacobs, and thus he controlled boxing.

Questionable Title Bouts. Carbo and Jacobs's domination of boxing had little effect (except financially) on the heavyweight championship. Louis was so popular that the bosses wanted him to remain champion, and he was such a good fighter that he needed no help from fight fixers to retain his championship. Only two of his seventeen title defenses during the 1940s ended in controversial decisions, and there was no suggestion that either was fixed. On 23 May 1941 Louis fought Buddy Baer, the younger brother of former champion Max Baer. The challenger fought more fiercely than anyone had predicted, knocking Louis out of the ring in the first round. By the end of the seventh the crowd at Madison Square Garden was cheering wildly, and Louis did not hear the bell that ended the round. He hit Baer after the bell had rung and knocked him out. When the challenger was unable to answer the bell for the eighth round, his handlers argued that Louis should be disqualified for hitting Baer after the seventh round had ended. Instead, referee Arthur Donovan, a former Jacobs employee, disqualified Baer for not being ready to begin the eighth round. Objections to the decision were to its form, not its substance. No one doubted that Louis was the better fighter.

Another Questionable Decision. The second questionable decision came in the next to last fight of Louis's career, on 5 December 1947 against "Jersey" Joe Walcott. The challenger was a few months older than the thirty-three-year-old champion and had been beaten by two of Louis's "Bums of the Month." He was a heavy underdog, but he knocked the champion down in the first round and again in the fourth. As the fight progressed, it was clear that Louis was on the decline as a fighter. In an attempt to protect his advantage, Walcott went on the defensive, backpedaling through the last rounds, and that tactic may have cost him the victory. When the fight was over, Louis left the ring dejectedly before the decision was announced; referee Ruby Goldstein had given the fight to Walcott. But the judges disagreed and handed Louis a split decision. Six months later in the rematch, Louis was behind on points when he knocked Walcott out in the eleventh round.

Rocky Graziano. Boxing in the lower weight divisions was not as simple. There was no crowd favorite comparable to Louis. Among middleweights, for example, and there were several able contenders — Tony Zale, Ken

Joe Louis and Billy Conn after their first fight, 1941

Overlin, and Billy Soose before the war; Zale, Rocky Graziano, La Motta, and Cerdan after the war. As a result, the promoters, who always had the upper hand in fight negotiations, could easily stage fights on their terms. Fixes were commonly used to set up promotable championship matches, and the fighters had to accept them if they wanted their careers to progress. Graziano testified in January 1947 that he was offered $100,000 to throw a fight late in 1946 against underdog Ruben Shank. Zale had knocked Graziano out in the sixth round of their September 1946 championship bout, and Graziano, who was the leading challenger with thirty-eight wins before the championship fight, was unwilling to compromise his reputation with a dive to a fighter of Shank's caliber. He was also unwilling to defy Carbo and Jacobs, so he feigned a back injury and withdrew from the contest. Nonetheless, shifting betting odds made New York Attorney General Frank Hogan, a crusader against boxing corruption, suspicious. His attention forced an inquiry by a grand jury. Graziano told them he had been offered bribes three times since May 1945 — once to throw a fight against Al Davis and twice to lose against Shank. In addition, there were allegations that an overweight match between Graziano and welterweight champion Marty Servo was fixed when Servo went from an underdog to a 10–1 favorite the day of the fight. Graziano refused to cancel the match and beat Servo badly, breaking his nose before knocking him out in the second round. After his testimony before the grand jury, the New York State Athletic Commission revoked Graziano's license to box, placing his rematch with Tony Zale in jeopardy. But boxing was ruled by state commissions, with no central control. So the Zale-Graziano fight was moved to Chicago (outside the control of Mike Jacobs), where the Illinois state boxing commission took a more lenient attitude toward the challenger's failure to report the attempts to bribe him. Graziano won the world middleweight championship on 16 July 1947 with

a sixth-round knockout in a fight that drew an indoor-fight record $422,918. New York continued to recognize Zale as champion. The success of that fight marked the beginning of the end of Mike Jacobs's control of the sport. In 1948 Graziano and Zale fought again, this time in Newark, New Jersey, just across the river from Manhattan and within range of the New York fight fans. Zale won this time with a knockout in the eighth round.

The Raging Bull. Jake La Motta (who had learned to box in the same reform school as Rocky Graziano) was a particularly anxious middleweight contender who often fought as a light heavyweight during this time. He was offered $100,000 to throw a fight against Tony Janiro in June 1947. He replied that he would do so only if he were guaranteed a championship fight. The bosses refused, and La Motta (weighing 155 pounds) took out his frustration on the good-looking Janiro, beating him mercilessly for ten rounds. A few months later, La Motta was offered his championship bid and, again, $100,000 if he would throw a fight against light-heavyweight contender Billy Fox, whose reputation was being bolstered for a challenge to Gus Lesnevich's light-heavyweight championship. La Motta (fighting at 170 pounds) accepted the deal and staged a lifeless fight against Fox for four rounds before the referee stopped the match and awarded Fox a victory. La Motta claimed his poor performance was the result of a broken rib he had suffered in training, but the New York State Athletic Commission was not convinced. They fined him $1,000, suspended his license, and kept his and Fox's purses for seven months before they rescinded their penalty under threat of a lawsuit. Finally, on 16 June 1949, La Motta got his middleweight title shot against Marcel Cerdan, the Frenchman who had taken the title from Zale the year before. To get the fight, La Motta had to pay Carbo and his associates $20,000. His purse was $19,000, but he made his money by betting $10,000 on himself to win. The rematch, which promised to be a big payday for La Motta, was canceled after Cerdan died in a plane crash on his way to the United States to train. (Fox was beaten twice by Lesnevich for the light-heavyweight title, after which he retired.)

Sweet as Sugar. Sugar Ray Robinson was one of the most active boxers in the history of the sport. He turned professional in 1940 at the age of twenty, having won all of his eighty-five amateur bouts and sixty-nine of them by knockout (forty of which were in the first round). His first professional fight was on 4 October 1940. Between that time and 31 October 1941 he fought twenty-six times, winning all his fights and twenty of them by knockout. Of his six decisions, three came in ten rounds, one against lightweight contender Sammy Angott five months before Angott won the lightweight championship; one against Fritzie Zivic three months after Zivic lost the welterweight championship to Red Cochrane; and one against Marty Servo, who became champion just after the war by beating Cochrane. By 1942 Robinson

In 1941 television became a factor, though telephoto lenses were not advanced enough to make boxing an attractive television sport until after World War II. Even so, there were some closed-circuit matches broadcast to limited receivers set up in public venues. The first such telecast was of the Ken Overlin–Billy Soose middleweight championship fight on 9 May 1941 at Madison Square Garden (in which Soose beat the champion in fifteen rounds). The fight was telecast to 1,400 paying fans at the New Yorker Theater, heralding a prominent role for television broadcasts in fight promotion. By 1948 the technical problems had been solved and there was a potential television audience of 1.75 million viewers. The stakes, which were already high, increased, as people who did not own their own sets were invited to bars and hotels to watch important events, such as championship boxing matches, on television.

was being called the best fighter pound for pound in boxing (except for Louis, of course), and by the end of the decade the qualification was dropped. Robinson suffered his first loss in his fortieth fight, on 5 February 1943, fighting out of his weight class against Jake La Motta, whom he had defeated four months earlier. He did not lose again for eight years. He became welterweight champion on 20 December 1946, beating Tommy Bell for the title vacated when Servo had his championship stripped because he refused to fight Robinson. When in 1947 he reported a bribe related to an attempt to arrange a fight with Servo, Robinson had his license suspended for thirty days. At one point he said he had been offered money to show up overweight at the weigh-in for a fight with Servo; at another point he said he had been offered money not to fight. The commission punished him for seeming to change his story.

A Champion's Attitude. After he became champion Robinson became a deficit spender. He drove flashy cars, including a pink Cadillac; he traveled with an entourage that rivaled Joe Louis's and included a golf partner, a hairdresser, and a dwarf mascot. His flamboyance cost him. The gangsters who ran boxing disapproved of him and gave the best fights to others first. Robinson could not make enough to pay his debts, and by midcareer he was in debt, despite good investments and a steady fight schedule. He was in the 88 percent tax bracket and had little left after his purses were distributed to meet his huge expenses. The need for money kept Robinson boxing until 1965 when he was forty-five years old. When he retired he had fought a total of 202 fights with eighteen defeats.

Louis and Conn. In the view of many fight fans, the fight of the decade and the most anticipated fight of the decade were the two matches between Billy Conn and Joe Louis, the first match six months before Louis joined the army and the second just after he was released from duty. Billy Conn was a handsome white fighter from a family of tough boxers. He won the light-heavyweight title in September 1939 from Melio Bettina and held it until June 1941, when he vacated the title to fight Louis. Fifty-five thousand fans showed up at the Polo Grounds in New York on 18 June 1941 to see the 170-pound contender take on the champion, who had trained down to 199 1/2 to avoid seeming too overpowering. Louis had fought six times since the end of January. He was tired and unprepared for the fighter who entered the ring with him that night. Conn took Louis's best punches, danced away, and countered with his own barrages for twelve rounds. Conn was clearly quicker than Louis, and he showed the stamina to slug with the champion. By the tenth round the fight seemed clearly to be Conn's, and Conn built on his lead in the eleventh and twelfth rounds. His corner advised him to fight defensively for the last three rounds, but he wanted to knock Louis out. In the thirteenth the two fighters traded punches evenly until the end of the round, when Louis slipped a punch and hit Conn with an overhand right followed by a left jab, a right uppercut, a left hook, and a right cross, in succession. Conn fell, and the referee began his count to ten. Two seconds after he finished counting Conn out, the bell rang to end the round.

Boxing and the War. Professional boxing was curtailed but hardly eliminated during the war, though its character changed. Big matches were promoted as war benefits. All major titles were frozen in 1941, and competition for them did not resume until early 1946. Four thousand professional boxers joined the military, including five world champions. Jacobs arranged for Louis to fight a benefit for the war effort with Buddy Baer, which ended in a one-round knockout. A further attempt to arrange a rematch of Louis's most exciting fight of the decade, against Conn, was aborted when Jacobs was criticized for negotiating to reserve for himself all seats in the first twenty rows of the arena so he could scalp the tickets. Amid plaudits for his patriotism, Joe Louis volunteered for the army on 10 January 1942 at the peak of his career "to fight them Japs . . . who are all lightweights, anyway," he told the press. His observation that "We will win because we are on God's side" became a popular patriotic slogan. At the end of March 1942 Private Louis defended his title in Madison Square Garden against Abe Simon, whom he knocked out in the sixth round. As a show of patriotism, Louis bought $3,000 worth of tickets for servicemen and donated his purse to the Army Emergency Relief Organization. It was the last heavyweight championship fight until 1946. The total of Louis's donations to war-relief organizations in 1942 was $111,082, an amount the IRS later ruled was taxable at a rate of 90

Pvt. Joe Louis says_

"We're going to do our part ...and we'll win because we're on God's side"

Army poster, 1942

percent. Louis and other champions staged exhibitions during the war and fought at military benefits, but professional boxing was at a virtual standstill until the war ended.

Louis-Conn II. There was not enough time before the war-related suspension of championship boxing to arrange a rematch between Louis and Conn, but the appetite for that fight increased with time. By 1946 Mike Jacobs was promoting the most anticipated match of the era. Ringside seats sold for an all-time high of $100, and total revenue was just under $2 million. The live audience of 45,266 saw Louis beat Conn decisively with an eighth-round knockout. The fight was a disappointment, and though Conn's performance was criticized by the press, they were impressed by the size of Louis's purse. The numbers have been variously reported, but it is clear that although Louis earned a record $625,916 for the fight, after the proceeds were divided he was left with little to show for his effort. He owed Jacobs $170,000 for money lent him during the war; he had borrowed $41,000 from his manager, John Roxborough. He owed the IRS $115,992 in back taxes and an additional $247,056 in taxes on his fight earnings. He had recently divorced his wife, Marva, and he owed her a $25,000 settlement. That is a total debt of $598,048, leaving Louis some $28,000

to cover his expenses, which included the support of twenty-three people in his entourage. His biggest payday was not big enough.

Tournament of Champions and the IBC. In 1946 professional boxing was revived, and Jacobs remained king, a position he maintained until poor health forced him into semiretirement at the end of 1947. By that time Madison Square Garden revenues alone were $1.25 million per year. In mid 1947 a rival promotional organization, Tournament of Champions, was established with backing from Columbia Broadcasting System. At about the same time, Joe Louis decided to retire after a near defeat by the lightly regarded "Jersey" Joe Walcott, and with substantial backing the champion formed Joe Louis Enterprises to orchestrate the succession of the title. Joe Louis Enterprises bought the rights to promote the four major contenders for the heavyweight title. Louis fought once more, a rematch with Walcott in June 1948 that ended in an eleventh-round knockout, then he stepped down. By 1949 Joe Louis Enterprises had merged with Tournament of Champions to form the International Boxing Club (IBC) and had bought out Jacobs's rights to promote at Madison Square Garden. After the merger Louis was left with a 20 percent share of the IBC (which was worth little because his partners owned the facilities where IBC fights were held and skimmed off most of the profits in rent) and a $20,000-per-year employment contract to work for the organization. In 1950 the IBC controlled half of the championship bouts in the United States, and, in the words of sports historian Jeffrey T. Sammons, "the dominant individual entrepreneur . . . gave way to the faceless corporation."

Sources:

Joe Louis Barrow, Jr., and Barbara Munder, *Joe Louis: 50 Years an American Hero* (New York: McGraw-Hill, 1988);

Jake La Motta, *Raging Bull: My Story* (Englewood Cliffs, N.J.: Prentice-Hall, 1970);

Chris Mead, *Joe Louis: Black Hero in White America* (New York: Scribners, 1985);

Jeffrey T. Sammons, *Beyond the Ring: The Role of Boxing in American Society* (Urbana & Chicago: University of Illinois Press, 1988).

FOOTBALL, COLLEGE

Rule Changes. College football began its modern period in the 1940s, when the game took on basic qualities that it retains fifty years later. College football was revolutionized by one major rule change — the free-substitution rule — and one major tactical innovation — the refinement of the T-formation to exploit the passing game that stimulated a flood of lesser rule changes.

Free Substitution. The free-substitution rule, which went into effect in 1941, had repercussions far beyond those intended. Before the war eleven men on a football team played the entire game, offense and defense. Only injury was grounds for substituting. The new rule allowed players to substitute for one another at any time, except during the last two minutes of the first half. During the

SPORTS   **549**

Frank Sinkwich, University of Georgia quarterback, 1942

war free substitution was the salvation of college football, allowing weakened teams to continue playing. When the war was over and veteran players returned to college football, coaches used the rule for strategic purposes. They introduced the platoon system, in which players specialized in a single aspect of the game — short-yardage offense, passing offense, corresponding defenses, and special teams.

Platooning. The first attempt at platooning came on 13 October 1945 when the University of Michigan met Army. Underdog Michigan was largely manned by eighteen-year-old freshmen, and the Wolverine staff knew they were in for a long afternoon. To keep the score as close as possible, head coach Fritz Crisler decided to play eleven players offensively and another eleven defensively. Michigan held the West Pointers to a 7–7 tie going into the fourth quarter before losing 28–7, but the value of rotating offensive and defensive players was proven. Soon such specialists had swelled the size of major teams to one hundred or more men, and coaching staffs increased accordingly to as many a ten coaches per team. As a result football became a very expensive sport to play, causing many colleges to rethink whether they could afford to field a team. During the war about 350 colleges abandoned football, led by Robert Hutchins's announcement that the University of Chicago would disband its team. Some schools revived their teams after the war; others gave up intercollegiate competition permanently, in many cases because free substitution had made the game too expensive.

Strategy. During the same time, tacticians were changing the character of the sport from a game in which offensive players sought to overpower the defense with brute strength to a game of finesse, in which the forward pass was used to avoid contact with tacklers. By early 1940 Stanford University coach Clark Shaughnessy had taken the game's oldest offensive alignment, redesigned it, and become the father of the modern T-formation — with grand success. Unlike the double wing, the Rockne shift (named after Notre Dame coach Knute Rockne), and the Meyer spread-and-wing (named after Texas Christian coach Dutch Meyer), which tried to split the defense, Shaughnessy's T-formation used fakes, brush blocks, and shifting linemen to befuddle the defense. Shaughnessy also used a man in motion, a flanker, and a quarterback under center to the formation. This allowed liberal use of the forward pass, mixed with end runs and quick runs up the middle. Prompted by Shaughnessy's success, a revision of the rules in 1945 gave the quarterback more freedom of movement when passing, transforming college football in the 1940s into a wide-open, offense-oriented game that packed fans into the stands. No longer was an incomplete fourth-down pass into the opponent's end zone considered a touchback; now a team in scoring position could chance a touchdown pass without the risk of giving up field position in the event of an incompletion. The penalty for roughing the passer was increased. The most important stimulus to the passing game came in 1945 with the elimination of the rule that the quarterback must be at least five yards behind the line of scrimmage when he passed the ball. It was one of the most significant of all the forward-pass rules, offering pass-oriented quarterbacks the option to run if circumstances warranted.

The Penalty Flag. The 1940s were notable for one other important innovation. For several years it had been obvious that the referees needed a way to indicate a penalty without stopping play. Officials blowing whistles and horns to signal penalties caused confusion and often did not accomplish their purpose. On 16 October 1941, during a game between Oklahoma City and Youngstown State, Coach Dwight "Dike" Beede of Youngstown State talked the officials into using a red-and-white cloth flag loaded with drapery weights to indicate a penalty. The experiment worked, and the penalty flag was born.

Powerhouse Teams. The early years of the decade were dominated by a handful of teams. In the Big Ten Conference Minnesota, led by running backs George Franck and Bruce Smith, went undefeated in 1940 and 1941 and was ranked number one in the nation both years by the Associated Press. The revised T-formation was tailor-made for Minnesota's starting backfield. Early in the season their win over seventh-ranked Nebraska served notice of the potential of the new style of play. On 16 November 1940, a week after Minnesota replaced Cornell as the top team in the country, Dartmouth snapped Cornell's eighteen-game winning streak when,

Army's "Mr. Inside" and "Mr. Outside": Glenn Davis and Doc Blanchard

highlight of the year was the running of Frank Sinkwich of Georgia, the prototype of the modern tailback. That year he was the first player to accumulate more than 2,000 yards in total offense, with 2,187 total yards. Sinkwich led the 11–1 Georgia Bulldogs to their first Southeastern Conference title and won the Heisman Trophy. By 1943 almost two hundred colleges had discontinued football. Gasoline rationing and transportation restrictions curtailed travel, and many teams simply played nearby schools.

Army. Many of the nation's best eligible athletes were at West Point in 1944, and the Army team was bolstered by their presence. That year they averaged 56 points per game, a modern record, and rushed for an average 298.6 yards per game. While other teams struggled to field a team, Army coach Earl Blaik had so many players on his squad he used two separate teams. Glenn Davis and Felix "Doc" Blanchard started making football history that year as the finest one-two offensive punch in college football. Known as Mr. Outside (Davis) and Mr. Inside (Blanchard), the pair led Army to 9–0 records in 1944 and 1945 and a 9–0–1 record in 1946. Blanchard took home the Heisman Trophy in 1945, the first player to win as a junior, and Davis was the winner in 1946.

Notre Dame. With the war at an end and the soldiers back on campus, the high point of the 1946 season was the grudge match between Notre Dame and Army. Notre Dame wanted to avenge the humiliating defeats of the last two years, and Army needed to prove it was capable of winning against teams not weakened by war. The hard-fought game, which ended 0–0, included one of the finest collections of college talent ever assembled on a football field. The two squads included fourteen future or current all-American players and ten future Hall of Famers. At season's end Notre Dame was by a narrow margin named national champion by the Associated Press. By 1947 and 1948 Notre Dame and Michigan were the teams to beat. Both went undefeated each year, with Notre Dame repeating as national champion in 1947 and Michigan taking the honors and the Rose Bowl in 1948. During the 1947 season only Northwestern was able to score more than once against the Irish of Notre Dame. Michigan, on the other hand, was stocked with war veterans, now seniors, who used a modern-day two-platoon system. The decade ended with Notre Dame still on top, going undefeated again, even though thirteen players had graduated the previous year. The Notre Dame attack produced an average of 434.8 yards per game to lead the nation. Two-time all-American Leon Hart of Notre Dame won the Heisman Trophy and the Maxwell Award as the player of the year. That same year Oklahoma, led by their young coach Bud Wilkinson, moved into the spotlight with an 11–0 season. During his seventeen-year career Wilkinson fashioned a 145–29–4 record.

Blacks' Bowls. In 1941 the first annual Steel Bowl in Birmingham, Alabama, pitted midwestern champion

with only two seconds left in the game, the referee lost track of the action and Dartmouth scored on fifth down to win 7–3. That same day Georgetown's unbeaten streak of twenty-three games ended at the hands of Boston College. In 1941 Minnesota once again finished 8–0 in a year memorable for trick plays, innovative formations, and the running of their Heisman Trophy winner Bruce Smith. Oregon State defeated Duke in the Rose Bowl, which was moved from Pasadena, California, to Durham, North Carolina, because large gatherings were prohibited on the West Coast after the bombing of Pearl Harbor.

The War Years. As the wartime need for fighting men depleted the ranks of football, several new powers emerged. In 1942 coach Paul Brown brought Ohio State to dominance with a 9–1 record. His teams were fast and always in excellent physical shape, providing Ohio State with a fourth-quarter advantage in the days before platoons. Their only loss was to Wisconsin after twenty-one players became ill on the way to the game. The other

Bill Osmanski (9) running for a touchdown in the Chicago Bears' 1940 championship rout of the Washington Redskins, 73–0

Wilberforce against Morris Brown of Atlanta in a contest to determine the national black college title. Wilberforce scored first, but after that it was all Morris Brown, which decisively claimed the win, 19–3. The following year, for the first time in the history of black college football, the top team in the Colored Intercollegiate Athletic Association met the champion of the Southeastern Intercollegiate Athletic Association in a postseason game. Morris Brown's unbeaten and untied team was pitted against North Carolina College in the Peach Blossom Classic in Columbus, Georgia. In the third quarter of that game, played on 6 December, Morris Brown mounted a sustained drive to score and eventually win both the game, 7–6, and the national Negro college championship. On the train trip home the North Carolina College team was told that Pearl Harbor had been attacked. Thirteen of the thirty-three-man squad were eligible for the draft.

Sources:

Ocania Chalk, *Black College Sport* (New York: Dodd, Mead, 1976);

Dave Newhouse, *Heisman: After the Glory* (Saint Louis: Sporting News, 1985);

Tom Perrin, *Football: A College History* (Jefferson, N.C.: McFarland, 1987).

FOOTBALL, PROFESSIONAL

Taking the Title. The 1940 title game between the Chicago Bears (8–3) and the Washington Redskins (9–2) was billed as a game between equally great passing teams, featuring two of the game's premier quarterbacks: Sid Luckman of the Bears and Sammy Baugh of the Redskins. The two teams had met in the final game of the season, a low-scoring affair won by the Redskins, 7–3, and fans were prepared for a close game. Few were prepared for the 73–0 blowout of Washington by the Bears. It did not happen by accident. In preparing for the championship game, Bear coaches refined the T-formation the team had been using and introduced some new concepts, including a series of counter plays to take advantage of the Redskins' propensity to shift their defensive line toward the motion of the backfield. It was a coach's win.

Franchise Players. Creating heroes was essential to the commercial success of the National Football League (NFL), and Sammy Baugh of the Washington Redskins was the preeminent pro football hero of the day. Baugh, who joined the Redskins in 1937, posed little threat as a runner, but his pinpoint passing changed the game. Working the tailback position in the single-wing formation, Baugh could throw the football from a variety of angles and for long, short, and medium gains. Professional rules permitted passing from anywhere behind the scrimmage line, and Baugh took full advantage of the opportunity. He was known for his rapid release and his

Otto Graham, Dante Lavelli, Paul Brown, and Mac Speedie of the 1949 Cleveland Browns

willingness to throw the ball on every down. Considered the first modern passer, Baugh played until 1952, when he was forty, remaining with the Redskins the entire time. Another quarterback who captured the public's attention during the decade was Sid Luckman of the Chicago Bears. More than any other quarterback, Luckman exploited the modern T-formation, as he demonstrated in the 1940 championship-game rout of the Redskins.

The War Takes Its Toll. The 1941 championship game also featured the Chicago Bears, and once again they delivered a sound beating, this time to the New York Giants, 37–9. Even though their team did not make it to the championship game that year, two of the best players in the league were Don Hutson of the Green Bay Packers, who led the league in scoring and pass receiving, and Cecil Isbell, the Packers' quarterback, who led the league in passing. Isbell became the first quarterback to throw for more than 2,000 yards and more than 20 touchdowns in a single season. Unlike the year before, when national radio broadcast of the championship attracted national attention, the 1941 championship, which took place two weeks after the attack on Pearl Harbor, seemed a distraction. Only 13,341 fans showed up for the contest. Two players in the game, Bears quarterback Young Bussey and Jack Lumins of the Giants, were later killed in the war. During the next four years 638 NFL players entered military service, and 21 gave their lives.

Combining to Compete. The NFL managed to limp through the war by relying on overaged or draft-deferred players and an array of merged teams. In 1943 the Cleveland Rams suspended play, and the Pittsburgh Steelers merged with the Philadelphia Eagles, creating the Phil-Pitt Eagles or Steagles; they were joined by the Cardinals in 1944, forming the Card-Pitt Team. Reduced to only eight teams, the NFL was still remarkably popular, with attendance averaging 23,644 per game in 1943, up 39 percent from the previous season. One of the greatest players of that era was Bill Dudley, the last of the great offensive and defensive players and the only football player voted most valuable in college, the armed services, and the professional ranks. A star at the University of Virginia, he signed with the Pittsburgh Steelers in 1942 and led the league in yards gained on the ground before going into the service. When he returned in 1945, he signed with the Detroit Lions for $20,000, the highest salary ever paid at that time for a professional football player.

Postwar Prosperity. The postwar economy put large amounts of money into professional football. The 1946 championship between the New York Giants and the Chicago Bears drew 58,000, the largest football gate of that era. Under the rules of that day, the players divided the largest pot ever offered, with each member of the winning club taking home almost $2,000 extra. Televi-

In a severe blow to college football, late in 1939, President Robert Hutchins of the University of Chicago announced that the school was dropping its varsity football program. Hutchins explained, "there is no doubt that football has been a major handicap to education in the United States . . . (and has) done much to originate the popular misconceptions of what a university is." He summed up his position by stating, "I think it is a good thing for this country to have one important university discontinue football." In 1940 the University of Chicago converted the locker rooms beneath the deserted football stadium, Stagg Field, into a secret laboratory for the federally funded Manhattan Project, devoted to building the atomic bomb. On 2 December 1942 physicist Enrico Fermi achieved the first controlled release of nuclear energy in his lab underneath the stadium.

Source: John R. Thelin, *Games Colleges Play: Scandal and Reform in Intercollegiate Athletics* (Baltimore: Johns Hopkins University Press, 1994).

Byron Nelson and Harold "Jug" McSpaden, 1945

sion began showing interest in football, and Commissioner Bert Bell ruled that local areas should be blacked out of broadcasts to make sure fans continued to show up at the stadium.

AAFC. The biggest financial issue was the emergence of a new league. Many players back from the war found themselves wooed by both the NFL and the new All-American Football Conference (AAFC). Organized by *Chicago Tribune* editor Art Ward, the AAFC had attracted wealthy owners for every franchise and enthusiastically ignored the boundaries of the NFL draft to lure rookies and veterans alike to the new league. Before the war, players got an average of $150 a game; by 1949 the average minimum salary for a ten-game season was $5,000, and most players earned much more. Led by former Notre Dame star Jim Crowley, the AAFC brought football franchises to New York, Brooklyn, Buffalo, Miami, Cleveland, Chicago, and San Francisco. The NFL met the challenge by hiring Bert Bell, part owner of the Pittsburgh Steelers, as its commissioner. Bell led the NFL through fourteen years of tremendous growth. In 1946 both leagues located teams in California; the NFL Rams moved from Cleveland to Los Angeles, and the AAFC placed teams in San Francisco and Los Angeles. Pro football thus became the first major league sport to come to the West Coast. But the economy would not support this ambitious two-league structure, and financial stress in 1947 forced the two leagues to merge.

The Brown Years. The closing years of the decade were shaped by Paul Brown, coach of the Cleveland Browns. He turned football into a serious study and required that all of his players be students of the game.

Players were expected to learn elaborate playbooks and follow different assignments for their positions on each play. Brown called every play for the quarterback from the sidelines, introducing a type of blueprinting that reshaped the game.

Sources:
Peter King, *Football: A History of the Professional Game* (Birmingham, Ala.: Oxmoor House, 1993);

David M. Nelson, *Anatomy of a Game: Football, the Rules, and the Men who Made the Game* (Newark: University of Delaware Press, 1994);

Robert Smith, *Illustrated History of Pro Football* (New York: Madison Square, 1970).

GOLF

The Golfers' Sacrifice. Americans enjoyed their golf throughout the war, although in a limited fashion. Three-quarters of the clubs in the United States remained open without interruption. Only a few took the suggestion of the United States Golf Association (USGA) and plowed their roughs into victory gardens for club members. Yet thousands joined in the recycling craze to find quality golf equipment without affecting war supplies. The Black Rock Club in Atlanta, like many courses, drained its lake and rescued sixteen thousand balls for reprocessing. For the first time members caddied for themselves when bag-toting caddies joined the military; members also pitched in to maintain their courses when the army of groundskeepers who kept the fairways and greens in playable shape went to war. Power mowers were at a premium; when they broke, parts were unavailable to fix them. Quality golf balls, of the type most duffers had grown accustomed to, were unavailable.

The Pros at War. From 1942 to 1945 all major USGA events — including the Open, the Amateur, the Women's Amateur, and the Amateur Public Links Championship — were suspended; even so, there were plenty of tour events for civilian golfers. When the U.S. Open was canceled in 1942, it was quickly replaced by the Hale America Open, played in Chicago as a benefit for the war, raising $20,000. In 1943 the Augusta National Golf Course, home of the suspended Masters, was turned over to grazing cattle in order to help the war effort. By that time golf stars Sam Snead, Lawson Little, Jimmy Demaret, and Lloyd Mangrum were among 350 Professional Golfers' Association (PGA) members in military service. That year their professional association sent them each a carton of cigarettes as a Christmas gift.

Byron Nelson. Golf in the war years was unquestionably the era of Byron Nelson. His performances in 1944 and 1945, when he swept twenty-six of fifty-one starts, with eight tournament victories in 1944 and eighteen in 1945, persuaded thousands that he was at least the peer of the immortal Bobby Jones. It is difficult to measure Nelson's greatness because he played during the war years when competition was light. Yet during that time the steady and consistent Nelson dominated not only the world of golf, but the courses themselves. Assuming that par on the courses he played averaged 71, Nelson was approximately 320 under par for 1945 tournament play. Nelson's average score for eighteen holes over his 120 tournament rounds was 68.33, one of the most remarkable golfing achievements of the decade.

Money. In 1945 alone, Nelson collected $66,000 in war bond prizes, the largest being the $13,600 for winning at Tam O'Shanter. The cash value of his year's winnings, $52,511, was a record, topping his 1944 total of $35,000. Despite his bad back, Nelson had been in the money in every tournament he had entered and was able to double Ben Hogan's record of finishing in the money in fifty-six consecutive tournaments. During one stretch Nelson won eleven tournaments in a row, with Harold "Jug" McSpaden his closest competitor. In 1945 the average total purse in an official PGA event was $12,183; ten years later it had grown to $21,722, and forty years later to $538,000. Professional golf was not yet a major sport in the 1940s.

WPA and LPGA. The Women's Professional Golfers' Association (WPA) was formed in 1946 by a pioneer woman pro named Hope Seignious, with the help of her father. The event was a modest success, and the Seigniouses published a magazine that served as the association's house organ. Yet the WPA failed to serve as a unifying organization. In 1949 the rival Ladies' Professional Golf Association (LPGA) was headed by Babe Didrikson Zaharias's manager Fred Corcoran, who had formerly guided the growth of the men's PGA. He provided the leadership and promotional expertise to stimulate the development of the women's tour. During those early days Alvin Handmacher, the entrepreneur who founded Weathervane clothing, helped bring money and exposure to the sport. Handmacher used the LPGA to promote his products nationally through a four-stop transcontinental tournament with a total purse of $15,000 and a $5,000 bonus for the winner. The tourna-

Seventeen-year-old winner of the Olympic gold medal in the decathlon, Bob Mathias

ment started in San Francisco and went to Chicago, Cleveland, and New York. Helen Lengfeld, publisher of the *National Golfer* magazine, later subsidized the spring tour with an additional $15,000. Two golfers, Patty Berg and Zaharias, dominated the tournament in those days and set the standard for play in the 1950s.

Sources:

Editors of *Golf Magazine, Golf Magazine's Encyclopedia of Golf* (New York: HarperCollins, 1993);

Herb Graffis, *The PGA* (New York: Crowell, 1975);

Herbert Warren Wind, *The Story of American Golf* (New York: Knopf, 1975).

THE OLYMPICS

Canceled Games. The International Olympic Committee faced awesome difficulties planning the 1940 Olymiad. The games were first scheduled to be held in Japan, but in 1938 the Japanese were preoccupied by their conflict with the Chinese and withdrew as the host country. The IOC then awarded the games to Helsinki, Finland, whose plans were interrupted when the Russians invaded in 1939. By that time it was clear that world events were too chaotic to allow for the Olympics. The war forced cancellation of the 1940 and 1944 games, and many believed that the depth of international hatred aroused by the war would end the Olympics altogether. But in 1945 the International Olympic Committee met in bomb-scarred London to plan the 1948 games for that city. The German blitz had devastated much of London;

housing was at a premium; everything from food to transportation was rationed. Critics and naysayers abounded. The bickering set a new Olympic record for acrimony, and ultimately Japan, Germany, and Italy were barred from competing. The Soviet Union, which had not participated in an Olympiad since the Russian Revolution of 1917, did not participate this time either.

Summer Olympics. London was ill-prepared but eager for the Olympics. For the most part the games were held in existing facilities as the British could spare neither the money nor the materials to construct an Olympic village. Male athletes stayed at an army camp in Uxbridge; the women, in dormitories at Southland College. The weather did not cooperate. It rained almost every day during the competition, and on the rare occasions when the sky was clear the track remained soggy. Eager to put the war behind them, fifty-nine countries entered the 1948 games, more than in any other Olympiad, but relatively few records were set. The conditions were less than ideal, and many of the world's best athletes were either injured, distracted, or out of condition because of war.

1948 Summer Games. In men's track and field, the core of the games, the United States demonstrated convincingly that it still had world-class talent. The Americans won eleven events, Sweden five, and eight other countries one each. For the first time in Olympic history, no competitor won more than one individual track and field event. The darling of the Olympics was clearly the American boy wonder, Bob Mathias. Only seventeen, Mathias earned the title of world's greatest amateur athlete during the 1948 Olympics by winning the grueling decathlon. Since the days of Jim Thorpe, the decathlon had been the supreme test of track and field ability and versatility. A natural athlete, Mathias trained for only a month before his first decathlon competition against college stars, and he won. Six weeks later he was in the Olympics, competing against experienced athletes from around the world. When asked, after the gold medal ceremony, "What are you going to do to celebrate?" Mathias answered, "Start shaving, I guess." He also won the United States decathlon championship in 1949 and 1950. He became the star running back for the Stanford football team in 1951 and returned to the Olympics in 1952 to win a second gold medal in Helsinki. The Olympics were also a special time for American sprinter Harrison "Bones" Dillard, who not only took home the gold in the 100-meter, but defeated Mel Patton, holder of the world record in that event. In the 1952 Olympics Dillard won the 110-meter high hurdles as well, adding another gold medal to his collection. Two military men were gold medal victors: U.S. Army Air Force Sergeant Mal Whitfield broke the world record in the 800-meter run, and Sammy Lee, a Korean-American who served as an eye, ear, and nose specialist in the U.S. Army Medical Corps, won the high-diving event. The U.S. basketball team, led by Bob "Foothills" Kurland, won easily, and in

heavyweight weight lifting the American hero was John Henry Davis, a Brooklyn mechanic who hoisted a combined 997 pounds in the military press, the snatch, and the clean and jerk. He was a repeat winner in 1952.

Winter Olympics. At the Winter Olympics in Saint Moritz, Switzerland, the United States took gold medals in skiing and figure skating for the first time in Olympic history. Gretchen Fraser won the slalom, while eighteen-year-old Dick Button glided to victory in the men's figure skating, becoming a favorite of spectators. Button, from Englewood, New Jersey, was not only the first American to win a gold medal in figure skating, he produced the highest point total in Olympic history: 994.7 in compulsory figures and 191.77 in free skating. When the games ended in February, the United States took home three gold medals, four silver, and two bronze, the best American showing in Winter Olympic history. The United States finished behind only Sweden and Switzerland.

Sources:

William Oscar Johnson, *The Olympics: A History of the Games* (Montgomery, Ala.: Oxmoor House, 1978);

John Kieran and Arthur Daley, *The Story of the Olympic Games, 776 B.C. to 1972* (Philadelphia: Lippincott, 1973);

Dick Schaap, *An Illustrated History of the Olympics* (New York: Knopf, 1975).

TENNIS

USLTA versus PLTA. There was an uneasy alliance between amateurs and professionals in American tennis during the 1940s. The conservative, upper-class traditions of the sport were protected by the United States Lawn Tennis Association (USLTA), a member of the International Lawn Tennis Association (ILTA), which provided standardized rules throughout the world and declared itself an organization of amateurs only. Professional tennis coaches began to appear in the 1920s, and they had formed an alliance called the Professional Lawn Tennis Association (PLTA) to declare their adherence to USLTA standards, even though they charged to teach tennis. In 1928 the Palm Beach Tennis Club staged the first exhibition by professional tennis players, many of whom were PLTA members, but the event did not stimulate much enthusiasm. By the 1940s there were touring professionals who played for small audiences — the Bill

Tilden tour was the most successful — and the USLTA had modified its charter to allow one annual open tournament a year in which amateurs and professionals played each other. For the most part, though, the tennis purists paid only passing interest to those who would stoop to accept pay for their games, despite the credibility lent to the professional circuit when popular champions Fred Perry of Great Britain and Ellsworth Vines of the United States joined the Bill Tilden tour in 1937 and grossed $412,181 for sixty-one matches.

Jack Kramer. A flashy and personable player named Jack Kramer changed fans' attitudes toward professional tennis. He won the United States Outdoor Championship in 1946 and 1947 and Wimbledon singles and doubles titles in 1947, all amateur championships. A promoter named Jack Harris offered him a $50,000-per-year guarantee for two years against 35 percent of the gate receipts to turn pro, and Kramer snapped at the opportunity. In 1948 he played a series of eighty-nine matches in the United States and abroad with Bobby Riggs, who had been Wimbledon champion in 1939, United States outdoor champion in 1939 and 1941, and United States professional champion in 1946 and 1947. The tour revived professional tennis, which had been in a steady decline from its high point in 1937 until 1942, when it was suspended for the war. Gross revenues were $383,000, considered a huge success. The tour traveled five thousand miles a month and carried its own equipment to set up courts. Kramer won the pro championship in 1948 and lost to Riggs in 1949.

Gorgeous Gussie. Amateur tennis made the headlines when Augusta Moran, better known as Gorgeous Gussie, posed a threat at Wimbledon after winning the United States Indoor Championship in 1949. She was the fourth-ranked player in the world, and number one in the hearts of the sports press for her good looks and vivacious spirit. When she showed up on center court at staid Wimbledon with lace panties under her designer tennis dress, she was front-page news in London for five days straight. When she lost to a diminutive Chinese player in the third round, John M. Ross, editor of *American Lawn Tennis Magazine,* observed in *Collier's* with barely restrained excitement that "her opponent's height was somewhat less than twice the circumference of the most expressive part of Gussie's sweater." She took her sex appeal to the pros in 1950, joining Riggs, Kramer, and an international array of tennis stars on the Harris tour.

Sources:
"The Big Pro Show," *Newsweek,* 30 (29 December 1947): 58;

Official Encyclopedia of Tennis (New York: Harper & Row, 1972);

John M. Ross, "Good Gussy," *Collier's,* 124 (3 September 1949): 30, 71–72;

"Villain's Victory," *Time,* 51 (5 January 1948), 47.

THE WAR AND SPORTS

War Effects. World War II affected every aspect of

American life in the early 1940s, including sports. For the first time directors of athletic events had to consider the impact of using "war-necessary materials" — which included able-bodied athletes — and the possibility of invasion — which resulted in the relocation of the Rose Bowl from the West Coast to the East. As the war progressed so did its impact on sports.

Athletes Respond. In 1941 Minnesota running back Bruce Smith, winner of the Heisman Trophy as the best player in college football, was the 119th player taken in the professional football draft; Smith was 1-A (the draft board designation for men eligible for immediate induction into the military), and professional teams were unwilling to take the risk of drafting a player who might not return from the war. The spirit of patriotism that swept the nation left little room for the special privileges athletes were accustomed to. As the best physical specimens in the nation, they were expected to do their part to defend their country, and they responded admirably. Every member of the New Mexico State Teachers College football and basketball teams, for example, quit to enter military service in 1941, and other college athletes responded similarly.

Rule Changes. The resulting lack of athletes on the playing fields brought rule changes that altered major games in significant ways. College football introduced a rule that allowed teams to substitute players for one another at any time. Although it was rescinded in 1953, the player-substitution rule set the stage for platoon football. Freshmen were allowed to compete as varsity players for the first time in most college sports. The Cincinnati Reds allowed fifteen-year-old left-hander Joe Nuxhall to pitch in a pro game in 1944 (he threw to seven batters in one game; two of them got hits and the rest walked; Nuxhall retired that year with an earned-run average of 67.50, though he returned to baseball eight years later and played until 1966, mostly with the Reds). Sixteen-year-old Tommy "Buckshot" Brown played shortstop in forty-six games for the Brooklyn Dodgers in 1944, the first of his sixteen years in the major leagues. Congress defeated a law to allow seventeen-year-olds to box.

Accommodation. But the changes calculated to allow the continuation of sports in wartime were inadequate in some cases. By 1943 more than two hundred colleges had abandoned football, and those teams that remained were composed of players of predraft age and deferments. The 1942 season of the American Hockey Association was suspended for lack of players; many major golf tournaments were eliminated. *Newsweek* abandoned its all-American polls during the war. The nation's 17 million bowlers received the mixed news that the cost of a game was frozen at the March 1942 level by the federal government — along with many other prices in wartime America — but bowling pins were in short supply as all available wood went for army and navy shoemakers, and girls begin taking jobs as pinsetters to the chagrin of traditionalists who preferred pin boys. The tons of rubber used to make tennis and golf balls prior to the war were diverted to equipping army trucks. Under wartime conditions manufacturers began producing "victory balls," made of synthetic rubber, that were often soggy and unresponsive. Because of severe travel restrictions imposed on the nation, the 1942 wartime version of the Army-Navy football game was shifted from Philadelphia's Municipal Stadium (capacity 102,000) to Thompson Field (22,000), and tickets were limited to people living within ten miles of the statehouse in Annapolis, Maryland. So serious were the travel restrictions that half the Annapolis student body was delegated to cheer for Army, whose cadets were denied transportation from West Point. Underdog Navy used its home-field advantage to rout Army 14–0.

Warrior Athletes. As the war wore on, the War Mobilization office cracked down on all professional athletes between the ages of eighteen and twenty-six, requesting that the Selective Service review their draft status. "They prove to thousands by their great physical feats upon the football or baseball field that they are physically fit and as able to perform military services as are the 11,000,000 men in uniform," Director of War Mobilization James F. Byrnes said. He ordered all horse racing suspended, "to prevent the use of critical materials, services, and transportation in the operations of these tracks." Jockeys were offered jobs in airplane manufacturing plants, where they could crawl into tiny places even women could not go. As a result of Byrnes's suggestions that athletes were evading the draft, a sports story began listing athletes' deferment status. In 1945, for example, *Newsweek* magazine wrote: "Before the discharge of Samuel Jackson Snead (bad back) from the Navy last fall, the 1944–5 grapefruit circuit of the PGA looked like an easy spoon shot for Byron Nelson (hemophiliac and 4-F)." But few accused athletes of being slackers. The official death toll for just one sport,

---

the National Football League, reached twenty-one players killed in action in 1944.

Money and Supplies. Those who could not join the military were encouraged to raise money for the war effort. In golf the U.S. Open was replaced by a fund-raiser, the Hale America Open Tournament in Chicago. The directors of college basketball's two rival, competing end-of-year tournaments, the NCAA and the NIT, arranged a Red Cross war-benefit challenge game between the two tournament winners. In professional football a series of National Football League exhibition games raised $680,384 for war-relief charities in 1942, the first full year of the war. Joe Louis was one several boxers who donated the proceeds of fights to the war effort, though Louis was most generous, directing some $111,000 of his boxing proceeds in 1941 and 1942 to war-support causes. In some cases athletic events were used to gather war supplies. When scrap metal was in short supply in September 1942, baseball fans were admitted free if they brought along scrap metal to games. In Chicago the price was two pounds of scrap; in Brooklyn the metal tariff was ten pounds per free seat; Brooklyn Dodger fans were admitted free to games in July and August 1943 if they brought one-half pound of kitchen fat, and children were admitted free to games in 1944 if they brought waste paper; in that same year baseball's bible, the record book, was not published because of paper shortage. Some 4.5 million service men and women did not need anything but their uniforms to get admitted free to major league and minor league baseball games from 1941 to 1945.

Source:
Douglas A. Noverr and Lawrence E. Ziewacz, *The Games They Played: Sports in American History, 1865–1980* (Chicago: Nelson-Hall, 1983).

HEADLINE MAKERS

EDDIE ARCARO

1916-

JOCKEY

Young Jockey. Eddie Arcaro quit school at age fourteen to ride racehorses, and he became one of the most successful jockeys in the history of the sport, the only rider ever to win two Triple Crowns. Five feet, two inches tall and weighing 114 pounds, Arcaro developed powerful hands and the ability to use the whip with either hand early in his career. With experience he gained the knowledge to judge pace to become the finest "money boy" in the game. During his twenty-six-year career his mounts won over $24 million.

Success. Arcaro learned to ride almost by instinct, he once said, and rarely credited himself with a great ride, preferring to praise the horses. "You seldom hear of a jockey getting into a slump riding good horses," he explained. He rode in his first race in May 1931 and had not ridden a winner for forty-five races when he brought Eagle Bird to the wire in first place at Agua Caliente in January 1932. After Arcaro sustained two fractured ribs and a punctured lung in 1934, stable owner Clarence Davison, who had given Arcaro his first chance to ride, paying him $20 per week, sold his contract for $5,000 to Calumet Farms. There he had access to the best horses in racing and made his reputation, beginning with a winning ride on Larwin in the 1938 Kentucky Derby, the first of a record five Kentucky Derby wins.

Two Triple Crowns. For Calumet, Arcaro rode the great Whirlaway, one of the fastest racehorses ever to take the track, but who had the bad habit of drifting wide on the turns. Arcaro was able to keep Whirlaway under control, and in 1941 he rode him to a track record in the Kentucky Derby and a Triple Crown. In 1942 Arcaro was suspended for a year for trying to force Cuban jockey Vincent Nodarse over the fence aqueduct. He admitted his mistake and used the time off to gather his resources.

He returned better and more determined than ever. In 1945 he won another Kentucky Derby and the Belmont Stakes, and in 1946 he rode 160 winners, who collected over $1 million in purses, the most ever won by a single jockey in a year. The peak of Arcaro's career was in 1948, when he rode Citation to the Triple Crown; that year Arcaro had 188 winners and won $1.68 million in purses. By 1952 more than half his 15,665 mounts had finished in the money. In 1958 he became the third jockey to amass more than 4,000 victories. After his retirement Arcaro worked as a sports journalist, providing race commentary on radio and television.

PATRICIA "PATTY" BERG

1918-

GOLFER

Young Athlete. One of the leading woman golfers from the 1940s through the 1960s, Patty Berg developed professional women's golf in the United States. Berg grew up in Minneapolis and was athletic as a young girl, playing sandlot baseball and quarterback for a boys' football team. She placed third in a national "midget" ice skating race while in high school and was a track star at her high school. Berg began playing golf in 1932 and excelled under her father's teaching. Within a year she qualified to compete in the state championship tournament. In 1935 she won the first of three Minnesota state championships and reached the finals in the U.S. Women's National Amateur Tournament. At age seventeen Berg attracted national attention when she lost 3 and 2 that same year to the well-known Glenna Collet Vare. In 1937 Berg made it to the finals again, but lost 6 and 5 to Estelle Lawson Page.

Golf Success. Patty Berg rose in the amateur golf world by playing tournaments as a student at the University of Minnesota. In 1938 she won the U.S. Women's Amateur Tournament, the Women's Western, the

Trans-Mississippi, and the Women's Western Derby events. Berg won a total of forty amateur tournaments and played on two Curtis Cup teams before she signed as a professional with Wilson Sporting Goods Company of Chicago in 1940. Women had little status as professional golfers at the time, and no professional tour. Berg and Babe Zaharias were among the first women professional golfers. She went on to win the Western Women's Open title in 1941, 1943, and 1948. She also won the first U.S. Women's National Open in 1946.

Pro Tour. When the first women's pro tour was established in 1948, Patty Berg was one of the first three players. Berg served as the first president of the Ladies' Professional Golf Association from 1948 until 1952 and helped develop the LPGA, winning thirty-nine tournaments by 1958. Berg averaged 75.5 strokes per round in those years, and though she lost some power after cancer surgery in 1971, her average went up only three strokes. By 1981, when she stopped competing, Berg had won eighty-three pro tournaments.

FELIX "DOC" BLANCHARD

1924-

FOOTBALL PLAYER

"Mr. Inside." Felix "Doc" Blanchard was one of Army's "Touchdown Twins," along with Glenn Davis. They dominated college football in the mid 1940s, earning the nicknames of Mr. Inside (Blanchard) and Mr. Outside (Davis). From 1944 to 1946 the one-two punch of Blanchard and Davis led Army to twenty-seven victories, one tie, and no losses, even though cadets were forced to complete a four-year curriculum in three years to meet the country's need for military officers. Moreover, Blanchard's size, strength, and versatility made him a formidable player during the last days when men played the entire game, both offense and defense. The combination of Blanchard's strength and Davis's speed molded new concepts about how a highly explosive football offense would be formed, dramatically lifting fan interest.

Army Man. Originally enrolled at North Carolina to be near his ailing father, Blanchard was recruited to West Point after he was drafted following his freshman year. Because of the war, athletes who had lettered at other universities could receive appointments to the United States Military Academy, where three more seasons of eligibility awaited. As a result, Army was awesome during those years, when many college teams were forced to terminate their programs for lack of players or compete with a combination of freshmen and 4-F squads filled with men rejected by the army. Throughout his career the 205-pound fullback hammered relentlessly at opponents,

normally between the tackles, while Davis flew around the ends from a T-formation offense. In 1944 this combination of power and speed allowed Army to produce the most explosive offense in college football history, averaging 56 points per game, setting an NCAA record. In the duo's first game together in 1944, against Blanchard's old North Carolina team, the Touchdown Twins spearheaded an offense that produced a 46–0 victory and set the tone for the remainder of the year. The most impressive game of that national championship season was a 59–0 thrashing of Notre Dame, which had held Army scoreless in every game they had played since 1938 and winless since 1931. *New York Times* sports reporter Allison Danzig wrote the next day, "It was Blanchard who sent kickoffs into the end zone, who punted when (quarterback Doug) Kenna was not on the field, who intercepted passes and was even more poisonous on the defense than when he was in running with the ball." After Army's victory over Navy, Army assistant coach Herman Hickman said that Blanchard "is the only man who runs his own interference."

The Team. There had never been a football backfield with such a combination of brute strength and blinding speed as Blanchard and Davis provided. Together during their three years, the pair produced 3,989 yards rushing, 1,317 yards receiving, and 89 touchdowns. In 1945 Army repeated as national champion, and the duo appeared on the cover of *Time* magazine. A year later the two made the cover of *Life* magazine, and shortly after graduation each played himself in a widely panned movie of their football careers, *Spirit of West Point.* That year Blanchard scored 19 touchdowns, averaged 7.1 yards per rush, and caught four passes for 166 yards, his finest season. Finishing third in the Heisman Trophy balloting as a plebe, he won in 1945; Davis finished second. Blanchard was the first junior to win the Heisman, the award given to the nation's best football player, and the first athlete to win both the Heisman and James Sullivan Award, given to the nation's finest amateur athlete. He was also the first football player to win the James Sullivan Award. During his final year at Army, Blanchard was injured, yet he still averaged 5.1 yards per rush, caught seven passes for 166 yards, scored 10 touchdowns, and finished fourth in the Heisman voting, won that year by his running mate, Davis. During his three West Point years, Blanchard accumulated 1,666 yards rushing and 38 touchdowns. In the off-season Blanchard took up the shot put so (according to legend) he could continue to enjoy the food provided for the track team. He became a three-time consensus all-American in track and field.

Life after Football. Upon graduation Blanchard, Davis, and Army end Barney Poole all hoped to continue their football-playing days in either the National Football League or the All-American Football Conference, which operated from 1946–1949. The Pittsburgh Steelers of the NFL and the San Francisco 49ers, then of the AAFC, held Blanchard's draft rights. But with war still underway, and recognizing the visibility and popularity of the football players, Secretary of War Robert P. Patterson rejected their request for a three-month furlough. "The War Department," he said, "cannot favorably consider granting extended leave of absence for engaging in private enterprise . . . any other decision would be inimical to the best interests of the service." Blanchard entered the Army Air Corps, where he stayed for twenty-five years as a pilot; Davis resumed his football career, playing two years for Los Angeles before an injury forced his retirement.

MILDRED "BABE" DIDRIKSON

1911-1956

OLYMPIC MEDALIST, GOLFER

Babe. As a young girl, Mildred Didrikson was such a powerful home run hitter on the baseball field that her friends nicknamed her "Babe," after Babe Ruth. The name stuck. Didrikson grew up near Port Arthur, Texas, and showed her athletic talent early. A high-school all-American basketball star, Didrikson went on to play in an industrial athletic league, leading her team to two finals and a national championship. She once scored 106 points in a basketball game. Didrikson then turned to track and qualified for the United States team at the 1932 Olympics. Described variously in the press as Whatta-Gal Didrikson, the Texas Tornado, and the Terrific Tomboy, she won gold medals in the javelin, with a world-record throw, and the 80-meter hurdles, in which she set a U.S. outdoor record time. She tied the winner in the high jump but was given a second-place silver medal because of her unconventional style. At the 1932 Amateur Athletic Union (AAU) championships, she entered eight of ten events and won five.

Rounded Athlete. In the 1930s there was no competitive setting in which a woman athlete could earn a living. Didrikson was suspended from the AAU in 1932 for allegedly appearing in a Chrysler Corporation advertisement, and she decided to turn professional. She toured with a mixed-gender basketball team called Babe Didrikson's All Americans and pitched at major league baseball spring-training games in 1934. She earned $1,500 a month and played some four hundred games with a male baseball team called the House of David. She once struck out New York Yankee great Joe DiMaggio. Sportswriter Grantland Rice described her as "the most flawless specimen of muscle harmony, of complete mental and physical coordination the world of sport has ever known"; in his opinion she was the greatest athlete of either sex in the history of American sports.

Golf. Didrikson took up golf in 1932, and in November 1934 she shot seventy-five to qualify in her first tournament, the Fort Worth Women's Invitational. Her first tournament victory was in April 1935, when she won the Texas Women's Amateur Championship, and the United States Golf Association immediately made her a professional, a disappointment because there were only two professional golf tournaments for women at the time. In 1938 she married George Zaharias, a professional wrestler and promoter, who began to manage her career. He arranged for her to sit out of professional play for three years, between 1940 and 1943, to regain her amateur status. During that time she played in professional tournaments but refused cash prizes. Once the tournaments resumed after the war, Zaharias played a full schedule and won a series of fourteen consecutive titles, including the British Women's Amateur Championship, the first ever won by an American, in 1947. Though she was known for her long drives, it was her precise short game that won tournaments for her.

LPGA. Babe Didrikson Zaharias turned professional again in August 1947 and founded the Ladies' Professional Golf Association in January 1948. From 1949 to 1951 she was the top LPGA money winner. In 1953 she won her third United States Women's Open by 13 strokes, her last victory. She died of cancer in 1956. Babe Didrikson Zaharias was named Athlete of the Year by the Associated Press in 1932 for track and in 1944–1946 and 1950 for golf. In 1950 she was named the greatest female athlete of the first half of the twentieth century by the AP.

Source:
Elizabeth A. Lynn, *Babe Didrikson Zaharias* (New York: Chelsea House, 1989).

JOE DiMAGGIO

1914-

BASEBALL PLAYER

Career. One of the most popular and fabled players to compete in Yankee Stadium, Joe DiMaggio was winner of three Most Valuable Player awards. His 1941 hitting streak of 56 games was one of the most closely watched achievements in baseball history, and he was so beloved by his fans that Japanese attempting to insult American soldiers on World War II battlefields called out insults to DiMaggio. His career batting average was .325, and he hammered 361 home runs. In 1949 he became the American League's first $100,000 player.

Before the Yankees. Son of Italian immigrant parents, Giuseppe Paolo DiMaggio Jr. grew up in the San Francisco area with his four brothers and four sisters. At seventeen DiMaggio elected to play minor league base-ball with the San Francisco Seals, the team on which his brother was making his professional debut near the end of the 1932 season. With a salary of $250 a month, 6-foot-2-inch DiMaggio became a Bay Area celebrity in 1933, hitting safely in 61 consecutive games, an all-time record for professional baseball, while hitting .340 and driving in 169 runs. A year later DiMaggio hit .341 and was purchased by the New York Yankees for $25,000 and five minor league players. An impressive .398 batting average earned him a Yankee tryout in 1936, where he was billed as the next Babe Ruth. DiMaggio's debut was delayed because of an injury, yet when he appeared on the field for the first time, on 3 May 1936, 25,000 cheering, flag-waving Italian residents of New York showed up to welcome him to the team.

"Joltin Joe, the Yankee Clipper." By 1936 "Joltin' Joe," as he was called, led the league with a career-high 46 home runs. Even with the depth of the left field fence in Yankee Stadium, DiMaggio hit 361 career home runs, placing him fifth on the major league all-time home run list when he retired in 1951. In 1937 he batted an impressive .346, driving in 167 runs. The next season DiMaggio hit .324, followed in 1939 with a .381 and his first batting championship and the league Most Valuable Player award. Late in the 1939 season DiMaggio was hitting at a .412 pace, but eye trouble, and possibly the pressure, kept him from staying above the .400 mark.

The Streak. During the 1940 season DiMaggio captured his second consecutive batting title with a .352, but for the first time since he had joined the Yankees his team failed to win the pennant — setting the stage for the 1941 season that would make baseball history. DiMaggio's 56-game hitting streak during the 1941 season began on 15 May, when he singled home a run, and ended on 17 July. In between he hit .406, and fans all over the country anxiously checked each game day to see if the Yankee Clipper had kept the streak going. People jammed the ballpark; radio programs were interrupted for "DiMag" bulletins, the U.S. Congress designated a page boy to rush DiMaggio bulletins to the floor, and newspaper switchboards lit up every afternoon with the question of the day, "Did DiMaggio get his hit?" Immediately after Cleveland pitchers Al Smith and Jim Bagby held DiMaggio hitless on 17 July, with the help of two great plays at third base by Ken Keltner, he started another hitting streak that ran 17 games. At the same time, twenty-two-year-old Red Sox slugger Ted Williams was setting a modern-age batting average of .406. During that same year, young pitcher Bob Feller won 25 games for the Cleveland Indians, and veteran pitcher Lefty Grove won his 300th game. In 1941 DiMaggio won his second Most Valuable Player award and like the rest of the nation began to feel the pressure of a nation readying itself for war. During the 1942 season DiMaggio batted .305 and was drafted into the army along with thousands of other young men. During his three years in the army

DiMaggio played baseball in the Pacific and across the United States. The 1946 season was a disappointment (he batted .290), but by 1947 he was back in form, hitting .315 to win his third Most Valuable Player award and lead his team to the pennant.

Hall of Famer. Aided by the media machine of New York City and his own powerful statistics, DiMaggio became a national hero after the war — even though he played for the often-hated Yankees. He was even immortalized in a song called "Joltin' Joe DiMaggio," recorded by the Les Brown Orchestra. In 1948 DiMaggio had returned to the height of this form, winning the home run title with 39, the RBI crown with 155, and the batting title with a .320 average. DiMaggio sat out the first two months of the 1949 season with a bone spur in his heel, but as always his return was memorable. Although playing in pain, during his first games for new manager Casey Stengel, DiMaggio belted four homers in three games that broke the back of the league-leading Red Sox and helped the Yankees bring home another pennant. In 1951, with another soon-to-be Yankee superstar, young Mickey Mantle, on the scene, DiMaggio's average slipped to .263 with only 12 homers. Announcing his retirement at age thirty-seven in 1952, he turned down a fourth consecutive $100,000 contract because "when baseball is no longer fun, it's no longer a game." The Yankees, whose history is replete with heroes, retired his uniform, the world-famous pinstripe number five. In later years DiMaggio hosted pregame television shows, made television commercials, and was briefly married to the voluptuous Hollywood actress Marilyn Monroe. He was elected to the Baseball Hall of Fame in 1955, and in 1969 he was named the "Greatest Living Player" in a centennial poll of sportswriters.

Sources:

Maury Allen, *Where Have You Gone, Joe DiMaggio? The Story of America's Last Hero* (New York: Dutton, 1975);

Jack B. Moore, *Joe DiMaggio: A Bio-Bibliography* (Westport, Conn.: Greenwood Press, 1986);

Michael Seidel, *Streak: DiMaggio and the Summer of '41* (New York: McGraw-Hill, 1988).

JOE LOUIS

1914-1981

BOXER

Childhood. Joe Louis Barrow was born in a sharecropper's shack in Lexington, Alabama, the seventh of eight children. Two years after his birth his father was committed to Searcy State Hospital for the Colored Insane, where he died twenty years later. Mrs. Barrow remarried a man who had five children of his own, and moved her family in with his. The children slept three to a bed. In 1926, when Joe

Louis was twelve, his stepfather moved the family to Detroit and went to work at the Ford plant. Louis was already behind in school, and the transition to a new setting only complicated his education. It seemed clear to teachers that he was not a candidate for graduation, so they referred him to Bronson Trade School, where he stayed until age seventeen, to learn cabinet making. In an attempt to keep her son off the streets, Louis's mother saved up to buy him a violin and pay for music lessons. He took the money and used it to rent a locker at the Brewster Recreation Center, where he could box. He took the ring name Joe Louis when he filled out his application for amateur competition. The space for his name was small, and Louis wrote big, so only his first two names would fit. Amateur boxers were paid in merchandise certificates for as much as $25, which they could redeem for goods at local stores. In 1933 Louis helped support his family by fighting more than once a week. At the end of the year he had won fifty of fifty-four fights, forty-three by knockout. That record attracted the attention of John Roxborough, a racketeer who had served time for manslaughter and was boss of the Detroit numbers racket; he signed up his friend Julian Black as Louis's manager. Under their management Louis won the light-heavyweight Golden Gloves championship and then the National Amateur Athletic Union championship. He turned pro on 4 July 1934.

Mike Jacobs. Joe Louis won ten of twelve fights by knockout in his first year as a professional and developed a reputation in the Detroit area as a devastating puncher. Boxing promoter Mike Jacobs discovered him and saw the opportunity to make a fortune. He negotiated an exclusive contract with Louis to promote all his fights; then he lined up a match in New York City with perhaps the most overrated fighter of the time, the huge Italian Primo Carnera. The prefight publicity was masterful: a primitive black man against a white giant. There was speculation about a race war if Louis beat the white fighter; the Ku Klux Klan opposed the fight and sent death threats to Louis supporters. On 25 June 1935, sixty thousand people filed in to Yankee Stadium to see the much smaller Louis punish Carnera before knocking him out in the sixth round. Louis earned his nickname "The Brown Bomber" that night, and on 22 June 1937 he knocked out James J. Braddock in the eighth round.

Schmeling. On 19 June 1936 Louis fought Max Schmeling for the right to take on heavyweight champion James J. Braddock. In the fight with Schmeling, Louis was more than a representative of his race on fight night; he was an American hero fighting against a German champion when the anti-Semitism of the Nazis was already apparent. It was assumed Louis would win easily, and when he was knocked out in the twelfth round, the loss took on uncommon significance. He had been fighting for two years, and his record was twenty-seven wins, with twenty-two knockouts, and one loss. He had to fight another year, eleven more fights with ten more

knockouts, before he got his championship shot. On 22 June he knocked out Braddock in the eighth round and received a purse of $103,684 on gate receipts of $715,470. Joe Louis was the youngest heavyweight champion in history and the first black champion since Jack Johnson in 1915. He was also the most popular heavyweight boxer in history. In an era of undisguised racism, Louis fascinated white fans who were awed by his stony ferocity and raw power, and he stood as a symbol of racial pride for blacks. His fights were broadcast over radio and were heard by as many as two-thirds of all the radio listeners in America, audiences of as many as fifty million, and he attracted millions of tens of thousands to the arenas for his every fight. In the most corrupt of all sports he maintained a reputation as a man untainted by scandal, whose natural talent made him unbeatable — except against Schmeling. When he fought Schmeling again, two years and three days after their first fight, he declared, "There ain't going to be any decision in this fight." Seventy thousand fans paid over $1 million at Yankee Stadium to see Louis fight the man now openly promoted as the Nazi champion, and Louis gave them what they wanted with a knockout in two minutes and four seconds of the first round. He had defeated Germany for them and for millions of radio listeners. Heywood Broun wrote the next day in the *New York World-Telegram* that Louis had "exploded the Nordic myth with a bombing glove."

Champ. For eleven years he fought all comers — ninety-two matches, including eighteen exhibitions during the war, and he took a year off when he was serving in the military. He won more than $4 million in purses, but owed money when he retired. As a champion Louis was magnanimous. He supported more than twenty friends and family during the 1940s, and when his large purses were divided, he had little left over for himself. When he retired, he rebelled against promoter Mike Jacobs, who had used his right to promote Louis's fights to establish a dynasty and make a fortune. Louis went into fight promotions himself, and he became a partner in the International Boxing Club (IBC), which superseded Jacobs's Twentieth Century Sporting Club as the dominant power in professional boxing, but Louis's partners saw to it that his 20 percent share of IBC was not worth much, as they drained profits for themselves. Louis was a celebrity though, and he survived on value of his name, though money went out faster than it came in and the IRS took whatever it could to discharge the income-tax debt Louis had accumulated during his salad days. By early 1960 he was reduced to acting as a greeter at Las Vegas casinos, first at the Thunderbird Hotel and then at Caesar's Palace. He began smoking, drinking to excess, and taking drugs, a habit that nearly killed him when he overdosed in 1969. He died on 12 April 1981 after a long illness punctuated by periods of dementia.

Death. Joe Louis laid in state at Caesar's Palace Sports Pavilion, where thousands of former fans paid their respects, and then at the Nineteenth Street Baptist Church in Washington, D.C., where he was flown in Air Force One, the presidential plane. Jesse Jackson delivered the eulogy before Louis was buried at Arlington National Cemetery.

Sources:

Joe Louis Barrow, Jr., and Barbara Munder, *Joe Louis: 50 Years an American Hero* (New York: McGraw-Hill, 1988);

Chris Mead, *Joe Louis: Black Hero in White America* (New York: Scribners, 1985).

LARRY MACPHAIL

1890-1975

MAJOR LEAGUE BASEBALL OWNER

Businessman. Often-fired Brooklyn Dodger manager Leo Durocher said of his boss, team owner Larry MacPhail, "There is a thin line between genius and insanity, and in Larry's case it was sometimes so thin you could see him drifting back and forth." Volatile, egotistical, and driven, Larry MacPhail pioneered the movement among major league baseball owners to approach the game as a business that provides sports entertainment. Like any good businessman engaged in selling to the public, MacPhail believed in promotion. To him a baseball team owner's job was to attract ticket-buying fans to the stadium and give them a good show.

Entering Baseball. MacPhail was a student athlete at the University of Michigan and earned his law degree at the age of twenty from Georgetown University. After a successful military career in World War I, during which he just missed in an attempt to kidnap Kaiser Wilhelm II, he returned to civilian life as an entrepreneur. In 1934 his friend Branch Rickey recommended him to the owner of the Cincinnati Reds, who was looking for someone to revive his floundering team. As vice-president of the Reds from 1934 to 1937, MacPhail turned the team into a money-making winner. He painted the park orange to create excitement; he introduced usherettes in the stadium and night baseball; and he hired an enthusiastic radio announcer, Red Barber, to stir fans' spirits while keeping them in touch with their team. He started a farm system to recruit and develop talented players, laying the foundation for Cincinnati's National League pennant in 1939 and World Series championship in 1940.

The Dodgers. After a year in a family investment business MacPhail accepted the offer of the Brooklyn Trust Company in 1938 to try to rescue the Brooklyn Dodgers, who has amassed a debt of some $500,000 due, in part, to poor management. MacPhail agreed and made an immediate impact, transforming a team of losers who had won only three pennants in the twentieth century into profitable winners. He renovated Ebbets Field and bought first-rate players, including first baseman Dolph Camilli. He hired Red Barber from the Reds, violating a gentleman's agreement among owners not to hire one another's employees. Under MacPhail's leadership each Dodger game was promoted as a grudge match, and the result was unprecedented fan support. Within three years he delivered his fans a National League pennant. More significant to him, after five seasons the team's entire debt to the Brooklyn Trust Company was paid off, at a time when many teams claimed to be losing money.

The Yankees. MacPhail left the Dodgers in 1942 to join the army, where he was commissioned as a colonel in charge of public relations. When the war was over, he returned to baseball with a flourish. He; Dan Topping, owner of the professional football Brooklyn Tigers; and millionaire builder Del E. Webb bought the New York Yankees for $2.8 million, and MacPhail served as president of the organization. He installed a king-size floodlight system at Yankee Stadium, where night baseball had been taboo, and hired attractive young women to stage a fashion show on the field. At one game he gave away 500 pairs of nylon stockings. For wealthy customers he created a first-class saloon, a forerunner of the sky box. He even suggested that the Yankees might draw more fans if they were not so home run oriented, despite the fact that power hitting had brought New York fourteen pennants and ten world championships from 1921 to 1943. After the Yankees won the World Series in 1947, MacPhail publicly crossed the line from genius to madness. He got drunk, made insulting remarks to reporters and to his partners in the locker room, and punched a sportswriter. Just after that he sold his interest in the Yankees for $2 million to Topping and Webb. When MacPhail left the Yankees he left baseball for horseracing. He raised horses in Maryland and later served as president of Bowie Race Track. He died in 1975 at the age of eighty-five. He attributed his longevity to having left baseball before the excitement killed him.

JACKIE ROBINSON

1919-1972

FIRST BLACK IN MAJOR LEAGUE BASEBALL

Childhood. Jackie Robinson was born in Georgia, the youngest of five children of Mallie and Jerry Robinson. His father deserted the family when Jackie was six months old, and his mother moved the family to Pasadena, California, in search of opportunity. Mallie Robinson, a domestic, purchased a home in a white Pasadena neighborhood with the help of a welfare agency. The neighbors petitioned unsuccessfully to have the Robinsons removed and then offered to buy the family out. Mrs. Robinson refused. Jackie Robinson remembered that "Pasadena regarded us as intruders. My brothers and I were in many a fight that started with a racial slur on the very street we lived on. We saw movies from segregated balconies, swam in the municipal pool only on Tuesdays, and were permitted in the YMCA only one night a week."

Youth. Athletics became a passion for the two Robinson boys, Jackie and his older brother Mack, who won a silver medal in the 1936 Berlin Olympics, finishing second to Jesse Owens in the 200-meter dash. Jackie Robinson attended UCLA, and in his senior year he was not named to either of the top all-division teams, despite leading the conference in scoring for two seasons. As one observer commented, "It's purely the case of a coach refusing to recognize a player's ability . . . out of prejudice." Robinson was a remarkable all-around athlete. He was UCLA's first four-letter man, excelling in football, basketball, track, and baseball. One coach called him "the best basketball player in the United States." In football in his junior year he averaged eleven yards a carry. He was the NCAA broad jump champion in 1940. Robinson dropped out of UCLA in his senior year to help support his mother and worked as a coach for the National Youth Administration, supplementing his income by playing baseball.

Army. Jackie Robinson was drafted into the army in 1942, where he fought segregation from the beginning. When he was barred from officer's training school, he fought to have the decision reversed, and he continued to oppose segregation in sports recreation and at his base PX. In 1944 his insistence on equal treatment landed him in military court facing court-martial for insubordination. He had refused a southern bus driver's order to sit in the back of a military bus, knowing that the army had just ordered the desegregation of base transportation. When the police and the provost of the base took the bus driver's side at the trial, the judges ruled that Robinson had acted within his rights, and he received an honorable discharge in November 1944.

First Meeting with Rickey. When Brooklyn Dodger general manager Branch Rickey searched in 1945 for a player to cross the color line and integrate professional baseball, Jackie Robinson was identified as the man for the experiment. In their first meeting Rickey grilled Robinson on the insults and indignities he would face as the first black major league ballplayer. In a role-playing exercise, Rickey confronted Robinson as the abusive teammate, the hostile opponent, and the insulting fan. Robinson remembered that "[Rickey's] acting was so convincing that I found myself chain-gripping my fingers behind my back." Finally, Robinson responded, "Mr. Rickey, do you want a ballplayer who's afraid to fight back?" Rickey replied, "I want a player with guts enough not to fight back." At that meeting Branch Rickey impressed upon Robinson the importance of passive resistance and told him it was essential that he avoid all confrontation until

he was established in the major leagues. Robinson agreed. He signed a contract for a monthly salary of $600 plus a bonus of $3,500 to play for the Montreal Royals, the Dodgers' best farm club, in preparation for his introduction into the major leagues. Robinson was sworn to secrecy, with the exception of his fiancée and his mother. Robinson married his college sweetheart, Rachel Isum, on 10 February 1946.

The Great Experiment. The news was made public at a signing ceremony on 23 October 1945 in Montreal. When Robinson addressed the crowd at the signing he expressed delight at being chosen as the first black man in the major leagues. He pointed out that most of his playing was on integrated teams, and, anticipating the problems that lay ahead, Robinson affirmed, "I'm ready to take the chance. Maybe I'm doing something for my race." For two years with the Royals, Robinson encountered what his wife described as the worst name-calling she and her husband had ever endured, and she feared for his life. But they did endure, and Robinson began the 1947 season as a Brooklyn Dodger.

On the Field. Robinson's performance surpassed expectations in his 1947 season: he batted .297 and led the Dodgers with 29 stolen bases and 125 runs scored. In 1948 he was moved to the position of second baseman, and from 1953 until he stopped playing in 1957 Robinson shifted between the outfield and the infield. Jackie Robinson's best year was 1949. He won the National League's Most Valuable Player award, with a .342 batting average, 37 stolen bases, 122 runs scored, and 124 RBIs. Robinson's triumph engendered a winning team spirit, and the Dodgers won six pennants in the late 1940s. He was traded to the New York Giants in 1956, and within a month of the trade he announced his retirement to become an executive with the Chock Full O'Nuts restaurant chain. He was elected to the Baseball Hall of Fame in Cooperstown, New York, in 1962, the first year he was eligible.

Later Years. Breaking the color barrier took a personal toll on Jackie Robinson. After he retired from the team in 1957, he became a vociferous critic of organized baseball's treatment of blacks. Robinson's 1964 memoir, *Baseball Has Done It*, is a litany of complaints about the inequity in salary and opportunity for black players. Robinson, who personified the rags-to-riches myth, believed in a liberal dream of integration for blacks. He advocated black capitalism and participated in black-owned business ventures in Harlem. Independent in his political positions, Robinson supported Republican presidential candidate Richard Nixon in 1960 and resigned from the NAACP in 1967 because he objected to the organization's failure to include younger, progressive blacks. Jackie Robinson died of a heart attack in 1972 at the age of fifty-three.

Sources:
David Falkner, *Great Time Coming: The Life of Jackie Robinson, From Baseball to Birmingham* (New York: Simon & Schuster, 1995);

Elliott J. Gorn and Warren Goldstein, *A Brief History of American Sports* (New York: Hill & Wang, 1993);

Jules Tygiel, *Baseball's Great Experiment: Jackie Robinson and His Legacy* (New York: Oxford University Press, 1983).

PEOPLE IN THE NEWS

At age thirty **Eddie Arcaro** joined an elite horse-racing circle in 1945, winning his third Kentucky Derby, riding Hoop Jr. His previous victories had been on Lawrin in 1938 and Whirlaway in 1941.

When **Citation** won the eightieth running of the Belmont Stakes in 1948 (worth $77,700 to the winner), he became the eighth horse to win the Triple Crown since 1919. It was the second Triple Crown for both jockey Eddie Arcaro and Calumet Farms, who won with Whirlaway in 1941.

In 1941 **Ken Bartholomew** captured the North American speed-skating championship.

In 1942 Saint Louis Cardinal pitcher **Johnny Beazley** won 21 games, including two in the World Series, to attain the best rookie record since Peter Alexander won 28 in 1911.

In 20 August 1945 seventeen-year-old Brooklyn Dodgers shortstop **Tommy Brown** hit a home run off Preacher Roe of the Pittsburgh Pirates to become the youngest person to hit a major league home run.

In 1941 the AAU selected swimmer **Gloria Callen** as the outstanding woman athlete of 1940.

Gerald Cote won the sixth annual Yonkers Marathon in 1940 to win the national AAU championship. He finished in 2:34:06.2.

In 1943 **Gerald Cote** won the forty-seventh Boston Marathon, running the 26-mile course in 2:28:25 4/5.

In 1945 eighteen-year-old **Ann Curtis** won the grand slam of the women's national free-style swimming championships, capturing the 100-, 400-, 800-, and 1,500-yard races during a single meet; Curtis became the first woman and first swimmer to win the James E. Sullivan Memorial Award as outstanding athlete of the year.

In 1940 female skipper **Katherine Dewey** guided the AAU senior national bobsledding championship team at Lake Placid, New York. The rest of the Sno Birds team were **Leo Martin, Pat Martin,** and **Lawrence Straight.**

In 1943 the AAU's James E. Sullivan Memorial Trophy was awarded to miler **Gilbert H. Dodds**.

In 1940 **David Freeman** of Pasadena, California, successfully defended his men's national badminton championship title, previously won in 1939.

In 1945, with manpower shortages at their height, Saint Louis Cardinals baseball team called up one-armed player **Peter Gray**; he appeared in 77 games and collected 51 hits in 234 at bats for a .218 batting average.

In 1943 twenty-year-old **Lorraine Heinisch** of Kenosha, Wisconsin, became the first woman to umpire a major professional event, the National Semi-Pro Baseball Tournament, played in Wichita, Kansas.

In 1940 **Russ Hoogerhyde** of Northbrook, Illinois, won the individual national archery championship for the sixth time in a tournament held at Massachusetts State College. **Ann Weber** of Bloomfield, New Jersey, set records in all events, winning the women's individual championship.

In 1941 **Willie Hoppe** won the world three-cushion billiard title for the second consecutive year.

In 1949 **Willie Hoppe,** at age sixty-one, won his sixth world three-cushion billiard title without a loss since 1937; Hoppe began playing in 1906.

On 30 June 1948 Detroit Tiger pitcher **Bob Lemon** threw the first no-hitter recorded in Detroit's twenty-six league years and the first night no-hitter in American League history.

In 1948 handball champion **Gus Lewis** drew a capacity crowd of 300, at $10 a head, to capture his second straight National AAU title without the loss of a game.

In 1941 **Toni Matt** won the national combined ski championship.

In 1940 **Marion Miley,** ranked number two among women golfers in 1939 and winner of numerous national tournaments, was murdered by an unidentified masked man.

In 1941 **Clarence Parker** was named the most valuable player in the NFL in 1940 by the Professional Football Writers Association of America.

In 1940 **Samuel Reshevsky** of New York won his third national chess tournament held by the United States Chess Federation.

In 1941 long distance runner **Gregory Rice** received the AAU's James E. Sullivan Memorial Trophy as outstanding athlete of 1940.

In 1945 **Maurice Richard,** the high-scoring right winger of the Montreal Canadiens, set a new modern goal-scoring record with 44 goals in one season.

In 1942 sixty-year-old Branch Rickey of the Saint Louis Cardinals took the general manager's job with the Brooklyn Dodgers, succeeding another legend of baseball, **Larry MacPhail.** Rickey's reported salary is $40,000.

In 1941 jockey **Alfred "Robby" Robertson** won six out of seven horse races in Jamaica, New York, the first time that record had been accomplished on a New York track.

In 1948 **Matt Sassone** of Saint Mary's Academy pitched a no-hitter, but lost 1–0 to **Ray Lappointe** of Glens Falls High, who also turned in a no-hitter.

In 1949 **Red Schoendienst** set a National League record for a second baseman by handling the ball 320 consecutive times without an error.

In 1947 **Joe Verdeur** from LaSalle University set a world record in the 200-yard breaststroke, then broke his own record four times.

In 1946 **Babe Didrikson Zaharias** won the Associated Press's Best Athlete of the Year award for the second time, the first time based on her Olympic track prowess, the second for her excellence in golf.

AWARDS

1940

Major League Baseball World Series — Cincinnati Reds (National League), 4 vs. Detroit Tigers (American League), 3

National Football League Championship — Chicago Bears, 73 vs. Washington Redskins, 0

Collegiate Football National Champion — University of Minnesota

Heisman Trophy, Collegiate Football — Tom Harmon (University of Michigan)

Cotton Bowl — Clemson University, 6 vs. Boston College, 3

Orange Bowl — Georgia Tech, 21 vs. University of Missouri, 7

Rose Bowl — University of Southern California, 14 vs. University of Tennessee, 0

Sugar Bowl — Texas A&M, 14 vs. Tulane University, 13

National Collegiate Athletic Association Basketball — Indiana University, 60 vs. University of Kansas, 42

National Hockey League Stanley Cup — New York Rangers

Kentucky Derby, Horse Racing — Gallahadion (Carroll Bierman, jockey)

Preakness, Horse Racing — Bimelech (F. A. Smith, jockey)

Belmont Stakes, Horse Racing — Bimelech (F. A. Smith, jockey)

Masters Golf Tournament — Jimmy Demaret

Professional Golfers' Association Championship — Byron Nelson

U.S.G.A. Open Championship — W. Lawson Little, Jr.

U.S.G.A. Amateur Championship — Richard Chapman

U.S.G.A. Women's Amateur Championship — Betty Jameson

U.S. National Tennis Tournament, Men's Singles — W. Donald McNeill

U.S. National Tennis Tournament, Women's Singles — Alice Marble

A.A.A. National Auto Champion — Rex Mays

Indianapolis 500 Auto Race Champion — Wilbur Shaw

1941

Major League Baseball World Series — New York Yankees (American League), 4 vs. Brooklyn Dodgers (National League), 1

National Football League Championship — Chicago Bears, 37 vs. New York Giants, 9

Collegiate Football National Champion — University of Minnesota

Heisman Trophy, Collegiate Football — Bruce Smith (University of Minnesota)

Cotton Bowl — Texas A&M, 13 vs. Fordham University, 12

Orange Bowl — Mississippi State University, 14 vs. Georgetown University, 7

Rose Bowl — Stanford University, 21 vs. University of Nebraska, 13

Sugar Bowl — Boston College, 19 vs. University of Tennessee, 13

National Collegiate Athletic Association Basketball — University of Wisconsin, 39 vs. Washington State University, 34

National Hockey League Stanley Cup — Boston Bruins

Kentucky Derby, Horse Racing — Whirlaway (Eddie Arcaro, jockey)

Preakness, Horse Racing — Whirlaway (Eddie Arcaro, jockey)

Belmont Stakes, Horse Racing — Whirlaway (Eddie Arcaro, jockey)

Masters Golf Tournament — Craig Wood

Professional Golfers' Association Championship — Vic Ghezzi

U.S.G.A. Open Championship — Craig Wood

U.S.G.A. Amateur Championship — Marvin Ward

U.S.G.A. Women's Amateur Championship — Betty Hicks Newell

U.S. National Tennis Tournament, Men's Singles — Bobby Riggs

U.S. National Tennis Tournament, Women's Singles — Sarah Palfrey Cooke

A.A.A. National Auto Champion — Rex Mays

Indianapolis 500 Auto Race Champions — Floyd Davis and Mauri Rose

1942

Major League Baseball World Series — Saint Louis Cardinals (National League), 4 vs. New York Yankees (American League), 1

National Football League Championship — Washington Redskins, 14 vs. Chicago Bears, 6

Collegiate Football National Champion — Ohio State University

Heisman Trophy, Collegiate Football — Frank Sinkwich (University of Georgia)

Cotton Bowl — University of Alabama, 29 vs. Texas A&M, 21

Orange Bowl — University of Georgia, 40 vs. Texas Christian University, 26

Rose Bowl — Oregon State University, 20 vs. Duke University, 16

Sugar Bowl — Fordham University, 2 vs. University of Missouri, 0

National Collegiate Athletic Association Basketball — Stanford University, 53 vs. Dartmouth College, 38

National Hockey League Stanley Cup — Toronto Maple Leafs

Kentucky Derby, Horse Racing — Shut Out (Wayne Wright, jockey)

Preakness, Horse Racing — Alsab (Basil James, jockey)

Belmont Stakes, Horse Racing — Shut Out (Eddie Arcaro, jockey)

Masters Golf Tournament — Byron Nelson

Professional Golfers' Association Championship — Sam Snead

U.S.G.A. Open Championship — No tournament because of war

U.S.G.A. Amateur Championship — No tournament because of war

U.S.G.A. Women's Amateur Championship — No tournament because of war

U.S. National Tennis Tournament, Men's Singles — Frederick "Ted" Schroeder, Jr.

U.S. National Tennis Tournament, Women's Singles — Pauline Betz

Indianapolis 500 Auto Race Champion — No race because of war

1943

Major League Baseball World Series — New York Yankees (American League), 4 vs. Saint Louis Cardinals (National League), 1

National Football League Championship — Chicago Bears, 41 vs. Washington Redskins, 21

Collegiate Football National Champion — Notre Dame University

Heisman Trophy, Collegiate Football — Angelo Bertelli (Notre Dame University)

Cotton Bowl — University of Texas, 14 vs. Georgia Tech, 7

Orange Bowl — University of Alabama, 37 vs. Boston College, 21

Rose Bowl — University of Georgia, 9 vs. University of California, Los Angeles, 0

Sugar Bowl — University of Tennessee, 14 vs. University of Tulsa, 7

National Collegiate Athletic Association Basketball — University of Wyoming, 46 vs. Georgetown University, 34

National Hockey League Stanley Cup — Detroit Red Wings

Kentucky Derby, Horse Racing — Count Fleet (Johnny Longden, jockey)

Preakness, Horse Racing — Count Fleet (Johnny Longden, jockey)

Belmont Stakes, Horse Racing — Count Fleet (Johnny Longden, jockey)

Masters Golf Tournament — No tournament because of war

Professional Golfers' Association Championship — No tournament because of war

U.S.G.A. Open Championship — No tournament because of war

U.S.G.A. Amateur Championship — No tournament because of war

U.S.G.A. Women's Amateur Championship — No tournament because of war

U.S. National Tennis Tournament, Men's Singles — Joseph Hunt

U.S. National Tennis Tournament, Women's Singles — Pauline Betz

Indianapolis 500 Auto Race Champion — No race because of war

1944

Major League Baseball World Series — Saint Louis Cardinals (National League), 4 vs. Saint Louis Browns (American League), 2

National Football League Championship — Green Bay Packers, 14 vs. New York Giants, 7

Collegiate Football National Champion — Army

Heisman Trophy, Collegiate Football — Leslie Horvath (Ohio State University)

Cotton Bowl — University of Texas, 7 vs. Randolph Field, 7

Orange Bowl — Louisiana State University, 19 vs. Texas A&M, 14

Rose Bowl — University of Southern California, 29 vs. University of Washington, 0

Sugar Bowl — Georgia Tech, 20 vs. University of Tulsa, 18

National Collegiate Athletic Association Basketball — University of Utah, 42 vs. Dartmouth College, 40

National Hockey League Stanley Cup — Montreal Canadiens

Kentucky Derby, Horse Racing — Pensive (Conn McCreary, jockey)

Preakness, Horse Racing — Pensive (Conn McCreary, jockey)

Belmont Stakes, Horse Racing — Bounding Home (G. L. Smith, jockey)

Masters Golf Tournament — No tournament because of war

Professional Golfers' Association Championship — Bob Hamilton

U.S.G.A. Open Championship — No tournament because of war

U.S.G.A. Amateur Championship — No tournament because of war

U.S.G.A. Women's Amateur Championship — No tournament because of war

U.S. National Tennis Tournament, Men's Singles — Frank Parker

U.S. National Tennis Tournament, Women's Singles — Pauline Betz

Indianapolis 500 Auto Race Champion — No race because of war

1945

Major League Baseball World Series — Detroit Tigers (American League), 4 vs. Chicago Cubs (National League), 3

National Football League Championship — Cleveland Rams, 15 vs. Washington Redskins, 14

Collegiate Football National Champion — Army

Heisman Trophy, Collegiate Football — Felix "Doc" Blanchard (Army)

Cotton Bowl — Oklahoma A&M, 34 vs. Texas Christian University, 0

Orange Bowl — University of Tulsa, 26 vs. Georgia Tech, 12

Rose Bowl — University of Southern California, 25 vs. University of Tennessee, 0

Sugar Bowl — Duke University, 29 vs. University of Alabama, 26

National Collegiate Athletic Association Basketball — Oklahoma A&M, 49 vs. New York University, 45

National Hockey League Stanley Cup — Toronto Maple Leafs

Kentucky Derby, Horse Racing — Hoop Jr. (Eddie Arcaro, jockey)

Preakness, Horse Racing — Polynesian (Wayne Wright, jockey)

Belmont Stakes, Horse Racing — Pavot (Eddie Arcaro, jockey)

Masters Golf Tournament — No tournament because of war

Professional Golfers' Association Championship — Byron Nelson

U.S.G.A. Open Championship — No tournament because of war

U.S.G.A. Amateur Championship — No tournament because of war

U.S.G.A. Women's Amateur Championship — No tournament because of war

U.S. National Tennis Tournament, Men's Singles — Frank Parker

U.S. National Tennis Tournament, Women's Singles — Sarah Palfrey Cooke

Indianapolis 500 Auto Race Champion — No race because of war

1946

Major League Baseball World Series — Saint Louis Cardinals (National League), 4 vs. Boston Red Sox (American League), 3

National Football League Championship — Chicago Bears, 24 vs. New York Giants, 14

All-American Football Conference — Cleveland Browns, 14 vs. New York Yankees, 9

Collegiate Football National Champion — Notre Dame

Heisman Trophy, Collegiate Football — Glenn Davis (Army)

Cotton Bowl — University of Texas, 40 vs. University of Missouri, 27

Orange Bowl — University of Miami, 13 vs. College of the Holy Cross, 6

Rose Bowl — University of Alabama, 34 vs. University of Southern California, 14

Sugar Bowl — Oklahoma A&M, 33 vs. Saint Mary's College, 13

National Collegiate Athletic Association Basketball — Oklahoma A&M, 43 vs. University of North Carolina, 40

National Hockey League Stanley Cup — Montreal Canadiens

Kentucky Derby, Horse Racing — Assault (Warren Mehrtens, jockey)

Preakness, Horse Racing — Assault (Warren Mehrtens, jockey)

Belmont Stakes, Horse Racing — Assault (Warren Mehrtens, jockey)

Masters Golf Tournament — Herman Keiser

Professional Golfers' Association Championship — Ben Hogan

U.S.G.A. Open Championship — Lloyd Mangrum

United States Women's Open Golf Championship — Patty Berg

U.S.G.A. Amateur Golf Championship — Ted Bishop

U.S.G.A. Women's Amateur Golf Championship — Babe Didrikson Zaharias

U.S. National Tennis Tournament, Men's Singles — Jack Kramer

U.S. National Tennis Tournament, Women's Singles — Pauline Betz

A.A.A. National Auto Champion — Ted Horn

Indianapolis 500 Auto Race Champion — George Robson

1947

Major League Baseball World Series — New York Yankees (American League), 4 vs. Brooklyn Dodgers (National League), 3

National Football League Championship — Chicago Cardinals, 28 vs. Philadelphia Eagles, 21

All-American Football Conference — Cleveland Browns, 14 vs. New York Yankees, 3

Collegiate Football National Champion — Notre Dame

Heisman Trophy, Collegiate Football — Johnny Lujack (Notre Dame)

Cotton Bowl — Louisiana State University, 0 vs. University of Arkansas, 0

Orange Bowl — Rice University, 8 vs. University of Tennessee, 0

Rose Bowl — University of Illinois, 45 vs. University of California, Los Angeles, 14

Sugar Bowl — University of Georgia, 20 vs. University of North Carolina, 10

Basketball Association of America Championship — Philadelphia, 4 vs. Chicago, 1

National Collegiate Athletic Association Basketball — College of the Holy Cross, 58 vs. University of Oklahoma, 47

National Hockey League Stanley Cup — Toronto Maple Leafs

Kentucky Derby, Horse Racing — Jet Pilot (Eric Guerin, jockey)

Preakness, Horse Racing — Faultless (Doug Dodson, jockey)

Belmont Stakes, Horse Racing — Phalanx (Ruperto Donosco, jockey)

Masters Golf Tournament — Jimmy Demaret

Professional Golfers' Association Championship — Jim Ferrier

Ryder Cup Professional Golf Match — United States, 11 vs. Great Britain, 1

U.S.G.A. Open Championship — Lew Worsham

United States Women's Open Golf Championship — Betty Jameson

U.S.G.A. Amateur Championship — Robert Riegel

U.S.G.A. Women's Amateur Championship — Louise Suggs

U.S. National Tennis Tournament, Men's Singles — Jack Kramer

U.S. National Tennis Tournament, Women's Singles — A. Louise Brough

A.A.A. National Auto Champion — Ted Horn

Indianapolis 500 Auto Race Champion — Mauri Rose

1948

Major League Baseball World Series — Cleveland Indians (American League), 4 vs. Boston Braves (National League), 2

National Football League Championship — Philadelphia Eagles, 7 vs. Chicago Cardinals, 0

All-American Football Conference — Cleveland Browns, 49 vs. Buffalo Bills, 7

Collegiate Football National Champion — University of Michigan

Heisman Trophy, Collegiate Football — Doak Walker (Southern Methodist University)

Cotton Bowl — Pennsylvania State University, 13 vs. Southern Methodist University, 13

Orange Bowl — Georgia Tech, 20 vs. University of Kansas, 14

Rose Bowl — University of Michigan, 49 vs. University of Southern California, 0

Sugar Bowl — University of Texas, 27 vs. University of Alabama, 7

Basketball Association of America — Baltimore Bullets, 4 vs. Philadelphia Warriors, 2

National Collegiate Athletic Association Basketball — University of Kentucky, 58 vs. Baylor University, 42

National Hockey League Stanley Cup — Toronto Maple Leafs

Kentucky Derby, Horse Racing — Citation (Eddie Arcaro, jockey)

Preakness, Horse Racing — Citation (Eddie Arcaro, jockey)

Belmont Stakes, Horse Racing — Citation (Eddie Arcaro, jockey)

Masters Golf Tournament — Claude Harmon

Professional Golfers' Association Championship — Ben Hogan

U.S.G.A. Open Championship — Ben Hogan

United States Women's Open Golf Championship — Babe Didrikson Zaharias

U.S.G.A. Amateur Championship — Willie Turnesa

U.S.G.A. Women's Amateur Championship — Grace Lenczyk

U.S. National Tennis Tournament, Men's Singles — Pancho Gonzales

U.S. National Tennis Tournament, Women's Singles — Margaret Osborne du Pont

A.A.A. National Auto Champion — Ted Horn

Indianapolis 500 Auto Race Champion — Mauri Rose

1949

Major League Baseball World Series — New York Yankees (American League), 4 vs. Brooklyn Dodgers (National League), 1

National Football League Championship — Philadelphia Eagles, 14 vs. Los Angeles Rams, 0

All-American Football Conference — Cleveland Browns, 21 vs. San Francisco 49ers, 7

Collegiate Football National Champion — Notre Dame

Heisman Trophy, Collegiate Football — Leon Hart (Notre Dame)

Cotton Bowl — Southern Methodist University, 21 vs. University of Oregon, 13

Orange Bowl — University of Texas, 41 vs. University of Georgia, 28

Rose Bowl — Northwestern University, 20 vs. University of California, 14

Sugar Bowl — University of Oklahoma, 14 vs. University of North Carolina, 6

Basketball Association of America — Minneapolis, 4 vs. Washington, 2

National Collegiate Athletic Association Basketball — University of Kentucky, 40 vs. Oklahoma A&M, 36

National Hockey League Stanley Cup — Toronto Maple Leafs

Kentucky Derby, Horse Racing — Ponder (Steve Brooks, jockey)

Preakness, Horse Racing — Capot (Theodore "Ted" Adkinson, jockey)

Belmont Stakes, Horse Racing — Capot (Theodore "Ted" Adkinson, jockey)

Masters Golf Tournament — Sam Snead

Professional Golfers' Association Championship — Sam Snead

U.S.G.A. Open Championship — Cary Middlecoff

United States Women's Open Golf Championship — Louise Suggs

U.S.G.A. Amateur Championship — Charles Coe

U.S.G.A. Women's Amateur Championship — Dorothy Porter

Ryder Cup Professional Golf Match — United States, 7 vs. Great Britain, 5

U.S. National Tennis Tournament, Men's Singles — Pancho Gonzales

U.S. National Tennis Tournament, Women's Singles — Margaret Osborne du Pont

A.A.A. National Auto Champion — Johnny Parsons

Indianapolis 500 Auto Race Champion — Bill Holland

DEATHS

Sam Baroudi, 21, boxer, 26 February 1948.

Charles Behan, professional football player, killed in war, 1944.

Charles W. Bidwell, 51, owner of the Chicago Cardinals football team, in Chicago, Illinois, 19 April 1947.

Jack "Chappie" Blackburn, 58, trainer of heavyweight champion Joe Louis and lightweight boxer from 1900 to 1923, Chicago, Illinois, 23 April 1943.

Al Blozis, New York Giant tackle, killed in war, 1945.

Ernest Edward "Tiny" Bonham, 36, baseball pitcher, in Pittsburgh, Pennsylvania, 15 September 1949.

Caleb S. Bragg, 56, automobile racer, 24 October 1943.

William Gibbons Bramham, 72, president of the National Association of Professional Baseball Leagues from 1932 to 1946, in Durham, North Carolina, 8 July 1947.

Sam Breadon, 72, owner of the Saint Louis Cardinals baseball club, in Saint Louis, Missouri, 10 May 1949.

Roger Bresnahan, 64, baseball player, 4 December 1944.

Jack Burke, boxer who fought the longest (110 rounds) gloved boxing match in history in 1893, in Plainfield, New Jersey, 14 February 1942.

Christian K. "Red" Cagle, 37, all-American halfback at Army, in New York City, 23 December 1942.

Frank Calder, 65, president of the National Hockey League, in Montreal, Canada, 4 February 1943.

Hal Chase, 64, former professional baseball player, in Colusa, California, 18 May 1947.

James J. "Jimmy" Collins, baseball player, 6 March 1943.

Harry H. "Jasper" Davis, 74, former baseball player, in Philadelphia, Pennsylvania, 11 August 1947.

Jack Delaney, 48, light-heavyweight boxing champion of the world (1926–1927), in Katonah, New Jersey, 27 November 1948.

Alfred De Oro, 86, former world champion billiards player, in North Pelham, New York, 23 April 1948.

Jimmy Doyle, boxer, 25 June 1947.

Vince Dundee, 41, middleweight boxing champion of the world in 1933–1934, in Glendale, California, 27 July 1949.

John Joseph Evers, 65, former professional baseball player, in Albany, New York, 28 March 1947.

Alexander H. Findlay, 76, golf enthusiast credited with introducing the game to the United States, in Germantown, Pennsylvania, 16 April 1942.

Robert T. Fisher, 53, former Harvard University football star and coach, in Newton, Massachusetts, 7 July 1942.

John B. Foster, 77, baseball writer, 29 September 1941.

Hugh Fullerton, 72, baseball writer who broke the Chicago "Black Sox" scandal in 1919, in Dunedin, Florida, 27 December 1945.

Joseph Garber, senior national singles handball champion, killed in war, 1945.

Elmer Gedeon, baseball player with the Washington Senators, killed in war, 1944.

Lou Gehrig, 37, former New York Yankees baseball player, in New York City, 2 June 1941.

Benjamin Griffith, 68, athletic director at Bucknell University, 18 March 1945.

Bill Harmon, golfer, killed in war, 1945.

Ralph Hepburn, race car driver, in Indianapolis, Indiana, 16 May 1948.

J. W. Hinton, professional football player, killed in war, 1944.

Thomas Hitchcock, Sr., 80, sportsman, 29 September 1941.

Tommy Hitchcock, 44, polo player, killed in war, 19 April 1944.

William Ingram, 46, college football coach, killed in war, 2 June 1943.

Jack Johnson, 68, baseball pitcher, Raleigh, North Carolina, 10 June 1946.

Smiley Johnson, Green Bay Packers guard, killed in war, 1945.

Walter Johnson, 59, former Hall of Fame baseball pitcher, 10 December 1946.

William M. "Little Bill" Johnston, 51, tennis champion, 1 May 1946.

Howard Harding Jones, 55, football coach, 27 July 1941.

Nile Kinnick, 24, all-American halfback at the University of Iowa, 2 June 1943.

Kenesaw Mountain Landis, 78, baseball commissioner, in Chicago, Illinois, 25 November 1944.

Col. Emery Ellsworth Larson, 46, former football coach at the U.S. Naval Academy, in Atlanta, Georgia, 7 November 1945.

Emanuel Lasker, 72, former world chess champion, 11 January 1941.

Tony Lazzeri, 42, former New York Yankee second baseman, 7 August 1946.

Barney "Battling Levinsky" Lebrowitz, 59, world light heavyweight boxing champion (1916–1920), in Philadelphia, Pennsylvania, 12 February 1949.

Benny Leonard, 51, lightweight boxing world champion (1917–1925), 18 April 1947.

Ben Loving, golfer, killed in war, 1945.

Man o' War, 30, race horse, 1 November 1947.

Frank James Marshall, 67, chess expert, 10 November 1944.

Graham McNamee, noted NBC sports announcer, in New York City, 9 May 1943.

Marion Miley, 37, the number-two ranked professional golfer in 1939, 28 September 1941.

Jim Mooney, professional football player, killed in war, 1944.

William G. Morgan, 72, the originator of the game of volleyball, in Lockport, New York, 27 December 1942.

Stanley Grafton Mortimer, 56, amateur tennis champion, in New York City, 5 April 1947.

John A. "Jack" Munroe, 67, prizefighter, in Toronto, Canada, 13 February 1942.

Berna "Barney" Eli Oldfield, race car driver, 4 October 1946.

Charles William Paddock, 42, track star, killed in war, 21 July 1943.

Herb Pennock, 53, baseball player, in New York City, 30 January 1948.

Thomas Pettit, 86, tennis player, 17 October 1946.

Jake Powell, 40, former baseball player, in Washington, D.C., 4 November 1948.

Amos Rusie, 71, pitcher for the New York Giants in the 1890s, in Seattle, Washington, 6 December 1942.

George Herman "Babe" Ruth, 53, baseball player, in New York City, 16 August 1948.

Tommy Ryan, former welterweight and middleweight boxing champion of the world, in Granada Hills, California, 3 August 1948.

Alex Santilli, Fordham University football great, killed in war, 1944.

Richard D. Sears, 81, tennis champion, 8 April 1943.

John Shimkonis, golfer, killed in war, 1945.

Henry W. Slocum, 86, former American tennis champion, in New York City, 22 January 1949.

George F. Slosson, 95, billiards player, 21 June 1949.

Gus Sonnenberg, 44, former Dartmouth football star and professional wrestler, 12 September 1944.

Stephen Stavers, swimmer, killed in war, 1944.

Louis E. Stoddard, 70, former international polo star and chairman of the U.S. Polo Association from 1922 to 1936, in Los Angeles, California, 9 March 1948.

John Sutherland, 59, Pittsburgh Steelers coach, in Pittsburgh, Pennsylvania, 12 April 1948.

Joe Tinker, 68, former baseball player with the Chicago Cubs, in Orlando, Florida, 27 July 1948.

Torger Tokle, holder of twenty-four snow ski records, killed in war, 1945.

Michael "Smiling Mickey" Welch, 82, New York pitching star in the 1880s and 1890s and winner of three hundred major league baseball games, in Nashua, New Hampshire, 30 July 1941.

Chet Wetterlund, professional football player, killed in war, 1944.

Col. Matt J. Winn, 88, Kentucky Derby promoter, 6 October 1949.

Fielding Harris Yost, 75, college football coach, 20 August 1946.

Lou Zamperini, 25, star miler, killed in war, 27 May 1943.

PUBLICATIONS

Louis Henry Baker, *Do You Know Your Football?* (New York: Barnes, 1946);

Baker, *Football Facts and Figures* (New York: Farrar & Rinehart, 1945);

Gordon Arnold Campbell, *Ninth Series of Famous American Athletes of Today* (Boston: Page, 1946);

Allison Danzig and Peter Brandwein, eds., *Sports' Golden Age, A Close-up of the Fabulous Twenties* (New York: Harper, 1948);

Joe DiMaggio and Red Barber, *Baseball for Everyone: A Treasury of Baseball Lore and Instruction for Fans and Players* (New York: Whittlesey House, 1948);

Ray Oscar Duncan, *Six Man Football* (New York: Barnes, 1940);

Nat Fleischer, *The Heavyweight Championship: an Informal History of Heavyweight Boxing from 1719 to the Present Day* (New York: Putnam, 1949);

Stanley Bernard Frank, ed., *Sports Extra; Classics of Sports Reporting* (New York: Barnes, 1944);

Arnold Gingrich, ed., *Esquire's Second Sports Reader* (New York: Barnes, 1946);

Herbert Butler Graffis, ed., *Esquire's First Sports Reader* (New York: Barnes, 1945);

Frank Graham, *The Brooklyn Dodgers* (New York: Putnam, 1945);

Harry Grayson, *They Played the Game, the Story of Baseball Greats* (New York: Barnes, 1946);

John V. Grumbach, *The Saga of Sock: A Complete Story of Boxing* (New York: Barnes, 1949);

Edwin L. Haislet, *Boxing* (New York: Ronald, 1940);

Gertrude Hawley, *An Anatomical Analysis of Sports* (New York: Barnes, 1941);

Harold Kaese, *Eighty Stories of Famous American Athletes of Today* (Boston: Page, 1942);

Harold Keith, *Sports and Games* (New York: Crowell, 1941);

John Kieran, *The American Sporting Scene* (New York: Macmillan, 1942);

Frank William Leahy, *Notre Dame Football: The T Formation* (New York: Prentice-Hall, 1949);

Ira Lepouce Lee, *Low and Inside: A Book of Baseball Anecdotes, Oddities, and Curiosities* (Garden City, N.Y.: Doubleday, 1949);

Frederick George Lieb, *The Story of the World Series, An Informal History* (New York: Putnam, 1949);

Thomas Meany, *Baseball's Greatest Teams* (New York: Barnes, 1949);

Frank Grant Menke, *The New Encyclopedia of Sports* (New York: Barnes, 1947);

Margaret Hinkel Meyer, *Technic of Team Sports for Women* (Philadelphia: Saunders, 1942);

James Joseph Aloysius Powers, *Baseball Personalities, the Most Colorful Figures of All Time* (New York: Field, 1949);

Harold Rice, *Within the Ropes: Championship Action* (New York: Stephen-Paul, 1946);

Don Cash Seaton, *Safety in Sports* (New York: Prentice-Hall, 1948);

J. G. Taylor Spinks, *Life Story of Amos Alonzo Stagg: Grand Old Man of Football* (Saint Louis: Spinks, 1946);

William Stern, *Favorite Baseball Stories* (Garden City, N.Y.: Blue Ribbon, 1949);

Thomas Louis Stix, *"Say It Ain't So Joe"* (New York: Boni & Gaer, 1947);

Dorothy Sumption, *Sports for Women* (New York: Prentice-Hall, 1940);

John Roberts Tunis, *Sport for the Fun of It* (New York: Barnes, 1940);

Tunis, *Yea! Wildcats!* (New York: Harcourt, Brace, 1944);

Archie Ward, *Frank Leahy and the Fighting Irish: The Story of Notre Dame Football* (New York: Putnam, 1944);

Stanley Woodward, *Sports Page* (New York: Simon & Schuster, 1949);

Rachel Dunaven Yocum, *Individual Sports for Men and Women* (New York: Barnes, 1947).

GENERAL REFERENCES

GENERAL

John Brooks, *The Great Leap: The Past Twenty-five Years in America* (New York: Harper & Row, 1966);

Mary Kupiec Cayton, Elliott J. Gorn, and Peter T. Williams, eds. *Encyclopedia of American Social History,* 3 volumes (New York: Scribners, 1993);

Chronicle of the 20th Century (Mount Kisco, N.Y.: Chronicle, 1987);

Current Biography Yearbook (New York: Wilson, [various years]);

John Patrick Diggins, *The Proud Decades* (New York: Norton, 1988);

John W. Dodds, *Everyday Life in Twentieth Century America* (New York: Putnam, 1965);

Paul Johnson, *Modern Times: From the Twenties to the Nineties,* revised edition (New York: HarperCollins, 1991);

Thomas M. Leonard, *Day by Day: The Forties* (New York: Facts On File, 1977);

Charles D. Lowery and John F. Marszalek, eds., *Encyclopedia of African-American Civil Rights: From Emancipation to the Present* (Westport, Conn.: Greenwood Press, 1992);

Iwan W. Morgan and Neil A. Wynn, *America's Century: Perspective on U.S. History Since 1900* (New York: Holmes & Meier, 1993);

Michael Downey Rice, *Prentice-Hall Dictionary of Business, Finance, and Law* (Englewood Cliffs, N.J.: Prentice-Hall, 1983);

Barbara Sicherman, Carol Hurd Green with Ilene Kantrov and Hariette Walker, eds., *Notable American Women: The Modern Period, A Biographical Dictionary* (Cambridge, Mass.: Harvard University Press, 1980);

This Fabulous Century, 1940–1949 (Alexandria, Va.: Time-Life Books, 1969);

Time Lines on File (New York: Facts On File, 1988);

James Trager, *The People's Chronology* (New York: Holt, Rinehart & Winston, 1979);

Claire Walter, *Winners: The Blue Ribbon Encyclopedia of Awards* (New York: Facts On File, 1982);

Leigh Carol Yuster and others, eds., *Ulrich's International Periodicals Directory: A Classified Guide to Current Periodicals, Foreign and Domestic, 1986–1987,* twenty-fifth edition, 2 volumes (New York & London: R.R. Bowker, 1986).

ART

H. Harvard Arnason, *History of Modern Art: Painting, Sculpture, Photography,* third edition (Englewood Cliffs, N.J.: Prentice-Hall, 1986);

Whitney Balliett, *American Musicians: Fifty Portraits in Jazz* (New York: Oxford University Press, 1986);

Cedric Belfrage, *The American Inquisition, 1945–1960* (New York: Thunder's Mouth Press, 1989);

James E. B. Breslin, *Mark Rothko: A Biography* (Chicago: University of Chicago Press, 1993);

Humphrey Carpenter, *A Serious Character: The Life of Ezra Pound* (Boston: Houghton Mifflin, 1988);

Patrick Carr, ed., *The Illustrated History of Country Music* (Garden City, N.Y.: Doubleday, 1980);

Virginia Carr, *The Lonely Hunter: A Biography of Carson McCullers* (New York: Doubleday, 1975);

Riva Castleman and Guy Davenport, eds., *Art of the Forties* (New York: Metropolitan Museum of Art, 1991);

Samuel B. Charters and Leonard Kunstadt, *Jazz: A History of the New York Scene* (Garden City, N.Y.: Doubleday, 1962);

Gilbert Chase, *America's Music: From the Pilgrims to the Present,* revised third edition (Chicago: University of Illinois Press, 1987);

Jonathan Coe, *Humphrey Bogart: Take It and Like It* (New York: Grove Weidenfeld, 1991);

Malcolm Cowley, *A Second Flowering* (New York: Penguin, 1984);

Francis Davis, *The History of the Blues* (New York: Hyperion, 1995);

Emile De Antonio and Mitch Tuchman, *Painters Painting: A Candid History of the Modern Art Scene, 1940–1970* (New York: Abbeville, 1984);

Agnes de Mille, *America Dances* (New York: Macmillan, 1980);

de Mille, *Martha: The Life and Work of Martha Graham* (New York: Random House, 1991);

Thomas Doherty, *Projections of War* (New York: Columbia University Press, 1993);

Philip H. Ennis, *The Seventh Stream: The Emergence of Rocknroll in American Popular Music* (Hanover, N.H.: University Press of New England, 1992);

Rusty E. Frank, *Tap!: The Greatest Tap Dance Stars and Their Stories, 1900–1955* (New York: William Morris, 1990);

Francis Frascina, ed., *Pollock and After: The Critical Debate* (New York: HarperCollins, 1985);

Otto Friedrich, *City of Nets* (New York: Harper and Row, 1986);

John Gassner, ed., *Best American Plays: Third Series, 1945–1951* (New York: Crown, 1952);

Addison Gayle, *Richard Wright: Ordeal of a Native Son* (Garden City, N.Y.: Anchor/Doubleday, 1980);

Gary Giddins, *Celebrating Bird* (New York: Beech Tree Books, 1987);

Ira Gitler, *Jazz Masters of the Forties* (New York: Macmillan, 1966);

Gitler, *Swing to Bop: An Oral History of The Transition in Jazz in the 1940s* (New York: Oxford University Press, 1985);

Lois G. Gordon and Alan Gordon, *American Chronicle: Six Decades in American Life* (New York: Atheneum, 1987);

Martha Graham, *Blood Memory* (New York: Doubleday, 1991);

Thomas B. Hess, *Six Painters* (Houston, Tex.: Rice University Press, 1968);

James Howard, *The Complete Films of Orson Welles* (New York: Citadel Press, 1991);

John Howlett, *Frank Sinatra* (London: Plexus, 1980);

H. W. Janson, *History of Art*, fifth edition (New York: Abrams, 1995);

Barry D. Karl, *The Uneasy State* (Chicago: University of Chicago Press, 1983);

Frederick R. Karl, *American Fictions, 1940–1980* (New York: Harper & Row, 1983);

Clayton Koppes and Gregory Black, *Hollywood Goes to War* (New York: Free Press, 1987);

Allan Lewis, *American Plays and Playwrights of the Contemporary Theatre* (New York: Crown, 1965);

Richard R. Lingeman, *Don't You Know There's A War On?: The American Home Front, 1941–1945* (New York: Putnam, 1970);

Bill C. Malone, *Country Music, U.S.A.* (Austin: University of Texas, 1985);

Edward Margolies, *Native Sons* (New York: Lippincott, 1968);

Joseph H. Mazo, *Prime Movers: The Makers of Modern Dance in America* (Princeton, N.J.: Princeton Book Company, 1977);

Don McDonagh, *The Complete Guide to Modern Dance* (Garden City, N.Y.: Doubleday, 1976);

McDonagh, *George Balanchine* (Boston: Twayne, 1983);

Anna Moszynska, *Abstract Art* (New York: Thames & Hudson, 1990);

Steven Naifeh and Gregory White Smith, *Jackson Pollock: An American Saga* (New York: HarperCollins, 1991);

Paul Oliver, Max Harrison, and William Bolcom, *The New Grove Gospel, Blues and Jazz* (New York: Norton, 1986);

Richard H. Pells, *The Liberal Mind in a Conservative Age* (New York: Harper & Row, 1985);

Regenia Perry, *Free Within Ourselves* (Washington, D.C.: National Museum of American Art, Smithsonian Institution, in association with Pomegranate Artbooks, 1992);

James A. Porter, *Modern Negro Art* (Washington, D.C.: Howard University Press, 1992);

David Revill, *The Roaring Silence: John Cage: A Life* (New York: Arcade, 1992);

Nikos Sangos, *Concepts of Modern Art* (New York: Thames & Hudson, 1994);

Russell Sanjek, *American Popular Music and Its Business Vol. III, From 1900 to 1984* (New York: Oxford University Press, 1988);

Moira Shearer, *Balletmaster: A Dancer's View of George Balanchine* (London: Sidgwick & Jackson, 1986);

Alain Silver and Elizabeth Ward, *Film Noir: An Encyclopedic Reference to the American Style*, third edition (Woodstock, N.Y.: Overlook Press, 1992);

Ernestine Stodelle, *Deep Song: The Dance Story of Martha Graham* (New York: Schirmer, 1984);

David Stowe, *Swing Changes* (Cambridge, Mass.: Harvard University Press, 1994);

Vera Stravinsky and Robert Craft, *Stravinsky in Pictures and Documents* (New York: Simon & Schuster, 1978);

Nicholas E. Tawa, *Serenading the Reluctant Eagle: American Musical Life, 1925–1945* (New York: Schirmer, 1984);

Nick Tosches, *Country: Living Legends and Dying Metaphors in America's Biggest Music* (London: Secker & Warburg, 1985);

Katrina Vanden Heuvel, ed., *The Nation, 1865–1990* (New York: Thunder's Mouth Press, 1990);

Edmund Wilson, *The Forties: From Notebooks and Diaries of the Period* (New York: Farrar, Straus & Giroux, 1983);

William Wright, *Lillian Hellman: The Image, the Woman* (New York: Simon & Schuster, 1986).

BUSINESS AND THE ECONOMY

John Brooks, *The Autobiography of American Business* (Garden City, N.Y.: Doubleday, 1974);

Keith L. Bryant, Jr., ed., *Encyclopedia of American Business History and Biography: Railroads in the Age of Regulation, 1900–1980* (Columbia, S.C.: Bruccoli Clark Layman / New York: Facts On File, 1988);

Bryant, and Henry C. Dethloff, *A History of American Business* (Englewood Cliffs, N.J.: Prentice-Hall, 1983);

Edward F. Denison, *The Sources of Economic Growth in the United States and the Alternatives Before Us* (New York: Committee for Economic Development, 1962);

John M. Dobson, *A History of American Enterprise* (Englewood Cliffs, N.J.: Prentice Hall, 1988);

John Kenneth Galbraith, *Economic Development* (Cambridge, Mass.: Harvard University Press, 1964);

George Gilder, *The Spirit of Enterprise* (New York: Simon & Schuster, 1984);

Charles E. Gilland, Jr., ed., *Readings in Business Responsibility* (Braintree, Mass.: D. H. Mark, 1969);

James R. Green, *The World of the Worker: Labor in Twentieth-Century America* (New York: Hill & Wang, 1980);

William M. Leary, ed., *Encyclopedia of American Business History and Biography: The Airline Industry* (Columbia, S.C.: Bruccoli Clark Layman / New York: Facts On File, 1992);

Ann R. Markusen, *The Rise of the Gunbelt: The Military Remapping of Industrial America* (New York: Oxford University Press, 1991);

George S. May, ed., *Encyclopedia of American Business History and Biography: Banking and Finance, 1913–1989* (Columbia, S.C.: Bruccoli Clark Layman / New York: Facts On File, 1990);

Glenn Porter, ed., *Encyclopedia of American Economic History: Studies of the Principal Movements and Ideas,* 3 volumes (New York: Scribners, 1980);

Joseph C. Pusateri, *A History of American Business* (Arlington Heights, Ill.: Harlan Davidson, 1984);

John B. Rae, *The American Automobile: A Brief History* (Chicago & London: University of Chicago Press, 1965);

Sidney Ratner, James H. Soltow, and Richard Sylla, *The Evolution of the American Economy* (New York: Basic Books, 1979);

Graham Robinson, *Pictorial History of the Automobile* (New York: W. H. Smith, 1987);

Larry Schweikart, ed., *Encyclopedia of American Business History and Biography: Banking and Finance, 1913–1989* (Columbia, S.C.: Bruccoli Clark Layman / New York: Facts On File, 1990);

Bruce Seely, ed., *Encyclopedia of American Business History and Biography: Iron and Steel in the Twentieth Century* (Columbia, S.C.: Bruccoli Clark Layman / New York: Facts On File, 1993);

Herbert Alexander Simon, *The New Science of Management Decision* (New York: Harper & Row, 1960).

FASHION

Pierre Balmain, *My Years and Seasons* (London: Cassell, 1964);

Michael Batterberry and Ariane Batterberry, *Mirror, Mirror: A Social History of Fashion* (New York: Holt, Rinehart & Winston, 1977);

Helen L. Brockman, *The Theory of Fashion Design* (New York: Wiley, 1965);

The Changing American Woman: 200 Years of American Fashion (New York: Fairchild, 1976);

Mila Contini, *Fashion: From Ancient Egypt to the Present Day* (New York: Odyssey, 1965);

Maryanne Dolan, *Vintage Clothing, 1880–1960: Identification and Value Guide* (Florence, Ala.: Books Americana, 1984);

Elizabeth Ewing, *History of Twentieth Century Fashion* (Totowa, N.J.: Barnes & Noble, 1986);

Harper's Bazaar: 100 Years of the American Female (New York: Random House, 1967);

Sandra Ley, *Fashion for Everyone: The Story of Ready-to-Wear, 1870–1970s* (New York: Scribners, 1975);

Valerie Lloyd, *The Art of Vogue Photographic Covers: Fifty Years of Fashion and Design* (New York: Harmony, 1986);

Lloyd, *Fabric and Fashion: Twenty Years of Costume Council Gifts* (Los Angeles: Los Angeles County Museum of Art, 1974);

Lloyd, *McDowell's Directory of Twentieth Century Fashion* (Englewood Cliffs, N.J.: Prentice-Hall, 1985);

Mary Shaw Ryan, *Clothing: A Study in Human Behavior* (New York: Holt, Rinehart & Winston, 1966);

Donald Stowell and Erin Wertenberger, *A Century of Fashion 1865–1965* (Chicago: Encyclopedia Britannica, 1987);

Jane Trahey, ed., *Harper's Bazaar: 100 Years of the American Female* (New York: Random House, 1967);

Trahey, *The Mode in Costume* (New York: Scribners, 1958);

Barry James Wood, *Show Windows: Seventy-five Years of the Art of Display* (New York: Congdon & Weed, 1982).

GOVERNMENT AND POLITICS

Gar Alperovitz, *Atomic Diplomacy: Hiroshima and Potsdam* (New York: Simon & Schuster, 1965);

Stephen E. Ambrose, *Rise to Globalism,* seventh revised edition (New York: Penguin, 1993);

Harry Elmer Barnes, *Perpetual War For Perpetual Peace: A Critical Examination of the Foreign Policy of Franklin Delano Roosevelt* (New York: Greenwood Press, 1969);

Richard J. Barnet, *The Roots of War* (New York: Atheneum, 1972);

John Morton Blum, *V Was For Victory: Politics and American Culture During World War II* (New York: Harcourt Brace Jovanovich, 1976);

Robert A. Dallek, *Franklin D. Roosevelt and American Foreign Policy, 1932–1945* (New York: Oxford University Press, 1981);

Robert A. Divine, *Roosevelt and World War II* (Baltimore: Johns Hopkins University Press, 1969);

Robert J. Donovan, *Conflict and Crisis: The Presidency of Harry S. Truman, 1945–1948* (New York: Norton, 1977);

Henry L. Feingold, *The Politics of Rescue: The Roosevelt Administration and the Holocaust, 1938–1945,* expanded and updated edition (New York: Holocaust Library, 1980);

Herbert Feis, *The Road To Pearl Harbor* (Princeton: Princeton University Press, 1971);

Richard M. Freeland, *The Truman Doctrine and the Origins of McCarthyism: Foreign Policy, Domestic Politics, and Internal Security, 1946–1948* (New York: Schocken, 1974);

Frank Freidel, *FDR: Launching the New Deal* (Boston: Little, Brown, 1973);

John Lewis Gaddis, *The Long Peace: Inquiries into the History of the Cold War* (New York: Oxford University Press, 1987);

Gaddis, *The United States and the Origins of the Cold War, 1941–1947* (New York: Columbia University Press, 1972);

John Kenneth Galbraith, *The Affluent Society* (Boston: Houghton Mifflin, 1960);

Eric F. Goldman, *A Rendezvous With Destiny: A History of Modern American Reform* (New York: Knopf, 1952; revised and abridged edition, New York: Vintage, 1956);

Doris Kearns Goodwin, *No Ordinary Time: Franklin and Eleanor Roosevelt: The Homefront in World War II* (New York: Simon & Schuster, 1994);

William Graebner, *The Age of Doubt: American Thought and Culture in the 1940s* (Boston: Twayne, 1990);

Alonzo L. Hamby, *Beyond the New Deal: Harry S Truman and American Liberalism* (New York: Columbia University Press, 1973);

Hamby, ed., *Harry S Truman and the Fair Deal* (Lexington, Mass.: Heath, 1974);

Richard Hofstadter, *The American Political Tradition and the Men Who Made It* (New York: Knopf, 1948);

Jeanne Wakatsuki Houston and James D. Houston, *Farewell to Manzanar: A True Story of Japanese-American Experience during and after the World War II Internment* (Boston: Houghton Mifflin, 1973);

William R. Keylor, *The Twentieth-Century World: An International History* (New York: Oxford University Press, 1984);

Walter LaFeber and others, *The American Century* (New York: McGraw-Hill, 1990);

Melvyn P. Leffler, *A Preponderance of Power: National Security, the Truman Administration, and the Cold War* (Stanford, Cal.: Stanford University Press, 1992);

Richard Lingeman, *Don't You Know There's a War on? The American Home Front, 1941–1945* (New York: Putnam, 1970);

Haskell Lookstein, *Were We Our Brothers Keepers?: The Public Response of American Jews to the Holocaust, 1938–1944* (New York: Hartmore House, 1985);

Thomas McCormick, *America's Half-Century: United States Foreign Policy in the Cold War* (Baltimore: Johns Hopkins University Press, 1989);

Seymour Melman, *Pentagon Capitalism: The Political Economy of War* (New York: McGraw-Hill, 1970);

Melman, *The Permanent War Economy: American Capitalism in Decline* (New York: Simon & Schuster, 1974);

Arnold A. Offner, *American Appeasement: United States Foreign Policy and Germany, 1933–1938* (New York: Norton, 1976);

Geoffrey Perrett, *Days of Sadness, Years of Triumph: The American People, 1939–1945* (Madison: University of Wisconsin Press, 1985);

Richard Polenberg, *War and Society: The United States, 1941–1945* (Philadelphia: Lippincott, 1972);

Bruce M. Russett, *No Clear and Present Danger* (New York: Harper & Row, 1972);

Arthur M. Schlesinger, Jr., *The Age of Roosevelt,* 3 volumes (Boston: Houghton Mifflin, 1956–1960);

Schlesinger, ed., *The History of American Presidential Elections, 1789–1968* (New York: Chelsea House, 1971);

Schlesinger, ed., *History of U.S. Political Parties* (New York: Chelsea House, 1973);

Edward H. Spicer, Asael T. Hansen, Katherine Luomala, and Marvin K. Opler, *Impounded People: Japanese-Americans in the Relocation Centers* (Tucson: University of Arizona Press, 1969);

C. L. Sulzberger, *The American Heritage Picture History of World War II* (New York: American Heritage Publishing, 1966);

James L. Sundquist, *Dynamics of the Party System: Alignment and Realignment of Political Parties in the United States,* revised edition (Washington, D.C.: Brookings Institution, 1983);

William Appleman Williams, *The Contours of American History* (Chicago: Quadrangle Books, 1966);

John E. Wiltz, *From Isolation to War, 1931–1941* (New York: Crowell, 1968);

Allan M. Winkler, *Home Front U.S.A.: America During World War II* (Arlington Heights, Ill.: Harlan Davidson, 1986);

David S. Wyman, *The Abandonment of the Jews: America and the Holocaust, 1941–1945* (New York: Pantheon, 1984);

Daniel Yergin, *Shattered Peace: The Origins of the Cold War and the National Security State* (Boston: Houghton Mifflin, 1977);

Howard Zinn, *Postwar America, 1945–1971* (Indianapolis: Bobbs-Merrill, 1973).

LAW

John C. Armor and Peter Wright, *Manzanar* (New York: New York Times Books, 1988);

Allan Bosworth, *America's Concentration Camps* (New York: Norton, 1967);

Harold W. Chase, *Security and Liberty; The Problem of Native Communists, 1947–1955* (Garden City, N.Y.: Doubleday, 1955);

Steven Chin, *When Justice Failed: The Fred Korematsu Story* (Austin, Tex.: Raintree Steck-Vaughn, 1993);

Commission On The Bicentennial Of The United States, *The Supreme Court Of The United States — Its Beginnings And Its Justices 1790–1991* (Washington, D.C.: Commission On The Bicentennial Of The United States, 1992);

Robert F. Cushman, *Leading Constitutional Decisions* (Englewood Cliffs, N.J.: Prentice-Hall, 1977);

William O. Douglas, *The Court Years, 1939–1975* (New York: Random House, 1980);

Kermit L. Hall, ed., *The Oxford Companion to the Supreme Court* (New York: Oxford University Press, 1992);

Maureen Harrison and Steve Gilbert, eds., *Landmark Decisions Of The United States Supreme Court II* (Beverly Hills: Excellent Books, 1992);

Alger Hiss, *Recollections Of A Life* (New York: Holt, 1988);

Alfred H. Kelly, Winfred A. Harbison, and Herman Belz, *The American Constitution, Its Origins and Development — Volume II,* seventh edition (New York: Norton, 1991);

Jethro K. Lieberman, *The Enduring Constitution, A Bicentennial Perspective* (New York: West, 1987);

Robert G. McCloskey, *The American Supreme Court* (Chicago: University of Chicago Press, 1960);

Robert Morris, ed., *Encyclopedia of American History,* sixth edition (New York: Harper & Row, 1982);

Jay Robert Nash, *Bloodletters And Badmen* (New York: Evans, 1973);

Bernard Schwartz, *The American Heritage History of The Law In America* (New York: McGraw-Hill, 1974);

John Tateishi, *And Justice For All — An Oral History Of The Japanese American Detention Camps* (New York: Random House, 1984);

Telford Taylor, *The Anatomy Of The Nuremberg Trials* (New York: Knopf, 1992);

Treaties And Alliances Of The World (New York: Scribners, 1968);

Sanford J. Ungar, *FBI* (Boston: Atlantic Monthly Press/Little, Brown, 1976).

LIFESTYLES AND SOCIAL TRENDS

Michael Barone, *Our Country: The Shaping of America from Roosevelt to Reagan* (New York: Free Press, 1990);

A. Russell Buchanan, *Black Americans in World War II* (Santa Barbara & London: Clio, 1977);

William Chafe, *The American Woman: Her Changing Social, Economic, and Political Roles, 1920–1970* (New York: Oxford University Press, 1972);

Stephanie Coontz, *The Way We Never Were: American Families and the Nostalgia Trap* (New York: Basic Books, 1992);

John P. Diggins, *The Proud Decades: America in War and in Peace, 1941–1960* (New York: Norton, 1988);

Diggins, *Up From Communism: Conservative Odysseys in American Intellectual History* (New York: Harper & Row, 1975);

Andreas Feininger, *New York in the Forties* (New York: Dover, 1978);

Peter G. Filene, *Him/Her/Self: Sex Roles in Modern America* (New York: Harcourt Brace Jovanovich, 1974);

John Hope Franklin and Isidore Starr, *The Negro in Twentieth Century America* (New York: Random House, 1967);

Estelle B. Freedman and John D'Emilio, *Intimate Matters: A History of Sexuality in America* (New York: Harper & Row, 1988);

Susan M. Hartmann, *The Home Front and Beyond: American Women in the 1940s* (Boston: Twayne, 1982);

Kenneth T. Jackson, *Crabgrass Frontier: The Suburbanization of the United States* (New York: Oxford University Press, 1985);

Ulysses Lee, *The Employment of Negro Troops,* United States Army in World War II Special Studies no. 8 (Washington, D.C.: Office of the Chief of Military History, United States Army, 1966);

Elaine Tyler May, *Homeward Bound: American Families in the Cold War Era* (New York: Basic Books, 1988);

Steven Mintz and Susan Kellogg, *Domestic Revolutions: A Social History of American Family Life* (New York: Free Press, 1988);

John Modell, *Into Own's Own: From Youth to Adulthood in the United States, 1920–1975* (Berkeley: University of California Press, 1989);

Rosalind Rosenberg, *Divided Lives: American Women in the Twentieth Century* (New York: Hill & Wang, 1992).

MEDIA

Association of National Advertisers, *Magazine Circulation and Rate Trends: 1940–1967* (New York: ANA, 1969);

Charles O. Bennett, *Facts Without Opinion: First Fifty Years of the Audit Bureau of Circulation* (Chicago: ABC, 1965);

Mike Benton, *The Comic Book in America: An Illustrated History* (Dallas: Taylor, 1989);

Tim Brooks, *The Complete Directory to Prime Time TV Stars: 1946–Present* (New York: Ballantine, 1987);

Robert Campbell, *The Golden Years of Broadcasting: A Celebration of the First 50 Years of Radio and TV on NBC* (New York: Scribners, 1972);

Harry Castleman and Walter J. Podrazik, *Watching TV: Four Decades of American Television* (New York: McGraw-Hill, 1982);

John Dunning, *Tune in Yesterday: The Ultimate Encyclopedia of Old-Time Radio 1925–1976* (Englewood Cliffs, N.J.: Prentice-Hall, 1976);

Walter B. Emery, *National and International Systems of Broadcasting: Their History, Operation, and Control* (East Lansing: Michigan State University Press, 1969);

Amy Janello and Brennon Jones, *The American Magazine* (New York: Abrams, 1991);

Laurence W. Lichty and Malachi Topping, *American Broadcasting: A Source Book on the History of Radio and Television* (New York: Hastings House, 1975);

J. Fred MacDonald, *Don't Touch That Dial: Radio Programming in American Life from 1920 to 1960* (Chicago: G. K. Hall, 1979);

MacDonald, *Television and the Red Menace* (New York: Praeger, 1985);

Alexander McNeil, *Total Television: A Comprehensive Guide to Programming from 1948–1980* (New York: Penguin, 1980);

Christopher Sterling, ed., *Broadcasting and Mass Media: A Survey Bibliography* (Philadelphia: Temple University Press, 1974);

Sterling, ed., *The History of Broadcasting: Radio to Television,* 32 volumes (New York: New York Times/Arno, 1972);

Sterling, ed., *Telecommunications,* 34 volumes (New York: New York Times/Arno, 1974);

Vincent Terrace, *The Complete Encyclopedia of Television Programs: 1947–1979,* second edition (New York: Barnes, 1980);

Antoon J. van Zuilen, *The Life Cycle of Magazines: A Historical Study of the Decline and Fall of the General Interest Mass Audience Magazine in the United States During the Period 1946–1972* (Ulthoorn, The Netherlands: Graduate Press, 1977).

MEDICINE AND HEALTH

Leonard Berkowitz, *Aggression: A Psychological Analysis* (New York: McGraw-Hill, 1962);

The Cambridge World History of Human Disease (New York: Cambridge University Press, 1993);

Rick J. Carlson, *The End of Medicine* (New York: Wiley, 1975);

Frederic Fox Cartwright, *Disease and History* (New York: Crowell, 1972);

James H. Cassedy, *Medicine in America: A Short History* (Baltimore: Johns Hopkins University Press, 1991);

Faith Clark, ed., *Symposium III: The Changing Patterns of Consumption of Food,* International Congress of Food Science and Technology, Proceedings of the Congress

Symposia, 1962, vol. 5 (New York: Gordon & Breach Science, 1967);

Companion Encyclopedia of the History of Medicine (London: Routledge, 1993);

Bernard Dixon, *Beyond the Magic Bullet* (New York: Harper & Row, 1978);

John Patrick Dolan, *Health and Society: A Documentary History of Medicine* (New York: Seabury, 1978);

Martin Duke, *The Development of Medical Techniques and Treatments: From Leeches to Heart Surgery* (Madison, Conn.: International Universities Press, 1991);

Esmond R. Long, *A History of Pathology* (New York: Dover, 1965);

Albert S. Lyons, *Medicine: An Illustrated History* (New York: Abrams, 1978);

William A. Nolen, *A Surgeon's World* (New York: Random House, 1972);

Sherwin B. Nuland, *Doctors: the Biography of Medicine* (New York: Knopf, 1988);

John R. Paul, *A History of Poliomyelitis* (New Haven & London: Yale University Press, 1971);

Stanley Joel Reiser, *Medicine and the Reign of Technology* (New York: Cambridge University Press, 1978);

Rosemary Stevens, *American Medicine and the Public Interest* (New Haven: Yale University Press, 1971);

Elliot S. Valenstein, *Great and Desperate Cures* (New York: Basic Books, 1986).

RELIGION

Sydney E. Ahlstrom, *A Religious History of the American People*, 2 volumes (Garden City, N.Y.: Doubleday, 1975);

Catherine Albanese, *America, Religions and Religious* (Belmont, Cal.: Wadsworth, 1981);

Nancy T. Ammerman, *Bible Believers: Fundamentalists in the Modern World* (New Brunswick, N.J.: Rutgers University Press, 1987);

Bernham P. Beckwith, *The Decline of U.S. Religious Faith, 1912–1984* (Palo Alto, Cal.: Beckwith, 1985);

Robert N. Bellah and Frederick E. Greenspahn, eds., *Uncivil Religion: Irreligious Hostility in America* (New York: Crossroads, 1987);

Robert Benne, *Defining America; A Christian Critique of the American Dream* (Philadelphia: Fortress Press, 1974);

John C. Bennett, *Christians and the State* (New York: Scribners, 1958);

Charles C. Brown, *Niebuhr and His Age: Reinhold Niebuhr's Prophetic Role in the Twentieth Century* (Philadelphia: Trinity Press International, 1992);

Jackson W. Carroll, *Beyond Establishment: Protestant Identity in a Post-Protestant Age* (Louisville, Ky.: Westminster/John Knox, 1993);

Samuel McCrea Cavert, *The American Churches in the Ecumenical Movement, 1900–1968* (New York: Association Press, 1968);

John Cooney, *The American Pope: The Life and Times of Francis Cardinal Spellman* (New York: New York Times Books, 1984);

Jay P. Dolan, *The American Catholic Experience: A History from Colonial Times to the Present* (Garden City, N.Y.: Doubleday, 1985);

Robert F. Drinan, *Religion, the Courts, and Public Policy* (New York: McGraw-Hill, 1963);

John L. Eighmy, *Churches in Cultural Captivity: A History of the Social Attitudes of Southern Baptists* (Knoxville: University of Tennessee Press, 1987);

Henry L. Feingold, *A Time for Searching: Entering the Mainstream, 1920-1945* (Baltimore: Johns Hopkins University Press, 1992);

James Hennesey, *American Catholics: A History of the Roman Catholic Community in the United States* (New York: Oxford University Press, 1981);

Arthur Hertzberg, *The Jews in America: Four Centuries of an Uneasy Encounter: A History* (New York: Simon & Schuster, 1989);

Darryl Hudson, *The Ecumenical Movement in World Affairs* (London: Weidenfeld and Nicolson, 1969);

Winthrop S. Hudson, *Religion in America: An Historical Account of the Development of American Religious Life* (New York: Scribners, 1981);

William R. Hutchinson, *The Modernist Impulse in American Protestantism* (Cambridge: Harvard University Press, 1976);

Donald G. Jones and Russell E. Richey, eds., *American Civil Religion* (San Francisco: Mellen Research University Press, 1990);

Edward L. Long, *The Christian Response to the Atomic Crisis* (Philadelphia: Westminster, 1950);

Martin Marty, *Pilgrims in Their Own Land: 500 Years of Religion in America* (Boston: Houghton Mifflin, 1984);

Leo Pfeiffer, *Church, State, and Freedom*, second edition (Boston: Beacon, 1967);

Russell E. Richey, *American Civil Religion* (New York: Harper & Row, 1974);

Ralph Lord Roy, *Apostles of Discord, A Study of Organized Bigotry and Disruption on the Fringes of Protestantism* (Boston: Beacon, 1953);

Mark Silk, *Spiritual Politics: Religion and America since World War II* (New York: Simon & Schuster, 1988);

Ronald H. Stone, *Reinhold Niebuhr: Prophet to Politicians* (Nashville: Abingdon, 1972);

Joseph Tussman, ed., *The Supreme Court on Church and State* (New York: Oxford University Press, 1962);

Brooks R. Walker, *Christian Fright Peddlers* (Garden City, N.Y.: Doubleday, 1964);

Edmund Wilson, *The Dead Sea Scrolls, 1947–1969* (New York: Oxford University Press, 1969);

Robert Wuthnow, *The Restructuring of American Religion: Society and Faith Since World War II* (Princeton: Princeton University Press, 1988).

SCIENCE AND TECHNOLOGY

Gary M. Abshire, ed., *The Impact of Computers on Society and Ethics: A Bibliography* (Morristown, N.J.: Creative Computing, 1980);

Garland Allen, *Life Science in the Twentieth Century* (Cambridge: Cambridge University Press, 1978);

Jack Belzer, Albert G. Holzman, and Allen Kent, eds., *Encyclopedia of Computer Science and Technology,* 16 volumes (New York: Marcel Dekker, 1975–1981);

Paul Boyer, *By the Bomb's Early Light: American Thought and Culture at the Dawn of the Nuclear Age* (New York: Pantheon, 1985);

Arthur Holly Compton, *Atomic Quest: A Personal Narrative* (New York: Oxford University Press, 1956);

Joseph J. Corn, *The Winged Gospel: America's Romance with Aviation, 1900–1950* (New York: Oxford University Press, 1983);

Hamilton Cravens, *The Truimph of Evolution: American Scientists and the Heredity-Environment Controversy, 1900–1941* (Philadelphia: University of Pennsylvania Press, 1978);

Carl N. Degler, *In Search of Human Nature: the Decline and Revival of Darwinism in American Social Thought* (New York: Oxford University Press, 1991);

Laura Fermi, *Illustrious Immigrants: The Intellectual Migration from Europe* (Chicago: University of Chicago Press, 1968);

Donald Fleming and Bernard Bailyn, eds., *The Intellectual Migration* (Cambridge, Mass.: Harvard University Press, 1969);

Charles Coulston Gillespie, ed., *Dictionary of Scientific Biography,* 18 volumes (New York: Scribners, 1970–1990);

Herman H. Goldstein, *The Computer from Pascal to von Neumann* (Princeton: Princeton University Press, 1972);

Leslie R. Groves, *Now It Can Be Told: The Story of the Manhattan Project* (New York: Harper, 1962);

J. Haugelan, *Artificial Intelligence: The Very Idea* (Cambridge, Mass.: MIT Press, 1985);

G. Kass-Simon and Patricia Farnes, eds., *Women of Science* (Bloomington: University of Indiana Press, 1990);

Leslie Katz, ed., *Fairy Tales for Computers* (Boston: Nonpareil Books, 1969);

Evelyn Fox Keller, *A Feeling for the Organism: The Life and Work of Barbara McClintock* (New York: Freeman, 1983);

Daniel J. Kevles, *In the Name of Eugenics: Genetics and the Uses of Human Heredity* (New York: Knopf, 1985);

Kevles, *The Physicists: The History of a Scientific Community in Modern America* (New York: Knopf, 1978);

Anthony O. Lewis, ed., *Of Men and Machines* (London: Dutton, 1963);

Ernst Mayr and William B. Provine, *The Evolutionary Synthesis: Perspectives on the Unification of Biology* (Cambridge, Mass.: Harvard University Press, 1980);

Frank McGill, *Great Events From History II,* Science and Technology Series; Volume 3, 1931–1952 (Pasadena, Cal.: Salem Press, 1991);

McGraw-Hill Encyclopedia of Science and Technology, fourth edition, 14 volumes (New York: McGraw-Hill, 1977);

Sam Mescowitz, ed., *The Coming of Robots* (New York: Collier, 1963);

N. Metropolis, ed., *A History of Computing in the Twentieth Century* (New York: Academic Press, 1980);

Lewis Mumford, *The Myth of the Machine: The Pentagon of Power* (New York: Harcourt Brace Jovanovich, 1964);

Science & Technology Desk Reference, edited by Carnegie Library of Pittsburgh, Science and Technology Department (Detroit: Gale Research, 1993);

Martin J. Sherwin, *A World Destroyed: The Atomic Bomb and the Grand Alliance* (New York: Knopf, 1975);

Robert Silverberg, ed., *Men and Machines* (New York: Meredith Press, 1968);

Herbert Alexander Simon, *Sciences of the Artificial* (Cambridge, Mass.: MIT Press, 1969);

C. P. Snow, *The Two Cultures and the Scientific Revolution* (New York: Cambridge University Press, 1961);

Arnold Thrachray, Jeffrey Sturchio, P. Thomas Carroll, and Robert Bush, *Chemistry in America, 1876–1976* (Dordrecht, Holland: Reidel, 1985).

SPORTS

Charles C. Alexander, *Our Game: An American Baseball History* (New York: Holt, 1991);

Arthur R. Ashe, Jr., *A Hard Road to Glory: A History of the African-American Athlete Since 1946* (New York: Warner, 1988);

William J. Baker and John M. Carrol, eds., *Sports in Modern America* (Saint Louis: River City, 1981);

Jim Benagh, *Incredible Olympic Feats* (New York: McGraw-Hill, 1976);

Edwin H. Cady, *The Big Game: College Sports and American Life* (Knoxville: University of Tennessee Press, 1978);

Roger Caillois, *Man, Play, and Games* (London: Thames & Hudson, 1962);

Erich Camper, *Encyclopedia of the Olympic Games* (New York: McGraw-Hill, 1972);

John Durant, *Highlights of the Olympics* (New York: Hastings House, 1965);

Ellen W. Gerber, Jan Feshlin, Pearl Berlin, and Waneen Wyrick, *The American Woman in Sport* (Reading, Mass.: Addison-Wesley, 1974);

Elliott J. Gorn, *The Manly Art* (Ithaca, N.Y.: Cornell University Press, 1986);

Peter J. Graham and Horst Ueberhorst, eds., *The Modern Olympic Games* (Cornwall, N.Y.: Leisure Press, 1976);

Will Grimsley, *Golf: Its History, People and Events* (Englewood Cliffs, N.J.: Prentice-Hall, 1966);

Grimsley, *Tennis: Its History, People and Events* (Englewood Cliffs, N.J.: Prentice-Hall, 1971);

Allen Guttman, *A Whole New Ball Game: An Interpretation of American Sports* (Chapel Hill: University of North Carolina Press, 1988);

Dorothy V. Harris, ed., *Women and Sports* (University Park: Pennsylvania State University Press, 1972);

Robert J. Higgs, *Sports: A Reference Guide* (Westport, Conn.: Greenwood Press, 1982);

Neil D. Isaacs, *All the Moves: A History of College Basketball* (Philadelphia: Lippincott, 1975);

Bill James, *The Bill James Historical Baseball Abstract* (New York: Villard, 1986);

William O. Johnson, *All That Glitters Is Not Gold* (New York: Putnam, 1972);

Roger Kahn, *The Boys of Summer* (New York: Harper & Row, 1972);

Kahn, *The Era: 1947–1956, When the Yankees, the Giants, and the Dodgers Ruled the World* (New York: Ticknor & Fields, 1993);

Ivan N. Kaye, *Good Clean Violence: A History of College Football* (Philadelphia: Lippincott, 1973);

Richard D. Mandel, *Sport: A Cultural History* (New York: Columbia University Press, 1984);

Robert Mechicoff and Steven Estes, *A History and Philosophy of Sport and Physical Education* (Dubuque, Iowa: William C. Brown, 1993);

James A. Michener, *Sports in America* (New York: Random House, 1976);

Jack Olsen, *The Black Athlete: A Shameful Story* (New York: Time-Life Books, 1968);

Robert W. Peterson, *Only the Ball Was White* (Englewood Cliffs, N.J.: Prentice-Hall, 1970);

Benjamin G. Rader, *American Sports: From the Age of Folk Games to the Age of Spectators* (Englewood Cliffs, N.J.: Prentice-Hall, 1983);

Martin Ralbovsky, *Destiny's Darlings* (New York: Hawthorn Books, 1974);

Steven A. Riess, ed., *The American Sporting Experience* (West Point, N.Y.: Leisure Press, 1984);

William F. Russell, *Go Up for Glory* (New York: Coward-McCann, 1966);

Leverett T. Smith, Jr., *The American Dream and the National Game* (Bowling Green: Bowling Green University Popular Press, 1975);

Betty Spears and Richard A. Swanson, *History of Sport and Physical Education*, third edition (Dubuque, Iowa: William C. Brown, 1983);

Jules Tygel, *Baseball's Great Experiment* (New York: Oxford University Press, 1983);

David Q. Voigt, *America Through Baseball* (Chicago: Nelson-Hall, 1976);

Herbert Warren Wind, *The Gilded Age of Sport* (New York: Simon & Schuster, 1961);

Wind, *The Realm of Sport* (New York: Simon & Schuster, 1966);

Earle F. Zeigler, ed., *A History of Physical Education and Sport in the United States and Canada* (Champaign, Ill.: Stipes, 1975).

CONTRIBUTORS

ARTS	DAVID MCLEAN *Santa Barbara, California*
BUSINESS AND THE ECONOMY	PHILLIP G. PAYNE *Ohio State University*
EDUCATION	ROBERT T. LAMBDIN *University of South Carolina* LAURA C. LAMBDIN *Francis Marion University* VICTOR BONDI *University of Massachusetts — Boston*
FASHION	JANE GERHARD *Brown University*
GOVERNMENT AND POLITICS	PAUL ATWOOD *University of Massachusetts — Boston*
LAW AND JUSTICE	MICHAEL L. PIERCE *Wakefield, Massachusetts*
LIFESTYLES AND SOCIAL TRENDS	MARGO HORN *Los Altos, California*
MEDIA	VICTOR BONDI *University of Massachusetts — Boston* DARREN HARRIS-FAIN *Bruccoli Clark Layman, Inc.* JAMES W. HIPP *Bruccoli Clark Layman, Inc.*
MEDICINE AND HEALTH	JOAN D. LAXSON *Boston, Massachusetts*
RELIGION	VICTOR BONDI *University of Massachusetts — Boston* DONALD L. JONES *University of South Carolina*
SCIENCE AND TECHNOLOGY	MARGO HORN *Los Altos, California*
SPORTS	SCOTT DERKS *Columbia, South Carolina* MARGO HORN *Los Altos, California*

INDEX OF PHOTOGRAPHS

INDEX

A

A.A.A. National Auto Championship 568, 570–572
A. C. Nielsen company 359
Aalto, Alvar 170, 182–183
Aaron, Hank 538
Abbé Practical Workshop 52
Abbott, Bud 29, 31, 55, 59
ABC. *See* American Broadcasting Company
Abelson, Philip 505
Abortion 328
Abrams, Georgie 513
"Absent Minded Moon" (Dorsey with Eberly) 29
Abstract Expressionism 35, 41, 43–47, 90
Abt, Dr. Isaac A. 436
Abyssinian Baptist Church, Harlem, New York 467
Academy Awards (Oscars) 57, 59–60, 63, 74, 76, 80–82, 86, 88, 90, 190
"Ac-cent-tchu-ate the Positive" (Andrews Sisters) 33
Acheson, Dean 212, 252, 255, 332, 384
Ackerman, Carl William 153
Across the River and Into the Trees (Hemingway) 53
Action in the North Atlantic 31, 57
Acuff, Roy 28, 30, 32–34, 67, 71
Adair, Dr. Frank E. 431
Adair, Eleanor 117
Adakian 370
Adam Opel AG 188
Adam's Rib 38
Adams, Ace 517
Adams, Ansel 47, 296
Adams, Connie 179
Adams, Herbert D. 431
Adams, Léonie 80

Adams, Williams 31
Addams, Frankie 79
Addams, Jane 279
Adkinson, Theodore "Ted" 571
Adler, Larry 49
Adler, Mortimer 140–141, 154, 157–158, 452
Adlow, Elijah 33
Adolescent dating 318, 330, 340–341
Adrian 170, 179–181, 193, 198
Adrian Room, Gunthers 170
Adrian, Ltd. 179
Aeschylus 75
Afonsky, Nicholas 390
African Americans 32, 35, 41, 45–46, 51, 53, 63, 66, 71, 77, 82–83, 88–89, 96, 104, 131, 136, 147, 149–150, 159–161, 208, 212, 218, 242–245, 254, 266–273, 275–276, 279, 283, 288, 301–303, 313, 317, 321–322, 326–330, 332, 341, 343–347, 349–350, 352, 354–355, 374, 381–382, 401, 403, 410–411, 415, 425, 433, 449, 466–467, 470, 476, 510–511, 520, 523–525, 527–530, 534, 536–539, 542, 545, 563, 565
The African Queen 74
Afrika Korps 231–232, 293
Aga Khan 84
Against the American Grain (Macdonald) 78
The Age of Anxiety (Auden) 86
Age of Innocence (Bernstein) 38
Agee, James 70, 380
Agricultural Adjustment Act 127, 284
Aguilar, Ernesto 517
"Ah, But It Happens" (Laine) 37
Ahnfeldt, Lt. Col. A. L. 408
Aida 35

Aiken, Conrad 80
Aiken, Howard 481, 490
"Ain't Misbehavin'" (Waller) 91
Air Force 398
Aitken, Robert Ingersoll 88
Ajemian, Maro 38
The Alamo 181
Albany Movement (1963) 470
Albee, Edward 79
Albee, Fred H. 439
Albert Lasker Awards 427, 435–436
Alcatraz Prison 296, 311
Aldanov, Mark 32
Aldrich, C. Anderson 437
Alexander, Peter 566
Alexander, William 519
Alexei, Metropolitan of Leningrad 446
Algren, Nelson 30, 38, 53
Alien Registration Act (Smith Act) 202, 216, 240, 292, 295, 297, 301, 308–309, 332, 375
"All Alone in the World" (Arnold) 35
"All I Need Is You" (Shore) 30
All My Sons (Miller) 36, 51
All Star Bowling tournament 515
All Star Quintet 66
"All That Glitters Is Not Gold" (Shore) 34
All the King's Men (Warren) 35, 38, 52–53, 86–87
All Thy Conquests (Hays) 35
All-American Football Conference (AAFC) 519, 521, 523, 527, 529, 554, 560, 570–571
All-American Girls Baseball League (AAGBL) 124, 530, 539–540
Allegheny Ludlum Steel Corporation 125
Allen, Laurence Edmund 388
Allen, Lewis 439

Allen, Robert S. 385–386

Allentown Morning Call 392

Allied Chalmers plant 94

Allied Chemical 496

Allied Expeditionary Force 274

Allison's House (Glaspell) 89

Almanac Singers 68

Almodovar, Louisa 311

Almodovar, Terry 311–312

"Along the Santa Fe Trail" (Miller & Orchestra with Eberly) 28

L'Alouette (Anouilh) 76

Alpher, Ralph Asher 487

Alsab 514, 568

Alternative to Futility (Trueblood) 474

Aluminum City Terrace Housing, Pennsylvania 166, 184, 193

Aly Khan 84, 190

"Am I Asking Too Much?" (Washington) 37

Amalgamated Clothing Workers of America 119, 288

"Amapola" (Dorsey & Orchestra) 28

Amateur Athletic Union (AAU) 511, 514–517, 520–521, 524–525, 561, 563, 566–567

Amateur Bicycle League of America 510

Amazing Stories 355, 392

Ambassador College (Pasadena, California) 475

Ambler, Eric 62

Amerasia 387

America 473

America First Committee 166, 172

American Abstract Artists Association 42

American Academy of Arts and Letters 28, 34, 36, 38, 84–85

American Academy of Dental Medicine 399

American Academy of Design 89

American Academy of Poets 84

American Anthropological Association 345

American Artists' Congress 380

American Association for Labor Legislation 412

American Association for the Advancement of Science 390, 396

American Association of Science Workers 401

American Association of Teachers Colleges 162

American Association of University Women 149

American Automobile Association 199

American Ballet Theater 48

American Baseball Guild 522

American Bible Society 445, 457

American Booksellers' Association 85

American Broadcasting Company (ABC) 362, 372, 376–377

American Business Consultants 365, 360

American Can Company 126

American Cancer Society 399–402, 427

American Chemical Society 396–400, 433, 502

American Civil Liberties Union 315, 318–319

American Civil War 69, 253, 298, 301–302, 322, 349, 371, 457

American College of Surgeons 396

American Committee for Cultural Freedom 156

American Communist Party (Communist Party USA) 63, 76, 78, 82–83, 138, 155, 215, 239, 265, 270, 272, 285, 295, 303–304, 308–309, 468

American Council on Education 132

American Council on Race Relations 317

American Cyanamide Company 432

American Dental Association 402

An American Dilemma: The Negro Problem of Modern Democracy (Myrdal) 272, 345

American Document (Graham) 74

American Economic Foundation 125

American Education Fellowship (Progressive Education Association) 131

American Expeditionary Force 289

American Federation of Labor (AFL) 94–96, 98–101, 116, 119, 121, 125, 214, 244, 269, 286, 468

American Federation of Musicians 31–32, 84, 363–364, 387

American Federation of Teachers 138

American Film Institute Life Achievement Award 81

American Football Coaches Association 510, 529

American Freedom and Catholic Power (Blanshard) 463

American Friends Service Committee 162, 476

American Fund for Public Service 302

American Geographic Society 400

American Gothic (Wood) 91

American Heart Association 401

American Hockey Association (AHA) 558

American Hospital Association 414

American Institute of Architects (AIA) 167, 194, 198

American Institute of Decorators 171

American Jewish Committee 323

American Jewish Congress 287, 447, 475–476

American Journal of Anatomy 391

American Lawn Tennis Magazine 557

American League (baseball) 510, 512–514, 518, 520, 522, 524, 527–528, 534–536, 538, 539, 561, 566–571

American League Most Valuable Player Award 510, 514–515, 517–518, 520, 524, 529, 534–535, 539, 562

American Legion 199, 254, 289, 301, 307, 365

American Locomotive Companies 101

American Medical Association (AMA) 96, 101, 396–399, 401–404, 412–414, 425, 431–433, 435

American Medical Society 411

American Olympic Commission 510

American Professional Football League 510

American Psychiatric Association 401, 429

American Public Health Association 433, 436

American Red Cross 174, 178, 197, 397–398, 415, 425, 541–542, 558

American Scholar 464

American Smelting and Refining 126

American Social Hygiene Association 396, 400

American Socialist Party 470

American Society for the Control of Cancer 431
American Society for the Prevention of Cruelty to Animals 355
American Society of Composers, Authors and Publishers (ASCAP) 31, 71, 358, 362–364, 387
American Society of Newspaper Editors 153
American Steel Foundries 127
American Syncopated Orchestra 88
American Telephone and Telegraph Company (AT&T) 101, 215
An American Tragedy (Dreiser) 88
American Workers Party 156
American Writers' Congress 29
American-Anglo-Transvaal corporation 113
Americans for Democratic Action (ADA) 269, 471
Americans for Intellectual Freedom 156
Ames, Joseph S. 488
Amherst College 317, 425
Amos Alonzo Stagg Award 510
Amos and Andy 377
Anaconda Copper Mining company 113
Analog Science Fact — Science Fiction 381
Anastasia, Albert 319
Anchors Aweigh 34, 48–49, 81
And Keep Your Powder Dry (Mead) 486
And Now Tomorrow (Field) 30
Andersen, Hendrick Christian 353
Anderson, Carl 390
Anderson, Dr. H. W. 431
Anderson, Harold MacDonald 390
Anderson, Ivy 88
Anderson, Jack 385, 386
Anderson, Maceo 49
Anderson, Marian 327
Anderson, Maxwell 41, 51
Anderson, Sherwood 88
The Andrews Sisters 28–30, 33–36, 38, 65
Andrews, Bert 389
Andrews, Dana 32
Andrews, Dr. George C. 431
Angels With Dirty Faces 73
Angle, Paul M. 123
Anglo-Russian Treaty (1942) 252
Angott, Sammy 513–515, 544–547
Animal Comics 359
Animal Crackers 89

Animal Farm (Orwell) 34–35
Anna and the King of Siam 34
Anne of Green Gables (Montgomery) 90
Annie Get Your Gun 36, 48–49, 69
"Anniversary Song" (Beneke, Miller & Orchestra) 36
Another Part of the Forest (Hellman) 76
Anouilh, Jean 76
An Anthology of Famous English and American Poetry 35
Anthony, Susan B. 36, 70, 354
Anthropology 482, 486–487, 491, 507
Anti-Semite and Jew (Sartre) 463
Anti-Communist League of America 138
Anti-Inflation Act 101
Antibiotics 405, 416–417, 421–423, 429–430, 433–434, 436, 480, 501
Antihistamines 406–407
Aperture 47
The Apollo, Harlem, New York 49
The Apostle (Asch) 31, 462
Apostoli, Fred 518
Appalachian Spring (Graham) 34, 49, 69, 75, 86
Appling, Luke 528
Arab-Israeli War 272
Arcaro, Eddie 512, 525, 530, 559, 566, 568–571
The Arch of Triumph (Remarque) 35
Archaeology 486–487
Archie (Montana) 359, 370
Architects Collaborative 171
Architectural Forum 199
Architecture 166–173, 182–185, 193–195, 197
Arden, Elizabeth 117–118, 197
Arden, Eve 377
Arena, John 321
Arendt, Hannah 158, 348
Aristocrat records 71
Mr. Arkadin (Welles) 82
Arlington National Cemetery 239, 275, 278, 564
Arliss, George 88
Armour Laboratories 403
Armstrong, Edwin H. 358
Armstrong, Henry 511, 544
Armstrong, Herbert W. 475
Armstrong, Louis 35, 65, 77
"The Army's Made a Man Out of Me" (Berlin) 51
Arnaud, Dean Leopold 167

Arnold, Eddy 33, 35, 37, 67
Arrival and Departure (Koestler) 31
The Arsenal of Democracy (Nelson) 123
Arsenic and Old Lace 33, 62, 88
The Art of Living (Peale) 471
Art of This Century Gallery 31–32, 36, 42, 44
Artists in Exile exhibit 30, 43
Artists' Gallery, New York 30, 43
"As Sweet As You" (Lund) 36
ASCAP. *See* American Society of Composers, Authors and Publishers
Asch, Sholem 31, 462–463
Asimov, Isaac 380–381
Associated Klans of Georgia 354
Associated Press 94, 239, 388–389, 392, 513, 515, 519, 521–523, 527, 542–543, 550–551, 561, 567
Association for the Advancement of Research on Multiple Sclerosis 400
Association of American Colleges 146, 161
Association of American Medical Colleges 433
Association of Catholic Trade Unionists (ACTU) 451
Association of Comics Magazine Publishers 360
Astaire, Fred 48–49, 166, 190
Astor, Mary 29, 60
Astounding Science-Fiction 369, 380–381
Astronomy 139, 487–488, 506–507
At Heaven's Gate (Warren) 31
Atanasoff, John Vincent 480, 500
Atanasoff Berry Computer (ABC) 480, 500
Athenagoras I, Archbishop 448, 475
Atherton, Gertrude Franklin 88
Atkinson, Brooks 389
Atkinson, Ted 530
Atlanta Journal 389
Atlantic Charter 204, 223, 263, 313, 453, 472
Atlee, Clement 250
Atomic bomb 35, 40, 56, 118, 132, 135, 138, 149, 157–158, 169, 190, 195, 203, 210–212, 216–217, 236–237, 250–252, 254, 256–258, 276–277, 282–284, 289, 332–333, 370, 381, 384, 400, 404, 407, 431, 446, 450, 454–455, 460, 463–464, 469,

Brady, William 73
Bragg, Caleb S. 572
Brahms 49
Brandeis, Louis D. 288, 323
Brandenburg, William 162
Brando, Marlon 52
Branham, William Gibbons 572
Braque, Georges 90
Brattain, Walter H. 482, 499
Bratton, Rufus 226
Braun, Wernher von 485, 497–498
Breadon, Sam 524, 572
Breakfast at Sardi's 390
Breckinridge, Sophonisba Preston 353
Breen, Joseph 54–55
Breger, David 371
Brenda Starr (Messick) 367
Breneman, Tom 88, 390
Bresnahan, Roger 572
Breton, Andre 42–43
Bretton Woods Conference 97, 112, 127, 208, 252, 286, 293
Breuer, Marcel 166, 169, 172, 182, 184, 193–194
Brewster Recreation Center 563
Bricker, John 208, 286
Brideshead Revisited (Waugh) 35
Bridges, Harry 280
Bridgman, Percy Williams 506
Brief Encounter 34
Brigadoon 41
Brigance, Tom 180
Briggs corporation 97
Brill, Dr. Abraham Arden 354, 439
Britannica 141
British Broadcasting Corporation (BBC) 374
British Film Institute 81
British Red Cross 385
British Royal Air Force (RAF) 222
British Women's Amateur Championship (golf) 561
Broadcast Music Incorporated (BMI) 67, 71, 358, 362–364
Broadway 31, 33–34, 36–38, 41, 48–52, 55, 64, 69, 79, 85, 88, 90, 354, 392, 439, 546
Broadway's Like That 73
Brock, Dr. R. C. 431
Bromfield, Louis 30–31
Bronson Trade School 563
Brookhaven National Laboratory 439
Brooklyn College 348, 519
Brooklyn Dodgers 329, 353, 511–513, 515, 517–518, 520–524,

526, 528–530, 534–539, 557–558, 564–567, 570–571, 574
Brooklyn Tigers 564
Brooklyn Trust Company 564
Brooks, Emerson 354
Brooks, Milton 388
Brooks, Steve 571
Brookwood Labor College 468
Broonzy, Big Bill 66
Brother Orchid 73
Brotherhood of Sleeping Car Porters 95, 243
Brough, Louise 515, 517, 524
Broun, Heywood 563
Browder, Earl 265–266
Brown, Anne 354
Brown, Clarence "Gatemouth" 66
Brown, Harry 33, 53
Brown, Les 33, 65
Brown, Morris 551–552
Brown, Lt. Paul 519, 551, 554
Brown, Roy 67
Brown, Tom 522
Brown, Tommy "Buckshot" 557, 566
Brown, Walter 543
Brown, Wesley A. 149
Brown, Dr. William Adams 475
Brown, Mrs. William Adams 354
Brown School 354
Brown University 163
Brown v. *Board of Education* 136, 150, 303, 312, 318
Bruff, Nancy 34
Brush, George DeForest 88
Bryan, Raymond "Slug" 510
Bryn Mawr College 353, 507
Bryson, Lyman 444
"Bubbles in My Beer" (Wills) 68
Buber, Martin 457, 460
Buchanan, Scott 140
Buchanan Brothers 35, 494
Buchenwald concentration camp 242, 380
Buck, Gene 387
Buck, Pearl S. 30, 37–38
Buck Privates 29, 55
Bucknell University 573
Buckner, Thomas A. 126
Buddhist Churches of America 444
Buddhist Mission of North America 444
Budenz, Louis 455
Budge, Don 514, 521, 528
Buffalo Bill's Wild West Show 69
Buffalo Bills 571
Bugs Bunny Nips the Nips 367

Buhlig, Richard 71
Buick airplane engine plant, Illinois 184
Buick Motor Car Company 126–127
The Build Up (Williams) 35
Bullets or Ballots 73
Bunau-Varilla, Philippe-Jean 288
Bunche, Ralph 272–273
Bunker, Earle L. 388
Bunker Hill 210
Burck, Jacob 388
Burger, Warren 274
Burgess, Warren Randolph 125
Burgess, William Starling 199
Burke, Jack 572
Burke, John J. 451
Burkett, Jesse 521
Burkhart, Dr. Harvey J. 439
Burkholder, Dr. Paul R. 423
Burleigh, Col. G. W. 323
Burleigh, Harry Thacker 88
Burnett, Whit 78
Burns, John Horne 36, 41, 53
Burns, Sister Leopoldina 439
Burton, Harold H. 293, 414
Busch, Adolf 70
Bush, George 343
Bush, Dr. Vannevar 132, 135, 158, 203, 480–481, 493, 496, 501, 504
Business Week 359
Bussey, Young 553
Bustanoby, Jacques 354
Butler, Frank E. 390
Butler, Nicholas Murray 162
Butler, Smedley Darlington 222, 288
Button, Dick 525, 556
"Buttons and Bows" (Shaw) 37
"By the Light of the Silvery Moon" (Edwards) 88
"By-U, By-O" (Herman & Orchestra with Lane) 29
Byrnes, James F. 70, 96, 211, 261, 264, 286, 292, 321, 336, 519, 558

C

"Cabaret" (Clooney) 38
Cabrini, Mother Frances Xavier 475
Cacchione, Peter V. 354
Caesar, Julius 278
Caesar, Sid 377
Caesar and Christ (Durant) 462
Caesar's Palace, Las Vegas 563
Café des Beaux Arts 354

Cleveland Indians 511, 521–522, 524, 526, 529, 534, 538–539, 562, 571

Cleveland Rams 512, 516, 520–521, 553, 569

Cleveland Stadium 539

Clifford, Clark 213, 269

Clift, Montgomery 38

Climenko, Dr. David R. 431

Clock Without Hands (McCullers) 79

Clooney, Rosemary 38, 65

Clothing Workers Union 319

Clytemnestra (Aeschylus) 75

Clytemnestra (Graham) 75

Coates, Robert 35, 44

"Coax Me a Little Bit" (Andrews Sisters) 35

Cobb, Lee J. 365

Cobb, Ty 539

Coburn, Julia 197

Coca, Imogene 377

Coca-Cola Company 112, 125, 260

Cochran, Negley Dakin 390

Cochran, Ray 514

Cochrane, Freddie 512

Cochrane, Red 544, 547

Cocking, Walter Dewey 130

"Code of Wartime Practices for American Broadcasters" (NAB) 359

Coe, Charles 572

Coe, Franklin 390

Cofall, Stanley B. 352

Coffin, Henry Sloane 446

Coffin, William Haskell 390

Cohan, George M. 88–89

Cohen, Maurice 311

Cohen, Morris R. 162

Cohen, Dr. Philip 431

Cohen, Seymour Stanley 482

"Cohens and the Kellys" series 90

Cohn, Edwin Joseph 438

Cohn, Roy 455

Cohon, Rabbi Beryl D. 464

Colbert, Claudette 31–32, 59

"Cold, Cold Heart" (Williams) 68

Cold War 40, 60–63, 76, 102, 104, 110–111, 118, 122, 125, 132, 139, 156–158, 218, 245, 247, 250–253, 255–256, 258, 268–270, 273, 275, 277–278, 285–286, 297, 304, 307, 329, 331–333, 336, 346–347, 364, 371, 383, 455, 468, 471, 474, 484, 493, 495, 503, 505

Cole, Jack 370

Cole, Lester 304

Cole, Nat King 35, 38

Collected Poems (Van Doren) 86

College Entrance Examination Board 130

College of the City of New York 315

College of the Holy Cross 570

College of the Pacific 517

Collegiate Football National Championship 560, 567–571

Collier's 287, 392, 557

Collins, J. Lawton 277

Collins, James J. "Jimmy" 572

Collins, Nathaniel 353

Collins, Ted 516

Colman, Ronald 30, 36, 87

The Color Curtain (Wright) 83

Colored Intercollegiate Athletic Association 552

Columbia Broadcasting System (CBS) 71, 358, 360, 362–363, 372–378, 387, 498–499, 549

Columbia College, Chicago 162

Columbia Pictures 54, 87

Columbia Records 364

Columbia University 36, 78, 131, 137, 140, 143, 149, 153–157, 163, 167, 214, 273–275, 279, 323, 351, 355, 379, 389–390, 425, 433, 448, 468, 485, 502, 507

Comic books 358–360, 362, 366, 369–370, 380–381, 391

Comic strips 359, 366, 369, 391–392

Comics and Sequential Art (Eisner) 382

"Comin' In on a Wing and a Prayer" (Song Spinners) 32

Comintern 256

The Commies Are After Your Kids 132, 137

Commission on Hospital Care 414

Committee for Cultural Freedom 133

Committee of Catholics for Human Rights 354

Committee on the Cause and Cure of War 162

Committee on Women in World Affairs 326

Committee to Defend America by Aiding the Allies 102, 287, 289

The Common Ventures of Life: Marriage, Birth, Work, and Death (Trueblood) 474

The Commonsense Book of Baby and Child Care (Spock) 329

Commonweal 452

Communicable Disease Center 399

Communism 36, 39–40, 60–61, 63, 68, 76, 78, 81–83, 100, 103, 111–112, 114, 122, 133, 135–141, 151, 155–156, 158–159, 161, 211–213, 215–216, 218–220, 223, 234, 237, 239, 244, 246–251, 255–259, 265–266, 268–270, 272–273, 275–276, 278, 280, 283, 285–287, 294, 297, 303–304, 308, 310, 316, 321, 330–332, 346–348, 354, 360, 362, 364–365, 371, 375, 383–384, 387, 413, 450–452, 454–455, 459, 468, 472–473, 495, 503–504

Communism and the Conscience of the West (Sheen) 455

The Communist Manifesto (Marx & Engel) 454

Como, Perry 32, 34–36, 38, 65

Compton, Arthur H. 463, 502, 505

Compton, Karl 501

Computer science 480–481, 483, 490–491, 500

Conan Doyle, Sir Arthur 89

Conant, James B. 131, 135, 138, 158, 496, 501, 504

Concerto for Clarinet and String Orchestra (Copland) 65

Conditioned Reflexes (Pavlov) 428

Condon, Eddie 35

Condon, Frank 390

Conference for Progressive Labor Action (CPLA) 468

Conference on Jewish Relations 348

Conference on Science, Philosophy and Religion 132

Conference on Science, Philosophy, and Religion in Their Relation to the Democratic Way of Life 444

"Confess" (Page) 37

"Confessin' the Blues" (McShann & Orchestra) 29

Confessions of a Nazi Spy 55

The Congress of American Mothers 287

Congress of Industrial Organizations (CIO) 94–95, 97, 99–100, 116, 119, 121–122, 216, 238, 244, 262, 266, 269, 287–288, 475

Congress of Partisans for Peace 156

Eden Theological Seminary 470
Edey, Mrs. Birdsall Otis 354
Edmondson, William 45
"Education and the United Nations" 130
Education for Freedom (Hutchins) 140
Educational broadcasting 367–368
Educational Reviewer (Crain) 137
Edwards, Gus 88
Edwards, Jonathan 74
Edwards, Dr. Waldo B. 432
Ehrenfest, Paul 502–503
Ehrlich, Dr. Paul 432
Eichmann, Adolf 348
Eichmann in Jerusalem: A Report on the Banality of Evil (Arendt) 348
Einstein, Albert 161, 257, 370, 484–485, 487
Einstein, Alfred 70
Eisenhower, Dwight D. 105, 112, 143, 205–207, 209–210, 214, 217, 231–233, 237, 240, 269, 274–277, 279, 283, 285, 333, 336, 448, 454, 474
Eisenhower, Mamie 196
Eisenhower, Milton 240
Eisenstein, Serge 76, 88
Eisler, Gerhart 321
Eisler, Hans 70
Eisner, Will 358, 366, 381–382
Eli Lilly and Company 396
Eliot, George 161
Eliot, Martha M. 437
Eliot, T. S. 38, 79–80
Ellery Queen's Mystery 358
Ellington, Edward Kennedy "Duke" 33, 41, 49, 65, 71, 84
Elliot, Maud Howe 88
Elliot, Maxine 88
Elliott, Bob 524
Elliott, Harriet Wiseman 162
Elliott, John Lovejoy 354
Ellis Island, New York 85
Ellison, Ralph 83
Elliston, Herbert 389
Eltinge, Julian 89
Ely, Richard T. 126
Emergency Maternity and Infant Care Program (EMIC) 327
Emergency Price Control Act 205, 338
Emerson, Haven 436
Emery, Dr. Clyde K. 432
Emory University 476
Employment Act (1946) 98, 110, 211

Emporia Gazette (Kansas) 393
Encounter 78, 156
Encyclopaedia Britannica 141, 154
Enders, Dr. John F. 418, 432, 482, 505
"Enemies List" (Nixon) 386
Engel, Friedrich 454
ENIAC (Electronic Numerical Integrator and Computer) 481, 490, 500
"Enoch Arden" (Tennyson) 117
Enola Gay 494
Equitable Savings and Loan building, Portland 183
Erla work camp 380
Erlanger, Joseph 435
Ernst, Max 42, 44
Erskine, John 140, 154, 462
Erwin, Charles 188
Espionage Act (1917) 475
Esquire 77–78, 327–328, 360
"The Essentials of a Good Peace" 453
ESSO (Standard Oil of New Jersey) 496
Ethridge, Mark 244
Etten, Nick 536
European Common Market 112, 114
European Food Program 141
European Theater of Operations 67, 234
"Europe's Twelve Greatest Men" (Pearson) 385
Eustis, Dorothy Harrison 354
Evangelical Church of the Prussian Union 473
Evangelical Lutheran Synod 449
Evangelical Theological Society 458
Evans, Gil 65
Evans, Luther H. 80
Evans, Walter 380
The Eve of St. Mark (Anderson) 51
Evening World (New York) 386
Evers, John Joseph 521, 572
Everson, Arch 462
Everson v. *Board of Education of Ewing Township* 462
Everybody's Shakespeare (Welles) 81
"Everything Happens to Me" (Dorsey with Sinatra) 29
Evins, David 198
Ewing, Dr. James 435, 439
Executive Order 8802 95, 243, 326, 343, 345

Executive Order 9066 205, 240, 305, 318, 327, 341
Executive Order 9809 212, 245, 329
Executive Order 9835 294
Executive Order 9981 345
Existentialism 40, 53, 62, 83, 460
Expansionism 111, 220, 252, 255–256, 283, 303, 383
Experimental Researches in Electricity (Faraday) 141, 154
Expressionism 40, 42, 46, 48–49, 74, 90
Eyes of the Navy 55

F

F. W. Dodge Corporation 392
Fables (Saroyan) 29
Fables For Our Time 49
Fackenthal, Dr. Frank Diehl 389
Fadiman, Clifton 140
Fagan, Sadie 76
Fagley, Richard M. 464
Fair de Graff, Robert 369
Fair Deal 210, 282
Fair Employment Practices Commission (FEPC) 267, 270, 345
Fair Employment Practices Committee (FEPC) 203, 243–245, 292, 317, 326, 343, 345
Fair Labor Standards Act 94, 203, 216, 280
Fairbank, John K. 139
Fairbanks, Douglas, Jr. 57
Fairbanks, Richard M. 391
Fairfax, Beatrice 354
Fairfield University 473
Faith and History: A Comparison of Christian and Modern Views of History (Niebuhr) 471
Faith Is the Answer (Peale) 471
Falconer, Mrs. M. P. 323
Falk, Lee 366
Fall River Legend 48
Falter, Clement 472
Fanfare for the Common Man (Copland) 32
Fantasia 28, 55, 85
Faraday, Michael 141, 154
"Faraway Places" (Crosby & Ken Darby Choir) 37
Farben, I. G. 103
Farewell, My Lovely (Chandler) 62
Farley, James A. 260–261
Farmer, James 326, 350, 469
The Farmer's Daughter 36, 87

Isolationism 55, 76, 102–103, 202, 217–218, 221–224, 227, 236, 261–262, 265, 280, 284, 288, 297, 384, 452–453, 472, 475
Isum, Rachel 565
"It Won't Be Long" (Acuff) 30
It's a Wonderful Life 34
It's Up to You 49
Italian Communist Party 234, 247
Italian Socialist Party 310
"Italy Betrayed" 85
"Italy My Country" 85
Ivanhoe (Scott) 161
Ives, Burl 365
Ives, Charles E. 86

J

J. P. Morgan and Company 126
Jack, Beau (Sidney Walker) 515–517, 544
Jack the Bear (Ellington) 65
Jackson, Charles 33
Jackson, Dr. Chevalier 435
Jackson, Jesse 564
Jackson, Mahalia 68
Jackson, Robert Houghwout 292, 296, 306, 312, 317–318
Jackson, Shirley 38, 84
Jacobs, Dr. Melville 432
Jacobs, Mike 545–549, 563
Jaffe, Philip 387
James, Basil 568
James, Charles 197
James, Harry 30, 32, 65, 80, 84, 145
James, William Roderick 89
James E. Sullivan Award 519, 521, 525, 561
Jameson, Betty 567, 571
Jane Coffin Childs Memorial Fund 354
Jane Eyre (film) 82
Janiro, Tony 547
Janney, Russell 462
Jansky, Karl 487
Japanese Americans 56, 58, 184, 205, 240, 241, 286, 289, 292–293, 296, 301, 304–306, 318, 327, 332, 341–343
Japanese Foreign Ministry 226
Japanese Imperial Army 226–228, 233
Japanese Imperial Navy 226–227, 237, 267
Japanese Supreme Council 236
Jaques, Francis 199
Jarvis, Anna M. 354

Jaspers, Karl 348
"Java Jive" (Ink Spots) 28
Jazz 35, 40–41, 48–49, 64–66, 69, 76–77, 84, 89
"Jeannie With the Light Brown Hair" (Foster) 364
Jefferson, Thomas 168, 170, 504
Jefferson Memorial 168, 170
Jeffries, Edward 344
Jelliffe, Dr. Smith Ely 439
Jenkins, Lew 513
Jet 382
Jet Pilot 118, 570
Jet Propulsion Laborary (JPL) 498
Jew Süss 81
Jewell, Edward Alden 43–44
Jewish Americans 348, 410–411
Jewish Social Studies, Jewish Frontier 348
Jewish Theological Seminary 460
Jim Crow laws 149–150, 243, 245, 268–269, 283, 301–303, 312, 382, 467, 469
Jimmie Dale books (Packard) 90
Jitterbug 48–49, 64, 84
"Jivin' Jacks and Jills" film series 49
Joan of Arc 37, 76
Joe F. Carr Trophy 519
Joe Louis Enterprises 549
John Brown's Body (Bénet) 88
John F. Kennedy International Airport 195
John Street Church, New York City 476
Johnny Belinda 37, 87
Johnny Eager 30
Johnny Got His Gun (Trumbo) 85
"Johnny Zero" (Song Spinners) 32
Johns, George Sibley 391
Johns Hopkins University 138, 159, 162–163, 402, 424, 433, 438, 474, 488
Johnson, Crockett 359, 366
Johnson, Jack 563, 573
Johnson, John H. 359, 382
Johnson, Lady Bird 196
Johnson, Laurence 365–366
Johnson, Louis 276
Johnson, Lyndon B. 258, 284–286, 504
Johnson, Malcolm 389
Johnson, Philip 169, 171, 182–183
Johnson, Smiley 573
Johnson, Van 32, 38, 59
Johnson, Walter 573
Johnson, William 45

Johnson, William E. "Pussyfoot" 354
Johnson, William Gary "Bunk" 89
Johnston, William M. "Little Bill" 573
Joint Panel on the Medical Aspects of Atomic Warfare 495
Joint Research and Development Board 501
Jolliffe, Dr. Norman 416
Jonathan Edwards (Miller) 463
Jones, Billy 391
Jones, Bobby 511, 555
Jones, Carmen 32
Jones, E. Stanley 444
Jones, Howard Harding 573
Jones, James 81
Jones, Jennifer 31, 38, 59, 87
Jones, Jo 66
Jones, Lois 45
Jones, R. T. 387
Jones, Rufus 162
Jones, Spike 30
Jones, Thomas Elsa 147, 161
Jones Beach, Long Island 352
Joplin, Scott 75
Jordan, Elizabeth 199
Jordan, Louis 32, 34, 66
Joslin, Dr. Elliot P. 435
Joslin, Theodore Goldsmith 391
Joslyn, George A. 355
Joslyn, Sarah H. 355
Journal of the American Medical Association 397–400, 426, 432
Journey in the Dark (Flavin) 86
Journey into Fear (Ambler) 62
Journey of Reconciliation (1947) 469
Joyce, James 29, 40, 79, 89
Joyce, William "Lord Haw Haw" 372
Judaism 55, 70, 119, 162, 217, 242, 266, 272, 276, 279, 287–288, 296, 348, 355, 364, 375, 410–411, 444–446, 449–450, 452–453, 455–461, 463–465, 469, 471, 473, 475–476, 487, 502, 504, 542
Judaism and Christianity: The Differences (Weiss-Rosmarin) 445
Juilliard School of Music 32, 66, 78, 89, 163
Julia Lee and Her Boyfriends 36
Julius Caesar (Shakespeare) 82
"Jump For Joy" (Ellington with Jeffries) 29
Jung, Carl 74

L

Labor Temple, New York City 469
Labor unions 37, 50, 71, 82, 85, 99–100, 102–103, 115–117, 119, 121–122, 126, 208, 238–239, 244, 246, 263, 266–268, 270, 272–273, 280, 284–285, 287, 293, 322, 335, 360, 375, 425, 451–452, 455, 473, 539
Ladd, Alan 30, 34, 54, 59
Ladies' Home Journal 428
Ladies Professional Golf Association (LPGA) 555, 560
Lady Chatterley's Lover (Lawrence) 328
Lady in the Dark 29
Lady Sings the Blues (Holiday) 77
Lafayette, Marie-Joseph-Paul-Yves-Roch-Gilbert du Motier, Marquis de 426
La Guardia, Fiorello 70, 138, 166, 177, 179, 242, 262, 287, 289
La Guardia Airport, New York 482
Laidlaw, Harriet Burton 355
Laine, Frankie 37
Lake Shore Drive Apartments 183
Lake, Veronica 30, 34, 166, 176–177
Lamarr, Hedy 109
Lambert, Albert Bond 439
Lambert, Eleanor 197
Lambert Pharmaceutical Company 439
Lamentation (Graham) 74
Lamont, Thomas William 127
La Motta, Jake 516, 528, 544, 546–548
Lamour, Dorothy 30
Lamp at Midnight (Stavis) 52
Lampell, Millard 365
"The Lamplighter's Serenade" (Miller with Eberly) 30
Land, Charlie 321
Land, Edwin 482
"Land of Love" (Cole) 38
Landi, Elissa 89
Landis, Carole 89
Landis, Kenesaw Mountain 518, 536, 538, 573
Landon, Alf 384
Landowska, Wanda 70
Landsteiner, Karl 436, 440
Lane, Muriel 29
Lane v. *Wilson* 302
Laney, Lucy 349

Lang, Fritz 34, 41
Langdon, Harry 89
Langmuir, Irving 492
Langston University 161
Languir, Irving 492
Lansky, Meyer 319
LaPorte Herald (Indiana) 386
Lappointe, Ray 567
Lardner, Rex 391
Lardner, Ring, Jr. 37, 304
The Lark (Hellman) 76
Larkin, Tippy 515
Larsen, Roy E. 134
Larson, Col. Emery Ellsworth 573
Larwin (racehorse) 559
LaSalle University 567
Lasker, Emmanuel 573
Lasker, Mrs. Albert D. (Mary) 426–427
Lassaw, Ibram 46
The Last Tycoon (Fitzgerald) 29
Lattimore, Owen 159
Latin Quarter, New York 70
"Laughing on the Outside" (Shore) 35
Laura 32
Laurence, William L. 389
Lavagetto, Cookie 539
Lavender Mist (Pollock) 45
Lawrence, D. H. 33, 79, 328
Lawrence, Dr. Ernest O. 432, 502
Lawrence, Jacob 45–46
Lawrin 566
Lawson, James 469
Lawson, John Howard 63
Layden, Elmer 521
Lazzeri, Tony 573
Le Rallec, Blanche 355
Lea Act 360
Lead, Kindly Light: Gandhi and the Way (Sheean) 463
League of Broke Husbands 181
League of Nations 114, 233, 288, 297, 313, 323
Leahy, Frank 529
Leahy, William D. 237
Lean, David 34, 36
The Leaning Tower and Other Stories (Porter) 33
Leatherneck 239
Lebrowitz, Barney "Battling Levinsky" 573
Ledbetter, Huddie "Leadbelly" 68, 89, 355
Lederle Laboratories 402
Lee, Dr. Sammy 556
Lee, Julia 36

Lee, Peggy 34, 37
Leeds University 159
Lefft, Dr. Harold H. 432
Legislative Reorganization Act 212
Lehman, Herbert 242
Lehman Brothers company 125
Leichtentritt, Hugo 70
Leinsdorf, Erich 70
LeMay, Curtis 276
Lemon, Bob 566
Lemos, Richie 513
Lenczyk, Grace 571
Lend-Lease program 96, 99, 203, 218, 222–223, 236, 246, 266, 282, 453
Lengfield, Helen 555
Lenin, Vladimir I. 78, 413
Leonard, Benny 573
Leonard, Buck 537
Leonard, Dr. Veador 440
Leonard, Dutch 536
Lepke, Louis 273, 319, 322, 546
Lerch, Walter 437
Lerner, Max 64, 239
Les Brown Orchestra 562
Leser, Tina 198
Lesnevich, Gus 512, 521, 525–526, 528, 545, 547
Lessing, Bruno (Randolph Block) 391
Lester Hofheimer Research Award 433
"Let It Snow! Let It Snow! Let I Snow!" (Monroe & Orchestra) 34
"Let's Knock the Hit out of Hitler" 64
Let There Be Light 59
Let Us Now Praise Famous Men (Evans) 380
Letter to the World (Graham) 74
Letter to Three Wives 38, 87
Letters That Didn't Reach You (PWB) 374
Levi, Primo 466
Levine, Philip 436
Levinson, Dr. Sidney O. 432
Levitt, Abraham 116, 173, 186, 330
Levitt, Alfred 116, 186, 330
Levitt, William 116, 330
Levitt and Sons 116, 170, 185
Levittown 116, 170, 173, 185–186, 330, 347
Levy, Fred, Jr. 512
Lewin, Albert 34
Lewin, Kurt 491
Lewis, Gus 566

MacFarlane, W. E. 391
Mach, Ernst 489
Machen, J. Gresham 457
Mackay, John 461
MacKenzie, Catherine 437
MacLean, Dr. J. Arthur 432
MacLeish, Archibald 36, 80, 374
MacMitchell, Leslie 513
MacNair, Harley F. 162
MacPhail, Larry 511, 515, 519, 524, 564, 567
Macy's department store 78
Madame Bovary 38
Mademoiselle Merit Award 194
Madison Avenue Methodist Church, New York City 462
Madison Square Garden, New York City 30, 242, 510, 514, 516, 541–543, 545–546, 548–549
Magazine of Fantasy and Science Fiction 361, 381
Magazine Publishers Association 383
Magee, John Benjamin 162
Magidoff, Jacob 392
Maginnis, Charles D. 199
The Magnificent Ambersons 30, 82, 88
Mahoney, Mrs. Daniel (Florence) 427
Mahoney, John Friend 436
Maier, Walter A. 448
Mailer, Norman 37, 41, 53, 310
Mainbocher 178, 180, 197
Major League Baseball World Series 510, 513, 515, 517–518, 520, 522, 524, 526, 528, 534–536, 538–539, 564, 567–571
Make Believe Ballroom 363
Malaria 279, 399, 407–409, 417, 432, 437, 501
Malcahyl, Hugh 535
Malcolm X (Malcolm Little) 466
Male and Female: A Study of the Sexes in a Changing World (Mead) 482
Mallarmé, Stéphane 75
Mallory, Dr. Frank Barr 440
Malta Conference 277
The Maltese Falcon (film) 29, 60–61, 73
Maltz, Albert 304
Mamakos, Steve 511
"Mam'selle" (Lund) 36
A Man for All Seasons (film) 82
The Man from Nazareth as His Companions Saw Him (Fosdick) 463
Man o' War 109, 524, 573

"The Man Who Lived Underground" (Wright) 83
The Man With the Golden Arm (Algren) 38, 53
"Mañana" (Lee) 37
The Manatee (Bruff) 34
Mandrake the Magician (Falk) 366
Maney, Joseph 517
Mangrum, Lloyd 555, 570
Manhattan Center, New York 28
Manhattan College 542
Manhattan Project 195, 237, 257, 381, 407, 463, 481, 485, 493, 495–496, 502–506, 554
Mankiewicz, Herman 82
Mankiewicz, Joseph L. 38, 87
Mann, Thomas 37–38, 41, 52, 84, 138
Mann Act 84
Mannheim, Karl 147
Manpower 60
"Mansion on the Hill" (Williams) 37
Mantle, Mickey 562
Manzanar internment camp 296, 305–306
Mao Tse-tung 211, 216, 258, 384
Maple Leaf Rag (Graham) 75
Marble, Alice 567
Marble Collegiate Church, New York City 471
March, Frederic 87
March of Dimes 427
March On Washington Movement (MOWM) 243
Marching Song (Welles) 81
"Maria Elena" (Dorsey with Eberly) 29
Marion, Martin 518
Maritain, Jacques 158, 445, 452, 457
Marker, Russell 433
Marmon, Howard C. 199
Marmon Motor Company 199
Marquand, John P. 29, 31, 34, 38
Marquette University 439
Marsh, Wayne 32
Marshall, Bruce 462
Marshall, Catherine 463
Marshall, Frank James 573
Marshall, George C. 99–100, 113–114, 210–213, 215, 226–227, 231, 237, 243, 255, 274, 276–278, 283, 294, 336, 371
Marshall, Rev. Peter 463, 476
Marshall, Thurgood 302, 316

Marshall Plan 100, 104, 112–114, 125, 139, 213, 252, 255–256, 260, 269, 277–278, 283, 294, 364
"A Marshmallow World" (Crosby) 38
Marston, Dr. William Moulton 440
Martha Graham Dance Company 75
Martial et Armand salon 196
Martin, Clyde F. 351
Martin, Dean 65
Martin, Freddie 29
Martin, Leo 566
Martin, Mary 38
Martin, Pat 566
Martinu, Bohuslav 70
Marx, Karl 78, 156, 365, 454
Marx-Engels Institute 156
Marxism 78, 121, 156, 272, 460, 470, 474
Mary (Asch) 463
Mary Adelaide Nutting Award 437
Mary Lee Fashions 195–196
Mary Worth (Connor & Saunders) 366
Mason, James 38
Mason, Joseph Warren Teets 392
Mason, William 322
Mason-Dixon Line 244
Massachusetts General Hospital 440
Massachusetts Handicap, Suffolk Downs 514
Massachusetts Institute of Technology (MIT) 135, 142, 170, 182–183, 194–195, 380, 431, 480, 491, 497, 501
Massachusetts State College 566
Masserman, Jules H. 437
Masses 393
Masson, André 42
Masters Golf Tournament 511, 527, 555, 567–572
Mathematics 137, 145–146, 317, 484–485, 493, 500–501, 504
Mathews, Rev. Shailer 476
Mathias, Bob 526, 556
Matisse, Pierre 90
Matt, Toni 566
Matta, Robert 42
Matthiessen, F. O. 139
Mauchly, John W. 481, 490, 500
"Maud Humphrey Baby" (Humphrey) 73
Mauer, John 542
Maugham, Somerset 33

Michigan Civil Rights Act 313
Michigan State University 520
Michigan Wolverines 550
The Middle of the Journey (Trilling) 36
Middlecoff, Cary 572
Midgley, Thomas, Jr. 507
Mies van der Rohe, Ludwig 166, 169–171, 173, 183
Mies van der Rohe (Johnson) 169
The Migration of the Negro (Lawrence) 45
Mikan, George 541–544
Milburn, Amos 67
Mildred Pierce 34, 87
Miley, Jack 545
Miley, Marion 566, 573
Milhaud, Darius 70
Military draft 84, 130, 135, 145–146, 202, 204, 236, 238, 244, 247, 266, 292, 294, 326, 334, 336–337, 340, 445, 453, 466, 469, 496, 501, 530, 535–536, 541, 552–554, 557–558, 560, 562
Military Supply Act 202
Military uniforms 166, 176–178, 194, 197, 558
Milky Way galaxy 487
Milland, Ray 34, 87
Miller, Alice Duer 89
Miller, Ann 49
Miller, Arthur 36, 38, 41, 51, 86
Miller, Francis 453
Miller, Frieda 335
Miller, Glenn 28, 30, 32–33, 36, 64, 89
Miller, Harry A. 199
Miller, Perry 463
Miller, Rabbi Irving 475
Millinery Fashion Inspiration, Inc. 196
Millis, Harry Alvin 127
Mills, Freddie 521, 526, 528, 545
Mills, Frederick 90
Mills Brothers 29–30, 33, 37, 68
Mills College 163
Milwaukee Sentinel 392
Minami, Dale 318
Minersville School District v. *Gobitis* 298–301, 316
Minkowski, Rudolph 485
Minneapolis General Hospital 426
Minneapolis Lakers 525, 543
Minneapolis Times Tribune 392
Minneapolis Tribune 389
Minnesota Health Department 426
Minot, Dr. George R. 435

Minton, Sherman 216, 295, 304
Minton's Playhouse, Manhattan 66
The Miracle 473
The Miracle of the Bells (Janney) 462
Miracle on 34th Street 36
Mission to Moscow 31, 60
Mississippi State University 568
Missouri ex. rel. Gaines v. *Canada* 149
Missouri Valley Conference 525
Mr. Adam (Frank) 35
Mr. Chairman (Hobby) 276
Mr. Jones, Meet the Master (Marshall) 463
Mr. Lucky 31
Mister Roberts (Heggen) 51, 89
Mr. Smith Goes to Washington 88
Mitchell, Arthur 302
Mitchell, Margaret 90
Mitchell v. *United States* 302
Mitchum, Robert 84
Mitropoulos, Dimitri 31
Mitsubishi company 227
Mix, Tom 90
Mize, Johnny 539
Moby Dick (play) 82
Modern Negro Art (Porter) 41, 45–46
Modern Quarterly 390
Modernism 35, 40–42, 44, 52–53, 70, 79, 83, 391, 451–452, 456–457, 460, 473
Moffatt, Rev. James 476
Moffett, W. Edwin 433
Moholy-Nagy, Laszlo 182
Molyneaux, Joseph W. 355
Mondrian, Piet 28, 33, 42–43, 90
Mongol Journeys (Lattimore) 159
Moniz, Antonio 435
Moniz, Dr. Egas 420
Monk, Thelonious 66
Monroe, Bill 35–36
Monroe, Jimmy 77
Monroe, Marilyn 181, 562
Monroe, Vaughn 30, 34, 65
Monroe's Uptown House, Manhattan 66
Monsanto Chemical Corporation 496
Monsieur Verdoux 36
Montagu, William P. 445
Montague, James Jackson 392
Montana, Bob 370
Monte Cassino monastery 233
Monte-San, Vincent 198

Montefiore Hospital, New York 396
Monteil, Germaine 197
Montgomery, Gen. Bernard 231–232, 274
Montgomery, Bob 516–517, 524, 544
Montgomery, Lucy Maud 90
Montgomery Ward 97, 208, 322
Montreal Canadiens 518, 521, 523, 567, 569–570
Montreal Royals 537, 565
Montserrat (Hellman) 76
The Moon Is Down (Steinbeck) 30–31
Mooney, Jim 573
"Moonlight Serenade" (Miller) 89
Moore, C. L. 381
Moore, John Bassett 323
Moore, Lou 532
Moore, William Emmet 392
Moorhead, Agnes 59
Mooring, Mark 198
Moral Man and Immoral Society (Niebuhr) 470
Moran, Augusta "Gussie" 530, 557
More Washington Merry-Go-Round 385
Morehouse College 447
Morgan, Edmund N. 307
Morgan, Frank 31
Morgan, Helen 90
Morgan, John Pierpont 127
Morgan, T. H. 507
Morgan, Truman Spencer 392
Morgan, William G. 573
Morgan v. *Commonwealth of Virginia* 211, 302
Morgenstern, Oskar 493
Morgenthau, Henry R. 209, 242–243, 253, 287
Morris, George L. K. 78
Morris, Mary 355
Morris, Roland 163
Morris Brown College 511
Morrison, C. C. 453
Morrison, Philip 257
Morse, Ella Mae 67
Morse, Wayne 267
The Mortal Storm 28, 55
Mortimer, Lee 81
Mortimer, Stanley Grafton 573
Mosconi, Willie 515, 558
Moses, Robert 351–352
Mother India (Mayo) 89
The Mother of Us All (Thomson) 36, 70

Motherwell, Robert 33, 41, 44–45

Motion Picture Committee Cooperating for Defense 55

Motion Picture Herald 31

Mott, Frank 317

Moulton, Charles (William Moulton Marston) 358, 392

Mount Holyoke College 163, 279

Mount Palomar Observatory, California 482, 485, 487

Mount Rushmore (Borglum) 88

Mount Sinai Hospital, New York City 432–433

Mount Wilson Observatory, California 485, 487

The Mountain Lion (Stafford) 36

"Move It On Over" (Williams) 36

Move On Up a Little Higher (Jackson) 68

Mrs. Miniver 30, 57, 59, 87

Mrs. Parkington (Bromfield) 31

Muck, Karl 90

Muckerman, Richard 520, 527

Muhammad, Elijah (Robert Poole) 466

Muir, Jean 365

Muller, Herman J. 435

Muller, Paul H. 435

Mumford, Lewis 197, 464

Munch, Edvard 90

Munich Conference (1938) 220, 380, 384

Municipal Stadium, Philadelphia 558

Munroe, John A. "Jack" 573

Munsey's Magazine 393

Murder, Inc. 273, 319, 546

Murder My Sweet 62

Murders in the Rue Morgue (Poe) 85

Murlin, Dr. John 433

Muroc Army Base, California 481

Murphey, Frederick E. 392

Murphy, Audie 84

Murphy, Frank W. 241, 304, 312, 318, 323

Murphy, J. Edwin 392

Murray, Charlie 90

Murray, Philip 94, 121–122, 238, 266, 269, 287

Murrow, Edward R. 362, 374, 377

Museum of Modern Art 28, 32–33, 37, 44, 47, 166, 169, 194–195, 355

Museum of Non-Objective Painting 42

Musial, Stan 517, 522, 526–527, 530, 534–535, 539

Musician's Emergency Fund 163

Mussolini, Benito 79, 156, 207, 223, 231–232, 234, 247, 262, 311, 383, 469

Muste, Abraham Johannes 326, 350, 450, 468–470

Musto, Tony 511

Mutual Broadcasting Network 372, 374, 541

Mutual Defense Assistance Act 216

My Days of Anger (Farrell) 31

My Heart's in the Highlands (Saroyan) 51

My Little Chickadee 28

"My Most Humiliating Jim Crow Experience" 382

"My Sweet Hunk of Trash" (Holiday & Armstrong) 77

Myers, Howard 199

Myers, Ruth 49

Myrdal, Gunnar 272, 345

Mystici Corporis (Pope Pius XII) 445, 451

N

Nabokov, Vladimir 29

Nagasaki 210, 236–237, 257, 284, 332, 400, 407, 432, 454, 460, 463–464, 482, 494–495, 502–504

Nakama, Keo 515

The Naked and the Dead (Mailer) 37, 53

Nakia, Reuben 46

Nash, Charles W. 127, 199

Nash, John 493

Nash, Paul 90

Nash Motor Company 127, 199, 329

Nast, Conde 90

Nathan, Robert 29

Nation 138, 156, 243, 348, 393

Nation of Islam (Black Muslims) 466

National Academy of Design 198

National Academy of Sciences 432, 501, 505

National American Woman Suffrage Association 280, 354

National Association for Stock Car Auto Racing (NASCAR) 533, 534

National Association for the Advancement of Colored People (NAACP) 63, 136, 149, 243–

245, 302–303, 316–317, 326, 382, 425, 565

National Association of Broadcasters (NAB) 359, 363

National Association of Evangelicals (NAE) 458

National Association of Intercollegiate Athletics (NAIA) 542

National Association of Professional Baseball Leagues 572

National Baptist Convention of America 466

National Basketball Association (NBA) 528, 543–544

National Basketball League (NBL) 525, 528, 543

National Board of Medical Examiners 410

National Book Award 53

National Boxing Association (NBA) 510, 513

National Broadcasting Company (NBC) 84–85, 91, 362, 372, 374, 376–377, 385, 498–499, 573

National Broadcasting Company v. *United States* 359

National Cancer Institute 402, 434

National Cartoonists Society 360

National Catholic Education Association 447

National Citizens Commission for Public Schools 134

National City Bank of New York 125

National Collegiate Athletic Association (NCAA) 511, 514, 516, 518–519, 521–523, 525, 527, 541–542, 558, 560, 565, 567–571

National Committee Against Mental Illness 437

National Conference for the Improvement of Teachers 133

National Conference of Christians and Jews 475

National Council for American Education 132, 137–138

National Council of Churches 456

National Council of Congregational Churches 476

National Council of Negro Women 349

National Education Association (NEA) 132, 134, 138, 146, 155, 160–163

National Eucharistic Congress 472

National Federation of Employees 351

National Football League (NFL) 322, 512–513, 515–517, 520–522, 527, 529, 552–554, 558, 560, 566–571

National Football League Most Valuable Player Award 519, 523

National Foundation for Infantile Paralysis 396–398, 401, 426, 439

National Gallery of Art 29, 85

National Golfer 555

National Health Institute 433

National Health Survey of 1936 427

National Heart Institute 404

National Hockey League (NHL) 511, 514, 516, 518, 567–572

National Hockey League Most Valuable Player Award 523

National Hockey League Stanley Cup 511, 514, 516, 518–519, 521, 523, 525, 528, 567–571

National Housing Agency 184

National Institute of Arts and Letters 84

National Institute of Mental Health (NIMH) 402, 404, 419

National Institutes of Health (NIH) 419, 437

National Interfraternity Council 131, 149

National Invitational Tournament (NIT) 541–542, 558

National Jewish Hospital 431

National Jewish Welfare Board 445

National League (baseball) 511, 518, 520, 522, 528, 534, 536–539, 564–565, 567–571

National League Most Valuable Player Award 515, 517–518, 520, 522, 524, 527, 529, 534, 537–538, 565

National League Player of the Year Award 518

National League Rookie of the Year Award 537, 538

National Lutheran Council 445

National Medical Association 403

National Mental Health Act 399, 419

National Negro College Championship 552

National Negro Congress 35

National Negro League 272

National Opinion Research Center 446, 461

National Periodical Publications 367, 370, 387

National Recovery Act (NRA) 281

National Recovery Administration 122, 124, 158

National Research Council 351, 398, 425, 486, 490

National Science Foundation (NSF) 495, 501

National Security Act 213, 216, 256, 294

National Semi-Pro Baseball tournament 566

National Stewardship Institute 447

National Stock Car championship 527

National Student Association 133

National Teachers' Association 142

National Tennis Championships 517

National Urban League 354

National Velvet 32

National Youth Administration (NYA) 145, 349, 565

National-American Football League 529

Native Americans 44, 74, 88, 397, 411

Native Son (Wright) 28, 41, 53

The Nature and Destiny of Man (Niebuhr) 461, 471

Nausea (Sartre) 38

Naval Supply Act 202

Navarro, Theodore "Fats" 66

Navy Day, 27 October 1941 223

The Nazi Strike 59

Nazism 40, 55–56, 59–60, 64, 70, 76, 102, 105, 131, 139, 149, 153, 157, 166, 179, 182, 188, 193, 208, 210, 219, 222–223, 225, 231–232, 235, 242–243, 245–246, 252, 255, 262, 274, 278–279, 286–288, 293–294, 296, 299, 303, 307–308, 313, 318, 321, 332, 345, 348, 355, 364, 367, 372, 375, 379, 385, 410–411, 445, 450, 453–455, 457–460, 464–465, 469, 473, 476, 484–485, 504, 536, 563

NBC. *See* National Broadcasting Company

NEA Service 388

"Near You" (Andrews Sisters) 36

Nebraska State Journal 389

Nebrit, James M., Jr. 302

Nef, John 158

Neff, Wallace 197

Negro American League (baseball) 526–527

Negro Baseball Leagues 537, 539

Negro Baseball World Series 515

Negro Digest 63, 359, 382

Negro National League (baseball) 512, 527

The Negro Soldier 63

Nehru on Gandhi (Nehru) 463

Nehru, Jawaharlal 463

Nelson, Byron 517, 519–522, 555, 558, 567–568, 570

Nelson, Donald M. 95, 106, 123

Nervi, Pier Luigi 194

Neutra, Richard 184

Neuwelt, Dr. Frank 432

"Never Again (Will I Knock on Your Door)" (Williams) 35

Never Come Morning (Algren) 30

Nevins, Allan 161

New American Library (NAL) 369

New Brunswick Theological Seminary 468

New Deal 42, 69, 102–103, 105, 114, 117, 119, 121–124, 127, 144–145, 158, 218–219, 236, 253, 256–257, 259–263, 265–269, 271, 273, 279–284, 288–289, 296, 312, 315, 317, 331, 364, 379, 383, 413, 416, 451

New Directions Press 38

New Jersey Agricultural Experiment Station 430, 438

New Masses 393

New Methods vs. Old in American Education 130

New Mexico State Teachers College 557

The New Republic 261, 285

New School for Social Research 156

New York Academy of Medicine 411

New York American 546

New York Americans 511

New York Athletic Club 511

New York Avenue Presbyterian Church 476

New York Board of Education 137

New York Board of Regents 161

New York City Ballet 48

New York City Bureau of Municipal Research 351

New York Commission on Secondary-School Curriculum 130

New York Committee on Safety 279

New York County Medical Society 402

Republican Party 55, 101, 115, 117, 121, 202, 206, 208, 212, 214, 218–219, 222, 242, 256–259, 261–263, 265–271, 273–274, 280, 283–289, 308, 323–324, 342, 346, 350, 352, 360, 383–384, 387, 391, 413, 474, 565
Reshevsky, Samuel 567
Reston, James 389
Reuben Award 360
Reuther, Walter 123, 216, 269
Reveille with Beverly 81
Revenue Act of 1942 95, 109
Review of Politics 348
Rex Morgan, M.D. (Dallis) 367
Rhee, Syngman 215
Rhinelander, Maj. Philip 355
Rhoads, Dr. C. P. 434
Rhodes, Ted 525
Rhythm Wranglers 67
Ribbentrop, Joachim von 308
Rice, Charles O. 451
Rice, Elmer 41, 51
Rice, Grantland 561
Rice, Gregory 510–511, 514, 516, 567
Rice, Julian 542
Rice University 570
Rich, Charles Alonzo 199
Richard, Maurice 523, 567
Richards, Dr. Alfred Newton 416–417, 436
Richards, George 375
Richardson, Dr. Garwood 433
Richmond Golf Club (Virginia) 525
Richmond Times Dispatch 389
Rickard, Tex 545
Rickey, Branch 515, 517–520, 530, 534, 536–539, 564–565, 567
Ridge, Lola 90
Ridgely, Henry 323
Ridgway, Matthew 277
Riefenstahl, Leni 59
Riegel, Robert 571
Riegger, Wallingford 71
Rieseman, David 242
Rieveschl, Dr. George, Jr. 406
Riggs, Bobby 510, 512, 514, 521, 526, 528, 531, 557, 568
Riggs, Lynn 69
Ring 521
Ringling Brothers Circus 30, 48, 463
Rip Kirby (Raymond) 360
Ripley, Robert LeRoy 49, 355, 392
Riter, Franklin 307

Ritter, Father Joseph E. 149
Ritter, Tex 35, 37
River Road (Keys) 35
River Rouge Ford plant 94
Riverside Church, New York City 475
RKO Studios 37, 54, 63, 82, 87
Roach, Max 66
Road to Morocco 30
The Road to Singapore 28
The Rubber Bridegroom (Welty) 30
Robbins, Frederick 482, 505
Robbins, Harold 38
Robbins, Jerome 48
Robbins, Dr. William 433
The Robe (Douglas) 462
Robelto, Joe 516
Roberts, Kenneth 36
Roberts, Mary M. 438
Roberts, Oral 462
Roberts, Owen J. 293
Roberts, Theophilus 161
Roberts, William Carman 392
Robertson, Alfred (Robby) 567
Robeson, Paul 353
Robinson, Bill 49
Robinson, Edward G. 28, 73
Robinson, Holton D. 199
Robinson, Jackie 329, 353, 520, 523–524, 529–530, 537–539, 564–565
Robinson, Jerry 564
Robinson, Luther Bill "Bojangles" 90
Robinson, Mack 565
Robinson, Mallie 564, 565
Robinson, Sugar Ray 515–516, 523–526, 528, 530, 544, 547–548
Robinson, T. L. 323
Robinson House, Massachusetts 169, 182, 194
Robinson-Patman Act 117
Robles, Emmanuel 76
Robson, George 532, 570
Rochester Royals 525
Rochester Society of Free Thinkers 148
Rochester University 433
Rock, John 437
Rock 'n' roll 71
"Rock Island Line" (Ledbetter) 89
Rock Island Railroad 302
Rockefeller, Abby Greene 355
Rockefeller, David 273
Rockefeller, Godfrey 557
Rockefeller, John D., Jr. 355, 433
Rockefeller, Sterling 557

Rockefeller Foundation 351, 396
Rockefeller Institute for Medical Research 431, 438, 489
Rockford Peaches (Illinois) 539–540
Rockne, Knute 550
Rodeo 31, 48, 69, 84
Rodgers, Richard 69, 71, 85
Rodin 90
Roe, Preacher 566
Rogers, Ginger 31, 66
Rogers, Roy 59
Rogers, Will 90
Rolland, Romaine 90
Romeo and Juliet (Shakespeare) 81
Rommel, Gen. Erwin 231, 274, 278, 293
Romulo, Carlos P. 388
Rooney, Betty Jane 338
Rooney, Mickey 31, 338
The Roosevelt I Knew (Perkins) 280
Roosevelt, Eleanor 55, 134, 138, 143, 148, 211, 243, 261, 287, 310, 349, 353, 382, 473
Roosevelt, Franklin D. 28–29, 49, 55–56, 81, 94–96, 102–106, 108–110, 112, 115–127, 131, 141, 143, 159, 166–169, 172, 174, 188, 197, 202–209, 217–219, 222–224, 226–227, 231, 234–244, 246–250, 253–254, 257, 259–271, 273–275, 277, 279–289, 292–293, 296, 305, 308, 312–313, 315–318, 321–322, 326–327, 331–332, 336, 338, 341, 343–345, 349, 360, 363, 372–375, 379, 391–392, 404, 413, 416, 418, 433, 444, 446, 453, 465, 472, 475, 480–481, 485, 493, 496, 501, 503–504, 519, 530, 536, 545
Roosevelt, Theodore 288, 289
Roosevelt, Theodore, Jr. 289
Roosevelt Medal 507
Roper, Jim 534
Roper Polls 266
Roscoe B. Jackson Memorial Laboratory for Cancer Research 432
Rose, Mauri 523, 526, 532, 568, 571
Rose Bowl 513, 523, 551, 557, 567–571
Rose Bowl Parade 358
Roseland Ballroom, New York 49
Rosen, Joseph 319
Rosenberg, Alfred 308
Rosenberg, Ethel 258

Schermerhorn, James 392
Schine, David 455
Schmeling, Max 563
Schmidt, Otto 392
Schmitt, Gladys 462
Schmitz, Andrew 518
Schnabel, Artur 70
Schocken Books 348
Schoenberg, Arnold 70–71, 158
Schoendienst, "Red" 567
Schoenstein, Paul 388
School Lunch Program 141
Schroeder, Frederick "Ted", Jr. 515, 568
Schultz, Dr. Edwin W. 433
Schuman, William 70, 86
Schwellenbach, Lewis-Baxter 127
Schwerdt, Dr. C. E. 433
Schwinger, Julian 505
Schwoegler, Connie 515
Science 390, 398, 434
Science: The Endless Frontier (Bush) 132
Science and Invention 355, 392
Science Illustrated 494
Science Press 390
Scopes Monkey Trial 323, 457
Scotia Seminary 349
Scott, Col. Robert L. 462
Scott, Sir Walter 161
Scottsboro Nine 469
Scoundrel Time (Hellman) 76
Scoville, Mildred C. 437
Scowcroft, Richard 462
Scranton Times (Pennsylvania) 389
"Scrapple from the Apple" (Parker) 66
"The Scream" (Munch) 90
Screen Directors Guild 36, 330
Scripps-Howard Newspapers 386, 388, 390, 392
Scruggs, Earl 68
Scudder, Janet 90
Seabiscuit (race horse) 514
Seabloom, Clark 353
Seaborg, Glenn Theodore 480
The Searching Wind (Hellman) 51, 76
Searcy State Hospital for the Colored
Insane 562
G. D. Searle & Company 402
Sears, Richard D. 573
Sears, Roebuck and Company 106, 123, 141
The Seasons (Cage) 71
Seattle Open Golf Tournament 520

Second Vatican Council 452, 473
The Secret Life of Walter Mitty 36
Secular Cantata no. 2 ("A Free Song") (Schumann) 86
Securities and Exchange Commission 192, 275
Sedway, Morris 319–320
See It Now 377
Seeger, Pete 68
The Seeing Eye, Inc. 354
Segrè, Emilio 484
Segregation 41, 63, 71, 133, 136, 142, 149, 150, 152, 160, 213–215, 240, 242–245, 266, 268, 272, 273, 283, 301–303, 312, 326, 332, 335, 343–345, 347, 350, 466, 469, 536, 565
Seibolds, Geraldine 386
Seidel, Emil 355
Seignious, Hope 555
Seivers, Roy 529
Selective Service 161, 202, 206, 214, 223, 236, 262, 292, 294, 429, 445, 469, 536, 558
Seligsberg, Alice J. 355
Selznick, David O. 59
Selznick International 86
"Sentimental Journey" (Brown & Orchestra with Day) 33
Seraph on the Suwanee (Hurston) 37, 53
"Serenity Prayer" (Niebuhr) 470
Serge millinery house 196
Sergeant York 29, 55, 87
Servo, Marty 544, 547–548
Sessions, Roger 70
Sessler, Charles 85
Seton, Hall 514
Sevareid, Eric 373–374
The Seven Storey Mountain (Merton) 463
Seventeen 359
Sex 81, 137, 330, 340–341, 345–346, 350–351, 369–370, 421, 429, 454, 530, 557
Sex discrimination 117, 152, 240, 280, 328, 332, 335, 343, 345, 410, 446, 530
Sexual Behavior in the Human Female (Kinsey) 350–351
Sexual Behavior in the Human Male (Kinsey) 350–351, 401, 482
Seyfert, Carl 506
Seyfert Galaxies 506
Seymour, Charles 161
Seymour, Forrest W. 388
"The Shadow" 82, 368, 376

Shakespeare, William 50, 81, 88
The Shaking of the Foundations (Tillich) 474
The Shame of the States (Deutsch) 419
Shank, Ruben 547
Shapiro, Jacob 319
Shapiro, Karl 80, 86
Shapley, Harlow 139
Sharpe, D. P. 437
Sharton, Alexander R. 392
Shasta Dam 120
Shaughnessy, Clark 550
Shaw, Artie 29, 77
Shaw, George Bernard 34
Shaw, Irwin 37, 41, 53
Shaw, Wilbur 532, 567
Shawn, Ted 74
The She-Wolf (Pollock) 33
She Wore a Yellow Ribbon 38
Shea, George Beverly 445
Sheahan, Marion W. 437
Shean, Al 90
Sheean, Vincent J. 463
Sheehan, Winfield 90
Sheen, Fulton J. 445, 452, 455, 463
Sheffield Scientific School, Yale University 118
Sheil, Bernard 453
Sheldon, Edward Brewster 90
Shell Corporation 496
Shelley Memorial Prize for Poetry 90
Shelley v. *Kraemer* 303
The Sheltering Sky (Bowles) 38
Shelton, Dr. Don Odell 476
Sheppard and Enoch Pratt Hospital 429
Sherman Antitrust Act 97, 397
Sherwood, Robert E. 51, 56, 73, 86
Shifrin, Lt. Commander Leo 421
Shimkonis, John 573
Shinn, Dr. Milicent W. 440
Shintoism 139
Shirer, William 362
Shockley, William 482, 499
Shoemaker, Vaughn 389
Sholtz, James 527
Shor, Toots 70
Shore, Dinah 30, 34–35, 37–38, 65
Short, Elizabeth (Black Dahlia) 309
Short, Gen. Walter C. 205, 224, 226–227
Shostakovich, Dimitri 32–33
Shotton, Burt 523, 526
Showboat 49, 88–89